ORDNANCE SURVEY

STREET ATLAS

Derbyshire

Contents

IV Key to maps

VI Administrative boundaries

1 Street maps

266 Index explanation and abbreviations

267 Index of towns, villages and rural localities

268 Index of street names

PHILIP'S

First edition published 1995 by

Ordnance Survey
Romsey Road
Maybush
Southampton SO16 4GU

and

Philip's
an imprint of Reed Books
Michelin House, 81 Fulham Road, London, SW3 6RB
and Auckland, Melbourne, Singapore and Toronto

ISBN 0-540-06137-9 (Philip's, hardback)
ISBN 0-540-06138-7 (Philip's, softback)
ISBN 0-319-00565-8 (Ordnance Survey, hardback)
ISBN 0-319-00566-6 (Ordnance Survey, softback)

To the best of the Publishers' knowledge, the information in this atlas was correct at the time of going to press. No responsibility can be accepted for any errors or their consequences.

The representation in this atlas of a road, track or path is no evidence of the existence of a right of way.

Printed and bound in Great Britain by
Bath Press, Bath

Key to map symbols

	British Rail station
	Private railway station
	Bus or coach station
H	**Heliport**
	Police station (may not be open 24 hours)
	Hospital with casualty facilities (may not be open 24 hours)
	Post office
+	**Place of worship**
	Important building
P	**Parking**
174	**Adjoining page indicator**
	No adjoining page
	Motorway
	Dual carriageway
	Main or through road
A27	**Road numbers** (Department of Transport)
	Gate or obstruction to traffic (restrictions may not apply at all times or to all vehicles)
	All paths, bridleways, BOAT's, RUPP's, dismantled railways, etc.
	Track

The representation in this atlas of a road, track or path is no evidence of the existence of a right of way

Amb Sta	**Ambulance station**	LC	**Level crossing**
Coll	**College**	Liby	**Library**
FB	**Footbridge**	Mus	**Museum**
F Sta	**Fire station**	Sch	**School**
Hospl	**Hospital**	TH	**Town hall**

0 | 1/4 | 1/2 | 3/4 | 1 mile

0 | 250m | 500m | 250m | 1 Kilometre

The scale of the maps is 3½ inches to 1 mile (1:18103)

The small numbers around the edges of the maps identify the 1 kilometre National Grid lines

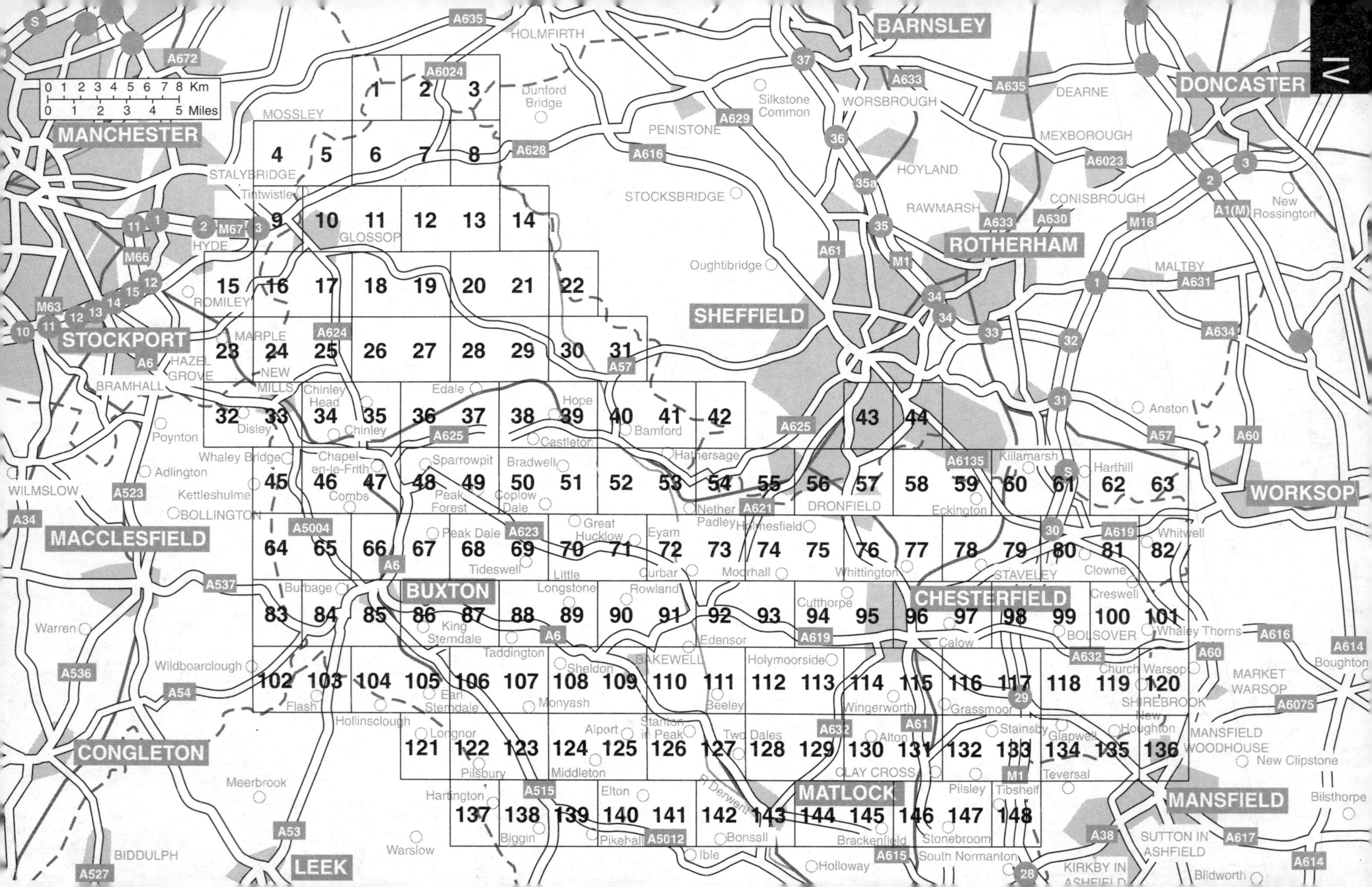
MANCHESTER
STOCKPORT
MACCLESFIELD
CONGLETON
LEEK
BUXTON
SHEFFIELD
ROTHERHAM
BARNSLEY
DONCASTER
WORKSOP
CHESTERFIELD
MATLOCK
MANSFIELD
0 1 2 3 4 5 6 7 8 Km
0 1 2 3 4 5 Miles
HOLMFIRTH
MOSSLEY
STALYBRIDGE
Tintwistle
GLOSSOP
HYDE
ROMILEY
MARPLE
HAZEL GROVE
NEW MILLS
BRAMHALL
Poynton
Disley
Whaley Bridge
Adlington
Kettleshulme
BOLLINGTON
WILMSLOW
Warren
Wildboarclough
Meerbrook
BIDDULPH
Warslow
Hollinsclough
Flash
Burbage
Chinley Head
Chinley
Chapel-en-le-Frith
Combs
Edale
Hope
Castleton
Bamford
Hathersage
Sparrowpit
Peak Forest
Bradwell
Coplow Dale
Peak Dale
Great Hucklow
Tideswell
Little Longstone
Eyam
Curbar
Rowland
Nether Padley
Holmesfield
Moorhall
DRONFIELD
Whittington
Eckington
Killamarsh
Harthill
Whitwell
Clowne
STAVELEY
Creswell
BOLSOVER
Whaley Thorns
Calow
Cutthorpe
Edensor
BAKEWELL
Holymoorside
King Sterndale
Taddington
Sheldon
Monyash
Earl Sterndale
Beeley
Longnor
Pilsbury
Middleton
Aiport
Stanton in Peak
Two Dales
Wingerworth
Grassmoor
Alton
CLAY CROSS
Stainsby
Glapwell
Teversal
Church Warsop
SHIREBROOK
New Houghton
MARKET WARSOP
MANSFIELD WOODHOUSE
New Clipstone
Bilsthorpe
SUTTON IN ASHFIELD
KIRKBY IN ASHFIELD
Bildworth
Boughton
Hartington
Biggin
Elton
Pikehall
R Derwent
Bonsall
Ible
Holloway
Brackenfield
Stonebroom
South Normanton
Pilsley
Tibshelf
Dunford Bridge
PENISTONE
Silkstone Common
WORSBROUGH
HOYLAND
STOCKSBRIDGE
Oughtibridge
RAWMARSH
MEXBOROUGH
DEARNE
CONISBROUGH
MALTBY
New Rossington
Anston
A635
A672
A6024
A628
A629
A616
A633
A61
M1
A630
A6023
M18
A1(M)
A631
A634
A57
A60
A625
A6135
A621
A619
A623
A6
A5004
A624
M67
M66
M63
A523
A34
A537
A536
A54
A53
A527
A515
A5012
A615
A632
A38
A617
A614
A616
A6075

Key to map pages

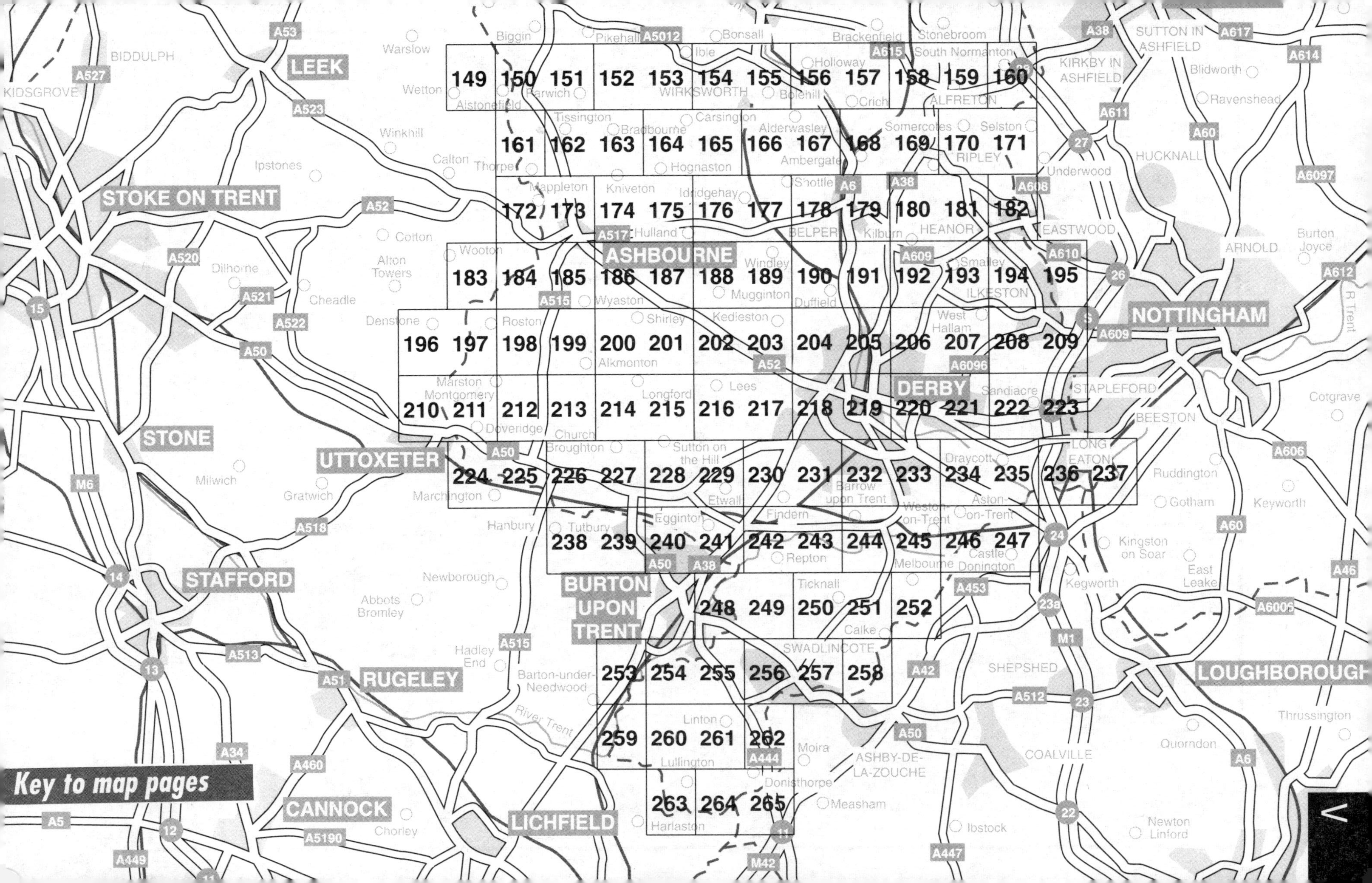

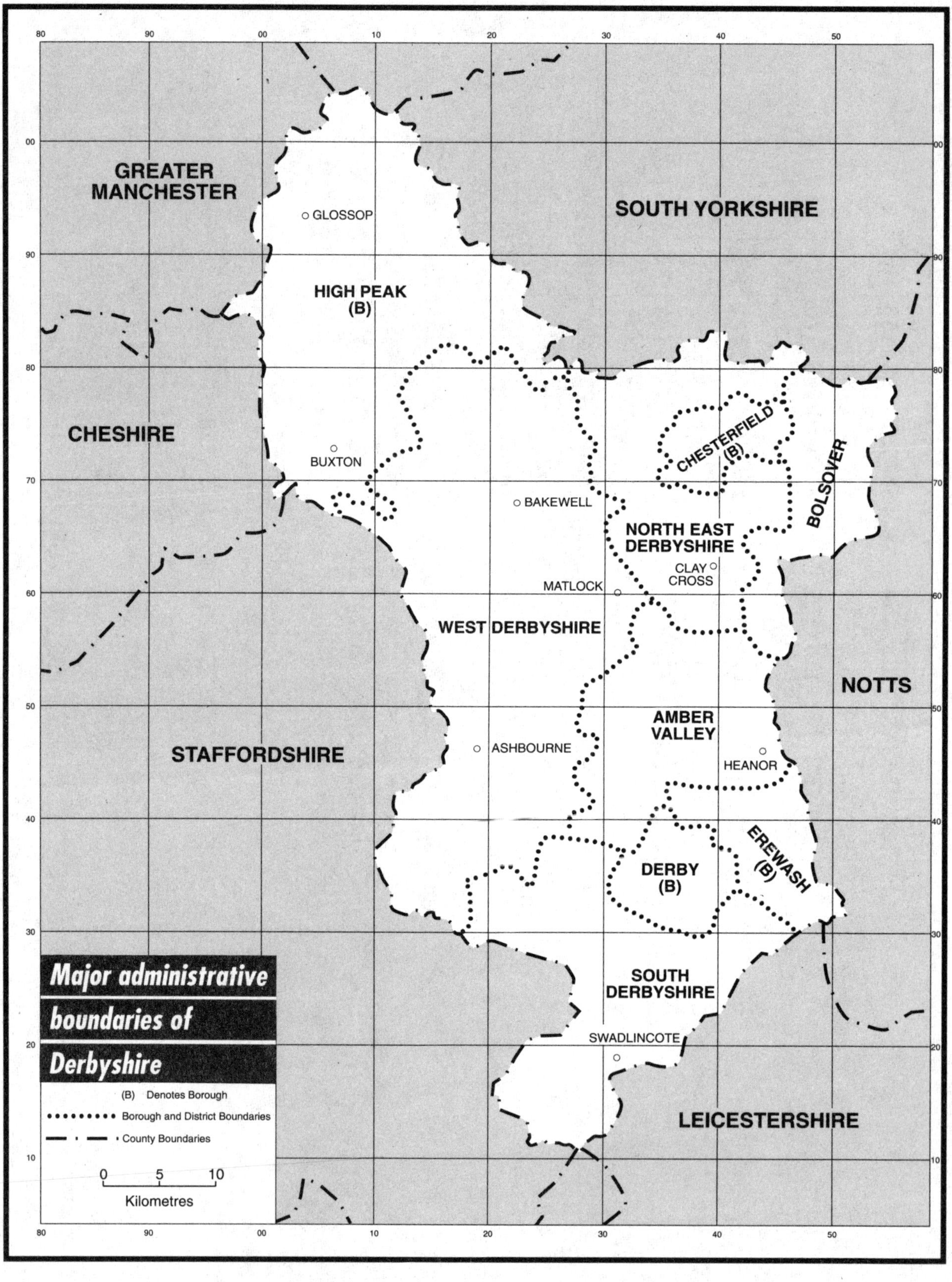

GREATER MANCHESTER
SOUTH YORKSHIRE
GLOSSOP
HIGH PEAK (B)
CHESHIRE
BUXTON
BAKEWELL
CHESTERFIELD (B)
BOLSOVER
NORTH EAST DERBYSHIRE
CLAY CROSS
MATLOCK
WEST DERBYSHIRE
NOTTS
AMBER VALLEY
STAFFORDSHIRE
ASHBOURNE
HEANOR
EREWASH (B)
DERBY (B)
SOUTH DERBYSHIRE
SWADLINCOTE
LEICESTERSHIRE
Major administrative boundaries of Derbyshire
(B) Denotes Borough
Borough and District Boundaries
County Boundaries
0 5 10
Kilometres

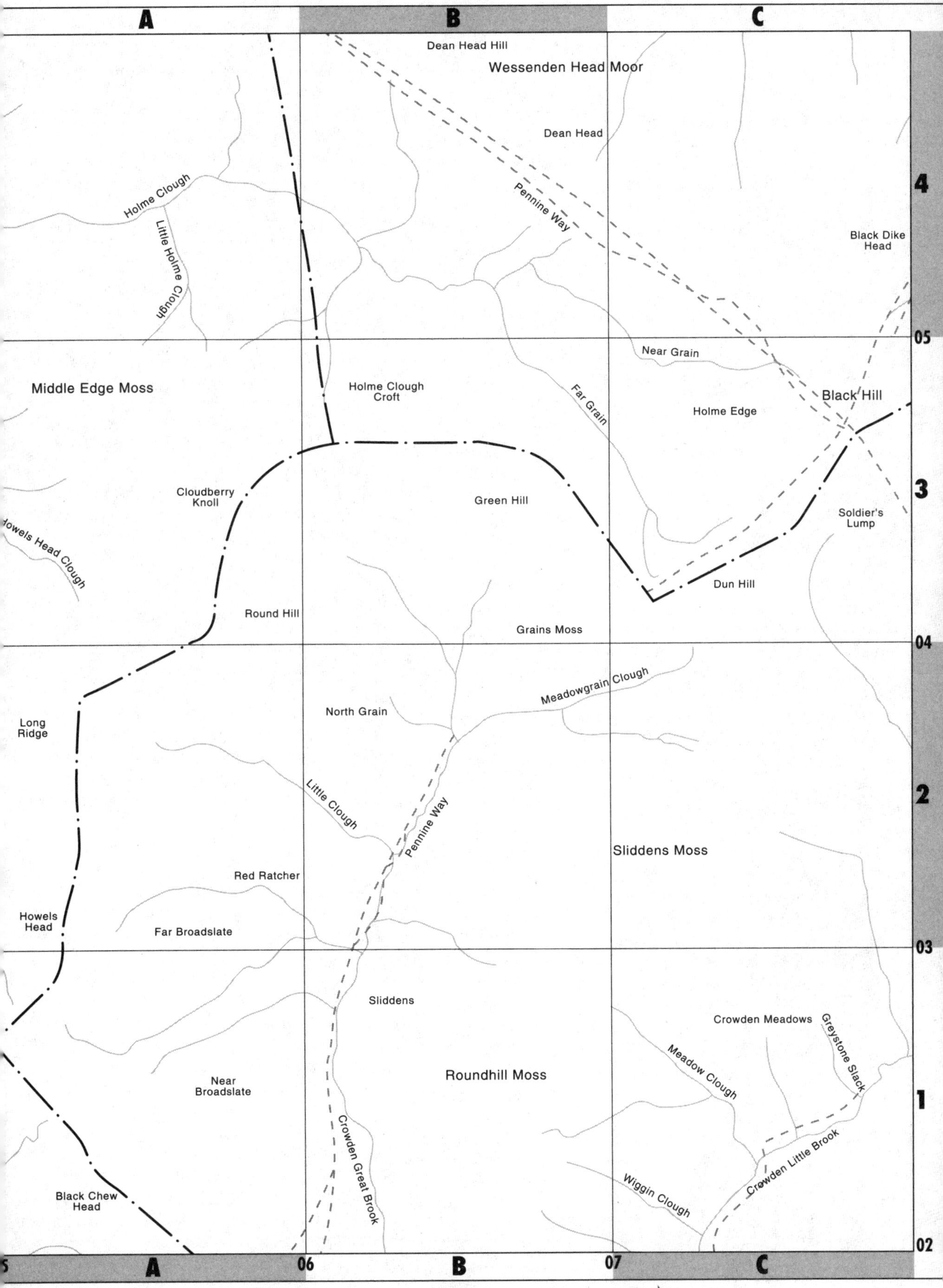
A
B
C
Dean Head Hill
Wessenden Head Moor
Dean Head
Pennine Way
Holme Clough
Little Holme Clough
Black Dike Head
4
05
Near Grain
Middle Edge Moss
Holme Clough Croft
Far Grain
Black Hill
Holme Edge
Cloudberry Knoll
Green Hill
3
Soldier's Lump
Howels Head Clough
Dun Hill
Round Hill
Grains Moss
04
Meadowgrain Clough
North Grain
Long Ridge
Little Clough
Pennine Way
2
Sliddens Moss
Red Ratcher
Howels Head
Far Broadslate
03
Sliddens
Crowden Meadows
Greystone Slack
Meadow Clough
Roundhill Moss
Near Broadslate
1
Crowden Great Brook
Crowden Little Brook
Wiggin Clough
Black Chew Head
02
06
07
A
B
C

1

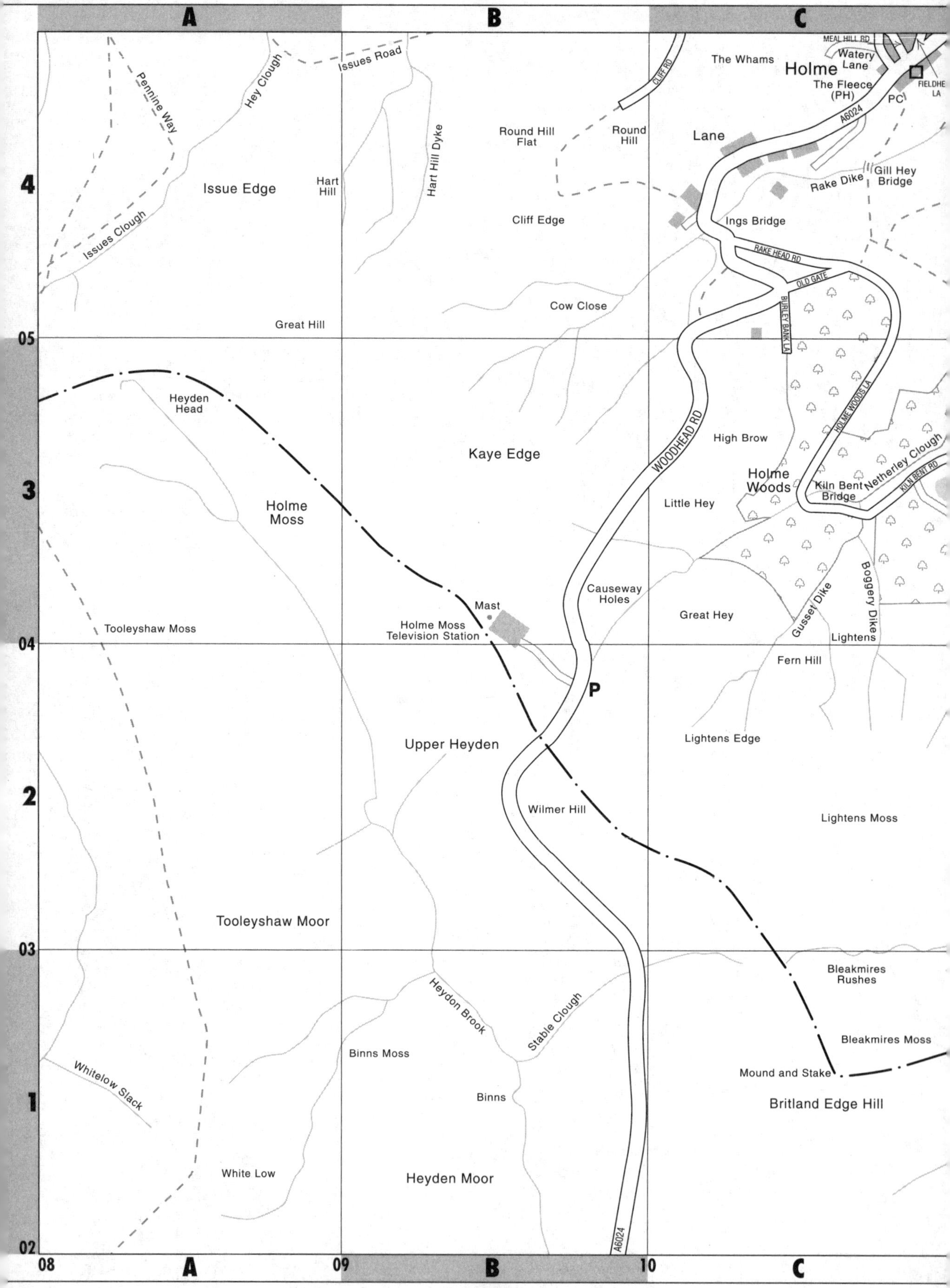
A
B
C
Issues Road
Hey Clough
Pennine Way
Issue Edge
Hart Hill
Hart Hill Dyke
Issues Clough
Great Hill
Round Hill Flat
Round Hill
CLIFF RD
Cliff Edge
Cow Close
The Whams
Holme
MEAL HILL RD
Watery Lane
The Fleece (PH)
FIELDHEAD LA
PC
A6024
Lane
Rake Dike
Gill Hey Bridge
Ings Bridge
RAKE HEAD RD
OLD GATE
BURLEY BANK LA
HOLME WOODS LA
High Brow
Netherley Clough
KILN BENT RD
Holme Woods
Kiln Bent Bridge
Little Hey
Kaye Edge
WOODHEAD RD
Heyden Head
Holme Moss
Causeway Holes
Great Hey
Gusset Dike
Boggery Dike
Lightens
Mast
Holme Moss Television Station
Tooleyshaw Moss
Fern Hill
P
Lightens Edge
Upper Heyden
Wilmer Hill
Lightens Moss
Tooleyshaw Moor
Bleakmires Rushes
Heydon Brook
Stable Clough
Bleakmires Moss
Binns Moss
Mound and Stake
Whitelow Slack
Binns
Britland Edge Hill
White Low
Heyden Moor
A6024
05
04
03
02
4
3
2
1
08
09
10

1
7

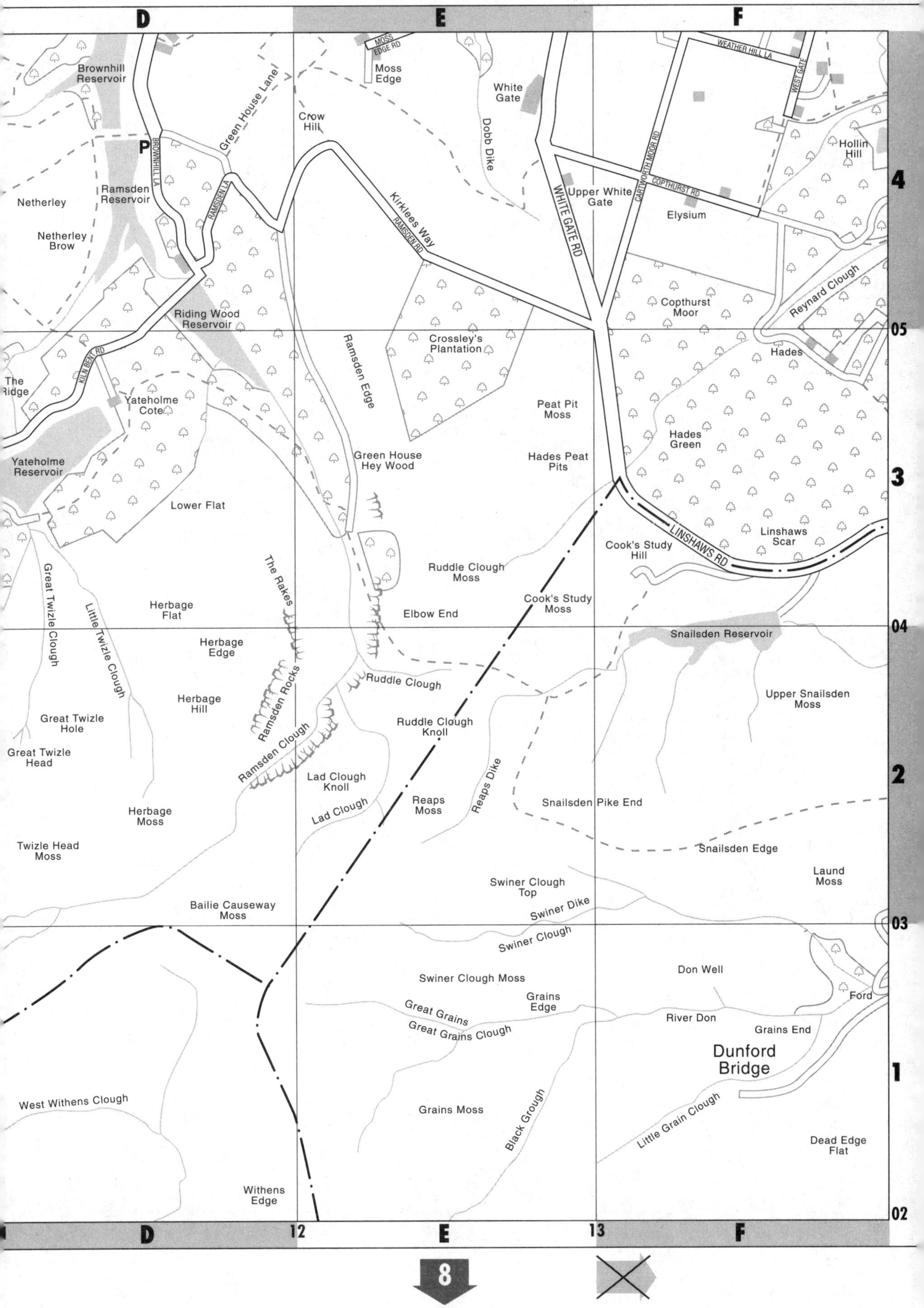
D
E
F
Brownhill Reservoir
Moss Edge
MOSS EDGE RD
White Gate
WEATHER HILL LA
WEST GATE
Green House Lane
Crow Hill
Netherley
Netherley Brow
Ramsden Reservoir
BROWNHILL LA
RAMSDEN LA
Kirklees Way
RAMSDEN RD
Dobb Dike
Upper White Gate
WHITE GATE RD
CARTWORTH MOOR RD
COPTHURST RD
Elysium
Hollin Hill
Copthurst Moor
Reynard Clough
Riding Wood Reservoir
Crossley's Plantation
Ramsden Edge
Hades
The Ridge
KILN BENT RD
Yateholme Cote
Peat Pit Moss
Hades Green
Yateholme Reservoir
Green House Hey Wood
Hades Peat Pits
Lower Flat
Linshaws Scar
LINSHAWS RD
Cook's Study Hill
Ruddle Clough Moss
The Rakes
Herbage Flat
Elbow End
Cook's Study Moss
Great Twizle Clough
Little Twizle Clough
Herbage Edge
Snailsden Reservoir
Ruddle Clough
Herbage Hill
Upper Snailsden Moss
Ramsden Rocks
Great Twizle Hole
Ruddle Clough Knoll
Great Twizle Head
Ramsden Clough
Lad Clough Knoll
Reaps Dike
Reaps Moss
Lad Clough
Snailsden Pike End
Herbage Moss
Twizle Head Moss
Snailsden Edge
Laund Moss
Swiner Clough Top
Bailie Causeway Moss
Swiner Dike
Swiner Clough
Don Well
Swiner Clough Moss
Grains Edge
Ford
Great Grains
River Don
Great Grains Clough
Grains End
Dunford Bridge
West Withens Clough
Grains Moss
Black Grough
Little Grain Clough
Dead Edge Flat
Withens Edge
4
05
3
04
2
03
1
02
12
13
D
E
F

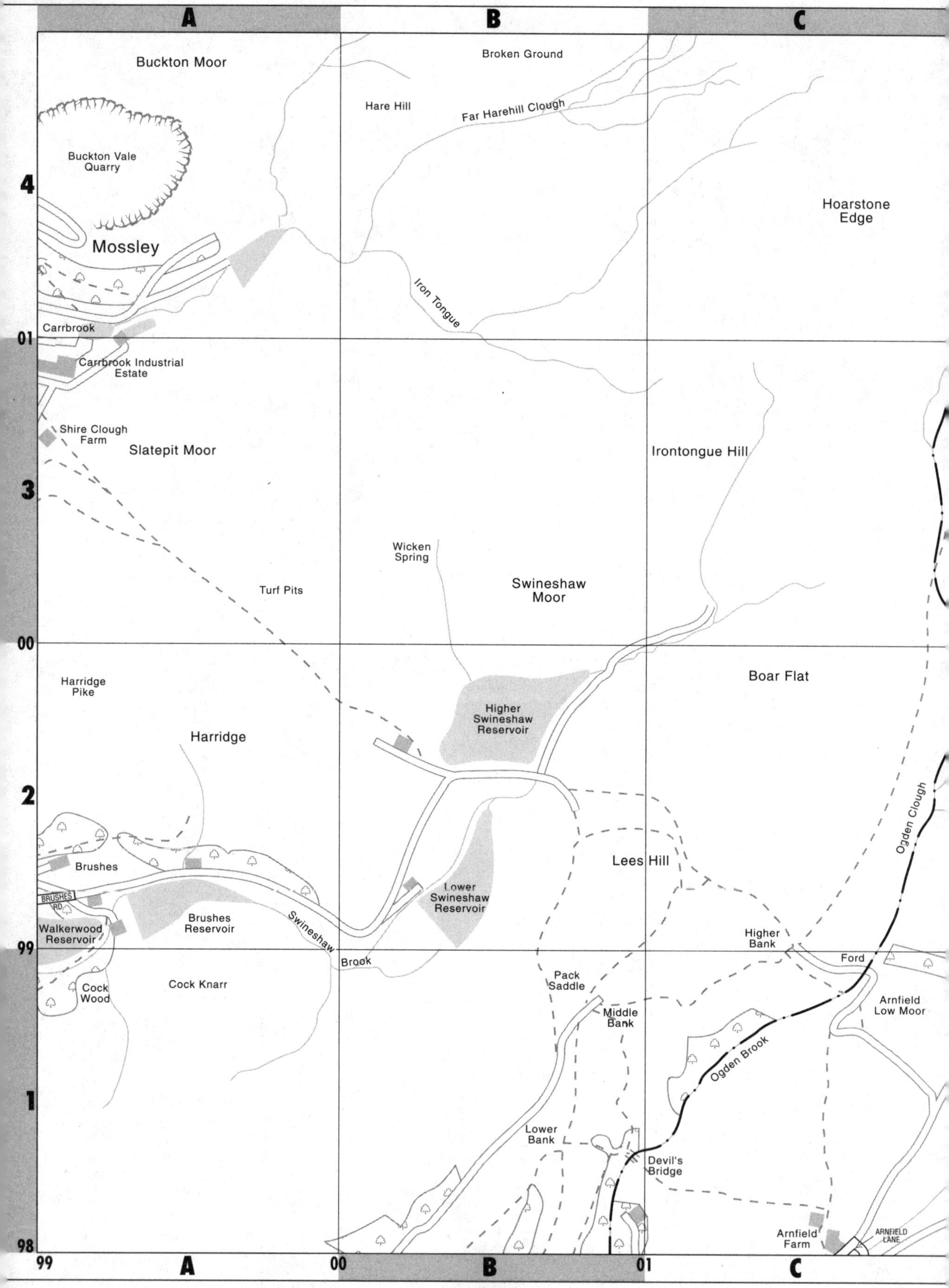
A
B
C
Buckton Moor
Broken Ground
Hare Hill
Far Harehill Clough
Buckton Vale Quarry
4
Hoarstone Edge
Mossley
Iron Tongue
Carrbrook
01
Carrbrook Industrial Estate
Shire Clough Farm
Slatepit Moor
Irontongue Hill
3
Wicken Spring
Swineshaw Moor
Turf Pits
00
Harridge Pike
Boar Flat
Higher Swineshaw Reservoir
Harridge
2
Ogden Clough
Lees Hill
Brushes
BRUSHES RD
Lower Swineshaw Reservoir
Brushes Reservoir
Swineshaw
Walkerwood Reservoir
Higher Bank
99
Brook
Ford
Pack Saddle
Cock Wood
Cock Knarr
Arnfield Low Moor
Middle Bank
Ogden Brook
1
Lower Bank
Devil's Bridge
Arnfield Farm
ARNFIELD LANE
98
99
A
00
B
01
C

6

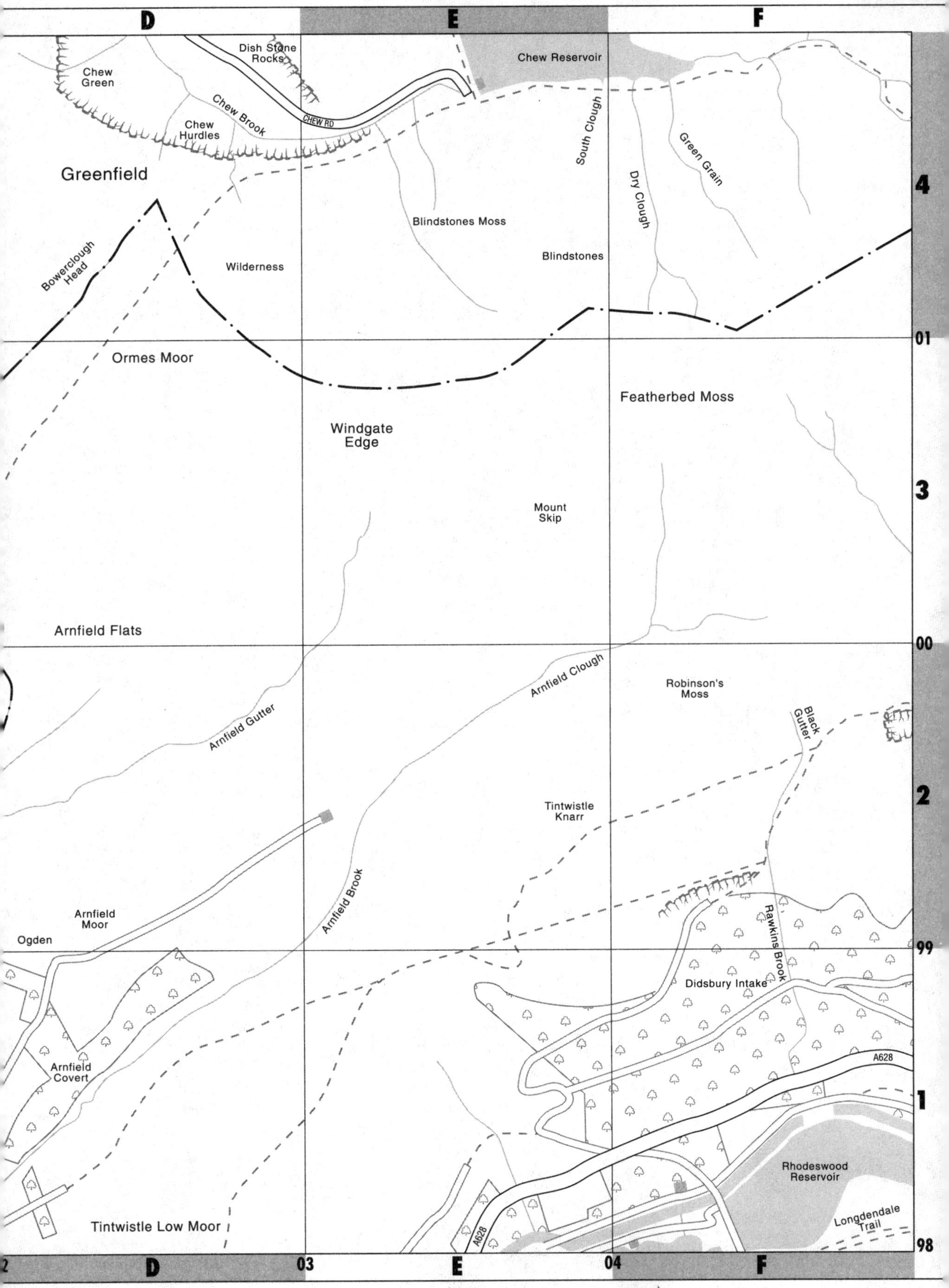
D
E
F
Chew Reservoir
Dish Stone Rocks
Chew Green
Chew Brook
CHEW RD
Chew Hurdles
Greenfield
South Clough
Dry Clough
Green Grain
Blindstones Moss
Blindstones
Bowerclough Head
Wilderness
4
01
Ormes Moor
Featherbed Moss
Windgate Edge
Mount Skip
3
Arnfield Flats
00
Arnfield Clough
Robinson's Moss
Black Gutter
Arnfield Gutter
2
Tintwistle Knarr
Arnfield Brook
Arnfield Moor
Ogden
Rawkins Brook
99
Didsbury Intake
Arnfield Covert
A628
1
Rhodeswood Reservoir
Longdendale Trail
A628
Tintwistle Low Moor
98
2
D
03
E
04
F

10
6

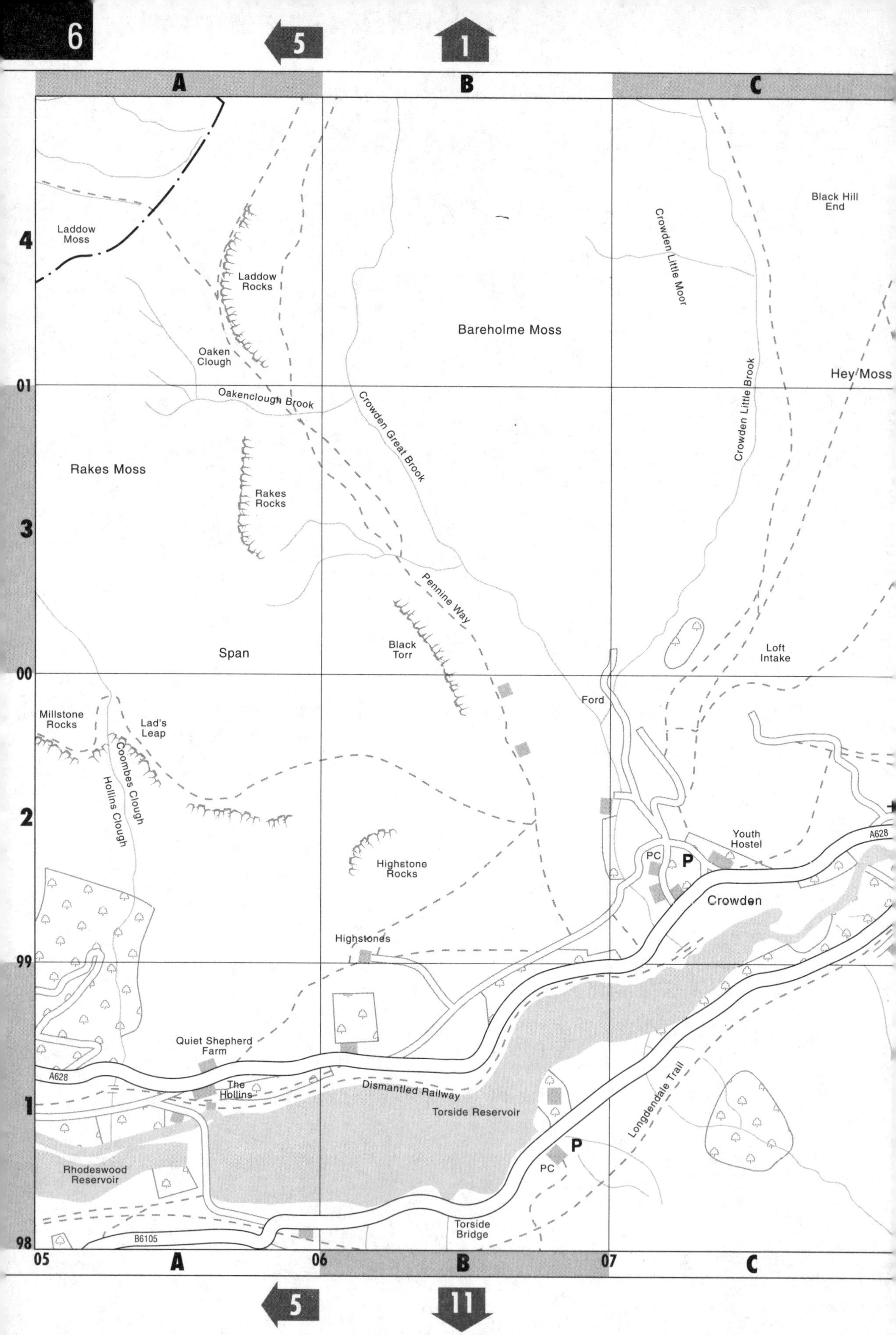
5
1
A
B
C
Laddow Moss
Laddow Rocks
Oaken Clough
Oakenclough Brook
Bareholme Moss
Crowden Little Moor
Black Hill End
Hey Moss
Crowden Little Brook
Crowden Great Brook
Rakes Moss
Rakes Rocks
Pennine Way
Black Torr
Span
Loft Intake
Ford
Millstone Rocks
Lad's Leap
Coombes Clough
Hollins Clough
Youth Hostel
PC
P
A628
Highstone Rocks
Crowden
Highstones
Quiet Shepherd Farm
The Hollins
Dismantled Railway
Torside Reservoir
Longdendale Trail
Rhodeswood Reservoir
PC
P
Torside Bridge
B6105
4
01
3
00
2
99
1
98
05
06
07
5
11

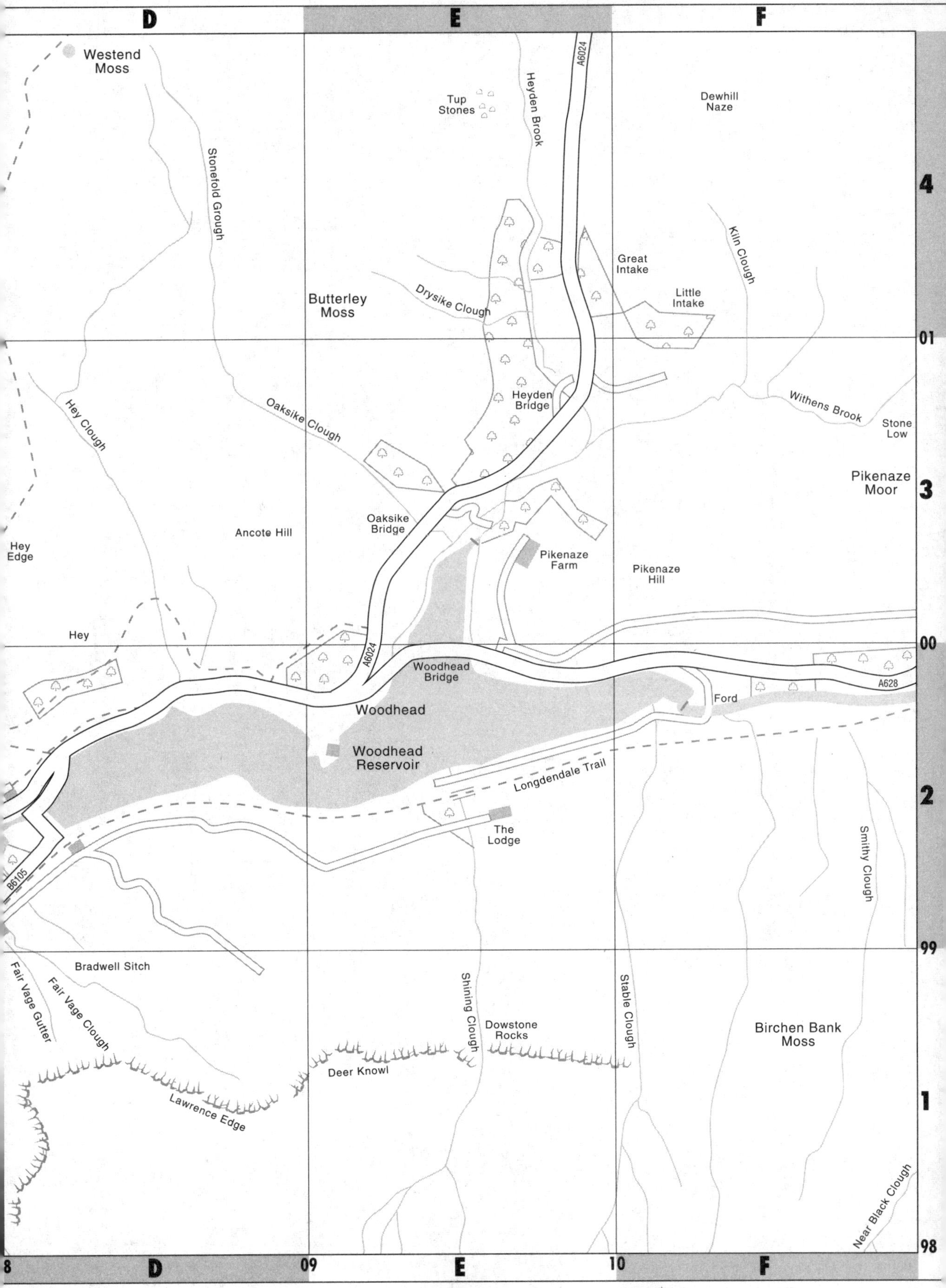
D
E
F
Westend Moss
Tup Stones
Heyden Brook
A6024
Dewhill Naze
Stonefold Grough
4
Kiln Clough
Great Intake
Little Intake
Butterley Moss
Drysike Clough
01
Heyden Bridge
Withens Brook
Stone Low
Hey Clough
Oaksike Clough
Pikenaze Moor
3
Oaksike Bridge
Hey Edge
Ancote Hill
Pikenaze Farm
Pikenaze Hill
Hey
00
Woodhead Bridge
A628
Ford
Woodhead
Woodhead Reservoir
Longdendale Trail
2
The Lodge
Smithy Clough
B6105
99
Bradwell Sitch
Fair Vage Gutter
Fair Vage Clough
Shining Clough
Stable Clough
Dowstone Rocks
Birchen Bank Moss
Deer Knowl
1
Lawrence Edge
Near Black Clough
98
8
09
10

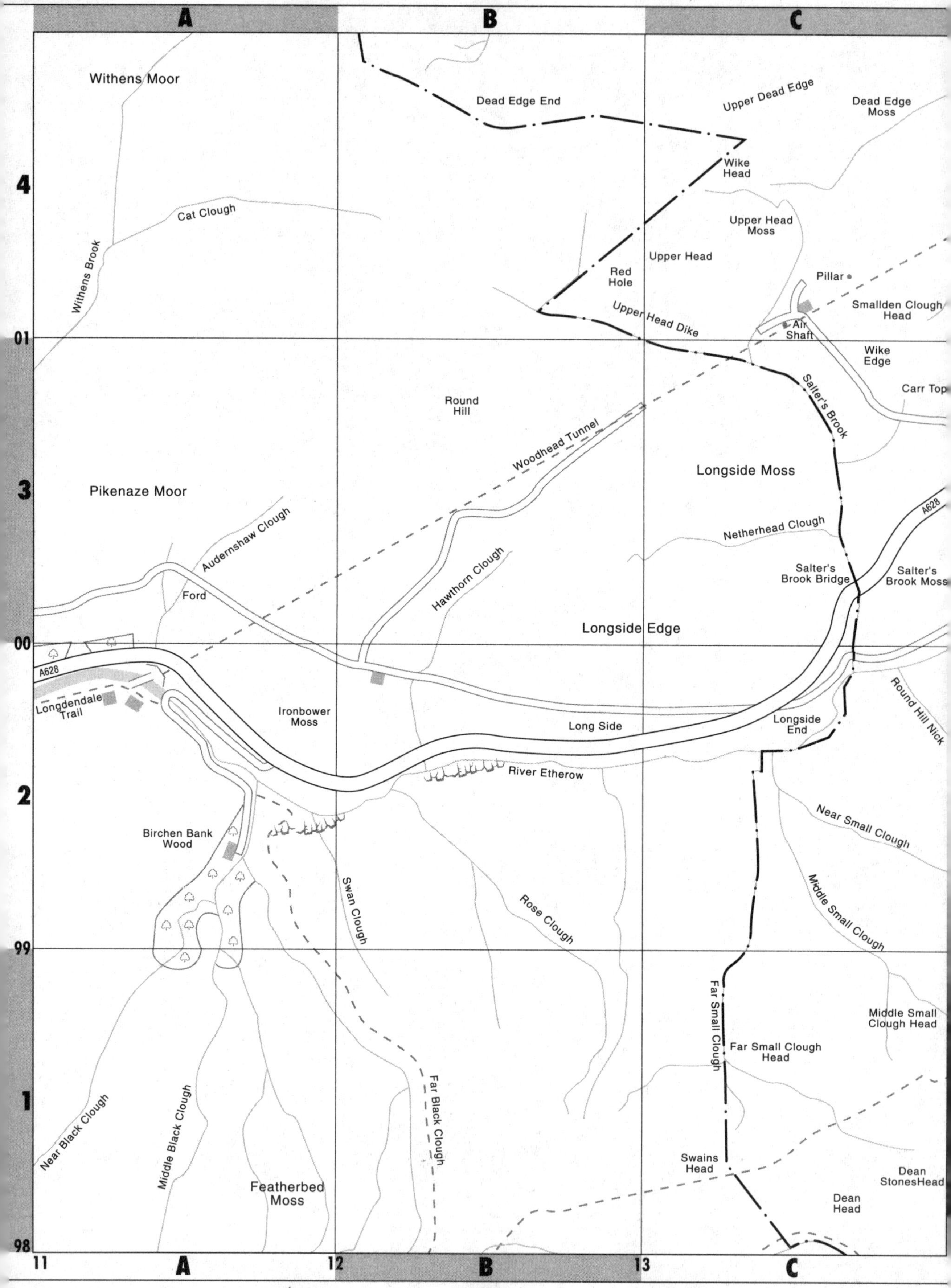
A
B
C
Withens Moor
Dead Edge End
Upper Dead Edge
Dead Edge Moss
Wike Head
Cat Clough
Withens Brook
Upper Head Moss
Upper Head
Red Hole
Pillar
Smallden Clough Head
Upper Head Dike
Air Shaft
Wike Edge
Carr Top
Round Hill
Salter's Brook
Woodhead Tunnel
Longside Moss
Pikenaze Moor
Audernshaw Clough
Netherhead Clough
A628
Hawthorn Clough
Salter's Brook Bridge
Salter's Brook Moss
Ford
Longside Edge
A628
Round Hill Nick
Longdendale Trail
Ironbower Moss
Long Side
Longside End
River Etherow
Birchen Bank Wood
Near Small Clough
Swan Clough
Middle Small Clough
Rose Clough
Far Small Clough
Middle Small Clough Head
Far Small Clough Head
Far Black Clough
Near Black Clough
Middle Black Clough
Swains Head
Dean StonesHead
Featherbed Moss
Dean Head
4
01
3
00
2
99
1
98
11
12
13
A
B
C

4
10

D
E
F
Hollingworth Hall Farm
Hollingworthall Moor
Hobson Moor Road
Hall Farm
Moorside Farm
Landslow Green
Hobson Moor
Widowscroft Farm
Hollingworth Brook
Arnfield Reservoir
Crossgates Farm
ARNFIELD LA
CROSSGATE LA
MANCHESTER RD
WOOLLEY MILL LA
WOOLLEY LA
HOBSON MOOR RD
Hardtimes Farm
Lumb Farm
Thorncliffe Farm
Thorncliffe Hall
Meadowbank Farm
Millbrook Bridge
Sewage Works
Ind Est
Mill
Works
Dismantled Railway
Hollingworth
Sch
GREEN LA
MARKET ST
DEWSNAP LA
Rabbit La
Mottram Old Hall
Coach Road
Nettle Hall Farm
MOTTRAM RD
A57
A628
A6018
BACK MOOR
STALYBRIDGE RD
HYDE RD
Mottram in Longdendale
Woolley Bridge
Woolley
WOOLLEY BRIDGE RD
HADFIELD RD
Brookfield
NEWSHAW LA
CARRHOUSE LA
Carr House
River Etherow
Melandra Castle ROMAN FORT
Cemy
Warhill
Hattersley
Targeton Hill
Mudd
Lower Mudd Farm
LITTLEMOOR RD
BROADBOTTOM RD
CHURCH RD
The Hague
Sewage Works
Carrhouse Lane
Lower Gamesley
Gamesley
Glossop Brook
SHAW LA
DINTING RD
Dinting Vale
Dinting Viaduct
Resrs
Mottram Hill
Hague Road
Pingot Lane
GORSEY BROW
HILLEND LA
Robin Wood
Bankwood Mill
Robinwood Farm
GLOSSOP RD
A626
97
96
95
94
4
3
2
1
00
01

16
10

9
5

A
B
C
4
97
3
96
2
95
1
94
02
03
04
Townhead Farm
Valehouse Wood
Valehouse Reservoir
Old House
Deepclough
B6105
Higher Deepclough
A628
WOODHEAD RD
Tintwistle
LOWER SQ
HIGHER SQ
ARNFIELD LA
OLD RD
THE STOCKS
CHAPEL BROW
CHURCH ST
A628
Cockerhill
Valehouse Farm
Sch
BANK LA
NEW RD
Devil's Elbow
Nell's Pike
Ogden Clough
Tintwistle Bridge
Bottoms Reservoir
GODDARD LA
WATERSIDE
PETER ST
BROSSCROFT VIL
BROSSCROFT
THE LODGE
Longdendale Trail
Reservoir
Reservoir
Peak Naze
BANKBOTTOM
JONES ST
OSBORNE PL
STATION RD
Hadfield
1 THE CROSS
2 WARHURST FOLD
3 OLD HALL SQ
JACKSON ST
PADFIELD MAIN RD
PEEL ST
Sch
RHODES ST
BARBER ST
POST ST
REGENT ST
TEMPLE ST
TEMPLE AVE
Padfield
Reservoir
WOODHEAD RD
Blackshaw
Little Padfield Farm
LEES ROW
PLATT ST
Sch
Liby
PC
CHAPEL LA
RAILWAY ST
Hadfield Station
Hadfield Mills
MARLOW ST
Upper Swineshaw Resr
Sch
CHURCH ST
QUEEN ST
SOUTH MARLOW
PARK RD
REDGATE
ST ANDREWS CT
GLADSTONE ST
MARLOW BROW
PARK RD
Cemy
PC
Swineshaw Resr
THE AVENUE
LITTLEBROOK CL
BANKSWOOD CL
GODDARD RD
Banks Wood
Castlehill Wood
Bettenhill
CEMETERY RD
Cat Wood
Broom Hill
Sch
Mast
Mouselow
NORTH RD
Reservoir
Laneside Farm
HILLTOP RD
SHAW LA
Wimberryhill
The Heath
Mouselow Quarry
Hilltop
Hospl
Hospl
BEXLEY CL
BOWDEN RD
KINGSMOOR FIELDS
SHIRE WAY
CASTLE HILL
BUTE ST
HOPE ST
CHARLES LA
Moorside
PARK CRES
Howard Park
HAYWARDS CL
FERNHILL CL
HEATH RD
HOPE ST
Dinting Junction
GLOSSOP
PC
Sch
RAMSDEN CL
Sch
THORPE ST
DUNNE LA
BACKSHAW
WELL GATE
WATER ST
SMEDLEY PL
WESLEY ST
HOWARD CL
CHURCH ST
CHURCH WLK
CHURCH ST S
SHEPLEY ST
Shell Brook
Higher Dinting
ASHES LA
TALBOT RD
HALL MEADOW RD
KINGSMOOR RD
Sch
Old Glossop
Dinting Station
Mus
BIRCHSIDE AVE
ELM GR
ASHLEIGH AVE
SPIRE HOLLIN
Sch
OLD HALL CL
KING'S PARK CL
CHURCH CL
MANOR PARK VIEW
Hall Fold Farm
MANOR PARK RD
Manor Park
Shire Hill
LC
DINTING RD
TEN FOOT CL
Trad Est
DINTING LA
CEDAR CL
SPINNEY CL
Sch
FAUVEL RD
NORFOLK ST
KENT RD
ROYLE AVE
Sch
Works
Lower Dinting Mill
Liby
LORD ST
FAUVEL PL
Off
TALBOT ST
FITZALAN ST
BOOTH'S CT
DROVERS WLK
PC
A57
DINTING VALE
WREN NEST RD
GOSBROOK RD
SURREY ST
HOWARD ST
CHARLES ST
KING EDWARD AVE
RIVERSIDE CL
Sch
JORDAN ST
YORK ST
PYEGROVE RD
WOODCOCK GR
QUEEN'S DR
PYEGROVE
Sch
PC
HIGH ST W
WREN NEST TERR
HALL'S CT
EDWARD ST
ARUNDEL ST
PC
Sta
B6105
ELLISON ST
SMITHY CL
QUARRY CL
MANOR ST
REGENT ST
CORN ST
PC
SHEFFIELD RD
A57
ARNFIELD GRANGE
SIMMONDLEY LA
ARNFIELD GRNG
PRIMROSE LA
A6016
HUGH ST
SPRING ST
COOPER ST
SUMMERS PL
QUEEN ST
SUNLAWS ST
Sch
ST MARY'S RD
BROOK ST
GEORGE ST
Amb Sta
BERNARD ST
CROSS ST
MARKET ST
HENRY ST
STATION ST
NRFLK SQ
VCTRA ST
SMITHY FOLD
Off
HIGH ST E
MILLTOWN
SHIREBROOK DR
CROFT MANOR
SILK ST
THOMAS ST
BIRCH GREEN
BROOK MEADOW
COWBROOK AVE
DOVEDALE CT
PARTINGTON CT
MILLERSDALE CT
HILLWOOD DR
HURSTBROOK CL
HURST RD
FAIRWAYS CL
HATHERSAGE DR
A
B
C
9
17

6
12

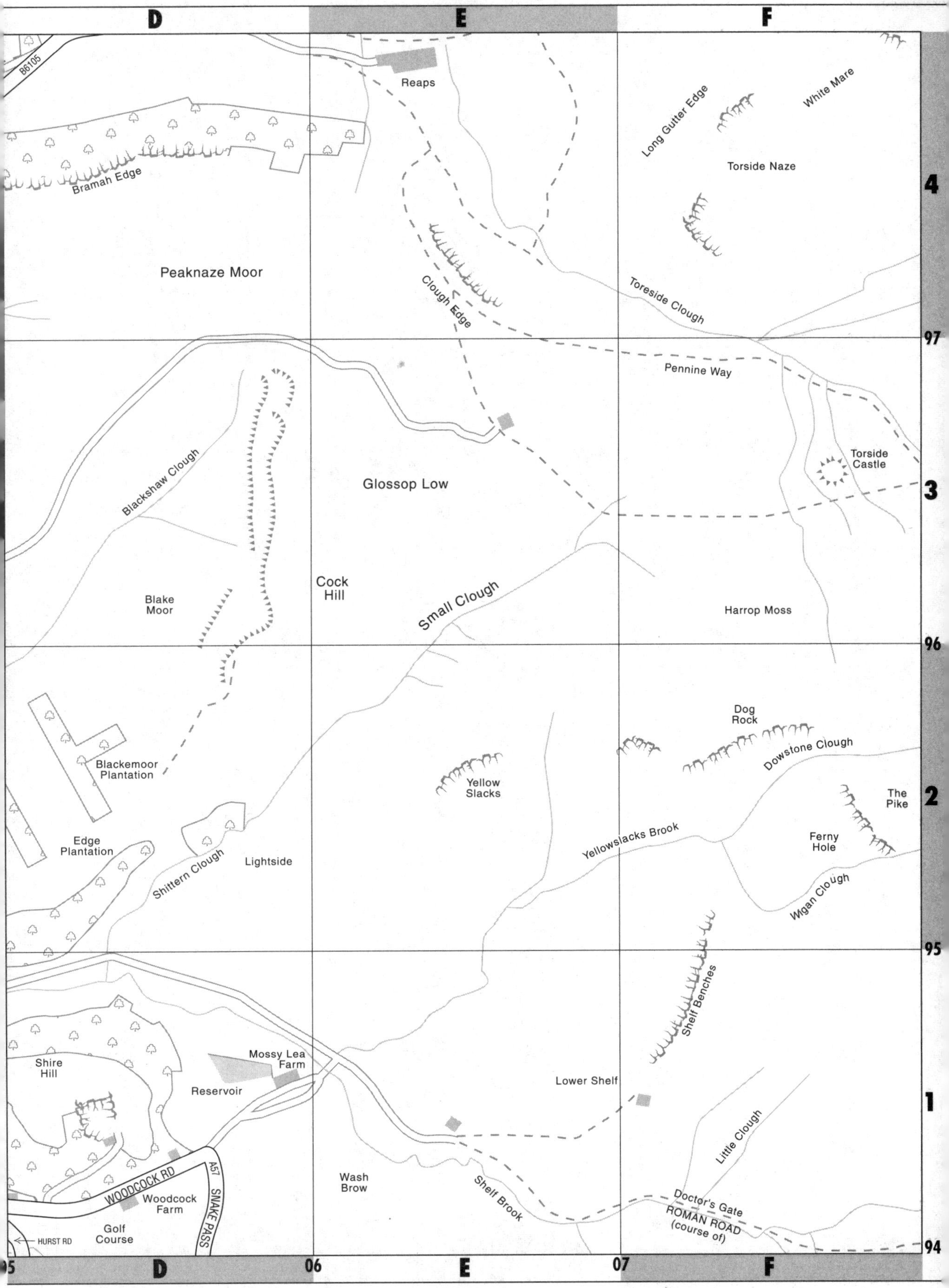
D
E
F
B6105
Reaps
Bramah Edge
Peaknaze Moor
Long Gutter Edge
White Mare
Torside Naze
Clough Edge
Toreside Clough
4
97
Pennine Way
Blackshaw Clough
Glossop Low
Torside Castle
3
Cock Hill
Blake Moor
Small Clough
Harrop Moss
96
Dog Rock
Dowstone Clough
Blackemoor Plantation
Yellow Slacks
The Pike
2
Edge Plantation
Yellowslacks Brook
Ferny Hole
Shittern Clough
Lightside
Wigan Clough
95
Shelf Benches
Mossy Lea Farm
Shire Hill
Reservoir
Lower Shelf
1
Little Clough
WOODCOCK RD
A57
SNAKE PASS
Woodcock Farm
Wash Brow
Shelf Brook
Doctor's Gate
ROMAN ROAD (course of)
HURST RD
Golf Course
94
05
06
07

18
12

11
7

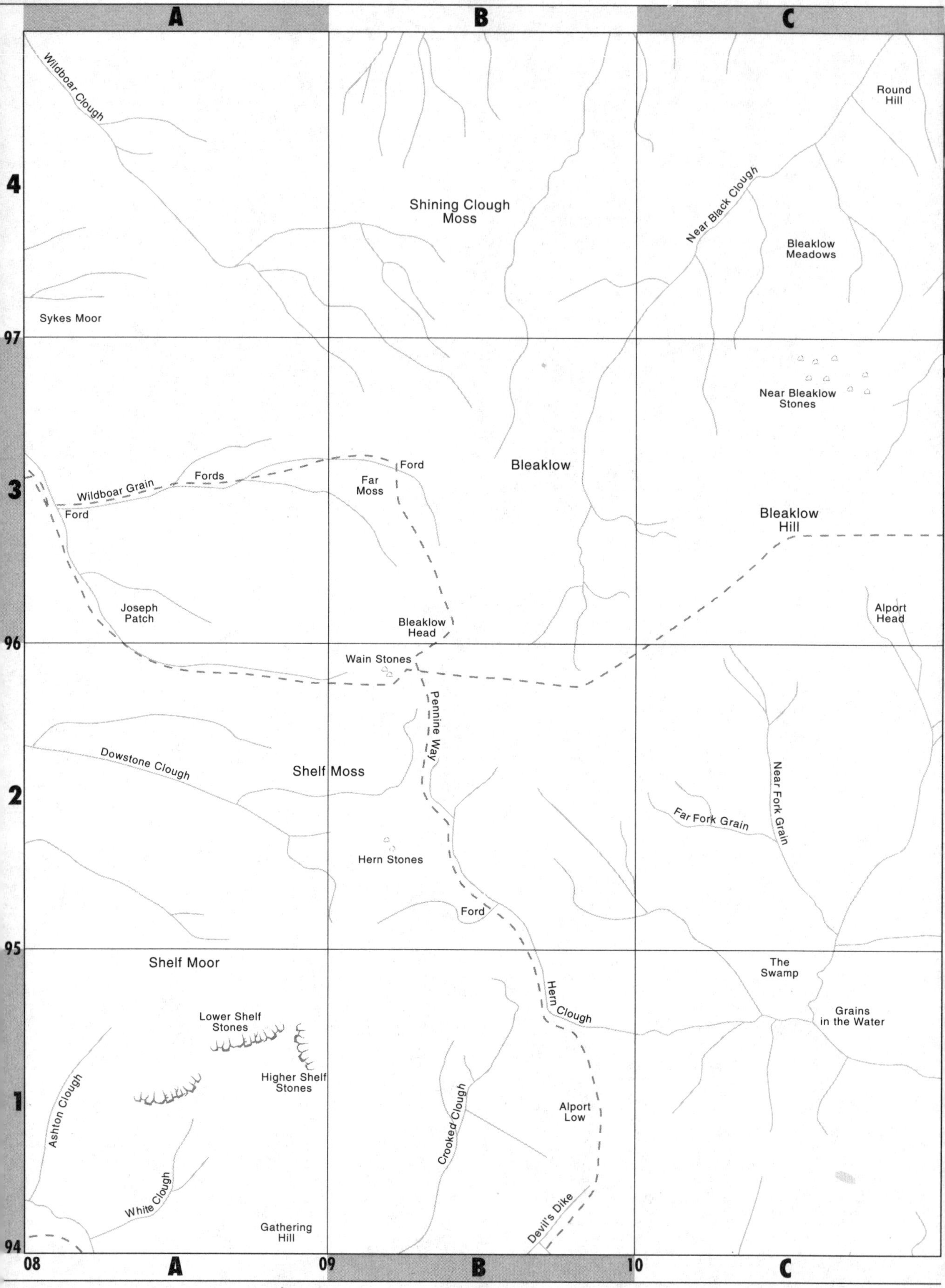
A
B
C
Wildboar Clough
Round Hill
4
Shining Clough Moss
Near Black Clough
Bleaklow Meadows
Sykes Moor
97
Near Bleaklow Stones
Ford
Bleaklow
Fords
Far Moss
3
Wildboar Grain
Ford
Bleaklow Hill
Joseph Patch
Bleaklow Head
Alport Head
96
Wain Stones
Pennine Way
Dowstone Clough
Shelf Moss
2
Near Fork Grain
Far Fork Grain
Hern Stones
Ford
95
Shelf Moor
The Swamp
Hern Clough
Lower Shelf Stones
Grains in the Water
Higher Shelf Stones
1
Ashton Clough
Crooked Clough
Alport Low
White Clough
Devil's Dike
Gathering Hill
94
08
A
09
B
10
C

11
19

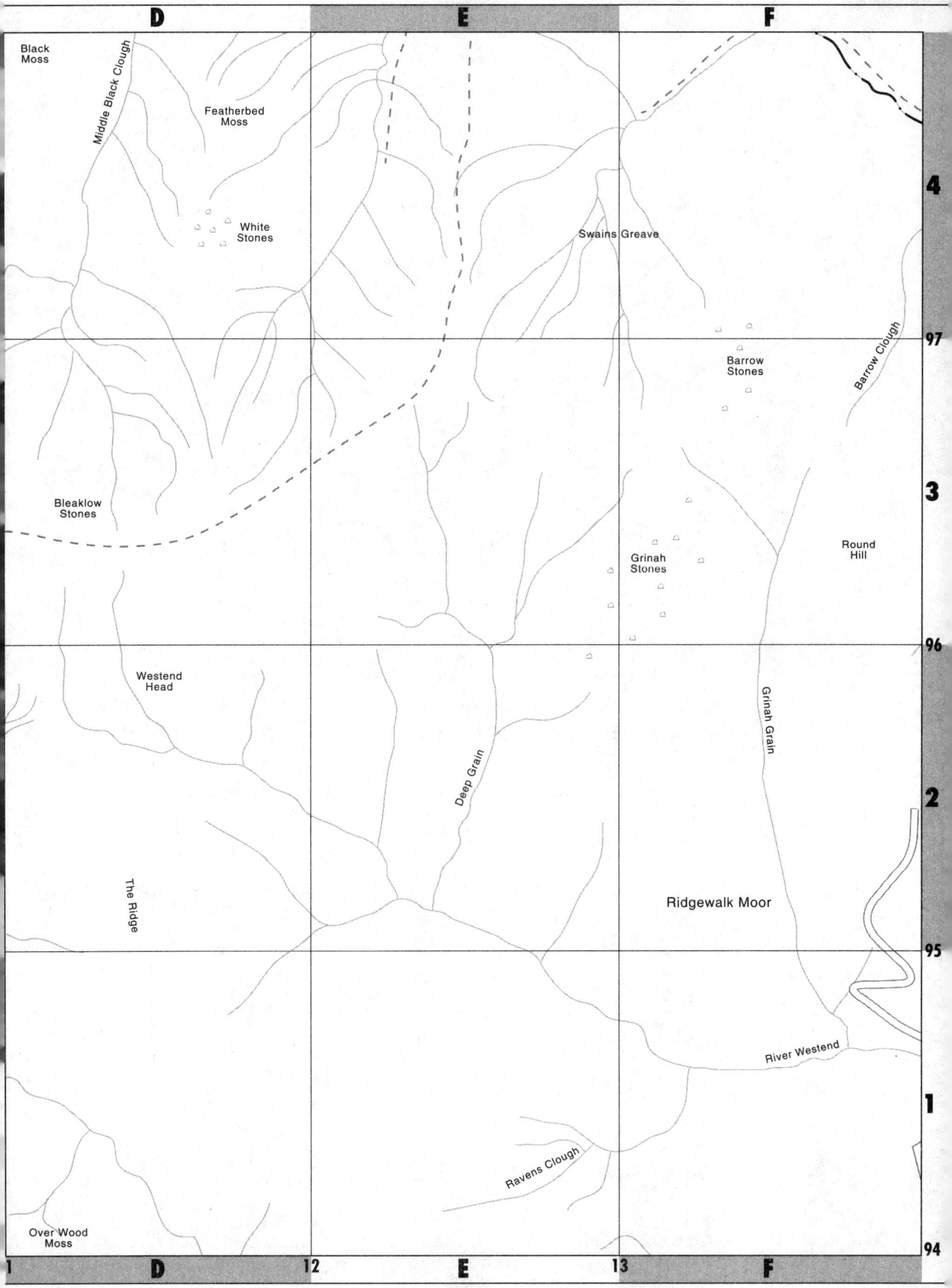
D
E
F
Black Moss
Middle Black Clough
Featherbed Moss
White Stones
Swains Greave
4
97
Barrow Stones
Barrow Clough
Bleaklow Stones
3
Grinah Stones
Round Hill
96
Westend Head
Grinah Grain
Deep Grain
2
The Ridge
Ridgewalk Moor
95
River Westend
1
Ravens Clough
Over Wood Moss
94
1
D
12
E
13
F

A B C

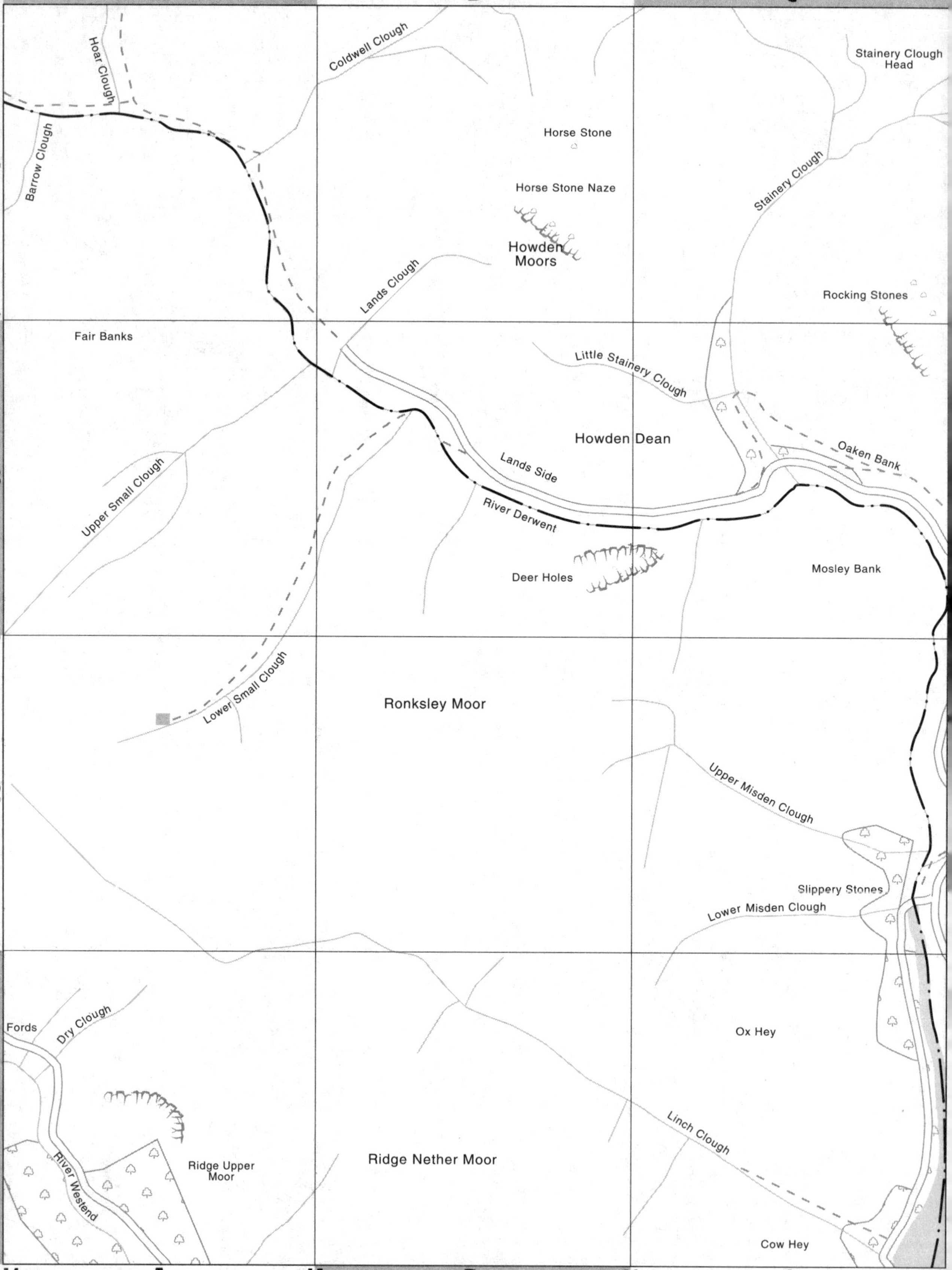
Coldwell Clough
Hoar Clough
Stainery Clough Head
Horse Stone
Barrow Clough
Horse Stone Naze
Stainery Clough
Howden Moors
Lands Clough
Rocking Stones
Fair Banks
Little Stainery Clough
Howden Dean
Oaken Bank
Lands Side
Upper Small Clough
River Derwent
Deer Holes
Mosley Bank
Lower Small Clough
Ronksley Moor
Upper Misden Clough
Slippery Stones
Lower Misden Clough
Ox Hey
Fords
Dry Clough
Linch Clough
River Westend
Ridge Upper Moor
Ridge Nether Moor
Cow Hey
4
97
3
96
2
95
1
94
14
15
16

A B C

16

D E F

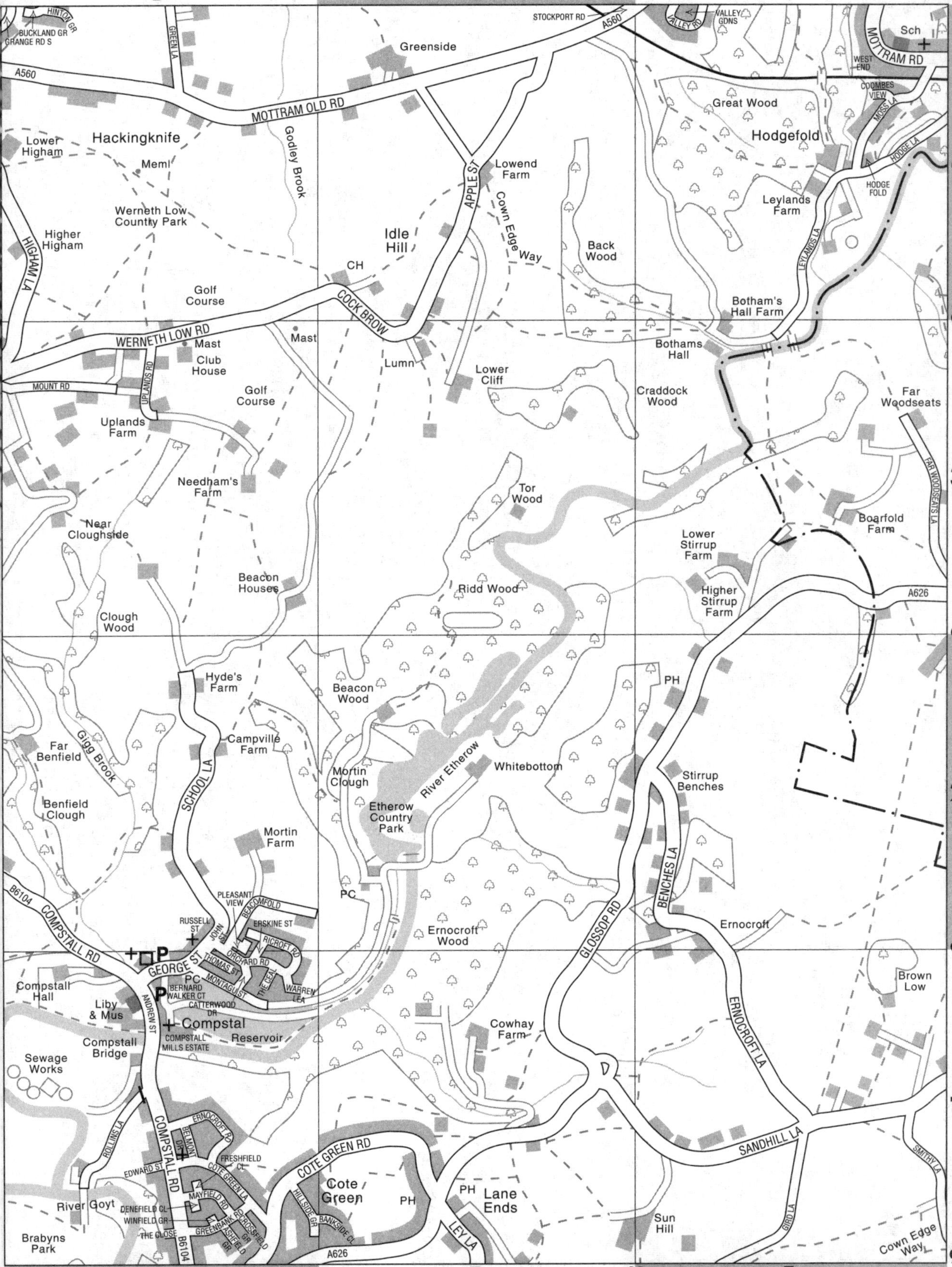

D E F

23

16

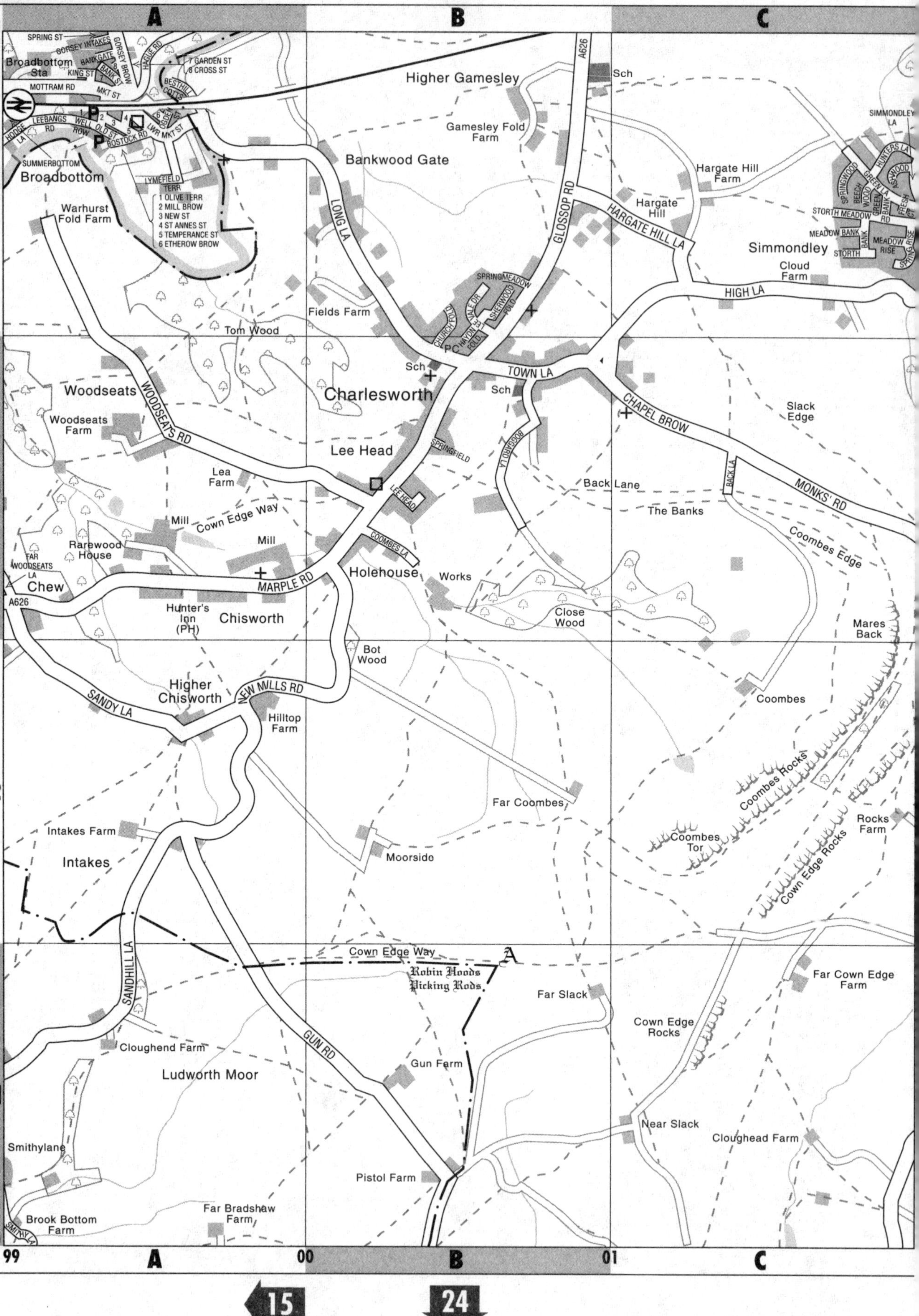
A
B
C
Broadbottom Sta
Broadbottom
SPRING ST
GORSEY INTAKES
GORSEY BROW
HAGUE RD
7 GARDEN ST
8 CROSS ST
MOTTRAM RD
MKT ST
BESTHILL COTTS
LEEBANGS RD
HODGE LA
WELL OLD ST
BOSTOCK RD
LWR MKT ST
SUMMERBOTTOM
LYMEFIELD TERR
1 OLIVE TERR
2 MILL BROW
3 NEW ST
4 ST ANNES ST
5 TEMPERANCE ST
6 ETHEROW BROW
Warhurst Fold Farm
Higher Gamesley
Gamesley Fold Farm
Bankwood Gate
Sch
A626
GLOSSOP RD
LONG LA
Hargate Hill Farm
Hargate Hill
HARGATE HILL LA
SIMMONDLEY LA
Simmondley
Cloud Farm
HIGH LA
STORTH MEADOW RD
MEADOW BANK
MEADOW RISE
Fields Farm
Tom Wood
CHURCH FOLD
SPRING MEADOW
SHERWOOD FOLD
PC
TOWN LA
Woodseats
Woodseats Farm
WOODSEATS RD
Charlesworth
Lee Head
SPRINGFIELD
CHAPEL BROW
Slack Edge
Lea Farm
Back Lane
BACK LA
MONKS' RD
The Banks
Mill
Cown Edge Way
Rarewood House
FAR WOODSEATS LA
Chew
MARPLE RD
COOMBES LA
Holehouse
Works
Coombes Edge
Hunter's Inn (PH)
Chisworth
Close Wood
Mares Back
Bot Wood
Higher Chisworth
NEW MILLS RD
SANDY LA
Hilltop Farm
Coombes
Coombes Rocks
Far Coombes
Intakes Farm
Intakes
Moorside
Coombes Tor
Rocks Farm
Cown Edge Rocks
Cown Edge Way
Robin Hoods Picking Rods
Far Slack
Far Cown Edge Farm
SANDHILL LA
Cown Edge Rocks
Cloughend Farm
GUN RD
Ludworth Moor
Gun Farm
Near Slack
Cloughead Farm
Smithylane
Pistol Farm
Far Bradshaw Farm
Brook Bottom Farm
4
93
3
92
2
91
1
90
99
00
01

10
18

D
E
F
4
3
2
1
93
92
91
90
2
03
04
Schs
Sch
Mun Bdg
PC
The Bank
Whitfield
Bridgefield
Simmondley
Old Lane
Hobroyd Farm
Works
F Sta
Charlestown
Lees Hall Farm
Lees Hall
Whiteley Nab
Herod Farm
Oak Wood
Sitch
Cown Edge Rocks
Long Clough
Shaw Moor Plantation
Chunal
Lane Ends Farm
Gnat Hole
LEAN TOWN
Whitfield Barn Farm
Carr Farm
Brownhill
Jumble
Hurstnook Farm
Moorfield
The Twitchlings
Worm Stones
Shaw Moor
Whitethorn Clough
Shooting Cabin
Chunal Moor
Higher Plainstead Farm
Plainsteads Farm
Butcher's Piece Farm
Knarrs Nook
Near Plainsteads
Hollingworth Head Farm
The Grouse (PH)
Chunal Plantation
Harry Hut
Knarrs
Matley Moor
Burnt Hill
A6016
A624
SIMMONDLEY LA
SIMMONDLEY NEW RD
SIMMONDLEY GR
HIGH LA
HIGHVIEW
PRIMROSE LA
PRIMROSE CRES
PRIMROSE HILL
SLATELANDS RD
SLATELANDS AVE
HOLLIN CROSS LA
TURNLEE RD
TURNLEE CL
CHARLESTOWN RD
CHARLESTOWN
CHUNAL LA
GLOSSOP RD
MONK'S RD
VICTORIA ST
GLADSTONE ST
HAGUE ST
CLIFFE RD
KIDD RD
DERBYSHIRE LEVEL
MORLEY ST
HIGHFIELD RD
UPLANDS RD
WHITFIELD CROSS
WHITFIELD AVE
PADFIELD GATE
KING CHARLES CT
CROSSLANDS CL
LOWER BANK
CROSS CLIFFE
SHREBROOK DR
SLANT CL
PHILIP HOWARD RD
MARKET ST
GEORGE ST
ST MARY'S RD
TREDCROFT ST
QUEEN ST
PIKE'S LA
SUNLAWS ST
CHADWICK ST
SUNNY BANKS
BROOKSIDE
LONGCLOUGH DR
BRENDON
BOWLAND RD
ARUNDEL GRANGE
BEECH AVE
PENNINE RD
COTSWOLD CL
SIMONS CL
SIMONS WLK
ARDEN CL
HIGHWOOD CL
HEATHER BANK
LONGMOOR RD
WERNETH RD
MELANIE CL
TARNSIDE FOLD
THE GREEN
STORTH MEADOW RD
DINGLE CL
PEAKNAZE CL
WILSON'S TERR
KINDER
ASHTON ST
JACKSON ST
RIVERVIEW COTTS
LEE MOUNT
TURNLEE DR
YORK TERR
UNITY WLK
EBENEZER ST
FREETOWN
KERSHAW ST
WOOD ST
TODD ST
NURSERY
SOUDERBY ST
SEFTON
PARK TERR
DUKES
PRINCESS
STAFFORD CL
GORSE WAY
SANDIWAY
WORCESTER GR
LEICESTER
YORKSHIRE
HAMPSHIRE CL
WILTSHIRE
SHROPSHIRE
RIVERBANK
WINGFIELD
HIGHBANK RD
BRACKEN WAY
SOUTH VIEW RD
LINACRE WAY
HATHERSAGE DR
WARWICK CL
GLOUCESTER WAY
HEBDEN CL
WINNATS CL
PEVERIL CT
DERWENT CL
FURNESS CL
ASHBOURNE

25
18

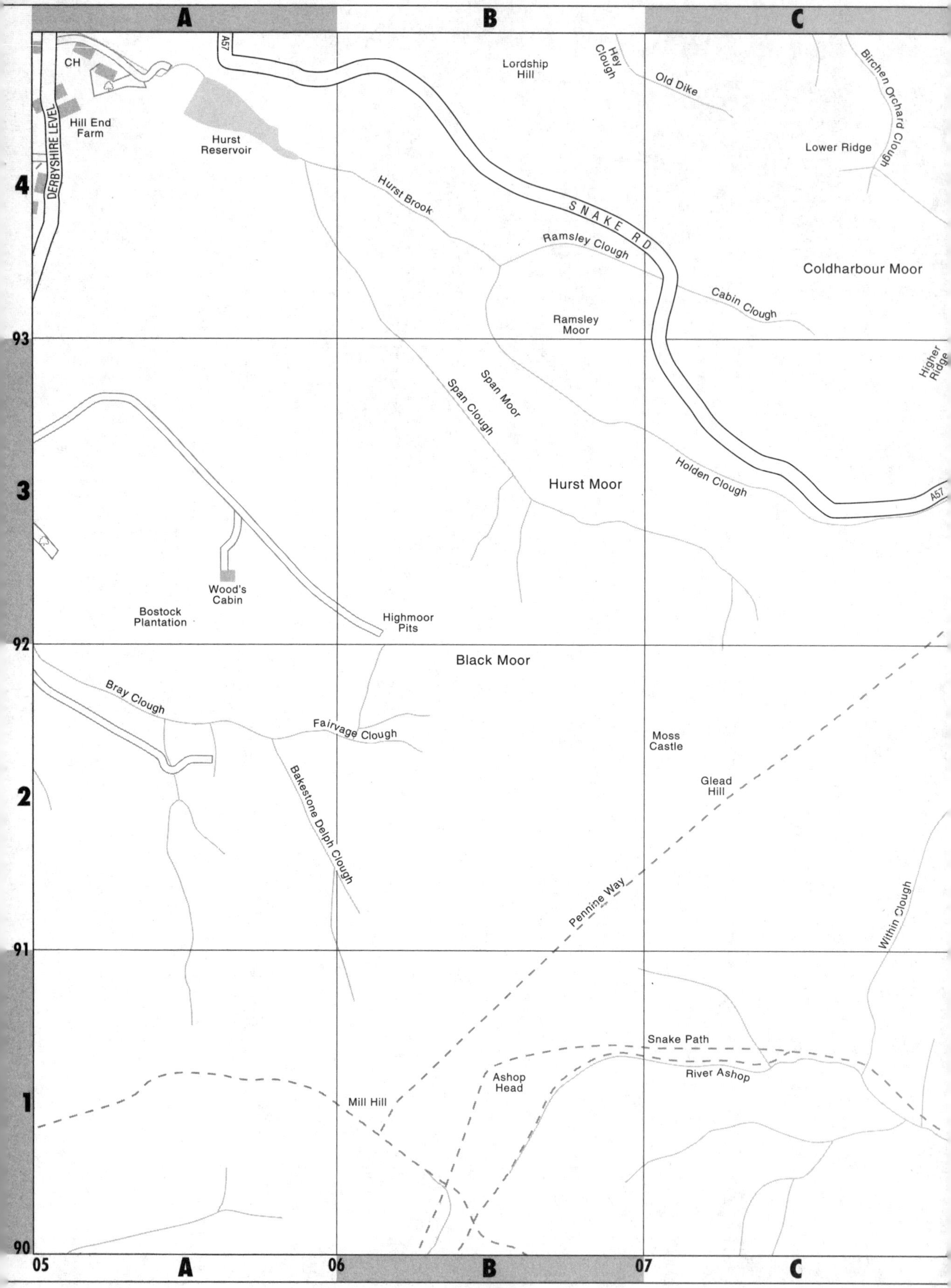
A
B
C
CH
Hill End Farm
DERBYSHIRE LEVEL
A57
Hurst Reservoir
Lordship Hill
Hey Clough
Old Dike
Birchen Orchard Clough
Lower Ridge
Hurst Brook
SNAKE RD
Ramsley Clough
Coldharbour Moor
Cabin Clough
Ramsley Moor
Higher Ridge
Span Moor
Span Clough
Hurst Moor
Holden Clough
A57
Wood's Cabin
Bostock Plantation
Highmoor Pits
Black Moor
Bray Clough
Fairvage Clough
Moss Castle
Glead Hill
Bakestone Delph Clough
Pennine Way
Within Clough
Snake Path
Ashop Head
River Ashop
Mill Hill
4
93
3
92
2
91
1
90
05
06
07

12 20

D
E
F
Rose Clough
Crooked Clough
Devil's Dike
Upper North Grain
Doctor's Gate
ROMAN ROAD
(course of)
Urchin Clough
Old Woman
Pennine Way
Snake Pass
Doctor's Gate
Culvert
SNAKE RD
ROMAN ROAD
Nether North Grain
Thomason's Hollow
Featherbed
Moss
Lady Clough Moor
Featherbed
Top
Salvin Ridge
Within Clough
Lady Clough
Upper Gate Clough
Snake
Plantations
Nether Gate Clough
Red Clough
Saukin Ridge
A57
Ashop Clough
Rough Bank
Urchin Clough
Snake Path
River Ashop
Black Ashop Moor
4
93
3
92
2
91
1
90
8
09
10
P

27 20

19
13

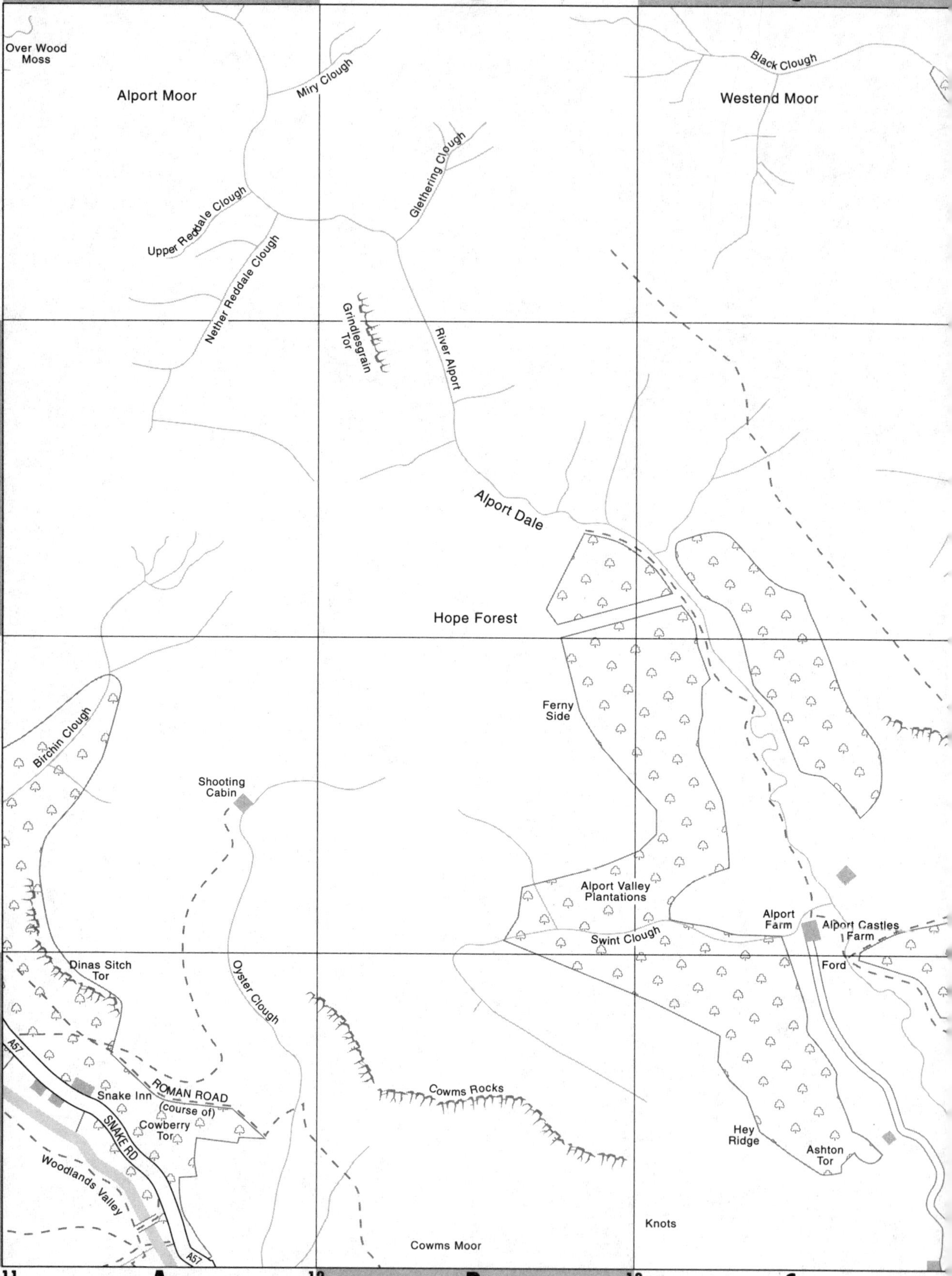
A
B
C
Over Wood Moss
Alport Moor
Miry Clough
Black Clough
Westend Moor
4
Glethering Clough
Upper Reddale Clough
Nether Reddale Clough
93
Grindlesgrain Tor
River Alport
3
Alport Dale
Hope Forest
92
Ferny Side
Birchin Clough
2
Shooting Cabin
Alport Valley Plantations
Alport Farm
Alport Castles Farm
Swint Clough
91
Dinas Sitch Tor
Oyster Clough
Ford
A57
Snake Inn
ROMAN ROAD (course of)
Cowms Rocks
1
Cowberry Tor
SNAKE RD
Hey Ridge
Ashton Tor
Woodlands Valley
Knots
Cowms Moor
90
A57
11
12
13
A
B
C

19
28

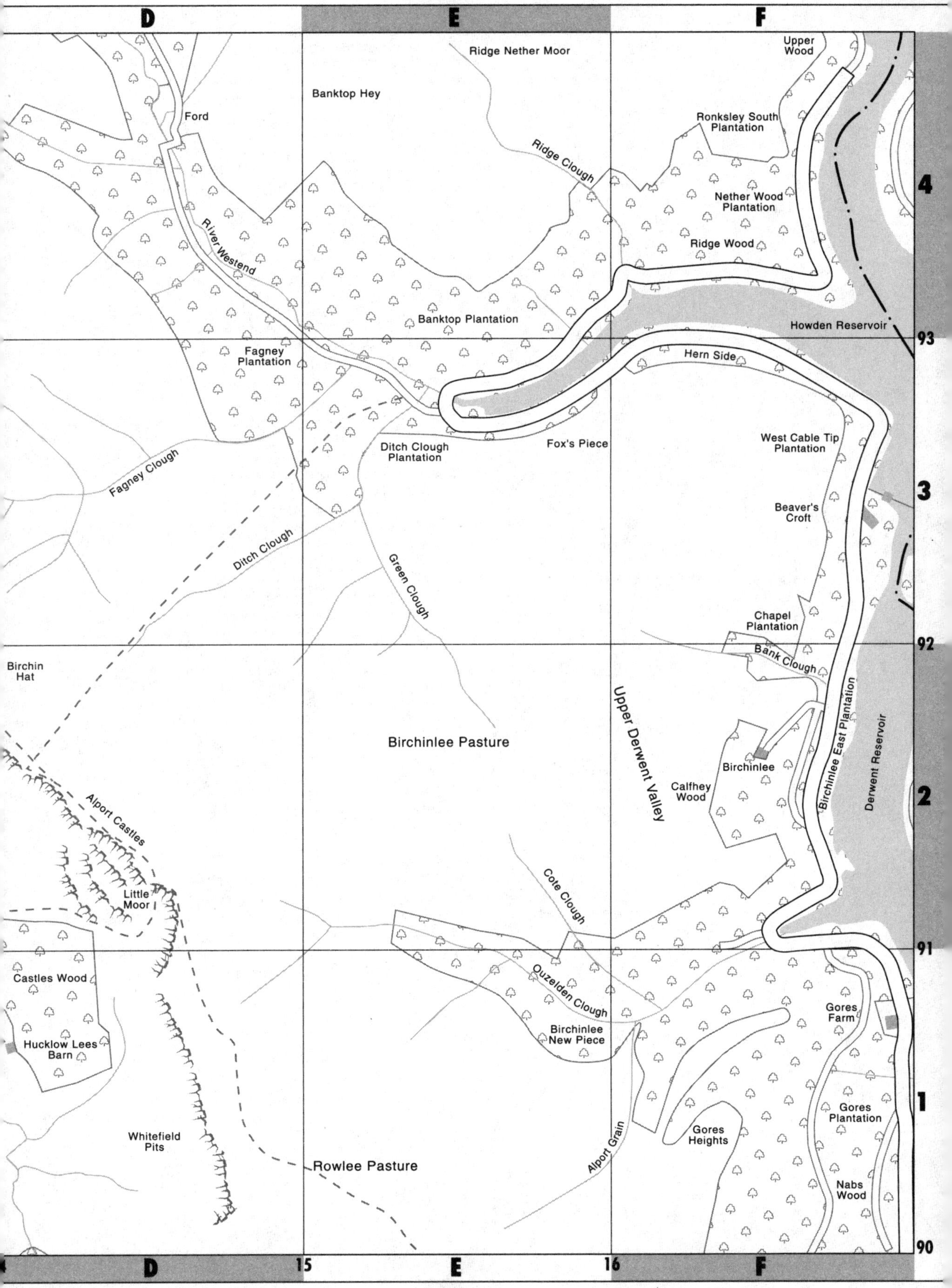
D
E
F
Ridge Nether Moor
Banktop Hey
Upper Wood
Ford
Ronksley South Plantation
Ridge Clough
Nether Wood Plantation
River Westend
Ridge Wood
Banktop Plantation
Howden Reservoir
Fagney Plantation
Hern Side
Ditch Clough Plantation
Fox's Piece
West Cable Tip Plantation
Fagney Clough
Beaver's Croft
Ditch Clough
Green Clough
Chapel Plantation
Birchin Hat
Bank Clough
Upper Derwent Valley
Birchinlee East Plantation
Birchinlee Pasture
Derwent Reservoir
Birchinlee
Calfhey Wood
Alport Castles
Cote Clough
Little Moor
Ouzelden Clough
Castles Wood
Gores Farm
Birchinlee New Piece
Hucklow Lees Barn
Gores Plantation
Whitefield Pits
Gores Heights
Alport Grain
Rowlee Pasture
Nabs Wood
4
93
3
92
2
91
1
90
15
16

21

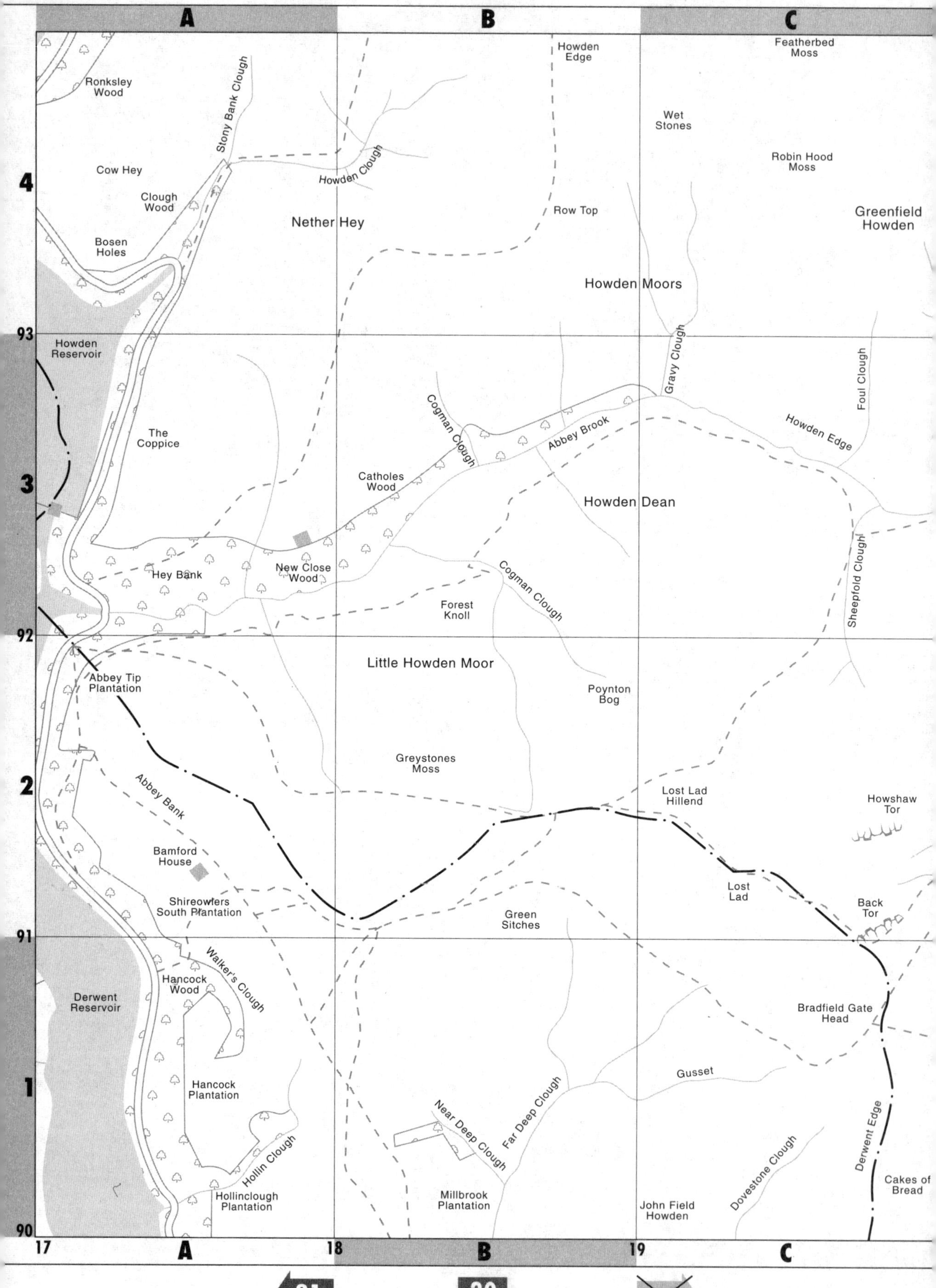
A
B
C
Featherbed Moss
Howden Edge
Ronksley Wood
Stony Bank Clough
Wet Stones
Robin Hood Moss
Cow Hey
Howden Clough
Clough Wood
Nether Hey
Row Top
Greenfield Howden
Bosen Holes
Howden Moors
Howden Reservoir
Gravy Clough
Foul Clough
Cogman Clough
Howden Edge
The Coppice
Abbey Brook
Catholes Wood
Howden Dean
Sheepfold Clough
Hey Bank
New Close Wood
Cogman Clough
Forest Knoll
Little Howden Moor
Abbey Tip Plantation
Poynton Bog
Greystones Moss
Abbey Bank
Lost Lad Hillend
Howshaw Tor
Bamford House
Lost Lad
Back Tor
Shireowlers South Plantation
Green Sitches
Walker's Clough
Hancock Wood
Derwent Reservoir
Bradfield Gate Head
Gusset
Hancock Plantation
Far Deep Clough
Near Deep Clough
Derwent Edge
Hollin Clough
Dovestone Clough
Cakes of Bread
Hollinclough Plantation
Millbrook Plantation
John Field Howden
4
93
3
92
2
91
1
90
17
18
19

21
30

15
24

D
E
F
Marple Bridge
Brabyns Park
Marple Locks
Marple Station
A626 GLOSSOP RD
COMPSTALL RD
COTE GREEN RD
LOWER FOLD
TOWN ST
BRABYNS BROW
STATION RD
B6101
ARKWRIGHT RD
HOLLINS LA
HIGH WOOD FOLD
OAKLANDS AVE
LEIGHTON DR
CLEMENT RD
TOWNSCLIFFE LA
LONGHURST LA
PARKSIDE LA
OLD HALL LA
LOW LEA RD
LAKES RD
Hare & Hounds (PH)
MILL BROW
HOLLYWOOD RD
Sportsmans Farm
Mill Brow
Greenhill
Mellor Hall
Townscliffe Farm
Vicarage
Sch
Lower Hall
Podnor
CHURCH RD
KNOWLE RD
DOVE BANK
MOOR END RD
Mellor
PC
PH
Bottom's Bridge
Reservoir
Damsteads Farm
Tarden
GIBB LA
Bottom's Hall
Linnet Clough
CH
Whetmorhurst
WHETMORHURST RD
Cobden Farm
Cobdenedge Farm
Cobden Edge
Snape Hey
Mellor Moor
Golf Course
The Banks
Black Lane
Cown Edge Way
River Goyt
Peak Forest Canal
STRINES RD
MARPLE
Hill Top Farm
Strawberry Hill
Richmond Farm
Goyt Way
RIDGE RD
THE RIDGE
BARLOW WOOD DR
PLUCKSBRIDGE RD
Marpleridge
Sportsman's Arms PH
Lower Cliffe
Capstone
Greenclough Farm
Shaw Farm
High Cliff Poultry Farm
Strines
Works
Romper PH
Ridge End
RIDGE END FOLD
HOLLYWOOD RD
Fox Inn (PH)
Brook Bottom
BROOK BOTTOM RD
STATION RD
WHITECROFT RD
Strines Station
Whitecroft Farm
Lea Cote Farm
Turf Lee Farm
TURF LEA RD
WYBERSLEY RD
B6101
89
88
87
86
4
3
2
1
97
98

32
24

23
16
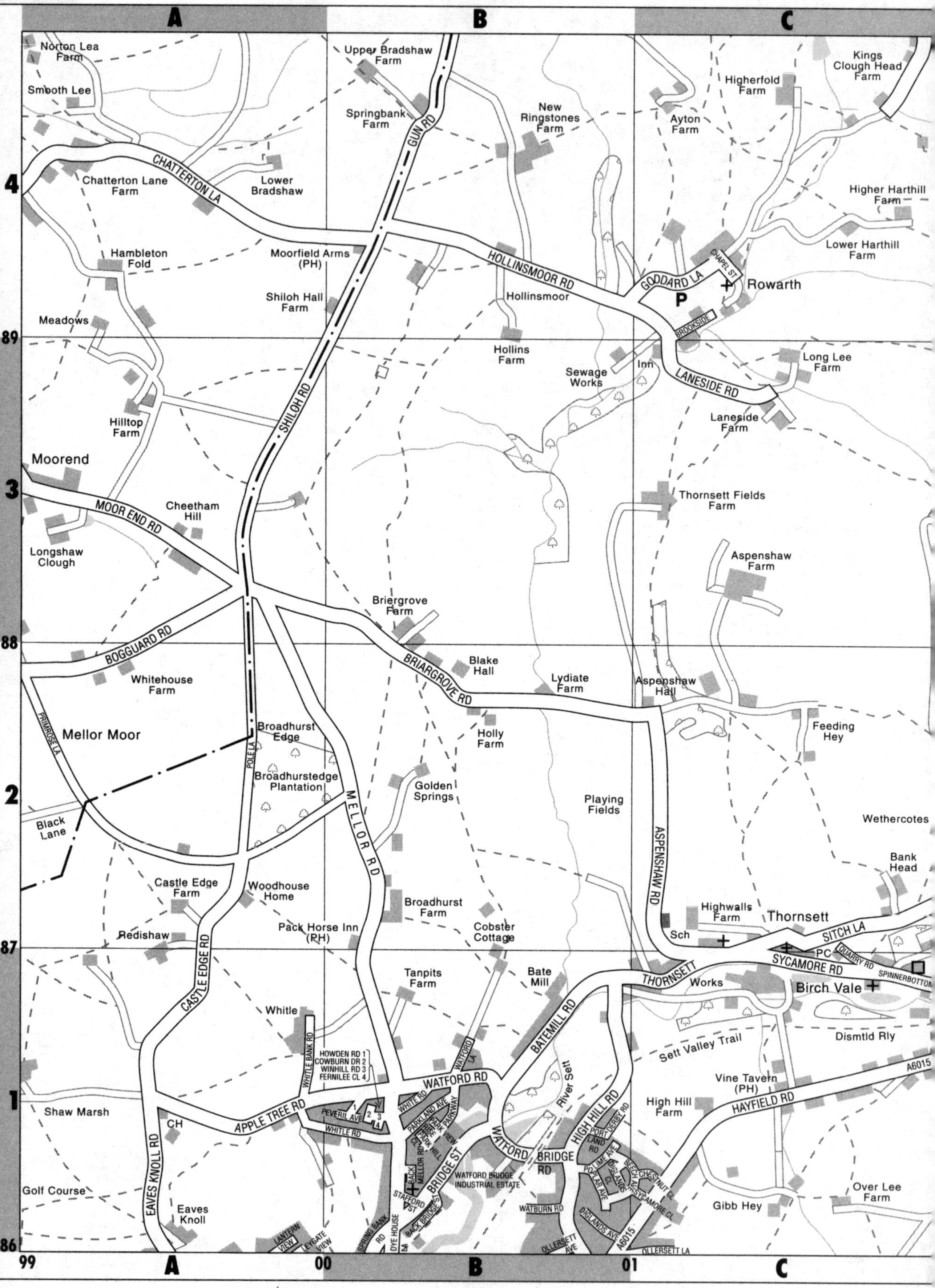
A
B
C
4
3
2
1
89
88
87
86
99
00
01
Norton Lea Farm
Smooth Lee
Upper Bradshaw Farm
Springbank Farm
GUN RD
New Ringstones Farm
Higherfold Farm
Ayton Farm
Kings Clough Head Farm
CHATTERTON LA
Chatterton Lane Farm
Lower Bradshaw
Higher Harthill Farm
Lower Harthill Farm
Hambleton Fold
Moorfield Arms (PH)
HOLLINSMOOR RD
GODDARD LA
CHAPEL ST
Rowarth
P
Shiloh Hall Farm
Hollinsmoor
Meadows
BROOKSIDE
Hollins Farm
Sewage Works
Inn
Long Lee Farm
LANESIDE RD
Laneside Farm
SHILOH RD
Hilltop Farm
Moorend
MOOR END RD
Cheetham Hill
Thornsett Fields Farm
Longshaw Clough
Aspenshaw Farm
Briergrove Farm
BOGGUARD RD
BRIARGROVE RD
Blake Hall
Lydiate Farm
Aspenshaw Hall
Whitehouse Farm
PRIMROSE LA
Mellor Moor
Broadhurst Edge
POLE LA
Holly Farm
Feeding Hey
Broadhurstedge Plantation
Golden Springs
MELLOR RD
Playing Fields
Black Lane
ASPENSHAW RD
Wethercotes
Bank Head
Castle Edge Farm
Woodhouse Home
Broadhurst Farm
Highwalls Farm
Thornsett
Pack Horse Inn (PH)
Cobster Cottage
Sch
SITCH LA
Redishaw
PC
QUARRY RD
SYCAMORE RD
Tanpits Farm
Bate Mill
THORNSETT
Works
Birch Vale
SPINNERBOTTOM
CASTLE EDGE RD
BATEMILL RD
Whitle
Dismtld Rly
Sett Valley Trail
WHITE BANK RD
HOWDEN RD 1
COWBURN DR 2
WINHILL RD 3
FERNILEE CL 4
WATFORD LA
River Sett
WATFORD RD
Vine Tavern (PH)
A6015
Shaw Marsh
High Hill Farm
HAYFIELD RD
APPLE TREE RD
PEVERIL AVE
WHITE RD
PARKLAND AVE
PARKWAY
HIGH HILL RD
DERBY RD
PORTLAND RD
CH
WHITLE RD
BRIDGE ST
WATFORD BRIDGE RD
LIME AVE
BEECH AVE
CHESTNUT CL
POPLAR AVE
SYCAMORE CL
DIGLANDS CL
EAVES KNOLL RD
WATFORD BRIDGE INDUSTRIAL ESTATE
Golf Course
MELLOR RD
BACK
STAFFORD ST
BACK BRIDGE ST
Over Lee Farm
Gibb Hey
Eaves Knoll
WATBURN RD
DIGLANDS AVE
SPRING BANK RD
DYE HOUSE LA
OLLERSETT AVE
A6015
LANTERN VIEW
LEYGATE VIEW
OLLERSETT LA
23
33

17
26

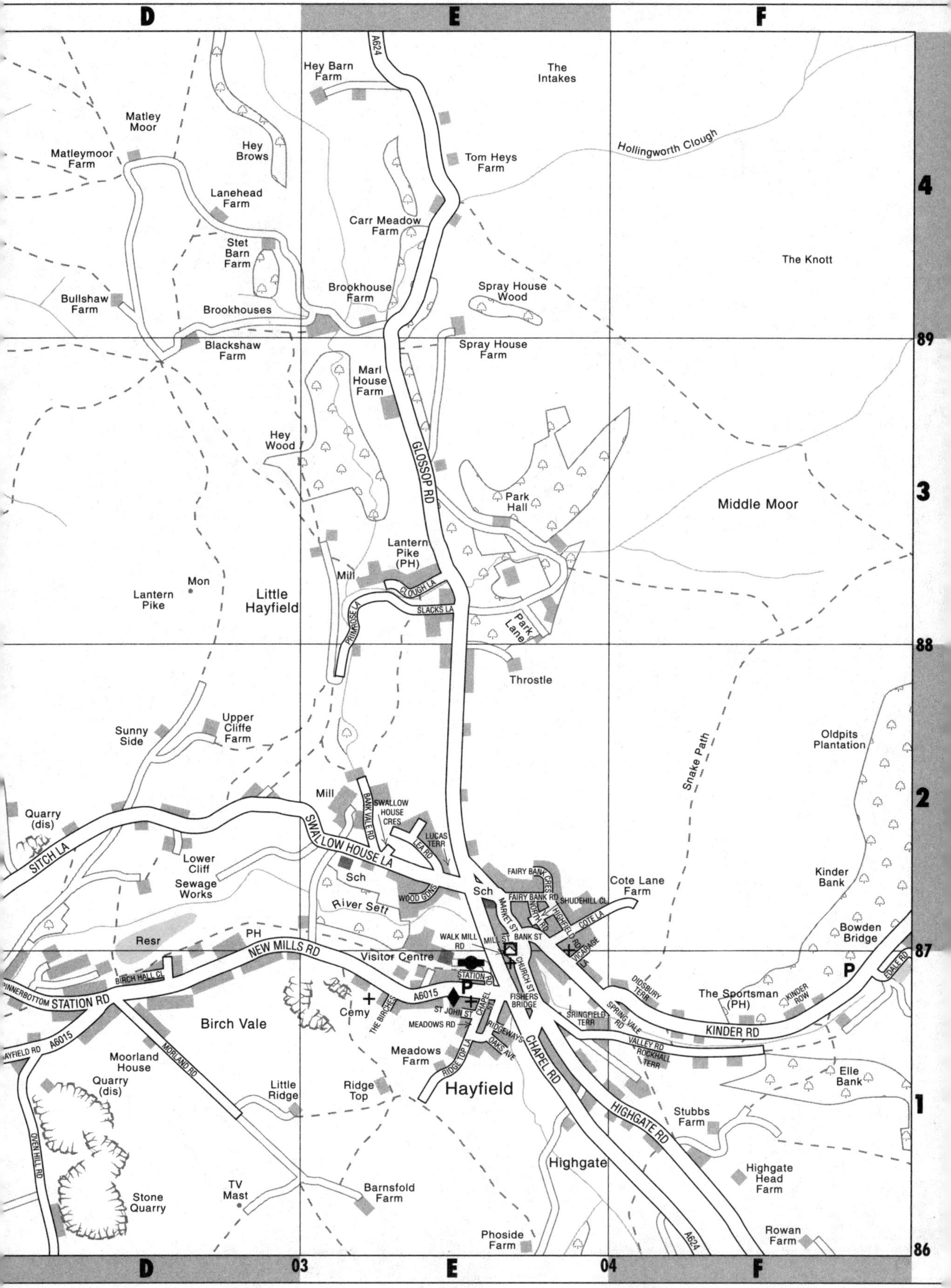
D
E
F
A624
Hey Barn Farm
The Intakes
Matley Moor
Hey Brows
Matleymoor Farm
Tom Heys Farm
Hollingworth Clough
Lanehead Farm
Carr Meadow Farm
Stet Barn Farm
The Knott
Brookhouse Farm
Spray House Wood
Bullshaw Farm
Brookhouses
Blackshaw Farm
Spray House Farm
Marl House Farm
Hey Wood
GLOSSOP RD
Park Hall
Middle Moor
Lantern Pike (PH)
Mon
Lantern Pike
Little Hayfield
Mill
CLOUGH LA
SLACKS LA
PRIMROSE LA
Park Lane
Throstle
Upper Cliffe Farm
Sunny Side
Snake Path
Oldpits Plantation
Mill
SWALLOW HOUSE CRES
BANK VALE RD
Quarry (dis)
SWALLOW HOUSE LA
LUCAS TERR
LEA RD
SITCH LA
Lower Cliff
Sch
Sewage Works
WOOD GDNS
Sch
FAIRY BANK CRES
FAIRY BANK RD
SHUDEHILL CL
Cote Lane Farm
Kinder Bank
River Sett
MARKET ST
NORTH RD
HIGHFIELD RD
COTE LA
Bowden Bridge
Resr
PH
WALK MILL RD
MILL ST
BANK ST
VICARAGE
NEW MILLS RD
Visitor Centre
CHURCH ST
STATION RD
EDALE RD
P
BIRCH HALL CL
DIDSBURY TERR
The Sportsman (PH)
KINDER ROW
SPINNERBOTTOM
STATION RD
A6015
P
Cemy
FISHERS BRIDGE
SPRINGFIELD TERR
SPRING VALE RD
KINDER RD
Birch Vale
THE BIRCHES
ST JOHN ST
CHAPEL ST
MEADOWS RD
RIDGEWAYS
VALLEY RD
ROCKHALL TERR
HAYFIELD RD
A6015
MORLAND RD
Moorland House
Meadows Farm
OAKS AVE
CHAPEL RD
Elle Bank
Quarry (dis)
Little Ridge
Ridge Top
RIDGE TOP LA
Hayfield
HIGHGATE RD
Stubbs Farm
OVEN HILL RD
Highgate
Highgate Head Farm
TV Mast
Stone Quarry
Barnsfold Farm
Phoside Farm
A624
Rowan Farm
89
88
87
86
4
3
2
1
03
04
D
E
F

34
26

25
18

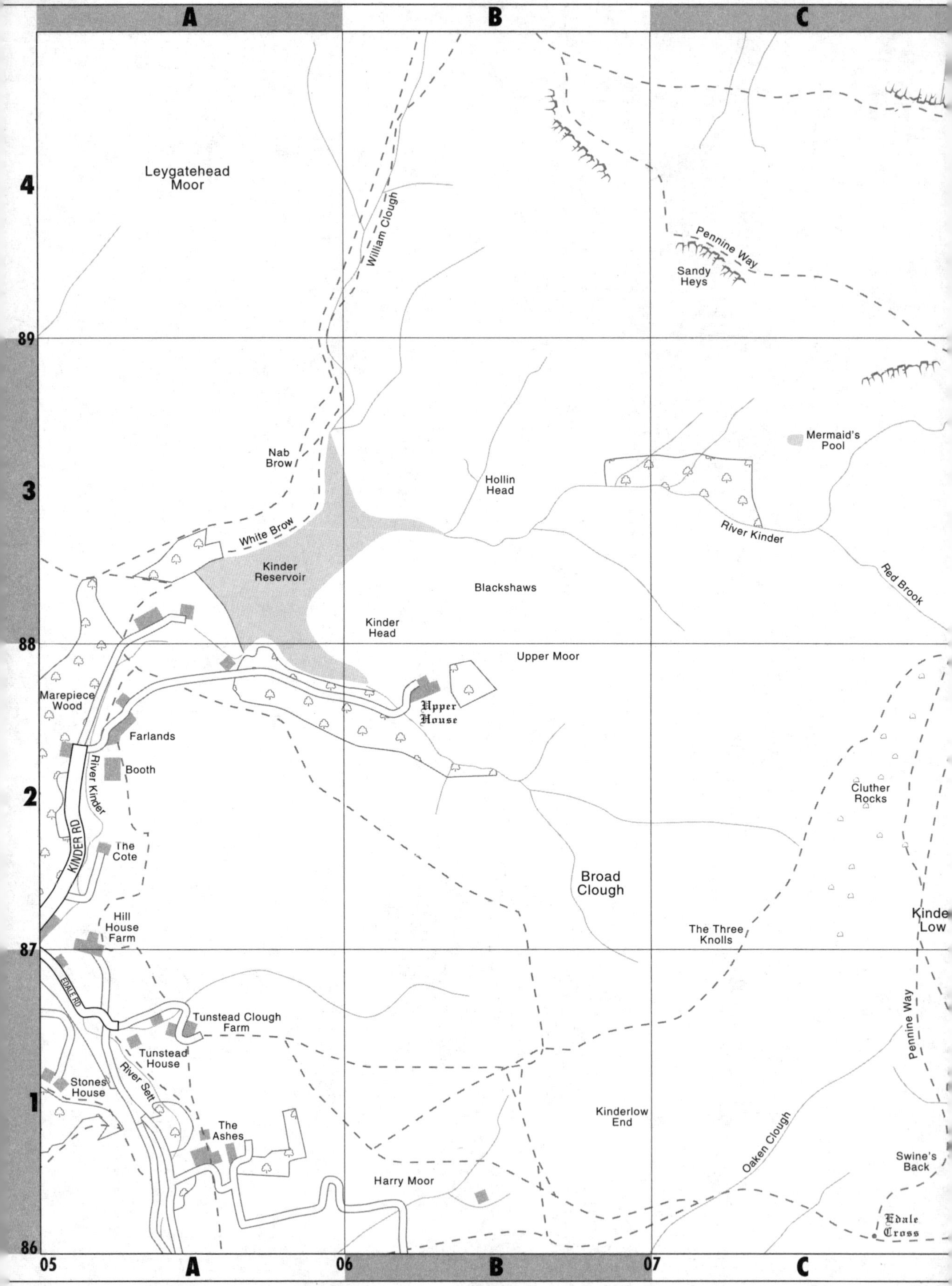
A
B
C
Leygatehead Moor
William Clough
Pennine Way
Sandy Heys
4
89
Nab Brow
Hollin Head
Mermaid's Pool
3
White Brow
Kinder Reservoir
River Kinder
Blackshaws
Red Brook
Kinder Head
88
Upper Moor
Marepiece Wood
Upper House
Farlands
Booth
River Kinder
KINDER RD
2
Cluther Rocks
The Cote
Broad Clough
Hill House Farm
The Three Knolls
Kinde Low
87
EDALE RD
Tunstead Clough Farm
Pennine Way
Tunstead House
River Sett
Stones House
1
The Ashes
Kinderlow End
Oaken Clough
Swine's Back
Harry Moor
Edale Cross
86
05
06
07
A
B
C

25
35

19
28

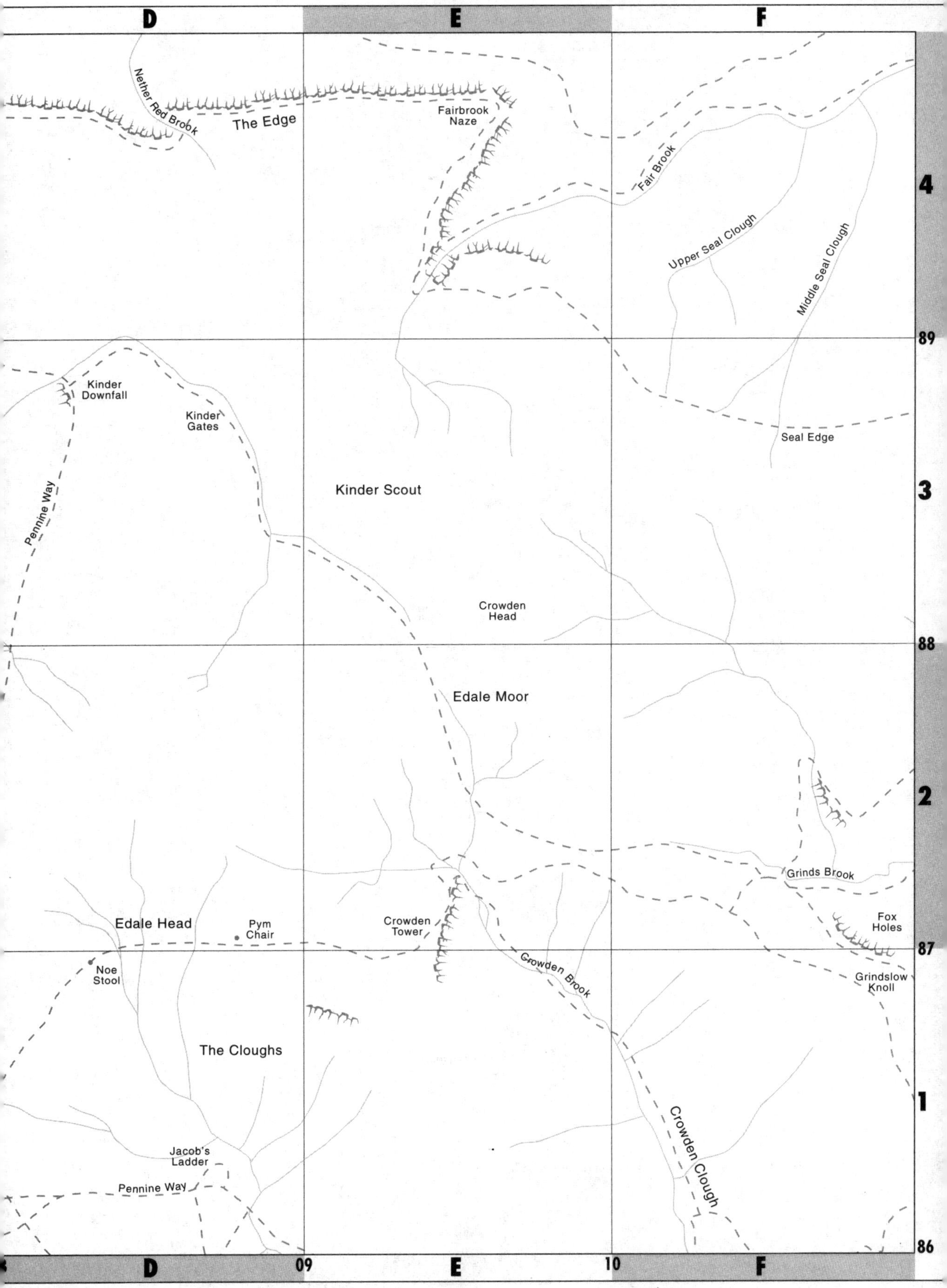
D
E
F
Nether Red Brook
The Edge
Fairbrook
Naze
Fair Brook
Upper Seal Clough
Middle Seal Clough
4
89
Kinder
Downfall
Kinder
Gates
Seal Edge
Pennine Way
Kinder Scout
3
Crowden
Head
88
Edale Moor
2
Grinds Brook
Fox
Holes
Edale Head
Pym
Chair
Crowden
Tower
87
Noe
Stool
Crowden Brook
Grindslow
Knoll
The Cloughs
1
Crowden
Clough
Jacob's
Ladder
Pennine Way
86
D
09
E
10
F

36
28

27
20

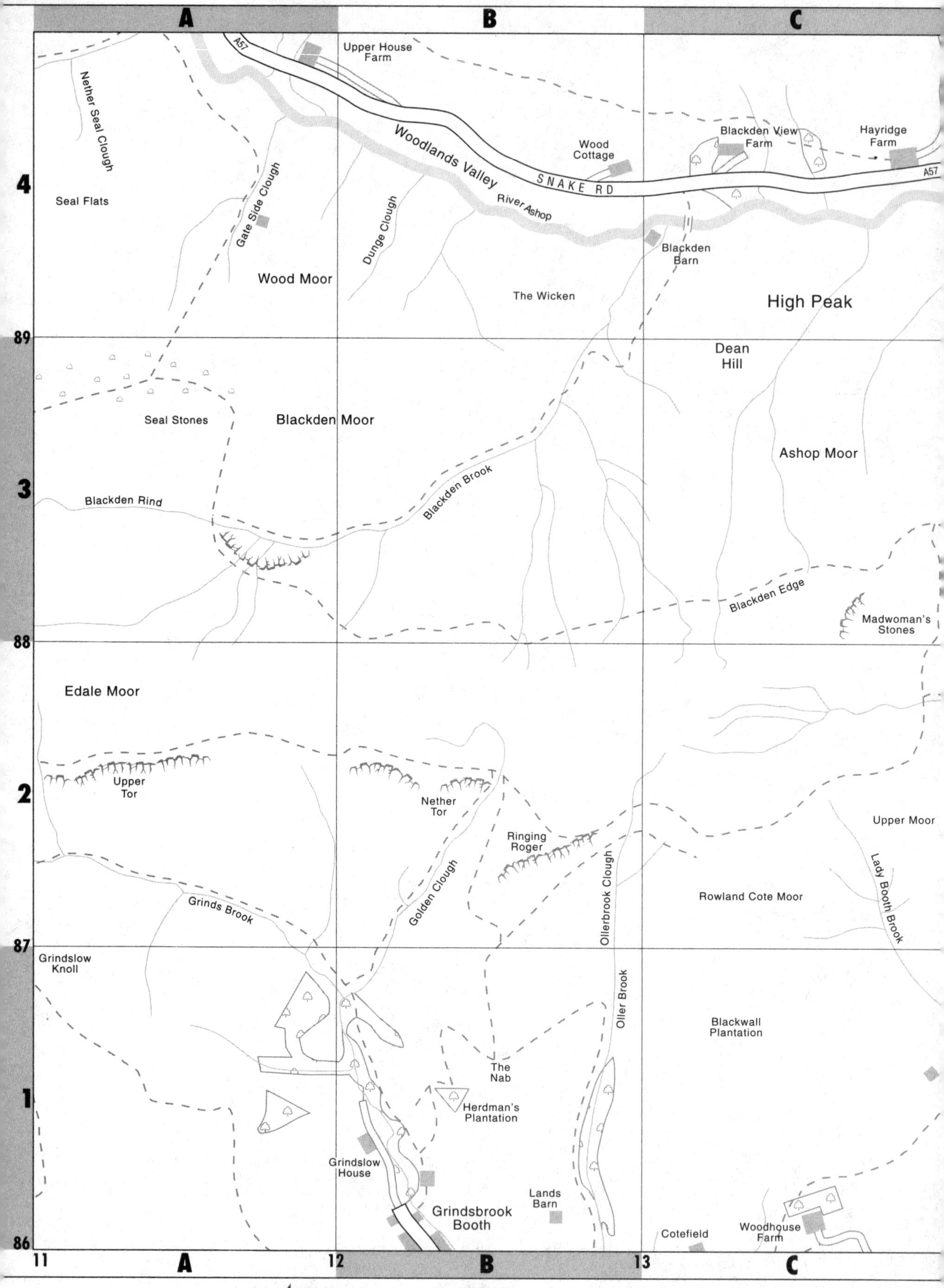
A
B
C
4
89
3
88
2
87
1
86
11
12
13
A57
Upper House Farm
Nether Seal Clough
Woodlands Valley
SNAKE RD
Wood Cottage
Blackden View Farm
Hayridge Farm
A57
Seal Flats
Gate Side Clough
Dunge Clough
River Ashop
Blackden Barn
Wood Moor
The Wicken
High Peak
Dean Hill
Seal Stones
Blackden Moor
Ashop Moor
Blackden Rind
Blackden Brook
Blackden Edge
Madwoman's Stones
Edale Moor
Upper Tor
Nether Tor
Ringing Roger
Upper Moor
Golden Clough
Ollerbrook Clough
Lady Booth Brook
Grinds Brook
Rowland Cote Moor
Grindslow Knoll
Oller Brook
Blackwall Plantation
The Nab
Herdman's Plantation
Grindslow House
Lands Barn
Grindsbrook Booth
Cotefield
Woodhouse Farm

27
37

21
30

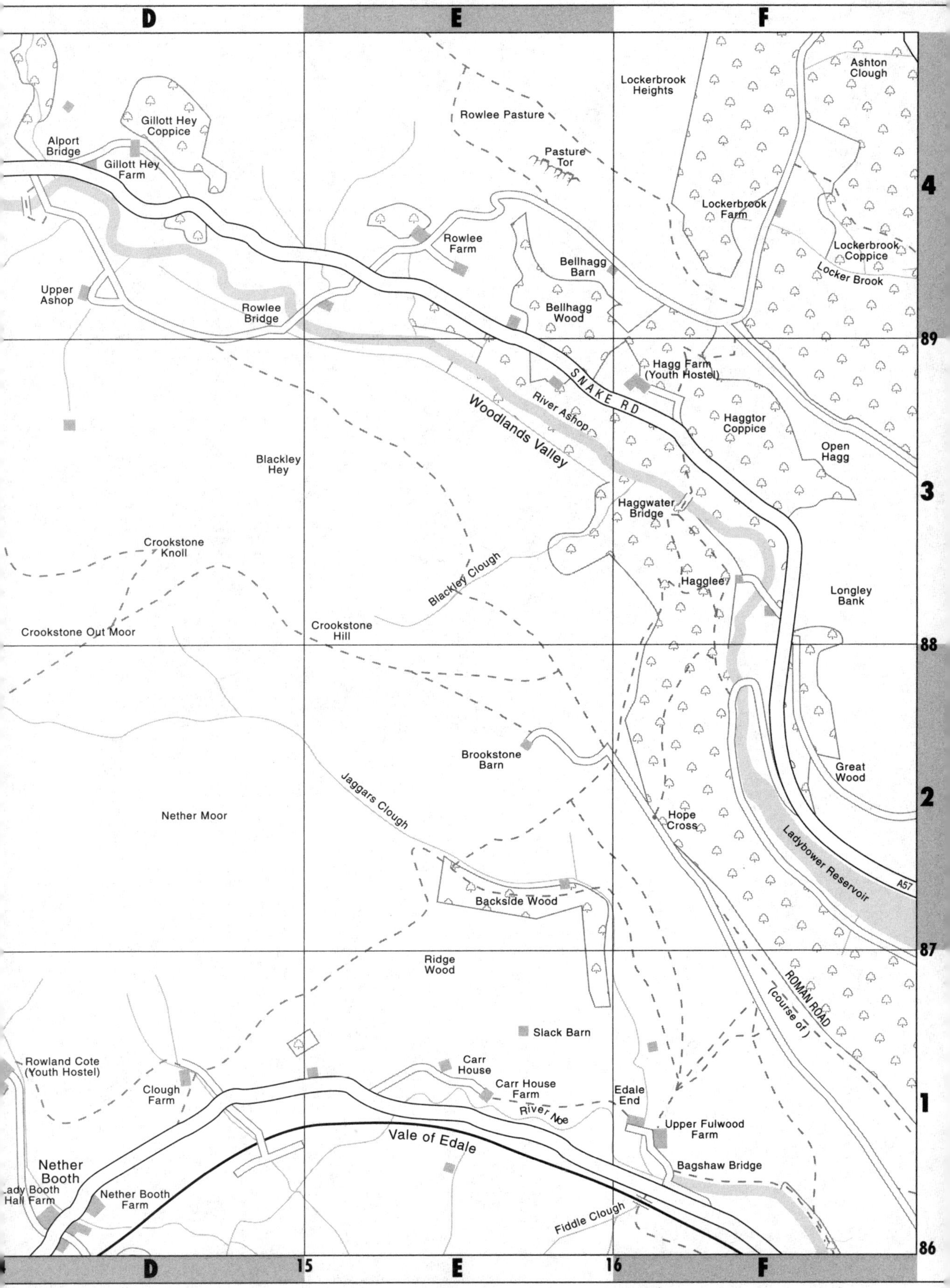
D
E
F
Lockerbrook Heights
Ashton Clough
Rowlee Pasture
Gillott Hey Coppice
Alport Bridge
Gillott Hey Farm
Pasture Tor
4
Lockerbrook Farm
Rowlee Farm
Lockerbrook Coppice
Locker Brook
Bellhagg Barn
Upper Ashop
Rowlee Bridge
Bellhagg Wood
89
Hagg Farm (Youth Hostel)
SNAKE RD
River Ashop
Woodlands Valley
Haggtor Coppice
Open Hagg
Blackley Hey
3
Haggwater Bridge
Crookstone Knoll
Blackley Clough
Hagglee
Longley Bank
Crookstone Out Moor
Crookstone Hill
88
Brookstone Barn
Great Wood
Nether Moor
Jaggars Clough
2
Hope Cross
Ladybower Reservoir
A57
Backside Wood
87
Ridge Wood
ROMAN ROAD (course of)
Slack Barn
Rowland Cote (Youth Hostel)
Carr House
Clough Farm
Carr House Farm
Edale End
1
River Noe
Upper Fulwood Farm
Vale of Edale
Nether Booth
Bagshaw Bridge
Lady Booth Hall Farm
Nether Booth Farm
Fiddle Clough
86
15
16

38
30

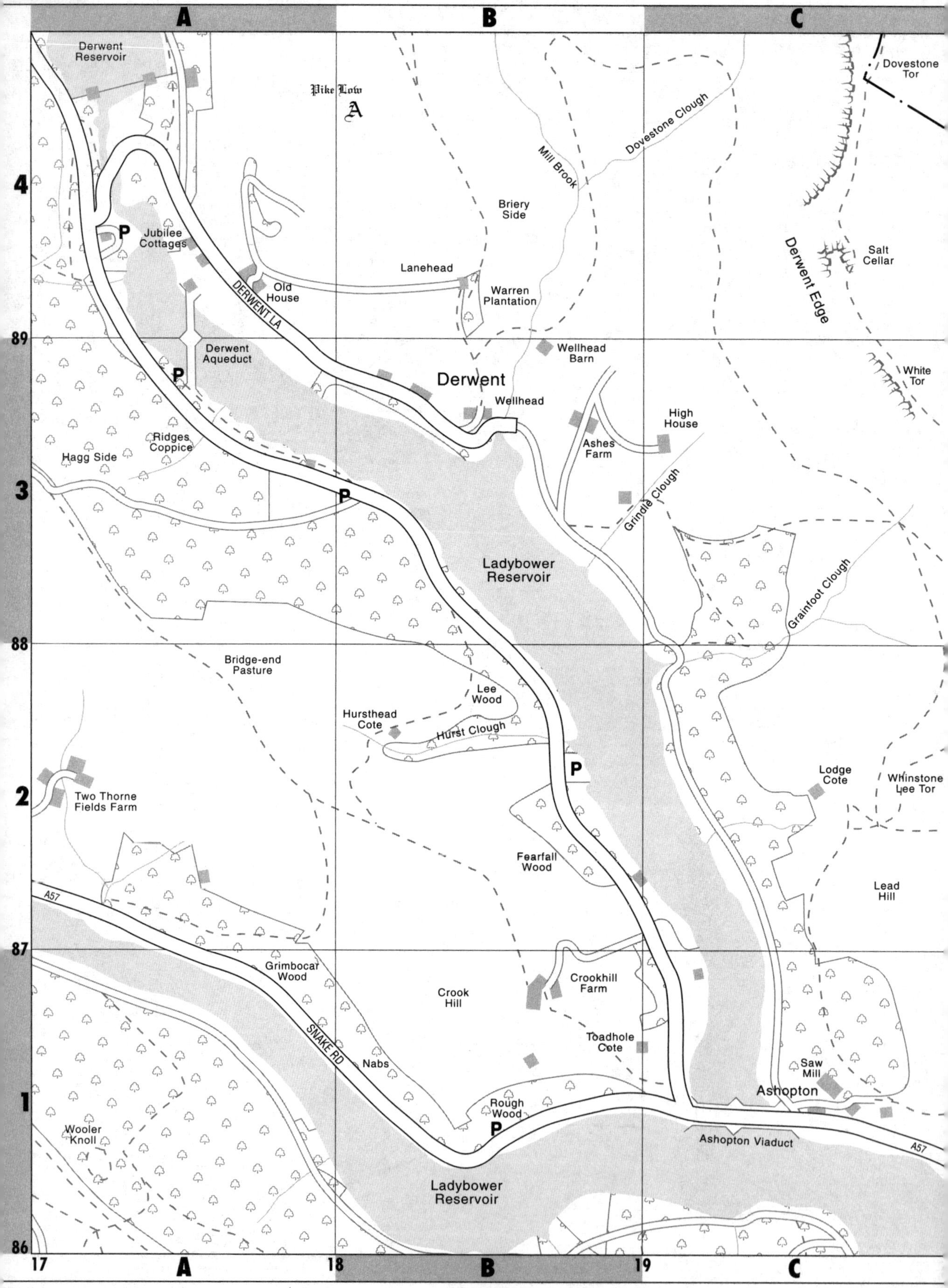
A
B
C
4
3
2
1
89
88
87
86
17
18
19
Derwent Reservoir
Pike Low
Dovestone Tor
Dovestone Clough
Mill Brook
Briery Side
Jubilee Cottages
P
Salt Cellar
Derwent Edge
Lanehead
Old House
DERWENT LA
Warren Plantation
Derwent Aqueduct
Wellhead Barn
Derwent
Wellhead
White Tor
High House
Ashes Farm
Ridges Coppice
Hagg Side
Grindle Clough
Ladybower Reservoir
Grainfoot Clough
Bridge-end Pasture
Lee Wood
Hursthead Cote
Hurst Clough
Lodge Cote
Whinstone Lee Tor
Two Thorne Fields Farm
Fearfall Wood
Lead Hill
A57
Grimbocar Wood
Crook Hill
Crookhill Farm
SNAKE RD
Toadhole Cote
Nabs
Saw Mill
Ashopton
Rough Wood
Wooler Knoll
Ashopton Viaduct
Ladybower Reservoir

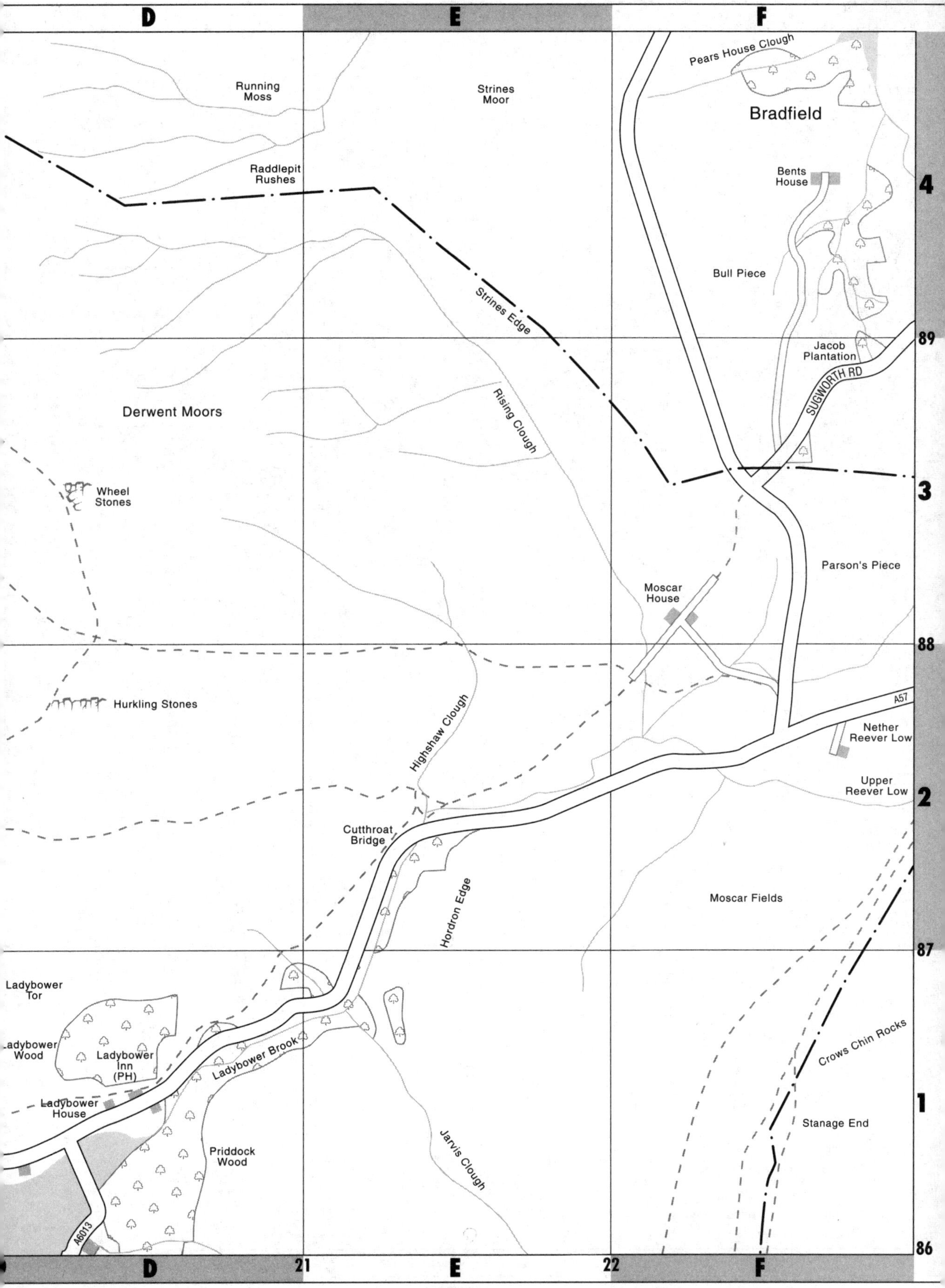
D
E
F
Pears House Clough
Running Moss
Strines Moor
Bradfield
Raddlepit Rushes
Bents House
4
Bull Piece
Strines Edge
89
Jacob Plantation
SUGWORTH RD
Rising Clough
Derwent Moors
Wheel Stones
3
Parson's Piece
Moscar House
88
A57
Hurkling Stones
Highshaw Clough
Nether Reever Low
Upper Reever Low
2
Cutthroat Bridge
Moscar Fields
Hordron Edge
87
Ladybower Tor
Ladybower Wood
Ladybower Inn (PH)
Ladybower Brook
Crows Chin Rocks
Ladybower House
1
Stanage End
Priddock Wood
Jarvis Clough
A6013
86
D
21
E
22
F

23

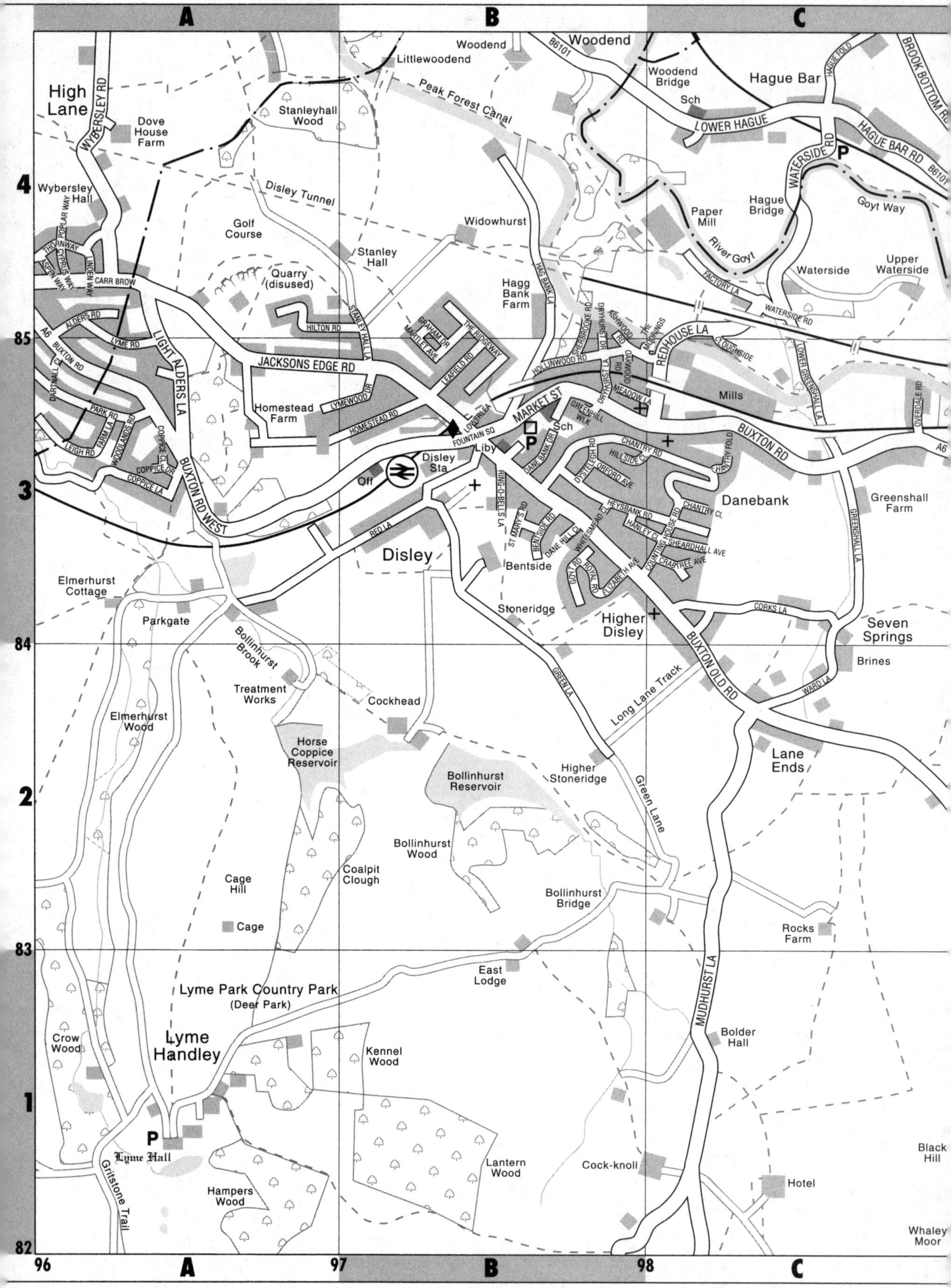
A
B
C
High Lane
Wybersley Rd
Dove House Farm
Wybersley Hall
Poplar Way
Thornway
Cypress Way
Aspen Way
Linden Way
Carr Brow
Alders Rd
Lyme Rd
A6
Buxton Rd
Dartnall Cl
Light Alders La
Park Rd
Farm La
Woodlands Rd
Leigh Rd
Coppice Cl
Coppice Dr
Coppice La
Buxton Rd West
Stanleyhall Wood
Disley Tunnel
Golf Course
Quarry (disused)
Hilton Rd
Stanley Hall
Stanley Hall La
Jacksons Edge Rd
Homestead Farm
Lymewood Dr
Homestead Rd
Littlewoodend
Woodend
Peak Forest Canal
Widowhurst
Graham Dr
Martlet Ave
The Ridgeway
Leafield Rd
Lower La
Fountain Sq
Disley Sta
Off
Liby
Red La
Disley
Hagg Bank Farm
Hag Bank La
B6101
Woodend
Woodend Bridge
Sch
Hague Bar
Lower Hague
Hague Fold
Brook Bottom Rd
Hague Bar Rd
Waterside Rd
P
Paper Mill
Hague Bridge
Goyt Way
River Goyt
Waterside
Upper Waterside
Factory La
Waterside Rd
Redhouse La
Cloughside
Lower Greenshall La
The Moorings
Ashwood Rd
Oakwood Rd
Drywood Dr
Dryhurst La
Sherbrooke Rd
Hollinwood Rd
Market St
Greenhill Wlk
Meadow La
Sch
Mills
Overdale Rd
Buxton Rd
A6
Dane Bank Dr
Chantry Rd
Hillside Cl
Dystelegh Rd
Orford Ave
Chantry Fold
Ring-o-Bells La
St Mary's Rd
Bentside Rd
Dane Hill Cl
Whitesmead Cl
Heysbank Rd
Hanley Cl
Counting House Rd
Chantry Cl
Sheardhall Ave
Crabtree Ave
Goyt Rd
Royal Rd
Elizabeth Ave
Danebank
Greenshall Farm
Greenshall La
Bentside
Stoneridge
Higher Disley
Corks La
Seven Springs
Brines
Ward La
Buxton Old Rd
Elmerhurst Cottage
Parkgate
Bollinhurst Brook
Treatment Works
Cockhead
Elmerhurst Wood
Horse Coppice Reservoir
Green La
Long Lane Track
Lane Ends
Higher Stoneridge
Bollinhurst Reservoir
Green Lane
Bollinhurst Wood
Coalpit Clough
Cage Hill
Cage
Bollinhurst Bridge
Rocks Farm
East Lodge
Lyme Park Country Park
(Deer Park)
Mudhurst La
Crow Wood
Lyme Handley
Kennel Wood
Bolder Hall
Lyme Hall
Gritstone Trail
Hampers Wood
Lantern Wood
Cock-knoll
Hotel
Black Hill
Whaley Moor
4
85
3
84
2
83
1
82
96
97
98

24
34

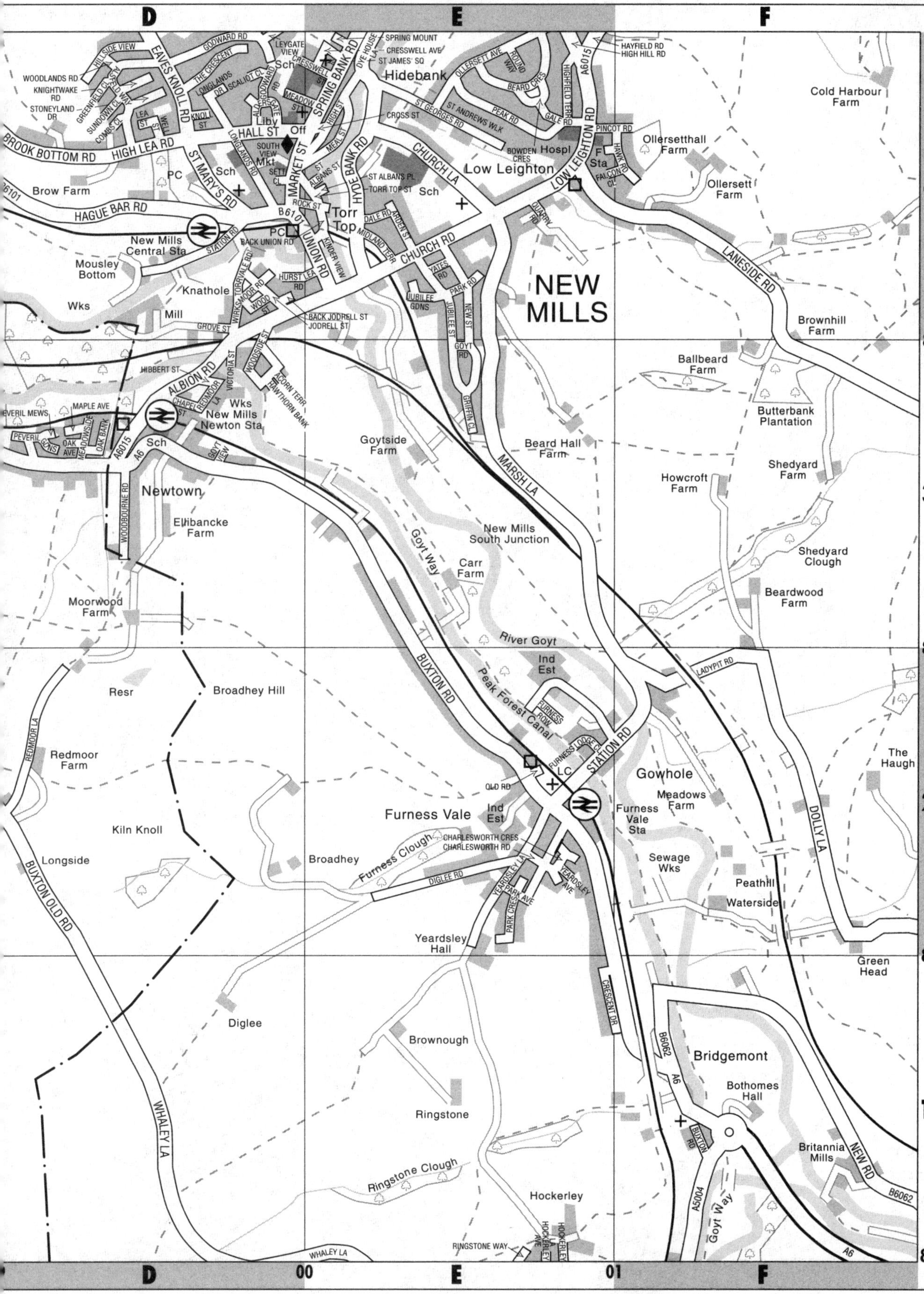
D
E
F
NEW MILLS
Hidebank
Low Leighton
Torr Top
Brow Farm
HAGUE BAR RD
BROOK BOTTOM RD
HIGH LEA RD
EAVES KNOLL RD
HILLSIDE VIEW
WOODLANDS RD
KNIGHTWAKE RD
STONEYLAND DR
GREENFIELD CL
SUNDOWN CL
COMBS CL
GODWARD RD
THE CRESCENT
LONGLANDS
SCALIOT CL
LEYGATE VIEW
CRESSWELL
SPRING BANK RD
DYE HOUSE LA
SPRING MOUNT
CRESSWELL AVE
ST JAMES' SQ
OLLERSETT AVE
ROUND WAY
BEARD CRES
HIGHFIELD TERR
A6015
HAYFIELD RD
HIGH HILL RD
ST GEORGES RD
ST ANDREWS WLK
PEAK RD
GALE RD
CROSS ST
PINCOT RD
HAWK RD
FALCON CL
LOW LEIGHTON RD
BOWDEN CRES
Hospl
F Sta
Ollersetthall Farm
Ollersett Farm
Cold Harbour Farm
HALL ST
Liby
Off
Mkt
SOUTH VIEW
MARKET ST
MEAL ST
ST ALBANS ST
ST ALBANS PL
TORR TOP ST
HYDE BANK RD
CHURCH LA
Sch
PC
ST MARY'S RD
LONGLANDS RD
B6101
ROCK ST
New Mills Central Sta
STATION RD
BACK UNION RD
UNION RD
KINDER VIEW
DALE RD
ARDEN ST
MIDLAND TERR
CHURCH RD
YATES RD
PARK RD
QUARRY RD
LANESIDE RD
Mousley Bottom
Knathole
Wks
Mill
HURST LEA RD
TORRVALE RD
MOOR RD
WOOD ST
WIRKSMOOR RD
BACK JODRELL ST
JODRELL ST
GROVE ST
JUBILEE GDNS
JUBILEE ST
NEW ST
GOYT RD
GRIFFIN CL
Brownhill Farm
Ballbeard Farm
Butterbank Plantation
HIBBERT ST
ALBION RD
VICTORIA ST
WOODSIDE ST
ACORN TERR
HAWTHORN BANK
REDMOOR LA
CHAPEL ST
MAPLE AVE
PEVERIL MEWS
PEVERIL GDNS
MEADOWSIDE
OAK AVE
OAK BANK
A6015
A6
New Mills Newton Sta
GOYT VIEW
Newtown
WOODBOURNE RD
Ellibancke Farm
Goytside Farm
Beard Hall Farm
MARSH LA
Howcroft Farm
Shedyard Farm
New Mills South Junction
Goyt Way
Carr Farm
Shedyard Clough
Beardwood Farm
Moorwood Farm
River Goyt
Ind Est
Resr
Broadhey Hill
BUXTON RD
Peak Forest Canal
FURNESS ROW
FURNESS LODGE CL
STATION RD
LADYPIT RD
Redmoor Farm
REDMOOR LA
LC
OLD RD
Gowhole
Meadows Farm
The Haugh
Furness Vale
Ind Est
Furness Vale Sta
DOLLY LA
Kiln Knoll
Longside
BUXTON OLD RD
Broadhey
Furness Clough
CHARLESWORTH CRES
CHARLESWORTH RD
DIGLEE RD
YEARDSLEY LA
PARK AVE
PARK CRES
YEARDSLEY AVE
Sewage Wks
Peathill
Waterside
Yeardsley Hall
Green Head
CRESCENT DR
Diglee
Brownough
Bridgemont
B6062
A6
Bothomes Hall
Ringstone
BUXTON RD
Britannia Mills
NEW RD
WHALEY LA
Ringstone Clough
Hockerley
A5004
Goyt Way
HOCKERLEY AVE
HOCKERLEY LA
RINGSTONE WAY
WHALEY LA
4
85
3
84
2
83
1
82
00
01

45
34

33
25

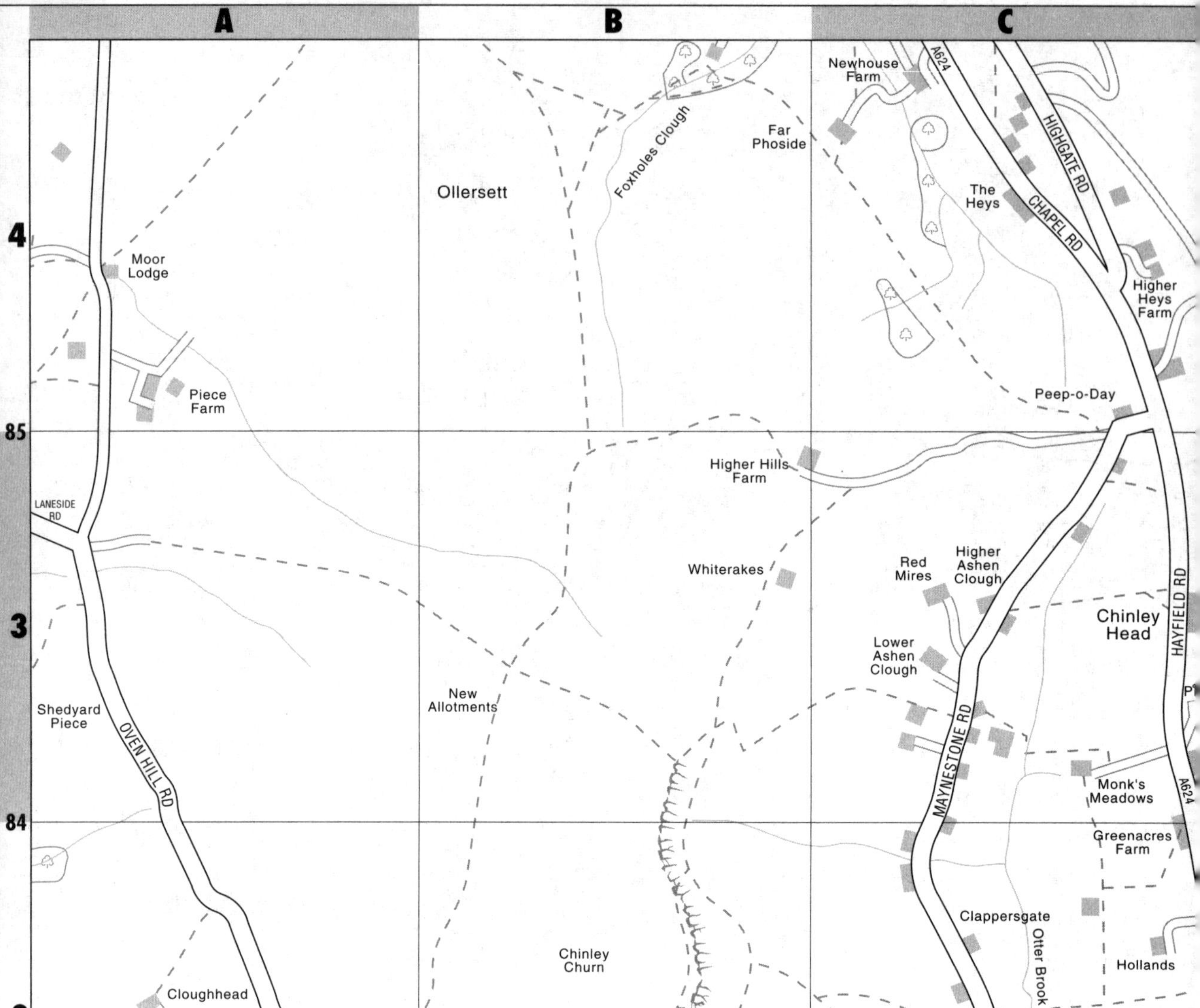
A
B
C
4
85
3
84
2
83
1
82
02
03
04
Newhouse Farm
A624
Far Phoside
Foxholes Clough
Ollersett
HIGHGATE RD
The Heys
CHAPEL RD
Moor Lodge
Higher Heys Farm
Piece Farm
Peep-o-Day
Higher Hills Farm
LANESIDE RD
Whiterakes
Red Mires
Higher Ashen Clough
HAYFIELD RD
Chinley Head
Lower Ashen Clough
New Allotments
Shedyard Piece
OVEN HILL RD
MAYNESTONE RD
Monk's Meadows
Greenacres Farm
Clappersgate
Otter Brook
Chinley Churn
Hollands
Cloughhead
Cracken Edge
The Naze
Throstle Bank
Laneside Farm
Hill Farm
Mosley House
Alders Farm
Ancoats
Dryclough
ALDERS LA
LYME PARK
Chinley Houses
Cotebank
Tithe Barn
Stubbins
STUBBINS LA
RUTLAND WAY
ALPHA RD
ALDER BROOK
Hotel
BUXTON RD
Chinley Station
STATION RD
PORTLAND GR
B6062
PIKE VIEW CL
DOLLY LA
Brierley Green
CRACKEN CL
MANNERS CL
PRINCES RD
Hollin Wood
LOWER LA
BELGRADE AVE
ALDERS AVE
STOCKTON DR
Buxworth
DOLLY WOOD CL
BRIERLEY PK
DEVONSHIRE DR
RHUDDLAN PL
DERWENT SQ
GREEN LA
Knowltop
Leaden Knowle
White Hall
DERWENT DR
HAWTHORN CL
ASH GR
Chinley
B6062
STATION RD
WHITEHALL TERR
HUNTERS GN
HARRINGTON DR
GRANBY AVE
NEW RD
Sch
JANE LA
Works
Black Brook
WHITEHOUGH HEAD LA
FORGE TERR
Mill
BROOKSIDE
Inn
A6
Inn

26
36

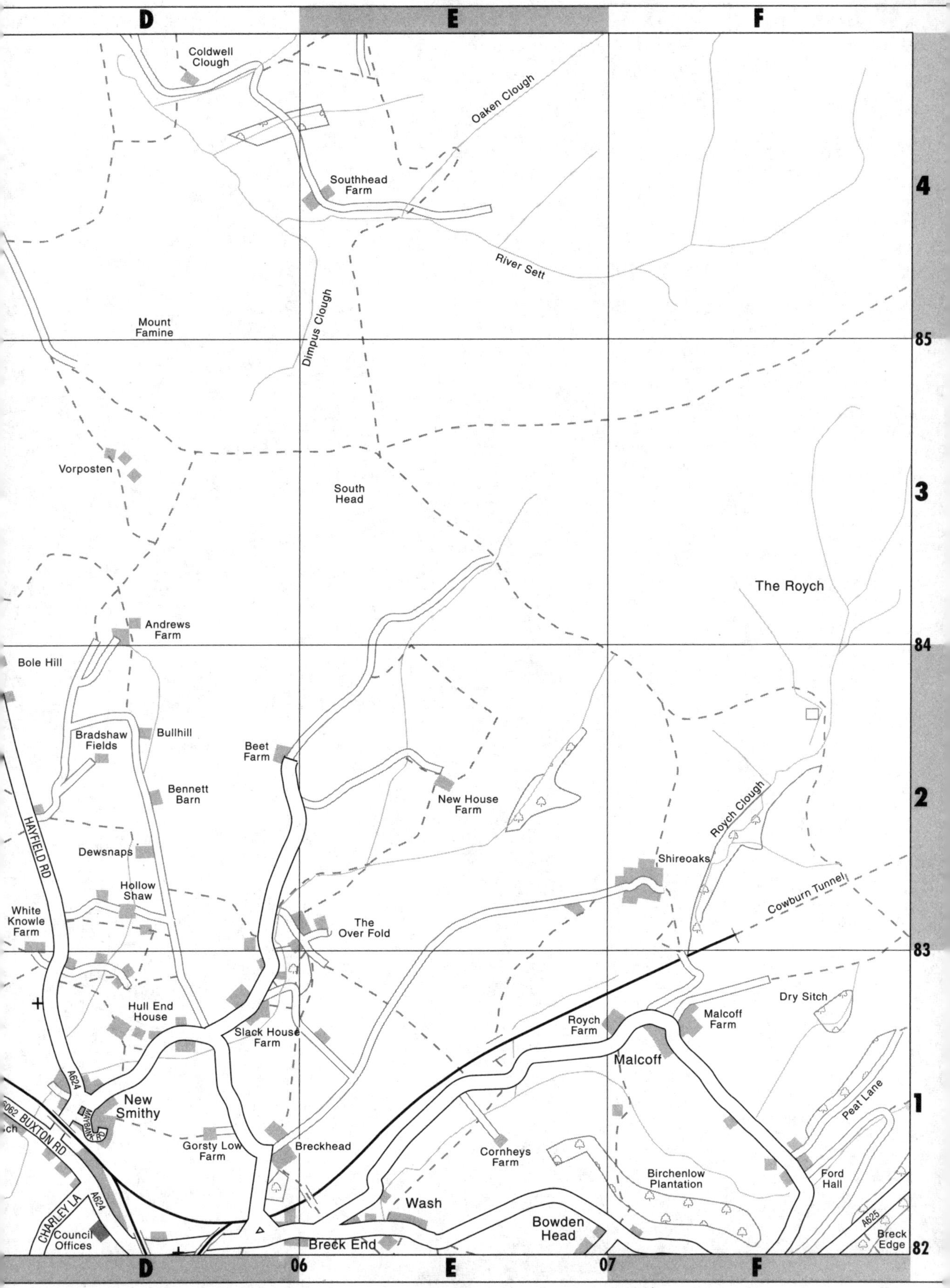
D
E
F
Coldwell Clough
Oaken Clough
Southhead Farm
River Sett
Mount Famine
Dimpus Clough
Vorposten
South Head
The Roych
Andrews Farm
Bole Hill
Bradshaw Fields
Bullhill
Beet Farm
Bennett Barn
New House Farm
Roych Clough
Dewsnaps
Shireoaks
Hollow Shaw
Cowburn Tunnel
White Knowle Farm
The Over Fold
Dry Sitch
Hull End House
Roych Farm
Malcoff Farm
Slack House Farm
Malcoff
HAYFIELD RD
A624
New Smithy
Peat Lane
BUXTON RD
MAYBANK CL
Gorsty Low Farm
Breckhead
Cornheys Farm
Birchenlow Plantation
Ford Hall
CHARLEY LA
A624
Wash
Council Offices
Bowden Head
A625
Breck Edge
Breck End
4
85
3
84
2
83
1
82
06
07

47
36

35
27

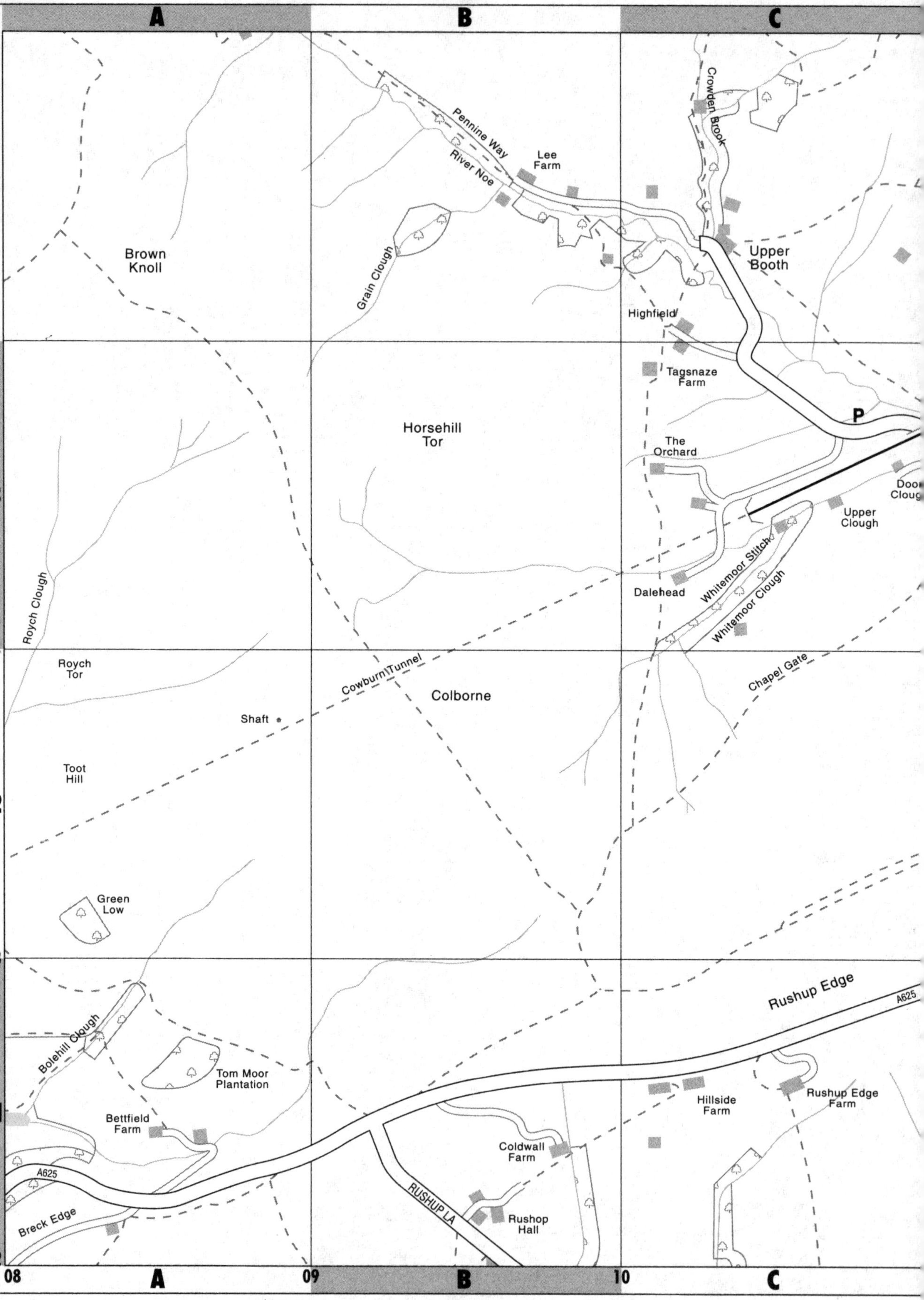
A
B
C
4
85
3
84
2
83
1
82
08
09
10
Pennine Way
River Noe
Lee Farm
Crowden Brook
Upper Booth
Brown Knoll
Grain Clough
Highfield
Tagsnaze Farm
Horsehill Tor
P
The Orchard
Upper Clough
Dalehead
Whitemoor Stitch
Whitemoor Clough
Roych Clough
Roych Tor
Cowburn Tunnel
Colborne
Chapel Gate
Shaft
Toot Hill
Green Low
Rushup Edge
A625
Bolehill Clough
Tom Moor Plantation
Bettfield Farm
Hillside Farm
Rushup Edge Farm
Coldwall Farm
RUSHUP LA
Rushop Hall
Breck Edge

35
48

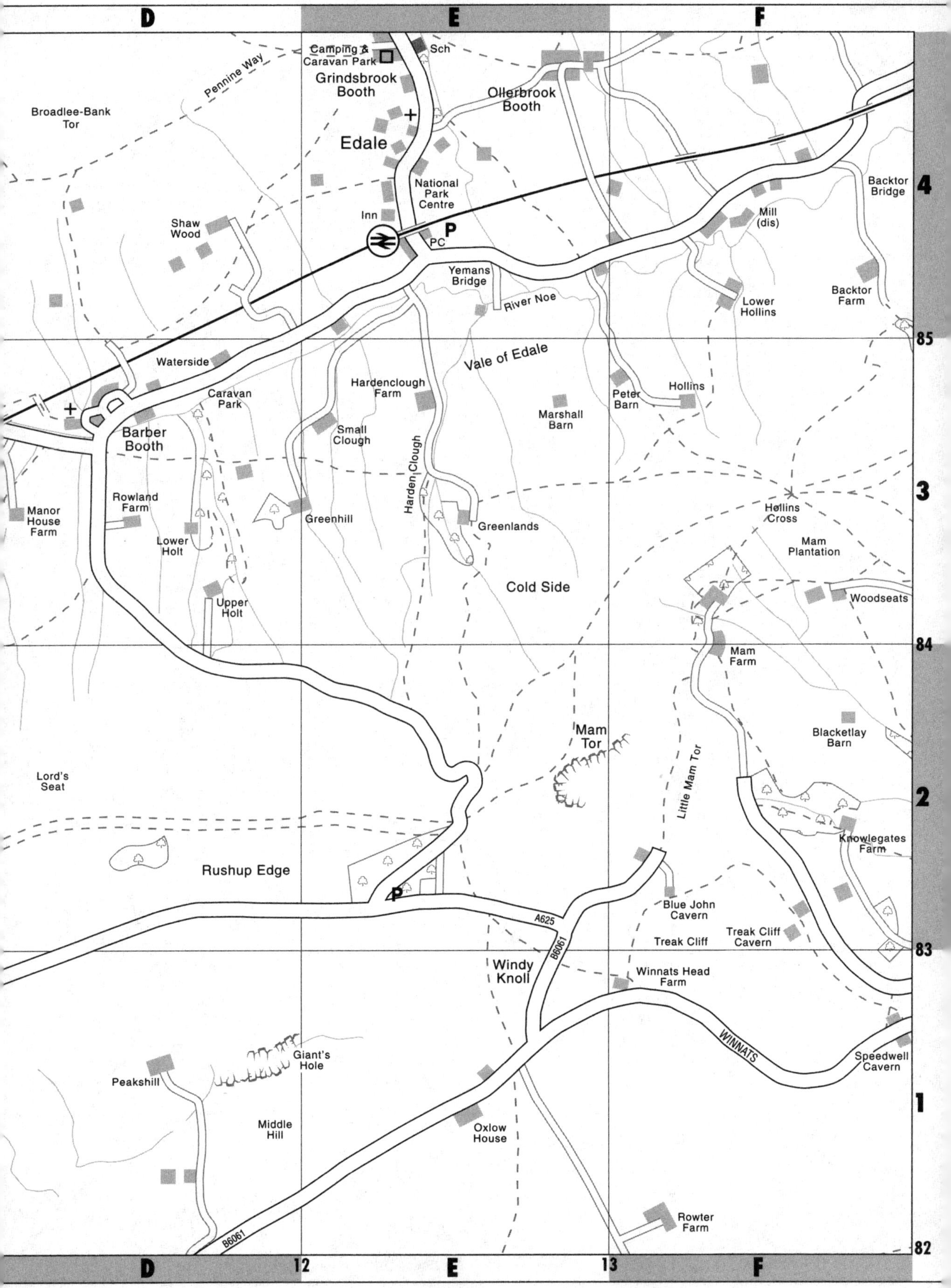
D
E
F
Camping &
Caravan Park
Sch
Grindsbrook
Booth
Pennine Way
Ollerbrook
Booth
Broadlee-Bank
Tor
Edale
National
Park
Centre
Backtor
Bridge
4
Mill
(dis)
Inn
Shaw
Wood
P
PC
Yemans
Bridge
River Noe
Lower
Hollins
Backtor
Farm
85
Vale of Edale
Waterside
Hardenclough
Farm
Caravan
Park
Hollins
Peter
Barn
Marshall
Barn
Barber
Booth
Small
Clough
Harden Clough
3
Manor
House
Farm
Rowland
Farm
Greenhill
Greenlands
Hollins
Cross
Lower
Holt
Mam
Plantation
Cold Side
Upper
Holt
Woodseats
84
Mam
Farm
Mam
Tor
Blacketlay
Barn
Lord's
Seat
Little Mam Tor
2
Knowlegates
Farm
Rushup Edge
P
Blue John
Cavern
A625
Treak Cliff
Cavern
Treak Cliff
B6061
83
Windy
Knoll
Winnats Head
Farm
WINNATS
Giant's
Hole
Speedwell
Cavern
Peakshill
1
Middle
Hill
Oxlow
House
Rowter
Farm
B6061
82
12
13

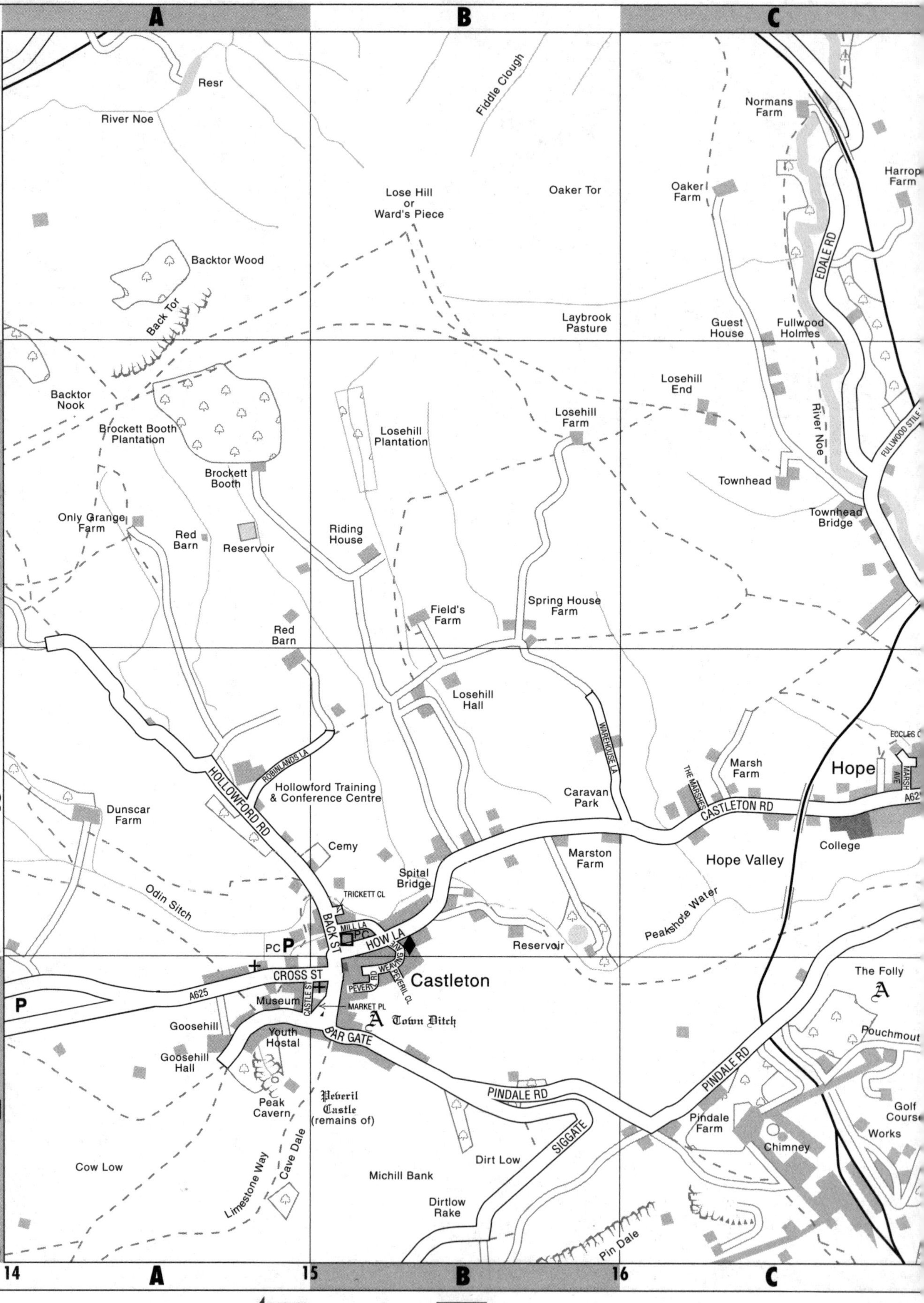
A
B
C
4
85
3
84
2
83
1
82
14
15
16
Resr
River Noe
Fiddle Clough
Normans Farm
Harrop Farm
Lose Hill or Ward's Piece
Oaker Tor
Oaker Farm
Backtor Wood
Back Tor
EDALE RD
Laybrook Pasture
Guest House
Fullwood Holmes
Backtor Nook
Losehill End
Brockett Booth Plantation
Losehill Farm
Losehill Plantation
River Noe
FULLWOOD STILE
Brockett Booth
Townhead
Only Grange Farm
Red Barn
Reservoir
Riding House
Townhead Bridge
Spring House Farm
Field's Farm
Red Barn
Losehill Hall
WAREHOUSE LA
ECCLES
Hope
MARSH AVE
Marsh Farm
THE MARSHES
ROBINLANDS LA
HOLLOWFORD RD
Hollowford Training & Conference Centre
Caravan Park
CASTLETON RD
A625
Dunscar Farm
Cemy
Marston Farm
Hope Valley
College
Odin Sitch
Spital Bridge
TRICKETT CL
Peakshole Water
MILL LA
PC
BACK ST
HOW LA
PC
P
WEAVING AVE
Reservoir
CROSS ST
Castleton
The Folly
P
A625
PEVERIL RD
PEVERIL CL
Museum
CASTLE ST
MARKET PL
Town Ditch
Pounchmout
Goosehill
Youth Hostal
BAR GATE
Goosehill Hall
PINDALE RD
PINDALE RD
Peak Cavern
Peveril Castle (remains of)
SIGGATE
Pindale Farm
Golf Course
Works
Chimney
Dirt Low
Cow Low
Cave Dale
Limestone Way
Michill Bank
Dirtlow Rake
Pin Dale

30
40

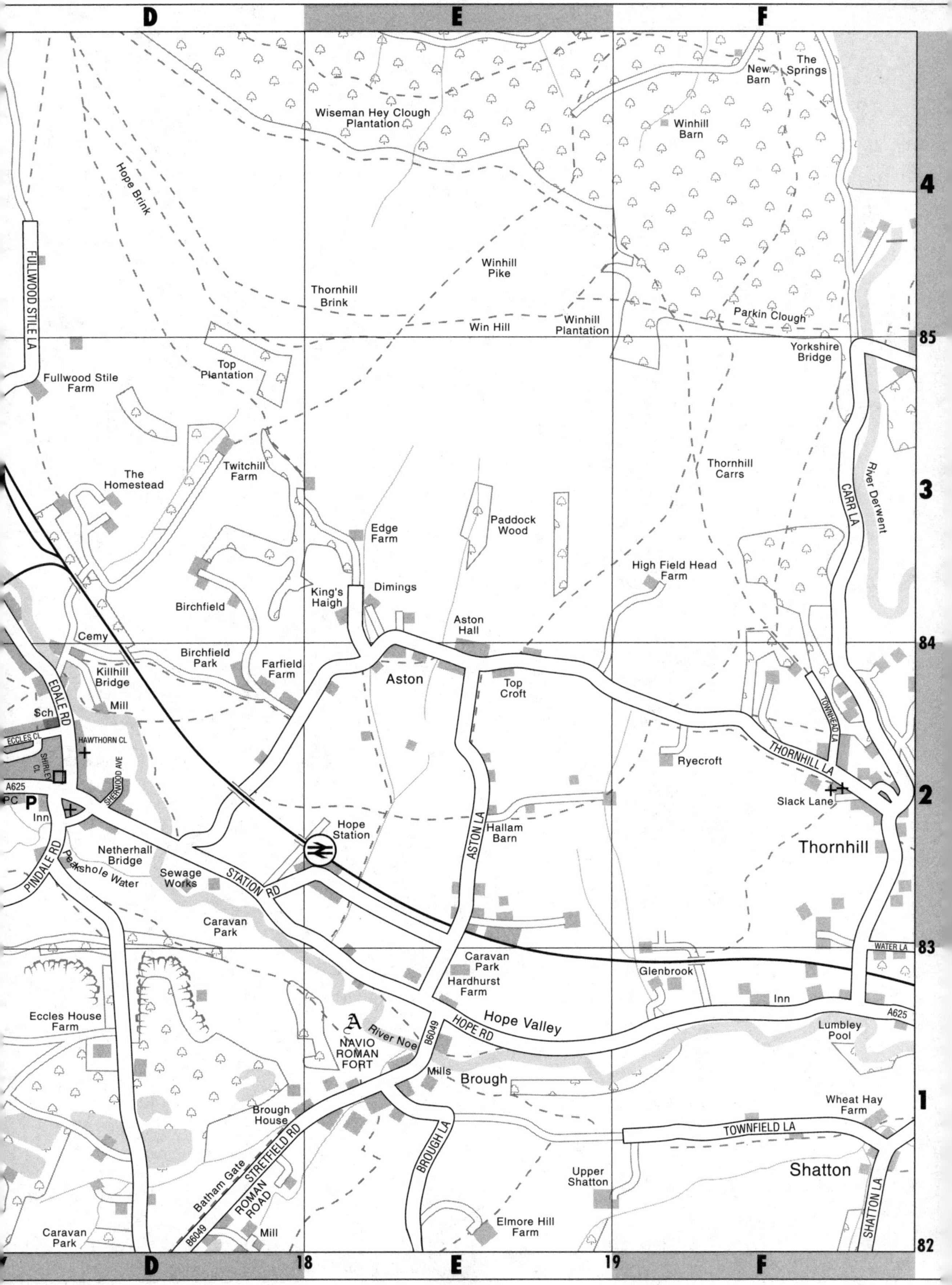
D
E
F
Wiseman Hey Clough Plantation
New Barn
The Springs
Winhill Barn
Hope Brink
FULLWOOD STILE LA
Winhill Pike
Thornhill Brink
Win Hill
Winhill Plantation
Parkin Clough
Yorkshire Bridge
Fullwood Stile Farm
Top Plantation
The Homestead
Twitchill Farm
Thornhill Carrs
CARR LA
River Derwent
Paddock Wood
Edge Farm
High Field Head Farm
Birchfield
King's Haigh
Dimings
Aston Hall
Cemy
Birchfield Park
Farfield Farm
Killhill Bridge
Aston
Top Croft
EDALE RD
Mill
Sch
HAWTHORN CL
ECCLES CL
SHIRLEY CL
SHERWOOD AVE
TOWNHEAD LA
THORNHILL LA
Ryecroft
A625
PC
P
Inn
Slack Lane
Hope Station
Hallam Barn
ASTON LA
Thornhill
Netherhall Bridge
PINDALE RD
Peakshole Water
Sewage Works
STATION RD
Caravan Park
WATER LA
Caravan Park
Hardhurst Farm
Glenbrook
Inn
Eccles House Farm
Hope Valley
HOPE RD
B6049
River Noe
NAVIO ROMAN FORT
Lumbley Pool
Mills
Brough
Brough House
STRETFIELD RD
BROUGH LA
Wheat Hay Farm
TOWNFIELD LA
Batham Gate
ROMAN ROAD
Upper Shatton
Shatton
SHATTON LA
Caravan Park
Mill
Elmore Hill Farm
18
19
4
85
3
84
2
83
1
82

51
40

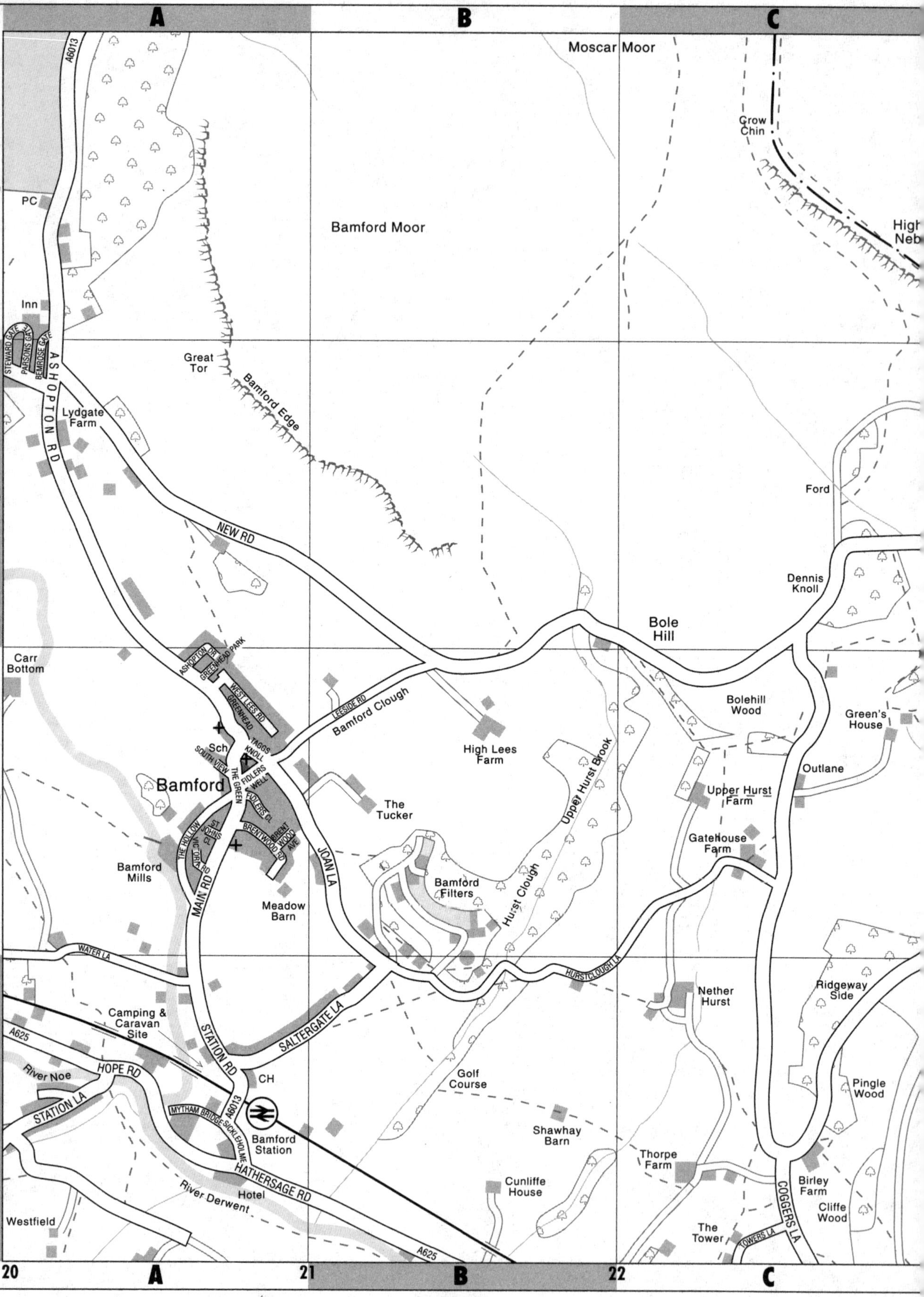
A
B
C
Moscar Moor
Crow Chin
High Neb
Bamford Moor
PC
Inn
STEWARD GATE
PARSONS GATE
BEMROSE GATE
ASHOPTON RD
A6013
Great Tor
Bamford Edge
Lydgate Farm
NEW RD
Ford
Dennis Knoll
Bole Hill
Carr Bottom
ASHOPTON DR
GREENHEAD PARK
WEST LEES RD
GREENHEAD
LEESIDE RD
Bamford Clough
TAGGS KNOLL
Sch
SOUTH VIEW
THE GREEN
FIDLERS WELL
FIDLERS CL
Bamford
High Lees Farm
Bolehill Wood
Green's House
Outlane
Upper Hurst Brook
Upper Hurst Farm
The Tucker
THE HOLLOW
ST JOHNS CL
VICTORIA RD
BRENTWOOD RD
BRENT WOOD AVE
Bamford Mills
JCAN LA
Gatehouse Farm
Bamford Filters
Hurst Clough
MAIN RD
Meadow Barn
WATER LA
HURSTCLOUGH LA
Nether Hurst
Ridgeway Side
Camping & Caravan Site
A625
SALTERGATE LA
STATION RD
HOPE RD
River Noe
CH
Golf Course
Pingle Wood
STATION LA
MYTHAM BRIDGE
SICKLEHOLME
Bamford Station
Shawhay Barn
HATHERSAGE RD
Hotel
River Derwent
Thorpe Farm
Cunliffe House
Birley Farm
COGGERS LA
Cliffe Wood
Westfield
The Tower
TOWERS LA
4
85
3
84
2
83
1
82
20
21
22

42

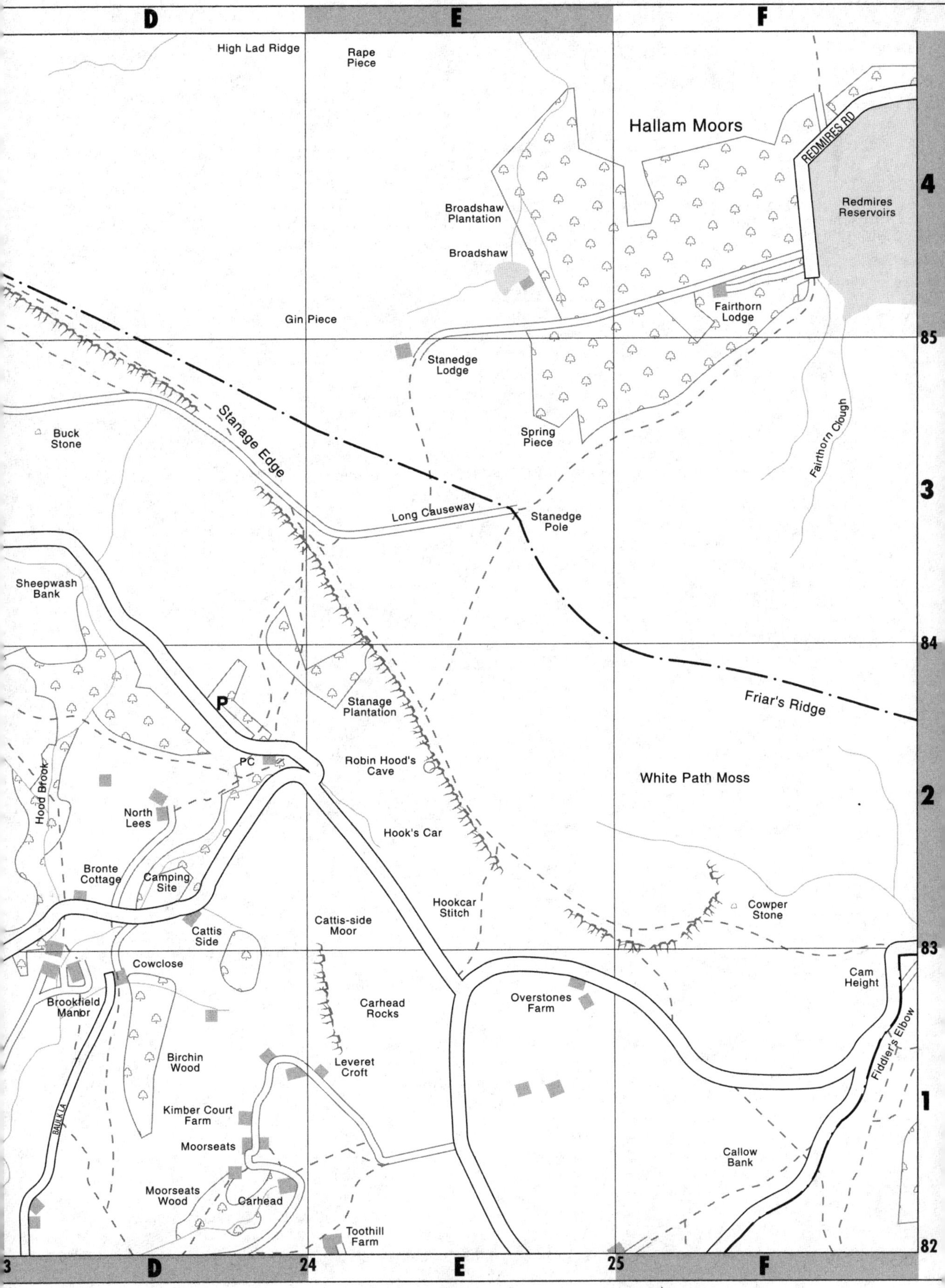
D
E
F
High Lad Ridge
Rape Piece
Hallam Moors
REDMIRES RD
Redmires Reservoirs
Broadshaw Plantation
Broadshaw
Fairthorn Lodge
Gin Piece
Stanedge Lodge
Buck Stone
Stanage Edge
Spring Piece
Fairthorn Clough
Long Causeway
Stanedge Pole
Sheepwash Bank
Friar's Ridge
Stanage Plantation
P
PC
Robin Hood's Cave
White Path Moss
Hood Brook
North Lees
Hook's Car
Bronte Cottage
Camping Site
Hookcar Stitch
Cowper Stone
Cattis Side
Cattis-side Moor
Cowclose
Cam Height
Brookfield Manor
Carhead Rocks
Overstones Farm
Fiddler's Elbow
Birchin Wood
Leveret Croft
Kimber Court Farm
BAULK LA
Moorseats
Callow Bank
Moorseats Wood
Carhead
Toothill Farm
85
84
83
82
4
3
2
1
24
25

53
42

A
B
C
Lodge Moor
Hospl
LODGE MOOR RD
Wyming Brook Farm
Reservoir Cottages
REDMIRES RD
WYMING BROOK DR
Redmires Plantaion
Works
Wyming Brook Farm
SOUGHLEY LA
Soughley
Redmires Conduit
BROWN HILLS LA
Peat Farm
ROPER HILL
Redmires Reservoirs
Fulwood Grange Farm
Brownhills Farm
Birk's Green Farm
HARRISON LA
Fulwood Booth
FULWOOD HEAD RD
Knoll Top Farm
MAYFIELD RD
Douse Croft Farm
GORSE LA
Mill Lane Farm
Fulwood Head
Wagg Lane
DOUSE CROFT LA
Yarncliffe House Farm
FOXHALL LA
HARROP LA
BASSETT LA
ANDWELL LA
Green House Farm
White Stones
FULWOOD LA
GREENHOUSE LA
CLOUGH LA
Bassett
Rud Hill
Brown Edge Farm
Porter Clough
Clough Hollow
Hallam Moors
Moorfield Farm
Brown Edge
Ringinglow
RINGINGLOW RD
Lady Canning's Plantation
Upper Burbage Bridge
Ox Stones
Burbage Rocks
Burbage Moor
HOUNDKIRK RD
JUMBLE RD
SHEEPHILL RD
Ford
Houndkirk Moor
4
85
3
84
2
83
1
82
26
27
28
A
B
C

44

D
E
F
SHEFFIELD
Highfield
Lowfield
Black Bank
Norfolk Park
Crematorium
Cemetery
Arbourthorne
Deep Pit
Sports Ground
Arbourthorne Estate
Hurlfield Campus
Newfield Green
Buck Wood
Meersbrook Park
Meersbrook
Allot Gdns
Meers Brook
Rollestone
Hurl Field
Norton Lees
Norton Woodseats
Gleadless Valley
Rollestone Wood
Leeshall Wood
Golf Course
Hemsworth
Herdings
The Lumb
Club House
Bolehill
Bolehill Farm
Blackmoor
Graves Park
Oakes Park
Grange Farm
Oakes-in-Norton
Wet Lands
Lightwood Farm
Hospital
EAST BANK RD
GLEADLESS RD
CITY RD
NORTON AVE
BOCHUM PARKWAY
HEMSWORTH RD
DERBYSHIRE LA
LEIGHTON RD
BLACKSTOCK RD
NORTON LEES LA
LIGHTWOOD LA
NORTON LA
PARK GRANGE RD
SPENCER RD
HEELEY BANK RD
CARFIELD AVE
A6102
A6135
B6388
B6388
85
84
83
82
4
3
2
1
36
37

57

44

43

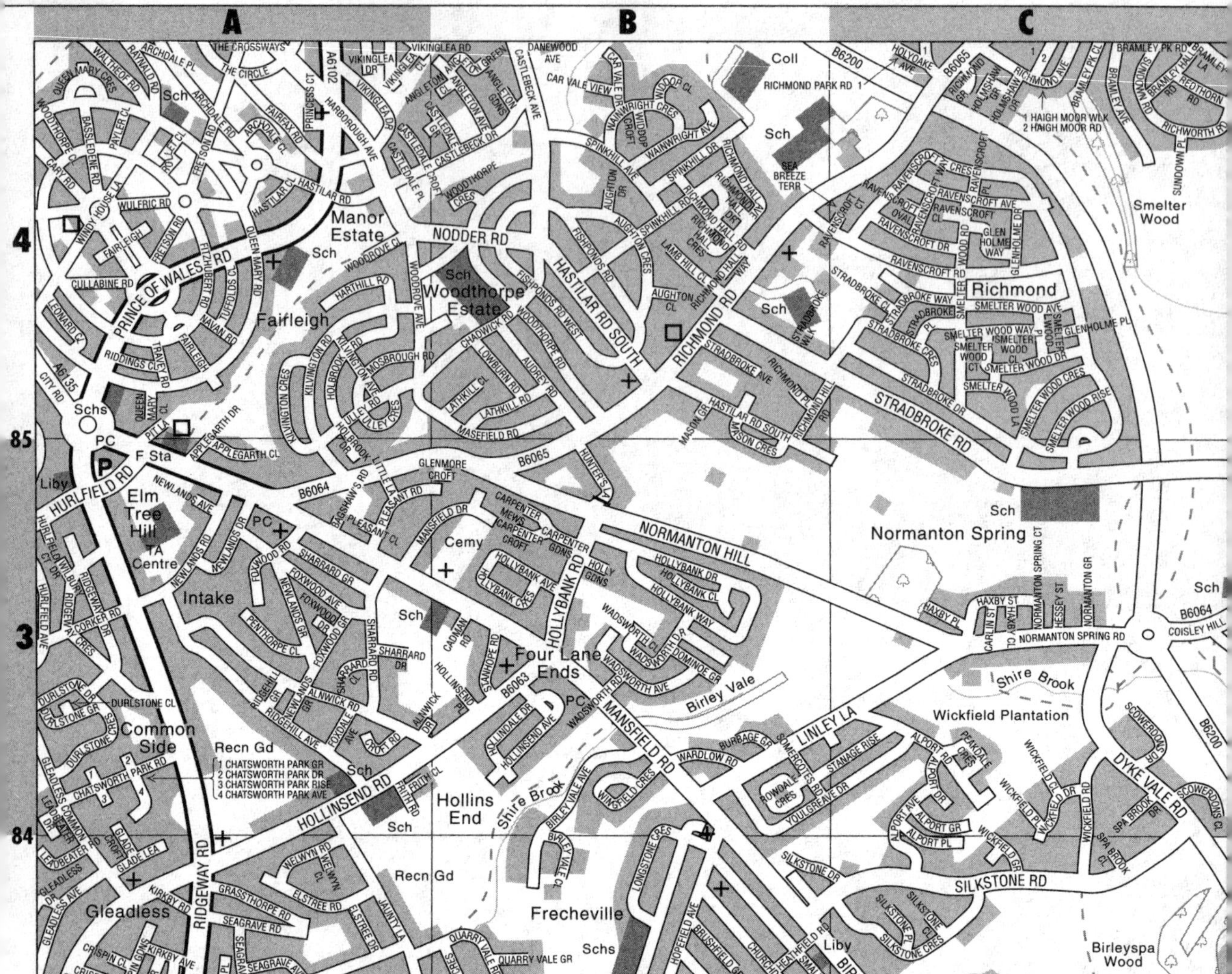
A
B
C
4
85
3
84
2
83
1
82
38
39
40
Manor Estate
Woodthorpe Estate
Fairleigh
Richmond
Smelter Wood
Normanton Spring
Elm Tree Hill
TA Centre
Intake
Cemy
Four Lane Ends
Birley Vale
Wickfield Plantation
Shire Brook
Common Side
Recn Gd
Hollins End
Gleadless
Frecheville
Birleyspa Wood
Base Green
Gleadless Townend
Birley
Whitelane End
Birleywood Farm
Charnock Hall
Golf Course
Sunny Bank
Carter Lodge
Birley Wood
Stoneley Wood
Birdfield
Highlane
Robin Brook
Coll
Sch
Schs
Liby
F Sta
PC
PH
PRINCE OF WALES RD
NODDER RD
HASTILAR RD SOUTH
RICHMOND RD
STRADBROKE RD
NORMANTON HILL
NORMANTON SPRING RD
HOLLINSEND RD
MANSFIELD RD
HURLFIELD RD
RIDGEWAY RD
LINLEY LA
SILKSTONE RD
BIRLEY MOOR RD
THORNBRIDGE DR
OCCUPATION LA
BIRLEY SPA LA
DYKE VALE RD
SHEFFIELD RD
FOX LA
BIRLEY LA
WHITE LA
HIGH LA
CARTERHALL LA
B6064
B6065
B6063
B6054
B6200
B6388
A6102
A6135
1 CHATSWORTH PARK RD
2 CHATSWORTH PARK DR
3 CHATSWORTH PARK RISE
4 CHATSWORTH PARK AVE
1 HAIGH MOOR WLK
2 HAIGH MOOR RD
MOORTHORPE WAY 1
MOORTHORPE GREEN 2
MOORTHORPE GDNS 3
DEANHEAD DR 4
DARFIELD CL 5

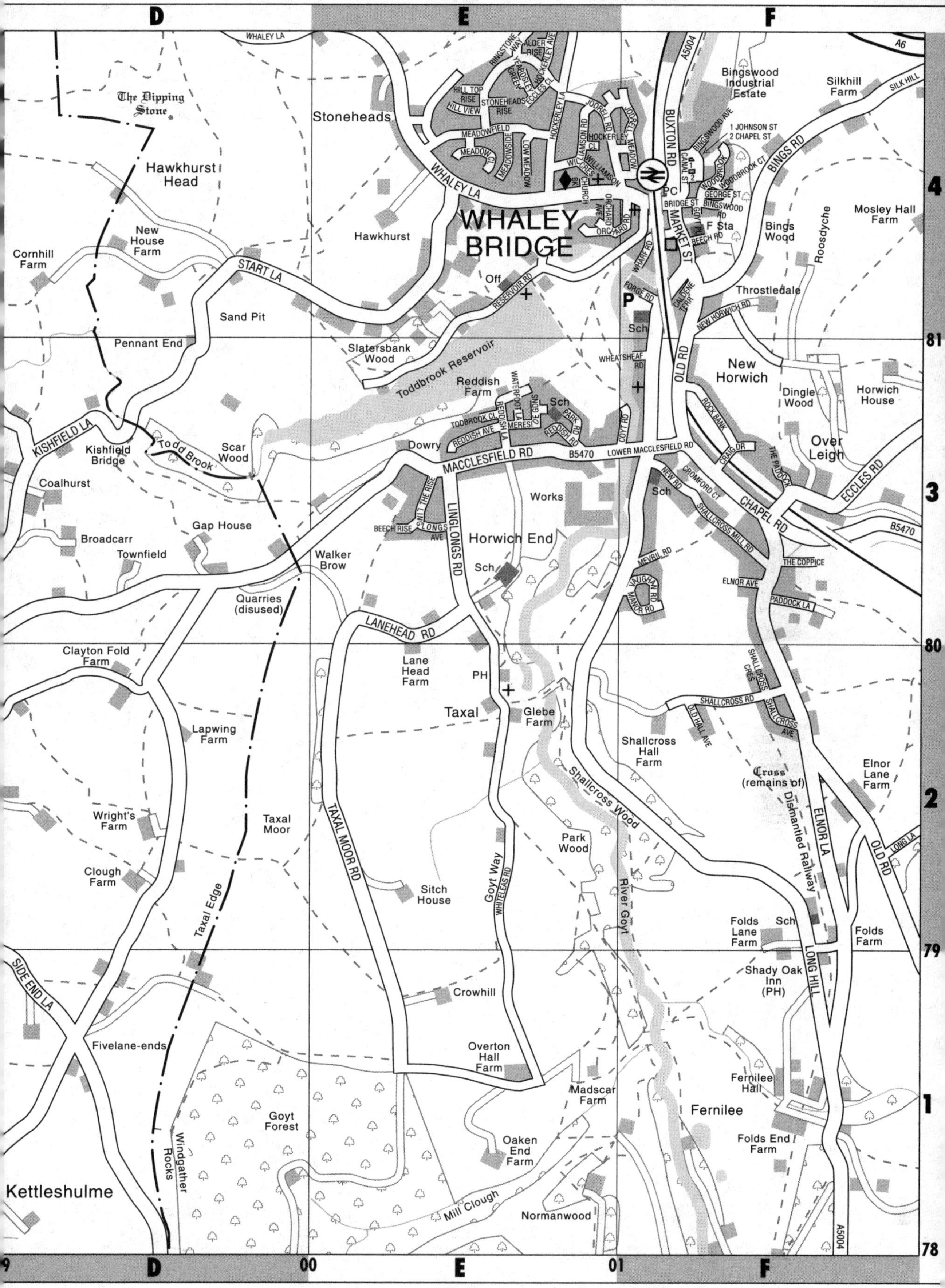
D
E
F
WHALEY LA
The Dipping Stone
Hawkhurst Head
Stoneheads
RINGSTONE WAY
ALDER RISE
HOCKERLEY AVE
YEARDSLEY GREEN
ECCLES CL
HILL TOP RISE
HILL VIEW
STONEHEADS RISE
MEADOWFIELD
MEADOW CL
MEADOWSIDE
LOW MEADOW
HOCKERLEY LA
WILLIAMSON RD
JODRELL RD
JODRELL MEADOW
HOCKERLEY CL
WILLIAMSON CRES
WILLIAMSON AVE
CHURCH AVE
ORCHARD AVE
ORCHARD RD
WHALEY LA
WHALEY BRIDGE
A5004
BUXTON RD
A6
Bingswood Industrial Estate
Silkhill Farm
SILK HILL
1 JOHNSON ST
2 CHAPEL ST
BINGSWOOD AVE
CANAL ST
WOODBROOK
WOODBROOK CT
BINGS RD
GEORGE ST
BRIDGE ST
BINGSWOOD RD
GOYT PL
BEECH RD
MARKET ST
PC
F Sta
Bings Wood
Roosdyche
Mosley Hall Farm
New House Farm
Hawkhurst
Cornhill Farm
START LA
Off
RESERVOIR RD
WHARF RD
FORGE RD
CALDENE TERR
Throstledale
NEW HORWICH RD
Sand Pit
P
Sch
Pennant End
Slatersbank Wood
Toddbrook Reservoir
WHEATSHEAF RD
OLD RD
New Horwich
Dingle Wood
Horwich House
Reddish Farm
WATERFOOT LA
SNIPE CL
Sch
TODBROOK CL
REDDISH LA
MERES
PARK RD
REDDISH RD
GOYT RD
ROCK BANK
KISHFIELD LA
Kishfield Bridge
Todd Brook
Scar Wood
Dowry
REDDISH AVE
MACCLESFIELD RD
B5470
LOWER MACCLESFIELD RD
CRAIG DR
THE PADDOCK
Over Leigh
ECCLES RD
Coalhurst
NEW RD
CROMFORD CT
CHAPEL RD
Works
Sch
SHALLCROSS MILL RD
B5470
Broadcarr
Gap House
Townfield
KNIT THE RISE
BEECH RISE
LONGS AVE
LINGLONGS RD
Horwich End
MEVRIL RD
THE COPPICE
ELNOR AVE
Walker Brow
Sch
VAUGHAN RD
MANOR RD
PADDOCK LA
Quarries (disused)
LANEHEAD RD
Clayton Fold Farm
Lane Head Farm
PH
SHALLCROSS CRES
SHALLCROSS RD
Taxal
Glebe Farm
OLD HALL AVE
SHALLCROSS AVE
Lapwing Farm
Shallcross Hall Farm
Cross (remains of)
Elnor Lane Farm
Shallcross Wood
Wright's Farm
Taxal Moor
TAXAL MOOR RD
Park Wood
Dismantled Railway
ELNOR LA
OLD RD
LONG LA
Clough Farm
Goyt Way
WHITELEAS RD
Sitch House
River Goyt
Taxal Edge
Folds Lane Farm
Sch
Folds Farm
SIDE END LA
LONG HILL
Shady Oak Inn (PH)
Crowhill
Fivelane-ends
Overton Hall Farm
Fernilee Hall
Madscar Farm
Fernilee
Goyt Forest
Oaken End Farm
Folds End Farm
Windgather Rocks
Kettleshulme
Mill Clough
Normanwood
A5004
4
81
3
80
2
79
1
78
9
00
01
D
E
F

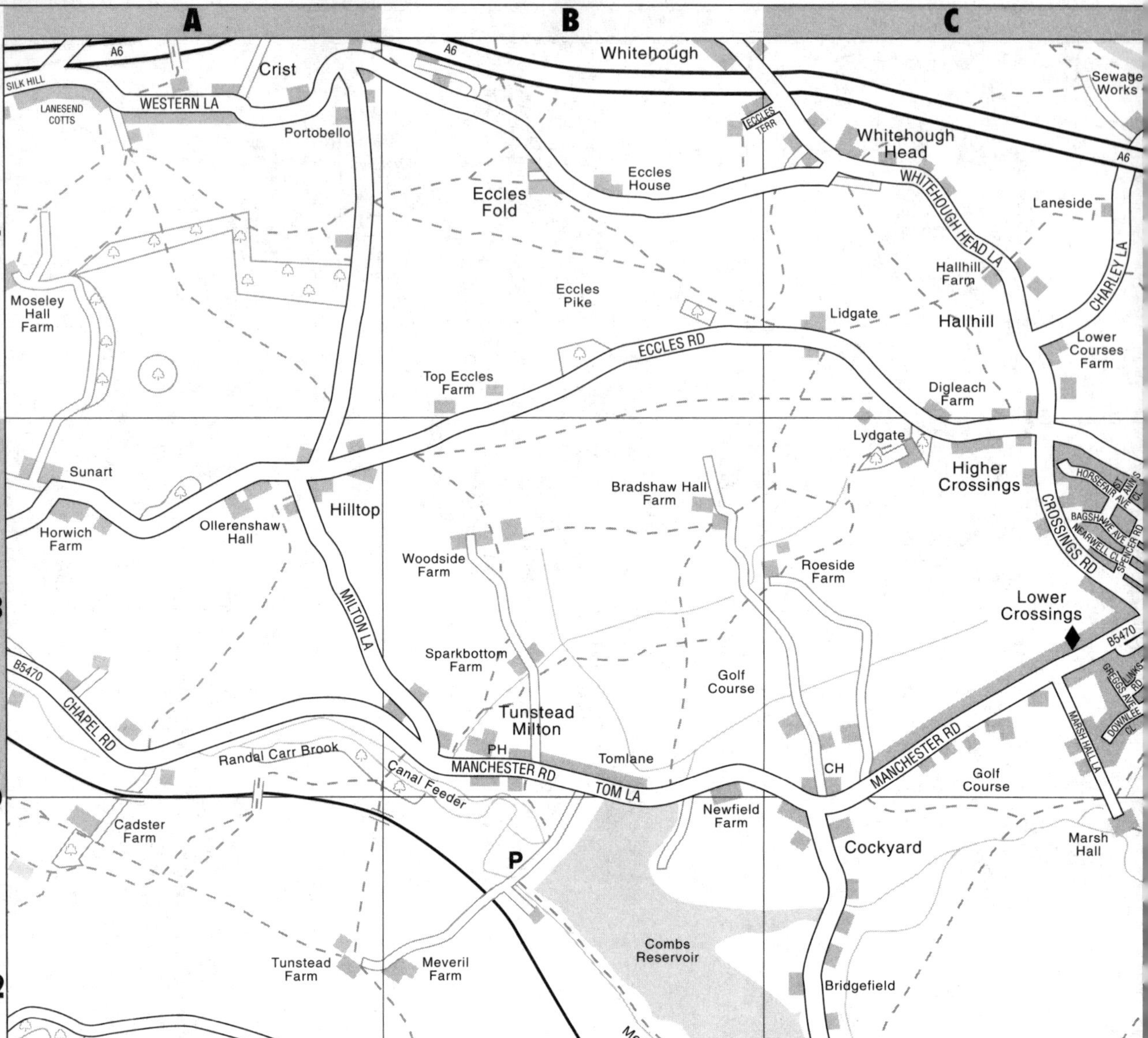
A
B
C
A6
Whitehough
Crist
SILK HILL
WESTERN LA
LANESEND COTTS
Portobello
Sewage Works
ECCLES TERR
Whitehough Head
A6
Eccles House
Eccles Fold
WHITEHOUGH HEAD LA
Laneside
CHARLEY LA
Hallhill Farm
Moseley Hall Farm
Eccles Pike
Lidgate
Hallhill
Lower Courses Farm
ECCLES RD
Top Eccles Farm
Digleach Farm
Lydgate
Sunart
Higher Crossings
HORSEFAIR AVE
Hilltop
Bradshaw Hall Farm
BAGSHAWE AVE
NEARWELL CL
SPENCER RD
CROSSINGS RD
Horwich Farm
Ollerenshaw Hall
Woodside Farm
Roeside Farm
Lower Crossings
MILTON LA
B5470
B5470
Sparkbottom Farm
Golf Course
GREGGS AVE
LINKS RD
DOWNLEE CL
CHAPEL RD
Tunstead Milton
MARSH HALL LA
MANCHESTER RD
PH
Randal Carr Brook
Tomlane
CH
Canal Feeder
MANCHESTER RD
TOM LA
Golf Course
Newfield Farm
Cadster Farm
Cockyard
Marsh Hall
P
Combs Reservoir
Tunstead Farm
Meveril Farm
Bridgefield
Meveril Brook
COMBS RD
LONG LA
Ladder Hill
Owlgreave Farm
Black Edge Plantation
Television Station
Spire Hollins Farm
Thorney Lee
THE AVENUE
PH
Old Brook House
Long Edge Plantation
OLD RD
Pritchard Green Farm
Whitehills
Haylee House
P
Combs
COMBS LA
RIDGE LA
Overhill Farm
COWLOW LA
Rye Flatt Farm
Haylee Farm
4
81
3
80
2
79
1
78
02
03
04
A
B
C

D
E
F
Bridgeholm Green
Mill
CHARLEY LA
A624
CROSS KEYS ROW
Chapel Milton
HAYFIELD RD
Bowden Hall
Slackhall Farm
A625
Slackhall
Mag Low
Maglow Farm
BOWDEN LA
Bowden Hey Farm
Slacke Hall
SHEFFIELD RD
Higher Courses Farm
Wks
THE CRESCENT
Black Brook
Bagshaw Hall Farm
Bagshaw
POPLAR TERR
HAYFIELD RD EAST
Burrfields
Townend
A6
Laneside
BURRFIELDS RD
DANESWAY
CHURCH LA
PICKFORD PL
ROEBUCK PL
MARKET PL
CHURCH BR
TERRACE RD
MARKET ST
QUENTIN RD
BARLOW RD
HEYWORTH RD
BERESFORD RD
ELDON
ANCHOR AVE
NETHERFIELD RD
BROOKLANDS AVE
BROOKLANDS RD
B5470
BLACKBROOK LA
Blackbrook
Peaslows Farm
STATION RD
ECCLES RD
HORSE FAIR AVE
SPENCER RD
CROSSINGS AVE
ECCLES FOLD
MELLOR LA
CROSS ST
HIGH ST
PC
TH
PARK VIEW DR
F Sta
Sch
Smithfield
GREEN PARK DR
EASTBROOK CL
LONGSON RD
ANCHOR FOLD
ASHFIELD RD
Schs
MANCHESTER RD
B5470
Chapel-en-le-Frith
JUBILEE RD
HORDERNS RD
HORDERNS LA
GRANGE PARK RD
PARK RD
THORNBROOK RD
WESTBROOK CL
LOWER EAVES VIEW
WARMBROOK RD
MOSS VIEW RD
THORNELL CL
WILSHAW CL
BURDEKIN CL
BERESFORD AVE
JOHNSON WAY
PARK CRES
GRANGE AVE
Blackbrook Farm
High Leigh
LINKS RD
FRITH VIEW
ELMFIELD
LANESIDE CL
HORDERNS PARK RD
WILLOW DR
GRANGE PARK AVE
OAK CL
Lower Eaves
ASHBOURNE LA
BUXTON RD
CROMWELL AVE
KNOWLE AVE
HOLLIN DR
ROWTON GRANGE RD
BROOKSIDE RD
Sch
ALSTON RD
EISBOURNE DR
LEEFIELD RD
WOODLANDS RD
THE HAWTHORNS
LONGMEADE DR
SYCAMORE RD
BRIDGEWAY
Warm Brook
Marshgreen Farm
Eaves Hall
Eaves Tunnel
Lower Plumpton
Windy Wall Farm
Barmoor Clough
Bolt Edge
LONG LA
Paradise Farm
Higher Plumpton
Down Lee Farm
Hollinknoll
LC
Chapel-en-le-Frith Station
Platting Farm
A623
Ridge Lodge
Martinside
Tunnel
Sittinglow
HIGHER HALLSTEADS
Ridge Reservoirs
Top Lodge
Ridge Farm
Hallsteads Farm
MEADOW LA
Bank Hall
Ridge Hall
Dove Holes Tunnel
Cow Low
COWLOW LA
BEELOW CL
HALLSTEADS
Cowlow
Dove Holes
HIGHFIELD AVE
HALLSTEADS CL
Castle Naze
Combs Edge
Short Edge
Lady Low
MEADOW CL
Sch
Bull Ring Henge
Meadows Farm
STATION RD
ALEXANDER RD
HORSESHOE AVE
Dove Holes Station
A6
4
81
3
80
2
79
1
78
05
06
07

47 36

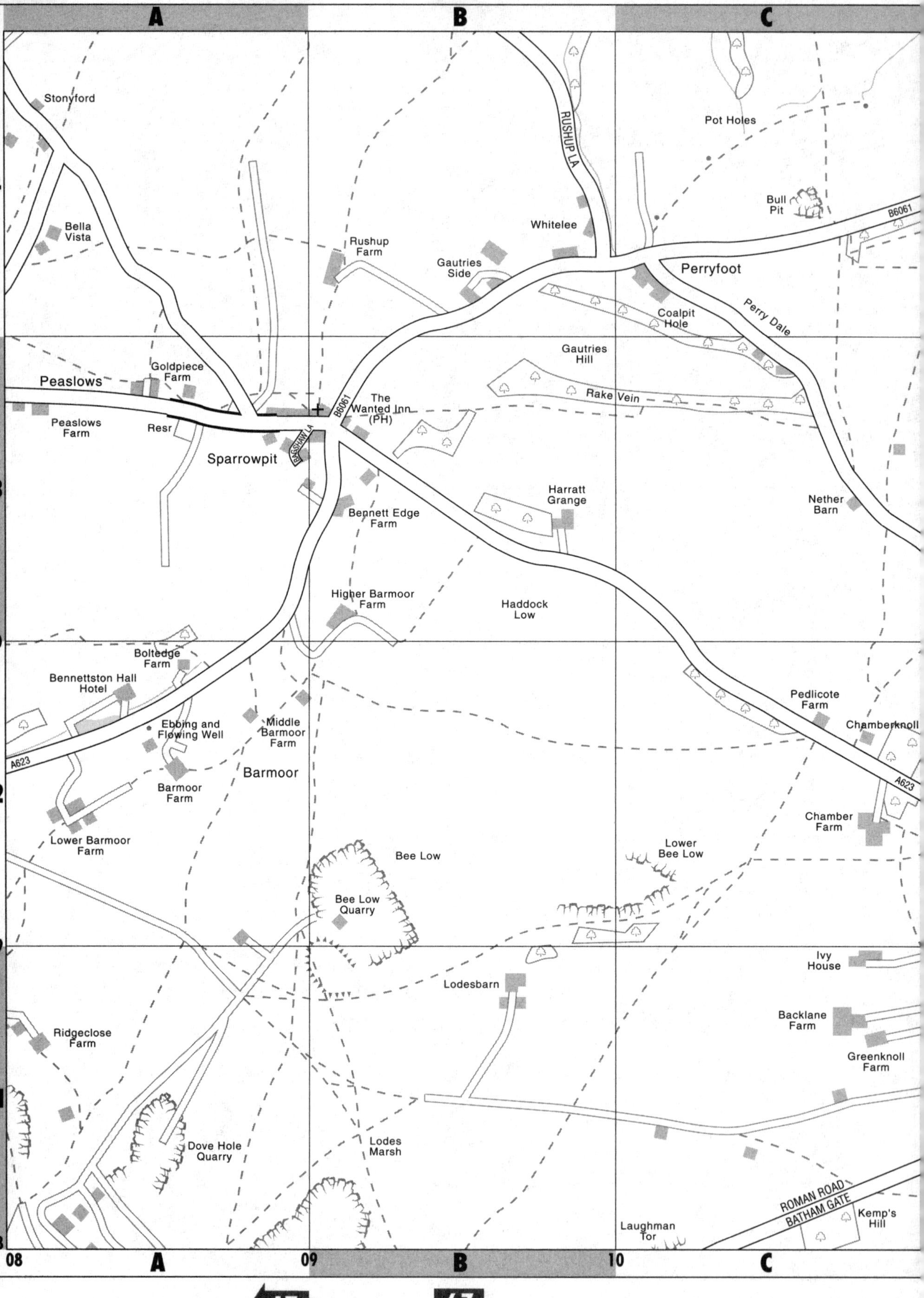
A
B
C
Stonyford
Bella Vista
Rushup Farm
RUSHUP LA
Whitelee
Gautries Side
Pot Holes
Bull Pit
B6061
Perryfoot
Perry Dale
Coalpit Hole
Gautries Hill
Rake Vein
Goldpiece Farm
Peaslows
Peaslows Farm
Resr
Sparrowpit
BAGSHAW LA
The Wanted Inn (PH)
Bennett Edge Farm
Harratt Grange
Nether Barn
Higher Barmoor Farm
Haddock Low
Boltedge Farm
Bennettston Hall Hotel
Ebbing and Flowing Well
Middle Barmoor Farm
Barmoor
Barmoor Farm
A623
Lower Barmoor Farm
Pedlicote Farm
Chamberknoll
Chamber Farm
Bee Low
Bee Low Quarry
Lower Bee Low
Lodesbarn
Ivy House
Backlane Farm
Greenknoll Farm
Ridgeclose Farm
Dove Hole Quarry
Lodes Marsh
Laughman Tor
ROMAN ROAD
BATHAM GATE
Kemp's Hill
4
81
3
80
2
79
1
78
08
09
10

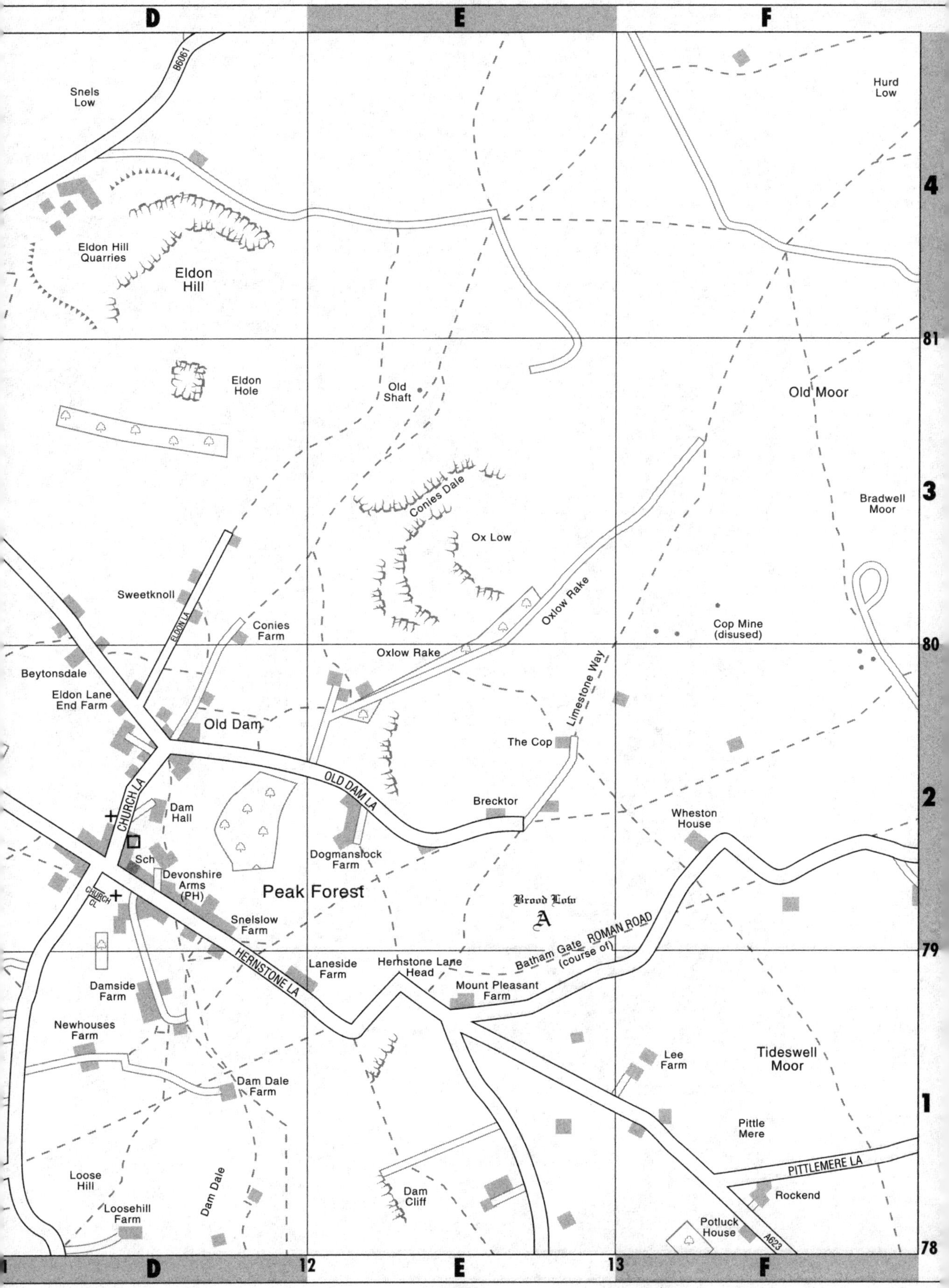
D
E
F
B6061
Snels Low
Hurd Low
4
Eldon Hill Quarries
Eldon Hill
81
Eldon Hole
Old Shaft
Old Moor
3
Conies Dale
Bradwell Moor
Ox Low
Sweetknoll
ELDON LA
Oxlow Rake
Conies Farm
Cop Mine (disused)
80
Oxlow Rake
Beytonsdale
Limestone Way
Eldon Lane End Farm
Old Dam
The Cop
CHURCH LA
OLD DAM LA
2
Brecktor
Dam Hall
Wheston House
Sch
Dogmanslock Farm
Devonshire Arms (PH)
CHURCH CL
Peak Forest
Brood Low
Snelslow Farm
ROMAN ROAD
Batham Gate (course of)
79
HERNSTONE LA
Laneside Farm
Hernstone Lane Head
Damside Farm
Mount Pleasant Farm
Newhouses Farm
Lee Farm
Tideswell Moor
Dam Dale Farm
1
Pittle Mere
PITTLEMERE LA
Loose Hill
Dam Dale
Dam Cliff
Rockend
Loosehill Farm
Potluck House
A623
78
12
13

49
38

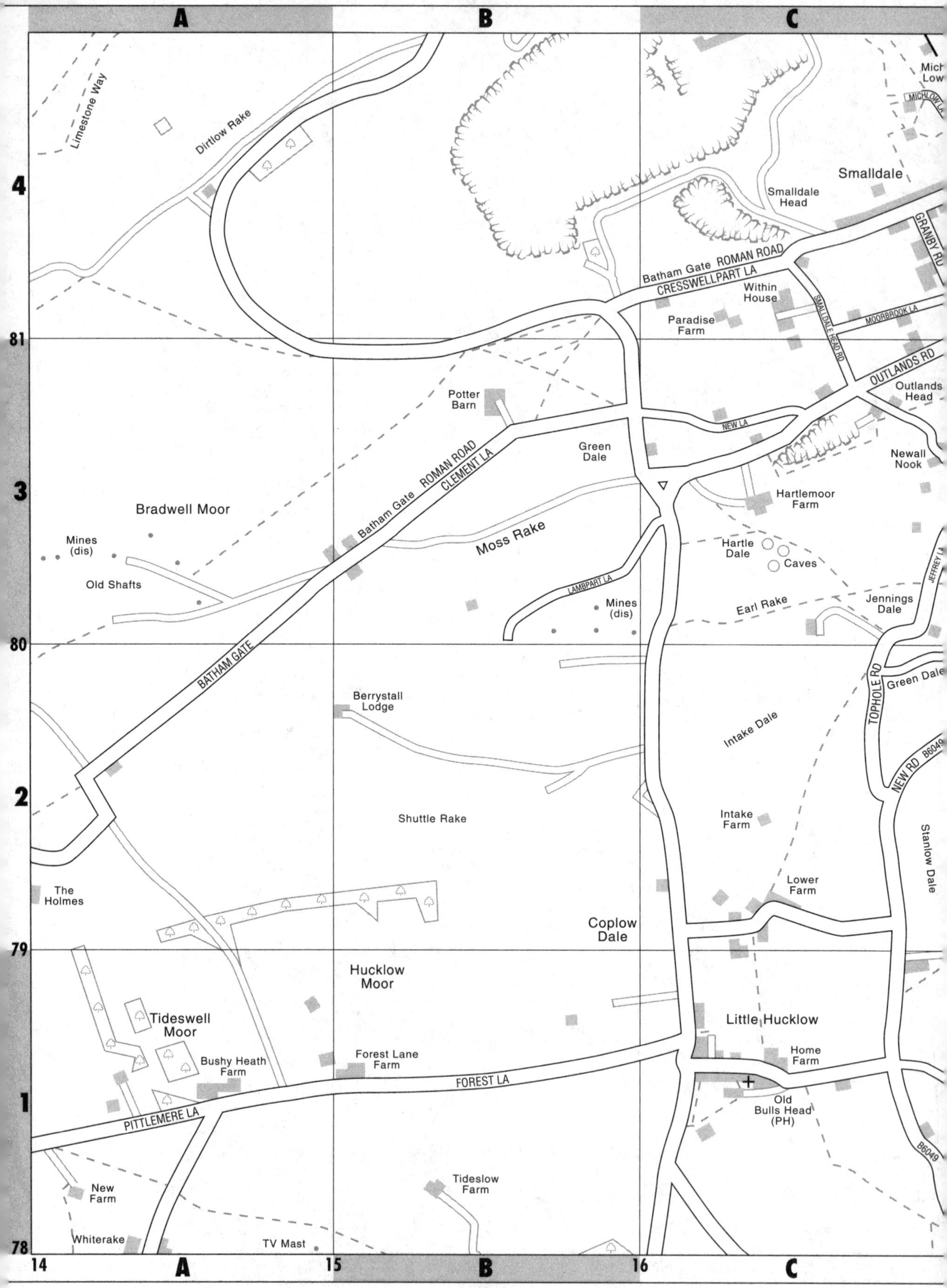
A
B
C
4
81
3
80
2
79
1
78
14
15
16
Limestone Way
Dirtlow Rake
Smalldale
Smalldale Head
Mich Low
MICHLOW LA
GRANBY RD
Batham Gate ROMAN ROAD
CRESSWELLPART LA
Within House
Paradise Farm
SMALLDALE HEAD RD
MOORBROOK LA
OUTLANDS RD
Outlands Head
Potter Barn
NEW LA
Green Dale
Newall Nook
Batham Gate ROMAN ROAD
CLEMENT LA
Bradwell Moor
Hartlemoor Farm
Moss Rake
Hartle Dale
Caves
Mines (dis)
Old Shafts
LAMBPART LA
Mines (dis)
Earl Rake
Jennings Dale
JEFFREY LA
BATHAM GATE
Berrystall Lodge
TOPHOLE RD
Green Dale
Intake Dale
NEW RD B6049
Shuttle Rake
Intake Farm
Stanlow Dale
The Holmes
Lower Farm
Coplow Dale
Hucklow Moor
Tideswell Moor
Little Hucklow
Bushy Heath Farm
Forest Lane Farm
Home Farm
FOREST LA
PITTLEMERE LA
Old Bulls Head (PH)
B6049
New Farm
Tideslow Farm
Whiterake
TV Mast

49
69

39
52
D
E
F
Caravan Park
Lee House
Brough Lee
Batham's Farm
ROMAN ROAD
Batham Gate
STRETFIELD RD
B6049
GORE LA
MAIN RD
TOWN LA
Grey Ditch
The Car
Overdale Brook
BROUGH LA
Shatton Moor
TV Mast
SHATTON LA
Shatton Edge
Sch
Wks
Sta
Smithy-Hill
Bradwell
NETHERSIDE
CHURCH ST
PC
Rebellion Knoll
Dale End
Bagshawe Cavern
Bradwell Hills
BESSIE LA
THE HILLS
THE GREEN
JEFFREY LA
Bradwell Dale
Bradwell Edge
Over Dale
Burton Bole End
Burton Bole
Siney Sitch
Wolf's Pit
Hill Rake
Robin Hood's Cross
Hazlebadge Hall
DUPER LA
NEW RD
Fold Farm
Abney
Ash House Farm
Abney Moor
Bleak Knoll
Deadmans Clough
Quarters Farm
Cockey Farm
Durham Edge
Nether Water Farm
Camphill (Gliding Field)
Abney Grange
Grange Farm
Gliding Club
Bretton Brook
Burrs Mount
Broad Low
Hucklow Edge
Youth Hostel
4
81
3
80
2
79
1
78
18
19
70
52

51
40

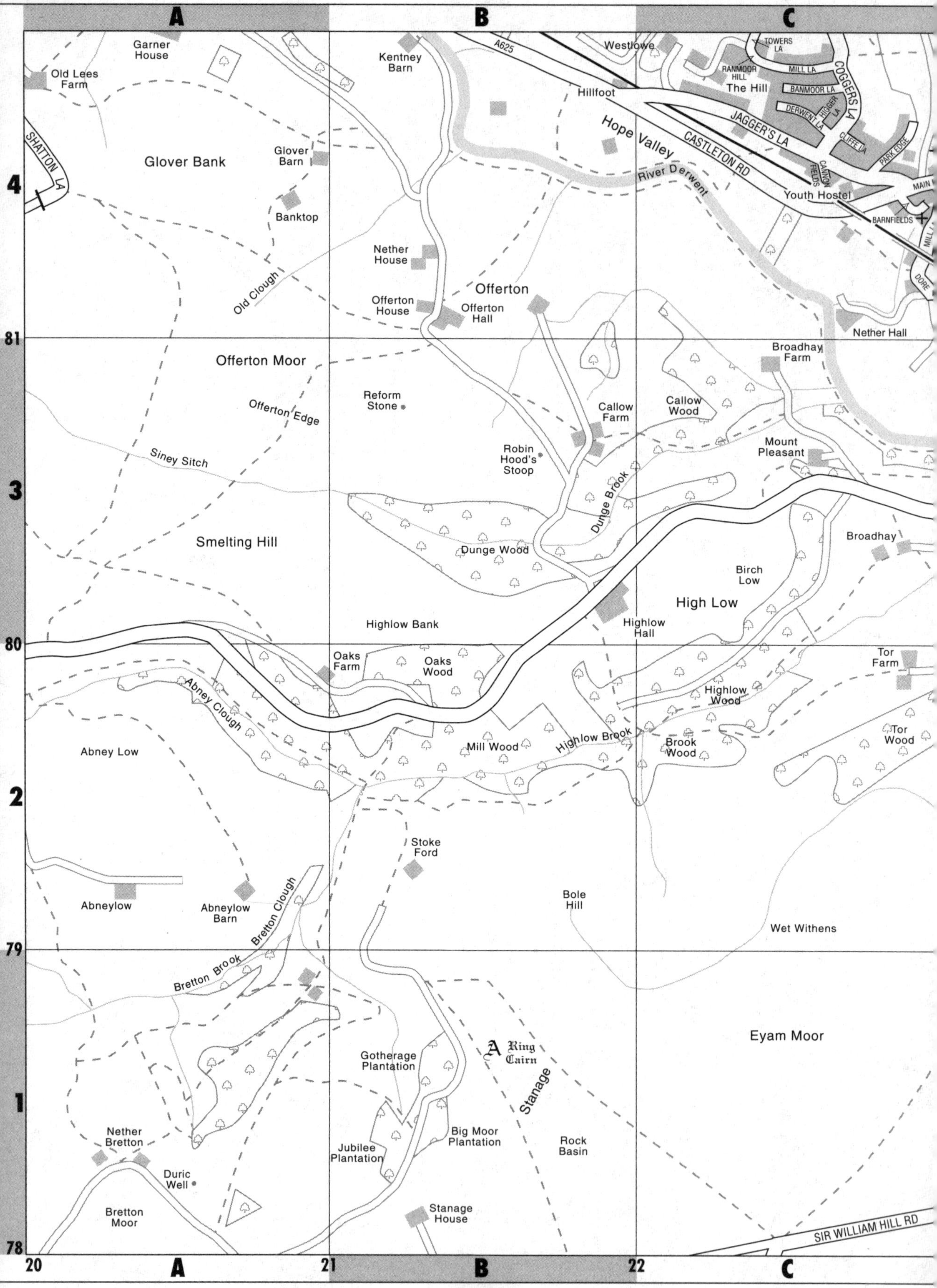
A
B
C
Garner House
Old Lees Farm
Kentney Barn
A625
Westlowe
TOWERS LA
RANMOOR HILL
MILL LA
The Hill
BANMOOR LA
COGGERS LA
Hillfoot
DERWENT LA
HIGGER LA
JAGGER'S LA
CLIFFE LA
PARK EDGE
Hope Valley
CASTLETON RD
SHATTON LA
Glover Bank
Glover Barn
River Derwent
CANNON FIELDS
Youth Hostel
MAIN
BARNFIELDS
Banktop
Nether House
DORE
Offerton
Old Clough
Offerton House
Offerton Hall
Nether Hall
Offerton Moor
Broadhay Farm
Reform Stone
Callow Farm
Callow Wood
Offerton Edge
Mount Pleasant
Siney Sitch
Robin Hood's Stoop
Dunge Brook
Broadhay
Smelting Hill
Dunge Wood
Birch Low
High Low
Highlow Bank
Highlow Hall
Oaks Farm
Oaks Wood
Tor Farm
Abney Clough
Highlow Wood
Tor Wood
Highlow Brook
Mill Wood
Brook Wood
Abney Low
Stoke Ford
Bole Hill
Abneylow
Abneylow Barn
Bretton Clough
Wet Withens
Bretton Brook
Eyam Moor
Ring Cairn
Gotherage Plantation
Stanage
Big Moor Plantation
Nether Bretton
Jubilee Plantation
Rock Basin
Duric Well
Stanage House
Bretton Moor
SIR WILLIAM HILL RD
4
81
3
80
2
79
1
78
20
21
22

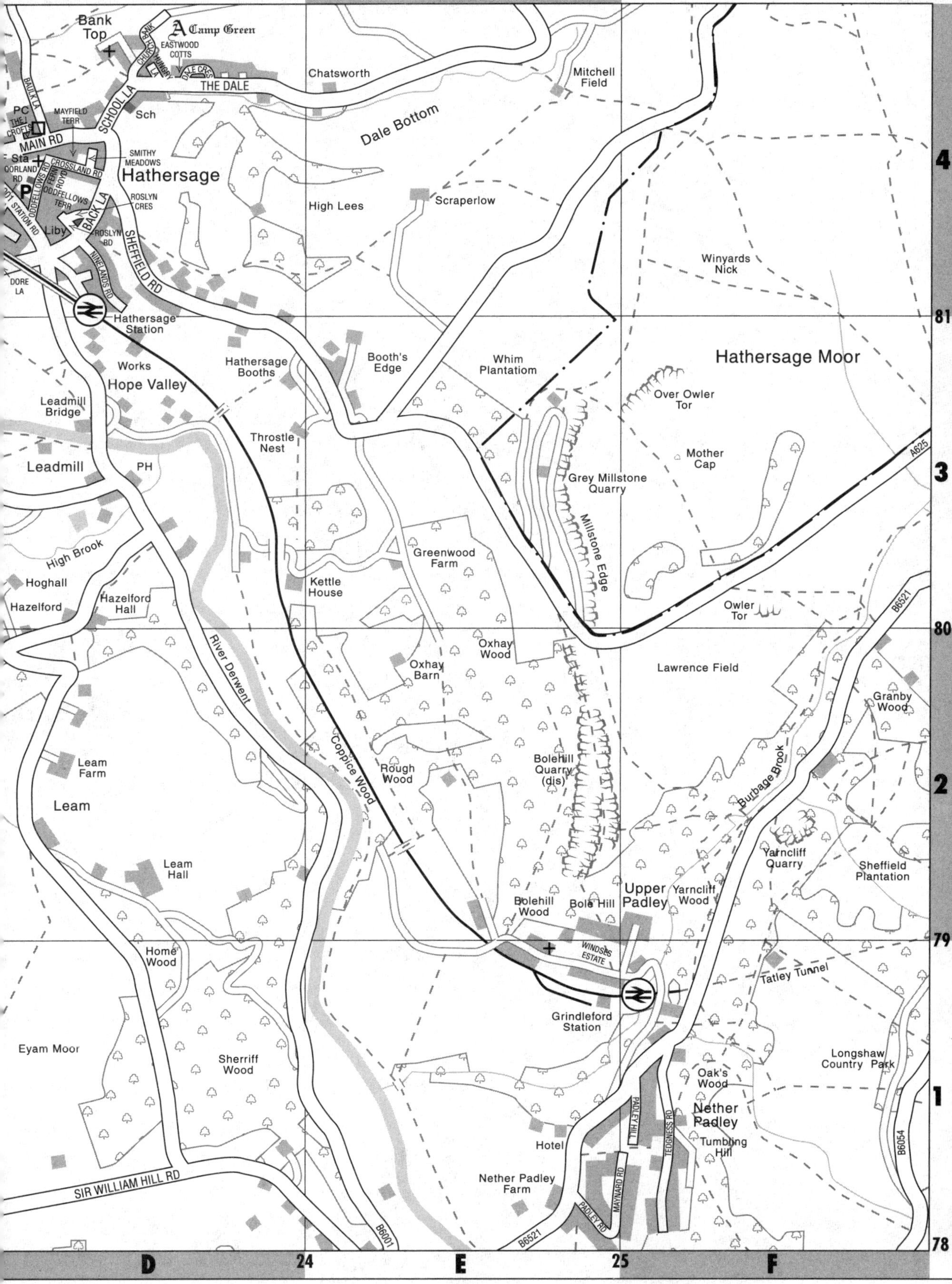
D
E
F
Bank Top
Camp Green
EASTWOOD COTTS
THE DALE
Chatsworth
Mitchell Field
Dale Bottom
Sch
MAIN RD
Hathersage
High Lees
Scraperlow
Winyards Nick
Hathersage Station
Hathersage Booths
Booth's Edge
Whim Plantatiom
Hathersage Moor
Works
Hope Valley
Leadmill Bridge
Over Owler Tor
Throstle Nest
Mother Cap
Leadmill
PH
Grey Millstone Quarry
A625
High Brook
Greenwood Farm
Millstone Edge
Hoghall
Kettle House
Hazelford Hall
Hazelford
Owler Tor
B6521
Oxhay Wood
Lawrence Field
Oxhay Barn
River Derwent
Granby Wood
Leam Farm
Rough Wood
Bolehill Quarry (dis)
Burbage Brook
Coppice Wood
Leam
Yarncliff Quarry
Leam Hall
Sheffield Plantation
Upper Padley
Yarncliff Wood
Bolehill Wood
Bole Hill
Home Wood
WINDSOR ESTATE
Tatley Tunnel
Grindleford Station
Eyam Moor
Longshaw Country Park
Sherriff Wood
Oak's Wood
Nether Padley
Tumbling Hill
Hotel
B6054
Nether Padley Farm
SIR WILLIAM HILL RD
B6001
B6521
PADLEY RD
MAYNARD RD
PADLEY HILL
TEDGNESS RD
4
81
3
80
2
79
1
78
24
25

53
42

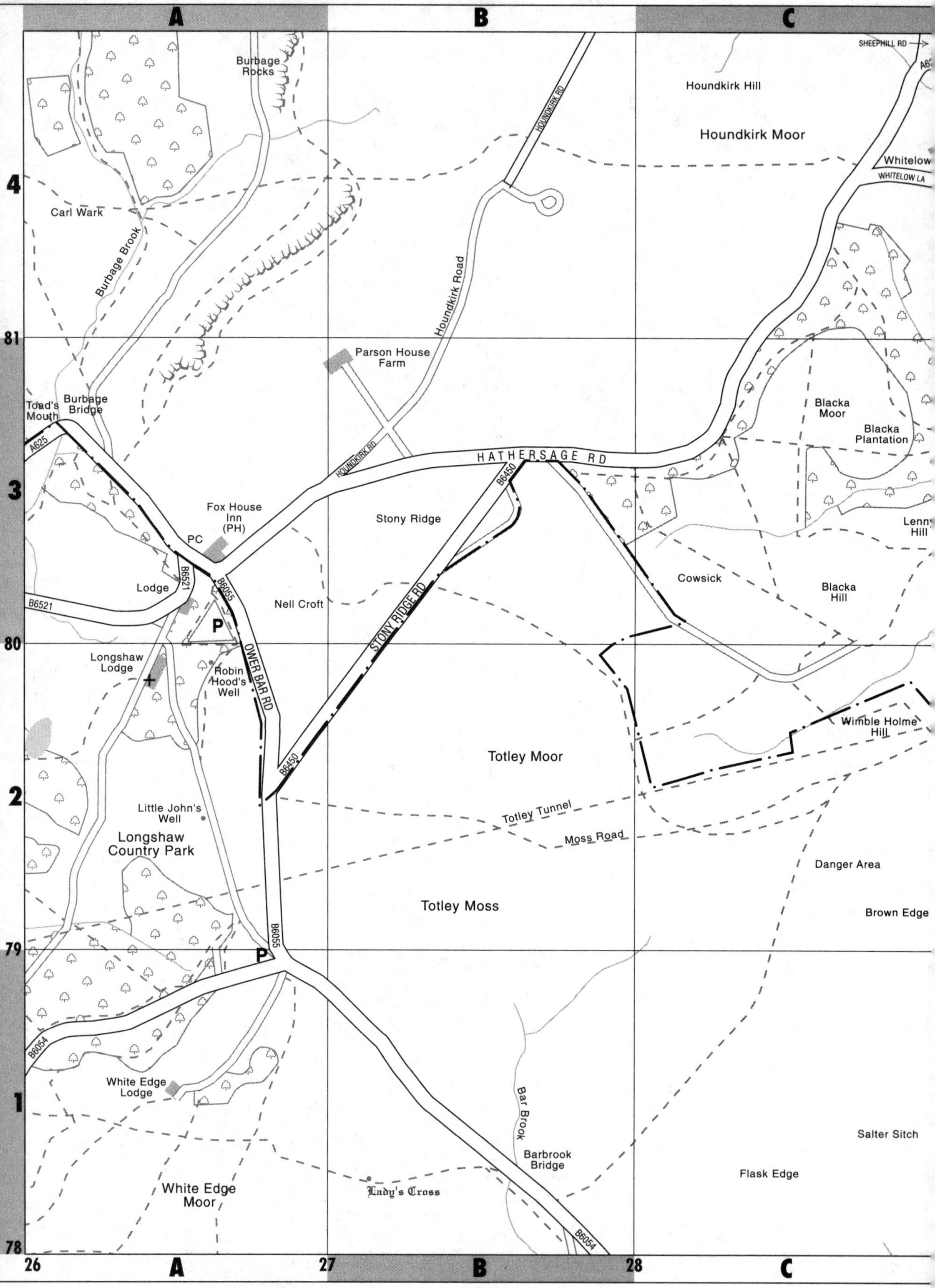
A
B
C
SHEEPHILL RD
Burbage Rocks
Houndkirk Hill
Houndkirk Moor
HOUNDKIRK RD
Whitelow
WHITELOW LA
4
Carl Wark
Burbage Brook
Houndkirk Road
81
Parson House Farm
Toad's Mouth
Burbage Bridge
Blacka Moor
Blacka Plantation
A625
HATHERSAGE RD
HOUNDKIRK RD
B6450
3
Fox House Inn (PH)
PC
Stony Ridge
Lenny Hill
B6521
Lodge
B6055
Cowsick
Blacka Hill
B6521
Nell Croft
STONY RIDGE RD
P
80
Longshaw Lodge
Robin Hood's Well
OWER BAR RD
Wimble Holme Hill
Totley Moor
B6450
2
Little John's Well
Totley Tunnel
Longshaw Country Park
Moss Road
Danger Area
Totley Moss
Brown Edge
B6055
79
P
B6054
White Edge Lodge
1
Bar Brook
Salter Sitch
Barbrook Bridge
Flask Edge
White Edge Moor
Lady's Cross
B6054
78
26
A
27
B
28
C

56

D
E
F
Fern Glen Farm
HATHERSAGE RD
A625
BRICKHOUSE LA
CROSS LA
Brick Houses
LIMB LA
Picnic Area
Limb Hill
Ecclesall Wood
Limb Brook
Ryecroft Glen
Ryecroft Farm
KERWIN RD
KERWIN CL
KERWIN DR
PARKERS LA
CAUSEWAY GDNS
CAUSEWAY HEAD RD
CAUSEWAY GLADE
RUSHLEY CL
RUSHLEY RD
RUSHLEY DR
RUSHLEY AVE
RYECROFT VIEW
KINGSCROFT CL
RYECROFT GLEN RD
NEWFIELD LA
NEWFIELD CFT
NEWFIELD CRES
HEATHER LEA AVE
HEATHER LEA PL
THE CAUSEWAY
MEADWAY DR
THE MEADWAY
Causeway Head
PC
LEYFIELD RD
DEVONSHIRE TERRACE RD
HIGH ST
RUSHLEIGH CT
DORE HALL CROFT
DORE RD
Dore
VICARAGE LA
SAVAGE LA
Whitelow Farm
New Whitelow Farm
WHITELOW LA
High Greave
Recreation Ground
TOWNHEAD RD
HIGH TREES
DRURY LA
CHURCH LA
MIDDLEFIELD CL
MIDDLEFIELD CFT
OVERDALE RISE
OVERDALE GDNS
BLACKA MOOR RD
BLACKA MOOR CRES
BLACKA MOOR VIEW
Townhead
Schs
Roundseats Farm
Redcar Brook
SHORTS LA
Fairthorn
OLD HAY GDNS
OLD HAY LA
Broadstorth
OLDHAY CL
Sch
FURNISS AVE
BURLINGTON GR
ASHFURLONG RD
THORNSETT GDNS
VICTOR RD
CAVENDISH AVE
BURLINGTON RD
GILLEYFIELD AVE
BURLINGTON GLEN
BURLINGTON CT
DEVONSHIRE DR
ASHFURLONG CL
ASHFURLONG DR
ABBEYDALE PARK RISE
Abbeydale Park
ABBEYDALE PARK CRES
DEVONSHIRE RD
DEVONSHIRE GR
DEVONSHIRE GLEN
BUSHEY WOOD RD
WYVERN GDNS
DUNVALE CT
MERCIA DR
VERNON RD
CHATSWORTH RD
BRINKBURN VALE RD
BRINKBURN CT
BRINKBURN DR
BRINKBURN CL
ABBEYDALE RD S
A621
WEST VIEW LA
WEST VIEW CL
Hallfield Farm
Avenue Farm
Oldhay Brook
TOTLEY BROOK GLEN
TOTLEY BROOK GR
KINGS COPPICE
TOTLEY BROOK WAY
TOTLEY BROOK CL
TOTLEY BROOK CROFT
WESSEX GDNS
Totley Brook
KING EGBERT RD
SHERWOOD CHASE
TOTLEY BROOK RD
WOODLAND PL
MILL LA
MILLDALE RD
GROVE RD
GROVE CT
HOUSE CT
HAYBROOK
AKLEY BANK CL
OAKBANK CT
MOUNT FORD
MARSTON CRES
STONECROFT RD
PROSPECT RD
Totley Rise
QUEEN VICTORIA RD
Totley Bents
Hillfoot
HILLFOOT RD
QUARRY RD
TERREY RD
THE QUADRANT
THE CRES
STRAWBERRY LEE LA
Bolehill Lodge
Taylor's Hill
PENNY LA
GROVE AVE
TOTLEY GRANGE CL
THE GROVE
Totley
LAVERDENE RD
LAVERDENE CL
LAVERDENE WAY
GLOVER RD
LAVERDENE AVE
ole Hill
Moss Road
Totley Tunnel
MOSS RD
BENTS RD
CHAPEL LA
BUTTS HILL
TOTLEY GRANGE DR
TOTLEY GRANGE RD
THE GREEN
LEMONT RD
LAVERDENE DR
Needham's Dike
Sch
SUMMER LA
GREEN OAK CRES
Liby
New Totley
ALDAM RD
MICKLEY LA
WOLLATON RD
LONGFORD DR
LONGFORD RD
LONGFORD SPINNEY
LANE HEAD RD
BASLOW RD
OVERCROFT RISE
OLDWELL CL
STOCKS GREEN DR
STOCKS GREEN CT
TOTLEY HALL LA
MEADOW GROVE RD
SUNNYVALE AVE
SUNNYVALE RD
MEADOW GROVE
MAIN AVE
GREEN OAK AVE
GREEN OAK DR
GREEN OAK GR
GREEN OAK RD
ALDAM CL
ALDAM WAY
ALDAM CROFT
ROWAN TREE DELL
Rifle Range
DANGER AREA
Brown Edge
Hollin Hill
Coll
St George's Farm
Little Wood
Works
Gillfield Wood
Woodthorpe Hall
Moor Edge Farm
Totley Brook
Moorwood's Farm
Thickwood Lodge
Moorwood's Hall Farm
MOORWOOD AVE
Owler Lee
Holmesfield Park Wood
Storth Lodge
Old Hall
Fanshaw Gate
FANSHAW GATE LA
Storth House
HOB LA
Owler Bar
Peacock Inn
A621
B6054
4
81
3
80
2
79
1
78
30
31

74

56

55

A
B
C
Mill Pond
Mus
Golf Course
Ecclesall Wood
Limb Brook
River Sheaf
Ladies' Spring Wood
Limb Bridge
Beauchief Hall
Beauchief
Parkbank Wood
Cockshutt Farm
Gulleys Wood
Beauchief Park
Dore and Totley Station
CH
Golf Course
Old Park Wood
DORE RD
ABBEYDALE RD S
WOODLAND VIEW
LADIES SPRING DR
LADIES SPRING GR
BEAUCHIEF DR
BEAUCHIEF ABBEY LA
COCKSHUTT DR
CRAWSHAW AVE
WINGERWORTH AVE
OLD PARK RD
OLD PARK AVE
WESTWICK GR
WESTWICK RD
WESTWICK CRES
BOCKING LA
WALTON CL
CHANCET WOOD RD
ROXTON AVE
GREENHILL AVE
MEADOW HEAD AVE
ROBERT RD
SCHOOL LA
RENEY RD
Liby
Sch
Greenhill
PARKWAY
Sport Groun
JAMES ANDREW CRES
JAMES ANDREW CL
LUPTON RD
TOPPHAM DR
TOPPHAM WAY
GERVASE AVE
GERVASE DR
GERVASE RD
GERVASE WLK
LOWEDGES RD
LOWEDGES CRES
GRESLEY RD
GRESLEY WLK
Greenhill Park
HEMPER LA
GREENHILL PARKWAY
RENEY AVE
RENEY CRES
RENEY WLK
HASLAM CRES
ATLANTIC RD
ATLANTIC DR
BECKET AVE
BOLAND RD
EDMUND AVE
EDMUND CL
FOX LA
ELWOOD RD
BRADWAY RD
Lower Bradway
F Sta
CH
Bradway
Bradway Tunnel
BIRCHITT RD
BIRCHITT CL
BRADWAY GRANGE RD
CONALAN AVE
KENWELL DR
Poynton Wood
POYNTON WOOD CRES
ROSAMOND GLADE
CASTLEROW DR
CASTLE ROW
TWENTYWELL DR
TWENTYWELL LA
TWENTYWELL RISE
TWENTYWELL VIEW
Bradway Bank
ST QUENTIN VIEW
ST QUENTIN MOUNT
ST QUENTIN RISE
ST QUENTIN DR
6 LADYBOWER CT
7 DERWENT CT
8 CELANDINE CT
9 ST QUENTIN CL
Sch
1 FIVE TREES AVE
2 FIVE TREES DR
3 FIVE TREES CL
BRINKBURN DR
ROSAMOND PL
ROSAMOND AVE
ROSAMOND DR
EVERARD AVE
Totley Rise
PROSPECT RD
WOLLATON AVE
WOLLATON RD
LONGFORD CRES
TOTLEY LA
IVY CLOSE AVE
B6054
BRADWAY RD
Upper Bradway
10 PROSPECT CT
11 MOORVIEW CT
PROSPECT RD
LONGFORD DR
1 QUEEN VICTORIA RD
2 PROSPECT PL
3 EVERARD GLADE
4 WOLLATON DR
5 LONGFORD CL
A621
Border View Farm
Golf Course
PCs
PC
Upper Birchitt
Bowshaw Farm
Bowshaw
ROD MOOR RD
Mickley Farm
MICKLEY LA
Works
Barnes Lane
Mickley
Barnes Farm
Summerwood Top
STUBLEY HOLLOW
PH
HOLMLEY LA
B6056
SHEFFIELD RD
WREAKES LA
NORTHERN COMMON
Rod Moor
BARNES AVE
BARNES LA
STUBLEY CL
STUBLEY LA
SUMMERWOOD LA
GREEN LEA
LONGCROFT RD
CROFT LEA
ORCHARD SQ
SMITHY CROFT
LONGCROFT AVE
Sch
STUBLEY DR
SUMMERWOOD PL
DRONFIELD
Gosforth Valley
Birchin Lee Farm
Dronfield Woodhouse
STAFFORD CL
LONGCROFT CRES
WELBECK CL
OARR LA
PCs
Nursery
Sch
HOLMESFIELD RD
Holmesfield Park Wood
B6056
SOLWAY RISE
FORTH AVE
ALPORT RISE
MORAY PL
TAY CL
LORNE CL
15 BUCKINGHAM CL
16 CHATSWORTH PL
17 BURBAGE CL
18 MILLSTONE CL
19 MONTROSE PL
ULLSWATER PARK
ULLSWATER DR
SHEARDS CL
SHEARDS DR
SHEARDS WAY
WEST ST
VICTORIA ST
PCs
Liby
BEECHWOOD RD
REPTON PL
DALBURY RD
WINDSOR DR
WENTWORTH RD
SHERWOOD RD
PENTLAND RD
Sch
10 SHERWOOD PL
11 GARDOM CL
12 LYNWOOD CL
13 BIRCHEN CL
14 HEATON CL
KENDAL DR
CONISTON RD
ENNERDALE CL
BUTTERMERE DR
CASTLERIGG WAY
TURNER CL
GOSFORTH LA
GOSFORTH DR
East Hollow
ELVASTON CL
MELBOURNE AVE
LEABROOK RD
ROCKINGHAM CL 1
NEWSTEAD CL 2
MAPPERLEY RD 3
HAZELWOOD CL 4
INGLEBY CL 5
IVAN BROOK CL 6
ARUNDEL CL 7
BRADWELL CL 8
ASHFORD RD 9
KILBURN RD
RAVENSDALE RD
SNELSTON CL
NORBURY CL
HAWKSHEAD AVE
Sch
GRASMERE RD 1
KENTMERE CL 2
BOWNESS CL 3
PATTERDALE CL 4
WINDERMERE AVE
ESKDALE CL
ROTHAY CL
RYDAL
ROSTON CL
HAYFIELD CL
GOSFORTH DR
B6054 MAIN RD
A61
HEATHFIELD CL
CROFTON RISE
LOWRY DR
81
80
79
78
4
3
2
1
32
33
34

55

75

43
58

D E F

D E F

76
58

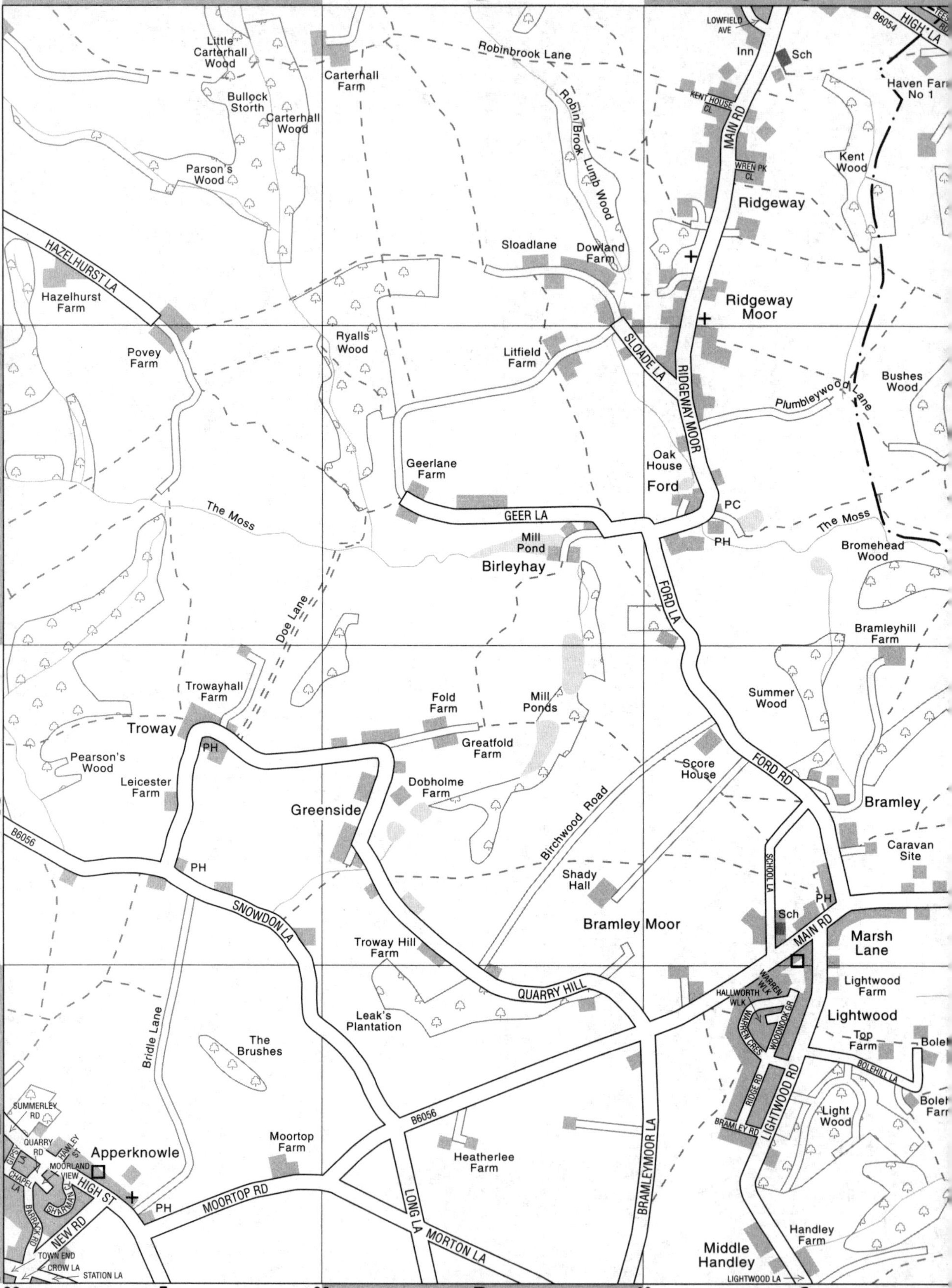
A
B
C
Little Carterhall Wood
Robinbrook Lane
Carterhall Farm
Bullock Storth
Carterhall Wood
Parson's Wood
Robin Brook
Lumb Wood
LOWFIELD AVE
B6054
HIGH LA
Inn
Sch
Haven Farm No 1
KENT HOUSE CL
MAIN RD
Kent Wood
WREN PK CL
Ridgeway
HAZELHURST LA
Hazelhurst Farm
Sloadlane
Dowland Farm
Ridgeway Moor
Povey Farm
Ryalls Wood
Litfield Farm
SLOADE LA
RIDGEWAY MOOR
Plumbleywood Lane
Bushes Wood
Oak House
Ford
Geerlane Farm
The Moss
PC
GEER LA
Mill Pond
PH
Bromehead Wood
Birleyhay
FORD LA
Doe Lane
Bramleyhill Farm
Trowayhall Farm
Fold Farm
Mill Ponds
Summer Wood
Troway
Greatfold Farm
Score House
FORD RD
Pearson's Wood
Leicester Farm
Dobholme Farm
Birchwood Road
Bramley
Greenside
B6056
SCHOOL LA
Caravan Site
Shady Hall
SNOWDON LA
Bramley Moor
Sch
Marsh Lane
Troway Hill Farm
QUARRY HILL
Lightwood Farm
HALLWORTH WLK
WARREN WLK
WARREN CRES
WOODNOOK GR
Lightwood
Leak's Plantation
Top Farm
Bridle Lane
The Brushes
BOLEHILL LA
RIDGE RD
LIGHTWOOD RD
SUMMERLEY RD
Light Wood
QUARRY RD
HAWLEY ST
Apperknowle
Moortop Farm
BRAMLEY RD
GIPSY LA
MOORLAND VIEW
Heatherlee Farm
CHAPEL LA
SHARMAN CL
HIGH ST
BRAMLEYMOOR LA
MOORTOP RD
LONG LA
BARRACK RD
NEW RD
MORTON LA
Handley Farm
Middle Handley
TOWN END
CROW LA
STATION LA
LIGHTWOOD LA
4
81
3
80
2
79
1
78
38
39
40

D
E
F
Mosborough
Plumbley
West Mosborough
Halfway
Westfield
Eckington
Plumbleylane Farm
Plumbleywood Lane
Bowercinder Hill
Cadman Wood
Ladybank Wood
Twelve Acre Wood
The Moss
Lady Ida's Drive
Eckington Park
High Bramley Wood
Ince Piece Wood
Eckington Hall
Beighton Hill
Cemy
Danes Balk
Windmill Hill
The Moss Brook (PH)
Ridgeway Arms (PH)
Resr
Playing Fields
Swallow's Lane
Back Lane
Ravencar Farm
Low Farm
Eckington Marsh
Marsh Farm
Golf Course
Coldwell Plantation
Willowbed Plantation
Renishaw Hall
Renishaw Park
Mill
River Rother
Civic Centre
Hotel
Liby
Sch
Wks
PH
PC
F Sta
Off
Pumbleywood Lane
QUARRY HILL
MOSBOROUGH MOOR
A6135
B6058
STATION RD
HIGH ST
QUEEN ST
SCHOOL ST
SOUTH ST
CHAPEL ST
DUKE ST
PLUMBLEY LA
PLUMBLEY HALL RD
MOSS WAY
ECKINGTON WAY
ROTHERHAM RD
WINDMILL GREENWAY
SHEFFIELD RD
GASHOUSE LA
HILL RD
CHURCH ST
B6052
LITTLEMOOR
B6053
PIPWORTH LA
ROTHERSIDE RD
PINFOLD ST
SOUTHGATE
STATION RD
HIGH ST
WEST ST
DRONFIELD RD
B6056
MAIN RD
RAVENCAR RD
BERRY AVE
SETCUP LA
STAVELEY LA
CHESTERFIELD RD
BOLEHILL LA
1 BISHOPDALE RISE
2 BISHOPDALE DR
3 PARKGATE CL
4 PARKGATE DR
5 PARKGATE CROFT
1 SHORTBROOK BANK
2 SHORTBROOK CF
3 SHORTBROOK WLK
4 SHORTBROOK CL
5 EASTCROFT WAY
1 MURRAYFIELD DR
2 STONEGRAVELS CROFT
81
80
79
78
4
3
2
1
42
43

A
B
C
Holbrook
Rother Valley Country Park
Killamarsh Meadows
Works
Short Brook
MEADOWBROOK INDUSTRIAL ESTATE
STATION RD
B6058
Nether Moor
Nether Green
Barber's Lane
Canal (disused)
Angle Inn (PH)
Norwood
Norwood Industrial Estate
Highmoor Farm
Sewage Works
Netherthorpe
Sheepcote Hill
SHEFFIELD RD
BRIDGE ST
HIGH ST
KIRKCROFT LA
The Crown (PH)
Church Town
Dale Farm
Gannow Hill
MANSFIELD RD
High Moor
Killamarsh
Oxclose Farm
River Rother
Dismantled Railway
Upperthorpe
UPPERTHORPE RD
WESTTHORPE RD
Traveller's Rest (PH)
West End Hotel (PH)
Westthorpe Green
Westthorpe
BOILEY LA
HUT LA
High Moor Colliery
Boiley Farm
Mine (dis)
Comberwood Farm
Park Brook
GREEN LA
SPINKHILL RD
Chaplewheel Dam
Birley Farm
Spring Wood
Parkhall Farm
STATION RD
Mill Farm
A6135
College
Park Hall (Hotel)
PARKHILL LA
Spinkhill
Quarrydam Cottages
High Wood
River Rother
SPINKHILL LA
Bridge House
Sch
Top Farm
THE AVENUE
THE LANE
Park Farm
Sewage Works
Hotel
Smithy Brook
Ingdale Farm
Quarrydam Wood
MAIN RD
Renishaw
SYDAY LA
4
81
3
80
2
79
1
78
44
45
46

62

D
E
F
4
81
3
80
2
79
1
78
48
49
M1
Nor Wood
Baugy Hill
Broad Bridge Dike
Hard Field
HARD LA
MANOR RD
Top Farm
Poplar Farm
WALSEKER LA
Woodall Pond
North House
Beehive Farm
NORTHLANDS
CASSON DR
HUDSON CL
GLEBE AVE
THORPE RD
GLEBE FARM CL
The Flats
CHAPEL YD
UNION ST
RECTORY GDNS
STREET FARM CL
llamarsh Pond
Woodall
Broad Bridge
JACKYS LA
WOODALL LA
ORCHARD
LEE
KYE LA
Harthill
KILLAMARSH LA
Low Plantation
Sewage Works
DOWCARR LA
GREYSTONES CT
DARLEY CL
CARVER WAY
CARVER CL
DE SUTTON PL
DISHWELL LA
SOUTH FARM AVE
SERLAY LA
OSBORNE CROFT
DE WARREN PL
DOCTOR LA
Sch
WOODALL RD
Woodall Bottoms
Stone Hill
PRYOR MEDE
PRIORY CT
PEREGRIN WAY
CRESCENT
WINNEY HILL
THE HOP INGE
THE DOWNINGS
SERLBY DR
COMMON RD
Woodall Service Area
Harthill Reservoir
HEWITT PL
FIRVALE
HARTHILL FIELD RD
Woodall Common
A618
NSFIELD RD
Fir Hill
Birkenhead Wood
Carr Farm Cottage
WINNEY LA
Carr Farm
The Pebley (PH)
Pebleygrove Farm
Pebley Oaks
Pebley Reservoir
Harthill Field
ROTHERHAM RD
Crabtree Wood
Car Plantation
Hawke Wood
Nitticarhill Wood
Garden Plantation
HARTHILL LA
High Wood
Sch
WARD LA
Nitticarhill Rd
Nitticarhill
Butcherlawn Pond
Longrybank Wood
A618

80
62

61

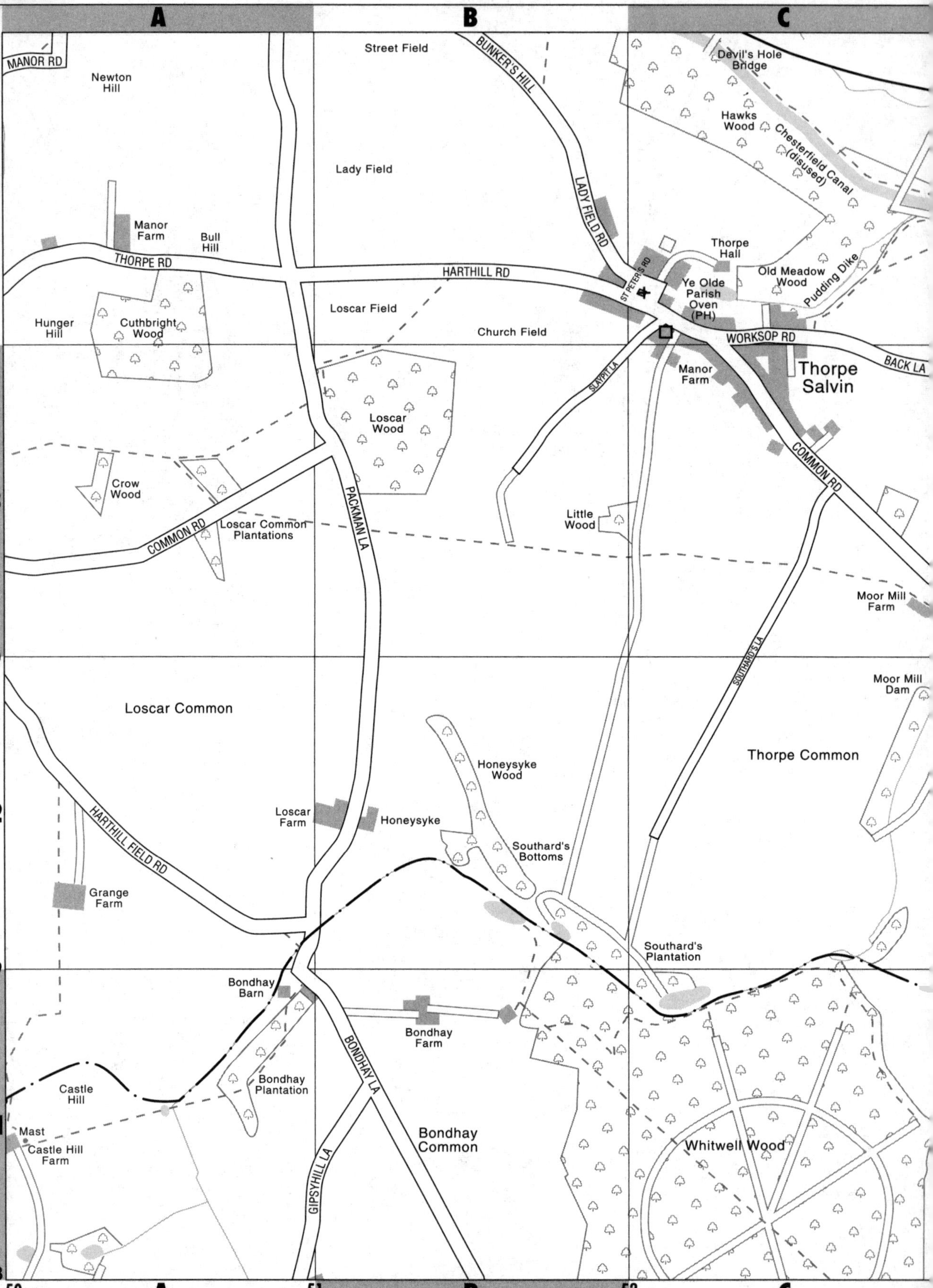
A
B
C
MANOR RD
Newton Hill
Street Field
BUNKER'S HILL
Devil's Hole Bridge
Hawks Wood
Chesterfield Canal (disused)
Lady Field
LADY FIELD RD
4
Manor Farm
Bull Hill
THORPE RD
HARTHILL RD
ST PETER'S RD
Thorpe Hall
Old Meadow Wood
Pudding Dike
Ye Olde Parish Oven (PH)
Hunger Hill
Cuthbright Wood
Loscar Field
Church Field
WORKSOP RD
BACK LA
81
Manor Farm
Thorpe Salvin
SLAYPIT LA
Loscar Wood
COMMON RD
3
Crow Wood
Loscar Common Plantations
COMMON RD
PACKMAN LA
Little Wood
Moor Mill Farm
80
SOUTHARD'S LA
Moor Mill Dam
Loscar Common
Thorpe Common
Honeysyke Wood
2
Loscar Farm
Honeysyke
HARTHILL FIELD RD
Southard's Bottoms
Grange Farm
Southard's Plantation
79
Bondhay Barn
Bondhay Farm
BONDHAY LA
Bondhay Plantation
Castle Hill
1
Mast
Castle Hill Farm
Bondhay Common
Whitwell Wood
GIPSYHILL LA
78
50
51
52

61
81

D
E
F
Fan Field
Dismtd Rly
Fan Field Farm
Quarry (dis)
Brancliffe Grange
Canal Feeder
Low Spring Wood
Potters Nook Bridge
Old Spring Wood
Turnerwood Bridge
Broad Wood
Turnerwood
Chesterfield Canal (disused)
Sch
BRANCLIFFE LA
CARTWRIGHT ST
GLENTHORN CL
SHIREOAKS COMM
Shireoaks Station
WOODSIDE RD
ELMTREE CL
LEEDS RD
CORNWALL RD
WALNUT AVE
CHERRY TREE AVE
YORK PL
PEMBROKE RD
LC
BETHEL TERR
SHIREOAKS ROW
BACK LA
Allot Gdns
Hatfield Farm
Colliery
Shireoaks
LITTLE LA
Bondhay Dyke
Bottom Farm
THORPE LA
Shireoaks Park
SHIREOAKS RD
Ford
Lob Wells Wood
Netherthorpe
Top Farm
The Hall
Netherthorpe Airfield
Oak Wood
Top Hall
Shireoaks Park Wood
NETHER THORPE RD
SPRING LA
Holme Carr Wood
WHITWELL RD
Holme Carr
DUMB HALL LA
Scratts Wood
Whitwell Road
Silver Birches
STEETLEY LA
Works
SCRATTA LA
Dumb Hall
Armstrong Quarry
Steetley Farm Cottages
Firbeck Farm
Firbeck House
Steetley House
Firbeck Common
FEATHERBED LA
Darfoulds
Worksop
Firbeck Lane
A619
Arrow Farm
Harness Grove
4
81
3
80
2
79
1
78
54
55

82

45

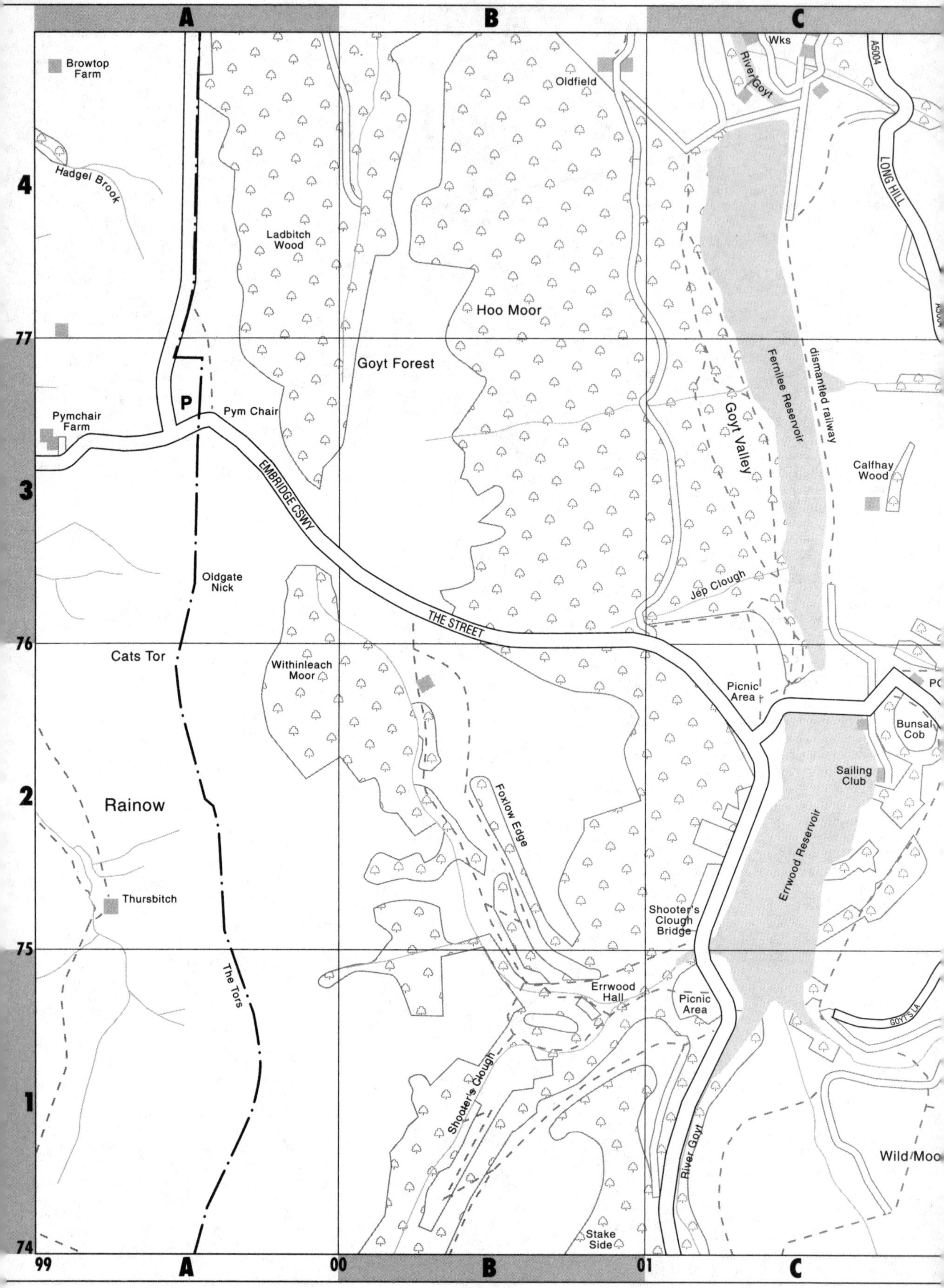
A
B
C
Browtop Farm
Hadgel Brook
Ladbitch Wood
Oldfield
Wks
River Goyt
A5004
LONG HILL
Hoo Moor
Goyt Forest
P
Pym Chair
Pymchair Farm
EMBRIDGE CSWY
Fernilee Reservoir
dismantled railway
Goyt Valley
Calfhay Wood
Oldgate Nick
Jep Clough
THE STREET
Cats Tor
Withinleach Moor
Picnic Area
Bunsal Cob
Sailing Club
Rainow
Foxlow Edge
Errwood Reservoir
Thursbitch
Shooter's Clough Bridge
The Tors
Errwood Hall
Picnic Area
GOYT'S LA
Shooter's Clough
River Goyt
Wild Moo
Stake Side
4
77
3
76
2
75
1
74
99
00
01

83

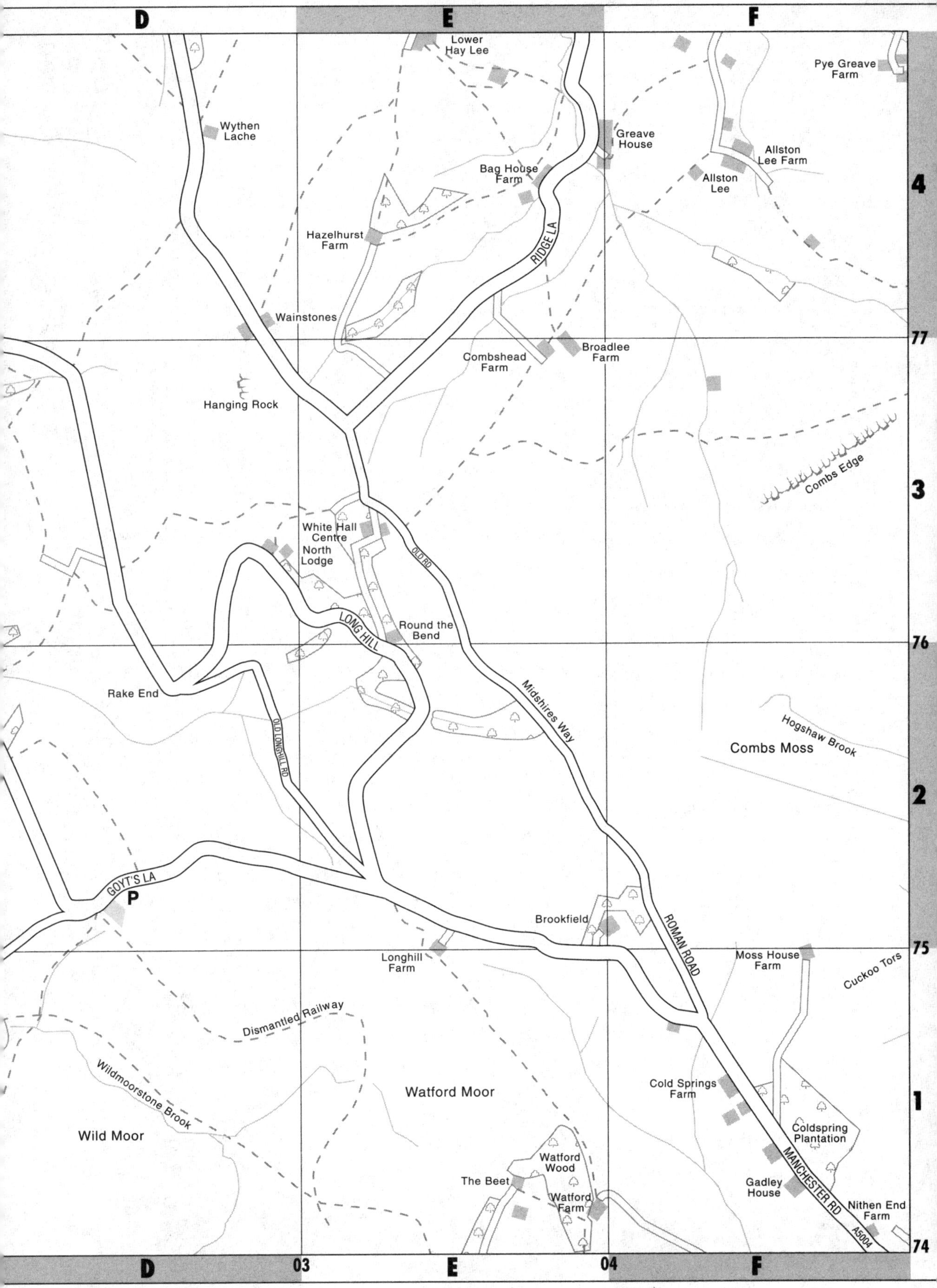
D
E
F
Lower Hay Lee
Pye Greave Farm
Wythen Lache
Greave House
Allston Lee Farm
Bag House Farm
Allston Lee
4
Hazelhurst Farm
RIDGE LA
Wainstones
77
Combshead Farm
Broadlee Farm
Hanging Rock
Combs Edge
3
White Hall Centre
North Lodge
OLD RD
LONG HILL
Round the Bend
76
Rake End
Midshires Way
Hogshaw Brook
Combs Moss
OLD LONGHILL RD
2
GOYT'S LA
P
Brookfield
ROMAN ROAD
75
Longhill Farm
Moss House Farm
Cuckoo Tors
Dismantled Railway
Wildmoorstone Brook
Watford Moor
Cold Springs Farm
1
Wild Moor
Coldspring Plantation
Watford Wood
The Beet
Watford Farm
Gadley House
MANCHESTER RD
Nithen End Farm
A5004
74
D
03
E
04
F

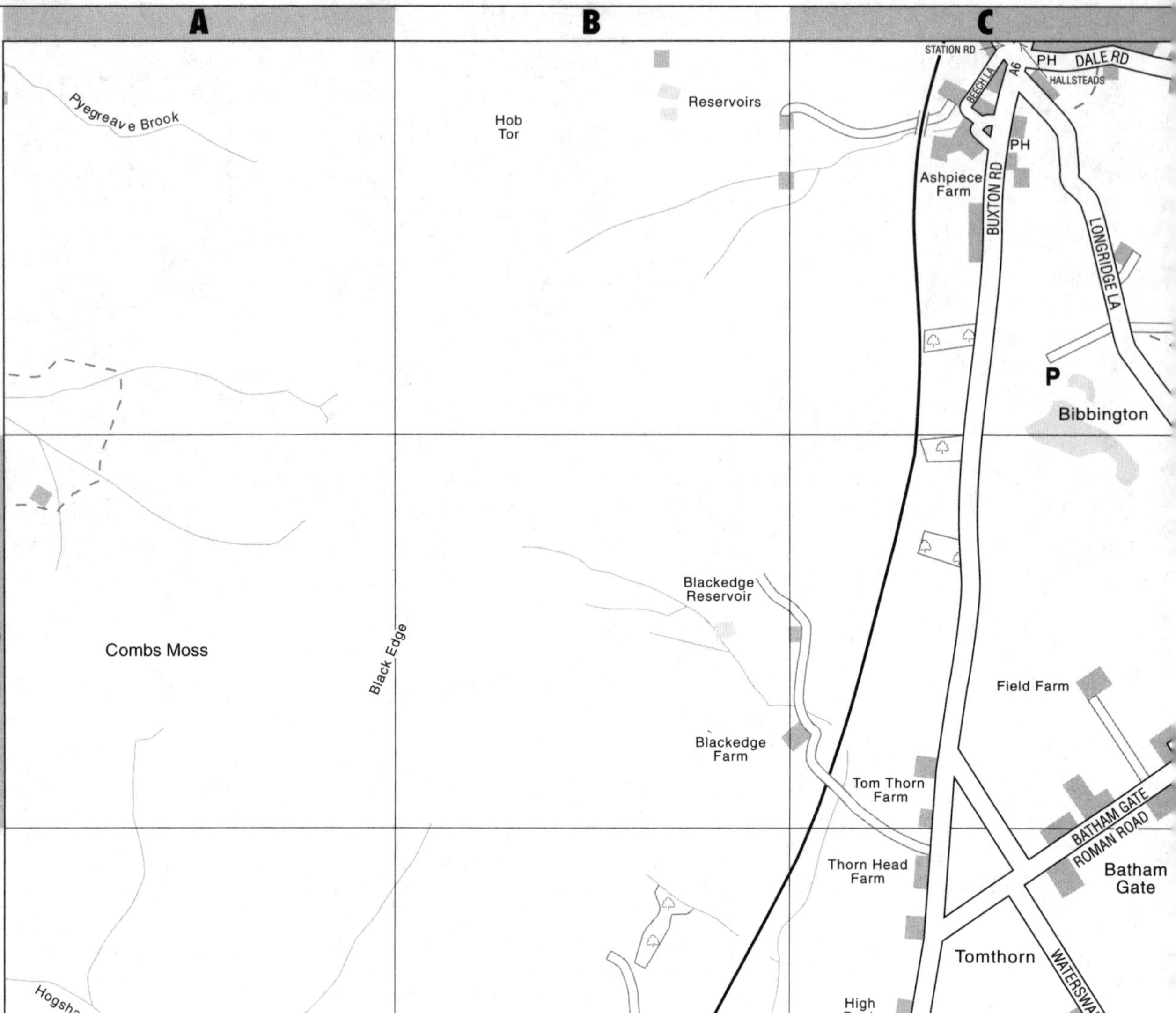
A
B
C
4
77
3
76
2
75
1
74
05
06
07
STATION RD
PH
DALE RD
HALLSTEADS
BEECH LA
A6
Reservoirs
Hob Tor
Pyegreave Brook
PH
Ashpiece Farm
BUXTON RD
LONGRIDGE LA
P
Bibbington
Blackedge Reservoir
Combs Moss
Black Edge
Field Farm
Blackedge Farm
Tom Thorn Farm
BATHAM GATE
ROMAN ROAD
Thorn Head Farm
Batham Gate
Tomthorn
WATERSWALLOWS LA
High Peak Nurseries
Hogshaw Brook
Television Station
Brownedge Plantation
Reservoirs
Turner Lodge
Brookhouse Farm
Lightwood Reservoirs
Brook House
Breezemount Farm
Light Wood
Frome Lodge
Waterswallows Green
Works
The Barms Farm
DAISYMERE LA
Hogshaw Brook
NURSERY DR
BROWN EDGE RD
Golf Course
Fairfield Common
WATERSWALLOWS RD
LIGHTWOOD RD
Corbar Hill
Nunsfield Farm
LADYCROFT
WATERSWALLOWS MEWS
DAKIN CT
Sch
CORBAR RD
WILLIAMSON AVE
BARMS WAY
Townend Farm
Corbar Woods
Sch
CORBARWOODS LA
Sch
LANSDOWNE RD
Sch
NUNSFIELD RD
GLENMOOR RD
ST PETER'S RD
NORTH RD
FAIRFIELD RD
DAKIN
CROSS ST
FOXES YD
MONTPELIER PL
CHERRY TREE DR
ASHWOOD RD
TOWN END
CH
LESSER LA
LASCELLES RD

48
68

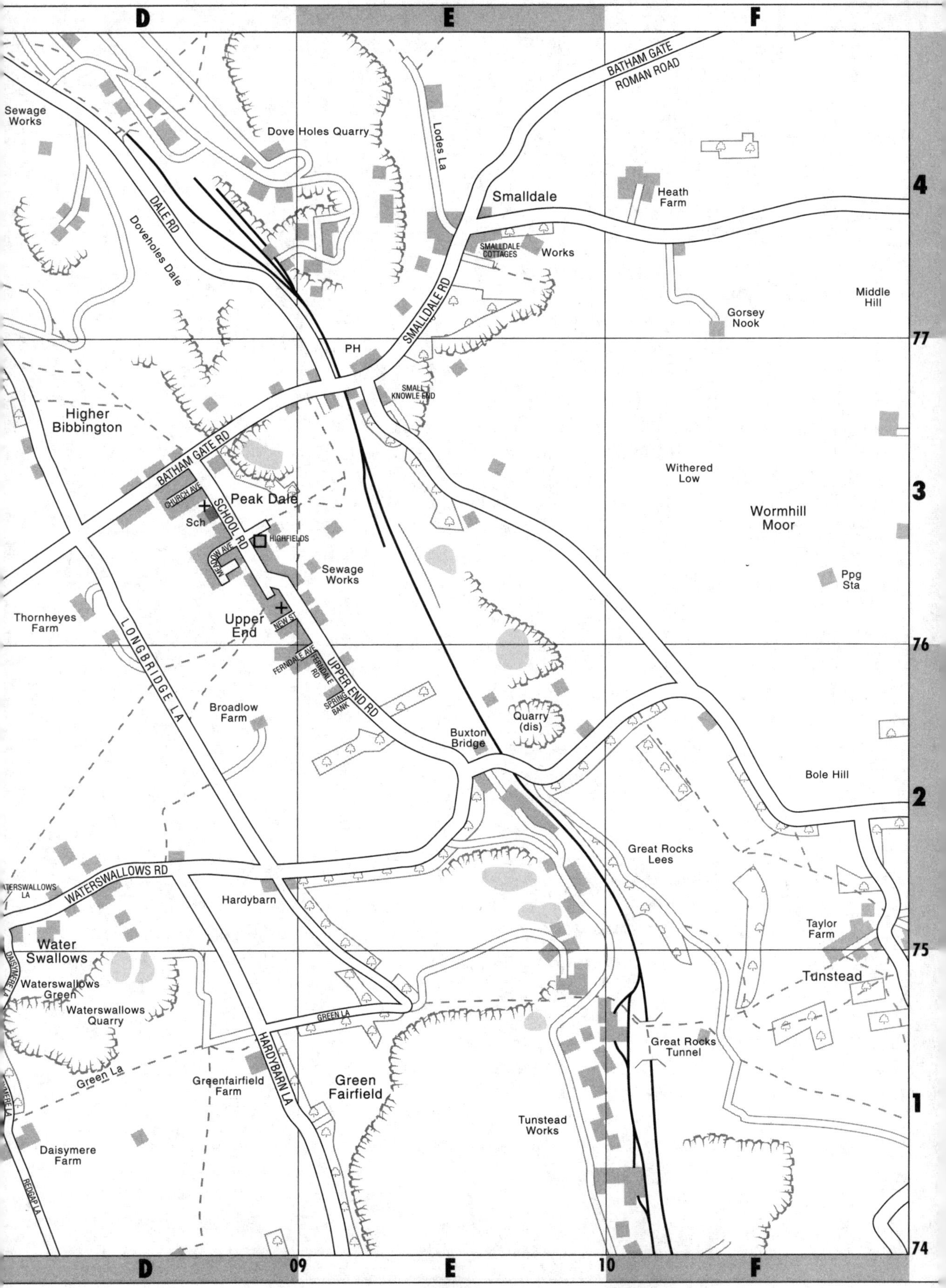
D
E
F
Sewage Works
Dove Holes Quarry
Lodes La
BATHAM GATE
ROMAN ROAD
Smalldale
Heath Farm
DALE RD
Doveholes Dale
SMALLDALE COTTAGES
Works
SMALLDALE RD
Middle Hill
Gorsey Nook
PH
SMALL KNOWLE END
Higher Bibbington
BATHAM GATE RD
CHURCH AVE
SCHOOL RD
Peak Dale
Sch
HIGHFIELDS
MEADOW AVE
Withered Low
Wormhill Moor
Sewage Works
Ppg Sta
Thornheyes Farm
Upper End
NEW ST
FERNDALE AVE
FERNDALE RD
SPRING BANK
UPPER END RD
LONGBRIDGE LA
Broadlow Farm
Quarry (dis)
Buxton Bridge
Bole Hill
Great Rocks Lees
WATERSWALLOWS RD
WATERSWALLOWS LA
Hardybarn
Taylor Farm
Water Swallows
Tunstead
Waterswallows Green
Waterswallows Quarry
DAISYMERE LA
GREEN LA
Great Rocks Tunnel
HARDYBARN LA
Green La
Greenfairfield Farm
Green Fairfield
Tunstead Works
Daisymere Farm
REDGAP LA
4
77
3
76
2
75
1
74
09
10

86
68

67
49

A
B
C
Kempshill Farm
Lower Kempshill Farm
Stone Lea Farm
Dam Dale
A623
4
77
Hay Dale
Dale Head Farm
Dale Head
WATER LA
Bottom Farm
Sitch House
3
Wheston
Hall
The Top Farm
Peter Dale
76
Limestone Way
Cherryslack
2
Hargatewall
Hayward Farm
Wind Low
Hargate Hall
Monksdale House
Tunstead
75
Hill Top Farm
Wormhill Hill
MONKSDALE LA
Monk's Dale
1
Old Hall Farm
Wormhill
Nature Reserve
Wormhill Hall
74
11
12
13

D
E
F
Whiterake
Tides Low
Tideslow Rake
WASHHOUSE BOTTOM
High Rake
Poyntoncross Barn
Windmill
B6049
Poyntoncross House
Rising Sun Farm
4
Grundy House
Wall Cliff
Wallcliffe Reservoir
77
Highfield House
Brook Bottom
Benstor House
WATER LA
Holmelacy Farm
Anchor Farm
Brook Villa
MANCHESTER RD
Anchor Farm
Cemy
3
Lane Head
B6049
Anchor Inn (PH)
BANK VIEW
CONDLIFF RD
ALMA RD
Town Head
LOWER TERR RD
TERRACE RD
MEVERILL RD
WHITECROSS AVE
WHITECROSS RD
RECREATION RD
Sch
76
A623
WHESTON BANK
Crossgate Farm
MARKET SQUARE
PURSEGLOVE RD
ST JOHN'S RD
Liby
PH
HIGH ST
MONKSDALE CL
MARKET PL
CHANTRY LA
PURSEGLOVE DR
CONJOINT LA
SHERWOOD COPSE
COMMERCIAL RD
CHANTRY CT
PARKE RD
NICHOLSON CT
Summer Cross
SUMMER CROSS
Tideswell
CHURCH ST
CHURCH AVE
CLIFF LA
FOUNTAIN SQUARE
PC
Litton Edge
SHERWOOD RD
QUEEN ST
CHERRY TREE SQUARE
CHURCH LA
2
SUNNY BANK LA
Sterndale House
BUXTON RD
Town End
Litton
TITHE BARN CL
GORDON RD
STERNDALE CL
PINFOLD CRES
PINFOLD RD
Sch
Slancote Lane
LITTLE LA
DALE VIEW
MIRES LA
RICHARD LA
THE LODGE
HALL LA
The Farm
Dale House
Heathydale Ward
75
Eastsides Lane
Litton Dale
MEADOW LA
Sewage Works
BOARSLACK LA
Meadow Farm
BOTTOMHILL RD
1
Tideswell Dale
Cemy
Mines (dis)
P
Long Meadow Lane
PC
Monksdale Lane
Lunch La
B6049
74
D
15
E
16
F

69
51

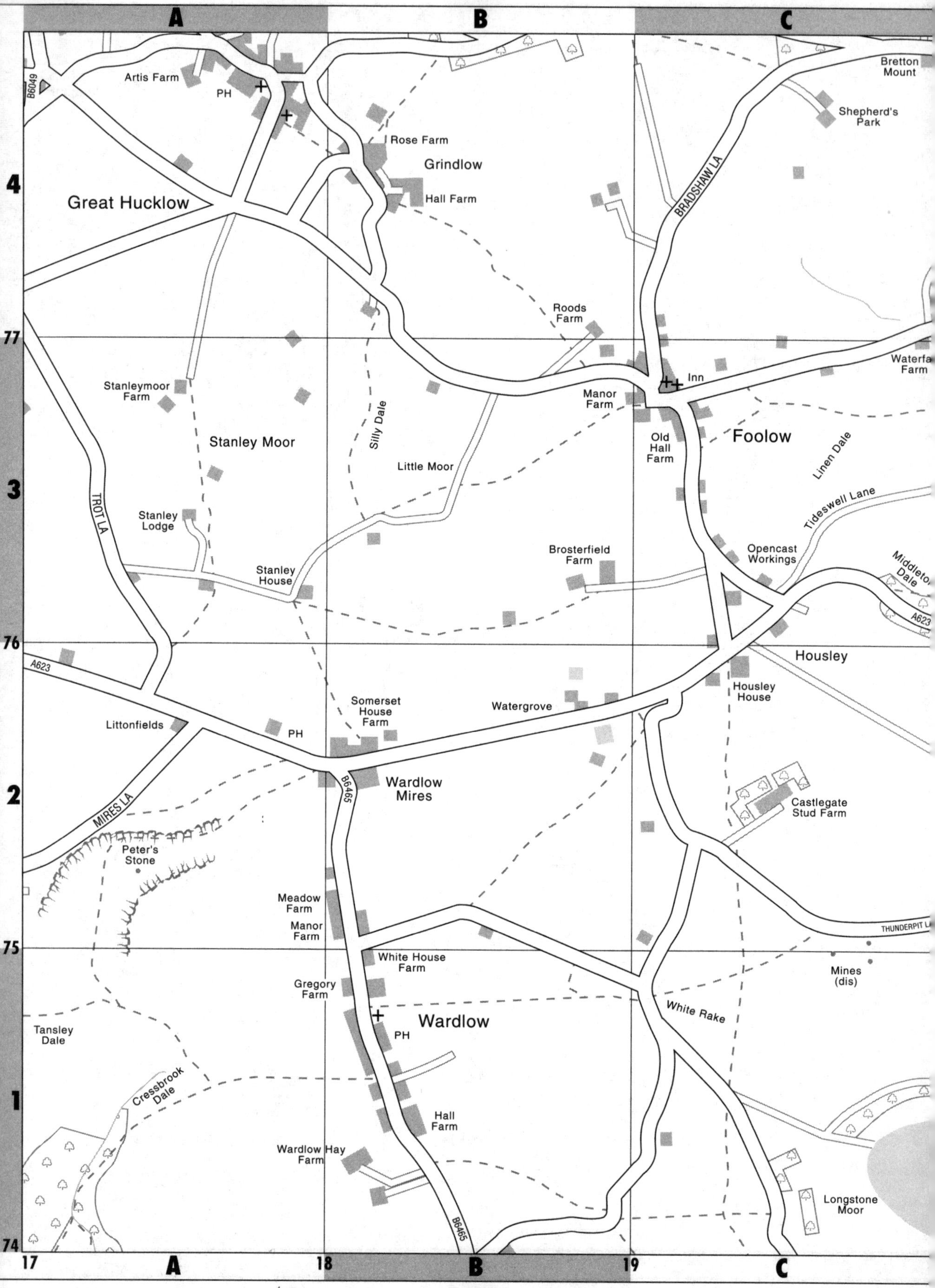
A
B
C
4
77
3
76
2
75
1
74
17
18
19
B6049
Artis Farm
PH
Rose Farm
Grindlow
Hall Farm
Great Hucklow
Bretton Mount
Shepherd's Park
BRADSHAW LA
Roods Farm
Inn
Manor Farm
Waterfa Farm
Stanleymoor Farm
Stanley Moor
Silly Dale
Little Moor
Old Hall Farm
Foolow
Linen Dale
Tideswell Lane
TROT LA
Stanley Lodge
Stanley House
Brosterfield Farm
Opencast Workings
Middleto Dale
A623
Housley
Housley House
Watergrove
Somerset House Farm
Littonfields
PH
Wardlow Mires
B6465
Castlegate Stud Farm
MIRES LA
Peter's Stone
Meadow Farm
Manor Farm
THUNDERPIT L
White House Farm
Mines (dis)
Gregory Farm
Wardlow
PH
White Rake
Tansley Dale
Cressbrook Dale
Hall Farm
Wardlow Hay Farm
Longstone Moor
B6465

69
89

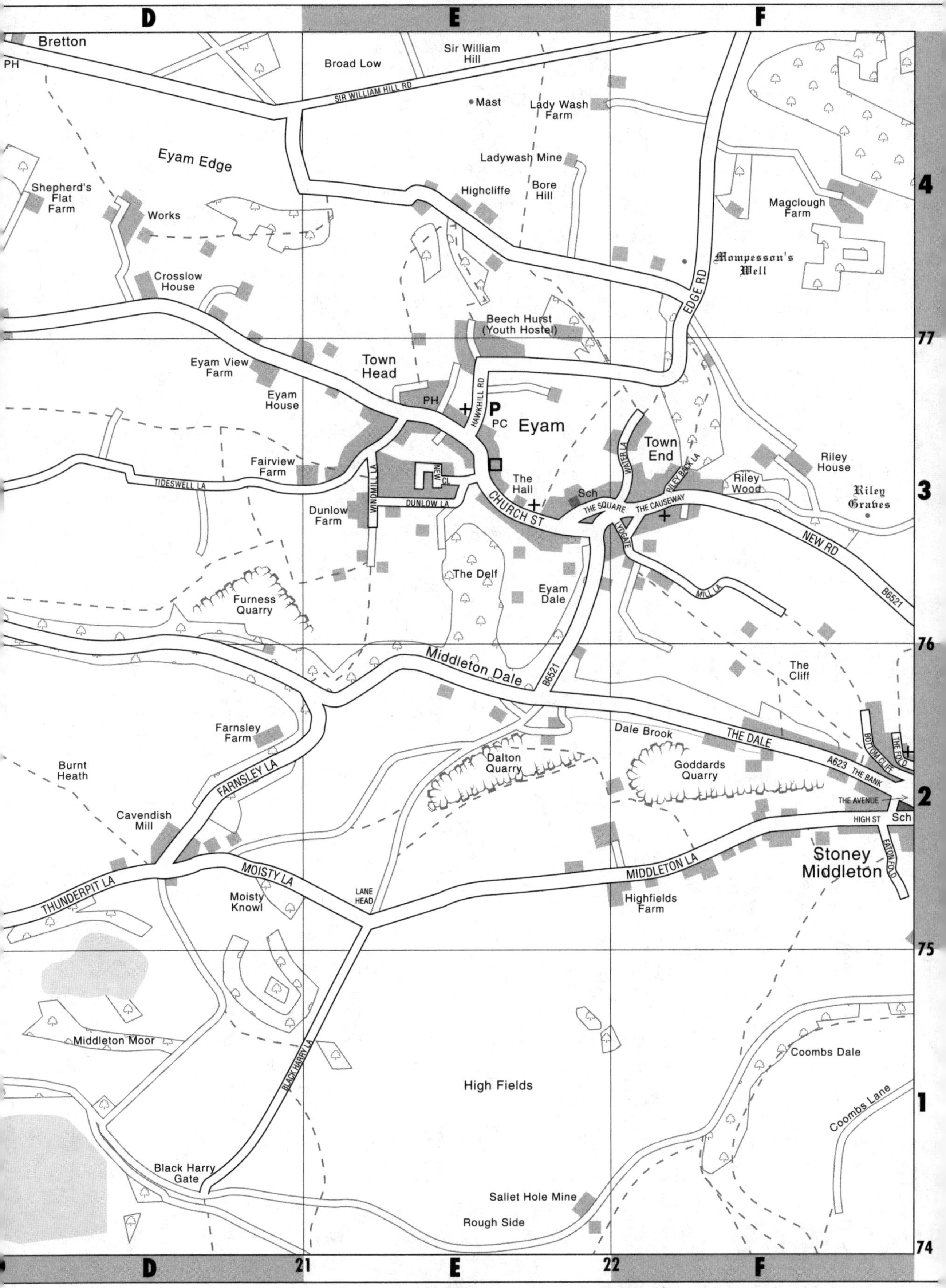
D
E
F
Bretton
PH
Broad Low
Sir William Hill
SIR WILLIAM HILL RD
Mast
Lady Wash Farm
Eyam Edge
Ladywash Mine
Shepherd's Flat Farm
Works
Highcliffe
Bore Hill
Magclough Farm
Mompesson's Well
Crosslow House
EDGE RD
Beech Hurst (Youth Hostel)
Town Head
Eyam View Farm
Eyam House
PH
HAWKHILL RD
P
PC
Eyam
Town End
Fairview Farm
TIDESWELL LA
WINDMILL LA
NEW CL
The Hall
WATER LA
RILEY BACK LA
Riley Wood
Riley House
Riley Graves
Dunlow Farm
DUNLOW LA
CHURCH ST
Sch
THE SQUARE
THE CAUSEWAY
LYDGATE
NEW RD
The Delf
Eyam Dale
MILL LA
B6521
Furness Quarry
Middleton Dale
B6521
The Cliff
Farnsley Farm
Dale Brook
THE DALE
BOTTOM CLIFF
THE FOLD
Burnt Heath
Dalton Quarry
Goddards Quarry
A623 THE BANK
FARNSLEY LA
THE AVENUE
Cavendish Mill
HIGH ST
Sch
Stoney Middleton
EATON FOLD
MOISTY LA
MIDDLETON LA
THUNDERPIT LA
Moisty Knowl
LANE HEAD
Highfields Farm
Middleton Moor
BLACK HARRY LA
Coombs Dale
High Fields
Coombs Lane
Black Harry Gate
Sallet Hole Mine
Rough Side
4
77
3
76
2
75
1
74
D
21
E
22
F

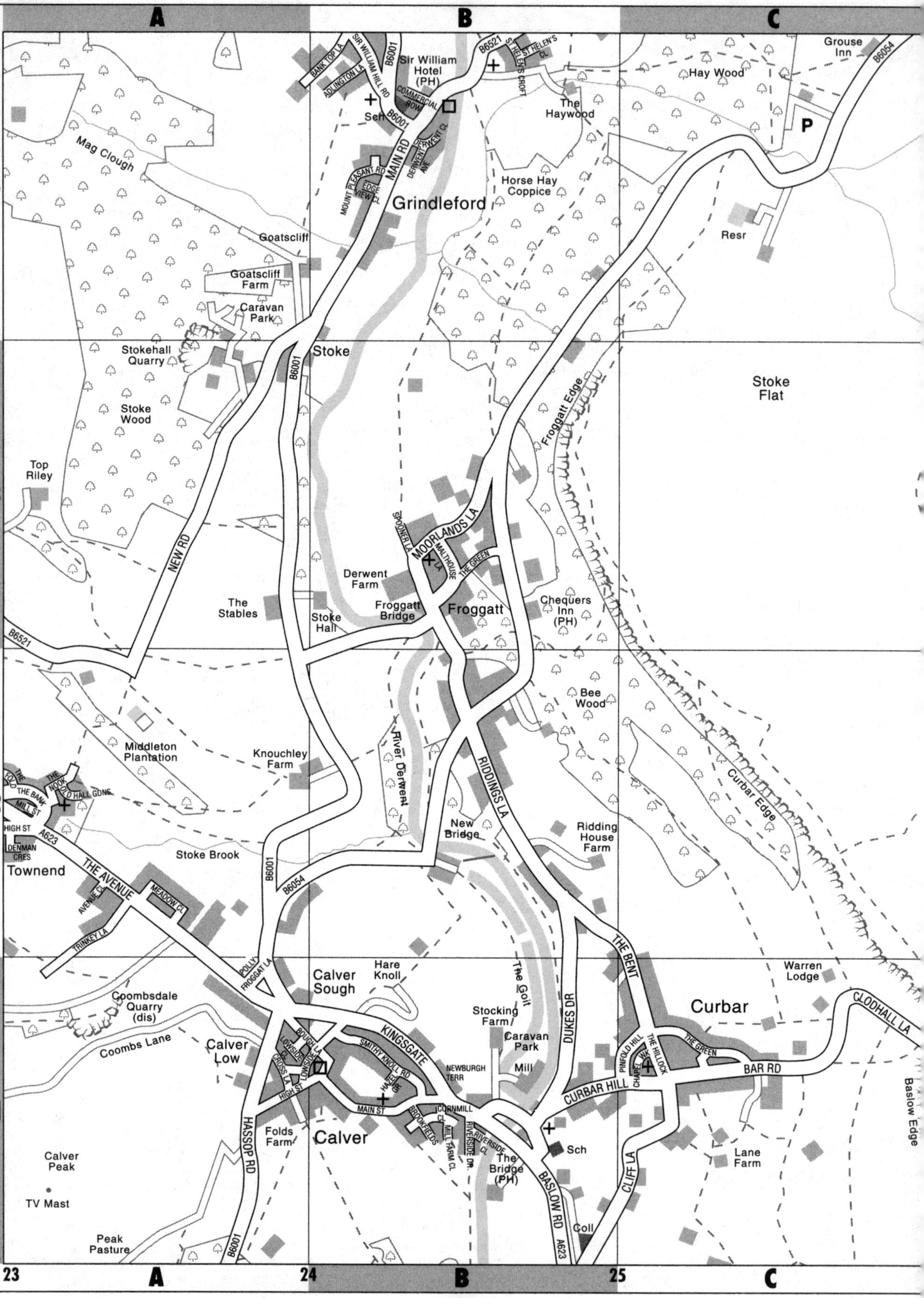
A
B
C
Grouse Inn
B6054
Hay Wood
BANK TOP LA
SIR WILLIAM HILL RD
B6001
Sir William Hotel (PH)
B6521
ST HELEN'S CROFT
ST HELEN'S CL
ADLINGTON LA
COMMERCIAL ROW
Sch
The Haywood
P
Mag Clough
MAIN RD
DERWENT CL
DERWENT AVE
MOUNT PLEASANT RD
EDGE VIEW CL
Horse Hay Coppice
Grindleford
Resr
Goatscliff
Goatscliff Farm
Caravan Park
Stokehall Quarry
Stoke
Stoke Flat
Stoke Wood
Froggatt Edge
Top Riley
MOORLANDS LA
SPOONER LA
MALTHOUSE LA
THE GREEN
NEW RD
Derwent Farm
The Stables
Froggatt Bridge
Stoke Hall
Froggatt
Chequers Inn (PH)
B6521
Bee Wood
Middleton Plantation
Knouchley Farm
River Derwent
RIDDINGS LA
Curbar Edge
THE FOLD
THE NOOK
THE BANK
MILL ST
OLD HALL GDNS
HIGH ST
A623
DENMAN CRES
New Bridge
Ridding House Farm
Stoke Brook
Townend
THE AVENUE
MEADOW CL
AVENUE CL
B6054
TRINKEY LA
POLLY FROGGAT LA
Calver Sough
Hare Knoll
The Goit
THE BENT
Warren Lodge
Curbar
CLODHALL LA
Coombsdale Quarry (dis)
Stocking Farm
Caravan Park
DUKES DR
Coombs Lane
Calver Low
BOUGH LA
LOWSIDE
LOWSIDE CL
CROSS LA
KINGSGATE
SMITHY KNOLL RD
HAZEL GR
NEWBURGH TERR
Mill
PINFOLD HILL
THE HILLOCK
CHAPEL WK
THE GREEN
BAR RD
CURBAR HILL
Baslow Edge
HIGH ST
MAIN ST
CORNMILL CL
BROOKFIELDS
MILL FARM CL
RIVERSIDE DR
RIVERSIDE CL
Folds Farm
Calver
Sch
HASSOP RD
The Bridge (PH)
BASLOW RD
CLIFF LA
Lane Farm
Calver Peak
TV Mast
Peak Pasture
Coll
A623
4
77
3
76
2
75
1
74
23
24
25

54
74

D
E
F
White Edge Moor
Hurkling Stone
Bar Brook
B6054
Saltersitch Bridge
Bucka Hill
4
A621
Barbrook Reservoir
77
Works
Greaves's Piece
White Edge
Car Top
CAR RD
3
Big Moor
76
Bar Brook
2
Ramsley Moor
Ramsley Lodge
Swine Sty
75
P
Ramsley Reservoir
Sandyford Brook
1
Leash Fen
Blake Brook
Eaglestone Flat
A621
74
D
27
E
28
F

92
74

73
55

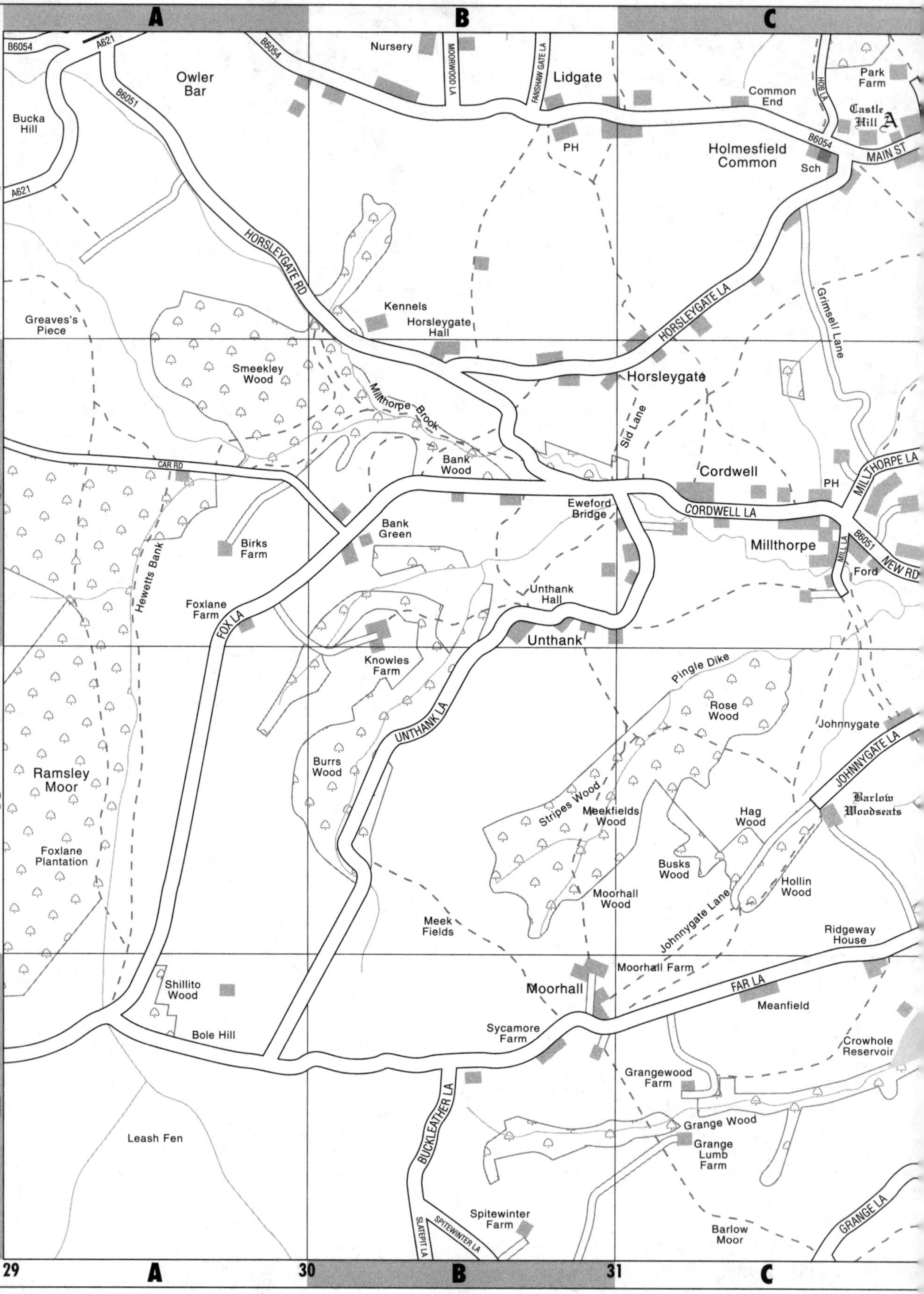
A
B
C
4
77
3
76
2
75
1
74
29
30
31
B6054
A621
Owler Bar
Bucka Hill
B6051
Nursery
MOORWOOD LA
FANSHAW GATE LA
Lidgate
Common End
HOB LA
Park Farm
Castle Hill
PH
Holmesfield Common
B6054
MAIN ST
Sch
HORSLEYGATE RD
HORSLEYGATE LA
Greaves's Piece
Kennels
Horsleygate Hall
Grimsell Lane
Smeekley Wood
Horsleygate
Millthorpe Brook
Sid Lane
CAR RD
Bank Wood
Cordwell
MILLTHORPE LA
PH
CORDWELL LA
Eweford Bridge
Birks Farm
Bank Green
Millthorpe
B6051
MILL LA
NEW RD
Ford
Hewetts Bank
Foxlane Farm
FOX LA
Unthank Hall
Unthank
Knowles Farm
Pingle Dike
Rose Wood
UNTHANK LA
Johnnygate
JOHNNYGATE LA
Ramsley Moor
Burrs Wood
Stripes Wood
Meekfields Wood
Hag Wood
Barlow Woodseats
Foxlane Plantation
Busks Wood
Hollin Wood
Moorhall Wood
Johnnygate Lane
Meek Fields
Ridgeway House
Moorhall Farm
Shillito Wood
Moorhall
FAR LA
Meanfield
Sycamore Farm
Bole Hill
Crowhole Reservoir
Grangewood Farm
BUCKLEATHER LA
Grange Wood
Leash Fen
Grange Lumb Farm
Spitewinter Farm
SPITEWINTER LA
SLATEPIT LA
GRANGE LA
Barlow Moor

73
93

56
76

D
E
F
Cowley Bar
B6054
PARK RISE
WOODSIDE VIEW
THE CRESCENT
VICARAGE CL
WOODSIDE AVE
MAIN RD
PARK AVE
PH
Four Acres
Kirk Farm
Green Farm
Holmesfield
PH
CARTLEDGE LA
Cartledge Hall
Cartledge
Cartledge Hall Farm
MILLTHORPE LA
BRADWELL CL
ASHFORD CL
ASHFORD RD
ALTON CL
HATTON CL
CONISTON RD
MARSTON CL
DRAYCOTT PL
GOSFORTH DR
Kitchen Wood
Spring Wood
Cowley Hall
GAINSBOROUGH RD
CONSTABLE CL
LANDSEER CL
REYNOLDS CL
ROTHAY CL
Hills Farm
HOLBEIN CL
HEATHFIELD CL
HOGARTH RISE
CURZON AVE
A61
UNSTONE DRONFIELD BY PASS
GARTH WAY
HANBURY CL
CAVENDISH RISE
DEVONSHIRE CL
GOSFORTH LA
COWLEY BOTTOM
Shirecliffe Farm
Hilltop Farm
School Wood
BARLOW LEES LA
Cowley
Greenfield Farm
COWLEY LA
4
77
Peakley Hill
DOBBIN LA
Black Car Lumb
Peakley Hill Farm
Lees Wood
Grasscroft Wood
Great Brind Wood
Little Brind Wood
Barlow Lees
Lees Common
3
Barlow Lees Farm
Monk Wood
GATELAND LA
Highlightley Farm
NEW RD
HIGHLIGHTLEY LA
Brindwoodgate
76
Lees Plantation
JOHNNYGATE LA
Dobmeadow Wood
Bradleylane Farm
Dunston Brook
BRADLEY LA
Crowhole
Broombank Plantation
Sewage Works
Broadmeadow Wood
Lee Bridge
2
KEEPERS LA
VALLEY RD
MILL ST
OVERLEES
BROOK VALE CL
SPRINGFIELD RD
VALLEY RISE
Mill
Farlane Farm
Crowhole Brook
Rumbling Street
FAR LA
SMELTINGHOUSE LA
MILLCROSS LA
Sch
Common Side
Rutland Terrace
Barlow Common
FURNACE LA
75
Wildaygreen Farm
Wellspring Farm
COMMONSIDE RD
Church Farm
Elm Tree Farm
WILDAYGREEN LA
Wilday Green
Holme Farm
Springwell Farm
Crowhole Reservoir
Bolehill
Barlow
The Peacock (PH)
WILKIN HILL
1
HACKNEY LA
Newgate Farm
Newgate
Sudbrook Farm
GRANGE LA
MELLOR LA
Grangehouse Farm
Oaks Lane
Ford
Green Lane
Oxton Rake Hall Farm
Sud Brook
COMMON LA
BARLOW RD B6051
74
D
33
E
34
F

94
76

75
57

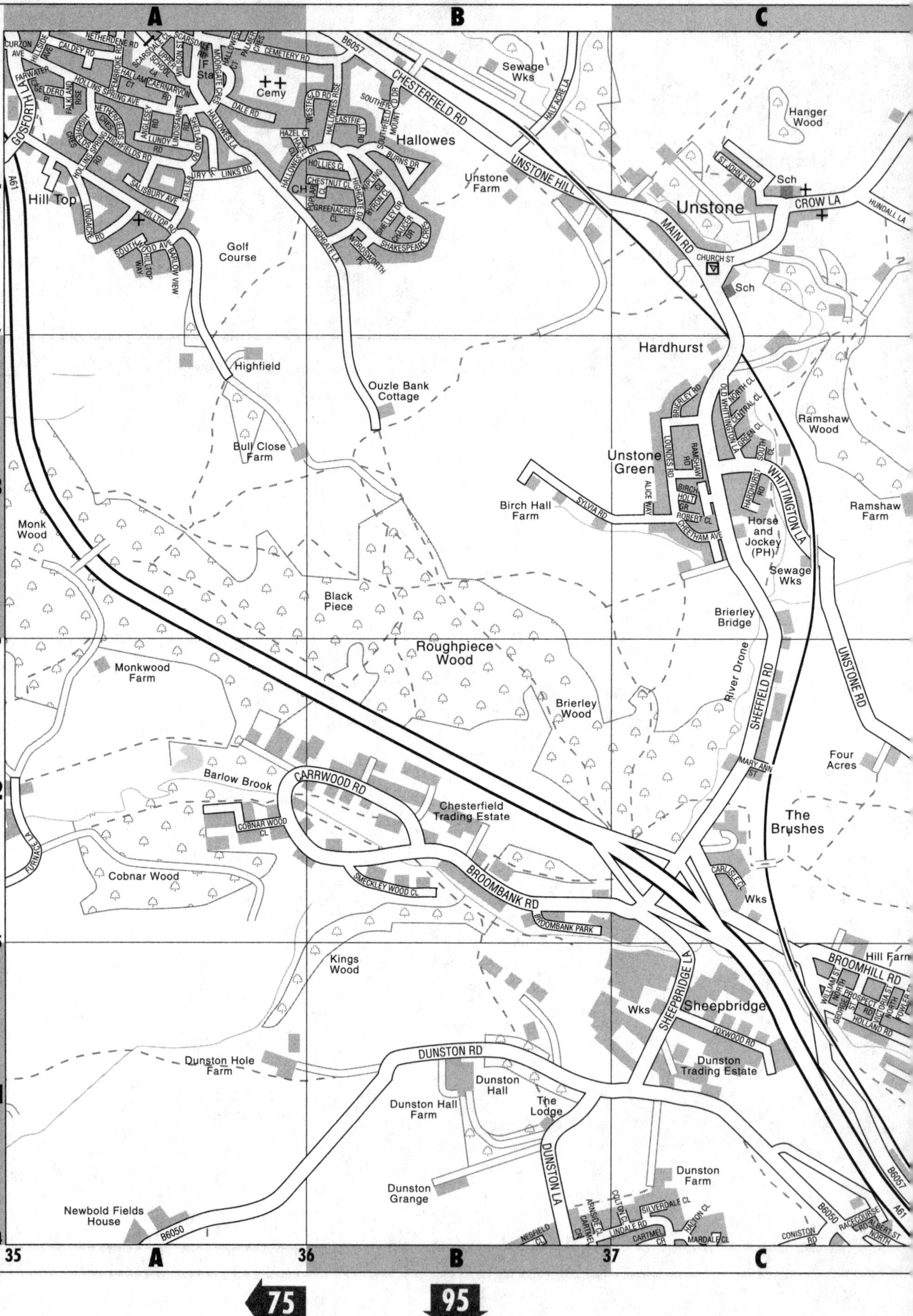
A
B
C
Hallowes
Cemy
Sta
Hill Top
Golf Course
Sewage Wks
Hanger Wood
Unstone Farm
Unstone
Sch
Hardhurst
Highfield
Ouzle Bank Cottage
Bull Close Farm
Ramshaw Wood
Unstone Green
Birch Hall Farm
Ramshaw Farm
Monk Wood
Horse and Jockey (PH)
Sewage Wks
Black Piece
Brierley Bridge
Roughpiece Wood
Monkwood Farm
Brierley Wood
River Drone
Four Acres
Barlow Brook
Chesterfield Trading Estate
The Brushes
Cobnar Wood
Wks
Kings Wood
Hill Farm
Wks
Sheepbridge
Dunston Hole Farm
Dunston Trading Estate
Dunston Hall
Dunston Hall Farm
The Lodge
Dunston Farm
Dunston Grange
Newbold Fields House
CHESTERFIELD RD
UNSTONE HILL
MAIN RD
CROW LA
HUNDALL LA
CHURCH ST
ST JOHN'S RD
HALF ACRE LA
B6057
A61
GOSFORTH LA
CEMETERY RD
DALE RD
HALLOWES LA
LINKS RD
SALISBURY AVE
HILLTOP RD
LONGACRE RD
SOUTHWOOD AVE
BARLOW VIEW
HIGHGATE LA
HIGHGATE DR
WORDSWORTH PL
SHAKESPEARE CRES
BURNS DR
SHEFFIELD RD
WHITTINGTON LA
UNSTONE RD
SYLVIA RD
ALICE WAY
LOUNDES RD
BRIERLEY RD
ROBERT CL
CHEETHAM AVE
HARDHURST RD
MARY ANN ST
CARRWOOD RD
COBNAR WOOD CL
SMECKLEY WOOD CL
BROOMBANK RD
BROOMBANK PARK
FURNACE LA
CARLISLE CL
BROOMHILL RD
HOLLAND RD
SHEEPBRIDGE LA
FOXWOOD RD
DUNSTON RD
DUNSTON LA
B6050
SILVERDALE CL
LINDALE RD
CARTMEL CR
MARDALE CL
NESFIELD CL
CONISTON RD
RACECOURSE RD
ALBERT ST NORTH
4
77
3
76
2
75
1
74
35
36
37

75
95

D
E
F
STATON LA
SHEPHERD'S ROW
CROW LA
Grange Farm
Unstone Grange
Manor Farm
HUNDALL LA
Hundall
Miner's Arms (PH)
Hall Farm
Butchersick Farm
Stubbing Wood
POOL'S LA
LONG LA
ASH LA
Ash Lane Farm
West Handley
MORTON LA
BRAMLEYMOOR LA
CAVENDISH SQ
MAIN RD
Manor Farm
Sewage Works
LIGHTWOOD LA
PH
Middle Handley
WESTFIELD LA
Southgate Lodge
B6052
Nether Handley
STAVELEY LA
Binkley Wood
Binkley Cottages
SLAG LA
Springwell House
SPRINGWELL HILL
South View Farm
Eyries Farm
Works
WINDMILL LA
Mast
Hardwick Cottage
Grasscroft Wood
Poultry Farm
Glasshouse Common
ECKINGTON RD
Parkgate Farm
Opencast Works
GLENAVON CL
HANDLEY RD
PARKGATE LA
Caravan Site
CAMERORY WAY
DALVEY WAY
HIGHLAND RD
CRAGGON DR
CAIRNGORM CL
BALMORAL WAY
CROMDALE AVE
BRAEMAR CL
CAIRN DR
GLASSHOUSE LA
Glasshouse Farm
Parkhouse Farm
HUNDALL LA
Hospl
BATEMAN CL
FLINTSON AVE
STONE LA
REDHOUSE CL
WHITTINGTON RD
WHITTINGTON RD
PC
MEADOW CT 1
SPRINGWOOD CT 2
BAMFORD ST 3
CROSS LONDON ST
CROWN CL
New Whittington
CROSS WELLINGTON ST
UNSTONE RD
Manor Syck Farm
Whittington Grange
Green Farm
HIGH ST
Sch
P
LONDON ST
BACK SOUTH ST
SOUTH ST N
WELLINGTON ST
DEVONSHIRE AVE N
ALBERT RD
DEVONSHIRE RD N
MITCHELL WAY
Handleywood Farm
1 LINNET HOUSE
2 BUNTING HOUSE
3 KINGFISHER HOUSE
4 FIELDFARE HOUSE
5 GOLDCREST HOUSE
6 ASHLEIGH CL
RODGE CROFT
CHURCH ST N
CHURCH LA N
Sch
Sch
BREARLEY ST
Brearley Park
COMPASS CRES
SIMS CROFT
MAY AVE
DURHAM AVE
BREARLEY AVE
DALE BANK CRES
LITTLEFIELD RD
GARDEN CL
BLUEBANK VIEW
DURHAM CL
CAXTON CL
HARDWICK AVE
SOUTH ST N
CHESTERFIELD AVE
STAVELEY RD
ANDERSON CL
Merrians Farm
LAUREL GARTH CL
GLOSSOP'S CROFT
BURNBRIDGE RD
MEADOW CL
HIGH ST
PC
Mus
HOWARD DR
IVY CL
HIGH ST
BOWER FARM RD
ROECAR CL
PYNOT RD
OAK BANK AVE
ASHCROFT DR
LAURENCE CL
BROOMHILL RD
WEBSTER CROFT
RUTLAND ST
SWANWICK ST
PROSPECT RD
HOLLAND RD
THE GLEBE WAY
OLD BAKERY CL
HILLTOP RD
DANBY AVE
GIPSY LA
STATION LA
STATION LA IND EST
River Rother
Dismtd Rly
Hounsfield Bridge
CAVENDISH ST N 1
DOVERIDGE CL 2
WHITTINGTON HILL
NEWBRIDGE ST
LANGTREE AVE
Old Whittington
NEWBRIDGE LA
1 HARTLAND WAY
2 BURSDON CL
3 LYDFORD AVE
Sewage Works
Chesterfield Canal (dis)
Bluebank Wood
NEWBRIDGE CT
1 SHEFFIELD RD
2 BRIMINGTON RD N
WHITTING VALLEY RD
LAYTON DR
B6052
STATION RD
Dismtd Rly
BILBY LA
COW LA
STATION RD
New Brimington
DORSET DR 1
SYCAMORE RD 2
DORSET CL
ELM ST
UPPER KING ST
KING ST
VICTORIA ST
PETERDALE RD
CHERWELL CL
BOURNE CL
QUEEN ST
ARMYTAGE IND EST
4
77
3
76
2
75
1
74
39
40

77
59

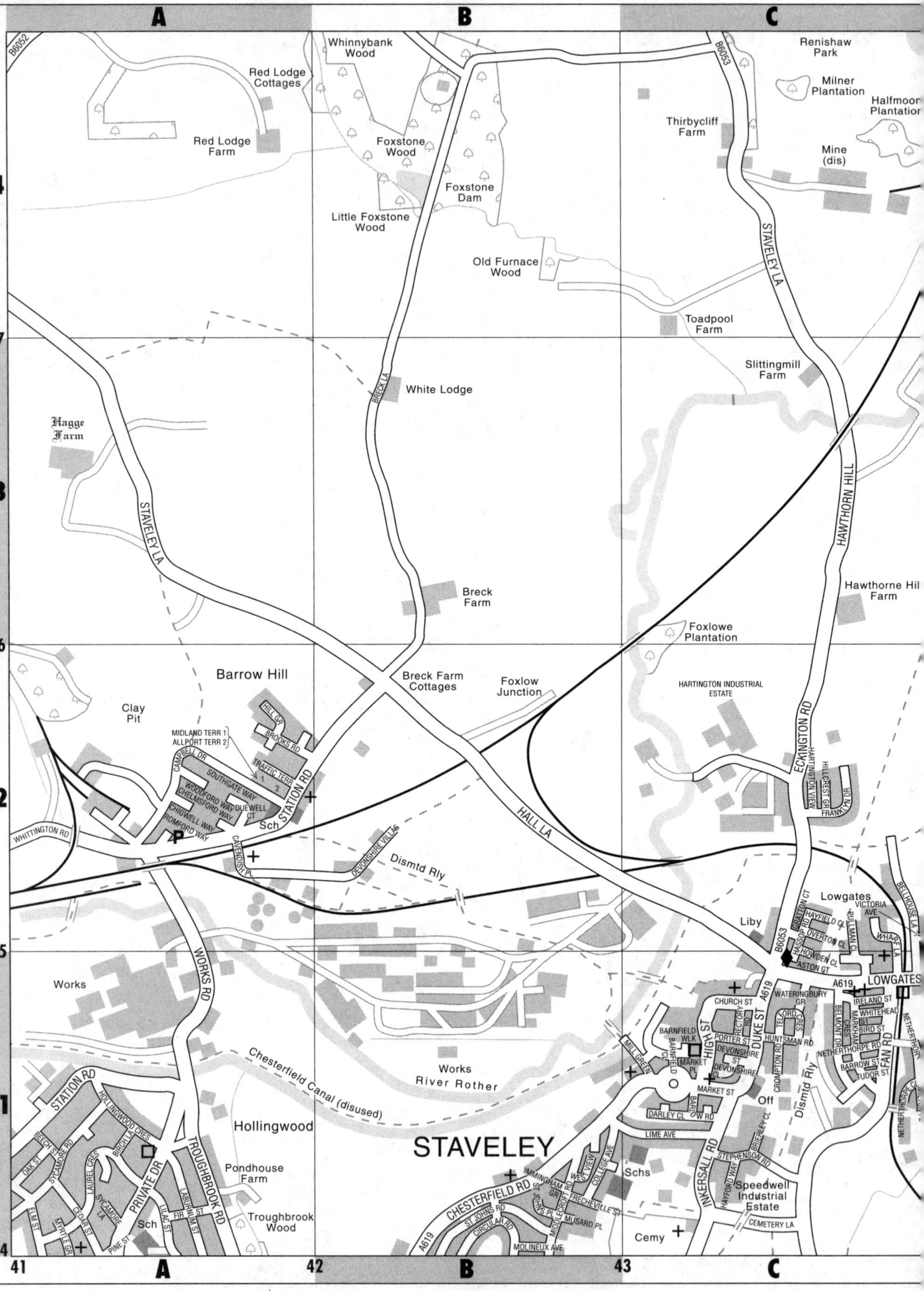
A
B
C
4
77
3
76
2
75
1
74
41
42
43
B6052
B6053
Whinnybank Wood
Red Lodge Cottages
Red Lodge Farm
Foxstone Wood
Foxstone Dam
Little Foxstone Wood
Renishaw Park
Milner Plantation
Halfmoor Plantation
Thirbycliff Farm
Mine (dis)
STAVELEY LA
Old Furnace Wood
Toadpool Farm
Slittingmill Farm
BRECK LA
White Lodge
Hagge Farm
HAWTHORN HILL
Breck Farm
Hawthorne Hill Farm
Foxlowe Plantation
Barrow Hill
Breck Farm Cottages
Foxlow Junction
HARTINGTON INDUSTRIAL ESTATE
Clay Pit
HILL GR
BROOKS RD
MIDLAND TERR 1
ALLPORT TERR 2
CAMPBELL DR
TRAFFIC TERR
SOUTHGATE WAY
WOODFORD WAY
CHELMSFORD WAY
DUEWELL CT
STATION RD
CHIGWELL WAY
ROMFORD WAY
Sch
WHITTINGTON RD
CAVENDISH PL
DEVONSHIRE VILLAS
Dismtd Rly
HALL LA
ECKINGTON RD
HARTINGTON VIEW
HILLCREST GR
FRANKLYN DR
Lowgates
VICTORIA AVE
BELLHOUSE LA
GRATTON CT
HAYFIELD CL
PULLMAN CL
OVERTON CL
HOWDEN CL
ASTON CT
WHARF LA
Liby
B6053
WORKS RD
Works
A619
LOWGATES
WATERINGBURY GR
CHURCH ST
RECTORY RD
DUKE ST
TELFORD CRES
IRELAND ST
WHITEHEAD ST
MARKHAM CRES
BELMONT DR
BIRD ST
NETHERTHORPE RD
FAN RD
BARRNFIELD WLK
BARNFIELD CL
HIGH ST
PORTER ST
DEVONSHIRE ST
HUNTSMAN RD
MILL GREEN
MARKET PL
DEVONSHIRE
BARROW ST
TUDOR ST
Chesterfield Canal (disused)
Works
River Rother
MARKET ST
CROMPTON RD
Off
STATION RD
HOLLINGWOOD CRES
DARLEY CL
BARLOW RD
Hollingwood
BEECH ST
SYCAMORE RD
BIRCH LA
LIME AVE
STAVELEY
OAK ST
LAUREL CRES
PRIVATE DR
TROUGHBROOK RD
BRIERLEY CL
STEPHENSON RD
Pondhouse Farm
Schs
SYCAMORE LA
LABURNUM ST
FIR ST
LILAC ST
IMMINGHAM GR
WEST VIEW
COLLEGE AVE
INKERSALL RD
HAYFORD WAY
Speedwell Industrial Estate
ELM ST
CEDAR ST
MYRTLE GR
PINE ST
Sch
Troughbrook Wood
CHESTERFIELD RD
ST JOHNS RD
ST JOHNS PL
MIDDLECROFT RD
FRECHEVILLE ST
MUSARD PL
CIRCULAR RD
A619
MOLINEUX AVE
Cemy
CEMETERY LA

77
97

60
80

D
E
F
45
46
77
76
75
74
4
3
2
1
Works
Smithy Brook
Hollinwood Farm
B6419
A6135
HAGUE AVE
CHURCH CL
MAIN RD
Sch
CIRCULAR DR
FIELD AVE
REYNARD CRES
EAST ST
CARRWOOD RD
Renishaw
EMMETT CARR LA
BROOK ST
EMMETT CARR CL
GARDEN AVE
THE WYND
SHEFFIELD RD
Blacksmiths Arms (PH)
SYDAY LA
Prince of Wales (PH)
Commonside Farm
LOW COMM
West Knoll
Hazelwood House
River Rother
The Hague
Emmett Carr
Barlborough Low Common
Low Common Farm
Garfield House
WESTFIELD LA
Beighton Fields
Dismtd Rly
A6135
Priory Farm
Westfield Farm
Dismantled Railway
HAGUE LA
Beightonfields Priory
M1
Robinson's Lumb
Sewage Works
Woodhouse Lane Farm
WOODHOUSE LA
Happy Valley
Pond Farm
Grange Farm
A619
Huggester Farm
River Doe Lee
Holbrook Farm
RENISHAW RD
WORKSOP RD
MILLER AVE
HAWTHORN AVE
ALMOND CRES
ROSE CRES
SHAMROCK PL
VALLEY RD
ASH GR
Norbriggs Cutting (disused)
LANSBURY AVE
BLUNT AVE
WILLOW DR
EDALE RD
HAZEL GR
Mastin Moor
Gate Inn (PH)
HOWELLS PL
DERWENT VIEW
ROWAN
CHERRY TREE GR
HILLSIDE DR
CARPENTER AVE
Romeley Wood
Caravan Site
Norbriggs
BENT LA
The Farm
THE PADDOCKS
Sch
CRANLEIGH RD
BURKITT DR
TOLLBRIDGE RD
THORPLEIGH RD
WHITE RD
MOOR VIEW RD
BOUNDARY RD
LOWGATES
F Sta
Netherthorpe
Norbriggs Cottages
Woodthorpe Hall Farm
SPENCER AVE
NORBRIGGS RD
Woodthorpe
BOLSOVER RD
Sch
WOODTHORPE RD
Wellsholme Farm
Bank House
LOWFIELDS
BRIDLE RD
The Albert Inn (PH)
SEYMOUR LA
Sch
B6419
Woodthorpe Grange
Oxcroft Junction
WOODTHORPE RD
M1

98
80

79
61

A
B
C
4
77
3
76
2
75
1
74
47
48
49
M1
WARD LA
Longrybank Wood
Coltsworth Lane
COLTSWORTH LA
A618
WALLS LA
Speetley Plantation
Eastwood Farm
Eastwood Cottage
Barlborough
Reservoirs
Whitebrick Moor
WESTFIELD BANK
RUTHYN AVE
CALIFORNIA LA
PARK ST
PARK VIEW
Sch
Speetley Farm
HIGH ST
De Rodes Arms (PH)
SHEFFIELD RD
WEST END
CHURCH ST
NEW RD
ORCHARD CL
WESTBRIDGE RD
RODWOOD AVE
MANOR RD
CHURCH VIEW
CLIFTON AVE
WEST VIEW
MANOR GR
ASHLEIGH RD
A619
A616
Mill Farm
Van Dyk Hotel
BOURNE HILL CL
BOWDON AVE
HAWTHORNE CL
THE CRESCENT
CLOWNE RD
FOREST CT
SLAYLEY VIEW RD
OCCUPATION CL
A6135
Hawthorns Farm
CHESTERFIELD RD
WHITECROFT VIEW
BRACKEN LA
Slayley Farm
Forrest's Plantation
ROTHERHAM RD
Barlborough Common
Opencast Workings
New Barlborough
Harlesthorpe
WORKSOP RD
Cemetery
MONNIES END
MASTIN AVE
SLAYLEY VIEW
HERITAGE DR
HUTCHINGS CRES
BARLBOROUGH RD
NEW BARLBOROUGH CL
BRAMLYN CT
BRAMLYN CL
HARLESTHORPE LA
Manor Farm
HICKINGWOOD LA
PARK VIEW
SOUTHGATE
WILSON AVE
HARLESTHORPE AVE
HICKINWOOD CR
Fire Station
Barlborough Common
CRESWELL RD
WEST LEA COTTAGES
Sch
SALVIN CRES
RECREATION CL
B6417
NORTH RD
STATION RD
BROOKBANK RD
RHODES COTTS
BROOK LA
BROOKHILL
CLUMBER CL
BARTON ST
GRAY ST
CHATSWORTH AVE
HEALEY ST
MITCHELL ST
DEVONSHIRE WAY
PORTLAND ST
BOUGHTON LA
CHESTNUT DR
P
PC
MILL ST
RECTORY RD
College
Hood Croft Farm
REGENT ST
ROMELEY CRES
PH
SLAYLEY HILL
CHURCH ST
MEADOW VIEW
CHURCH VIEW
RINGER WAY
Schs
CLIFF HILL
HIGH ST
B6418
CROWN ST
SUNNY BROOK CL
MANOR CT
SOUTHWOOD DR
ST JOHN'S CRES
CHURCH LA
NORTHFIELDS
ELMTON CL
Hoodcroft Lane
LOW RD
JOHN ST
CRAGGS DR
KING ST
ORCHARD CL
WELBECK CT
DUKERIES CT
BORDER LA
Clowne Common
Clowne
Stanfree Farm
Milking Lane
RINGER LA
COURT VIEW
ROOD LA
KINGS CL
FIELD VIEW
SOUTHFIELDS
BAMSBROOK DR
HIGH LEES RD
BEECH TREE DR
RIDGWAY
Low Common Farm
STERRY CL
ASH TREE RD
RAMPER AVE
PITCH CL
PAVILION CL
CRICKET VIEW
RIDGWAY
WILLOW TERR
OFFRIDGE CL
OAK TREE RD
Romeley Hall Farm
Sterry House Farm
MANSFIELD RD
High Ash Farm
Ringer House
Ringer Villa Farm
BORDER LA
BRIDLE RD
Appletree Inn (PH)
Stanfree Cottage
Congreave House
Border Farm
CLOWNE RD
APPLETREE RD
BAMSBROOK LA
Grange Farm
CHURCH RD
EAST AVE
Calow Farm
HILL LA
B6418
B6417

D
E
F
North Walls
South Walls
WALLS LA
Gipsyhill Farm
GIPSYHILL LA
Cinders Farm
Hawthorn Fields
BONDHAY LA
Woodnook
Whitwell Wood
Rob Nook
Commonside Farm
Springfield Farm
Whitwell Common
CLINTHILL LA
A619
B6043
PH
Whitwell Hall
DOLES LA
WORKSOP RD
GREENWAY
HIGH ST
SCOTLAND ST
MANOR FARM CT
HANGER HILL
STATION RD
PORTLAND ST
Lby
MASON ST
PORTLAND
TITCHFIELD ST
BUTT HILL
Hickin Wood
Highwood Farm
Whitwell
Claylands
HILLSIDE CL
JUBILEE PL
LAWRENCE VIEW
JUBILEE CRES
JUBILEE GDNS
JUBILEE RD
CLAYLANDS GR
CLAYLANDS RD
CLAYLANDS PL
PLANTATION CL
HILLSIDE ST
SOUTH VIEW
SOUTHFIELD LA
SOUTHFIELD CL
BAKESTONE MOOR
NEW ST
SANDY CL
THORPE AVE
FRANKLIN AVE
FRANKLIN CRES
LONGHURST VIEW
Hickingwood Farm
HICKINGWOOD LA
GAPSICK LA
HIGHWOOD LA
SOUTHGATE CRES
ASHLEA WLK
CLUNE ST
ROSE AVE
WEST ST
EAST ST
WILSON AVE
JAGO AVE
MARKLAND CRES
MARKLAND AVE
JUBILEE CRES
CHATSWORTH AVE
CRESWELL RD
THORESBY AVE
CAVENDISH DR
HADDON AVE
DUKE ST
BENTINCK DR
HARDWICK CL
PORTLAND ST
DEVONSHIRE WAY
WOODLAND GR
HARTINGTON CT
Bakestone Moor
Gorse Covert
Highfield House
Archaeological Trail
Peter More
Tunnel
Hollin Hill
HOLLIN HILL
Works
PETER MORE HILL
Mill Cottages
Lower Mill Farm
Hollinhill Grips
SHEFFIELD RD
Butcher's Wood
CHURCH LA
RIDGEWAY
BORDER LA
Markland Farm
Upper Mill Farm
Sch
HAZELMERE RD
MARKLAND VIEW
HAWTHORN AVE
NOBEL CL
CHESTNUT DR
HALDANE CL
SYCAMORE AVE
STEPHENSON CL
LINDEN RD
ORCHARD DR
ROWAN CL
Dismantled Rly
Hazelmere Farm
Brookside Farm
Markland Grips
Markland Plantation
MARKLAND LA
Archaeological Trail
SKINNER ST
Creswell
Cemy
BAKER ST
QUEENS CT
KINGS ST
QUEEN ST
KING ST
DOVER ST
WOLLEN CL
Bank House Farm
ROGERS AVE
TENNYSON AVE
SHAKESPEARE AVE
EYRE ST
WEST ST
EAST ST
SHERWOOD AVE
PORTLAND AVE
JOHN ST
ANN ST
ELMTON RD
PH
Sch
MODEL VILLAGE
Lby
CHURCH ST
WELBECK ST
TITCHFIELD ST
DUKE ST
HAZELBY RD
VICTORIA ST
LABURNUM CL
MANSFIELD RD
WILLOW CL
CRAGS VIEW
B6042
FIELDINGS
BEECH AVE
CRAGS RD
DUCHESS ST
A616
DEVONSHIRE DR
CHATSWORTH RD
MANSE AVE
BENTINCK CL
WOOD AVE
MANSE CL
BANK CL
HOLBECK ST
4
77
3
76
2
75
1
74
51
52

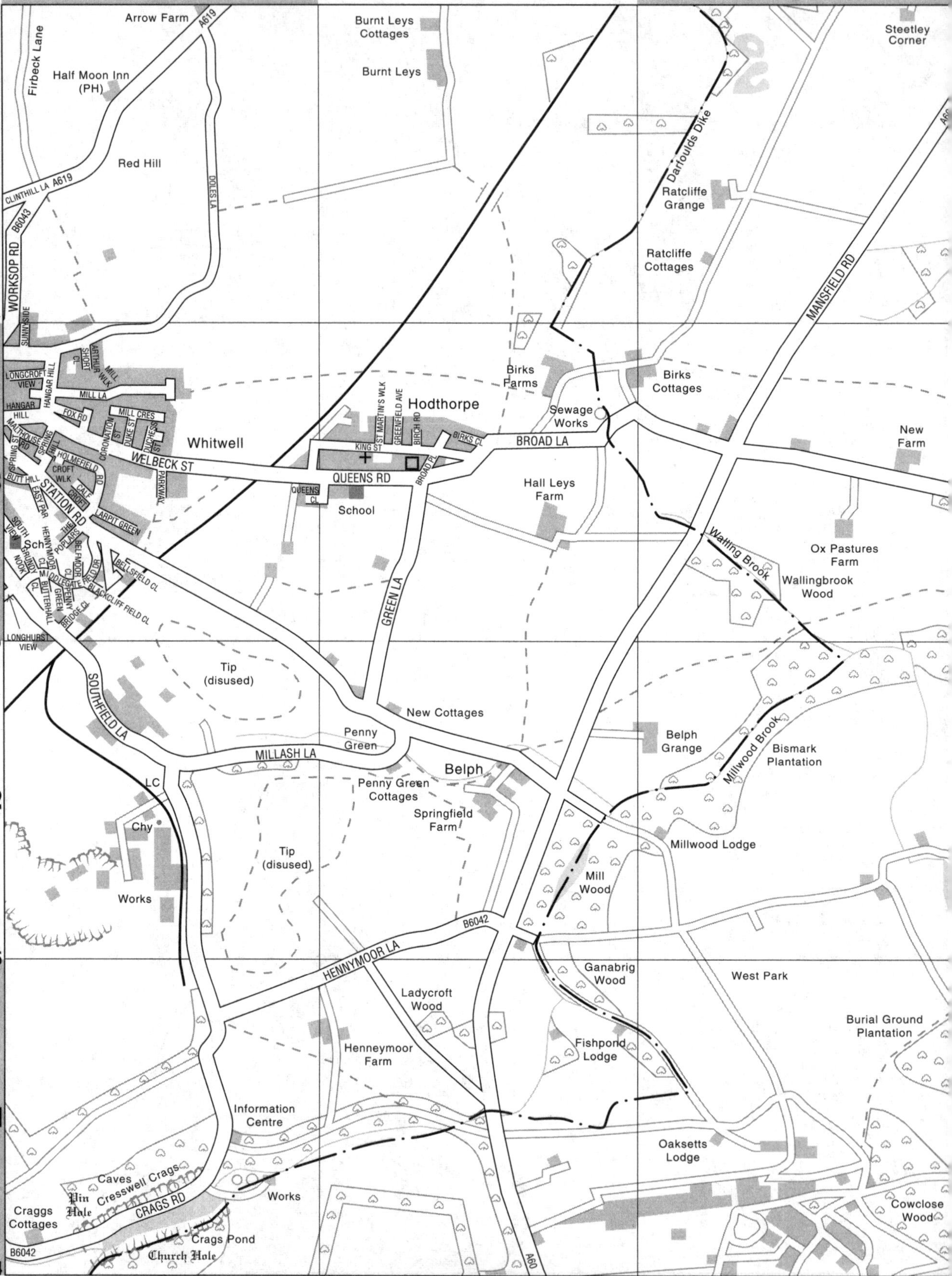
A B C
4 3 2 1
77 76 75 74
53 54 55
Arrow Farm
A619
Firbeck Lane
Half Moon Inn (PH)
Red Hill
Burnt Leys Cottages
Burnt Leys
Steetley Corner
Dartoulds Dike
Ratcliffe Grange
Ratcliffe Cottages
CLINTHILL LA A619
B6043
WORKSOP RD
DOLES LA
MANSFIELD RD
SUNNYSIDE
SHORT CL
ARTHUR WLK
MILL WLK
LONGCROFT VIEW
HANGAR HILL
MILL LA
FOX RD
MILL CRES
CORONATION ST
DUKE ST
DUCHESS ST
MALTHOUSE RD
SPRING ST
HOLMEFIELD RD
Whitwell
WELBECK ST
PARKWAY
CROFT WLK
BUTT HILL
STATION RD
EASY PAR
CAFE CROFT
LARPIT GREEN
SOUTH VIEW
Sch
NOOK
HENNYMOOR CL
THE POPLARS
BELFMOOR CL
MIDDLEGATE FIELD DR
BELLSFIELD CL
BLACKCLIFF FIELD CL
BUTTERHALL
PENNY GREEN
BRIDGE CL
LONGHURST VIEW
Hodthorpe
ST MARTIN'S WLK
GREENFIELD AVE
BIRCH RD
KING ST
BIRKS CL
BROAD LA
BROAD PL
QUEENS RD
QUEENS CL
School
Birks Farms
Birks Cottages
Sewage Works
New Farm
Hall Leys Farm
Walling Brook
Ox Pastures Farm
Wallingbrook Wood
GREEN LA
Tip (disused)
SOUTHFIELD LA
New Cottages
Penny Green
MILLASH LA
Belph
Belph Grange
Millwood Brook
Bismark Plantation
LC
Chy
Penny Green Cottages
Springfield Farm
Millwood Lodge
Works
Mill Wood
B6042
HENNYMOOR LA
Ganabrig Wood
West Park
Ladycroft Wood
Henneymoor Farm
Fishpond Lodge
Burial Ground Plantation
Information Centre
Oaksetts Lodge
Caves
Cresswell Crags
Pin Hole
Craggs Cottages
CRAGS RD
Works
Cowclose Wood
Crags Pond
Church Hole
A60

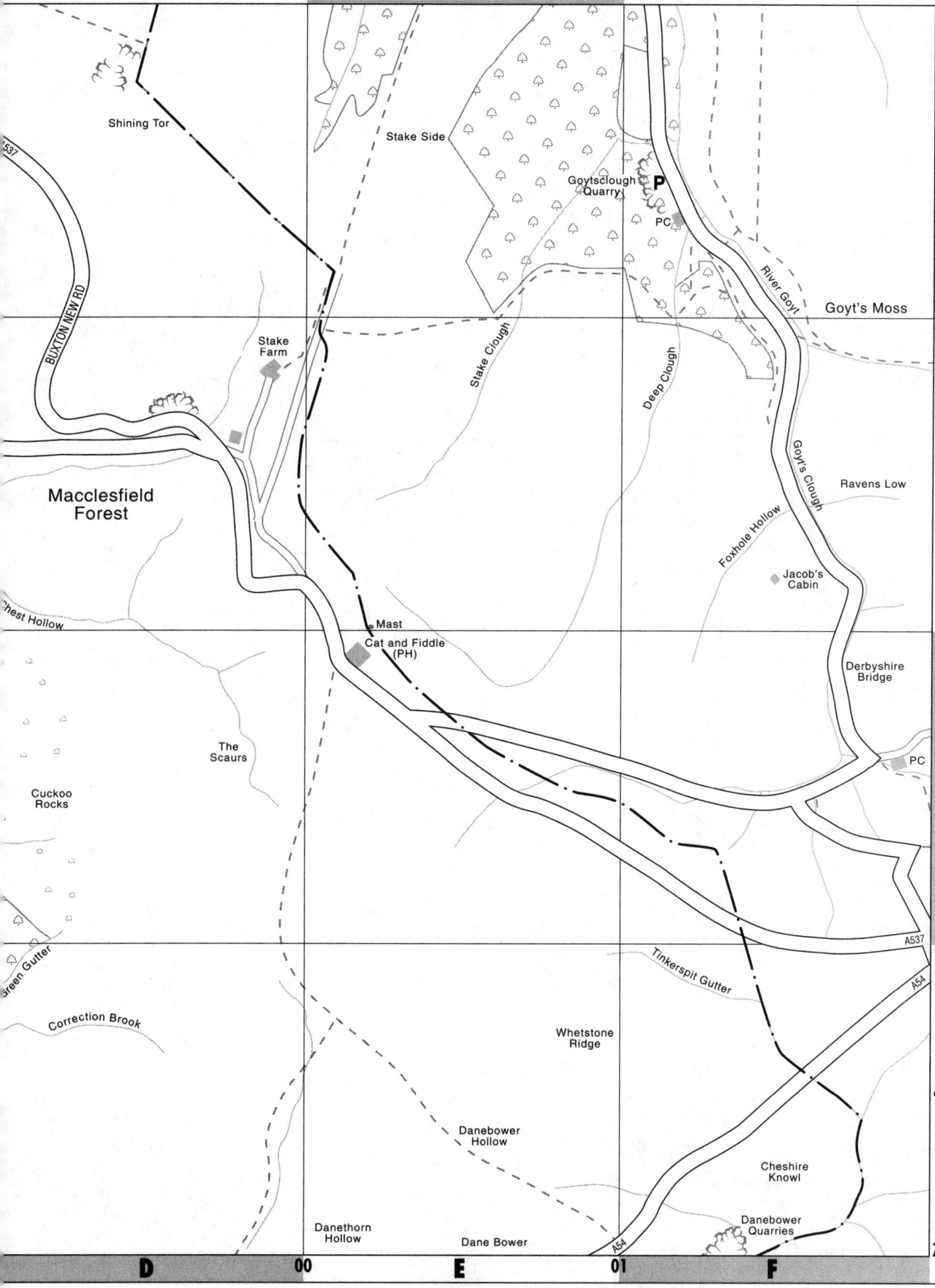
D
E
F
Shining Tor
Stake Side
Goytsclough Quarry
P
PC
River Goyt
Goyt's Moss
A537
BUXTON NEW RD
Stake Farm
Stake Clough
Deep Clough
Macclesfield Forest
Goyt's Clough
Ravens Low
Foxhole Hollow
Jacob's Cabin
Chest Hollow
Mast
Cat and Fiddle (PH)
Derbyshire Bridge
The Scaurs
PC
Cuckoo Rocks
A537
Green Gutter
Tinkerspit Gutter
A54
Correction Brook
Whetstone Ridge
Danebower Hollow
Cheshire Knowl
Danethorn Hollow
Dane Bower
Danebower Quarries
A54
4
73
3
72
2
71
1
70
D
00
E
01
F

83
65

A
B
C
4
73
3
72
2
71
1
70
02
03
04
Beet Wood
Tunnel Farm
Edgemoor
Plex Lodge
Plex Farm
Burbage Edge
Golf Course
Manchester Rd
Nithen End
CH
Gadley Cl
Carlisle Gr
Watford Rd
Gadley La
The Paddock
River's Vale
St John's Rd
Wyelands Cl
B5059
Macclesfield Rd
Bishops La
Bridge Farm
Nursery La
Arbor Gr
Turncliff Cl
Cavendish Ave
Girdon Cl
Dovedale Cres
Hargate Rd
Goytlands
Sch
Milldale Ave
Ecclesbourne Dr
Green La
Holmfield
PC
Duke St
Burbage
Shay Lodge
Dismtd Rly
Berry Clough
Burbage-edge Plantation
Goslin Bar Farm
Macclesfield Old Rd
Kennett Gr
Level La
Terret Gr
Anncroft Rd
Brookside Gr
Buxton Country Park
Poole's Cavern
Grin Plantation
Leek Rd
P
Caravan Park
PCs
Raven's Low Flat
Burbage Reservoir
A54
Macclesfield Main Rd
Canholes
PC
P
Bridgehouse Farm
The Terret
The Bungalow
Grin Low Rd
Terret Plantation
Ladmanlow
Stanley Moor
Stanley Moor Reservoir
Moss Chain
A537
A54
Feathered Moss
Thatch Marsh
Axe Edge Moor
River Dane
Dane Head
Axe Edge
A53
Turncliff Common
Anthony Hill
Turncliff

83
103

66
86

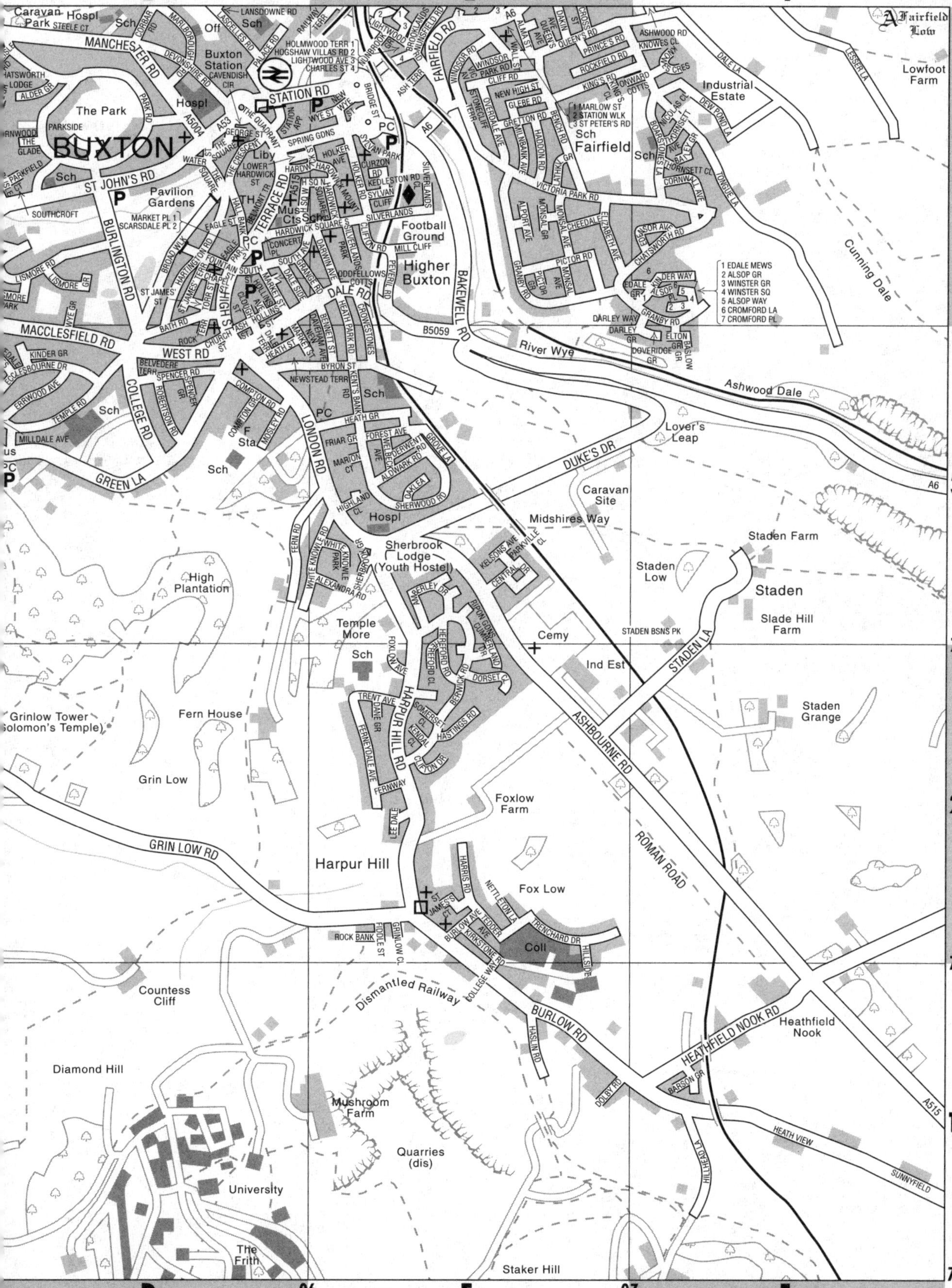
D
E
F
BUXTON
Buxton Station
Caravan Park
Hospl
Sch
Off
The Park
Pavilion Gardens
Liby
Mus
Cts
Football Ground
Higher Buxton
Fairfield
Industrial Estate
Lowfoot Farm
Fairfield Low
Cunning Dale
River Wye
Ashwood Dale
Lover's Leap
Caravan Site
Midshires Way
Staden Farm
Staden Low
Staden
Slade Hill Farm
Sherbrook Lodge (Youth Hostel)
High Plantation
Temple More
Cemy
Ind Est
Staden Grange
Grinlow Tower (Solomon's Temple)
Fern House
Grin Low
Foxlow Farm
Harpur Hill
Fox Low
Coll
Countess Cliff
Dismantled Railway
Heathfield Nook
Diamond Hill
Mushroom Farm
Quarries (dis)
University
The Frith
Staker Hill
MANCHESTER RD
STATION RD
ST JOHN'S RD
BURLINGTON RD
TERRACE RD
MACCLESFIELD RD
WEST RD
COLLEGE RD
GREEN LA
LONDON RD
DALE RD
HIGH ST
FAIRFIELD RD
BAKEWELL RD
VICTORIA PARK RD
DUKE'S DR
ASHBOURNE RD
HARPUR HILL RD
STADEN LA
GRIN LOW RD
ROMAN ROAD
BURLOW RD
HEATHFIELD NOOK RD
HEATH VIEW
A6
A515
A5004
A53
B5059
1 EDALE MEWS
2 ALSOP GR
3 WINSTER GR
4 WINSTER SQ
5 ALSOP WAY
6 CROMFORD LA
7 CROMFORD PL
1 MARLOW ST
2 STATION WLK
3 ST PETER'S RD
HOLMWOOD TERR 1
HOGSHAW VILLAS RD 2
LIGHTWOOD AVE 3
CHARLES ST 4
4
73
3
72
2
71
1
70
06
07

104
86

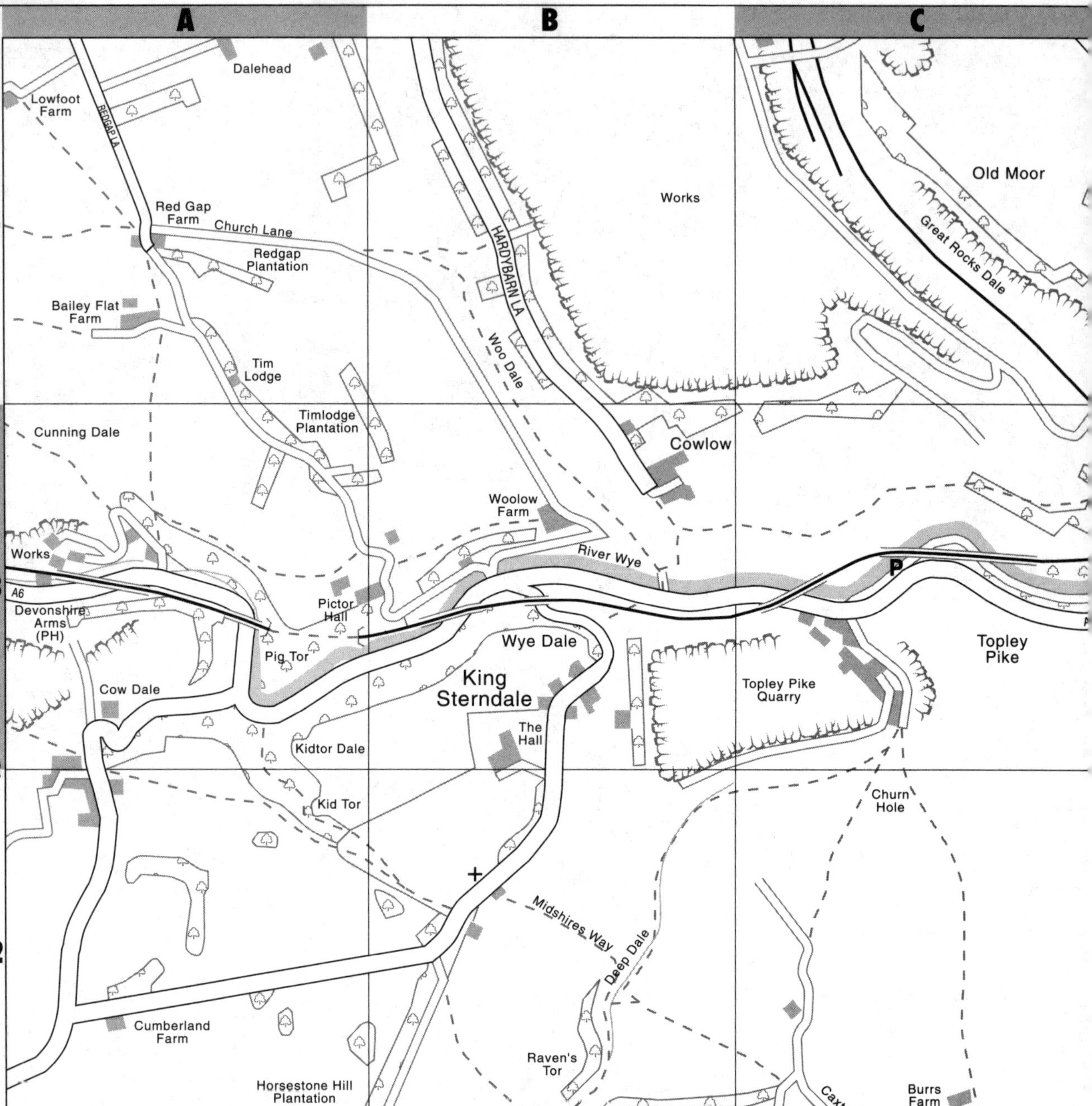
A
B
C
Dalehead
Lowfoot Farm
REDGAP LA
Red Gap Farm
Church Lane
Redgap Plantation
Bailey Flat Farm
Tim Lodge
Timlodge Plantation
Cunning Dale
Works
Old Moor
Great Rocks Dale
HARDYBARN LA
Woo Dale
Cowlow
Woolow Farm
River Wye
Works
A6
Devonshire Arms (PH)
Pictor Hall
Pig Tor
Wye Dale
King Sterndale
P
Topley Pike
Topley Pike Quarry
Cow Dale
The Hall
Kidtor Dale
Kid Tor
Churn Hole
Midshires Way
Deep Dale
Cumberland Farm
Raven's Tor
Horsestone Hill Plantation
Caxterway Lane
Burrs Farm
Arden Villas
A527
Priest's Way
Back Dale
Horseshoe Dale
OLD COALPIT LA
COMMON LA
A515
Sewage Works
Bullhay Dale
Shallow Grange
Brierlow Dale
A5270
4
73
3
72
2
71
1
70
08
09
10

D
E
F
Chapelsteads Farm
Hassop Farm
Flag Dale
Knot Low
Glebe Farm
Old Moor
River Wye
Meadow Wood
Chee Tor
Chee Dale
Monsal Trail
P
PC
PH
B6049
Millers Dale
Meadow
Mosley Farm
Dismantled Railway
Blackwell Dale
LONG LA
Blackwell Hall
Blackwell
Cottage Farm
Topleyhead Farm
Lydgate Farm
Priestcliffe
Priestcliffe Hall
Limestone Way
A5270
Calton Farm
Highcliff Farm
PRIESTCLIFFE RD
Rock Lodge Farm
Priestcliff Ditch
B6049
Mines (disused)
HOLLOW OF THE MOOR
Calton Hill
Chelmorton Flat
Senners Lane
The Waterloo (PH)
A6
MAIN RD
SCHOOL LA
Sch
Rock House Farm
Sough Lane
SENNERS LA
COALPIT LA
Pillwell Gate
Sough Top
Fivewells Farms
Chelmorton Low
SLIPPERLOW LA
Taddington Moor
Moor Grange
SOUGH LA
Pillwell Lane
Shepley Farm
MOOR LA
Church Inn (PH)
Midshires Way
Sch
COMMON LA
Chelmorton
MAIN ST
CHURCH LA
GREEN LA
Bosley Fields
FLAT LA
4
73
3
72
2
71
1
70
12
13

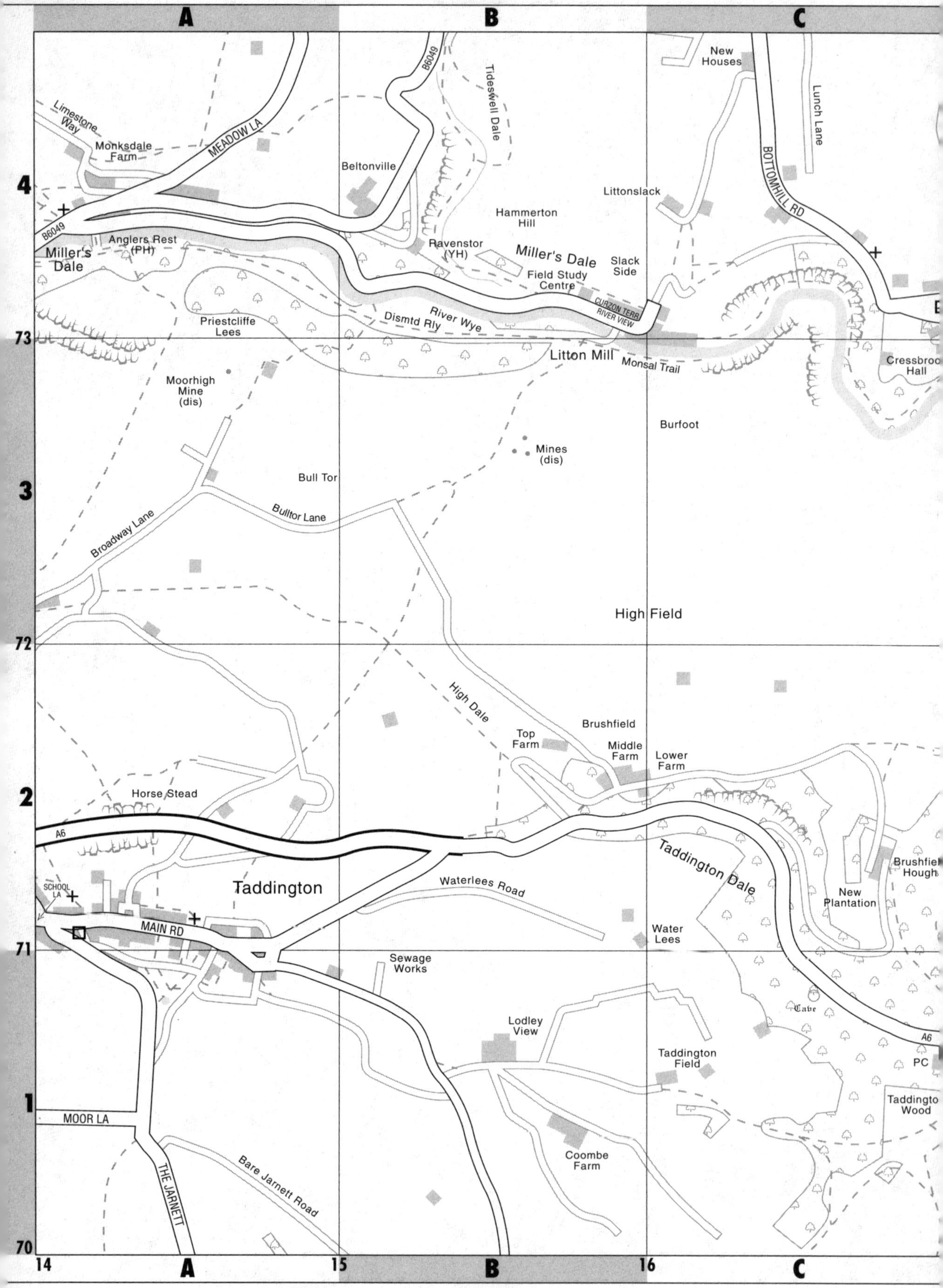
A
B
C
4
3
2
1
73
72
71
70
14
15
16
Limestone Way
Monksdale Farm
MEADOW LA
B6049
Tideswell Dale
New Houses
Lunch Lane
BOTTOMHILL RD
Beltonville
Littonslack
Hammerton Hill
Miller's Dale
Anglers Rest (PH)
Ravenstor (YH)
Miller's Dale
Slack Side
Field Study Centre
CURZON TERR
RIVER VIEW
Priestcliffe Lees
River Wye
Dismtd Rly
Litton Mill
Monsal Trail
Cressbrook Hall
Moorhigh Mine (dis)
Burfoot
Mines (dis)
Bull Tor
Bulltor Lane
Broadway Lane
High Field
High Dale
Top Farm
Brushfield
Middle Farm
Lower Farm
Horse Stead
A6
Taddington Dale
Brushfield Hough
Taddington
Waterlees Road
New Plantation
SCHOOL LA
MAIN RD
Water Lees
Sewage Works
Cave
Lodley View
Taddington Field
PC
MOOR LA
Taddington Wood
Coombe Farm
THE JARNETT
Bare Jarnett Road

70
90

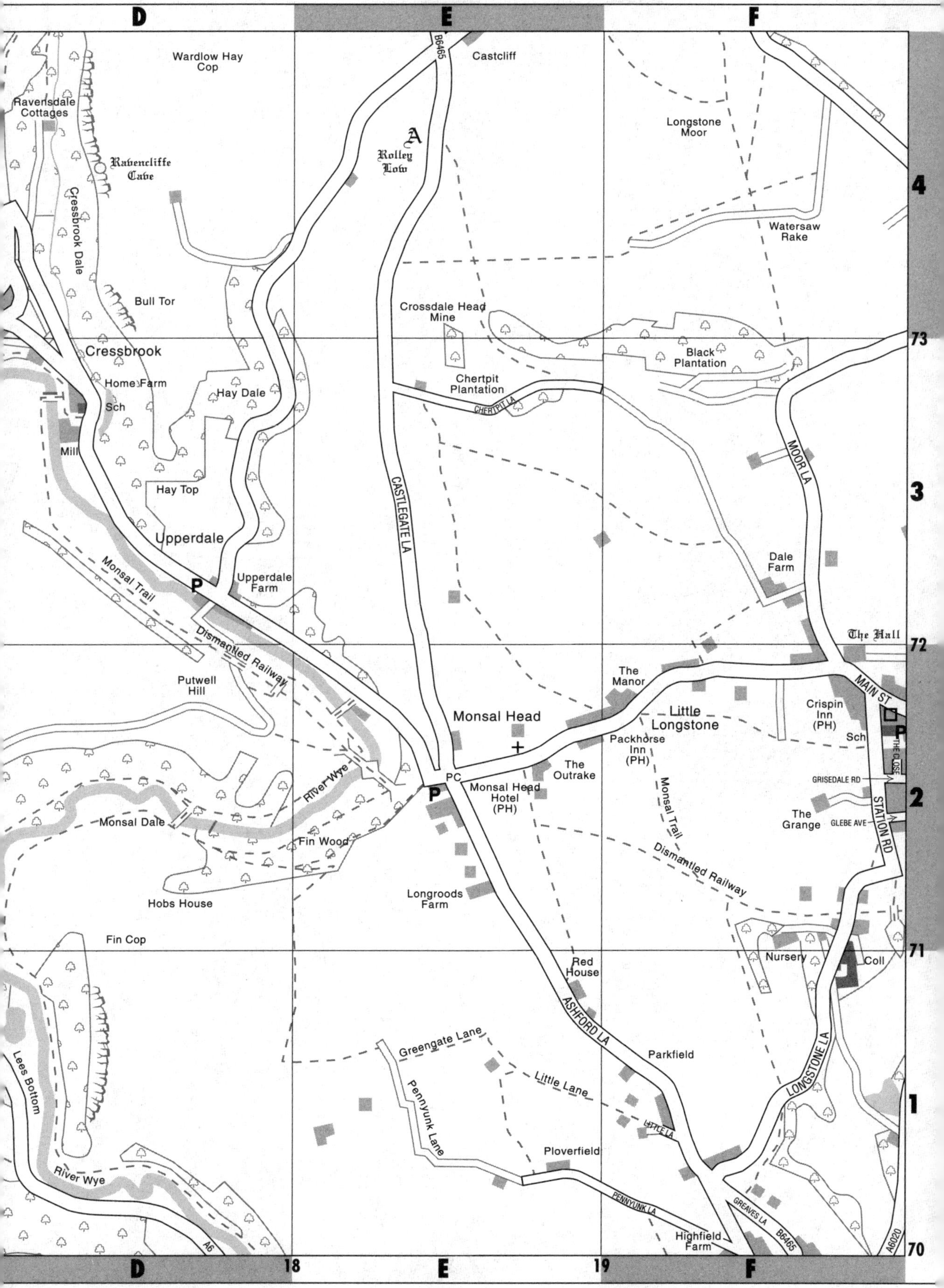
D
E
F
Wardlow Hay Cop
Castcliff
B6465
Ravensdale Cottages
Rolley Low
Longstone Moor
Ravencliffe Cave
Cressbrook Dale
Watersaw Rake
Bull Tor
Crossdale Head Mine
Cressbrook
Black Plantation
Home Farm
Hay Dale
Chertpit Plantation
CHERTPIT LA
Sch
Mill
MOOR LA
CASTLEGATE LA
Hay Top
Upperdale
Dale Farm
Monsal Trail
P
Upperdale Farm
Dismantled Railway
The Hall
Putwell Hill
The Manor
MAIN ST
Crispin Inn (PH)
Monsal Head
Little Longstone
Packhorse Inn (PH)
Sch
THE CLOSE
The Outrake
GRISEDALE RD
River Wye
PC
Monsal Head Hotel (PH)
Monsal Dale
Monsal Trail
STATION RD
The Grange
GLEBE AVE
Fin Wood
Dismantled Railway
Longroods Farm
Hobs House
Fin Cop
Red House
Nursery
Coll
ASHFORD LA
Lees Bottom
Greengate Lane
Parkfield
LONGSTONE LA
Little Lane
Pennyunk Lane
LITTLE LA
Ploverfield
River Wye
PENNYUNK LA
GREAVES LA
B6465
A6
Highfield Farm
A6020
4
73
3
72
2
71
1
70
18
19

108
90

89
71

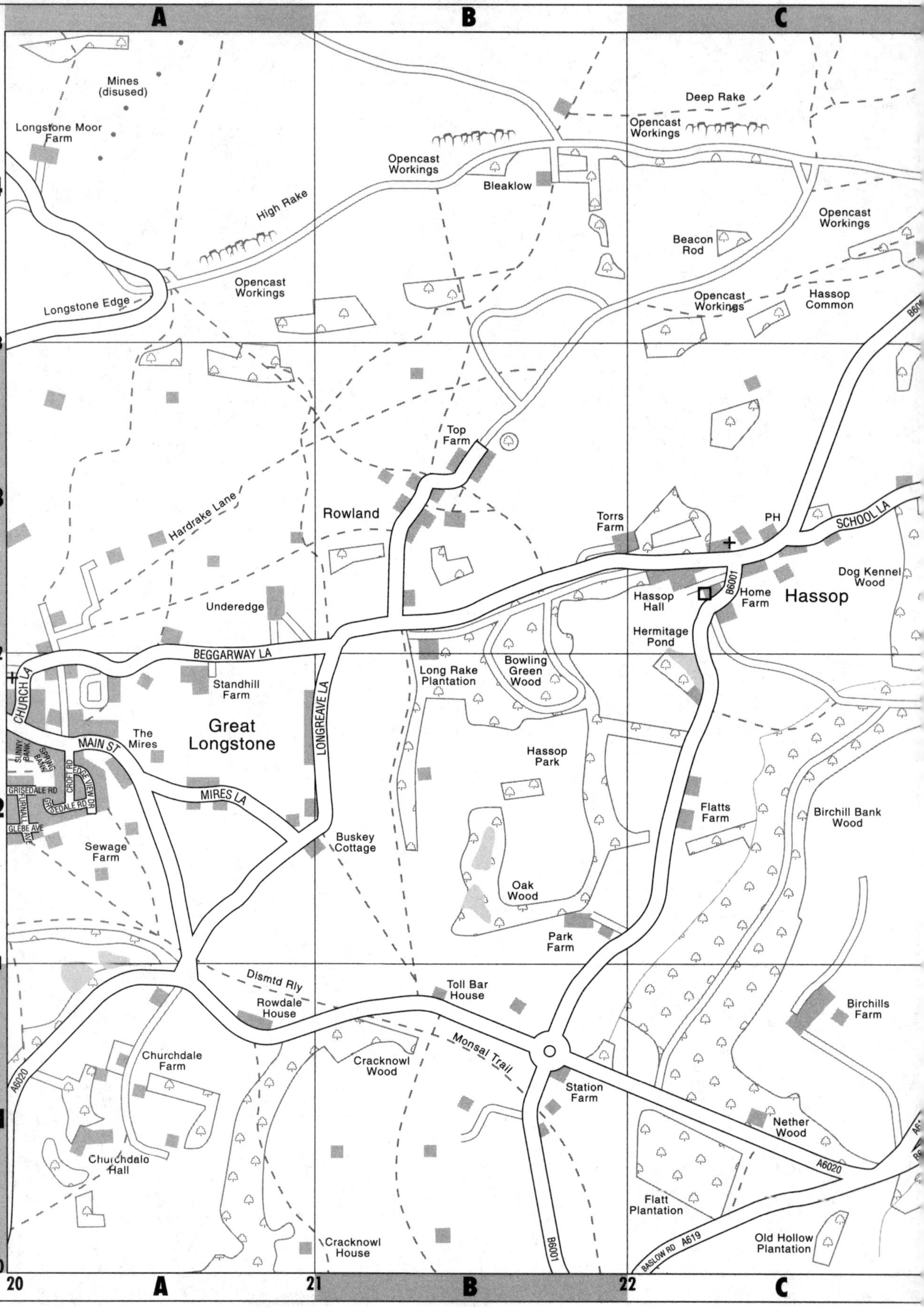
A
B
C
4
3
2
1
73
72
71
70
20
21
22
Mines
(disused)
Longstone Moor
Farm
High Rake
Opencast
Workings
Longstone Edge
Opencast
Workings
Bleaklow
Deep Rake
Opencast
Workings
Opencast
Workings
Beacon
Rod
Opencast
Workings
Hassop
Common
B6001
Top
Farm
Rowland
Hardrake Lane
Underedge
BEGGARWAY LA
Torrs
Farm
PH
SCHOOL LA
Dog Kennel
Wood
Hassop
Hall
B6001
Home
Farm
Hassop
Hermitage
Pond
CHURCH LA
Standhill
Farm
Great
Longstone
The
Mires
MAIN ST
SUNNY BANK
SPRING BANK
CROFT RD
EDGE VIEW DR
GRISEDALE RD
FURNALL AVE
GRISEDALE RD
GLEBE AVE
MIRES LA
LONGREAVE LA
Long Rake
Plantation
Bowling
Green
Wood
Hassop
Park
Flatts
Farm
Birchill Bank
Wood
Sewage
Farm
Buskey
Cottage
Oak
Wood
Park
Farm
Dismtd Rly
Rowdale
House
Toll Bar
House
Birchills
Farm
Monsal Trail
Churchdale
Farm
Cracknowl
Wood
Station
Farm
A6020
Nether
Wood
Churchdalo
Hall
A6020
Flatt
Plantation
B6001
Old Hollow
Plantation
Cracknowl
House
BASLOW RD A619

72
92

D E F

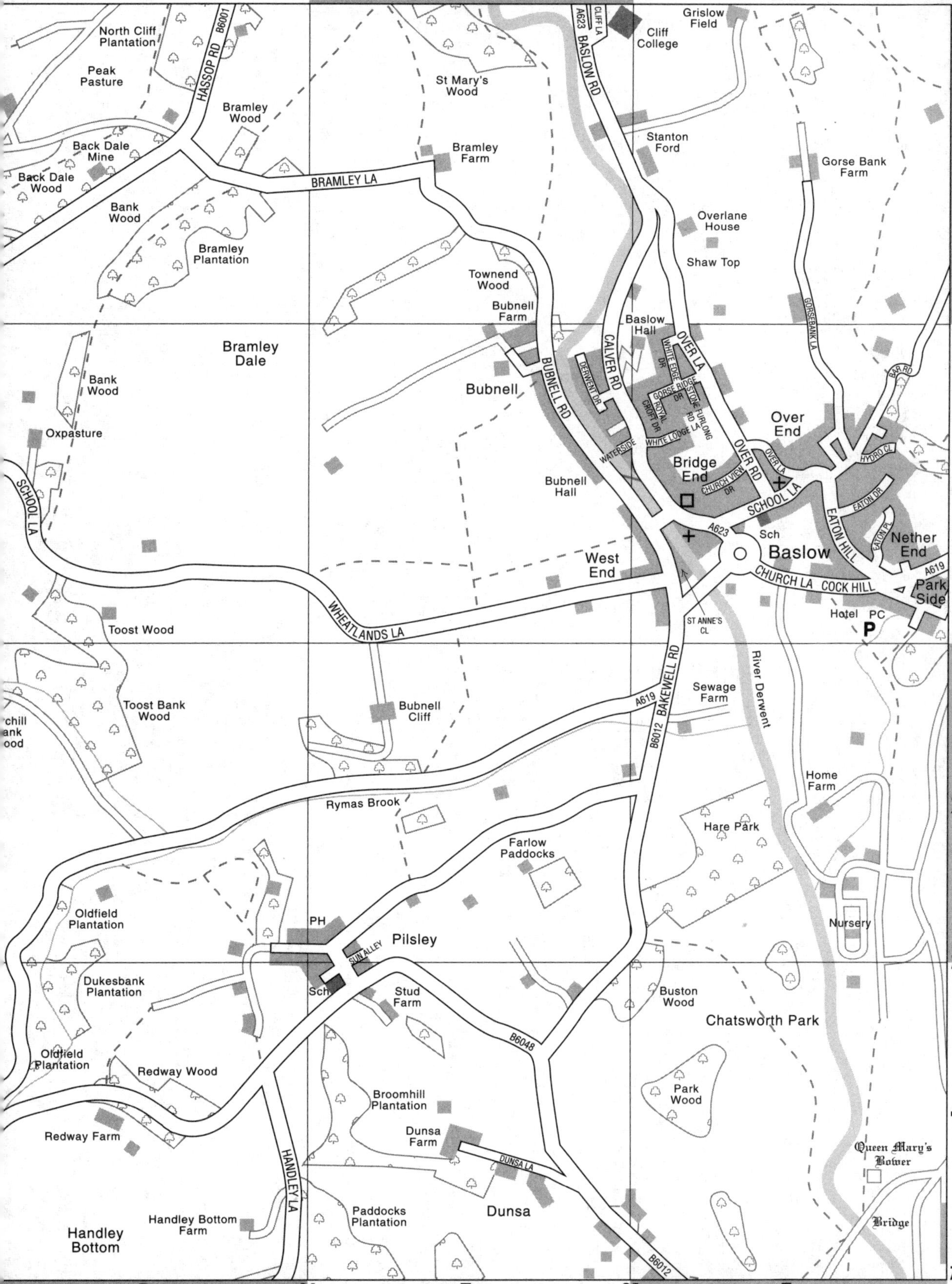

D E F

110
92

91
73

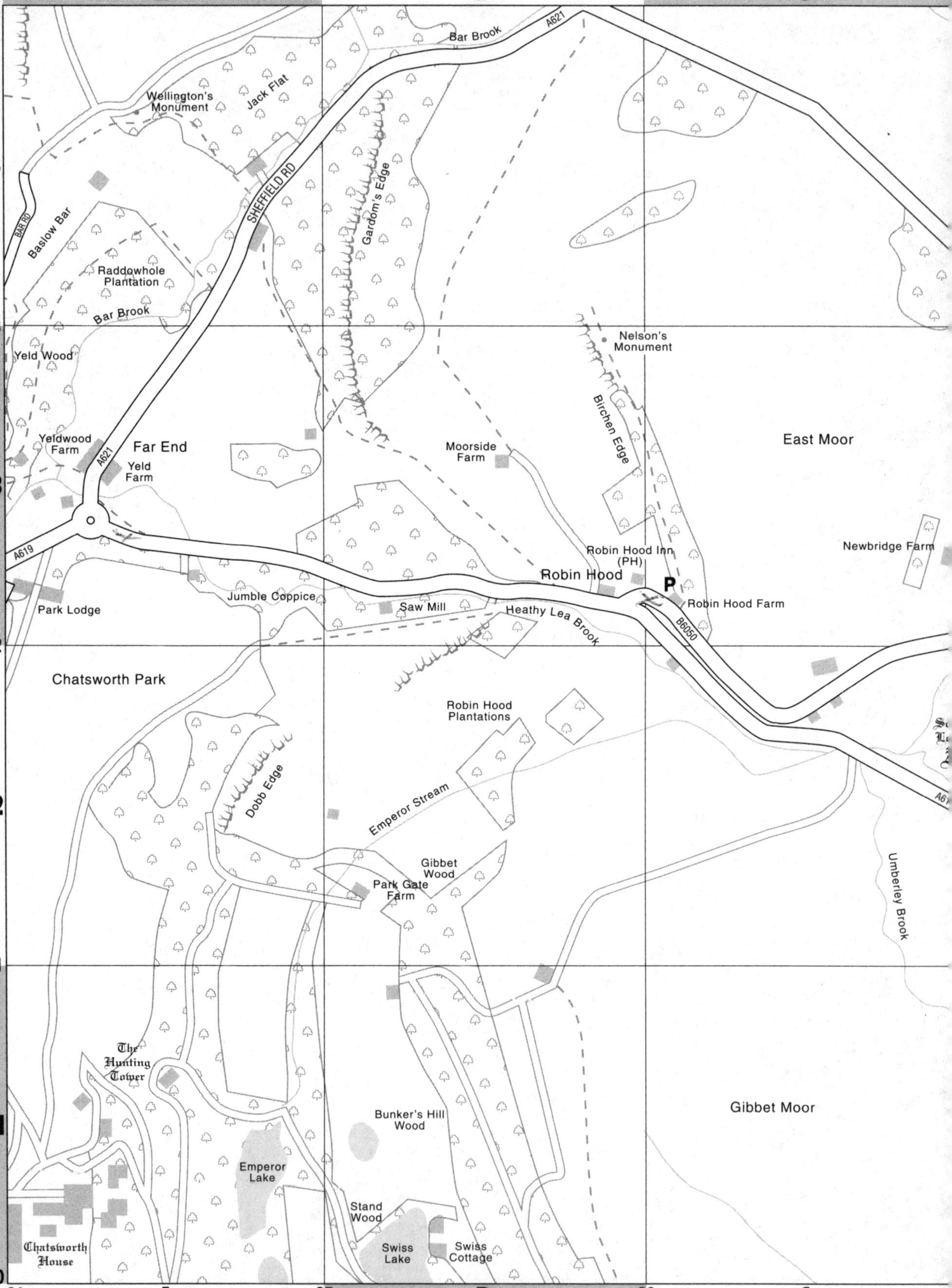
A
B
C
4
3
2
1
73
72
71
70
26
27
28
Bar Brook
A621
Wellington's Monument
Jack Flat
SHEFFIELD RD
Gardom's Edge
BAR RD
Baslow Bar
Raddowhole Plantation
Bar Brook
Yeld Wood
Nelson's Monument
Birchen Edge
Yeldwood Farm
Far End
A621
Yeld Farm
Moorside Farm
East Moor
A619
Robin Hood Inn (PH)
Robin Hood
Newbridge Farm
P
Robin Hood Farm
Park Lodge
Jumble Coppice
Saw Mill
Heathy Lea Brook
B6050
Chatsworth Park
Robin Hood Plantations
Dobb Edge
Emperor Stream
Gibbet Wood
Park Gate Farm
Umberley Brook
The Hunting Tower
Bunker's Hill Wood
Gibbet Moor
Emperor Lake
Stand Wood
Swiss Lake
Swiss Cottage
Chatsworth House

91
111

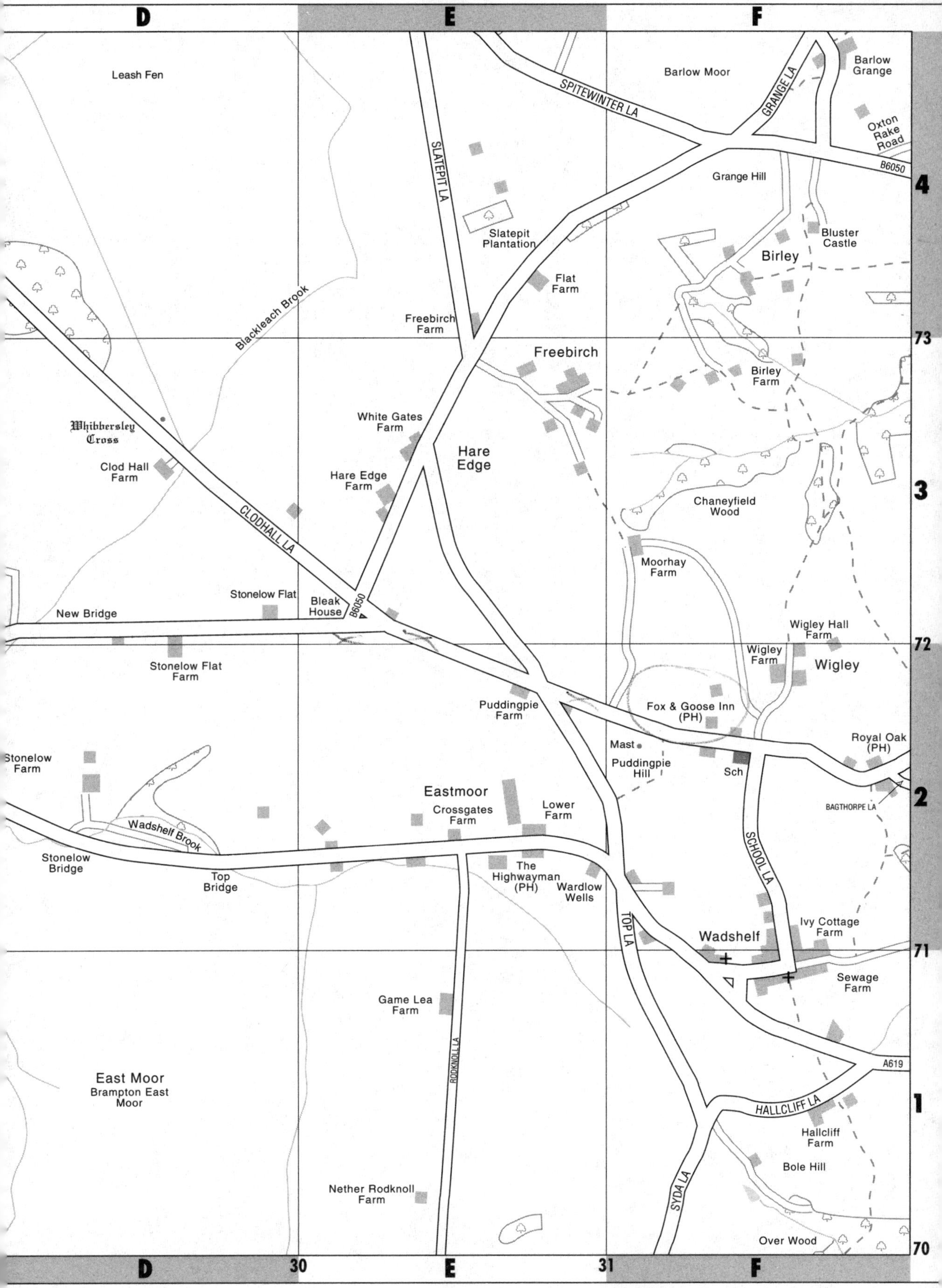
D
E
F
Leash Fen
Barlow Moor
Barlow Grange
SPITEWINTER LA
GRANGE LA
Oxton Rake Road
B6050
SLATEPIT LA
Grange Hill
Slatepit Plantation
Bluster Castle
Birley
Flat Farm
Blackleach Brook
Freebirch Farm
Freebirch
Birley Farm
White Gates Farm
Whibbersley Cross
Hare Edge
Clod Hall Farm
Hare Edge Farm
Chaneyfield Wood
CLODHALL LA
Moorhay Farm
Stonelow Flat
Bleak House
B6050
New Bridge
Wigley Hall Farm
Wigley Farm
Wigley
Stonelow Flat Farm
Puddingpie Farm
Fox & Goose Inn (PH)
Mast
Royal Oak (PH)
Stonelow Farm
Puddingpie Hill
Sch
BAGTHORPE LA
Eastmoor
Crossgates Farm
Lower Farm
Wadshelf Brook
SCHOOL LA
Stonelow Bridge
Top Bridge
The Highwayman (PH)
Wardlow Wells
TOP LA
Ivy Cottage Farm
Wadshelf
Sewage Farm
Game Lea Farm
A619
RODKNOLL LA
East Moor
Brampton East Moor
HALLCLIFF LA
Hallcliff Farm
Bole Hill
SYDA LA
Nether Rodknoll Farm
Over Wood
4
73
3
72
2
71
1
70
30
31

A
B
C
4
73
3
72
2
71
1
70
32
33
34
Green Lane
Oxton Rake Road
Oaks Lane
Oxton Rakes
OAKS LA
Jumble Hole
Salter Wood
Baines Wood
COMMON LA
Cutthorpe Common
Three Merry Lads (PH)
CUTTHORPE RD
B6050
Overgreen
Thorpe House
RIGGOTTS WAY
MAIN RD
Cow Close Farm
Gate Inn (PH)
Ingmanthorpe
Sch
Cutthorpe
Brockwell Lane
Pratthall
The Cottages
Cutthorpe Green
Pratthall Farm
Green Farm
GREEN LA
Cutthorpe Hall
Birley Wood
Kitchenflat Wood
Hall Farm
Birley Brook
Linacre Wood
Water Works
P
PC
Linacre Brook
Dumble Wood
Linacre Reservoirs
Priestfield Wood
Ducksick Wood
Woodnook Farm
Woodnook
Sims Wood
North Lane
WOODNOOK LA
The Grove
Sch
Upper Ashgate Farm
Hollins House
GROVE LA
ASHGATE RD
Brampton Hall
George & Dragon (PH)
Hollins
Hemmings Green
Old Brampton
Ashgate
Hospital
Nuttack Lane
Caushouse Farm
Offley Place
BAGTHORPE LA
Lady Wood
Bagthorpe Farm
Bramma Wood
The Birches
Frithhall Wood
PIPER LA
Broomhall Farm
Frith Hall
Leadhill Farm
Horse Wood
Westwick Farm
FRITHHALL LA
WESTWICK LA
Rufford Farm
Brookside
Rufford House
A619
Ladywoods
Fairfield
CHATSWORTH RD
BASLOW RD
Leagreave
Nether Chanderhill
Brookside Nurseries
HOLYMOOR RD
Cherry Trees
Hagg Wood
Chanderhill
CHANDER HILL LA
POCKNEDGE LA
Old Barn Farm
Foxbrook Farm
Belmont Park
WOODLAND WK
ASHURST CL
BRIARDENE CL
CAPTHORNE CL
WOODLEIGH CL
HAWTHORNE WAY
BRUSHFIELD RD
CORVE WAY
WHEATFIELD WAY
FOXBROOK CL
HARVEST WAY
THORNE CL
FAIRFIELD
MEADOW RISE
WESTBROOK DR
BROOKSIDE BAR
HOLLENS WAY
THE GRANGE
WOODNOOK WAY

D
E
F
Four Lane Ends
DUNSTON RD B6050
Upper Newbold
ABBEY CROFT
Cutthorpe Common End
Fields Farm
Over Newbold Farm
Brockwell Lane
Loundsley Green
Holme Brook
Playing Field
PH
Sch
Liby
Newbold
Newbold Moor
NEWBOLD RD B6051
HIGHFIELD LA
KESWICK DR
DUNSTON LA
LITTLEMOOR
SAINT JOHN'S RD
RACECOURSE RD
STAND RD
PEVERIL RD
TAPTON VIEW RD
LOUNDSLEY GREEN RD
LINACRE RD
PENNINE WAY
BROCKWELL LA
HAWKSLEY AVE
Brockwell
Ashgate
ASHGATE RD
Ashgate Plantation
Moor Lea
Amb Sta
CROSS ST
SALTERGATE
WEST BARS
Offs
OLD RD
OLD HALL RD
STORRS RD
CHATSWORTH RD
WALTON RD
Brampton
Wks
HUNLOKE AVE
BOYTHORPE RD
Boythorpe
Cemetery
Sports Gd
Brookside
SOMERSALL LA
River Hipper
PCs
Somersall Farm
TA Centre
Queen's Park
PC's
MARKHAM RD A619
A632
B6150
4
73
3
72
2
71
1
70
36
37

95
77

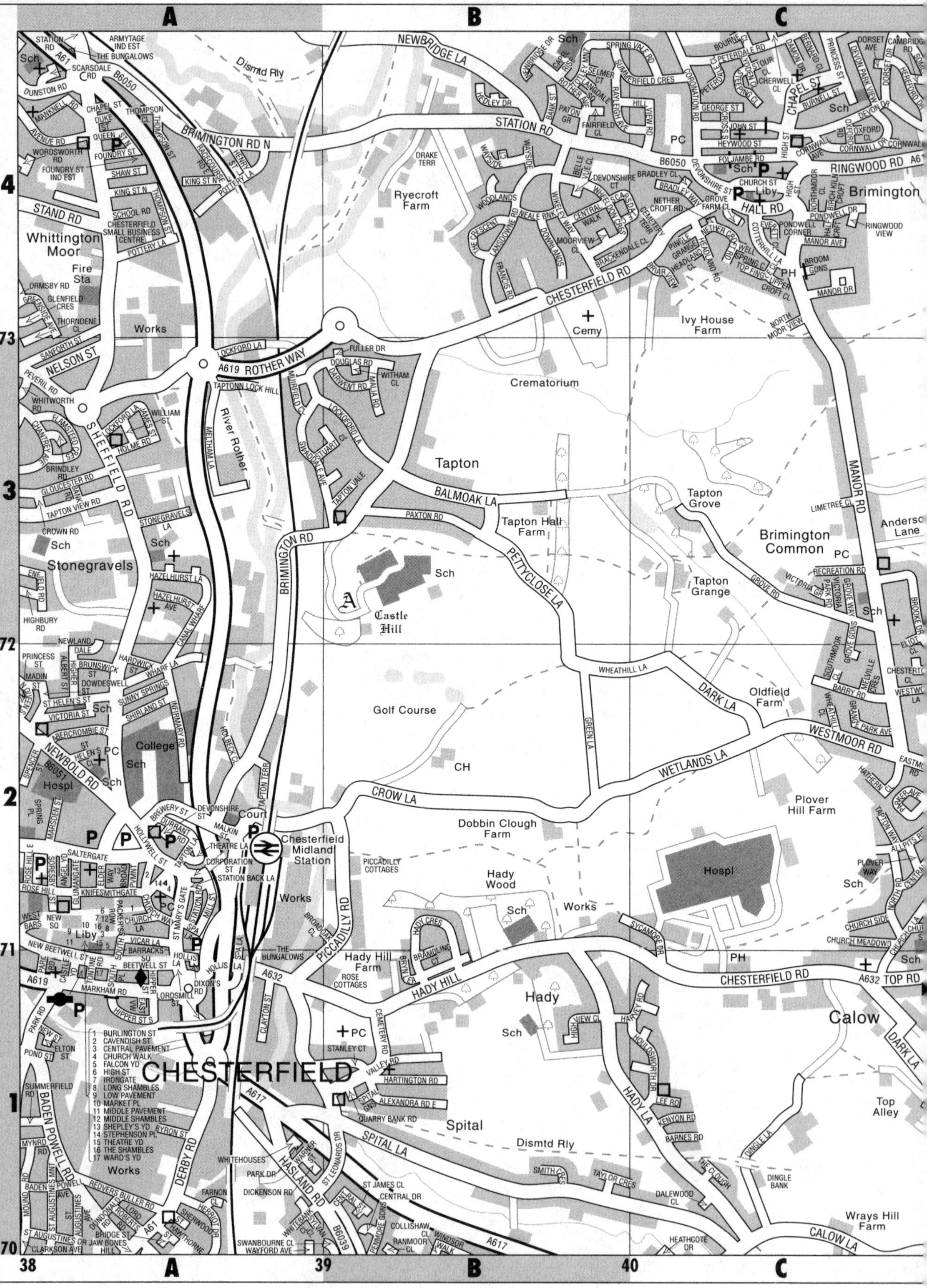
A
B
C
4
73
3
72
2
71
1
70
38
39
40
NEWBRIDGE LA
Dismtd Rly
ARMYTAGE IND EST
THE BUNGALOWS
STATION RD
BRIMINGTON RD N
B6050
Ryecroft Farm
DRAKE TERR
Brimington
RINGWOOD RD
HALL RD
CHESTERFIELD RD
Whittington Moor
Fire Sta
STAND RD
Works
NELSON ST
A619 ROTHER WAY
Cemy
Ivy House Farm
Crematorium
River Rother
SHEFFIELD RD
Tapton
BALMOAK LA
Tapton Grove
Tapton Hall Farm
MANOR RD
Brimington Common
PC
Stonegravels
BRIMINGTON RD
PETTYCLOSE LA
Sch
Tapton Grange
GROVE RD
Castle Hill
WHEATHILL LA
DARK LA
Oldfield Farm
WESTMOOR RD
Golf Course
GREEN LA
WETLANDS LA
CH
College
NEWBOLD RD
Hospl
CROW LA
Plover Hill Farm
Dobbin Clough Farm
Chesterfield Midland Station
PICCADILLY COTTAGES
Hady Wood
Works
Hospl
PICCADILLY RD
Hady Hill Farm
HADY HILL
CHESTERFIELD RD
PH
A632 TOP RD
Calow
Hady
CHESTERFIELD
SPITAL LA
Spital
Dismtd Rly
HADY LA
Top Alley
DINGLE BANK
Wrays Hill Farm
CALOW LA
DERBY RD
HASLAND RD
A617
A61
BADEN POWELL RD
1 BURLINGTON ST
2 CAVENDISH ST
3 CENTRAL PAVEMENT
4 CHURCH WALK
5 FALCON YD
6 HIGH ST
7 IRONGATE
8 LONG SHAMBLES
9 LOW PAVEMENT
10 MARKET PL
11 MIDDLE PAVEMENT
12 MIDDLE SHAMBLES
13 SHEPLEY'S YD
14 STEPHENSON PL
15 THEATRE YD
16 THE SHAMBLES
17 WARD'S YD

95
115

D
E
F
Troughbrook Rd
Troughbrook Hill
Chesterfield Rd
Private Dr
Maple St
PH
Ringwood Hall
Division St
A619
Sch
Cemy
Erin Rd
Staveley Rd
Spoil Heap
Poolsbrook Farm
Hobner Lane
Middlecroft
Middlecroft Rd
Sch
Ringwood Farm
Parker's Wood
Inkersall Green Rd
Inkersall Rd
Inkersall Green
Furnace Lane
West Wood
Furnace Farm
Opencast Workings
Inkersall
Inkersall Farm
Pools Brook
Trough Brook
West Croft House
Tom La
Dismantled Railway
Ladybower Wood
Bower Plantation
Blue Lodge Farm
Lodge Farm
Allpits Plantation
Bonne Vienne
Arkwright Arms (PH)
Cherry Tree Farm
Works Farm
A632
Sewage Works
Brook Farm
Moor Farm
Works La
Blacksmith La
Top Rd
Duckmanton
Caravan Site
Gorse Farm
Lodge Farm
Lodge Farm
Arkwright Town
Moortop Farm
Sch
Nursery Farm
Sutton La
Calow Oaks
Deepsick La
B6425
The Croft
Duckmanton Moor
Dark La
Bolehill
Back La
Moorfields
Cock Alley
Riddings House Farm
Moor La
Woodside Cottage
Spoil Heap
42
43
4
73
3
72
2
71
1
70

97
79

A
B
C
4
73
3
72
2
71
1
70
44
45
46
Seymour Junction
M1
MILL LA
B6419
Lodge Farm
POOLSBROOK AVE
POOLSBROOK VIEW
STAVELEY RD
THE GROVE
POOLSBROOK CRES
POOLSBROOK SQ
COTTAGE CL
Poolsbrook
Sch
PH
ERIN RD
WOODTHORPE RD
BENTINCK RD
Shuttlewood Common
Woodside
Shuttlewood
CLOWNE RD
WOODTHORPE CL
ADIN AVE
PRETORIA ST
BOLSOVER RD
VIVIAN ST
PATTISON ST
SHUTTLEWOOD
Opencast Workings
NORTH GR
POOLSBROOK RD
WEST CRES
NORTH CRES
WHITTON PL
EAST CRES
The Oaks
TOM LA
MARKHAM RD
DUCKMANTON RD
POOLSBROOK RD
SOUTH CRES
Duckmanton
Middle Farm
The Nunnery
Nunnery Farm
Wyandott Farm
CHESTERFIELD RD
Woodhouse Farm
Bolsover Woodhouse
Sewage Works
Off
Colliery
Works
Poplar Farm
OLD PEVEREL RD
Resr
ROBERTSON'S AVE
MARKHAM LA
Nether Woodhouse Farm
BUTTERMILK LA
CHERRY TREE DR
BEECH GR
ST PETERS CL
Manor Farm
RECTORY CL
Works
WOODHOUSE LA
BLIND LA
Over Woodhouse
NETHER SPRINGS RD
IRON CLIFF RD
BRIAR BRIGGS RD
MANOR COURT RD
SPRINGFIELD CRES
PEVERILL RD
FARMFIELDS
HOUFTON RD
HYNDLEY RD
DEEPDALE RD
HOULSWORTH CRES
DAVEY CT
HOUFTON CRES
HARVEY CT
HALDANE CRES
HASLAM CT
A632
B6418
CHESTERFIELD RD
River Doe Lea
Dismtd Rly
Long Duckmanton
Colliery
Railway Cottages
Lea-Holme
Mill Farm
STATION RD
OLD HILL
LONGCOURSE LA
VILLAS RD
Longcourse House
Longcourse Farm
New Bolsover
Sch
RUTLAND AVE
The Goit
Burton Barn
Dismantled Railway
NEW STATION RD
CHAPEL RD
CARR VALE RD
BAINBRIDGE RD
The Goit
Sewage Works
NORTH VIEW ST
DUMBLES RD
M1

97
117

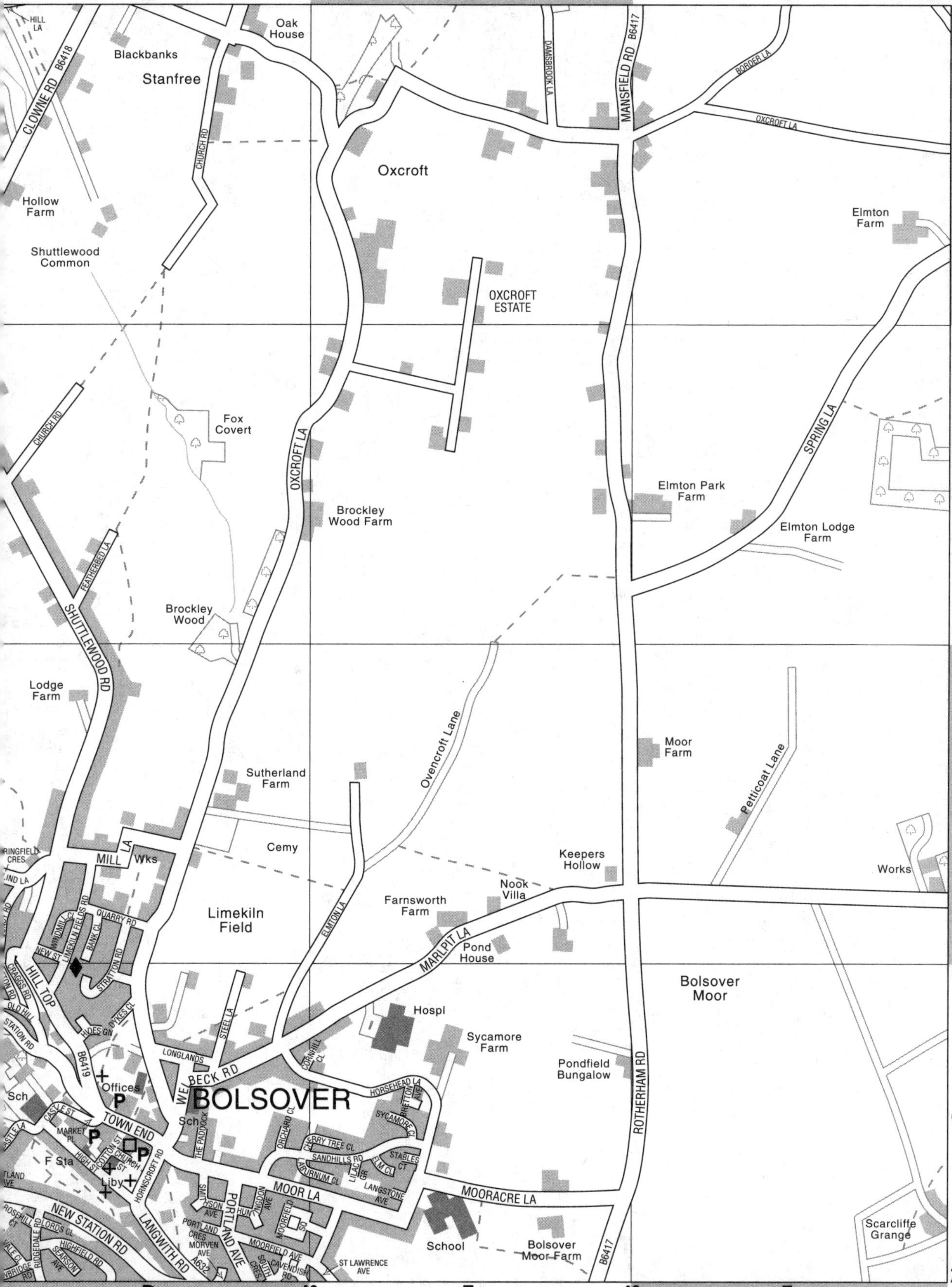
Oak House
Blackbanks
Stanfree
CLOWNE RD B6418
CHURCH RD
Hollow Farm
Shuttlewood Common
Oxcroft
OXCROFT ESTATE
DAMSBROOK LA
MANSFIELD RD B6417
BORDER LA
OXCROFT LA
Elmton Farm
Fox Covert
OXCROFT LA
Brockley Wood Farm
Elmton Park Farm
SPRING LA
Elmton Lodge Farm
FEATHERBED LA
SHUTTLEWOOD RD
Brockley Wood
Lodge Farm
Ovencroft Lane
Moor Farm
Petticoat Lane
Sutherland Farm
Cemy
MILL LA
Wks
Keepers Hollow
Works
Nook Villa
Limekiln Field
Farnsworth Farm
ELMTON LA
MARLPIT LA
Pond House
QUARRY RD
BANK CL
STRATTON RD
NEW ST
HILL TOP
CRAGGS RD
OLD HILL
STATION RD
DYKES CL
HIDES GN
B6419
LONGLANDS
STEEL LA
Hospl
Sycamore Farm
Bolsover Moor
Pondfield Bungalow
WELBECK RD
CORNHILL CL
HORSEHEAD LA
Offices
Sch
BOLSOVER
CASTLE ST
TOWN END
MARKET PL
HIGH ST
CHURCH ST
F Sta
Liby
HORNSCROFT RD
THE PADDOCK
ORCHARD CL
CHERRY TREE CL
SANDHILLS RD
LABURNUM CL
LILAC GR
ELM CL
STABLES CT
SYCAMORE CL
LANGSTONE AVE
MOOR LA
MOORACRE LA
ROTHERHAM RD
NEW STATION RD
LANGWITH RD
PORTLAND AVE
PORTLAND CRES
MORVEN AVE
MOORFIELD AVE
CAVENDISH RD
ST LAWRENCE AVE
School
Bolsover Moor Farm
B6417
A632
Scarcliffe Grange
ROSEHILL
LORDS CL
RIDGEDALE RD
HIGHFIELD RD
SEARSON AVE
HUNTINGDON AVE
TYSON AVE
4
73
3
72
2
71
1
70
48
49

99
81

A
B
C
Markland Farm
MARKLAND LA
Archaeological Trail
WOOD LA
CHATSWORTH RD
ELMTON RD
MODEL VILLAGE
Dismantled Railway
DUCHESS ST
MORVEN ST
WELBECK ST
Fox Green
Camp Hill
The Oaks
OXCROFT LA
Grange Farm
Elmton
SPRING LA
PH
Elm Tree Farm
Green Farm
FRITHWOOD LA
Colliery
Spoil Heap
Frithwood Farm
Frith Wood
The Old Hag
OXPASTURE LA
Whaley Moor
LC
MAG LA
Norwood Farm
Whaley Hall
WHALEY COMMON
Whaley Common
PH
Whaley
MOORFIELD
Bolsover Moor Quarry
Grave Wood
Whaley Farm
Mill Pond
P
Mill Farm
Country Park
Scarcliffe Park
Owl Sick
WHALEY RD
P
Apsley Grange
Owl Spring
Archaeological Trail
Dismtd Rly
River Poulter
A632
PH
DEVONSHIRE DR
LANGWITH MALTINGS
DALE CL
Scarcliffe Grange
4
73
3
72
2
71
1
70
50
51
52

82

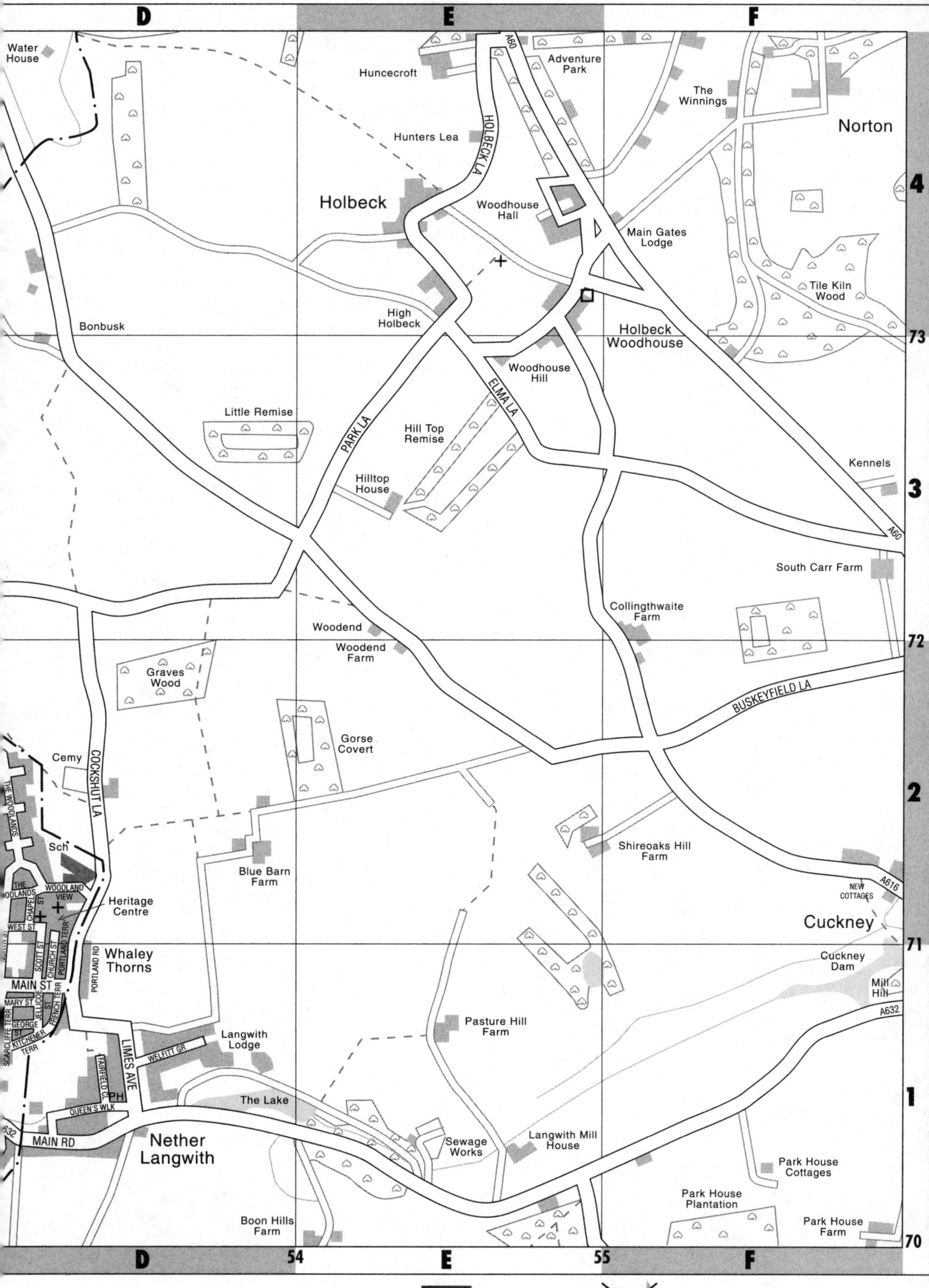
D
E
F
Water House
Huncecroft
Adventure Park
The Winnings
Norton
Hunters Lea
HOLBECK LA
A60
Holbeck
Woodhouse Hall
Main Gates Lodge
Tile Kiln Wood
Bonbusk
High Holbeck
Holbeck Woodhouse
Woodhouse Hill
ELMA LA
Little Remise
PARK LA
Hill Top Remise
Kennels
Hilltop House
A60
South Carr Farm
Collingthwaite Farm
Woodend
Woodend Farm
Graves Wood
BUSKEYFIELD LA
Gorse Covert
Cemy
COCKSHUT LA
THE WOODLANDS
Sch
Shireoaks Hill Farm
Blue Barn Farm
WOODLAND VIEW
Heritage Centre
NEW COTTAGES
A616
Cuckney
WEST ST
CHAPEL ST
SCOTT ST
CHURCH ST
PORTLAND TERR
PORTLAND RD
Whaley Thorns
Cuckney Dam
Mill Hill
MAIN ST
MARY ST
JELLICOE ST
FRENCH TERR
GEORGE ST
SCARCLIFFE TERR
KITCHENER TERR
A632
Pasture Hill Farm
Langwith Lodge
LIMES AVE
WELFITT GR
FAIRFIELD CL
PH
The Lake
QUEEN'S WLK
A632
MAIN RD
Nether Langwith
Sewage Works
Langwith Mill House
Park House Cottages
Park House Plantation
Boon Hills Farm
Park House Farm
4
73
3
72
2
71
1
70
54
55

120

83

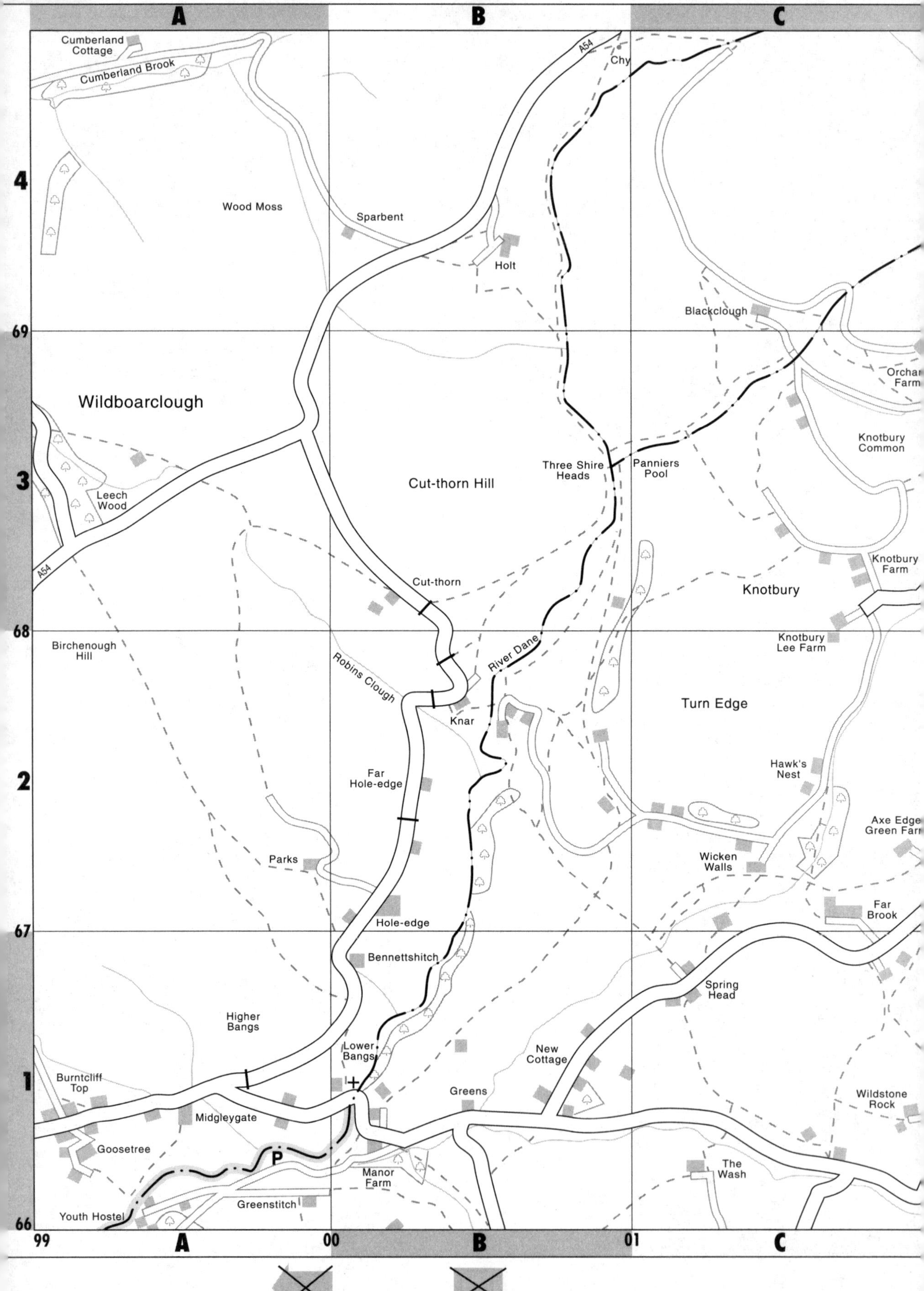
A
B
C
Cumberland Cottage
Cumberland Brook
A54
Chy
4
Wood Moss
Sparbent
Holt
Blackclough
69
Orchar Farm
Wildboarclough
Knotbury Common
3
Leech Wood
Cut-thorn Hill
Three Shire Heads
Panniers Pool
Knotbury Farm
A54
Cut-thorn
Knotbury
68
Birchenough Hill
Robins Clough
River Dane
Knotbury Lee Farm
Turn Edge
Knar
2
Far Hole-edge
Hawk's Nest
Axe Edge Green Farm
Parks
Wicken Walls
Hole-edge
Far Brook
67
Bennettshitch
Spring Head
Higher Bangs
New Cottage
Lower Bangs
1
Burntcliff Top
Greens
Wildstone Rock
Midgleygate
Goosetree
P
Manor Farm
The Wash
Youth Hostel
Greenstitch
66
99
A
00
B
01
C

D E F

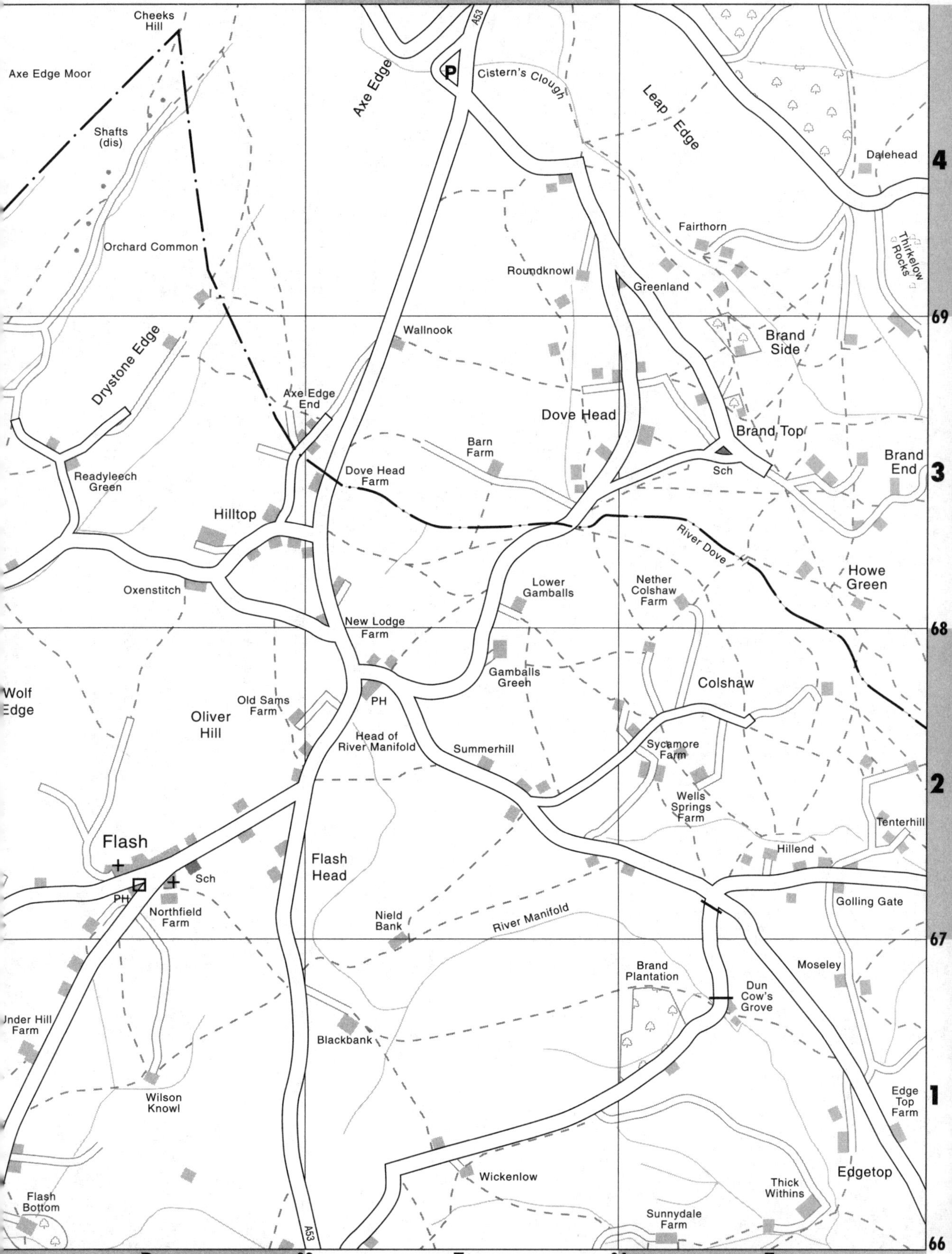
Cheeks Hill
Axe Edge Moor
Shafts (dis)
Orchard Common
Axe Edge
A53
P
Cistern's Clough
Leap Edge
Dalehead
Thirkelow Rocks
Fairthorn
Roundknowl
Greenland
Wallnook
Brand Side
Drystone Edge
Axe Edge End
Dove Head
Barn Farm
Brand Top
Sch
Brand End
Readyleech Green
Dove Head Farm
Hilltop
River Dove
Oxenstitch
Lower Gamballs
Nether Colshaw Farm
Howe Green
New Lodge Farm
Gamballs Green
Colshaw
Wolf Edge
Old Sams Farm
Oliver Hill
PH
Head of River Manifold
Summerhill
Sycamore Farm
Wells Springs Farm
Tenterhill
Flash
Hillend
Sch
Flash Head
PH
Northfield Farm
Nield Bank
River Manifold
Golling Gate
Brand Plantation
Moseley
Dun Cow's Grove
Under Hill Farm
Blackbank
Wilson Knowl
Edge Top Farm
Edgetop
Wickenlow
Thick Withins
Flash Bottom
Sunnydale Farm
A53
4
69
3
68
2
67
1
66
03
04

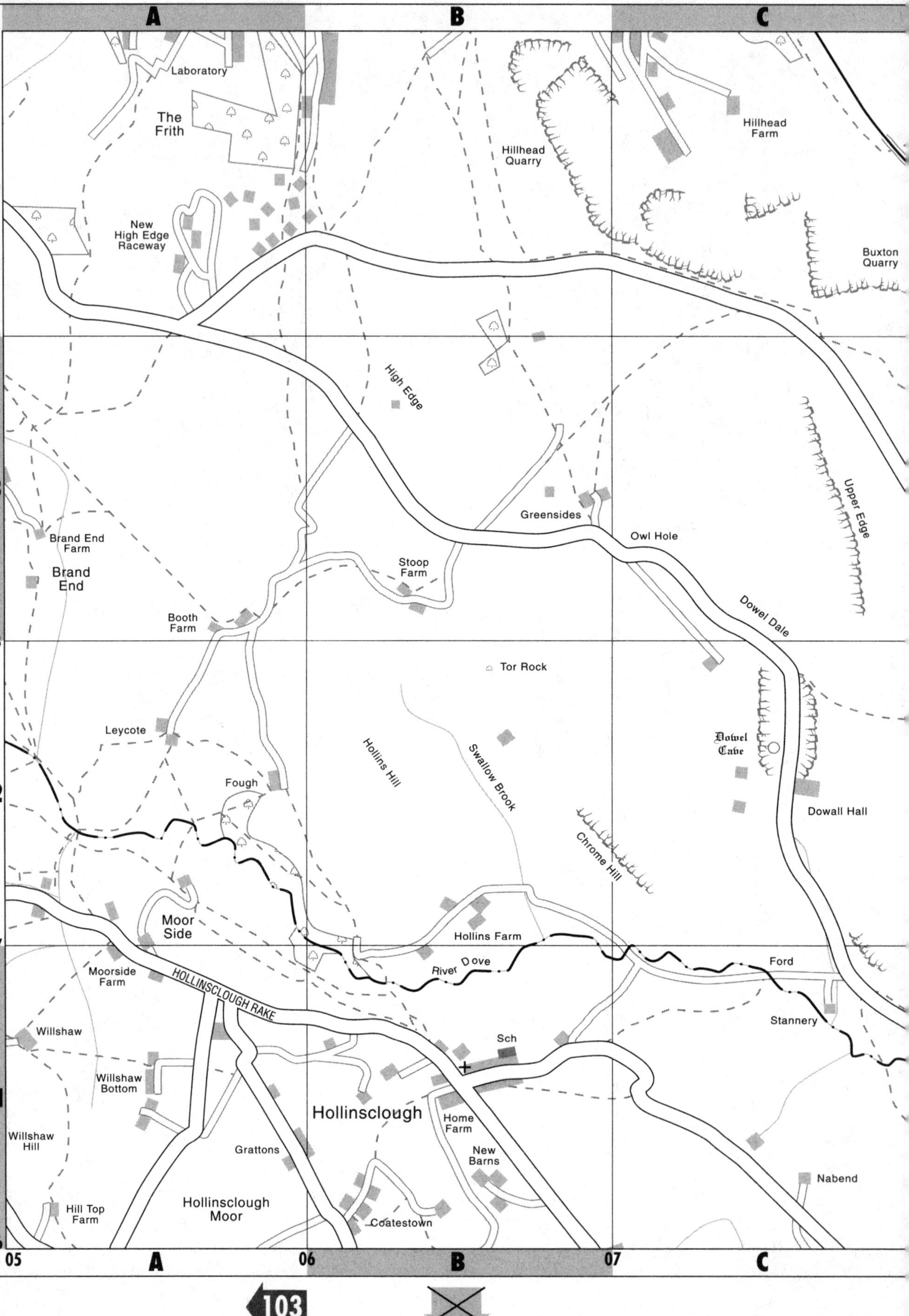
A
B
C
Laboratory
The Frith
Hillhead Quarry
Hillhead Farm
New High Edge Raceway
Buxton Quarry
High Edge
Greensides
Owl Hole
Upper Edge
Brand End Farm
Brand End
Stoop Farm
Booth Farm
Dowel Dale
Tor Rock
Leycote
Hollins Hill
Swallow Brook
Dowel Cave
Fough
Dowall Hall
Chrome Hill
Moor Side
Hollins Farm
River Dove
Ford
Moorside Farm
HOLLINSCLOUGH RAKE
Willshaw
Stannery
Sch
Willshaw Bottom
Hollinsclough
Home Farm
Willshaw Hill
Grattons
New Barns
Nabend
Hill Top Farm
Hollinsclough Moor
Coatestown
4
69
3
68
2
67
1
66
05
06
07

D
E
F
A515
Brierlow Bar Farm
BRIERLOW BAR
A5270
B5053
Farditch Farm
OLD COALPIT LA
THE DITCH
Netherlow Farm
Morland
Red Hurst
Hindlow
Buxton Quarry
Brierlow Grange
Nether Low
Hindlow Tunnel
Hind Low
STERNDALE MOOR
ROMAN ROAD (course of)
Blindlow Hollow
Brier Low
Great Low
Harley Grange
Greatlow
A515
Hindlow Quarry
Jericho Farm
Dismtd Rly
Dowlow Farm
Hatch-a-Way
Dowlow Works
Fernydale
Glutton Dale
DALE VIEW
Glutton
Earl Sterndale
Sch
Home Farm
Parkhouse Hill
Quiet Woman (PH)
Hall Farm
Braemar House
Hitter Hill
Underhill Farm
Abbotside Farm
Aldery Cliff
Glutton Bridge
River Dove
Fox Hole Cave
High Wheeldon
Wheeldon Trees
B5053
Underhill
Green Lane
4
69
3
68
2
67
1
66
D
09
E
10
F

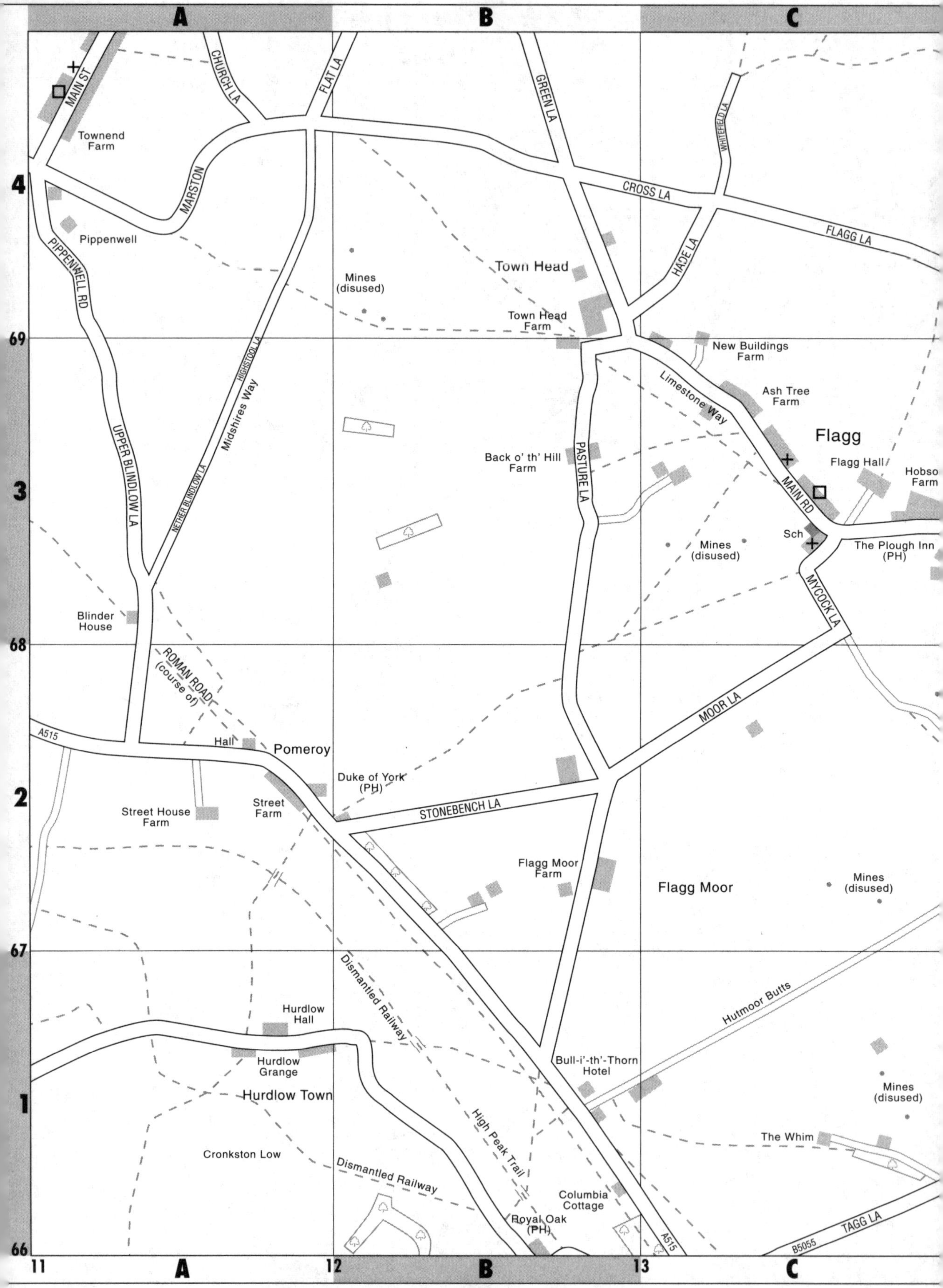
A
B
C
4
69
3
68
2
67
1
66
11
12
13
MAIN ST
CHURCH LA
FLAT LA
GREEN LA
WHITEFIELD LA
Townend Farm
MARSTON
CROSS LA
FLAGG LA
HADE LA
Pippenwell
PIPPENWELL RD
Mines (disused)
Town Head
Town Head Farm
New Buildings Farm
Limestone Way
Ash Tree Farm
Flagg
Flagg Hall
Hobso
Farm
HIGHSTOOL LA
Midshires Way
UPPER BLINDLOW LA
NETHER BLINDLOW LA
Back o' th' Hill Farm
PASTURE LA
MAIN RD
Sch
The Plough Inn (PH)
MYCOCK LA
Blinder House
ROMAN ROAD (course of)
MOOR LA
A515
Hall
Pomeroy
Duke of York (PH)
STONEBENCH LA
Street House Farm
Street Farm
Flagg Moor Farm
Flagg Moor
Dismantled Railway
Hutmoor Butts
Hurdlow Hall
Hurdlow Grange
Hurdlow Town
Bull-i'-th'-Thorn Hotel
High Peak Trail
The Whim
Cronkston Low
Dismantled Railway
Columbia Cottage
Royal Oak (PH)
B5055
TAGG LA

88
108

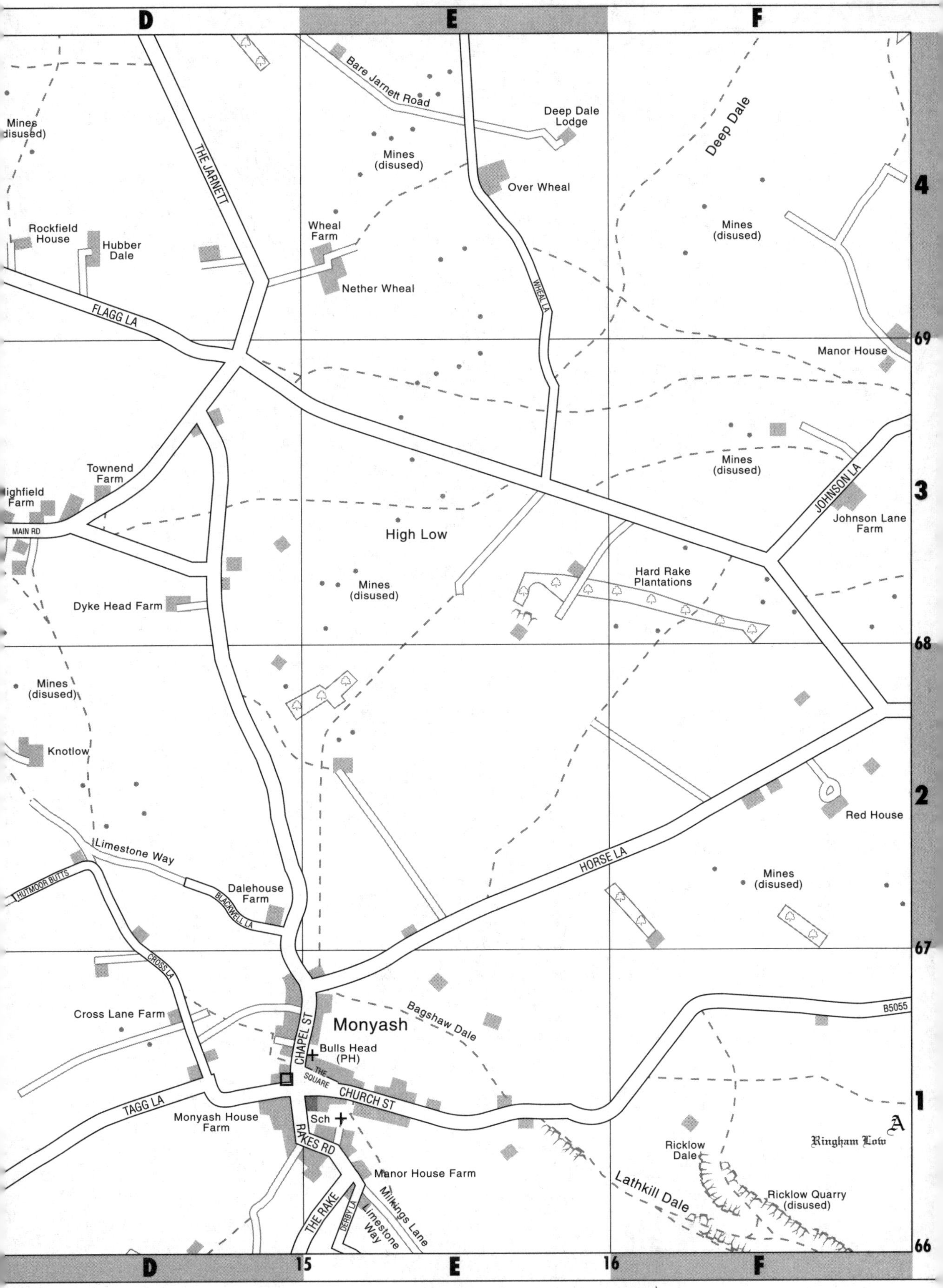

123
108

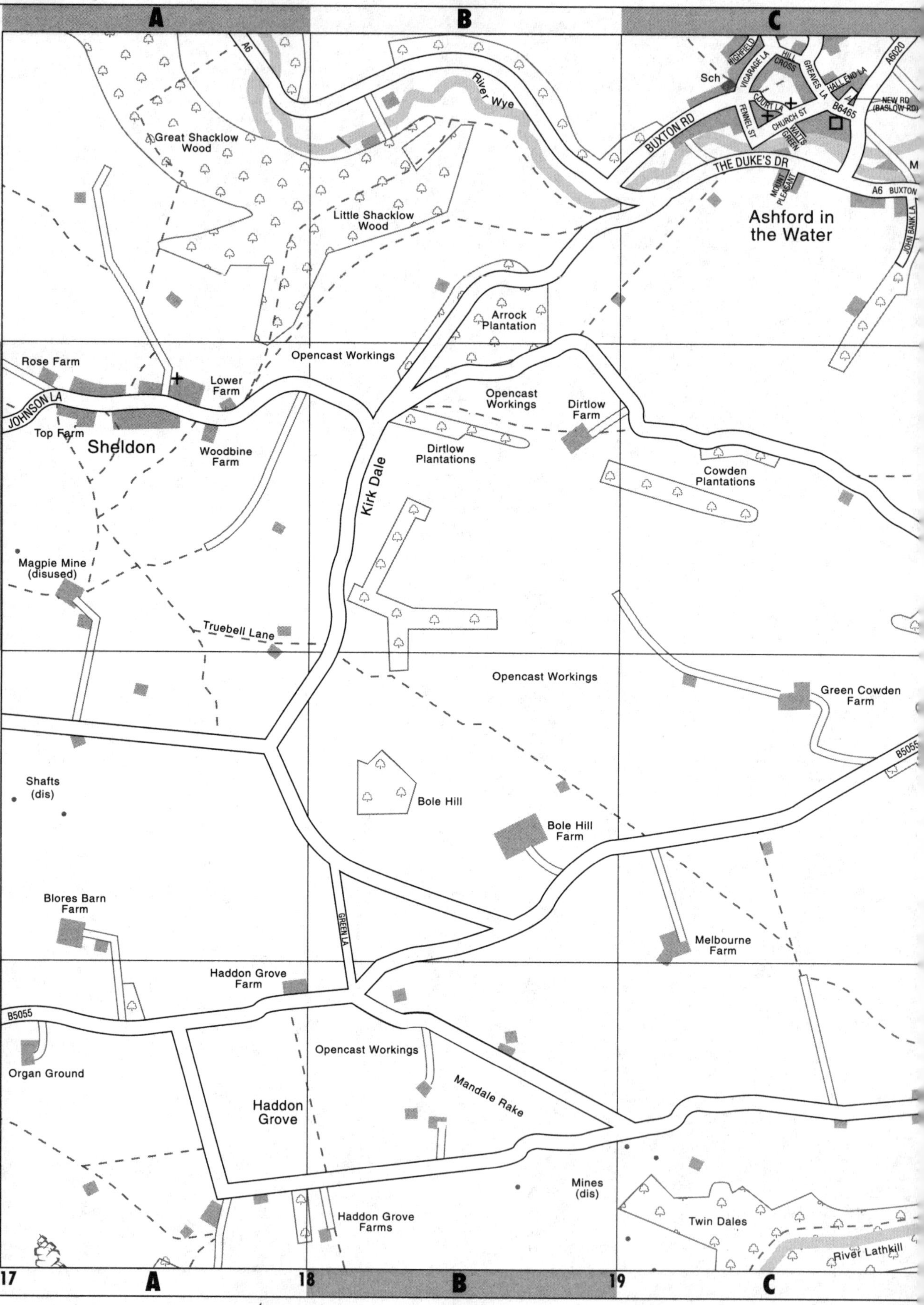
A
B
C
A6
River Wye
Great Shacklow Wood
Little Shacklow Wood
Arrock Plantation
Sch
HIGHFIELD
VICARAGE LA
HILL CROSS
GREAVES LA
HALL END LA
A6020
NEW RD (BASLOW RD)
COURT LA
FENNEL ST
CHURCH ST
WATTS GREEN
B6465
BUXTON RD
THE DUKE'S DR
MOUNT PLEASANT
A6 BUXTON
JOHN BANK LA
Ashford in the Water
4
69
Rose Farm
JOHNSON LA
Top Farm
Sheldon
Lower Farm
Woodbine Farm
Opencast Workings
Opencast Workings
Dirtlow Farm
Dirtlow Plantations
Kirk Dale
Cowden Plantations
3
Magpie Mine (disused)
Truebell Lane
68
Opencast Workings
Green Cowden Farm
B5055
2
Shafts (dis)
Bole Hill
Bole Hill Farm
Blores Barn Farm
GREEN LA
Melbourne Farm
67
Haddon Grove Farm
B5055
Opencast Workings
Organ Ground
Mandale Rake
1
Haddon Grove
Mines (dis)
Twin Dales
River Lathkill
Haddon Grove Farms
66
17
18
19
A
B
C

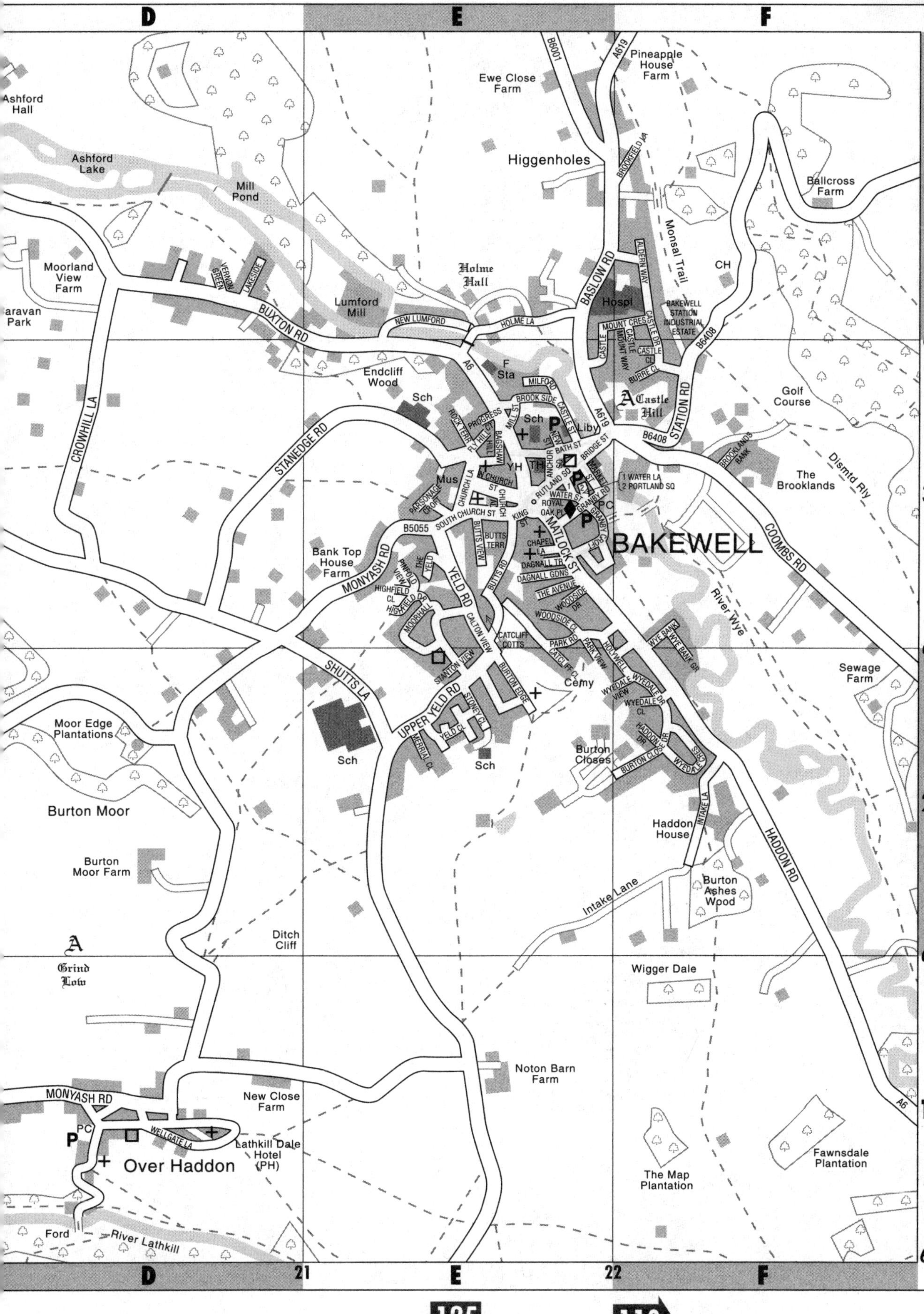
D
E
F
4
69
3
68
2
67
1
66
21
22
Ashford Hall
Ashford Lake
Mill Pond
Moorland View Farm
Caravan Park
Ewe Close Farm
Pineapple House Farm
Higgenholes
Ballcross Farm
Holme Hall
Lumford Mill
Monsal Trail
CH
Hospl
BAKEWELL STATION INDUSTRIAL ESTATE
Endcliff Wood
F Sta
Sch
Castle Hill
Golf Course
Liby
Mus
YH
TH
PC
The Brooklands
Dismtd Rly
BAKEWELL
Bank Top House Farm
River Wye
Cemy
Sewage Farm
Moor Edge Plantations
Sch
Sch
Burton Closes
Burton Moor
Haddon House
Burton Moor Farm
Burton Ashes Wood
Intake Lane
Ditch Cliff
Grind Low
Wigger Dale
Noton Barn Farm
New Close Farm
Lathkill Dale Hotel (PH)
Over Haddon
The Map Plantation
Fawnsdale Plantation
Ford
River Lathkill
BUXTON RD
VERNON GREEN
LAKESIDE
NEW LUMFORD
HOLME LA
CROWHILL LA
STANEDGE RD
BASLOW RD
BROOKFIELD LA
ALDERN WAY
MOUNT CRES
CASTLE DR
CASTLE CL
BURRE CL
MOUNT WAY
STATION RD
B6408
A619
B6001
A6
MILFORD
BROOK SIDE
CASTLE ST
PROGRESS
ROCK TERR
FLY HILL
BAGSHAW HILL
MILL ST
NEW ST
BATH ST
BRIDGE ST
ANCHOR SQ
RUTLAND SQ
WATER ST
ROYAL OAK PL
KING ST
MATLOCK ST
GRANBY RD
MARKET ST
GRANBY CROFT
1 WATER LA
2 PORTLAND SQ
N CHURCH ST
PARSONAGE CROFT
SOUTH CHURCH ST
CHURCH ALLEY
B5055
BUTTS VIEW
BUTTS TERR
BUTTS RD
CHAPEL LA
DAGNALL TR
DAGNALL GDNS
THE AVENUE
WOODSIDE DR
WOODSIDE CL
BROOKLANDS BANK
COOMBS RD
MONYASH RD
PINFOLD VIEW
THE YELD
YELD RD
HIGHFIELD CL
HIGHFIELD DR
MOORHALL
CALTON VIEW
CATCLIFF COTTS
PARK RD
PARK VIEW
HOLYWELL
CATCLIFF CL
WYE BANK
WYE BANK GR
WYEDALE VIEW
WYEDALE DR
WYEDALE CL
HADDON DR
BURTON CLOSE DR
WYEDALE CRES
INTAKE LA
HADDON RD
SHUTTS LA
STANTON VIEW
BURTON EDGE
UPPER YELD RD
STONEY CL
YELD CL
MERIAL CL
MONYASH RD
WELLGATE LA
PC

109
91

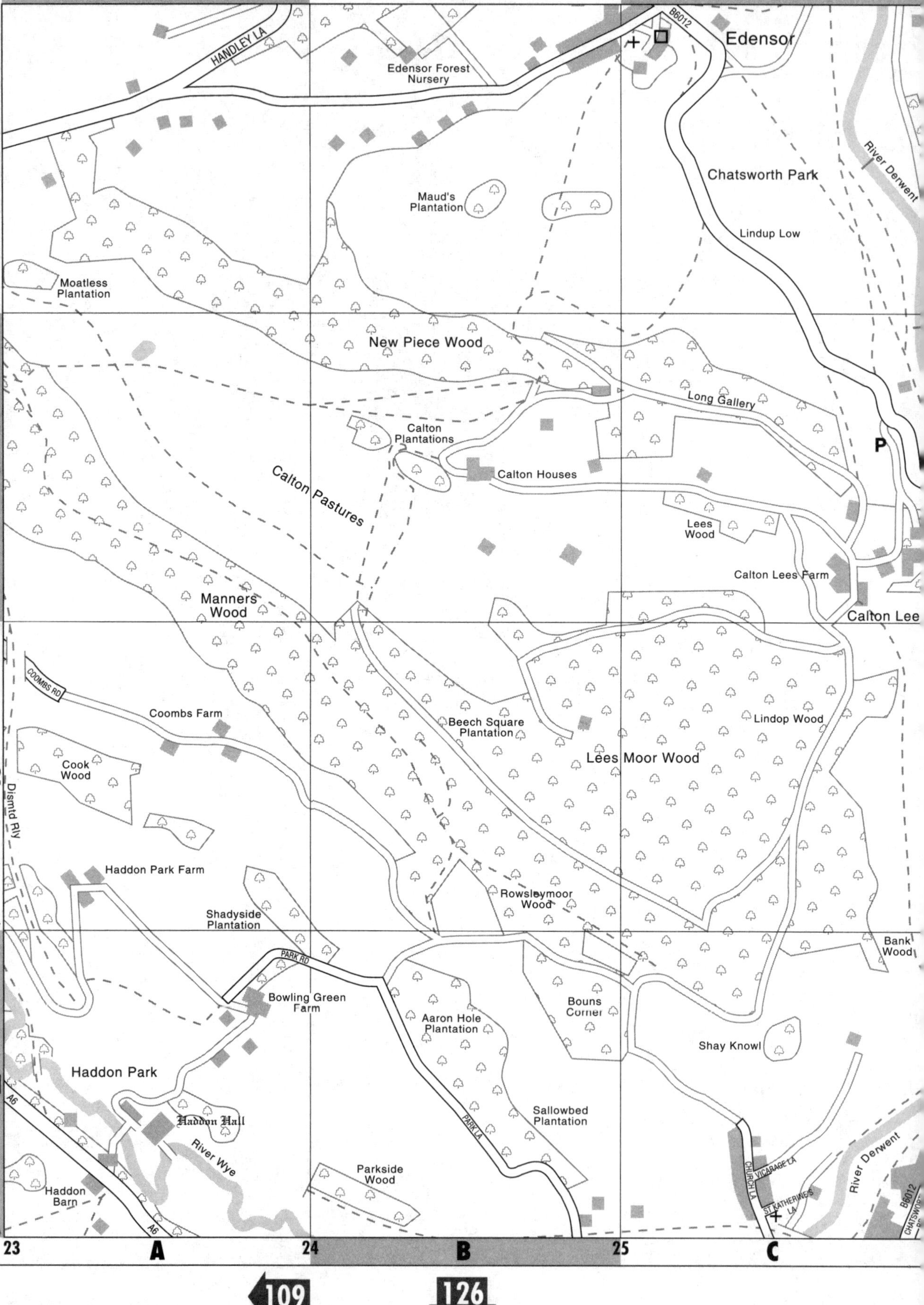

109
126

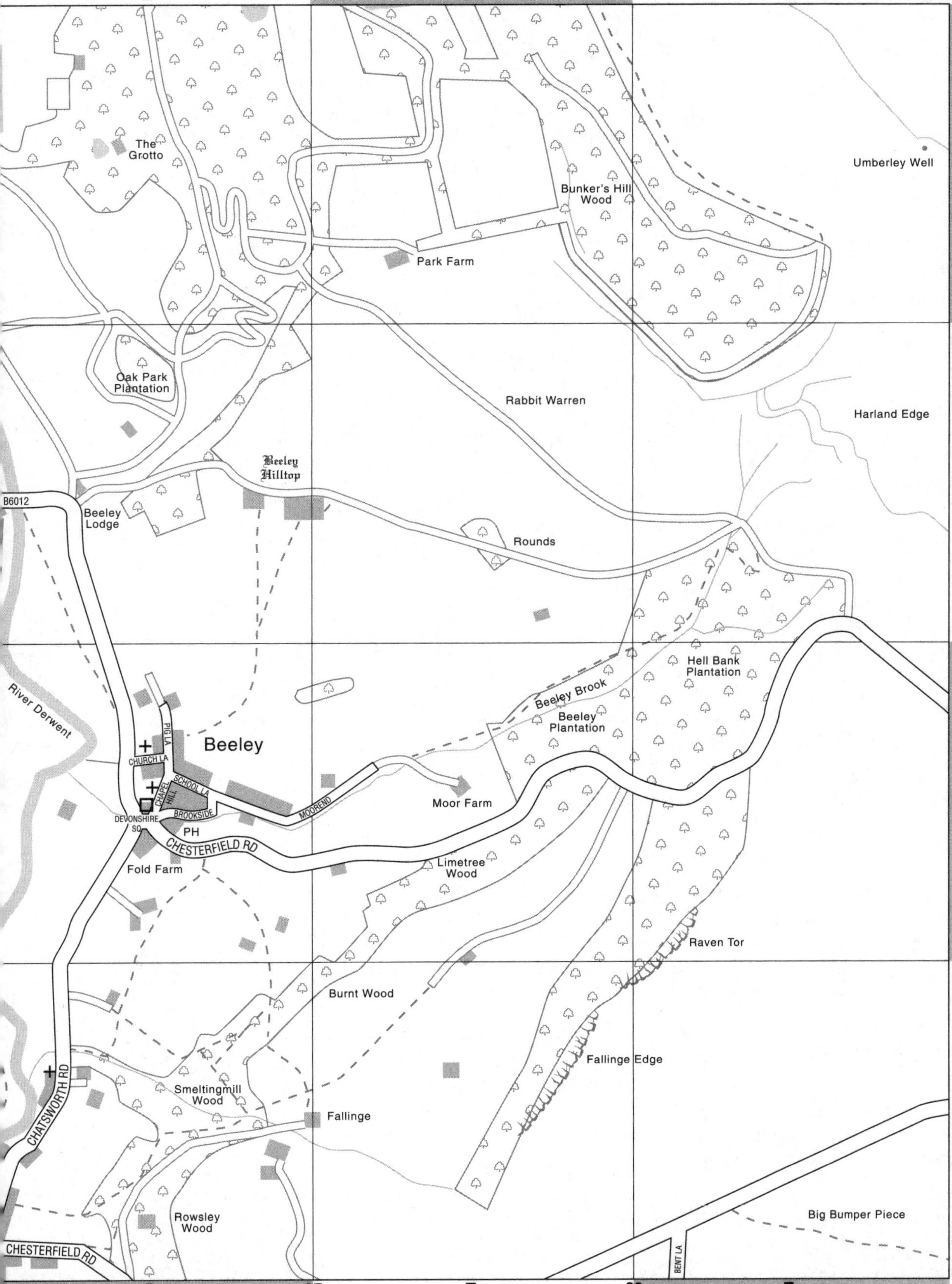
D
E
F
4
69
3
68
2
67
1
66
27
28
The Grotto
Umberley Well
Bunker's Hill Wood
Park Farm
Oak Park Plantation
Rabbit Warren
Harland Edge
Beeley Hilltop
B6012
Beeley Lodge
Rounds
Hell Bank Plantation
Beeley Brook
Beeley Plantation
River Derwent
Beeley
PIG LA
CHURCH LA
SCHOOL LA
CHAPEL HILL
BROOKSIDE
MOOREND
DEVONSHIRE SQ
PH
Moor Farm
CHESTERFIELD RD
Fold Farm
Limetree Wood
Raven Tor
Burnt Wood
Fallinge Edge
CHATSWORTH RD
Smeltingmill Wood
Fallinge
Rowsley Wood
Big Bumper Piece
BENT LA
CHESTERFIELD RD

111
93

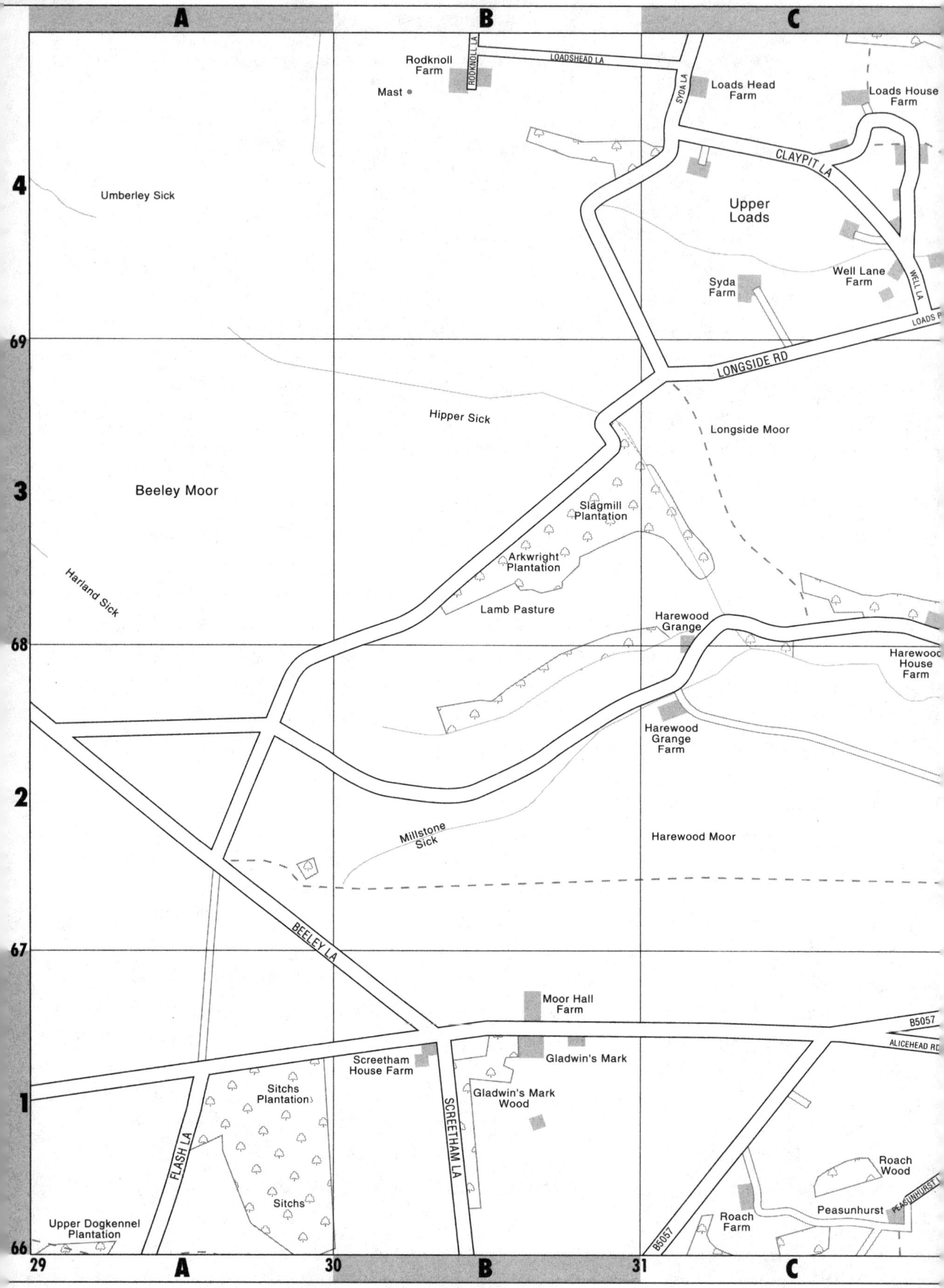

111
128

94
114

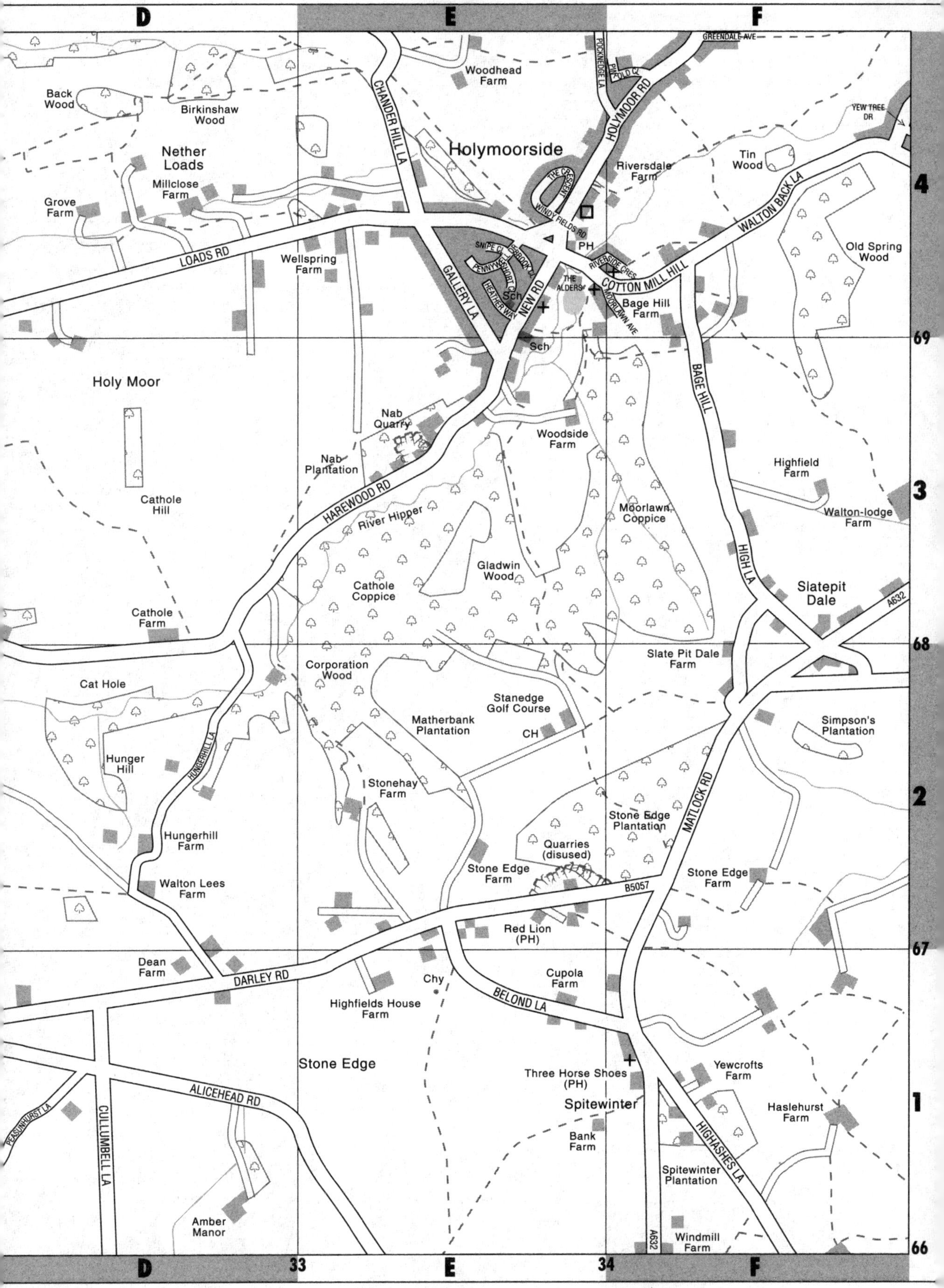

129
114

113
95

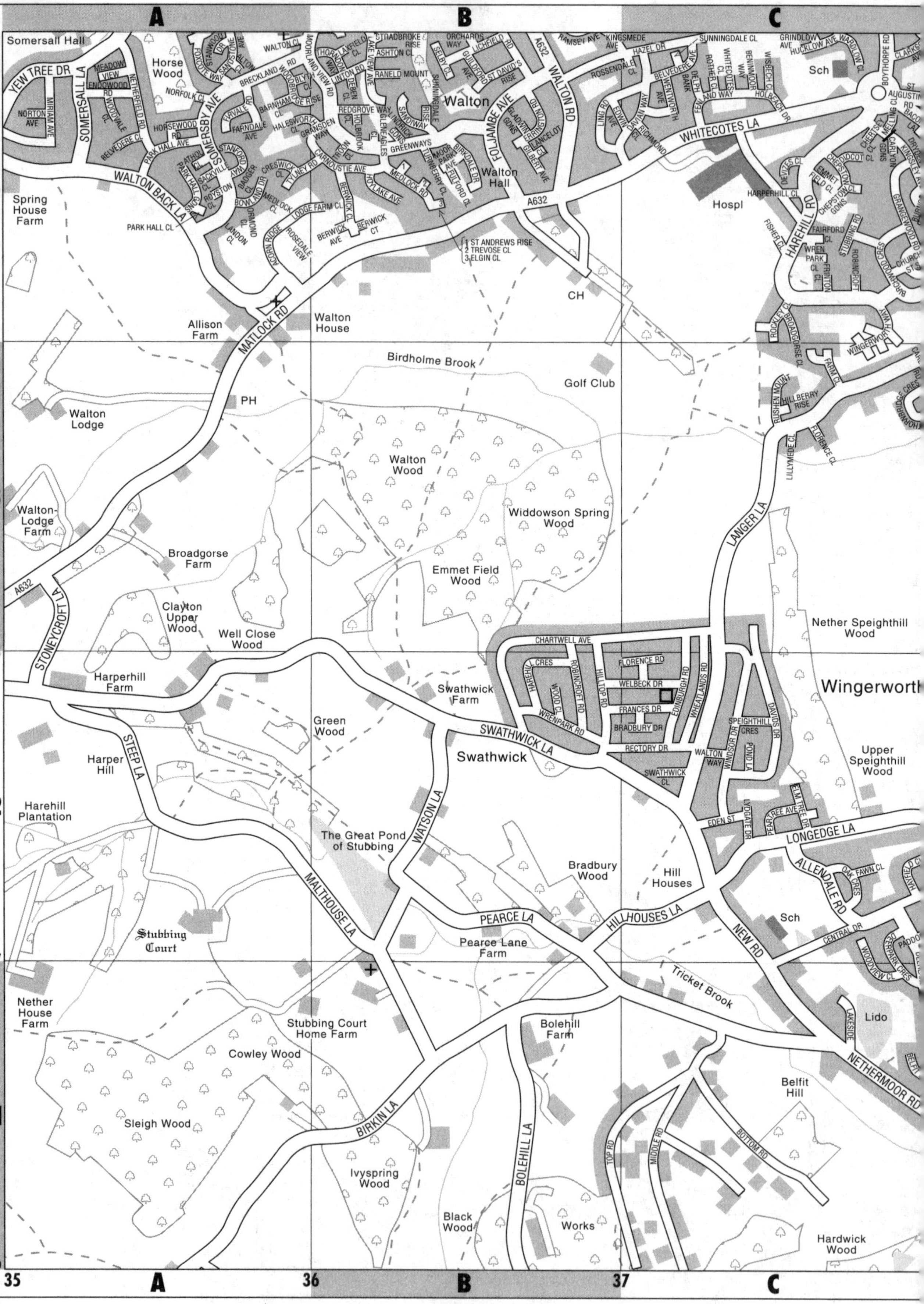
A
B
C
Somersall Hall
YEW TREE DR
SOMERSALL LA
MEADOW VIEW
ENDOWOOD RD
WOODVALE
NETHERFIELD RD
Horse Wood
NORFOLK CL
NORTON AVE
MIRIAM AVE
BELVEDERE CL
HORSEWOOD RD
PARK HALL AVE
SOMERSBY AVE
FOXCOTE WAY
STANWOOD DR
SANDSTONE AVE
DALTON
WALTON CL
BRECKLAND RD
MOORLAND VIEW RD
THORNDON
LAXFIELD CL
STRADBROKE RISE
ASHTON CL
ORCHARDS WAY
LICHFIELD RD
SELBY CL
GUILDFORD AVE
ST DAVID'S RISE
RANELD MOUNT
SUNNINGDALE
Walton
FAIRVALE RD
FARNDALE AVE
BARNHAM
HALESWORTH CL
GRANSDEN WAY
REDGROVE WAY
HOLBROOK
GLENEAGLES
SANDIWAY
GREENWAYS
FOLJAMBE AVE
GLADWIN GDNS
ERRINGTON RD
LANCELOT
GILBERT AVE
WALTON RD
A632
RAMSEY AVE
KINGSMEDE AVE
HAZEL DR
ROSSENDALE CL
SUNNINGDALE CL
BELVEDERE AVE
WENTWORTH
DELPH BANK
ROTHER CL
WHITECOTES CL
BENINGHOOD WAY
WISBECH CL
GRINDLOW AVE
HUCKLOW AVE
WARDLOW CL
Sch
BOYTHORPE RD
ST AUGUSTINES
LING RD
EDWIN AVE
DAVIAN WAY
FEN AND WAY
HOLBEACH DR
RICHMOND
WHITECOTES LA
STANFORD
ATHOLL CL
SACKVILLE CL
ROYSTON CL
BADGER
CRESWICK CL
TYLNEY RD
CARNOUSTIE AVE
TROON
BERWICK CL
HOYLAKE AVE
MEDLOCK RD
TURNBERRY CL
MOOR PARK AVE
BIRKDALE DR
FULFORD CL
Walton Hall
4
Spring House Farm
WALTON BACK LA
PARK HALL CL
BOWLAND DR
MEDLOCK CL
LODGE FARM CL
ORMOND CL
LANDON CL
ACORN RIDGE
ROSEDALE VIEW
BERWICK AVE
BERWICK CT
1 ST ANDREWS RISE
2 TREVOSE CL
3 ELGIN CL
A632
Hospl
HARPERHILL CL
DEVIZES CL
DIDCOT CL
EMMET FIELD CL
CHEPSTOW CL
CHEPSTOW GDNS
KINGSLEY AVE
GRANGEWOOD RD
FISHER CL
HAREHILL RD
FAIRFORD CL
WREN PARK CL
STUBBING RD
FRINTON CL
ROBINCROFT
CH
Allison Farm
MATLOCK RD
Walton House
ROCKLEY CL
BROADGORSE CL
WINGERWORTH WAY
69
Birdholme Brook
Golf Club
Walton Lodge
PH
RUSHEN MOUNT
HILLBERRY RISE
FARM CL
LILLYMEDE CL
FLORENCE CL
Walton Wood
3
Walton-Lodge Farm
Widdowson Spring Wood
LANGER LA
Broadgorse Farm
Emmet Field Wood
A632
STONEYCROFT LA
Clayton Upper Wood
Well Close Wood
Nether Speighthill Wood
68
CHARTWELL AVE
HAREHILL CRES
ROBINCROFT RD
HILLTOP RD
FLORENCE RD
WELBECK DR
EDINBURGH RD
WHEATLANDS RD
WOOD CL
FRANCES DR
WRENPARK RD
BRADBURY DR
RECTORY DR
Harperhill Farm
Swathwick Farm
Wingerworth
Green Wood
SWATHWICK LA
Swathwick
SPEIGHTHILL CRES
DAVIDS DR
WALTON WAY
WINDSOR DR
POND LA
SWATHWICK CL
STEEP LA
Harper Hill
Upper Speighthill Wood
2
Harehill Plantation
WATSON LA
EDEN ST
LYDGATE DR
PEARTREE AVE
ELM TREE DR
LONGEDGE LA
The Great Pond of Stubbing
Bradbury Wood
Hill Houses
ALLENDALE RD
OAK CRES
FAWN CL
MALTHOUSE LA
PEARCE LA
HILLHOUSES LA
Sch
Stubbing Court
Pearce Lane Farm
NEW RD
CENTRAL DR
WOODVIEW CL
67
Tricket Brook
Nether House Farm
Stubbing Court Home Farm
Bolehill Farm
LAKESIDE
Lido
Cowley Wood
NETHERMOOR RD
1
Belfit Hill
Sleigh Wood
BIRKIN LA
BOLEHILL LA
TOP RD
MIDDLE RD
BOTTOM RD
Ivyspring Wood
Black Wood
Works
Hardwick Wood
66
35
A
36
B
37
C

96
116

131
116

115
97

A
B
C
4
3
2
1
69
68
67
66
41
42
43
Nether House Farm
HALLEFLASH LA
CALOW LA
Calow Green
Calow Green Farm
BACK LA
MOOR LA
B6425
Spoil Heap
Sutton Lane Farm
Bull Paddock Farm
SUTTON LA
Woodnook Farm
Hall Farm
ROCK LA
Calow Brook
HASSOCKY LA
Sutton Springs Wood
Yewtree Farm
Springwood Farm
A617
Hill Farm
B6425
Muster Brook
SHIRE LA
B6039
TEMPLE NORMANTON BSNS PK
Bond's Main
SPRINGWOOD ST
ELM ST
POSTMANS LA
Sch
High House Farm
Grassmoor Country Park
CHURCH LA
Cemy
Temple Normanton
MANSFIELD RD
BIRKIN LA
P
Musterbrook Bridge
A617
Philadelphia
SLACK LA
High Top Poultry Farm
CHESTERFIELD RD
Williamthorpe Ponds (Nature Reserve)
MOORLAND DR
LILAC CL
GORSE BANK
BRAMBLE CL
BRACKEN AVE
HEATHER AVE
FERN CL
Lings Farm
Williamthorpe Industrial Park
Sewage Works
HEATH RD
PARK RD
PAVILION WORKSHOPS
Holmewood
CHESTERFIELD RD
SHELLEY ST
SHAKESPEARE ST
TENNYSON ST
SHAW ST
LAWRENCE AVE
DICKENS DR
MASEFIELD AVE
B6039
WOOD ST
HUNLOKE RD
COMPTON ST
DUKES CL
QUEENSWAY
CAVENDISH CL
DEVONSHIRE TERR
A6175
HARDWICK VIEW RD
ASTWITH CL
STAINSBY CL
B6038
P

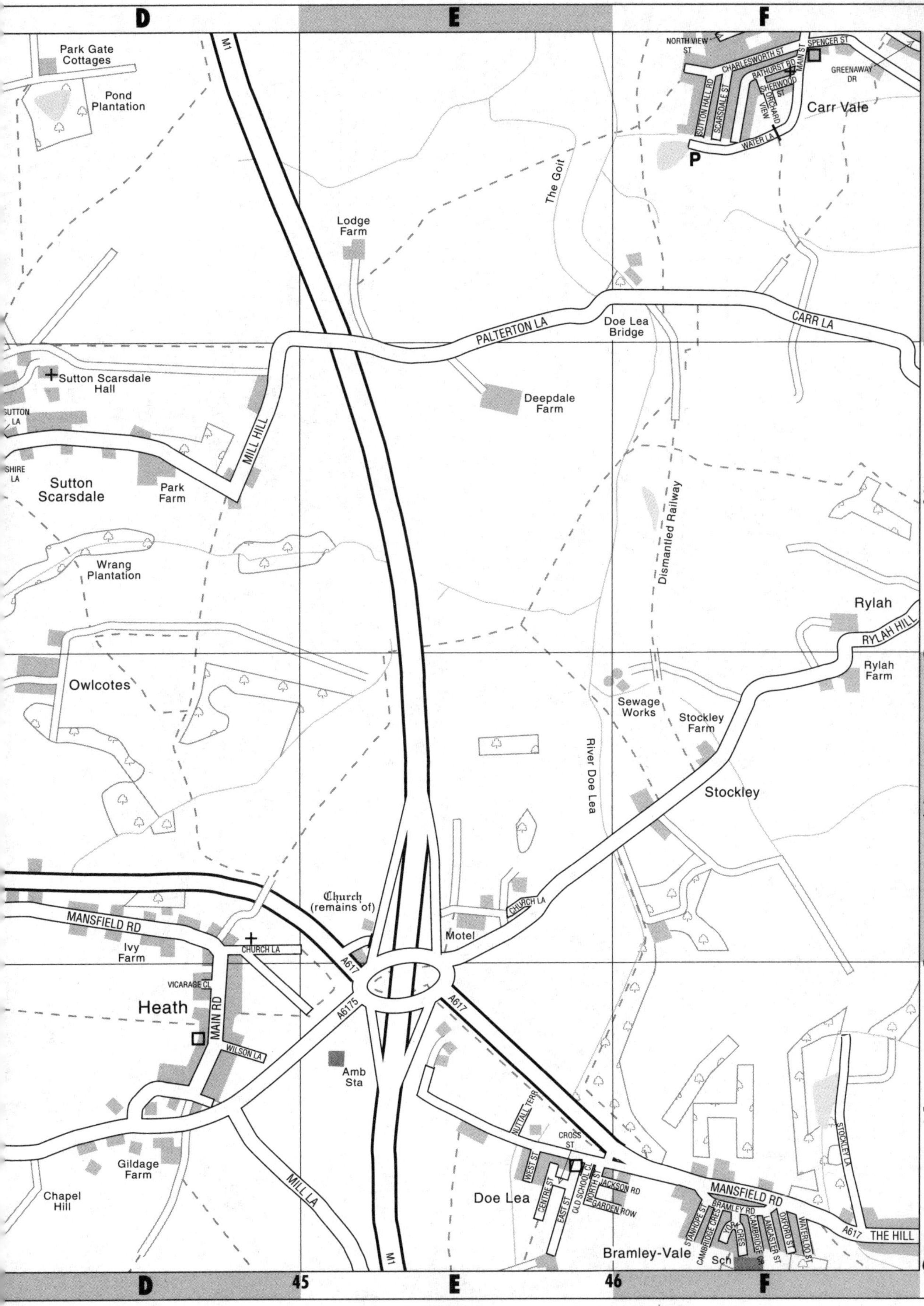
D
E
F
M1
Park Gate Cottages
Pond Plantation
NORTH VIEW ST
SPENCER ST
CHARLESWORTH ST
BATHURST RD
MAIN ST
SHERWOOD ST
ORCHARD VIEW
SUTTON HALL RD
SCARSDALE ST
WATER LA
GREENAWAY DR
Carr Vale
P
The Goit
4
Lodge Farm
PALTERTON LA
Doe Lea Bridge
CARR LA
69
Sutton Scarsdale Hall
SUTTON LA
Deepdale Farm
MILL HILL
SHIRE LA
Sutton Scarsdale
Park Farm
Dismantled Railway
3
Wrang Plantation
Rylah
RYLAH HILL
68
Owlcotes
Rylah Farm
Sewage Works
Stockley Farm
River Doe Lea
Stockley
2
Church (remains of)
CHURCH LA
Motel
MANSFIELD RD
Ivy Farm
CHURCH LA
A617
67
VICARAGE CL
Heath
MAIN RD
A6175
A617
WILSON LA
Amb Sta
1
NUTTALL TERR
CROSS ST
STOCKLEY LA
Gildage Farm
WEST ST
CENTRE ST
EAST ST
OLD SCHOOL CL
NORTH ST
JACKSON RD
GARDEN ROW
MANSFIELD RD
BRAMLEY RD
Chapel Hill
MILL LA
Doe Lea
STANHOPE ST
CAMBRIDGE CRES
YORK CRES
CAMBRIDGE DR
LANCASTER ST
OXFORD ST
WATERLOO ST
A617
THE HILL
Bramley-Vale
Sch
M1
66
D
45
E
46
F

A
B
C
4
69
3
68
2
67
1
66
47
48
49
BROOKFIELD RD
GREENWAY DR
MEADOW CL
VALLEY RD
SPITTAL GARDENS
AVONDALE RD
FAIRFIELD RD
RIDGEDALE RD
NEW STATION RD
COUNCIL TERR
EASTERN AVE
A632
CAVENDISH RD
PORTLAND AVE
TOWER CRES
ST LAWRENCE AVE
CROMWELL RD 1
POLYFIELDS LA 2
OWLCOTES VIEW
CRICH VIEW
STOCKLEY VIEW
HUDSON MOUNT
VICTORIA ST
CROSS ST
MIDDLE ST
WELLS ST
LANGWITH RD
NESBIT ST
SELWYN ST
SUTTON VIEW
DARWOOD LA
WEST VIEW
PH
Hillstown
CASTLE GREEN
PLEASANT AVE
The Meadows
B6417
ROTHERHAM RD
MOOR LA
Lidget Lane
Fox Hill
FOX HILL
MANSFIELD RD
NORTHFIELD LA
Scarcliffe
Sch
PH
MAIN ST
WOOD LA
STATION RD
CARR LA
The Elms Farm
THIRTEEN ROW
STEEL'S LA
Palterton
PENNINE VIEW
BACK LA
Sch
EAST ST
GANG LA
Meadowspot Farm
MANSFIELD RD
RYLAH HILL
MAIN ST
PH
Poulterwell Lane
Birch Hill Plantation
Hill Top Farm
TRANSVAAL TERR
LING LA
Roseland Wood
Fox Covert
LOSK LA
ROTHERHAM RD
Archaeological Trail
Lanes Farm
GLAPWELL LA
Terrace Wood
LOSK CNR
Water Lane
Houghton Bassett
WATER LA
Elm Tree Farm
GREER LA
Hall Farm
Car Wood
Greer Lane
Houghton Felley
Stony Houghton
THE PINFOLD
BACK LA
CEDAR CL
PARK AVE
BEECH CRES 1
CHESTNUT AVE 2
ROWTHORNE LA 3
GREEN LA
A617
THE HILL
PH
HILLTOP CL
MANSFIELD RD
A617
B6417

100
120

135
120

A
B
C
Park House Farm
Boon Hills Wood
Top Farm
Cuckney Hay Wood
Dismantled Railway
Lady's Grove
Warsop Wood
Minster Wood
Collier Spring
WOOD LA
LILAC GR
LIME CRES
BIRCH ST
SYCAMORE ST
Lord Stubbins Wood
William Wood Lane
Spoil Heap
Spring Lane
William Wood Farm
Warsop Cottage Farm
Parson's Wood
Askew Spa
Hills and Holes
HEWETT ST
KING ST
NORTH ST
WEST ST
Sch
1 MUSTERS ST
2 NEW LINDEN ST
3 MANVERS ST
4 MANVERS CT
LANGWITH RD
AUSTIN ST
STATION RD
HARDWICK ST
VERNON CT
VERNON ST
MERCHANTS ST
Sookholme Lodge Farm
PH
Warsop Vale
Sch
Sookholme Moor
Market Warsop
STONEBRIDGE
William Wood Bridge
CARTER LA
B6031
B6407
Bully Lane
Hammerwater Bridge
Works
SOOKHOLME RD
Spoil Heap
SOOKHOLME LA
River Meden
LONGSTER LA
Mill Farm
Colliery
Spring Farm
Spoil Heap
Sookholme
BATH LA
Bath Lane Farm
Mosscar Lane
Sookholme Bath
Spion Kop
WOOD LA
Rough Wood
MANSFIELD RD
GEORGE
SOOKHOLME RD
Ox Pasture Wood
Nettleworth Farm
B6047
A60
Spring Wood
4
69
3
68
2
67
1
66
53
54
55

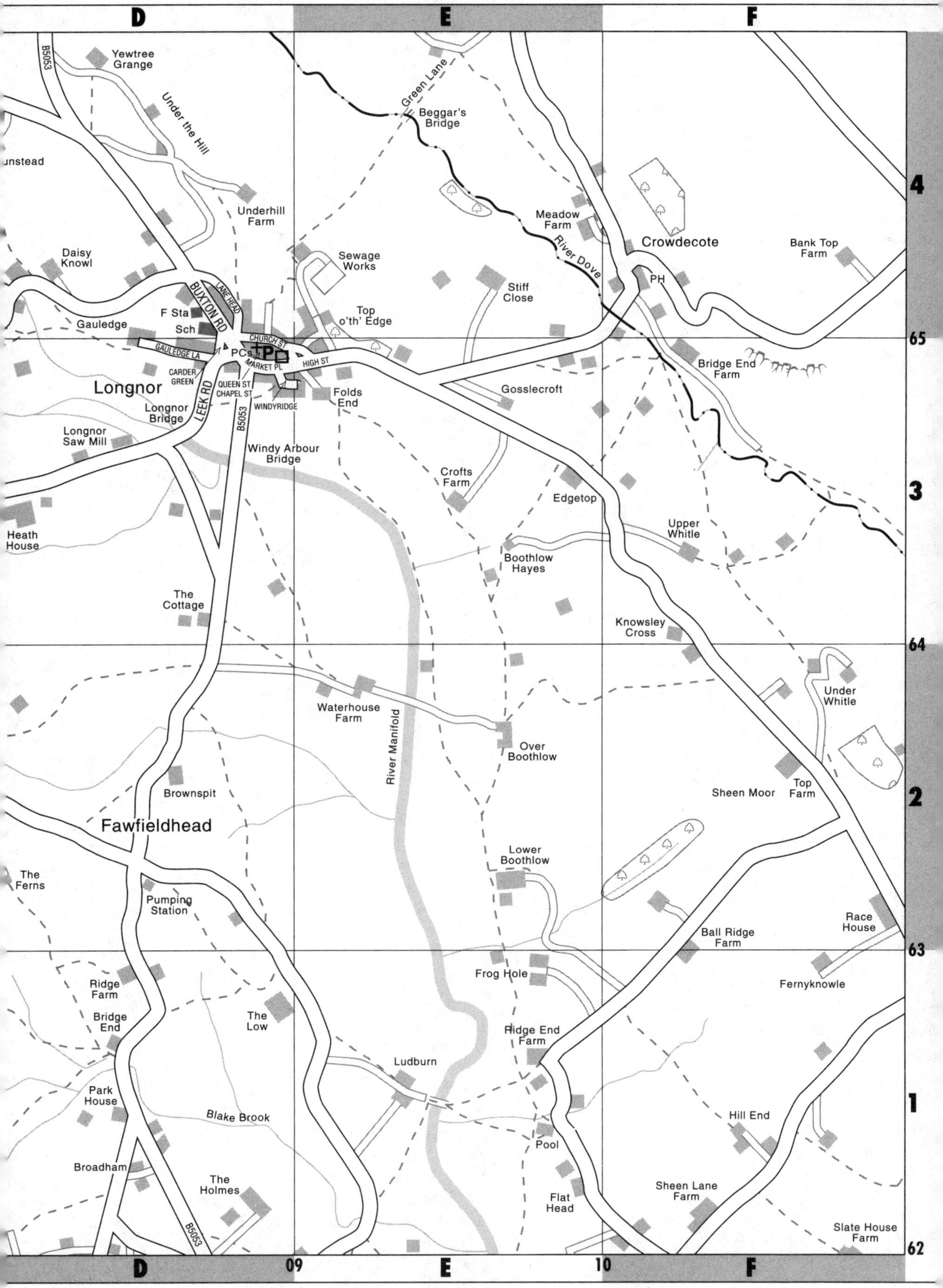
D
E
F
Yewtree Grange
Under the Hill
Green Lane
Beggar's Bridge
Underhill Farm
Meadow Farm
River Dove
Crowdecote
Bank Top Farm
Daisy Knowl
Sewage Works
PH
Stiff Close
Top o'th' Edge
F Sta
Sch
Gauledge
BUXTON RD
LANE HEAD
CHURCH ST
GAULEDGE LA
PCs
P
MARKET PL
HIGH ST
CARDER GREEN
QUEEN ST
CHAPEL ST
WINDYRIDGE
LEEK RD
B5053
Longnor
Longnor Bridge
Longnor Saw Mill
Folds End
Gosslecroft
Bridge End Farm
Windy Arbour Bridge
Crofts Farm
Edgetop
Heath House
Upper Whitle
Boothlow Hayes
The Cottage
Knowsley Cross
Under Whitle
Waterhouse Farm
Over Boothlow
River Manifold
Brownspit
Sheen Moor
Top Farm
Fawfieldhead
Lower Boothlow
The Ferns
Pumping Station
Ball Ridge Farm
Race House
Frog Hole
Fernyknowle
Ridge Farm
The Low
Bridge End
Ridge End Farm
Ludburn
Park House
Blake Brook
Hill End
Pool
Broadham
The Holmes
Flat Head
Sheen Lane Farm
Slate House Farm
4
65
3
64
2
63
1
62
09
10

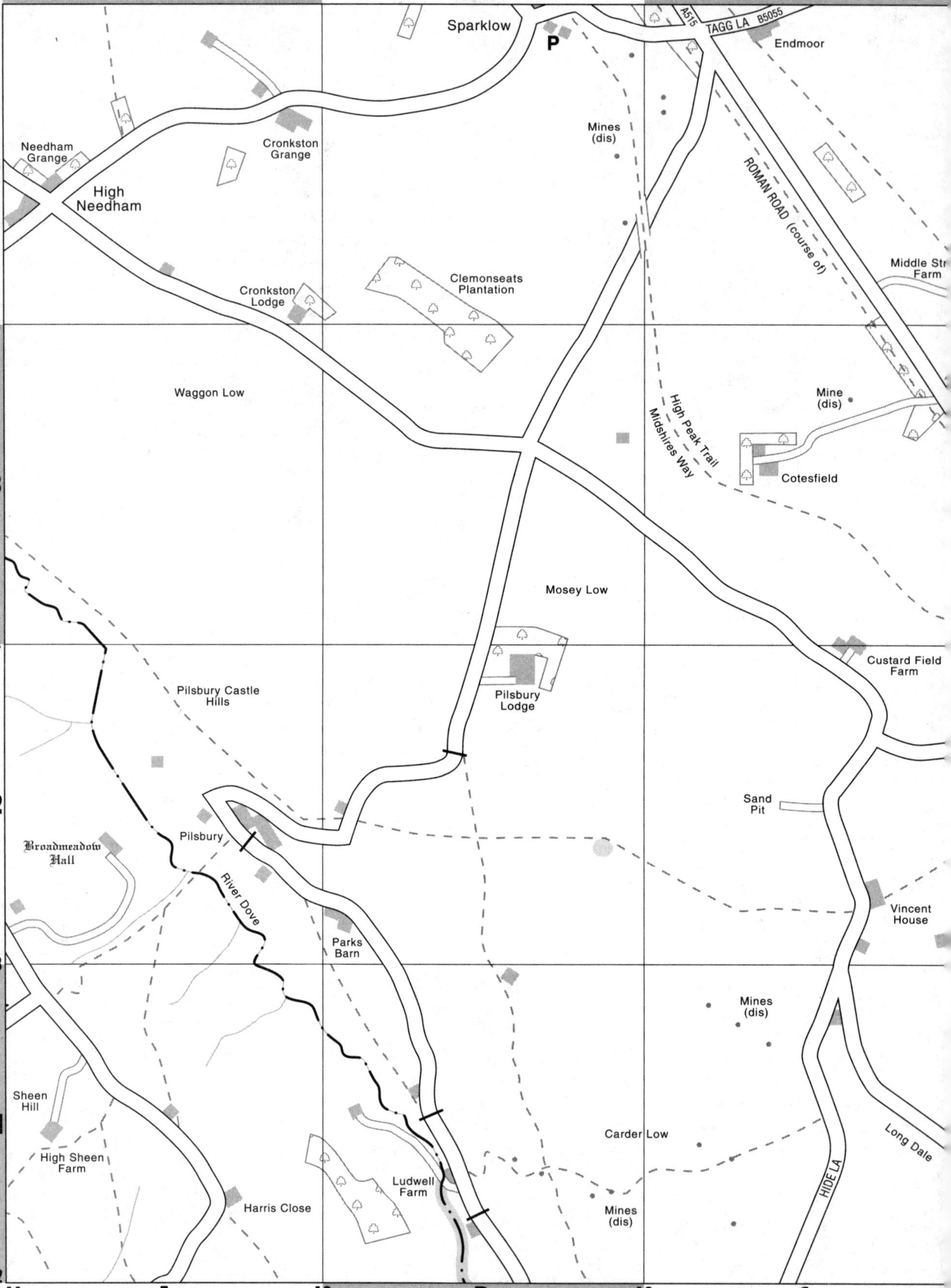
A
B
C
Sparklow
P
A515
TAGG LA
B5055
Endmoor
Mines (dis)
Needham Grange
Cronkston Grange
4
High Needham
ROMAN ROAD (course of)
Middle Str Farm
Clemonseats Plantation
Cronkston Lodge
65
Waggon Low
Mine (dis)
High Peak Trail
Midshires Way
Cotesfield
3
Mosey Low
64
Custard Field Farm
Pilsbury Castle Hills
Pilsbury Lodge
2
Sand Pit
Pilsbury
Broadmeadow Hall
River Dove
Vincent House
Parks Barn
63
Mines (dis)
Sheen Hill
1
Carder Low
Long Dale
High Sheen Farm
Ludwell Farm
HIDE LA
Harris Close
Mines (dis)
62
11
12
13

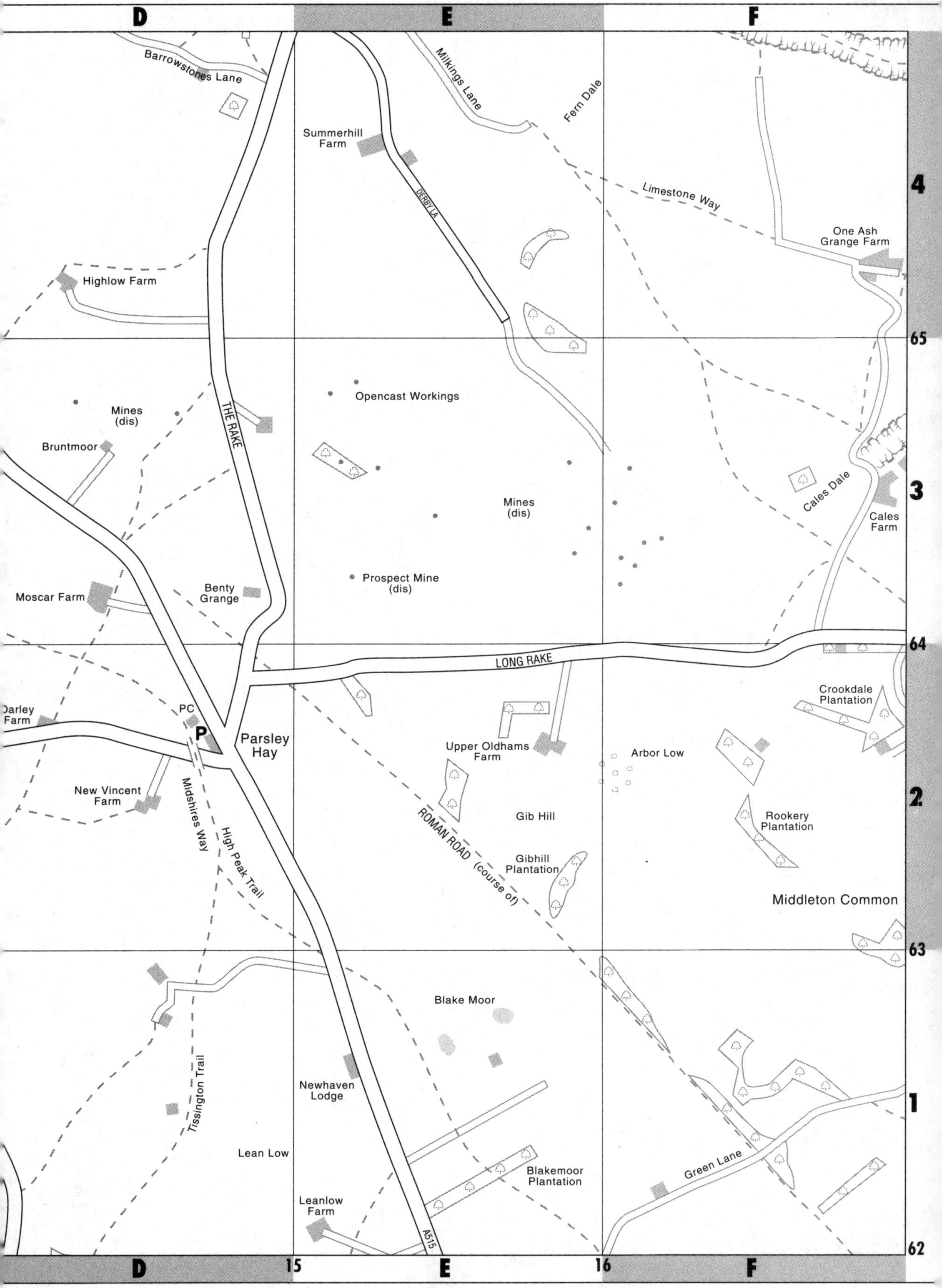
D
E
F
Barrowstones Lane
Milkings Lane
Fern Dale
Summerhill Farm
DERBY LA
Limestone Way
One Ash Grange Farm
Highlow Farm
Opencast Workings
Mines (dis)
Bruntmoor
THE RAKE
Mines (dis)
Cales Dale
Cales Farm
Prospect Mine (dis)
Benty Grange
Moscar Farm
LONG RAKE
Crookdale Plantation
Darley Farm
PC
P
Parsley Hay
Upper Oldhams Farm
Arbor Low
New Vincent Farm
Midshires Way
High Peak Trail
ROMAN ROAD (course of)
Gib Hill
Rookery Plantation
Gibhill Plantation
Middleton Common
Blake Moor
Newhaven Lodge
Tissington Trail
Lean Low
Blakemoor Plantation
Green Lane
Leanlow Farm
A515
4
65
3
64
2
63
1
62
15
16

123
108

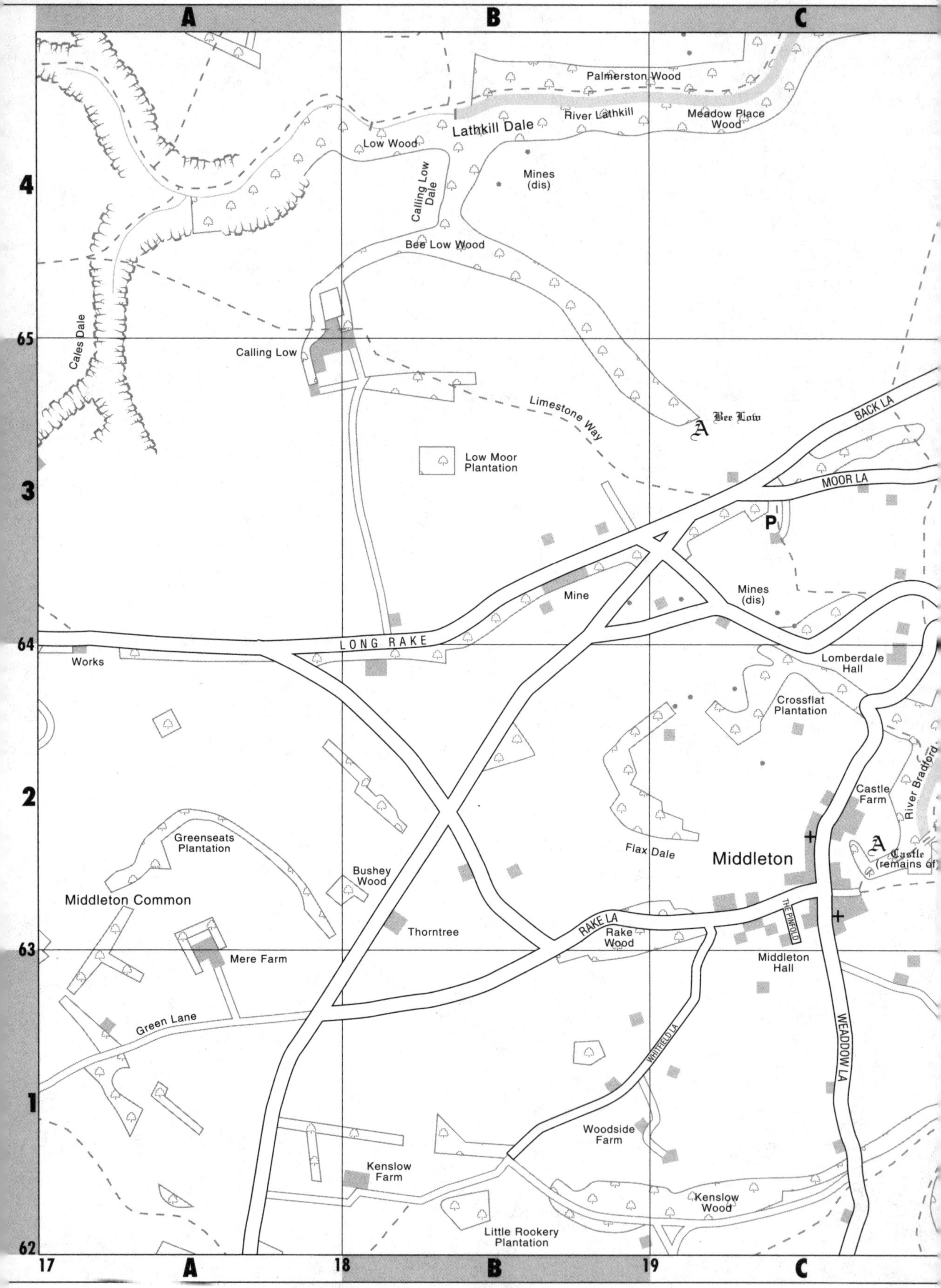

123
139

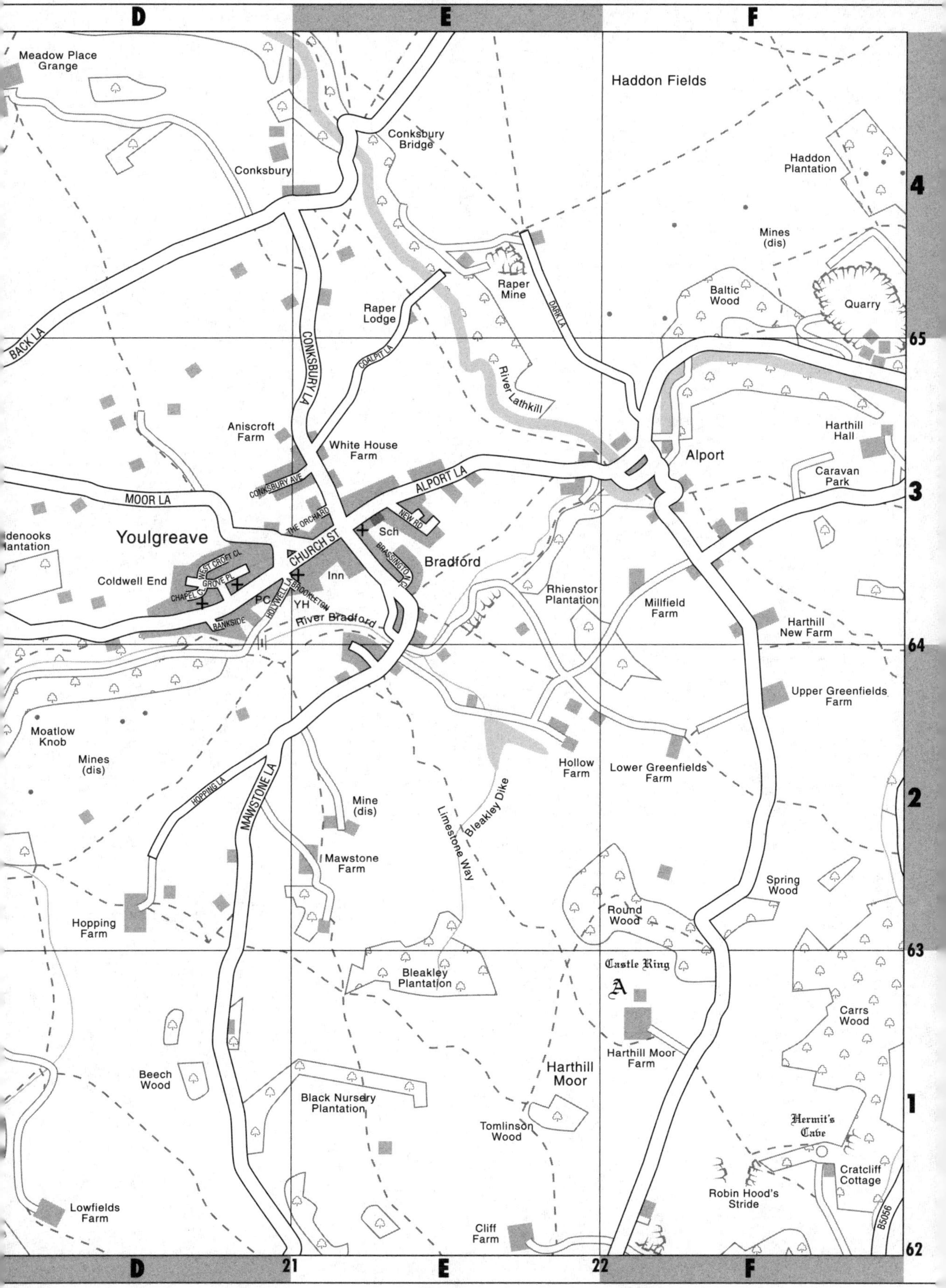
D
E
F
Meadow Place Grange
Haddon Fields
Conksbury Bridge
Haddon Plantation
Conksbury
4
Mines (dis)
Raper Mine
Baltic Wood
Quarry
Raper Lodge
DARK LA
BACK LA
CONKSBURY LA
COALPIT LA
65
River Lathkill
Aniscroft Farm
Harthill Hall
White House Farm
Alport
Caravan Park
MOOR LA
CONKSBURY AVE
ALPORT LA
3
THE ORCHARD
NEW RD
Youlgreave
Sch
idenooks lantation
CHURCH ST
BRASSINGTON
Bradford
WEST CROFT CL
GROVE PL
Coldwell End
Inn
Rhienstor Plantation
Millfield Farm
CHAPEL CL
PC
HOLYWELL LA
BROOKLETON
YH
BANKSIDE
River Bradford
Harthill New Farm
64
Upper Greenfields Farm
Moatlow Knob
Mines (dis)
Hollow Farm
Lower Greenfields Farm
HOPPING LA
MAWSTONE LA
Bleakley Dike
Mine (dis)
2
Limestone Way
Mawstone Farm
Spring Wood
Round Wood
Hopping Farm
63
Castle Ring
Bleakley Plantation
Carrs Wood
Harthill Moor Farm
Beech Wood
Harthill Moor
1
Black Nursery Plantation
Hermit's Cave
Tomlinson Wood
Cratcliff Cottage
Robin Hood's Stride
Lowfields Farm
Cliff Farm
B5056
62
D
21
E
22
F

125
110

125
141

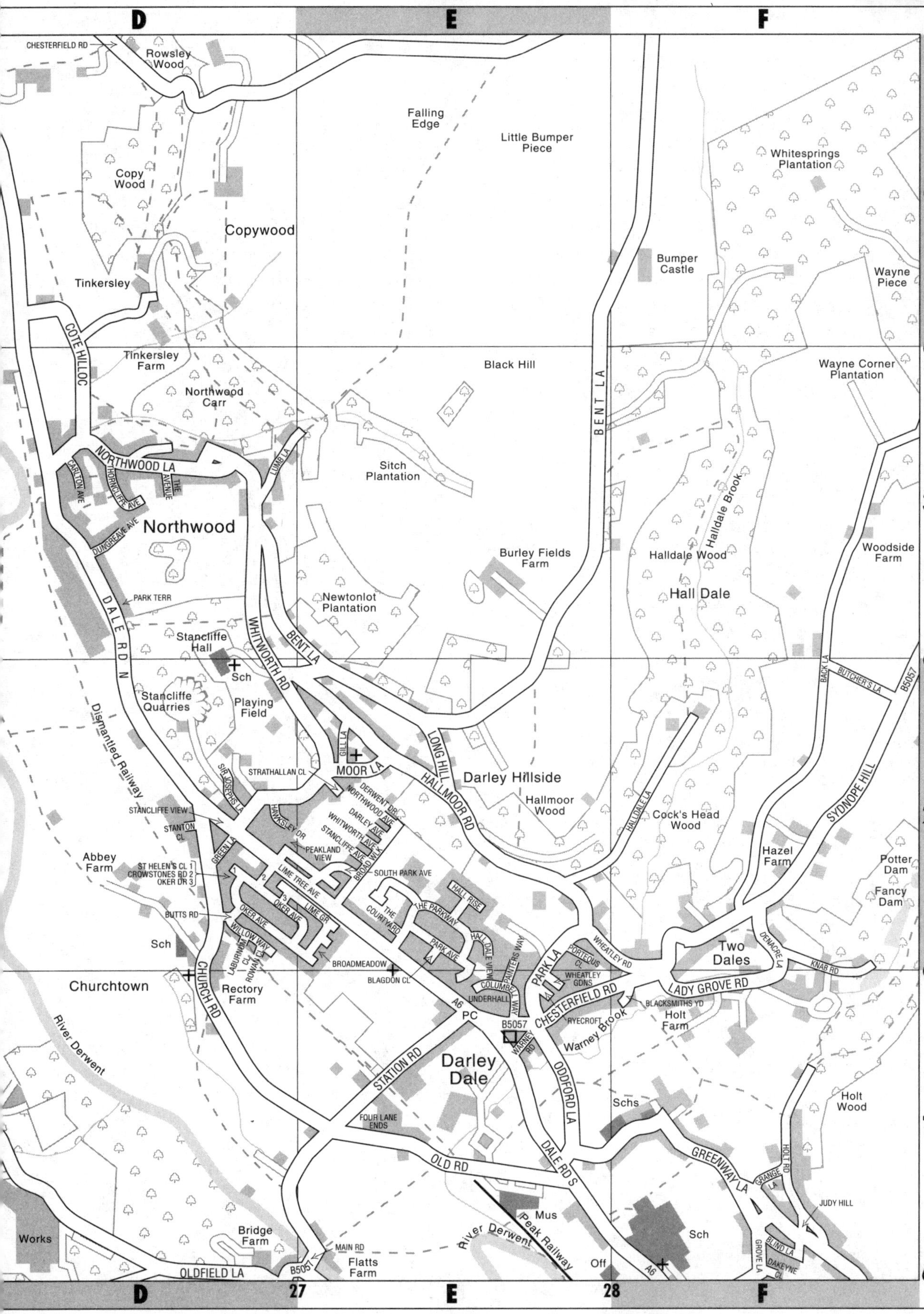
D
E
F
Rowsley Wood
Copy Wood
Copywood
Falling Edge
Little Bumper Piece
Whitesprings Plantation
Bumper Castle
Wayne Piece
Tinkersley
Tinkersley Farm
Northwood Carr
Black Hill
Wayne Corner Plantation
Sitch Plantation
Northwood
Burley Fields Farm
Halldale Wood
Hall Dale
Halldale Brook
Woodside Farm
Newtonlot Plantation
Stancliffe Hall
Sch
Stancliffe Quarries
Playing Field
Darley Hillside
Hallmoor Wood
Cock's Head Wood
Hazel Farm
Potter Dam
Fancy Dam
Abbey Farm
Two Dales
Churchtown
Rectory Farm
Holt Farm
Warney Brook
Darley Dale
Schs
Holt Wood
Dismantled Railway
River Derwent
Works
Bridge Farm
Flatts Farm
Mus
Peak Railway
Off
COTE HILL
NORTHWOOD LA
DALE RD N
WHITWORTH RD
BENT LA
LONG HILL
HALLMOOR RD
MOOR LA
CHURCH RD
STATION RD
OLD RD
DALE RD S
ODDFORD LA
CHESTERFIELD RD
LADY GROVE RD
SYDNOPE HILL
BUTCHER'S LA
BACK LA
B5057
GREENWAY LA
HOLT RD
OLDFIELD LA
B5051
A6
PC
CHESTERFIELD RD
PARK TERR
STRATHALLAN CL
STANCLIFFE VIEW
STANTON CL
ST HELEN'S CL 1
CROWSTONES RD 2
OKER DR 3
BUTTS RD
BROADMEADOW
BLAGDON CL
SOUTH PARK AVE
FOUR LANE ENDS
MAIN RD
JUDY HILL
BLACKSMITHS YD
RYECROFT
WHEATLEY RD
WHEATLEY GDNS
PORTEOUS CL
UNDERHALL
COLUMBELL WAY
KNAB RD
DENACRE LA
GRANGE LA
BLIND LA
GROVE LA
DAKEYNE CL
Sch
65
64
63
62
4
3
2
1
27
28

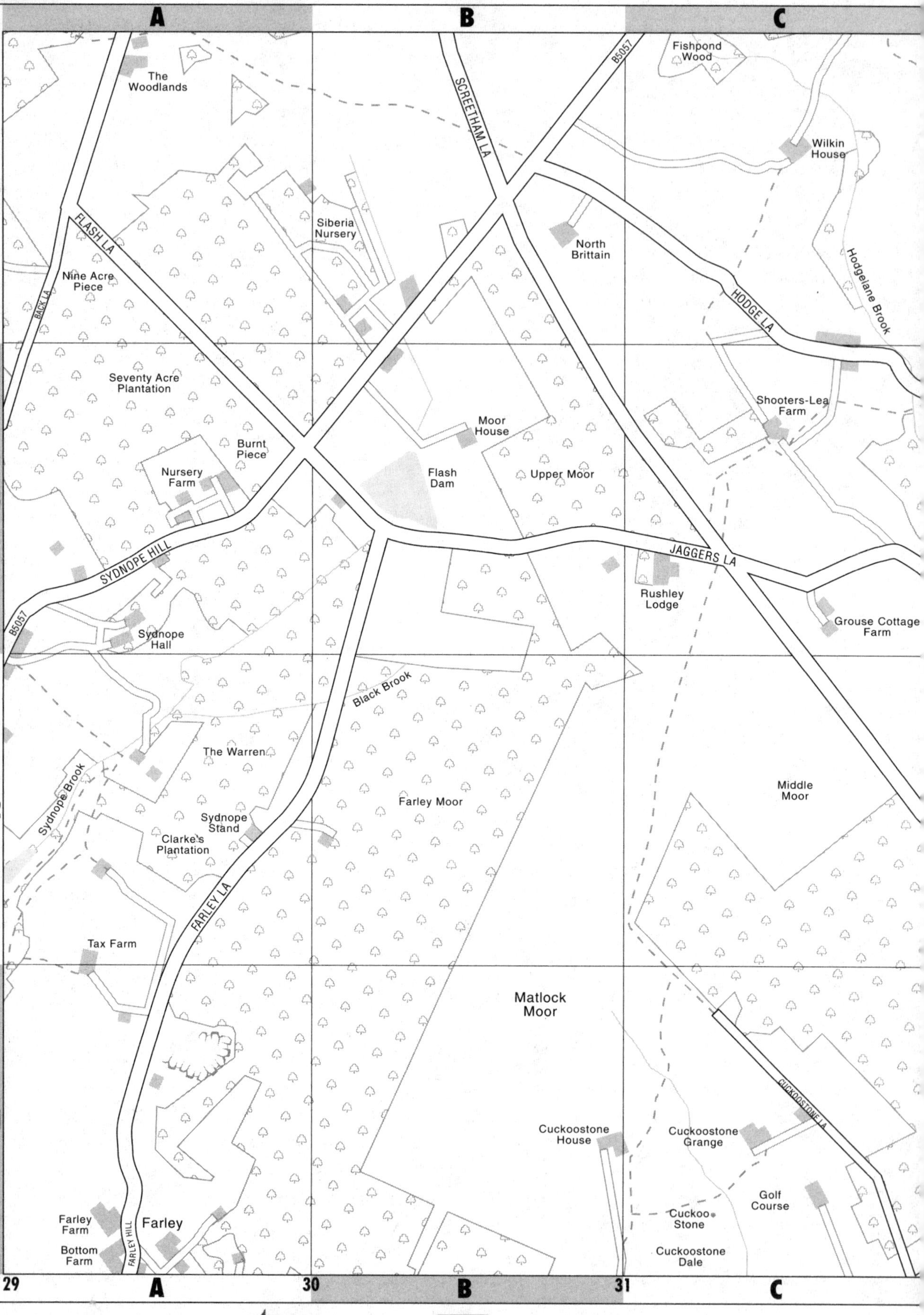
A
B
C
The Woodlands
Fishpond Wood
B5057
SCREETHAM LA
Wilkin House
Siberia Nursery
FLASH LA
North Brittain
Hodgelane Brook
Nine Acre Piece
BACK LA
HODGE LA
Seventy Acre Plantation
Shooters-Lea Farm
Moor House
Burnt Piece
Nursery Farm
Flash Dam
Upper Moor
JAGGERS LA
SYDNOPE HILL
Rushley Lodge
Grouse Cottage Farm
B5057
Sydnope Hall
Black Brook
The Warren
Sydnope Brook
Middle Moor
Farley Moor
Sydnope Stand
Clarke's Plantation
FARLEY LA
Tax Farm
Matlock Moor
CUCKOOSTONE LA
Cuckoostone House
Cuckoostone Grange
Golf Course
Farley Farm
Farley
Cuckoo Stone
Bottom Farm
FARLEY HILL
Cuckoostone Dale
4
65
3
64
2
63
1
62
29
30
31
A
B
C

D
E
F
Alicehead Farm
Alicehead
Highashes Farm
Spancarr
A632
HIGHASHES LA
Bunting Field
Alicehead Road Farm
ALICEHEAD RD
SHEEPLEA LA
Dryhurst Farm
CULLUMBELL LA
BUNTINGFIELD LA
SWINGER LA
Spancarr Farm
New Farm
BIRKIN LA
Sheeplea House Farm
LONG LA
Uppertown
Bath Lane Farm
HARDWICK LA
BATH LA
Smalley Brook
Well Six Farm
Hardwick Farm
MATLOCK RD
Hall Moor Farm
Hardwick
BROCKHURST LA
Brockhurst
Overend
Whitefield Farm
Prestedge Farm
WHITEFIELD LA
OAKS LA
Peglant
Brockhurst Farm
Bath House Farm
Yew Tree Farm
Robridding
Hodgelane Brook
KELSTEDGE LA
Henstone Cottage
CRIPTON LA
HILLTOP RD
HILL RD
Kelstedge Farm
PH
THE CAUSEWAY
WEST EDGE CL
B6036
Marsh Brook
CHAPEL HILL
MARSH GREEN LA
Vernonlane Farm
ROBRIDDING RD
Kelstedge
HILLSIDE
Amber House
Marsh Green
Rattle
PUDDING BAG LA
Quarry (dis)
ASHOVER RD
Ashover
MOOR RD
MALTHOUSE LA
PC
NARROWLEYS LA
Wire Stone
AMBER LA
West Edge
Sch
YEW TREE CL
Amberlane Farm
Amber Hill Cottage
DOVECOTES
P
Eddlestow Hall Farm
CHURCH ST
Eddlestow Lot
River Amber
Butts
BUTTS RD
B6036
Bottom Moor
Quarry (dis)
Amber Hill Farm
Goss Hall
PH
HOCKLEY LA
Mill (dis)
Slack
SLACK LA
Sycamore Farm
Hollow Lane
Salter Lane
Greenend
Quarry (dis)
Back Lane
Top Slack Farm
HOLESTONE GATE RD
Amber Hill
LANT LA
A632
CHESTERFIELD RD
Lantlodge Wood
Overton Cotts
Overton Hall
GIN LA
4
65
3
64
2
63
1
62
33
34
D
E
F

129
114

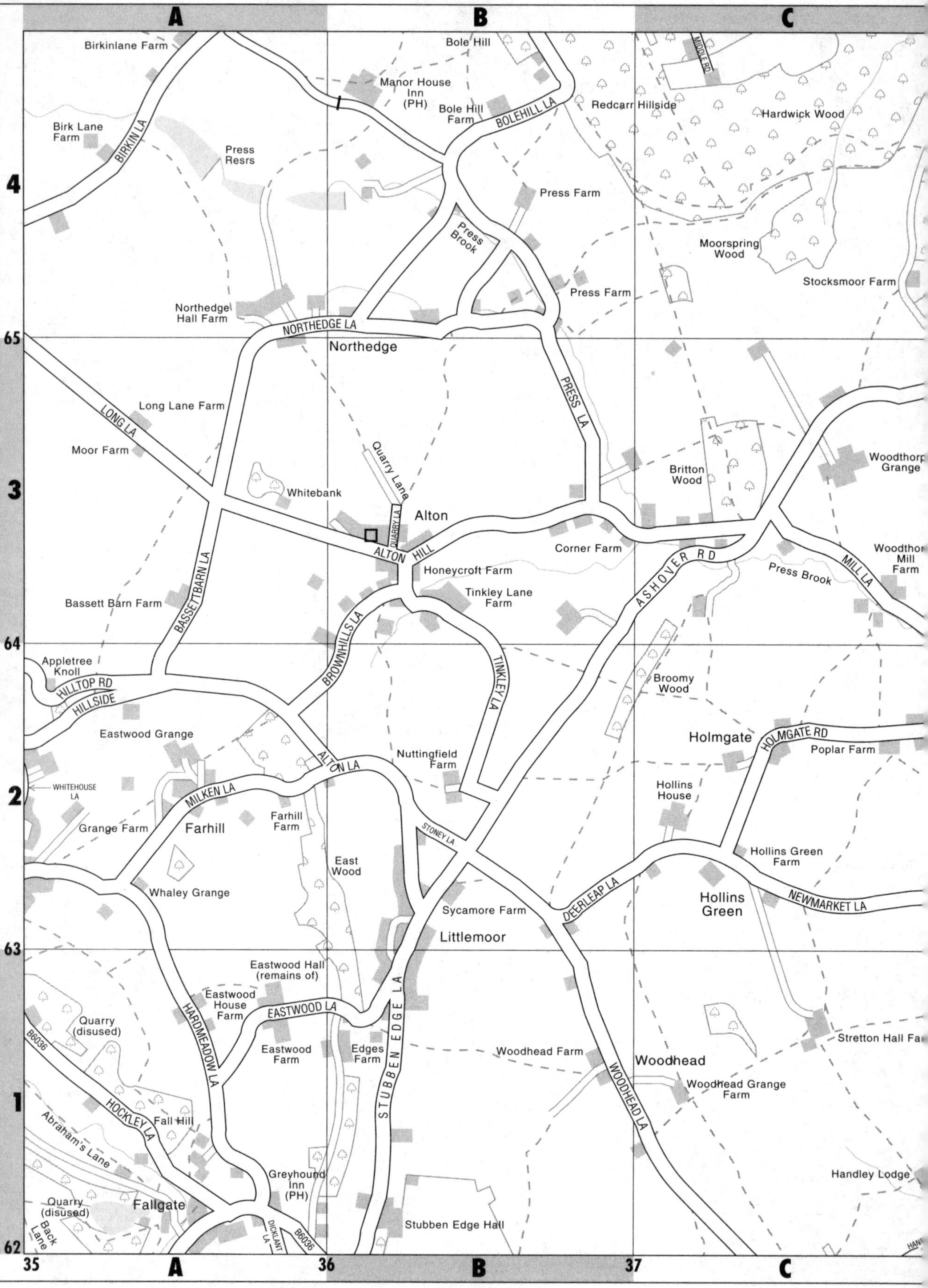

129
145

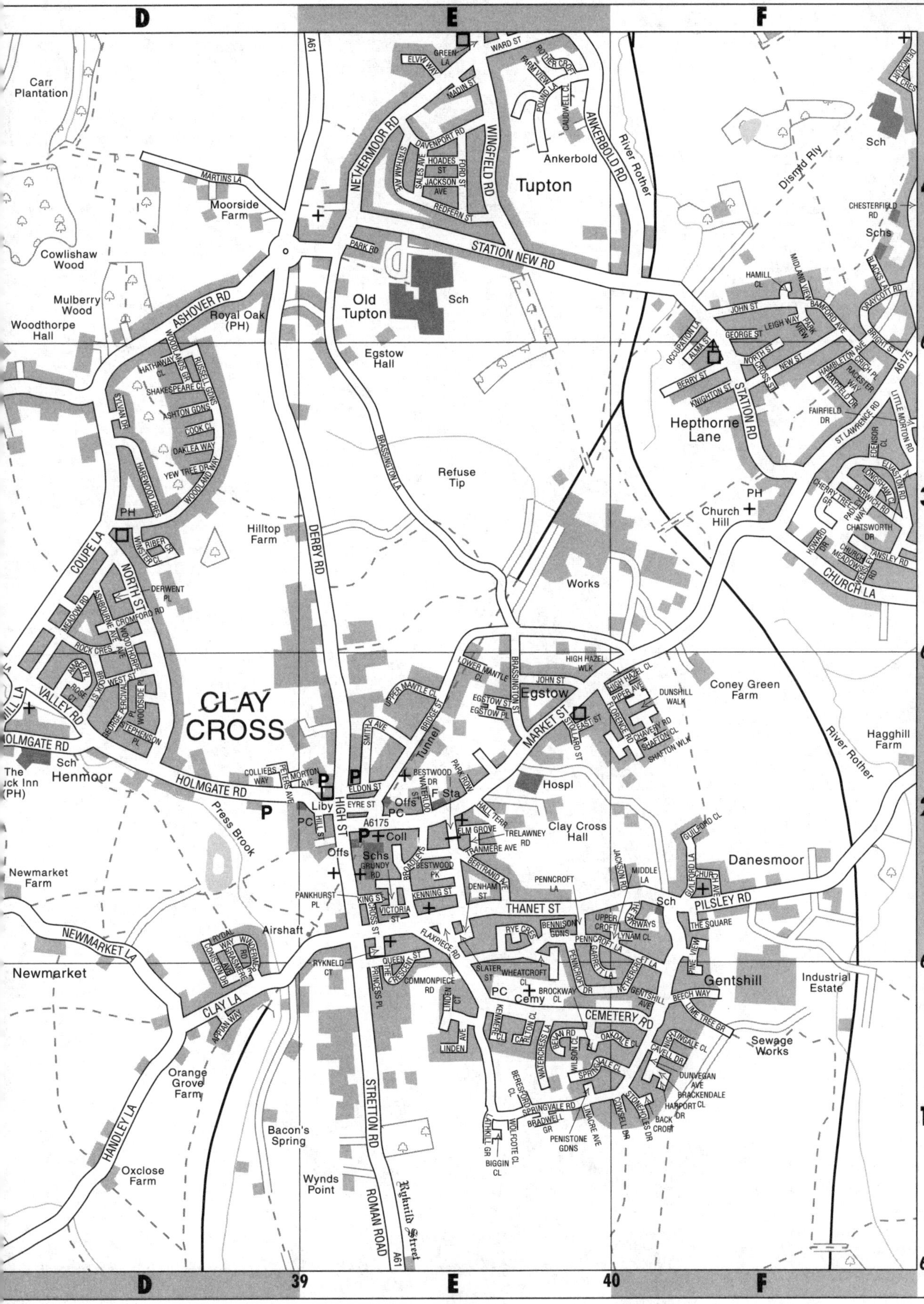
115
132
D
E
F
Carr Plantation
Moorside Farm
Cowlishaw Wood
Mulberry Wood
Woodthorpe Hall
Royal Oak (PH)
Tupton
Old Tupton
Ankerbold
Egstow Hall
Refuse Tip
Hepthorne Lane
Church Hill
Hilltop Farm
Works
CLAY CROSS
Coney Green Farm
Egstow
Hospl
Clay Cross Hall
Henmoor
Newmarket Farm
Newmarket
Airshaft
Danesmoor
Gentshill
Industrial Estate
Sewage Works
Haggill Farm
Orange Grove Farm
Bacon's Spring
Oxclose Farm
Wynds Point
River Rother
Press Brook
Rykneld Street
STATION NEW RD
ASHOVER RD
DERBY RD
HIGH ST
STRETTON RD
ROMAN ROAD
HOLMGATE RD
NEWMARKET LA
CLAY LA
HANDLEY LA
MARKET ST
THANET ST
PILSLEY RD
CEMETERY RD
CHURCH LA
STATION RD
NETHERMOOR RD
WINGFIELD RD
ANKERBOLD RD
BRASSINGTON LA
COUPE LA
NORTH ST
VALLEY RD
A61
A6175
146
132
39
40
62
63
1
2
3
4
64
65

131 116

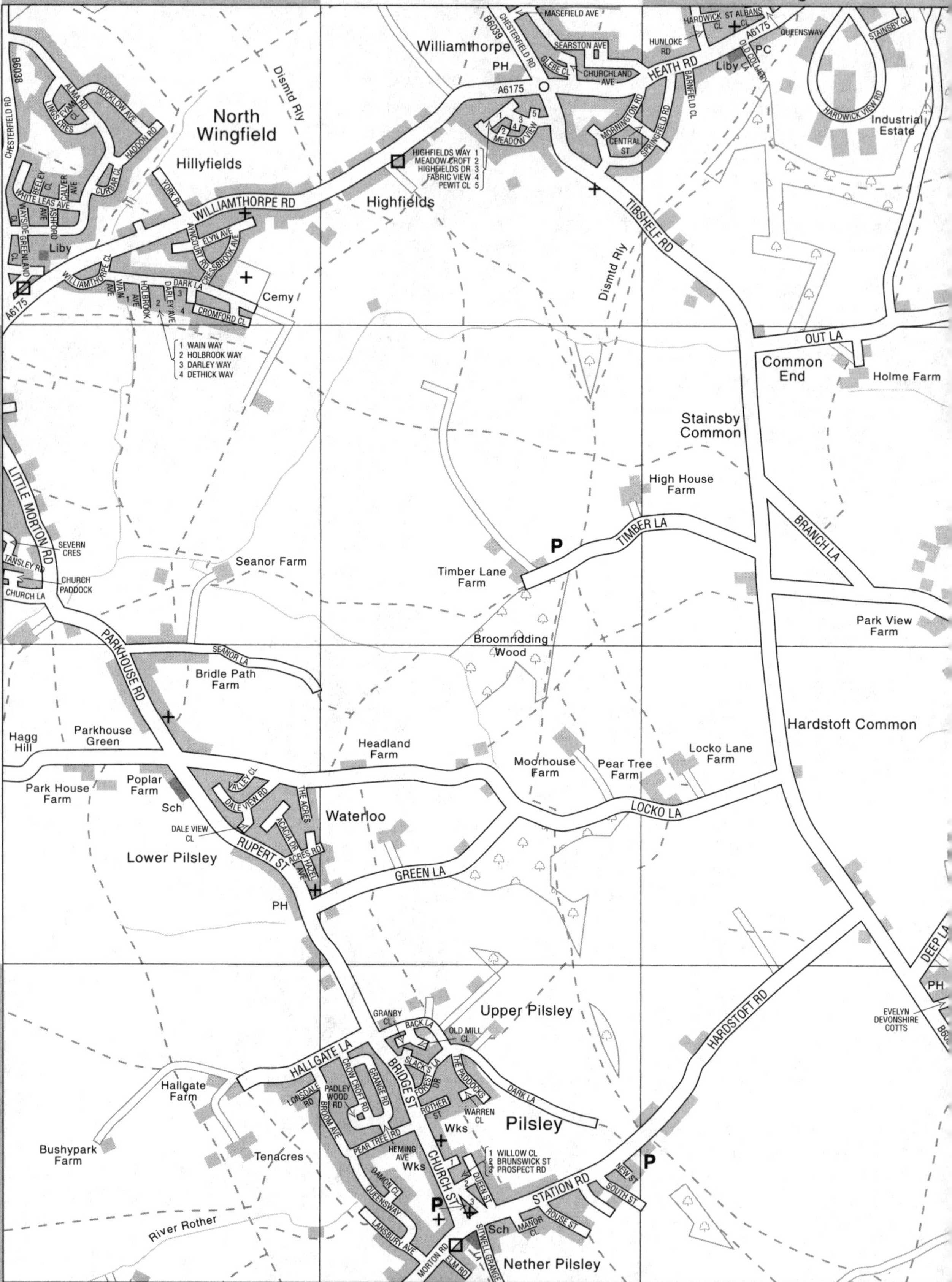

131 147

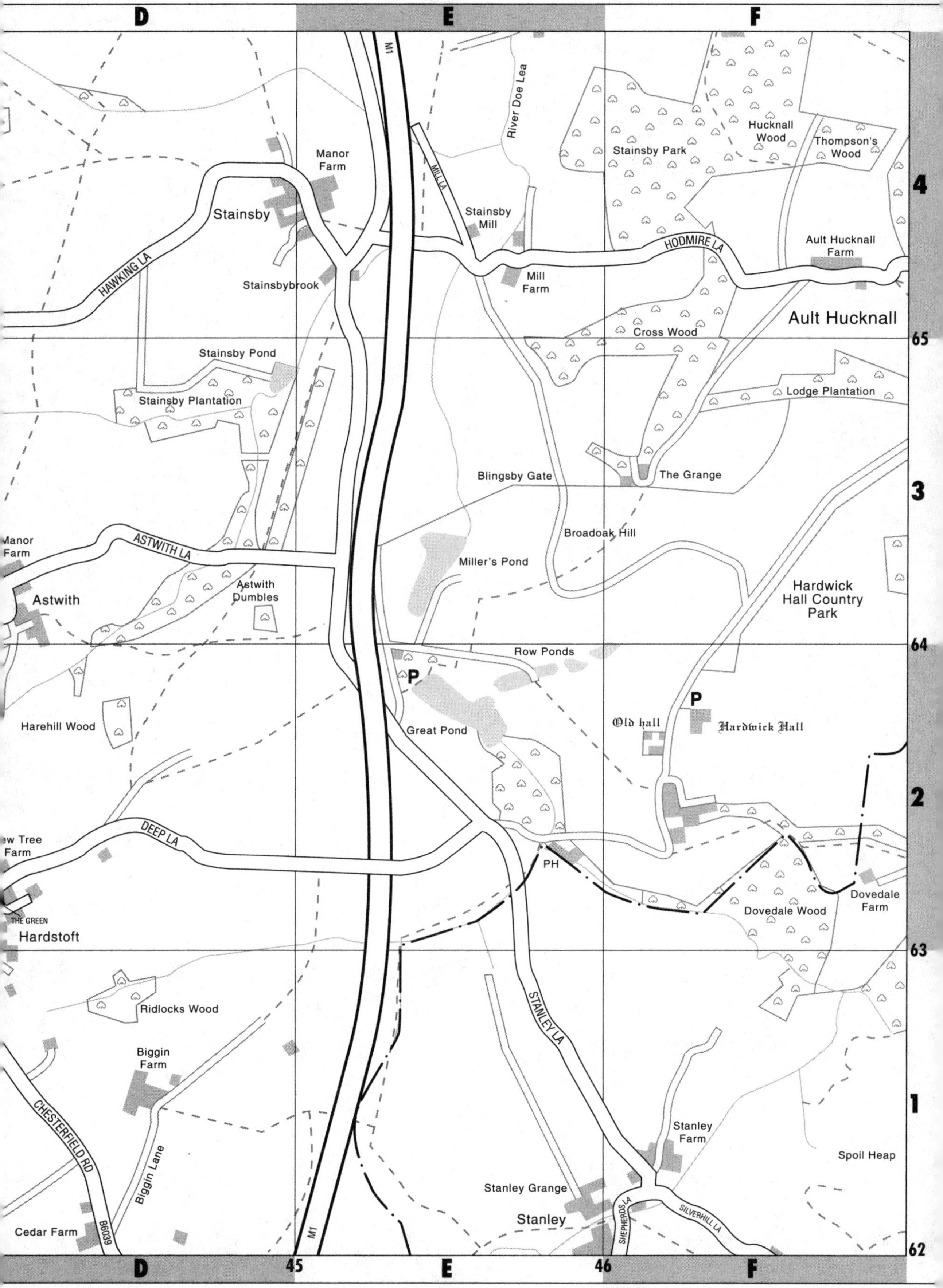
D
E
F
M1
River Doe Lea
Manor Farm
MILL LA
Stainsby
Stainsby Mill
HAWKING LA
Stainsbybrook
Mill Farm
Stainsby Park
Hucknall Wood
Thompson's Wood
HODMIRE LA
Ault Hucknall Farm
Ault Hucknall
Cross Wood
Stainsby Pond
Stainsby Plantation
Lodge Plantation
Blingsby Gate
The Grange
Broadoak Hill
Manor Farm
ASTWITH LA
Miller's Pond
Astwith
Astwith Dumbles
Hardwick Hall Country Park
Row Ponds
P
Harehill Wood
Great Pond
Old hall
Hardwick Hall
DEEP LA
Yew Tree Farm
PH
THE GREEN
Hardstoft
Dovedale Wood
Dovedale Farm
Ridlocks Wood
STANLEY LA
Biggin Farm
CHESTERFIELD RD
Biggin Lane
Stanley Farm
Spoil Heap
Stanley Grange
Stanley
SHEPHERDS LA
SILVERHILL LA
Cedar Farm
B6039
4
65
3
64
2
63
1
62
45
46

A
B
C
4
3
2
1
65
64
63
62
47
48
49
Glapwell
BEECH CRES
MAPLE GR
HARDWICK AVE
ORCHARD CRES
POPLAR DR
LIME TREE AVE
THE GREEN
HAWTHORN AVE
SYCAMORE AVE
CHURCH VIEW
LILAC GR
OAK TREE AVE
A617
MANSFIELD RD
GREEN LA
Strickle Brook
Dismtld Rly
Griff Wood
AULT HUCKNALL LA
ROWTHORNE LA
DALE LA
Longman Nook
Hill Top Farm
ROTHERHAM RD
B6417
New Houghton
Works
PAVILION GDNS
GARDEN AVE
CHURCH VIEW
VERNEY WAY
CORONATION AVE
OCCUPATION RD
MEDEN AVE
MOORGATE AVE
APPLEBY RD
CHESTERFIELD RD
PH
Sch
Top Farm
DUKE'S DR
Hall Farm
Rowthorne
P
FIELD LA
Car Plantation
Farfield Lane
LONGHEDGE LA
Spoil Heap
Car Ponds
Norcliff Wood
Merril Sick
Park Piece
Batley Farm
Dismantled Railway
BATLEY LA
Longedge Lane
NEWBOUNDMILL LA
Norwood
Hardwick Park Farm
Dismantled Railway
Newbound Farm
Newboundmill Farm
BAXTER HILL
MOORHAIGH LA
Crossley Plantation
NEWBOUND LA
Baxterhill
TOP LA
Hare Plantation
PEARTREE LA
Hill Farm
River Meden
Little Dawgates Wood
NEWGATES LA
Spoil Heap

D
E
F
Moorgate Hollow
B6407
Stuffynwood Farm
Lodge Farm
COMMON LA
Dismantled Railway
Forge Lane
Pleasley Park
Little Matlock
Mill
Pleasley Vale
Works
OUTGANG LA
River Meden
Mills (dis)
Warehouse
The Coppice
Dismtd Rly
Northfield House
ROTHERHAM RD
B6417
A617
B6407
CHESTERFIELD RD
CHURCH LA
Pleasley
Lower Radmanthwaite
Meden Lane
North Lodge Farm
BOOTH AVE
CHESTERFIELD RD
DEANSGATE
HOLBROOK CL
PH
MEDEN SQ
MEDEN BANK
CROW HILL
HIGH ST
MEDEN CL
HILL
LITTLE LA
CHURCH ST
BAGSHAW ST
POPLAR DR
TEVERSAL AVE
West Sidings
NEWBOUNDMILL LA
CROOKES AVE
SCHOOL LA
LEAS AVE
WILKINSON CL
Pleasleyhill
WOBURN LA
Sch
Cemy
NORTHFIELD LA
COMMON LA
NORTHFIELD AVE
Pleasleyhill Farm
CHESTERFIELD RD N
RADNOR PL
CARDALE RD
CAMBRIA RD
WOBURN RD
WOBURN PL
Radmanthwaite
HILLMOOR ST
CLARENCE ST
PH
NEW ENGLAND
CATOR RD
RADMANTHWAITE RD
CROMPTON RD
Radmanthwaite
Moorhaigh
SAMPSON'S LA
Sampson's Lane Farm
MOORHAIGH LA
Moorhaigh Farm
WATER LA
CRANMER GR
OXCLOSE LA
Penniment Bungalow Farm
WHARMBY AVE
WILSON ST
STACEY RD
Milehill Farm
GREEN LA
PENNIMENT LA
Sch
CARPENTER AVE
BROUGHAM AVE
FIELDEN AVE
BOOTH CRES
PEEL CRES
WILBERFORCE RD
BUTLER CRES
HOBHOUSE RD
BRIGHT SQ
CLUMBER CT
COTGRAVE CL
BURLINGTON DR
BALMORAL CL
CLUMBER DR
ILION ST
DEBDALE LA
A6075
LITTLE DEBDALE LA
BEECH HILL CRES
1 COBDEN PL
2 NIGHTINGALE DR
SHAFTESBURY AVE
Bull Farm
RUSKIN RD
ARMILO CRES
HAWTON CL
EMERALD CL
BEECH HILL DR
BEECH HILL AVE
CHESTERFIELD RD S
ABBOTT RD
ABBOTTS CROFT
BECKETT AVE
THORN AVE
OUNDLE DR
BUXTON
NEWPORT CRES
LANGLEY CL
DALESTORTH
ELSTON
SHELTON
CHERITON CL
MORTON ST
EVERTON ST
FAIRHOLME DR
Sch
PERLETHORPE AVE
A617
MARLBOROUGH RD
BROWNLOW RD
BOULD ST
ALBION ST
TOP LA
Moorhaigh Wood Farm
Water Lane Farm
SAUNBY AVE
CULLINGHAM
BLYTH
UPTON MOUNT
COLWICK
CHESTER ST
WOODBOROUGH RD
WYSALL CL
WESTFIELD DR
WESTFIELD LA
DRAYTON AVE 1
WAINWRIGHT AVE 2
PEMBLETON DR 3
PRATT CL 4
MELLORS RD 5
A6075
Penniment Farm
Penniment House Farm
PENNIMENT LA
4
65
3
64
2
63
1
62
51
52
D
E
F

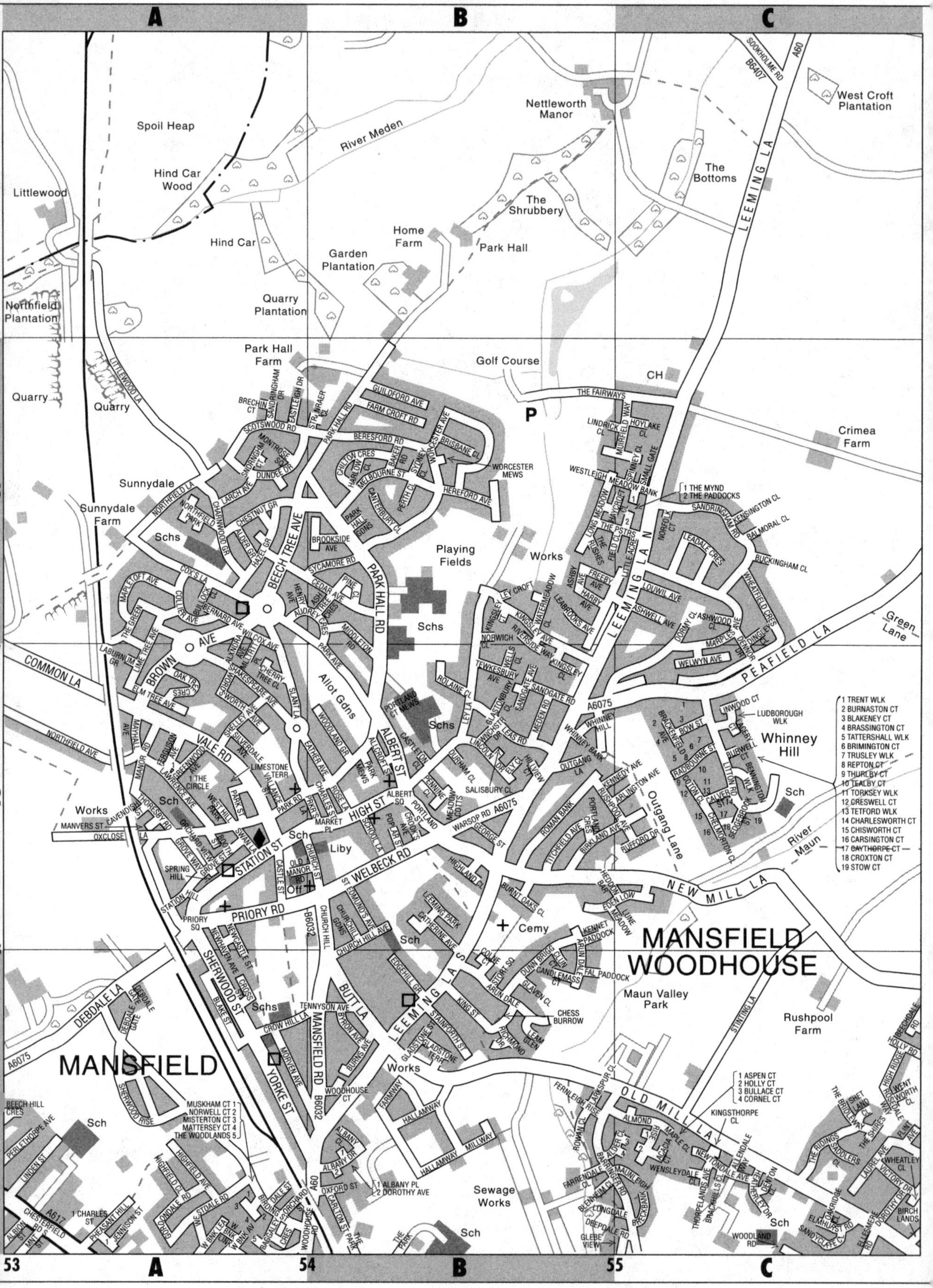
A
B
C
Spoil Heap
Hind Car Wood
Littlewood
Hind Car
River Meden
Nettleworth Manor
West Croft Plantation
The Bottoms
The Shrubbery
Home Farm
Park Hall
Garden Plantation
Quarry Plantation
Northfield Plantation
LEEMING LA
Park Hall Farm
Golf Course
CH
Quarry
Crimea Farm
Sunnydale
Sunnydale Farm
Schs
Playing Fields
Works
Green Lane
COMMON LA
Allot Gdns
PEAFIELD LA
Whinney Hill
Sch
Liby
Cemy
Outgang Lane
River Maun
NEW MILL LA
MANSFIELD WOODHOUSE
Maun Valley Park
Rushpool Farm
MANSFIELD
OLD MILL LA
Sewage Works
1 TRENT WLK
2 BURNASTON CT
3 BLAKENEY CT
4 BRASSINGTON CT
5 TATTERSHALL WLK
6 BRIMINGTON CT
7 TRUSLEY WLK
8 REPTON CT
9 THURLBY CT
10 TEALBY CT
11 TORKSEY WLK
12 CRESWELL CT
13 TETFORD WLK
14 CHARLESWORTH CT
15 CHISWORTH CT
16 CARSINGTON CT
17 CAYTHORPE CT
18 CROXTON CT
19 STOW CT
1 ASPEN CT
2 HOLLY CT
3 BULLACE CT
4 CORNEL CT
MUSKHAM CT 1
NORWELL CT 2
MISTERTON CT 3
MATTERSEY CT 4
THE WOODLANDS 5
1 THE MYND
2 THE PADDOCKS
1 ALBANY PL
2 DOROTHY AVE
53
54
55

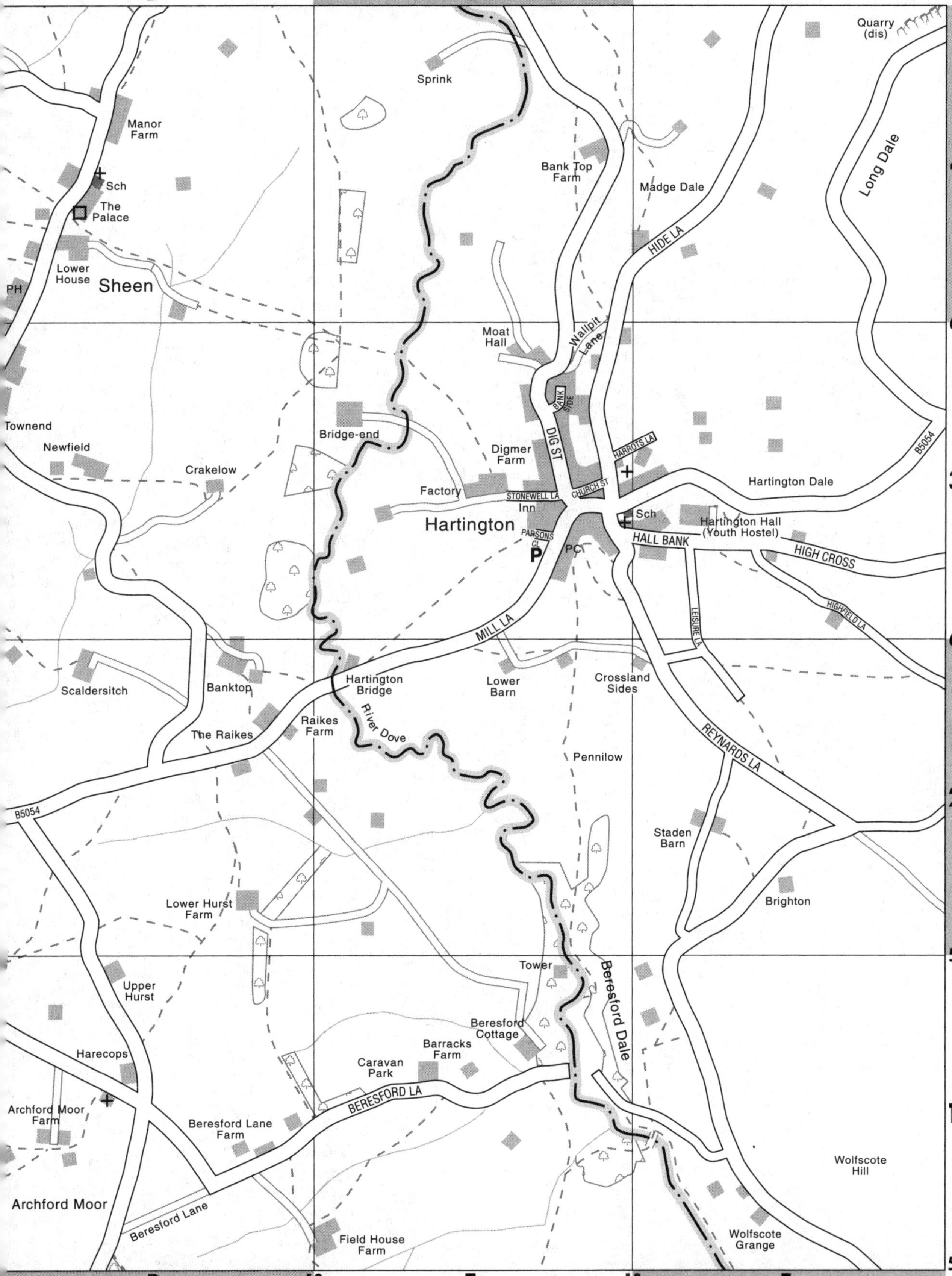
Quarry (dis)
Sprink
Manor Farm
Sch
The Palace
Lower House
Sheen
PH
Bank Top Farm
Madge Dale
Long Dale
HIDE LA
Moat Hall
Wallpit Lane
BANK SIDE
DIG ST
HARROTS LA
Townend
Newfield
Crakelow
Bridge-end
Digmer Farm
Factory
STONEWELL LA
CHURCH ST
Inn
Hartington
PARSONS CL
P
PC
Sch
Hartington Hall (Youth Hostel)
Hartington Dale
B5054
HALL BANK
HIGH CROSS
HIGHFIELD LA
LEISURE LA
MILL LA
Scaldersitch
Banktop
Hartington Bridge
Lower Barn
Crossland Sides
The Raikes
Raikes Farm
River Dove
Pennilow
REYNARDS LA
B5054
Staden Barn
Brighton
Lower Hurst Farm
Upper Hurst
Tower
Beresford Dale
Beresford Cottage
Barracks Farm
Harecops
Caravan Park
Archford Moor Farm
BERESFORD LA
Beresford Lane Farm
Wolfscote Hill
Archford Moor
Beresford Lane
Field House Farm
Wolfscote Grange
4
61
3
60
2
59
1
58
12
13

137
123

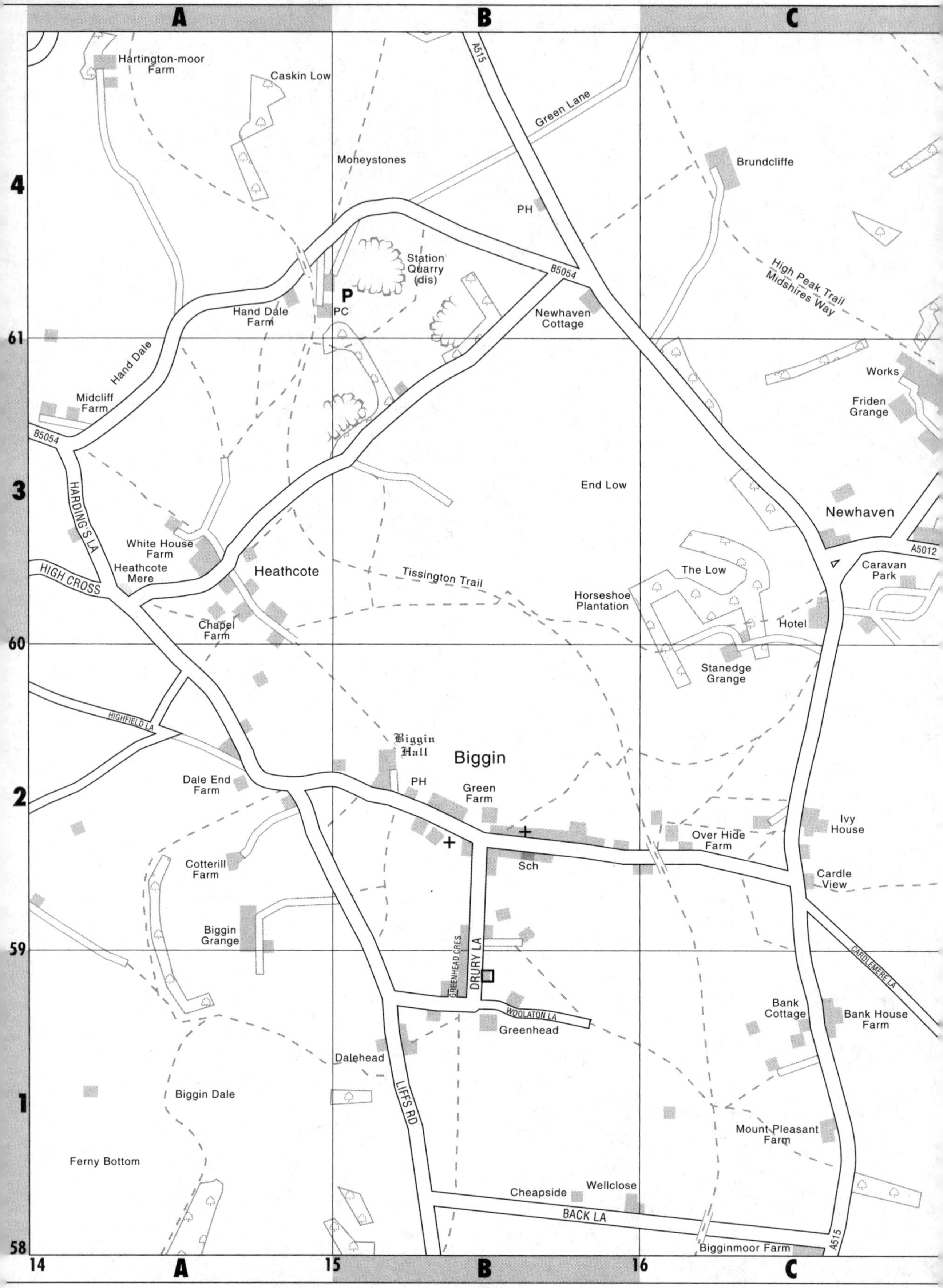

137
150

124
140

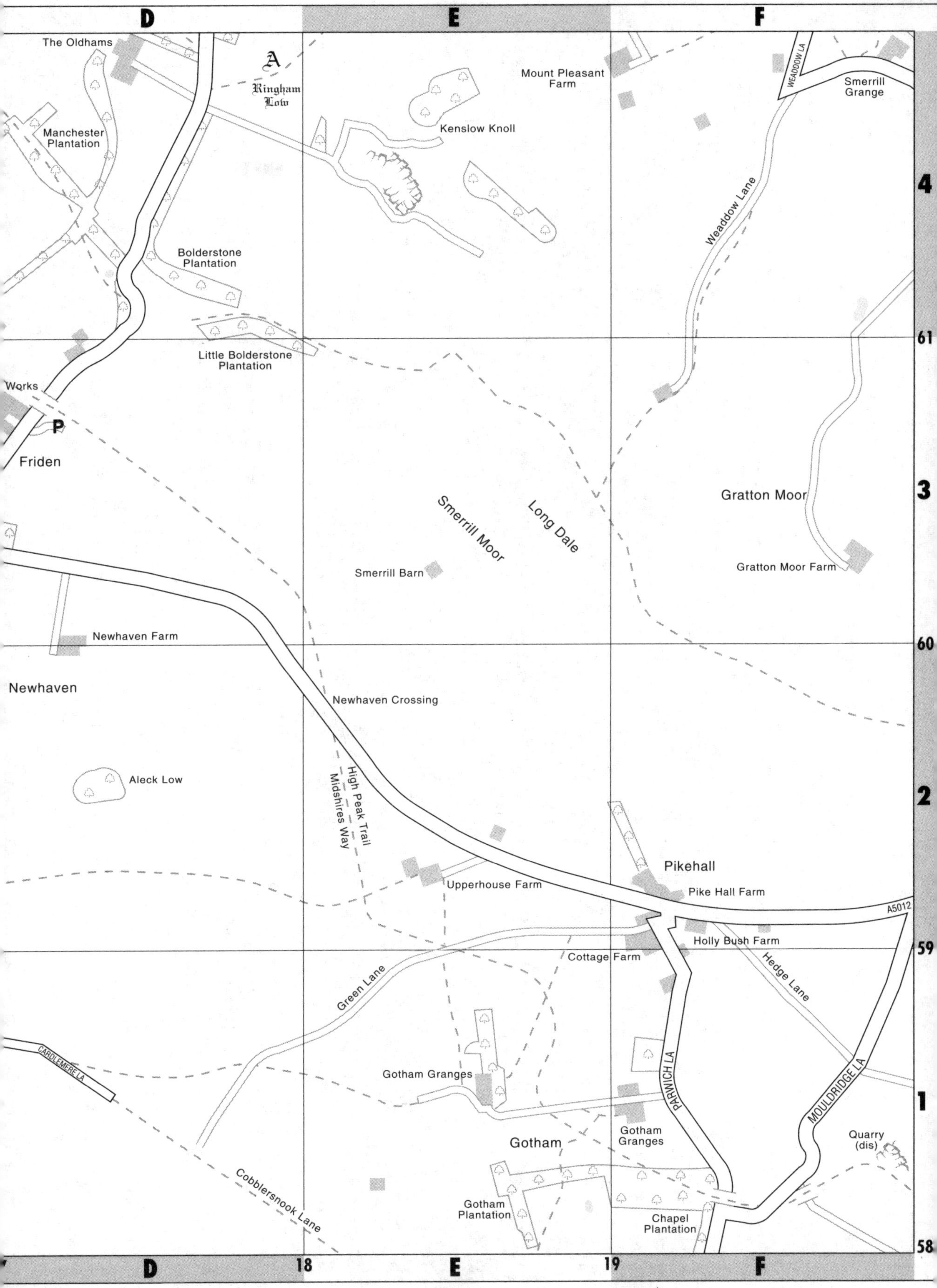

151
140

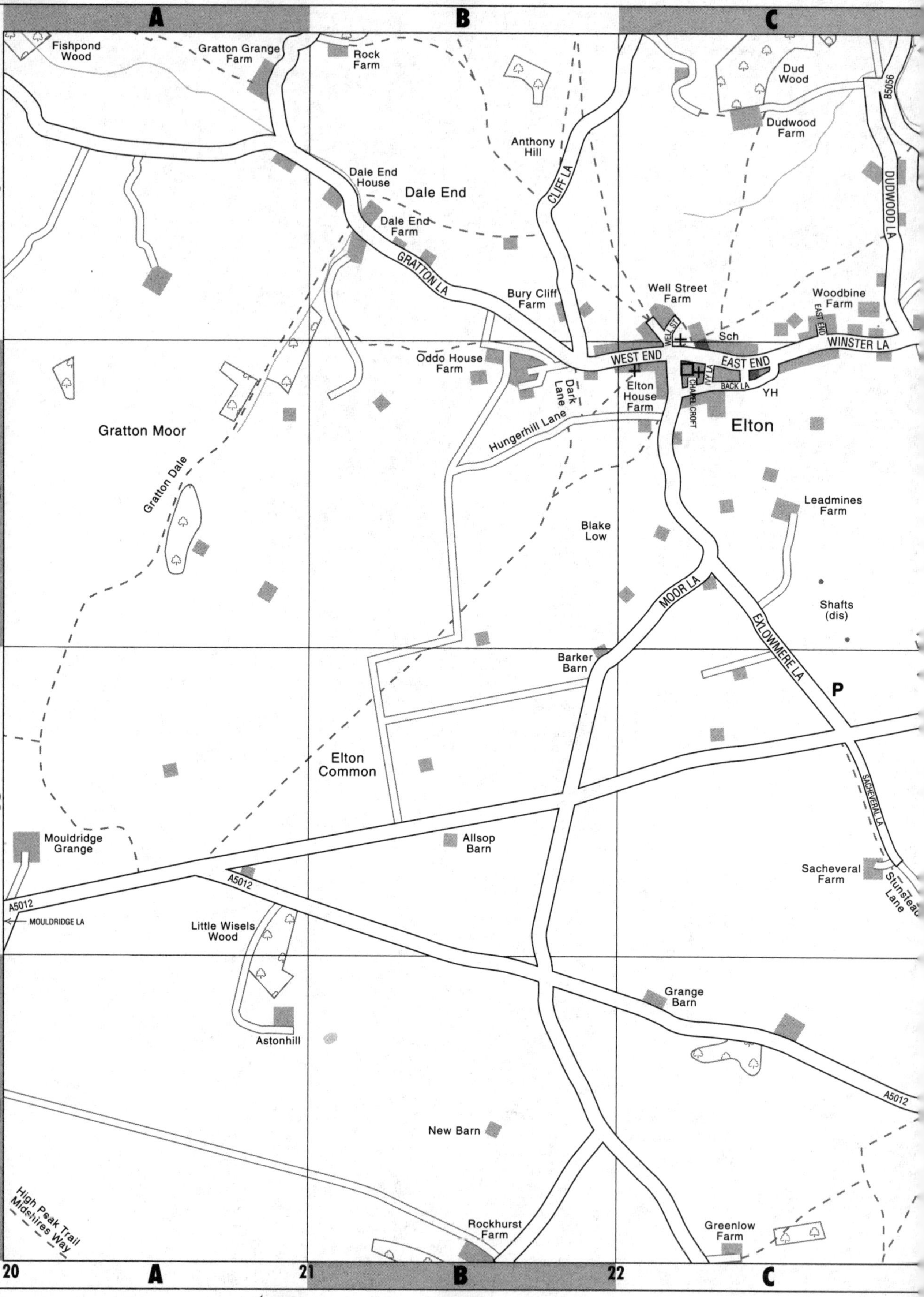
A
B
C
4
61
3
60
2
59
1
58
20
21
22
Fishpond Wood
Gratton Grange Farm
Rock Farm
Dud Wood
B5056
Dudwood Farm
Anthony Hill
Dale End House
Dale End
Dale End Farm
CLIFF LA
DUDWOOD LA
GRATTON LA
Bury Cliff Farm
Well Street Farm
Woodbine Farm
WELL ST
Sch
EAST END
WINSTER LA
WEST END
EAST END
Oddo House Farm
Dark Lane
Elton House Farm
BACK LA
YH
CHAPEL CROFT
Elton
Hungerhill Lane
Gratton Moor
Gratton Dale
Leadmines Farm
Blake Low
MOOR LA
Shafts (dis)
EXLOWMERE LA
Barker Barn
P
Elton Common
SACHEVERAL LA
Mouldridge Grange
Allsop Barn
Sacheveral Farm
A5012
A5012
MOULDRIDGE LA
Little Wisels Wood
Grange Barn
Astonhill
A5012
New Barn
High Peak Trail
Midshires Way
Rockhurst Farm
Greenlow Farm

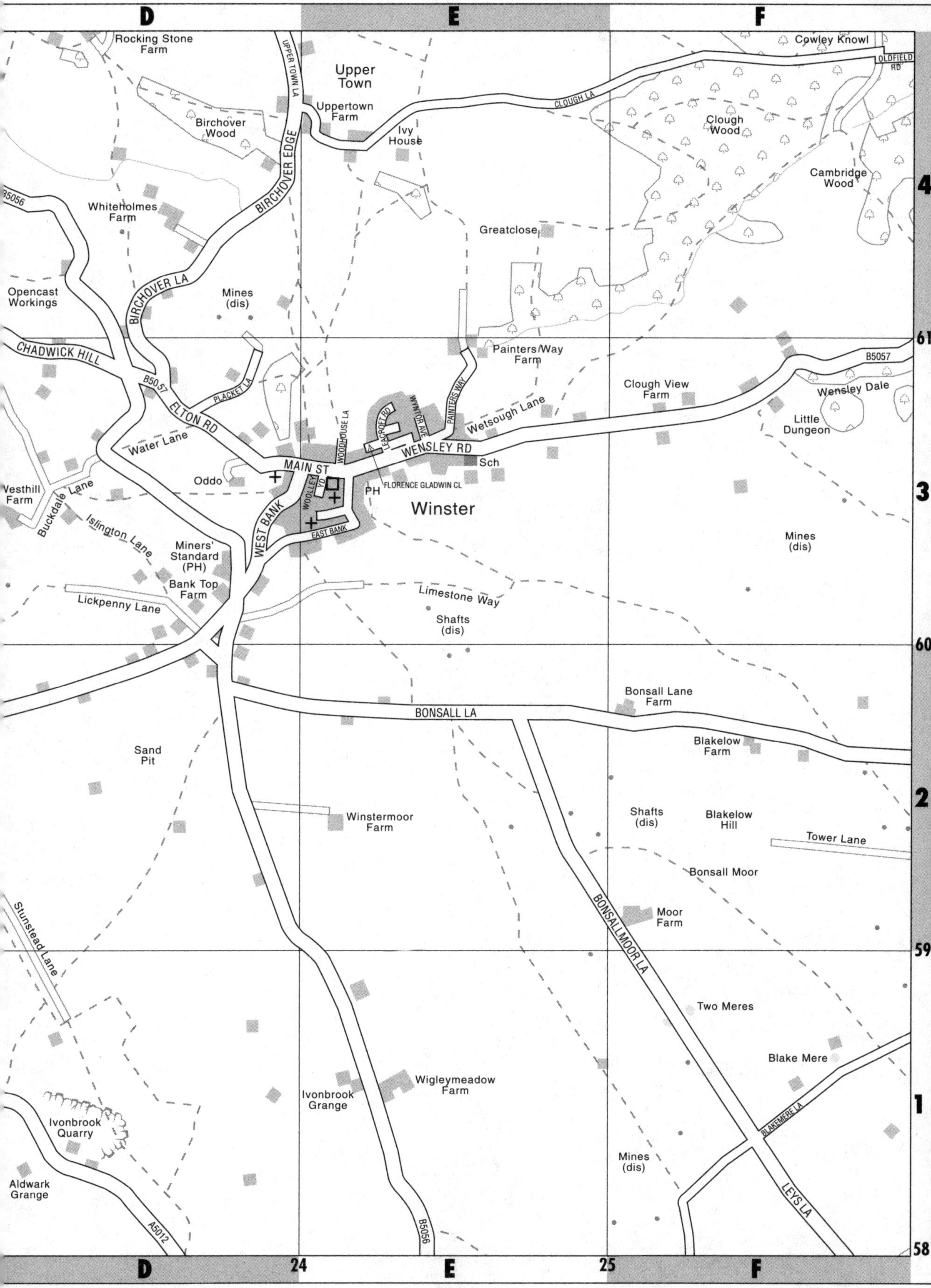
D
E
F
Rocking Stone Farm
Upper Town
Uppertown Farm
Ivy House
Cowley Knowl
OLDFIELD RD
CLOUGH LA
Clough Wood
Cambridge Wood
Birchover Wood
UPPER TOWN LA
BIRCHOVER EDGE
B5056
Whiteholmes Farm
Greatclose
Opencast Workings
BIRCHOVER LA
Mines (dis)
4
61
CHADWICK HILL
B5057
ELTON RD
PLACKET LA
Painters Way Farm
PAINTERS WAY
WYNTOR AVE
LEACROFT RD
WOODHOUSE LA
Clough View Farm
B5057
Wensley Dale
Little Dungeon
Wetsough Lane
Water Lane
WENSLEY RD
MAIN ST
Sch
Oddo
WOOLLEY YD
FLORENCE GLADWIN CL
PH
Winster
Vesthill Farm
Buckdale Lane
Islington Lane
WEST BANK
EAST BANK
3
Mines (dis)
Miners' Standard (PH)
Bank Top Farm
Lickpenny Lane
Limestone Way
Shafts (dis)
60
Bonsall Lane Farm
BONSALL LA
Blakelow Farm
Sand Pit
2
Winstermoor Farm
Shafts (dis)
Blakelow Hill
Tower Lane
Bonsall Moor
Moor Farm
BONSALLMOOR LA
Stunstead Lane
59
Two Meres
Blake Mere
Wigleymeadow Farm
Ivonbrook Grange
1
Ivonbrook Quarry
BLAKEMERE LA
Mines (dis)
Aldwark Grange
A5012
B5056
LEYS LA
58
D
24
E
25
F

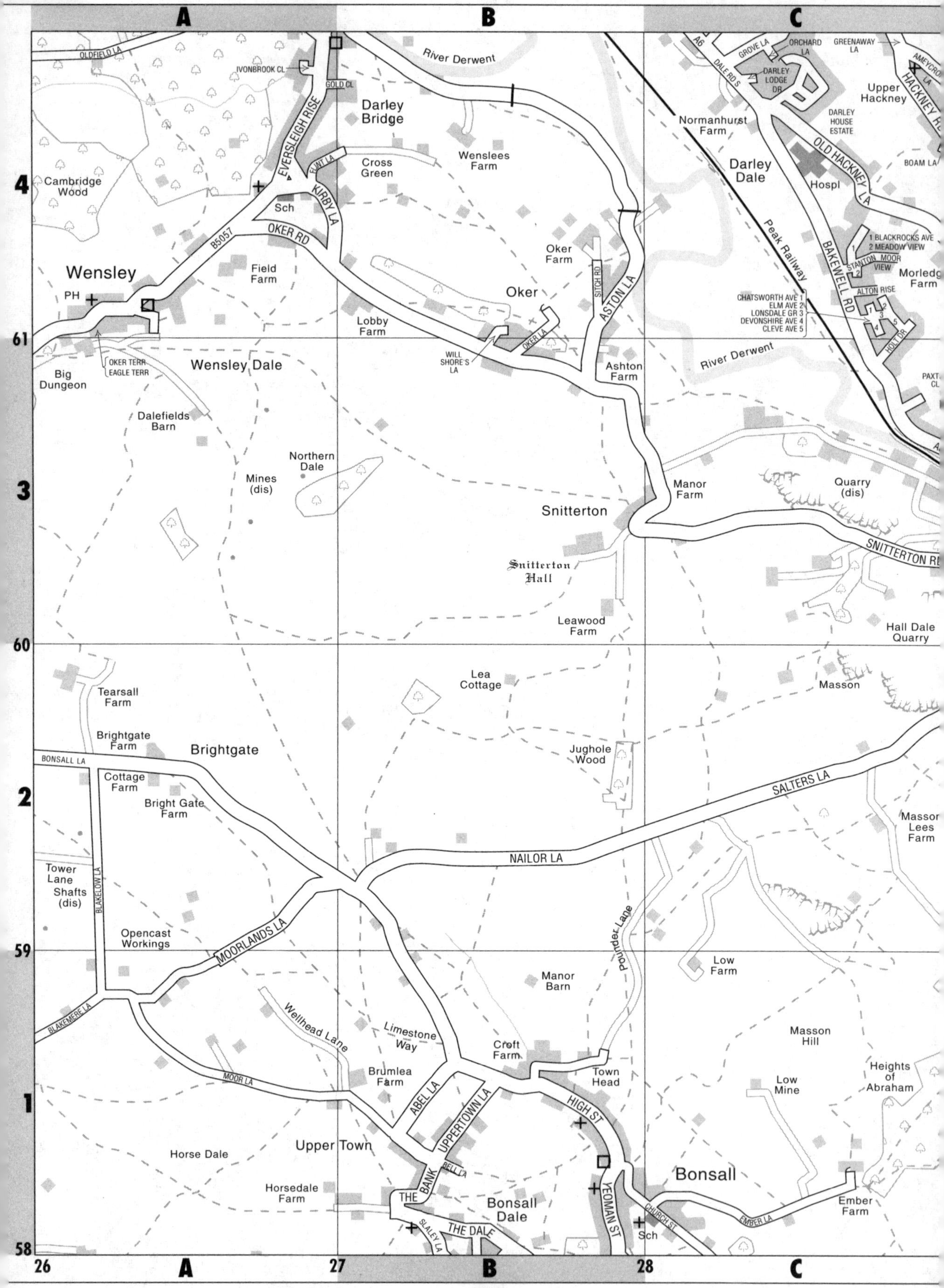
A
B
C
4
3
2
1
61
60
59
58
26
27
28
OLDFIELD LA
IVONBROOK CL
GOLD CL
EVERSLEIGH RISE
FLINT LA
KIRBY LA
Sch
B5057
OKER RD
River Derwent
Darley Bridge
Cross Green
Wenslees Farm
Cambridge Wood
Wensley
PH
Field Farm
Lobby Farm
WILL SHORE'S LA
OKER LA
Oker
Oker Farm
SITCH RD
ASTON LA
Ashton Farm
Big Dungeon
OKER TERR
EAGLE TERR
Wensley Dale
Dalefields Barn
Northern Dale
Mines (dis)
Snitterton
Snitterton Hall
Leawood Farm
Manor Farm
A6
DALE RD S
GROVE LA
ORCHARD LA
DARLEY LODGE DR
GREENAWAY LA
AMEYCROFT LA
HACKNEY RD
Upper Hackney
Normanhurst Farm
Darley Dale
DARLEY HOUSE ESTATE
OLD HACKNEY LA
BOAM LA
Hospl
Peak Railway
BAKEWELL RD
1 BLACKROCKS AVE
2 MEADOW VIEW
STANTON MOOR VIEW
Morledge Farm
ALTON RISE
CHATSWORTH AVE 1
ELM AVE 2
LONSDALE GR 3
DEVONSHIRE AVE 4
CLEVE AVE 5
HOLT DR
River Derwent
Quarry (dis)
SNITTERTON RD
Hall Dale Quarry
Masson
Tearsall Farm
Lea Cottage
Brightgate Farm
Brightgate
BONSALL LA
Cottage Farm
Bright Gate Farm
Jughole Wood
SALTERS LA
Masson Lees Farm
NAILOR LA
Tower Lane Shafts (dis)
BLAKELOW LA
Opencast Workings
MOORLANDS LA
Pounder Lane
Low Farm
Manor Barn
BLAKEMERE LA
Wellhead Lane
Limestone Way
Croft Farm
Masson Hill
Town Head
Heights of Abraham
MOOR LA
Brumlea Farm
ABEL LA
UPPERTOWN LA
HIGH ST
Low Mine
Horse Dale
Upper Town
THE BANK
BELL LA
Bonsall
Horsedale Farm
THE DALE
Bonsall Dale
YEOMAN ST
CHURCH ST
EMBER LA
Ember Farm
SLALEY LA
Sch

D E F

Bent Farm
AMEYCROFT LA
Upper Hackney
Mount Pleasant Farm
FARLEY HILL
BURNETT LA
HACKNEY RD
OLD HACKNEY LA
UNDERWOOD TERR
Goodwin's Wood
Sandy Lane Farm
SANDY LA
Golf Course
CH
Portland Grange Farm
Bentley Bridge
Springfield Farm
QUARRY LA
Lumshill Quarry (dis)
FOXHOLES LA
HEATHFIELD
PINEWOOD RD
HIGH RIDGE
HURKER RISE
WOLDS RISE
FALCON CROSS
CAVENDISH PARK
BENT LA
BIDSTON CL
MOORFIELD
The Wolds
WELLINGTON CL
BENTLEY CL
GRITSTONE RD
CHESTERFIELD RD
Sch
LUMSDALE
THE TERR
Bentley Brook
Sch
CROOK STILE
SMEDLEY ST W
QUARRY BANK
ACORN RIDGE
CAVENDISH RD
Coll
GEORGE RD
AMBERDENE
WEST CRES
HURDS HOLLOW
DRABBLES RD
THE CLOSE
SYCAMORE RD
JOHN ST
FAR GREEN
JACKSON TOR RD
JACKSON RD
COBDEN RD
WELLINGTON ST
Dimple
COLLINGWOOD CRES
SHERIFF DR
WILMOT'S
Sch
ALL SAINTS RD
MALPAS RD
WOOLLEY RD
SMEDLEY ST
WELLINGTON ST
CARSON CROFT
HOPEWELL R
RUTLAND ST
RUTLAND AVE
WELLFIELD
WELLFIELD ST
Coll
Convent
ASKER LA
BULL LA
WISHING STONE WAY
HAWLEYS CL
MOOREDGE DR
HIGHFIELD DR
SMITHS HILL RISE
DAYS MILL CL
DALESFIELD
MEGDALE
WYVERN CL
DIMPLE RD
ALLEN HILL
PROSPECT DR
DIMPLE CRES
MALVERN GDNS
Off
Off
Coll
SMEDLEY ST E
SPRINGFIELD RISE
FOXHOLES LA
Lumsdale Farm
Lumsdale
Oakedge House
OAKSEDGE LA
BAKEWELL RD
Peak Railway
MATLOCK
IMPERIAL RD
EDGE RD
EDGEFOLD RD
TH
BANK GDNS
BANK RD
NEW ST
HENRY ST
OAK RD
Sch
Matlock Bank
VICTORIA CT
SCHOOL RD
Schs
HILLTOPS VIEW
HAZEL GR
HURST RISE
LUMSDALE CRES
LILYBANK CL
POPE CARR RD
F Sta
TURNPIKE
THE LIMES CL
METTESFORD
FAIRHOLMES
OVERDALE
Matlock Station
SNITTERTON RD
CROWN SQ
A6
LIMES
GROVE WLK
FIRS PARADE
STEEP TURNPIKE
LIME TREE RD
LYNHOLMES RD
HURST RISE
PC
PARK HEAD RD
CAUSEWAY LA
Liby
1 ST JOSEPH'S ST
2 LIME GROVE AVE
Matlock Green
LINDEN GR
RIBER VIEW CL
Matlock Bridge
HOLT LA
DENE FIELDS CT
Amb Sta
OLD LIME CT
Mill
Mill
Mill
SALTERS LA
Masson Mount
OLDE DERWENT AVE
ENGLISH RD
A615
ST GILES WLK
SHERWOOD RD
MORNINGTON RISE
A632
SMUSE LA
Yewtree Farm
OLD COACH RD
Ind Est
BROOKFIELD WAY
Limestone Way
KNOWLESTON PL
MATLOCK GREEN
ALFRETON RD
STONEY WAY
Mon
CHURCH ST
BROOK LEA
PARK CL
Matlock Cliff
A615
Greenhills Farm
PIC TOR LA
Sch
Old Matlock
COMMON WOOD
Hilltop Farm
ST JOHN'S RD
THE SHORTLANDS
BLUEBELL CROFT
WHITE WOODS WAY
Sch
Shining Cliff
DALE RD
PC
River Derwent
High Tor Tunnel
TOR RISE
PUMP CL
Netherclose Farm
Riber Castle (Wildlife Park)
Riber
Masson Farm
Riber Hall Farm
High Tor
HIGH TOR RD
STARKHOLMES RD
Wards End
Riber Hill
Riber Hall
RIBER RD
Works
Rec Gd
Carr Lane Farm
CARR LA
Matlock Dale
Twr
Cable Car
RIBER RD
Sch
WHITE TOR RD
Starkholmes
Yew Tree Farm
Balk Wood
PC's
MASSON RD
HOPE TERR
HOLME RD
Matlock Bath Station
Hearthstone
HEARTHSTONE LA
LITTLEMOOR LA
Littlemoor Farm
UPPERWOOD RD
WEST BANK
WATERLOO RD
NORTH PARADE
BRUNSWOOD RD
PC's
Sitch Farm
Littlemoor
ORCHARD RD
TEMPLE RD
SOUTH PARADE
Jubilee Bridge
Matlock Bath
Caravan Park
Hearthstone Farm
Hearthstone Lane
Littlemoor Wood Farm
WILLERBLEY RD
Littlemoor Wood
Mus
PC
A6
DERBY RD
4
61
3
60
2
59
1
58
30
31

D E F

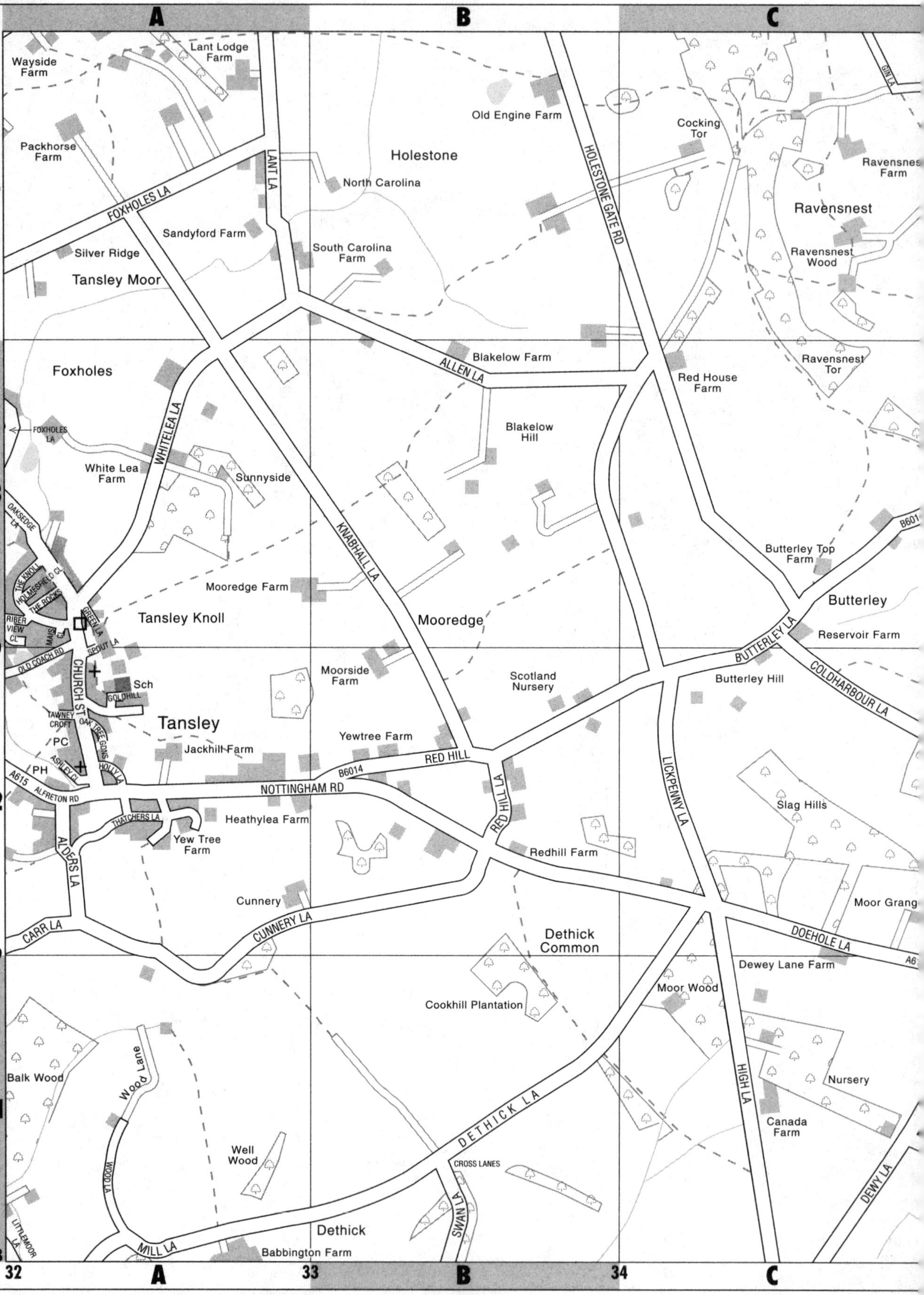
A
B
C
Wayside Farm
Lant Lodge Farm
Packhorse Farm
Old Engine Farm
Cocking Tor
Holestone
North Carolina
Ravensnest Farm
Ravensnest
FOXHOLES LA
LANT LA
HOLESTONE GATE RD
Sandyford Farm
South Carolina Farm
Ravensnest Wood
Silver Ridge
Tansley Moor
Foxholes
Blakelow Farm
ALLEN LA
Red House Farm
Ravensnest Tor
FOXHOLES LA
Blakelow Hill
WHITELEA LA
White Lea Farm
Sunnyside
KNABHALL LA
OAKSEDGE LA
THE KNOLL
HOLMESFIELD CL
THE ROCKS
Butterley Top Farm
B601
Mooredge Farm
Butterley
RIBER VIEW CL
MAIS CL
GREEN LA
Tansley Knoll
Mooredge
BUTTERLEY LA
Reservoir Farm
SPOUT LA
OLD COACH RD
CHURCH ST
Sch
GOLDHILL
Moorside Farm
Scotland Nursery
Butterley Hill
COLDHARBOUR LA
TAWNEY CROFT
OAK TREE GDNS
Tansley
PC
Yewtree Farm
Jackhill Farm
RED HILL
ASHLEY CL
HOLLY LA
B6014
PH
A615
ALFRETON RD
NOTTINGHAM RD
RED HILL LA
LICKPENNY LA
Slag Hills
THATCHERS LA
Heathylea Farm
Yew Tree Farm
ALDERS LA
Redhill Farm
Cunnery
Moor Grang
CARR LA
CUNNERY LA
Dethick Common
DOEHOLE LA
A6
Dewey Lane Farm
Moor Wood
Cookhill Plantation
Wood Lane
Balk Wood
Nursery
HIGH LA
DETHICK LA
Canada Farm
Well Wood
WOOD LA
CROSS LANES
DEWY LA
LITTLEMOOR LA
SWAN LA
Dethick
MILL LA
Babbington Farm
4
61
3
60
2
59
1
58
32
33
34

D
E
F
Stars Wood
Back La
Wash Farm
DICKLANT LA
B6036
STUBBEN EDGE LA
Ridgewell Farm
WOODHEAD LA
HANDLEY LA
Elmtree
HUNT LA
GIN LA
PH
SHEEPWASH LA
DALEBANK LA
Dalebank Farm
BADGER LA
Handley
BROWN LA
Dalebank
Milltown
ASHOVER NEW RD
HAWTHORNE CL
Sch
BERRISFORD LA
B6036
River Amber
PH
HAY LA
WHITE HORSE LA
Woolley Moor
TEMPERANCE HILL
B6014
Raven House
OAKSTEDGE LA
Woolley Farm
Fletcherhill
Boar Farm
Greenfield Farm
Chapel Farm
PH
P
PC
Hole Wood
Walnut Farm
STONEROWS LA
Smithy Cottage
Castle Farm
SOUTH HILL LA
Ashover Hay Farm
QUARRY LA
Ogston Sailing Club
BUTTERLEY LA
DARK LA
PC
P
Ashover Hay
Yew Tree Farm
Woolley
Coalpit Wood
Clattercotes Wood
Top Farm
Ogston Reservoir
HURST LA
Carr Brook
Berridge-lane Farm
BERRIDGE LA
WHITECARR LA
Whitecarr Farm
OGSTON NEW RD
Picnic Site
P
Ogston Carr
Ogston Hall
615
COLDHARBOUR LA
Highoredish Farm
Carr Farm
Trinity Chapel (rems of)
Trinity Farm
Sycamore Farm
Church Farm
Mathersgrave
CARR LA
Dewy Lane Farm
SCHOOL LA
SCHOOL LA
CHURCH LA
Brackenfield
Brackenfield Green
Broomhill
Home Farm
PH
DEWY LA
Dewdale Farm
Doehole
MATLOCK RD
MILLERS LA
Grange Farm
BRACKENFIELD LA
Green Farm
BUTTERFIELD LA
Shipman's Farm
Wiнny Brook
Butterfield Farm
Lindwaylane Farm
Roadnook Farm
Lindwaylane Farm
LINDWAY LA
Lindwaylane End Farm
A615
BACK LA
4
61
3
60
2
59
1
58
36
37

145
131

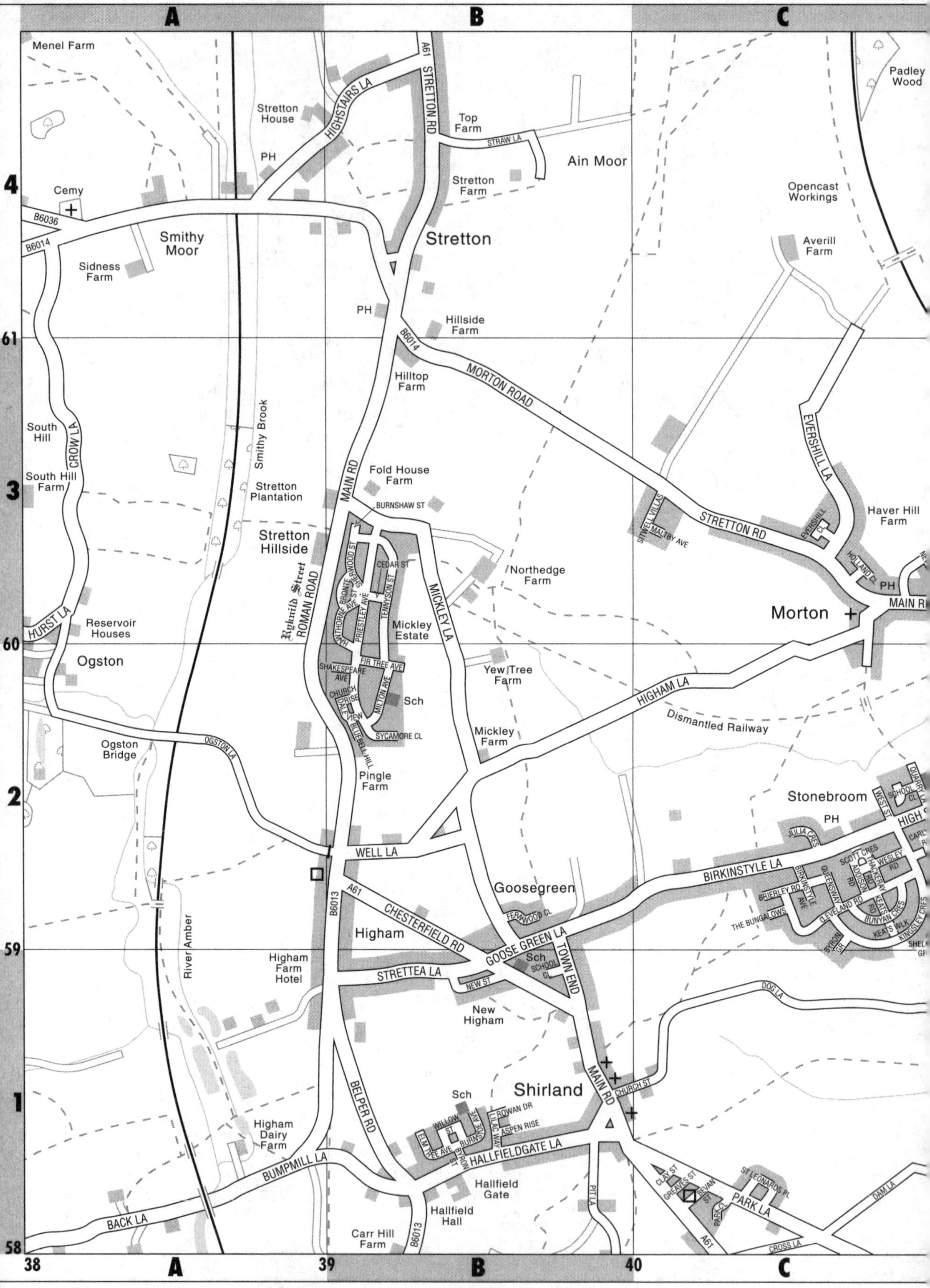

145
158

D E F

4
61
3
60
2
59
1
58

D 42 E 43 F

147
133

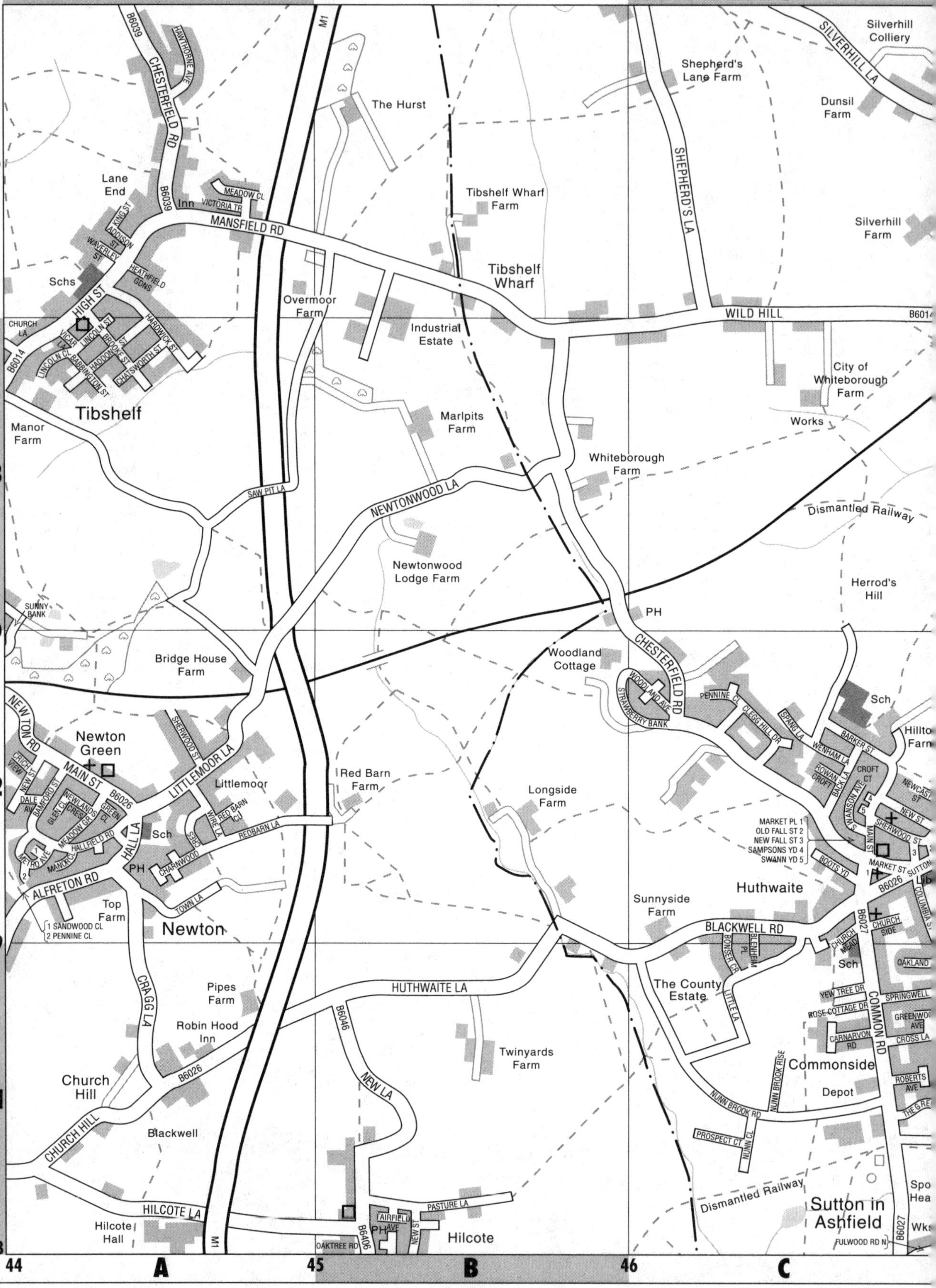
A
B
C
Tibshelf
Lane End
Schs
Inn
Manor Farm
Overmoor Farm
The Hurst
Tibshelf Wharf Farm
Tibshelf Wharf
Industrial Estate
Marlpits Farm
Whiteborough Farm
Shepherd's Lane Farm
Silverhill Colliery
Dunsil Farm
Silverhill Farm
City of Whiteborough Farm
Works
Dismantled Railway
Herrod's Hill
Newtonwood Lodge Farm
Bridge House Farm
Newton Green
Littlemoor
Red Barn Farm
Longside Farm
Woodland Cottage
PH
Sch
Huthwaite
Sunnyside Farm
Top Farm
Newton
Pipes Farm
Robin Hood Inn
Church Hill
Blackwell
Twinyards Farm
The County Estate
Commonside
Depot
Hilcote Hall
Hilcote
Sutton in Ashfield
Dismantled Railway
CHESTERFIELD RD
MANSFIELD RD
WILD HILL
SHEPHERD'S LA
SILVERHILL LA
NEWTONWOOD LA
SAW PIT LA
HIGH ST
LITTLEMOOR LA
MAIN ST
HALL LA
ALFRETON RD
TOWN LA
REDBARN LA
CHARNWOOD
HUTHWAITE LA
CRAGG LA
CHURCH HILL
HILCOTE LA
NEW LA
PASTURE LA
BLACKWELL RD
COMMON RD
NUNN BROOK RD
PROSPECT CT
M1
B6014
B6039
B6026
B6046
B6406
B6027
1 SANDWOOD CL
2 PENNINE CL
MARKET PL 1
OLD FALL ST 2
NEW FALL ST 3
SAMPSONS YD 4
SWANN YD 5
4
3
61
60
2
59
1
58
44
45
46

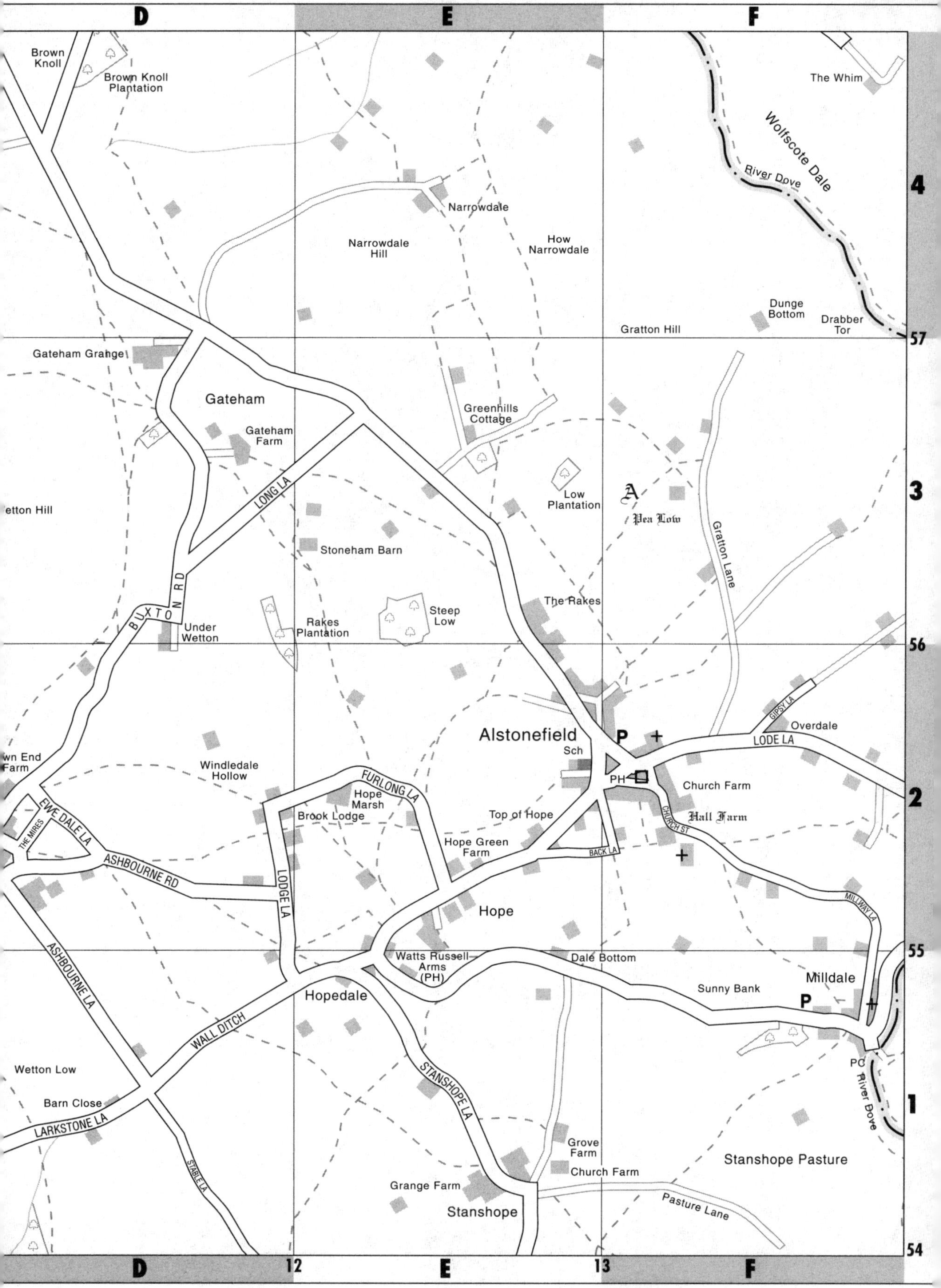
D
E
F
Brown Knoll
Brown Knoll Plantation
The Whim
Wolfscote Dale
River Dove
4
Narrowdale
Narrowdale Hill
How Narrowdale
Dunge Bottom
Drabber Tor
Gratton Hill
57
Gateham Grange
Gateham
Gateham Farm
Greenhills Cottage
LONG LA
Low Plantation
Pea Low
3
etton Hill
Stoneham Barn
Gratton Lane
BUXTON RD
The Rakes
Under Wetton
Rakes Plantation
Steep Low
56
Alstonefield
Sch
P
GIPSY LA
Overdale
LODE LA
wn End Farm
Windledale Hollow
FURLONG LA
Hope Marsh
PH
Church Farm
2
EWE DALE LA
THE MIRES
Brook Lodge
Top of Hope
CHURCH ST
Hall Farm
ASHBOURNE RD
Hope Green Farm
BACK LA
LODGE LA
Hope
MILLWAY LA
ASHBOURNE LA
Watts Russell Arms (PH)
Dale Bottom
55
Milldale
Hopedale
Sunny Bank
WALL DITCH
PC
Wetton Low
STANSHOPE LA
River Dove
Barn Close
1
LARKSTONE LA
Grove Farm
Stanshope Pasture
STABLE LA
Church Farm
Grange Farm
Pasture Lane
Stanshope
54
12
13

149
138

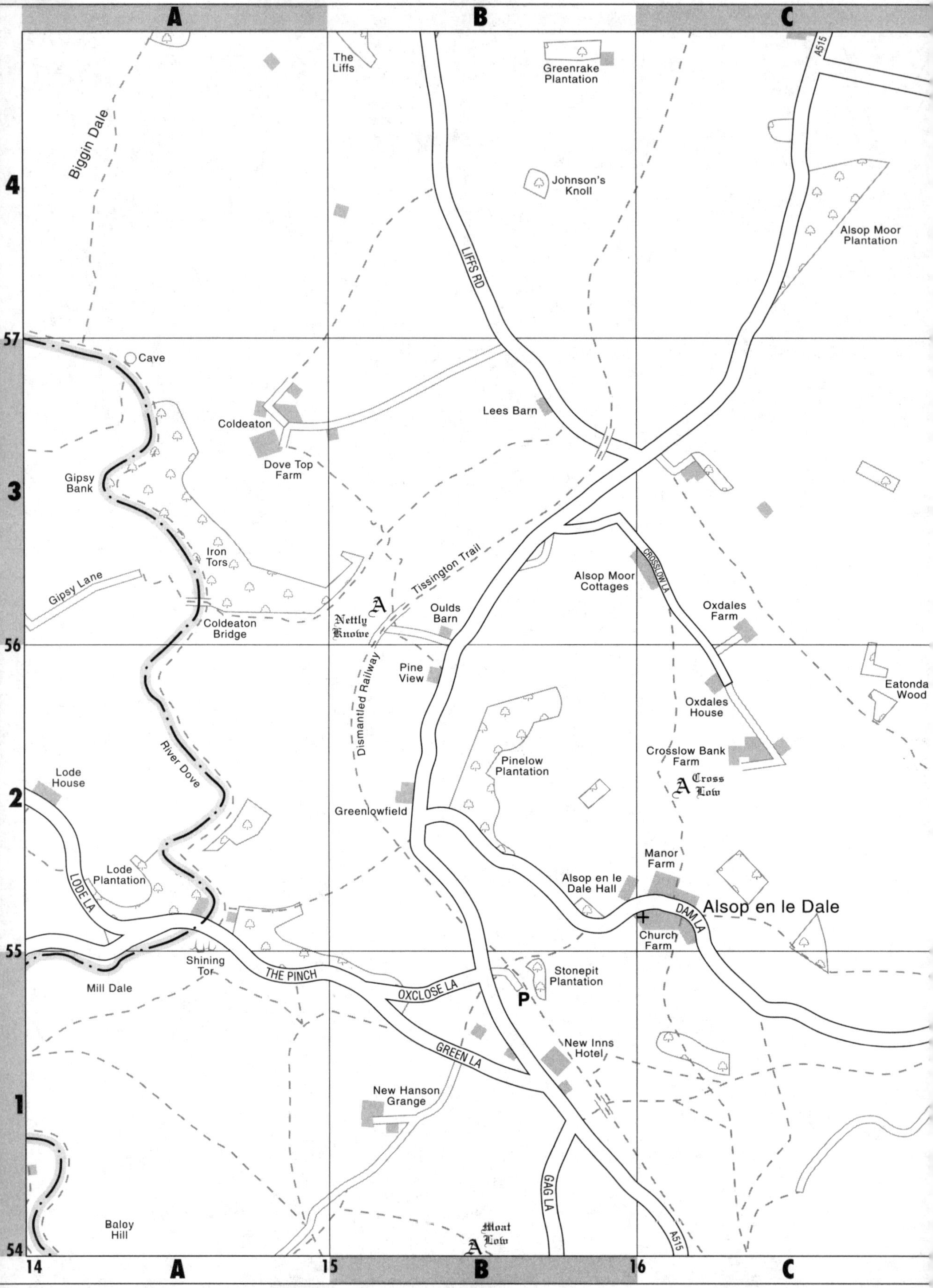

149
161

139
152

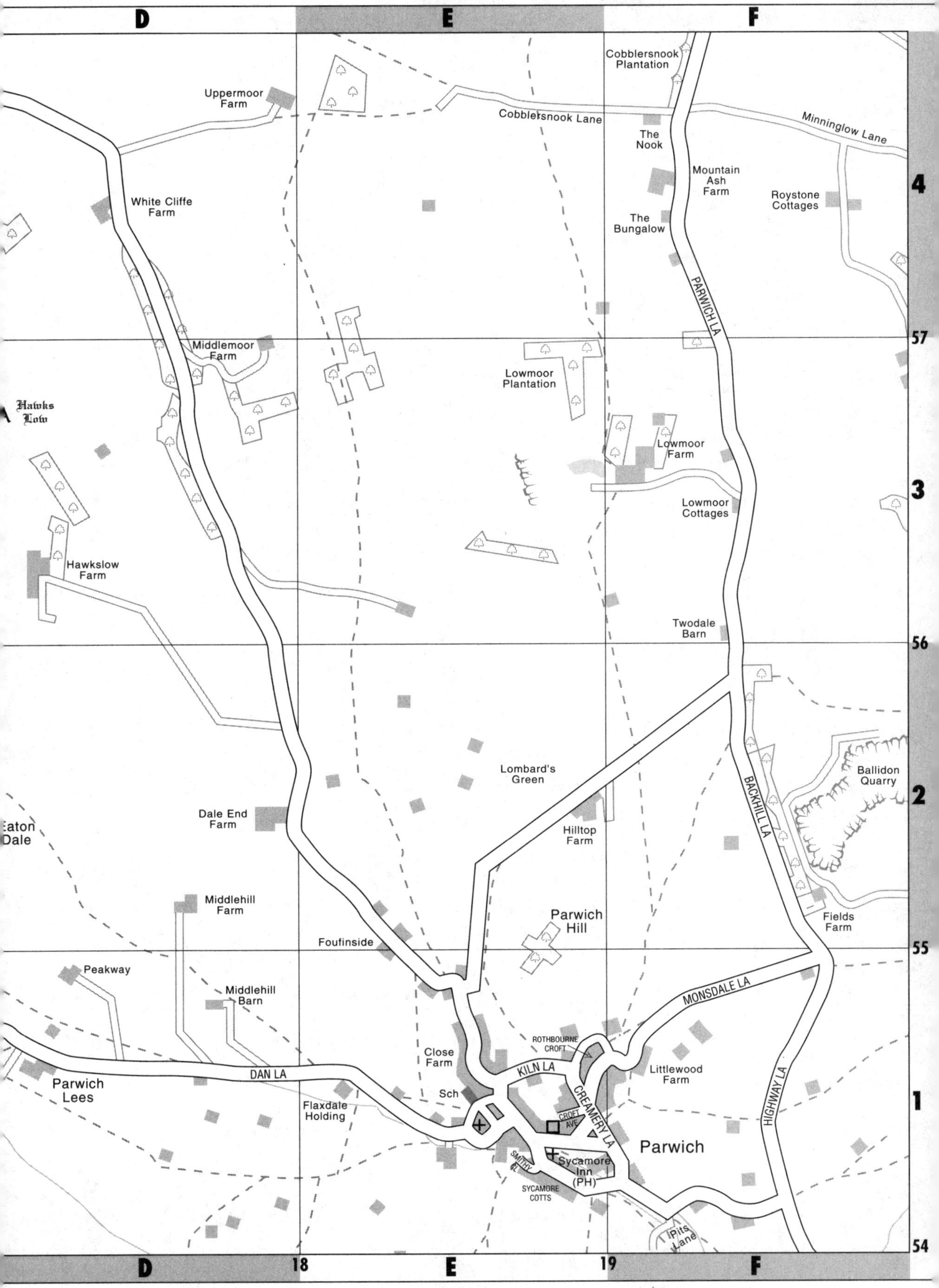

162
152

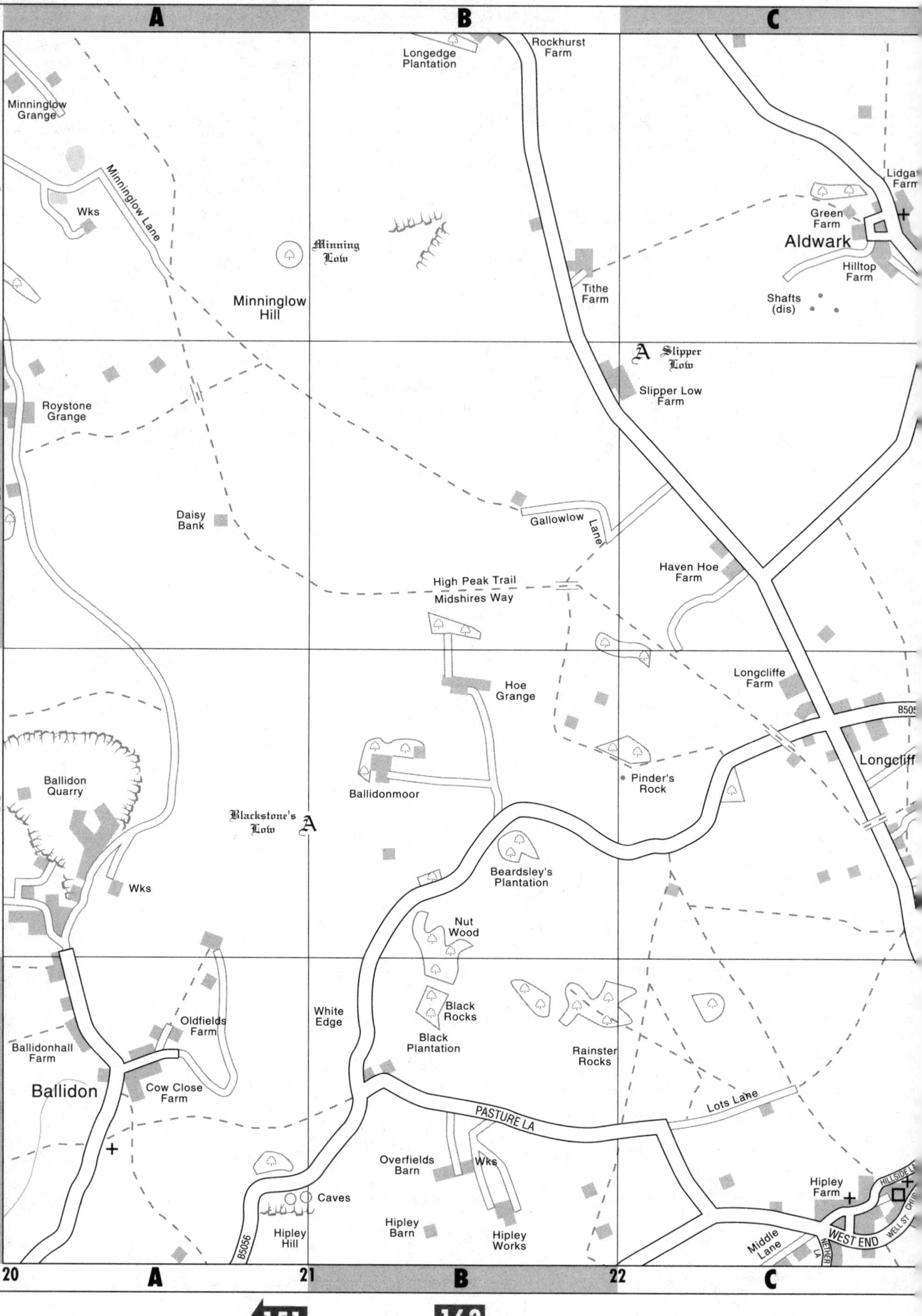
A
B
C
4
57
3
56
2
55
1
54
20
21
22
Longedge Plantation
Rockhurst Farm
Minninglow Grange
Wks
Minninglow Lane
Minning Low
Minninglow Hill
Lidgate Farm
Green Farm
Aldwark
Hilltop Farm
Tithe Farm
Shafts (dis)
Slipper Low
Slipper Low Farm
Roystone Grange
Daisy Bank
Gallowlow Lane
Haven Hoe Farm
High Peak Trail
Midshires Way
Hoe Grange
Longcliffe Farm
B5056
Longcliffe
Ballidon Quarry
Ballidonmoor
Pinder's Rock
Blackstone's Low
Wks
Beardsley's Plantation
Nut Wood
White Edge
Black Rocks
Black Plantation
Rainster Rocks
Oldfields Farm
Ballidonhall Farm
Ballidon
Cow Close Farm
PASTURE LA
Lots Lane
Overfields Barn
Wks
Caves
Hipley Farm
HILLSIDE LA
CHURCH ST
WELL ST
WEST END
NETHER LA
Middle Lane
Hipley Barn
Hipley Hill
Hipley Works
B5056

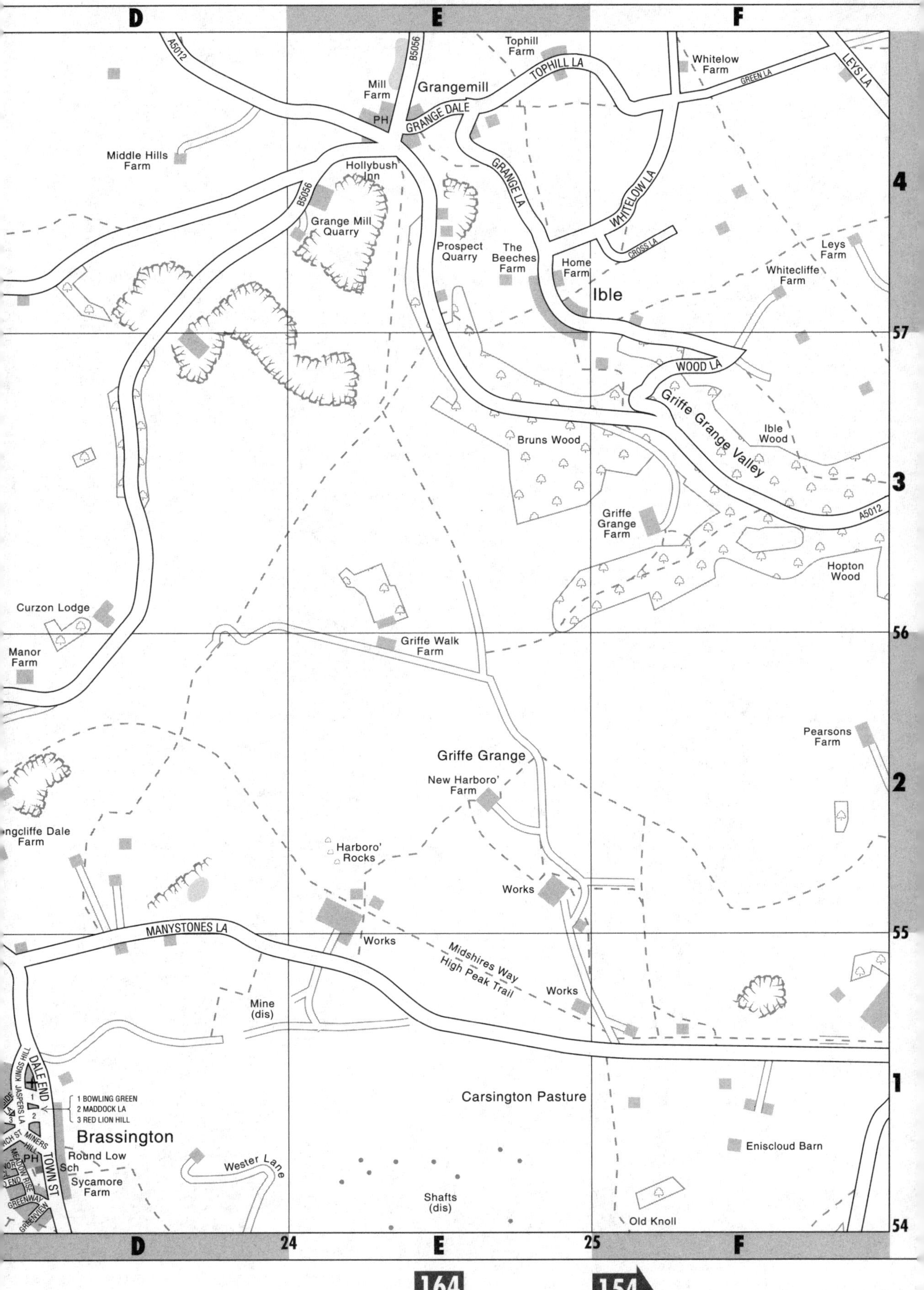
D
E
F
A5012
B5056
Tophill Farm
Whitelow Farm
GREEN LA
LEYS LA
Mill Farm
Grangemill
TOPHILL LA
PH
GRANGE DALE
Middle Hills Farm
Hollybush Inn
GRANGE LA
WHITELOW LA
4
Grange Mill Quarry
Prospect Quarry
The Beeches Farm
Home Farm
CROSS LA
Leys Farm
Whitecliffe Farm
Ible
57
WOOD LA
Griffe Grange Valley
Ible Wood
Bruns Wood
3
Griffe Grange Farm
Hopton Wood
Curzon Lodge
Manor Farm
56
Griffe Walk Farm
Pearsons Farm
Griffe Grange
New Harboro' Farm
2
ngcliffe Dale Farm
Harboro' Rocks
Works
MANYSTONES LA
55
Works
Midshires Way
High Peak Trail
Works
Mine (dis)
DALE END
1 BOWLING GREEN
2 MADDOCK LA
3 RED LION HILL
JASPERS LA
MINERS HILL
Carsington Pasture
1
Brassington
Round Low
PH
Sch
TOWN ST
Sycamore Farm
Wester Lane
Eniscloud Barn
Shafts (dis)
Old Knoll
GREENWAY
GREENVIEW
54
D
24
E
25
F

A
B
C
Leys
Bonsall Mines (dis)
LEYS LA
Sunnyside Farm
Byeway Lane
SLALEY LA
Fairy Lane
THE DALE
Slaley Farm
Sunnyside Farm
Slaley
Bonsall Wood
VIA GELLIA RD
Via Gellia
Black Tor
BLACK TOR RD
Study Farm
Town End Farm
CHURCH ST
CLATTERWAY
PH
Mill Pond
Works
Groaning Tor
Via Gellia Mill
Balleye Quarry
Bonsall Hollow
Slinter Wood
Griffe Grange Valley
Middleton Wood
A5012
B5023
NEW RD
Cemy
BURROWS LA
Hopton Wood
CHAPEL CROFT
DUKE ST
THE GREEN
THE HALL
WATER LA
KING ST
CHAPEL LA
CHURCHILL AVE
STILE CROFT
QUEEN ST
LONGLOAD LA
Dean Hollow
MAIN ST
THE MOOR
DOGHOLE LA
RAIN'S LA
Willowdene Farm
Middleton
THE FIELDS
HILLSIDE
THE ALLEY
Sch
Hopton Quarries
Middleton Moor
Works
Dismantled Railway
DARK LA
CROMFORD
B5035
Rise End
PORTER LA
PH
B5035
MALTHOUSE CL
STEEPLE GRANGE
Arm Lees Farm
Middleton Top Visitor's Centre
Ireland Farm
Intake Quarry
High Peak Trail Midshires Way
Middle Peak
Middlepeak
Wirksworth Industrial Estate
NEW RD
RAVENSTOR RD
Moor Farm
Middle Peak Quarry
OLD LA
CROMFORD LA
Broxendale Farm
SOUGH LA
B5036
Sch
Cemy
CEMETERY LA
Fire Sta
GREEN HILL
THE DALE
HARRISON DR 1
COLDWELL ST 2
CHURCH ST 3
MARKET PL 4
DALE END 5
NORTH END
Sch
Mines (dis)
Norbreck Farm
BOWLING GREEN LA
CROWN YD
B5023
CHAPEL LA
PO
TH
Sch
GREENWAY CROFT
B5035
WEST END
B5035
4
57
3
56
2
55
1
54
26
27
28

143
156

D E F

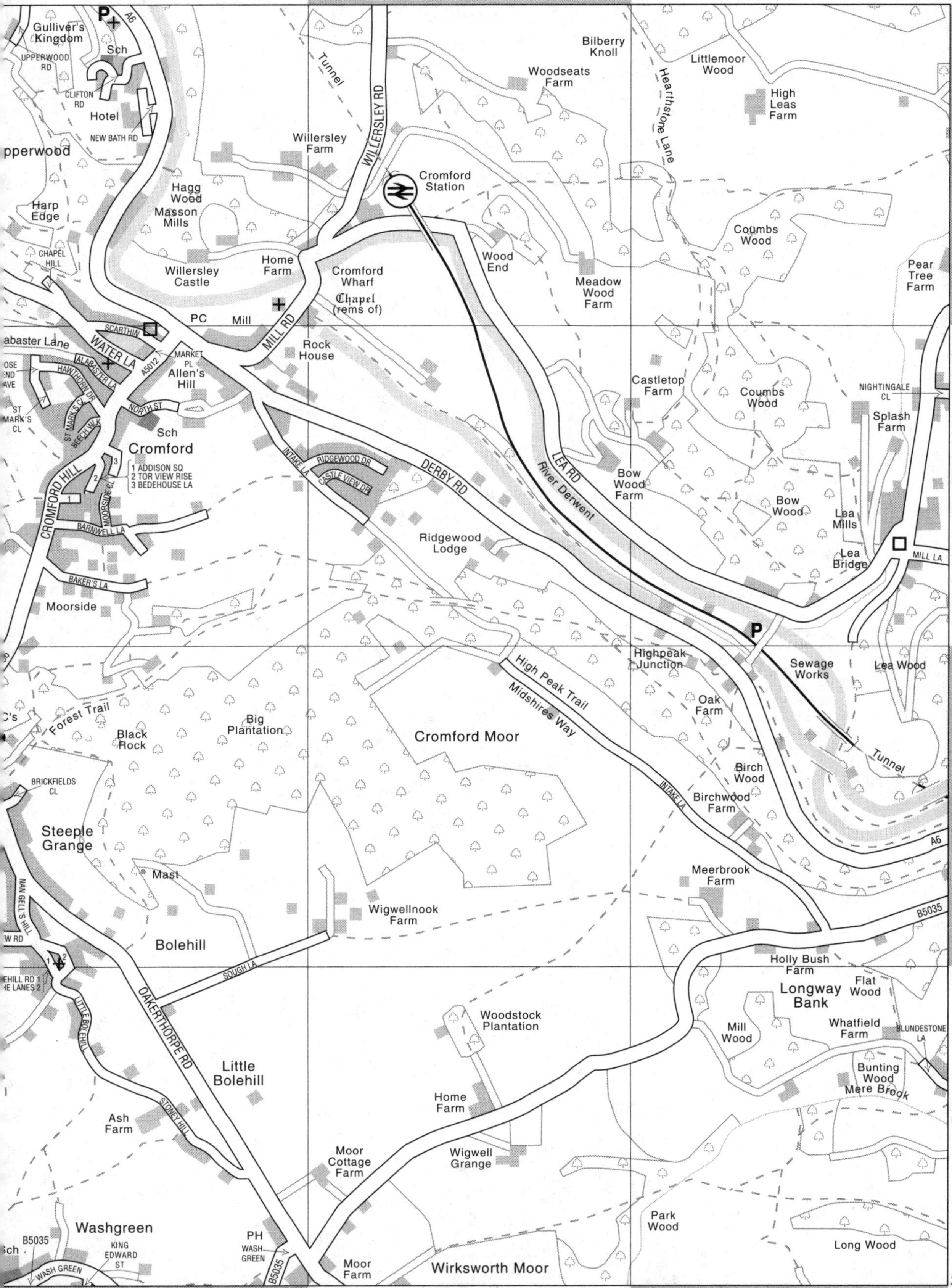

D E F

166
156

155
144

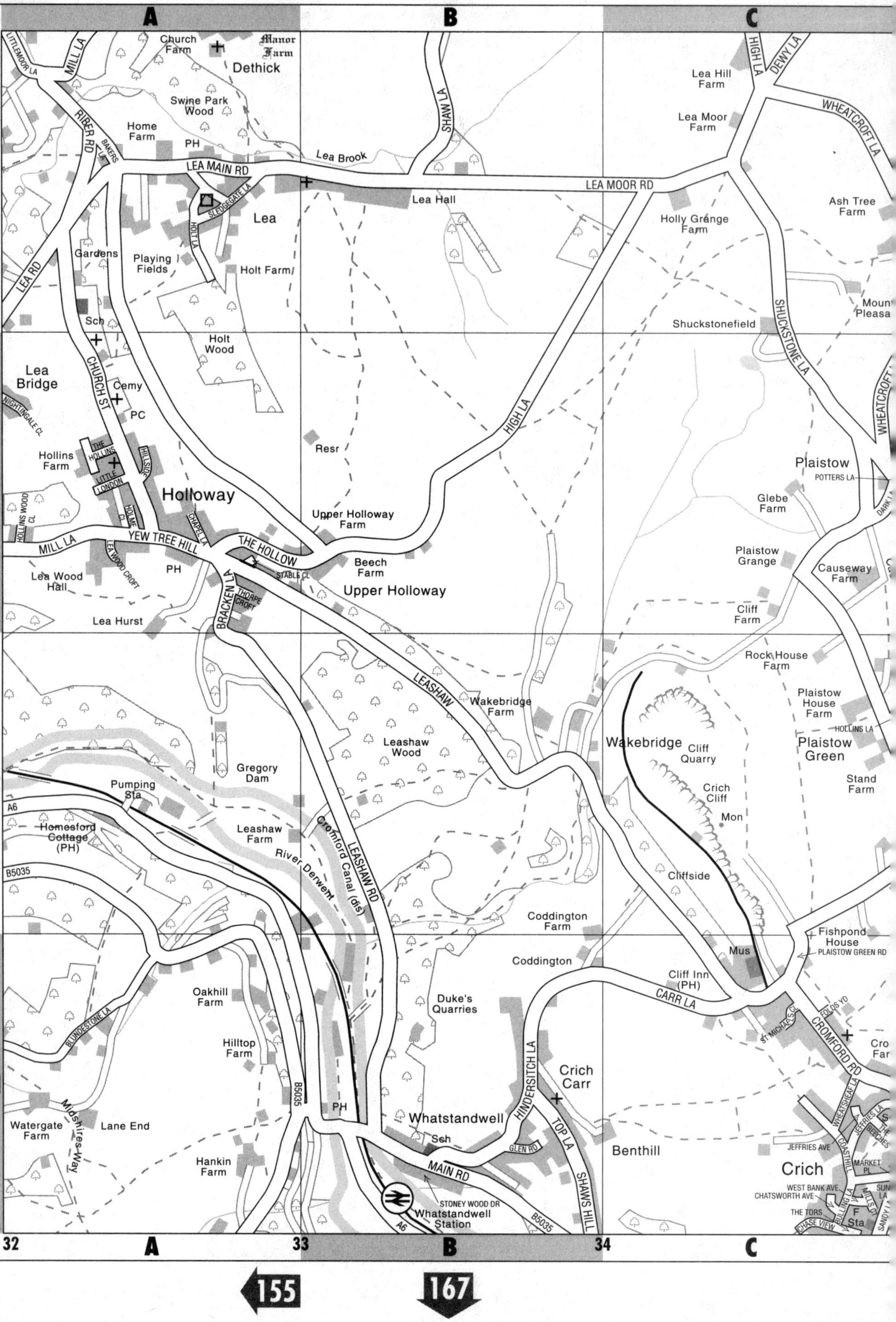

155
167

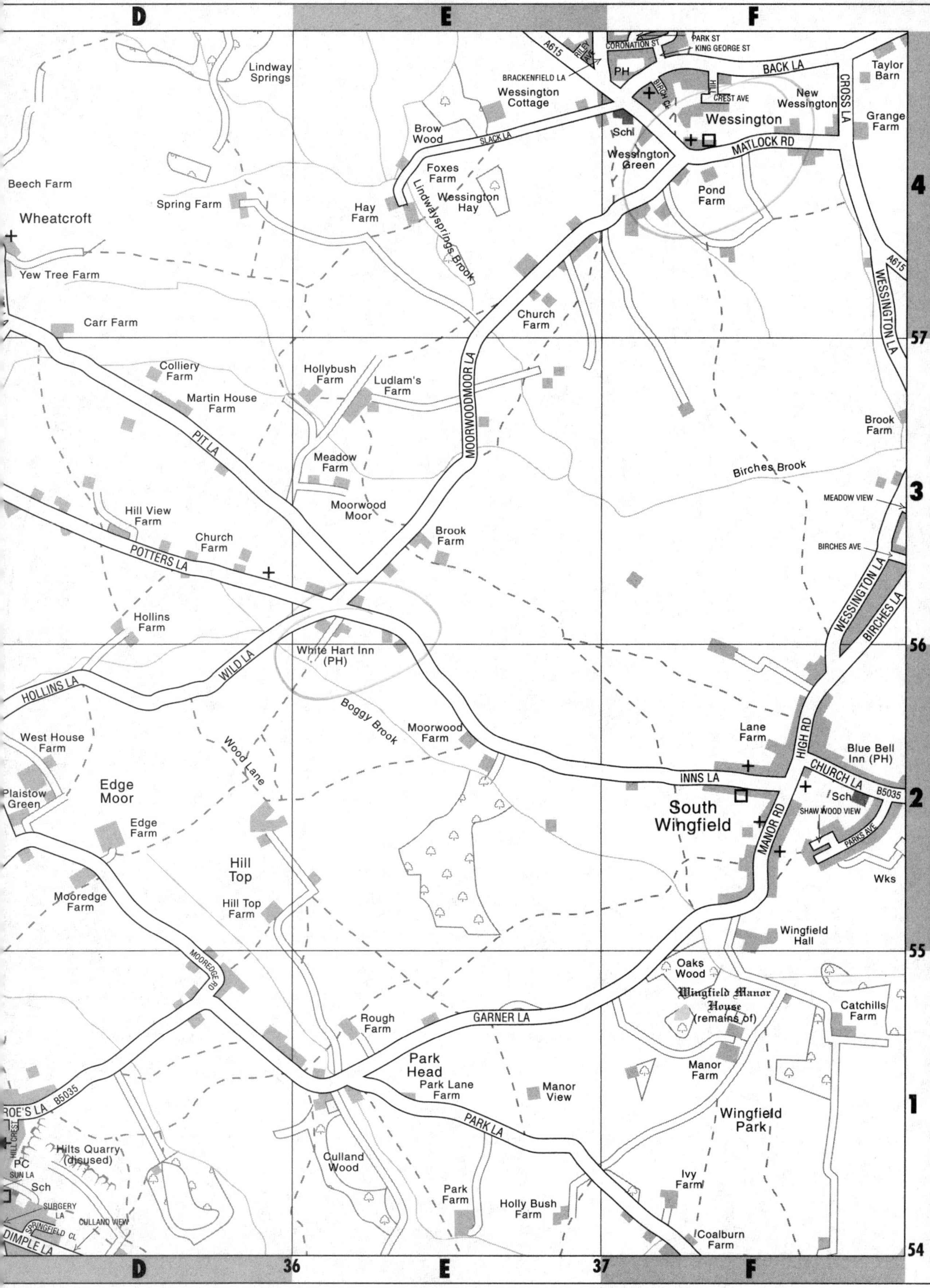
D
E
F
Lindway Springs
Beech Farm
Wheatcroft
Spring Farm
Yew Tree Farm
Carr Farm
Hay Farm
Brow Wood
SLACK LA
Foxes Farm
Wessington Hay
Lindwaysprings Brook
A615
RILEY
BRACKENFIELD LA
Wessington Cottage
CORONATION ST
PARK ST
KING GEORGE ST
PH
BACK LA
BIRCH CL
HILL
CREST AVE
New Wessington
Wessington
Schl
Wessington Green
MATLOCK RD
CROSS LA
Taylor Barn
Grange Farm
Pond Farm
A615
WESSINGTON LA
Church Farm
Colliery Farm
Martin House Farm
Hollybush Farm
Ludlam's Farm
MOORWOODMOOR LA
PIT LA
Meadow Farm
Moorwood Moor
Brook Farm
Birches Brook
Brook Farm
MEADOW VIEW
BIRCHES AVE
Hill View Farm
Church Farm
POTTERS LA
Hollins Farm
WILD LA
HOLLINS LA
White Hart Inn (PH)
WESSINGTON LA
BIRCHES LA
Boggy Brook
Moorwood Farm
Wood Lane
West House Farm
Plaistow Green
Edge Moor
Edge Farm
Lane Farm
HIGH RD
Blue Bell Inn (PH)
INNS LA
CHURCH LA
B5035
Sch
South Wingfield
MANOR RD
SHAW WOOD VIEW
PARKS AVE
Wks
Hill Top
Hill Top Farm
Mooredge Farm
MOOREDGE RD
Wingfield Hall
Oaks Wood
Wingfield Manor House (remains of)
Catchills Farm
GARNER LA
Rough Farm
Park Head
Park Lane Farm
Manor View
Manor Farm
ROE'S LA
B5035
PARK LA
Wingfield Park
Hilts Quarry (disused)
HILL CREST
PC
SUN LA
Sch
SURGERY LA
SPRINGFIELD CL
CULLAND VIEW
DIMPLE LA
Culland Wood
Park Farm
Holly Bush Farm
Ivy Farm
Coalburn Farm
4
57
3
56
2
55
1
54
36
37
D
E
F

157
146

A B C

A B C

157
169

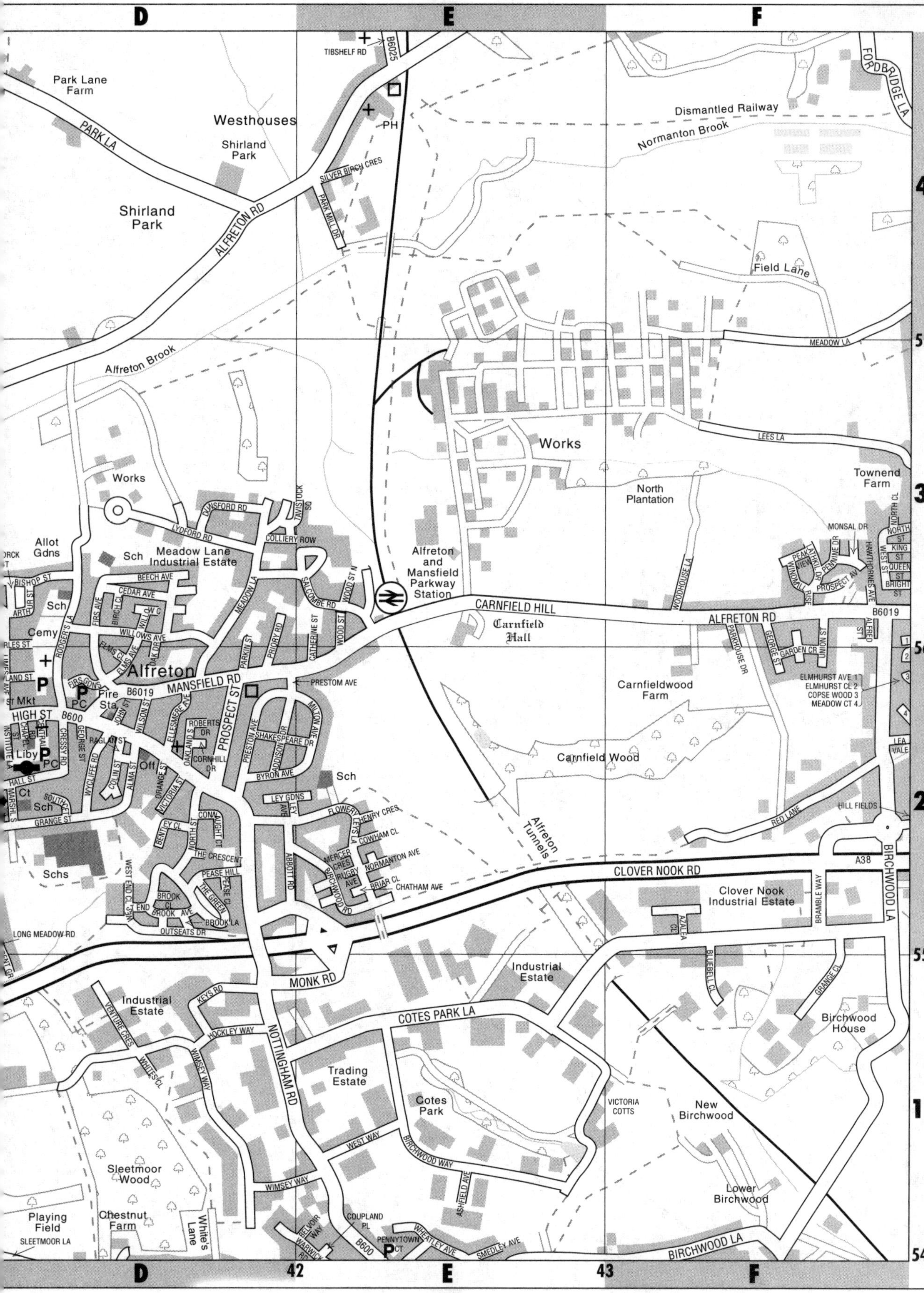

147
160
D
E
F
Park Lane Farm
PARK LA
Westhouses
Shirland Park
Shirland Park
ALFRETON RD
TIBSHELF RD
B6025
PH
SILVER BIRCH CRES
PARK MILL DR
Dismantled Railway
Normanton Brook
FORDBRIDGE LA
Field Lane
MEADOW LA
57
Alfreton Brook
LEES LA
Works
Works
Townend Farm
North Plantation
3
4
DANSFORD RD
TAVISTOCK SQ
LYDFORD RD
COLLIERY ROW
Allot Gdns
Sch
Meadow Lane Industrial Estate
Alfreton and Mansfield Parkway Station
MONSAL DR
BISHOP ST
BEECH AVE
CEDAR AVE
SALCOMBE RD
WOOD ST N
CARNFIELD HILL
WOODHOUSE LA
PROSPECT AV
ALFRETON RD
B6019
Carnfield Hall
Cemy
WILLOWS AVE
Alfreton
MANSFIELD RD
PRESTON AVE
PARKHOUSE DR
GEORGE ST
GARDEN CR
UNION ST
56
ELMHURST AVE 1
ELMHURST CL 2
COPSE WOOD 3
MEADOW CT 4
Mkt
HIGH ST
B600
B6019
Fire Sta
PC
Carnfieldwood Farm
Carnfield Wood
SHAKESPEARE DR
PROSPECT ST
Liby
PC
Ct
Sch
GRANGE ST
BYRON AVE
Sch
LEY GDNS
FLOWERY LEYS LA
HENRY CRES
COWHAM CL
RED LANE
HILL FIELDS
2
Alfreton Tunnels
NORMANTON AVE
CHATHAM AVE
Schs
THE CRESCENT
PEASE HILL
CLOVER NOOK RD
A38
BIRCHWOOD LA
Clover Nook Industrial Estate
BRAMBLE WAY
AZALEA CL
BROOK LA
OUTSEATS DR
LONG MEADOW RD
MONK RD
55
Industrial Estate
BLUEBELL CL
GRANGE CL
Industrial Estate
KEYS RD
COTES PARK LA
HOCKLEY WAY
NOTTINGHAM RD
Birchwood House
WHITES CL
WIMSEY WAY
Trading Estate
Cotes Park
VICTORIA COTTS
New Birchwood
1
WEST WAY
BIRCHWOOD WAY
Sleetmoor Wood
WIMSEY WAY
ASHFIELD AVE
Lower Birchwood
Playing Field
Chestnut Farm
White's Lane
SLEETMOOR LA
COUPLAND PL
PENNYTOWN CT
WHEATLEY AVE
SMEDLEY AVE
BIRCHWOOD LA
B600
54
D
42
E
43
F

159 148

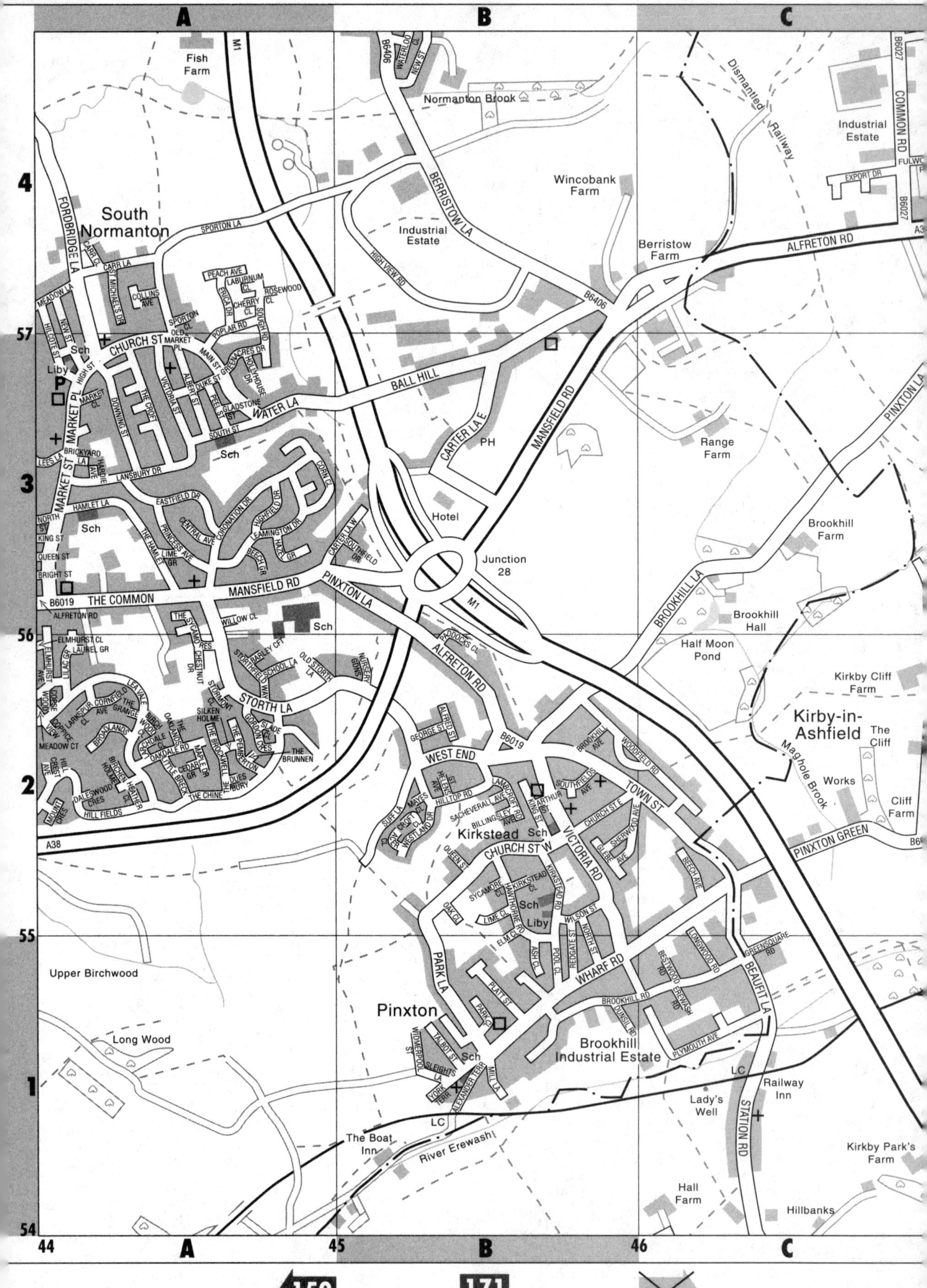
A
B
C
4
3
2
1
57
56
55
54
44
45
46
Fish Farm
M1
B6406
WATERLOO CL
NEW ST
Normanton Brook
Dismantled Railway
B6027
COMMON RD
Industrial Estate
FULWO
EXPORT DR
A3
Wincobank Farm
BERRISTOW LA
Industrial Estate
HIGH VIEW RD
South Normanton
SPORTON LA
FORDBRIDGE LA
CARR CL
CARR LA
ST MICHAEL'S DR
COLLINS AVE
PEACH AVE
LABURNUM CL
CHERRY CL
ROSEWOOD CL
ERICA DR
POPLAR RD
SOUGH RD
SPORTON CL
OLD MARKET PL
MEADOW LA
NEW ST
HILCOTE ST
Sch
CHURCH ST
MAIN ST
GREEN CRES
ACRES DR
HOLLINHOUSE DR
DUKE ST
Liby
HIGH ST
P
MARKET PL
MARKET CL
DOWNING ST
THE CROFT
VICTORIA ST
ALBERT ST
PEEL ST
GLADSTONE ST
SOUTH ST
WATER LA
BALL HILL
Berristow Farm
ALFRETON RD
B6406
MANSFIELD RD
CARTER LA E
PH
Range Farm
PINXTON LA
Sch
LEES LA
BRICKYARD LA
HARDIE AVE
MARKET ST
LANSBURY DR
CORN CL
EASTFIELD DR
HAMLET LA
NORTH ST
KING ST
Sch
THE HAMLET
CENTRAL AVE
CORONATION DR
HIGHFIELD DR
LEAMINGTON DR
HAZEL GR
BEECH GR
PRINCESS AVE
LIME GR
CARTER LA W
SOUTHFIELD DR
Hotel
Junction 28
QUEEN ST
BRIGHT ST
B6019
THE COMMON
MANSFIELD RD
PINXTON LA
ALFRETON RD
M1
Brookhill Farm
BROOKHILL LA
Brookhill Hall
Half Moon Pond
THE SYCAMORES
WILLOW CL
Sch
PADDOCKS CL
ELMHURST CL
LAUREL GR
ELMHURST AVE
LILAC GR
CHESTNUT DR
BARLEY CFT
STORTHFIELD WAY
SCHOOL LA
OLD STORTH LA
NURSERY GDNS
ALFRETON RD
Kirkby Cliff Farm
LEA VALE
CORNFIELD AVE
THE GRANGE
GORSE
WOOD VIEW
COPPICE
LARKSPUR CL
BIRCH WOOD
STORMONT CL
SILKEN HOLME
STORTH LA
ALFRED ST
GEORGE ST
Kirby-in-Ashfield
The Cliff
BROADLANDS
CHURCHDALE CT
OAKLANDS
THE SPINNEY
AVONDALE RD
OAKDALE RD
THE BROOKWELL
THE PEMBERTON
GORDON CRES
SLADE CL
THE BRUNNEN
B6019
BROOKHILL AVE
WOODFIELD RD
MEADOW CT
HILL CREST
BIRCHEN HOLME
LITTLE BRECK
CEDAR GR
MAPLE DR
THE DUES BURY
WEST END
ST HELENS AVE
LAMBCROFT RD
KING ST
ARTHUR ST
SOUTHFIELDS AVE
TOWN ST
Maghole Brook
Works
Cliff Farm
DALESWOOD CRES
HEATHER CL
THE CHINE
HILL FIELDS
MOUNT CRES
MAYES CT
HILLTOP RD
SACHEVERALL AVE
BILLINGSLEY AVE
CHURCH ST E
SHERWOOD AVE
A38
SUFF LA
ACRE
CROFT CL
WESTLAND DR
Kirkstead
Sch
CHURCH ST W
VICTORIA RD
GLEBE AVE
PINXTON GREEN
B6
QUEEN ST
BEECH AVE
SYCAMORE CL
HAWTHORNE RD
KIRKSTEAD CL
KIRKSTEAD RD
Sch
OAK CL
LIME CL
Liby
ELM CL
WILSON ST
NORTH ST
REDGATE ST
POOL CL
ASH CL
LONGWOOD RD
GREENSQUARE RD
BESTWOOD RD
Upper Birchwood
PARK LA
WHARF RD
PLATT ST
BROOKHILL RD
EREWASH RD
BEAUFIT LA
DUNSIL RD
Pinxton
PARK CL
Long Wood
WIDMERPOOL ST
TALBOT ST
Sch
Brookhill Industrial Estate
PLYMOUTH AVE
SLEIGHTS LA
LC
Railway Inn
YORK TERR
ALEXANDER TERR
MILL LA
Lady's Well
STATION RD
LC
The Boat Inn
River Erewash
Kirkby Park's Farm
Hall Farm
Hillbanks
A
B
C

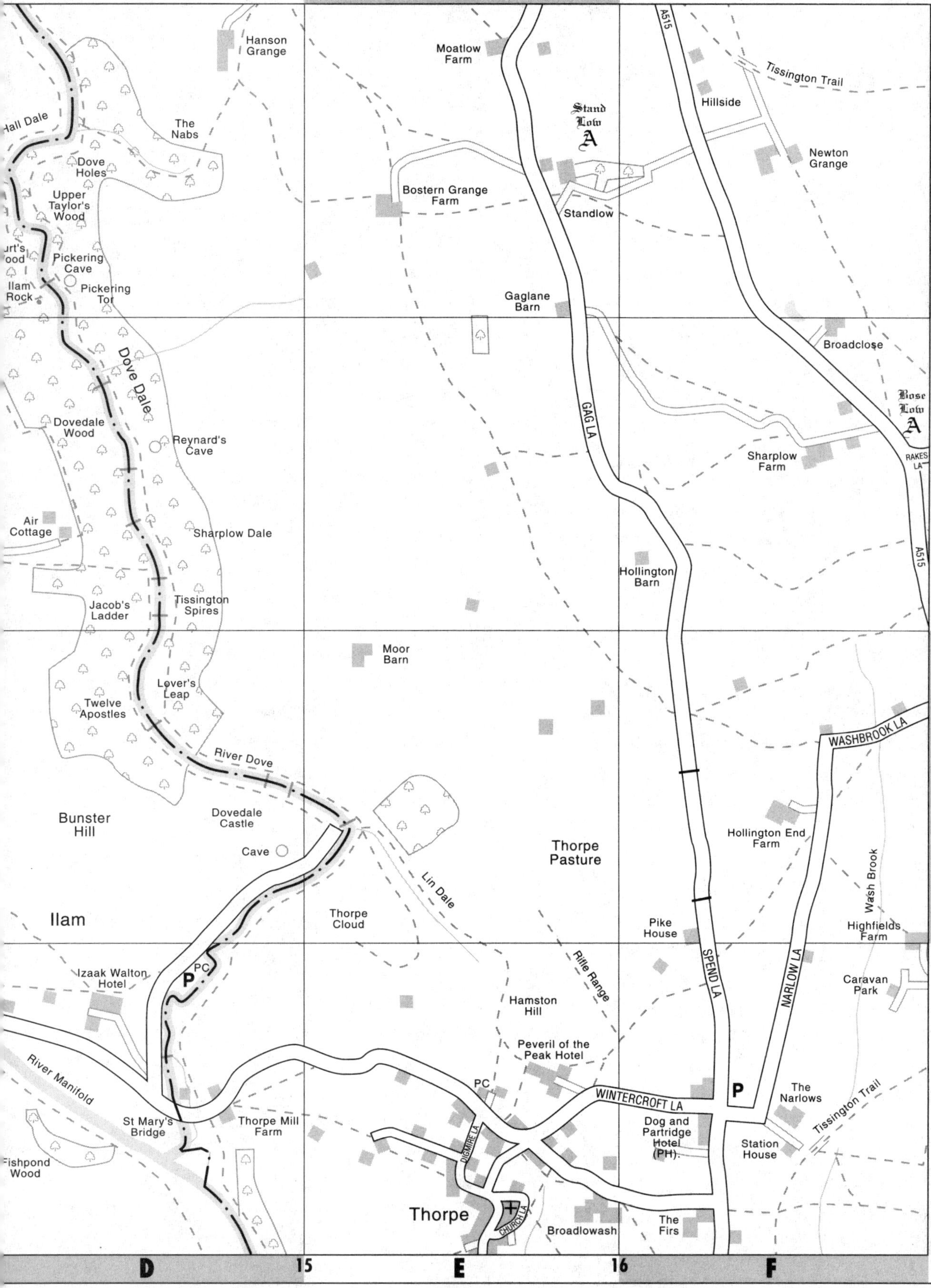
D
E
F
Hanson Grange
Moatlow Farm
Tissington Trail
Hillside
Stand Low
Hall Dale
The Nabs
Newton Grange
Dove Holes
Bostern Grange Farm
Standlow
Upper Taylor's Wood
Pickering Cave
Pickering Tor
Ilam Rock
Gaglane Barn
Broadclose
Dove Dale
Bose Low
Dovedale Wood
Reynard's Cave
GAG LA
Sharplow Farm
RAKES LA
A515
Air Cottage
Sharplow Dale
Hollington Barn
Jacob's Ladder
Tissington Spires
Moor Barn
Lover's Leap
Twelve Apostles
River Dove
WASHBROOK LA
Bunster Hill
Dovedale Castle
Hollington End Farm
Cave
Thorpe Pasture
Lin Dale
Wash Brook
Ilam
Thorpe Cloud
Pike House
Highfields Farm
Izaak Walton Hotel
PC
P
Rifle Range
SPEND LA
NARLOW LA
Caravan Park
Hamston Hill
River Manifold
Peveril of the Peak Hotel
WINTERCROFT LA
The Narlows
Tissington Trail
St Mary's Bridge
Thorpe Mill Farm
DIGMIRE LA
Dog and Partridge Hotel (PH)
Station House
Fishpond Wood
Thorpe
CHURCH LA
Broadlowash
The Firs
4
53
3
52
2
51
1
50
15
16

161
151

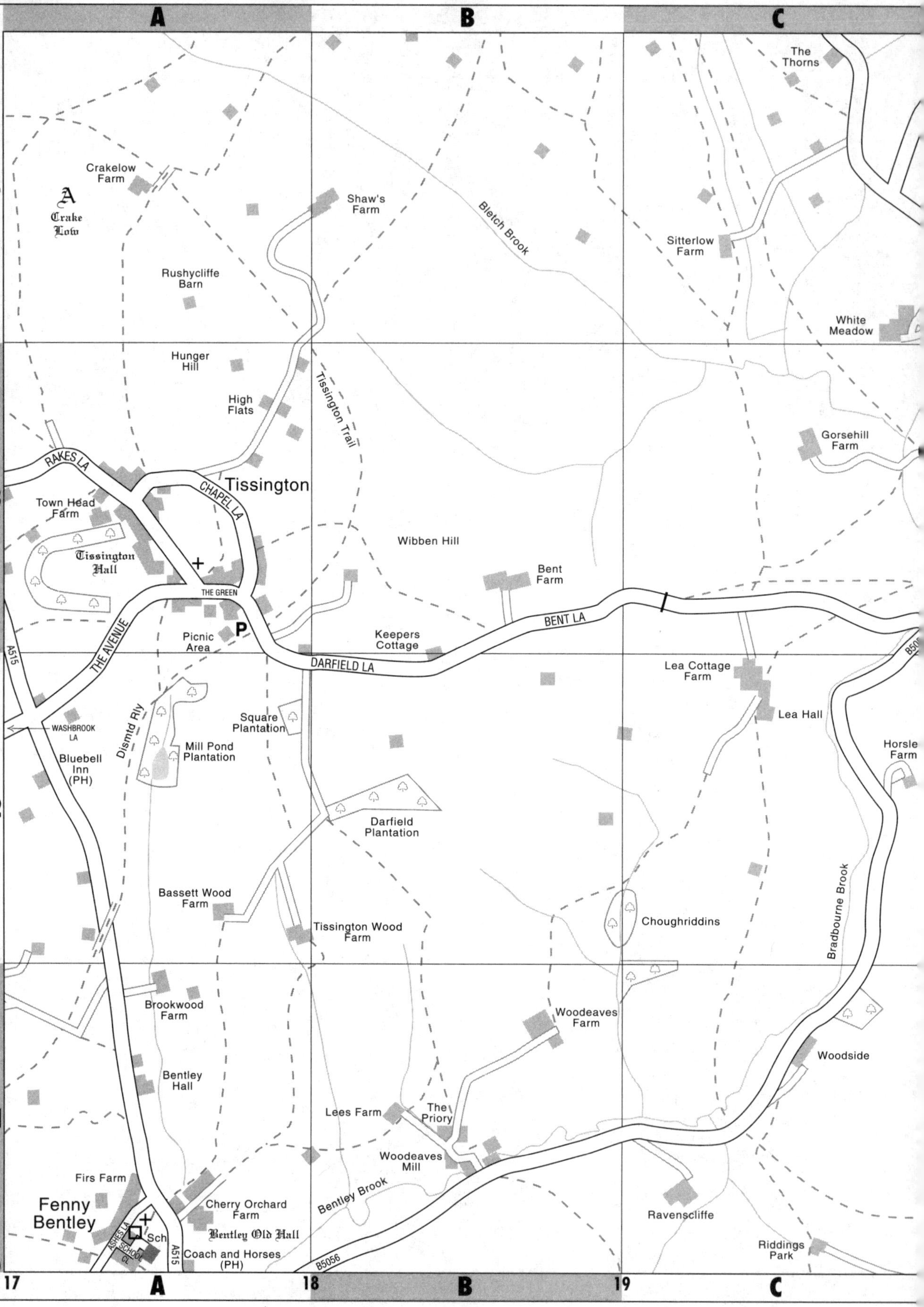

161
173

152
164

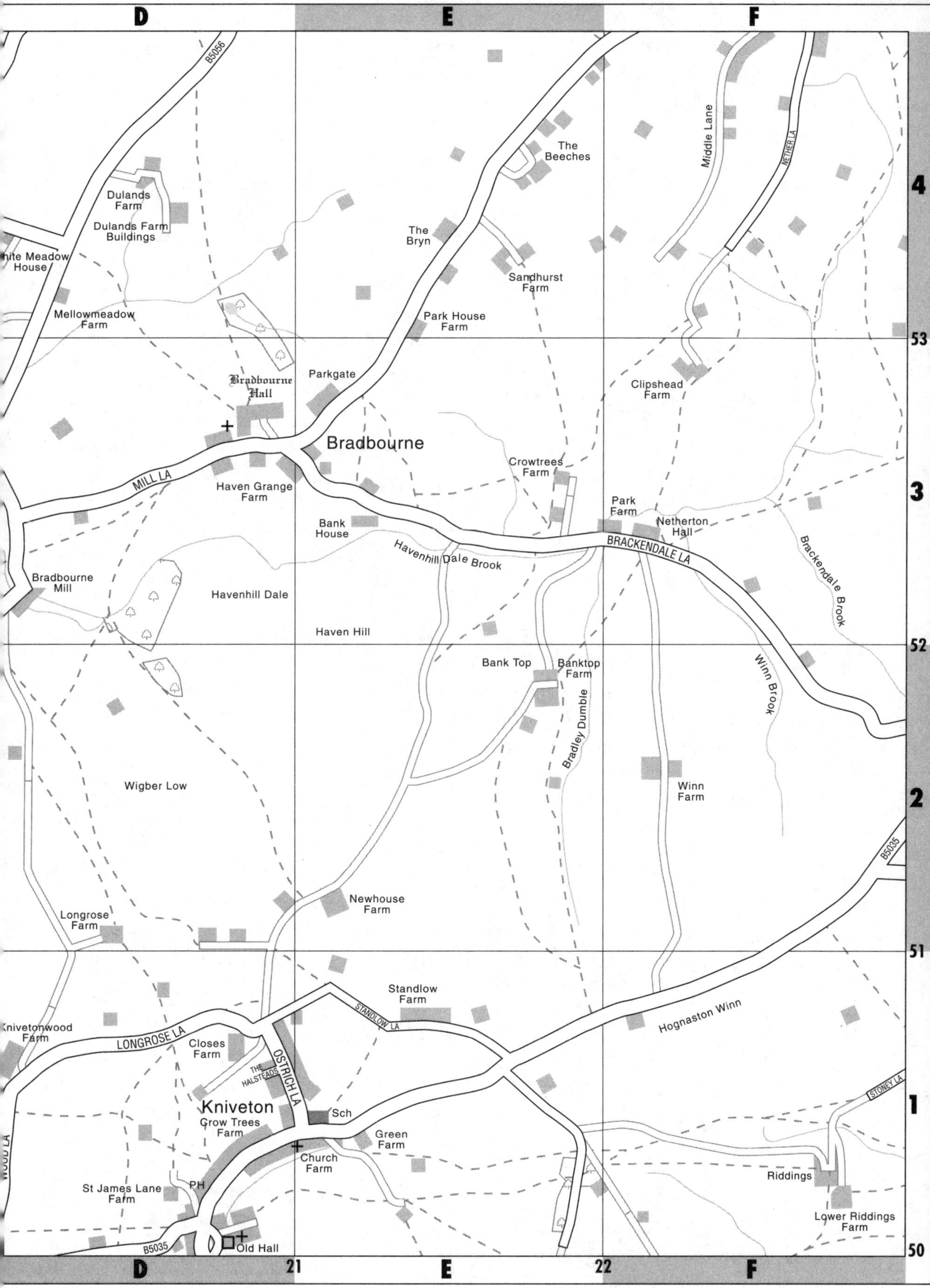

174
164

163
153

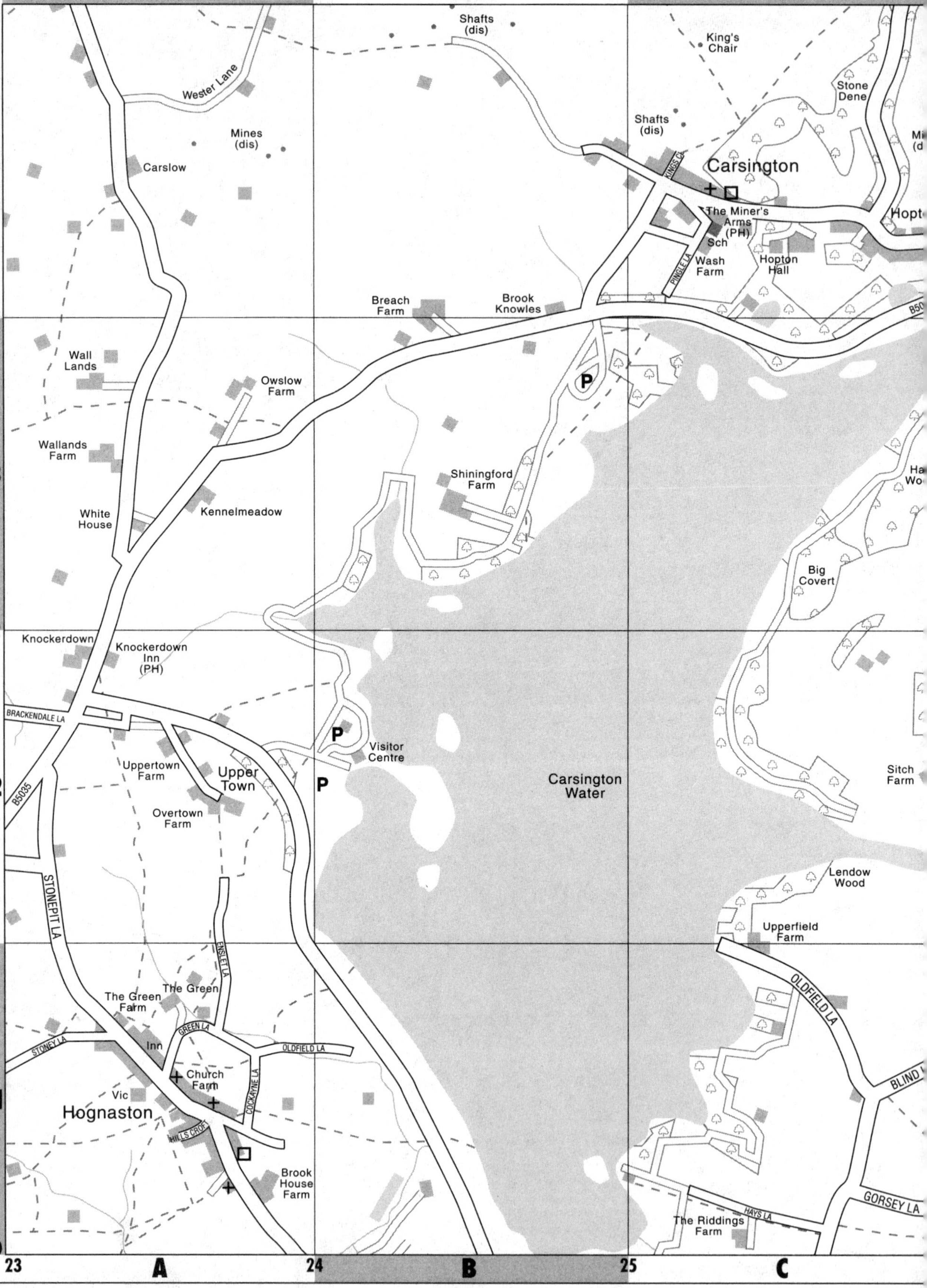
A
B
C
4
53
3
52
2
51
1
50
23
24
25
Shafts (dis)
King's Chair
Stone Dene
Wester Lane
Shafts (dis)
Mines (dis)
Carslow
Carsington
KINGS CL
The Miner's Arms (PH)
Sch
Wash Farm
PINGLE LA
Hopton Hall
Hopt
Breach Farm
Brook Knowles
B5035
Wall Lands
Owslow Farm
Wallands Farm
Shiningford Farm
White House
Kennelmeadow
Big Covert
Knockerdown
Knockerdown Inn (PH)
BRACKENDALE LA
Visitor Centre
Uppertown Farm
Upper Town
B5035
Carsington Water
Sitch Farm
Overtown Farm
Lendow Wood
STONEPIT LA
Upperfield Farm
ENSLET LA
OLDFIELD LA
The Green Farm
The Green
GREEN LA
STONEY LA
Inn
OLDFIELD LA
Church Farm
COCKAYNE LA
Vic
Hognaston
HILLS CROFT
BLIND
Brook House Farm
GORSEY LA
HAYS LA
The Riddings Farm

154
166

176
166

165
155

165
177

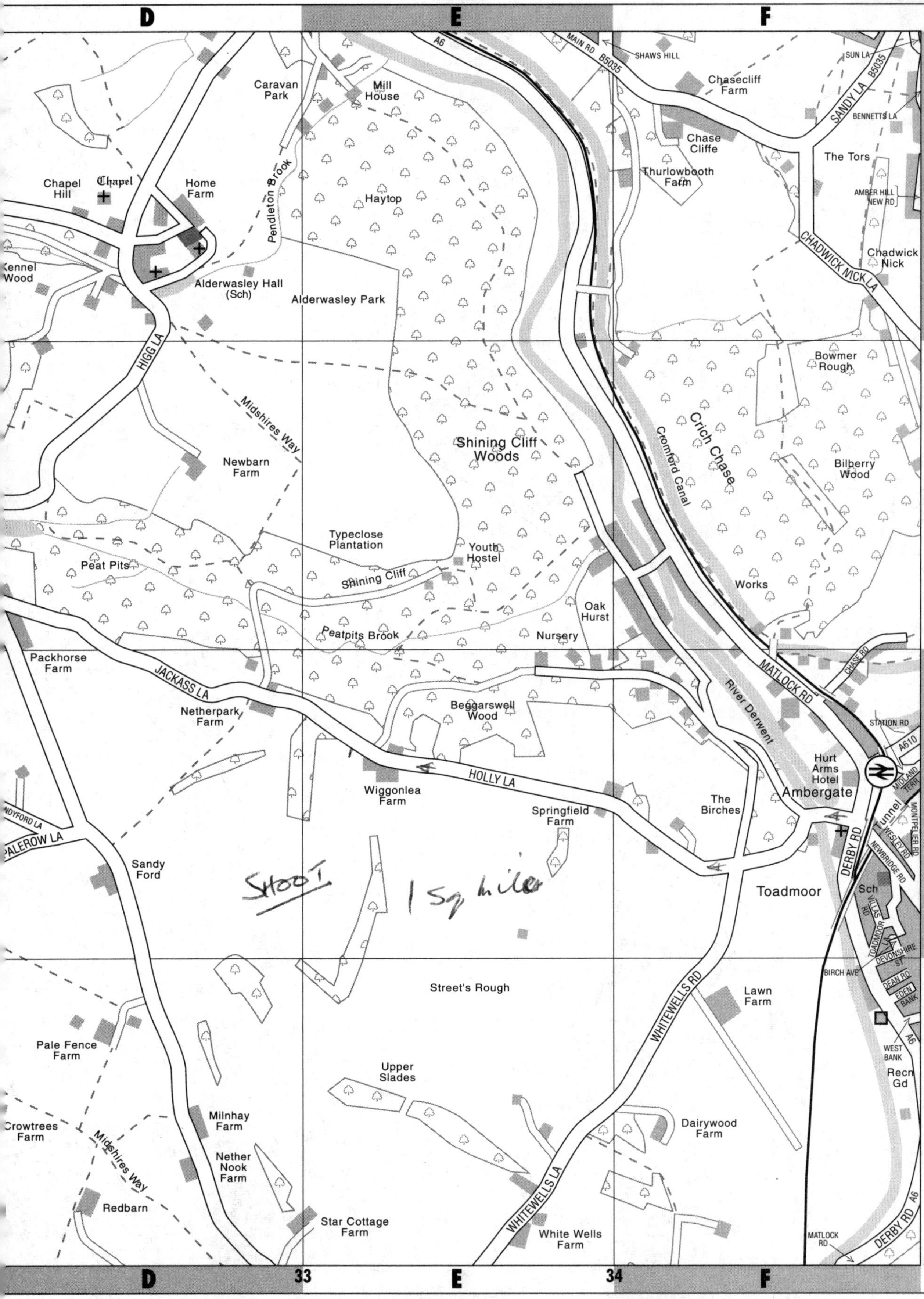
D
E
F
Caravan Park
Mill House
Chapel Hill
Chapel
Home Farm
Pendleton Brook
Haytop
Kennel Wood
Alderwasley Hall (Sch)
Alderwasley Park
HIGG LA
Midshires Way
Newbarn Farm
Shining Cliff Woods
Typeclose Plantation
Youth Hostel
Peat Pits
Shining Cliff
Peatpits Brook
Oak Hurst
Nursery
Packhorse Farm
JACKASS LA
Netherpark Farm
Beggarswell Wood
Wiggonlea Farm
HOLLY LA
Springfield Farm
PALEROW LA
Sandy Ford
Street's Rough
WHITEWELLS RD
Pale Fence Farm
Upper Slades
Milnhay Farm
Crowtrees Farm
Nether Nook Farm
Redbarn
Star Cottage Farm
WHITEWELLS LA
White Wells Farm
A6
MAIN RD
B5035
SHAWS HILL
Chasecliff Farm
SUN LA
SANDY LA
BENNETTS LA
Chase Cliffe
The Tors
Thurlowbooth Farm
AMBER HILL NEW RD
CHADWICK NICK LA
Chadwick Nick
Bowmer Rough
Crich Chase
Cromford Canal
Bilberry Wood
Works
MATLOCK RD
CHASE RD
River Derwent
STATION RD
A610
Hurt Arms Hotel
Ambergate
MIDLAND TERR
The Birches
Tunnel
WESLEY RD
MONTPELIER RD
DERBY RD
NEWBRIDGE RD
Toadmoor
Sch
VILLAS RD
TOADMOOR LA
DEVONSHIRE ST
BIRCH AVE
DEAN RD
EDEN BANK
Lawn Farm
WEST BANK
Recn Gd
Dairywood Farm
MATLOCK RD
DERBY RD
4
53
3
52
2
51
1
50
33
34
SHOOT

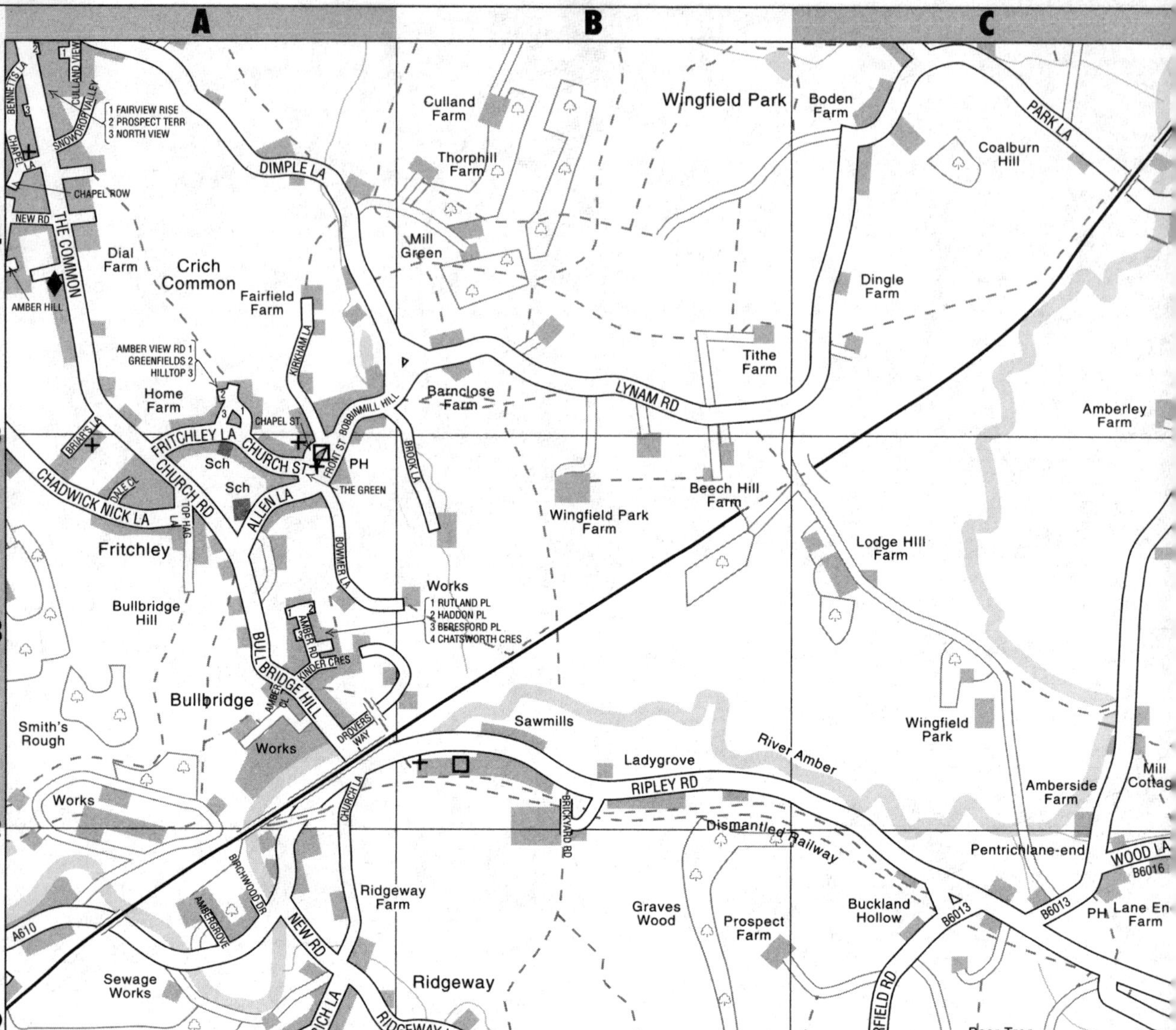
A
B
C
1 FAIRVIEW RISE
2 PROSPECT TERR
3 NORTH VIEW
BENNETTS LA
CULLAND VIEW
SNOWDROP VALLEY
CHAPEL LA
CHAPEL ROW
NEW RD
THE COMMON
AMBER HILL
Culland Farm
Thorphill Farm
Mill Green
Wingfield Park
Boden Farm
PARK LA
Coalburn Hill
DIMPLE LA
Dial Farm
Crich Common
Fairfield Farm
KIRKHAM LA
Dingle Farm
AMBER VIEW RD 1
GREENFIELDS 2
HILLTOP 3
Home Farm
CHAPEL ST
Barnclose Farm
BOBBINMILL HILL
LYNAM RD
Tithe Farm
Amberley Farm
BRIAR'S LA
FRITCHLEY LA
CHURCH ST
FRONT ST
BROOK LA
PH
Sch
THE GREEN
CHADWICK NICK LA
DALE CL
CHURCH RD
TOP HAG LA
ALLEN LA
BOWMER LA
Wingfield Park Farm
Beech Hill Farm
Lodge Hill Farm
Fritchley
Works
1 RUTLAND PL
2 HADDON PL
3 BERESFORD PL
4 CHATSWORTH CRES
Bullbridge Hill
AMBER RD
KINDER CRES
BULL BRIDGE HILL
AMBER PL
DROVERS WAY
Bullbridge
Smith's Rough
Sawmills
Wingfield Park
River Amber
Ladygrove
RIPLEY RD
Amberside Farm
Mill Cottag
CHURCH LA
BRICKYARD RD
Dismantled Railway
Pentrichlane-end
WOOD LA
B6016
BIRCHWOOD DR
AMBERGROVE
Ridgeway Farm
Graves Wood
Prospect Farm
Buckland Hollow
B6013
PH
Lane End Farm
A610
NEW RD
Sewage Works
Ridgeway
CHESTERFIELD RD
RIDGEWAY LA
HAWKINS DR
CRICH LA
Thacker's Wood
Pear Tree Farm
LYNTON RD
Starvehimvalley Bridge
Valley Farm
Gun Lane Farm
Ridgeway Farm
SLACK LA
Heage Hall
NODIN HILL LA
HALL LA
Nodin Hill Farm
NEWBRIDGE RD
GUN LA
CHURCH ST
Bond Lane Farm
WEST BANK
Heage Firs
MALTHOUSE LA
Windmill (disused)
BOND LA
Heage Firs Farm
SHOP LA
BANK VIEW RD
GUIDE POST
BROOK ST
DUNGLEY HILL
SCHOOL LA
The Gables Farm
SPANKER LA
PH
GADSBY RISE
Sch
West View Farm
Bent Farm
EAGLE ST
PC
THE CROFT
B6374
SPANKER TERR
BENTFIELD RD
Nether Heage
TENTER LA
Heage
A6 DERBY RD
Sewerage Farm
Works
BOWLING ALLEY
BROOK ST
Hartshay Hall Farm
Dunge Wood
PICKARD LA
BAKERS HILL
PH
Damstead Farm
OLD RD
1 EAST VIEW RD
2 THE ROCKERIES
NEW RD
Heage Common Farm
B6013
SCHOOL HOUSE HILL
PARKSIDE
4
53
3
52
2
51
1
50
35
36
37

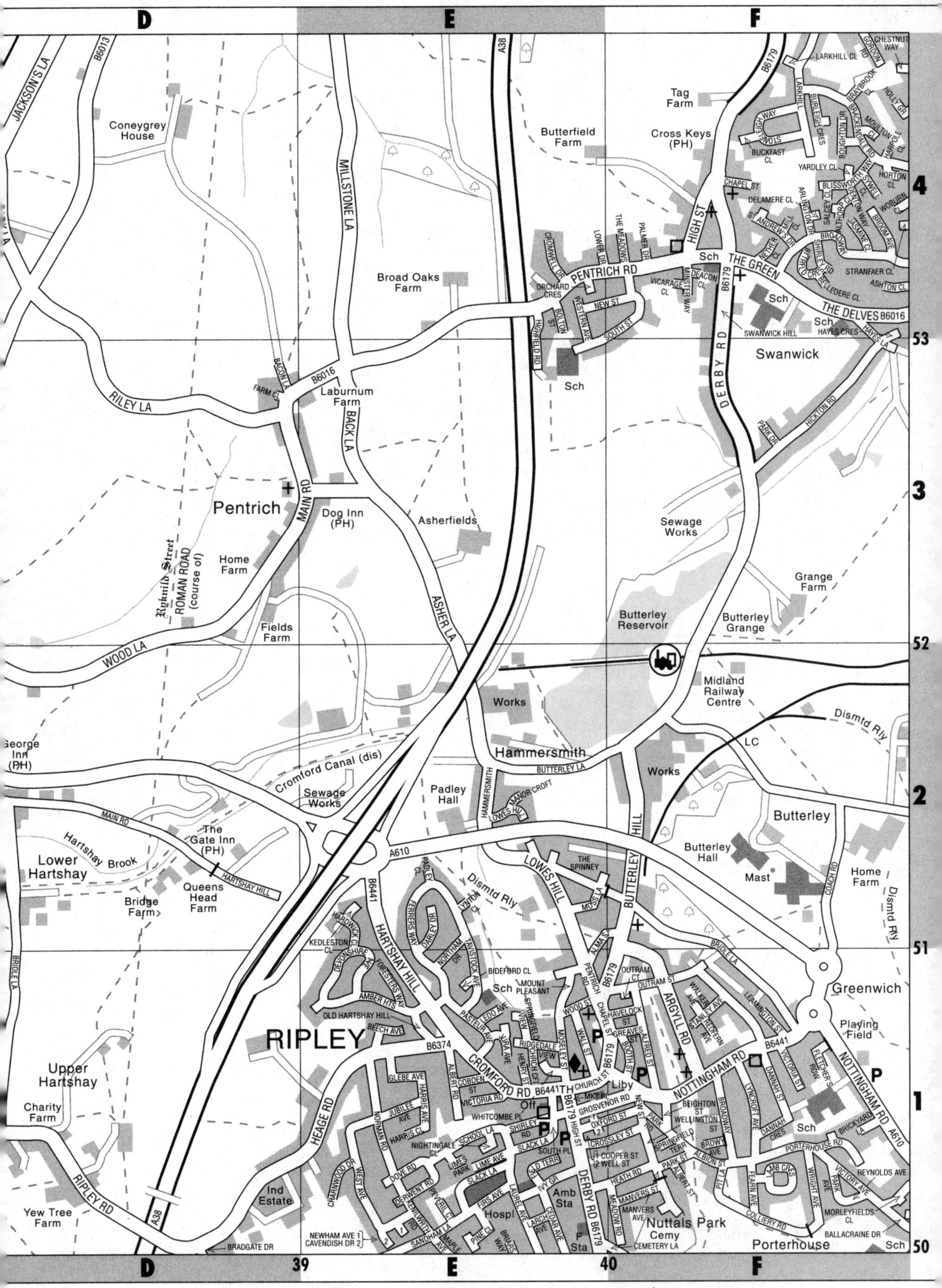
D
E
F
4
53
3
52
2
51
1
50
39
40
JACKSON'S LA
B6013
Coneygrey House
MILLSTONE LA
A38
Tag Farm
Butterfield Farm
Cross Keys (PH)
B6179
LARKHILL CL
CHESTNUT WAY
GORDON RD
LARKHILL
BURLEIGH CRES
BRAYBROOK CL
HOLLY GR
BRACKENDALE RD
MOULTON CL
HARPOLE CL
HORTON CL
BUCKFAST CL
YARDLEY CL
CHAPEL ST
DELAMERE CL
BLISSWORTH
ST ANDREWS DR
WOBURN CL
BROOM AVE
JASMINE CL
HIGH ST
CROMWELL DR
LOWER DR
THE MEADOWS
PALMER DR
Sch
THE GREEN
Broad Oaks Farm
PENTRICH RD
ORCHARD CRES
VICARAGE CL
DEACON CL
MINSTER WAY
STRANFAER CL
ASHTON CL
BELLEDERE CL
NEW ST
WESTERN AVE
BOLTON ST
SOUTH ST
HIGHFIELD RD
THE DELVES B6016
SWANWICK HILL
HAYES CRES
HAYES LA
DERBY RD
Swanwick
BACON LA
B6016
FARM CL
RILEY LA
Laburnum Farm
BACK LA
PARK DR
HICKTON RD
MAIN RD
Pentrich
Dog Inn (PH)
Asherfields
Sewage Works
Home Farm
Rykniild Street
ROMAN ROAD (course of)
ASHER LA
Grange Farm
Fields Farm
Butterley Reservoir
Butterley Grange
WOOD LA
Midland Railway Centre
Works
Dismtd Rly
George Inn (PH)
Hammersmith
LC
Cromford Canal (dis)
BUTTERLEY LA
Padley Hall
MANOR CROFT
HAMMERSMITH
LOWES HILL
Sewage Works
Butterley
MAIN RD
The Gate Inn (PH)
Hartshay Brook
Lower Hartshay
A610
Butterley Hall
Mast
Home Farm
COACH RD
Queens Head Farm
HARTSHAY HILL
Bridge Farm
B6441
PADLEY CL
LYNTON CL
THE SPINNEY
MOSS LA
BUTTERLEY HILL
BRIDLE LA
HARDWICK CL
FERRERS WAY
DARLEY DR
KEDLESTON CL
DEVONSHIRE AVE
FORESTERS WAY
NORTHAM DR
TAVISTOCK AVE
ALMA ST
BIDEFORD CL
OUTRAM CT
OUTRAM ST
Greenwich
MOUNT PLEASANT
PENTRICH RD
B6179
ARGYLL RD
WALKER AVE
TANTLEY AVE
REDFERN AVE
LEAMINGTON ST
AMBER HTS
OLD HARTSHAY HILL
BEECH AVE
PASTEUR AVE
LEDO AVE
SPRINGFIELD VIEW
WOOD ST
HAVELOCK ST
GREAVES ST
Playing Field
RIPLEY
B6374
JURA AVE
RIDGEDALE VIEW
MOSELEY ST
WALL ST
BOOTH ST
ALFRED ST
NOTTINGHAM RD
B6441
VICTORIA ST
FLETCHER ST
ROW
NOTTINGHAM RD
Upper Hartshay
GLEBE AVE
ALBERT RD
CROMFORD RD
HENRY ST
CHURCH CFT
CHURCH ST
Liby
COBDEN ST
B6441
MKT PL
Charity Farm
JUBILEE AVE
HARRIS AVE
VICTORIA RD
Off
GROSVENOR RD
BEIGHTON ST
WELLINGTON ST
BROADWAY
LYNCROFT AVE
DANNAH ST
Sch
BRICKYARD LA
HEAGE RD
NORMAN RD
HARRIS CL
WHITCOMBE PL
SHIRLEY RD
OXFORD ST
CROSSLEY ST
PARK RD
DANNAH CRES
A610
NIGHTINGALE CL
SCHOOL LA
SLACK LA
SOUTH PL
HIGH ST
SPRINGFIELD TERR
BROWN AVE
ALBION ST
PORTERHOUSE RD
REYNOLDS AVE
WEST AVE
LIMES PARK
LIME AVE
1 COOPER ST
2 WELL ST
PARK ST
PIT LA
CHARNWOOD DR
DOVE RD
DERWENT RD
SLACK LA
FIELD TERR
HEATH RD
ALBERT ST
FEARN AVE
LAMB CRES
WRIGHT AVE
VICTORY AVE
PARK
Ind Estate
RIPLEY RD
PEVERIL CL
FIRS AVE
LAUREL AVE
WY GR
Amb Sta
MANVERS ST
MORLEYFIELDS CL
Yew Tree Farm
KENILWORTH RD
Hospl
LARCH AVE
CEDAR AVE
DERBY RD B6179
MEADOW RD
MANVERS AVE
Nuttals Park
COLLIERY RD
A38
SANDHAM LA
MAPLE AVE
PINE CL
BRIARS WAY
F Sta
Cemy
CEMETERY LA
BALLACRAINE DR
NEWHAM AVE 1
CAVENDISH DR 2
BRADGATE DR
Porterhouse
Sch
BRIDLE LA

169
159

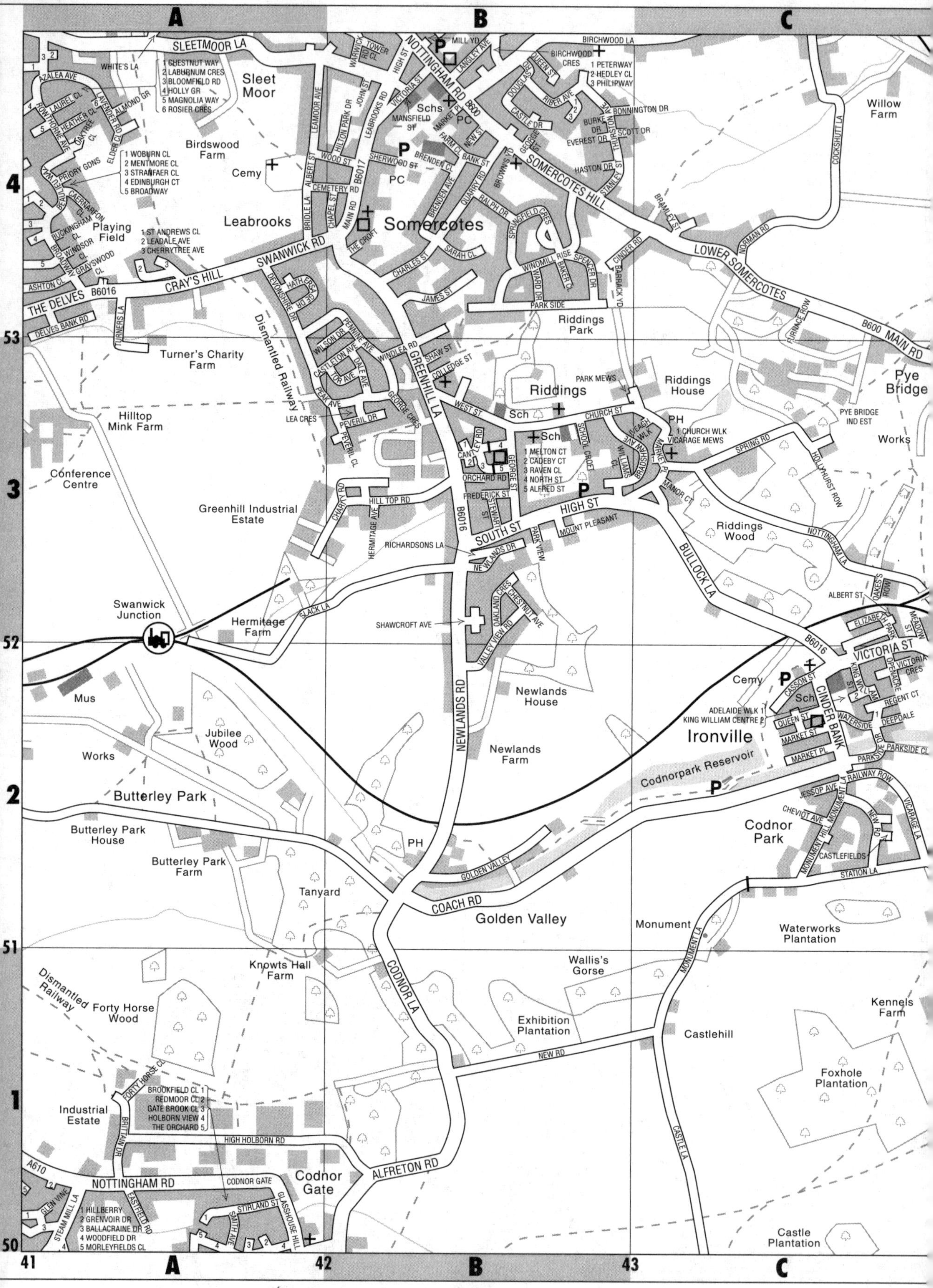
A
B
C
4
53
3
52
2
51
1
50
41
42
43
SLEETMOOR LA
WHITE'S LA
1 CHESTNUT WAY
2 LABURNUM CRES
3 BLOOMFIELD RD
4 HOLLY GR
5 MAGNOLIA WAY
6 ROSIER CRES
Sleet Moor
AZALEA AVE
ALMOND GR
Birdswood Farm
1 WOBURN CL
2 MENTMORE CL
3 STRANFAER CL
4 EDINBURGH CT
5 BROADWAY
Cemy
PRIORY GDNS
Leabrooks
Playing Field
1 ST ANDREWS CL
2 LEADALE AVE
3 CHERRYTREE AVE
SWANWICK RD
CRAY'S HILL
B6016
THE DELVES
DELVES BANK RD
ASHTON CL
TURNERS LA
Turner's Charity Farm
Dismantled Railway
Hilltop Mink Farm
Conference Centre
Greenhill Industrial Estate
Swanwick Junction
Hermitage Farm
SLACK LA
Mus
Jubilee Wood
Works
Butterley Park
Butterley Park House
Butterley Park Farm
Tanyard
Knowts Hall Farm
Forty Horse Wood
Industrial Estate
FORTY HORSE CL
BRITTAIN DR
BROOKFIELD CL 1
REDMOOR CL 2
GATE BROOK CL 3
HOLBORN VIEW 4
THE ORCHARD 5
HIGH HOLBORN RD
A610
NOTTINGHAM RD
CODNOR GATE
Codnor Gate
STIRLAND ST
SMITH AVE
GLASSHOUSE HILL
GLEN VINE
STEAM MILL LA
EASTFIELD RD
1 HILLBERRY
2 GRENVOIR DR
3 BALLACRAINE DR
4 WOODFIELD DR
5 MORLEYFIELDS CL
ALFRETON RD
CODNOR LA
NEW RD
Exhibition Plantation
Wallis's Gorse
Castlehill
CASTLE LA
MONUMENT LA
Monument
Golden Valley
COACH RD
GOLDEN VALLEY
PH
NEWLANDS RD
Newlands Farm
Newlands House
SHAWCROFT AVE
VALLEY VIEW RD
OAKLAND CRES
CHESTNUT AVE
NEWLANDS DR
RICHARDSONS LA
HERMITAGE AVE
HILL TOP RD
CHARTY RD
SOUTH ST
PARK VIEW
MOUNT PLEASANT
HIGH ST
BULLOCK LA
NOTTINGHAM RD
MILL YD
HIGH ST
WARWICK RD
TOWER CL
LANGLEY AVE
BIRCHWOOD LA
BIRCHWOOD CRES
1 PETERWAY
2 HEDLEY CL
3 PHILIPWAY
QUEEN ST
RIBER AVE
BONNINGTON DR
Schs
PC
MANSFIELD ST
SHERWOOD ST
B6017
Somercotes
SOMERCOTES HILL
CASTLE DR
EVEREST DR
SCOTT DR
HASTON DR
STANLEY ST
BRAMLEY ST
LOWER SOMERCOTES
NORMAN RD
CINDER RD
BARRACK YD
Willow Farm
COCKSHUTT LA
THE CROFT
CHARLES ST
SARAH CL
JAMES ST
WINDMILL RISE
SPENCER DR
PARK SIDE
Riddings Park
GREENHILL LA
WINDLEA RD
SHAW ST
COLLEDGE ST
WEST ST
Riddings
PARK MEWS
Riddings House
CHURCH ST
PH
1 CHURCH WLK
VICARAGE MEWS
Sch
1 MELTON CT
2 CADEBY CT
3 RAVEN CL
4 NORTH ST
5 ALFRED ST
ORCHARD RD
FREDERICK ST
GEORGE ST
SCHOOL CROFT
WILLIAMS CL
SPRING RD
HOLLYHURST ROW
MANOR CT
FURNACE ROW
B600 MAIN RD
Pye Bridge
PYE BRIDGE IND EST
Works
Riddings Wood
NOTTINGHAM LA
ALBERT ST
OAKES'S ROW
VICTORIA ST
Cemy
CASSON ST
CINDER BANK
ADELAIDE WLK 1
KING WILLIAM CENTRE 2
QUEEN ST
MARKET ST
MARKET PL
Ironville
REGENT CT
DEEPDALE
WATERSIDE
PARKSIDE CL
PARKSIDE DR
RAILWAY ROW
Codnorpark Reservoir
JESSOP AVE
CHEVIOT AVE
MONUMENT HILL
NEW RD
VICARAGE ROW
Codnor Park
CASTLEFIELDS
STATION LA
Waterworks Plantation
Kennels Farm
Foxhole Plantation
Castle Plantation

D
E
F
Sewage Works
Hobsic Farm
HOBSIC LA
PH
Hall Green
Hillbank Farm
COMMON SIDE
Commonside
Hall Green Farm
BRIDGE END AVE
River Erewash
Crimea Farm
Pye Bridge Junction
Dismantled Railway
CHURCH LA
HOMECROFT DR
STONEY LA
Rosemaryhill
1 ALBERTA AVE
2 CHESTNUT DR
3 CEDAR DR
B6018
Selston Green
Selston
MANSFIELD RD
Pinfold Farm
Liby
Sch
ALFRETON RD
Pye Bridge
B600
MAIN RD
EREWASH ST
RIVER VIEW
Sleepy Hole
CHAPEL RD
HOOLEY ST
VICTORIA RD
HOLLY HILL RD
PEACH AVE
GREEN FARM RD
HOME FM CT
CRESCENT RD
NOTTINGHAM RD
Dove Green
Golf Course
B6016
Ashes Farm
Allen's Green
HANSTUBBIN RD
WOOD NOOK CL
Toadhole
LANGTON HOLLOW
Handstubbing
INKERMAN RD
INKER MAN ST
ALMA RD
Barrows Green
Barrows Hill
Home Farm
Lea Farm
SELSTON RD
BARROWS HILL LA
NEW ROW
Pye Hill
TOP ROW
WAGSTAFF LA
PROVIDENCE RD
LAVERICK RD
FRANKLIN RD
PYE HILL RD
PALMERSTON ST
New Westwood
Bagthorpe Brook
Bagthorpe
Shepherds Rest (PH)
Manor Farm
Jacksdale
THE ORCHARDS
Gate Inn (PH)
LOWER BAGTHORPE
Westwood
Brookside Farm
FLATTS LA
Wansley Hall
Westwood Farm
Yewtree Farm
Cromford Canal (disused)
MAIN RD
WILHALLOW LA
Underwood Green
PLAINSPOT RD
Plain Spot
Underwood Hill
Hole in the Wall (PH)
PRIMROSE AVE
Plain Spot Farm
BRINSLEY HILL
FRANCES ST
HIGH ST
CLUMBER AVE
MAIN ST
BROAD LA
New Brinsley
Pollington House
Oaktree Farm
WINTER CLOSES
A608
RED LA
WINDSMOOR RD
4
53
3
52
2
51
1
50
45
46

161

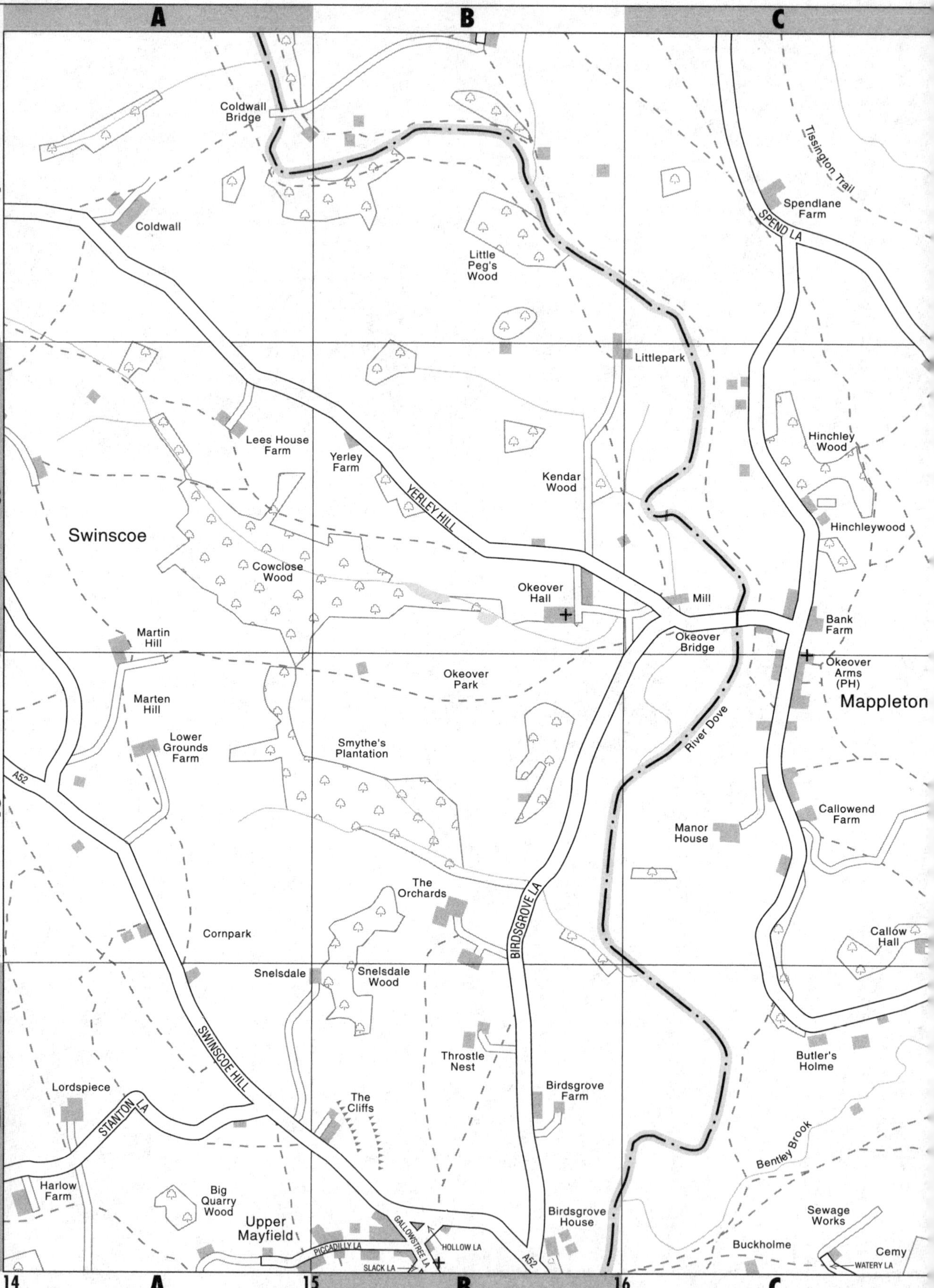
A
B
C
Coldwall Bridge
Coldwall
Little Peg's Wood
Tissington Trail
Spendlane Farm
SPEND LA
Littlepark
Lees House Farm
Yerley Farm
YERLEY HILL
Kendar Wood
Hinchley Wood
Hinchleywood
Swinscoe
Cowclose Wood
Okeover Hall
Mill
Okeover Bridge
Bank Farm
Okeover Arms (PH)
Mappleton
Martin Hill
Marten Hill
Okeover Park
Lower Grounds Farm
Smythe's Plantation
River Dove
A52
Manor House
Callowend Farm
The Orchards
BIRDSGROVE LA
Cornpark
Callow Hall
Snelsdale
Snelsdale Wood
SWINSCOE HILL
Throstle Nest
Butler's Holme
Lordspiece
The Cliffs
Birdsgrove Farm
STANTON LA
Bentley Brook
Harlow Farm
Big Quarry Wood
Upper Mayfield
Birdsgrove House
Sewage Works
GALLOWSTREE LA
HOLLOW LA
PICCADILLY LA
SLACK LA
A52
Buckholme
Cemy
WATERY LA
4
49
3
48
2
47
1
46
14
15
16
A
B
C

184

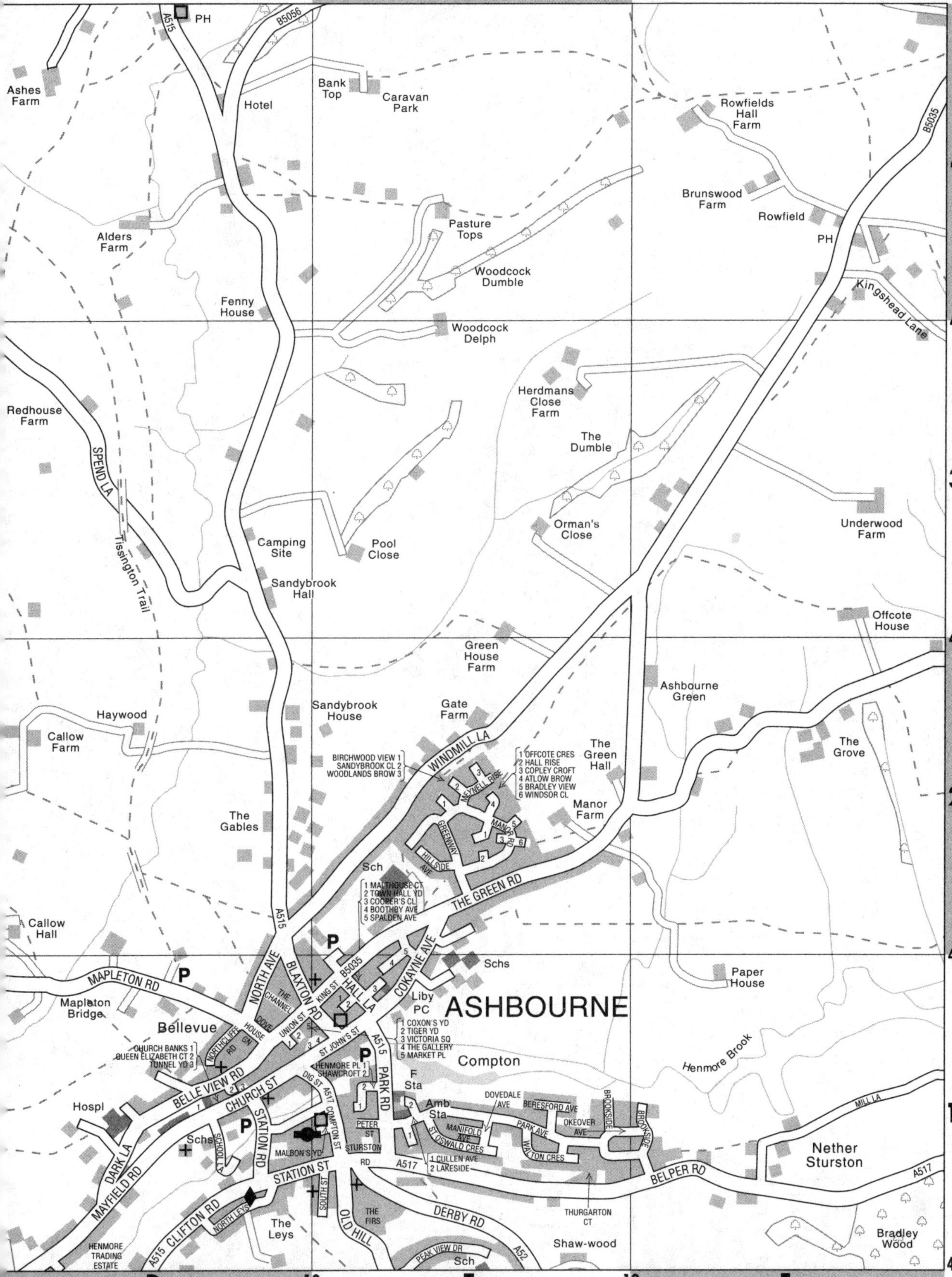
PH
A515
B5056
Ashes Farm
Hotel
Bank Top
Caravan Park
Rowfields Hall Farm
B5035
4
Brunswood Farm
Rowfield
PH
Alders Farm
Pasture Tops
Woodcock Dumble
Kingshead Lane
Fenny House
Woodcock Delph
49
Herdmans Close Farm
Redhouse Farm
SPEND LA
The Dumble
3
Tissington Trail
Orman's Close
Underwood Farm
Camping Site
Pool Close
Sandybrook Hall
Offcote House
48
Green House Farm
Ashbourne Green
Sandybrook House
Gate Farm
Haywood
Callow Farm
The Grove
The Green Hall
WINDMILL LA
BIRCHWOOD VIEW 1
SANDYBROOK CL 2
WOODLANDS BROW 3
1 OFFCOTE CRES
2 HALL RISE
3 COPLEY CROFT
4 ATLOW BROW
5 BRADLEY VIEW
6 WINDSOR CL
MEYNELL RISE
2
Manor Farm
The Gables
GREENWAY
MANOR RD
HILLSIDE AVE
Sch
1 MALTHOUSE CT
2 TOWN HALL YD
3 COOPER'S CL
4 BOOTHBY AVE
5 SPALDEN AVE
THE GREEN RD
Callow Hall
A515
47
Schs
MAPLETON RD
NORTH AVE
BLAXTON RD
B5035
KING ST
HALL LA
COKAYNE AVE
Paper House
Mapleton Bridge
THE CHANNEL
Liby
PC
ASHBOURNE
Bellevue
DOVE HOUSE GN
UNION ST
NORTHCLIFFE RD
ST JOHN'S ST
1 COXON'S YD
2 TIGER YD
3 VICTORIA SQ
4 THE GALLERY
5 MARKET PL
A515
CHURCH BANKS 1
QUEEN ELIZABETH CT 2
TUNNEL YD 3
Compton
Henmore Brook
HENMORE PL 1
SHAWCROFT 2
PARK RD
BELLE VIEW RD
CHURCH ST
DIG ST
A517
F Sta
Hospl
Amb Sta
DOVEDALE AVE
BERESFORD AVE
BROOKSIDE
MILL LA
1
STATION RD
PETER ST
COMPTON ST
MANIFOLD AVE
PARK AVE
OKEOVER AVE
Schs
ST OSWALD CRES
WALTON CRES
Nether Sturston
DARK LA
MALBON'S YD
STURSTON RD
1 CULLEN AVE
2 LAKESIDE
A517
STATION ST
BELPER RD
A517
SOUTH ST
MAYFIELD RD
CLIFTON RD
NORTH LEYS
THE FIRS
DERBY RD
THURGARTON CT
The Leys
OLD HILL
Bradley Wood
A515
HENMORE TRADING ESTATE
PEAK VIEW DR
Sch
A52
Shaw-wood
46
18
19

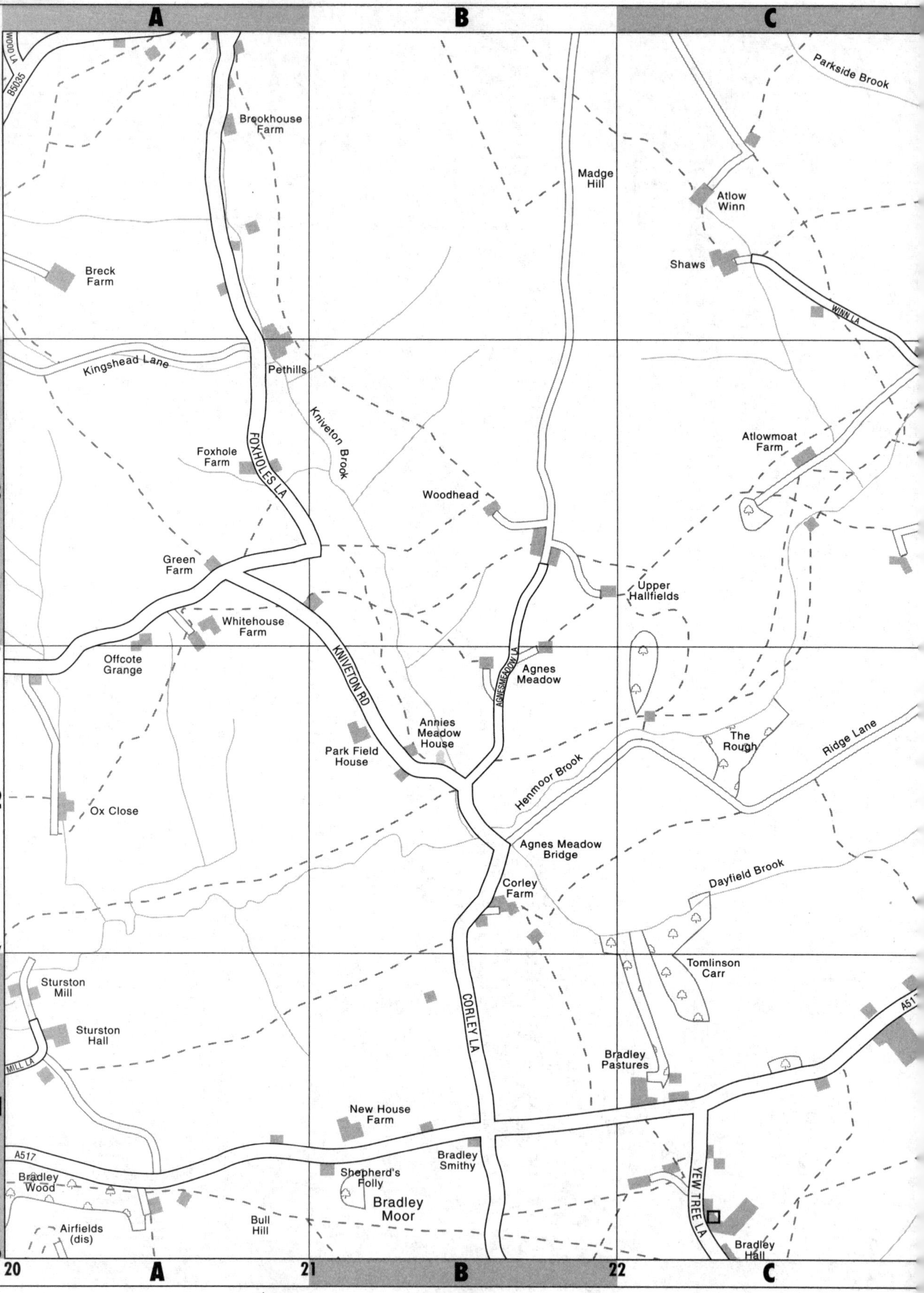
A
B
C
WOOD LA
B5035
Brookhouse Farm
Parkside Brook
Madge Hill
Atlow Winn
4
Breck Farm
Shaws
WINN LA
49
Kingshead Lane
Pethills
Kniveton Brook
FOXHOLES LA
Foxhole Farm
Atlowmoat Farm
3
Woodhead
Green Farm
Upper Hallfields
Whitehouse Farm
48
Offcote Grange
KNIVETON RD
AGNESMEADOW LA
Agnes Meadow
Annies Meadow House
The Rough
Park Field House
Ridge Lane
Henmoor Brook
2
Ox Close
Agnes Meadow Bridge
Dayfield Brook
Corley Farm
47
Sturston Mill
Tomlinson Carr
CORLEY LA
A517
Sturston Hall
MILL LA
Bradley Pastures
1
New House Farm
A517
Bradley Smithy
Bradley Wood
Shepherd's Folly
Bradley Moor
YEW TREE LA
Airfields (dis)
Bull Hill
Bradley Hall
46
20
21
22

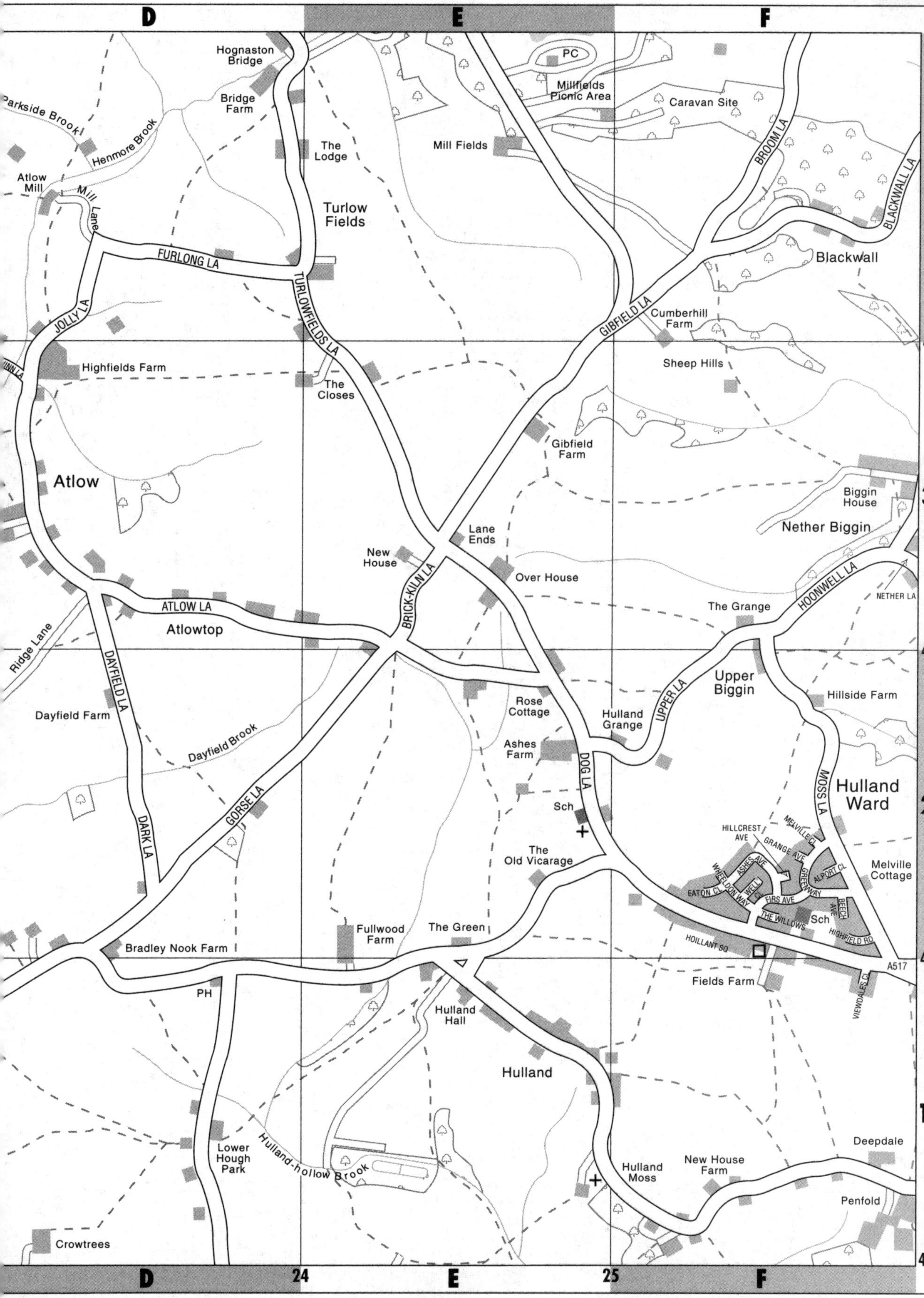
D
E
F
Hognaston Bridge
Bridge Farm
Parkside Brook
Henmore Brook
Atlow Mill
Mill Lane
The Lodge
Turlow Fields
Mill Fields
PC
Millfields Picnic Area
Caravan Site
BROOM LA
BLACKWALL LA
Blackwall
FURLONG LA
JOLLY LA
TURLOWFIELDS LA
GIBFIELD LA
Cumberhill Farm
Sheep Hills
Highfields Farm
The Closes
Gibfield Farm
Atlow
Biggin House
Nether Biggin
Lane Ends
New House
Over House
HOONWELL LA
NETHER LA
BRICK-KILN LA
ATLOW LA
Atlowtop
The Grange
Ridge Lane
DAYFIELD LA
Upper Biggin
Hillside Farm
Dayfield Farm
Rose Cottage
Hulland Grange
UPPER LA
Dayfield Brook
Ashes Farm
DOG LA
MOSS LA
Hulland Ward
GORSE LA
Sch
DARK LA
HILLCREST AVE
MELVILLE CL
GRANGE AVE
The Old Vicarage
ASHES AVE
WHEELDON WAY
WELL CL
GREENWAY
ALPORT CL
Melville Cottage
EATON CL
FIRS AVE
THE WILLOWS
BEECH AVE
Sch
HIGHFIELD RD
HOILLANT SQ
Fullwood Farm
The Green
Bradley Nook Farm
A517
VIEWDALES CL
Fields Farm
PH
Hulland Hall
Hulland
Lower Hough Park
Hulland-hollow Brook
Hulland Moss
New House Farm
Deepdale
Penfold
Crowtrees
4
49
3
48
2
47
1
46
24
25

175
165

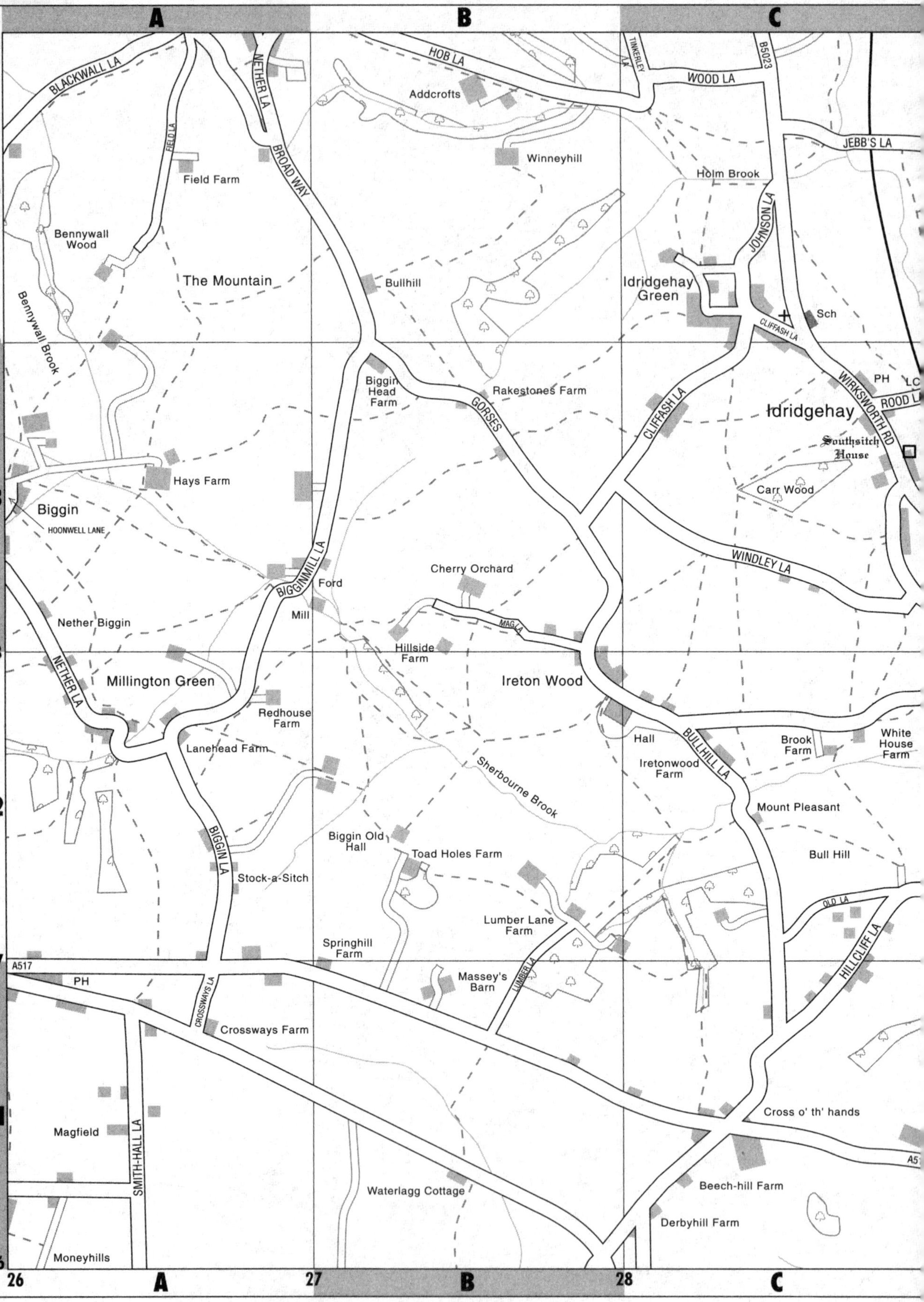

175
188

166
178

189
178

177
167

177
190

168
180

191
180

179
169

179
192

170
182

193
182

A
B
C
Gin Farm
Dismtd Rly
Hobsic
Brinsley Gin
Lower Stoneyford Farm
BOAT LA
Inn
Stoneyford
The Moor
Sch
Hall Farm
Crowfields Farm
Brinsley
HALL LA
PH
Park Farm
River Erewash
New Farm
STONEY LA
Coneygrey Plantation
Brinsley Brook
Crow Wood
ALDERCAR LA
Greasley
A610
CROMFORD RD
MANSFIELD RD
Dismtd Rly
Hall Farm
Aldercar
COCKERHOUSE RD
Eastwood Hall
UPPER DUNSTEAD RD
LOWER DUNSTEAD RD
Langley Mill
Nether Green Brook
EASTWOOD
GREENHILLS RD
DERBY RD
STATION RD
Langley Mill Station
Heanor
MANSFIELD RD
A608
Bailey Grove
NOTTINGHAM RD
MILNHAY RD
Erewash Canal
Sewage Works
Works
CHURCH ST
Langley
HAND'S RD
LACEY FIELDS RD
BREACH RD
LEE LA
Lacey Fields Farm
TINSLEY RD
Cemy
CHEWTON ST
4
49
3
48
2
47
1
46
44
45
46

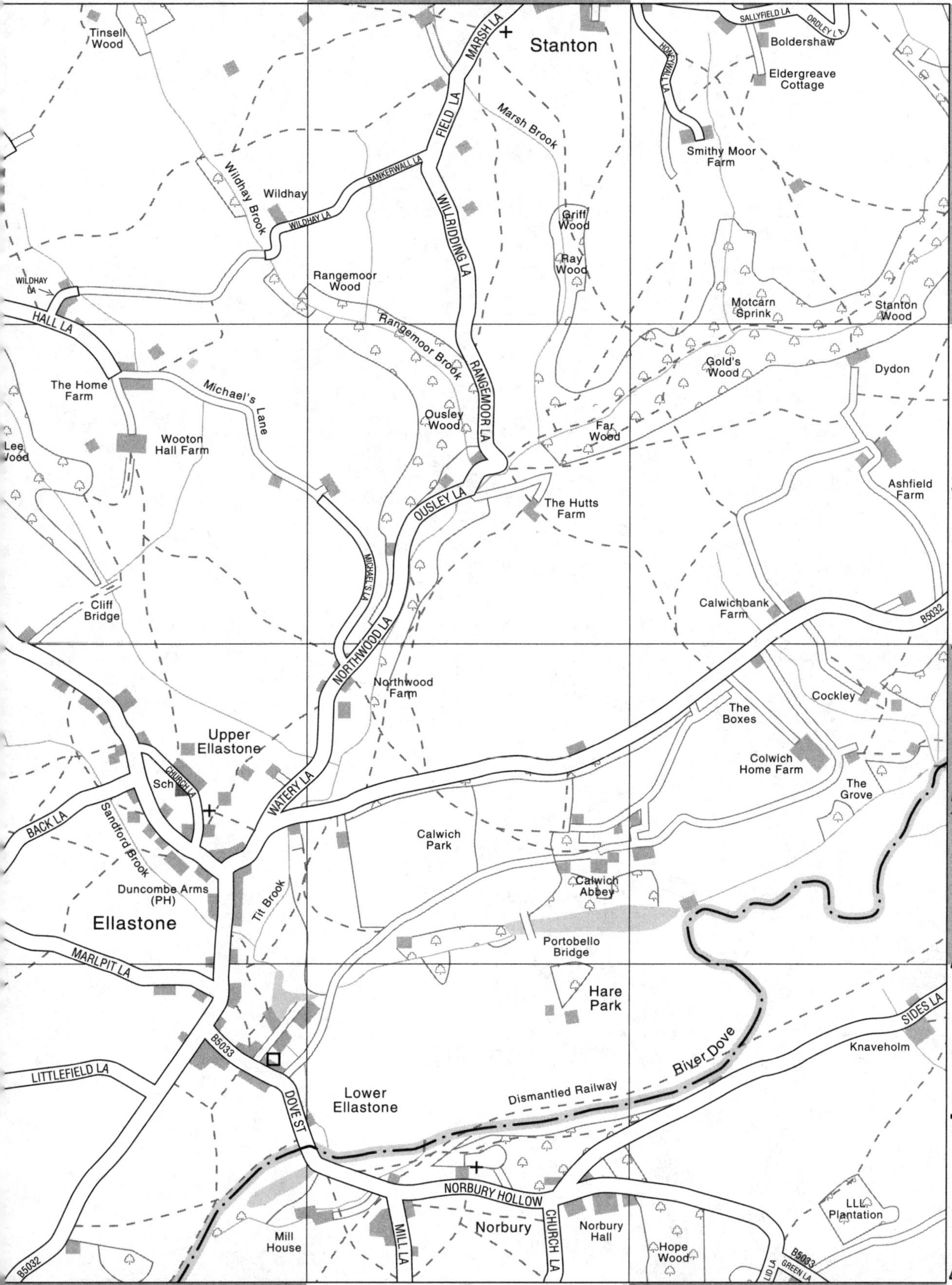
D
E
F
Tinsell Wood
Stanton
MARSH LA
SALLYFIELD LA
ORDLEY LA
Boldershaw
HONEYWALL LA
Eldergreave Cottage
FIELD LA
Marsh Brook
Smithy Moor Farm
BANKERWALL LA
Wildhay Brook
Wildhay
WILDHAY LA
WILLRIDDING LA
Griff Wood
Ray Wood
WILDHAY LA
Rangemoor Wood
HALL LA
Rangemoor Brook
Motcarn Sprink
Stanton Wood
Gold's Wood
Dydon
The Home Farm
Michael's Lane
RANGEMOOR LA
Ousley Wood
Far Wood
Lee Wood
Wooton Hall Farm
Ashfield Farm
OUSLEY LA
The Hutts Farm
MICHAEL'S LA
Cliff Bridge
Calwichbank Farm
B5032
NORTHWOOD LA
Northwood Farm
Cockley
The Boxes
Upper Ellastone
CHURCH LA
Colwich Home Farm
Sch
WATERY LA
The Grove
BACK LA
Sandford Brook
Calwich Park
Tit Brook
Calwich Abbey
Duncombe Arms (PH)
Ellastone
Portobello Bridge
MARLPIT LA
Hare Park
SIDES LA
B5033
River Dove
Knaveholm
LITTLEFIELD LA
Dismantled Railway
DOVE ST
Lower Ellastone
NORBURY HOLLOW
LLL Plantation
Norbury
CHURCH LA
Norbury Hall
MILL LA
Mill House
Hope Wood
B5032
LID LA
GREEN LA
B5033
4
45
3
44
2
43
1
42
12
13

183
172

183
198

D
E
F
MAYFIELD RD
A515
GEORGE ST
LODGE AVE
HIGHFIELD RD
CLIFTON RD
OLD HILL
PEAK VIEW DR
Sch
MUMFORD DR
SPRINGFIELD AVE
BROADMEADOW
LAMBOURNE AVE
BLORE CL
CAVENDISH DR
HADDON CT
STANTON RD
MILLDALE CT
ILAM CT
SPENDER CL
WEAVER CL
OLD DERBY RD
Spitalhill
BRICKYARD COTTAGES
ROWAN
Sch
POPLAR CRES
DERWENT GDNS
HAWTHORN CL
MAPLE DR
WILLOW MEADOW RD
OAK CRES
PINE CROFT
CHESTNUT DR
CEDAR CL
Westwood
Lodge Farm
Bank Cottages
Hilltop
DERBY RD
WHITLEY WAY
MOOR FARM RD W
Industrial Park
BLENHEIM RD
MOOR FARM RD E
Airfield (dis)
4
SNIPESMOOR LA
Caravan Park
45
Golf Course
Whitemeadow
A52
WYASTON RD
MOOR LA
The Hollies
3
Blake House
Briery House
Glebe House
DOBBINHORSE LA
Tinker's Inn
Osmaston Fields Farm
New House Farm
44
Sch
CHURCH LA
The Holts
Osmaston
New Buildings Farm
2
Osmaston Pastures
QUILOW LA
Quilow Farm
A515
Scardale Covert
43
EDLASTON LA
Wyaston Brook
Edlaston Hall
Copse Hill
PH
Edlaston
Church Farm
Wyaston
1
ORCHARD LA
Wyaston Grove
Airfield (dis)
The Hole
RODSLEY LA
42
D
18
E
19
F

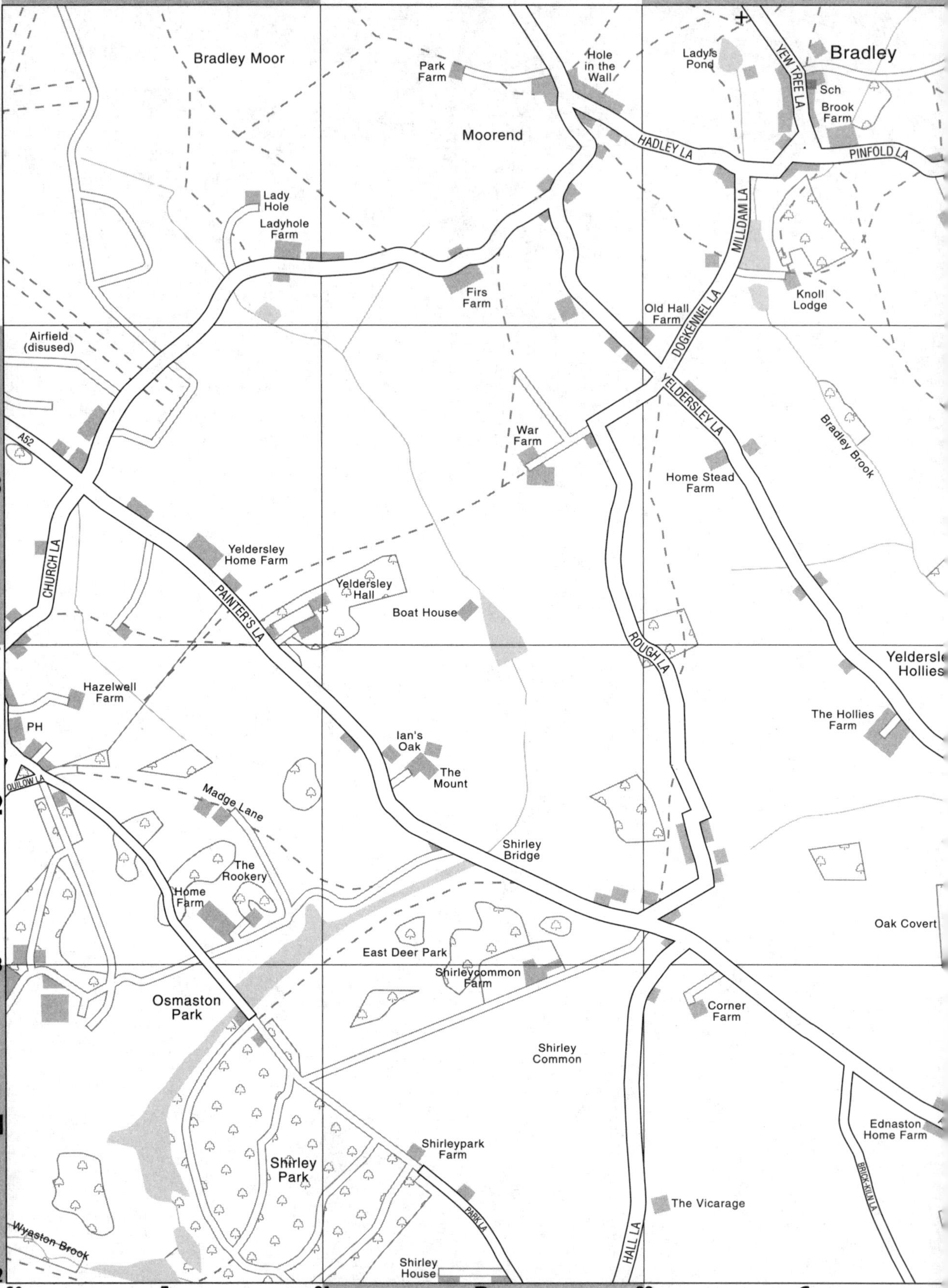
A
B
C
Bradley Moor
Park Farm
Hole in the Wall
Lady's Pond
YEW TREE LA
Bradley
Sch
Brook Farm
Moorend
HADLEY LA
PINFOLD LA
MILLDAM LA
Lady Hole
Ladyhole Farm
Firs Farm
Knoll Lodge
Old Hall Farm
DOGKENNEL LA
Airfield (disused)
YELDERSLEY LA
War Farm
Bradley Brook
A52
Home Stead Farm
CHURCH LA
Yeldersley Home Farm
Yeldersley Hall
PAINTER'S LA
Boat House
ROUGH LA
Yeldersley Hollies
Hazelwell Farm
PH
The Hollies Farm
Ian's Oak
The Mount
QUILOW LA
Madge Lane
Shirley Bridge
The Rookery
Home Farm
Oak Covert
East Deer Park
Shirleycommon Farm
Osmaston Park
Corner Farm
Shirley Common
Ednaston Home Farm
Shirleypark Farm
Shirley Park
BRICK-KILN LA
PARK LA
The Vicarage
Wyaston Brook
HALL LA
Shirley House
4
45
3
44
2
43
1
42
20
21
22

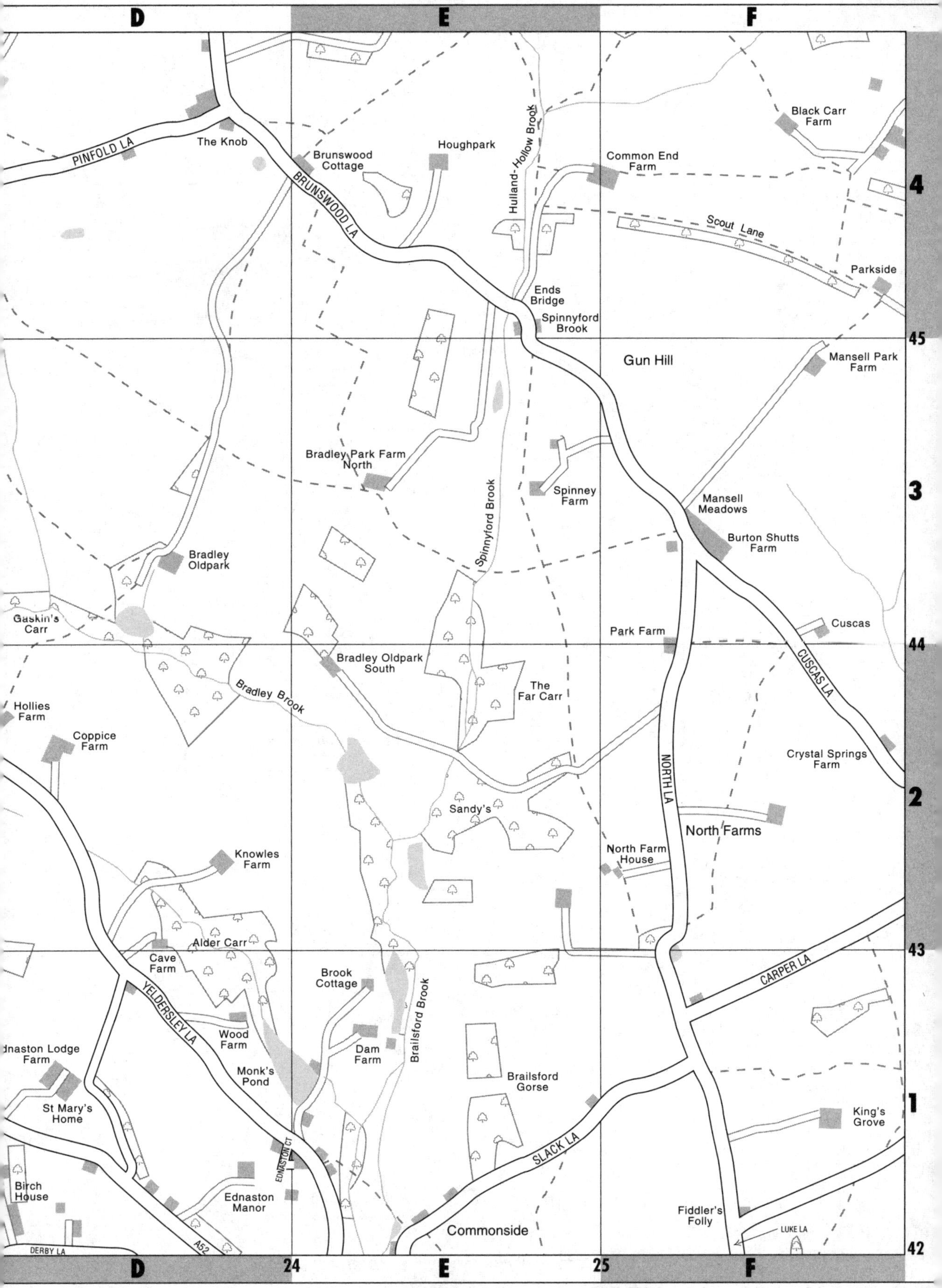
D
E
F
PINFOLD LA
The Knob
Brunswood Cottage
BRUNSWOOD LA
Houghpark
Hulland-Hollow Brook
Common End Farm
Black Carr Farm
Scout Lane
Parkside
Ends Bridge
Spinnyford Brook
Gun Hill
Mansell Park Farm
Bradley Park Farm North
Spinnyford Brook
Spinney Farm
Mansell Meadows
Burton Shutts Farm
Bradley Oldpark
Gaskin's Carr
Park Farm
Cuscas
CUSCAS LA
Bradley Oldpark South
The Far Carr
Bradley Brook
Hollies Farm
Coppice Farm
Crystal Springs Farm
NORTH LA
Sandy's
North Farms
Knowles Farm
North Farm House
Alder Carr
Cave Farm
CARPER LA
YELDERSLEY LA
Brook Cottage
Brailsford Brook
Wood Farm
Dam Farm
dnaston Lodge Farm
Monk's Pond
Brailsford Gorse
St Mary's Home
King's Grove
EDNASTON CT
SLACK LA
Birch House
Ednaston Manor
Fiddler's Folly
LUKE LA
Commonside
DERBY LA
A52
4
45
3
44
2
43
1
42
24
25

187
176

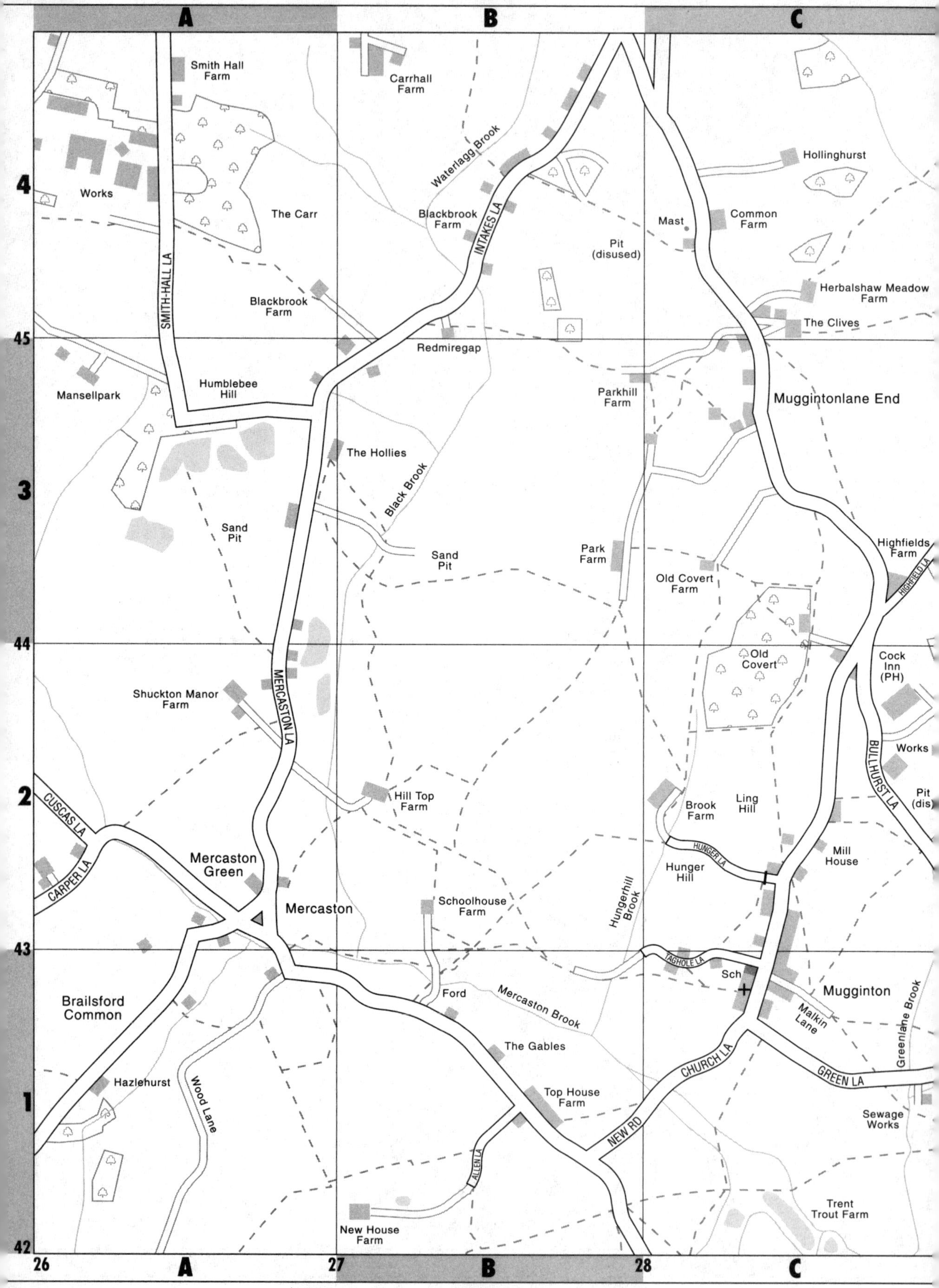
A
B
C
4
3
2
1
45
44
43
42
26
27
28
Smith Hall Farm
Carrhall Farm
Waterlagg Brook
Hollinghurst
Works
The Carr
Blackbrook Farm
INTAKES LA
Mast
Common Farm
Pit (disused)
SMITH-HALL LA
Blackbrook Farm
Herbalshaw Meadow Farm
The Clives
Redmiregap
Mansellpark
Humblebee Hill
Parkhill Farm
Muggintonlane End
The Hollies
Black Brook
Sand Pit
Sand Pit
Park Farm
Highfields Farm
HIGHFIELD LA
Old Covert Farm
Old Covert
Cock Inn (PH)
Shuckton Manor Farm
MERCASTON LA
Works
BULLHURST LA
CUSCAS LA
Hill Top Farm
Brook Farm
Ling Hill
Pit (dis
HUNGER LA
Mill House
CARPER LA
Mercaston Green
Hunger Hill
Hungerhill Brook
Schoolhouse Farm
Mercaston
TAGHOLE LA
Sch
Mugginton
Malkin Lane
Brailsford Common
Ford
Mercaston Brook
Greenlane Brook
The Gables
CHURCH LA
GREEN LA
Hazlehurst
Wood Lane
Top House Farm
Sewage Works
NEW RD
ALLEN LA
New House Farm
Trent Trout Farm

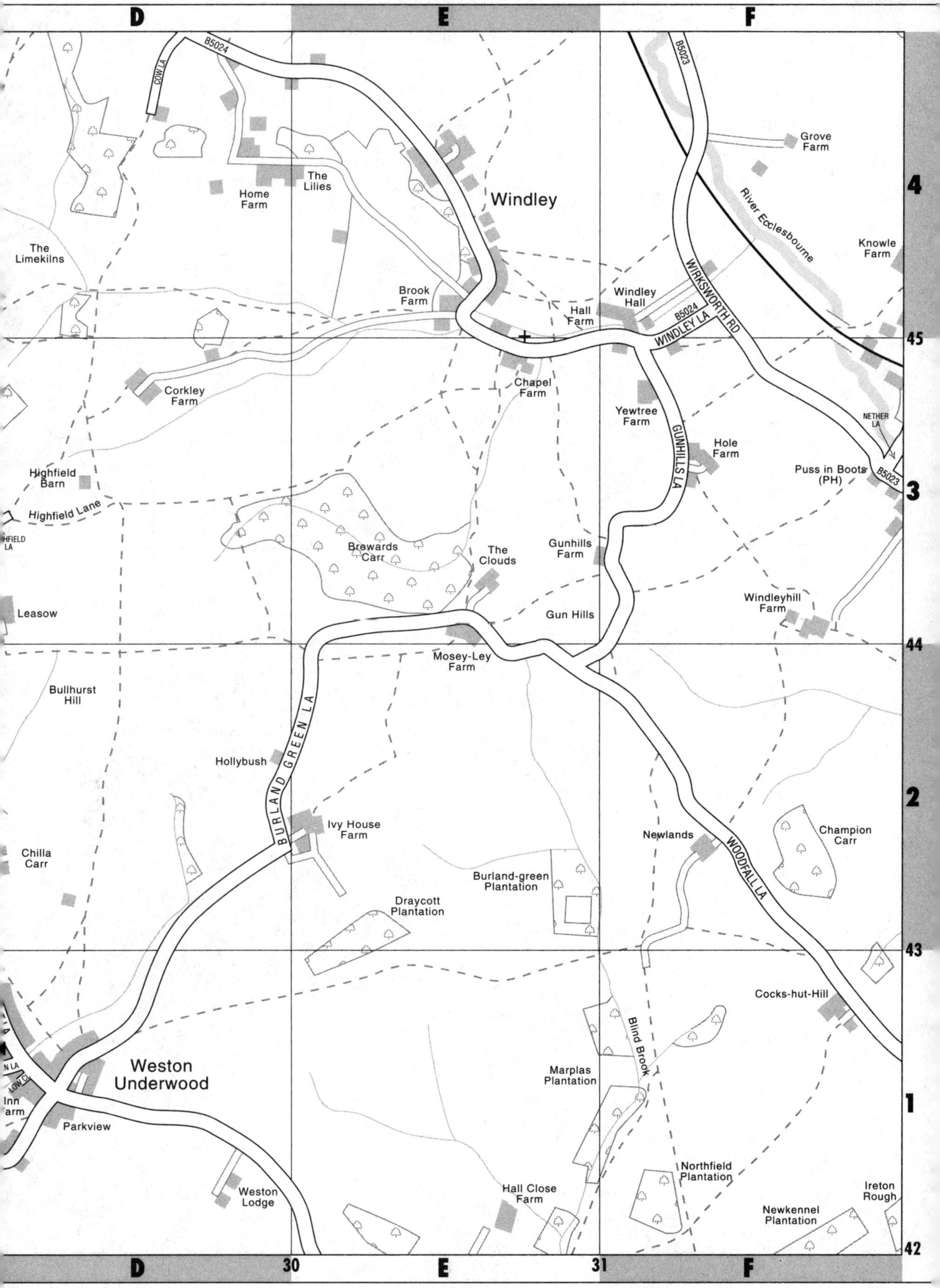
D
E
F
B5024
COW LA
B5023
Grove Farm
Home Farm
The Lilies
Windley
River Ecclesbourne
Knowle Farm
The Limekilns
Brook Farm
Windley Hall
Hall Farm
WIRKSWORTH RD
B5024
WINDLEY LA
Corkley Farm
Chapel Farm
Yewtree Farm
NETHER LA
GUNHILLS LA
Hole Farm
Puss in Boots (PH)
B5023
Highfield Barn
Highfield Lane
Brewards Carr
The Clouds
Gunhills Farm
Leasow
Gun Hills
Windleyhill Farm
Mosey-Ley Farm
Bullhurst Hill
BURLAND GREEN LA
Hollybush
Ivy House Farm
Newlands
WOODFALL LA
Champion Carr
Chilla Carr
Burland-green Plantation
Draycott Plantation
Cocks-hut-Hill
Blind Brook
Weston Underwood
Marplas Plantation
Parkview
Northfield Plantation
Weston Lodge
Hall Close Farm
Newkennel Plantation
Ireton Rough
4
45
3
44
2
43
1
42
30
31

189
178

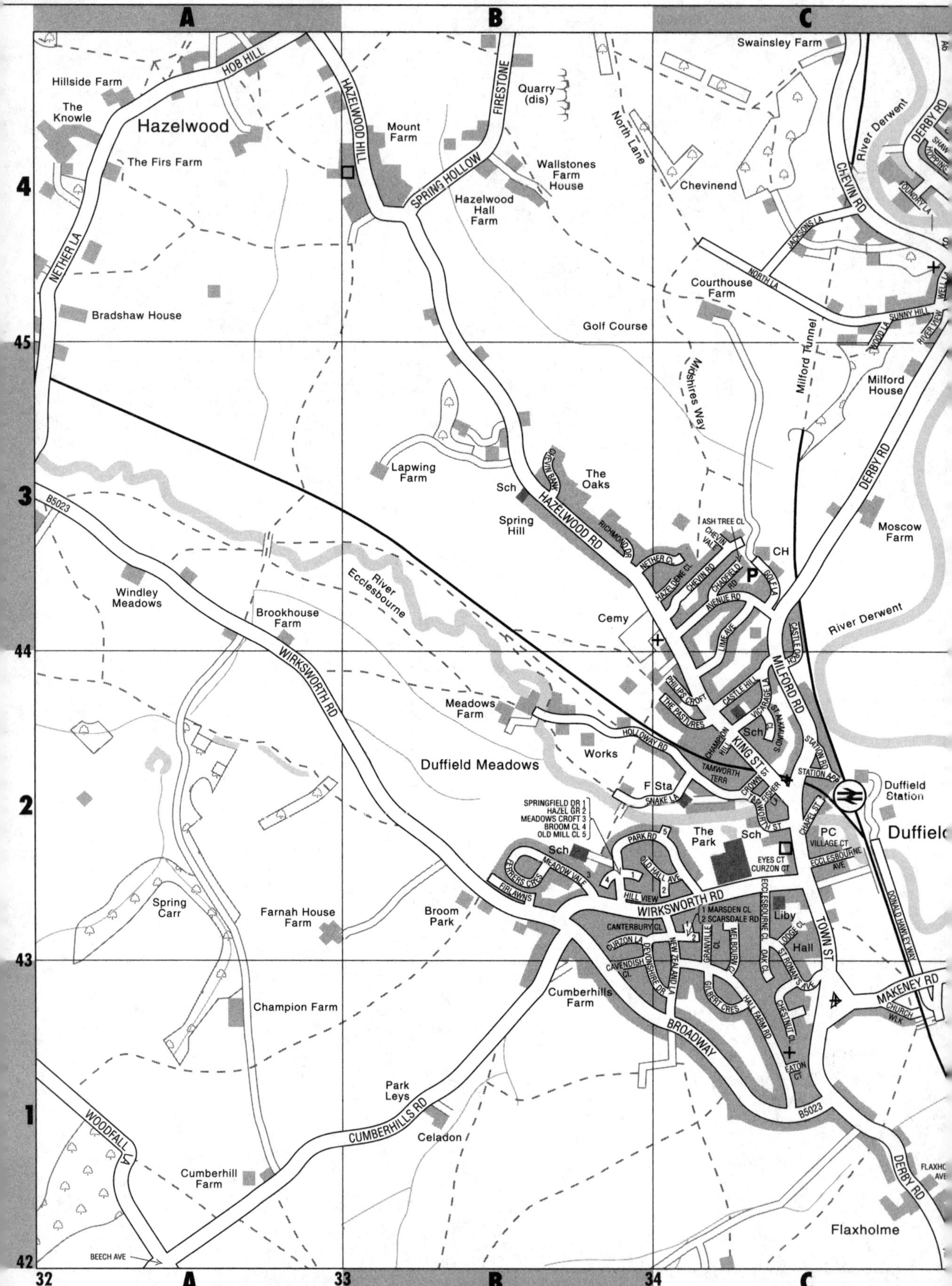

189
204

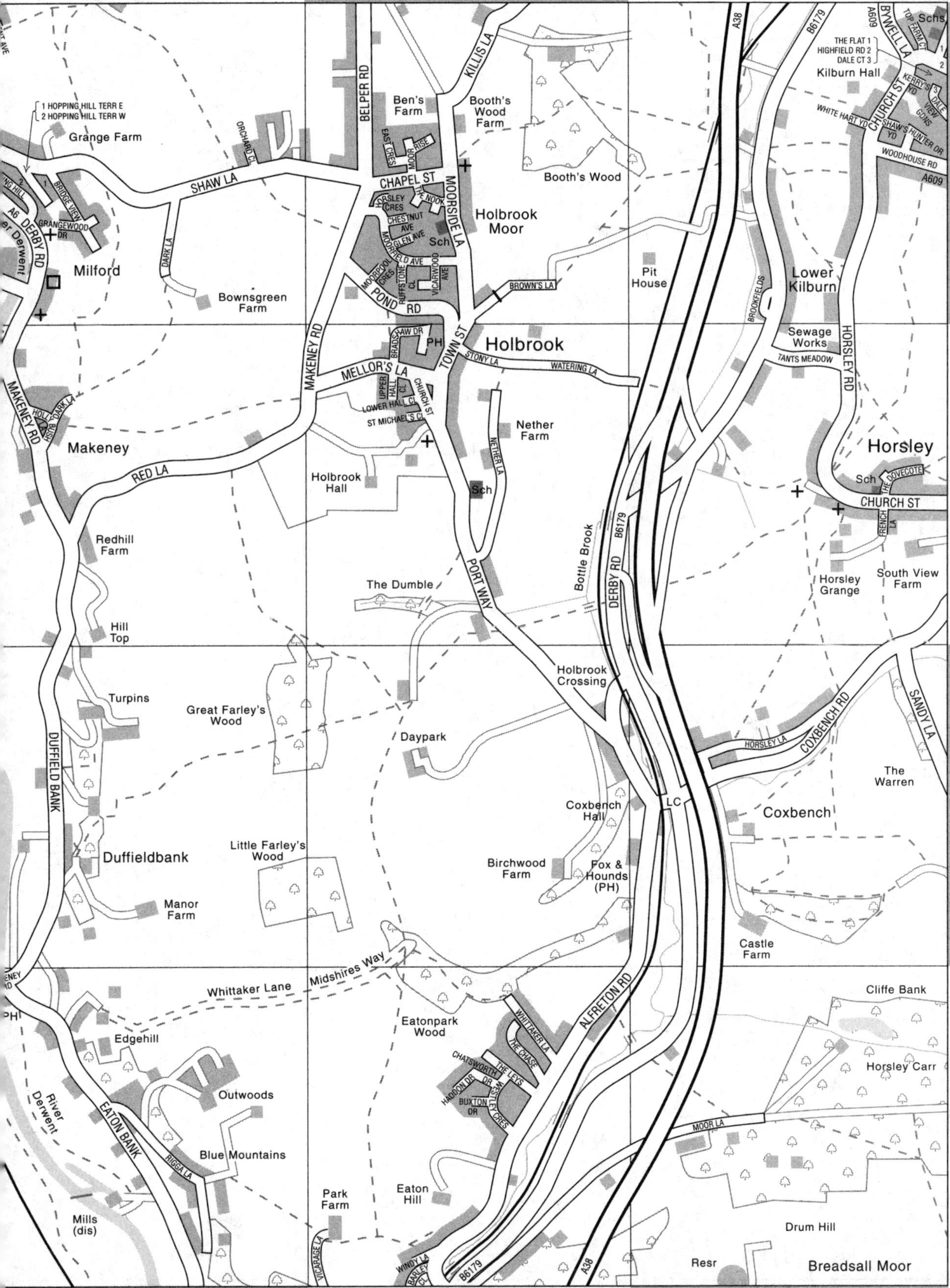
D
E
F
Grange Farm
Milford
Bownsgreen Farm
Makeney
Redhill Farm
Hill Top
Turpins
Duffieldbank
Manor Farm
Edgehill
Outwoods
Blue Mountains
Mills (dis)
River Derwent
Ben's Farm
Booth's Wood Farm
Booth's Wood
Holbrook Moor
Holbrook
Nether Farm
Holbrook Hall
The Dumble
Great Farley's Wood
Daypark
Little Farley's Wood
Holbrook Crossing
Coxbench Hall
Birchwood Farm
Fox & Hounds (PH)
Whittaker Lane
Midshires Way
Eatonpark Wood
Eaton Hill
Park Farm
Pit House
Lower Kilburn
Kilburn Hall
Sewage Works
Horsley
Horsley Grange
South View Farm
The Warren
Coxbench
Castle Farm
Cliffe Bank
Horsley Carr
Drum Hill
Breadsall Moor
Resr
Bottle Brook
SHAW LA
RED LA
MAKENEY RD
BELPER RD
KILLIS LA
MOORSIDE LA
TOWN ST
PORT WAY
DERBY RD
ALFRETON RD
DUFFIELD BANK
EATON BANK
COXBENCH RD
HORSLEY RD
SANDY LA
MOOR LA
CHURCH ST
MELLOR'S LA
STONY LA
WATERING LA
BROWN'S LA
POND RD
CHAPEL ST
A38
A6
A609
B6179
36
37
42
43
44
45
1
2
3
4

191 180

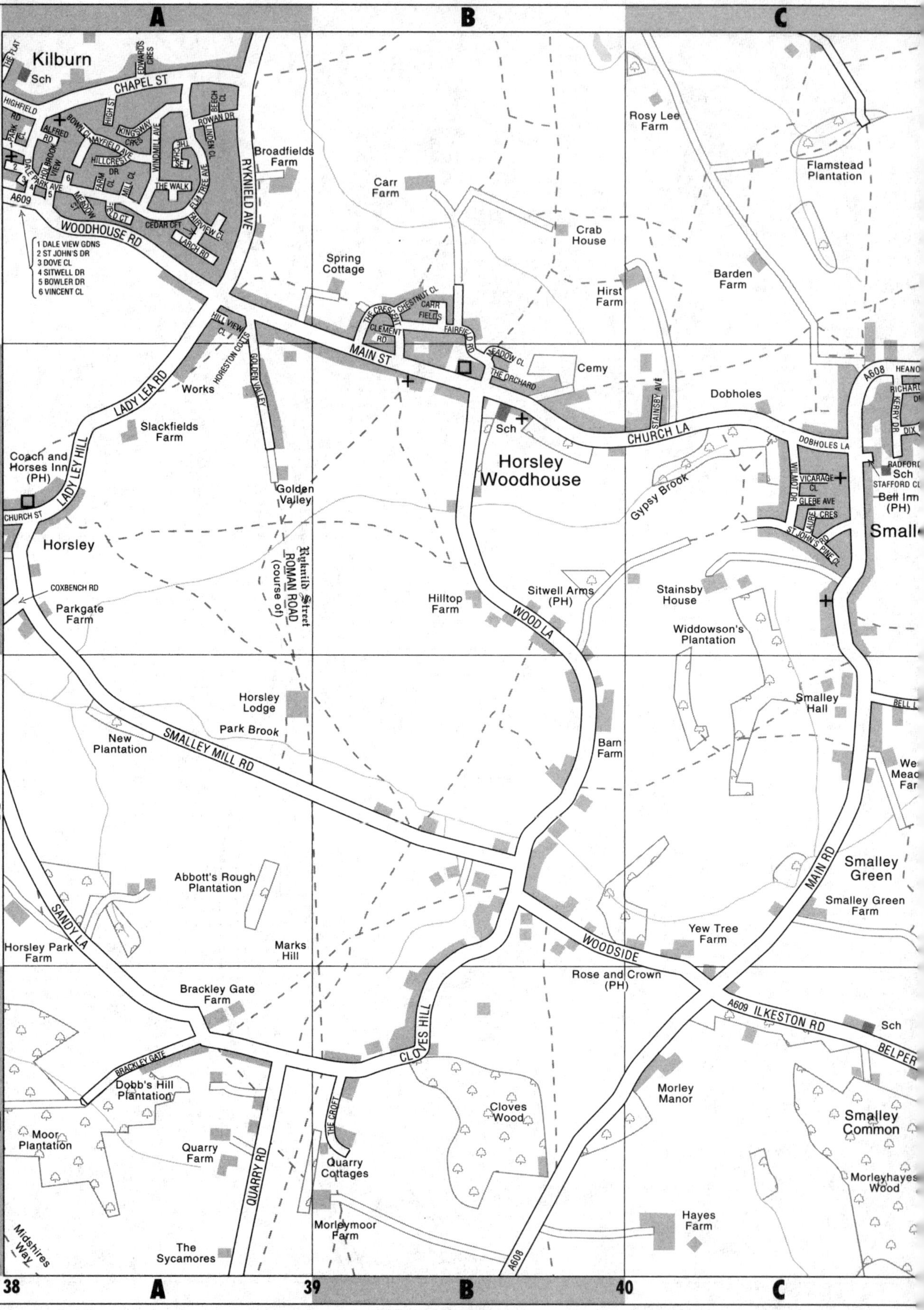

A
B
C
4
45
3
44
2
43
1
42
38
39
40
Kilburn
Sch
CHAPEL ST
HIGHFIELD RD
ALFRED RD
PARK CL
HOLBROOK VIEW
DALE PARK AVE
MAYFIELD AVE
HILLCREST DR
HIGH ST
KINGSWAY CRES
WINDMILL AVE
BEECH CL
ROWAN DR
LINDEN CL
THE WALK
ELM TREE AVE
FAIRVIEW CL
CEDAR CFT
LARCH RD
FARM CL
MILL CL
MEADOW ST
FIELD CT
A609
WOODHOUSE RD
RYKNIELD AVE
EDWARDS CRES
THE FLAT
1 DALE VIEW GDNS
2 ST JOHN'S DR
3 DOVE CL
4 SITWELL DR
5 BOWLER DR
6 VINCENT CL
Broadfields Farm
Carr Farm
Spring Cottage
Crab House
Rosy Lee Farm
Flamstead Plantation
Barden Farm
Hirst Farm
THE CRESCENT
CHESTNUT CL
CARR FIELDS
CLEMENT RD
FAIRFIELD RD
MEADOW CL
THE ORCHARD
MAIN ST
HILL VIEW CL
HORESTON COTTS
GOLDEN VALLEY
LADY LEA RD
Works
Cemy
STAINSBY AVE
Dobholes
A608
HEANOR
RICHARD
KERRY DR
DIX
Slackfields Farm
Sch
CHURCH LA
DOBHOLES LA
Horsley Woodhouse
Coach and Horses Inn (PH)
LADY LEY HILL
CHURCH ST
Golden Valley
Gypsy Brook
WILMOT DR
VICARAGE CL
GLEBE AVE
LAUREL CRES
ST JOHN'S RD
PINE CL
RADFORD
Sch
STAFFORD CL
Bell Inn (PH)
Small
Horsley
COXBENCH RD
Parkgate Farm
Rykneld Street ROMAN ROAD (course of)
Hilltop Farm
Sitwell Arms (PH)
WOOD LA
Stainsby House
Widdowson's Plantation
Horsley Lodge
Park Brook
New Plantation
SMALLEY MILL RD
Barn Farm
Smalley Hall
BELL L
We Mead Far
Abbott's Rough Plantation
SANDY LA
Marks Hill
Horsley Park Farm
MAIN RD
Smalley Green
Smalley Green Farm
Yew Tree Farm
WOODSIDE
Rose and Crown (PH)
Brackley Gate Farm
A609 ILKESTON RD
Sch
BELPER
BRACKLEY GATE
CLOVES HILL
Dobb's Hill Plantation
THE CROFT
Cloves Wood
Morley Manor
Moor Plantation
Quarry Farm
QUARRY RD
Quarry Cottages
Smalley Common
Morleyhayes Wood
Hayes Farm
Morleymoor Farm
Midshires Way
The Sycamores
A608

181
194

207
194

193
182

193
208

D
E
F
Newthorpe Common
Giltbrook
Kimberley
Depot
Gilt Hill Farm
Sch
A610
B6010
A6096
GILT HILL
EASTWOOD RD
MAWS LA
HARDY ST
HIGH SPANIA
MAIN ST
HIGH ST
Coll
Hogs Head (PH)
Sewage Works
Dismantled Railway
GIN CLOSE WAY
AWSWORTH LA
Grasscroft Farm
Swingate
Manor Farm
Awsworth
THE LANE
Babbington Hall
Babbington
BABBINGTON LA
Viaduct
Stenson's Lock
NEWTON'S LA
WESTBY LA
Babbington House Farm
Swingate Farm
Cossall Common
AWSWORTH RD
Common Farm
Strelley Park Farm
Cossall Marsh
Spring Wood
River Erewash
Erewash Canal
CORONATION RD
Nottingham Canal (disused)
Works
THE ROPEWORK SEEDBED CENTRE
CHURCH LA
Cossall
Manor Farm
Grange Farm
ROBINETTES LA
Turkey Fields Farm
Oldmoor Farmhouse
MILL LA
DEAD LA
48
49
4
45
3
44
2
43
1
42

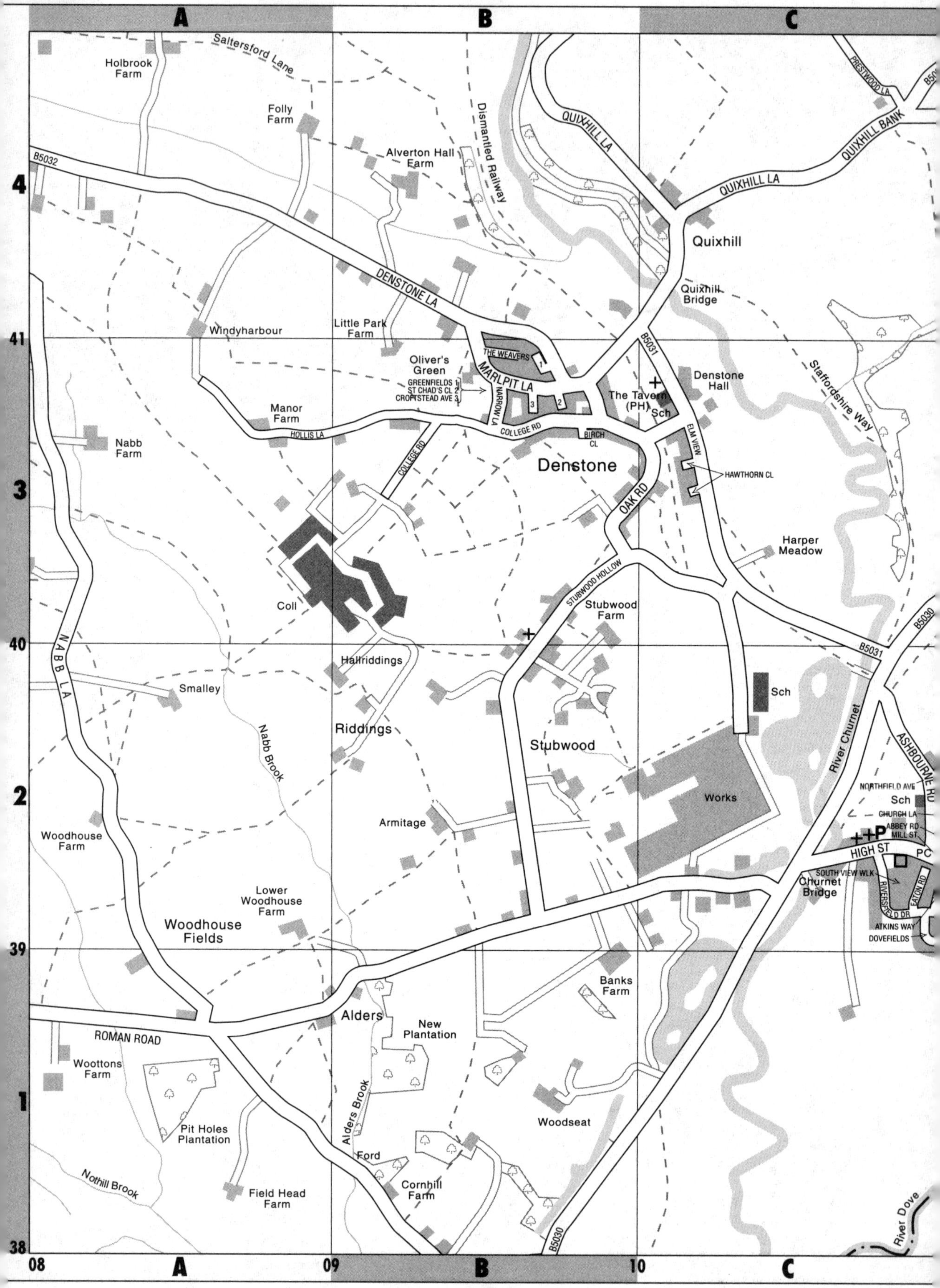
A
B
C
Saltersford Lane
Holbrook Farm
Folly Farm
Alverton Hall Farm
Dismantled Railway
QUIXHILL LA
PRESTWOOD LA
QUIXHILL BANK
Quixhill
Quixhill Bridge
B5032
DENSTONE LA
Windyharbour
Little Park Farm
Oliver's Green
GREENFIELDS 1
ST CHAD'S CL 2
CROFTSTEAD AVE 3
THE WEAVERS
MARLPIT LA
NARROW LA
Manor Farm
HOLLIS LA
COLLEGE RD
BIRCH CL
B5031
The Tavern (PH)
Sch
Denstone Hall
ELM VIEW
HAWTHORN CL
Staffordshire Way
Nabb Farm
Denstone
OAK RD
Coll
STUBWOOD HOLLOW
Stubwood Farm
Harper Meadow
NABB LA
Hallriddings
Smalley
Riddings
Nabb Brook
Stubwood
River Churnet
ASHBOURNE RD
Works
NORTHFIELD AVE
CHURCH LA
ABBEY RD
MILL ST
HIGH ST
PC
Woodhouse Farm
Armitage
SOUTH VIEW WLK
Churnet Bridge
RIVERSFIELD DR
EATON RD
Lower Woodhouse Farm
Woodhouse Fields
ATKINS WAY
DOVEFIELDS
Banks Farm
Alders
New Plantation
ROMAN ROAD
Woottons Farm
Pit Holes Plantation
Alders Brook
Woodseat
Ford
Nothill Brook
Cornhill Farm
Field Head Farm
B5030
River Dove
4
41
3
40
2
39
1
38
08
09
10

D
E
F
B 5030
Ivy Cottages
Osier Plantation
Four Acre Plantation
Green Lane Farm
B 5033
GREEN LA
Woodend
Riverside Centre
Alfross House
MILL LA
CHURCH LA
LID LA
Sch
Leigh's Plantation
Dismantled Railway
MEADOW LA
New House Farm
BAG LA
Inge Cottages
Swinholm Farm
Roston Inn (PH)
Roston
THE HOLLOW
Squashly Farm
UNDERTOWN LA
Dalesgap
Dovecliff
arrowhill
Highfields House
Doveflats
River Dove
Shield House Farm
Hurd's Barn
The Shawleys
ORTHFIELD AVE
DOVE LA
RONATION CRES
CHURCH LA
Sch
Rocester
Longchimneys
BEY RD
WEST VIEW
Marston Park
MILL ST
Park Holme
Valley View Walk
Rocester Bridge
ERSFIELD DR
White House
Marston Lodge
VEFIELDS
Daisybank Farm
Alder Carrs
Springfield House
Clowneholme Farm
Marstonbank Farm
Staffordshire Way
Abbotsholme (Sch)
Thurvaston
CUBLEY LA
Monk's Clownholme
Barway Cottages
THURVASTON RD
Sedsall Rough
Marstonbrook Farm
Marston House Farm
WESTON BANK
41
40
39
38
4
3
2
1
12
13

197
184

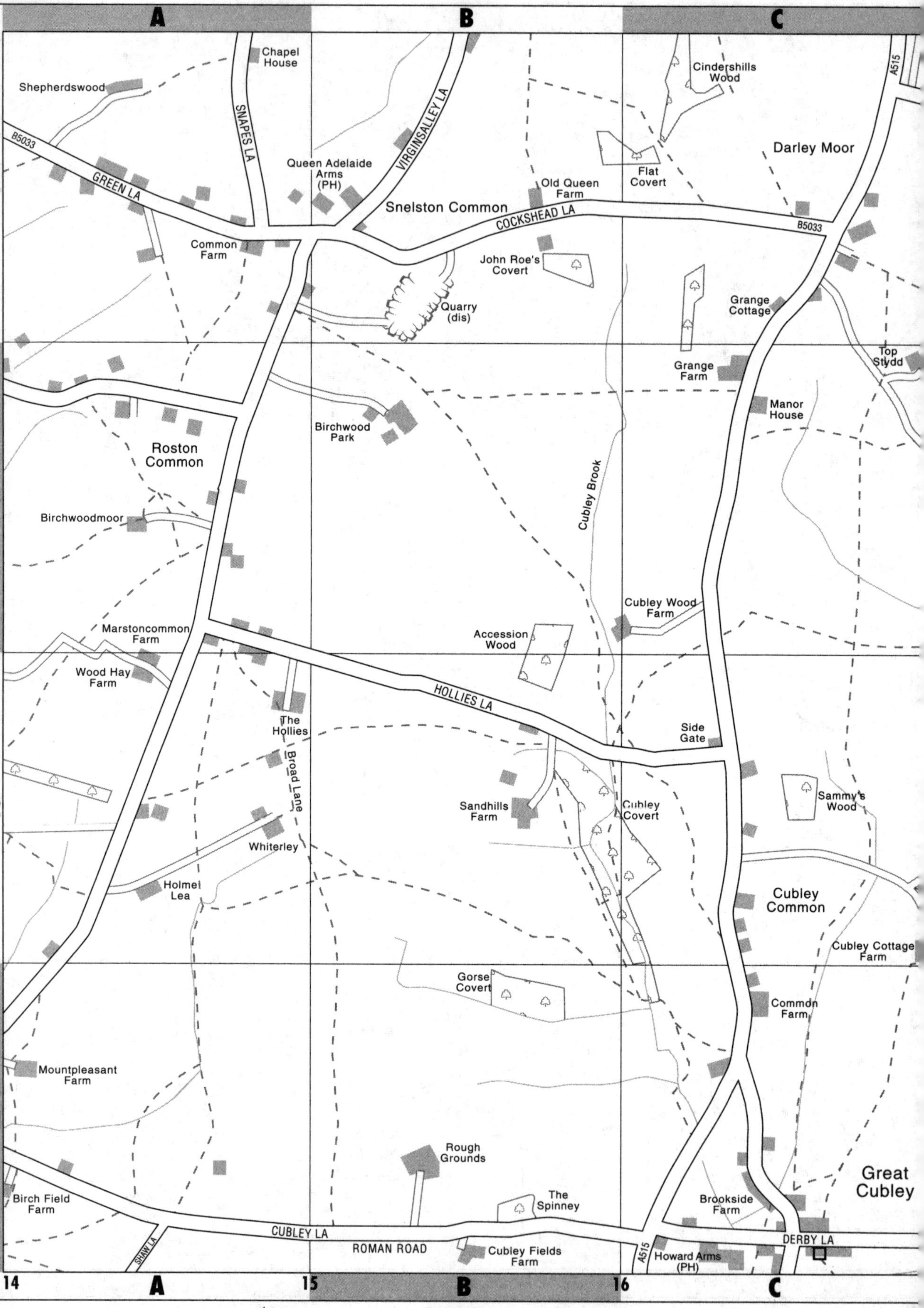
A
B
C
4
3
2
1
41
40
39
38
14
15
16
Chapel House
Shepherdswood
SNAPES LA
B5033
GREEN LA
Queen Adelaide Arms (PH)
VIRGINSALLEY LA
Snelston Common
Old Queen Farm
COCKSHEAD LA
Cindershills Wood
Flat Covert
Darley Moor
A515
B5033
Common Farm
John Roe's Covert
Quarry (dis)
Grange Cottage
Top Stydd
Grange Farm
Manor House
Birchwood Park
Roston Common
Birchwoodmoor
Cubley Brook
Cubley Wood Farm
Accession Wood
Marstoncommon Farm
Wood Hay Farm
HOLLIES LA
The Hollies
Side Gate
Broad Lane
Sandhills Farm
Cubley Covert
Sammy's Wood
Whiterley
Holmel Lea
Cubley Common
Cubley Cottage Farm
Gorse Covert
Common Farm
Mountpleasant Farm
Rough Grounds
Great Cubley
Birch Field Farm
The Spinney
Brookside Farm
CUBLEY LA
DERBY LA
ROMAN ROAD
SHAW LA
A515
Cubley Fields Farm
Howard Arms (PH)

D
E
F
RODSLEY LA
Wyastoncommon Farm
Shirley Oldpark Farm
Hales Green
Knob Farm
Brown's Brook
Rodsley Cottage
RODSLEY LA
4
Leasowes
Swallowtail Farm
Rodsleywood
41
Bentley Brook
Park Farm
3
PRIORY CL
RODSLEY LA
PH
Sch
GRAVELLY BANK MEWS
Yeaveley
Eddishes
Ivy House Farm
Stydd Hall
Bull Lane
40
Cemy
The Old Vicarage
Riddings
Styddhouse Farm
Leapley Mount Farm
Boothay Farm
2
Bog Plantation
LEAPLEY LA
Bentley Cottage Farm
39
Home Farm
Bentley Brook
Bentley Fields Farm
Alkmonton House
1
Alkmonton
Alkmonton Bottoms
ROMAN ROAD
RBY LA
Bentley Hall
Top House Farm
38
D
18
E
19
F

199
186

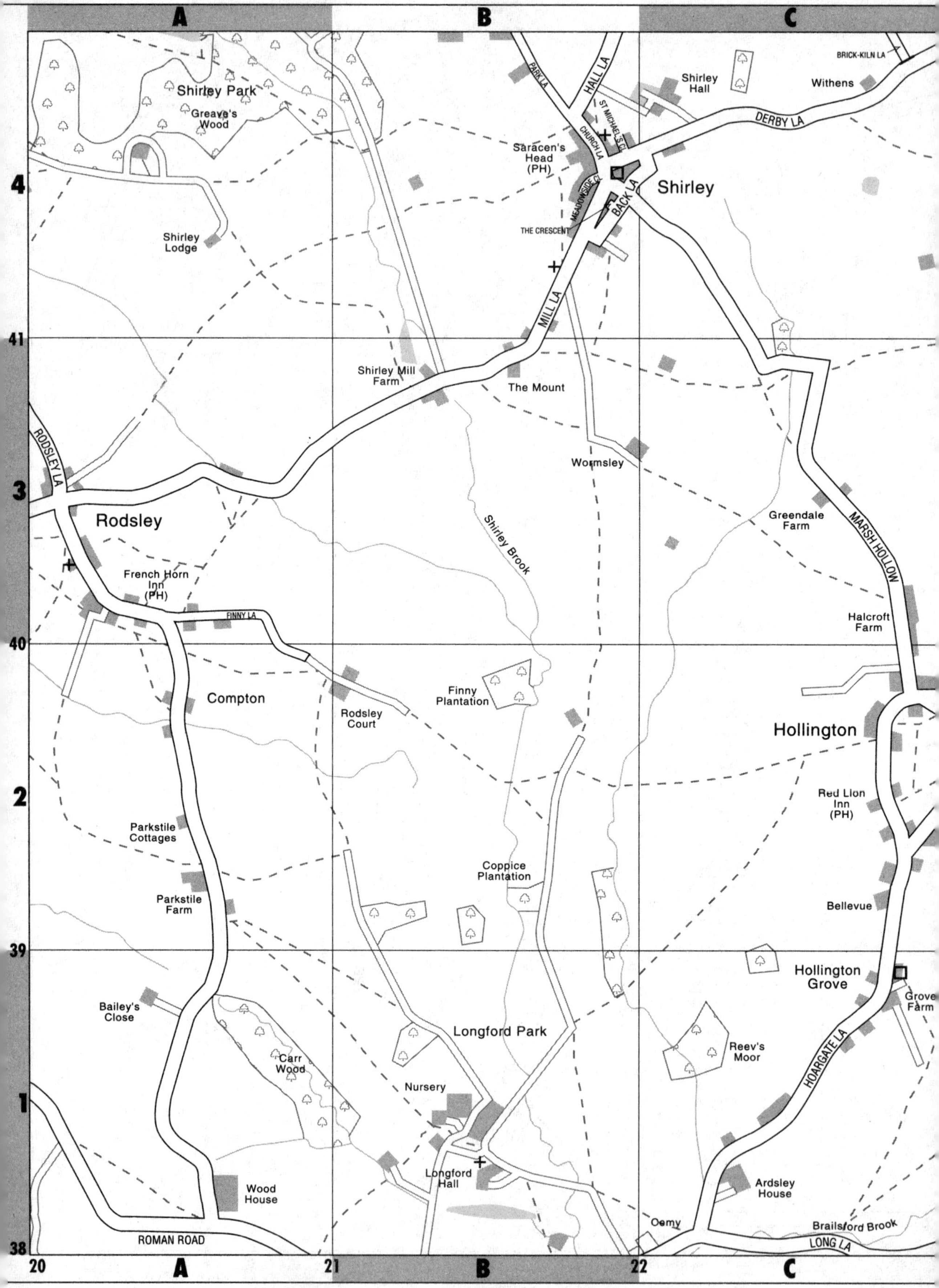

199
214

187
202

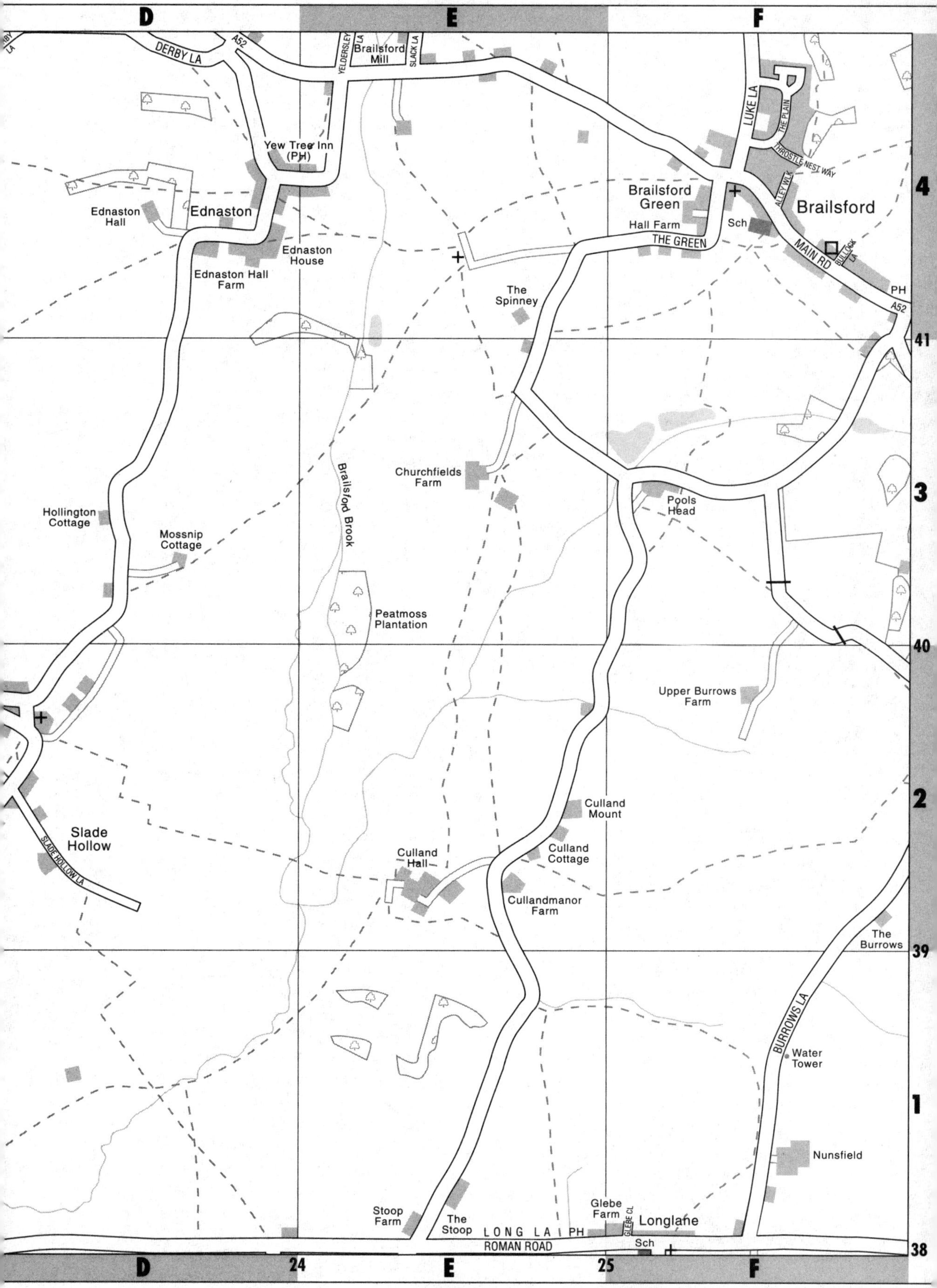

215
202

201
188

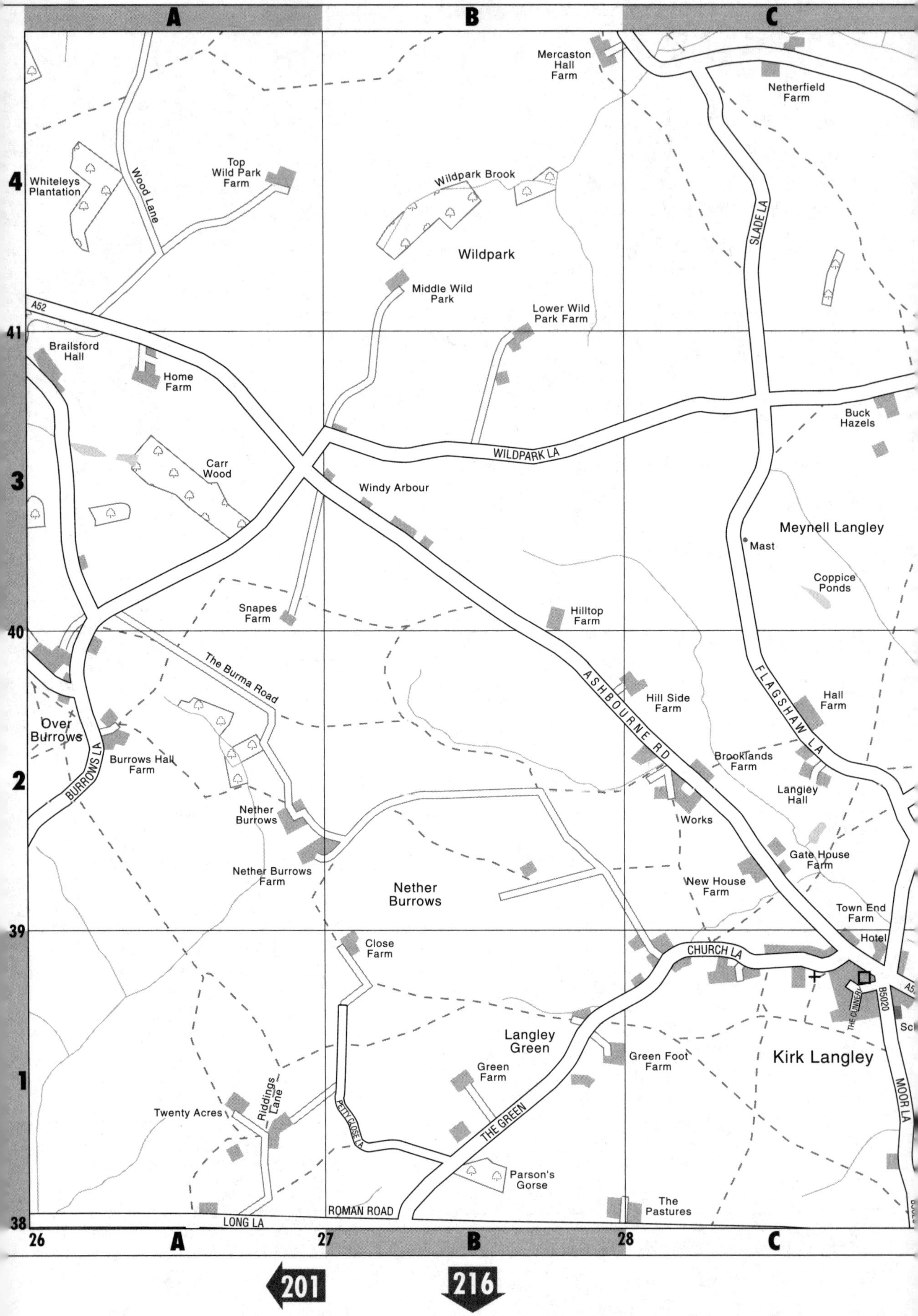
A
B
C
Mercaston Hall Farm
Netherfield Farm
Top Wild Park Farm
Whiteleys Plantation
Wood Lane
Wildpark Brook
Wildpark
SLADE LA
Middle Wild Park
A52
Lower Wild Park Farm
Brailsford Hall
Home Farm
Buck Hazels
Carr Wood
WILDPARK LA
Windy Arbour
Meynell Langley
Mast
Coppice Ponds
Snapes Farm
Hilltop Farm
The Burma Road
ASHBOURNE RD
Hill Side Farm
FLAGSHAW LA
Hall Farm
Over Burrows
BURROWS LA
Burrows Hall Farm
Brooklands Farm
Langley Hall
Nether Burrows
Works
Nether Burrows Farm
Gate House Farm
New House Farm
Nether Burrows
Town End Farm
Close Farm
CHURCH LA
Hotel
B5020
THE GUNNERY
Langley Green
Green Foot Farm
Kirk Langley
Green Farm
Riddings Lane
Twenty Acres
PETTY CLOSE LA
THE GREEN
MOOR LA
Parson's Gorse
The Pastures
ROMAN ROAD
LONG LA
4
41
3
40
2
39
1
38
26
27
28

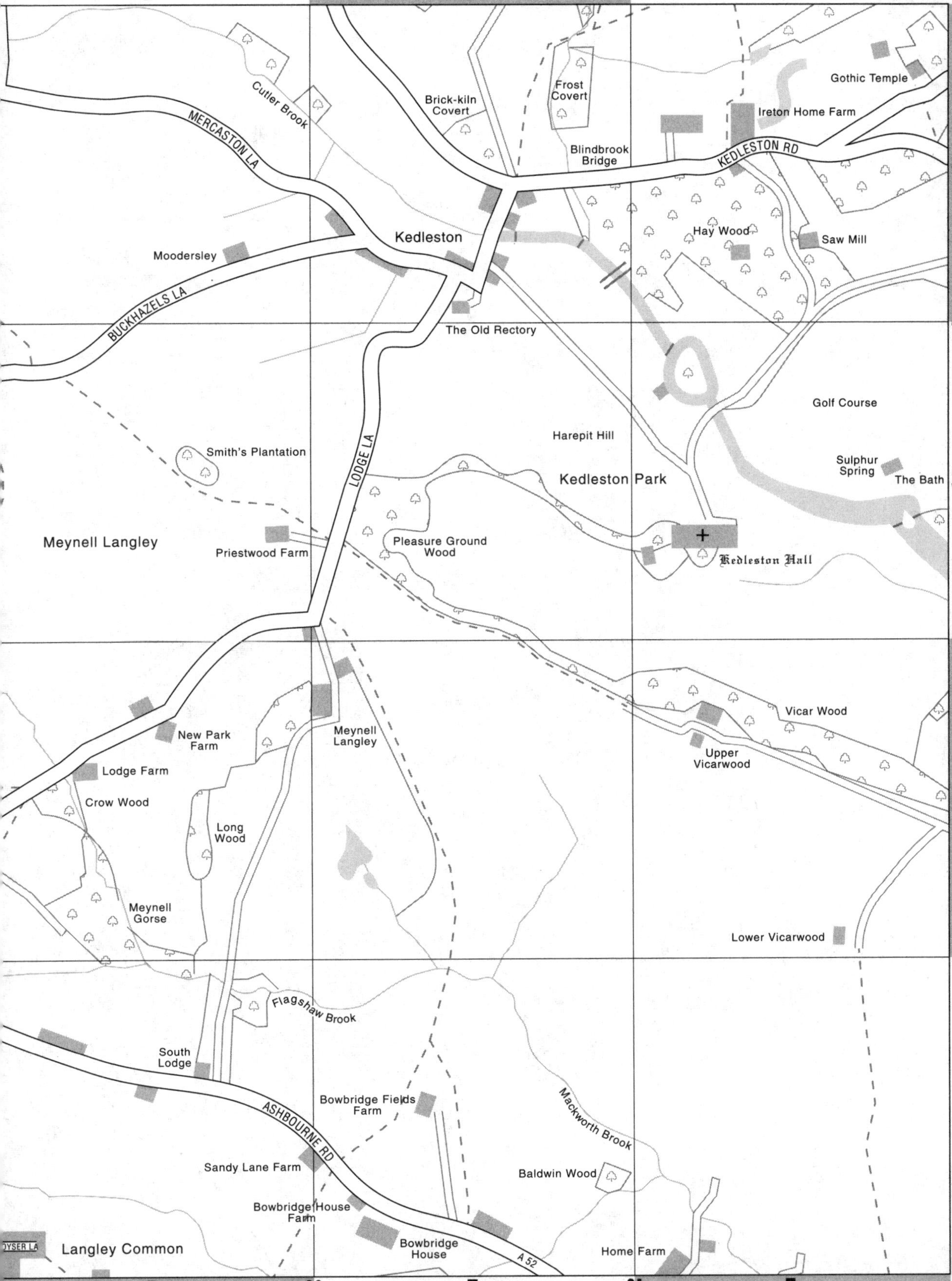

D
E
F
Cutler Brook
MERCASTON LA
Brick-kiln Covert
Frost Covert
Blindbrook Bridge
KEDLESTON RD
Gothic Temple
Ireton Home Farm
4
Kedleston
Moodersley
BUCKHAZELS LA
Hay Wood
Saw Mill
The Old Rectory
41
Golf Course
Harepit Hill
Smith's Plantation
LODGE LA
Kedleston Park
Sulphur Spring
The Bath
3
Meynell Langley
Priestwood Farm
Pleasure Ground Wood
Kedleston Hall
40
New Park Farm
Meynell Langley
Vicar Wood
Upper Vicarwood
Lodge Farm
Crow Wood
2
Long Wood
Meynell Gorse
Lower Vicarwood
39
Flagshaw Brook
South Lodge
ASHBOURNE RD
Bowbridge Fields Farm
Mackworth Brook
1
Sandy Lane Farm
Baldwin Wood
Bowbridge House Farm
OYSER LA
Langley Common
Bowbridge House
A 52
Home Farm
38
30
31

203 190

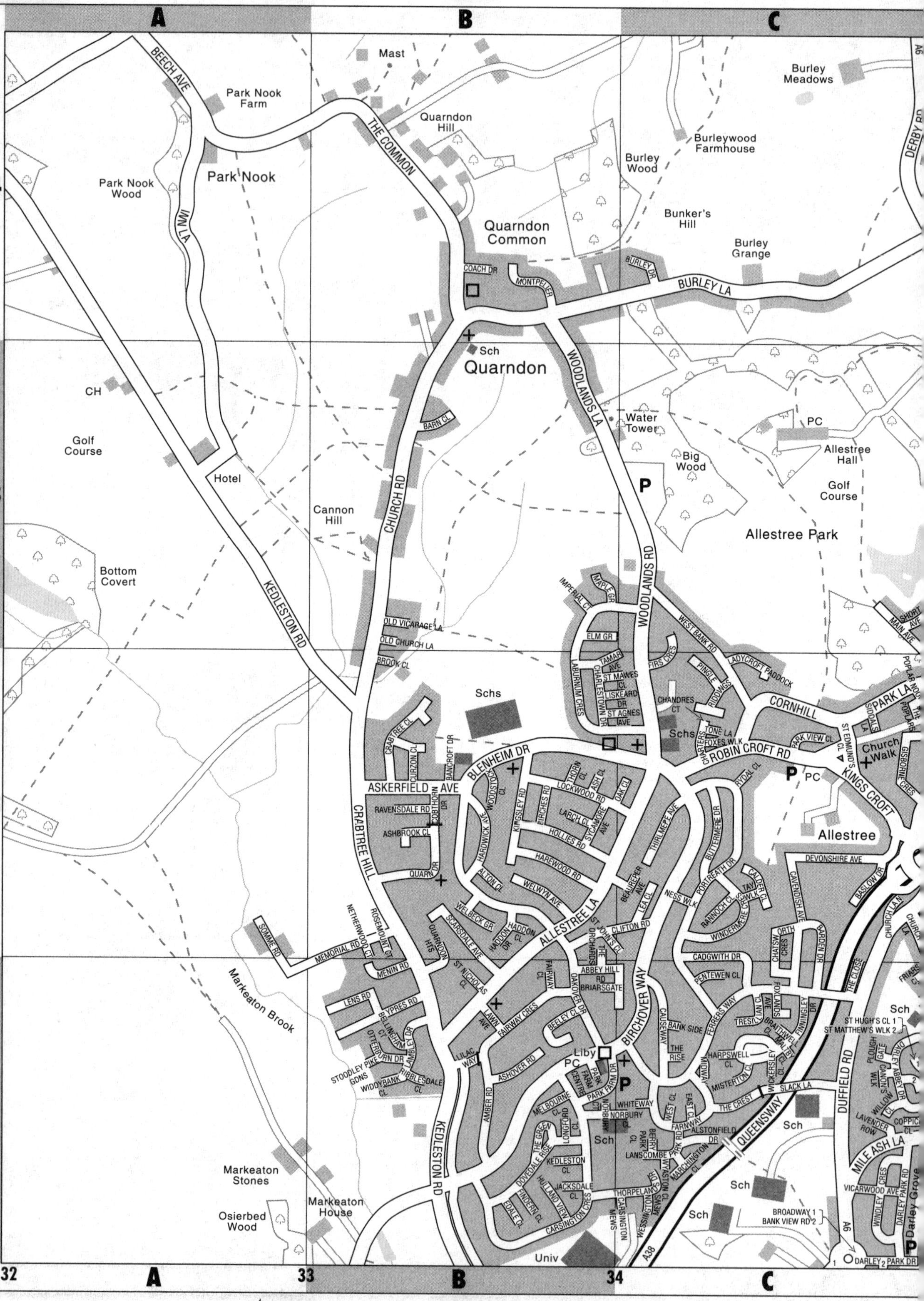
A
B
C
4
41
3
40
2
39
1
38
32
33
34
Mast
Park Nook Farm
Park Nook
Park Nook Wood
BEECH AVE
INN LA
THE COMMON
Quarndon Hill
Quarndon Common
Burley Wood
Bunker's Hill
Burley Grange
Burley Meadows
Burleywood Farmhouse
DERBY RD
BURLEY LA
BURLEY DR
COACH DR
MONTPELIER
Sch
Quarndon
WOODLANDS LA
Water Tower
Big Wood
P
PC
Allestree Hall
Golf Course
Allestree Park
CH
Golf Course
Hotel
BARN CL
CHURCH RD
Cannon Hill
Bottom Covert
KEDLESTON RD
WOODLANDS RD
IMPERIAL CT
MAPLE GR
ELM GR
TAMAR AVE
ST MAWES CL
LISKEARD DR
ST AGNES AVE
CHARLESTOWN DR
LABURNUM CRES
WEST BANK RD
FIRS CRES
PINGLE
RIDDINGS
LADYCROFT PADDOCK
CHANDRES CT
CHARTERS
TONE LA
FOXES WLK
Schs
CORNHILL
ROBIN CROFT RD
PARK VIEW CL
ST EDMUND'S CL
Church Walk
PARK LA
SIDDALS LA
POPLAR NOOK
GISBORNE CRES
KINGS CROFT
SHORT AVE
MAIN AVE
OLD VICARAGE LA
OLD CHURCH LA
BROOK CL
Schs
CRABTREE CL
CURZON CL
BANCROFT DR
BLENHEIM DR
ASKERFIELD AVE
RAVENSDALE RD
COBTHORN DR
ASHBROOK CL
QUARN DR
CRABTREE HILL
WOODSTOCK CL
HARDWICK AVE
KINGSLEY RD
BIRCHES RD
THORN CL
ASH CL
LOCKWOOD RD
OAK CL
LARCH CL
SYCAMORE AVE
HOLLIES RD
HAREWOOD RD
THIRLMERE AVE
BUTTERMERE DR
RYDAL CL
Allestree
DEVONSHIRE AVE
BASLOW DR
ALTON CL
WELWYN AVE
WELBECK GR
HADDON DR
HADDON CL
BEAUPERE AVE
LEA CL
NESS WLK
PORTREATH DR
RANNOCH CL
TAY CL
CALDER CL
WINDERMERE CRES
CAVENDISH AVE
CHATSWORTH CRES
BARDEN DR
ALLESTREE LA
CLIFTON RD
ST JOHN'S CL
THE ORCHARDS
NETHERWOOD CT
ROSEMOUNT CT
SOMME RD
MEMORIAL RD
MENIN RD
QUARNDON HTS
SCARSDALE AVE
ST NICHOLAS CL
FAIRWAY CL
ABBEY HILL RD
BRIARSGATE
DAKOVER DR
BIRCHOVER WAY
CAUSEWAY
CADGWITH DR
PENTEWEN CL
FERRERS WAY
TRESILIAN CL
FOXLANDS AVE
FINNINGLEY DR
THE CLOSE
CHURCH LA
FRIARS
Sch
ST HUGH'S CL 1
ST MATTHEW'S WLK 2
Markeaton Brook
LENS RD
YPRES RD
BELLINGHAM CT
LAMBLEY DR
OTTERBURN DR
STOODLEY PIKE GDNS
WIDDYBANK CL
RIBBLESDALE CL
LAWN AVE
FAIRWAY CRES
BEELEY CL
LILAC WAY
ASHOVER RD
Liby
PC
PARK FARM CENTRE
PARK FARM DR
P
BANK SIDE
THE RISE
HARPSWELL CL
WICKERSLEY CL
BRAITHWELL CL
MISTERTON CL
SLACK LA
THE CREST
MIDWAY
AMBER RD
MELBOURNE CL
NORBURY WAY
NORBURY CL
WHITEWAY
WEST CL
EAST CL
FARNWAY
ALSTONFIELD DR
QUEENSWAY
Sch
DUFFIELD RD
PLOUGH GATE
DARLEY ABBEY DR
CANON'S WLK
WILLOW CL
LAVENDER ROW
COPPICE CL
MILE ASH LA
THE GREEN
LONGFORD CL
DOVEDALE RISE
KEDLESTON CL
Sch
BERRY PARK CL
LANSCOMBE PARK RD
MARCHINGTON CL
Sch
HULLAND VIEW
JACKSDALE CL
EDALE CL
FINDERN CL
CARSINGTON CRES
THORPELANDS DR
CARSINGTON MEWS
WESSINGTON MEWS
WYASTON CL
A38
Sch
BROADWAY 1
BANK VIEW RD 2
A6
VICARWOOD AVE
WINDLEY CRES
DARLEY PARK RD
Darley Grove
P
DARLEY PARK DR
Univ
Markeaton Stones
Markeaton House
Osierbed Wood
A6

D
E
F
4
41
3
40
2
39
1
38
36
37
Sewage Works
Quarry (dis)
CROFT END
CRAB TREE HILL
BARLEY CL
OLD BARN CL
WOODLANDS CL
VICARAGE LA
PARK CL
Little Eaton
BROOKS HOLLOW
MORLEY LA
HOLM AVE
DUFFIELD RD
NEW HIGHFIELD RD
Sch
THE TOWN
LC
CHURCH LA
STATION RD
Burley Hill
BURLEY HILL
Jackson's Dumble
Golf Course
Resr
CAMP WOOD CL
NEW INN LA
ALFRETON RD
BERMUDA AVE
Breadsall Lodge
Glebe Farm
Works
Resr
Boosemoor Brook
Ryknild Street
ROMAN ROAD
Gorses' Wood
Allestree
EATON CL
EATON AVE
CHESTER AVE
Refuse Tip
FORD LA
Peg Low
RECTORY LA
MOOR RD
DUFFIELD RD
EVANS AVE
RUSHUP CL
CUCKMERE CL
FROGGATT CL
MEDWAY DR
WAVENEY CL
WINDRUSH CL
PADLEY CL
SPENBECK DR
SWALE CL
DERWENT CL
WHARFEDALE CL
FARNBOROUGH GDNS
ROCKINGHAM CL
VANBROUGH DR
B6179
A38
A61
Sch
DERWENT AVE
CHURCH WLK
DRIWNT AVE
ABBEY HILL
HOME FARM DR
WOODSIDE DR
PORTWAY CL
GEMA CL
FOUNTAINS CL
ASH TREE CL
CHURCH LA
MOORWAY
Breadsall
Sch
Mill Plantation
Dam Brook
River Derwent
BEECHCROFT
BROOKFIELDS DR
STATION RD
PALL MALL
BROOKSIDE RD
CROFT LA
Holme Nook
Dismantled Railway
1 MAIN AVE
2 PARK LA
3 POPLAR NOOK
4 GISBORNE CRES
The Windmill (PH)
A608
MANSFIELD RD
CHARTERHOUSE CL
QUEENSWAY
Croft Wood
NEARWOOD DR
HILL TOP
NORTH AVE
NUTWOOD CL
Sch
SOUTH AVE
LEAFENDEN CL
FRIARS CL
THSTLDWN CL
Nut Wood
CHURCH LA
ABBEYFIELDS CL
WATERSIDE CL
SPINNEY CL
Breadsall Hilltop
SIR FRANK WHITTLE RD
ALFRETON RD
FOXGLOVE DR
PRIMROSE CL
DIAMOND DR
FIELDGATE DR
STONESBY CL
CHAPTER CL
ABBOT CL
MINSTER RD
ALDER CL
ACER CROFT
BLACKTHORN CL
DEACON CL
KINGSLAND
BCKMNSTR CL
SDGBRK CL
BISHOP'S DR
CROFTERS CT
PADDOCK CROFT
SOMERBY WAY 1
GARTHORPE CT 2
TWEEDS MUIR CL 3
PYKESTONE CL 4
HOUGHTON CT
ULLSWATER CL 1
ENNERDALE WLK 2
RETFORD CL 3
KNUTSFORD GREEN 4
MORPETH GDNS 5
LYCHGATE CL
CORBEL CL
CHIME CL
STEEPLE CL
CEDARWOOD CT 1
BURDOCK CL 2
RIDGEWOOD CT
CRINGLE MEWS
FOXFIELDS DR
TROWBRIDGE CL
BRAINTREE CL
PENRITH PL
STRATFORD RD
BARNARD RD
RADSTOCK GDNS
Schs
WEIRFIELD RD
Toll
ST HUGH'S CL
OLD LA
HASLAM'S LA
Works
ELMWOOD DR
HAWKSHEAD AVE
LIME AVE
LYTHAM CL
MANSFIELD RD
SALTBURN CL
WHITBY AVE
SCARBOROUGH RISE
HARROGATE CR
LANGDALE DR
MILLOM PL
WELSHPOOL RD
OAKHAM CL
HORNCASTLE RD
PERTH ST
GRANTHAM AVE
ROTHBURY PL
ST ANDREWS VIEW
LONGSTOCK CL
1 ROSS WLK
2 HEXHAM WLK
3 EVESHAM CL
4 SANDRINGHAM RD
Schs
YOULGREAVE CL
TANSLEY RISE
WINGFIELD DR
MAPLETON AVE
MATLOCK RD
BUXTON RD
SHIRLEY RD
WINSTER RD
TIDESWELL RD
WOLLATON RD S
TADDINGTON RD
BRSSNGTN RD
8 KENDAL WLK
9 LEDBURY PL
MALVERN WAY
CAMBORNE CL
PEARTREE CT
LATHBURY CL
CONSETT CL
HORNSEA RD
MALTON PL
CHATTERIS DR
DAWSMERE CL
FINCHAM CL
STAITHES WLK 1
SKIPTON GREEN 2
HALIFAX CL 3
PICKERING RISE 4
BLYTH PL 5
REDCAR GDNS 6
SEASCALE CL 7
OLD MANSFIELD RD
A608
A61
Sch
WOODHURST CL
WALSHAM CT
1 DOWER CL
2 WEST ROW
3 NORTH ROW
4 THE HILL
5 THE SQUARE
6 THE HILL SQ
ABBEY LA
BRICK ROW
DARLEY ST
NEW RD
ABBEY YD
POPLAR ROW
FOLLY RD
PCs
Darley Abbey
Works

205
192

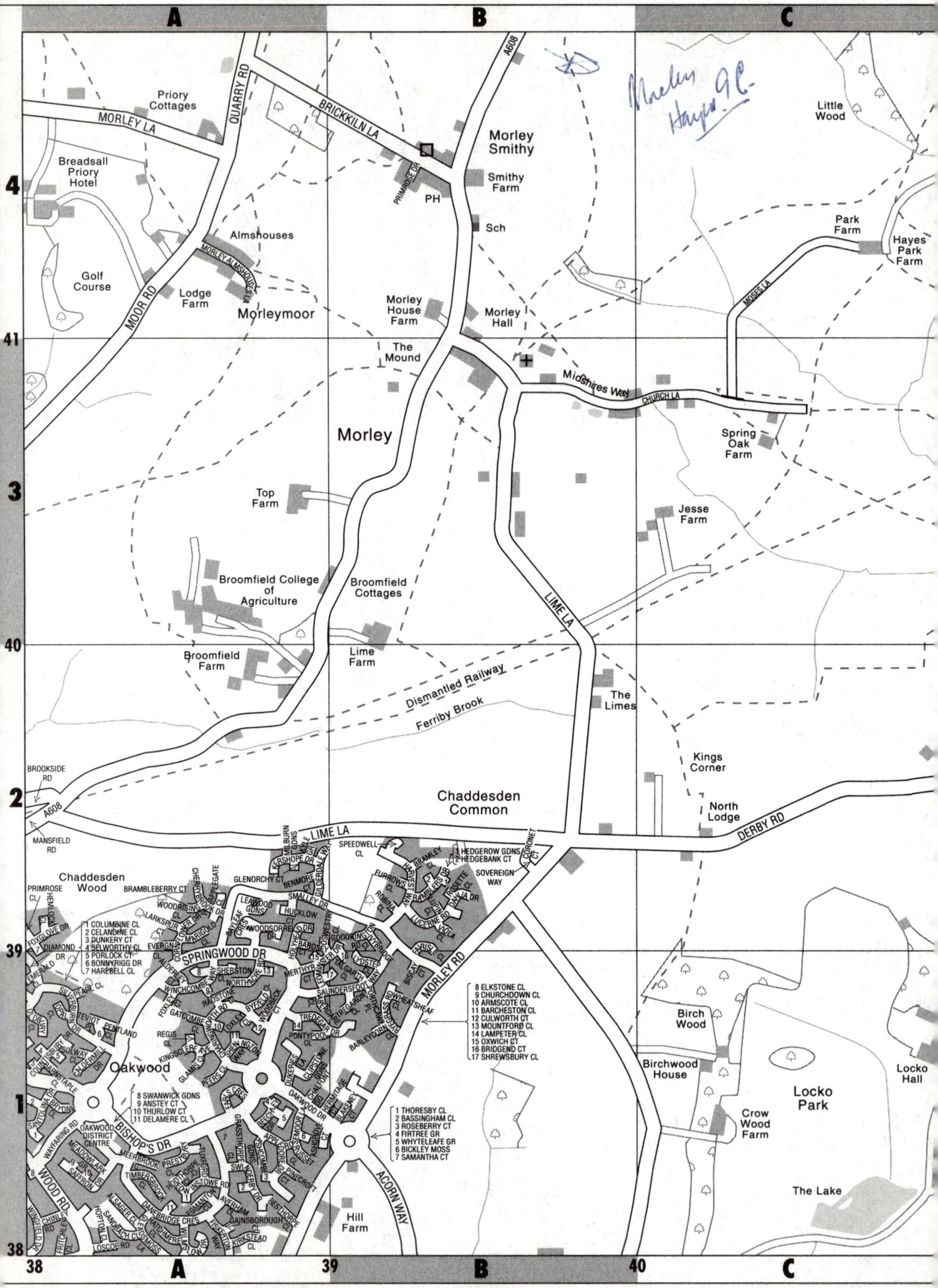
A
B
C
4
41
3
40
2
39
1
38
38
39
40
A608
MORLEY LA
QUARRY RD
BRICKKILN LA
Priory Cottages
Breadsall Priory Hotel
Golf Course
MOOR RD
Lodge Farm
Almshouses
MORLEY ALMSHOUSES LA
Morleymoor
PRIMROSE DR
PH
Morley Smithy
Smithy Farm
Sch
Morley House Farm
Morley Hall
The Mound
Midshires Way
CHURCH LA
Little Wood
Park Farm
Hayes Park Farm
MOSES LA
Spring Oak Farm
Morley
Top Farm
Jesse Farm
Broomfield College of Agriculture
Broomfield Cottages
LIME LA
Broomfield Farm
Lime Farm
Dismantled Railway
Ferriby Brook
The Limes
Kings Corner
BROOKSIDE RD
Chaddesden Common
North Lodge
DERBY RD
MANSFIELD RD
Chaddesden Wood
SPEEDWELL CL
1 HEDGEROW GDNS
2 HEDGEBANK CT
SOVEREIGN WAY
CORONET CT
GLENORCHY CT
BRAMBLEBERRY CT
PRIMROSE CL
HEMLOCK CL
FOXGLOVE DR
DIAMOND DR
1 COLUMBINE CL
2 CELANDINE CL
3 DUNKERY CT
4 SELWORTHY CL
5 PORLOCK CT
6 BONNYRIGG DR
7 HAREBELL CL
SPRINGWOOD DR
MORLEY RD
8 ELKSTONE CL
9 CHURCHDOWN CL
10 ARMSCOTE CL
11 BARCHESTON CL
12 CULWORTH CT
13 MOUNTFORD CL
14 LAMPETER CL
15 OXWICH CT
16 BRIDGEND CT
17 SHREWSBURY CL
Birch Wood
Birchwood House
Locko Hall
Locko Park
Crow Wood Farm
The Lake
Oakwood
8 SWANWICK GDNS
9 ANSTEY CT
10 THURLOW CT
11 DELAMERE CL
OAKWOOD DISTRICT CENTRE
BISHOP'S DR
WOOD RD
1 THORESBY CL
2 BASSINGHAM CL
3 ROSEBERRY CT
4 FIRTREE GR
5 WHYTELEAFE GR
6 BICKLEY MOSS
7 SAMANTHA CT
ACORN WAY
Hill Farm
LOSCOE RD

193
208

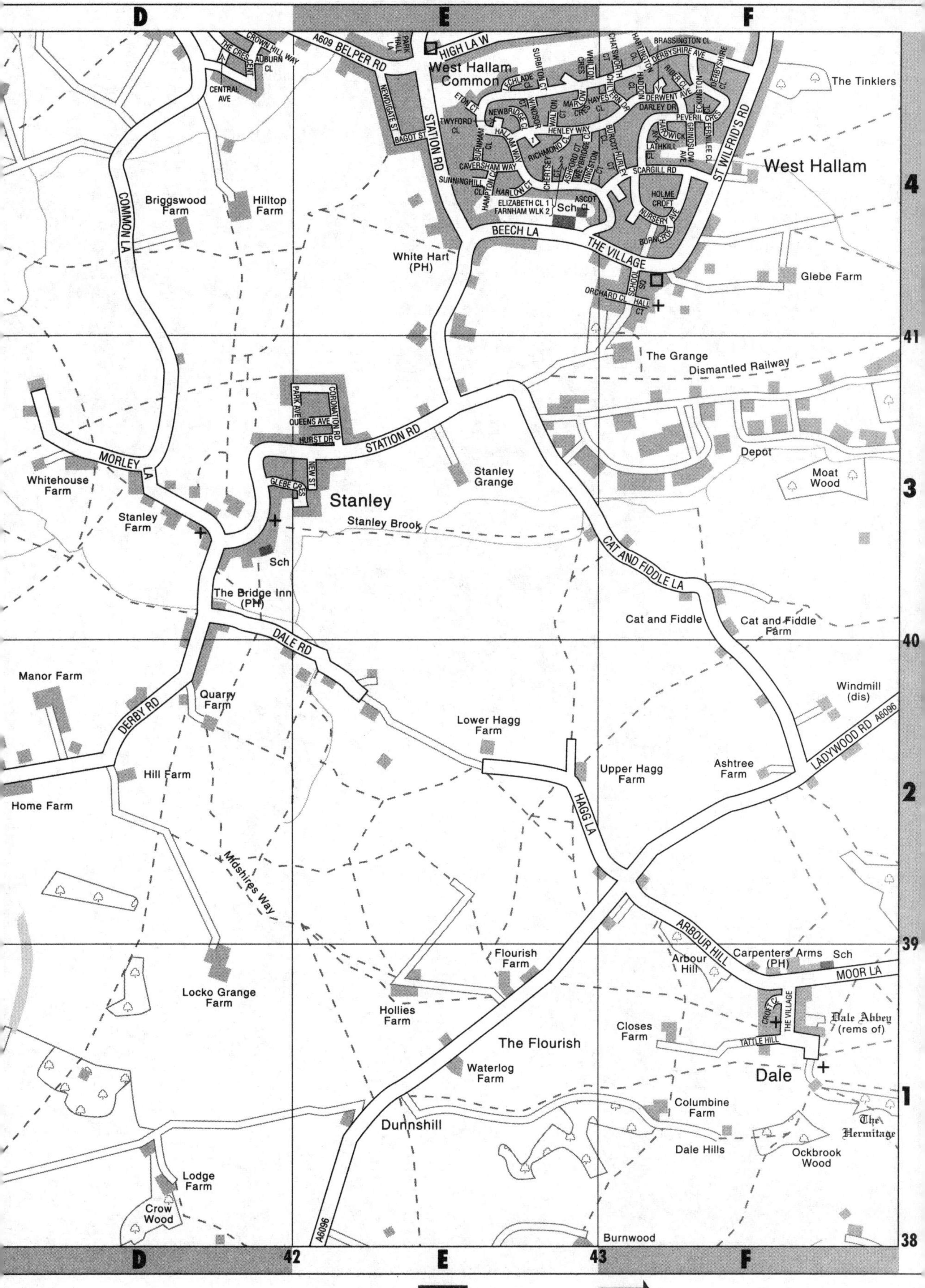
D
E
F
West Hallam Common
West Hallam
The Tinklers
A609 BELPER RD
HIGH LA W
STATION RD
ST WILFRID'S RD
BEECH LA
THE VILLAGE
Briggswood Farm
Hilltop Farm
COMMON LA
White Hart (PH)
Glebe Farm
Sch
The Grange
Dismantled Railway
Depot
Moat Wood
MORLEY LA
Whitehouse Farm
Stanley Farm
Stanley
Stanley Grange
Stanley Brook
CAT AND FIDDLE LA
The Bridge Inn (PH)
Cat and Fiddle
Cat and Fiddle Farm
DALE RD
Manor Farm
Quarry Farm
Windmill (dis)
Lower Hagg Farm
LADYWOOD RD A6096
DERBY RD
Hill Farm
Upper Hagg Farm
Ashtree Farm
Home Farm
HAGG LA
Midshires Way
ARBOUR HILL
Arbour Hill
Carpenters' Arms (PH)
MOOR LA
Flourish Farm
Locko Grange Farm
Hollies Farm
Closes Farm
Dale Abbey (rems of)
The Flourish
TATTLE HILL
Waterlog Farm
Dale
Columbine Farm
Dunnshill
The Hermitage
Dale Hills
Ockbrook Wood
Lodge Farm
Crow Wood
A6096
Burnwood
4
41
3
40
2
39
1
38
42
43

207
194

A
B
C
4
3
2
1
41
40
39
38
44
45
46
A609
HIGH LA E
Paddock Farm
Whitefurrows
Dismantled Railway
Thacker Barn Cottages
Thacker Barn
Golf Course
Straw's Bridge
DERBY RD
KNIVETON PARK
MANOR FIELDS DR
CH
Sch
WEST END DR
WEST END CRES
SCARBOROUGH AVE
DRUMMOND RD
KING GEORGE AVE
B6007
WHARNCLIFFE RD
OAKWELL DR
CHARTER PARK
P
F Sta
TA Cen
Liby
TH
Mus
Off
PC
PIMLICO
ST ANDREW'S
QUEEN'S DR
DARWIN AVE
MOSS RD
CEDAR PARK
ALBERT ST
SOUTH ST
A6007
QUEEN ST
WEST ST
GLADSTONE ST
CORONATION ST
MARKET ST
BATH ST
WILMOT ST
GREGORY ST
JACKSON AVE
ST MARY ST
BURNS ST
NEW LAWN RD
THE ALBION CENTRE
BURR LA
EAST ST
ANCHOR ROW
MARKET PL
HIGH ST
CHALONS WAY
GRESLEY RD
CANTELUPE RD
VINCENT AVE
MARGARET AVE
PARK RD
GRAHAM ST
LIME ST
WHITE LION SQ
A6096
REGENT ST
NOTTINGHAM RD
OXFORD ST
PERCY ST
DALE ST
1ST AVE
2ND AVE
3RD AVE
LISSETT AVE
BELPER ST
HAVELOCK ST
FIELD RD
UNION RD
STANLEY ST
ILKESTON
ALLENDALE
CHURCH VIEW
DALE VIEW
STANTON RD
BLACK HILLS DR
HOBSON DR
DERBYSHIRE DR
SPINNEY RD
NURSERY HOLLOW
APPLEBY CL
LOWER STANTON RD
Coll
Schs
CATHERINE AVE
CAVENDISH RD
INGLE RD
KIRKBY AVE
LOWER WHITWORTH RD
LITTLE HALLAM LA
LITTLE HALLAM HILL
Little Hallam
BIRDCROFT LA
HERMITAGE WLK
GARDEN AVE
LONGFIELD CRES
LONGFIELD LA
QUARRY HILL RD
Quarry Hill Industrial Park
EAGLE RD
KESTREL CL
MERLIN WAY
Foxhole Farm
PRIORY CL
ABBOT RD
SHARP CL
FRIARS CL
BUNTING CL
DUMBLES CL
WYNDALE DR
LOCK CL
GODFREY DR
LIMETREE RISE
CHERRY TREE CL
OLIVER RD
WESTFIELD CL
BRAEFIELD CL
VINE FARM CL
BELVOIR CL
EATON AVE
BANKFIELD DR
SUNNINGDALE DR
CROSS HILL DR
HIGHFIELD DR
RIDGEWAY DR
LADYWOOD RD
Kirk Hallam
GOOLE AVE
POPLAR WAY
WELBECK AVE
HEMLOCK LA
VALLEY RD
VALLEY VIEW
QUEEN ELIZABETH WAY
HARDWICK PL
CHATSWORTH
HILLARY PL
RIBBLESDALE
AVONDALE RD
ASCOT
TUDOR PL
BROOK PL
MEER RD
FESTIVAL RD
MACDONALD SQ
HENSHAW AVE
KENILWORTH DR
CONISTON DR
BALMORAL RD
ELIOT DR
KESWICK CL
WINDERMERE AVE
DEPEDALE AVE
SANDRINGHAM PL
TILTON GR
GLENDON RD
ST NORBERT DR
WIRKSWORTH RD
MUTHALL CIRC
BUCKMINSTER RD
WOODSTHORPE CRES
NUTBROOK CRES
GOODWOOD CRES
DALLIMORE RD
TRENT RD
WINDSOR CRES
Club
Ladywood Lodge Farm
A6096
Lady Wood
Ladywood Farm
Nutbrook Canal (dis)
Sow Brook
Sowbrook Farm
SOWBROOK BROOK
SOWBROOK LA
Stanton Bridge
ILKESTON RD
New Stanton
Works
Bassett Farm
LOW'S LA
LC
MOOR LA
Dale Moor
WOODPECKER HILL
Stanton Grove
Spoil Heap
Furnace Pond Farm
Grove Farm
DALE RD
Moorfield Farm
Thacker Wood
Hermit's Wood
POTATO PIT HILL
HIXON'S LA
Boyah Grange
Dalemoor Farm
LITTLEWELL LA
CHURCH LA
STANHOPE ST
PEPPER LA
FLAKE LA
PH
The Manor House

195

D
E
F
Larklands
Gallows Inn
Hallam Fields
Stanton-by-Dale
Trowell
Strelley
Oldmoor Wood
Robbinetts Arm (dis)
River Erewash
Shortwood Farm
Field House
Meadow Farm
Grange Wood
Nottingham Canal (disused)
Trowell Service Area
Robin Hood Way
Trowell Moor
Shortwood House
Moor Cottages
Uplands Farm
Trowell Junction
Factories
Hallam Fields Lock
Crompton Road Industrial Estate
Sewage Works
Erewash Canal
Trowell Hall
Potter's Plantation
Swancar Farm
Dismtd Rly
Works
Stanton Works
Junction Lock
Field Farm
Stapleford Hill
Golf Course
Stanton Gate
NOTTINGHAM RD
ILKESTON RD
COSSALL RD
STAPLEFORD RD
TROWELL RD
MOORBRIDGE LA
PASTURE RD
HICKINGS LA
LOW'S LA
GOLF CLUB RD
SEVEN OAKS RD
CORPORATION RD
HALLAM FIELDS RD
CROMPTON RD
M1
A6007
B6003
B6004
A6002
4
41
3
40
2
39
1
38
48
49

223

196

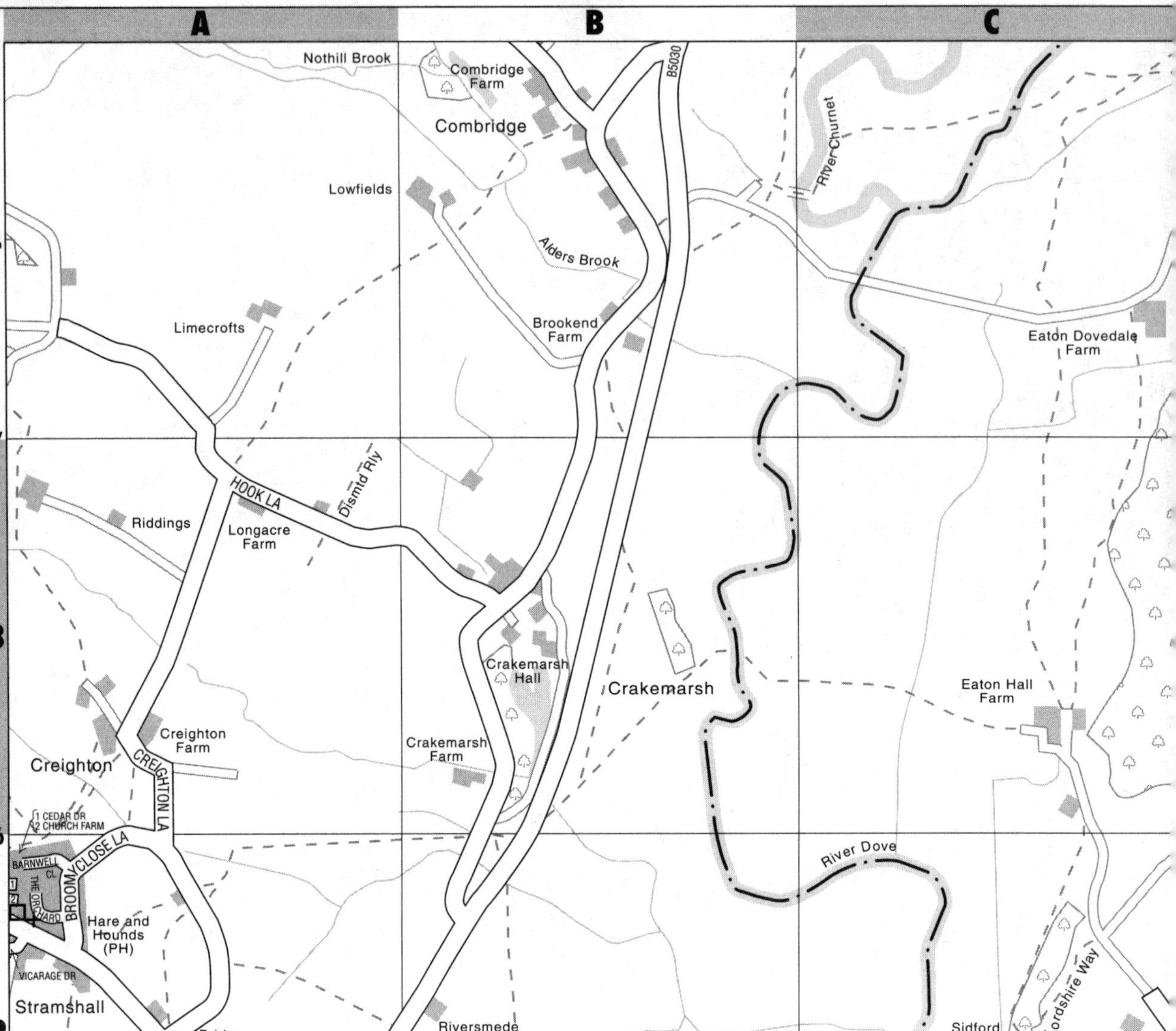

A
B
C
4
37
3
36
2
35
1
34
08
09
10
Nothill Brook
Combridge Farm
Combridge
B5030
Lowfields
River Churnet
Alders Brook
Brookend Farm
Limecrofts
Eaton Dovedale Farm
HOOK LA
Dismtd Rly
Riddings
Longacre Farm
Crakemarsh Hall
Crakemarsh
Eaton Hall Farm
Creighton Farm
Creighton
CREIGHTON LA
Crakemarsh Farm
1 CEDAR DR
2 CHURCH FARM
BROOM CLOSE LA
BARNWELL CL
THE ORCHARD
Hare and Hounds (PH)
VICARAGE DR
Stramshall
River Dove
Riversmede
Bridge Farm
River Tean
Sidford Wood
Staffordshire Way
Spath
ASHBOURNE RD
Spath Cottage Farm
Leasows Farm
Cottonmill Farm
A50
BENTLEY RD
THE MEADOWS
GREENACRES DR
BADGERY
STANLEY CRES
WEAVER RD
PARK AVE
A522
NEW RD
NORTHFIELD
The Heath
HOWITT CRES
JOHNSON RD
Sewage Works
Noah's Ark
UTTOXETER
A518
DERBY RD
Dove Bridge
GARDNER PL
REDFERN RD
SCHOOL RD
GRANGE RD
ORCHARD CL
APPLEWOOD CL
PRINCESS RD
MOSLEY DR
PENNYCROFT RD
COPES WAY
WINDSOR RD
HOLLY RD
CHEADLE RD
ST MARY'S CRES
WESTWARD CL
HEATH RD
CLARKE'S CL
HARVEY PL
SLADE FIELDS
PARK ST
Amb Sta
F Sta
The Wharf
PENNYCROFT LA
CROFT GR
CHOLTON
THE HORNBEAMS
HEATHLANDS DR
Sch
LIGHTFOOT RD
HEATH CROSS
SUNNYSIDE RD
GAS ST
EATON ST

197
212

224
212

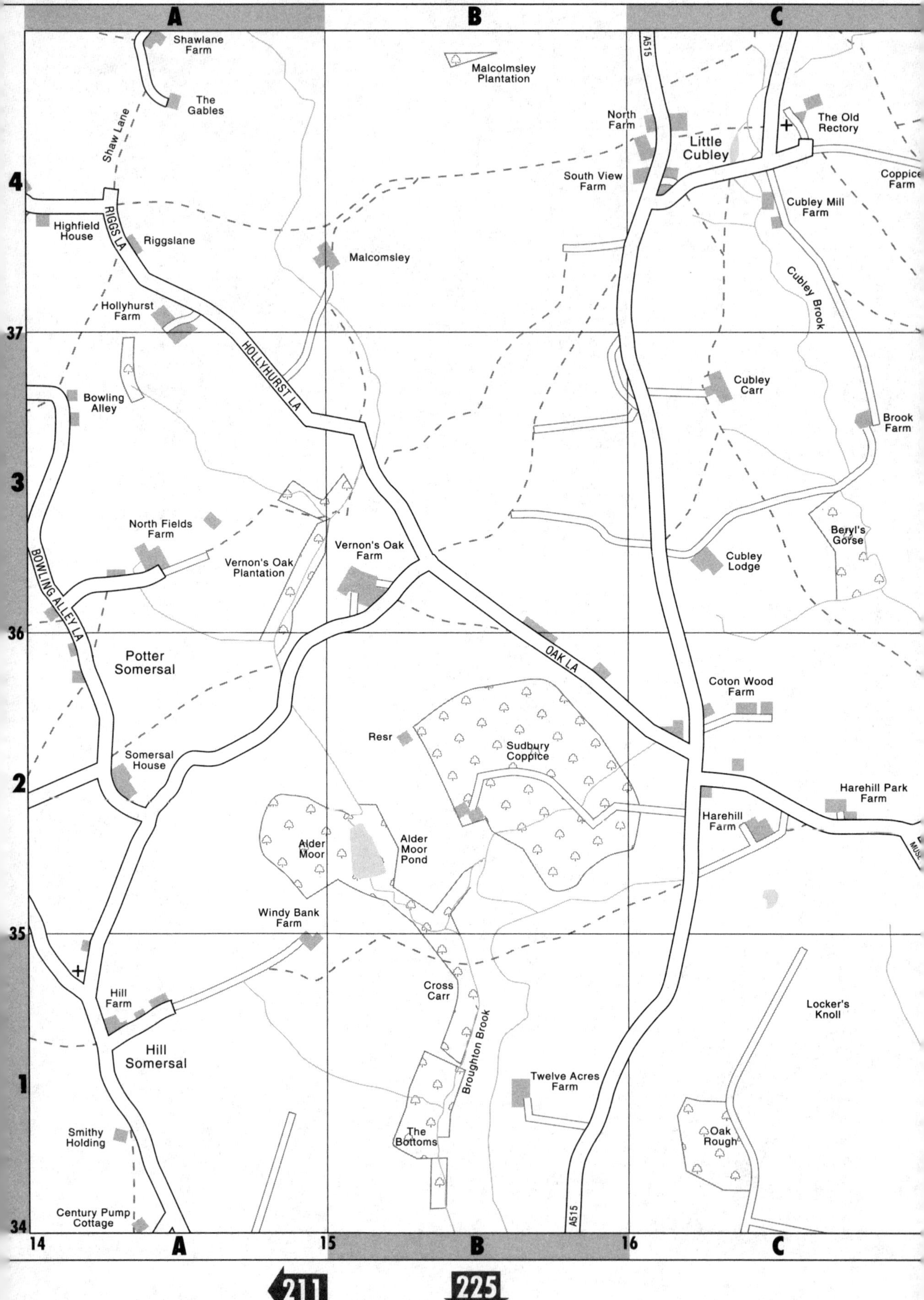
A
B
C
Shawlane Farm
The Gables
Shaw Lane
Malcolmsley Plantation
A515
North Farm
Little Cubley
The Old Rectory
South View Farm
Coppice Farm
Cubley Mill Farm
Highfield House
RIGGS LA
Riggslane
Malcomsley
Cubley Brook
Hollyhurst Farm
HOLLYHURST LA
Bowling Alley
Cubley Carr
Brook Farm
North Fields Farm
Vernon's Oak Plantation
Vernon's Oak Farm
Beryl's Gorse
Cubley Lodge
BOWLING ALLEY LA
OAK LA
Potter Somersal
Coton Wood Farm
Resr
Sudbury Coppice
Somersal House
Harehill Park Farm
Harehill Farm
Alder Moor
Alder Moor Pond
Windy Bank Farm
Cross Carr
Locker's Knoll
Hill Farm
Hill Somersal
Broughton Brook
Twelve Acres Farm
Smithy Holding
The Bottoms
Oak Rough
Century Pump Cottage
A515
4
37
3
36
2
35
1
34
14
15
16

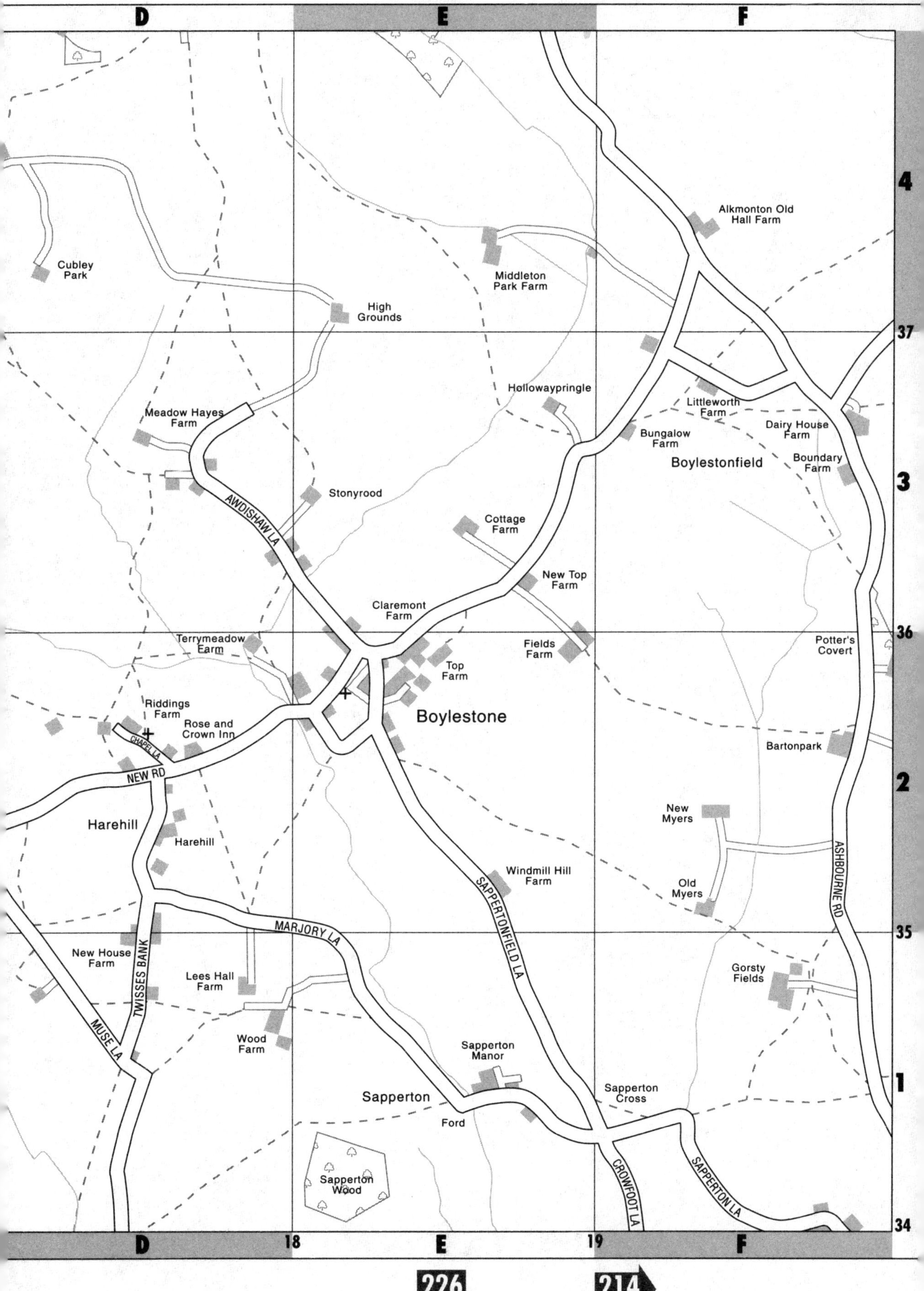
D
E
F
4
3
2
1
37
36
35
34
18
19
Cubley Park
High Grounds
Middleton Park Farm
Alkmonton Old Hall Farm
Hollowaypringle
Littleworth Farm
Bungalow Farm
Dairy House Farm
Boundary Farm
Boylestonfield
Meadow Hayes Farm
Stonyrood
Cottage Farm
New Top Farm
AWDISHAW LA
Claremont Farm
Terrymeadow Farm
Fields Farm
Top Farm
Potter's Covert
Riddings Farm
Rose and Crown Inn
CHAPEL LA
Boylestone
Bartonpark
NEW RD
Harehill
Harehill
New Myers
Windmill Hill Farm
Old Myers
ASHBOURNE RD
SAPPERTONFIELD LA
MARJORY LA
New House Farm
TWISSES BANK
Lees Hall Farm
Gorsty Fields
MUSE LA
Wood Farm
Sapperton Manor
Sapperton
Sapperton Cross
Ford
CROWFOOT LA
SAPPERTON LA
Sapperton Wood

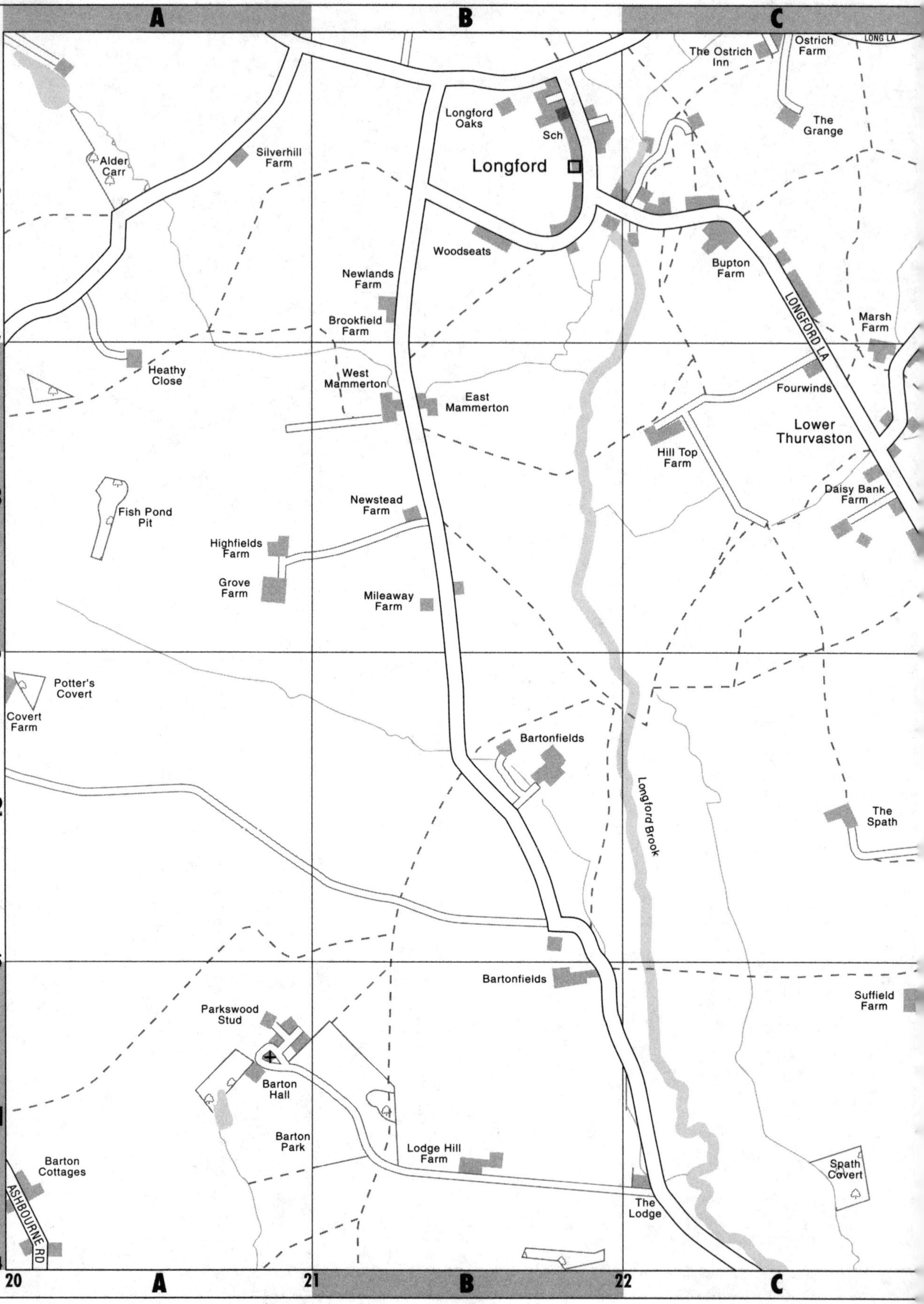
A
B
C
Ostrich Farm
LONG LA
The Ostrich Inn
Longford Oaks
Sch
Longford
The Grange
Silverhill Farm
Alder Carr
Woodseats
Bupton Farm
Newlands Farm
Brookfield Farm
LONGFORD LA
Marsh Farm
Heathy Close
West Mammerton
East Mammerton
Fourwinds
Lower Thurvaston
Hill Top Farm
Daisy Bank Farm
Newstead Farm
Fish Pond Pit
Highfields Farm
Grove Farm
Mileaway Farm
Potter's Covert
Covert Farm
Bartonfields
Longford Brook
The Spath
Bartonfields
Suffield Farm
Parkswood Stud
Barton Hall
Barton Park
Lodge Hill Farm
Barton Cottages
ASHBOURNE RD
Spath Covert
The Lodge
4
37
3
36
2
35
1
34
20
21
22

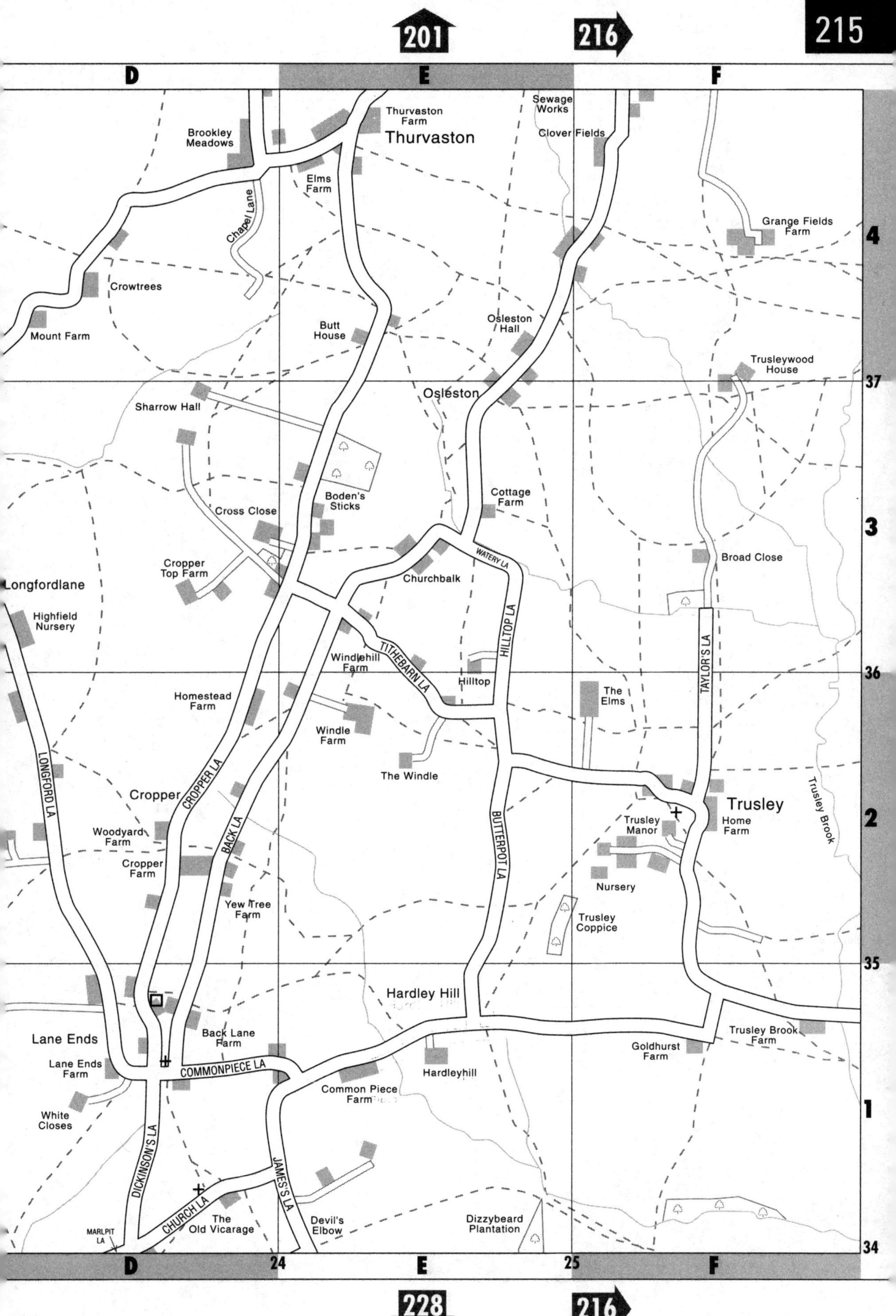
201
216
D
E
F
Thurvaston Farm
Thurvaston
Sewage Works
Clover Fields
Brookley Meadows
Elms Farm
Chapel Lane
Grange Fields Farm
Crowtrees
Mount Farm
Butt House
Osleston Hall
Trusleywood House
Osleston
Sharrow Hall
Boden's Sticks
Cottage Farm
Cross Close
Cropper Top Farm
WATERY LA
Broad Close
Churchbalk
Longfordlane
Highfield Nursery
HILLTOP LA
TITHEBARN LA
Windlehill Farm
Hilltop
TAYLOR'S LA
The Elms
Homestead Farm
Windle Farm
LONGFORD LA
The Windle
CROPPER LA
Cropper
Trusley
Trusley Brook
Woodyard Farm
BACK LA
BUTTERPOT LA
Trusley Manor
Home Farm
Cropper Farm
Nursery
Yew Tree Farm
Trusley Coppice
Hardley Hill
Lane Ends
Back Lane Farm
Trusley Brook Farm
Goldhurst Farm
Lane Ends Farm
COMMONPIECE LA
Hardleyhill
Common Piece Farm
White Closes
DICKINSON'S LA
JAMES'S LA
CHURCH LA
The Old Vicarage
Devil's Elbow
Dizzybeard Plantation
MARLPIT LA
4
37
3
36
2
35
1
34
24
25
228
216

A
B
C
LONG LA
ROMAN ROAD
Cherry Tree Farm
Poplar Grove Farm
Nunsclough Brook
Lees Hall
Lees
PH
Sewage Works
Black Fir Tree Farm
Hillside Farm
Foxfields Farm
Corner Farm
Rock House Farm
Hinckley Farm
Foxfield Plantation
Woodhouse Lane
Thatched Farm
Radbourne
Old Park Farm
Woodhouse Farm
Ravensdale Lodge
Cunnery Pond
Ravensdale
Daysclose Plantation
Birch Wood
Dog Kennel Pond
Radbourne Hall
The Rough
Radbourne Brook
The Rookery
Seedpiece Plantation
Rookhills Farm
Terrel Hays
White House Farm
Sandpit Wood
Dalbury Hollow
Smerrills Farm
Bearwardcote Hall
HEAGE LA
Manor Farm
Top Farm
Dalbury
Dismantled Railway
The Cottage
Bannell's Lane
4
37
3
36
2
35
1
34
26
27
28

D
E
F
Langley Common
Bowbridge Wood
Wind Pump
Brunhouse Farm
PH
BRUN LA
A52
JARVEY'S LA
Mackworth Brook
Wheathills Farm
LOWER RD
ASHBOURNE RD
CHURCH LA
Works
Mackworth
Squire's Nursery
Brun Wood
The Mackworth Hotel
ALDERSGATE 1
SYDENHAM RD 2
Ash House Farm
EMBANKMENT CL
Schs
Radbourne Common
Brickyard Wood
Pilldock Wood
ENDSLEIGH GDNS 1
CROYDON WLK 2
Water Twr
Resr
Brickyard Wood Farm
Skitteridge's Wood
MOORGATE 1
CHELSEA CL 2
FARRINGDON CL 3
HIGHBURY CL 4
MILBANK CL 5
EPPING CL 6
Ivy House Farm
Mackworth Fields
RADBOURNE LA
B5020
Coll
Moorcroft Farm
Silverhill Farm
Dismantled Railway
Silverhill Wood
Hackwood Farm
The Great Northern (PH)
Works
Sch
Potlocks Farm
Slade Plantation
Dismantled Railway
STATION RD
Black Wood
Bean Hole Plantation
Univ
Coll
Mickleover
WESTERN RD
Osierbed Wood
Sch
Recn Gd
PARK RD
UTTOXETER RD
BRIERFIELD WAY
Amb Sta
Sch
Hospl
KIPLING DR
A38
A516
CH
1 HOLMESFIELD DR
2 LITTLE LONGSTONE CL
3 ABNEY CL
1 ALL SAINTS CT
2 UFFA MAGNA
Brown Cross Plantation
Orchard Plantation
Bonehill Farm
Golf Course
4
37
3
36
2
35
1
34
30
31

217
204

A B C

A B C

217
231

DERBY
Little Chester
City Road Ind Park
Racecourse Park
Chaddesden
Derby Junction
Sand & Gravel Pit
River Derwent
The Holmes
Derby Station
Locomotive Works
Litchurch
Depot
Spoil Tip
Works
Mast
Wilmorton
Coll
Alvaston Park
Rose Hill
Football Ground
Osmaston Park Ind Est
Cemy
Sch
Schs
Offs
PCs
Mkt
Hospi
ALFRETON RD
MANSFIELD RD
SIR FRANK WHITTLE RD
STORES RD
HAMPSHIRE RD
HEREFORD RD
MAX RD
NOTTINGHAM RD
WILTSHIRE RD
ST ALKMUND'S WAY
STATION APP
RAILWAY TERR
LONDON RD
LITCHURCH LA
OSMASTON RD
NORMANTON RD
PEAR TREE RD
DAIRY HOUSE RD
ST THOMAS RD
TRAFFIC ST
CHARNWOOD ST
LEOPOLD ST
DOUGLAS ST
BATEMAN ST
ASCOT DR
CHEQUERS RD
THE PENTAGON
EASTGATE
A6
A61
A52
A514
A601
A608
B6000
36
37
4
3
2
1
34
35

A
B
C
4
37
3
36
2
35
1
34
38
39
40
South Lodge
Brunswood Farm
Spondon Wood
Lees Brook
ACORN WAY
LOCKO RD
Springfield Farm
MORLEY RD
WOOD RD
MAX RD
RUPERT RD
POYSER AVE
FIELD LA
GERTRUDE RD
CROMFORD RD
HASSOP RD
MATLOCK RD
GRINDLOW RD
WARDLOW AVE
LATHKILL RD
MONYASH CL
GLEADMOSS LA
COPES WAY
KIBWORTH CL
FISKERTON WAY
SEAGRAVE CL
SANDFIELD CL
MORLEY GDNS
MARTIN DR
MONCRIEFF CRES
AUDREY DR
STONEY FLATTS CRES
KEVIN CL
BROOKFIELD AVE
WILLETTS RD
MOIRA CL
DEBORAH DR
OAKRIDGE AVE
LAWRENCE AVE
Schs
Sch
WILSTHORPE RD
REGINALD RD S
CHAPEL LA
VICARAGE DR
APPLETON CL
KENNEDY CL
TENNESSEE RD
DULUTH AVE
CHALLIS AVE
MAINE DR
CHADDESDEN LA
TUDOR RD
CHURCH LA
RAINIER DR
Liby
ISMAY RD
MosseyYard Plantation
TRENTON GRN
TRENTON GREEN DR
PC
Chaddesden Park
Chaddesden Brook
ATCHISON GDNS
ALBEMARLE RD
ELLENDALE RD
ENNIS CL
CARSON RD
WASHINGTON AVE
WINSLOW GRN
ROOSEVELT AVE
VERMONT DR
EVANSTON GDNS
CHARLESTON RD
MARYLAND RD
DENISON GDNS
BRIDGEPORT RD
BOSTON CL
MICHIGAN CL
OREGON WAY
DAYTON CL
LEXINGTON RD
LANSING GDNS
HOUSTON CL
GRANT AVE
CHEYENNE GDNS
SPRINGFIELD RD
PARKSIDE RD
PATERSON AVE
SANDERSON RD
NEWHAVEN RD
VALLEY RD
SUNNY GR
Cherrytree Hill
CYPRESS WALK
LYNDHURST GR
SOUTH DR
ST JOHN'S DR
CLEVELAND AVE
ST JOHN'S AVE
ELIZABETH CL
ELM GR
LIME GR
COROVILLE CL
LEWISTON RD
EADLEY CL
BRIAR CL
JASMINE CL
ENOCH STONE DR
NOTTINGHAM RD
AUTUMN GR
EVELYN GR
EDWARD AVE
HILLSIDE AVE
STANLEY RD
HOWTH CL
ALBERT RD
EDEN RD
CHERRY TREE MEWS
BELFAST WALK
FOYLE AVE
MEADOW LA
Sch
A52
DONEGAL WALK
WATERFORD DR
CAVAN DR
KILDARE RD
LIMERICK RD
MEATH AVE
COLERAINE CL
GALWAY AVE
ALBERT CRES
A5111
A6005
DERBY RD
ROMAN ROAD
ASPEN DR
THE SIDINGS
WYVERN WAY
The Wyvern
DERBY RD
MEGALOUGHTON LA
CELANESE RD
Amb Sta
WEST SERVICE RD
EAST SERVICE RD
RAYNESWAY
HOLME LA
Water Reclamation Works
Sewage Works
Works
River Derwent
Mast
P
RAYNESWAY PK DR
Nature Reserve
Electricity Generating Station
Chy
Fire and Amb Sta
LONGLEY LA
HEYWOOD DR
AVONDALE RD
ROYAL HILL RD
CHARLES AVE
MARINA DR
SUNNINGDALE AVE
Sch
WEST RD
DEVAS GDNS
BEECHES AVE
PARK RD
ST WERBURGH'S VIEW
CHURCH MEWS
CHURCH ST
CHURCH HILL
POTTER ST
HALL DYKE
CHAPEL ST
Schs
POPLAR AVE
Liby
SITWELL ST
MERCIAN MEWS
MERCHANT AVE
PRIESTLAND AVE
GASCOIGNE DR
FOWLER AV
GILBERT
ST WERBURGH CL
LODGE LA
SITWELL CL
AYR CL
BORROWASH BY-PASS
BAMBURGH CL
SILVEY GR
LEEWAY
DRURY AVE
VANCOUVER AVE
A6096
WILLOWCROFT RD
DERBY RD
GREENBANK
DERWENT RD
STATION RD
Spondon Station
LC
STONEY CROSS
CONISTON AVE
ULLSWATER
BRECON CL
WINDERMERE DR
CHAPEL LA
LOCKO CT
CHAPEL SIDE
BRUNSWOOD CL
STRATHAVEN CT
OXFORD ST
GLADSTONE RD
BROCKLEY
COYTON CL
MOOR ST
READER ST
GRASMERE AVE
RUTLAND DR
FRAZER CL
ORCHARD CL
STEWART CL
NICHOLAS CL
CHESTERTON
STONE CL
PC
LOUISE GREAVES LA
SANDCROFT RD
MOOR END
HAMLET
GERARD CL
CLAYTON RD
CROFT CL
FELLSIDE
DALE RD
A6096
FARNINGHAM CL
LAWNSIDE
DREYFUS CL
CAERNARVON CL
BEAUMARIS CL
DEER PARK VIEW
WILLOW RD
CHAFFINCH
GOLDCREST DR
LINNET CL
REDSTART CL
BADGER CL
GREENFINCH CL
BARTON CL
HUNTLEY AVE
HOLYROOD
BRACKLEY DR
Cemy
PC
STONEY LA
LUDLOW CL
ARUNDEL DR
CLOVER CL
Schs
RANNOCH CL
SANDRINGHAM RD
LOCHINVER
BANKFIELD DR
BURNSIDE DR
WINGERWORTH PARK RD
SOUTH AVE
MEADOW CL
HILL CL
THE COVERT
GRAVEL PIT LA
THE PINGLE
HILLSIDE RD
HILLSIDE CRES
ASTERDALE VIEW
MOULT AVE
Spondon
TREVERIS CL
DERWENT RISE
RISE
KIRK LEES AVE N
KIRK LEES AVE S
BERESFORD DR
LADYBOWER RD
VERNON DR
HADDON DR
BORROWASH RD
ORMSKIRK RISE
SUNDEW CL
PARK LEYS CT
CAMBRIDGE ST
ARNHEM TERR
CHESTER CT
CRADDOCK AVE
LANGLEY RD
VINCENT AVE
LOVEDALE RD
EDNUND RD
MONSAL DR
KIRK DALE AVE
WENSLEY DR
EDALE RD
DEEPDALE RD
SILVERHILL RD
BORROWFIELD RD
MILLDALE RD
LITTON DR
NOTTINGHAM RD
ANGLERS LA
A6005
DERBY
BURROWFIELD MEWS

207
222

234
222

221
208

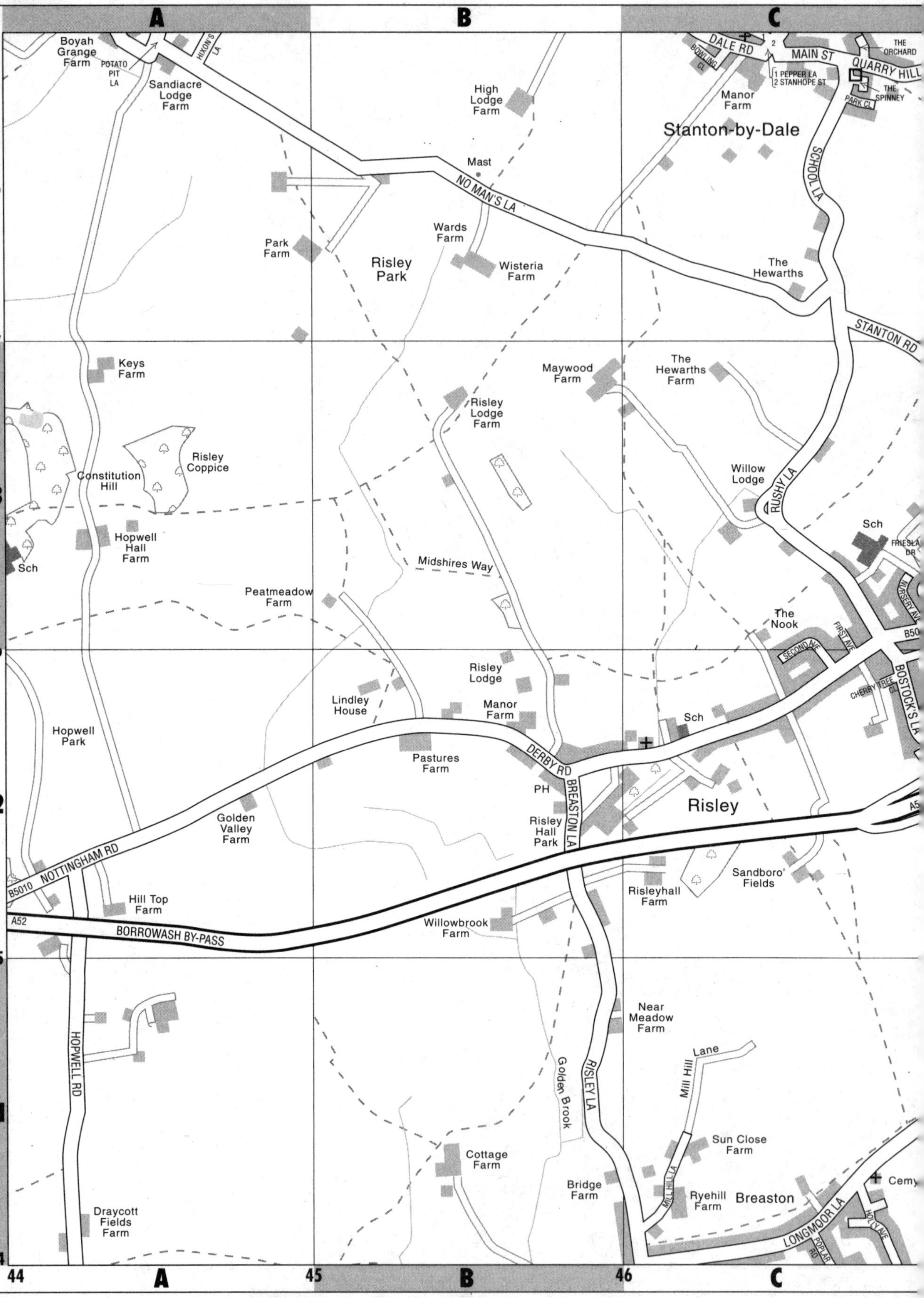

221
235

209

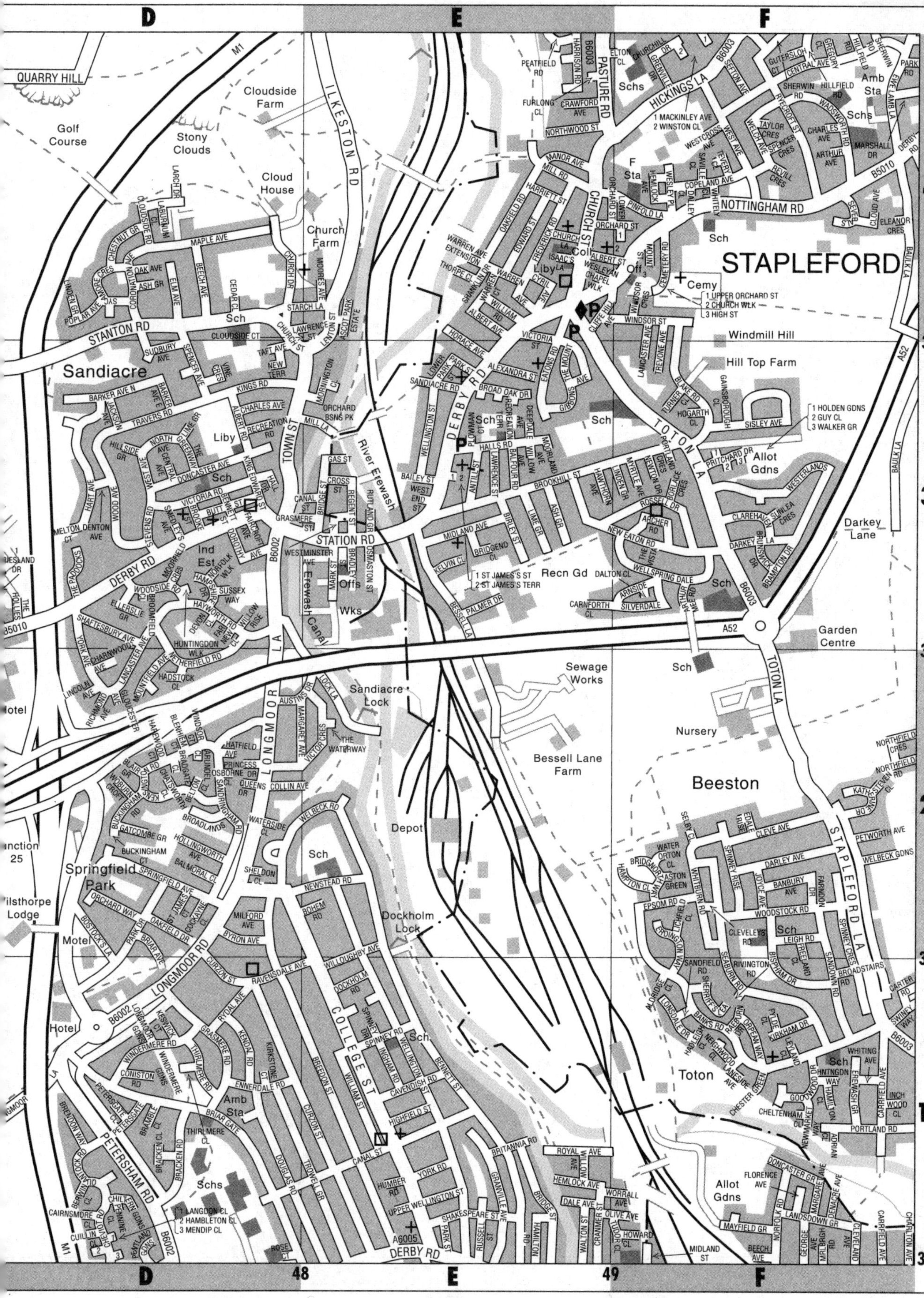
D
E
F
48
49
34
35
36
37
1
2
3
4
STAPLEFORD
Sandiacre
Beeston
Toton
Springfield Park
QUARRY HILL
M1
Golf Course
Cloudside Farm
Stony Clouds
Cloud House
Church Farm
ILKESTON RD
STANTON RD
DERBY RD
STATION RD
NOTTINGHAM RD
HICKINGS LA
TOTON LA
STAPLEFORD LA
LONGMOOR LA
LONGMOOR RD
COLLEGE ST
PETERSHAM RD
BROOKHILL ST
CHURCH ST
PASTURE RD
River Erewash
Erewash Canal
Sandiacre Lock
Dockholm Lock
Sewage Works
Bessell Lane Farm
Nursery
Garden Centre
Darkey Lane
Windmill Hill
Hill Top Farm
Recn Gd
Allot Gdns
Depot
Ind Est
Wks
Offs
Motel
Hotel
Amb Sta
Cemy
Liby
Sch
Schs
A52
B5010
B6002
B6003
A6005
1 UPPER ORCHARD ST
2 CHURCH WLK
3 HIGH ST
1 HOLDEN GDNS
2 GUY CL
3 WALKER GR
1 MACKINLEY AVE
2 WINSTON CL
1 ST JAMES'S ST
2 ST JAMES'S TERR
1 LANGDON CL
2 HAMBLETON CL
3 MENDIP CL

236

211

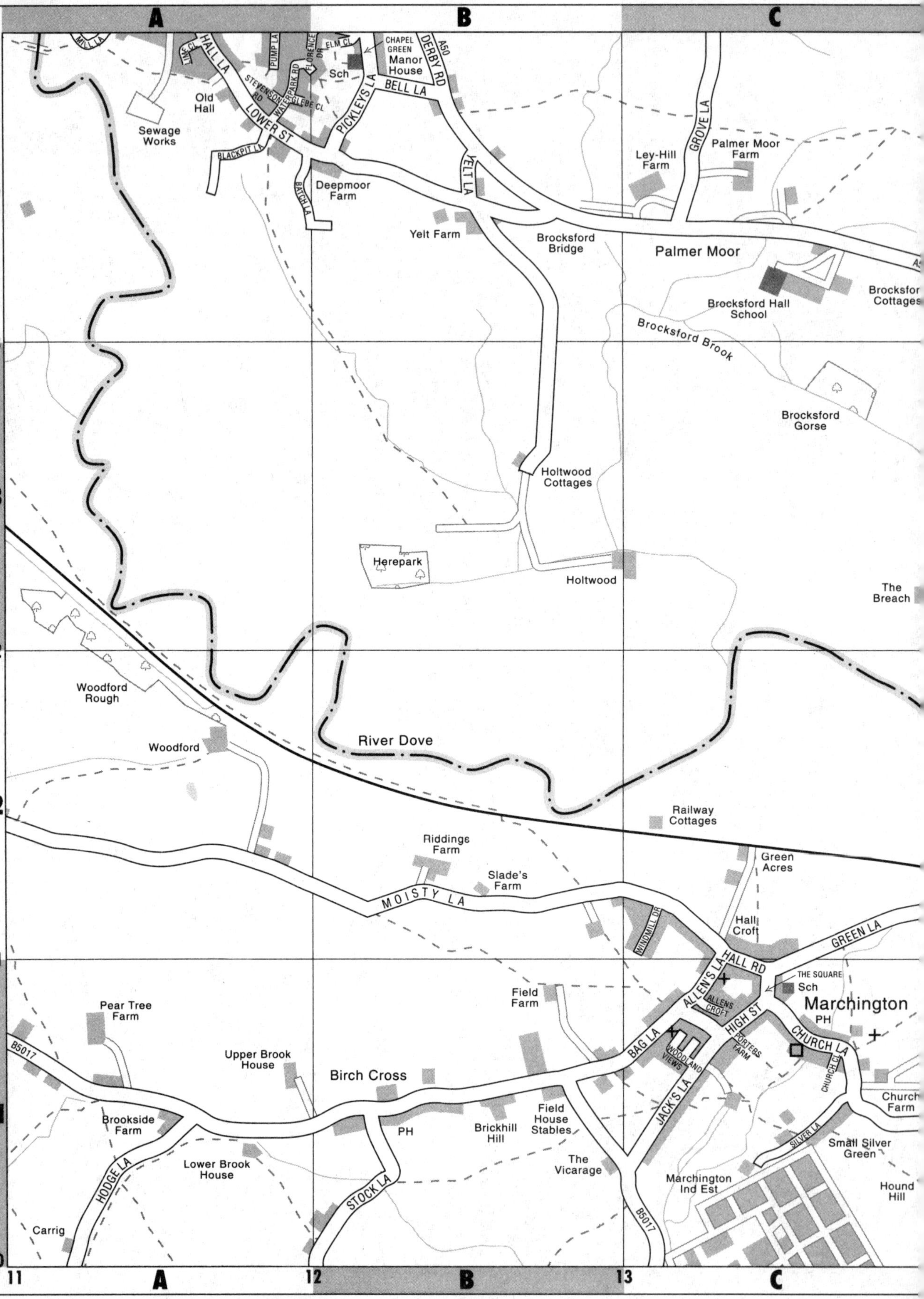

A
B
C
MILL LA
LIME CL
HALL LA
PUMP LA
FLORENCE DR
ELM CL
CHAPEL GREEN
Manor House
DERBY RD
A50
Sch
STEVENSON RD
WATERPARK RD
GLEBE CL
PICKLEYS LA
BELL LA
Old Hall
Sewage Works
LOWER ST
BLACKPIT LA
BATCH LA
Deepmoor Farm
YELT LA
Yelt Farm
Brocksford Bridge
GROVE LA
Ley-Hill Farm
Palmer Moor Farm
Palmer Moor
Brocksford Hall School
Brocksford Cottages
Brocksford Brook
Brocksford Gorse
Holtwood Cottages
Herepark
Holtwood
The Breach
Woodford Rough
Woodford
River Dove
Railway Cottages
Riddings Farm
Slade's Farm
Green Acres
MOISTY LA
WINDMILL DR
Hall Croft
GREEN LA
HALL RD
ALLEN'S LA
THE SQUARE
Sch
Marchington
PH
ALLENS CROFT
HIGH ST
CHURCH LA
PORTERS FARM
Field Farm
Pear Tree Farm
B5017
Upper Brook House
Birch Cross
BAG LA
WOODLAND VIEWS
JACK'S LA
CHURCH CL
Church Farm
Brookside Farm
PH
Brickhill Hill
Field House Stables
SILVER LA
Small Silver Green
HODGE LA
Lower Brook House
The Vicarage
Marchington Ind Est
Hound Hill
STOCK LA
Carrig
B5017
4
33
3
32
2
31
1
30
11
12
13

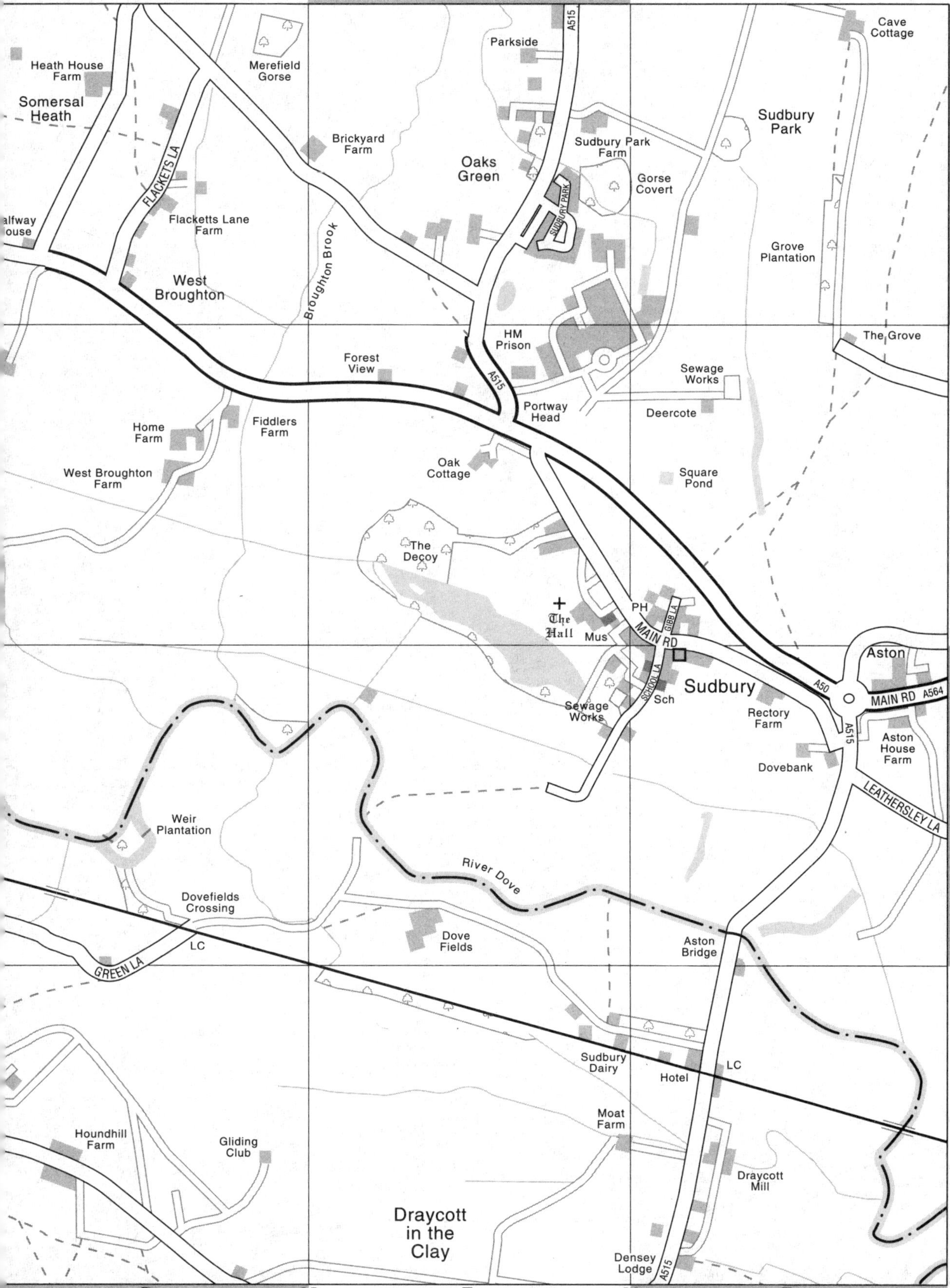
D
E
F
Heath House Farm
Somersal Heath
Merefield Gorse
Parkside
A515
Cave Cottage
Sudbury Park
Brickyard Farm
Oaks Green
Sudbury Park Farm
Gorse Covert
FLACKETS LA
SUDBURY PARK
alfway ouse
Flacketts Lane Farm
Grove Plantation
West Broughton
Broughton Brook
HM Prison
The Grove
Forest View
Sewage Works
Portway Head
Deercote
Home Farm
Fiddlers Farm
Oak Cottage
West Broughton Farm
Square Pond
The Decoy
PH
The Hall
Mus
MAIN RD
GIBB LA
Aston
SCHOOL LA
Sch
Sudbury
A50
MAIN RD
A564
Sewage Works
Rectory Farm
Aston House Farm
Dovebank
LEATHERSLEY LA
Weir Plantation
River Dove
Dovefields Crossing
Dove Fields
Aston Bridge
LC
GREEN LA
Sudbury Dairy
Hotel
LC
Moat Farm
Houndhill Farm
Gliding Club
Draycott Mill
Draycott in the Clay
Densey Lodge
4
33
3
32
2
31
1
30
15
16

A
B
C
4
33
3
32
2
31
1
30
17
18
19
Mackley House
Fox Hole
Sapperton Brook
The Homestead
SAPPERTON
Dale Brook
MUSE LA
Muselane Farm
Foston Mill Farm
MILL LA
CROWFOOT LA
Crowfoot Farm
Cotefield Farm
WOODHOUSE LA
Dalebrook
Aston Heath Farm
Ford
Aston Heath
Broomhill Farm
Foston Brook
Conygree Wood
Aston Heath Farm
BREACH LA
Haylane Farm
HAY LA
COPLOW LA
Sailor's Holme
Rough Wood
ASTON LA
Breach Gorse
WOODYARD LA
Home Farm
Lawn Farm
MAIN RD
A564
Foston
Aston
UTTOXETER RD
UTTOXETER RD
HM Detention Centre
Maidensley Farm
WOODLAND DR
Dale Brook
Lemon's Holme
Fishpond Plantation
Cote House
Roundabout Covert
Puddingbag Covert
Sewage Works
Leathersley Farm
The Churchleys
LEATHERSLEY LA
BROOM'S LA
WATERY LA
Sweet Holme
Scropton
Ivy House Farm
River Dove
Brookside Farm
PH
SCROPTON RD
River Dove
Dismantled Tramway
Brookhouse Farm
LC
MILL
A
B
C

D
E
F
Church Broughton
CHURCH RD
ASHBOURNE RD
TIPPER'S LA
BROUGHTON CL
AUDEN CL
CHAPEL LA
MAIN ST
PH
Sch
OLD HALL LA
1 FEARN CL
2 MEADOW RISE
BOGGY LA
Badder Green Farm
Badder Green
Bent Brook
Bent House
Sutton Heath
Longford Brook
COMMON LA
Mount Pleasant
SCHOOLPIECE LA
SUTTON RD
LITTLEFIELD RD
Broughton House Farm
The Bent
Limbersitch Brook
Littlemeadow Lane
Claypit Hill
Heath Top Farm
Heathtop
Dark Lane
BENT LA
LIMBERSITCH LA
Limbersitch Farm
Birchill's Farm
Hatton Fields Farm
Hatton Fields
Heath House
Hoon Drive Farm
Airfield (dis)
MIRY LA
SUTTON LA
Pennywaste Wood
Heath Cottage Farm
A50
Newlands Farm
CHURCH BROUGHTON RD
Works
Sycamore Farm
Hoon Mount Farm
BREACH LA
Hockley Farm
A564
UTTOXETER RD
MALTHOUSE LA
Hoon Hall
Heath Farm
BROOK LA
Guinea Farm
UTTOXETER RD
A50
A516
DERBY RD
A516
SAWPIT LA
PH
Yew Tree Farm
PH
THE SHIELING
THE HAYS
BROOK CL
BIRCH GR
BRADSHAW MEADOW
GRANVILLE CL
LIME CL
COOPERS CROFT
LEY CROFT
YEW TREE RD
RYE FLATTS LA
The Fields
FLAX CROFT
APPLETREE RD
WOODMANS CROFT
STATION RD
Liby
RUSSET CL
BRAMBLEY CT
HOLME CL
HEATH WAY
Sch
Cherry Cottage
The Firs Farm
Netherclose Lane
SCROPTON RD
Sch
FIELD AVE
A50
CHURCH MEWS
4
33
3
32
2
31
1
30
21
22
D
E
F

227
215

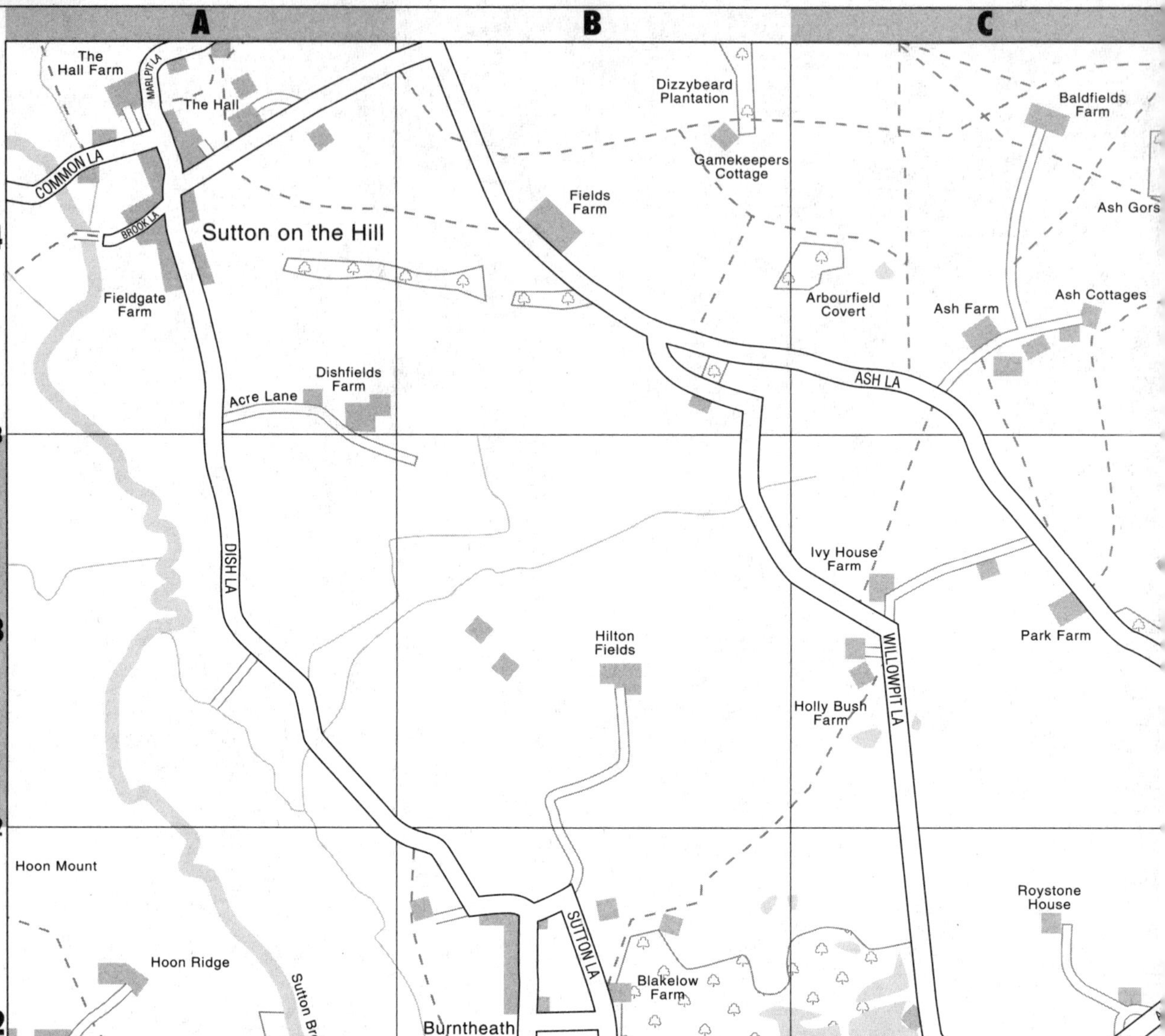
A
B
C
The Hall Farm
MARLPIT LA
The Hall
COMMON LA
BROOK LA
Sutton on the Hill
Fieldgate Farm
Dizzybeard Plantation
Gamekeepers Cottage
Fields Farm
Baldfields Farm
Ash Gors
Arbourfield Covert
Ash Farm
Ash Cottages
ASH LA
Dishfields Farm
Acre Lane
DISH LA
Ivy House Farm
Park Farm
Hilton Fields
WILLOWPIT LA
Holly Bush Farm
Hoon Mount
Roystone House
SUTTON LA
Hoon Ridge
Sutton Brook
Blakelow Farm
Burntheath
Hilton Gorse
Lodge Farm
DERBY RD
Hilton Lodge
A564
Hallcroft
Industrial Estate
Hoon Villa Farm
A516
DALE END RD
WEST AVE
SHADY GR
CHERRY TREE CL
DERBY GARTH
ELM DR
OAK DR
WILLOWFIELDS
NEW RD
LUCAS LA
Moorend
PERCY WOOD CL
Elm Tree Farm
A5132
MAIN ST
Hilton Common
Sch
WILLOW BROOK CL
MILL LA
DOVE RISE
FIELD CL
PEACROFT LA
Hargate Lodge
BACK LA
BANCROFT CL
Hilton
BLOOMFIELD CL
IVY CT
HAWTHORN CL
MARSTON LA
Hilton Brook
EGGINGTON RD
Hargate Hou Farm
Depot
Hargate Manor
4
33
3
32
2
31
1
30
23
24
25

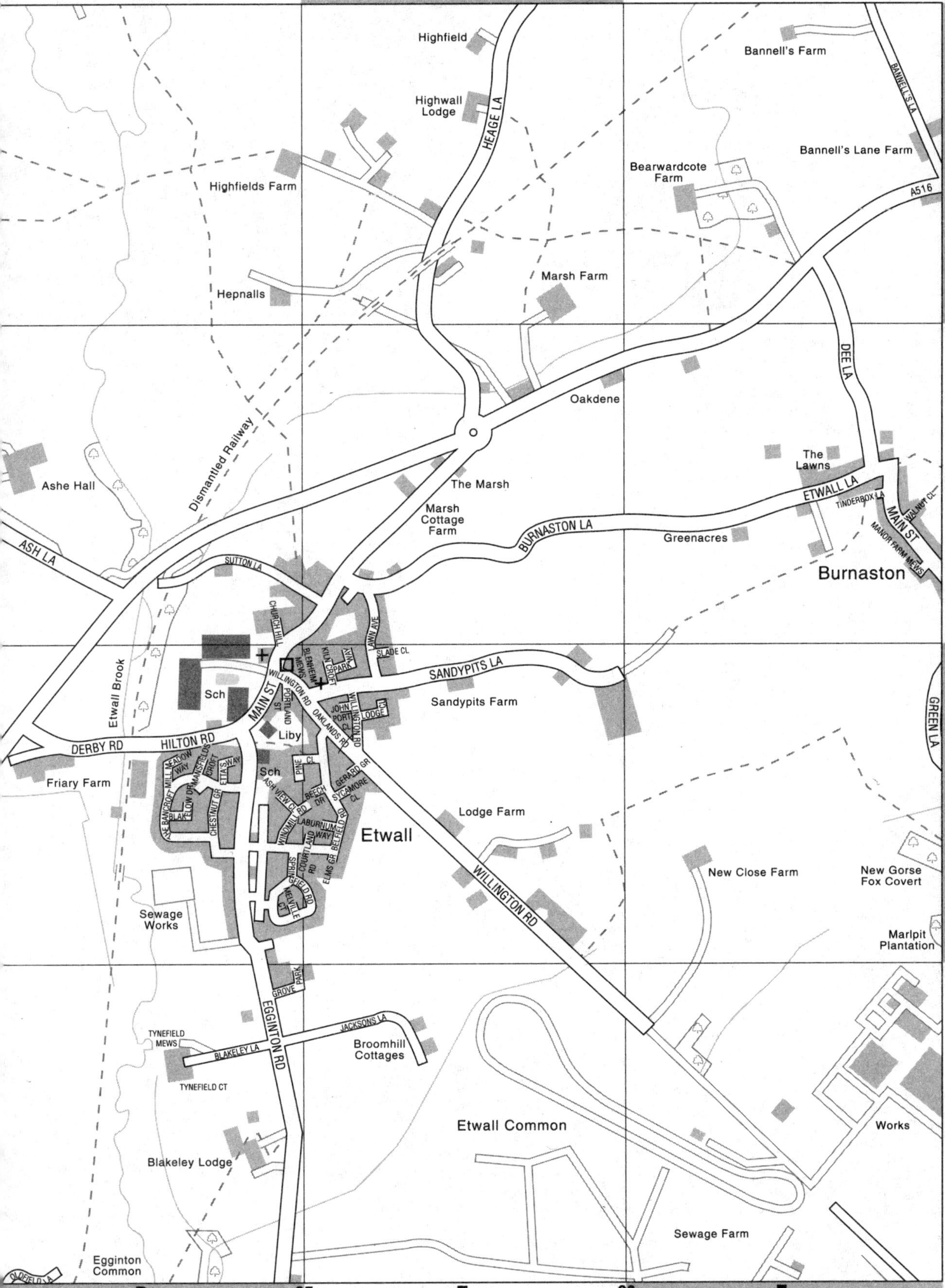
D
E
F
Highfield
Bannell's Farm
BANNELL'S LA
Highwall Lodge
HEAGE LA
Bannell's Lane Farm
Bearwardcote Farm
Highfields Farm
A516
Marsh Farm
Hepnalls
33
DEE LA
Oakdene
Dismantled Railway
The Lawns
Ashe Hall
The Marsh
ETWALL LA
TINDERBOX LA
MAIN ST
Marsh Cottage Farm
BURNASTON LA
Greenacres
ASH LA
SUTTON LA
Burnaston
CHURCH HILL
LAWN AVE
SLADE CL
32
SANDYPITS LA
Etwall Brook
Sch
Sandypits Farm
GREEN LA
DERBY RD
HILTON RD
Liby
Friary Farm
Lodge Farm
2
Etwall
WILLINGTON RD
New Close Farm
New Gorse Fox Covert
Sewage Works
Marlpit Plantation
31
GROVE
PARK
EGGINTON RD
JACKSONS LA
TYNEFIELD MEWS
BLAKELEY LA
Broomhill Cottages
TYNEFIELD CT
Etwall Common
Works
1
Blakeley Lodge
Sewage Farm
Egginton Common
OLDFIELD LA
30
27
28

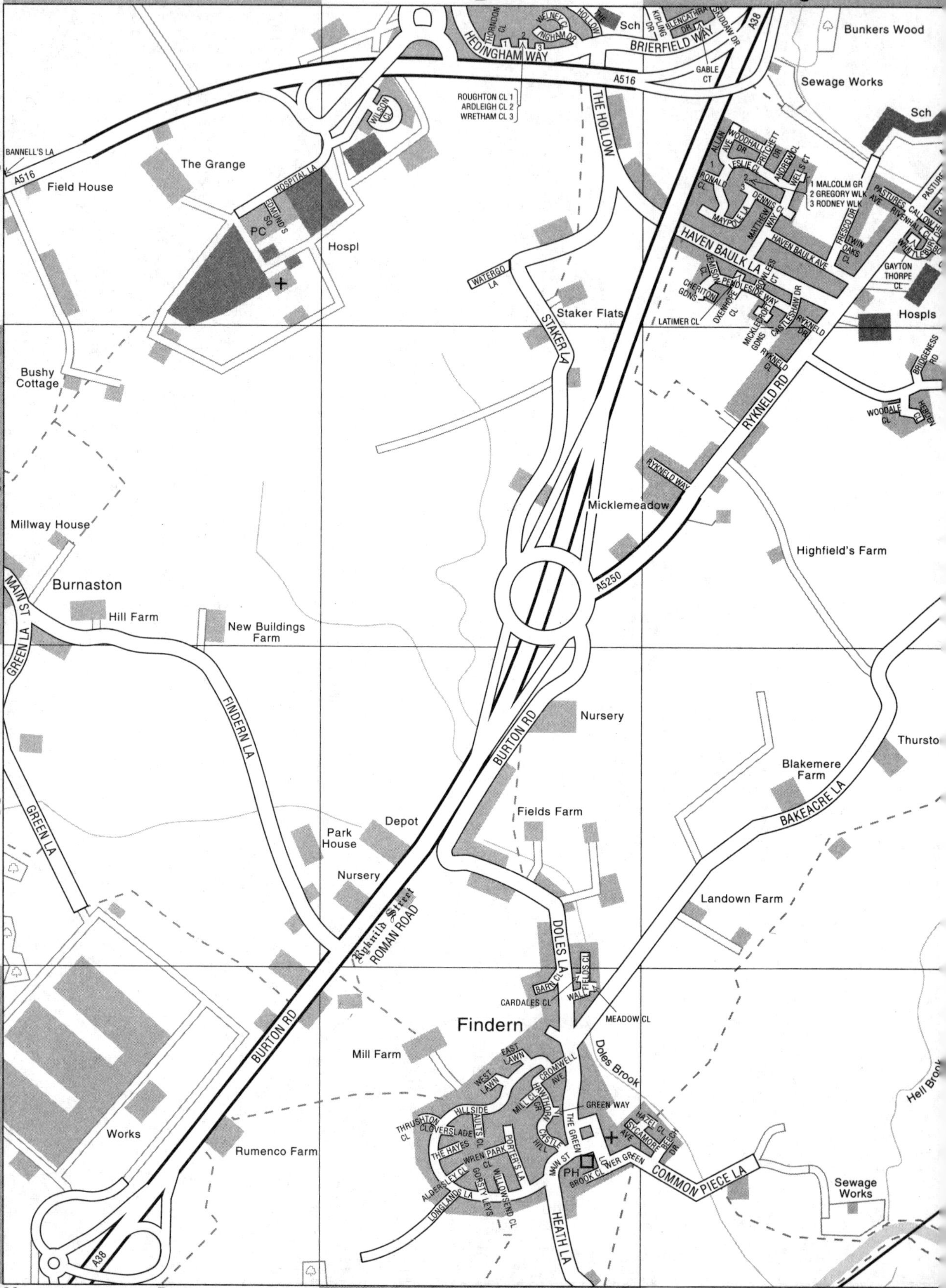
A
B
C
Bunkers Wood
Sewage Works
Sch
HEDINGHAM WAY
BRIERFIELD WAY
A516
THE HOLLOW
A38
GABLE CT
ROUGHTON CL 1
ARDLEIGH CL 2
WRETHAM CL 3
BANNELL'S LA
The Grange
Field House
HOSPITAL LA
PC
Hospl
WATERGO LA
Staker Flats
STAKER LA
HAVEN BAULK LA
HAVEN BAULK AVE
MAYPOLE LA
1 MALCOLM GR
2 GREGORY WLK
3 RODNEY WLK
LATIMER CL
RYKNELD RD
Hospls
GAYTON THORPE CL
TWIN OAKS CL
FRESCO DR
WOODALE CL
BRIDGENESS RD
Bushy Cottage
Millway House
Burnaston
Hill Farm
New Buildings Farm
MAIN ST
GREEN LA
RYKNELD WAY
Micklemeadow
A5250
Highfield's Farm
FINDERN LA
BURTON RD
Nursery
Thursto
Blakemere Farm
BAKEACRE LA
Fields Farm
Depot
Park House
Nursery
Landown Farm
Ryknild Street
ROMAN ROAD
DOLES LA
CARDALES CL
MEADOW CL
Findern
Mill Farm
Doles Brook
Hell Brook
CROMWELL AVE
EAST LAWN
WEST LAWN
HILLSIDE
GREEN WAY
THRUSHTON CL
CLOVERSLADE
THE HAYES
WREN PARK CL
PORTER'S LA
GORSTY LEYS
WILLOWSEND CL
ALDERSLEY CL
LONGLANDS LA
MAIN ST
PH
BROOK CL
LOWER GREEN
COMMON PIECE LA
SYCAMORE AVE
HAZEL CL
BEECH DR
HEATH LA
Sewage Works
Works
Rumenco Farm
A38
4
33
3
32
2
31
1
30
29
30
31

D
E
F
Littleover
Sch
PC
PASTURES HILL
A5250
THE HOLLOW
HILLSWAY
FERNWOOD CL
BRAYFIELD RD
TRAFFORD WAY
1 NORMANTON LA
2 BEECHWOOD CRES
3 LITTLEOVER CRES
4 BRAYFIELD AVE
5 OVAL CT
6 HEADINGLEY CT
7 TRENT BRIDGE CT
8 CRICKETERS CT
WARWICK AVE A511
LITTLEOVER LA
Cemy
KENILWORTH AVE
VILLAGE ST
A511
1 THE CROFT
2 WOOD CROFT
3 RABOWN AVE
DORRIEN AVE 1
BYNG AVE 2
NEWDIGATE ST 3
HAVELOCK RD 4
NEWLYN DR 5
Schs
Normanton
Hillcross
REGENCY CL 1
SOUTH BRAE CL 2
DATCHET CL
COTTISFORD CL
FINMERE CL
GREENACRES
WEST VIEW AVE
LOTHLORIEN CL
PLOUGHFIELD CL
BRIARWOOD WAY
NORBURY CRES
DALBURY WLK
DOVERIDGE WLK
BLAGREAVES LA
OAKLANDS AVE
Sunny Hill
Liby
MOORWAY LA
Hall Pastures Farm
Recreation Ground
GOODSMOOR RD
1 KATRINE WLK
2 AVIEMORE WAY
Sinfin
SINFIN LA
GRAMPIAN WAY
STENSON RD
Sch
Hell Brook
Hell Meadow
REDWOOD RD
Schs
P
Playing Fields
Moorfield
SINFIN MOOR LA
WALTHAM AVE 1
CHATSWORTH CT 2
Stenson Fields Farm
Stenson Fields
ARLESTON LA
THE EYRIE
KINGFISHER WLK
1 VETCHFIELD CL
2 WILLOWHERB CL
TAVISTOCK CL 1
PADSTOW CL 2
1 BANKHOLMES CL
2 KNIGHTS CL
3 HUNTERS CROFT
WILTON CL 1
SOUTHDOWN CL 2
OAKWOOD CL 3
ALBRIGHTON AVE 4
LEDBURY CHASE 5
GARRY CL 6
DUNVEGAN CL 7
TRENT CL 8
HAMBLEDON DR 9
COWDRAY CL 10
BLANKNEY CL 11
WRAGLEY WAY
CASTLECRAIG CT
DUNBAR CL
DEEP DALE LA
Stenson House
PH
Marina
Trent and Mersey Canal
Stenson
Ashlea Farm
4
33
3
32
2
31
1
30
33
34

231
219

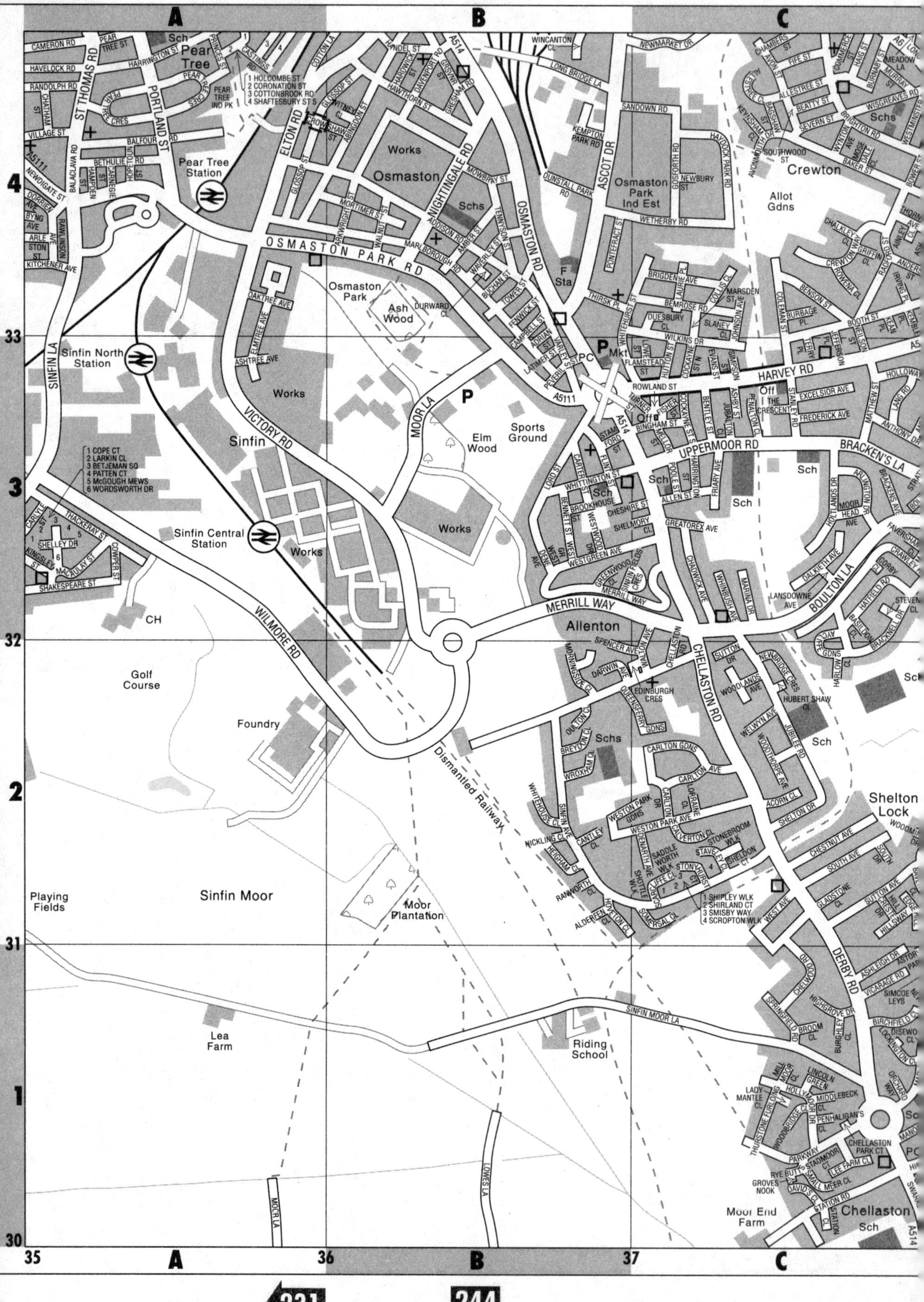
A
B
C
4
33
3
32
2
31
1
30
35
36
37
Pear Tree
Pear Tree Station
Osmaston
Works
Schs
Osmaston Park
Ash Wood
Osmaston Park Ind Est
Crewton
Allot Gdns
F Sta
Sinfin North Station
Sinfin Central Station
Sinfin
Works
Elm Wood
Sports Ground
Allenton
Golf Course
Foundry
Dismantled Railway
Playing Fields
Sinfin Moor
Moor Plantation
Lea Farm
Riding School
Moor End Farm
Chellaston
Shelton Lock
CH
Sch
OSMASTON PARK RD
VICTORY RD
WILMORE RD
SINFIN LA
MOOR LA
MERRILL WAY
OSMASTON RD
CHELLASTON RD
DERBY RD
HARVEY RD
UPPERMOOR RD
BOULTON LA
SINFIN MOOR LA
LOWES LA
NIGHTINGALE RD
ST THOMAS RD
PORTLAND ST
ASCOT DR
A5111
A514
1 HOLCOMBE ST
2 CORONATION ST
3 COTTONBROOK RD
4 SHAFTESBURY ST S
1 COPE CT
2 LARKIN CL
3 BETJEMAN SQ
4 PATTEN CT
5 McGOUGH MEWS
6 WORDSWORTH DR
1 SHIPLEY WLK
2 SHIRLAND CT
3 SMISBY WAY
4 SCROPTON WLK

D
E
F
4
33
3
32
2
31
1
30
39
40
Alvaston
RAYNESWAY
RAYNESWAY PARK DR
A5111
A6
LONDON RD
HARVEY RD
BOULTON LA
Boulton
Sch
Schs
PC
Liby
ELVASTON LA
SHARDLOW RD
KELDHOLME LA
HOLBROOK RD
HOLT AVE
1 DENTDALE CT
2 WENSLEYDALE WLK
3 COVERDALE WLK
1 STONESDALE CT
2 SWALEDALE CT
3 AIREDALE WLK
4 ARKENDALE WLK
5 FARNDALE CT
6 GLAISDALE NOOK
7 NIDDERDALE CT
8 ESKDALE WLK
9 GARSDALE CT
River Derwent
Home Farm
Bedford Drive
The Park
The Lake
Elvaston Castle
Oak Flat
Elvaston Castle Country Park
The Cottage
Coronation Plantation
Avenue Farm
CASTLE CT
SILVER LA
Thulston
B5010
OAK RD
BROAD LA
Grove Farm
PH
Moor Farm
End Farm
Boulton Moor
Thulston Fields Farm
Stubble Close
ASTORVILLE PARK RD
SNELSMOOR LA
Fox Covert Farm
Chellaston Covert
Marsh Flatts
HIGH ST
Chellaston
ASTON LA
CHELLASTON LA
Aston Hill
PRIORY CL

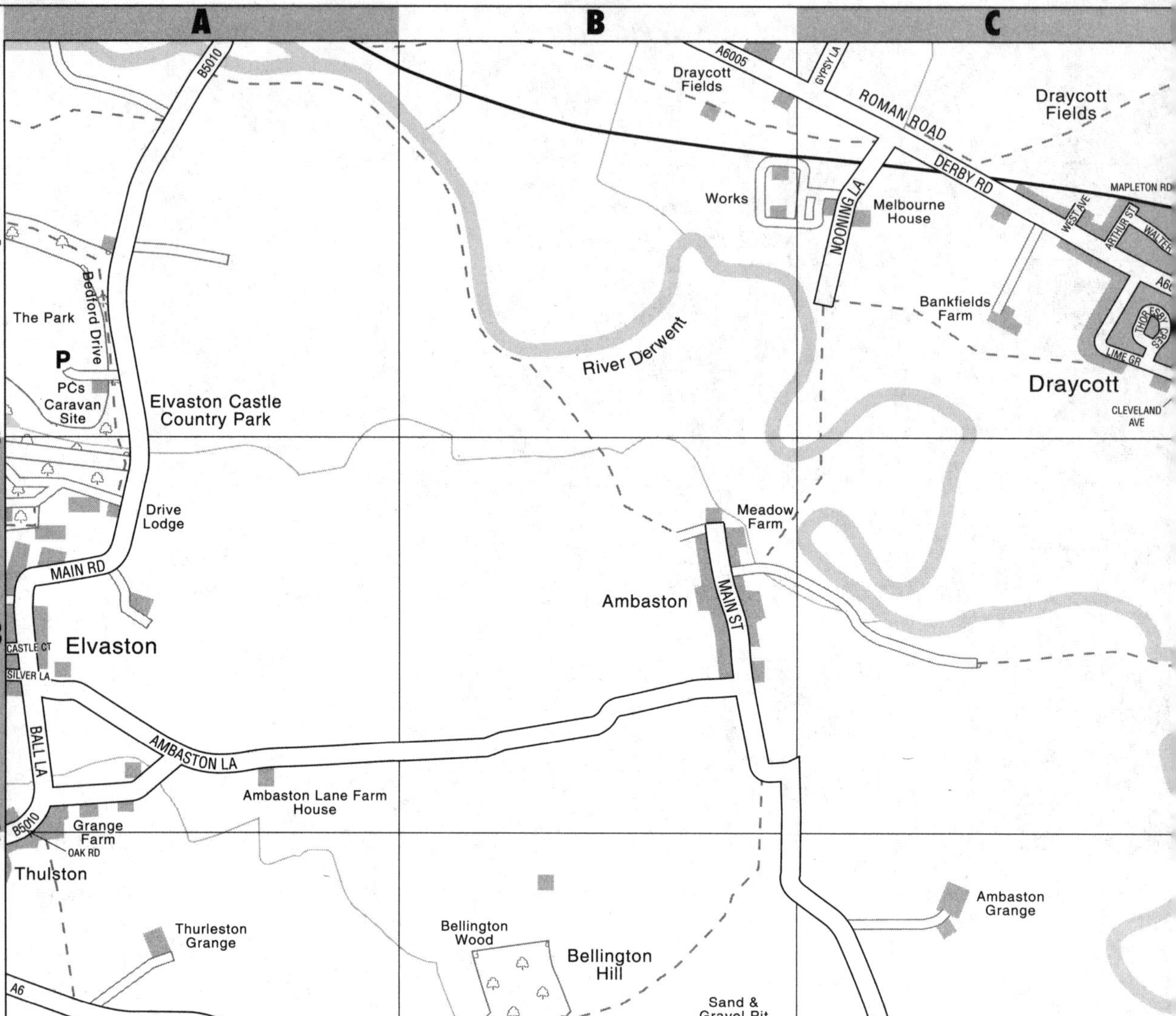
A
B
C
Draycott Fields
A6005
GYPSY LA
ROMAN ROAD
DERBY RD
Draycott Fields
MAPLETON RD
Works
NOONING LA
Melbourne House
WEST AVE
ARTHUR ST
WALTER
Bankfields Farm
LIME GR
Draycott
CLEVELAND AVE
B5010
Bedford Drive
The Park
P
PCs
Caravan Site
Elvaston Castle Country Park
River Derwent
Drive Lodge
Meadow Farm
MAIN RD
Ambaston
MAIN ST
CASTLE CT
Elvaston
SILVER LA
BALL LA
AMBASTON LA
Ambaston Lane Farm House
B5010
Grange Farm
OAK RD
Thulston
Ambaston Grange
Thurleston Grange
Bellington Wood
Bellington Hill
A6
Sand & Gravel Pit
Bellington Farm
AMBASTON LA
DERBY RD
Glebe Farm
Shardlow Moor
Moor Farm
Sch
Shardlow
Fox Covert Farm
Elms Farm
Manor Farm
CLOVER CT
GLENN WAY
Shardlow Hall
Hospl
ALTS NOOK WAY
WEST END DR
LONDON RD
WAKELYN CL
Brickyard Plantation
Bird's Nest Farm
COWLISHAW CL
Aston Moor
Alderslade Farm
ALDERSLADE CL
ASTON LA
Trent & Mersey Canal
4
33
3
32
2
31
1
30
41
42
43

D
E
F
4
33
3
32
2
31
1
30
45
46
Breaston
Liby
Sch
Cemy
Works
Off
Wks
PC
PH
The Elms
Attewell House
Elms Lodge
Wilne Cross
Poplar Farm
Breaston Fields Farm
LC
Church Wilne Reservoir
Gravel Pit
Sawley Grange Farm
Midshires Way
River Derwent
Church Wilne
Ivy House Farm
Great Wilne
Sewage Works
Porter's Bridge
Long Horse Bridge
Trent and Mersey Canal
River Trent
Sawley Cut
Hemington Fields House
HOPWELL RD
DRAYCOTT RD
STATION RD
SAWLEY RD
MAIN ST
WILSTHORPE RD
A6005
RISLEY LA
WILNE RD
WILNE LA
LONDON RD
CANAL BANK
THE WHARF
CAVENDISH CL
LONG ROW
MILLFIELD
THE MALTINGS
CAVENDISH CT
A6
B6540
TAMWORTH RD
NETHERFIELD LA
WARREN LA
M1
GREGORY AVE
STEVENSON AVE
HILLS RD
HIND AVE
SPRING CL
FESTIVAL AVE
ALBERT RD
HAYES AVE
MARLBOROUGH RD
THE CRESCENT
BRIDGE FIELD
BELL CL
FAR CROFT
EARLSWOOD CL
DELAMERE CL
CHURCHILL CL
PLACKETT CL
GRANGE AVE
LAWRENCE AVE
BURLINGTON CL
SHIRLEY CRES
WARD'S LA
MANOR CT
BLIND LA
THE GREEN
CHURCH VIEW
BOURNE SQ
MEADOW CL
FAIRFIELD AVE
RECTORY RD
CHERRY CL
MAYLANDS AVE
BELMONT AVE
PARK ST
GROSVENOR AVE
THE GROVE
WILLOUGHBY CL
POPLAR RD
BEECH AVE
HAWTHORN AVE
HOLLY AVE
MAPLE GR
ORCHARD CL
MAXWELL ST
MOUNT ST
HARRIMANS DR
HEATHER CRES
WOODLANDS AVE
BIRCHWOOD AVE
FIELD CL
VICTORIA RD
ROMAN RD
SOUTH ST
MILLS CL
LODGE ST
GILLIVER GDNS
WALK
MARKET ST
DERBY RD
MILNER AVE
HOLLY CL
ST CHAD'S CL
DERWENT ST
THE CROFT
ST MARY'S
NEW ST
SYDNEY ST
TOWN END RD
ELVASTON ST
VILLA ST
HARRINGTON ST
FOWLER ST
ATTEWELL CL
DRAYCOTT RD
BERESFORD RD
TWYFORD RD
HILTON CL
MELBOURNE CT
HARDWICK CT
HADDON WAY
INGLEBY RD
REPTON RD
WESTON CRES
WILNE CL
SUDBURY CT 1
ELVASTON DR 2
OVERDALE CL
PURDY MEADOW
OSMASTON CL
MATLOCK CT
HATHERSAGE AVE
PEVERIL CRES
WINSTER

A
B
C
LONG EATON
Wilsthorpe
West Park
Golden Brook
Trent College
Cemy
Nature Reserve
New Sawley
Long Eaton Station
Allot Gdns
Sawley
Schs
Ind Est
Erewash Canal
TAMWORTH RD
FIELDS FARM RD
WILSTHORPE RD
DERBY RD
NOTTINGHAM RD
HIGH ST
MAIN ST
STATION RD
MEADOW LA
DRAYCOTT RD
WILNE RD
PLANT LA
LOCK LA
WARREN LA
Stadium
Factory
Wks
Trent Rifle Lodge
Rifle Range
South Junction
Trent Farm
Sheetstores Junction
Golf Course
Narrow Bridge
Cranfleet Farm
Trent Junction
Trentlock
Trent Navigation Inn (PH)
Grounds Farm
Church Farm
Harrington Bridge
River Trent
Club
Sailing Club
Cranfleet Canal
Sawley Cut
Sawley Bridge Marina
River Soar
Red Hill
Redhill Lock
Redhill Farm
Thrumpton Park
Wood Hill
Ratcliffe on Soar Power Station
Ratcliffe Junction
Lockington Grounds Farm
1 HATTON CROFTS
2 RAD MEADOWS
3 OZIER HOLT
4 COCKLEYS
4 MALVERN GDNS
5 MICKLEDON CL
6 COTSWOLD CL
INGLEBOROUGH 1 GDNS
BREDON CL 2
BRECON CL 3
ALEXANDRA RD 1
EDWARD RD 2
1 WILNE AVE
2 CHURCH AVE
M1
A6005
B6002
B6540
4
33
3
32
2
31
1
30
47
48
49

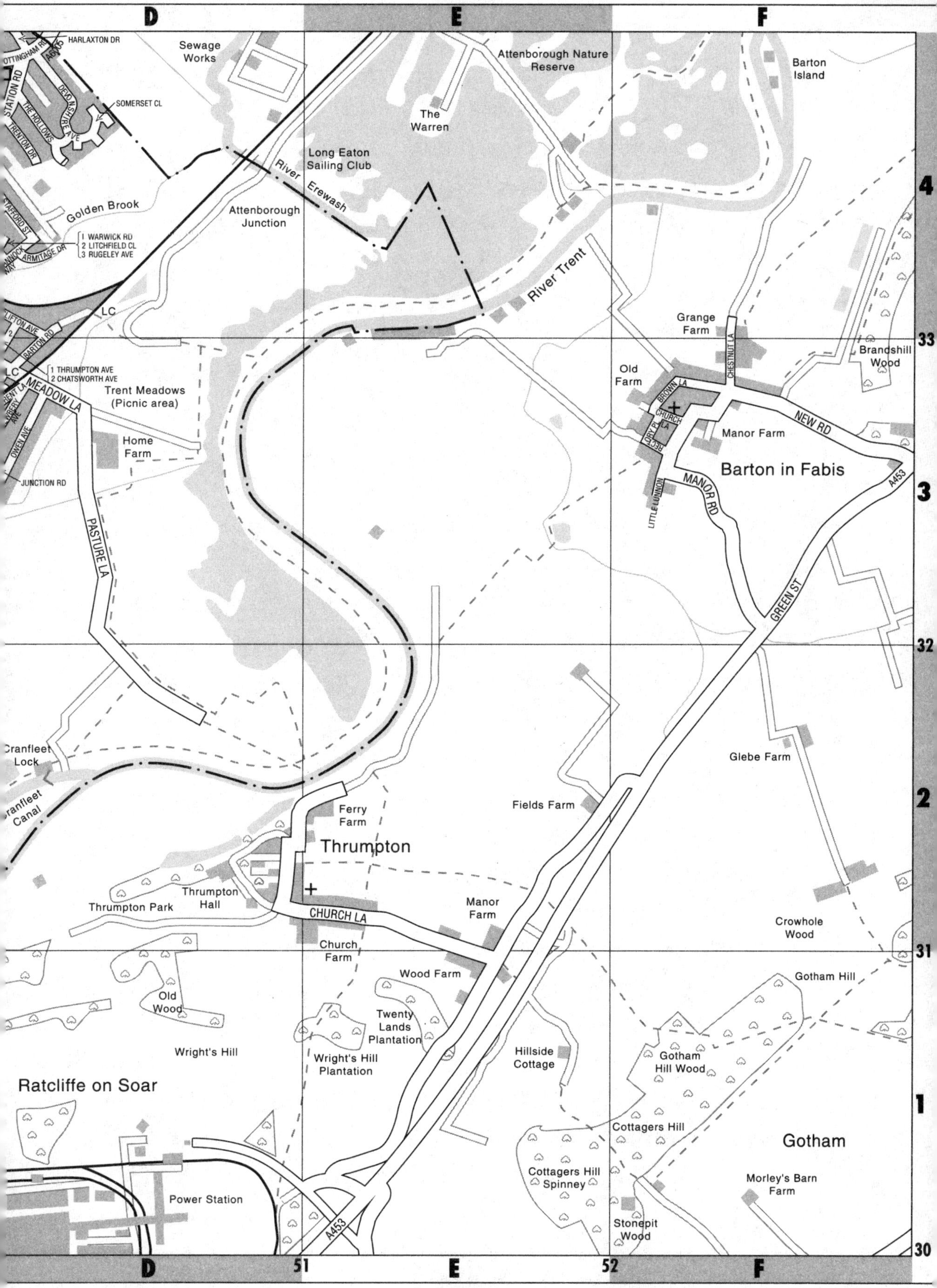
D
E
F
Sewage Works
HARLAXTON DR
NOTTINGHAM RD
A6005
STATION RD
DEVONSHIRE AVE
THE HOLLOWS
SOMERSET CL
TRENTON DR
STAFFORD ST
Golden Brook
1 WARWICK RD
2 LITCHFIELD CL
3 RUGELEY AVE
ARMITAGE DR
Attenborough Nature Reserve
The Warren
Long Eaton Sailing Club
River Erewash
Attenborough Junction
Barton Island
River Trent
LC
Grange Farm
CHESTNUT LA
Brandshill Wood
BARTON RD
1 THRUMPTON AVE
2 CHATSWORTH AVE
MEADOW LA
Trent Meadows (Picnic area)
Old Farm
BROWN LA
CHURCH LA
NEW RD
Manor Farm
Home Farm
OWEN AVE
JUNCTION RD
Barton in Fabis
MANOR RD
LITTLE LUNNON
A453
PASTURE LA
GREEN ST
Cranfleet Lock
Cranfleet Canal
Glebe Farm
Ferry Farm
Fields Farm
Thrumpton
Thrumpton Hall
Thrumpton Park
CHURCH LA
Manor Farm
Church Farm
Crowhole Wood
Wood Farm
Gotham Hill
Old Wood
Twenty Lands Plantation
Wright's Hill
Wright's Hill Plantation
Hillside Cottage
Gotham Hill Wood
Ratcliffe on Soar
Cottagers Hill
Gotham
Power Station
Cottagers Hill Spinney
Morley's Barn Farm
A453
Stonepit Wood
4
33
3
32
2
31
1
30
51
52

226

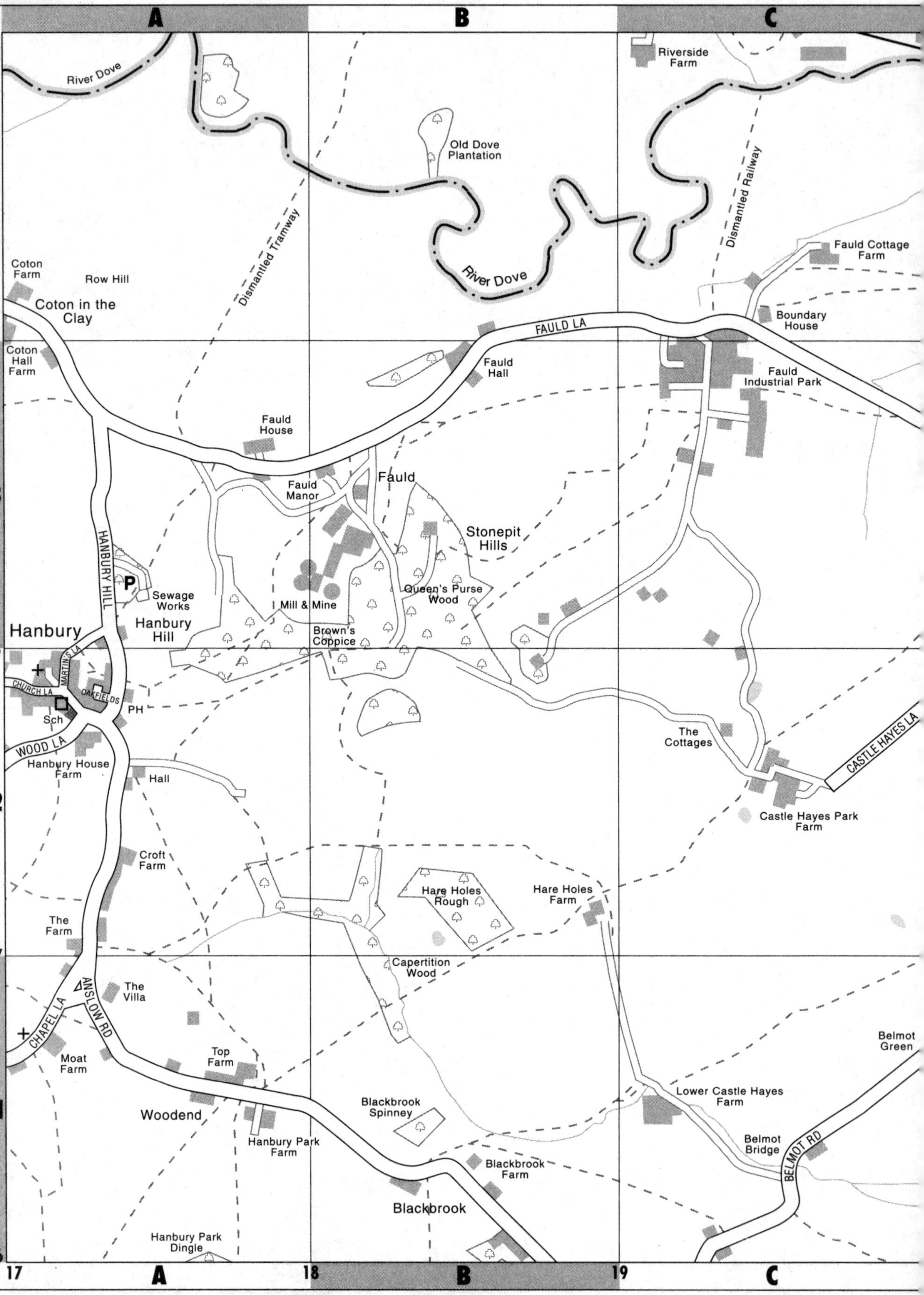
A
B
C
River Dove
Riverside Farm
Old Dove Plantation
Dismantled Tramway
Dismantled Railway
River Dove
Fauld Cottage Farm
Coton Farm
Row Hill
Coton in the Clay
Boundary House
FAULD LA
Coton Hall Farm
Fauld Hall
Fauld Industrial Park
Fauld House
Fauld Manor
Fauld
Stonepit Hills
HANBURY HILL
P
Sewage Works
Queen's Purse Wood
Mill & Mine
Hanbury
Hanbury Hill
Brown's Coppice
MARTIN'S LA
CHURCH LA
OAKFIELDS
Sch
PH
WOOD LA
Hanbury House Farm
Hall
The Cottages
CASTLE HAYES LA
Castle Hayes Park Farm
Croft Farm
Hare Holes Rough
Hare Holes Farm
The Farm
Capertition Wood
The Villa
ANSLOW RD
CHAPEL LA
Moat Farm
Top Farm
Belmot Green
Woodend
Blackbrook Spinney
Lower Castle Hayes Farm
Hanbury Park Farm
Belmot Bridge
Blackbrook Farm
BELMOT RD
Blackbrook
Hanbury Park Dingle
4
29
3
28
2
27
1
26
17
18
19

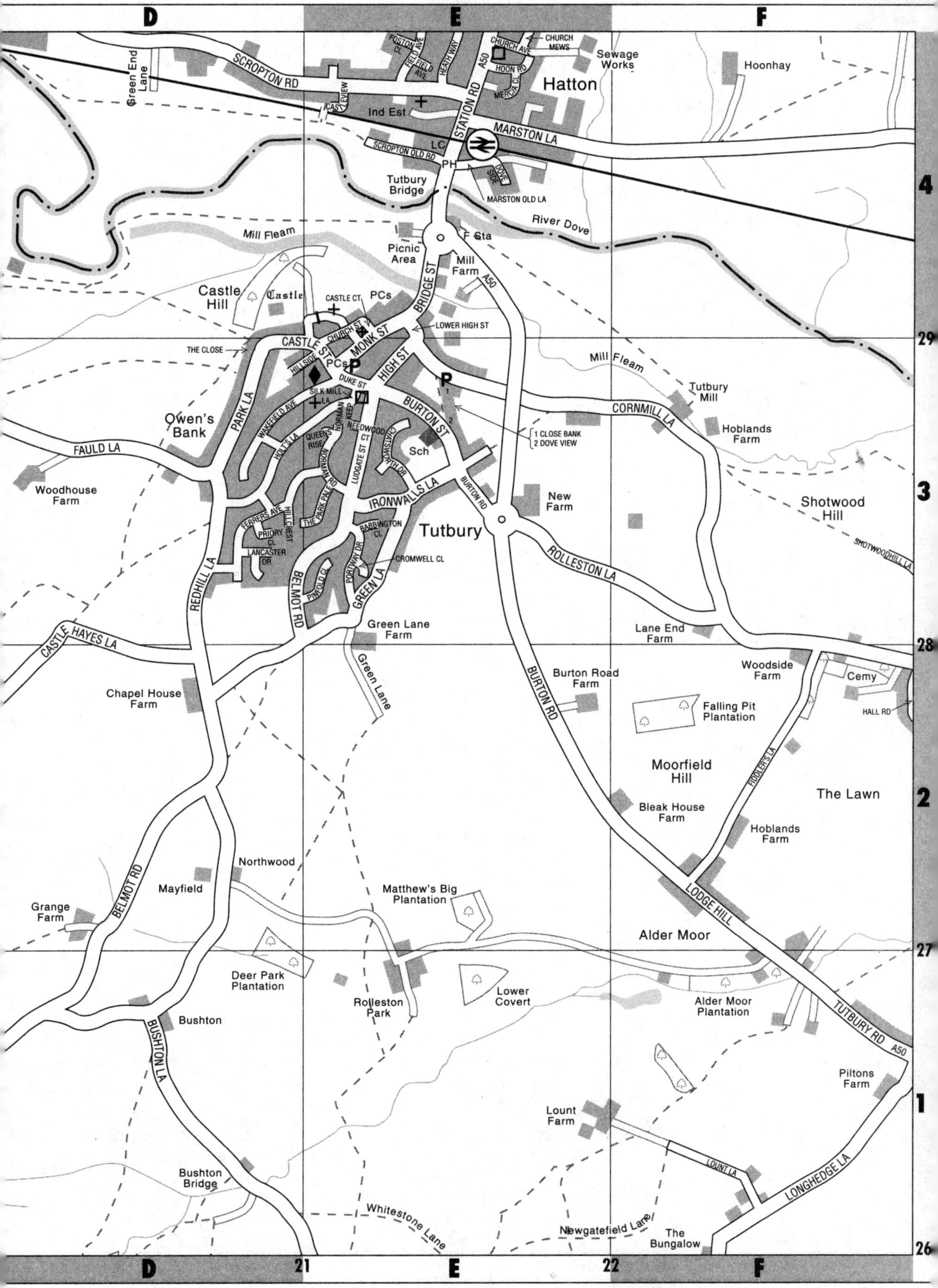
D
E
F
Green End Lane
SCROPTON RD
FOSTON CL
FIELD AVE
HEATH WAY
CHURCH AVE
CHURCH MEWS
HOON RD
MERCIA CL
Sewage Works
Hoonhay
Hatton
CASTLEVIEW
Ind Est
STATION RD
A50
MARSTON LA
SCROPTON OLD RD
LC
PH
DOVE SIDE
Tutbury Bridge
MARSTON OLD LA
River Dove
4
Mill Fleam
F Sta
Picnic Area
Mill Farm
BRIDGE ST
Castle Hill
Castle
CASTLE CT
PCs
LOWER HIGH ST
CASTLE ST
CHURCH ST
MONK ST
THE CLOSE
29
HILLSIDE
PCs
HIGH ST
DUKE ST
SILK MILL LA
WAKEFIELD AVE
Owen's Bank
PARK LA
KEEP
BURTON ST
Mill Fleam
Tutbury Mill
CORNMILL LA
Hoblands Farm
1 CLOSE BANK
2 DOVE VIEW
NEEDWOOD CT
CHATSWORTH DR
QUEENS RISE
HOLT'S LA
NORMAN RD
Sch
FAULD LA
Woodhouse Farm
LUDGATE ST
IRONWALLS LA
THE PARK PALE
BURTON RD
New Farm
3
Shotwood Hill
FERRERS AVE
HILLCREST
PRIORY CL
BABBINGTON CL
Tutbury
SHOTWOODHILL LA
LANCASTER DR
CROMWELL CL
PORTWAY DR
PINFOLD CL
ROLLESTON LA
REDHILL LA
BELMOT RD
GREEN LA
Green Lane Farm
Lane End Farm
CASTLE HAYES LA
28
Woodside Farm
Cemy
Burton Road Farm
Chapel House Farm
Green Lane
Falling Pit Plantation
HALL RD
BURTON RD
FIDDLER'S LA
Moorfield Hill
The Lawn
2
Bleak House Farm
Hoblands Farm
Northwood
BELMOT RD
Mayfield
Matthew's Big Plantation
LODGE HILL
Grange Farm
Alder Moor
27
Deer Park Plantation
Lower Covert
Rolleston Park
Alder Moor Plantation
Bushton
BUSHTON LA
TUTBURY RD
A50
Piltons Farm
Lount Farm
1
LOUNT LA
LONGHEDGE LA
Bushton Bridge
Whitestone Lane
Newgatefield Lane
The Bungalow
26
D
21
E
22
F

239
228

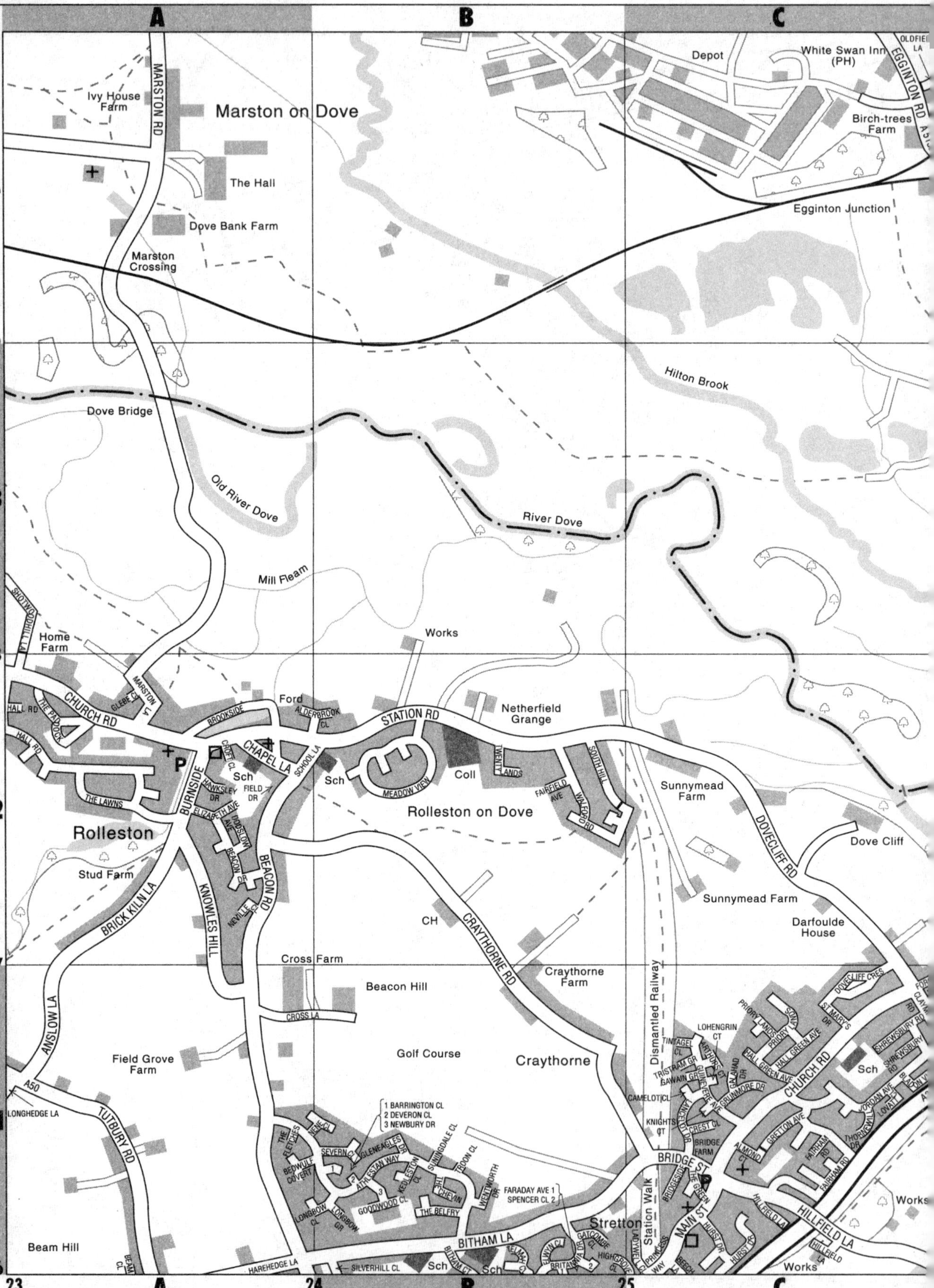
A
B
C
Marston on Dove
Ivy House Farm
MARSTON RD
The Hall
Dove Bank Farm
Marston Crossing
Depot
White Swan Inn (PH)
OLDFIELD LA
EGGINTON RD
Birch-trees Farm
Egginton Junction
Hilton Brook
Dove Bridge
Old River Dove
River Dove
Mill Fleam
Home Farm
Works
Ford
Netherfield Grange
STATION RD
CHURCH RD
HALL RD
THE PADDOCK
GLEBE CL
MARSTON LA
BROOKSIDE
ALDERBROOK CL
CHAPEL LA
SCHOOL LA
CROFT CL
Sch
Coll
MEADOW VIEW
TWENTY LANDS
SOUTH HILL
FAIRFIELD AVE
WALFORD RD
Sunnymead Farm
DOVECLIFF RD
Dove Cliff
Rolleston on Dove
Rolleston
BURNSIDE
HAWKSLEY DR
FIELD DR
ELIZABETH AVE
DODSLOW AVE
BEACON DR
BEACON RD
THE LAWNS
Stud Farm
BRICK KILN LA
KNOWLES HILL
NEVILLE CL
CH
CRAYTHORNE RD
Darfoulde House
Cross Farm
Beacon Hill
CROSS LA
Craythorne Farm
Dismantled Railway
Golf Course
Craythorne
Field Grove Farm
ANSLOW LA
A50
LONGHEDGE LA
TUTBURY RD
1 BARRINGTON CL
2 DEVERON CL
3 NEWBURY DR
THE FLETCHES
BEOWULF COVERT
SEVERN CL
GLENEAGLES DR
ATHELSTAN WAY
KEDLESTON CL
SUNNINGDALE CL
CHEVIN
TROON CL
WENTWORTH DR
LONGBOW CL
LONGBOW GR
GOODWOOD CL
THE BELFRY
FARADAY AVE 1
SPENCER CL 2
BITHAM LA
HAREHEDGE LA
SILVERHILL CL
BITHAM CT
BRITANNIA DR
GATCOMBE CL
HIGHGROVE CL
Stretton
Station Walk
PRINCESS WAY
MAIN ST
BRIDGE ST
BRIDGESIDE
THE GREEN
Beam Hill
BEAM CL
LOHENGRIN CT
TINTAGEL CL
TRISTRAM GR
GAWAIN GR
CAMELOT CL
KNIGHTS CT
GUINEVERE AVE
GALAHAD DR
GRUNMORE DR
CREST CL
BRIDGE FARM
PRIORY LANDS
PRIORY LA
HALL GREEN AVE
CHURCH RD
ST MARY'S DR
SHREWSBURY RD
DOVECLIFF CRES
Sch
GRETTON AVE
ALMOND CT
FAIRHAM RD
THORNEWILL DR
JORDAN AVE
HILLFIELD LA
HURST DR
Works
23
24
25
26
27
28
29
1
2
3
4

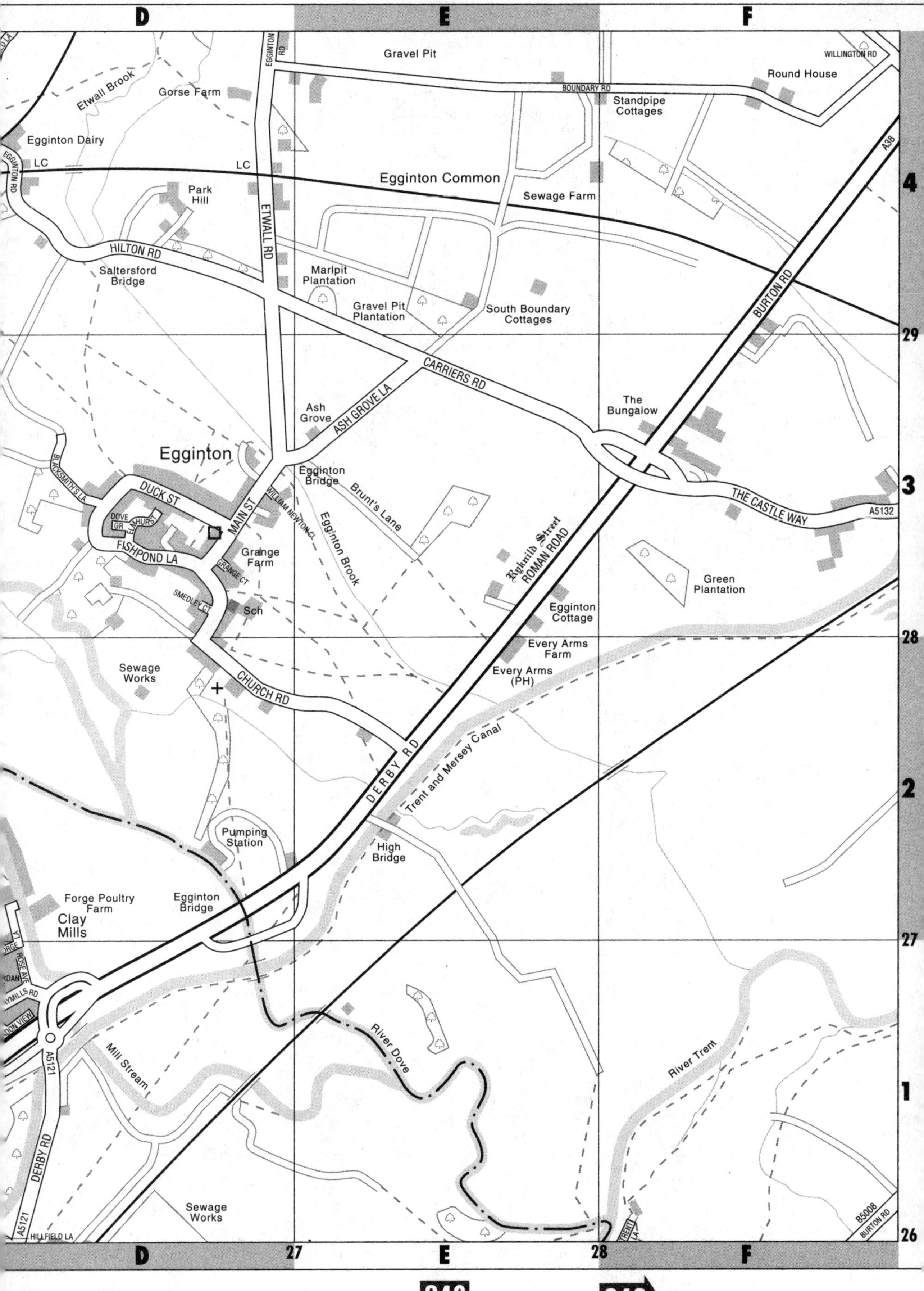
D
E
F
Gravel Pit
WILLINGTON RD
Round House
BOUNDARY RD
Standpipe Cottages
Etwall Brook
Gorse Farm
EGGINTON RD
Egginton Dairy
LC
LC
Egginton Common
Sewage Farm
Park Hill
ETWALL RD
A38
4
HILTON RD
Saltersford Bridge
Marlpit Plantation
Gravel Pit Plantation
South Boundary Cottages
BURTON RD
29
CARRIERS RD
ASH GROVE LA
Ash Grove
The Bungalow
Egginton
BLACKSMITH'S LA
DUCK ST
MAIN ST
WILLIAM NEWTON CL
Egginton Bridge
Brunt's Lane
Egginton Brook
THE CASTLE WAY
A5132
3
DOVE GR
ELMHURST
FISHPOND LA
Grange Farm
GRANGE CT
Ryknild Street
ROMAN ROAD
Green Plantation
SMEDLEY CT
Sch
Egginton Cottage
Every Arms Farm
28
Sewage Works
Every Arms (PH)
CHURCH RD
Trent and Mersey Canal
DERBY RD
2
Pumping Station
High Bridge
Forge Poultry Farm
Egginton Bridge
Clay Mills
27
ROSE AVE
A5121
River Dove
Mill Stream
River Trent
1
DERBY RD
Sewage Works
B5008
BURTON RD
TRENT LA
HILLFIELD LA
A5121
26
D
27
E
28
F

241
230

241
249

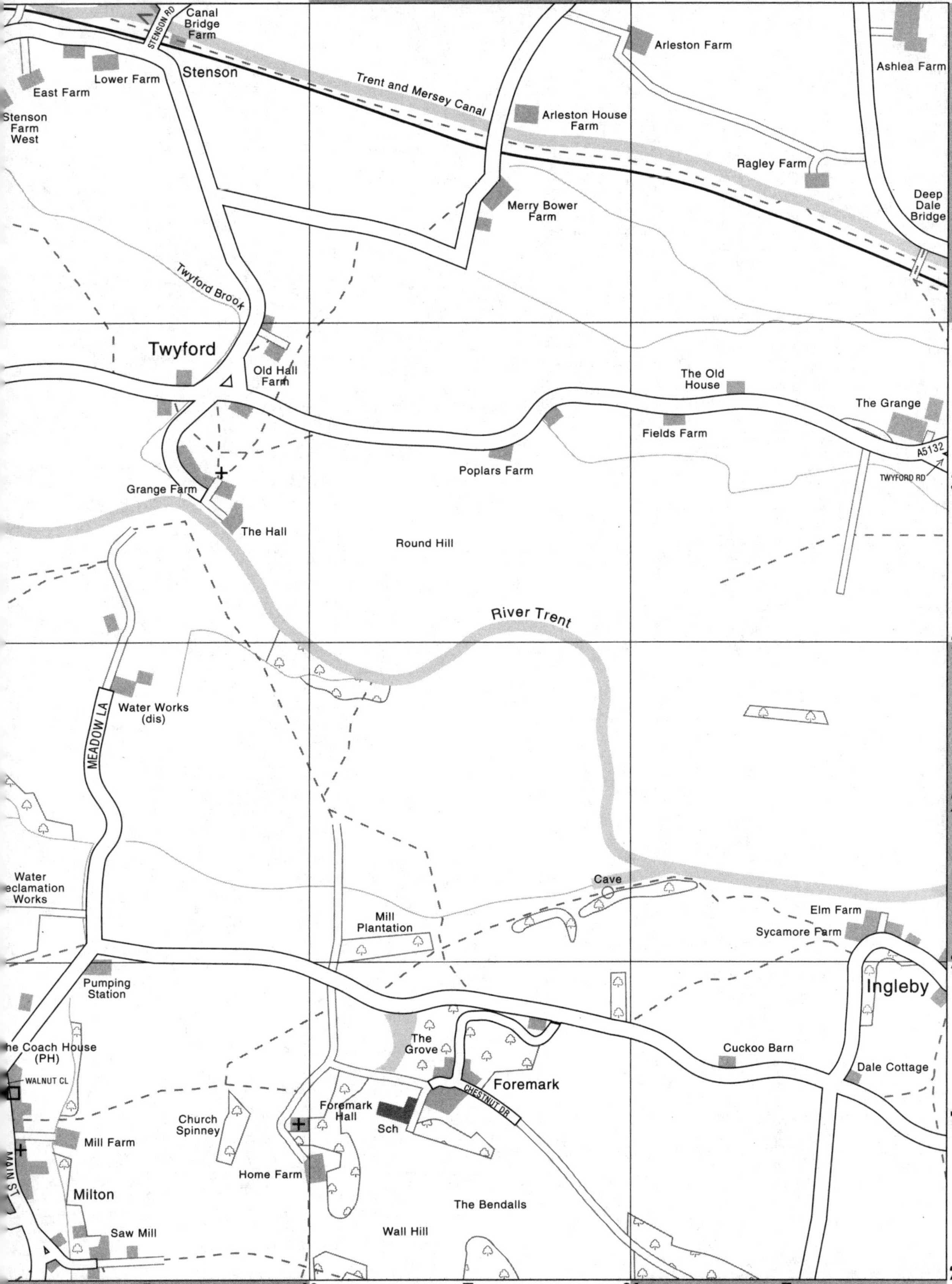
D
E
F
Canal Bridge Farm
STENSON RD
Stenson
East Farm
Lower Farm
Stenson Farm West
Trent and Mersey Canal
Arleston Farm
Ashlea Farm
Arleston House Farm
Ragley Farm
Deep Dale Bridge
Merry Bower Farm
Twyford Brook
Twyford
Old Hall Farm
The Old House
The Grange
Fields Farm
A5132
TWYFORD RD
Poplars Farm
Grange Farm
The Hall
Round Hill
River Trent
Water Works (dis)
MEADOW LA
Water eclamation Works
Cave
Elm Farm
Sycamore Farm
Mill Plantation
Ingleby
Pumping Station
The Grove
Cuckoo Barn
he Coach House (PH)
Foremark
Dale Cottage
WALNUT CL
CHESTNUT DR
Foremark Hall
Sch
Church Spinney
Mill Farm
Home Farm
MAIN ST
Milton
The Bendalls
Saw Mill
Wall Hill
4
29
3
28
2
27
1
26
33
34

243
232

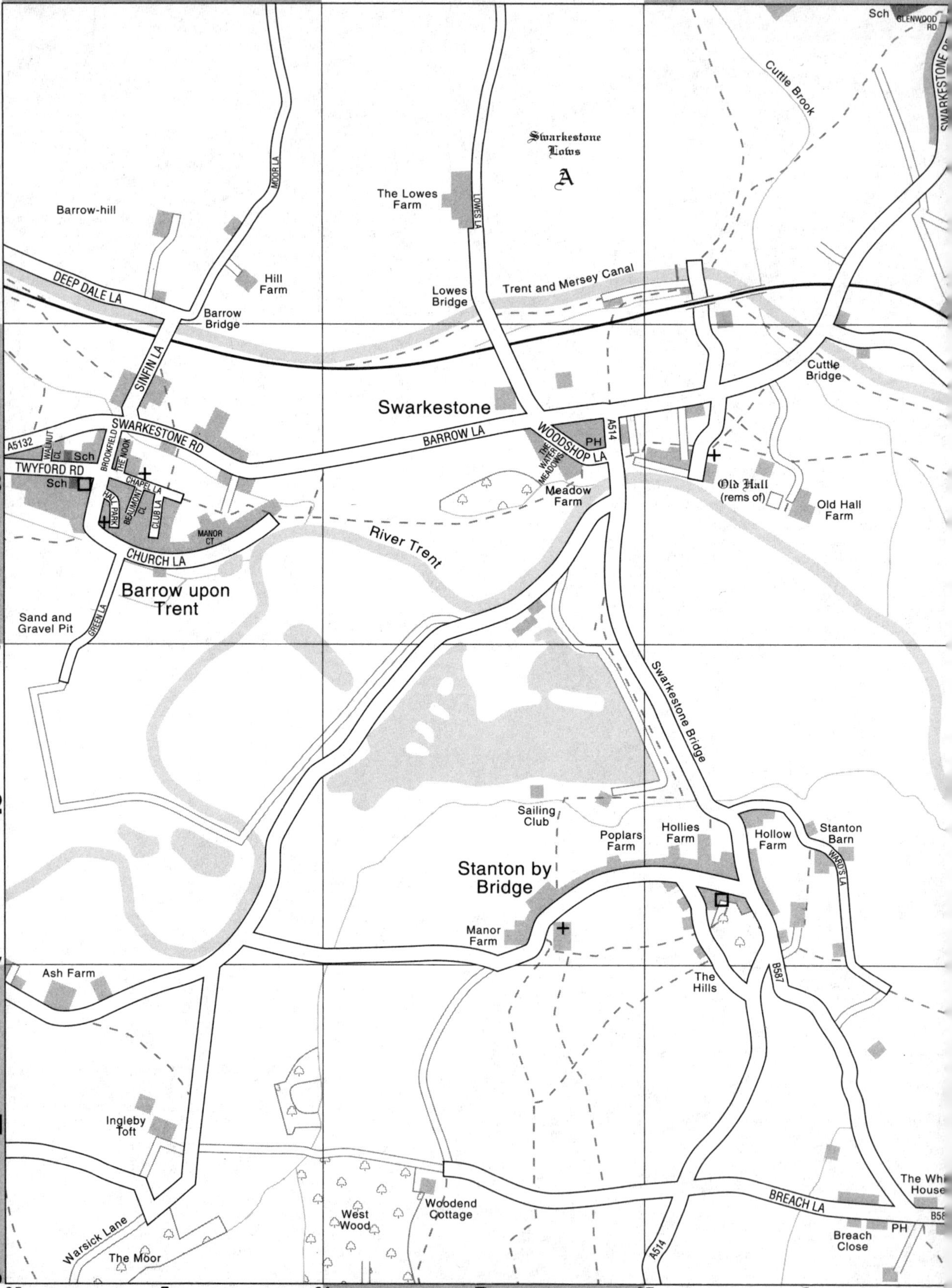

243
251

233
246

252
246

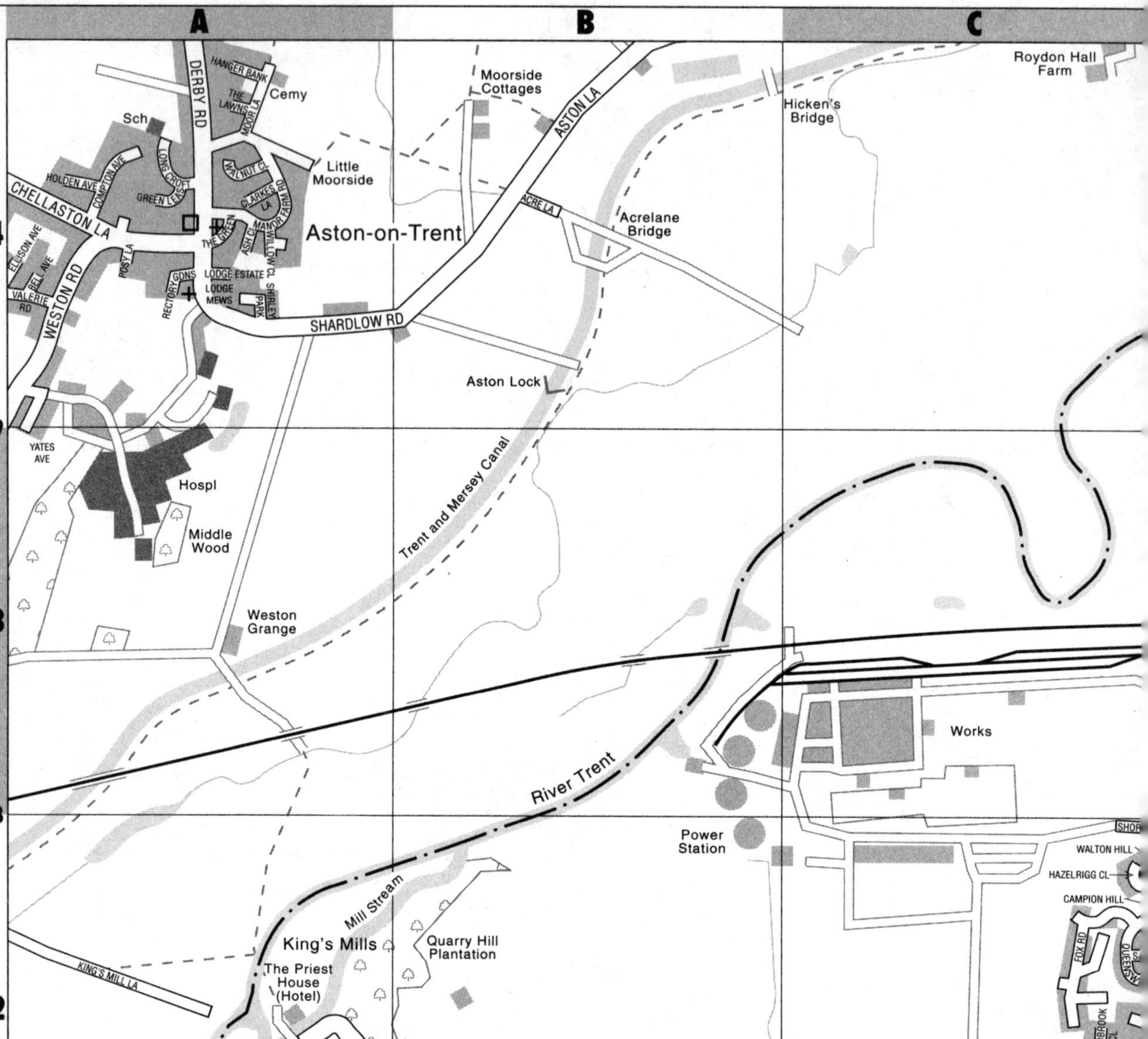
A
B
C
4
3
2
1
29
28
27
26
41
42
43
DERBY RD
HANGER BANK
THE LAWNS
MOOR LA
Cemy
Sch
LONG CROFT
HOLDEN AVE
COMPTON AVE
GREEN LEAS
CHELLASTON LA
WALNUT CL
CLARKES LA
MANOR FARM RD
THE GREEN
ASH CL
WILLOW CL
Aston-on-Trent
ELLISON AVE
BEL AVE
VALERIE RD
WESTON RD
POSY LA
RECTORY GDNS
LODGE ESTATE
LODGE MEWS
SHIRLEY PARK
SHARDLOW RD
Little Moorside
Moorside Cottages
ASTON LA
ACRE LA
Acrelane Bridge
Hicken's Bridge
Roydon Hall Farm
Aston Lock
YATES AVE
Hospl
Middle Wood
Trent and Mersey Canal
Weston Grange
River Trent
Works
Power Station
SHOR
WALTON HILL
HAZELRIGG CL
CAMPION HILL
FOX RD
QUEENSW
STUDBROOK CL
Mill Stream
King's Mills
Quarry Hill Plantation
KING'S MILL LA
The Priest House (Hotel)
PC
Home Farm
Highfields
PARK LA
Innisfree
STARKIE AVE
PARK A
SHIELDS
BOSWORTH RD
ADDOCK CL
Boathouse Walk Plantation
The Shrubbery
Captain's Gorse
Studbrook Hollow
Stud Brook
Donington Hall
Dalby's Covert
Donington Park (Deer Park)
Hill T Far
All Hooks
Thirteen Acre Plantation
Holly Wood
Starkey's Bridge
Motor Racing Circuit
Gallows Flesh Wood
Coppice Wood
B6

D
E
F
Cavendish Bridge
A6
River Trent
LONDON RD
The Cavendish Arms (PH)
TAMWORTH RD
B6540
M1
Sand and Gravel Pit
NETHERFIELD LA
DONNINGTON LA
BACK LA
4
29
A6
RYCROFT RD
Willow Farm
LC
Trent Farm
Hanover Estate
SYCAMORE RD
Sewage Works
3
STATION RD
New Delight Cottages
WILLOW RD
NEWBOLD DR
TRENT LA
MAIN ST
Hemington
Lockington
Lockington Park
HEMINGTON LA
MAIN ST
LOCKINGTON RD
Lockington Hall
HAWTHORN RD
STATION RD
VICTORIA ST
Hotel
Sch
DALEACRE AVE
KINGS GATE
28
CHURCH ST
Daleacre Hill
SPITTAL
TANYARD CL
CAMPION HILL
RAWDON CL
QUEENSWAY
LOUDOUN PL
War Meml
CHURCH LA
HUNTINGDON DR
HAULTON DR
HARCOURT PL
HILLSIDE
CASTLE HILL
THE MOAT
HEMINGTON HILL
The Dumps
SCHOOL LA
THE SPINNEY
SELINA CL
MONTEITH PL
P
Sch
GRANGE DR
BONDGATE
THE HOLLOW
THE BARROON
Cemy
2
THE GREEN
LOTHIAN PL
TIPNALL RD
CARRS CL
BOROUGH ST
CHURCH ST
THE BIGGIN
CHARNWOOD AVE
ORCHARD AVE
PEARTREE CL
MARKET ST
ST ANNE'S LA
CLAPGUN ST
GARDEN CRES
MOIRA DALE
PARK LA
APIARY GATE
King Street Plantation
DOVE COTE
EASTWAY
PC
DELVEN LA
MOUNT PLEASANT
Sch
TOWLES PASTURES
BARN CL
Liby
Coll
Castle Donington
COOKS AVE
HALL FARM CL
EATON RD
27
ROUTH AVE
ORLY AVE
CEDAR RD
HASTINGS ST
CAVENDISH CL
BAKEWELL DR
HALLAM FIELDS RD
HARVEY RD
HIGH ST
CRABTREE CL
MEADOW CRES
WINDMILL CL
ST EDWARD'S RD
STONEHILL
Field Farm
1
DISEWORTH RD
Mast
East Midlands Airport
26
45
46

241

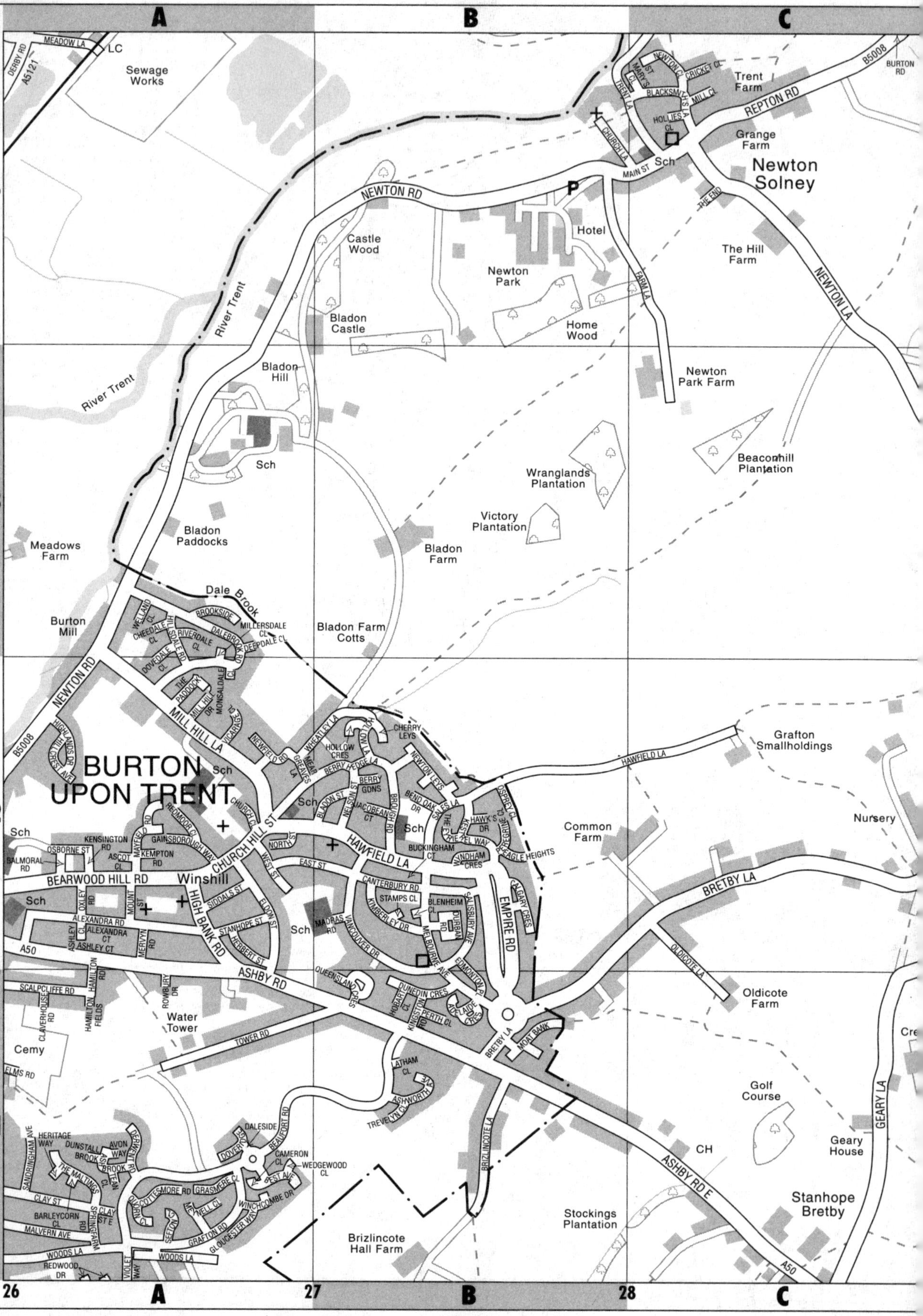
A
B
C
4
3
2
1
25
24
23
22
26
27
28
MEADOW LA
LC
DERBY RD
A5121
Sewage Works
River Trent
River Trent
NEWTON RD
Castle Wood
Bladon Castle
Bladon Hill
Sch
Bladon Paddocks
Meadows Farm
Burton Mill
Dale Brook
Newton Park
Hotel
Home Wood
P
Newton Park Farm
Wranglands Plantation
Victory Plantation
Bladon Farm
Bladon Farm Cotts
Beaconhill Plantation
NEWTON CL
CRICKET CL
MARY'S
TRENT LA
BLACKSMITHS LA
MILL CL
HOLLIES CL
CHURCH LA
MAIN ST
Sch
Trent Farm
Grange Farm
REPTON RD
B5008
BURTON RD
Newton Solney
THE END
The Hill Farm
FARM LA
NEWTON LA
BROOKSIDE
WELLAND CL
CHEEDALE CL
HILLSDALE RD
RIVERDALE CL
DALEBROOK RD
MILLERSDALE CL
DEEPDALE CL
DOVEDALE CL
THE PADDOCK
MILL HILL DR
MONSALDALE CL
VICARAGE CL
NEWTON RD
B5008
HIGHLANDS DR
HILLCREST AVE
MILL HILL LA
BURTON UPON TRENT
Sch
NEWFIELD RD
WHEATLEY LA
HOLLOW CRES
CHERRY LEYS
MEADOW LA
GREAVES LA
BERRY HEDGE LA
BERRY GDNS
NEWTON LEYS
BEND OAK DR
SALES LA
OSPREY CL
HAWFIELD LA
Grafton Smallholdings
Nursery
Sch
CHURCH HILL ST
BLADON ST
NELSON ST
JACOBEAN CT
BROUGH RD
Sch
THE EYRIE
KESTREL WAY
HAWK'S DR
PEREGRINE CL
EAGLE HEIGHTS
BUCKINGHAM CT
WYNDHAM CRES
Common Farm
Sch
KENSINGTON RD
OSBORNE ST
BALMORAL RD
ASCOT CL
MAYFIELD RD
REDMOOR CL
GAINSBOROUGH WAY
KEMPTON RD
NORTH ST
HAWFIELD LA
WEST ST
EAST ST
BEARWOOD HILL RD
Winshill
CANTERBURY RD
STAMPS CL
BLENHEIM CL
KIMBERLEY DR
DURBAN RD
SALISBURY AVE
EMPIRE RD
CALGARY CRES
BRETBY LA
Sch
OXLEY RD
MOUNT ST
HIGH BANK RD
SIDDALS ST
ELTON ST
STANHOPE ST
HERBERT ST
ALEXANDRA RD
ALEXANDRA CT
ASHLEY CL
ASHLEY CT
MERVYN RD
Sch
MADRAS RD
VANCOUVER DR
MELBOURNE AVE
EDMONTON PL
OLDICOTE LA
A50
ASHBY RD
QUEENSLAND CRES
DUNEDIN CRES
ADELAIDE CRES
HOBART CL
KINGSTON RD
PERTH CL
SCALPCLIFFE RD
CLAVERHOUSE RD
HAMILTON RD
HAMILTON FIELDS
ROWBURY DR
Water Tower
Oldicote Farm
BRETBY LA
MOAT BANK
Cemy
TOWER RD
ELMS RD
LATHAM CL
ASHWORTH AVE
TREVELYN CL
Golf Course
Cre
GEARY LA
BEAUFORT RD
DALESIDE
DOVERIDGE
CAMERON CL
WEDGEWOOD CL
BRIZLINCOTE LA
CH
ASHBY RD E
Geary House
Stanhope Bretby
HERITAGE WAY
DUNSTALL BROOK
AVON WAY
DERWENT RD
THE MALTINGS
SANDRINGHAM AVE
ASH BROOK
TEAN CL
CLAY ST
BARLEYCORN CL
SPRINGFARM RD
CLAY ST E
MALVERN AVE
WOODS LA
REDWOOD DR
VIOLET WAY
WOODS LA
MORE RD
GRASMERE CL
BEST AVE
WINCHCOMBE DR
GLOUCESTER WAY
GRAFTON RD
SEFTON
MELL CL
Stockings Plantation
Brizlincote Hall Farm
A50

255

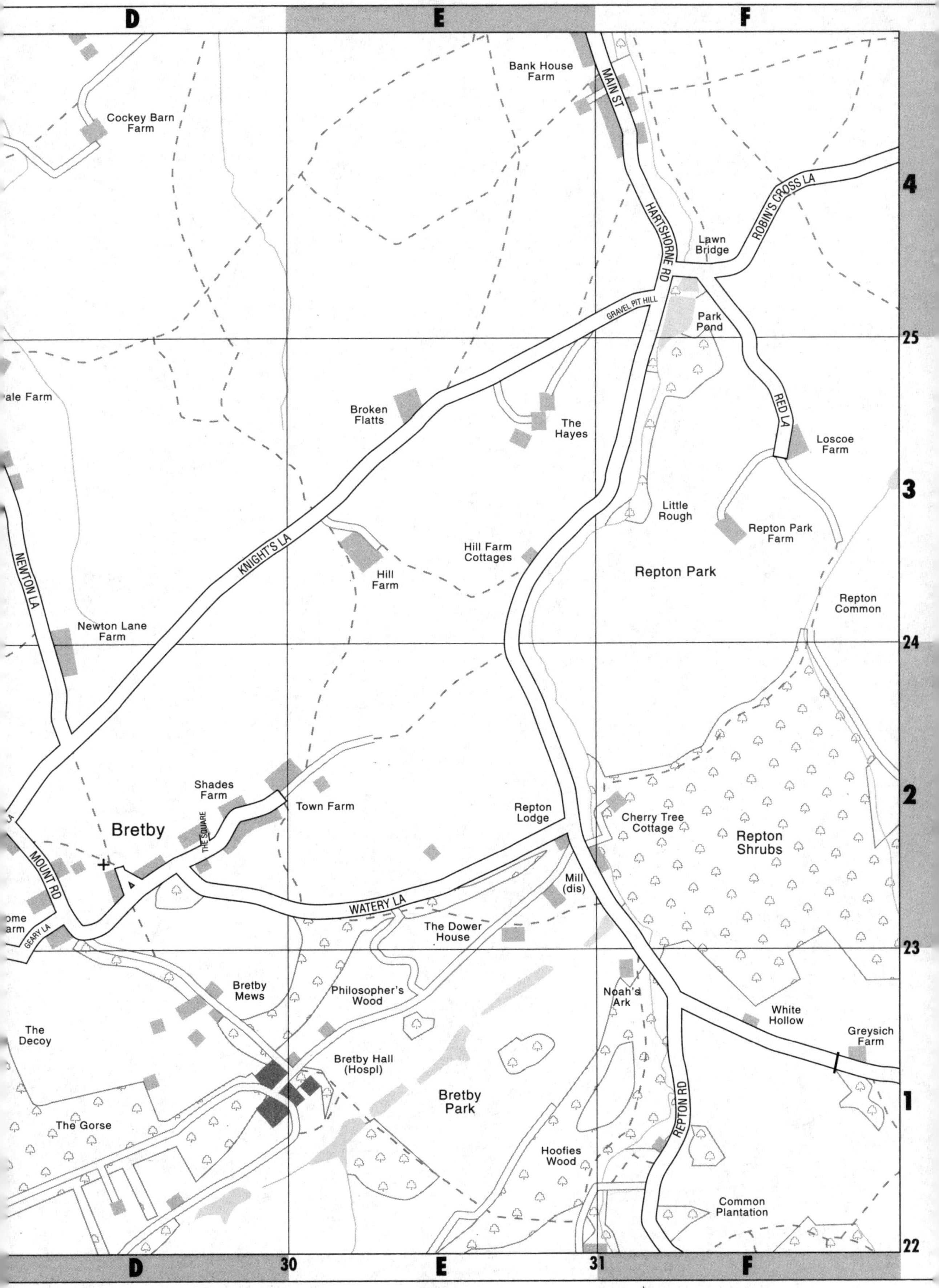
D
E
F
Bank House Farm
MAIN ST
Cockey Barn Farm
ROBIN'S CROSS LA
HARTSHORNE RD
Lawn Bridge
GRAVEL PIT HILL
Park Pond
ale Farm
Broken Flatts
The Hayes
RED LA
Loscoe Farm
Little Rough
Repton Park Farm
KNIGHT'S LA
Hill Farm Cottages
Hill Farm
Repton Park
Repton Common
NEWTON LA
Newton Lane Farm
Shades Farm
Town Farm
Repton Lodge
THE SQUARE
Bretby
Cherry Tree Cottage
Repton Shrubs
MOUNT RD
Mill (dis)
WATERY LA
ome arm
GEARY LA
The Dower House
Bretby Mews
Philosopher's Wood
Noah's Ark
White Hollow
The Decoy
Greysich Farm
Bretby Hall (Hospl)
Bretby Park
REPTON RD
The Gorse
Hoofies Wood
Common Plantation
4
25
3
24
2
23
1
22
30
31

249
243

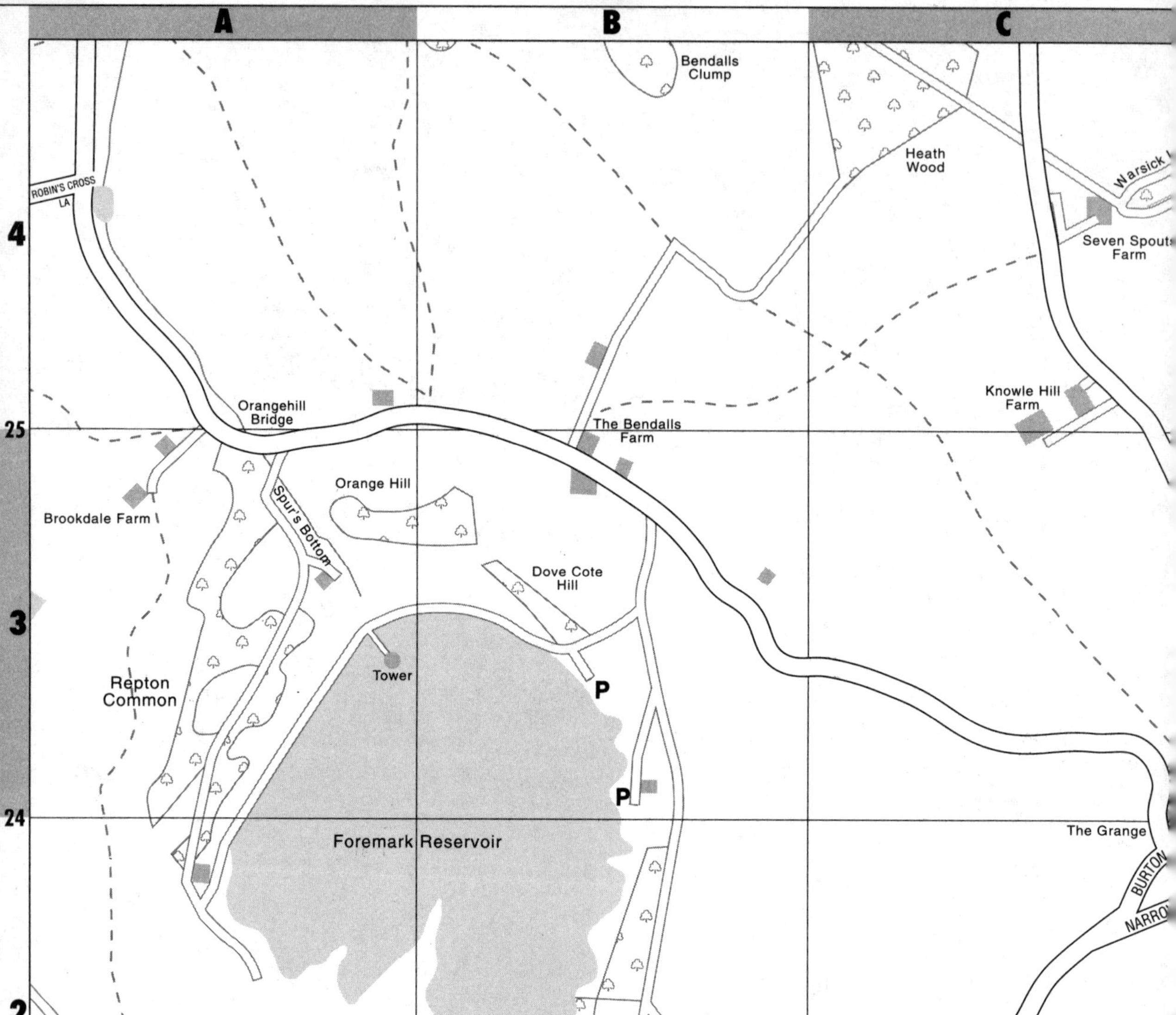

249
257

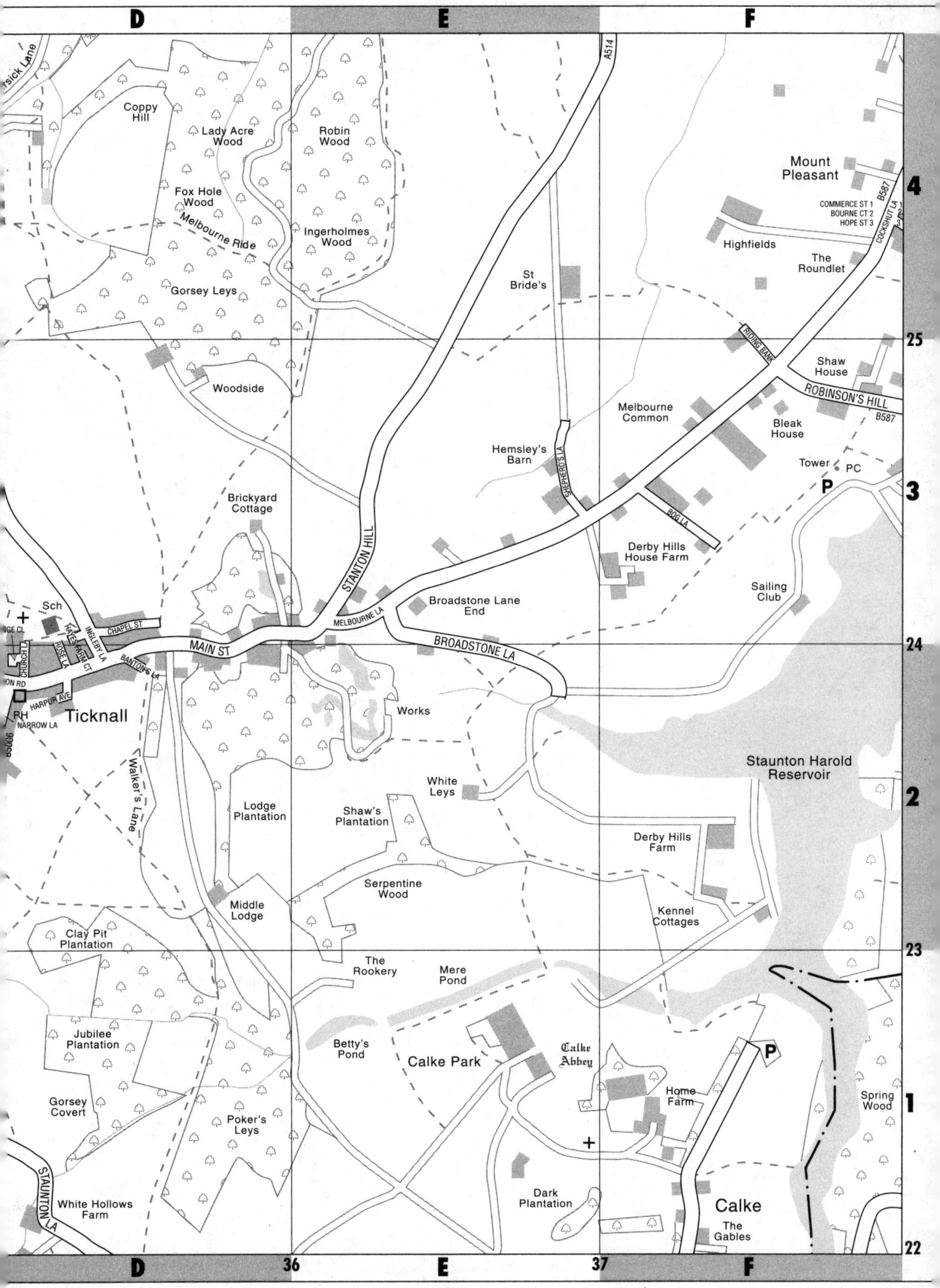
D
E
F
Coppy Hill
Lady Acre Wood
Robin Wood
Fox Hole Wood
Melbourne Ride
Ingerholmes Wood
Gorsey Leys
Woodside
Brickyard Cottage
St Bride's
A514
Mount Pleasant
Highfields
The Roundlet
COMMERCE ST 1
BOURNE CT 2
HOPE ST 3
B587
COCKSHUT LA
RIDING BANK
Shaw House
ROBINSON'S HILL
B587
Bleak House
Tower
PC
P
Melbourne Common
Hemsley's Barn
SHEPHERD'S LA
BOG LA
Derby Hills House Farm
Sailing Club
STANTON HILL
MELBOURNE LA
Broadstone Lane End
BROADSTONE LA
MAIN ST
Sch
CHAPEL ST
INGLEBY LA
HAYES FARM CT
ROSE LA
CHURCH LA
BANTON'S LA
HARPUR AVE
PH
NARROW LA
B5006
Ticknall
Works
Walker's Lane
Staunton Harold Reservoir
White Leys
Shaw's Plantation
Lodge Plantation
Derby Hills Farm
Serpentine Wood
Kennel Cottages
Middle Lodge
Clay Pit Plantation
The Rookery
Mere Pond
Jubilee Plantation
Betty's Pond
Calke Park
Calke Abbey
P
Home Farm
Spring Wood
Gorsey Covert
Poker's Leys
Dark Plantation
STAUNTON LA
White Hollows Farm
Calke
The Gables
4
25
3
24
2
23
1
22
36
37

A
B
C
4
25
3
24
2
23
1
22
38
39
40
Melbourne
Lilypool
New York
Hall
The Pool
The Intake
Woodhouse Farm
Pool Farm
Woodhouses
Staunton Harold Reservoir
Works
High Wood
The Common Farm
Melbourne Parks
Quarry Wood
Square Plantation
Paddock Pool
Gorse Covert
Melbourne Plantation
The Coppice
Coppice Nook
Spring Wood
Springwood Farm
Scotland
Scotlands Farm
Chestnut Park
Park Farm
Golf Course
Hobbes' Hole
The Bulwarks
Fort
Breedon Hill
Breedon on the Hill
Charity Farm
Nurseries
Wilson
Melbourne View
Ramsley Brook
Dismantled Railway
Forty Foot Lane
Carr Brook
Green Lane
Cemy
Schs
F Sta
PC
PH
CH
Sch
B587
ASHBY RD
DERBY RD
COCKSHUT LA
PACK HORSE RD
STATION RD
JAWBONE LA
MAIN ST
CHAPEL ST
CASTLE ST
CASTLE LA
HIGH ST
CHURCH ST
BLACKWELL LA
POOL RD
PENN LA
PENISTON RISE
CHURCH SQ
ROBINSON'S HILL
SIR HENRY'S LA
BURNEY LA
NOTTINGHAM RD
A453
A42
SQUIRREL LA
WORTHINGTON LA
DOCTOR'S LA
SLADE LA
SHORT HILL
DOG LA
WILSON RISE
HOLLOW RD
THE DELPH
MELBOURNE LA
RECTORY CL
CROSS ST
HILLSIDE CT
THE CRESCENT
HASTINGS CL
STUDFARM CL
THE DOVECOTE
SMITH AVE
OAKLANDS WAY
BLAKEMORE AVE
GRANGE CL
QUEENSWAY
CORONATION
WOODLANDS
MELTON AVE
WINDSOR AVE
HARD ACRE CL
ACACIA DR
BLACKTHORN CL
SPINNEY HILL
REDWAY CFT
VICTORIA ST
NORTH ST
SOUTH ST
ALMA ST
COMMERCE ST
UNION ST
GEORGE ST
DUNCLIFFE LA
THE PINGLE
ORCHARD CL
MOIRA ST
QUICK CL
THOMAS COOK CL
MARKET PL
POTTER ST
THE MEWS
JUBILEE CL
PALMERSTON CT
THE LILYPOOLS
CASTLE MILLS
CASTLE MEWS
SALISBURY LA
SELINA ST
WASHINGTON CL
BEECH AVE
LAMPAD CL
BOURNE CT
HOPE ST
HATTON CT

254

D
E
F
Tatenhill
DARK LA
MAIN ST
PH
Manor Farm
TATENHILL LA
Yews Bridge
Lawns Farm Cottage
BRANSTON RD
Robinson's Plantation
Brookfields Farm
Branston Lock
A38
WELLINGTON RD
Bean's Covert
HARCOURT RD
SPINNEY RD
CLEWLEY RD
WARWICK CL
MERLIN CRES
HARWOOD AVE
LYNWOOD RD
LYNWOOD CL
FESTIVAL RD
CLAYS LA
COTSWOLD RD
BRIDEFORD AVE
Branston Bridge
PH
A512
Sch
LEAMINGTON RD
CHURCH RD
Branston
LINGFIELD RD
MAIN ST
A512
TATENHILL LA
COURT FARM LA
MAIN ST
OLD RD
BRAMELL CL
WARREN LA
BURTON RD
RIVERSIDE DR
LANSDOWNE RD
4
21
Branston Water Park
Nature Reserve
Tatenhill Lock
3
Works
Gallow Bridge
Ppg Sta
ack Meadow Wood
Trent & Mersey Canal
Works
20
Works
Gorse Hall
LICHFIELD RD
Drakelow Power Station
Gorsehall Plantation
Works
Ryknild Street
ROMAN ROAD
2
Dunstall
River Trent
ewbold Manor Farm
Tucklesholme Farm
19
Sewage Works
Warren Hill
Depot
Warren Farm
Hotel
1
STATION RD
harf uses
Rylance Farm
Barr Hall
Walton Bridge
Barton-under-Needwood
BARTON TURN
B5016
STATION LA
MAIN ST
CADLE END LA
Walton-on-Trent
BELLS END RD
RIVERSIDE
ORCHARD CL
COTON RD
LEEDHAMS CROFT
HARRIN RD
Barton Turn
Inn
MEWIES CL
A38
18
D
21
E
22
F

259
254

A
B
C
Birmingham Curve Junction
Ferry Bridge
Upper Mills Farm
Stapenhill
Golf Course
River Trent
The Rookery
The Wilderness
Factory
Home Farm
Drakelowe House
Heath Farm
WALTON RD
ROSLISTON RD S
ROSLISTON RD
BURTON RD
ANGLESEY RD
BRANSTON RD
MAIN ST
SAXON ST
STANTON RD
Drakelow Power Station
Stapenhill Fields Farm
Flint Mill
Barn Farm
Royle Farm
Grove Wood
Grove Farm
Hill Covert
Morris Croft
Ashleigh House Farm
Sch
A5121
A444
4
3
2
1
21
20
19
18
23
24
25

D
E
F
Model Dairy Farm
VIOLET WAY
ASHDALE CL
ORCHID CL
CLEMATIS CRES
JASMINE CL
HONEYSUCKLE VIEW
GENISTA CL
Sch
Sch
BRETLANDS WAY
MEAD WLK
MEAD CRES
MANOR CRES
STANTON RD
MANOR RD
MANOR CL
PIDDOCKS RD
Piddocks Road
Stanton Manor
Hill Farm
Stanton
Sch
BRIDLE LA
WOODLAND RD
B5353
Stanton House
Dismantled Railway
Dismantled Railway
Dismantled Railway
HALLFIELDS RD
Hall Fields Farm
Council Farm
Cadley Hill
Breach Farm
Breach Cottage
Grasmere
SANDY LA
COTON PARK
New Barn Farm
Stanhope Arms (PH)
GEARY LA
ASHBY RD E
A50
THORN TREE LA
BRETBY BSNS PK
Works
Windmill Spinney
SUNNYSIDE
Schs
ROSE TREE LA
THORN TREE LA
WOOD LA
BIRCH AVE
PEAR TREE AVE
YEW TREE RD
BRETBY RD
WILLOW DR
HAWTHORN RISE
LABURNUM RD
LARCH RD
HIGH ST
CHESTERFIELD AVE
MAIN ST
HIGGINS RD
ASH TREE CL
PC
B5353
CHAPEL ST
APPLETON
ORCHARD ST
ROSELEIGH CRES
CHERRY TREE CL
Newhall
BROOK ST
NEW RD
NEW RD
PARLIAMENT ST
THE CROFT
THE CRESCENT
OVERSETTS CT
1 OAKLEIGH AVE
2 ASHLEIGH AVE
ROBINSON RD
PINE GR
PLUMMER RD
MANTON CL
THE LEYS
JOHN ST
MAYFAIR
ALMA RD
ST CATHERINE'S RD
PINGLE FARM RD
KILBURN WAY
KAY DR
Newhall Wood
GRANGE RD
Oversetts
THE FAIRWAY
ST JOHN'S DR
CECIL RD
SOUTH DR
FIELD WAY
THE BURROWS
WATERY LA
DALES CL
ASHOVER RD
TIDESWELL GREEN
BAKEWELL GREEN
OVERSETTS RD
RENSHAW DR
ST EDWARDS CT
WESTWOOD PARK
FARM SIDE
THE RISE
BRIAR CL
STONEYDALE CL
FAIRFIELD CRES
CRICH WAY
PARK RD
COPPERAS RD
WOODVIEW RD
Sch
MEADOW VIEW RD
MEADOW LA
THE PASTURES 3
THE PADDOCKS 4
ALMOND GR
HALLFIELDS RD
Opencast Workings
Works
SOLNEY CL
B5005
Boardman Ind Est
CADLEY HILL RD
Cadley Hill Ind Est
RYDER CL
BOARDMAN RD
PH
HEARTHCOTE RD
HANDSACRE CL
BARDOLPH CL
TWYFORD
GRESLEY WOOD RD
B5005
APPLEBY GLADE
WESTACRE DR
LATHKILL DALE
ANDERBY GDNS
CLIFTON CL
WYE DALE
DARLEY DALE
WOLFSCOTE DALE
BERESFORD DALE
BRAMLEY DALE
Kids Rough
SWADLINCOTE LA
BURTON RD
Hall Wood
Gresley Old Hall
Sports Ground
Castle Gresley
PH
MOUNT RD
A444
CASTLE RD
A514
SPRING CL
4
21
3
20
2
19
1
18
D
27
E
28
F

255
249

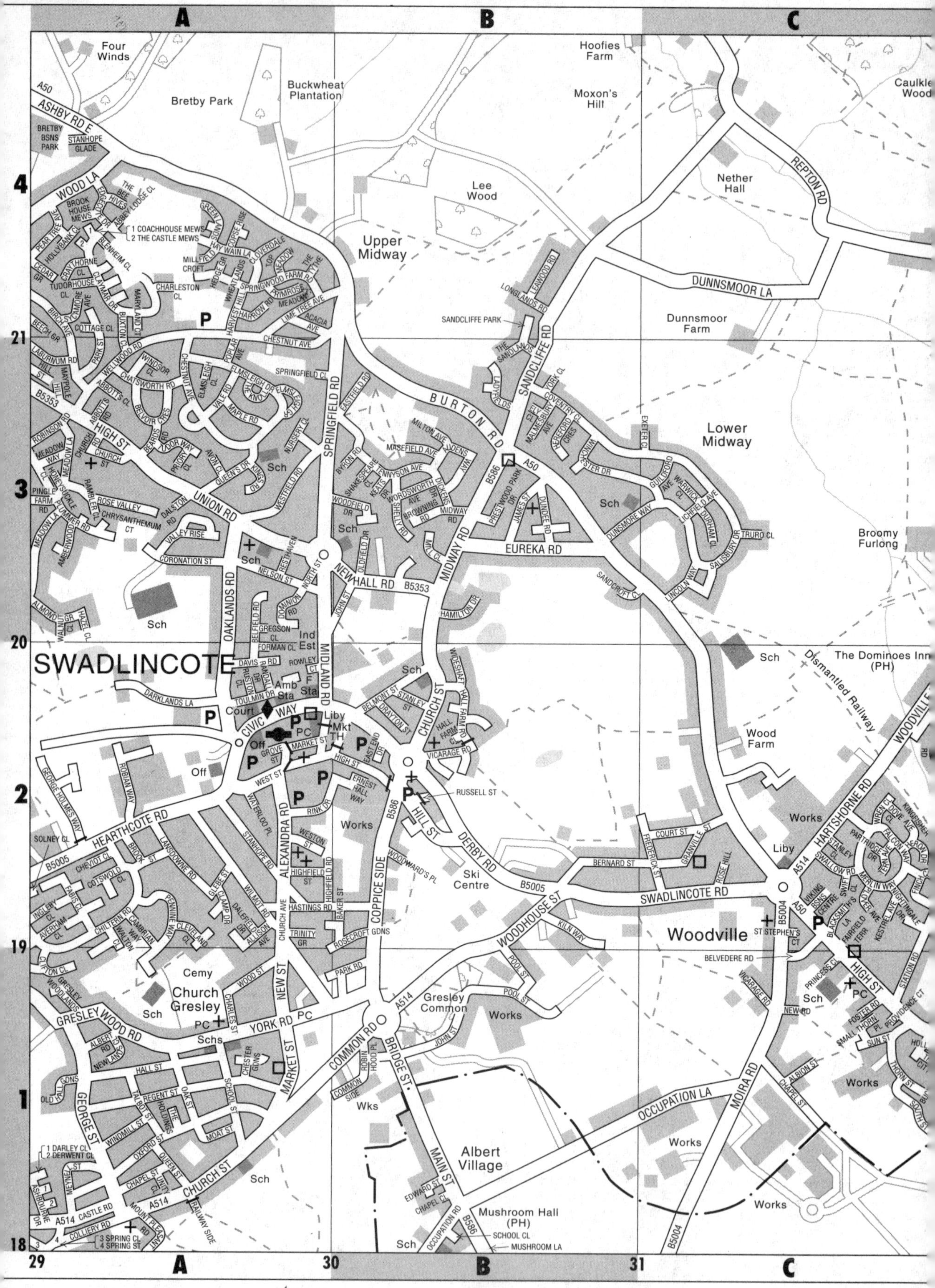

255
262

D
E
F
Wilder House
Spring Farm
SPRINGHILL
BROOK ST
PEAR TREE CL
KENDRICKS CL
REPTON RD
PH
TICKNALL LA
A514
Coppice House Farm
Coppice Farm
COAL LA
B5006
Henson's Coppice
White Hollows Farm
Shaw's Alders
Tadsor Farm
DERBY RD
MEREOAK LA
Ladyfields Plantation
Pisternhill Plantation
Manor Farm
Sch
Hartshorne
MAIN ST
CHURCH ST
Limehouse Dam
Daniel Hayes Farm
Long Alders
The Elms
P
SLACK LA
PH
TOWER RD
Horn Hill
Sharp's Bottom
Pistern Hill
WOODVILLE RD
Goseley Dale
Several Wood
MANCHESTER LA
Heath Farm
Hartshorne Heath
Short Hazels Farm
GOSELEY AVE
GOSELEY CRES
HARTSHILL RD
MOUNT RD
ELMSDALE RD
BRETBY VIEW
EDWARD ST
The Forties
HEATH LA
FORTIES LA
Hilltop Farm
Stonehouse Farm
Tithe Farm
NELSON PL
CHAPEL ST
MAIN ST
Manor Farm
PH
PH
BEECH DR
ASHBY RD
Boundary
Myrtle Lodge Farm
MILLFIELD ST
FIELD LA
HOLLY CT
A50
THE SHRUBBERY
ANNWELL LA
Tournament Field
Blackfordby House
HEATH LA
Scam-Hazel Farm
1 CANNER CL
2 THE CITY
3 THORN ST
BUTT LA
Sch
Annwell Place
PH
Hall
1 PARKERS CL
2 STRAWBERRY LA
3 CHURCH CL
Works
FENTON AVE
ELSTEAD LA
WELL LA
MAIN ST
VICARAGE CL
ASHBY LA
Blackfordby
Holywell Farm
A50
4
21
3
20
2
19
1
18
33
34

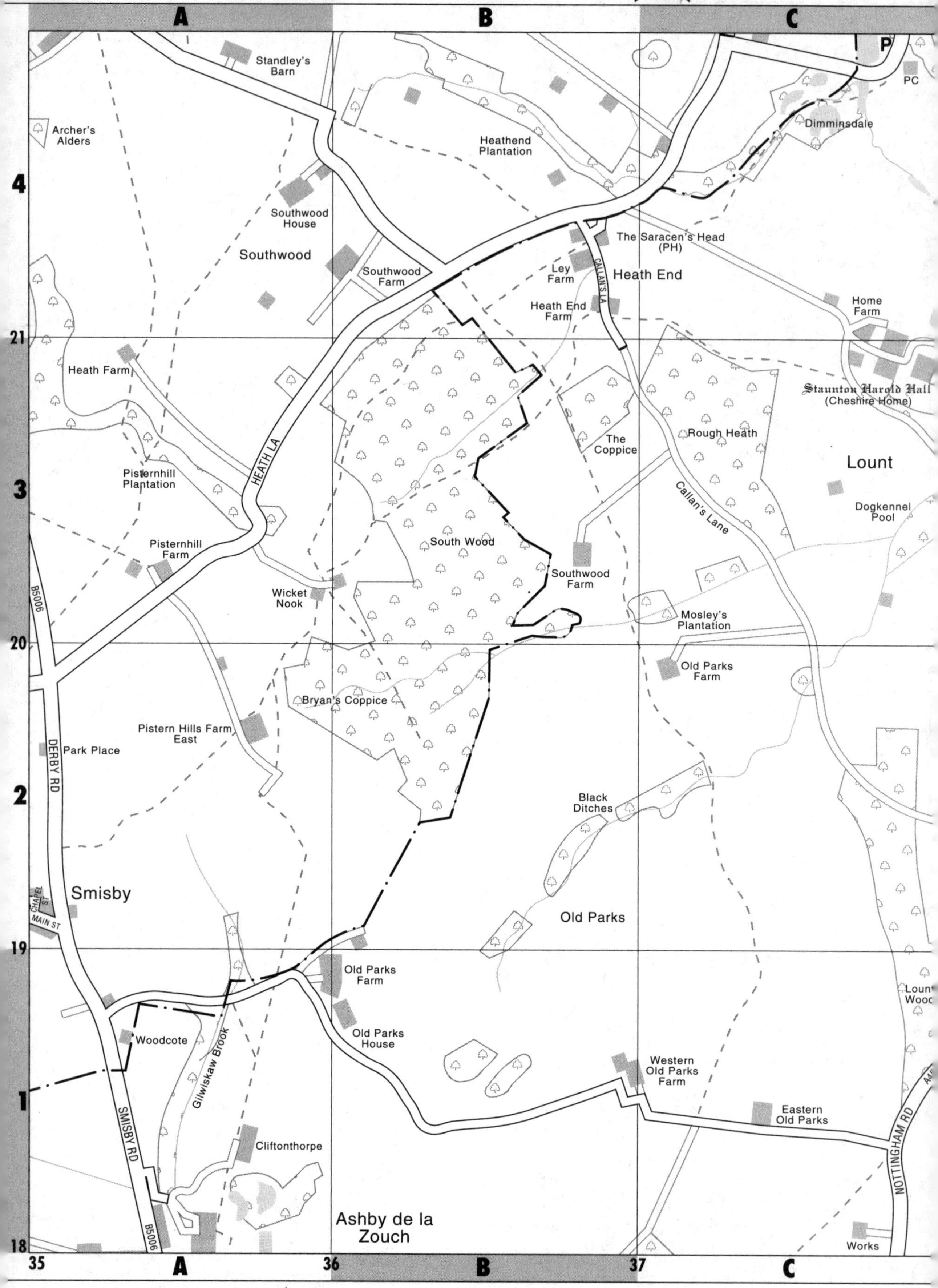
A
B
C
Standley's Barn
Archer's Alders
Heathend Plantation
P
PC
Dimminsdale
4
Southwood House
Southwood
The Saracen's Head (PH)
Southwood Farm
Ley Farm
CALLAN'S LA
Heath End
Heath End Farm
Home Farm
21
Heath Farm
Staunton Harold Hall (Cheshire Home)
The Coppice
Rough Heath
Pisternhill Plantation
HEATH LA
3
Lount
Callan's Lane
Dogkennel Pool
Pisternhill Farm
South Wood
Southwood Farm
B5006
Wicket Nook
Mosley's Plantation
20
Old Parks Farm
Bryan's Coppice
Pistern Hills Farm East
Park Place
DERBY RD
2
Black Ditches
Smisby
CHAPEL ST
MAIN ST
Old Parks
19
Old Parks Farm
Old Parks House
Woodcote
Gilwiskaw Brook
Western Old Parks Farm
1
Eastern Old Parks
SMISBY RD
Cliftonthorpe
NOTTINGHAM RD
B5006
Ashby de la Zouch
Works
18
35
36
37

D
E
F
LICHFIELD RD
LEEDHAMS CROFT
BELLS END RD
Fairfield
Walton Hall
Sch
STANDING BUTTS CL
ROSLISTON RD
tholme Farm
Old Hall
The Dumps
Marlpit Spinney
Old Barn Farm
Walton Hill Farm
Borough Hill
Coppershill Spinney
COTON RD
Ryelands Lodge
Walton Wood
Sand and Gravel Pit
Borough Holme
River Trent
Oaklands Farm
Borough Fields Farm
Old River Trent
Ryelands Plantation
Donkhill Cottages
The Rough
Cat Holme
Catton Hall
Cherry Holme
Catton Farm Cottages
Summerfields
Donkhill Plantation
Donkhill Farm
King's Covert
Catton Park
Mansditch Farm
Catton Wood
Croxall Wood
Pessall Lane
Pessall Brook
Edingale
Homestall Wood
4
17
3
16
2
15
1
14
21
22

259
254

259
263

D
E
F
SANDY LA
Hill Crest Farm
COTON PARK
Coton Park
Sewage Works
Dismantled Railway
MOUNT RD
THE SCOTTS
KNOB FIELDS
A444 BURTON RD
A514
CASTLE RD
A514
PRINCESS ST
STATION ST
BURTON RD
BRIDGE ST
CROSS ST
CHAPEL ST
High Cross Bank
LINTON RD
ARNOLD CL
Sch
MOUNT PLEASANT RD
BASS'S CRES
PINE WLK
ARTHUR ST
CEDAR RD
OAK CL
Mount Pleasant
HILLSIDE RD
Grange Farm
Manor Farm
PARK CL
Linton
CAULDWELL RD
PH
HIGHFIELDS DR
WARREN DR
GREEN FIELD DR
PEAR TREE DR
CHESTERFIELD DR
THE CREST
SEAL VIEW
CEDAR GR
HIGH ST
THE CLOSE
PRINCESS AVE
MAIN ST
CHARLTON CL
WINCHESTER DR
SYCAMORE CL
WINDSOR RD
PATRICK CL
EMBRY CL
HELSTON CL
WEATHERN FIELD
Sch
Longlands
Dismtd Rly
Greenfields
Waterfallows Farm
Linton Heath
LINTON HEATH
FIELDS LA
PARK RD
BURTON RD
A444
SEALWOOD LA
GREEN LA
Middle Hayes Farm
COLLIERY LA
SEALWOOD LA
Woodside Farm
Sealwood Farm
Botany Bay Farm
Park Farm
Green Lane
LULLINGTON RD
Potter's Wood
Grange Wood
Gunby Lea
GUNBY HILL
Grangewood Farm
Grangewood Hall
Gunby Farm
Woodfields Farm
Grangewood Lodge
LODGE RD
Woodside Farm
Grenvue
4
3
2
1
17
16
15
14
27
28

261 256

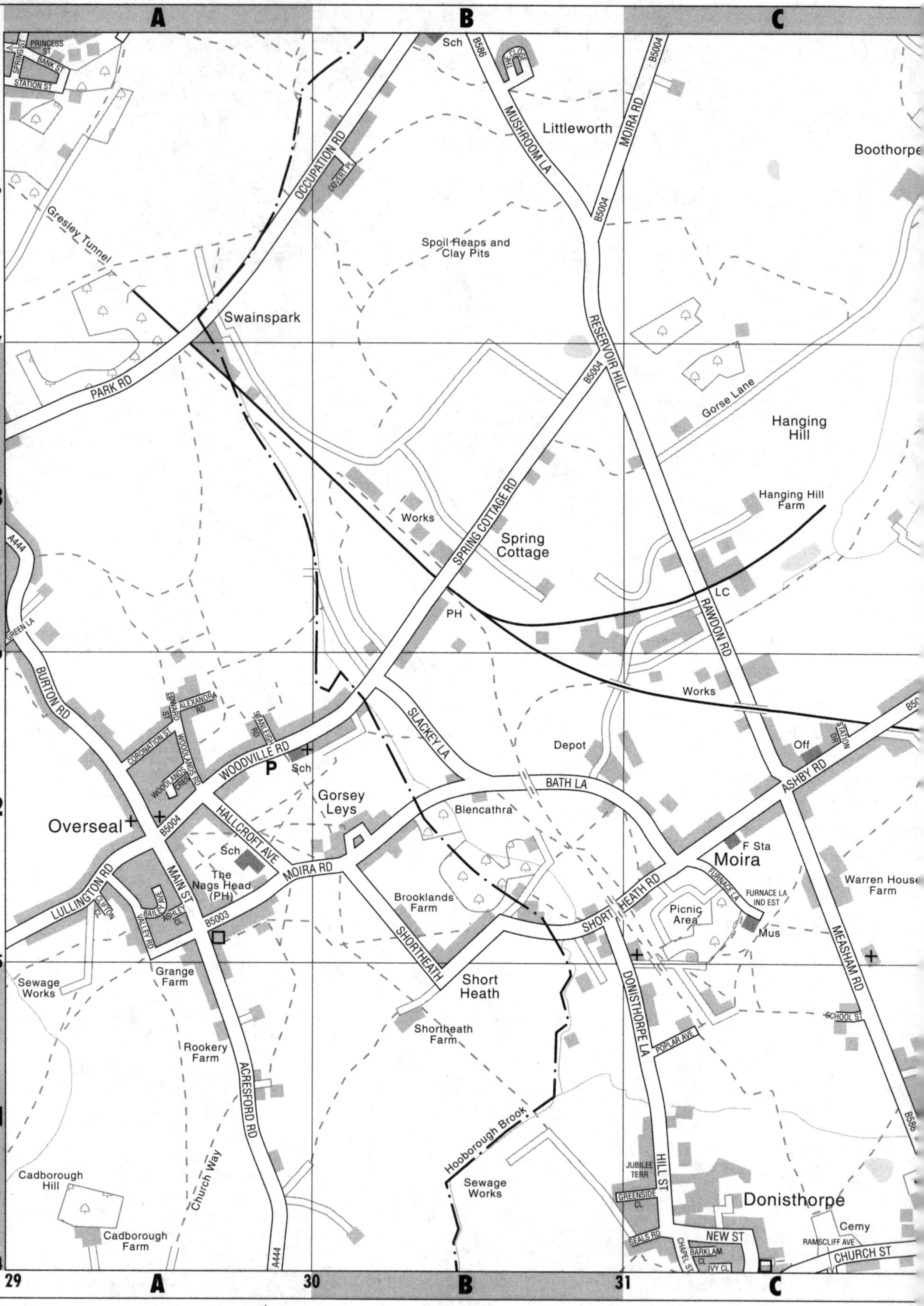

261 265

D
E
F
4
3
2
1
13
12
11
10
24
25
Lady Leys
Green Lane
Home Farm
Hall
PH
DAG LA
COLVILLE CL
Lullington
Woollens Plantation
Limes Farm
New Plantation
Edingale Fields Farm
Lullington Park
Westbrook Farm
Fox Covert
West Brook
Bald Hill's Farm
Seal Brook
River Mease
Mill Farm
LULLINGTON RD
PH
NETHERSEAL RD
MAIN ST
MEASE LA
Hall
TUDOR RISE
CHURCH ST
ST DAVID'S RD
ST ANDREW'S CL
Sch
Newhouse Farm
Haunton
SMITHY LA
CHESTNUT LA
Twizles Lane
Clifton Campville
SYERSCOTE LA
COPPICE LA

263
261

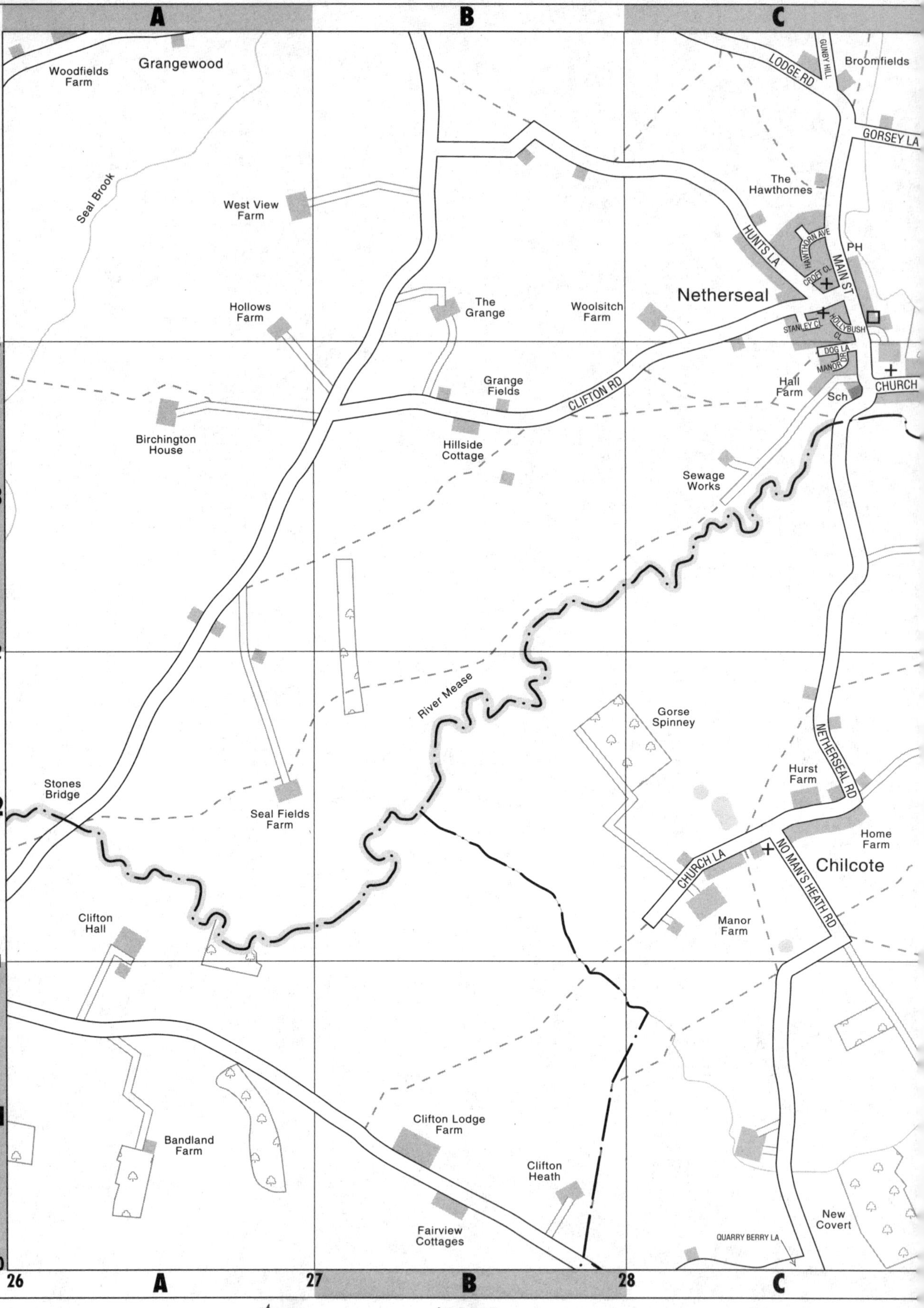
A
B
C
Woodfields Farm
Grangewood
Seal Brook
West View Farm
LODGE RD
GUNBY HILL
Broomfields
GORSEY LA
The Hawthornes
HUNTS LA
HAWTHORN AVE
CROFT CL
MAIN ST
PH
Netherseal
STANLEY CL
HOLLYBUSH CL
DOG LA
MANOR DR
Hollows Farm
The Grange
Woolsitch Farm
Grange Fields
CLIFTON RD
Hall Farm
Sch
CHURCH
Birchington House
Hillside Cottage
Sewage Works
River Mease
Gorse Spinney
Stones Bridge
Seal Fields Farm
Hurst Farm
NETHERSEAL RD
Home Farm
CHURCH LA
NO MAN'S HEATH RD
Chilcote
Clifton Hall
Manor Farm
Bandland Farm
Clifton Lodge Farm
Clifton Heath
Fairview Cottages
New Covert
QUARRY BERRY LA
4
13
3
12
2
11
1
10
26
27
28

263

262

D
E
F
4
13
3
12
2
11
1
10
30
31
MOUNT PLEASANT LA
A444
Seale
Pastures
GORSEY LA
Hooborough Brook
PH
Acresford
B5002
Eastfield
ACRESFORD RD
CHURCH ST
ACRESFORD RD
IVY CL
CHAPEL ST
CHURCH ST
NEW ST
RAMSCLIFF AVE
PH
TALBOT PL
HALL LA
Hall
Farm
Dismantled Railway
Saltersford Brook
STRETTON VIEW
CORONATION LA
Moneyhill
Farm
MEASHAM RD
Saltersford
Cottages
Mine
(dis)
CHAPEL ST
Stretton
Bridge
River Mease
Saltersford
Farm
Saltersford
Bridge
B5002
Oak
Villa
Mill
House
A42
Hall
Farm
Stretton en le Field
Manor House
Farm
Park
Farm
B5493
TAMWORTH RD
A42
MEASHAM RD
Heath
Lodge
Hill
Farm
A444
RECTORY LA
PARKFIELD CRES
B5493
M42
The Old
Rectory
Old House
CHURCH ST
STONEY LA
OLD END
ST MICHAEL'S DR

EXPLANATION OF THE STREET INDEX REFERENCE SYSTEM

Street names are listed alphabetically and show the locality, the page number and a reference to the square in which the name falls on the map page.

Example:	Marlpit La. Dens..196 B3
Marlpit La	This is the full street name, which may have been abbreviated on the map.
Dens	This is the abbreviation for the town, village or locality in which the street falls.
196	This is the page number of the map on which the street name appears.
B3	The letter and figure indicate the square on the map in which the centre of the street falls. The square can be found at the junction of the vertical column carrying the appropriate letter and the horizontal row carrying the appropriate figure.

ABBREVIATIONS USED IN THE INDEX

Road Names

Approach	App
Arcade	Arc
Avenue	Ave
Boulevard	Bvd
Buildings	Bldgs
Business Park	Bsns Pk
Broadway	Bwy
By-Pass	By-Ps
Causeway	Cswy
Circle	Circ
Circus	Cir
Close	Cl
Common	Comm
Corner	Cnr
Cottages	Cotts
Court	Ct
Courtyard	Ctyd
Crescent	Cres
Drive	Dri
Drove	Dro
East	E
Embankment	Emb
Esplanade	Espl
Gardens	Gdns
Grove	Gr
Heights	Hts
Industrial Estate	Ind Est
Junction	Junc
Lane	La
North	N
Orchard	Orch
Parade	Par
Passage	Pas
Place	Pl
Pleasant	Plea
Precinct	Prec
Promenade	Prom
Road	Rd
South	S
Square	Sq
Stairs	Strs
Steps	Stps
Street, Saint	St
Terrace	Terr
Walk	Wlk
West	W
Yard	Yd

Key to abbreviations of Town, Village and Rural locality names used in the index of street names.

bney	Abney	51	F2
ldercar	Ald	182	A2
lderwasley	Alder	166	C4
ldwark	Aldw	152	C4
lfreton	Alf	159	D2
lkmonton	Alk	199	E1
lsop en le Dale	A le Da	150	C2
lstonefield	Alst	149	E2
shbourne	Ashb	173	E1
shby-de-la-Zouch	Ash-Z	258	B1
shford in the Water	A in W	108	C4
shover	Ash	129	F2
ston-on-Trent	As on T	246	A4
tlow	Atlow	175	D3
ult Hucknall	Al Hu	133	F4
wsworth	Awsw	195	E2
akewell	Bake	109	F3
allidon	Ball	152	A1
amford	Bam	40	A2
arlborough	Barl	80	A4
arlow	Barlow	75	F1
arrow upon Trent	Ba on T	244	A3
arton in Fabis	B in F	237	F3
arton-under-Needwood	B-u-Ne	253	D1
aslow	Baslow	91	F3
eeley	Beeley	111	D2
eeston	Bees	223	F2
elper	Belper	179	D2
iggin	Biggin	138	B2
irchover	Bir	126	A1
lackfordby	Black	257	E1
olsover	Bols	99	D1
onsall	Bons	142	C1
oylestone	Boyl	213	E2
rackenfield	Brack	145	E1
radbourne	Brad	163	E3
radfield	Bradf	31	F4
radley	Bradl	186	C4
radwell	Bradw	51	D4
railsford	Brai	201	F4
ranston	Bran	253	F4
rassington	Brass	153	D1
readsall	Bread	205	C2
reaston	Brea	235	E4
reedon on the Hill	Br Hill	252	C1
retby	Bretby	249	D2
rinsley	Brin	182	C3
urnaston	Burn	229	F3
urton upon Trent	Bu on T	248	A2
uxton	Bux	85	D4
aldwell	Cald	260	C4
alke	Calke	251	F1
allow	Callow	165	D2
alow	Calow	96	C1
alver	Calver	72	B1
arsington	Cars	164	C4
astle Donington	C Don	247	E2
astleton	Cas	38	B1
hapel-en-le-Frith	C-Frith	47	D3
harlesworth	Cha	16	B3
helmorton	Chel	87	D1
hesterfield	Chest	96	A1
hilcote	Chil	264	C2
hinley	Chin	34	C1
hurch Broughton	Ch Bro	227	D4
lay Cross	Cl Cr	131	D2
lifton	Clif	184	C3
lifton Campville	C Camp	263	F1
lowne	Clowne	80	B2
odnor	Codnor	181	E4
ossall	Coss	195	E1
oton in the Elms	C Elms	260	B2
rich	Crich	156	C1
uckney	Cuck	101	F2
urbar	Curbar	72	C1
ale	Dale	207	F1
arley Dale	Da Da	127	E1
enby	Denby	180	B1
Denstone	Dens	196	B3
Derby	Derby	219	D3
Derwent	Der	30	B3
Disley	Disley	32	B3
Donisthorpe	Donis	262	C1
Doveridge	Dove	211	D1
Draycott	Dray	234	F4
Draycott in the Clay	Dr in C	225	E1
Dronfield	Dron	56	C1
Duffield	Duff	190	C2
Dunford Bridge	Dun Br	3	F1
Dunstall	Dun	253	D2
Earl Sterndale	E St	105	E2
Eastwood	East	182	C2
Eckington	Eck	59	E2
Edale	Edale	37	E4
Edensor	Eden	110	C4
Edingale	Edin	259	D1
Eggington	Eg	241	D3
Ellastone	Ella	183	D2
Elmton	Elmt	100	A4
Elton	Elton	140	C3
Elvaston	Elv	234	D3
Etwall	Etwall	229	E2
Eyham	Eyham	71	E3
Fawfieldhead	Fawf	121	D2
Fenny Bentley	F Bent	162	A1
Findern	Fin	230	B1
Flagg	Flagg	106	C3
Flash	Flash	103	D2
Foolow	Foolow	70	C3
Glapwell	Glap	134	B4
Glossop	Glos	10	A1
Gotham	Goth	237	F1
Grassmoor	Gra	115	F2
Greasley	Greas	182	C3
Great Cubley	G Cub	198	C1
Great Hucklow	G Huck	70	A4
Great Longstone	G Lo	90	A2
Greenfield	Green	5	D4
Grindleford	Grin	72	B4
Hallam Moors	Hal M	41	F4
Hanbury	Han	238	A3
Harthill	Hart	61	F3
Hartington	Hartin	137	E3
Hartshorne	Harts	257	D3
Hassop	Hassop	90	C3
Hathersage	Hath	53	D4
Hatton	Hatton	239	E4
Hayfield	Hay	25	E1
Hazelwood	Haz	190	A4
Heanor	Hean	181	E1
Heath	Heath	117	D1
High Lane	H La	32	A4
High Peak	H Pk	28	C4
Hilton	Hilton	228	B1
Hognaston	Hog	164	A1
Holbeck	Holb	101	E4
Holbrook	Holbr	191	E3
Hollington	Holl	200	C2
Hollinsclough	Hollin	104	B1
Holloway	Hollow	156	A3
Holme	Holme	2	C4
Holmesfield	Hol	75	D4
Holymoorside	Holy	113	E4
Hope	Hope	38	C2
Horsley	Hors	191	F3
Horsley Woodhouse	H Wood	192	B3
Hulland Ward	H Ward	175	F2
Ible	Ible	153	F4
Idridgehay	Idri	176	C3
Ilam	Ilam	161	D2
Ilkeston	Ilk	208	C4
Ingleby	Ingl	243	F1
Ironville	Iron	170	C2
Kettleshulme	Kettle	45	D1
Kilburn	Kilb	192	A4
Killamarsh	Kill	60	C3
Kimberley	Kim	195	F4
King Sterndale	K St	86	B3
Kirby-in-Ashfield	K-in-A	160	C2
Kirk Ireton	K Ire	165	E1
Kirk Langley	K Lang	202	C1
Kniveton	Kni	163	D1
Langley Mill	La Mill	182	A2
Lees	Lees	216	A4
Linton	Linton	261	E3
Little Eaton	Lit Ea	205	E4
Litton	Litton	69	F2
Lodge Moor	Lod M	42	C4
Long Duckmanton	L Duk	98	A2
Long Eaton	Lo Ea	236	B4
Longford	Longf	214	B4
Longnor	Long	121	D3
Lount	Lount	258	C3
Lullington	Lull	263	F4
Lyme Handley	L Han	32	A1
Macclesfield Forest	Mac For	83	D3
Mackworth	Mack	217	F4
Mansfield	Mans	136	A1
Mapperley	Mapp	193	F2
Mappleton	Mapple	172	C2
Marchington	March	224	C1
Market Warsop	Mar War	120	C2
Marple	Marple	23	D3
Marston Montgomery	M Mont	211	F4
Marston on Dove	M on D	240	A4
Matlock	Mat	143	D3
Matlock Bath	Mat Ba	143	D1
Mayfield	May	184	B4
Melbourne	Mel	252	A4
Middleton	Middle	124	C2
Middleton	Mid	154	B2
Moira	Moira	262	C2
Monyash	Mo	107	E1
Morley	Morley	206	B3
Morton	Morton	146	C3
Mosborough	Mosb	59	E1
Mossley	Mos	4	A4
Mottram in Longdendale	M in L	9	D2
Nether Langwith	Ne La	101	D1
Netherseal	Neth	264	C4
New Mills	N Mills	33	E4
Newton	Newt	148	A2
Newton Solney	N Sol	248	C4
North Wingfield	N Wing	132	A4
Northwood	North	127	D3
Norton	Nort	101	F4
Ockbrook	Ock	221	E3
Old Brampton	O Bram	94	B2
Osmaston	Osm	185	F2
Over Haddon	O Had	109	D1
Overseal	Over	262	A2
Parwich	Par	151	F1
Peak Forest	Pk F	49	D2
Pentrich	Pent	169	D3
Pilsley	Pils	132	B1
Pinxton	Pinx	160	B1
Pleasley	Plea	135	D3
Quarndon	Quar	204	B3
Radbourne	Radb	216	C3
Rainow	Rain	64	A2
Ratcliffe on Soar	R on S	237	D1
Repton	Rep	242	C1
Ripley	Ripley	169	E1
Risley	Risley	222	C2
Rocester	Roc	197	D2
Rodsley	Rods	200	A3
Rolleston	Rolle	240	A2
Rosliston	Rosl	260	B3
Roston	Rost	197	F4
Rowsley	Row	126	C4
Sandiacre	Sand	223	D3
Scarcliffe	Scarc	118	C3
Scropton	Scro	226	C1
Selston	Sels	171	F4
Shardlow	Shar	234	F1
Shatton	Shat	39	F1
Sheen	Sheen	137	D4
Sheffield	Shef	43	D4
Sheldon	Shel	108	A3
Shipley	Ship	194	A3
Shirebrook	Shireb	119	F2
Shireoaks	Shire	63	F3
Shirland	Shirl	146	B1
Shirley	Shir	200	C4
Shottle	Shot	177	F4
Smalley	Smal	192	C3
Smisby	Smisby	258	A2
Snelston	Snel	184	B2
Somercotes	Som	170	B4
Somersal Herbert	S Herb	211	F2
South Normanton	S Norm	160	A4
South Wingfield	S Wing	157	F2
Spout	Spout	166	B2
Stanley	Stanl	207	E3
Stanton	Stan	183	E4
Stanton by Bridge	St Br	244	B2
Stanton in Peak	St Pk	126	A3
Stanton-by-Dale	S-by-D	222	C4
Stapleford	Staple	223	F4
Staveley	Stav	78	B1
Stoney Middleton	St Mid	71	F2
Strelley	Stre	209	F4
Stretton	Stret	146	B4
Stretton en le Field	S Field	265	E2
Sudbury	Sud	225	F2
Sutton in Ashfield	S in A	148	C1
Sutton on the Hill	S Hill	228	A4
Swadlincote	Swad	256	A2
Swarkestone	Swark	244	B3
Swinscoe	Swin	172	A3
Taddington	Tadd	88	A2
Tansley	Tans	144	A2
Thornhill	Thor	39	F2
Thorpe	Thorpe	161	E1
Thorpe Salvin	Th Sa	62	C3
Thrumpton	Thrum	237	E2
Thurvaston	Thurv	215	E4
Tibshelf	Tibs	148	A3
Ticknall	Tick	251	D2
Tideswell	Tide	69	E2
Tintwistle	Tint	10	A4
Tissington	Tiss	162	A3
Totley	Totley	55	F3
Trowell	Trow	209	E3
Trusley	Trus	215	F2
Tupton	Tupton	131	E4
Turnditch	Turn	177	D1
Tutbury	Tut	239	E3
Twyford	Twy	243	D3
Unstone	Uns	76	C4
Uttoxeter	Utt	210	B1
Walton-on-Trent	Wa on T	253	F1
Wardlow	War	70	B1
Wensley	Wens	142	A4
West Hallam	We Ha	207	F4
Weston Underwood	W Und	189	D1
Weston-on-Trent	We on T	245	F3
Whaley Bridge	W Br	45	E4
Whitwell	Whit	81	F3
Wildboarclough	Wild	102	A3
Willington	Will	242	A3
Windley	Wind	189	E4
Wingerworth	Win	114	C2
Winster	Wins	141	E3
Wirksworth	Wirk	165	F4
Woodville	Wood	256	C2
Worksop	Work	63	F1
Wormhill	Wor	68	B1
Wyaston	Wya	185	E1
Yeaveley	Yea	199	E3
Youlgreave	Youl	125	D3

1st Ave. Ilk 208 C4
2nd Ave. Ilk 208 C4
3rd Ave. Ilk 208 C4
Abba Cl. Kim 195 F4
Abbey Brook Dr. Shef 56 C4
Abbey Croft. Chest 95 D4
Abbey Gdns. M in L 9 D2
Abbey Hill Rd. Derby 204 B1
Abbey Hill. Bread 205 D2
Abbey Hill. Derby 205 D2
Abbey La. Derby 205 D1
Abbey Lodge Cl. Swad 256 A4
Abbey St. Derby 218 C2
Abbey St. Ilk 194 C1
Abbey View Dr. Shef 43 D2
Abbey View Rd. Shef 43 D2
Abbey Yd. Derby 205 D1
Abbeydale Park Cres. Totley 55 F3
Abbeydale Park Rise. Totley 55 F3
Abbeydale Rd S. Shef 56 A4
Abbeydale Rd S. Totley 56 A4
Abbeydale Rd. Shef 43 D4
Abbeyfields Cl. Derby 205 D1
Abbeyhill Cl. O Bram 95 D2
Abbot Cl. Derby 205 F1
Abbot Rd. Ilk 208 B3
Abbot St. Awsw 195 E2
Abbots Gr. Belper 179 D3
Abbotsford Mews. Ilk 194 B2
Abbott Rd. Alf 159 D2
Abbott St. Hean 181 F1
Abbott St. Lo Ea 236 B3
Abbotts Barn Cl. Derby 218 C2
Abbotts Cl. Swad 256 A3
Abbotts Croft. Mans 135 F1
Abbotts Rd. Swad 256 A3
Abel La. Bons 142 B1
Abells. Denby 180 B1
Abercrombie St. Chest 96 A2
Aberdare Cl. Derby 206 A1
Abingdon St. Derby 232 B4
Abney Cl. Chest 95 E3
Abney Cl. Derby 217 F1
Abney Cl. Shef 43 E3
Abney Dr. Shef 43 E3
Abney Rd. Shef 43 E3
Acacia Ave. Derby 217 F1
Acacia Ave. Stav 97 D4
Acacia Ave. Swad 256 A4
Acacia Cres. Kill 60 A3
Acacia Ct. Mans 136 C1
Acacia Dr. Mel 252 A4
Acacia Dr. Pils 132 A2
Acer Cl. Kill 60 B3
Acer Cl. Pinx 160 B2
Acer Croft. Derby 205 F2
Acorn Ave. Greas 195 E4
Acorn Cl. Derby 232 C2
Acorn Dr. Belper 179 D3
Acorn Ridge. Chest 114 A4
Acorn Ridge. Mat 143 D3
Acorn Ridge. Shireb 119 E3
Acorn Terr. N Mills 33 D3
Acorn Way. Belper 179 D3
Acorn Way. Derby 220 B3
Acorn Way. Morley 220 B3
Acre La. As on T 246 B4
Acre St. Glos 17 E4
Acreage La. Shireb 119 F1
Acres Rd. Pils 132 A2
Acres The. Pils 132 A2
Acres View Cl. Chest 95 F4
Acresford Rd. Donis 265 E4
Acresford Rd. Neth 265 D3
Acresford Rd. Over 262 A1
Acton Ave. Lo Ea 236 C3
Acton Cl. Lo Ea 236 C3
Acton Gr. Lo Ea 236 C3
Acton Rd. Derby 217 F3
Acton Rd. Lo Ea 236 C3
Acton St. Lo Ea 236 C3
Adale Rd. Smal 193 D4
Adam Bede Cres. Wirk 165 F3
Adam St. Ilk 209 D3
Adam's Rd. K Lang 217 D4
Adams Cl. Ship 193 E4
Adams Ct. Ilk 194 C2
Adastral Ave. Shef 44 A1
Adderley Pl. Glos 9 F1
Adderley Rd. Glos 9 F1
Addison Dr. Alf 159 D2
Addison Rd. Derby 232 B4
Addison Rd. Shirl 146 C2
Addison Sq. Mat Ba 155 D3
Addison St. Tibs 148 A4
Addison Villas. East 182 C1
Adelaide Cl. Derby 217 F2
Adelaide Cl. Staple 209 F1
Adelaide Cres. Bu on T 248 B1
Adelaide Wlk. Iron 170 C2
Adin Ave. Bols 98 C3
Adlington Ave. Win 115 E1
Adlington La. Grin 72 B4
Admiral Cl. Hean 181 E1
Adrian Cl. Bees 223 F1
Adrian St. Derby 232 B3
Adwick Cl. Derby 217 E1
Agard St. Derby 218 C3
Agnesmeadow La. Kni 174 B2
Ainley Cl. Derby 232 C4
Ainsworth Dr. Derby 231 F4
Aintree Ave. Eck 59 D2
Aintree Cl. Kim 195 F4
Airedale Cl. Lo Ea 236 A3
Airedale Wlk. Derby 233 E3
Akley Bank Cl. Totley 55 F3
Alabaster La. Mat Ba 155 D3
Alandale Ave. Shireb 119 F3
Albany Cl. Mans 136 B1
Albany Ct. Staple 209 F1
Albany Dr. Mans 136 B1
Albany Pl. Mans 136 B1
Albany Rd. Derby 218 B2
Albany St. Ilk 209 D3
Albemarle Rd. Derby 220 A4
Albert Ave. Chest 77 F2
Albert Ave. Sels 171 D2
Albert Ave. Staple 223 E4
Albert Cres. Derby 220 A2
Albert Rd. Brea 235 D4
Albert Rd. Derby 220 A2
Albert Rd. Lo Ea 236 B4
Albert Rd. Ripley 169 E1
Albert Rd. Sand 223 D3
Albert Rd. Shef 43 D3
Albert Rd. Swad 256 A1
Albert Rd. Uns 77 E3
Albert St N. Chest 76 C1
Albert St. Belper 178 C2
Albert St. Derby 219 D3
Albert St. East 182 C2
Albert St. Eck 59 E1
Albert St. Glos 10 A3
Albert St. Ilk 208 C4
Albert St. Iron 170 C3
Albert St. Mans 136 B2
Albert St. Ripley 169 F1
Albert St. S Norm 160 A3
Albert St. Som 170 A4
Albert St. Staple 223 E4
Alberta Ave. Sels 171 F4
Albine Rd. Shireb 119 F3
Albion Centre The. Ilk 208 C4
Albion Rd. Chest 95 F2
Albion Rd. Lo Ea 236 C4
Albion Rd. N Mills 33 D3
Albion St. Derby 219 D3
Albion St. Ilk 194 C1
Albion St. Mans 135 F1
Albion St. Ripley 169 F1
Albion St. Wood 256 C1
Albrighton Ave. Derby 231 E1
Aldam Cl. Totley 55 F2
Aldam Croft. Totley 55 F2
Aldam Rd. Totley 55 F2
Aldam Way. Totley 55 F2
Alder Brook. Chin 34 C1
Alder Cl. Derby 205 F2
Alder Cl. Mans 136 C1
Alder Cl. Shireb 119 E3
Alder Gr. Bu on T 254 C4
Alder Gr. Bux 85 D4
Alder Gr. Mans 136 A3
Alder Rd. Belper 179 D2
Alder Rise. W Br 45 E4
Alder Way. Shireb 119 E2
Alderbrook Cl. Rolle 240 A2
Aldercar La. Ald 182 A3
Alderd Cl. Kill 60 C4
Alderfen Cl. Derby 232 B2
Alderley Ct. Derby 206 A1
Aldern Way. Bake 109 F4
Alderney Rd. Shef 43 D4
Alders Ave. Chin 34 C1
Alders La. Chin 34 C1
Alders La. Tans 144 A2
Alders Rd. H La 32 A4
Alders The. Holy 113 E4
Aldersgate. Derby 217 F4
Aldersgate. N Mills 33 D4
Alderslade Cl. As on T 234 A1
Aldersley Cl. Fin 230 B1
Alderson Pl. Shef 43 D4
Alderson Rd North. Shef 43 D4
Alderson Rd. Shef 43 D4
Aldred's La. Hean 182 A1
Aldridge Cl. Bees 223 F1
Aldwark Rd. Bux 85 E3
Aldwych. Derby 218 A3
Alexander Ave. Sels 171 E4
Alexander Rd. C-Frith 47 F1
Alexander St. East 182 C1
Alexander Terr. Pinx 160 B1
Alexandra Ave. Mans 136 A3
Alexandra Ct. Bu on T 248 A2
Alexandra Gdns. Derby 219 E1
Alexandra Rd E. Chest 96 B1
Alexandra Rd W. Chest 95 F2
Alexandra Rd. Bu on T 248 A2
Alexandra Rd. Bux 85 E3
Alexandra Rd. Dron 57 D1
Alexandra Rd. Lo Ea 236 B4
Alexandra Rd. Over 262 A2
Alexandra Rd. Shef 43 D4
Alexandra Rd. Swad 256 A2
Alexandra St. Staple 223 E3
Alexandre Cl. Derby 231 E3
Alford Cl. Chest 95 E2
Alfred Rd. Kilb 192 A4
Alfred St. Alf 158 C2
Alfred St. Pinx 160 B2
Alfred St. Ripley 169 F1
Alfred St. S Norm 159 F3
Alfred St. Som 170 B3
Alfreton Rd. Bread 205 E3
Alfreton Rd. Codnor 170 B1
Alfreton Rd. Derby 205 E3
Alfreton Rd. Holbr 191 E1
Alfreton Rd. Lit Ea 205 E3
Alfreton Rd. Mat 143 F2
Alfreton Rd. Newt 147 F1
Alfreton Rd. Pinx 160 B2
Alfreton Rd. Sels 171 E4
Alfreton Rd. Tans 143 F2
Alfreton Rd. Tibs 147 E2
Algar Cl. Shef 43 F4
Algar Dr. Shef 43 F4
Algar Pl. Shef 43 F4
Algar Rd. Shef 43 F4
Alice St. Derby 219 D3
Alice Way. Uns 76 C3
Alicehead Rd. Ash 113 E1
Alison Cl. Derby 219 F4
All Saints Ct. Derby 217 E1
All Saints Rd. Bu on T 254 B4
All Saints' Rd. Mat 143 D3
Allan Ave. Derby 230 C4
Allandale Rd. Hean 181 E1
Allcroft St. Mans 136 B2
Allen Hill. Mat 143 D3
Allen La. Ash 144 B3
Allen La. Crich 168 A3
Allen La. W Und 188 B1
Allen St. Derby 232 C3
Allen's Green Ave. Sels 171 F3
Allen's La. March 224 C1
Allenby Dr. Shef 56 C4
Allendale Rd. Win 114 C2
Allendale Way. Mans 136 C1
Allendale. Ilk 208 C4
Allens Croft. March 224 C1
Allestree Cl. Derby 232 C4
Allestree Dr. Shef 56 C4
Allestree La. Derby 204 B2
Allestree St. Derby 232 C4
Alley The. Mid 154 B2
Alley Wlk. Brai 201 F4
Allison Ave. Swad 256 A2
Allissa Ave. Ripley 180 C4
Allpits Rd. Calow 96 C2
Allport Terr. Newt 147 E1
Allport Terr. Stav 78 A2
Allsops Pl. Chest 95 F4
Allstone Lee. Belper 178 C3
Alma Cres. Dron 57 D2
Alma Hill. Kim 195 F4
Alma Hts. Derby 217 F1
Alma Rd. N Wing 132 A4
Alma Rd. Sels 171 F3
Alma Rd. Swad 255 F3
Alma Rd. Tide 69 E3
Alma St W. Chest 95 F1
Alma St. Alf 159 D2
Alma St. Bux 85 E4
Alma St. Derby 218 C2
Alma St. Mel 252 A4
Alma St. N Wing 131 F3
Alma St. Ripley 169 E2
Almond Ave. Ripley 180 B4
Almond Ave. Shireb 119 F3
Almond Cl. Calow 97 D2
Almond Cl. Kim 195 F4
Almond Cres. Stav 79 E2
Almond Ct. Bu on T 240 C1
Almond Dr. Kill 60 B3
Almond Gr. Som 170 A4
Almond Gr. Swad 256 A3
Almond Rise. Mans 136 C1
Almond St. Derby 218 C1
Alms Rd. Dove 211 E1
Alnwick Dr. Shef 44 A3
Alnwick Rd. Shef 44 A3
Alpha Rd. Chin 34 C1
Alpine Gr. Stav 97 D4
Alport Ave. Bux 85 E4
Alport Ave. Shef 44 C3
Alport Cl. Belper 179 D3
Alport Cl. H Ward 175 F2
Alport Dr. Shef 44 C3
Alport Gr. Shef 44 C3
Alport La. Spout 166 B2
Alport La. Youl 125 E3
Alport Pl. Shef 44 C3
Alport Rd. Shef 44 C3
Alport Rise. Dron 56 B1
Alsager Cl. Derby 206 A1
Alsfeld Way. N Mills 33 D4
Alsop Gr. Bux 85 F4
Alsop Pl. Bux 85 F4
Alsop Way. Bux 85 F4
Alston Rd. C-Frith 47 D3
Alstonfield Dr. Derby 204 C1
Althorp Cl. Som 169 F4
Alton Cl. Chest 114 A4
Alton Cl. Derby 204 B2
Alton Cl. Dron 75 E4
Alton Hill. Ash 130 B3
Alton La. Ash 130 B2
Alton Rd. Belper 179 E2
Alton Rise. Da Da 142 C4
Alts Nook Way. Shar 234 C1
Alum Chine Cl. Chest 115 E4
Alum Cl. Derby 233 E4
Alvaston St. Derby 233 D4
Alvenor St. Ilk 194 C1
Alverton Cl. Derby 217 E1
Alward's Cl. Derby 233 D3
Ambaston La. Elv 234 A3
Ambaston La. Shar 234 C2
Amber Cl. Ripley 168 A3
Amber Cres. Chest 95 E1
Amber Ct. Belper 179 D3
Amber Ct. Hean 181 F1
Amber Dr. Hean 182 A1
Amber Gr. Alf 158 C1
Amber Hill. Crich 168 A4
Amber Hts. Ripley 169 E1
Amber La. Ash 129 E2
Amber Pl. Cl Cr 131 D2
Amber Rd. Derby 204 B1
Amber Rd. Ripley 168 A3
Amber St. Derby 232 B4
Amber View Rd. Crich 168 A4
Amberdene. Mat 143 E3
Ambergrove. Ripley 168 A2
Amberley Dr. Bux 85 E3
Amberley Dr. Derby 231 F3
Amberwood. Swad 256 A3
Ambleside Cl. Chest 95 E4
Ambleside Cl. Mosb 59 F3
Ambleside Dr. East 182 B2
Ambrose St. Derby 219 D2
Ambrose Terr. Derby 218 C3
Amen Alley. Derby 219 D3
Amesbury Cl. Chest 95 F4
Amesbury La. Derby 205 F1
Ameycroft La. Da Da 143 D4
Amilda Ave. Ilk 208 C4
Amy St. Derby 218 C2
Anchor Ave. C-Frith 47 E3
Anchor Fold. C-Frith 47 E3
Anchor Rd. East 182 B1
Anchor Row. Ilk 208 C4
Anchor Sq. Bake 109 E3
Anderby Gdns. Swad 255 F1
Anderson Cl. Chest 77 F2
Anderson St. Derby 232 C4
Andrew Ave. Ilk 209 D4
Andrew Cl. Derby 230 C4
Andrew St. Marple 15 D1
Andrews Dr. La Mi 182 A2
Andrews Dr. Stanl 193 D1
Andwell La. Lod M 42 C3
Angel Yd. Chest 96 A2
Angerford Ave. Shef 43 D2
Anglers' La. Derby 220 C2
Anglesey Rd. Bu on T 254 A4
Anglesey Rd. Dron 76 A4
Anglesey St. Derby 219 E4
Angleton Ave. Shef 44 B4
Angleton Cl. Shef 44 B4
Angleton Gdns. Shef 44 B4
Angleton Green. Shef 44 B4
Ankerbold Rd. Tupton 131 E4
Ann St. Elmt 81 F1
Anncroft Rd. Bux 84 B3
Anne Potter Cl. Ock 221 E3
Annesley Cl. Chest 115 E4
Annesley Cl. Shef 56 C4
Annesley Rd. Shef 56 C4
Anns Rd N. Shef 43 D4
Anns Rd. Shef 43 D4
Annwell La. Smisby 257 F1
Anslow La. Rolle 240 A1
Anslow Rd. Han 238 A1
Anson Wlk. Ilk 194 C2
Anstee Rd. Lo Ea 236 B3
Anstey Ct. Derby 206 A1
Anthony Cres. Derby 232 C3
Anthony Dr. Derby 232 C3
Antill St. Staple 223 E3
Apiary Gate. C Don 247 D2
Appian Way. Cl Cr 131 E1
Appian Way. Derby 233 E3
Apple St. Marple 15 E4
Apple Tree Rd. N Mills 24 A1
Appleby Cl. Ilk 208 C3
Appleby Ct. Derby 218 C2
Appleby Glade. Linton 255 E1
Appleby Rd. Plea 134 C3
Appledore Dr. Derby 206 A1
Applegarth Cl. Shef 44 A3
Applegarth Dr. Shef 44 A3
Applegate Cl. Derby 206 A2
Appleton Cl. Derby 220 A4
Appleton Cl. Swad 255 F3
Appleton Dr. Belper 179 D3
Appleton Dr. Glos 17 F4
Appletree Cl. Ock 221 E1
Appletree Dr. Dron 57 D1
Appletree Rd. Bols 80 A1
Appletree Rd. Hatton 227 E1
Appletree Wlk. Dron 57 D
Applewood Cl. Belper 179 D
Applewood Cl. Utt 210 A
Arbor Cl. Derby 218 C
Arbor Gr. Bux 84 C
Arboretum Sq. Derby 219 D
Arboretum St. Derby 219 D
Arbour Cl. Chest 115 E
Arbour Hill. Dale 207 F
Arbourthorne Cotts. Shef 43 E
Arbourthorne Rd. Shef 43 F
Arcadia Ave. Shireb 119 F
Archdale Cl. Shef 44 A
Archdale Pl. Shef 44 A
Archdale Rd. Shef 44 A
Archer Rd. Staple 223 F
Archer St. Derby 219 F
Archer St. Ilk 194 C
Arden Cl. Chest 95 E
Arden Cl. Derby 218 C
Arden Cl. Glos 17 D
Arden St. N Mills 33 E
Ardleigh Cl. Derby 230 B
Ardsley Cl. Hean 182 A
Ardsley Cl. Shef 44 C
Ardsley Dr. Shef 44 C
Ardsley Gr. Shef 44 C
Ardsley Rd. Chest 95 D
Argyle Cl. Mar War 120 C
Argyle Cl. Shef 43 D
Argyle Rd. Shef 43 D
Argyle St. Derby 218 C
Argyle St. La Mi 182 B
Argyll Cl. Derby 220 C
Argyll Rd. Ripley 169 F
Arkendale Wlk. Derby 233 E
Arklow Cl. Chest 115 D
Arkwright Ave. Belper 179 E
Arkwright Dr. Marple 23 D
Arkwright Rd. Marple 23 D
Arkwright St. Derby 232 B
Arkwright St. Wirk 165 F
Arleston La. Derby 231 E
Arleston La. Derby 231 F
Arleston St. Derby 231 F
Arlington Ave. Mans 136 C
Arlington Dr. Derby 232 C
Arlington Dr. Som 169 F
Arlington Rd. Derby 218 B
Armitage Dr. Lo Ea 237 D
Arms Park Dr. Mosb 59 F
Armscote Cl. Derby 206 A
Armytage Ind Est. Chest 77 D
Arnfield La. Tint 9 F
Arnhem Terr. Derby 220 C
Arnold Ave. Lo Ea 236 A
Arnold Ave. Shef 44 A
Arnold Cl. Linton 261 F
Arnold Cres. Lo Ea 236 A
Arnold St. Derby 218 B
Arnside Cl. Chest 76 B
Arnside. Staple 223 F
Arran Cl. Derby 231 F
Arran Cl. Staple 209 F
Arran Ct. Tibs 147 F
Arridge Rd. Derby 219 F
Arrowscroft Way. M in L 9 E
Arthington St. Shef 43 D
Arthur Ave. Staple 223 F
Arthur Ct. Derby 219 D
Arthur Hind Cl. Derby 218 C
Arthur Mee Rd. Staple 223 F
Arthur Short Cl. Whit 82 A
Arthur St. Alf 159 D
Arthur St. Derby 219 D
Arthur St. Dray 234 C
Arthur St. Linton 261 F
Arthur St. Pinx 160 B
Arthurs Ct. Bu on T 240 C
Artic Way. Kim 195 E
Artisan View. Shef 43 D
Arun Dale. Mans 136 B
Arundel Ave. Derby 217 F
Arundel Cl. Chest 95 F
Arundel Cl. Sand 223 D
Arundel Cl. Shef 56 C
Arundel Dr. Derby 220 C
Arundel Grange. Glos 17 D
Arundel St. Derby 218 B
Arundel St. Glos 10 B
Ascot Ave. Kim 195 F
Ascot Cl. Bu on T 248 A
Ascot Cl. We Ha 207 E
Ascot Dr. Derby 232 B
Ascot Park Est. Sand 223 E
Ascot Pl. Ilk 208 B
Ash Cl. As on T 246 A
Ash Cl. Derby 204 B
Ash Cl. Kill 60 B
Ash Cl. M in L 9 D
Ash Cl. Pinx 160 B
Ash Cres. Eck 59 D
Ash Cres. Ripley 180 B
Ash Gr. Brin 182 B
Ash Gr. Chin 34 C
Ash Gr. Lo Ea 236 B
Ash Gr. Sand 223 D
Ash Gr. Sels 171 F

Ash Gr. Shireb 119 F3
Ash Gr. Staple 223 E3
Ash Gr. Stav 79 D2
Ash Grove La. Eg 241 E3
Ash La. Eck 57 F2
Ash La. Hilton 228 C4
Ash La. S Hill 228 C4
Ash La. Uns 57 F2
Ash La. Uns 77 E4
Ash Mount Rd. La Mi 182 A2
Ash St. Bux 85 D3
Ash St. Ilk 194 C2
Ash St. Mosb 59 E4
Ash Terr. Bux 85 E4
Ash Tree Cl. Bread 205 F2
Ash Tree Cl. Chest 95 E2
Ash Tree Cl. Duff 190 C3
Ash Tree Cl. Swad 255 F3
Ash Tree Cres. Mans 136 B3
Ash Tree Rd. Clowne 80 C1
Ash Vale. Chest 95 D2
Ash View Cl. Etwall 229 D2
Ashacre. Belper 179 E2
Ashbourne Ave. Cl Cr 131 D3
Ashbourne Cl. Chest 95 D3
Ashbourne Ct. Derby 218 C3
Ashbourne Ct. Glos 17 F4
Ashbourne Dr. Swad 256 A1
Ashbourne La. Alst 149 D1
Ashbourne La. C-Frith 47 E3
Ashbourne Rd. Alst 149 D2
Ashbourne Rd. Belper 178 B2
Ashbourne Rd. Bux 85 E2
Ashbourne Rd. Ch Bro 213 F2
Ashbourne Rd. Derby 218 B4
Ashbourne Rd. K Lang 202 B2
Ashbourne Rd. Mack 217 F4
Ashbourne Rd. May 184 B4
Ashbourne Rd. Roc 196 C2
Ashbourne Rd. Shot 177 E2
Ashbourne Rd. Turn 177 E2
Ashbourne Rd. Utt 210 A1
Ashbourne St. Scarc 119 F2
Ashbrook Ave. Ock 221 E1
Ashbrook Cl. Derby 204 B2
Ashbrook. Bu on T 248 A1
Ashbury Dr. Shef 43 E1
Ashbury La. Shef 43 E1
Ashby Ave. Mans 136 B3
Ashby La. Black 257 E1
Ashby Rd E. Bretby 248 C1
Ashby Rd. Black 257 E1
Ashby Rd. Br Hill 252 C1
Ashby Rd. Bu on T 248 A1
Ashby Rd. Mel 252 A3
Ashby Rd. Moira 262 C2
Ashby Rd. Tick 250 C1
Ashby St. Derby 232 C3
Ashcombe Gdns. Derby 206 A1
Ashcroft Cl. Derby 232 C4
Ashcroft Dr. Chest 77 D1
Ashdale Cl. Bu on T 255 D4
Ashdale Rd. Ilk 209 D3
Ashdown Dr. Chest 95 E1
Ashe Pl. Derby 218 C1
Asher La. Pent 169 E3
Ashes Ave. H Ward 175 F2
Ashes La. F Bent 162 A1
Ashes La. Glos 10 A1
Ashfield Ave. Derby 219 F4
Ashfield Ave. Som 159 E1
Ashfield Cl. Shef 43 F2
Ashfield Dr. Shef 43 F2
Ashfield Gr. Marple 15 D1
Ashfield Rd. C-Frith 47 E3
Ashfield Rd. Chest 115 E4
Ashfield Rd. Glos 9 F2
Ashford Ave. N Wing 132 A4
Ashford Cl. Dron 75 E4
Ashford Ct. We Ha 207 E4
Ashford La. A in W 89 E1
Ashford Mews. Glos 9 E1
Ashford Pl. Ilk 194 C3
Ashford Rd. Dron 75 E4
Ashford Rise. Belper 179 E3
Ashforth Ave. Hean 182 A1
Ashfurlong Cl. Totley 55 F4
Ashfurlong Dr. Totley 55 F4
Ashfurlong Rd. Totley 55 F4
Ashgate Ave. Chest 95 E2
Ashgate Rd. Chest 95 E2
Ashgate Rd. O Bram 95 E2
Ashgate Valley Rd. Chest 95 E2
Ashgrove Ct. Derby 206 A1
Ashland Rd. Eck 59 F2
Ashlea Dr. May 184 B4
Ashlea Wlk. Clowne 81 D3
Ashleigh Ave. Glos 10 A1
Ashleigh Ave. Shef 43 F3
Ashleigh Ave. Swad 255 F3
Ashleigh Cl. Chest 77 D2
Ashleigh Croft. Shef 43 F3
Ashleigh Ct. Eck 59 E1
Ashleigh Dr. Derby 232 C1
Ashleigh Dr. Shef 43 F3
Ashleigh Pl. Shef 43 F3
Ashleigh Rd. Barl 80 A4
Ashley Cl. Kill 60 B3
Ashley Cl. Over 262 A2
Ashley Cl. Tans 144 A2
Ashley Ct. Bu on T 248 A2
Ashley La. Kill 60 B3
Ashley St. Derby 218 B3
Ashlyn Rd. Derby 219 E3
Ashmeadow. Ock 221 D1
Ashmore Ave. Eck 59 D1
Ashop Rd. Belper 179 E3
Ashopton Ave. Derby 231 F4
Ashopton Dr. Bam 40 A2
Ashopton Rd. Bam 40 A3
Ashover New Rd. Stret 145 F4
Ashover Rd. Ash 129 F2
Ashover Rd. Ash 130 C3
Ashover Rd. Cl Cr 131 D4
Ashover Rd. Derby 204 B1
Ashover Rd. Derby 219 F4
Ashover Rd. Stav 97 E3
Ashover Rd. Swad 255 F3
Ashover Rd. Tupton 131 D4
Ashover Rd. Win 130 C3
Ashton Cl. Chest 114 B4
Ashton Cl. Derby 217 E2
Ashton Cl. Kill 60 B3
Ashton Cl. Som 170 A4
Ashton Gdns. Cl Cr 131 D3
Ashton Gdns. Glos 17 E4
Ashton St. Glos 17 E4
Ashton Way. Belper 179 E2
Ashtree Ave. Derby 232 A3
Ashurst Cl. Chest 94 C3
Ashview Cl. Lo Ea 236 A4
Ashwater Cl. Derby 231 F1
Ashwell Ave. Mans 136 C3
Ashwood Cl. Mans 136 C3
Ashwood Rd. Bux 66 C1
Ashwood Rd. Disley 32 B3
Ashwood. Glos 16 C4
Ashworth Ave. Bu on T 248 B1
Ashworth Ave. Derby 219 F3
Ashworth La. M in L 9 D2
Asker La. Mat 143 E3
Askerfield Ave. Derby 204 B2
Askew Gr. Rep 242 B1
Asline Rd. Shef 43 D4
Aspen Cl. Kill 60 B3
Aspen Ct. Mans 136 C1
Aspen Dr. Derby 220 B2
Aspen Rd. Eck 59 D1
Aspen Rise. Shirl 146 B1
Aspen Way. H La 32 A4
Aspenshaw Rd. N Mills 24 C2
Aspley Cl. Chest 95 F3
Astcote Cl. Hean 182 A1
Asterdale View. Derby 220 C2
Astil St. Bu on T 254 C4
Aston Cl. Derby 245 D4
Aston Cl. Dron 57 E2
Aston Ct. Ilk 194 C1
Aston Cl. Stav 78 C1
Aston Green. Bees 223 F2
Aston La. Derby 233 D1
Aston La. Hope 39 E2
Aston La. Shar 234 C1
Aston La. Sud 226 A3
Aston La. Wens 142 B4
Aston Rd. Derby 231 E3
Astorville Park Rd. Derby 232 C1
Astwith Cl. Heath 116 C1
Astwith La. Al Hu 133 D3
Atchison Gdns. Derby 220 A4
Atherfield Gdns. East 182 C2
Atherton Ave. M in L 9 D2
Atherton Cl. Shef 43 F3
Atherton Gr. M in L 9 D2
Atherton Rd. Ilk 194 B2
Atherton Rd. Shef 43 F3
Atherton Rd. Ship 194 B2
Athlestan Way. Bu on T 240 B1
Athlone Cl. Derby 219 E4
Athol Cl. Chest 114 A4
Athol Cl. Derby 231 F2
Atkin Pl. Shef 43 D4
Atkins Way. Roc 196 C2
Atlantic Dr. Shef 56 C3
Atlantic Rd. Shef 56 B3
Atlantic Way. Shef 56 C3
Atlantic Wlk. Shef 56 C3
Atlow Brow. Ashb 173 E2
Atlow Cl. Chest 95 D3
Atlow La. Atlow 175 D3
Atlow Rd. Derby 219 F4
Attewell Cl. Dray 235 D4
Attewell Rd. Awsw 195 D3
Attlebridge Cl. Derby 219 E4
Attlee Rd. Stav 97 D4
Auburn Cl. Stanl 207 D4
Auckland Cl. Derby 217 F2
Auden Cl. Ch Bro 227 D4
Audens Way. Swad 256 B3
Audrey Cres. Mans 136 B3
Audrey Dr. Derby 220 A4
Audrey Rd. Shef 44 B4
Aughton Cl. Shef 44 B4
Aughton Cres. Shef 44 B4
Aughton Dr. Shef 44 B4
Augusta St. Derby 219 D1
Aukland Dr. Mosb 59 F3
Aukland Rise. Mosb 59 F3
Aukland Way. Mosb 59 F3
Ault Hucknall La. Al Hu 134 A4
Aults Cl. Fin 230 B1
Austen Ave. Derby 231 D4
Austen Ave. Lo Ea 236 B3
Austin Sq. Derby 231 F4
Austin St. Shireb 120 A2
Austins Dr. Sand 223 D2
Autumn Gr. Derby 219 F3
Ave. Hean 193 F4
Avenue 1. Chest 115 D4
Avenue 2. Chest 115 D4
Avenue 3. Chest 115 D4
Avenue 4. Chest 115 D4
Avenue 5. Chest 115 D4
Avenue 6. Chest 115 D4
Avenue 7. Chest 115 D4
Avenue 8. Chest 115 D4
Avenue Cl. St Mid 72 A2
Avenue Rd. Chest 96 A4
Avenue Rd. Duff 190 C3
Avenue The. Bake 109 E3
Avenue The. Belper 178 C1
Avenue The. C-Frith 46 C1
Avenue The. Derby 219 D2
Avenue The. Derby 219 F3
Avenue The. Dron 57 D1
Avenue The. Eck 60 B1
Avenue The. Glos 10 A2
Avenue The. North 127 D3
Avenue The. St Mid 72 A2
Avenue The. Tiss 162 A3
Avenue The. We on T 245 F3
Averham Cl. Derby 206 A1
Averham Cl. Swad 256 A2
Aviemore Way. Derby 231 F2
Avis Ave. Hean 193 F4
Avon Cl. Derby 231 E1
Avon Cl. Dron 57 D2
Avon Cl. Swad 256 A3
Avon St. Derby 232 C4
Avon Way. Bu on T 248 A1
Avondale Cl. Lo Ea 236 A3
Avondale Rd. Bols 118 A4
Avondale Rd. Chest 95 F2
Avondale Rd. Derby 219 D2
Avondale Rd. Derby 220 B3
Avondale Rd. Ilk 208 B3
Avondale Rd. Stav 97 E4
Avonlea Cl. Ilk 209 D3
Avonmouth Dr. Derby 232 C4
Awdishaw La. Boyl 213 E3
Awsworth La. Awsw 195 E2
Awsworth La. Awsw 195 E3
Awsworth La. Kim 195 E3
Awsworth Rd. Ilk 194 C1
Aycliffe Gdns. Derby 232 C2
Aylesbury Ave. Derby 219 F4
Aylward Cl. Shef 43 F4
Aylward Rd. Shef 43 F4
Ayncourt Rd. N Wing 132 A4
Ayr Cl. Derby 220 B2
Azalea Ave. Som 170 A4
Azalea Cl. Alf 159 F2
Azalea Ct. Greas 195 E4

Babbacombe Cl. Derby 233 E4
Babbington Cl. Tut 239 E3
Babbington La. Kim 195 F2
Babbington St. Tibs 148 A3
Babbs La. Dove 211 E1
Babington Cl. Shef 43 F4
Babington La. Derby 219 D2
Bacchus Way. Morton 147 D3
Back Bridge St. N Mills 24 B1
Back Croft. Cl Cr 131 F1
Back Jodrell St. N Mills 33 D4
Back La. Alder 166 C4
Back La. Alst 149 F2
Back La. Biggin 138 E1
Back La. Brack 146 A1
Back La. C Don 247 D3
Back La. Calow 116 A4
Back La. Da Da 127 F2
Back La. Derby 233 D1
Back La. Ella 183 D2
Back La. Elton 140 C3
Back La. Glap 118 A1
Back La. Glos 16 C3
Back La. Hath 53 D4
Back La. Hean 181 F1
Back La. Hilton 228 B1
Back La. Ilk 194 C1
Back La. M in L 9 D2
Back La. Pent 169 E3
Back La. Pils 132 B1
Back La. S in A 148 C2
Back La. S Wing 157 F4
Back La. Scarc 118 A3
Back La. Shir 200 B4
Back La. Spout 166 B2
Back La. Th Sa 63 D3
Back La. Thurv 215 D2
Back La. Tibs 147 F3
Back La. Uns 57 F1
Back La. Youl 125 D3
Back Mellor Rd. N Mills 24 B1
Back Moor. M in L 9 D2
Back Rd. Uns 57 F1
Back Sitwell St. Derby 219 D2
Back South St. Uns 77 E3
Back St. Cas 38 B2
Back Union Rd. N Mills 33 E4
Back Wyver La. Belper 178 C3
Backhill La. Par 151 F2
Backhouse La. Ock 221 E3
Backmoor Cres. Shef 43 E1
Backmoor Rd. Shef 43 E1
Bacon Cl. Greas 195 D4
Bacon La. Pent 169 D3
Bacons La. Chest 115 D4
Baden Powell Ave. Chest 96 A1
Baden Powell Rd. Chest 96 A1
Badger Cl. Chest 114 A4
Badger Cl. Derby 220 C3
Badger La. Ash 145 E4
Badgery Cl. Utt 210 A1
Bag La. March 224 C1
Bag La. Rost 197 F4
Bage Hill. Holy 113 F3
Baggaley Cres. Mans 136 A1
Bagot St. We Ha 207 E4
Bagshaw Hill. Bake 109 E3
Bagshaw La. C-Frith 48 A3
Bagshaw St. Derby 232 C4
Bagshaw St. Mans 135 D2
Bagshaw's Rd. Shef 44 A3
Bagshawe Ave. C-Frith 46 C3
Bagthorp La. O Bram 94 A2
Bagthorpe La. O Bram 94 A2
Bailey Ave. Over 262 A2
Bailey Brook Cres. La Mi 182 A2
Bailey Brook Dr. La Mi 182 A2
Bailey Brook Ind Est. Hean 182 A1
Bailey Brook Wlk. La Mi 182 A2
Bailey Dr. Kill 60 C4
Bailey Gr. Bux 85 F4
Bailey Grove Rd. East 182 B1
Bailey St. Derby 218 C2
Bailey St. Staple 223 E3
Bainbridge Rd. Bols 98 C2
Bainbridge St. Derby 219 D2
Baines Wood Cl. Chest 95 E4
Bains Dr. Ock 221 E1
Bakeacre La. Fin 230 C2
Baker Ave. Hean 193 F4
Baker Cl. Som 170 B4
Baker Cl. Stanl 193 D1
Baker Dr. Kill 60 B3
Baker Rd. Mans 136 B3
Baker St. Bu on T 254 C4
Baker St. Derby 232 C4
Baker St. Elmt 81 F1
Baker St. Ilk 194 C1
Baker St. Swad 256 B2
Baker's La. Dove 211 E1
Baker's La. Mat Ba 155 D3
Bakers Hill. Ripley 168 C1
Bakers La. Hollow 156 A4
Bakestone Moor. Whit 81 F3
Bakewell Cl. Derby 217 F2
Bakewell Dr. C Don 247 D1
Bakewell Green. Swad 255 F3
Bakewell Mews. Glos 9 E1
Bakewell Rd. Baslow 91 F2
Bakewell Rd. Bux 85 E4
Bakewell Rd. Da Da 142 C4
Bakewell Rd. Lo Ea 236 C3
Bakewell Rd. Mat 143 D3
Bakewell Rd. Stav 97 E3
Bakewell St. Derby 218 C2
Balaclava Rd. Derby 232 A4
Balfour Rd. Derby 232 A4
Balfour Rd. Staple 223 E3
Balham Wlk. Derby 218 A3
Ball Hill. S Norm 160 B3
Ball La. Elv 234 A3
Ballacraine Dr. Ripley 169 F1
Ballards Way. Ock 221 E1
Ballater Cl. Derby 231 F2
Balleny Cl. Derby 205 F1
Balmoak La. Chest 96 B3
Balmoral Cl. Derby 218 A1
Balmoral Cl. Mans 136 C3
Balmoral Cl. Sand 223 D2
Balmoral Cres. Dron 56 B1
Balmoral Dr. Mans 135 F1
Balmoral Rd. Bu on T 248 A2
Balmoral Rd. Ilk 208 B3
Balmoral Rd. Ock 221 E1
Balmoral Way. Chest 77 F2
Bamburgh Cl. Derby 220 B2
Bamford Ave. Derby 231 F4
Bamford Ave. N Wing 131 F4
Bamford La. Glos 9 F1
Bamford Mews. Glos 9 F1
Bamford Rd. Stav 97 E3
Bamford St. Chest 77 E2
Bamford St. Newt 148 A2
Bamford St. Ripley 180 B4
Bamsbrook La. Clowne 80 B1
Banbury Ave. Bees 223 F2
Bancroft Cl. Hilton 228 B1
Bancroft Dr. Derby 204 B2
Bancroft The. Etwall 229 D2
Bangor St. Derby 219 F4
Bank Cl. Bols 99 D2
Bank Cl. Elmt 100 B4
Bank Cl. Tibs 147 F3
Bank Gdns. Mat 143 E3
Bank La. Tint 10 A4
Bank Rd. Chest 96 A3
Bank Rd. Mat 143 D3
Bank Side. Derby 204 C1
Bank Side. Hartin 137 E3
Bank St. Chest 95 F2
Bank St. Chest 96 B4
Bank St. Glos 10 A3
Bank St. Glos 17 E4
Bank St. Hay 25 E2
Bank St. La Mi 182 B2
Bank St. Lo Ea 236 C4
Bank St. M in L 16 A4
Bank St. Som 170 B4
Bank St. Swad 262 A4
Bank The. Bons 142 B1
Bank The. St Mid 71 F2
Bank Top La. Grin 72 B4
Bank Vale Rd. Hay 25 E2
Bank View Rd. Derby 218 C4
Bank View Rd. Ripley 168 B1
Bank View. Tide 69 D3
Bank Wood Cl. Chest 95 D4
Bankbottom. Glos 10 A3
Bankerwall La. Stan 183 E4
Bankfield Dr. Derby 220 C2
Bankfield Dr. Ilk 208 A3
Bankgate. M in L 16 A4
Bankholmes Cl. Derby 231 F1
Banks Rd. Bees 223 F1
Banksburn Cl. Hean 181 E1
Bankside Cl. Marple 15 E1
Bankside. Youl 125 D3
Bankswood Cl. Glos 10 A2
Bankwood Cl. Shef 43 E3
Bankwood Rd. Shef 43 E3
Banmoor La. Hath 52 C4
Bannell's La. Etwall 229 F4
Bannels Ave. Derby 231 D4
Banton's La. Tick 251 D2
Banwell Cl. Derby 217 E2
Bar Gate. Cas 38 B1
Bar Rd. Baslow 91 F3
Bar Rd. Curbar 72 C1
Barber Cl. Ilk 194 C2
Barber St. Glos 10 A3
Barber's La. Kill 60 B4
Barbon Cl. Chest 95 F3
Barcheston Cl. Derby 206 A1
Barclay Ct. Ship 194 B2
Barden Dr. Derby 204 C2
Bardolph Cl. Swad 255 F2
Bardsey Ct. Derby 206 A2
Bare La. Ock 221 E3
Barf Cl. Derby 217 F1
Bargate Cl. Belper 179 E1
Bargate La. Will 242 A3
Bargate Rd. Belper 179 D1
Barholme Cl. Chest 95 D4
Barker Ave E. Sand 223 D3
Barker Ave N. Sand 223 D3
Barker Ave. Sels 171 D2
Barker Fold. Chest 95 E2
Barker Gate. Ilk 194 C1
Barker La. Chest 95 E2
Barker St. S in A 148 C2
Barklam Cl. Donis 262 C1
Barlborough Rd. Clowne 80 B3
Barley Cft. Derby 232 C1
Barley Cft. S Norm 160 A2
Barley Cl. Lit Ea 205 E4
Barley Dale Dr. Staple 209 E1
Barley La. O Bram 95 D3
Barleycorn Cl. Bu on T 248 A1
Barleycorn Cl. Derby 206 B1
Barleycroft. Glos 9 F2
Barling Dr. Ship 194 B1
Barlow Dr (N). Awsw 195 D2
Barlow Dr (S). Awsw 195 D2
Barlow Lees La. Dron 75 F4
Barlow Rd. Barlow 94 C4
Barlow Rd. C-Frith 47 E3
Barlow Rd. Stav 78 C1
Barlow St. Derby 219 E2
Barlow View. Dron 76 A4
Barlow Wood Dr. Marple 23 D2
Barms Way. Bux 66 B1
Barn Cl. C Don 247 D2
Barn Cl. Chest 95 E3
Barn Cl. Fin 230 B1
Barn Cl. Glos 17 E4
Barn Cl. Quar 204 B3
Barnard Ave. Dron 57 E2
Barnard Rd. Derby 205 E1
Barnes Ave. Dron 56 C1
Barnes Green. Derby 218 A4
Barnes La. Dron 56 B1
Barnes Rd. Chest 96 C1
Barnfield Cl. N Wing 132 C4
Barnfield Cl. Stav 78 C1
Barnfield Wlk. Stav 78 C1
Barnfields. Hath 52 C4

Barnham Cl. Chest 114 A4
Barnsley La. Idri 165 F1
Barnsley La. Spout 165 F1
Barnstaple Cl. Derby 206 A1
Barnwell Cl. Utt 210 A2
Barnwell La. Mat Ba 155 D3
Barnwood Cl. Derby 217 E1
Barrack Rd. Uns 58 A1
Barrack Yd. Som 170 B4
Barracks Sq. Chest 96 A2
Barratt Rd. Eck 59 E1
Barrett St. Derby 233 D4
Barrie Dr. Derby 231 F3
Barrington Cl. Bu on T 240 B1
Barron's Way. Ock 221 E1
Barroon The. C Don 247 D2
Barrow La. Swark 244 B3
Barrow St. Stav 78 C1
Barrows Hill La. Sels 171 E3
Barry Rd. Chest 96 C2
Barson Gr. Bux 85 F1
Bartle Ave. Shef 43 F2
Bartle Dr. Shef 43 F2
Bartle Rd. Shef 43 F2
Bartle Way. Shef 43 F2
Barton Cl. Derby 220 C3
Barton Cres. Chest 95 D3
Barton Hill. Bir 126 B1
Barton Knoll. Belper 179 E2
Barton Knowle. Belper 179 E2
Barton Rd. Lo Ea 237 D3
Barton Rd. Shef 43 D3
Barton St. Bu on T 254 B4
Barton St. Clowne 80 C2
Barton Turn. B-u-Ne 253 D1
Basegreen Ave. Shef 44 A2
Basegreen Cl. Shef 44 B2
Basegreen Cres. Shef 44 A2
Basegreen Dr. Shef 44 B2
Basegreen Pl. Shef 44 A2
Basegreen Rd. Shef 44 B2
Basegreen Way. Shef 44 B2
Basildon Cl. Derby 232 C3
Baslow Cl. Lo Ea 236 A3
Baslow Dr. Derby 204 C2
Baslow Gr. Bux 85 F3
Baslow Mews. Glos 9 F1
Baslow Rd. Bake 109 E4
Baslow Rd. Curbar 72 B1
Baslow Rd. Holy 94 B1
Baslow Rd. Totley 55 E2
Bass St. Derby 218 B3
Bass's Cres. Linton 261 F4
Bassett Cl. Kim 195 F4
Bassett La. Lod M 42 C3
Bassett Rd. Kim 195 F4
Bassett The. Shireb 119 E3
Bassettbarn La. Ash 130 A3
Bassford Ave. Hean 181 F1
Bassingham Cl. Derby 206 A1
Bassledene Rd. Shef 44 A4
Batch La. Dove 224 A4
Bateman Cl. Chest 77 E2
Bateman St. Derby 219 E2
Batemill Rd. N Mills 24 B1
Batemoor Cl. Shef 57 D3
Batemoor Dr. Shef 57 D3
Batemoor Pl. Shef 57 D3
Batemoor Rd. Shef 57 D3
Batemoor Wlk. Shef 57 D3
Bath La. Ash 129 F3
Bath La. Mar War 120 B1
Bath La. Moira 262 B2
Bath Rd. Bux 85 D3
Bath Rd. Derby 217 F1
Bath St. Bake 109 E3
Bath St. Derby 219 D3
Bath St. Ilk 194 C1
Batham Gate Rd. Bux 67 D3
Batham Gate. Bradw 50 A2
Batham Gate. Pk F 48 C1
Batham Rd. Bradw 51 D4
Bathurst Rd. Bols 117 F4
Bathurst Terr. Scarc 100 C1
Batley La. Al Hu 134 C2
Batt St. Shef 43 D4
Baulk La. Bees 223 F3
Baulk La. Bees 223 F4
Baulk La. Hath 41 D1
Baverstock Cl. Derby 232 C2
Baxter Hill. Mans 134 C2
Baxter Sq. Derby 231 F3
Bay Ct. Kill 60 B3
Bayleaf Cres. Derby 206 A2
Baysdale Croft. Mosb 59 E4
Bayswater Cl. Derby 217 F3
Bayswater Rd. Kim 195 F4
Bazley Rd. Shef 43 F3
Beackden Cl. Belper 179 F2
Beacomfold. Marple 15 D2
Beacon Dr. Rolle 240 A2
Beacon Rd. Rolle 240 A2
Beaconsfield St. Lo Ea 236 C4
Beam Cl. Bu on T 240 A1
Beard Cres. N Mills 33 E4
Beards Rd. Swad 256 A3
Bearwood Hill Rd. Bu on T 248 A2
Beatty St. Derby 232 C4
Beatty Wlk. Ilk 194 C2
Beauchief Abbey La. Shef 56 B4
Beauchief Dr. Shef 56 B4
Beaufit La. Pinx 160 C1
Beaufort Ct Ind Est. Derby 219 E4
Beaufort Rd. Bu on T 248 A1
Beaufort Rd. Derby 231 E1
Beaufort St. Derby 219 E4
Beaulieu Way. Som 170 A4
Beaumaris Ct. Derby 220 C3
Beaumont Cl. Ba on T 244 A3
Beaumont Cl. Belper 179 E2
Beaumont Cl. Staple 209 F1
Beaumont Wlk. Derby 231 F3
Beaurepaire Cres. Belper 179 D3
Beaureper Ave. Derby 204 C2
Beauvale Dr. Ilk 194 C3
Becher St. Derby 219 D1
Beckenham Way. Derby 218 A3
Becket Ave. Shef 56 B3
Becket Cres. Shef 56 C3
Becket Rd. Shef 56 C3
Becket St. Derby 219 D3
Becket Well La. Derby 219 D3
Becket Wlk. Shef 56 C3
Beckett Ave. Mans 135 F1
Beckford La. Fin 242 C4
Beckitt Cl. Derby 233 D4
Becksitch La. Belper 178 C1
Bedehouse La. Mat Ba 155 D3
Bedford Cl. Derby 218 B2
Bedford Ct. Staple 209 F1
Bedford Rd. Bu on T 254 B4
Bedford St. Derby 218 B2
Bedgrave Cl. Kill 60 C4
Bee Hives The. Swad 256 A4
Beech Ave. Alf 159 D3
Beech Ave. Brea 235 F4
Beech Ave. Derby 233 D4
Beech Ave. Elmt 81 F1
Beech Ave. Glos 17 D4
Beech Ave. H Ward 175 F2
Beech Ave. Lo Ea 223 F1
Beech Ave. Mel 252 A4
Beech Ave. N Mills 24 B1
Beech Ave. Ock 221 E2
Beech Ave. Pinx 160 C2
Beech Ave. Quar 204 A1
Beech Ave. Ripley 169 E1
Beech Ave. Sand 223 D4
Beech Ave. Will 242 A3
Beech Cl. Belper 179 D2
Beech Cl. Kilb 192 A4
Beech Cres. Eck 59 D1
Beech Cres. Glap 134 A4
Beech Cres. Kill 60 B3
Beech Dr. Ashb 185 E4
Beech Dr. Derby 218 C4
Beech Dr. Etwall 229 E2
Beech Dr. Fin 230 C1
Beech Dr. Wood 257 D1
Beech Gdns. Derby 233 D4
Beech Gr. S Norm 160 A3
Beech Gr. Stav 98 A2
Beech Gr. Swad 255 F4
Beech Hill Ave. Mans 135 F1
Beech Hill Cres. Mans 135 F1
Beech Hill Dr. Mans 135 F1
Beech La. Bu on T 240 C1
Beech La. C-Frith 66 C4
Beech La. We Ha 207 E4
Beech Rd. W Br 45 F4
Beech Rise. W Br 45 E3
Beech St. Stav 78 A1
Beech Tree Ave. Mans 136 A3
Beech Tree Dr. Clowne 80 C1
Beech Way. Cl Cr 131 F1
Beech Way. Dron 57 D2
Beech Wlk. Derby 218 B1
Beech Wlk. Mat Ba 155 D3
Beechcroft. Bread 205 E2
Beechdale Cl. Chest 95 E2
Beechdale Rd. Mans 136 C1
Beeches Ave. Derby 220 B3
Beeches Ave. Shef 43 E4
Beeches Dr. Shef 43 E4
Beeches The. Crich 156 C1
Beeches The. Hean 193 E4
Beechfield Rd. Glos 9 F2
Beechley Dr. Derby 206 A1
Beechwood Cres. Derby 231 E4
Beechwood Dr. Marple 23 D3
Beechwood Rd. Dron 56 C1
Beechwood. Glos 16 C4
Beehive Yd. Chest 95 E1
Beeley Cl. Derby 204 B1
Beeley Cl. Derby 205 F1
Beeley Cl. N Wing 132 A4
Beeley Cl. Stav 97 E3
Beeley La. Beeley 112 D2
Beeley Way. Stav 97 E3
Beelow Cl. C-Frith 47 F1
Beeston Cl. Dron 56 B1
Beetwell St. Chest 96 A1
Beggarway La. G Lo 90 A3
Beighton St. Ripley 169 F1
Beldon Cl. Shef 43 E4
Beldon Pl. Shef 43 E4
Beldon Rd. Shef 43 E4
Belfast Walk. Derby 220 A2
Belfield Ct. Hean 181 E2
Belfield Rd. Etwall 229 E2
Belfield Rd. Swad 256 A3
Belfit Dr. Win 114 C1
Belfmoor Cl. Whit 82 A3
Belfry Cl. Derby 217 F1
Belfry The. Bu on T 240 B1
Belgrade Ave. Chin 34 C1
Belgrave Sq. Shef 43 D4
Belgrave St. Derby 219 D2
Belklane Dr. Kill 60 C4
Bell Ave. As on T 246 A4
Bell La. Bons 142 B1
Bell La. Dove 224 B4
Bell La. Ship 193 E3
Bell La. Smal 193 E3
Belle Acre Cl. Belper 178 C2
Belle View Rd. Ashb 173 D1
Belle Vue Ave. Ripley 180 B3
Belle Vue Cl. Chest 96 B4
Belledere Cl. Som 169 F4
Bellhouse La. Stav 78 C2
Bellingham Ct. Derby 204 B1
Bells End Rd. Wa on T 253 E1
Bellsfield Cl. Whit 82 A3
Belmont Ave. Brea 235 F4
Belmont Dr. Marple 15 D1
Belmont Dr. Ock 221 D1
Belmont Dr. Stav 78 C1
Belmont St. Swad 256 B2
Belmont Terr. Bux 85 D4
Belmot Rd. Tut 238 C1
Belmot Rd. Tut 239 D2
Belond La. Ash 113 E1
Belper La. Belper 178 C3
Belper Rd. Ashb 173 F1
Belper Rd. Derby 218 C4
Belper Rd. Holbr 191 E4
Belper Rd. Kilb 179 F1
Belper Rd. Morley 192 C1
Belper Rd. Shirl 146 B1
Belper Rd. Stanl 193 D1
Belper Rd. We Ha 207 E4
Belper St. Ilk 208 C4
Belsize Cl. Derby 217 F3
Belton Cl. Sand 223 D2
Belton Cl. Shef 56 C4
Belvedere Ave. Chest 114 C4
Belvedere Cl. Chest 114 A4
Belvedere Cl. Derby 217 E2
Belvedere Rd. Wood 256 C1
Belvedere Terr. Bux 85 D3
Belvoir Cl. Brea 235 E4
Belvoir Cl. Ilk 208 B3
Belvoir Cl. Lo Ea 236 C3
Belvoir Cres. Swad 256 A3
Belvoir St. Derby 218 C1
Belvoir Way. Som 159 E1
Bembridge Dr. Derby 233 E3
Bemrose Gate. Bam 40 A3
Bemrose Rd. Derby 232 C4
Bench Rd. Bux 85 E4
Benches La. Marple 15 F2
Bend Oak Dr. Bu on T 248 B2
Bendall Green. Derby 231 E3
Beninmoor Way. Chest 114 C4
Benjamin Outram Bsns Centre. Ripley 180 C4
Benmore Ct. Derby 206 A2
Benner Ave. Ilk 209 D3
Bennerley Ave. Ilk 194 C2
Bennett St. Bux 85 E3
Bennett St. Derby 232 B3
Bennett St. Lo Ea 223 E1
Bennett St. M in L 9 E3
Bennett St. Sand 223 D3
Bennetts La. Crich 167 F4
Bennetts La. Crich 168 A4
Bennington Wlk. Mans 136 C2
Bennison Gdns. Cl Cr 131 E2
Bensley Cl. Derby 233 D1
Benson St. Derby 232 C4
Bent La. Ch Bro 227 E3
Bent La. Da Da 127 E3
Bent La. Mat 143 D4
Bent La. North 127 E3
Bent La. Spout 166 B3
Bent La. Stav 79 D2
Bent La. Tiss 162 B3
Bent La. Wirk 166 B3
Bent The. Curbar 72 C2
Bent's La. Dron 57 E1
Bentfield Rd. Ripley 168 B1
Bentham Rd. Chest 95 F3
Bentinck Dr. Clowne 81 D2
Bentinck Rd. Bols 98 C4
Bentink Cl. Elmt 81 E1
Bentley Cl. Alf 159 D2
Bentley Cl. Mat 143 E4
Bentley Rd. Utt 210 A1
Bentley St. Derby 232 C3
Benton Dr. Marple 23 E4
Bents Cres. Dron 57 E2
Bents La. Dron 57 E2
Bents Rd. Totley 55 E2
Bentside Rd. Disley 32 B3
Beowulf Covert. Bu on T 240 A1
Beresford Ave. Ashb 173 E1
Beresford Ave. C-Frith 47 E3
Beresford Cl. Cl Cr 131 E1
Beresford Dale. Swad 255 F1
Beresford Dr. Derby 220 C2
Beresford Dr. Ilk 194 C3
Beresford La. Alst 137 E1
Beresford Pl. Ripley 168 A3
Beresford Rd. C-Frith 47 E3
Beresford Rd. Lo Ea 236 A3
Beresford Rd. Mans 136 B3
Berkeley Ave. Lo Ea 236 B3
Berkeley Cl. Derby 231 E4
Berkshire St. Derby 219 E4
Berle Ave. Hean 181 F1
Bermuda Ave. Lit Ea 205 E3
Bernard Ave. Mans 136 A3
Bernard Cl. Chest 96 C4
Bernard St. Glos 10 B1
Bernard St. Swad 256 B2
Bernard Walker Ct. Marple 15 D1
Berners Cl. Shef 43 F3
Berners Dr. Shef 43 F3
Berners Pl. Shef 43 F3
Berners Rd. Shef 43 F3
Berridge La. Ash 145 D2
Berrisford La. Stret 145 E4
Berristow La. S Norm 160 B4
Berry Ave. Eck 59 E2
Berry Gdns. Bu on T 248 B2
Berry Hedge La. Bu on T 248 B2
Berry Park Cl. Derby 204 C1
Berry St. N Wing 131 F3
Bertrand Ave. Cl Cr 131 E2
Berwick Ave. Chest 114 B4
Berwick Ave. Derby 219 E4
Berwick Cl. Derby 233 D3
Berwick Rd. Bux 85 E2
Berwin Cl. Lo Ea 223 D1
Berwyn Cl. Chest 95 E3
Bessalone Dr. Belper 179 D3
Bessell La. Bees 223 E3
Bessell La. Staple 223 E3
Bessie La. Bradw 51 D3
Best Ave. Bu on T 248 A1
Besthill Cotts. M in L 16 A4
Besthorpe Cl. Derby 206 A1
Bestwick Ave. Hean 182 A1
Bestwood Dr. Cl Cr 131 E2
Bestwood Pk. Cl Cr 131 E2
Bestwood Rd. Pinx 160 C1
Bethel Terr. Shire 63 F3
Bethulie Rd. Derby 232 A4
Betjeman Sq. Derby 232 A3
Betlingspring La. Snel 184 B2
Betony Cl. Kill 60 A3
Bevan Dr. Stav 97 D4
Bevan Rd. Cl Cr 131 E1
Bevan St. Shirl 146 C1
Beverley Dr. Kim 195 F4
Beverley St. Derby 219 E1
Beverleys Rd. Shef 43 D2
Bewdley Cl. Derby 233 D2
Bexley Cl. Glos 10 B2
Bicester Ave. Derby 231 E1
Bickley Moss. Derby 206 A1
Bideford Cl. Ripley 169 E1
Bideford Dr. Derby 231 E3
Bidston Cl. Mat 143 E4
Bidworth La. Glos 9 E1
Biggin Cl. Cl Cr 131 E1
Biggin La. H Ward 176 A2
Biggin The. C Don 247 D2
Bigginmill Lane. K Ire 176 B3
Bilby La. Chest 77 F1
Billam St. Eck 59 D2
Billingsley Ave. Pinx 160 B2
Bingham St. Derby 232 C3
Bings Rd. W Br 45 F4
Bingswood Ave. W Br 45 F4
Bingswood Rd. W Br 45 F4
Binscombe La. Derby 205 F2
Birch Ave. Ilk 209 D4
Birch Ave. Ripley 167 F2
Birch Ave. Swad 256 A4
Birch Cl. Alf 159 D3
Birch Cl. Dens 196 B3
Birch Cl. Gra 115 F2
Birch Cl. Kill 60 B3
Birch Cl. Ripley 180 B4
Birch Cl. S Wing 157 F4
Birch Farm Ave. Shef 57 D4
Birch Gr. Hatton 227 E1
Birch Gr. Shireb 119 E3
Birch Green. Glos 10 C1
Birch Hall Cl. Hay 25 D1
Birch Holt Gr. Uns 76 C3
Birch Kiln Croft. Chest 96 C4
Birch La. Stav 78 A1
Birch Rd. Whit 82 B3
Birch St. Mar War 120 C3
Birch View Ct. Derby 218 C4
Birchen Cl. Chest 95 E3
Birchen Cl. Shef 56 C4
Birchen Holme. S Norm 160 A2
Birches Ave. S Wing 157 E3
Birches Fold. Dron 57 E2
Birches La. Dron 57 E2
Birches La. S Wing 158 A3
Birches Rd. Derby 204 B2
Birches The. Hay 25 E1
Birchfield Cl. Derby 232 C1
Birchfield Park. Hean 193 F4
Birchfield Rd. Bu on T 254 C
Birchitt Cl. Shef 56 B3
Birchitt Pl. Shef 56 B3
Birchitt Rd. Shef 56 B3
Birchitt View. Dron 57 D2
Birchlands Dr. Kill 60 B3
Birchlands. Mans 136 C
Birchover Edge. Bir 141 D4
Birchover La. Wins 141 D4
Birchover Pl. Ilk 194 C3
Birchover Rd. Bir 126 B2
Birchover Rd. St Pk 126 B2
Birchover Rise. Derby 205 F
Birchover Way. Derby 204 C
Birchside Ave. Glos 10 A
Birchvale Rd. Shef 44 C2
Birchwood Ave. Derby 231 E3
Birchwood Ave. Lo Ea 236 A4
Birchwood Ave. Lo Ea 236 B
Birchwood Cl. Mosb 59 F4
Birchwood Cl. S Norm 160 A
Birchwood Cres. Chest 114 C
Birchwood Cres. Som 170 B4
Birchwood Croft. Mosb 59 F4
Birchwood Dr. Ripley 168 A
Birchwood Gdns. Mosb 59 F4
Birchwood Gr. Mosb 59 F4
Birchwood La. Pinx 159 F2
Birchwood La. S Norm 159 F2
Birchwood La. Som 159 F2
Birchwood La. Som 170 B4
Birchwood Rd. Alf 159 E
Birchwood Rise. Mosb 59 F4
Birchwood View. Ashb 173 E
Birchwood View. Mosb 59 F4
Birchwood Way. Mosb 59 F4
Birchwood Way. Som 159 E
Bircumshaw's Rd. Hean 181 F
Bird St. Stav 78 C
Birdcage Wlk. Derby 217 F
Birdcroft La. Ilk 208 C
Birdholme Cres. Chest 115 D
Birding St. Mans 136 A
Birdsgrove La. May 172 B
Birdsgrove La. Swin 172 B
Birdwood St. Derby 218 C
Birkdale Cl. Derby 218 A
Birkdale Cl. Ilk 194 B
Birkdale Dr. Chest 114 B
Birkin Ave. Tupton 115 E
Birkin La W. Gra 115 F
Birkin La. Gra 115 F
Birkin La. Gra 116 A
Birkin La. Win 114 B
Birkinstyle Ave. Shirl 146 C
Birkinstyle La. Shirl 146 C
Birkland Ave. Mans 136 B
Birks Cl. Whit 82 B
Birley Brook Dr. Chest 95 D
Birley La. Shef 44 C
Birley Moor Ave. Shef 44 C
Birley Moor Cl. Shef 44 C
Birley Moor Cres. Shef 44 C
Birley Moor Dr. Shef 44 C
Birley Moor Pl. Shef 44 C
Birley Moor Rd. Shef 44 C
Birley Moor Way. Shef 44 C
Birley Spa La. Shef 44 C
Birley St. Staple 223 E
Birley Vale Ave. Shef 44 B
Birley Vale Cl. Shef 44 B
Biscay Ct. Derby 206 B
Bishop St. Alf 159 D
Bishop St. East 182 C
Bishop's Ct. Mel 252 A
Bishop's Dr. Derby 205 F
Bishopdale Cl. Lo Ea 236 A
Bishopdale Dr. Mosb 59 D
Bishopdale Rise. Mosb 59 D
Bishops Ct. Shef 43 D
Bishops La. Bux 84 C
Bishopscourt Rd. Shef 43 D
Bispham Dr. Bees 223 F
Bitham Ct. Bu on T 240 B
Bitham La. Bu on T 240 B
Blaby Cl. Derby 231 F
Black Harry La. St Mid 71 D
Black Hills Dr. Ilk 208 C
Black Tor Rd. Bons 154 B
Blacka Moor Cres. Totley 55 E
Blacka Moor Rd. Totley 55 E
Blacka Moor View. Totley 55 E
Blackberry Flats. Mosb 59 F
Blackbird Row. Holbr 179 E
Blackbrook La. C-Frith 47 F
Blackburn Pl. Ilk 194 C
Blackcliff Field Cl. Whit 82 A
Blackdown Ave. Chest 95 D
Blackmore St. Derby 231 F
Blackpit La. Dove 224 A
Blackpool St. Bu on T 254 B
Blackrocks Ave. Da Da 142 C

acks La. N Wing 131 F4
ackshaw Rd. Glos 10 C1
acksmith La. Calow 97 D2
acksmith's La. Eg 241 D3
acksmith's La. N Sol 248 C4
acksmith's La. Wood 256 C2
acksmiths Yd. Da Da 127 F1
ackstock Cl. Shef 43 E1
ackstock Cres. Shef 43 E1
ackstock Dr. Shef 43 E1
ackstock Rd. Shef 43 E2
ackthorn Cl. Chest 115 E4
ackthorn Cl. Derby 205 F1
ackthorn Cl. Mel 252 A4
ackthorn Rd. Bu on T 254 C3
ackthorne Cl. Kilb 179 F1
ackthorne Dr. East 182 B1
ackwall Lane. K Ire 176 A4
ackwell La. Mel 252 B4
ackwell La. Mo 107 D2
ackwell Rd. S in A 148 C2
adon St. Bu on T 248 B2
adon View. Bu on T 241 D1
agdon Cl. Da Da 127 E2
agreaves Ave. Derby 231 E3
agreaves La. Derby 231 E3
air Gr. Sand 223 D2
ake Ct. Lo Ea 236 A3
ake Rd. Staple 223 F3
ake St. Ilk 194 C1
ake St. Mans 136 A1
akebrook Dr. Derby 233 D2
akeley La. Etwall 229 D1
akelow Dr. Etwall 229 D2
akelow La. Bons 142 A2
akemere La. Bons 141 F1
akemore Ave. Mel 252 A4
akeney Ct. Derby 206 B1
akeney Ct. Mans 136 C2
anch Croft. Mel 252 A4
andford Ave. Lo Ea 236 A3
andford Cl. Derby 233 E3
anford Dr. Chest 95 F4
ankney Cl. Derby 231 E1
axton Rd. Ashb 173 D1
encathra Dr. Derby 230 C4
enheim Cl. Bu on T 248 B2
enheim Cl. Glos 10 A3
enheim Cl. Mans 136 B1
enheim Cl. Swad 256 A4
enheim Dr. Derby 204 B2
enheim Mews. Etwall 229 E2
enheim Pl. S in A 148 C2
enheim Rd. Ashb 185 F4
enhiem Ct. Sand 223 D2
ind La. Bols 98 C2
ind La. Brea 235 E4
ind La. Da Da 127 F1
ind La. K Ire 165 D1
ind La. Wirk 165 F4
issworth Way. Som 169 F4
thfield Gdns. Derby 233 D1
oom St. Derby 219 D2
oomfield Cl. Derby 219 D2
oomfield Cl. Hilton 228 B1
oomfield Rd. Som 170 A4
oomfield St. Derby 219 E2
oomgrove Rd. Ilk 194 C1
ore Cl. Ashb 185 E4
ossom Cres. Shef 44 A2
uebank View. Uns 77 E3
uebell Cl. Derby 231 E1
uebell Cl. Sels 171 F1
uebell Cl. Som 159 F1
uebell Croft. Mat 143 D2
uebell Hill. Shirl 146 B2
uestone La. Bu on T 255 D4
undestone La. Wirk 156 A1
unt Ave. Stav 79 E2
unt St. Stanl 193 D1
yth Cl. Chest 114 A4
yth Cl. Mans 135 E1
yth Pl. Derby 205 E1
oam La. Da Da 142 C4
oardman Rd. Swad 255 F1
oarslack La. Litton 69 F1
oarstones La. Bux 85 F4
oat La. Ald 182 A4
oatmans Cl. Ilk 194 C1
obbin Mill La. Chest 95 E1
obbinmill Hill. Crich 168 A4
ochum Parkway. Shef 57 E4
ocking La. Shef 56 C4
ocking Rise. Shef 56 C4
oden St. Derby 219 D1
odmin Way. Chest 95 E3
oggard La. Cha 16 B3
ogguard Rd. Marple 24 A3
oggy La. Ch Bro 227 D4
ohem Rd. Lo Ea 223 E2
oiley La. Kill 60 B2
oland Rd. Shef 56 B3
old La. Derby 219 D3
olehill La. Ash 130 B4
olehill La. Eck 58 C1
olehill La. Eck 59 D1
olehill La. Win 114 B1
olehill Rd. Wirk 155 D2
Bolsover Rd. Bols 98 C3
Bolsover Rd. Stav 79 E2
Bolton St. Som 169 E4
Boman's La. Shot 177 F4
Bonchurch Cl. Derby 233 E3
Bond La. Ripley 168 C1
Bond St. Stav 97 E4
Bondfield Rd. Stav 97 E4
Bondgate. C Don 247 D2
Bondhay La. Whit 62 B1
Bonner's Rd. Awsw 195 E2
Bonnington Dr. Som 170 B4
Bonnington Rise. Marple 23 D4
Bonnyrigg Dr. Derby 206 A1
Bonsall Ct. Chest 95 E4
Bonsall Dr. Derby 217 F2
Bonsall La. Alf 158 C2
Bonsall La. Bons 141 E2
Bonsall La. Wins 141 E2
Bonsall St. Lo Ea 236 C4
Bonsallmoor La. Bons 141 F1
Bonsalt Dr. Som 170 B4
Bonser Cres. S in A 148 C1
Boot Hill. Rep 242 B2
Booth Ave. Plea 135 D3
Booth Cres. Mans 135 E1
Booth St. Derby 232 C4
Booth St. M in L 9 E3
Booth St. Mans 136 A2
Booth St. Ripley 169 F1
Booth's Ct. Glos 10 B1
Boothby Ave. Ashb 173 E1
Boothgate. Ripley 179 F4
Boots Yd. S in A 148 C2
Border Cl. Clowne 80 C2
Border Cres. Derby 233 D3
Border La. Elmt 80 C1
Borlace Cres. Staple 223 F3
Borough St. C Don 247 D2
Borrowash By-pass. Derby 220 B2
Borrowash By-pass. Ock 221 E2
Borrowash By-pass. Risley 221 E2
Borrowash Rd. Derby 220 C2
Borrowdale Ave. Mosb 59 F3
Borrowdale Cl. Mosb 59 F3
Borrowdale Dr. Lo Ea 236 A3
Borrowdale Dr. Mosb 59 F3
Borrowdale Rd. Mosb 59 F3
Borrowfield Rd. Derby 220 C2
Borrowfields. Ock 221 D1
Boscastle Rd. Derby 233 D3
Boscowan Ct. Ilk 194 C2
Bosley Mews. Belper 178 C3
Bosnall Ave. Derby 231 E4
Bostock Rd. M in L 16 A4
Bostock's La. Sand 222 C2
Bostock's La. Sand 223 D2
Boston Cl. Derby 220 B3
Boswell Sq. Derby 231 F4
Bosworth Ave. Derby 231 F3
Bosworth Rd. C Don 246 C2
Bosworth Way. Lo Ea 236 C3
Botany Dr. Ilk 194 C3
Bothe Cl. Lo Ea 236 B3
Bottom Cliff. St Mid 71 F2
Bottom Rd. Win 114 C1
Bottomhill Rd. Litton 69 F1
Bough La. Calver 72 A1
Boughton Dr. Som 169 F4
Boughton La. Clowne 80 B2
Bould St. Mans 135 F1
Boulevard The. M in L 9 E2
Boulton Cl. Chest 95 D3
Boulton Dr. Derby 233 D3
Boulton La. Derby 232 C3
Boulton La. Derby 233 D3
Boundary Cl. Shireb 119 F3
Boundary Cl. Stav 79 D2
Boundary Gdns. Tibs 147 F3
Boundary La. East 182 B2
Boundary Rd. Derby 218 C2
Boundary Rd. Eg 241 E4
Boundary Wlk. Scarc 100 C1
Bourne Cl. Chest 96 C4
Bourne Ct. Mel 251 F4
Bourne Hill Cl. Barl 80 A3
Bourne Sq. Brea 235 F4
Bourne St. Derby 219 D2
Bournebrook Ave. Wirk 165 F4
Bow St. Mans 136 C2
Bowbridge Ave. Derby 231 E3
Bowden Cres. N Mills 33 E4
Bowden La. C-Frith 47 E4
Bowden Rd. Glos 10 B2
Bowdon Ave. Barl 80 A3
Bower Farm Rd. Chest 77 D1
Bower St. Derby 232 C4
Bowes Well Rd. Ilk 194 C1
Bowland Cl. Derby 217 F1
Bowland Dr. Chest 114 A4
Bowland Rd. Glos 17 D4
Bowlees Ct. Derby 230 C4
Bowler Dr. Kilb 192 A4
Bowler St. Ripley 180 B4
Bowling Alley La. M Mont 212 A3
Bowling Alley La. Sud 212 A3
Bowling Alley. Ripley 168 C1
Bowling Cl. S-by-D 222 C4
Bowling Green La. Wirk 154 C1
Bowling Green. Brass 153 D1
Bowman Cl. Shef 43 F1
Bowman Dr. Shef 44 A1
Bowmer La. Crich 168 A3
Bowmer Rd. Derby 219 F1
Bown Cl. Kilb 192 A4
Bowness Cl. Chest 95 E4
Bowness Cl. Dron 56 C1
Bowness Rd. Chest 95 E4
Bowns Hill. Crich 157 D1
Bowshaw Ave. Shef 57 D3
Bowshaw Cl. Shef 57 D3
Bowshaw View. Shef 57 D3
Boxmoor Cl. Derby 230 C4
Boyd Gr. Derby 245 D4
Boyer St. Derby 218 C2
Boyer Wlk. Derby 218 C2
Boylestone Rd. Derby 231 E3
Boythorpe Ave. Chest 95 F1
Boythorpe Cres. Chest 95 F1
Boythorpe Mount. Chest 95 F1
Boythorpe Rd. Chest 95 F1
Boythorpe Rise. Chest 95 F1
Brabyns Brow. Marple 23 D4
Bracken Ave. Heath 116 C1
Bracken Cl. Lo Ea 223 D1
Bracken Cl. M in L 9 E3
Bracken Cl. Marple 23 E4
Bracken La. Barl 80 A3
Bracken La. Hollow 156 A3
Bracken Rd. Lo Ea 223 D1
Bracken Way. Glos 17 F4
Bracken's La. Derby 232 C3
Brackendale Cl. Chest 96 B4
Brackendale Cl. Cl Cr 131 F1
Brackendale La. Brad 163 F3
Brackendale Rd. Som 169 F4
Brackenfield Ave. Mans 136 C2
Brackenfield Dr. Greas 195 D4
Brackenfield Gr. Shef 44 B2
Brackenfield La. Brack 145 E1
Brackenfield La. S Wing 157 E4
Brackens Ave. Derby 232 C3
Brackensdale Ave. Derby 218 A3
Brackenwood Rd. Bu on T 254 C3
Brackhills Cl. Mans 136 C1
Brackley Dr. Derby 220 C3
Brackley Gate. Morley 192 A1
Bracknell Dr. Derby 232 C3
Bradbourne Ct. Derby 218 C2
Bradbury Cl. Chest 95 F2
Bradbury Cl. Ock 221 E1
Bradbury Dr. Win 114 C2
Bradbury St. Shef 43 D3
Bradden Ave. Staple 209 F1
Bradgate Cl. Sand 223 D2
Bradgate Ct. Derby 231 F3
Bradgate Dr. Ripley 169 D1
Brading Cl. Derby 233 E3
Bradley Cl. Bir 126 A1
Bradley Cl. Chest 96 C4
Bradley Dr. Belper 179 D2
Bradley La. Barlow 75 E2
Bradley St. Bu on T 254 C3
Bradley St. Derby 218 C4
Bradley St. Sand 223 E3
Bradley View. Ashb 173 E2
Bradley Way. Chest 96 C4
Bradshaw Ave. Som 170 C3
Bradshaw Cres. Marple 23 D4
Bradshaw Croft. Belper 178 C3
Bradshaw Dr. Holbr 191 E3
Bradshaw La. Foolow 70 C4
Bradshaw Meadow. Hatton 227 E1
Bradshaw Rd. Marple 23 D4
Bradshaw Rd. Stav 97 D3
Bradshaw St. Lo Ea 236 A3
Bradshaw Way. Derby 219 D2
Bradway Cl. Shef 56 A3
Bradway Dr. Shef 56 A3
Bradway Grange Rd. Shef 56 B3
Bradway Rd. Shef 56 B3
Bradwell Cl. Derby 217 F1
Bradwell Cl. Greas 195 E4
Bradwell Cl. Shef 56 C4
Bradwell Gr. Cl Cr 131 E1
Bradwell Head Rd. Bradw 51 D4
Bradwell Pl. Stav 97 E4
Bradwell St. Shef 43 D3
Bradwell Way. Belper 179 D3
Braefield Cl. Ilk 208 B3
Braemar Ave. East 182 C1
Braemar Cl. Chest 77 E2
Brailsford Rd. Derby 219 F4
Braintree Cl. Derby 205 E1
Braithwell Cl. Derby 204 C1
Bramall La. Shef 43 D4
Bramble Cl. Heath 116 C1
Bramble Cl. Lo Ea 223 D1
Bramble Cl. Shireb 119 F3
Bramble Mews. Derby 217 E1
Bramble St. Derby 218 C3
Bramble Way. Kilb 179 F1
Brambleberry Ct. Derby 206 A2
Brambling Ct. Chest 96 B1
Bramell Cl. Bran 253 F4
Bramfield Ave. Derby 218 C2
Bramfield Ct. Derby 218 C2
Bramham Rd. Marple 23 D2
Bramley Ave. Shef 44 C4
Bramley Cl. Derby 206 B2
Bramley Cl. Mosb 59 E4
Bramley Ct. Hatton 227 E1
Bramley Ct. Kim 195 F3
Bramley Dale. Swad 255 F1
Bramley Hall Rd. Shef 44 C4
Bramley La. Baslow 91 E4
Bramley La. Hassop 91 E4
Bramley La. Shef 44 C4
Bramley Pk Cl. Shef 44 C4
Bramley Pk Rd. Shef 44 C4
Bramley Rd. Al Hv 117 F1
Bramley Rd. Eck 58 C1
Bramley St. Som 170 C4
Bramleymoor La. Eck 58 C1
Bramleymoor La. Uns 58 C1
Bramlyn Cl. Clowne 80 B3
Bramlyn Ct. Clowne 80 B3
Brampton Ave. Hean 182 A1
Brampton Cl. Derby 217 E2
Brampton Ct. Belper 179 E2
Brampton Dr. Staple 223 F3
Bramshill Rise. Chest 95 E1
Branch La. Al Hu 132 C3
Brancliffe La. Shire 63 F4
Brandene Cl. Calow 97 D2
Brandreth Dr. Greas 195 D4
Branklene Cl. Kim 195 F4
Branksome Ave. Derby 233 E4
Branksome Chine Ave.
Chest 115 E4
Bransdale Cl. Lo Ea 236 A3
Branston Rd. Bran 253 E4
Branston Rd. Bu on T 254 B4
Branton Cl. Chest 95 F1
Brassington Cl. Greas 195 D4
Brassington Cl. We Ha 207 F4
Brassington Cl. Youl 125 E3
Brassington Cres. Glos 9 E1
Brassington Ct. Mans 136 C2
Brassington La. Cl Cr 131 E3
Brassington Rd. Duff 205 D4
Brassington St. Cl Cr 131 E2
Braybrook Cl. Som 169 F4
Brayfield Ave. Derby 231 E4
Brayfield Rd. Derby 231 E4
Breach La. Hatton 227 E2
Breach La. Scro 226 B3
Breach La. St Br 244 C1
Breach Rd. Denby 181 D2
Breach Rd. Hean 194 A4
Breadsall Ct. Ilk 194 C2
Breamfield La. Wirk 166 A4
Brearley Ave. Uns 77 E3
Brearley St. Uns 77 E3
Breaston La. Risley 222 B2
Brechin Ct. Mans 136 A3
Breck La. Stav 78 B3
Breckbank. Mans 136 C1
Breckland Rd. Chest 114 A4
Brecon Cl. Chest 95 E3
Brecon Cl. Derby 220 C3
Brecon Cl. Lo Ea 236 A4
Bredon Cl. Lo Ea 236 A4
Breedon Ave. Derby 231 E3
Breedon Hill Rd. Derby 218 C2
Breedon St. Lo Ea 223 E1
Brenden Ave. Som 170 B4
Brenden Cl. Som 170 B4
Brendon Ave. Chest 95 E2
Brendon Cl. Glos 17 D4
Brendon Dr. Kim 195 F4
Brendon Way. Lo Ea 223 D1
Brent Cl. Chest 95 E3
Brentford Dr. Derby 218 A3
Brentwood Ave. Bam 40 A2
Brentwood Rd. Bam 40 A2
Bretby Bsns Pk. Bretby 255 F4
Bretby La. Bretby 248 C2
Bretby La. Bu on T 248 B1
Bretby Rd. Chest 95 D3
Bretby Rd. Swad 255 F4
Bretby Sq. Derby 231 E3
Bretby View. Harts 257 D2
Bretlands Way. Bu on T 255 D3
Bretton Ave. Bols 99 E1
Bretton Ave. Derby 218 B1
Bretton Gr. Shef 44 B2
Bretton Rd. Belper 179 F3
Brewery St. Chest 96 A2
Brewery St. Kim 195 F3
Breydon Cl. Derby 232 B2
Briar Ave. Sand 223 D2
Briar Briggs Rd. Bols 98 C2
Briar Cl. Alf 159 E2
Briar Cl. Chest 95 F3
Briar Cl. Derby 220 A2
Briar Cl. Ock 221 E1
Briar Cl. Swad 255 F3
Briar Gate. Lo Ea 223 D1
Briar Lea Cl. Derby 231 F2
Briar Rd. Greas 195 E4
Briar View. Chest 96 C4
Briar's La. Crich 168 A4
Briardene Cl. Chest 94 C3
Briargrove Rd. N Mills 24 B2
Briars Cl. Kill 60 B3
Briars Way. Ripley 180 B4
Briarsgate. Derby 204 B1
Briarwood Cres. Marple 23 D2
Briarwood Way. Derby 231 E3
Brick Kiln La. Rolle 240 A2
Brick Row. Derby 205 D1
Brick St. Derby 218 C3
Brick-kiln La. Brai 186 C1
Brick-Kiln La. H Ward 175 E3
Brickbridge Rd. Marple 23 D3
Brickfield St. Glos 10 A3
Brickfields Cl. Wirk 155 D2
Brickhouse La. Totley 55 E4
Brickhouse Yd. Chest 95 F2
Brickkiln La. Morley 206 B4
Brickyard Cottages. Ashb 185 E4
Brickyard La. Kilb 179 F1
Brickyard La. Ripley 169 F1
Brickyard La. S Norm 160 A3
Brickyard Rd. Ripley 168 B3
Brickyard The. Stanl 193 D1
Bridge Cl. Whit 82 A3
Bridge End Ave. Sels 171 F4
Bridge Farm. Bu on T 240 C1
Bridge Field. Brea 235 E4
Bridge Foot. Belper 178 C3
Bridge Hill. Belper 178 C3
Bridge St. Bake 109 E3
Bridge St. Belper 178 C2
Bridge St. Bradw 51 D4
Bridge St. Bu on T 240 C1
Bridge St. Bux 85 E4
Bridge St. Chest 96 A1
Bridge St. Cl Cr 131 E2
Bridge St. Derby 218 C3
Bridge St. Ilk 194 C2
Bridge St. Kill 60 B4
Bridge St. La Mi 182 B2
Bridge St. Linton 261 F4
Bridge St. Lo Ea 223 E1
Bridge St. N Mills 24 B1
Bridge St. Pils 132 B1
Bridge St. Sand 223 E3
Bridge St. Swad 256 B1
Bridge St. Tupton 115 E1
Bridge St. Tut 239 E4
Bridge St. W Br 45 F4
Bridge View. Belper 191 D4
Bridgend Cl. Staple 223 E3
Bridgend Ct. Derby 206 B1
Bridgeness Rd. Derby 230 C3
Bridgeport Rd. Derby 220 B3
Bridgeside. Bu on T 240 C1
Bridgewater St. Tupton 115 E1
Bridgeway. C-Frith 47 D2
Bridgnorth Way. Bees 223 F2
Bridgwater Cl. Derby 233 E4
Bridg ford Ave. Bran 253 F4
Bridle Cl. Derby 233 D1
Bridle La. Ripley 169 D1
Bridle La. Ripley 169 F1
Bridle La. Som 170 A4
Bridle La. Swad 255 D3
Bridle Rd. Bols 80 A1
Bridle Rd. Stav 79 D1
Bridle Stile Ave. Mosb 59 D4
Bridle Stile Cl. Mosb 59 E4
Bridle Stile. Mosb 59 E4
Bridleway The. Mans 136 C1
Brierfield Ave. Shef 44 A2
Brierfield Cres. Shef 44 A2
Brierfield Rd. Shef 44 A2
Brierfield Way. Derby 230 C4
Brierley Cl. Stav 78 C1
Brierley Pk. Chin 34 A1
Brierley Rd. Shirl 146 C2
Brierley Rd. Uns 76 C3
Brierlow Bar. Chel 105 D4
Brigden Ave. Derby 232 C4
Brighstone Cl. Derby 233 E3
Bright Sq. Mans 135 E1
Bright St. Derby 218 B3
Bright St. Ilk 194 C2
Bright St. N Wing 131 F3
Bright St. S Norm 159 F3
Brighton Rd. Derby 232 C4
Brigmor Wlk. Derby 218 B3
Brimington Ct. Mans 136 C2
Brimington Rd N. Chest 96 A4
Brimington Rd. Chest 96 A3
Brimmesfield Cl. Shef 43 F4
Brimmesfield Dr. Shef 43 F4
Brimmesfield Rd. Shef 43 F4
Brincliffe Cl. Chest 95 D1
Brindley Cl. Shef 43 D2
Brindley Cres. Shef 43 D2
Brindley Ct. Kill 60 B3
Brindley Rd. Chest 96 A3
Brindley Wlk. Derby 231 F1
Brinkburn Cl. Totley 55 F3
Brinkburn Ct. Totley 55 F3
Brinkburn Dr. Totley 55 F3
Brinkburn Vale Rd. Totley 55 F3
Brinsley Hill. Brin 171 E1
Brisbane Cl. Mans 136 B3
Brisbane Dr. Staple 209 F1

Brisbane Rd. Derby 217 F2
Briset Cl. Derby 231 F1
Bristol Dr. Derby 217 F1
Bristol Rd. Ilk 194 C1
Britannia Ave. Ripley 181 D4
Britannia Dr. Bu on T 240 B1
Britannia Rd. Chest 115 D4
Britannia Rd. Lo Ea 223 E1
Brittain Dr. Ripley 170 A1
Brizlincote La. Bu on T 248 B1
Broad Bank. Derby 218 C4
Broad La. Brin 182 C4
Broad La. Elv 233 F2
Broad La. Whit 82 B3
Broad La. Work 82 B3
Broad Oak Dr. Brin 182 C4
Broad Oak Dr. Staple 223 E3
Broad Pavement. Chest 96 A2
Broad Pl. Whit 82 B3
Broad St. Lo Ea 236 B4
Broad Way. K Ire 176 A4
Broad Wlk. Bux 85 D4
Broad Wlk. Da Da 127 E2
Broadbottom Rd. M in L 9 D2
Broadfield Rd. Shef 43 D4
Broadfields Cl. Derby 218 C4
Broadgorse Cl. Chest 114 C4
Broadholme La. Belper 179 D4
Broadlands. S Norm 160 A2
Broadlands. Sand 223 D2
Broadleaf Cl. Derby 205 F1
Broadleys. Cl Cr 131 E2
Broadmeadow. Da Da 127 E2
Broadoak Cl. Chest 96 B2
Broadstairs Rd. Bees 223 F1
Broadstone La. Tick 251 E2
Broadway Ave. Ripley 169 F1
Broadway St. Bu on T 254 B4
Broadway. Derby 218 C4
Broadway. Duff 190 C1
Broadway. Hean 181 F1
Broadway. Ilk 194 C2
Broadway. Ripley 169 F1
Broadway. Som 169 F4
Brockhall Rise. Hean 182 A1
Brockhurst La. Ash 129 E3
Brocklehurst Ave. Shef 57 E4
Brocklehurst Piece. Chest 95 E1
Brockley Ave. Bols 98 C3
Brockley. Derby 220 C3
Brockway Cl. Cl Cr 131 E1
Brockwell La. Chest 95 E2
Brockwell Pl. Chest 95 F2
Brockwell Terr. Chest 95 F2
Brockwell The. S Norm 160 A2
Bromehead Way. Chest 95 E4
Bromley St. Derby 218 C4
Brompton Rd. Derby 217 F3
Bromyard Dr. Derby 233 D2
Bronte Pl. Derby 231 D4
Bronte St. Shirl 146 B3
Brook Ave. Alf 159 D2
Brook Bottom Rd. N Mills 33 D4
Brook Cl. Alf 159 D2
Brook Cl. Fin 230 B1
Brook Cl. Hatton 227 E1
Brook Cl. Holy 113 E4
Brook Cl. Lo Ea 236 C3
Brook Cl. Quar 204 B2
Brook Cotts. Ilk 194 C2
Brook Ct. Hean 182 A1
Brook End. Rep 242 B2
Brook House Mews. Swad 256 A4
Brook La. Alf 159 D2
Brook La. Clowne 80 C2
Brook La. Crich 168 B3
Brook La. Hatton 227 E2
Brook La. Ripley 180 B4
Brook La. S Hill 228 A4
Brook Lea. Mat 143 E2
Brook Meadow. Glos 10 C1
Brook Rd. Elv 233 F2
Brook Rd. Ock 221 E1
Brook Rd. Shef 43 D3
Brook Side. Bake 109 E3
Brook St. Barl 79 E4
Brook St. Cl Cr 131 D2
Brook St. Derby 218 C3
Brook St. Glos 10 B1
Brook St. Harts 257 D4
Brook St. Hean 181 D3
Brook St. Ripley 168 B1
Brook St. Ripley 168 C1
Brook St. Swad 255 F3
Brook St. Swad 256 A2
Brook St. Tibs 148 A3
Brook Vale Cl. Barlow 75 E2
Brook Vale Rd. La Mi 182 B1
Brook Wlk. Derby 218 C3
Brook Yd. Chest 95 F2
Brookbank Ave. Chest 95 E2
Brookbank Rd. Clowne 80 C2
Brookdale Ave. Marple 23 D2
Brookdale Rd. Harts 257 D2
Brooke Dr. Chest 96 C3
Brooke St. Ilk 209 D3
Brooke St. Sand 223 D3
Brookfield Ave. Chest 95 D1
Brookfield Ave. Derby 220 A4
Brookfield Ave. Derby 231 E3
Brookfield Cl. Codnor 170 A1
Brookfield Cres. Shireb 119 F3
Brookfield La. Bake 109 F4
Brookfield Rd. Bols 118 A4
Brookfield Way. Tans 143 F2
Brookfield. Ba on T 244 A3
Brookfields Dr. Bread 205 E2
Brookfields. Calver 72 B1
Brookfields. Hors 191 F4
Brookhill Ave. Pinx 160 B2
Brookhill La. Pinx 160 C3
Brookhill Leys Rd. East 182 C1
Brookhill Rd. Pinx 160 B1
Brookhill St. Staple 223 E3
Brookhill. Clowne 80 C2
Brookhouse St. Derby 232 B3
Brooklands Ave. C-Frith 47 E3
Brooklands Ave. Hean 181 F1
Brooklands Ave. Wirk 165 F4
Brooklands Bank. Bake 109 F3
Brooklands Dr. Derby 231 E4
Brooklands Rd. C-Frith 47 E3
Brooklands. Bux 85 E4
Brookleton. Youl 125 E3
Brooklyn Dr. Chest 95 E2
Brooklyn Pl. Shef 43 D3
Brooklyn Rd. Shef 43 D3
Brooks Hollow. Lit Ea 205 E4
Brooks Rd. Stav 78 A2
Brookside Ave. Mans 136 B3
Brookside Bar. Chest 94 C1
Brookside Cl. Derby 218 C4
Brookside Cl. Glos 9 F2
Brookside Cl. Lo Ea 236 A4
Brookside Cl. Rep 242 B1
Brookside Glen. Chest 94 C1
Brookside Gr. Bux 84 B3
Brookside Rd. Bread 205 F2
Brookside Rd. C-Frith 47 D3
Brookside. Ashb 173 E1
Brookside. Beeley 111 D2
Brookside. Belper 178 C2
Brookside. Bradw 51 D4
Brookside. Bu on T 248 A3
Brookside. Chin 34 A1
Brookside. Glos 17 D4
Brookside. Greas 182 C2
Brookside. N Mills 24 C4
Brookside. Rolle 240 A2
Brookvale Ave. Codnor 181 D4
Brookvale Ave. Denby 180 A1
Brookvale Rd. Denby 180 A1
Brookvale Rise. Denby 180 A1
Brookview Ct. Dron 57 D2
Broom Ave. Pils 132 B1
Broom Ave. Som 169 F4
Broom Cl. Belper 178 C3
Broom Cl. Chest 95 E4
Broom Cl. Derby 231 F1
Broom Cl. Derby 232 C1
Broom Cl. Duff 190 B2
Broom Dr. Gra 115 F1
Broom Gdns. Chest 96 C4
Broom La. K Ire 175 F4
Broom's La. Scro 226 A1
Broombank Park. Chest 76 B2
Broombank Rd. Chest 76 B2
Broomfield Ave. Chest 115 E4
Broomfield Cl. Sand 223 D3
Broomhill Ave. Ilk 209 D3
Broomhill Cl. Derby 217 E2
Broomhill Cl. Eck 59 D2
Broomhill Rd. Chest 76 C1
Broomhills La. Rep 242 B1
Broomyclose La. Utt 210 A2
Brosscroft Village. Glos 10 A3
Brosscroft. Glos 10 A3
Brough La. Bradw 51 E4
Brough La. Shat 51 E4
Brough Rd. Bu on T 248 B2
Brough St. Derby 218 B3
Brougham Ave. Mans 135 E1
Broughton Ave. Derby 218 B1
Broughton Cl. Ch Bro 227 D4
Broughton Rd. Chest 95 E4
Brow Cres. Mosb 59 F4
Brown Ave. Mans 136 A2
Brown Edge Rd. Bux 66 B1
Brown Hills La. Lod M 42 B4
Brown La. Ash 145 D4
Brown La. B in F 237 F3
Brown La. Dron 57 E2
Brown's Flats. Kim 195 F3
Brown's La. Holbr 191 E4
Brown's Rd. Lo Ea 236 C4
Brown's Yd. Som 170 B4
Brownhill La. Holme 3 D4
Brownhills La. Ash 130 B2
Browning Circ. Derby 231 F4
Browning Rd. Swad 256 B3
Browning St. Derby 231 F4
Brownlow Rd. Mans 135 F1
Broxtowe Ave. Kim 195 E3
Brun La. K Lang 217 D4
Brun La. Mack 217 D4
Brunnen The. S Norm 160 A2
Brunner Ave. Shireb 119 F2
Brunswick Dr. Staple 223 F3
Brunswick St. Chest 96 A2
Brunswick St. Derby 231 F4
Brunswick St. Pils 132 B1
Brunswood Cl. Derby 220 C3
Brunswood La. Bradl 187 E4
Brunswood Rd. Mat Ba 143 D1
Brunton Cl. Derby 217 E1
Brushes Rd. M in L 4 A2
Brushfield Gr. Shef 44 B2
Brushfield Rd. Chest 94 C3
Brussels Terr. Ilk 194 C1
Bryn Lea. Chest 96 B1
Brynsmoor Rd. Brin 182 C4
Bryony Cl. Derby 206 A1
Bryony Cl. Kill 60 A3
Bsns Centre. Ripley 180 C4
Bubnell Rd. Baslow 91 E3
Buchan St. Derby 232 B4
Buchanan St. Derby 219 D3
Buck Wood View. Shef 43 E3
Buckden Cl. Chest 95 E2
Buckfast Cl. Som 169 F4
Buckhazels La. Mack 203 D4
Buckingham Ave. Derby 219 E4
Buckingham Cl. Dron 56 B1
Buckingham Cl. Mans 136 C3
Buckingham Cl. Som 170 A4
Buckingham Ct. Bu on T 248 B2
Buckingham Ct. Sand 223 D2
Buckingham Rd. Sand 223 D2
Buckland Cl. Derby 218 C3
Buckland Gr. Marple 15 D4
Buckleather La. Barlow 74 B1
Buckley Cl. Wood 256 C1
Buckminster Cl. Derby 205 F1
Buckminster Rd. Ilk 208 B2
Bull La. Mat 143 E3
Bullace Ct. Mans 136 C1
Bullbridge Hill. Ripley 168 A3
Buller St. Derby 218 C1
Buller St. Ilk 209 D3
Bullhill La. H Ward 176 C2
Bullhurst La. W Und 188 C2
Bulling La. Crich 156 C1
Bullivant Ave. Elmt 100 B4
Bullock Cl. Mans 136 A3
Bullock La. Brai 201 F4
Bullock La. Iron 170 C3
Bullock La. Som 170 C3
Bullpit La. Duff 205 D4
Bullsmore. Belper 179 E2
Bumpmill La. Shirl 146 A1
Bungalows The. Chest 95 E2
Bungalows The. Chest 95 F4
Bungalows The. Chest 96 A1
Bungalows The. Chest 96 A4
Bungalows The. Kill 60 B3
Bungalows The. Shirl 146 C2
Bunker S Hill. Kill 60 C3
Bunker's Hill. Th Sa 62 B4
Bunting Cl. Chest 95 D1
Bunting Cl. Ilk 208 B3
Bunting Cl. Shef 43 D1
Bunting House. Chest 77 D2
Bunting Nook. Shef 43 D1
Buntingfield La. Ash 129 D4
Buntings Cl. Derby 218 A2
Bunyan Cres. Shirl 146 C2
Bunyan Green Rd. Sels 171 E4
Burbage Cl. Belper 179 E3
Burbage Cl. Dron 56 B1
Burbage Gr. Shef 44 B3
Burbage Pl. Derby 232 C4
Burbage Rd. Stav 97 E4
Burcot Cl. We Ha 207 F4
Burdekin Cl. C-Frith 47 E3
Burdett Way. Rep 242 B2
Burdock Cl. Derby 205 F1
Burgess Cl. Chest 115 E4
Burghley Cl. Derby 232 C1
Burke Dr. Som 170 B4
Burkitt Dr. Stav 79 D2
Burland Green La. W Und 189 D2
Burleigh Cres. Som 169 F4
Burleigh Dr. Derby 218 C4
Burleigh St. Ilk 194 C1
Burley Bank La. Holme 2 C4
Burley Cl. Chest 115 D4
Burley Dr. Quar 204 C4
Burley Hill. Duff 205 D4
Burley La. Quar 204 C4
Burlington Ave. Shireb 119 F3
Burlington Cl. Brea 235 E4
Burlington Dr. Mans 135 F1
Burlington Glen. Totley 55 F4
Burlington Gr. Totley 55 F4
Burlington Rd. Bux 85 D4
Burlington Rd. Derby 217 F3
Burlington Rd. Totley 55 F4
Burlington St. Chest 96 A2
Burlington Way. Derby 217 E1
Burlow Ave. Bux 85 E2
Burlow Rd. Bux 85 E1
Burnaby St. Derby 232 C4
Burnage Ct. Derby 218 C2
Burnaston Cl. Shef 56 C4
Burnaston Ct. Mans 136 C2
Burnaston La. Etwall 229 E3
Burnbridge Rd. Uns 77 E3
Burncroft. We Ha 207 F4
Burnell St. Chest 96 C4
Burnett La. Da Da 143 D4
Burney La. Br Hill 252 B1
Burney La. Lount 252 B1
Burnham Cl. We Ha 207 E4
Burnham Dr. Derby 217 E1
Burns Ave. Mans 136 B1
Burns Cl. Chest 114 C4
Burns Cl. Derby 231 D4
Burns Dr. Dron 76 B4
Burns Dr. Gra 115 F2
Burns St. Ilk 208 C4
Burnshaw St. Shirl 146 B3
Burnside Ave. Shef 43 D3
Burnside Ave. Shirl 146 B1
Burnside Cl. Derby 231 E2
Burnside Dr. Derby 220 C2
Burnside St. Derby 233 D4
Burnside. Glos 9 F2
Burnside. Rolle 240 A2
Burnt House Rd. Hean 181 E1
Burnt Oaks Cl. Mans 136 B2
Burr La. Ilk 194 C1
Burre Cl. Bake 109 F3
Burrfields Rd. C-Frith 47 D3
Burrowfield Mews. Derby 220 C1
Burrows La. Brai 201 F1
Burrows La. Mid 154 B3
Burrows La. Trus 201 F1
Burrows The. Swad 255 F3
Bursdon Cl. Chest 77 D1
Burton Close Dr. Bake 109 F2
Burton Edge. Bake 109 E2
Burton Rd. Bran 254 A4
Burton Rd. C Elms 260 B2
Burton Rd. Derby 218 B1
Burton Rd. Fin 230 B2
Burton Rd. Linton 255 E1
Burton Rd. Over 262 A2
Burton Rd. Rep 242 A1
Burton Rd. Rosl 260 B3
Burton Rd. Swad 256 B3
Burton Rd. Tick 250 C2
Burton Rd. Tut 239 E2
Burton Rd. Will 241 F4
Burton St. Hean 181 F1
Burton St. Tut 239 E3
Burwell Cl. Glos 17 D4
Burwell Ct. Mans 136 C2
Bush Vale. Belper 178 C3
Bushey Wood Rd. Totley 55 F3
Bushton La. Bu on T 239 D1
Bushton La. Tut 239 D1
Buskeyfield La. Nort 101 F2
Butcher's La. Da Da 127 F2
Bute St. Glos 10 C2
Butler Cres. Mans 135 E1
Butler Way. Kill 60 B3
Butt Hill. Whit 81 F3
Butt La. Black 257 D1
Butt La. Mans 136 B1
Butt St. Sand 223 D3
Butterfield Cres. Som 169 F4
Butterfield La. Brack 145 F1
Butterhall Cl. Whit 82 A3
Butterley Croft Bsns Centre. Ripley 180 C4
Butterley Hill. Ripley 169 F2
Butterley La. Ash 144 C3
Butterley La. Ripley 169 E2
Buttermead Cl. Staple 209 E1
Buttermere Cl. Chest 95 E4
Buttermere Dr. Derby 204 C2
Buttermere Dr. Dron 56 C1
Buttermilk La. Bols 98 B2
Buttermilk La. L Duk 98 B2
Butterpot La. Thurv 215 E2
Butterton Cl. Ilk 209 D4
Butterton Dr. Chest 95 D3
Buttonoak Dr. Derby 233 D2
Butts Hill. Totley 55 E2
Butts Rd. Ash 129 F2
Butts Rd. Bake 109 E3
Butts Rd. Da Da 127 D2
Butts Terr. Bake 109 E3
Butts The. Belper 179 D2
Butts View. Bake 109 E3
Buxton Ave. Hean 193 F4
Buxton Cl. Swad 256 A4
Buxton Ct. Ilk 194 B1
Buxton Dr. Derby 217 F2
Buxton Dr. Lit Ea 191 E1
Buxton Mews. Glos 9 F1
Buxton New Rd. Mac For 83 D3
Buxton Old Rd. Disley 32 C2
Buxton Rd W. Disley 32 A3
Buxton Rd. A in W 108 C4
Buxton Rd. Alst 149 D3
Buxton Rd. Bake 109 D4
Buxton Rd. C-Frith 47 E3
Buxton Rd. C-Frith 66 C4
Buxton Rd. Chin 34 C1
Buxton Rd. Derby 219 F4
Buxton Rd. Disley 32 C3
Buxton Rd. H La 32 A
Buxton Rd. Long 121 D
Buxton Rd. Mans 135 E
Buxton Rd. N Mills 33 E
Buxton Rd. Tide 69 E
Buxton Rd. W Br 33 E
Buxton Terr. M in L 9 E
Byfield Cl. Derby 206 A
Byng Ave. Derby 231 F
Byron Ave. Alf 159 D
Byron Ave. Bu on T 254 C
Byron Ave. Lo Ea 223 D
Byron Ave. Mans 136 B
Byron Cl. Dron 76 B
Byron Cl. Gra 115 F
Byron Cres. Awsw 195 E
Byron Ct. Staple 209 F
Byron Gr. Shirl 146 C
Byron Rd. Chest 115 D
Byron Rd. Swad 256 B
Byron St. Bux 85 E
Byron St. Chest 96 A
Byron St. Derby 218 C
Byron St. Ilk 194 C
Byron St. Shireb 119 F
Byron St. Shirl 146 B
Bywell La. Kilb 179 F

Cacklehill La. Snel 184 B
Cadeby Ct. Som 170 B
Cadgwith Dr. Derby 204 C
Cadley Hill Rd. Swad 255 F
Cadman Ct. Mosb 59 E
Cadman Rd. Shef 44 E
Cadman St. Mosb 59 E
Cadwell Cl. Derby 233 E
Caerhays Ct. Derby 231 E
Caernarfon Cl. Som 170 A
Caernarvon Cl. Chest 95 E
Caernarvon Cl. Derby 220 C
Caernarvon Rd. Dron 76 A
Caesar St. Derby 219 D
Cairn Dr. Chest 77 E
Cairngorm Cl. Chest 77 E
Cairns Cl. Derby 217 F
Cairnsmore Cl. Lo Ea 223 D
Caldene Terr. W Br 45 F
Calder Cl. Derby 204 C
Calderdale Dr. Lo Ea 236 A
Caldermill Dr. Derby 206 A
Caldey Rd. Dron 76 A
Calf Croft. Whit 82 A
Calgary Cres. Bu on T 248 B
California Gdns. Derby 218 B
California La. Barl 80 A
Calladine La. Shot 177 E
Calladine Rd. Hean 181 E
Callan's La. Ash-Z 258 E
Callow Dr. Shef 43 E
Callow Hill Way. Derby 230 C
Callow La. Callow 165 E
Callow La. Wirk 165 E
Callow Mount. Shef 43 E
Callow Pl. Shef 43 E
Callow Rd. Shef 43 E
Callywhite La. Dron 57 E
Calow Brook Dr. Chest 115 F
Calow La Ind Est. Chest 115 F
Calow La. Calow 96 C
Calow La. Chest 115 E
Calton View. Bake 109 E
Calver Ave. N Wing 132 A
Calver Cl. Derby 205 F
Calver Cres. Stav 97 E
Calver Mews. Glos 9 F
Calver Rd. Baslow 91 E
Calver St. Mans 136 C
Calvert St. Derby 219 E
Calverton Cl. Derby 232 C
Calvin Cl. Derby 233 D
Camberwell Ave. Derby 218 A
Camborne Cl. Derby 205 F
Cambria Rd. Mans 135 E
Cambrian Cl. Chest 95 E
Cambrian Way. Swad 256 A
Cambridge Cres. Al Hv 117 F
Cambridge Cres. Al Hv 117 F
Cambridge Cres. Staple 209 E
Cambridge Rd. Chest 96 C
Cambridge Rd. Shef 43 D
Cambridge St. Derby 219 D
Cambridge St. Derby 220 C
Cambridge St. Newt 147 F
Camdale Rise. Mosb 44 C
Camdale View. Mosb 44 C
Camden St. Derby 218 E
Camellia Cl. Derby 217 E
Camelot Cl. Bu on T 240 C
Cameron Cl. Bu on T 248 A
Cameron Rd. Derby 231 F
Camerory Way. Uns 77 E
Camms Cl. Eck 59 E
Camp St. Derby 219 D
Camp Wood Cl. Lit Ea 205 E
Campbell Dr. Stav 78 A
Campbell St. Belper 178 C
Campbell St. Derby 232 E
Campbell St. La Mi 182 E

mpion Hill. C Don 247 D2
mpion St. Derby 218 B3
nada St. Belper 179 D1
nal Bank. Shar 235 D1
nal Br. Kill 60 B3
nal Bridge. Will 242 A3
nal St. Derby 219 D2
nal St. Ilk 195 D1
nal St. Lo Ea 223 E1
nal St. Marple 23 D3
nal St. Sand 223 E3
nal St. W Br 45 F4
nal Wharf. Chest 96 A3
nberra Cl. Derby 217 F1
nberra Cl. Staple 209 F1
ndlemass Ct. Mans 136 B1
nner Cl. Wood 257 D1
nnock Way. Lo Ea 237 D4
nnon Fields. Hath 52 C4
nnon St. M in L 9 E3
non Cl. Ilk 194 C3
non's Wlk. Derby 204 C1
ntelupe Rd. Ilk 209 D4
nterbury Cl. Duff 190 C2
nterbury Cl. Mans 136 B3
nterbury Rd. Bu on T 248 B2
nterbury Rd. Shef 43 D3
nterbury Rd. Wirk 165 F4
nterbury St. Derby 219 F4
nterbury Terr. Wirk 165 F4
ntley Cl. Derby 232 B2
ntley Rd. Som 170 B3
pel Rise. Chest 96 B4
pthorne Cl. Chest 94 C3
r Rd. Hol 74 A3
r Vale Dr. Shef 44 B4
r Vale View. Shef 44 B4
rdale Rd. Mans 135 E2
rdales Cl. Fin 230 B1
rder Green. Long 121 D3
rdigan St. Derby 219 E4
rdlemere La. Biggin 138 F1
rdrona Cl. Derby 205 F1
rfield Ave. Shef 43 D3
rfield La. Shef 43 E3
rfield Pl. Shef 43 D3
risbrooke Gdns. Derby 231 E3
rlin Cl. Brea 235 F4
rlin St. Shef 44 C3
rlisle Ave. Derby 231 D4
rlisle Cl. Chest 76 C2
rlisle Gr. Bux 85 D4
rlisle Rd. Bux 84 C4
rlton Ave. Derby 232 C2
rlton Ave. North 127 D3
rlton Cl. Cl Cr 131 E1
rlton Cl. Hean 182 A2
rlton Cl. Mosb 59 E3
rlton Dr. Derby 232 C2
rlton Gdns. Derby 232 C2
rlton Rd. Chest 115 D3
rlton Rd. Derby 218 C1
rlton Rd. Lo Ea 236 A3
rlton St. Mans 136 B1
rlyle Rd. Shirl 146 C2
rlyle St. Derby 231 F3
rlyle St. Hean 181 E2
rlyon Gdns. Chest 114 C4
rnarvon Rd. S in A 148 C1
rnegie St. Derby 232 A4
rnfield Hill. S Norm 159 E3
rnforth Cl. Derby 217 F1
rnforth Cl. Staple 223 E3
rnoustie Ave. Chest 114 B4
rnoustie Cl. Derby 217 F1
rol Cres. Derby 219 F3
roline Cl. Derby 233 E4
roline Ct. Ilk 209 D3
rpenter Ave. Mans 135 E1
rpenter Ave. Stav 79 D2
rpenter Croft. Shef 44 B3
rpenter Gdns. Shef 44 B3
rpenter Mews. Shef 44 B3
rper La. Brai 187 F1
rr Brow. H La 32 A4
rr Cl. S Norm 160 A4
rr Fields. H Wood 192 B4
rr La. Brack 145 E2
rr La. Crich 156 C1
rr La. Mat 143 F1
rr La. S Norm 160 A4
rr La. Scarc 117 F4
rr La. Thor 39 F3
rr Vale Rd. Bols 98 C2
rrfield Ave. Bees 223 F1
rrfield Ave. Lo Ea 223 F1
rrfield Ct. Shef 43 D3
rrfield Dr. Shef 43 D3
rrfield Rd. Shef 43 D3
rrfield St. Shef 43 D3
rrhouse La. M in L 9 E2
rriage Dr The. Glos 9 F3
rriers Rd. Eg 241 E3
rrington St. Derby 219 D2
rron Cl. Derby 231 F2
rrs Cl. C Don 247 D2
rrwood Rd. Chest 76 A2
rrwood Rd. Eck 79 D4
Carsington Cl. Chest 95 D3
Carsington Cres. Derby 204 B1
Carsington Ct. Mans 136 C2
Carsington Mews. Derby 204 C1
Carson Croft. Mat 143 E3
Carson Mount. Shef 44 A2
Carson Rd. Derby 220 A3
Carter La E. S Norm 160 B3
Carter La W. S Norm 160 B3
Carter La W. Shireb 119 E2
Carter La. Mar War 120 B2
Carter La. Shireb 119 F2
Carter Pl. Shef 43 D3
Carter Rd. Bees 223 F1
Carter Rd. Shef 43 D3
Carter St. Derby 232 B3
Carterhall La. Eck 44 B1
Carterhall La. Shef 44 B1
Carterhall Rd. Shef 44 A1
Cartledge La. Hol 75 D4
Cartmel Cl. Dron 56 C1
Cartmel Cres. Chest 95 F4
Cartworth Moor Rd. Holme 3 F4
Cartwright St. Shire 63 F4
Cary Rd. Eck 59 D2
Cary Rd. Shef 44 A4
Casson Ave. Derby 233 D3
Casson Dr. Hello 61 A1
Casson St. Iron 170 C2
Castings Rd. Derby 232 A4
Castle Cl. Bake 109 F3
Castle Croft. Derby 233 E3
Castle Ct. Elv 234 A3
Castle Ct. Tut 239 E4
Castle Dr. Bake 109 F4
Castle Dr. Codnor 181 F4
Castle Dr. Som 170 B4
Castle Edge Rd. N Mills 24 A1
Castle Green. Scarc 118 A4
Castle Hayes La. Tut 239 D3
Castle Hill Cl. Eck 59 E2
Castle Hill. C Don 247 D2
Castle Hill. Duff 190 C2
Castle Hill. Eck 59 E2
Castle Hill. Fin 230 B1
Castle Hill. Glos 10 C1
Castle House. Derby 219 E2
Castle La. Bols 99 D1
Castle La. Iron 170 C1
Castle La. Mel 252 A4
Castle Mews The. Swad 256 A4
Castle Mews. Mel 252 A4
Castle Mills. Mel 252 A4
Castle Mount Cres. Bake 109 E4
Castle Mount Way. Bake 109 F4
Castle Orch. Duff 190 C2
Castle Rd. Swad 255 F1
Castle Row. Shef 56 A3
Castle St. Bake 109 E3
Castle St. Bols 99 D1
Castle St. Cas 38 A1
Castle St. Derby 219 D2
Castle St. Glos 10 A2
Castle St. Mans 136 A2
Castle St. Mel 252 A4
Castle St. Tut 239 E3
Castle View Dr. Mat Ba 155 E3
Castle View. Ald 182 A2
Castle View. Eck 59 E2
Castle Way The. Will 241 F3
Castle Yd. Chest 96 A1
Castlebeck Ave. Shef 44 B4
Castlebeck Dr. Shef 44 B4
Castlecraig Ct. Derby 231 F1
Castledale Croft. Shef 44 A4
Castledale Gr. Shef 44 B4
Castledale Pl. Shef 44 A4
Castlefields. Iron 170 C2
Castlegate La. G Low 89 E3
Castlerigg Way. Dron 56 C1
Castlerow Cl. Shef 56 A3
Castlerow Dr. Shef 56 A3
Castleshaw Dr. Derby 230 C4
Castleton Ave. Derby 231 F4
Castleton Ave. Ilk 194 C3
Castleton Ave. Som 170 B3
Castleton Cl. Mans 136 B2
Castleton Cres. Glos 9 F1
Castleton Gr. Chest 97 D3
Castleton Rd. Hath 52 C4
Castleton Rd. Hope 38 C2
Castleview. Hatton 239 E4
Cat And Fiddle La. Dale 207 F3
Cat La. Shef 43 E3
Catchford View. Chest 95 D4
Catcliff Cl. Bake 109 E2
Catcliff Cotts. Bake 109 E3
Cathedral Rd. Derby 219 D3
Cathedral View. Derby 218 B1
Catherine Ave. Ilk 208 C3
Catherine Ave. Mans 136 B2
Catherine St. Alf 159 E2
Catherine St. Chest 95 F2
Catherine St. Derby 219 D1
Catholme La. B-u-Ne 259 D2
Catkin Dr. Greas 195 E4
Cator Rd. Mans 135 E2
Catterick Dr. Derby 217 E1
Catterwood Dr. Marple 15 D1
Catton La. Rosl 260 A3
Catton La. Wa on T 260 A3
Caudwell Cl. Tupton 131 E4
Cauldron Dr. Chest 95 D3
Cauldwell Rd. Cald 261 D3
Cauldwell Rd. Linton 261 D3
Causeway Gdns. Totley 55 E4
Causeway Head Rd. Totley 55 E4
Causeway La. Mat 143 E3
Causeway The. Eyam F3 71
Causeway The. Ash 129 E2
Causeway The. Totley 55 E4
Causeway The. Wirk 165 F4
Causeway. Derby 204 C1
Cavan Dr. Derby 220 A2
Cavell Dr. Cl Cr 131 F1
Cavendish Ave. Bux 84 C3
Cavendish Ave. Derby 204 C2
Cavendish Ave. Totley 55 F4
Cavendish Cir. Bux 85 D4
Cavendish Cl. C Don 247 D1
Cavendish Cl. Dove 211 E1
Cavendish Cl. Duff 190 B1
Cavendish Cl. N Wing 116 C1
Cavendish Cl. Shar 235 D1
Cavendish Cres. Staple 209 E1
Cavendish Ct. Derby 218 C3
Cavendish Ct. Shar 235 D1
Cavendish Dr. Ashb 185 E4
Cavendish Dr. Clowne 81 D2
Cavendish Dr. Ripley 169 E1
Cavendish Park. Mat 143 E4
Cavendish Pl. Stav 78 A2
Cavendish Rd. Bols 99 D1
Cavendish Rd. Ilk 208 C3
Cavendish Rd. Lo Ea 223 E1
Cavendish Rd. Mat 143 E3
Cavendish Rise. Dron 75 F4
Cavendish Sq. Uns 77 E4
Cavendish St N. Chest 77 D1
Cavendish St. Chest 96 A2
Cavendish St. Derby 218 C3
Cavendish St. Mans 136 A2
Cavendish St. Scarc 119 F4
Cavendish St. Stav 97 E4
Cavendish Way. Derby 217 F1
Caversfield Cl. Derby 231 D4
Caversham Way. We Ha 207 E4
Cavill Rd. Shef 43 D2
Cawdor Rd. Shef 43 F3
Caxton Cl. Uns 77 E3
Caxton Ct. Derby 231 F3
Caxton St. Derby 231 F3
Caxton St. Derby 231 F4
Caythorpe Ct. Mans 136 C2
Ceal The. Marple 15 D1
Cecil Ave. Dron 57 D1
Cecil Rd. Dron 57 D1
Cecil Rd. Swad 255 F3
Cecil St. Derby 218 B3
Cedar Ave. Alf 159 D3
Cedar Ave. Chest 95 E3
Cedar Ave. Lo Ea 236 B3
Cedar Ave. Mans 136 B3
Cedar Ave. Ripley 169 E1
Cedar Ave. Ripley 180 B4
Cedar Cl. Ashb 185 E4
Cedar Cl. Eck 59 D1
Cedar Cl. Glap 118 A1
Cedar Cl. Glos 10 A1
Cedar Cl. Kill 60 B3
Cedar Cl. Sand 223 D4
Cedar Croft. Kilb 192 A4
Cedar Dr. Ock 221 E2
Cedar Dr. Sels 171 F4
Cedar Dr. Utt 210 A2
Cedar Gr. Belper 179 D1
Cedar Gr. Linton 261 E3
Cedar Gr. S Norm 160 A2
Cedar Gr. Swad 256 A4
Cedar Park. Ilk 208 C4
Cedar Rd. C Don 247 D1
Cedar Rd. Linton 261 F4
Cedar St. Derby 218 C4
Cedar St. Shirl 146 B3
Cedar St. Stav 78 A1
Cedarwood Ct. Derby 205 F1
Celandine Cl. Derby 206 A1
Celandine Ct. Shef 56 A3
Celandine Gdns. Shef 56 A3
Celanese Rd. Derby 220 B2
Cemetery La. Ripley 169 F1
Cemetery La. Stav 78 C1
Cemetery La. Wirk 154 C1
Cemetery Rd. Belper 179 D3
Cemetery Rd. Chest 96 B1
Cemetery Rd. Cl Cr 131 F1
Cemetery Rd. Dron 76 A4
Cemetery Rd. Glos 10 B2
Cemetery Rd. Som 170 B4
Cemetery Rd. Staple 223 F4
Cemetery Terr. Chest 96 C4
Central Ave. Chest 95 F1
Central Ave. Elmt 100 B4
Central Ave. Ock 221 D1
Central Ave. S Norm 160 A3
Central Ave. Sand 223 D3
Central Ave. Stanl 207 D4
Central Ave. Staple 223 F4
Central Cl. Shireb 119 F2
Central Cl. Uns 76 C3
Central Dr. Bux 85 E3
Central Dr. Calow 96 C2
Central Dr. Chest 96 B1
Central Dr. Newt 147 F1
Central Dr. Shireb 119 F2
Central Dr. Win 114 C2
Central Pavement. Chest 96 A2
Central Rd. Alf 159 D2
Central St. Chest 96 B1
Central St. N Wing 132 C4
Central Walk. Chest 96 B4
Centre Ct. Derby 219 D2
Centre St. Al Hv 117 E1
Centurion Wlk. Derby 219 D4
Chaddesden Cl. Shef 56 C4
Chaddesden La End.
Derby 219 F3
Chaddesden La. Derby 220 A3
Chaddesden Park Rd.
Derby 219 F4
Chadfield Rd. Duff 190 C3
Chadwick Ave. Derby 232 C3
Chadwick Hill. Elton 141 D3
Chadwick Nick La. Crich 167 F4
Chadwick Rd. Shef 44 B4
Chadwick St. Glos 17 D4
Chaffinch Cl. Derby 220 C3
Chain La. Derby 218 A1
Chalfont Sq. Derby 206 A1
Chalkley Cl. Derby 232 C4
Challands Cl. Chest 115 E4
Challands Way. Chest 115 E4
Challis Ave. Derby 220 A4
Challoner Green. Mosb 59 F4
Challoner Way. Mosb 59 F4
Chalons Cl. Ilk 194 C1
Chalons Way. Ilk 194 C1
Chalons Way. Ilk 208 C4
Chambers Ave. Ilk 209 D4
Chambers Ct. M in L 9 D2
Chambers St. Derby 219 F1
Champion Dr. Kill 60 B3
Champion Hill. Duff 190 C2
Chancel Pl. Derby 218 C2
Chancery La. Derby 218 A3
Chancet Wood Cl. Shef 56 C4
Chancet Wood Dr. Shef 56 C4
Chancet Wood Rd. Shef 56 C4
Chancet Wood Rise. Shef 56 C4
Chancet Wood View. Shef 56 C4
Chander Hill La. Holy 113 E4
Chandlers Ford. Derby 205 F1
Chandos Cres. Kill 60 B3
Chandos Pole St. Derby 218 B3
Chandres Ct. Derby 204 C2
Chaneyfield Way. Chest 95 D4
Channel The. Ashb 173 D1
Chantrey Ave. Chest 96 A3
Chantrey Rd. Shef 43 D2
Chantry Cl. Derby 217 E1
Chantry Cl. Disley 32 C3
Chantry Cl. Lo Ea 236 A2
Chantry Ct. Tide 69 E2
Chantry Fold. Disley 32 C3
Chantry La. Tide 69 E2
Chantry Rd. Disley 32 B3
Chapel Brow. Cha 16 C3
Chapel Brow. Tint 10 A4
Chapel Cl. Moira 256 B1
Chapel Cl. Will 242 A3
Chapel Cl. Youl 125 D3
Chapel Croft. Elton 140 C3
Chapel Croft. Mid 154 B3
Chapel Green. Dove 224 B4
Chapel Hill. Ash 129 F2
Chapel Hill. Beeley 111 D2
Chapel Hill. Bons 155 D4
Chapel Houses. Marple 23 D3
Chapel La E. Chest 115 E4
Chapel La W. Chest 95 E1
Chapel La. Ba on T 244 A3
Chapel La. Bake 109 E3
Chapel La. Boyl 213 D2
Chapel La. Ch Bro 227 D4
Chapel La. Crich 168 A4
Chapel La. Derby 220 A4
Chapel La. Derby 220 C3
Chapel La. Derby 233 D1
Chapel La. Glos 9 F3
Chapel La. Han 238 A1
Chapel La. Hollow 156 A3
Chapel La. Mid 154 B3
Chapel La. Rolle 240 A2
Chapel La. Tiss 162 A3
Chapel La. Totley 55 E2
Chapel La. Uns 58 A1
Chapel La. Wirk 154 C1
Chapel Pl. Kim 195 F3
Chapel Rd. Bols 98 C2
Chapel Rd. Gra 115 F2
Chapel Rd. Hay 25 E1
Chapel Rd. Sels 171 F3
Chapel Rd. W Br 45 F3
Chapel Row. Crich 168 A4
Chapel Row. Ock 221 D1
Chapel Side. Derby 220 C3
Chapel St. Alf 159 D2
Chapel St. Belper 178 C2
Chapel St. Bux 85 D4
Chapel St. C Elms 260 B2
Chapel St. Chest 96 A4
Chapel St. Chest 96 C4
Chapel St. Crich 168 A3
Chapel St. Derby 219 D3
Chapel St. Derby 220 C3
Chapel St. Donis 265 F3
Chapel St. Donis 265 F4
Chapel St. Duff 190 C2
Chapel St. East 182 C1
Chapel St. Glos 10 B1
Chapel St. Hay 25 E1
Chapel St. Hean 194 A4
Chapel St. Holbr 191 E4
Chapel St. Ilk 194 C1
Chapel St. Kilb 192 A4
Chapel St. Kim 195 F3
Chapel St. Linton 261 F4
Chapel St. Lo Ea 236 C4
Chapel St. Long 121 D3
Chapel St. Mel 252 A4
Chapel St. Mo 107 D1
Chapel St. Mosb 59 E3
Chapel St. N Mills 24 C4
Chapel St. N Mills 33 D3
Chapel St. Ripley 169 E1
Chapel St. Scarc 101 D2
Chapel St. Shirl 147 D2
Chapel St. Smisby 257 F2
Chapel St. Som 169 F4
Chapel St. Som 170 B4
Chapel St. Swad 255 F3
Chapel St. Swad 256 A1
Chapel St. Tick 251 D3
Chapel St. W Br 45 F4
Chapel St. Wood 256 C1
Chapel Way. Tupton 115 E1
Chapel Wlk. Curbar 72 C1
Chapel Yd. Dron 57 D1
Chapman Ave. Derby 233 D3
Chapman La. Gra 115 F2
Chapter Cl. Derby 205 E1
Chardin Ave. Marple 23 E4
Charingworth Rd. Derby 206 A1
Chariot Cl. Derby 233 E3
Charity Rd. Som 170 B3
Charlbury Cl. Derby 231 D4
Charles Ashmore Rd. Shef 57 D4
Charles Ave. Derby 220 B3
Charles Ave. Sand 223 D3
Charles Ave. Staple 223 F4
Charles Cl. Ilk 209 D3
Charles La. Glos 10 C2
Charles St. Alf 159 D3
Charles St. Bux 85 E4
Charles St. Chest 95 F2
Charles St. Glos 10 B1
Charles St. Lo Ea 236 B3
Charles St. Mans 136 A1
Charles St. Mans 136 B2
Charles St. Som 170 B4
Charles St. Swad 256 A1
Charleston Cl. Swad 256 A4
Charleston Rd. Derby 220 B3
Charlestown Dr. Derby 204 B2
Charlestown Rd. Glos 17 E4
Charlestown. Glos 17 E3
Charlesworth Cres. W Br 33 E2
Charlesworth Ct. Mans 136 C2
Charlesworth Rd. W Br 33 E2
Charlesworth St. Bols 117 F4
Charley La. Chin 47 D4
Charlotte La. Bradw 51 D4
Charlotte Rd. Shef 43 D4
Charlotte St. Derby 219 D1
Charlton Ave. Lo Ea 223 F1
Charlton Cl. Linton 261 E3
Charnock Ave. Shef 44 A1
Charnock Cres. Shef 44 A2
Charnock Dale Rd. Shef 44 A1
Charnock Dr. Shef 44 A2
Charnock Gr. Shef 44 A1
Charnock Hall Rd. Shef 44 A1
Charnock View Rd. Shef 44 A1
Charnock Wood Rd. Shef 44 A1
Charnwood Ave. Belper 179 D2
Charnwood Ave. C Don 247 E2
Charnwood Ave. Derby 231 E3
Charnwood Ave. Lo Ea 236 A2
Charnwood Ave. Ock 221 E1
Charnwood Ave. Sand 223 D2
Charnwood Cres. Newt 148 A2
Charnwood Dr. Ripley 169 E1
Charnwood Gr. Mans 136 A3
Charnwood St. Derby 219 D2
Charter Park. Ilk 208 C4
Charterhouse Cl. Derby 205 F2
Charterstone La. Derby 204 C2
Chartwell Ave. Win 114 B3
Chartwell Dr. Derby 219 E3
Chase Rd. Ripley 167 F2
Chase The. Derby 231 F2
Chase The. Kilb 192 A4

Chase The. Lit Ea 191 E1
Chase View. Crich 156 C1
Chasecliff Cl. Chest 95 E3
Chatham Ave. Alf 159 E2
Chatham St. Derby 232 A4
Chatsworth Ave. Chest 95 D1
Chatsworth Ave. Clowne 80 C2
Chatsworth Ave. Crich 156 C1
Chatsworth Ave. Da Da 142 C4
Chatsworth Ave. Lo Ea 237 D3
Chatsworth Ave. Shireb 119 F3
Chatsworth Cl. Alf 158 C2
Chatsworth Cl. Sand 223 D2
Chatsworth Cres. Derby 204 C2
Chatsworth Cres. Ripley 168 A3
Chatsworth Ct. Derby 231 F2
Chatsworth Ct. Stav 97 E4
Chatsworth Ct. We Ha 207 F4
Chatsworth Dr. Derby 217 F2
Chatsworth Dr. Lit Ea 191 E1
Chatsworth Dr. N Wing 131 F3
Chatsworth Dr. Tut 239 E3
Chatsworth Lodge. Bux 85 D4
Chatsworth Park Ave. Shef 44 A3
Chatsworth Park Dr. Shef 44 A3
Chatsworth Park Gr. Shef 44 A3
Chatsworth Park Rd. Shef 44 A3
Chatsworth Park Rise. Shef 44 A3
Chatsworth Pl. Dron 56 B1
Chatsworth Pl. Ilk 208 A3
Chatsworth Rd. Bux 85 F4
Chatsworth Rd. Chest 95 E1
Chatsworth Rd. Elmt 81 E1
Chatsworth Rd. Row 111 D1
Chatsworth Rd. Swad 256 A3
Chatsworth Rd. Totley 55 F3
Chatsworth St. Derby 218 C1
Chatsworth St. Tibs 148 A3
Chatteris Dr. Derby 205 E1
Chatterton La. Marple 24 A4
Chaucer Dr. Dron 76 B4
Chaucer Rd. Chest 95 F4
Chaucer St. Ilk 194 C1
Chavery Rd. Cl Cr 131 F2
Cheadle Cl. Derby 218 A1
Cheadle Rd. Utt 210 A1
Cheam Cl. Derby 217 F3
Cheapside. Belper 178 C2
Cheapside. Derby 219 D3
Chedale Cl. Chest 95 E3
Chedworth Dr. Derby 233 E3
Cheedale Ave. Chest 95 E3
Cheedale Cl. Bu on T 248 A3
Cheedale. Bux 85 E4
Cheetham Ave. Uns 76 C3
Chellaston La. As on T 233 E1
Chellaston Park Ct. Derby 232 C1
Chellaston Rd. Derby 232 C2
Chelmarsh Cl. Derby 233 D2
Chelmorton Cl. Mans 136 C2
Chelmorton Pl. Derby 219 F4
Chelmsford Cl. Derby 217 E2
Chelmsford Way. Stav 78 A2
Chelsea Cl. Derby 217 F3
Cheltenham Cl. Bees 223 F1
Chelwood Rd. Derby 232 C1
Chepstow Cl. Chest 114 C4
Chepstow Gdns. Chest 114 C4
Chequer La. Shot 166 B1
Chequers La. Derby 219 E3
Chequers Rd. Derby 219 E3
Cheribough Rd. C Don 247 D2
Cheriton Cl. Mans 135 F1
Cheriton Dr. Ship 194 B2
Cheriton Gdns. Derby 230 C4
Cherry Bank Rd. Shef 43 D2
Cherry Cl. Brea 235 F4
Cherry Cl. S Norm 160 A4
Cherry Cl. Shireb 119 F3
Cherry Garth. Hilton 228 B1
Cherry Leys. Bu on T 248 B2
Cherry St S. Shef 43 D4
Cherry St. Shef 43 D4
Cherry Tree Ave. Belper 179 D3
Cherry Tree Ave. Ripley 180 B4
Cherry Tree Ave. Shire 63 F4
Cherry Tree Cl. Bols 99 E1
Cherry Tree Cl. Brin 182 C4
Cherry Tree Cl. Hilton 228 B1
Cherry Tree Cl. Ilk 208 B3
Cherry Tree Cl. Mans 136 A2
Cherry Tree Cl. Risley 222 C2
Cherry Tree Cl. Swad 255 F3
Cherry Tree Dr. Bux 66 B1
Cherry Tree Dr. Kill 60 B3
Cherry Tree Dr. Stav 98 A2
Cherry Tree Gr. N Wing 131 F3
Cherry Tree Gr. Stav 79 E2
Cherry Tree Mews. Derby 220 A2
Cherry Tree Sq. Tide 69 E2
Cherrybrook Dr. Derby 206 A2
Cherrytree Ave. Som 170 A4
Cherrytree Rd. Bu on T 254 C4
Chertpit La. G Low 89 E3
Chertsey Cl. Chest 114 C4
Chertsey Ct. We Ha 207 E4
Chertsey Rd. Derby 217 E1
Cherwell Cl. Chest 77 F1
Chesapeake Rd. Derby 220 A3
Cheshire St. Derby 232 C3
Cheshire Way. Sels 171 E2
Chess Burrow. Mans 136 B1
Chessel Cl. Shef 43 D2
Chester Ave. Derby 205 D3
Chester Ct. Derby 220 C2
Chester Gdns. Swad 256 A1
Chester Green Rd. Derby 219 D4
Chester Green. Bees 223 F1
Chester St. Chest 95 F2
Chester St. Mans 135 F1
Chesterfield Ave. Chest 77 F2
Chesterfield Ave. Lo Ea 236 C4
Chesterfield Ave. Swad 255 F3
Chesterfield Dr. Linton 261 E3
Chesterfield Rd N. Mans 135 E2
Chesterfield Rd S. Shef 57 D3
Chesterfield Rd. Alf 158 C3
Chesterfield Rd. Barl 80 A3
Chesterfield Rd. Beeley 111 D2
Chesterfield Rd. Belper 179 D2
Chesterfield Rd. Bols 98 C3
Chesterfield Rd. Calow 96 C1
Chesterfield Rd. Chest 96 B4
Chesterfield Rd. Da Da 127 E1
Chesterfield Rd. Dron 57 D1
Chesterfield Rd. Eck 59 D1
Chesterfield Rd. Gra 115 F1
Chesterfield Rd. L Duk 98 B2
Chesterfield Rd. Mat 143 E4
Chesterfield Rd. N Wing 116 B1
Chesterfield Rd. N Wing 132 A4
Chesterfield Rd. Plea 134 C4
Chesterfield Rd. Ripley 168 C2
Chesterfield Rd. Row 111 D1
Chesterfield Rd. S in A 148 C2
Chesterfield Rd. Shef 43 D3
Chesterfield Rd. Shirl 146 B2
Chesterfield Rd. Shirl 158 C3
Chesterfield Rd. Stav 97 D4
Chesterfield Rd. Tibs 133 D1
Chesterfield Rd. Uns 59 D1
Chesterfield Small Bsns Centre.
Chest 96 A4
Chesterman Cl. Awsw 195 D2
Chesterton Ave. Derby 231 F4
Chesterton Cl. Chest 96 C2
Chesterton Rd. Derby 220 C3
Chestnut Ave. Belper 179 D1
Chestnut Ave. Derby 217 E2
Chestnut Ave. Derby 219 D1
Chestnut Ave. Derby 232 C2
Chestnut Ave. Eck 59 D1
Chestnut Ave. Holbr 191 E4
Chestnut Ave. Kill 60 B3
Chestnut Ave. Ripley 180 B4
Chestnut Ave. Som 170 B3
Chestnut Ave. Swad 256 A3
Chestnut Bank. Hean 181 E1
Chestnut Cl. Dron 76 B4
Chestnut Cl. Duff 190 C1
Chestnut Cl. H Wood 192 B4
Chestnut Cl. N Mills 24 C1
Chestnut Dr. Ashb 185 E4
Chestnut Dr. Clowne 80 B2
Chestnut Dr. Elmt 81 F1
Chestnut Dr. Rep 243 E1
Chestnut Dr. S Norm 160 A2
Chestnut Dr. Sels 171 F4
Chestnut Dr. Shireb 119 E2
Chestnut Gr. Etwall 229 D2
Chestnut Gr. Mans 136 A3
Chestnut Gr. Ock 221 E2
Chestnut Gr. Sand 223 D4
Chestnut Gr. Tibs 147 F3
Chestnut La. B in F 237 F3
Chestnut La. C Camp 263 F1
Chestnut Rd. Bu on T 254 C4
Chestnut Rd. La Mi 182 A2
Chestnut Way. Rep 242 B1
Chestnut Way. Som 170 A4
Chestnuts The. Lo Ea 236 A4
Chevely Ct. Derby 219 E4
Cheverton Cl. Derby 233 E3
Chevin Ave. Derby 217 F1
Chevin Ave. Ock 221 E1
Chevin Bank. Duff 190 B3
Chevin Pl. Derby 218 C4
Chevin Rd. Belper 178 C1
Chevin Rd. Belper 190 C4
Chevin Rd. Derby 218 C4
Chevin Rd. Duff 190 C3
Chevin The. Bu on T 240 B1
Chevin Vale. Duff 190 C3
Chevin View. Belper 178 C2
Cheviot Ave. Iron 170 C2
Cheviot Cl. Swad 256 A2
Cheviot Rd. Lo Ea 223 D1
Cheviot St. Derby 218 B3
Cheviot Way. Chest 95 E3
Chew Rd. Green 5 D4
Chewton St. East 182 C1
Cheyenne Gdns. Derby 220 B3
Cheyne Wlk. Derby 218 B3
Chichester Cl. Ilk 209 D4
Chilson Dr. Derby 217 E2
Chiltern Cl. Chest 95 E2
Chiltern Cl. Gra 115 F2
Chiltern Dr. We Ha 207 F4
Chiltern Gdns. Lo Ea 223 D1
Chiltern Rd. Swad 256 A2
Chilton Cres. Mans 136 B3
Chime Cl. Derby 205 F1
Chine The. S Norm 160 A2
Chingford Ct. Derby 218 A3
Chinley Rd. Derby 206 A1
Chippinghouse Rd. Shef 43 D4
Chiswick Cl. Derby 217 F3
Chisworth Ct. Mans 136 C2
Chiverton Cl. Dron 57 D1
Chorlton Terr. Utt 210 B1
Christchurch Ct. Derby 219 D3
Chrysalis Way. East 182 B2
Chrysanthemum Ct. Swad 256 A3
Chunal La. Glos 17 E3
Church Alley. Bake 109 E3
Church Ave. Bux 67 D3
Church Ave. Cl Cr 131 F2
Church Ave. Hatton 239 E4
Church Ave. Lo Ea 236 A2
Church Ave. Swad 256 A2
Church Ave. Tide 69 E2
Church Bank. Hath 53 D4
Church Banks. Ashb 173 D1
Church Bk. W Br 45 E4
Church Broughton Rd.
Hatton 227 E2
Church Brow. C-Frith 47 D3
Church Cl. Black 257 D1
Church Cl. Bu on T 248 A2
Church Cl. Clowne 80 C2
Church Cl. Derby 233 D1
Church Cl. Eck 79 D4
Church Cl. Glos 10 C1
Church Cl. March 224 C1
Church Cl. Newt 147 E1
Church Cl. Pk F 49 D2
Church Cl. Stav 97 E4
Church Cl. Trow 209 E2
Church Cl. Will 242 A3
Church Cl. Win 115 D2
Church Cnr. K Ire 165 D1
Church Croft. C Elms 260 B2
Church Croft. Ripley 169 E1
Church Dr. Ilk 194 B2
Church Dr. Sand 223 D4
Church Dr. Shireb 119 F2
Church Farm. Utt 210 A2
Church Fold. Cha 16 B4
Church Hill Ave. Mans 136 B2
Church Hill St. Bu on T 248 A2
Church Hill. Derby 220 B2
Church Hill. Etwall 229 D3
Church Hill. Kim 195 F3
Church Hill. Mans 136 B2
Church Hill. Newt 148 A1
Church La N. Chest 77 D2
Church La N. Derby 204 C2
Church La. B in F 237 F3
Church La. Ba on T 244 A3
Church La. Bake 109 E3
Church La. Bake 109 E3
Church La. Baslow 91 F3
Church La. Beeley 111 D2
Church La. Belper 179 D2
Church La. Brack 145 E1
Church La. Bread 205 F2
Church La. Brin 182 C4
Church La. C Don 247 D2
Church La. C Don 247 F2
Church La. C-Frith 47 D3
Church La. Cald 260 C4
Church La. Calow 97 D2
Church La. Chel 106 A4
Church La. Chest 96 A2
Church La. Chil 264 C2
Church La. Clowne 80 C2
Church La. Coss 195 E1
Church La. Derby 205 D1
Church La. Derby 220 A3
Church La. Dove 211 D1
Church La. Ella 183 D2
Church La. G Lo 90 A2
Church La. Gra 116 A2
Church La. H Wood 192 C3
Church La. Han 238 A2
Church La. Heath 117 D2
Church La. Heath 117 E2
Church La. K Lang 202 C1
Church La. Kill 60 C3
Church La. Lit Ea 205 E4
Church La. Mack 217 F4
Church La. March 224 C1
Church La. Marple 23 D3
Church La. May 184 B3
Church La. Morley 206 C3
Church La. N Mills 33 E4
Church La. N Sol 248 B4
Church La. N Wing 131 F3
Church La. Osm 186 A3
Church La. Pk F 49 D2
Church La. Plea 135 D3
Church La. Ripley 168 A3
Church La. Roc 197 D2
Church La. Rost 197 E4
Church La. Row 110 C1
Church La. S Hill 215 D1
Church La. S Wing 157 F2
Church La. S-by-D 208 C1
Church La. Sels 171 E4
Church La. Shir 200 B4
Church La. Staple 223 E4
Church La. Thorpe 161 E1
Church La. Thrum 237 E2
Church La. Tibs 147 F3
Church La. Tick 251 D2
Church La. Tide 69 E2
Church La. Totley 55 E3
Church La. W Und 188 C1
Church Level. K Ire 165 D1
Church Mead. S in A 148 C2
Church Meadows. Calow 96 C2
Church Meadows. N Wing 131 F3
Church Mews. Derby 220 B2
Church Mews. Hatton 227 E1
Church Mews. Kill 60 C4
Church Mews. Mosb 59 E4
Church Paddock. N Wing 132 A3
Church Rd. Bols 99 D3
Church Rd. Bols 99 D4
Church Rd. Bran 253 F4
Church Rd. Bu on T 240 C1
Church Rd. Ch Bro 227 D4
Church Rd. Crich 168 A3
Church Rd. Da Da 127 D1
Church Rd. Eg 241 D2
Church Rd. M in L 9 E2
Church Rd. Marple 23 F3
Church Rd. N Mills 33 E4
Church Rd. Quar 204 B3
Church Rd. Rolle 240 A2
Church Rd. Snel 184 B2
Church Rd. Swad 256 A3
Church Rise. Shirl 146 B2
Church Row. M in L 9 D2
Church Side. Calow 96 C2
Church Side. S in A 148 C2
Church Sq. Hean 181 F1
Church Sq. Mel 252 A3
Church St E. Pinx 160 B2
Church St N. Chest 77 D2
Church St S. Chest 115 D4
Church St S. Glos 10 C1
Church St W. Chest 95 E1
Church St W. Pinx 160 B2
Church St. A in W 108 C4
Church St. Alf 158 C2
Church St. Alst 149 F2
Church St. Ash 129 F2
Church St. Ashb 173 D1
Church St. Barl 80 A4
Church St. Belper 179 D2
Church St. Bols 99 D1
Church St. Bons 142 B1
Church St. Bradw 51 D4
Church St. Brass 153 D1
Church St. Bux 85 D3
Church St. C Camp 263 F1
Church St. C Don 247 F2
Church St. C Elms 260 B2
Church St. Calow 96 C2
Church St. Chest 96 C4
Church St. Clowne 80 C2
Church St. Crich 168 A3
Church St. Denby 180 B1
Church St. Derby 218 B1
Church St. Derby 219 D1
Church St. Derby 220 B3
Church St. Derby 233 E4
Church St. Donis 262 C1
Church St. Dron 57 D1
Church St. East 182 C1
Church St. Eck 59 F2
Church St. Elmt 81 F1
Church St. Eyam 71 E3
Church St. Glos 10 A2
Church St. Glos 10 B1
Church St. Hartin 137 E3
Church St. Harts 257 D3
Church St. Hay 25 E1
Church St. Hean 181 F1
Church St. Holbr 191 E3
Church St. Hollow 156 A3
Church St. Hors 191 F3
Church St. Ilk 194 C2
Church St. Kilb 191 F4
Church St. Long 121 D3
Church St. Mans 135 D2
Church St. Mans 136 B2
Church St. Marple 23 D3
Church St. Mat 143 E2
Church St. Mel 252 A4
Church St. Mo 107 E1
Church St. Neth 264 C3
Church St. Ock 221 E2
Church St. Pils 132 B1
Church St. Ripley 168 B1
Church St. Ripley 169 E1
Church St. Ripley 181 D4
Church St. S Field 265 F1
Church St. S Norm 160 A3
Church St. Sand 223 D4
Church St. Scarc 101 D1
Church St. Shirl 146
Church St. Som 170
Church St. Staple 223
Church St. Stav 78
Church St. Swad 256
Church St. Swad 256
Church St. Swad 256
Church St. Tans 144
Church St. Tide 69
Church St. Tint 10
Church St. Tut 239
Church St. Uns 76
Church St. Wirk 165
Church St. Youl 125
Church View Dr. Baslow 91
Church View. Barl 80
Church View. Brea 235
Church View. Clowne 80
Church View. Glap 134
Church View. Hean 181
Church View. Ilk 208
Church View. Kill 60
Church View. Plea 134
Church Walk. Chest 96
Church Way. Chest 96
Church Wlk. Brin 182
Church Wlk. Derby 205
Church Wlk. Duff 190
Church Wlk. East 182
Church Wlk. Glos 10
Church Wlk. Som 170
Church Wlk. Staple 223
Churchdale Ave. Staple 209
Churchdale Rd. Shef 44
Churchdown Cl. Derby 206
Churchill Ave. Mid 154
Churchill Cl. Brea 235
Churchill Dr. Staple 223
Churchill Gdns. Mans 136
Churchland Ave. N Wing 132
Churchside La. Gra 115
Churchside. Gra 115
Churchside. Will 242
Churston Rd. Chest 95
Cinder Bank. Iron 170
Cinder La. Kill 60
Cinder La. Wirk 165
Cinder Rd. Som 170
Cinderhill La. Shef 57
Circle The. Derby 231
Circle The. Mans 136
Circle The. Shef 44
Circular Dr. Eck 79
Circular Rd. Chest 115
Circular Rd. Stav 78
City Rd. Derby 219
City Rd. Shef 43
City Rd. Shef 44
City The. Wood 256
City The. Wood 257
Civic Centre. Dron 57
Civic Way. Swad 256
Clamp Dr. Swad 256
Clapgun St. C Don 247
Clara Mount Rd. Hean 182
Clarehaven. Staple 223
Clarence Rd. Chest 95
Clarence Rd. Derby 218
Clarence Rd. Lo Ea 236
Clarence St. Chest 95
Clarence St. Mans 135
Clarence St. Shirl 147
Clarendon Rd. Stav 97
Clarke Ave. Hean 181
Clarke Dr. Lo Ea 236
Clarke St. Derby 219
Clarke's Cl. Utt 210
Clarkes La. As on T 246
Clarkson Ave. Chest 96
Clatterway. Bons 154
Claverhouse Rd. Bu on T 248
Claxton St. Hean 181
Claxton Terr. Hean 181
Clay La. Cl Cr 131
Clay La. Hean 181
Clay St E. Bu on T 248
Clay St. Bu on T 248
Clay St. Dray 235
Clay St. Shirl 146
Claye St. Lo Ea 236
Claylands Cl. M in L 9
Claylands Gr. Whit 81
Claylands Pl. Whit 81
Claylands Rd. Whit 81
Claymar Dr. Swad 256
Claymills Rd. Bu on T 241
Claypit La. Holy 112
Clays La. Bran 253
Clayton Gr. Hean 181
Clayton St. Chest 96
Clegg Hill Dr. S in A 148
Clematis Cres. Bu on T 255
Clement La. Bradw 50
Clement Rd. H Wood 192
Clement Rd. Marple 23
Cleve Ave. Bees 223
Cleve Ave. Da Da 142
Cleveland Ave. Derby 220

eveland Ave. Dray 235 D4
eveland Ave. Lo Ea 223 F1
eveland Cl. Swad 256 A2
eveland Rd. Shirl 146 C2
eveland Way. Chest 95 E3
eveleys Rd. Bees 223 F2
ewley Rd. Bran 253 F4
ff Bvd. Kim 195 F4
ff La. Curbar 72 C1
f La. Elton 140 B4
ff La. K in A 160 C2
ff La. Tide 69 E2
ff Rd. Bux 85 E4
ff Rd. Holme 2 C4
fash Lane. Idri 176 C3
fe Field Rd. Shef 43 D2
fe Hill Ave. Staple 223 E4
fe La. Hath 52 C4
fe Rd. Glos 17 E4
fe View Rd. Shef 43 D3
ford Cl. Chest 95 D1
ford Cl. Lo Ea 236 A2
ford St. Derby 219 E1
ford St. Lo Ea 236 C4
ton Ave. Barl 80 A4
ton Ave. Lo Ea 237 D4
ton Cl. Over 262 A2
ton Cl. Swad 256 A1
ton Dr. Bux 85 E2
ton Dr. Derby 217 F2
ton Rd. Bux 85 E4
ton Rd. Clif 185 D4
ton Rd. Derby 204 C2
ton Rd. Mat Ba 155 D4
ton Rd. Neth 264 B3
ton St. Chest 95 F2
ton St. Derby 219 E2
nthill La. Whit 81 F4
nton Ave. Brin 182 B3
nton St. Derby 219 E3
ostone Gdns. Derby 206 A1
dhall La. Curbar 72 C1
dhall La. O Bram 93 D3
onmore Croft. Shef 43 E1
onmore Dr. Shef 43 E1
se Bank. Tut 239 E3
se The. Derby 204 C1
se The. Derby 218 B1
se The. G Low 89 F2
se The. Linton 261 E3
se The. Marple 15 D1
se The. Mat 143 D3
se The. Moira 262 B4
se The. Shireb 119 F3
se The. Tut 239 D3
ud Ave. Staple 223 F4
udside Ct. Sand 223 D4
udside Rd. Sand 223 D4
udwood Cl. Derby 218 A1
ugh Ave. Marple 23 E3
ugh Bank. Shef 43 D4
ugh La. Bir 141 E4
ugh La. Hay 25 E3
ugh La. Lod M 42 C3
ugh La. Wens 141 E4
ugh Side. Marple 23 E4
ugh St. Bux 85 D4
ugh The. Chest 96 C1
ughside. Disley 32 C3
ver Cl. Derby 220 C3
ver Ct. Shar 234 C1
ver Ct. Shef 43 E1
ver Nook Rd. Pinx 159 F2
ver Nook Rd. S Norm ... 159 F2
ver Nook Rd. Som 159 F2
ver Rise. Greas 195 E4
verdale Dr. Derby 231 F1
verdale. Swad 256 A4
verslade. Fin 230 B1
ves Hill. Morley 192 B1
ves Hill. Smal 192 B1
wne Rd. Barl 80 B3
wne Rd. Bols 99 D4
b La. Ba on T 244 A3
bmill Terr. Chest 95 F2
mber Ave. Brin 171 F1
mber Cl. Clowne 80 C2
mber Ct. Ilk 194 C3
mber Ct. Mans 135 F1
mber Dr. Mans 135 F1
mber Pl. Stav 97 E3
mber St. Lo Ea 236 B4
n Ct. Mans 136 B1
ne St. Clowne 81 D3
ster Rd. Belper 178 C2
sters The. Belper 178 C2
operative St. Derby 218 C1
operative St. Lo Ea 236 C3
ach Dr. Greas 182 C2
ach Dr. Quar 204 B4
ach Rd. Iron 170 B2
ach Rd. M in L 9 E3
ach Rd. Ripley 169 F2
ach Rd. Ripley 170 B2
ach Rd. Som 170 B2
achhouse Mews. Swad . 256 A4
achways. Mapp 193 F2
al La. Harts 257 E4
Coal La. Tick 257 E4
Coalpit La. C Elms 260 C2
Coalpit La. Youl 125 E3
Coasthill. Crich 156 C1
Coatsby Rd. Kim 195 F4
Cobden Pl. Mans 135 F1
Cobden Rd. Chest 95 F2
Cobden Rd. Mat 143 E3
Cobden St. Derby 218 B3
Cobden St. Derby 218 B3
Cobden St. Lo Ea 236 C4
Cobden St. Ripley 169 E1
Cobham Cl. Derby 231 E2
Cobnar Ave. Shef 43 D1
Cobnar Dr. Chest 95 E4
Cobnar Dr. Shef 43 D1
Cobnar Rd. Shef 43 D1
Cobnar Wood Cl. Chest 76 A2
Cobthorn Dr. Derby 204 B2
Cock Brow. Marple 15 E4
Cock Hill. Baslow 91 F3
Cock Pitt The. Derby 219 D3
Cockayno Cl. Sand 223 D2
Cockayne La. Hog 164 A1
Cockayne St N. Derby 232 C3
Cockayne St S. Derby 232 C3
Cockerhouse Rd. East 182 C2
Cockleys. Lo Ea 236 B3
Cockshead La. Snel 198 B4
Cockshut La. Holb 101 D2
Cockshut La. Mel 251 F4
Cockshut La. Ne La 101 D2
Cockshutt Ave. Shef 56 B4
Cockshutt Dr. Shef 56 B4
Cockshutt Dr. Shef 56 B4
Cockshutt La. Som 170 C4
Cockshutt Rd. Shef 56 B4
Cod Beck Cl. Derby 233 E3
Codnor Denby La. Codnor 181 D3
Codnor Denby La. Denby .. 181 D3
Codnor Gate. Codnor 170 A1
Codnor La. Som 170 B1
Coffin La. K Ire 165 D1
Coggers La. Hath 52 C4
Coisley Hill. Shef 44 C3
Cokayne Ave. Ashb 173 E1
Coke St. Derby 218 B3
Coldharbour La. Ash 145 D2
Coldstream Wlk. Derby 231 F2
Coldwell St. Wirk 154 C1
Cole La. Ock 221 E2
Coleman St. Derby 232 C4
Coleraine Cl. Derby 220 A2
Coleridge St. Derby 231 F3
Coleridge St. Derby 231 F4
Colin Ave. Codnor 181 D4
Colin St. Alf 159 D2
Coliseum Centre The.
Derby 219 D2
Colledge St. Som 170 B3
College Mews. Derby 218 C3
College Pl. Derby 219 D3
College Rd. Bux 85 D3
College Rd. Dens 196 B3
College Rd. Eck 60 B1
College St. Lo Ea 223 E1
College Way. Bux 85 E1
Collier Ave. Mans 136 A3
Collier La. Ock 221 E2
Collier St. Glos 17 E4
Colliers Way. Cl Cr 131 D2
Colliery La. Neth 261 E2
Colliery Rd. Alf 158 C1
Colliery Rd. Newt 147 F1
Colliery Rd. Ripley 169 F1
Colliery Rd. Swad 256 A1
Colliery Row. Alf 159 D3
Collin Ave. Sand 223 D2
Collingham Gdns. Derby 218 A3
Collingham Rd. Mans 135 E1
Collingwood Cres. Mat 143 D3
Collingwood Rd. Lo Ea 236 C3
Collins Ave. S Norm 160 A4
Collis Cl. Derby 232 C4
Collishaw Cl. Chest 115 E4
Collumbell Ave. Ock 221 E3
Colne Ct. Mans 136 B1
Colombo St. Derby 219 D1
Colonsay Cl. Staple 209 E2
Colton Cl. Chest 76 C1
Coltsfoot Dr. Derby 231 F1
Coltsworth La. Barl 80 C4
Columbell Way. Da Da 127 E1
Columbia St. S in A 148 C2
Columbine Cl. Derby 206 A1
Colver Rd. Shef 43 D4
Colvile St. Derby 218 B3
Colville Cl. Lull 263 E4
Colwell Dr. Derby 233 E3
Colwick Cl. Mans 135 F1
Colwyn Ave. Derby 218 B1
Colyear St. Derby 219 D3
Combs Cl. N Mills 33 D4
Combs La. C-Frith 46 C1
Combs Mews. Glos 9 E1
Combs Rd. C-Frith 46 C2
Commerce St. Derby 232 C4
Commerce St. Mel 252 A4
Commercial Rd. Tide 69 E2
Commercial Row. Grin 72 B4
Common La. Chel 87 D1
Common La. Mans 136 A2
Common La. O Bram 94 C4
Common La. Plea 119 E2
Common La. S Hill 228 A4
Common La. Scarc 119 E2
Common La. Shireb 119 E2
Common La. Stanl 207 D4
Common Piece La. Fin 230 C1
Common Rd. Hart 62 A3
Common Rd. S in A 148 C1
Common Rd. Swad 256 B1
Common Rd. Th Sa 62 C3
Common Side. Sels 171 F4
Common Side. Swad 256 B1
Common The. Crich 168 A4
Common The. Quar 204 B4
Common The. S Norm 160 A3
Common Wood. Mat Ba 143 D2
Commonpiece La. S Hill ... 215 D1
Commonpiece Rd. Cl Cr ... 131 E2
Commons Cl. Greas 195 D4
Commonside Rd. Barlow 75 E1
Compass Cres. Uns 77 E3
Compstall Mills Est. Marple . 15 D1
Compstall Rd. Marple 15 D1
Compton Ave. As on T 246 A4
Compton Cl. Derby 233 E3
Compton Gr. Bux 85 D3
Compton Rd. Bux 85 D3
Compton St. Ashb 173 E1
Compton St. Chest 95 F2
Compton St. N Wing 116 C1
Compton St. Scarc 119 F4
Conalan Ave. Shef 56 A3
Concert Pl. Bux 85 D4
Condliff Rd. Tide 69 D3
Conduit St. Tint 9 F4
Coniston Ave. Derby 220 C3
Coniston Cres. Derby 205 E1
Coniston Dr. Cl Cr 131 D1
Coniston Dr. Ilk 208 B3
Coniston Rd. Chest 95 F4
Coniston Rd. Dron 56 C1
Coniston Rd. Lo Ea 223 D1
Coniston Way. Chest 95 F4
Conksbury Ave. Youl 125 E3
Conksbury La. Youl 125 E3
Connaught Ct. Alf 159 D2
Connaught Rd. Derby 218 B2
Connelly Ct. Chest 95 F2
Consett Cl. Derby 205 E1
Constable Ave. Derby 218 B2
Constable Cl. Dron 56 C1
Constable Cl. Shef 43 F1
Constable Dr. Derby 218 A1
Constable Dr. Marple 23 D4
Constable Dr. Shef 43 E1
Constable La. Derby 218 B2
Constable Pl. Shef 43 F1
Constable Rd. Shef 43 E1
Constable Way. Shef 43 E1
Convent Cl. Bu on T 254 C4
Conway Ave. Ock 221 E1
Conway St. Lo Ea 236 C4
Conygree La. May 184 B4
Cook Cl. Belper 179 F3
Cook Cl. Cl Cr 131 D3
Cook Dr. Ilk 209 D3
Cook La. Dove 211 D1
Cookfield. Ripley 179 F4
Cookham Cl. Derby 217 E1
Cooks Ave. C Don 247 D2
Coombes La. Cha 16 B3
Coombes View. Marple 15 F4
Coombs Rd. Bake 109 F3
Cooper St. Derby 218 B3
Cooper St. Glos 10 A1
Cooper St. Ripley 169 E1
Cooper's Cl. Ashb 173 E1
Coopers Cl. Ock 221 E1
Coopers Croft. Hatton 227 E1
Cope Ct. Derby 232 A3
Copeland Ave. Staple 223 F4
Copeland St. Derby 219 D2
Copes Way. Derby 220 A4
Copes Way. Utt 210 A1
Copley Croft. Ashb 173 E2
Coplow La. Scro 226 B3
Copper Yd. Denby 180 C1
Copperas Rd. Swad 255 E3
Coppice Ave. Ilk 194 B3
Coppice Cl. Chest 115 E3
Coppice Cl. Derby 204 C1
Coppice Cl. Disley 32 A3
Coppice Dr. Disley 32 A3
Coppice Dr. East 182 B2
Coppice Dr. Hean 193 F4
Coppice La. C Camp 263 F1
Coppice La. Disley 32 A3
Coppice Side. Swad 256 B2
Coppice The. Shireb 119 E2
Coppice The. W Br 45 F3
Coppice View. S Norm 160 A2
Copse Cl. Wirk 165 F4
Copse Rise. Swad 256 A4
Copse The. Ilk 194 B3
Copse The. Marple 23 E4
Copseside Cl. Lo Ea 236 A4
Copsewood. S Norm 160 A2
Copthurst Rd. Holme 3 F4
Corbar Rd. Bux 66 A1
Corbarwoods La. Bux 66 A1
Corbel Cl. Derby 205 F1
Corby Cl. Hello 232 A1
Corden Ave. Derby 218 A1
Corden St. Derby 219 D1
Cordville Cl. Derby 220 A3
Cordwell Ave. Chest 95 E4
Cordwell Cl. C Don 246 C2
Cordwell Cl. Stav 97 E4
Cordwell La. Hol 74 C3
Cordy La. Brin 182 C4
Cordy La. Sels 182 C4
Corfe Cl. Derby 231 E3
Corfield Ave. Hean 193 F4
Corinium Cl. Derby 233 E3
Corker Rd. Shef 44 A3
Corks La. Disley 32 C3
Corley La. Bradl 174 B1
Corn Cl. S Norm 160 A3
Corn Market. Derby 219 D3
Corn St. Glos 10 B1
Cornel Ct. Mans 136 C1
Cornfield Ave. S Norm 160 A2
Cornfield Cl. O Bram 95 D3
Cornfield Rd. Kim 195 F4
Cornflower Dr. Derby 206 A2
Cornhill Cl. Bols 99 D1
Cornhill Dr. Alf 159 D2
Cornhill. Derby 204 C2
Cornmill Cl. Calver 72 B1
Cornmill La. Tut 239 F3
Cornwall Ave. Bux 85 F4
Cornwall Ave. Chest 96 C4
Cornwall Cl. Chest 96 C4
Cornwall Cl. Sels 171 E2
Cornwall Dr. Chest 96 C4
Cornwall Dr. Gra 115 F2
Cornwall Rd. Bu on T 254 C3
Cornwall Rd. Derby 219 E3
Cornwall Rd. Shire 63 F4
Cornwallis Cl. Lo Ea 236 B3
Coronation Ave. Belper 179 D3
Coronation Ave. Derby 233 E3
Coronation Ave. Plea 134 C4
Coronation Ave. Sand 223 D4
Coronation Cl. Mel 252 A4
Coronation Cres. Roc 197 D2
Coronation Dr. S Norm 160 A3
Coronation Dr. Shireb 119 F1
Coronation La. Donis 265 F3
Coronation Rd. Chest 96 C4
Coronation Rd. Coss 195 D1
Coronation Rd. Mapp 193 F2
Coronation Rd. Stanl 207 E3
Coronation St. Derby 232 A4
Coronation St. Ilk 208 C4
Coronation St. Over 262 A2
Coronation St. Swad 256 A3
Coronation St. Whit 82 A3
Coronet Ct. Derby 206 B2
Corporation Rd. Ilk 209 D3
Corporation St. Chest 96 A2
Corporation St. Derby 219 D3
Corve Way. Chest 94 C3
Cossall Rd. Cross 209 E3
Cossall Rd. Trow 209 E3
Cote Bottom La. Ch Bro 227 D4
Cote Green La. Marple 15 D1
Cote Green Rd. Marple 15 E1
Cote Hilloc. North 127 D3
Cote La. Hay 25 E2
Cotes Park La. Som 159 E1
Cotgrave Rd. Mans 135 F1
Cotman Dr. Marple 23 E4
Cotmanhay Rd. Ilk 194 C2
Coton Cl. Mans 136 C2
Coton La. Rosl 260 B3
Coton Park. Linton 255 E1
Coton Rd. Wa on T 259 F3
Cotswold Cl. Chest 95 E3
Cotswold Cl. Derby 231 E4
Cotswold Cl. Glos 17 D4
Cotswold Cl. Lo Ea 236 A4
Cotswold Cl. Swad 256 A2
Cotswold Dr. Gra 115 F2
Cotswold Rd. Bran 253 F4
Cottage Cl. Ilk 194 B2
Cottage Cl. Stav 98 A4
Cottage Cl. Swad 256 A4
Cottage Garden La. Hean . 181 E1
Cottage La. Glos 9 F1
Cottam Cres. Marple 23 D4
Cotterhill La. Chest 96 C4
Cottesmore Rd. Bu on T ... 248 A1
Cottisford Cl. Derby 231 D4
Cotton Brook Rd. Derby 219 D1
Cotton La. Derby 219 E1
Cotton Mill Hill. Holy 113 F4
Cotton St. Bols 99 D1
Counduit Rd. Bols 118 A4
Counting House Rd. Disley . 32 C3
Countisbury Dr. Derby 206 A1
Coupe La. N Wing 131 D3
Coupe St. Ripley 180 C4
Coupland Pl. Som 159 E1
Court Farm La. Bran 253 F4
Court La. A in W 108 C4
Court Pl. Stav 97 E4
Court St. Swad 256 C2
Court The. Derby 233 D3
Court View. Clowne 80 C2
Courtland Dr. Derby 233 D3
Courtland Rd. Etwall 229 E2
Courtney Way. Belper 179 E3
Courtyard The. Da Da 127 E2
Courtyard The. M in L 9 E3
Coventry Cl. Swad 256 B3
Coventry La. Bees 209 F1
Coverdale Wlk. Derby 233 E4
Covert Pl. Moira 262 B4
Covert The. Derby 220 C2
Cow La. Chest 77 F1
Cow La. Turn 189 D4
Cowbrook Ave. Glos 10 C1
Cowburn Dr. N Mills 24 B1
Cowdray Cl. Derby 231 E1
Cowham Cl. Alf 159 E2
Cowley Bottom. Hol 75 F4
Cowley Gdns. Mosb 59 F4
Cowley La. Hol 75 E4
Cowley St. Derby 218 C4
Cowlishaw Cl. Shar 234 C1
Cowlow La. C-Frith 47 E1
Cowper Rd. Greas 195 D4
Cowper St. Derby 232 A3
Cowsell Dr. Cl Cr 131 F1
Cowsley Rd. Derby 219 E4
Cox's La. Mans 136 A3
Coxbench Rd. Hors 191 F2
Coxon St. Derby 220 C3
Coxon's Yd. Ashb 173 D1
Coyt Rd. W Br 45 F3
Crab Tree Hill. Lit Ea 205 E4
Crabtree Ave. Disley 32 C3
Crabtree Cl. C Don 247 D1
Crabtree Cl. Derby 204 B2
Crabtree Cl. Wirk 165 F4
Crabtree Hill. Derby 204 B2
Cracken Cl. Chin 34 B1
Craddock Ave. Derby 220 C2
Craddock Rd. Shef 43 F4
Cragdale Gr. Mosb 59 E4
Cragg La. Newt 148 A1
Craggon Dr. Chest 77 E2
Craggs Dr. Clowne 80 C2
Craggs Rd. Bols 99 D1
Craglands Gr. Chest 95 D3
Crags Rd. Elmt 82 A1
Crags Rd. Whit 82 A1
Crags View. Elmt 81 F1
Craig Dr. W Br 45 F3
Craig St. Lo Ea 236 C4
Cranborne Rd. Chest 95 F4
Cranbourne Cl. Staple 209 E1
Cranleigh Rd. Stav 79 D2
Cranmer Gr. Mans 135 E2
Cranmer Rd. Derby 219 E3
Cranmer St. Ilk 194 C1
Cranmer St. Lo Ea 223 E1
Craven Rd. Chest 95 F3
Crawford Ave. Staple 223 E4
Crawford Rd. Shef 43 D2
Crawley Rd. Derby 232 C3
Crawshaw Ave. Shef 56 B4
Cray's Hill. Som 170 A4
Crayford Rd. Derby 233 D3
Craythorne Cl. Swad 256 A4
Craythorne Rd. Bu on T 240 B2
Craythorne Rd. Rolle 240 B2
Creamery La. Par 151 E1
Crecy Cl. Derby 218 B2
Creighton La. Utt 210 A3
Crescent Dr. W Br 33 E1
Crescent Rd. Sels 171 E3
Crescent The. Alf 159 D2
Crescent The. Barl 80 B3
Crescent The. Br Hill 252 C1
Crescent The. Bradw 51 D4
Crescent The. Brea 235 E4
Crescent The. Bux 85 D4
Crescent The. C-Frith 47 E4
Crescent The. Chest 96 B4
Crescent The. Cl Cr 131 E1
Crescent The. Derby 219 F3
Crescent The. Derby 232 C3
Crescent The. H Wood 192 B4
Crescent The. Hol 75 D4
Crescent The. Holy 113 E4
Crescent The. May 184 B4
Crescent The. N Mills 33 D4
Crescent The. Rep 242 B1
Crescent The. Shir 200 B4
Crescent The. Shireb 119 F3
Crescent The. Stanl 207 D4
Crescent The. Staple 209 F1
Crescent The. Swad 255 F3
Crescent The. Totley 55 F3
Cressbrook Ave. N Wing ... 132 A4
Cresswell Ave. N Mills 33 E4
Cresswell St. N Mills 33 E4

Cresswellpart La. Bradw 50 C4
Cressy Rd. Alf 159 D2
Crest Cl. Bu on T 240 C1
Crest The. Derby 204 C1
Crest The. Linton 261 E3
Creswell Ct. Mans 136 C2
Creswell Rd. Clowne 80 C2
Creswick Cl. Chest 114 A4
Crewe St. Derby 218 C1
Crewton Way. Derby 232 C4
Crich Ave. Derby 218 B1
Crich Circ. Derby 218 B1
Crich La. Belper 179 D4
Crich La. Ripley 168 A2
Crich Pl. N Wing 131 F3
Crich Rd. Stav 97 E4
Crich View. Bols 118 A4
Crich View. Newt 148 A2
Crich View. Ripley 179 F4
Crich Way. Swad 255 F3
Cricket Cl. N Sol 248 C4
Cricket View. Clowne 80 C1
Cricketers Cl. Bu on T 254 C4
Cricketers Ct. Derby 231 E4
Cricklewood Rd. Derby 218 A3
Cringle Mews. Derby 205 F1
Cripton La. Ash 129 F3
Crispin Cl. Shef 44 A2
Crispin Dr. Shef 44 A2
Crispin Gdns. Shef 44 A2
Crispin Rd. Shef 44 A2
Critch's Flats. Kim 195 F3
Critchley St. Ilk 194 C1
Croft Ave. Par 151 E1
Croft Cl. Dale 207 F1
Croft Cl. Derby 220 C3
Croft Cl. Neth 264 C4
Croft Cl. Ock 221 E2
Croft Cl. Pinx 160 B2
Croft Cl. Rolle 240 A2
Croft Cres. Awsw 195 E3
Croft Ct. S in A 148 C2
Croft End. Lit Ea 205 E4
Croft Gr. Utt 210 B1
Croft La. Bread 205 E2
Croft Lea. Dron 56 B1
Croft Manor. Glos 10 C1
Croft Rd. G Lo 90 A2
Croft Rd. Shef 44 A3
Croft The. Belper 179 E1
Croft The. Bu on T 254 C4
Croft The. Derby 231 E4
Croft The. Dray 235 D3
Croft The. Glos 10 A3
Croft The. Morley 192 B1
Croft The. Ripley 168 C1
Croft The. S Norm 160 A3
Croft The. Som 170 B4
Croft The. Swad 255 F3
Croft View. Stav 97 E3
Croft Wlk. Whit 82 A3
Crofters Ct. Derby 205 F1
Crofton Cl. Dron 56 C1
Crofton Rise. Dron 56 C1
Crofts The. Hath 53 D4
Croftstead Ave. Dens 196 B3
Cromarty Cl. Derby 231 F2
Cromarty Rise. Dron 56 B1
Cromdale Ave. Chest 77 E2
Cromer Cl. Derby 217 E1
Cromford Cl. Ald 182 A2
Cromford Cl. Lo Ea 236 A3
Cromford Cl. N Wing 132 A4
Cromford Ct. Chest 95 E4
Cromford Ct. W Br 45 F3
Cromford Dr. Derby 217 F2
Cromford Dr. Stav 97 E4
Cromford Hill. Mat Ba 155 D3
Cromford La. Bux 85 F4
Cromford La. Wirk 154 C1
Cromford Pl. Bux 85 F4
Cromford Rd. Ald 181 F3
Cromford Rd. Ald 182 A2
Cromford Rd. Cl Cr 131 D3
Cromford Rd. Crich 156 C1
Cromford Rd. Derby 220 A4
Cromford Rd. Ripley 169 E1
Crompton Rd. Mans 135 E2
Crompton Rd. Ilk 209 D2
Crompton St. Derby 219 D2
Crompton St. Plea 134 C4
Cromwell Ave. C-Frith 47 D3
Cromwell Ave. Fin 230 B1
Cromwell Ave. Ilk 209 D3
Cromwell Ave. Newt 147 F1
Cromwell Cl. Tut 239 E3
Cromwell Dr. Som 169 E4
Cromwell Rd. Bols 118 A4
Cromwell Rd. Chest 95 F2
Cromwell Rd. Derby 218 C1
Cromwell St. Greas 195 E4
Crook Stile. Mat 143 D4
Crook's Ave. Mans 136 B2
Crookes Ave. Plea 135 D3
Cropper La. Thurv 215 D2
Cropton Cl. Derby 233 E3
Crosby St. Derby 218 B2
Cross Chantrey Rd. Shef 43 D2
Cross Cl. Derby 231 E4
Cross Cliffe. Glos 17 F4
Cross Keys Row. Chin 47 D4
Cross La. Calver 72 A1
Cross La. Codnor 181 D4
Cross La. Dron 57 D1
Cross La. Dron 57 E2
Cross La. Flagg 106 C4
Cross La. Ible 153 F4
Cross La. Mo 107 D1
Cross La. Rolle 240 A1
Cross La. S in A 148 C1
Cross La. S Wing 157 F4
Cross La. Shirl 158 C4
Cross La. Totley 55 E4
Cross Lanes. Hollow 144 B1
Cross London St. Uns 77 E3
Cross Myrtle Rd. Shef 43 D4
Cross Park Rd. Shef 43 D3
Cross Rd. Utt 210 A1
Cross Rise. Glos 17 F4
Cross Side. Clif 184 C4
Cross St. Al Hv 117 E1
Cross St. Br Hill 252 C1
Cross St. Bux 85 E4
Cross St. C-Frith 47 D3
Cross St. Cas 38 A1
Cross St. Chest 95 F2
Cross St. Chest 96 C4
Cross St. Cl Cr 131 E2
Cross St. Derby 218 B3
Cross St. Glos 10 A3
Cross St. Gra 115 F2
Cross St. Kill 60 C4
Cross St. Linton 261 F4
Cross St. Lo Ea 236 C4
Cross St. M in L 9 E2
Cross St. M in L 16 A4
Cross St. Mans 136 A1
Cross St. N Mills 33 E4
Cross St. N Wing 131 F3
Cross St. Sand 223 E3
Cross St. Scarc 118 B4
Cross The. Glos 10 A3
Cross Wellington St. Uns 77 E3
Crossfield Gr. Marple 15 D1
Crossgate La. Tint 9 F4
Crosshill Dr. Ilk 208 B3
Crosshill. Codnor 181 D3
Crossings Ave. C-Frith 47 D3
Crossings Rd. C-Frith 46 C3
Crossland Dr. Shef 44 A2
Crossland Pl. Shef 44 A2
Crossland Rd. Hath 53 D4
Crosslands Cl. Glos 17 E4
Crossley St. Ripley 169 E1
Crosslow La. A le Da 150 C3
Crossways La. H Ward 176 A1
Crossways The. Shef 44 A4
Crow Croft Rd. Pils 132 B1
Crow Hill La. Mans 136 A1
Crow Hill. Mans 135 D3
Crow La. Chest 96 B2
Crow La. Stret 146 A3
Crow La. Uns 76 C4
Crowestones. Bux 85 E3
Crowfoot La. Ch Bro 226 C4
Crowhill La. Bake 109 D3
Crown Cl. Uns 77 E3
Crown Hill Way. Stanl 207 D4
Crown Mews. Derby 218 C2
Crown Rd. Chest 96 A3
Crown Sq. Mat 143 D3
Crown St. Clowne 80 C2
Crown St. Derby 218 C2
Crown St. Duff 190 C2
Crown St. Marple 23 D2
Crown Terr. Belper 178 C2
Crown Yd. Wirk 154 C1
Crowshaw St. Derby 232 A4
Crowstones Rd. Da Da 127 D2
Croxton Ct. Mans 136 C2
Croydon Wlk. Derby 217 F3
Cruck Cl. Dron 56 C1
Cubley La. G Cub 198 B1
Cubley La. M Mont 198 B1
Cuckmere Cl. Derby 205 D3
Cuckoostone La. Mat 128 F1
Cuillin Cl. Lo Ea 223 D1
Cullabine Rd. Shef 44 A4
Culland View. Crich 168 A4
Cullen Ave. Ashb 173 E1
Cullumbell La. Ash 129 D4
Culworth Cl. Belper 179 E2
Culworth Ct. Derby 206 A1
Cumberhills Rd. Duff 190 B1
Cumberland Ave. Derby 219 F3
Cumberland Cl. Sels 171 E2
Cumberland Cres. Ock 221 D1
Cumberland Dr. Bux 85 E2
Cumberland Rd. Bu on T 254 B3
Cumbria Wlk. Derby 217 E1
Cummings St. Derby 219 D1
Cundy Rd. Bols 99 D2
Cunliffe St. Dron 57 E2
Cunnery La. Tans 144 A2
Cunnery The. K Lang 202 C1
Curbar Cl. N Wing 132 A4
Curbar Curve. Stav 97 E3
Curbar Hill. Curbar 72 B1
Curborough Dr. Derby 233 E3
Curlew Ave. Eck 59 D2
Curtis Gr. Glos 10 A3
Curzon Ave. Dron 75 F4
Curzon Cl. Derby 204 B2
Curzon Cl. Kill 60 B3
Curzon Ct. Duff 190 C2
Curzon La. Derby 233 D4
Curzon La. Duff 190 B2
Curzon Rd. Bux 85 E4
Curzon Rd. Derby 219 F4
Curzon St. Derby 218 C3
Curzon St. Lo Ea 223 D1
Curzon Terr. Litton 88 B4
Cuscas La. Brai 187 F2
Cut La. Derby 219 D4
Cutholme Cl. Chest 95 D2
Cutler Cl. Kill 60 A4
Cuttholme Rd. Chest 95 E2
Cuttholme Way. Chest 95 E2
Cutthorpe Grange. Chest 95 D4
Cutthorpe Rd. Chest 95 D4
Cuttlebrook Cl. Derby 231 F3
Cypress Ave. Shef 43 E1
Cypress Cl. Kill 60 B3
Cypress Walk. Derby 220 A3
Cyprus Rd. Shef 43 D3
Cyprus Way. H La 32 A4
Cyril Ave. Staple 223 E4

Dade Ave. Stav 97 E3
Dag La. Lull 263 F4
Dagnall Gdns. Bake 109 E3
Dagnall Terr. Bake 109 E3
Dagnam Cl. Shef 43 F3
Dagnam Cres. Shef 43 F3
Dagnam Dr. Shef 43 F4
Dagnam Pl. Shef 43 F3
Dagnam Rd. Shef 43 F4
Dahlia Dr. Derby 206 B2
Dairy House Rd. Derby 219 D1
Daisy Farm Rd. Greas 195 E4
Daisymere La. Bux 67 D1
Dakeyne Cl. Da Da 127 F1
Dakin Ave. Bux 85 E4
Dakin Ct. Bux 66 C1
Dalbury Rd. Shef 56 C4
Dalbury Wlk. Derby 231 E3
Dale Ave. Lo Ea 223 E1
Dale Ave. Newt 148 A2
Dale Ave. Som 170 B3
Dale Bank Cres. Uns 77 E3
Dale Cl. Brea 235 E4
Dale Cl. Crich 168 A3
Dale Cl. Scarc 100 C1
Dale Cl. Scarc 119 F4
Dale Cl. Shirl 147 D2
Dale Cl. Stav 97 E4
Dale Cres. Hath 53 D4
Dale Cres. Tupton 115 E1
Dale Ct. Kilb 191 F4
Dale End Rd. Hilton 228 B1
Dale End. Brass 153 D1
Dale End. Wirk 154 C1
Dale La. Al Hu 134 B4
Dale La. Bux 85 F4
Dale Park Ave. Kilb 192 A4
Dale Rd N. Da Da 127 D3
Dale Rd N. North 127 D3
Dale Rd N. Row 126 C4
Dale Rd S. Da Da 127 E1
Dale Rd. Bux 67 D4
Dale Rd. Bux 85 E4
Dale Rd. C-Frith 66 C4
Dale Rd. Dale 221 D3
Dale Rd. Derby 218 C1
Dale Rd. Derby 220 C3
Dale Rd. Derby 233 E4
Dale Rd. Dron 76 A4
Dale Rd. Kill 60 C3
Dale Rd. Kim 195 F3
Dale Rd. Mat Ba 143 D2
Dale Rd. N Mills 33 E4
Dale Rd. S-by-D 208 B1
Dale Rd. Stanl 207 E2
Dale Rd. Tupton 115 E1
Dale Side. Bux 85 D4
Dale St. Ilk 208 C4
Dale St. Mans 136 A1
Dale Terr. Bux 85 D3
Dale The. Bons 142 B1
Dale The. Hath 53 D4
Dale The. St Mid 71 F2
Dale The. Wirk 154 C1
Dale View Cl. Pils 132 A2
Dale View Gdns. Kilb 191 F4
Dale View Gdns. Kilb 192 A4
Dale View Rd. Pils 132 A2
Dale View. E St 105 D2
Dale View. Ilk 208 C4
Dale View. Litton 69 F2
Dale View. Shirl 146 B2
Daleacre Ave. C Don 247 F3
Dalebank La. Ash 145 D4
Dalebrook Rd. Bu on T 248 A3
Dalefield Dr. Swad 256 A2
Dales Cl. Swad 255 F3
Dalesfield. Mat 143 D3
Daleside. Bu on T 248 A1
Dalestorth Ave. Mans 135 E1
Daleswood Cres. S Norm 160 A2
Dalewood Cl. Chest 96 C1
Dalkeith Ave. Derby 232 C3
Dalley Cl. Staple 223 F4
Dalley La. Belper 178 B3
Dallimore Rd. Ilk 208 B2
Dalston Rd. Swad 256 A3
Dalton Ave. Derby 218 B2
Dalton Cl. Staple 223 F3
Daltons Cl. Ald 182 A2
Dalvey Way. Uns 77 E3
Dam La. A le Da 150 C2
Dam La. Shirl 146 C1
Damon Cl. Pils 132 B1
Damon Dr. Chest 96 C4
Damsbrook Dr. Clowne 80 C2
Dan La. Par 151 D1
Danbury Gr. Gra 115 F2
Danby Ave. Chest 77 D1
Dane Bank Dr. Disley 32 B3
Dane Gr. Bux 85 E2
Dane Hill Cl. Disley 32 B3
Danebridge Cres. Derby 206 A1
Danesby Cres. Denby 180 A1
Danesby Rise. Denby 180 A1
Danesway. C-Frith 47 D3
Danewood Ave. Shef 44 B4
Dannah Cres. Ripley 169 F1
Dannah St. Ripley 169 F1
Darby St. Derby 218 C1
Darcy Rd. Eck 59 E2
Daresbury Cl. Shef 43 E3
Daresbury Dr. Shef 43 E3
Daresbury Pl. Shef 43 E3
Daresbury Rd. Shef 43 E3
Daresbury View. Shef 43 E3
Darfield Ave. Shef 44 C1
Darfield Cl. Shef 44 C1
Darfield Dr. Hean 182 A1
Darfield La. Tiss 162 B2
Dark La. Ash 145 E3
Dark La. Ashb 173 D1
Dark La. Bradl 175 D2
Dark La. Callow 165 E2
Dark La. Calow 96 C1
Dark La. Chest 96 C2
Dark La. Crich 156 C3
Dark La. Dun 253 D4
Dark La. Holbr 191 D4
Dark La. Mat Ba 154 C2
Dark La. N Wing 132 A4
Dark La. Pils 132 B1
Dark La. Youl 125 E4
Darkey La. Staple 223 F3
Darklands La. Swad 256 A2
Darley Abbey Dr. Derby 204 C1
Darley Ave. Bees 223 F2
Darley Ave. Da Da 127 E2
Darley Ave. N Wing 132 A4
Darley Cl. Stav 78 C1
Darley Cl. Swad 256 A1
Darley Dale. Swad 255 F1
Darley Dr. Lo Ea 236 A3
Darley Dr. Ripley 169 E2
Darley Dr. We Ha 207 F4
Darley Gr. Bux 85 E3
Darley Gr. Derby 219 D4
Darley House Est. Da Da 142 C4
Darley La. Derby 219 D3
Darley Lodge Dr. Da Da 142 C4
Darley Park Dr. Derby 204 C1
Darley Park Rd. Derby 204 C1
Darley Rd. Ash 113 E2
Darley Sq. Ilk 194 C3
Darley St. Derby 205 D1
Darley Way. Bux 85 F4
Darley Way. N Wing 132 A4
Darsway. C Don 246 C2
Dartford Pl. Derby 233 D3
Dartnall Cl. H La 32 A3
Darwent Rd. Chest 96 B3
Darwin Ave. Bux 85 E4
Darwin Ave. Chest 95 F3
Darwin Ave. Derby 232 B2
Darwin Ave. Ilk 208 C4
Darwin Pl. Derby 219 D3
Darwin Rd. Chest 95 F2
Darwin Rd. Derby 217 F2
Darwin Rd. Lo Ea 236 A3
Darwood La. Bols 118 A4
Dashwood St. Derby 219 D2
Datchet Cl. Derby 231 D4
Daveham Ave. Bux 85 E3
Davenport Rd. Derby 232 B4
Davenport Rd. Tupton 131 E4
Daventry Cl. Derby 217 E2
Davey Ct. Bols 98 C2
Davian Way. Chest 114 C4
David's Cl. Derby 232 C1
Davids Dr. Win 114 C2
Davis Rd. Swad 256 A2
Dawber La. Kill 60 C4
Dawlish Ct. Derby 233 E4
Dawlish Ct. East 182 B2
Dawn View. Staple 209
Dawsmere Cl. Derby 205
Dawver Rd. Kim 195
Day Gr. M in L 9
Dayfield La. Atlow 175
Daylesford Cl. Derby 231
Days La. Belper 178
Days Mill Cl. Mat 143
Dayton Cl. Derby 220
Deacon Cl. Derby 205
Deacon Cl. Som 169
Dead La. Cross 209
Deadman's La. Derby 219
Deamon St. Newt 147
Dean Cl. Derby 218
Dean Rd. Ripley 167
Dean St. Derby 218
Dean St. La Mi 182
Deanhead Dr. Shef 44
Deans Dr. Ock 221
Deansgate. Plea 135
Debdale Gate. Mans 136
Debdale La. Mans 136
Deben Cl. Chest 114
Deborah Dr. Derby 220
Dee Cl. Derby 231
Dee La. Burn 229
Deep Dale La. Ba on T 231
Deep Dale La. Ba on T 244
Deep Dale La. Derby 231
Deep La. Al Hu 133
Deepdale Ave. Ock 221
Deepdale Ave. Staple 223
Deepdale Cl. Bu on T 248
Deepdale Ct. Hean 181
Deepdale La. Snel 184
Deepdale Rd. Belper 179
Deepdale Rd. Bols 98
Deepdale Rd. Derby 220
Deepdale Rd. Lo Ea 236
Deepdale Rd. Mans 136
Deepdale. Iron 170
Deepsick La. L Duk 97
Deepwell Ave. Kill 60
Deepwell Ave. Mosb 59
Deepwell Bank. Mosb 59
Deepwell Ct. Mosb 59
Deepwell View. Mosb 59
Deer Park View. Derby 220
Deerlands Rd. Chest 95
Deerlands Rd. Win 114
Deerleap La. Ash 130
Deerleap La. Cl Gr 130
Deerpark Cres. Win 114
Degge St. Derby 219
Deincourt Cl. Derby 221
Deincourt Cres. N Wing 131
Delamere Cl. Brea 235
Delamere Cl. Derby 206
Delamere Cl. Som 169
Dell The. Chest 95
Delph Bank. Chest 114
Delph St. Shef 43
Delph The. Br Hill 252
Delven La. C Don 247
Delves Bank Rd. Som 170
Delves Cl. Chest 95
Delves Rd. Hean 193
Delves Rd. Ship 193
Delves The. Som 169
Denacre Ave. Lo Ea 223
Denacre La. Da Da 127
Denarth Ave. Derby 232
Denbigh St. Derby 219
Denby Common. Denby 180
Denby La. Denby 180
Dene Fields Ct. Mat 143
Denefield Cl. Marple 15
Denham St. Cl Cr 131
Denison Cl. Shef 43
Denison Gdns. Derby 220
Denman Cres. St Mid 72
Denmark Rd. Shef 43
Dennis Cl. Derby 230
Dennor Dr. Mans 136
Denstone Dr. Derby 233
Denstone La. Dens 196
Dent La. Shef 44
Dentdale Ct. Derby 233
Denton Ave. Sand 223
Denton Cl. Mans 136
Denton Way. Som 169
Denver Ct. Staple 209
Denver Rd. Derby 217
Depedale Ave. Ilk 208
Depot St. Derby 219
Derby La. Brai 201
Derby La. Derby 231
Derby La. G Cub 198
Derby La. Mo 123
Derby La. Shir 200
Derby Pl. Shef 43
Derby Rd. Alder 167
Derby Rd. Alf 158
Derby Rd. As on T 234
Derby Rd. Ashb 185
Derby Rd. Belper 190
Derby Rd. Bu on T 241

rby Rd. Chest 115 D3
rby Rd. Cl Cr 131 E3
rby Rd. Dale 206 C2
rby Rd. Denby 180 B2
rby Rd. Derby 220 B2
rby Rd. Derby 232 C1
rby Rd. Dove 211 E1
rby Rd. Dray 234 C4
rby Rd. Duff 190 C1
rby Rd. Duff 204 C4
rby Rd. East 182 B2
rby Rd. East 182 C1
rby Rd. Eg 241 E2
rby Rd. Elv 234 A1
rby Rd. Hatton 227 F1
rby Rd. Hean 181 E1
rby Rd. Hilton 228 C2
rby Rd. Hors 191 E3
rby Rd. Ilk 208 B4
rby Rd. Kilb 179 F1
rby Rd. Lo Ea 236 A4
rby Rd. M on D 228 A1
rby Rd. Mat Ba 155 E3
by Rd. Mel 252 A4
by Rd. N Mills 24 B1
by Rd. Ock 221 D1
by Rd. Ripley 167 F2
by Rd. Ripley 180 B2
rby Rd. Risley 222 B2
rby Rd. Sand 223 D3
rby Rd. Smisby 258 A2
rby Rd. Som 169 F3
rby Rd. Stanl 207 D2
rby Rd. Staple 223 E3
rby Rd. Staple 223 F4
by Rd. Swad 256 B2
by Rd. Tick 257 F4
by Rd. Tupton 131 E3
by Rd. Utt 210 B1
by Rd. Win 115 D3
by Rd. Wirk 165 F3
by Small Bsns Centre.
Derby 219 D2
by St. Glos 17 E4
by St. Ilk 208 C4
by St. Shef 43 E3
by Terr. Shef 43 E3
by Trading Est. Derby .. 219 D4
byshire Ave. Trow 209 E2
byshire Ave. We Ha 207 F4
byshire Cl. We Ha 207 F4
byshire Dr. Ilk 208 C3
byshire Dr. Sels 171 E2
byshire La. Shef 43 D2
byshire Level. Glos 17 F3
rington Leys. Derby 233 E3
ventio Cl. Derby 219 D4
went Ave. Belper 179 D1
went Ave. Derby 205 D2
went Ave. Grin 72 B4
went Ave. Ilk 194 B1
went Ave. Ock 221 E2
went Ave. We Ha 207 F4
went Cl. Derby 205 D2
went Cl. Dron 57 D2
went Cl. Glos 17 F4
went Cl. Grin 72 B4
went Cl. Swad 256 A1
went Cres. Chest 95 E4
went Croft. Will 242 A3
went Ct. Shef 56 A3
went Dr. Baslow 91 E3
went Dr. Chin 34 C1
went Dr. Da Da 127 E2
went Dr. Derby 231 E1
went Dr. Tibs 147 F3
went Gdns. Ashb 185 E4
went Gr. Alf 158 C1
went La. Der 30 A4
went La. Hath 52 C4
went Pl. Cl Cr 131 D3
went Rd. Bu on T 248 A1
went Rd. Bux 85 E3
went Rd. Derby 220 B2
went Rd. Dron 57 D2
went Rd. Ripley 169 E1
went Rise. Derby 220 C2
went Sq. Chin 34 C1
went St. Belper 178 C2
went St. Derby 219 D3
went St. Dray 235 D4
went St. Lo Ea 236 B3
went Vale. Belper 178 C1
went View. Belper 178 C3
went View. Stav 79 E2
borough Rd. Sels 171 E4
nick La. Hollow 144 B1
nick Way. N Wing 132 A4
as Gdns. Derby 220 B3
eron Cl. Bu on T 240 B1
eron Rd. Mosb 59 F4
izes Cl. Chest 114 C4
on Cl. Bu on T 254 C3
on Cl. Derby 219 E3
on Cl. Gra 115 F1
on Cl. Sand 223 D3
on Dr. Chest 96 C4
on Park View. Chest 96 C4
Devon St. Ilk 209 D3
Devonshire Av. Lo Ea 237 D4
Devonshire Ave E. Chest 115 E4
Devonshire Ave N. Chest 77 F2
Devonshire Ave. Da Da 142 C4
Devonshire Ave. Derby 204 C2
Devonshire Ave. Ock 221 E1
Devonshire Cl. Chest 95 F4
Devonshire Cl. Dron 75 F4
Devonshire Cl. Ilk 194 C3
Devonshire Cl. Stav 78 C1
Devonshire Cl. Totley 55 F3
Devonshire Ct. Chest 96 B4
Devonshire Dr. Chin 34 B1
Devonshire Dr. Derby 217 F2
Devonshire Dr. Duff 190 B1
Devonshire Dr. East 182 C1
Devonshire Dr. Elmt 81 E1
Devonshire Dr. Scarc 119 F4
Devonshire Dr. Som 170 A4
Devonshire Dr. Staple 209 E1
Devonshire Dr. Totley 55 F4
Devonshire Glen. Totley 55 F3
Devonshire Gr. Totley 55 F3
Devonshire Rd E. Chest 115 E4
Devonshire Rd N. Uns 77 E3
Devonshire Rd. Bux 85 D4
Devonshire Rd. Totley 55 F3
Devonshire Sq. Beeley 111 D2
Devonshire St. Chest 96 A2
Devonshire St. Chest 96 C4
Devonshire St. Plea 135 D4
Devonshire St. Ripley 167 F2
Devonshire St. Stav 78 C1
Devonshire Terr. N Wing 116 C1
Devonshire Terrace Rd.
Totley 55 E4
Devonshire Villas. Chest 95 F4
Devonshire Villas. Stav 78 B2
Devonshire Way. Clowne 81 D2
Dew Pond La. Bux 85 E4
Dewint Ave. Marple 23 D4
Dewsnap La. M in L 9 D3
Dewy La. Ash 144 C1
Dewy La. Crich 144 C1
Dexter St. Derby 219 E1
Dialstone. Bradw 51 D4
Diamond Dr. Derby 205 F2
Diamond Jubilee Cotts. Clif 184 C4
Dickens Dr. N Wing 116 B1
Dickens Dr. Swad 256 B3
Dickens Sq. Derby 231 F4
Dickenson Rd. Chest 96 A1
Dickinson St. Derby 219 E1
Dickinson's La. S Hill 215 D1
Dicklant La. Ash 145 D4
Didcot Cl. Chest 114 C4
Didsbury Terr. Hay 25 F1
Dig St. Ashb 173 E1
Dig St. Hartin 137 E3
Digby St. Coss 195 D1
Digby St. Kim 195 E4
Diglands Ave. N Mills 24 B1
Diglands Cl. N Mills 24 B1
Diglee Rd. W Br 33 E2
Digmire La. Thorpe 161 E1
Dimple Cres. Mat 143 D3
Dimple La. Crich 168 A4
Dimple Rd. Mat 143 D3
Dingle Bank. Calow 96 C1
Dingle Cl. Glos 17 D4
Dingle La. Calow 96 C1
Dingle The. Bu on T 254 C4
Dingley Cl. Mans 136 C3
Dinting La. Glos 10 A1
Dinting Lodge Ind Est. Glos .. 9 F1
Dinting Rd. Glos 10 A1
Dinting Vale. Glos 10 A1
Diseworth Rd. C Don 247 D1
Dish La. S Hill 228 A3
Ditch The. Chel 105 F4
Division Rd. Shireb 119 F2
Division St. Stav 97 E4
Dix Ave. Smal 192 C3
Dixie St. Sels 171 D2
Dixon's Rd. Chest 96 A1
Dobbin La. Barlow 75 E3
Dobbinhorse La. Clif 185 D3
Dobholes La. Smal 192 C3
Dobson Pl. Stav 97 D3
Dock Wlk. Chest 95 F1
Dockholm Rd. Lo Ea 223 E1
Doctor's La. Br Hill 252 C1
Dodslow Ave. Rolle 240 A2
Doe Hill La. Tibs 147 E3
Doehole La. Ash 144 C2
Dog La. Br Hill 252 C3
Dog La. H Ward 175 E2
Dog La. Neth 264 C3
Dog La. Shirl 146 C1
Doghole La. Mid 154 B2
Dogkennel La. Osm 186 C4
Dolby Rd. Bux 85 E1
Doles La. Fin 230 B2
Doles La. Whit 82 A4
Dolly La. Chin 34 A1
Dolly Wood Cl. Chin 34 A1
Dolphin Cl. Derby 221 D3
Dominion Rd. Swad 256 A3
Dominoe Gr. Shef 44 B3
Donald Hawley Way. Duff . 190 C2
Doncaster Ave. Sand 223 D3
Doncaster Gr. Lo Ea 223 F1
Donegal Wlk. Derby 220 A2
Donisthorpe La. Moira 262 C1
Donner Cres. Ilk 194 C3
Donnington Cl. Derby 231 F3
Donnington Dr. Derby 231 F3
Donnington La. C Don 247 E4
Dorchester Ave. Derby 219 F4
Dorchester Rd. Kim 195 F4
Dore Cl. Totley 56 A4
Dore Hall Croft. Totley 55 E4
Dore La. Hath 53 D4
Dore Rd. Totley 55 F4
Doris Rd. Ilk 209 D4
Dorking Rd. Derby 218 A3
Dormy Cl. Mans 136 C3
Dorothy Ave. Mans 136 B1
Dorothy Ave. Sand 223 D3
Dorothy Dr. Mans 136 C1
Dorothy Vale. Chest 95 E2
Dorrien Ave. Derby 232 A4
Dorset Ave. Chest 96 C4
Dorset Cl. Bu on T 254 C3
Dorset Cl. Bux 85 E2
Dorset Cl. Chest 77 F1
Dorset Dr. Chest 96 C4
Dorset St. Derby 219 E3
Dorterry Cres. Ilk 209 D3
Douglas Ave. Awsw 195 E3
Douglas Ave. Hean 181 E1
Douglas Rd. Chest 96 B3
Douglas Rd. Lo Ea 223 D1
Douglas Rd. Som 170 B4
Douglas St. Derby 219 D1
Douse Croft La. Lod M 42 C3
Dove Bk. Marple 23 F3
Dove Cl. Derby 218 A2
Dove Cl. Kilb 192 A4
Dove Cl. Wood 256 C2
Dove Gr. Eg 241 D3
Dove House Green. Ashb . 173 D1
Dove La. Lo Ea 236 B4
Dove La. Roc 197 D2
Dove Rd. Ripley 169 E1
Dove Rise. Hilton 228 B1
Dove Side. Hatton 239 E4
Dove St. Ella 183 D1
Dove View. Tut 239 E3
Dovecliff Cres. Bu on T 240 C1
Dovecliff Rd. Bu on T 240 C2
Dovecliff Rd. Rolle 240 C2
Dovecote Dr. Ock 221 D1
Dovecote The. Br Hill 252 C1
Dovecote The. Hors 191 F3
Dovecote. C Don 247 D2
Dovecotes. Ash 129 F2
Dovedale Ave. Ashb 173 E1
Dovedale Ave. Chest 97 D3
Dovedale Ave. Derby 233 E4
Dovedale Ave. Lo Ea 236 A3
Dovedale Circ. Ilk 194 C3
Dovedale Cl. Bu on T 248 A3
Dovedale Cl. Ripley 180 B3
Dovedale Cres. Belper 179 D3
Dovedale Cres. Bux 84 C3
Dovedale Ct. Chest 95 F4
Dovedale Ct. Glos 10 C1
Dovedale Ct. Lo Ea 236 A3
Dovedale Rd. Derby 220 C2
Dovedale Rise. Derby 204 B1
Dovefields. Roc 196 C2
Dover Ct. Derby 219 D1
Dover St. Derby 219 D1
Dover St. Elmt 81 F1
Doveridge Cl. Chest 77 D1
Doveridge Gr. Bux 85 F3
Doveridge Wlk. Derby 231 E3
Doveridge. Bu on T 248 A1
Doveside. May 184 B4
Dowdeswell St. Chest 96 A2
Dower Cl. Derby 205 D1
Downham Cl. Derby 217 F1
Downing Cl. Derby 217 F3
Downing Cl. Derby 218 A3
Downing Rd. Derby 219 E3
Downing Rd. Shef 56 C4
Downing St. S Norm 160 A3
Downlands. Chest 96 B4
Downlee Cl. C-Frith 46 C3
Downmeadow. Ripley 179 F4
Drabbles Rd. Mat 143 D3
Drage St. Derby 219 D4
Drake Terr. Chest 96 B4
Draycott Cl. Hean 181 E2
Draycott Ct. Ilk 194 C2
Draycott Dr. Derby 217 E2
Draycott Pl. Dron 75 E4
Draycott Rd. Brea 235 E4
Draycott Rd. Lo Ea 236 A2
Draycott Rd. N Wing 131 F4
Draycott Rd. Ock 221 E1
Drayton Ave. Derby 217 F3
Drayton Ave. Mans 135 E1
Drayton St. Swad 256 B2
Dresden Cl. Derby 217 E1
Drewery La. Derby 218 C2
Dreyfus Cl. Derby 220 C3
Drive The. Haz 177 F2
Dronfield Pl. Ilk 194 C3
Dronfield Rd. Eck 59 D1
Drovers Way. Ripley 168 A3
Drovers Wlk. Glos 10 B1
Drummond Rd. Ilk 194 C1
Drury Ave. Derby 220 B2
Drury La. Biggin 138 E1
Drury La. Dron 57 E2
Drury La. Totley 55 E4
Dryden Ave. Chest 115 D4
Dryden Ct. Staple 209 F1
Dryden St. Derby 231 F4
Dryhurst Dr. Disley 32 B3
Dryhurst La. Disley 32 B3
Drysdale Rd. Derby 217 E2
Duchess St. Elmt 81 F1
Duchess St. Whit 82 A3
Duck St. Eg 241 D3
Duckmanton Rd. Stav 98 A3
Duckworth Sq. Derby 219 D3
Dudwood La. Elton 140 C4
Duesbury Cl. Derby 232 C4
Duesbury The. S Norm 160 A2
Duewell Ct. Stav 78 A2
Duffield Bank. Duff 191 D2
Duffield Cl. Lo Ea 236 A3
Duffield Rd. Derby 204 C1
Duffield Rd. Derby 205 D3
Duffield Rd. Lit Ea 205 D4
Duke St. Bux 84 C3
Duke St. Chest 96 A4
Duke St. Clowne 81 D2
Duke St. Derby 219 D3
Duke St. Elmt 81 F1
Duke St. Ilk 194 C2
Duke St. Mid 154 B3
Duke St. Mosb 59 E3
Duke St. S Norm 160 A3
Duke St. Stav 78 C1
Duke St. Whit 82 A3
Duke's Dr The. A in W 108 C4
Duke's Dr. Al Hu 134 A4
Duke's Dr. Bux 85 E3
Dukeries Ct. Clowne 80 C1
Dukeries La. Derby 206 A1
Dukes Cl. N Wing 116 C1
Dukes Dr. Chest 95 F3
Dukes Dr. Curbar 72 B1
Dukes Pl. Ilk 194 C2
Dukes St. Glos 17 E4
Duluth Ave. Derby 220 A4
Dulverton Ave. Derby 231 E1
Dulwich Rd. Derby 217 F3
Dumb Hall La. Shire 63 D2
Dumb Hall La. Th Sa 63 D2
Dumbles Cl. Ilk 208 B3
Dumbles La. Denby 180 C1
Dumbles Rd. Bols 98 C2
Dumbleton Rd. Kill 60 C3
Dunbar Cl. Derby 231 F1
Duncan Cl. Belper 179 D3
Duncan Rd. Derby 231 F4
Duncliffe La. Mel 252 A4
Dundee Dr. Mans 136 A3
Dundee Rd. Swad 256 B3
Dundonald Rd. Chest 96 A1
Dunedin Cl. Derby 217 F2
Dunedin Cres. Bu on T 248 B1
Dunedin Glen. Mosb 59 F3
Dunedin Gr. Mosb 59 F3
Dungley Hill. Ripley 168 B1
Dungreave Ave. North 127 D3
Dunkery Ct. Derby 206 A1
Dunkirk. Derby 218 C2
Dunlow La. Eyam 71 E3
Dunn Brigg. Mans 136 B1
Dunne La. Glos 10 C1
Dunnsmoor La. Harts 256 C4
Dunoon Cl. Derby 231 F2
Dunsa La. Eden 91 E1
Dunsford Rd. Alf 159 D3
Dunshill Wlk. Cl Cr 131 F2
Dunsil Rd. Pinx 160 B1
Dunsmore Dr. Derby 205 F1
Dunsmore Way. Swad 256 B3
Dunstall Brook. Bu on T 248 A1
Dunstall Park Rd. Derby 232 B4
Dunston Cl. Lo Ea 236 C4
Dunston La. Chest 76 B1
Dunston La. Chest 95 E4
Dunston Rd. Chest 76 B1
Dunton Cl. Derby 219 E3
Dunvegan Ave. Cl Cr 131 F1
Dunvegan Cl. Derby 231 E1
Duper La. Abney 51 F3
Durban Rd. Bu on T 248 B2
Durham Ave. Derby 219 F3
Durham Ave. Gra 115 F1
Durham Ave. Uns 77 E3
Durham Cl. Mans 136 B2
Durham Cl. Swad 256 C3
Durham Cl. Uns 77 E3
Durham St. Ilk 194 C1
Durley Chine Dr. Chest 115 E4
Durley Cl. Derby 233 E4
Durlstone Cl. Shef 44 A3
Durlstone Cres. Shef 44 A3
Durlstone Dr. Shef 44 A3
Durlstone Gr. Shef 44 A3
Durrant Rd. Chest 96 A2
Durvale Ct. Totley 55 F3
Durward Cl. Derby 232 B4
Dyche Cl. Shef 57 D3
Dyche Dr. Shef 57 D3
Dyche La. Dron 57 D3
Dyche La. Shef 57 D3
Dyche Pl. Shef 57 D3
Dyche Rd. Shef 57 D3
Dye House La. N Mills 33 E4
Dyke Vale Rd. Shef 44 C3
Dykes Cl. Bols 99 D1
Dymond Gr. Gra 115 F2

E Nelson St. Hean 181 F1
Each Well La. Alf 158 C2
Eagle Heights. Bu on T 248 B2
Eagle Par. Bux 85 D4
Eagle Rd. Ilk 208 C2
Eagle St. Bux 85 D4
Eagle St. Ripley 168 C1
Eagle Terr. Bir 126 A1
Eagle Terr. Wens 142 A4
Ealing Cl. Derby 218 A3
Eardley Cl. Derby 220 A3
Earls Cres. Derby 206 A1
Earlswood Cl. Brea 235 E4
Earnshaw St. M in L 9 E2
Easedale Cl. Chest 94 C3
East Ave. Bols 80 A1
East Ave. Derby 217 F2
East Bank Cl. Shef 43 E3
East Bank Pl. Shef 43 E3
East Bank Rd. Shef 43 E3
East Bank View. Shef 43 E3
East Bank Way. Shef 43 E3
East Bank. Wins 141 E3
East Cl. Derby 204 C1
East Cres. Holbr 191 E4
East Cres. Stav 98 A3
East Croft Ave. Derby 231 E3
East Dr. Dove 211 D1
East End Dr. Swad 256 B2
East End. Elton 140 C3
East Glade Ave. Shef 44 C2
East Glade Cl. Shef 44 C2
East Glade Cres. Shef 44 C2
East Glade Pl. Shef 44 C2
East Glade Rd. Shef 44 C2
East Glade Sq. Shef 44 C2
East Glade Way. Shef 44 C2
East Lawn. Fin 230 B1
East Rd. Shef 43 D4
East Service Rd. Derby 220 A2
East St. Al Hv 117 E1
East St. Bu on T 248 B2
East St. Cl Cr 131 E2
East St. Clowne 81 D3
East St. Derby 219 D3
East St. Eck 79 D4
East St. Elmt 81 E1
East St. Hean 194 A4
East St. Ilk 208 C4
East St. Lo Ea 236 C4
East St. Scarc 118 C3
East Vale. Marple 23 D3
East View Ave. Eck 59 E1
East View Rd. Ripley 168 C1
East View. Shireb 119 F3
Eastbrae Rd. Derby 231 E4
Eastbrook Cl. C-Frith 47 E3
Eastcliffe Ct. Shef 43 E4
Eastcliffe. Shef 43 E4
Eastcroft Cl. Mosb 59 F4
Eastcroft Dr. Mosb 59 F4
Eastcroft Glen. Mosb 59 F4
Eastcroft View. Mosb 59 F4
Eastcroft Way. Mosb 59 F4
Eastern Ave. Bols 118 A4
Eastern Ave. Shef 43 F4
Eastern Cres. Shef 43 E3
Eastern Dr. Shef 43 E4
Eastern Wlk. Shef 43 E4
Eastfield Dr. S Norm 160 A3
Eastfield Rd. Dron 76 B4
Eastfield Rd. Ripley 170 A1
Eastfield Rd. Swad 256 B3
Eastgate. Derby 219 E3
Eastleigh Ct. Chest 115 E4
Eastleigh Dr. Derby 217 F1
Eastleigh Dr. Mans 136 A3
Eastmoor Rd. Chest 96 C2
Eastway. C Don 247 D2
Eastwood Ave. Derby 218 B1
Eastwood Cl. Chest 115 E4
Eastwood Cotts. Hath 53 D4
Eastwood Dr. Calow 97 D1
Eastwood Dr. Derby 218 B1
Eastwood La. Ash 130 A1
Eastwood Park Dr. Chest .. 115 E4
Eastwood Rd. Kim 195 F3
Easy Par. Whit 82 A3
Eather Ave. Mans 136 B2

Eaton Ave. Derby 205 D3
Eaton Ave. Ilk 208 B3
Eaton Bank. Lit Ea 191 D1
Eaton Cl. Derby 205 D3
Eaton Cl. H Ward 175 F2
Eaton Ct. Derby 218 C3
Eaton Ct. Duff 190 C1
Eaton Dr. Baslow 91 F3
Eaton Fold. St Mid 71 F2
Eaton Grange Dr. Lo Ea 236 A4
Eaton Hill. Baslow 91 F3
Eaton Pl. Baslow 91 F3
Eaton Rd. C Don 247 D2
Eaton Rd. Roc 196 C2
Eaton St. Utt 210 B1
Eatons Rd. Staple 223 E3
Eaves Knoll Rd. N Mills 24 A1
Ebenezer St. Glos 17 E4
Ebenezer St. Ilk 194 C2
Ebenezer St. La Mi 182 A2
Eccles Cl. Hope 39 D2
Eccles Cl. W Br 45 E4
Eccles Fold. C-Frith 47 D3
Eccles Rd. C-Frith 46 B4
Eccles Rd. C-Frith 47 D3
Eccles Rd. W Br 45 F3
Eccles Terr. C-Frith 46 B4
Ecclesbourne Ave. Duff 190 C2
Ecclesbourne Cl. Duff 190 C2
Ecclesbourne Dr. Bux 85 D3
Eckington Cl. We Ha 207 F4
Eckington Rd. Dron 57 E2
Eckington Rd. Eck 57 E2
Eckington Rd. Mosb 59 F4
Eckington Rd. Stav 78 C2
Eckington Rd. Uns 77 E3
Eckington Way. Mosb 59 F4
Edale Ave. Derby 217 E1
Edale Ave. Derby 218 C1
Edale Ave. Derby 233 D4
Edale Cl. Derby 204 B1
Edale Cl. Lo Ea 236 A3
Edale Cres. Glos 9 F1
Edale Ct. Chest 95 F4
Edale Dr. Derby 220 C2
Edale Gr. Bux 85 F4
Edale Rd. Hay 26 A1
Edale Rd. Hope 38 C4
Edale Rd. Stav 79 E2
Edale Rise. Bees 223 F2
Edale Sq. Ilk 194 C3
Edale Way. Belper 179 D3
Eden Bank. Ripley 167 F1
Eden Low. Mans 136 C2
Eden Rd. Derby 220 A2
Eden St. Derby 233 D4
Eden St. Win 114 C2
Edenhall Rd. Shef 43 F4
Edensor Ave. Bux 85 F4
Edensor Cl. N Wing 131 F3
Edensor Ct. Stav 97 E4
Edensor Dr. Belper 179 E3
Edensor Sq. Derby 218 C2
Edge Hill Ct. Lo Ea 236 B2
Edge Hill. Derby 232 C2
Edge Rd. Eyam 71 F4
Edge Rd. Mat 143 D3
Edge View Cl. Grin 72 B4
Edge View Dr. G Lo 90 A2
Edgecote Dr. Swad 256 A4
Edgefold Rd. Mat 143 D3
Edgehill Gr. Mans 136 B1
Edgewood Rd. Kim 195 F3
Edgware Rd. Derby 217 F3
Edinburgh Cres. Derby 232 C2
Edinburgh Ct. Som 170 A4
Edinburgh Rd. Chest 95 F3
Edinburgh Rd. Win 114 C2
Edith Wood Cl. Derby 233 D3
Edlaston La. Wya 185 D1
Edmonton Pl. Bu on T 248 B1
Edmund Ave. Shef 56 B3
Edmund Cl. Shef 56 B3
Edmund Dr. Shef 56 B3
Edmund Rd. Derby 220 C2
Edmund Rd. Shef 43 D4
Edmund St. Chest 95 F4
Edmund's Sq. Burn 230 A4
Ednaston Ave. Derby 231 E3
Edward Ave. Derby 220 A3
Edward Ave. Sels 171 D2
Edward Rd. Lo Ea 236 B4
Edward St. Ald 182 A2
Edward St. Belper 179 D2
Edward St. Derby 219 D3
Edward St. Eck 59 E2
Edward St. Glos 10 B1
Edward St. Harts 257 D2
Edward St. Marple 15 D1
Edward St. Moira 256 B1
Edward St. Over 262 A2
Edward St. Staple 223 E4
Edward St. Stav 97 E4
Edward Wlk. Tupton 115 E1
Edwards Cres. Kilb 192 A4
Edwin Ave. Chest 114 B4
Edwin Rd. Shef 43 E3
Edwinstowe Rd. Derby 206 A1
Egerton Dr. Staple 209 E1
Egerton Rd. Dron 57 D1
Eggesford Rd. Derby 231 E1
Eggington Rd. Hilton 228 C1
Egginton Rd. Etwall 229 D1
Egmanton Cl. Derby 206 A1
Egreaves Ave. Hean 181 E2
Egstow Pl. Cl Cr 131 E2
Egstow St. Cl Cr 131 E2
Eider Cl. Shireb 119 E2
Eland Cl. Derby 221 D3
Eland Rd. Shireb 119 F3
Elder Cl. Som 170 A4
Elder Ct. Kill 60 B3
Elder Way. Chest 96 A2
Eldon Cl. C-Frith 47 E3
Eldon La. Pk F 49 D2
Eldon St. Bu on T 248 A2
Eldon St. Cl Cr 131 E2
Eleanor Ave. Ilk 209 D3
Eleanor Cres. Staple 223 F4
Eley Wlk. Derby 218 C2
Elgar Dr. Lo Ea 236 A3
Elgin Ave. Derby 218 A1
Elgin Cl. Chest 114 B4
Eliot Cl. Chest 96 C3
Eliot Cl. Lo Ea 236 A3
Eliot Dr. Ilk 208 B3
Eliot Rd. Derby 231 D4
Elizabeth Ave. Bux 85 E4
Elizabeth Ave. Disley 32 B3
Elizabeth Ave. Rolle 240 A2
Elizabeth Cl. Derby 220 A3
Elizabeth Cl. We Ha 207 E4
Elizabeth Ct. Ilk 194 B1
Elizabeth Park. Iron 170 C3
Elkstone Cl. Derby 206 A1
Elkstone Rd. Chest 95 D3
Ella Bank Rd. Hean 182 A1
Ellastone Gdns. Derby 233 D4
Ellendale Rd. Derby 220 A4
Ellerslie Gr. Sand 223 D3
Ellesmere Ave. Alf 159 D2
Ellesmere Ave. Derby 219 E1
Ellesmere Dr. Trow 209 E3
Elliot Ave. Bradw 51 D4
Elliott Dr. Stav 97 E3
Ellis Cl. Lo Ea 236 B3
Ellison Ave. As on T 246 A4
Ellison Cl. M in L 9 E3
Ellison St. Glos 10 B1
Elm Ave. Belper 179 D1
Elm Ave. Da Da 142 C4
Elm Ave. Lo Ea 236 B4
Elm Ave. Sand 223 D4
Elm Cl. Bols 99 E1
Elm Cl. Chest 95 F4
Elm Cl. Dove 224 B4
Elm Cl. Kill 60 B3
Elm Cl. M in L 9 D2
Elm Cl. Pinx 160 B2
Elm Cres. Mosb 59 E4
Elm Dr. Hilton 228 B1
Elm Dr. Kill 60 B3
Elm Gr. Derby 204 B3
Elm Gr. Derby 220 A3
Elm Gr. Glos 10 B1
Elm Grove. Cl Cr 131 E2
Elm Park Ct. Derby 218 C4
Elm Rd. Eck 59 E1
Elm Rd. Pils 132 B1
Elm St. Gra 116 A2
Elm St. Ock 221 D1
Elm St. Stav 97 D4
Elm Tree Ave. Kilb 192 A4
Elm Tree Ave. Mans 136 A2
Elm Tree Ave. Shireb 119 E2
Elm Tree Ave. Shirl 146 B1
Elm Tree Cres. Dron 57 D2
Elm Tree Dr. Win 114 C2
Elm View. Dens 196 C3
Elma La. Holb 101 E3
Elmfield. C-Frith 47 D3
Elmhurst Ave. S Norm 160 A2
Elmhurst Cl. S Norm 160 A2
Elmhurst Rd. Mans 136 C1
Elmhurst. Eg 241 D3
Elms Ave. Alf 159 D2
Elms Ave. Derby 218 A1
Elms Ave. Ripley 180 B4
Elms Cl. Alf 159 D2
Elms Dr. Derby 218 A1
Elms Gr. Etwall 229 E2
Elms Rd. Bu on T 248 A1
Elms Rd. C Elms 260 B2
Elms St. Derby 218 C4
Elms The. Kim 195 F4
Elmsdale Rd. Harts 257 D2
Elmsfield Ave. Hean 182 A1
Elmslea Ave. C Elms 260 B2
Elmsleigh Cl. Swad 256 A3
Elmsleigh Dr. Swad 256 A3
Elmsleigh Gr. Swad 256 A3
Elmton Cl. Clowne 80 C2
Elmton Cl. Elmt 100 B4
Elmton La. Bols 99 E2
Elmton Rd. Elmt 81 F1
Elmtree Ave. Derby 232 A4
Elmtree Ave. Sels 171 F4
Elmtree Cl. Shire 63 F4
Elmwood Dr. Derby 205 E1
Elmwood Dr. Mosb 59 E3
Elnor Ave. W Br 45 F3
Elnor La. W Br 45 F2
Elnor St. La Mi 182 B2
Elsecar Cl. Belper 179 E3
Elstead La. Black 257 D1
Elston Cl. Mans 135 E1
Elstree Dr. Shef 44 A2
Elstree Rd. Shef 44 A2
Elton Cl. Staple 223 E4
Elton Gr. Bux 85 F3
Elton Rd. Derby 232 A4
Elton Rd. Wins 141 D3
Elton St. Chest 96 A1
Elton View. Stav 97 E4
Elvaston Cl. Dron 56 A1
Elvaston Dr. Lo Ea 236 A2
Elvaston La. Derby 233 E4
Elvaston Rd. N Wing 131 F3
Elvaston St. Dray 235 D4
Elvin Way. Tupton 131 E4
Elwood Rd. Shef 56 B3
Elwyn Cl. Bu on T 240 B1
Ely Cl. Mans 136 B2
Ely Cl. Swad 256 B3
Elyn Ave. N Wing 132 A4
Embankment Cl. Derby 217 F4
Ember La. Bons 142 C1
Embridge Cswy. Bux 64 A3
Emerald Cl. Derby 206 A1
Emerald Cl. Mans 135 F1
Emerson Sq. Derby 231 F3
Emery Cl. Linton 261 E3
Emmet Field Cl. Chest 114 C4
Emmett Carr Cl. Barl 79 E4
Emmett Carr La. Barl 79 E4
Empire Rd. Bu on T 248 B2
Empress Ave. Marple 23 D3
Empress Rd. Derby 218 C2
Emsworth Cl. Ship 194 B2
End The. N Sol 248 C4
Endowood Rd. Chest 114 A4
Endsleigh Gdns. Derby 217 F3
Enfield Rd. Chest 96 A3
Enfield Rd. Derby 218 A3
England Cres. Hean 182 A1
Englishe Rd. Mat 143 D2
Ennerdale Ave. Mosb 59 F3
Ennerdale Cl. Dron 56 C1
Ennerdale Cres. Chest 95 E4
Ennerdale Dr. Mosb 59 F3
Ennerdale Rd. Lo Ea 223 D1
Ennerdale Wlk. Derby 205 E1
Ennis Cl. Derby 220 B4
Enoch Stone Dr. Derby 220 A2
Enslet La. Hog 164 A2
Epping Cl. Derby 217 F3
Epsom Rd. Bees 223 F2
Epworth Dr. Derby 233 D2
Erdington Way. Bees 223 F2
Erewash Dr. Ilk 209 D3
Erewash Gr. Bees 223 F1
Erewash Rd. Pinx 160 C1
Erewash Sq. Ilk 209 D3
Erewash St. Ald 171 D3
Erewash St. Lo Ea 236 C4
Erica Dr. S Norm 160 A4
Erin Rd. Stav 98 A4
Ernest Hall Way. Swad 256 B2
Ernocroft La. Marple 15 F1
Ernocroft Rd. Marple 15 D1
Errington Ave. Shef 43 F3
Errington Cl. Shef 43 F3
Errington Cres. Shef 43 F3
Errington Rd. Chest 114 B4
Errington Rd. Shef 43 F3
Errington Way. Shef 43 F4
Errwood Ave. Bux 85 D3
Erskine Cres. Shef 43 E4
Erskine Rd. Shef 43 E4
Erskine St. Marple 15 D2
Erskine View. Shef 43 E4
Eskdale Cl. Dron 56 C1
Eskdale Cl. Lo Ea 236 A3
Eskdale Wlk. Derby 233 E3
Essendine Cres. Shef 43 D2
Essex Rd. Bu on T 254 B3
Essex St. Derby 219 E3
Essex St. East 182 C1
Essex St. Ilk 194 C1
Estwic Ave. East 182 C2
Etherow Brow. M in L 16 A4
Etherow Way. Glos 9 F3
Eton Ct. We Ha 207 E4
Eton St. Derby 219 F1
Etruria Gdns. Derby 219 D4
Etta's Way. Etwall 229 D2
Ettrick Cl. Chest 95 E3
Ettrick Dr. Derby 231 F1
Etwall Cl. Chest 95 D3
Etwall La. Burn 229 F3
Etwall Rd. Derby 217 E1
Etwall Rd. Eg 241 D4
Etwall Rd. Will 242 A4
Etwall St. Derby 218 C3
Eureka Rd. Swad 256 B3
Evans Ave. Derby 205 D3
Evans St. Derby 232 C3
Evanston Gdns. Derby 220 A3
Evelyn Devonshire Cotts.
Al Hu 132 C1
Evelyn Gr. Derby 220 A3
Everard Ave. Shef 56 A3
Everard Dr. Shef 56 A3
Everard Glade. Shef 56 A3
Everest Dr. Som 170 B4
Everett Cl. Chest 96 C4
Evergreen Cl. Derby 206 A2
Evershill Cl. Morton 146 C3
Evershill La. Morton 146 C3
Eversleigh Rise. Wens 142 A4
Everton St. Mans 135 F1
Evesham Ave. Glos 10 A3
Evesham Cl. Derby 205 F1
Ewart La. Alf 158 C2
Ewe Dale La. Alst 149 D2
Ewe Lamb Cl. Bees 209 F1
Ewe Lamb La. Staple 209 F1
Excelsior Ave. Derby 232 C3
Exchange St. Derby 219 D3
Exeter Cl. Swad 256 C3
Exeter Pl. Derby 219 D3
Exeter St. Derby 219 D3
Exlowmere La. Elton 140 C3
Export Dr. S in A 160 C4
Eyam Cl. N Wing 132 A4
Eyam La. Glos 9 E1
Eyam Mews. Glos 9 F1
Eyam Walk. Belper 179 D3
Eyes Ct. Duff 190 C2
Eyre Gdns. Chest 95 F2
Eyre St E. Chest 115 E4
Eyre St. Cl Cr 131 E2
Eyre St. Elmt 81 E1
Eyre's Gdns. Ilk 194 C1
Eyrie The. Bu on T 248 B2
Eyrie The. Derby 231 F1

Fabis Cl. Swad 256 A2
Fabric View. N Wing 132 B4
Factory La. Disley 32 C4
Factory La. Ilk 194 C1
Factory St. Chest 95 E1
Fair Lea Cl. Lo Ea 236 B3
Fair View. Chest 95 F2
Fair View. May 184 B4
Fairbourne Dr. Derby 217 E2
Faircroft Ave. Sand 223 D3
Fairdene. Derby 218 C1
Faire St. Derby 218 C2
Faires Cl. Ock 221 E1
Fairfax Rd. Derby 218 C1
Fairfield Ave. Brea 235 F4
Fairfield Ave. Newt 148 B1
Fairfield Ave. Ock 221 E2
Fairfield Ave. Rolle 240 B2
Fairfield Ave. Shirl 147 D2
Fairfield Cl. Chest 96 B4
Fairfield Cl. Ne La 101 D1
Fairfield Cres. Lo Ea 236 A2
Fairfield Cres. Swad 255 F3
Fairfield Ct. O Bram 94 C2
Fairfield Dr. O Bram 94 C2
Fairfield Rd. Bols 118 A4
Fairfield Rd. Bux 85 E4
Fairfield Rd. Chest 95 F2
Fairfield Rd. Derby 218 C1
Fairfield Rd. H Wood 192 B4
Fairfield Terr. Wood 256 C2
Fairford Cl. Chest 114 C4
Fairham Rd. Bu on T 240 C1
Fairholme Dr. Mans 135 F1
Fairholmes. Mat 143 E3
Fairisle Cl. Derby 206 B2
Fairleigh. Shef 44 A4
Fairview Ave. Sels 171 F1
Fairview Cl. Derby 231 D4
Fairview Cl. Kilb 192 A4
Fairview Rd. Dron 57 D2
Fairview Rise. Crich 168 A4
Fairway Cl. Derby 204 B1
Fairway Cres. Derby 204 B1
Fairway The. Swad 255 F3
Fairway. Bran 254 A4
Fairways Cl. Glos 10 C1
Fairways The. Cl Cr 131 F2
Fairways The. Mans 136 B3
Fairwinds Cl. Dron 57 D1
Fairwood Dr. Derby 233 E3
Fairy Bank Cres. Hay 25 E2
Fairy Bank Rd. Hay 25 E2
Fal Paddock. Mans 136 B1
Falcon Cl. N Mills 33 E4
Falcon Ct. Ilk 194 B1
Falcon Rd. Dron 57 E2
Falcon Rise. Dron 57 E2
Falcon Way. Derby 231 F1
Falcon Way. Wood 256 C2
Falcon Yd. Chest 96 A2
Falkland Rise. Dron 76 A4
Fall Rd. Hean 181 F2
Fallow Rd. Derby 220 C3
Fallowfield Rd. Uns 77 E3
Falmouth Rd. Derby 233
Fan Rd. Stav 78
Fanny Ave. Kill 60
Fanshaw Ave. Eck 59
Fanshaw Bank. Dron 57
Fanshaw Cl. Eck 59
Fanshaw Dr. Eck 59
Fanshaw Gate La. Totley 55
Fanshaw Rd. Dron 57
Fanshaw Rd. Eck 59
Fanshaw Way. Eck 59
Far Croft. Brea 235
Far Cross. Mat 143
Far Green. Mat 143
Far Hill. Bradw 51
Far La. Barlow 75
Far La. Ock 221
Far Laund. Belper 179
Far New Cl. Sand 223
Far Woodseats La. Cha 15
Faraday Ave. Bu on T 240
Faraday Ct. Staple 209
Farfield Rd. Ilk 209
Farish Pl. Shef 43
Farley Hill. Da Da 143
Farley La. Da Da 128
Farley Rd. Derby 218
Farm Cl. Belper 179
Farm Cl. Chest 114
Farm Cl. Dron 57
Farm Cl. Ilk 209
Farm Cl. Kilb 192
Farm Cl. Lo Ea 236
Farm Cl. Pent 169
Farm Cl. Shef 44
Farm Cl. Som 170
Farm Cres. Mosb 59
Farm Croft Rd. Mans 136
Farm Dr. Derby 233
Farm La. Disley 32
Farm La. N Sol 248
Farm Side. Swad 255
Farm St. Derby 218
Farm View. Tupton 131
Farm Walk. Mosb 59
Farmfields Cl. Bols 98
Farmhouse Rd. Derby 231
Farmilo Cres. Mans 135
Farmlands La. Derby 231
Farmstead Cl. Shef 43
Farmway. Mans 136
Farnah Green Rd. Belper 178
Farnborough Gdns. Derby 205
Farncombe La. Derby 205
Farndale Ave. Chest 114
Farndale Cl. Lo Ea 236
Farndale Ct. Derby 233
Farndon Dr. Bees 223
Farneworth Rd. Derby 217
Farnham Cl. Derby 217
Farnham Wlk. We Ha 207
Farningham Cl. Derby 220
Farnon Cl. Chest 96
Farnsley La. St Mid 71
Farnsworth St. Chest 115
Farnway. Derby 204
Farrendale Cl. Mans 136
Farringdon Cl. Derby 217
Farthing Ct. Lo Ea 236
Farwater Cl. Dron 76
Farwater La. Dron 56
Fauld La. Han 238
Fauld La. Tut 238
Fauld La. Tut 239
Fauvel Pl. Glos 10
Fauvel Rd. Glos 10
Faversham Cl. Derby 232
Fawn Cl. Win 114
Fay Gdns. Glos 9
Faywood Dr. Marple 23
Fearn Ave. Ripley 169
Fearn Cl. Ch Bro 227
Fearn Cl. Lo Ea 236
Featherbed La. Bols 99
Featherbed La. Work 63
Fellbrigg Rd. Shef 43
Fellside. Belper 179
Fellside. Derby 220
Fenchurch Wlk. Derby 218
Fenland Way. Chest 114
Fennel St. A in W 108
Fenton Ave. Black 257
Fenton Rd. Derby 217
Fenton St. Eck 59
Fenwick St. Derby 232
Ferguson Ave. Mans 136
Fern Ave. Stav 97
Fern Ave. Will 242
Fern Bank Ave. Newt 147
Fern Cl. Eck 59
Fern Cl. Heath 116
Fern Cl. Shireb 119
Fern Cl. Will 242
Fern Cres. East 182
Fern Lea. M in L 9
Fern Rd. Bux 85
Fern Royd. Hath 53
Fern Way. Eck 59

ernbank Dr. Eck 59 D2
ernbank. Bradw 51 D4
erncroft Ave. Mosb 59 E4
erndale Ave. Bux 67 E2
erndale Cl. Dron 57 E2
erndale Rd. Bux 67 E2
erndale Rd. Dron 57 E2
erndale Rise. Dron 57 E2
erneydale Ave. Bux 85 E2
ernhill Cl. Glos 10 B2
ernhill Ct. Derby 233 D2
ernhill. Marple 23 D3
ernilee Cl. N Mills 24 B1
ernilee Cl. We Ha 207 F4
ernilee Gdns. Duff 205 D4
ernlea Cl. Glos 9 F2
ernleigh Rise. Mans 136 B1
ernway. Bux 85 E2
ernwood Cl. Chest 115 F4
ernwood Cl. Derby 231 E4
ernwood Cl. Shirl 146 B2
ernwood. Marple 23 E4
errers Ave. Tut 239 D3
errers Cl. C Don 247 D2
errers Cres. Duff 190 B2
errers Way. Derby 204 C1
errers Way. Ripley 169 E2
erry Green. Will 242 A3
erry St. Bu on T 254 C4
erry Vale Cl. Bu on T 254 C4
estival Ave. Brea 235 E4
estival Rd. Bran 253 F4
estival Rd. Ilk 208 B3
iddle St. Bux 85 E2
iddler's La. Rolle 239 F2
idlers Cl. Bam 40 A2
idlers Well. Bam 40 A2
ield La. Stan 183 E4
ield Ave. Eck 79 D4
ield Ave. Hatton 239 E4
ield Cl. Brea 235 F4
ield Cl. Dron 56 B1
ield Cl. Hilton 228 B1
ield Cl. Mans 136 B3
ield Cl. Ock 221 D2
ield Cres. Derby 233 D3
ield Ct. Kilb 192 A4
ield Dr. Derby 233 D3
ield Dr. Rolle 240 A2
ield Dr. Shireb 119 F1
ield End. Brass 153 D1
ield House La. Marple 23 D3
ield La. Al Hu 134 B3
ield La. Belper 178 C2
ield La. Black 257 E1
ield La. Derby 220 A4
ield La. Derby 233 D3
eld La. K Ire 176 A4
eld Rd. Ilk 208 C4
eld Rise. Derby 231 E4
eld Row. Belper 178 C2
eld St. Codnor 181 D4
ield Terr. Ripley 169 E1
eld The. Ship 194 A3
eld View Cl. Derby 233 D3
eld View. Clowne 80 C2
ield Way. Swad 255 F3
ielden Ave. Mans 135 E1
ieldfare House. Chest 77 D2
ieldgate Dr. Derby 205 F1
ieldhead La. Holme 2 C4
ieldhead Rd. Shef 43 D4
ieldhead Way. Chest 95 E3
ieldings Rd. Elmt 81 F1
elds Cres. M in L 9 E3
ields Farm Rd. Lo Ea 236 C3
ields Gr. M in L 9 E3
ields La. Kill 60 A3
ields La. Linton 261 F3
elds The. Mid 154 B2
fe St. Derby 232 C4
nch Cl. Wood 256 C2
ncham Cl. Derby 205 E1
nchley Ave. Derby 217 F3
ndern Cl. Belper 179 E3
ndern Cl. Derby 204 B1
ndern La. Burn 230 A2
ndern La. Will 242 A3
ndern St. Derby 218 B3
nmere Cl. Derby 231 D4
nningley Dr. Derby 204 C1
nny La. Rods 200 A3
nsbury Ave. Derby 218 A3
nsley Wlk. Derby 231 F3
r Cl. Shireb 119 E3
r Pl. Kill 60 B3
r Rd. Eck 59 E1
r St. Stav 78 A1
r Tree Ave. Shirl 146 B2
restone. Haz 178 B1
rlawns. Duff 190 B2
rs Ave. Alf 159 D3
rs Ave. H Ward 175 F2
rs Ave. Ripley 169 E1
rs Cres. Derby 204 C2
rs Gdns. Alf 159 D2
rs Parade. Mat 143 E3
rs St. Lo Ea 236 A2
Firs The. Ashb 173 E1
First Ave. Risley 222 C3
Firthwood Ave. Dron 57 E2
Firthwood Cl. Dron 57 E2
Firthwood Rd. Dron 57 E2
Firtree Gr. Derby 206 A1
Firvale Rd. Chest 114 A4
Fisher Cl. Chest 114 C4
Fisher Cl. Rep 242 B1
Fisher Ct. Ilk 194 C2
Fisher La. Duff 190 C2
Fisher St. Derby 232 C3
Fishers Bridge. Hay 25 E1
Fishpond La. Eg 241 D3
Fishponds Cl. Win 115 D2
Fishponds Rd W. Shef 44 B4
Fishponds Rd. Shef 44 B4
Fiskerton Way. Derby 206 A1
Fitzalan St. Glos 10 B1
Fitzhubert Rd. Shef 44 A4
Fitzroy Rd. Shef 43 D3
Five Lamps Ct. Derby 218 C3
Five Lands Rd. Bu on T 254 C4
Five Trees Ave. Totley 56 A3
Five Trees Cl. Totley 56 A3
Five Trees Dr. Totley 56 A3
Flackets La. Dove 225 D4
Flackets La. Sud 225 D4
Flagg La. Flagg 106 C4
Flagshaw La. K Lang 202 C2
Flake La. S-by-D 208 C1
Flamstead Ave. Hean 181 E2
Flamstead La. Denby 180 C1
Flamstead Rd. Ilk 194 C1
Flamstead St. Derby 232 C3
Flamsteed Cres. Chest 96 A3
Flash La. Da Da 128 D4
Flat La. Chel 106 B4
Flat The. Kilb 191 F4
Flatts La. Sels 171 E2
Flax Croft. Hatton 227 E1
Flaxholme Ave. Duff 190 C1
Flaxpiece Rd. Cl Cr 131 E2
Fleet Cres. Belper 178 C2
Fleet Park. Belper 179 D2
Fleet St. Derby 219 D1
Fleet The. Belper 178 C2
Fletcher Ave. Dron 57 D1
Fletcher St. Hean 181 F1
Fletcher St. Lo Ea 236 B4
Fletcher's Row. Ripley 169 F1
Fletches The. Bu on T 240 A1
Flint Ave. Mans 136 C1
Flint La. Wens 142 A4
Flint St. Derby 232 B3
Flintson Ave. Chest 77 E2
Flixton Rd. Kim 195 F4
Flood St. Ock 221 E2
Florence Ave. Lo Ea 223 F1
Florence Cl. Chest 114 C3
Florence Ct. Ilk 194 C1
Florence Dr. Dove 211 E1
Florence Gladwin Cl. Wins 141 E3
Florence Rd. Cl Cr 131 F2
Florence Rd. Win 114 C2
Florence Way. M in L 9 E3
Florin Gdns. Lo Ea 236 A4
Flowery Leys La. Alf 159 E2
Fluery Cl. Shef 43 F2
Fluery Cres. Shef 43 F2
Fluery Pl. Shef 43 F2
Fluery Rd. Shef 43 F2
Fluery Rise. Shef 43 F2
Fly Hill. Bake 109 E3
Foggs Entry. Wirk 165 F4
Fold The. St Mid 71 F2
Folds Yd. Crich 156 C1
Foljambe Ave. Chest 114 B4
Foljambe Rd. Chest 96 C4
Folkestone Dr. Derby 233 D3
Folly Rd. Derby 205 D1
Foolow Ave. Chest 95 F1
Forbes Cl. Lo Ea 236 C3
Ford Ave. Hean 181 E2
Ford Cl. Dron 56 C1
Ford Cl. Ripley 180 B4
Ford Gr. M in L 9 D2
Ford La. Derby 205 D3
Ford La. Eck 58 C3
Ford La. Will 242 B3
Ford Rd. Eck 58 C2
Ford St. Belper 178 C2
Ford St. Bu on T 254 C4
Ford St. Derby 218 C3
Ford St. Tupton 131 E4
Fordbridge La. S Norm 160 A4
Fordwells Cl. Derby 231 D4
Foremark Ave. Derby 231 F4
Forest Ave. Bux 85 E3
Forest Cl. Belper 179 D3
Forest Ct. Barl 80 A3
Forest Dr. Pils 132 B1
Forest La. G Huck 50 B1
Forester St. Derby 219 D2
Foresters Way. Ripley 169 E1
Forge Cl. Rep 242 B1
Forge La. Bu on T 241 D1
Forge La. Kill 60 A4
Forge Rd. W Br 45 F4
Forge Terr. C-Frith 34 C1
Forge The. Trow 209 D3
Forman Cl. Swad 256 A2
Forman St. Derby 218 C3
Forrester Ave. We on T 245 F3
Forrester's La. Dron 57 E2
Forth Ave. Dron 56 B1
Forties La. Smisby 257 F2
Forty Horse Cl. Ripley 170 A1
Forum Cl. Derby 233 E3
Fosbrooke Dr. Lo Ea 236 B3
Fossett's Ave. Sels 171 F4
Foster Rd. Wood 256 C1
Foston Cl. Hatton 239 E4
Foston Dr. Chest 95 D3
Foundary La. Belper 190 C4
Foundry St Ind Est. Chest 96 A4
Foundry St. Chest 96 A4
Fountain Sq. Disley 32 B3
Fountain Sq. Tide 69 E2
Fountain St. Bux 85 D4
Fountains Cl. Derby 205 D2
Four Lane Ends. Da Da 127 E1
Four Lanes. M in L 9 D2
Fowler Ave. Derby 220 B2
Fowler St. Chest 76 C1
Fowler St. Derby 218 C3
Fowler St. Dray 235 D4
Fox Cl. Derby 231 E1
Fox Cl. Lo Ea 236 B3
Fox Croft. Tibs 147 F3
Fox Hill. Scarc 118 C4
Fox La. Hol 74 A3
Fox La. Shef 44 B2
Fox La. Shef 56 B3
Fox Rd. C Don 246 C2
Fox Rd. Whit 82 A3
Fox St. Derby 219 E3
Foxbrook Cl. Chest 94 C3
Foxcote Way. Chest 114 A4
Foxcroft Chase. Kill 60 B3
Foxcroft Dr. Kill 60 B3
Foxcroft Gr. Kill 60 B3
Foxdale Ave. Shef 44 A3
Foxes Wlk. Derby 204 C2
Foxes Yd. Bux 66 B1
Foxfields Dr. Derby 205 F1
Foxglove Ave. Bu on T 255 D4
Foxglove Cl. Calow 97 D2
Foxglove Rd. Greas 195 E4
Foxhall La. Lod M 42 C3
Foxholes La. Kni 174 A3
Foxholes La. Tans 144 A4
Foxlands Ave. Derby 204 C1
Foxley Ct. Derby 206 A1
Foxlow Ave. Bux 85 E2
Foxpark View. Tibs 147 F3
Foxstone Cl. Stav 97 E4
Foxwood Ave. Shef 44 A3
Foxwood Cl. Chest 115 E3
Foxwood Dr. Shef 44 A3
Foxwood Gr. Shef 44 A3
Foxwood Rd. Chest 76 C1
Foxwood Rd. Shef 44 A3
Foyle Ave. Derby 220 A2
Framlingham Pl. Shef 43 E4
Framlingham Rd. Shef 43 E4
Frances Dr. Win 114 C2
Frances St. Sels 171 E1
Franchise St. Derby 218 C2
Francis Rd. Chest 96 B4
Francis St. Derby 219 E3
Franklin Ave. Whit 81 F3
Franklin Cres. Whit 81 F3
Franklin Rd. Sels 171 D2
Franklyn Dr. Derby 233 D3
Franklyn Dr. Stav 78 C2
Franklyn Rd. Chest 95 F2
Frazer Cl. Derby 220 C3
Frecheville St. Stav 78 B1
Frederic Ave. Hean 193 F4
Frederick Ave. Derby 232 C3
Frederick Ave. Ilk 209 D3
Frederick Rd. Staple 223 E4
Frederick St. Alf 159 D3
Frederick St. Bu on T 254 C4
Frederick St. Derby 218 B3
Frederick St. Gra 115 F2
Frederick St. Lo Ea 236 C4
Frederick St. Som 170 B3
Frederick St. Swad 256 C2
Freebirch View. Chest 95 D4
Freeby Ave. Mans 136 B3
Freehold St. Derby 218 C2
Freeland Cl. Bees 223 F2
Freeman Ave. Derby 231 F3
Freemantle Rd. Derby 217 F2
Freesia Cl. Derby 217 F1
Freetown. Glos 17 E4
French La. Hors 191 F3
French St. Derby 218 C1
French St. Ilk 209 D3
French Terr. Scarc 101 D1
Fresco Dr. Derby 230 C4
Fresh Ct. Glos 16 C4
Freshfield Cl. Marple 15 D1
Fretson Rd. Shef 44 A4
Freydon Way. Calow 97 D2
Friar Gate Ct. Derby 218 C3
Friar Gate. Derby 218 C3
Friar Gr. Bux 85 E3
Friar St. Lo Ea 236 B4
Friars Cl. Derby 205 D1
Friars Ct. Ilk 208 B3
Friary Ave. Derby 232 C3
Friary St. Derby 218 C3
Friesland Dr. Sand 223 D3
Frinton Cl. Chest 114 C4
Frisby Ave. Lo Ea 236 C3
Fritchley Cl. Derby 206 A1
Fritchley La. Crich 168 A4
Frith Cl. Shef 44 A3
Frith Rd. Shef 44 A3
Frith View. C-Frith 47 D3
Frithhall La. O Bram 94 B1
Frithwood La. Elmt 100 B4
Frizams La. Fin 242 C4
Froggatt Cl. Derby 205 D3
Froggatt Cl. Stav 97 E3
Front St. Crich 168 A3
Frost Ave. La Mi 182 A2
Fryar Rd. Greas 182 C2
Fulbrook Rd. Derby 231 D4
Fulford Cl. Chest 114 B4
Fulham Rd. Derby 218 A3
Full St. Derby 219 D3
Fuller Dr. Chest 96 B3
Fullwood Ave. Ilk 194 C1
Fullwood St. Ilk 194 C1
Fullwood Stile La. Hope 39 D4
Fulmar Cl. Derby 218 A2
Fulwood Head Rd. Hal M 42 B4
Fulwood La. Lod M 42 C3
Fulwood Rd N. S in A 148 C1
Fulwood Rd S. S in A 160 C4
Furlong Cl. Staple 223 E4
Furlong La. Alst 149 E2
Furlong La. Atlow 175 D4
Furnace Cl. Gra 115 F1
Furnace La Ind Est. Moira 262 C2
Furnace La. Barlow 75 F2
Furnace La. Hean 181 E2
Furnace La. Moira 262 C2
Furnace Rd. Ilk 209 D3
Furnace Row. Som 170 C4
Furnall Ave. G Lo 90 A2
Furness Cl. Glos 17 F4
Furness Lodge Cl. W Br 33 E2
Furness Row. W Br 33 E2
Furniss Ave. Totley 55 E3
Furrows Cl. Derby 206 B2
Fyfield Rd. Bu on T 254 C3
Fylde Cl. Bees 223 F1

Gable Ct. Derby 230 C4
Gadley Cl. Bux 84 C4
Gadley La. Bux 84 C4
Gadsby Rise. Ripley 168 B1
Gag La. Tiss 161 E3
Gainborough Cl. Derby 206 A1
Gainsborough Ave. Marple 23 D4
Gainsborough Cl. Staple 223 F3
Gainsborough Rd. Dron 75 F4
Gainsborough Way. Bu on T 248 A2
Gairloch Cl. Derby 231 E1
Galahad Dr. Bu on T 240 C1
Gale Rd. N Mills 33 E4
Gallery La. Holy 113 E4
Gallery The. Ashb 173 E1
Gallows Inn Cl. Ilk 209 D3
Gallowstree La. May 172 B1
Gallowstree La. May 184 B4
Galway Ave. Derby 220 A2
Gang La. Scarc 118 C3
Gannow Cl. Kill 60 C4
Gapsick La. Whit 81 D3
Garden Ave. Eck 79 D4
Garden Ave. Ilk 208 C3
Garden Ave. Plea 134 C4
Garden Ave. Shireb 119 F2
Garden Cl. Uns 77 E3
Garden Cr. S Norm 159 F2
Garden Cres. C Don 247 D2
Garden Rd. East 182 C2
Garden Row. Al Hv 117 E1
Garden St. Derby 218 C3
Garden St. M in L 16 A4
Gardens The. Hean 181 E2
Gardens The. Ripley 180 B4
Gardner Pl. Utt 210 A1
Gardom Cl. Shef 56 C4
Garfield Ave. Dray 235 D4
Garfield Cl. Derby 231 E3
Garfield Cl. Staple 209 F1
Garland Cl. Mosb 59 F4
Garland Croft. Mosb 59 F4
Garland Way. Mosb 59 F4
Garner La. S Wing 157 E1
Garnett Ave. Hean 181 F1
Garrett La. Cl Cr 131 E1
Garrick St. Derby 233 D4
Garry Cl. Derby 231 E4
Garsdale Ct. Derby 233 E3
Garth Cres. Derby 233 D3
Garth Rd. Marple 23 D3
Garth Way Cl. Dron 56 C1
Garth Way. Dron 56 C1
Garthorpe Ct. Derby 205 F1
Gartrice Gdns. Kill 60 A3
Gary Cl. Derby 231 E3
Gas St. M in L 9 E3
Gas St. Sand 223 E3
Gas St. Utt 210 B1
Gascoine Dr. Derby 220 B2
Gashouse La. Eck 59 E3
Gashouse La. Mosb 59 E3
Gaskell Ave. Derby 231 F4
Gatcombe Cl. Bu on T 240 B1
Gatcombe Cl. Derby 206 A1
Gatcombe Gr. Sand 223 D2
Gate Brook Cl. Codnor 170 A1
Gatefield Cl. Chest 95 E4
Gateland La. Barlow 75 F3
Gauledge La. Long 121 D3
Gaunt Cl. Shef 43 E2
Gaunt Dr. Shef 43 E2
Gaunt Pl. Shef 43 E2
Gaunt Rd. Shef 43 E2
Gaunt Way. Shef 43 E2
Gawain Gr. Bu on T 240 C1
Gawsworth Cl. Glos 10 A3
Gayton Ave. Derby 231 E3
Gayton Thorpe Cl. Derby 230 C4
Geary La. Bretby 248 C1
Geer La. Eck 58 B3
Gelderd Pl. Dron 76 A4
Gema Cl. Derby 205 D2
Genista Cl. Bu on T 255 D4
Gentshill Ave. Cl Cr 131 F1
George Ave. Lo Ea 223 F1
George Cres. Som 170 B3
George Holmes Way. Swad 256 A2
George Percival Pl. Cl Cr 131 D2
George Rd. Mat 143 E3
George St. Alf 159 D2
George St. Ashb 185 D4
George St. Belper 178 C2
George St. Bux 85 D4
George St. Chest 76 C1
George St. Chest 96 C4
George St. Derby 218 C3
George St. Glos 17 E4
George St. La Mi 182 A2
George St. Mans 136 B2
George St. Mar War 120 C1
George St. Marple 15 D1
George St. Mel 252 A4
George St. N Wing 131 F4
George St. Pinx 160 B2
George St. S Norm 159 F3
George St. Scarc 101 D1
George St. Som 170 B3
George St. Som 170 B4
George St. Swad 256 A1
George St. W Br 45 F4
Gerard Cl. Chest 95 E1
Gerard Cl. Derby 220 C3
Gerard Cl. Shef 43 D3
Gerard Ct. Derby 218 C2
Gerard Gr. Etwall 229 E2
Gerard St. Derby 218 C2
Gerard St. Shef 43 D3
Gertrude Rd. Derby 220 A4
Gertrude Rd. Dray 235 D4
Gervase Ave. Shef 56 C3
Gervase Dr. Shef 56 C3
Gervase Pl. Shef 56 C3
Gervase Rd. Shef 56 C3
Gervase Wlk. Shef 56 C3
Gibb La. Marple 23 F3
Gibb La. Sud 225 F3
Gibb St. Lo Ea 236 C4
Gibbons Ave. Staple 223 E3
Gibbons Dr. Shef 43 F1
Gibbons Way. Shef 43 F1
Gibfield La. Belper 178 C1
Gibfield La. Hog 175 E3
Gibfield La. K Ire 175 E3
Gifford Rd. Shef 43 D4
Gilbert Ave. Chest 114 B4
Gilbert Cl. Derby 220 B2
Gilbert Cres. Duff 190 C1
Gilbert St. Derby 233 D3
Gilderdale Way. Derby 206 A2
Gill La. Da Da 127 E2
Gill's La. Gra 115 F1
Gillamoor Ct. Derby 233 E3
Gilleyfield Ave. Totley 55 F4
Gilliver Gdns. Dray 235 D4
Gillot St. Hean 194 A4
Gilt Hill. Kim 195 E4
Giltbrook Cres. Greas 195 E4
Giltway. Greas 195 E4
Gimson Cl. Ilk 194 B2
Gin Close Way. Awsw 195 E3
Gin Close Way. Kim 195 E3
Gin La. Ash 144 C4
Gipsy La. Alst 149 F2
Gipsy La. Chest 77 D1
Gipsy La. Uns 58 A1
Gipsyhill La. Whit 81 D4

Gird La. Marple 15 F1
Girdon Cl. Bux 84 C3
Gisborne Cl. Derby 217 F2
Gisborne Cres. Derby 204 C2
Gisborne Green. Derby 218 C3
Gisbourne Dr. C-Frith 47 D3
Glade Cl. Chest 95 F3
Glade Croft. Shef 44 A2
Glade Lea. Shef 44 A2
Glade The. Bux 85 D4
Glade The. Chest 95 E2
Gladstone Ave. Hean 181 F1
Gladstone Ave. Newt 147 F1
Gladstone Cl. Derby 232 C2
Gladstone Dr. Brin 182 C4
Gladstone Rd. Alf 158 C2
Gladstone Rd. Chest 95 F2
Gladstone Rd. Derby 220 C3
Gladstone St E. Ilk 208 C4
Gladstone St. Derby 218 C1
Gladstone St. Glos 10 A2
Gladstone St. Glos 17 E4
Gladstone St. Hean 181 F1
Gladstone St. Ilk 208 C4
Gladstone St. La Mi 182 B2
Gladstone St. Lo Ea 236 B3
Gladstone St. Mans 136 B1
Gladstone St. S Norm 160 A3
Gladstone Terr. Mans 136 B1
Gladwin Gdns. Chest 114 B4
Glaisdale Nook. Derby 233 E3
Glamis Cl. Derby 206 A1
Glapwell La. Glap 118 A1
Glasshouse Hill. Codnor 181 D4
Glasshouse La. Uns 77 E3
Glastonbury Cl. Mans 136 B2
Glastonbury Rd. Derby 233 E4
Glaven Cl. Mans 136 B1
Gleadless Ave. Shef 44 A2
Gleadless Bank. Shef 43 F2
Gleadless Comm. Shef 44 A3
Gleadless Cres. Shef 43 F3
Gleadless Ct. Shef 43 D3
Gleadless Dr. Shef 43 F2
Gleadless Mount. Shef 44 A2
Gleadless Rd. Shef 43 E3
Glebe Ave. G Lo 90 A2
Glebe Ave. Hart 61 F4
Glebe Ave. Pinx 160 B2
Glebe Ave. Ripley 169 E1
Glebe Ave. Smal 192 C3
Glebe Cl. C Elms 260 B2
Glebe Cl. Dove 224 A4
Glebe Cl. N Wing 132 B4
Glebe Cl. Rolle 240 A2
Glebe Cl. Thurv 201 F1
Glebe Cres. Ilk 209 D4
Glebe Cres. Stanl 207 D3
Glebe Farm Cl. Hart 61 F4
Glebe Rd. Bux 85 E4
Glebe Rise. Derby 218 B1
Glebe St. Swad 256 A2
Glebe The. Awsw 195 D2
Glebe The. Rosl 260 B3
Glebe Way The. Chest 77 D1
Gledhill Cl. Dron 57 D1
Glen Ave. Holbr 191 E4
Glen Cl. Newt 148 A2
Glen Rd. Crich 156 B1
Glen View Rd. Shef 56 C4
Glen View. Belper 178 C1
Glen Vine. Ripley 170 A1
Glenavon Cl. Uns 77 E3
Glenbrook Hill. Glos 10 B1
Glencoe Way. Chest 95 D2
Glencroft Dr. Derby 231 E2
Glendale Dr. Derby 220 C3
Glendon Rd. Derby 231 E2
Glendon Rd. Ilk 208 B2
Glendon St. Stanl 193 D1
Gleneagles Cl. Chest 114 B4
Gleneagles Cl. Derby 217 F1
Gleneagles Dr. Bu on T 240 B1
Glenfield Ave. Kim 195 E4
Glenfield Cres. Chest 96 A4
Glenfield Cres. Derby 217 E1
Glenfield Rd. Lo Ea 236 B3
Glengarry Way. Derby 231 F2
Glenholme Dr. Shef 44 C4
Glenholme Pl. Shef 44 C4
Glenholme Way. Shef 44 C4
Glenmoor Rd. Bux 66 B1
Glenmore Croft. Shef 44 B3
Glenmoy Cl. Derby 231 E4
Glenn Way. Shar 234 C1
Glenorchy Ct. Derby 206 A2
Glenthorn Cl. Shire 63 F4
Glenthorne Cl. Chest 95 E1
Glenwood Rd. Derby 245 D4
Glinton Ave. Newt 147 F1
Glossop Brook Rd. Glos 10 A1
Glossop Rd. Cha 16 B4
Glossop Rd. Glos 9 F1
Glossop Rd. Hay 25 E3
Glossop Rd. Marple 15 E2
Glossop St. Derby 232 A4
Glossop's Croft. Chest 77 D1
Gloster St. Derby 219 F1
Gloucester Ave. Chest 95 F3
Gloucester Ave. Sand 223 D2
Gloucester Rd. Chest 95 F3
Gloucester Way. Bu on T 248 A1
Gloucester Way. Glos 17 F4
Glover Rd. Shef 43 D4
Glover Rd. Totley 55 F3
Gloves La. Newt 147 E1
Gloves La. Tibs 147 E1
Glumangate. Chest 96 A2
Goathland Rd. Derby 231 E1
Goddard La. Glos 10 A3
Goddard La. N Mills 24 C4
Goddard Rd. Glos 10 A2
Godfrey Dr. Ilk 208 B3
Godfrey St. Hean 181 F1
Godkin Dr. Ald 182 A2
Godward Rd. N Mills 33 D4
Gold Cl. Wens 142 A4
Gold La. Mack 217 F4
Goldcrest Dr. Derby 220 C3
Goldcrest House. Chest 77 D2
Golden Valley. H Wood 192 A3
Golden Valley. Som 170 B2
Golders Green Wlk. Derby 218 A3
Goldhill. Tans 144 A2
Golf Club Rd. S-by-D 209 D1
Golf La. Duff 190 C3
Gomersal La. Dron 57 D1
Goodale St. Derby 219 D1
Goodman Cl. Greas 195 E4
Goodrington Rd. Derby 206 B2
Goods Rd. Belper 178 C1
Goodsmoor Rd. Derby 231 F3
Goodwin Dr. Kim 195 F3
Goodwin Rd. Shef 43 D3
Goodwin's La. Haz 178 B1
Goodwood Cl. Bu on T 240 B1
Goodwood Cres. Ilk 208 B2
Goodwood Dr. Bees 223 F1
Goodwood Dr. Derby 233 E3
Gooker La. Alf 158 C2
Goole Ave. Ilk 208 B3
Goose Green La. Shirl 146 B2
Goose La. Codnor 181 E4
Gordon Ave. Shef 43 D1
Gordon Cres. S Norm 160 A2
Gordon Rd. Derby 218 C2
Gordon Rd. Ock 221 D1
Gordon Rd. Som 169 F4
Gordon Rd. Tide 69 E2
Gordon St. Ilk 195 D1
Gordondale Rd. Mans 136 A1
Gore La. Bradw 51 D4
Gorman Cl. Chest 95 F4
Gorse Bank. Heath 116 C1
Gorse Cl. Derby 231 E3
Gorse Cl. Greas 195 E4
Gorse Dr. Kill 60 B3
Gorse La. Bradl 175 D2
Gorse La. Lod M 42 C4
Gorse Ridge Dr. Baslow 91 F3
Gorse Valley Rd. Chest 115 F4
Gorse Valley Way. Chest 115 F4
Gorse Way. Glos 17 F4
Gorsebank La. Baslow 91 F4
Gorses. Alder 178 B4
Gorses. Idri 176 B3
Gorsey Bank. Wirk 165 F4
Gorsey Brigg. Shef 56 C4
Gorsey Brow. M in L 9 D1
Gorsey Cl. Belper 178 C3
Gorsey Intakes. M in L 16 A4
Gorsey La. K Ire 165 D1
Gorsey La. Neth 265 D4
Gorsty Leys. Fin 230 B1
Gosber Rd. Eck 59 F2
Gosber St. Eck 59 E2
Goseley Ave. Harts 257 D2
Goseley Cres. Harts 257 D2
Gosforth Cl. Dron 56 C1
Gosforth Cres. Dron 56 C1
Gosforth Dr. Dron 56 C1
Gosforth Green. Dron 56 C1
Gosforth La. Dron 56 C1
Gosforth Rd. Derby 232 C4
Gower Cres. Chest 95 E3
Gower St. Derby 219 D2
Goyt Pl. W Br 45 F4
Goyt Rd. Disley 32 B3
Goyt Rd. N Mills 33 E3
Goyt Side Rd. Chest 95 F1
Goyt View. N Mills 33 D3
Goyt's La. Bux 65 D2
Goytlands. Bux 84 C3
Grace Cres. Hean 181 F1
Grafham Cl. Derby 233 D2
Grafton Rd. Bu on T 248 A1
Grafton St. Derby 218 C1
Graham Cl. Bu on T 254 B4
Graham Dr. Disley 32 B3
Graham St. Ilk 208 C4
Grammer St. Hean 181 D2
Grampian Cres. O Bram 95 D2
Grampian Way. Derby 231 F2
Grampian Way. Lo Ea 236 A4
Granary Cl. Chest 95 D4
Granby Ave. Chin 34 C1
Granby Cl. Pils 132 B1
Granby Croft. Bake 109 E3
Granby Rd. Bake 109 E3
Granby Rd. Bradw 50 C4
Granby Rd. Bux 85 E4
Granby St. Ilk 194 C1
Grandfield St. Hean 181 E2
Grandstand Rd. Derby 219 E3
Grange Ave. Brea 235 E4
Grange Ave. C-Frith 47 D3
Grange Ave. Derby 231 F4
Grange Ave. Dron 56 C1
Grange Ave. H Ward 175 F2
Grange Cl. Mel 252 A4
Grange Cl. Som 159 F1
Grange Cl. Tick 251 D2
Grange Ct. Eg 241 D3
Grange Dale. Ible 153 E4
Grange Dr. C Don 247 D2
Grange Dr. Lo Ea 236 C4
Grange La. Barlow 75 D1
Grange La. Da Da 127 F1
Grange La. Ible 153 E4
Grange Park Ave. C-Frith 47 D3
Grange Park Ave. Chest 96 C2
Grange Park Rd. C-Frith 47 D3
Grange Rd S. Marple 15 D4
Grange Rd. Bux 85 E4
Grange Rd. Derby 233 D3
Grange Rd. Lo Ea 236 C4
Grange Rd. Pils 132 B1
Grange Rd. Swad 255 F3
Grange Rd. Utt 210 A1
Grange St. Alf 159 D2
Grange St. Derby 219 D1
Grange The. O Bram 94 C2
Grange The. S Norm 160 A2
Grange The. Smal 193 E4
Grange View. East 182 C2
Grange Walk. Gra 115 F1
Grangewood Ave. Ilk 208 C4
Grangewood Dr. Belper 191 D4
Grangewood Rd. Chest 114 C4
Gransden Way. Chest 114 B4
Gransden Way. Chest 114 B4
Grant Ave. Derby 220 A3
Grantham Ave. Derby 205 F1
Grantham Cl. Greas 195 E4
Granville Ave. Lo Ea 223 E1
Granville Cl. Chest 115 E4
Granville Cl. Duff 190 C2
Granville Cl. Hatton 227 E1
Granville St. Derby 218 C3
Granville St. Swad 256 C2
Grasmere Ave. Cl Cr 131 D2
Grasmere Ave. Derby 220 C3
Grasmere Cl. Bu on T 248 A1
Grasmere Cl. Chest 95 E4
Grasmere Cres. Derby 231 F2
Grasmere Rd. Dron 56 C1
Grasmere Rd. Lo Ea 223 D1
Grasmere St. Sand 223 D3
Grass St. Ilk 194 C2
Grasscroft Cl. Chest 95 E3
Grassdale View. Shef 44 C2
Grassmoor Cl. Shef 43 F3
Grassmoor Cres. Glos 9 E1
Grassthorpe Cl. Derby 206 A1
Grassthorpe Rd. Shef 44 A2
Gratton Ct. Stav 78 C2
Gratton La. Elton 140 B4
Gravel Pit Hill. Rep 249 F4
Gravel Pit La. Derby 220 C2
Gravelly Bank Mews. Yea 199 E3
Graves Trust Homes. Shef 57 D4
Gray St. Clowne 80 C2
Gray St. Mosb 59 E4
Grayling St. Derby 219 D1
Grayswood Cl. Som 170 A4
Great Croft. Dron 56 B1
Great Northern Rd. Derby 218 C3
Great Northern Rd. East 182 B1
Greatorex Ave. Derby 232 C3
Greaves La. A in W 108 C4
Greaves St. Ripley 169 F1
Greaves St. Shirl 146 C1
Green Ave. Derby 233 D1
Green Bank. Glos 16 C4
Green Chase. Eck 59 E2
Green Cl. Mat 143 D3
Green Cl. Newt 148 A2
Green Cl. Stav 97 E3
Green Cl. Uns 76 C3
Green Cl. Will 242 A3
Green Cres. Sels 171 F3
Green Cross. Dron 57 D1
Green Farm Cl. Chest 95 E3
Green Farm Rd. Sels 171 E3
Green Glen. Chest 95 E1
Green Hill. Wirk 154 C1
Green La. Ba on T 244 A3
Green La. Bake 108 B2
Green La. Barl 60 B2
Green La. Belper 178 C2
Green La. Bons 153 F4
Green La. Br Hill 252 C3
Green La. Burn 230 A2
Green La. Bux 67 E1
Green La. Bux 85 D3
Green La. Chel 106 B4
Green La. Chest 96 B2
Green La. Chin 34 C1
Green La. Clif 184 C4
Green La. Da Da 127 D2
Green La. Derby 219 D2
Green La. Derby 233 E4
Green La. Disley 32 B2
Green La. Dron 57 D1
Green La. Glos 9 F2
Green La. Glos 16 C4
Green La. Hog 164 A1
Green La. Ilk 209 D4
Green La. Kill 60 B2
Green La. M in L 9 E3
Green La. Mans 135 D1
Green La. March 225 D1
Green La. Marple 15 D4
Green La. O Bram 94 C4
Green La. Ock 221 E3
Green La. Over 261 F2
Green La. Pils 132 B2
Green La. Plea 134 B4
Green La. Rost 198 A4
Green La. Tans 144 A3
Green La. Tiss 150 B1
Green La. Tupton 115 E1
Green La. Tut 239 E3
Green La. W Und 188 C1
Green La. Whit 82 B3
Green Lands. Swad 256 A4
Green Lea. Dron 56 B1
Green Leas. As on T 246 A4
Green Oak Ave. Totley 55 F2
Green Oak Cres. Totley 55 F2
Green Oak Dr. Totley 55 F2
Green Oak Gr. Totley 55 F2
Green Oak Rd. Totley 55 F2
Green Park Dr. C-Frith 47 D3
Green Park. Derby 218 A3
Green Rd The. Ashb 173 E2
Green St. B in F 237 F3
Green St. Chest 77 D1
Green The. Al Hu 133 D2
Green The. Alf 159 D2
Green The. As on T 246 A4
Green The. Bam 40 A2
Green The. Belper 179 D3
Green The. Bir 126 A1
Green The. Br Hill 252 C1
Green The. Bradw 51 D3
Green The. Brai 201 F4
Green The. Brea 235 E4
Green The. Bu on T 240 C1
Green The. C Don 247 D2
Green The. Chest 115 E4
Green The. Crich 168 A3
Green The. Curbar 72 B3
Green The. Curbar 72 C1
Green The. Derby 204 B1
Green The. Derby 217 E1
Green The. Dray 235 D4
Green The. Fin 230 B1
Green The. Glap 134 A4
Green The. Glos 17 D4
Green The. K Lang 202 B1
Green The. Mans 136 A3
Green The. Marple 23 D2
Green The. Mid 154 B3
Green The. S in A 148 C1
Green The. Som 169 F4
Green The. Tiss 162 A3
Green The. Totley 55 E2
Green The. Will 242 A3
Green Way. Fin 230 B1
Green Way. Win 115 E1
Greenacre Ave. Hean 182 A2
Greenacre The. Clif 184 C4
Greenacres Cl. Dron 76 B4
Greenacres Dr. S Norm 160 A3
Greenacres Dr. Utt 210 A1
Greenacres. Derby 231 D4
Greenbank Dr. Chest 95 E2
Greenbank Rd. Marple 15 D1
Greenbank. Derby 220 B2
Greenburn Cl. Derby 231 E3
Greendale Ave. Holy 113 F4
Greendale Ct. Dron 57 D1
Greendale Shopping Centre. Dron 57 D1
Greenfell Ave. Derby 231 F3
Greenfield Ave. Whit 82 B3
Greenfield Cl. N Mills 33 D4
Greenfield Cl. Shef 56 C4
Greenfield Dr. Linton 261 E3
Greenfield Dr. Shef 56 C4
Greenfield Rd. Shef 56 C4
Greenfield St. Glos 10 A3
Greenfields Ave. Derby 231 D4
Greenfields. Ald 182 A2
Greenfields. Dens 196 B3
Greenfields. Eck 59 E2
Greenfinch Cl. Derby 220 C3
Greengate Cl. Chest 95 E1
Greenhall Rd. Eck 59 E2
Greenhead Cres. Biggin 138 E1
Greenhead Park. Bam 40 A2
Greenhead. Bam 40 A
Greenhill Ave. Ripley 180 C
Greenhill Ave. Shef 56 C
Greenhill La. Som 170 B
Greenhill Main Rd. Shef 56 C
Greenhill Parkway. Shef 56 C
Greenhill Wlk. Disley 32 B
Greenhills Rd. East 182 C
Greenhouse La. Lod M 42 C
Greenland Ave. Derby 218 A
Greenland Cl. N Wing 132 A
Greens Ct. Ilk 194 B
Greens La. Kim 195 F
Greenshall La. Disley 32 C
Greenside Ave. Chest 96 A
Greenside Cl. Donis 262 C
Greenside Cl. Lo Ea 236 C
Greenside Ct. Derby 217 E
Greensquare Rd. K in A 160 C
Greenvale Cl. Bu on T 254 C
Greenview. Brass 153 D
Greenway Cl. Ock 221 D
Greenway Croft. Wirk 154 C
Greenway Dr. Bols 118 A
Greenway La. Da Da 127 F
Greenway The. Sand 223 D
Greenway The. Shef 56 C
Greenway. Ashb 173 E
Greenway. Brass 153 D
Greenway. H Ward 175 F
Greenway. Whit 81 F
Greenways. Chest 114 B
Greenwich Dr N. Derby 218 B
Greenwich Dr S. Derby 218 A
Greenwood Ave. Derby 219 F
Greenwood Ave. Ilk 209 D
Greenwood Ave. Mans 136 A
Greenwood Ave. S in A 148 C
Greenwood Cl. Derby 232 B
Greenwood Ct. Derby 219 D
Greenwood Rd. Bu on T 254 C
Greer La. Scarc 118 B
Gregg Ave. Hean 181 F
Greggs Ave. C-Frith 46 C
Gregors Way. Belper 179 E
Gregory Ave. Ald 182 A
Gregory Ave. Brea 235 E
Gregory Ave. La Mi 182 A
Gregory Cl. Staple 223 F
Gregory Rd. Shef 43 D
Gregory St. Ilk 208 C
Gregory Wlk. Derby 230 C
Gregson Cl. Swad 256 A
Grenville Dr. Ilk 194 C
Grenville Dr. Staple 223 F
Grenvoir Dr. Ripley 170 A
Gresham Rd. Derby 232 E
Gresley Rd. Ilk 194 C
Gresley Rd. Shef 56 C
Gresley Wlk. Shef 56 C
Gresley Wood Rd. Wood 256 A
Gresley Woodlands. Swad 256 A
Gretton Ave. Bu on T 240 C
Gretton Rd. Bux 85 E
Grey St. Derby 218 C
Griffin Cl. Derby 232 C
Griffin Cl. N Mills 33 E
Griggs Gdns. Wirk 165 F
Grimshaw Ave. Derby 233
Grin Low Rd. Bux 85 D
Grindlow Ave. Chest 95 F
Grindlow Cl. Shef 43 E
Grindlow Dr. Shef 43 E
Grindlow Rd. Derby 220 A
Grindon Cl. Chest 95 E
Grindslow Ave. We Ha 207 F
Grinlow Cl. Bux 85 E
Grisedale Rd. G Lo 90 A
Grisedale Wlk. Dron 56 C
Gritstone Rd. Mat 143 E
Groome Ave. Hean 181 E
Grosvenor Ave. Brea 235 F
Grosvenor Ave. Lo Ea 236 A
Grosvenor Rd. East 182 C
Grosvenor Rd. Marple 23
Grosvenor Rd. Ripley 169 E
Grosvenor St. Derby 232 E
Grove Ave. Totley 55 E
Grove Cl. Elv 233 F
Grove Ct. Ripley 180 C
Grove Farm Cl. Chest 96 C
Grove Gdns. Chest 96 C
Grove House Ct. Totley 55 F
Grove La. Bux 85 E
Grove La. Da Da 127 F
Grove La. Dove 224 C
Grove La. O Bram 94 A
Grove La. S Herb 211 F
Grove Mews. East 182 C
Grove Park. Etwall 229
Grove Pl. Youl 125
Grove Rd. Chest 96
Grove Rd. Totley 55 F
Grove St. Chest 115
Grove St. Derby 219
Grove St. Mans 136 A
Grove St. N Mills 33
Grove St. Swad 256 A

rove The. Brea 235 F4
rove The. Derby 217 F1
rove The. Glos 9 F2
rove The. Stav 98 A4
rove The. Totley 55 E2
rove Way. Chest 96 C3
rove Way. Mans 136 A2
roves Nook. Derby 232 C1
rundy Ave. Sels 171 E4
rundy Nook. Whit 82 A3
rundy Rd. Cl Cr 131 E2
runmore Dr. Bu on T 240 C1
uernsey Rd. Shef 43 D4
uide Post. Ripley 168 B1
uildford Ave. Chest 114 B4
uildford Ave. Mans 136 B3
uildford Ave. Shef 43 E4
uildford Ave. Swad 256 C3
uildford Cl. Shef 43 E4
uildford Dr. Shef 43 E4
uildford Rise. Shef 43 F4
uildford Way. Shef 43 F4
uilford Cl. Cl Cr 131 F2
uilford La. Cl Cr 131 F2
uinevere Ave. Bu on T 240 C1
un La. Ripley 168 B1
un Rd. Cha 16 B1
un Rd. Marple 16 B1
unby Hill. Neth 261 F1
unhills La. Wind 189 F3
urney Ave. Derby 231 E3
utersloh Ct. Staple 223 F4
y Cl. Staple 223 F3
ypsy La. Drayc 221 F1

ackney La. Barlow 75 F1
ackney Rd. Da Da 143 D4
ackthorne Rd. Shef 43 D2
addon Ave. Clowne 81 D2
addon Cl. Alf 158 C2
addon Cl. Chest 95 E1
addon Cl. Derby 204 B2
addon Cl. Dron 57 D1
addon Cl. We Ha 207 F4
addon Ct. Ashb 185 E4
addon Dr. Bake 109 F2
addon Dr. Derby 204 B2
addon Dr. Derby 217 F2
addon Dr. Derby 220 C2
addon Dr. Lit Ea 191 E1
addon Nurseries. Ilk 194 C2
addon Pl. Ripley 168 A3
addon Pl. Shireb 119 E3
addon Pl. Stav 97 E4
addon Rd. Bake 109 F2
addon Rd. Bux 85 E4
addon Rd. N Wing 132 A4
addon St. Derby 218 C1
addon St. Ilk 194 C2
addon St. Tibs 148 A3
addon Way. Lo Ea 235 F2
ade La. Flagg 106 C4
adfield Pl. Glos 17 E4
adfield Rd. Glos 9 F2
adfield Sq. Glos 17 E4
adfield St. Glos 17 E4
adfields Ave. M in L 9 E3
adleigh Cl. Bees 223 F1
adley La. Bradl 186 C4
adley St. Ilk 209 D3
adstock Cl. Sand 223 D2
ady Cres. Chest 96 B2
ady Hill. Chest 96 B1
ady La. Chest 96 B1
ag Bank La. Disley 32 B4
ag La. Wind 177 E1
agg La. Dale 207 E2
ague Ave. Eck 79 D4
ague Bar Rd. N Mills 33 D4
ague Fold. N Mills 32 C4
ague La. Eck 79 D4
ague Rd. M in L 16 A4
ague St. Glos 17 E4
aig Memorial Homes. Shef 57 D4
aig St. Derby 232 C4
aigh Moor Rd. Shef 44 C4
aigh Moor Wlk. Shef 44 C4
ailsham Cl. Derby 217 E2
aines Cl. Derby 231 F2
alcyon App. Win 115 E1
alcyon Cl. Shef 44 C2
aldane Cl. Elmt 81 F1
aldane Cres. Bols 98 C1
alesworth Cl. Chest 114 A4
aley Cl. Kim 195 E3
alf Acre La. Dron 76 B4
alf Croft. Chest 96 C4
alfmoon La. Callow 165 D2
alfmoon La. K Ire 165 D2
alfway Centre. Mosb 59 F4
alfway Dr. Mosb 59 F4
alfway Gdns. Mosb 59 F4
alifax Cl. Derby 205 E1
all Bank. Bux 85 D4
all Bank. Hartin 137 F3
all Cl. Dron 56 B1
all Cl. M in L 9 D3
all Ct. We Ha 207 F4
Hall Dale View. Da Da 127 E2
Hall Dr. Dove 211 D1
Hall Dr. M in L 9 D3
Hall Dr. Sand 223 D3
Hall Dyke. Derby 220 B3
Hall End La. A in W 108 C4
Hall Farm Cl. C Don 247 D2
Hall Farm Cl. Swad 256 B2
Hall Farm Rd. Duff 190 C1
Hall Farm Rd. Swad 256 B2
Hall Gate View. Bradw 51 D4
Hall Green Ave. Bu on T 240 C1
Hall La. Ashb 173 E1
Hall La. Brin 182 B3
Hall La. Donis 265 F4
Hall La. Dove 224 A4
Hall La. Litton 69 F2
Hall La. Newt 148 A2
Hall La. Ripley 168 B2
Hall La. Shir 200 B4
Hall La. Stan 183 D3
Hall La. Stav 78 B2
Hall La. Will 242 A3
Hall Leys La. Mel 245 E1
Hall Meadow Rd. Glos 10 B1
Hall Park. Ba on T 244 A3
Hall Rd. Ald 182 B2
Hall Rd. Chest 96 C4
Hall Rd. March 224 C1
Hall Rd. Rolle 239 F2
Hall Rise. Ashb 173 E2
Hall Rise. Da Da 127 E2
Hall St. Alf 159 D2
Hall St. Derby 233 D4
Hall St. N Mills 33 D4
Hall St. Swad 256 A1
Hall Terr. Cl Cr 131 E2
Hall The. Mid 154 B3
Hall Walk. Tupton 115 E1
Hall's Ct. Glos 10 B1
Hall's Row. Chest 95 E1
Hallam Ct. Dron 76 A4
Hallam Fields Rd. Ilk 209 D2
Hallam Fields. C Don 247 D1
Hallam Way. We Ha 207 E4
Hallamway. Mans 136 B1
Hallcliff La. O Bram 93 F1
Hallcroft Ave. Over 262 A2
Hallcroft Rd. Ilk 208 C4
Halldale La. Da Da 127 F2
Hallfield Cl. Win 115 D2
Hallfield Rd. Newt 148 A2
Hallfieldgate La. Shirl 146 B1
Hallfields Rd. Swad 255 E2
Hallfields Rd. Swad 255 F2
Hallflash La. Calow 116 A4
Hallgate La. Pils 132 A1
Hallington Dr. Hean 181 E1
Hallmoor Rd. Da Da 127 E2
Hallowes Ct. Dron 57 D1
Hallowes Dr. Dron 76 B4
Hallowes La. Dron 76 A4
Hallowes Rise. Dron 76 B4
Halls La. Greas 195 D4
Halls Rd. Staple 223 E3
Hallsteads Cl. C-Frith 47 F1
Hallsteads. C-Frith 47 F1
Hallum Ct. Ilk 194 C2
Hallworth Wlk. Eck 58 C1
Hallyburton Cl. Shef 43 E3
Hallyburton Dr. Shef 43 E3
Hallyburton Rd. Shef 43 E3
Halsteads The. Kni 163 D1
Halstock Dr. Derby 233 E4
Halton Cl. Chest 76 C1
Hambledon Cl. Chest 95 E3
Hambledon Dr. Derby 231 E1
Hambleton Ave. N Wing 131 F3
Hambleton Cl. Lo Ea 223 D1
Hamblin Cres. Derby 231 F2
Hamill Cl. N Wing 131 F4
Hamilton Cl. Bees 223 F1
Hamilton Cl. Derby 217 F2
Hamilton Dr. Swad 256 B3
Hamilton Fields. Bu on T 248 A1
Hamilton Rd. Bu on T 248 A1
Hamilton Rd. Derby 218 C1
Hamilton Rd. Derby 220 C3
Hamilton Rd. Lo Ea 223 E1
Hamilton Terr. Will 242 A3
Hamlet La. S Norm 160 A3
Hamlet The. Hean 181 F2
Hamlet The. S Norm 160 A3
Hammersmith. Ripley 169 E2
Hammonds Ct. Wirk 165 F4
Hampden St. Derby 232 A4
Hampden St. Greas 195 E4
Hampshire Ct. Glos 17 F4
Hampshire Ct. Sels 171 D2
Hampshire Dr. Sand 223 D3
Hampshire Rd. Derby 219 E4
Hampstead Dr. Derby 218 A3
Hampton Cl. Bees 223 F2
Hampton Cl. Derby 220 C3
Hampton Cl. We Ha 207 E4
Hampton St. Chest 115 E4
Hanbury Cl. Chest 95 D3
Hanbury Cl. Dron 56 C1
Hanbury Hill. Han 238 A3
Hanbury Rd. Derby 219 F3
Hand's Rd. Hean 182 A1
Handby St. Chest 115 E4
Handel St. Derby 232 B4
Handford Ct. Derby 218 B3
Handford St. Derby 218 B3
Handley La. Cl Cr 131 D1
Handley La. Eden 91 D1
Handley La. Stret 145 F4
Handley Rd. Uns 77 E3
Handsacre Cl. Swad 255 F2
Handyside St. Derby 219 D3
Hangar Hill. Whit 82 A3
Hanger Bank. As on T 246 A4
Hanley Cl. Disley 32 B3
Hanover Sq. Derby 218 A3
Hansard Gate. Derby 219 E3
Hanslynn. Elv 233 F2
Hanstubbin Rd. Sels 171 F3
Hanwell Way. Derby 218 A3
Harbin Rd. Wa on T 253 E1
Harborough Ave. Shef 44 A4
Harby Ave. Mans 136 B3
Harcourt Pl. C Don 247 D2
Harcourt Rd. Bran 253 F4
Harcourt St. Derby 219 D2
Hardacre Cl. Mel 252 A4
Hardhurst Rd. Derby 233 D3
Hardhurst Rd. Uns 76 C3
Hardie Ave. S Norm 160 A3
Hardie Pl. Stav 97 E4
Harding's La. Biggin 138 D3
Hardmeadow La. Ash 130 A1
Hardstoft Rd. Al Hu 132 C1
Hardstoft Rd. Pils 132 C1
Hardwick Ave. Derby 204 B2
Hardwick Ave. Shireb 119 F2
Hardwick Ave. Uns 77 E3
Hardwick Ave. We Ha 207 F4
Hardwick Cl. Clowne 81 D2
Hardwick Cl. Dron 57 E1
Hardwick Cl. N Wing 132 C4
Hardwick Cl. Ripley 169 E2
Hardwick Ct. Lo Ea 235 F2
Hardwick Dr. Derby 217 F1
Hardwick La. Ash 129 E3
Hardwick Mount. Bux 85 E4
Hardwick Pl. Ilk 208 B3
Hardwick Square E. Bux 85 E4
Hardwick Square N. Bux 85 E4
Hardwick Square S. Bux 85 D4
Hardwick Square W. Bux 85 D4
Hardwick St. Bux 85 D4
Hardwick St. Chest 96 A2
Hardwick St. Derby 232 B4
Hardwick St. L Duk 97 E1
Hardwick St. Scarc 119 F4
Hardwick St. Shireb 120 A2
Hardwick St. Tibs 148 A4
Hardwick View Rd. Heath 132 C4
Hardwick's Yd. Chest 95 F1
Hardy Barn. Ship 194 A4
Hardy Cl. Lo Ea 236 B3
Hardy Cres. Codnor 181 D4
Hardy St. Alf 158 C3
Hardy St. Kim 195 F4
Hardybarn La. Bux 86 B4
Harebell Cl. Derby 206 A2
Harehedge La. Bu on T 240 A1
Harehill Cres. Win 114 B2
Harehill Rd. Chest 114 C4
Harepit Cl. Derby 233 D3
Harewood Cres. Cl Cr 131 D3
Harewood Ct. Sand 223 D2
Harewood Rd. Derby 204 B2
Harewood Rd. Holy 113 E3
Hargate Hill La. Glos 16 C4
Hargate Rd. Bux 84 C3
Hargrave Ave. Ock 221 E3
Harlaxton Dr. Lo Ea 237 D4
Harlech Cl. Derby 221 D3
Harlequin Ct. East 182 B2
Harlesden Ave. Derby 218 A4
Harlesthorpe Ave. Clowne 80 C3
Harlesthorpe La. Clowne 80 C3
Harlow Cl. Derby 232 C2
Harlow Cl. Mans 136 B3
Harlow Ct. We Ha 207 E4
Harold Ave. Ald 182 A2
Harperhill Cl. Chest 114 C4
Harpole Cl. Som 169 F4
HarportDr. Cl Cr 131 F1
Harpswell Cl. Derby 204 C1
Harpur Ave. Derby 231 D4
Harpur Ave. Tick 251 D2
Harpur Hill Rd. Bux 85 E2
Harrier Way. Derby 231 F4
Harriet St. Derby 219 D2
Harriett St. Staple 223 E4
Harrimans Dr. Brea 235 F4
Harringay Gdns. Derby 218 B3
Harrington Ave. Ock 221 E1
Harrington Rd. Derby 218 B1
Harrington Rd. Shef 43 D4
Harrington St. Derby 232 A4
Harrington St. Derby 232 C3
Harrington St. Dray 235 D4
Harrington St. Lo Ea 236 A3
Harris Ave. Ripley 169 E1
Harris Cl. Ripley 169 E1
Harris Rd. Bux 85 E2
Harrison Dr. Wirk 154 C1
Harrison La. Lod M 42 C4
Harrison La. Tibs 147 F3
Harrison Rd. Staple 223 E4
Harrison St. Derby 218 C2
Harrogate Cres. Derby 205 E1
Harrop La. Lod M 42 C3
Harrots La. Hartin 137 E3
Harrow Dr. Bu on T 254 B4
Harrow Rd. Swad 256 A4
Harrow St. Derby 219 F1
Hart Ave. Sand 223 D3
Hartfield Cl. Chest 115 D4
Hartford Cl. Shef 43 D2
Hartford Rd. Shef 43 D2
Harthill Field Rd. Hart 62 A2
Harthill Rd. Shef 44 A4
Harthill Rd. Th Sa 62 B4
Hartington Cl. We Ha 207 F4
Hartington Ct. Clowne 81 D2
Hartington Ct. Dron 57 D1
Hartington Dr. Chin 34 C1
Hartington Ind Est. Stav 78 C2
Hartington Pl. Ilk 194 C3
Hartington Rd. Bux 85 D4
Hartington Rd. Chest 96 B1
Hartington Rd. Dron 57 D1
Hartington St. Derby 219 D2
Hartington St. Scarc 119 F4
Hartington View. Stav 78 C2
Hartington Way. Derby 217 E1
Hartland Dr. Derby 231 F3
Hartland Way. Chest 77 D1
Hartley St. Shef 43 D4
Hartopp Ave. Shef 43 E3
Hartopp Cl. Shef 43 E3
Hartopp Dr. Shef 43 E3
Hartopp Rd. Shef 43 E3
Hartshay Hill. Ripley 169 E1
Hartshill Rd. Harts 257 D2
Hartshorne Rd. Derby 231 E3
Hartshorne Rd. Rep 249 F4
Hartshorne Rd. Wood 256 C2
Hartside Cl. Chest 95 E3
Hartside Gdns. Lo Ea 236 A4
Hartwood Dr. Staple 209 E1
Harvest Hill. Swad 256 A4
Harvest Way. Derby 206 B2
Harvest Way. O Bram 95 D3
Harvey Clough Rd. Shef 43 D2
Harvey Croft. Trow 209 E2
Harvey Ct. Bols 98 C1
Harvey Pl. Utt 210 A1
Harvey Rd. C Don 247 D1
Harvey Rd. Chest 96 C1
Harvey Rd. Derby 232 C3
Harwood Ave. Bran 253 F4
Harwood Cl. Shef 43 D4
Harwood St. Shef 43 D4
Haslam Cres. Shef 56 C3
Haslam Ct. Bols 98 C1
Haslam's La. Derby 205 D1
Hasland Rd. Chest 96 A1
Hasland Rd. Chest 115 E4
Haslemere Ct. Derby 219 D1
Haslemere Rd. Lo Ea 236 A4
Haslin Rd. Bux 85 E1
Hassock La N. Ship 194 A4
Hassock La S. Ship 194 B3
Hassocky La. Calow 116 A3
Hassocky La. Gra 116 A3
Hassop Rd. Calver 72 A1
Hassop Rd. Derby 220 A4
Hassop Rd. Stav 78 C2
Hastilar Cl. Shef 44 A4
Hastilar Rd S. Shef 44 B4
Hastilar Rd. Shef 44 B4
Hasting St. C Don 247 D1
Hastings Cl. Br Hill 252 C1
Hastings Cl. Chest 95 E3
Hastings Rd. Bux 85 E2
Hastings Rd. Swad 256 A2
Hastings St. Derby 219 D1
Haston Dr. Som 170 B4
Hatchmere Cl. Derby 206 A1
Hatfield Ave. Sand 223 D2
Hatfield Rd. Derby 232 C3
Hathaway Cl. Cl Cr 131 D3
Hathern Cl. Chest 96 C2
Hathern Cl. Derby 231 F3
Hathern Cl. Lo Ea 236 B3
Hathersage Ave. Derby 231 F4
Hathersage Ave. Lo Ea 235 F3
Hathersage Cres. Glos 9 F1
Hathersage Dr. Glos 17 F4
Hathersage Dr. Som 170 A4
Hathersage Rd. Bam 40 A1
Hathersage Rd. Totley 54 B3
Hatton Cl. Dron 75 E4
Hatton Crofts. Lo Ea 236 B3
Hatton Ct. Mel 252 A4
Hatton Dr. Chest 95 D3
Haulton Dr. C Don 247 D2
Havelock Rd. Derby 231 F4
Havelock Rd. Derby 232 A4
Havelock St. Ilk 208 C4
Havelock St. Ripley 169 F1
Haven Baulk Ave. Derby 230 C4
Haven Baulk La. Derby 230 C4
Haven Ct. Derby 233 E3
Havercroft Tr. Kill 60 A4
Hawfield La. Bu on T 248 B2
Hawfield La. N Sol 248 C2
Hawk Green Rd. Marple 23 D2
Hawk Rd. N Mills 33 F4
Hawk's Dr. Bu on T 248 B2
Hawke St. Derby 218 B3
Hawkeshead Ave. Dron 56 C1
Hawkhill Rd. Eyam 71 E3
Hawking La. Al Hu 133 D4
Hawkins Ct. Ilk 194 C2
Hawkins Dr. Ripley 168 A2
Hawkshead Ave. Derby 205 E1
Hawksley Ave. Chest 95 F2
Hawksley Dr. Da Da 127 D2
Hawksley Dr. Rolle 240 A2
Hawksway. Shef 59 D2
Hawley St. Uns 58 A1
Hawleys Cl. Mat 143 F3
Hawthorn Ave. Brea 235 F4
Hawthorn Ave. Derby 233 D4
Hawthorn Ave. Elmt 81 F1
Hawthorn Ave. Glap 134 A4
Hawthorn Ave. Neth 264 C4
Hawthorn Ave. Ripley 180 B4
Hawthorn Ave. Staple 223 E3
Hawthorn Ave. Stav 79 E2
Hawthorn Bank. Glos 9 F2
Hawthorn Bank. N Mills 33 D3
Hawthorn Cl. Ashb 185 E4
Hawthorn Cl. Chin 34 C1
Hawthorn Cl. Dens 196 C3
Hawthorn Cl. Dove 211 D1
Hawthorn Cl. Hilton 228 B1
Hawthorn Cl. Hope 39 D2
Hawthorn Cr. Fin 230 B1
Hawthorn Cres. Bu on T 254 C4
Hawthorn Dr. Mat Ba 155 D3
Hawthorn Gr. M in L 9 E3
Hawthorn Rd. C Don 247 D3
Hawthorn Rd. Eck 59 D1
Hawthorn Rise. Swad 255 F4
Hawthorn St. Derby 232 B4
Hawthorne Ave. Dron 57 D2
Hawthorne Ave. Lo Ea 236 B3
Hawthorne Ave. Ock 221 E1
Hawthorne Ave. Shireb 119 E2
Hawthorne Ave. Shirl 146 B3
Hawthorne Ave. Tibs 148 A4
Hawthorne Cl. Barl 80 A3
Hawthorne Cl. Kilb 179 F1
Hawthorne Cl. Kill 60 B3
Hawthorne Cl. Stret 145 E4
Hawthorne Rd. Pinx 160 B2
Hawthorne Rise. Awsw 195 D2
Hawthorne St. Chest 96 A1
Hawthorne Way. Chest 94 C3
Hawthornes Ave. S Norm 159 F3
Hawthorns The. Belper 179 E3
Hawthorns The. C-Frith 47 D2
Hawton Cl. Mans 135 F1
Hawtrey Gdns. Derby 233 D3
Haxby Cl. Shef 44 C3
Haxby Pl. Shef 44 C3
Haxby St. Shef 44 C3
Hay La. Ash 145 D4
Hay La. Scro 226 C3
Hay La. Spout 166 B3
Hay La. Wirk 166 B3
Hay Wain La. Swad 256 A4
Haybrook Ct. Totley 55 F3
Haycroft Cl. Mans 136 C3
Haydn Fold. Cha 16 B4
Haydn Rd. Derby 219 F4
Haydock Cl. Kim 195 F4
Haydock Park Rd. Derby 232 C4
Hayes Ave. Brea 235 D4
Hayes Ave. Derby 231 E4
Hayes Cl. Pinx 160 B2
Hayes Cl. We Ha 207 F4
Hayes Cres. Som 169 F4
Hayes Ct. Mosb 59 F3
Hayes Dr. Mosb 59 F3
Hayes Farm Ct. Tick 251 D2
Hayes La. Som 169 F4
Hayes The. Fin 230 B1
Hayes Wood Rd. Stanl 193 D1
Hayfield Cl. Belper 179 D3
Hayfield Cl. Shef 56 C4
Hayfield Cl. Stav 78 C2
Hayfield Cl. Win 114 C2
Hayfield Cres. Shef 44 B2
Hayfield Dr. Shef 44 B2
Hayfield Pl. Shef 44 B2
Hayfield Rd East. C-Frith 47 E3
Hayfield Rd. C-Frith 35 D1
Hayfield Rd. C-Frith 47 D4
Hayfield Rd. N Mills 24 C1
Hayfield View. Eck 59 E2
Hayford Way. Stav 78 C1
Hayling Cl. Ship 194 B2
Haynes Ave. Trow 209 E3

Hays La. K Ire 164 C1
Hays The. Hatton 227 E1
Haywards Cl. Glos 10 B2
Haywood Cl. Derby 233 D3
Hayworth Rd. Sand 223 D3
Hazel Ave. Derby 231 E3
Hazel Ave. Kill 60 B3
Hazel Ave. Pils 132 A2
Hazel Cl. Ashb 185 E4
Hazel Cl. Dron 76 A4
Hazel Cl. Fin 230 C1
Hazel Cl. Hean 181 E1
Hazel Cl. Swad 256 A3
Hazel Cres. Shireb 119 E2
Hazel Ct. Dron 76 A4
Hazel Dr. Chest 114 C4
Hazel Dr. Derby 221 D3
Hazel Dr. Win 115 D2
Hazel Gr. Calver 72 B1
Hazel Gr. Duff 190 C2
Hazel Gr. Mans 136 A3
Hazel Gr. Mat 143 E3
Hazel Gr. S Norm 160 A3
Hazel Gr. Stav 79 E2
Hazel Rd. Eck 59 E1
Hazelbadge Cres. Shef 44 C2
Hazelby Rd. Elmt 100 C4
Hazeldene Cl. Duff 190 C3
Hazelhurst Ave. Chest 96 A3
Hazelhurst La. Chest 96 A3
Hazelhurst. Gra 115 E3
Hazelmere Rd. Elmt 81 E2
Hazelrigg Cl. C Don 246 C2
Hazelwood Cl. Shef 56 C4
Hazelwood Hill. Haz 190 B4
Hazelwood Rd. Bu on T 254 C3
Hazelwood Rd. Derby 219 F4
Hazelwood Rd. Duff 190 B3
Hazelwood Rd. Haz 190 B3
Hazlebarrow Cl. Shef 57 E3
Hazlebarrow Cres. Shef 57 E4
Hazlebarrow Ct. Shef 57 D4
Hazlebarrow Dr. Shef 57 D4
Hazlebarrow Gr. Shef 57 E4
Hazlebarrow Rd. Shef 57 D4
Hazlehurst La. Eck 57 F4
Headingley Ct. Derby 231 E4
Headland Cl. Chest 96 C4
Headland Rd. Chest 96 C4
Heage La. Etwall 229 E4
Heage Rd. Ripley 169 E1
Healaugh Way. Chest 115 D4
Heale St. Clowne 80 C2
Heanor Gate Rd. Hean 193 E4
Heanor Gate Rd. Ship 193 E4
Heanor Rd. Codnor 181 D4
Heanor Rd. Denby 181 D2
Heanor Rd. Hean 181 E1
Heanor Rd. Hean 181 E2
Heanor Rd. Ilk 194 B2
Heanor Rd. Smal 193 D4
Hearthcote Rd. Swad 256 A2
Hearthstone La. Mat 143 E1
Heath Ave. Derby 218 B1
Heath Ave. Kill 60 B3
Heath Cross. Utt 210 A1
Heath Ct. Derby 231 F2
Heath Gdns. Lo Ea 236 A4
Heath Gr. Bux 85 E3
Heath La. Black 257 E1
Heath La. Fin 242 B4
Heath La. Harts 257 F2
Heath La. Smisby 258 A3
Heath La. Tick 258 A3
Heath Park Rd. Bux 85 E3
Heath Rd. Bu on T 254 C4
Heath Rd. Glos 10 B1
Heath Rd. N Wing 116 C1
Heath Rd. N Wing 132 C4
Heath Rd. Ripley 169 F1
Heath Rd. Utt 210 A1
Heath St. Bux 85 D3
Heath The. Greas 195 D4
Heath View. Bux 85 F1
Heath Way. Hatton 227 E1
Heathcote Cl. Derby 233 E3
Heathcote Dr. Chest 115 F4
Heather Ave. Heath 116 C1
Heather Bank Cl. Glos 17 D4
Heather Cl. Calow 97 D2
Heather Cl. Derby 231 E1
Heather Cl. S Norm 160 A2
Heather Cl. Som 170 A4
Heather Cres. Brea 235 F4
Heather Cres. Derby 231 E3
Heather Gr. M in L 9 E3
Heather Lea Ave. Totley 55 E4
Heather Lea Pl. Totley 55 E4
Heather Vale Cl. Chest 115 F4
Heather Way. Holy 113 E4
Heatherley Dr. Mans 136 C1
Heathervale Rd. Chest 115 E4
Heathfield Ave. Chest 95 E2
Heathfield Ave. Ilk 209 D4
Heathfield Cl. Dron 75 F4
Heathfield Cl. Win 115 D2
Heathfield Gdns. Tibs 148 A4
Heathfield Nook Rd. Bux 85 F1
Heathfield Rd. Shef 44 B2
Heathfield. Mat 143 E4
Heathlands Dr. Utt 210 A1
Heaton Cl. Shef 56 C4
Heaton St. Chest 95 E1
Heavygate La. Shot 177 F4
Hebden Cl. Derby 230 C3
Hebden Dr. Glos 17 F4
Heddon Bar. Mans 136 C2
Hedge Gr. Swad 256 A4
Hedgebank Ct. Derby 206 B2
Hedgerow Gdns. Derby 206 B2
Hedingham Way. Derby 230 B4
Hedley Cl. Som 170 B4
Hedley Dr. Chest 96 B4
Heeley Arches. Shef 43 D4
Heeley Bank Rd. Shef 43 D4
Heeley Grn. Shef 43 D3
Heigham Cl. Derby 232 B2
Helmsley Ave. Mosb 59 F4
Helmton Dr. Shef 43 D2
Helmton Rd. Shef 43 D1
Helston Cl. Chest 115 D4
Helston Cl. Derby 233 D3
Helston Cl. Linton 261 E3
Heming Ave. Pils 132 B1
Hemington Hill. C Don 247 E2
Hemington La. C Don 247 F3
Hemlock Ave. Lo Ea 223 E1
Hemlock Ave. Staple 223 F4
Hemlock Cl. Derby 206 A2
Hemlock La. Ilk 208 B3
Hemp Yd. K Ire 165 D1
Hemper Gr. Shef 56 B4
Hemper La. Shef 56 B3
Hemsley Dr. East 182 B2
Hemsworth Rd. Shef 43 E1
Hendon Way. Derby 218 A3
Henley Ave. Shef 57 E4
Henley Gdns. Staple 209 F1
Henley Green. Derby 217 F3
Henley Way. We Ha 207 E4
Henmore Pl. Ashb 173 E1
Henmore Trading Est. Ashb 173 D1
Hennymoor Cl. Whit 82 A3
Hennymoor La. Whit 82 B1
Henry Ave. Mans 136 A3
Henry Ave. Mat 143 E3
Henry Cres. Alf 159 E2
Henry St. Chest 96 A4
Henry St. Derby 218 C3
Henry St. Eck 59 E2
Henry St. Glos 10 B1
Henry St. Gra 115 F2
Henry St. Ripley 169 E1
Henshaw Ave. Ilk 208 B3
Henshaw Pl. Ilk 194 C2
Herbert St. Bu on T 248 A2
Herdings Ct. Shef 44 A2
Herdings Rd. Shef 44 A2
Herdings View. Shef 44 A2
Hereford Ave. Mans 136 B3
Hereford Cl. Bux 85 E2
Hereford Cres. Swad 256 B3
Hereford Dr. Chest 96 C4
Hereford Rd. Bux 85 E2
Hereford Rd. Derby 219 E4
Hereward's Rd. Shef 43 E1
Herewood Cl. Shireb 119 F2
Heriot Dr. Chest 96 A1
Heritage Dr. Clowne 80 B3
Heritage Way. Bu on T 248 A1
Hermitage Ave. Ock 221 E1
Hermitage Ave. Som 170 B3
Hermitage Ct. Derby 206 A1
Hermitage Wlk. Ilk 208 C3
Hernstone La. Pk F 49 D1
Heron Dr. Wood 256 C2
Heron Way. Derby 218 A1
Heronswood Dr. Derby 220 B3
Herriot Dr. Chest 115 D4
Hessey St. Shef 44 C3
Hewett St. Mar War 120 B3
Hexham Ave. Ilk 209 D2
Hexham Wlk. Derby 205 F1
Hey St. Lo Ea 236 B2
Heyford Ct. Hean 182 A1
Heysbank Rd. Disley 32 B3
Heywood St. Chest 96 C4
Heyworth Rd. C-Frith 47 E3
Heyworth St. Derby 218 B3
Hibbert St. N Mills 33 D3
Hickings La. Staple 223 F4
Hickingwood La. Clowne 81 D3
Hickinwood Cres. Clowne 80 C3
Hickling Cl. Derby 232 B2
Hickton Rd. Som 169 F3
Hide La. Hartin 137 F4
Hides Green. Bols 99 D1
Higg La. Alder 167 D3
Higger La. Hath 52 C4
Higgins Rd. Swad 255 F3
High Bank Rd. Bu on T 248 A2
High Bank. Denby 180 C1
High Cross. Biggin 138 D3
High Cross. Hartin 137 F3
High Edge Dr. Ripley 179 F4
High Edge Mews. Belper 179 D3
High Hazel Cl. Cl Cr 131 F2
High Hazel Wlk. Cl Cr 131 F2
High Hill Rd. N Mills 24 B1
High Holborn Rd. Codnor 170 A1
High Holborn Rd. Ripley 170 A1
High Holborn. Ilk 194 C2
High La Central. We Ha 193 F1
High La E. We Ha 208 A4
High La E. WeHa 194 A1
High La W. We Ha 193 F1
High La. Cha 16 C4
High La. Eck 44 C1
High La. Glos 16 C4
High La. Hollow 144 C1
High La. Hollow 156 B3
High La. Holy 113 F3
High Lea Rd. N Mills 33 D4
High Lees Rd. Clowne 80 C1
High Pavement. Belper 179 D2
High Rd. S Wing 157 F2
High Ridge. Mans 136 C1
High Ridge. Mat 143 E4
High Spania. Kim 195 F4
High St E. Glos 10 B1
High St W. Glos 10 A1
High St. Alf 159 D2
High St. Barl 80 A4
High St. Belper 179 D2
High St. Bols 99 D1
High St. Bons 142 B1
High St. Brin 171 E1
High St. Bux 85 D4
High St. C Don 247 D1
High St. Dron 57 D1
High St. C-Frith 47 D3
High St. Calver 72 A1
High St. Chest 77 E2
High St. Chest 96 A2
High St. Chest 96 C4
High St. Cl Cr 131 E2
High St. Clowne 80 B2
High St. Codnor 181 D4
High St. Derby 233 D1
High St. Dove 211 D1
High St. Eck 59 E2
High St. Hean 181 E2
High St. Hean 181 F1
High St. Ilk 208 C4
High St. Kilb 192 A4
High St. Kill 60 B3
High St. Kim 195 F3
High St. Linton 261 E3
High St. Lo Ea 236 C4
High St. Long 121 E3
High St. Mans 135 D3
High St. Mans 136 B2
High St. March 224 C1
High St. Mel 252 A4
High St. Mosb 59 E4
High St. N Mills 33 E4
High St. Rep 242 B1
High St. Ripley 169 E1
High St. Roc 196 C2
High St. S Norm 160 A3
High St. Shirl 147 D2
High St. Som 169 F4
High St. Som 170 B3
High St. Som 170 B4
High St. St Mid 71 F2
High St. Staple 223 F4
High St. Stav 78 C1
High St. Swad 256 A3
High St. Swad 256 B2
High St. Tibs 147 F3
High St. Tibs 148 A4
High St. Tick 251 D2
High St. Tide 69 E2
High St. Totley 55 E4
High St. Tut 239 E3
High St. Uns 58 A1
High St. Whit 81 F3
High St. Wood 256 C1
High Tor Rd. Mat 143 D1
High Trees. Totley 55 E4
High View Cl. Chest 96 B1
High View Rd. S Norm 160 B4
High Wood Fold. Marple 23 E4
Higham La. Marple 15 D4
Higham La. Shirl 146 C2
Highashes La. Ash 113 F1
Highbank Rd. Glos 17 F4
Highbury Cl. Derby 217 F3
Highbury Rd. Chest 95 F3
Highcliffe Ave. Shireb 119 E2
Highcroft Cl. Lo Ea 236 C3
Higher Albert St. Chest 96 A2
Higher Barn Rd. Glos 9 F2
Higher Halsteads. Pk F 47 F2
Higher Sq. Tint 10 A4
Highfield Ave. C-Frith 47 F1
Highfield Ave. Chest 95 F3
Highfield Ave. Mans 136 A1
Highfield Ave. Shireb 119 E3
Highfield Cl. Bake 109 E3
Highfield Cl. Hean 181 D3
Highfield Cl. Mans 136 A1
Highfield Cotts. Derby 219 F3
Highfield Dr. Bake 109 E3
Highfield Dr. Ilk 208 A3
Highfield Dr. Mat 143 E3
Highfield Dr. S Norm 160 A3
Highfield Gdns. Derby 218 C4
Highfield Gdns. M in L 9 E3
Highfield La. Biggin 138 D2
Highfield La. Chest 95 F3
Highfield La. Derby 219 F3
Highfield La. Hartin 137 F3
Highfield La. W Und 188 C3
Highfield Mews. Derby 219 F3
Highfield Pl. Shef 43 D4
Highfield Rd. Ashb 185 D4
Highfield Rd. Belper 178 C1
Highfield Rd. Bols 99 D1
Highfield Rd. Chest 95 F3
Highfield Rd. Derby 218 C4
Highfield Rd. Derby 231 E4
Highfield Rd. Glos 17 E4
Highfield Rd. H Ward 175 F2
Highfield Rd. Hay 25 E2
Highfield Rd. Kilb 191 F4
Highfield Rd. Lit Ea 205 E4
Highfield Rd. Marple 23 D3
Highfield Rd. Som 169 E4
Highfield Rd. Swad 256 A2
Highfield St. Lo Ea 223 E1
Highfield St. Swad 256 A2
Highfield Terr. Chest 95 F3
Highfield Terr. N Mills 33 E4
Highfield View Rd. Chest 95 F3
Highfield Way. Ripley 180 B4
Highfield. A in W 108 C4
Highfields Cres. Dron 76 A4
Highfields Dr. Linton 261 E3
Highfields Dr. N Wing 132 B4
Highfields Rd. Dron 76 A4
Highfields Way. N Wing 132 B4
Highfields. Bux 67 D3
Highfields. Codnor 181 D4
Highgate Dr. Dron 76 B4
Highgate Dr. Ship 194 B2
Highgate Green. Derby 218 A3
Highgate La. Dron 76 B4
Highgate Rd. Hay 25 F1
Highgrove Cl. Bu on T 240 B1
Highgrove Dr. Derby 232 C1
Highland Cl. Bux 85 E3
Highland Cl. Mans 136 B2
Highland Rd. Chest 77 E2
Highlands Dr. Bu on T 248 A2
Highlightley La. Barlow 75 E3
Highlow Cl. Chest 95 E3
Highstairs La. Stret 146 B4
Highstool La. Chel 106 A3
Highview. Glos 17 D4
Highway La. Par 151 F1
Highwood Ave. Belper 179 E1
Highwood Cl. Glos 17 D4
Highwood La. Whit 81 E3
Highwood Pl. Eck 59 E2
Hilary Cl. Belper 179 F3
Hilcote La. Newt 148 A1
Hilcote St. S Norm 160 A3
Hilderstone Cl. Derby 233 E3
Hill Brow. Derby 219 D2
Hill Cl. Derby 220 C2
Hill Cl. Stanl 193 D1
Hill Cl. Turn 177 D1
Hill Crest Rd. Derby 219 E4
Hill Crest. Crich 157 D1
Hill Crest. Shireb 119 E2
Hill Cross Ave. Derby 231 E4
Hill Cross Dr. Derby 231 D4
Hill Cross. A in W 108 C4
Hill Fields. S Norm 160 A2
Hill Gr. Stav 78 A2
Hill Green Cl. C Elms 260 B2
Hill Park Cl. Derby 218 A1
Hill Rd. Ash 129 F2
Hill Rd. Eck 59 F2
Hill Rd. Hean 181 E1
Hill Rise Cl. Derby 231 E4
Hill Rise. Trow 209 E2
Hill Sq The. Derby 205 D1
Hill St. Bu on T 254 C4
Hill St. Cl Cr 131 E2
Hill St. Donis 262 C1
Hill St. Mans 135 D3
Hill St. Shef 43 D4
Hill St. Swad 255 F3
Hill St. Swad 256 B2
Hill The. Derby 205 D1
Hill The. Glap 118 A1
Hill Top Ave. Shireb 119 F2
Hill Top Rd. Som 170 B3
Hill Top Rise. W Br 45 E4
Hill Top. Bols 99 D1
Hill Top. C Don 247 D1
Hill Top. Derby 205 F2
Hill View Cl. H Wood 192 A4
Hill View Cl. Kilb 192 A4
Hill View Rd. Chest 96 C4
Hill View. Duff 190 B2
Hill View. Rep 242 C1
Hill View. W Br 45 E4
Hillary Pl. Ilk 208 A3
Hillberry Rise. Chest 114 C3
Hillberry. Ripley 170 A
Hillcliff La. H Ward 176 C
Hillcrest Ave. Bu on T 248 A
Hillcrest Ave. H Ward 175 F
Hillcrest Ave. S Norm 160 A
Hillcrest Dr. Codnor 181 D
Hillcrest Dr. Kilb 192 A
Hillcrest Gr. Stav 78 C
Hillcrest Rd. Chest 115 E
Hillcrest. Tut 239 D
Hillcreste Dr. Derby 232 C
Hillcroft Dr. Ock 221 E
Hillend La. M in L 9 D
Hillend. M in L 9 D
Hillfield La. Bu on T 240 C
Hillfield Rd. Staple 209 F
Hillfoot Rd. Totley 55 E
Hillhead La. Bux 85 F
Hillhouses La. Win 114 C
Hillman Dr. Stav 97 E
Hillmoor St. Mans 135 E
Hillock The. Curbar 72 C
Hills Croft. Hog 164 A
Hills Rd. Brea 235 E
Hills The. Bradw 51 D
Hillsdale Rd. Bu on T 248 A
Hillside Ave. Ashb 173 E
Hillside Ave. Derby 220 A
Hillside Ave. Dron 76 A
Hillside Cl. Disley 32 E
Hillside Cl. Glos 9 F
Hillside Cl. Whit 81 F
Hillside Cres. Derby 220 C
Hillside Ct. Br Hill 252 C
Hillside Dr. Chest 95 E
Hillside Dr. Lo Ea 236 A
Hillside Dr. Stav 79 E
Hillside Gr. Marple 15 D
Hillside Gr. Sand 223 D
Hillside La. Brass 152 C
Hillside Rd. Derby 220 C
Hillside Rd. Linton 261 E
Hillside Rise. Belper 178 C
Hillside View. N Mills 33 D
Hillside. Ash 130 A
Hillside. Bux 85 E
Hillside. C Don 247 D
Hillside. Fin 230 E
Hillside. Hollow 156 A
Hillside. La Mi 182 A
Hillside. Mid 154 E
Hillside. Mosb 59 E
Hillside. Tut 239 E
Hillside. Whit 81 F
Hillsway. Derby 218 A
Hillsway. Derby 232 C
Hillsway. Shireb 119 E
Hilltop Cl. Glap 118 A
Hilltop La. Thurv 215 E
Hilltop Rd. Ash 129 F
Hilltop Rd. Chest 77 D
Hilltop Rd. Dron 76 A
Hilltop Rd. Glos 10 A
Hilltop Rd. Pinx 160 E
Hilltop Rd. Win 114 E
Hilltop Way. Dron 76 A
Hilltop. Crich 168 A
Hilltops View. Mat 143 E
Hillview Ct. Mans 136 E
Hillwood Dr. Glos 17 F
Hilton Cl. Derby 217 E
Hilton Cl. Lo Ea 235 F
Hilton Park Dr. Som 170 E
Hilton Rd. Eg 241 D
Hilton Rd. Etwall 229 D
Hilton Rd. N Mills 32 A
Hind Ave. Brea 235 E
Hindersitch La. Crich 156 E
Hindscarth Cres. Derby 217 F
Hinton Gr. Marple 15 D
Hipley Cl. Chest 95 D
Hipper St S. Chest 96 A
Hipper St W. Chest 95 F
Hipper St. Chest 96 A
Hixon's La. S-by-D 208 A
Hoades St. Tupton 131 E
Hoargate La. Holl 200 C
Hob Hill. Haz 190 A
Hob La. K Ire 176 E
Hob La. Totley 55 F
Hobart Cl. Bu on T 248 E
Hobart Cl. Derby 217 F
Hobart Dr. Staple 209 F
Hobhouse Rd. Mans 135 E
Hobkirk Dr. Derby 231 F
Hobsic Cl. Brin 182 E
Hobsic La. Sels 171 F
Hobson Dr. Ilk 208 C
Hobson Moor Rd. M in L 9 E
Hockerley Ave. W Br 45 E
Hockerley Cl. W Br 45 E
Hockerley La. W Br 45 E
Hockley La. Ash 130 A
Hockley La. Win 115
Hockley Way. Som 159
Hodge Beck Cl. Derby 233
Hodge Fold. Marple 15 F
Hodge La. Ash 128 E

odge La. March 224 A1
odge La. Marple 15 F4
odmire La. Al Hu 133 F4
odthorpe Cl. Derby 206 A1
ogarth Cl. Staple 223 F3
ogarth Rd. Marple 23 D4
ogarth Rise. Dron 75 F4
oggbarn La. Hean 181 F3
oggs Field. East 182 C1
ogshaw Villas Rd. Bux 85 E4
oillant Sq. H Ward 175 F2
olbeach Dr. Chest 114 C4
olbeck Cl. Chest 96 A2
olbeck La. Holb 101 E4
olbeck St. Elmt 81 E1
olbein Cl. Dron 75 F4
olborn Dr. Derby 218 A4
olborn View. Codnor 170 A1
olbrook Ave. Mosb 59 F4
olbrook Ave. N Wing 132 A4
olbrook Cl. Chest 114 B4
olbrook Cl. Plea 135 D3
olbrook Dr. Shef 44 A3
olbrook Gn. Mosb 60 A4
olbrook Rd. Belper 178 C1
olbrook Rd. Derby 233 D3
olbrook Rd. Shef 44 A4
olbrook St. Hean 182 A1
olbrook View. Kilb 192 A4
olbrook Way. N Wing 132 A4
olburn Ave. Dron 57 D1
olcombe St. Derby 219 D1
olden Ave. As on T 246 A4
olden Gdns. Staple 223 F3
olderness Cl. Derby 231 E1
oldings The. Swad 256 A1
oldon Croft. Rosl 260 B3
olestone Gate Rd. Ash 129 E1
olker Ave. Bux 85 E4
olkham Cl. Ship 194 B2
olland Cl. Morton 146 C3
olland Meadow. Lo Ea 236 B3
olland Pl. Shef 43 D4
olland Rd. Chest 76 C1
olland Rd. Shef 43 D4
ollens Way. Chest 95 D3
ollies Cl. Clif 184 C3
ollies Cl. Dron 76 B4
ollies Cl. N Sol 248 C4
ollies Dr. Marple 23 D3
ollies La. G Cub 198 B2
ollies La. East 198 B2
ollies Rd. Derby 204 B2
ollies The. East 182 C1
ollies The. Sand 223 D3
ollin Cl. Chest 95 E4
ollin Cross La. Glos 17 E4
ollin Dr. C-Frith 47 D3
ollin Hill. Clowne 81 D2
ollindale Dr. Shef 44 B3
ollington Cl. Derby 219 F4
ollingwood Cres. Stav 78 A1
ollingworth Ave. Sand 223 D2
ollinhey Terr. M in L 9 E3
ollins Ave. Bux 85 D4
ollins La. Crich 157 D2
ollins La. Glos 9 E1
ollins La. Marple 23 E4
ollins Mews. Glos 9 E1
ollins Mt. Marple 23 D4
ollins Spring Ave. Dron 76 A4
ollins Spring Rd. Dron 76 A4
ollins St. Bux 85 D4
ollins The. Hollow 156 A3
ollins Wood Cl. Hollow 156 A3
ollinsclough Rake. Hollin 104 A1
ollinsend Ave. Shef 44 B3
ollinsend Pl. Shef 44 B3
ollinsend Rd. Shef 44 A3
ollinsmoor Rd. N Mills 24 B4
ollinwood Rd. Disley 32 B3
ollinwood Rd. Marple 23 D1
ollis La. Chest 96 A1
ollis La. Dens 196 A3
ollis St. Derby 233 D4
ollow Cres. Bu on T 248 B2
ollow Gate. Bradw 51 D4
ollow La. Bu on T 248 B2
ollow La. May 172 B1
ollow La. Mosb 59 F3
ollow Of The Moor. Tadd 87 F2
ollow Rd. Br Hill 252 C2
ollow The. Bam 40 A2
ollow The. C Don 247 D2
ollow The. Derby 217 E1
ollow The. Derby 230 B4
ollow The. Derby 231 E4
ollow The. Hollow 156 A3
ollow The. Rost 197 F3
olloway Rd. Derby 232 C3
olloway Rd. Duff 190 C2
ollowford Rd. Cas 38 A2
ollowood Ave. Derby 231 E4
ollows The. Lo Ea 237 D4
olly Ave. Brea 222 C1
olly Ave. Ripley 180 B4
olly Bank. M in L 9 E3
olly Bush La. Belper 191 D3
Holly Cl. Ashb 185 E4
Holly Cl. Dray 235 D4
Holly Cl. Kill 60 B3
Holly Ct. Derby 217 E1
Holly Ct. Mans 136 C1
Holly Ct. Wood 256 C1
Holly Gdns. Shef 44 B3
Holly Gr. Som 169 F4
Holly Green. Bu on T 254 C4
Holly Hill Rd. Sels 171 F3
Holly La. Alder 167 E2
Holly La. Tans 144 A2
Holly Rd. Kim 195 F4
Holly Rd. Mans 136 C1
Holly Rd. Utt 210 A1
Holly St. Bu on T 254 C4
Hollybank Ave. Shef 44 B3
Hollybank Cl. Shef 44 B3
Hollybank Cl. Swad 256 A4
Hollybank Cres. Shef 44 B3
Hollybank Dr. Shef 44 B3
Hollybank Rd. Shef 44 B3
Hollybank Way. Shef 44 B3
Hollybush Cl. Neth 264 C4
Hollyhouse Dr. S Norm 160 A3
Hollyhurst La. M Mont 212 A3
Hollyhurst Row. Som 170 C3
Hollymoor Dr. Derby 232 C1
Hollythorpe Cl. Chest 115 E4
Hollythorpe Cres. Shef 43 D2
Hollythorpe Rd. Shef 43 D2
Hollythorpe Rise. Shef 43 D2
Hollywell Ave. Codnor 181 D4
Hollywell St. Chest 96 A2
Hollywood Rd. Marple 23 F4
Holm Ave. Lit Ea 205 D4
Holm Cl. Dron 56 B1
Holm La. S Wing 158 A2
Holme Cl. Hatton 227 E1
Holme Cl. Hollow 156 A3
Holme Croft. We Ha 207 F4
Holme Farm Ave. Bu on T 254 C4
Holme Hall Cres. Chest 95 D3
Holme La. Bake 109 E4
Holme La. Derby 220 B2
Holme Park Ave. Chest 95 D4
Holme Rd. Chest 96 A3
Holme Rd. Mat Ba 143 D1
Holme Woods La. Holme 2 C3
Holmebank Cl. Chest 95 F2
Holmebank E. Chest 95 F2
Holmebank W. Chest 95 F2
Holmefield Cres. Ilk 209 D4
Holmefield Rd. Whit 82 A3
Holmes Bank. May 184 B4
Holmes Cl. La Mi 182 A2
Holmes Rd. Brea 235 E4
Holmes St. Derby 219 D1
Holmes St. Hean 181 E1
Holmesdale Cl. Dron 57 E2
Holmesdale Rd. Dron 57 E2
Holmesfield Cl. Tans 144 A3
Holmesfield Dr. Derby 217 F1
Holmesfield Dr. Ship 194 A4
Holmesfield Rd. Dron 56 A1
Holmewood Dr. Greas 195 D4
Holmfield. Bux 84 C3
Holmfield. Derby 231 F4
Holmgate Rd. Cl Gr 130 C2
Holmley Bank. Dron 57 D2
Holmley La. Dron 57 D2
Holmshaw Dr. Shef 44 C4
Holmshaw Gr. Shef 44 C4
Holmwood Terr. Bux 85 E4
Holt Ave. Derby 233 E3
Holt Dr. Da Da 142 C4
Holt La. Hollow 156 A4
Holt La. Mat 143 D2
Holt Rd. Da Da 127 F1
Holt's La. Tut 239 D3
Holtlands Dr. Derby 232 C3
Holyhead Dr. Derby 206 A2
Holymoor Rd. Holy 113 F4
Holyoake Ave. Shef 44 C4
Holyrood Cl. Derby 221 D3
Holywell La. Youl 125 D3
Holywell Rd. Ship 194 B2
Holywell. Bake 109 E3
Home Farm Cl. Ock 221 E3
Home Farm Dr. Derby 205 D2
Home Fm Ct. Sels 171 E3
Homecroft Dr. Sels 171 F4
Homer Dr. Marple 23 D4
Homestead Rd. Disley 32 B3
Homestead. Ald 182 A2
Honeyfield Dr. Ripley 180 C4
Honeysuckle Cl. Swad 256 A3
Honeysuckle View. Bu on T 255 D4
Honeywall La. Stan 183 F4
Honingham Rd. Ilk 194 B2
Hook La. Utt 210 A3
Hoole St. Chest 115 E4
Hooley Cl. Lo Ea 236 A3
Hooley St. Sels 171 F3
Hoon Rd. Hatton 239 E4
Hoonwell La. H Ward 175 F3
Hope Ave. Derby 217 E1
Hope Rd. Hope 39 E1
Hope Rd. Thor 39 E1
Hope St. Chest 95 F2
Hope St. Derby 219 D2
Hope St. Glos 10 C1
Hope St. Ilk 208 C4
Hope St. Mel 252 A4
Hope Terr. Mat Ba 143 D1
Hopedale Rd. Shef 44 B2
Hopefield Ave. Shef 44 B2
Hopetoun St. Derby 232 A4
Hopewell Rd. Mat 143 E3
Hopewell Wlk. Ilk 194 C3
Hopkins Ct. East 182 C2
Hopping Hill Terr E. Belper 191 D4
Hopping Hill Terr W. Belper 191 D4
Hopping Hill. Belper 190 C4
Hopping La. Youl 125 D2
Hopton Cl. Derby 206 A1
Hopwell Rd. Dray c 222 A1
Horace Ave. Staple 223 E3
Horderns La. C-Frith 47 D3
Horderns Park Rd. C-Frith 47 D3
Horderns Rd. C-Frith 47 D3
Horeston Cotts. H Wood 192 A4
Hornbeam Cl. Ilk 209 D4
Hornbeams The. Utt 210 A1
Horncastle Rd. Derby 205 E1
Horner Rd. Shef 43 D4
Hornscroft Rd. Bols 99 D1
Hornsea Rd. Derby 205 E1
Hornthorpe Rd. Eck 59 E1
Horridge St. Ilk 194 C2
Horse Fair Ave. C-Frith 47 D3
Horsehead La. Bols 99 E1
Horseshoe Ave. C-Frith 47 F1
Horsewood Rd. Chest 114 A4
Horsley Cl. Chest 95 D3
Horsley Cres. Holbr 191 E4
Horsley Cres. La Mi 182 A2
Horsley La. Hors 191 F2
Horsley Rd. Hors 191 F3
Horsley Rd. Kilb 191 F3
Horsleygate La. Hol 74 C4
Horsleygate Rd. Hol 74 A4
Horton Cl. Mosb 59 F4
Horton Cl. Som 169 F4
Horton Dr. Mosb 59 F4
Horton St. Derby 219 E1
Horwood Ave. Derby 218 B1
Hoselett Field Rd. Lo Ea 236 C3
Hospital La. Burn 230 A4
Houfton Cres. Bols 98 C2
Houfton Rd. Bols 98 C2
Houghton Ave. Ilk 194 B2
Houghton Ct. Derby 205 F1
Houldsworth Cres. Bols 98 C1
Houldsworth Dr. Chest 96 C1
Hoult St. Derby 218 B2
Houndkirk Rd. Totley 54 B4
Hounslow Rd. Derby 218 A3
Houston Cl. Derby 220 A3
Hoveton Cl. Derby 232 B2
How La. Cas 38 B2
Howard Cl. Glos 10 A1
Howard Cl. Lo Ea 223 F1
Howard Dr. Chest 77 D1
Howard Dr. N Wing 131 F3
Howard St. Derby 218 C1
Howard St. Glos 10 B1
Howden Cl. Derby 217 E1
Howden Cl. Stav 78 C2
Howden Rd. N Mills 24 B1
Howe St. Derby 218 B3
Howells Pl. Stav 79 D2
Howitt Cres. Utt 210 A1
Howitt St. Hean 181 F1
Howitt St. Lo Ea 236 C4
Howth Cl. Derby 220 A2
Hoylake Ave. Chest 114 B4
Hoylake Cl. Mans 136 C3
Hoylake Ct. Derby 217 E2
Hoylake Dr. Derby 217 E2
Hoyland Ct. Belper 179 F3
Hubert Shaw Cl. Derby 232 C2
Hucklow Ave. Chest 95 F1
Hucklow Ave. N Wing 132 A4
Hucklow Ave. Stav 97 E4
Hucklow Ct. Derby 206 A2
Hucknall Ave. Chest 95 E2
Hudson Cl. Hart 61 F4
Hudson Mount. Scarc 118 A4
Hufton's Ct. Ship 194 A4
Hufton's Dr. Ship 194 A4
Hugh La. Bradw 51 D4
Hugh St. Glos 10 A1
Hulland St. Derby 219 E2
Hulland View. Derby 204 B1
Humber Cl. Derby 233 E3
Humber Rd. Lo Ea 223 E1
Humbleton Dr. Derby 218 A3
Humphrey Rd. Shef 56 C4
Hundall La. Chest 77 D2
Hundall La. Uns 77 D4
Hunger La. W Und 188 C2
Hungerhill La. Holy 113 D2
Hungry La. Bradw 51 D3
Hungry La. Hath 53 D4
Hunloke Ave. Chest 95 F1
Hunloke Cres. Chest 95 F1
Hunloke Rd. N Wing 132 C4
Hunloke View. Win 115 D2
Hunsoon Rd. Eck 59 E2
Hunstone Ave. Shef 57 D4
Hunt Ave. Hean 181 F1
Hunt La. Ash 145 D4
Hunter Dr. Kilb 191 F4
Hunter Rd. Belper 179 E3
Hunter's La. Shef 44 B3
Hunters Croft. Derby 231 F1
Hunters Gn. Chin 34 C1
Hunters La. Glos 16 C4
Huntingdon Ave. Bols 99 D1
Huntingdon Dr. C Don 247 D2
Huntingdon Green. Derby 219 E3
Huntingdon Rd. Bu on T 254 B4
Huntingdon Way. Bees 223 F1
Huntingdon Wlk. Sand 223 D3
Huntley Ave. Derby 220 C3
Huntley Cl. Stav 97 D4
Hunts La. Neth 264 C4
Huntsman Rd. Stav 78 C1
Hurds Hollow. Mat 143 D3
Hurker Rise. Mat 143 E4
Hurl Dr. Shef 43 F3
Hurley Ct. We Ha 207 F4
Hurlfield Ave. Shef 44 A3
Hurlfield Ct. Shef 44 A3
Hurlfield Dr. Shef 43 F3
Hurlfield Hill. Shef 43 F3
Hurlfield Rd. Shef 43 F3
Hurst Dr. Bu on T 240 C1
Hurst Dr. Stanl 207 E3
Hurst La. Stret 146 A3
Hurst Lea Rd. N Mills 33 E4
Hurst Rd. Glos 10 C1
Hurst Rise. Mat 143 E3
Hurstbrook Cl. Glos 10 C1
Hurstclough La. Bam 40 B1
Hurstclough La. Hath 40 B1
Huss's La. Lo Ea 236 C4
Hut La. Kill 60 C2
Hutchings Cres. Clowne 80 B3
Huthwaite La. Newt 148 B1
Hutmoor Butts. Mo 107 D2
Hutton St. Derby 232 C3
Hyde Bank Rd. N Mills 33 E4
Hyde Park Rd. Derby 218 A3
Hyde Rd. M in L 9 D2
Hyde Way. M in L 9 D2
Hydro Cl. Baslow 91 F3
Hylton Cl. Bran 254 A4
Hyndley Rd. Bols 98 C2

Ian Ave. Wirk 165 F4
Ians Way. Chest 95 E2
Ibsley Cl. Derby 233 E3
Ida's Rd. Eck 59 E2
Ilam Cl. Stav 97 E3
Ilam Ct. Ashb 185 E4
Ilam Sq. Ilk 194 C3
Ilford Cl. Ship 194 B2
Ilford Rd. Derby 218 A3
Ilford Wlk. Derby 218 A3
Ilion St. Mans 135 F1
Ilkeston Rd. Hean 193 F4
Ilkeston Rd. S-by-D 208 C2
Ilkeston Rd. S-by-D 223 E4
Ilkeston Rd. Sand 223 E4
Ilkeston Rd. Smal 192 C1
Ilkeston Rd. Staple 209 F1
Ilkeston Rd. Trow 209 E3
Immingham Gr. Stav 78 B1
Imperial Ct. Derby 204 B3
Imperial Rd. Mat 143 D3
Inchwood Cl. Bees 223 F1
Independent Hill. Alf 158 C2
Industrial St. Derby 219 D1
Infirmary Rd. Chest 96 A2
Ingham Dr. Derby 230 B4
Ingham Rd. Lo Ea 223 E1
Ingle Cl. Derby 220 C3
Ingle's Channel. Belper 178 C2
Ingleborough Gdns. Lo Ea 236 A4
Ingleby Ave. Derby 231 F4
Ingleby Cl. Shef 56 C4
Ingleby Cl. Swad 256 A2
Ingleby La. Tick 251 D3
Ingleby Rd. Lo Ea 235 F2
Inglefield Rd. Ilk 209 D3
Ingleton Rd. Chest 115 D4
Inglewood Ave. Derby 217 E2
Ingliston Cl. Derby 233 E3
Inkerman Rd. Sels 171 F3
Inkerman St. Sels 171 F3
Inkersall Dr. Mosb 59 F4
Inkersall Green Rd. Stav 97 E4
Inkersall Rd. Stav 97 F4
Inn La. Quar 204 A4
Inns La. S Wing 157 F2
Institute La. Alf 159 D2
Instow Dr. Derby 231 E3
Intake La. Bake 109 F2
Intake La. Mat Ba 155 D3
Intake La. Mat Ba 155 F2
Intakes La. H Ward 188 B4
Inverary Cl. Derby 231 F2
Iona Cl. Derby 231 F2
Iona Cl. Tibs 147 F3
Iona Dr. Staple 209 E1
Ireland St. Stav 78 C1
Iron Cliff Rd. Bols 98 C2
Iron Gate. Derby 219 D3
Irongate. Chest 96 A2
Ironside Cl. Shef 43 E2
Ironside Pl. Shef 43 F2
Ironside Rd. Shef 43 F2
Ironside Wlk. Shef 43 E1
Ironwalls La. Tut 239 E3
Irving Pl. Derby 232 C4
Isaac's La. Staple 223 E4
Islay Cl. Staple 209 E2
Islay Rd. Derby 231 F2
Isleworth Dr. Derby 217 F3
Ismay Rd. Derby 219 F3
Ivan Brook Cl. Shef 56 C4
Ivanhoe Cl. Tupton 115 E1
Iveagh Wlk. Som 170 C3
Ivonbrook Cl. Wens 142 A4
Ivy Cl. Chest 77 D1
Ivy Cl. Donis 262 C1
Ivy Cl. Will 242 A3
Ivy Ct. Derby 217 E1
Ivy Ct. Hilton 228 B1
Ivy Gr. Ripley 169 E1
Ivy La. East 182 C1
Ivy La. Elton 140 C3
Ivy Lodge Cl. Bu on T 254 C4
Ivy Sq. Derby 219 E1
Ivybridge Cl. Derby 206 B2
Ivycroft. Glos 9 F2
Ivyside Cl. Kill 60 B3
Ivyside Gdns. Kill 60 B3

Jack's La. March 224 C1
Jackass La. Alder 167 D2
Jacksdale Cl. Derby 204 B1
Jackson Ave. Derby 218 A1
Jackson Ave. Ilk 208 C4
Jackson Ave. Sand 223 D3
Jackson Ave. Tupton 131 E4
Jackson Rd. Al Hv 117 F1
Jackson Rd. Cl Cr 131 F2
Jackson Rd. Mat 143 D3
Jackson St. Derby 218 C2
Jackson St. Glos 10 B3
Jackson St. Glos 17 E4
Jackson St. M in L 9 D2
Jackson Tor Rd. Mat 143 D3
Jackson's La. Belper 179 E4
Jackson's La. Pent 169 D4
Jackson's La. Ripley 179 E4
Jacksons Edge Rd. Disley 32 A3
Jacksons La. Belper 190 C4
Jacksons La. Etwall 229 E1
Jacobean Ct. Bu on T 248 B2
Jagger's La. Hath 52 C4
Jaggers La. Ash 128 F3
Jaggers La. Da Da 128 F3
Jago Ave. Clowne 81 D2
James Andrew Cl. Shef 56 C4
James Andrew Cres. Shef 56 C4
James Andrew Croft. Shef 56 C4
James St. Chest 96 A3
James St. Glos 17 E4
James St. Kim 195 F3
James St. Som 170 B4
James St. Swad 256 B3
James's La. S Hill 215 E1
Jane La. Chin 34 A1
Jarnett The. Flagg 107 D4
Jarvey's La. Mack 217 F4
Jarvis Rd. Derby 231 F1
Jasmin Cl. Shireb 119 E3
Jasmine Cl. Bu on T 255 D4
Jasmine Cl. Derby 220 A3
Jasmine Cl. Som 169 F4
Jaspers La. Brass 153 D1
Jaunty Ave. Shef 44 B2
Jaunty Cl. Shef 44 A2
Jaunty Cres. Shef 44 B2
Jaunty Dr. Shef 44 A2
Jaunty La. Shef 44 A2
Jaunty Mount. Shef 44 B2
Jaunty Pl. Shef 44 A2
Jaunty Rd. Shef 44 B2
Jaunty View. Shef 44 B2
Jaunty Way. Shef 44 A2
Jaw Bones Hill. Chest 115 D4
Jawbone La. Mel 252 B4
Jebb's La. Shot 177 D4
Jebb's Lane. Idri 176 C4
Jedburgh Cl. Derby 231 F1
Jefferson Pl. Derby 232 C4
Jeffery St. Shef 43 D3
Jeffrey La. Bradw 51 D3
Jeffries Ave. Crich 156 C1
Jeffries La. Crich 156 C1
Jellicoe St. Scarc 101 D1
Jemison Cl. Derby 230 C4
Jennison St. Mans 136 A1
Jephson Rd. Bran 254 A4
Jermyn Ave. Shef 44 C2
Jermyn Cl. Shef 44 C2
Jermyn Cres. Shef 44 C2

Jermyn Dr. Shef 44 C2
Jersey Rd. Shef 43 D4
Jervis Ct. Ilk 194 C2
Jervis Pl. Stav 97 D3
Jesses La. Belper 178 B4
Jessop Ave. Iron 170 C2
Jessop Dr. Derby 231 F1
Jessop St. Codnor 181 D4
Jessop St. Ripley 181 D4
Joan Ave. Hean 181 F1
Joan La. Bam 40 B2
Jodrell Ave. Belper 179 E2
Jodrell Meadow. W Br 45 F4
Jodrell Rd. W Br 45 E4
Jodrell St. N Mills 33 D4
John Bank La. A in W 108 C4
John Berrysford Cl. Derby 219 F3
John Dalton St. Glos 9 F3
John Eaton's Almshouses. Shef 43 D1
John Kennedy Gdn. M in L 9 D4
John Kennedy Rd. M in L 9 D2
John Lombe Dr. Derby 219 D4
John O'Gaunts Way. Belper 179 E2
John Port Cl. Etwall 229 E2
John St. Alf 159 D2
John St. Chest 95 F2
John St. Chest 96 C4
John St. Cl Cr 131 E2
John St. Clowne 80 B2
John St. Derby 219 D2
John St. Eck 59 E2
John St. Elmt 81 F1
John St. Glos 17 E4
John St. Hean 181 E1
John St. Ilk 194 C1
John St. Marple 15 D2
John St. Marple 23 D3
John St. Mat 143 D3
John St. N Wing 131 F4
John St. Som 170 B4
John St. Swad 255 F3
John St. Swad 256 B1
John St. Swad 256 B3
Johnnygate La. Barlow 75 D2
Johnson Ave. Derby 232 C4
Johnson Dr. Hean 181 F1
Johnson La. Shel 107 F3
Johnson Lane. Idri 176 C4
Johnson Rd. Utt 210 A1
Johnson St. W Br 45 F4
Johnson Way. C-Frith 47 E3
Johnstone Cl. Chest 95 F1
Jolly La. Atlow 175 D4
Jones St. Glos 10 A3
Jordan Ave. Bu on T 240 C1
Jordan St. Glos 10 C1
Jordanthorpe Parkway. Shef 57 E3
Joseph St. Belper 178 C2
Joseph St. Derby 219 D1
Joseph St. Eck 59 E2
Joseph St. Marple 23 D3
Joseph Wright Terr. Derby 219 D3
Joyce Ave. Bees 223 F2
Jubalton Cl. Derby 232 C3
Jubilee Ave. Ripley 169 E1
Jubilee Cl. Mel 252 A4
Jubilee Cres. Clowne 81 D2
Jubilee Cres. Kill 60 C4
Jubilee Cres. Whit 81 F3
Jubilee Ct. Belper 179 D1
Jubilee Ct. Wirk 165 F4
Jubilee Gdns. N Mills 33 E4
Jubilee Gdns. Whit 81 F3
Jubilee Pl. Whit 81 F3
Jubilee Rd. C-Frith 47 D3
Jubilee Rd. Derby 232 C2
Jubilee Rd. Whit 81 F3
Jubilee Sq. May 184 B4
Jubilee St. Kim 195 F4
Jubilee St. N Mills 33 E4
Jubilee Terr. Donis 262 C1
Judy Hill. Da Da 127 F1
Julia Cres. Shirl 146 C2
Julian Cl. Ilk 209 D3
Julie Ave. Hean 182 A1
Jumble Rd. Totley 42 C1
Junction Rd. Lo Ea 237 D3
Junction St. Derby 218 C2
Juniper Ct. Greas 195 E4
Juniper Rise. Kill 60 B3
Jura Ave. Ripley 169 E1
Jury St. Derby 218 C3
Katherine Dr. Bees 223 F2
Katrine Wlk. Derby 231 F2
Kay Dr. Swad 255 F3
Kean Pl. Derby 232 C4
Kearsley Rd. Shef 43 D4
Keats Ave. Derby 218 A1
Keats Cl. Lo Ea 236 A3
Keats Dr. Swad 256 B3
Keats Rd. Chest 95 F4
Keats Rd. Shirl 146 C2
Keats Way. Gra 115 F2
Keats Wlk. Shirl 146 C2
Keble Cl. Derby 219 D2
Kedleston Cl. Bu on T 240 B1
Kedleston Cl. Derby 204 B1
Kedleston Cl. Lo Ea 236 A3
Kedleston Cl. Ripley 169 E2
Kedleston Dr. Ilk 194 B2
Kedleston Gdns. Derby 218 C3
Kedleston Old Rd. Derby 218 B4
Kedleston Rd. Bux 85 E4
Kedleston Rd. Derby 204 A3
Kedleston Rd. Quar 204 A3
Kedleston Rd. W Und 203 F4
Kedleston St. Derby 218 C3
Keeling La. Bir 126 A1
Keepers La. Barlow 75 F2
Kegworth Ave. Derby 231 E3
Keilder Ct. Chest 95 E1
Kelburn Ave. Chest 95 E1
Keldholme La. Derby 233 E3
Kelmoor Rd. Derby 233 D4
Kelsons Ave. Bux 85 E3
Kelstedge La. Ash 129 E3
Kelvin Cl. Staple 223 E3
Kemble Pl. Derby 232 C4
Kemp Rd. Marple 23 E4
Kempton Cl. Kim 195 F4
Kempton Park Rd. Derby 232 B4
Kempton Rd. Bu on T 248 A2
Kendal Cl. Bux 85 E2
Kendal Dr. Dron 56 C1
Kendal Rd. Chest 95 F4
Kendal Rd. Lo Ea 223 D1
Kendal Wlk. Derby 205 E1
Kendon Ave. Derby 231 F3
Kendray Cl. Belper 179 E3
Kendricks Cl. Harts 257 D4
Kenilworth Ave. Derby 231 F4
Kenilworth Dr. Ilk 208 B3
Kenilworth Rd. Ripley 169 E1
Kenmere Cl. Cl Cr 131 E1
Kennedy Ave. Lo Ea 236 B3
Kennedy Ave. Mans 136 B2
Kennedy Cl. Derby 220 A4
Kennedy Dr. Staple 209 F1
Kennet Paddock. Mans 136 B2
Kennet Vale. Chest 95 E3
Kennett Gr. Bux 84 C3
Kenning St. Cl Cr 131 E2
Kenninghall Cl. Shef 43 E4
Kenninghall Dr. Shef 43 E4
Kenninghall Pl. Shef 43 E4
Kenninghall Rd. Shef 43 E4
Kensal Rise. Derby 218 A3
Kensington Cl. Mans 136 C3
Kensington Gdns. Ilk 208 C4
Kensington Rd. Bu on T 248 A2
Kensington Rd. Sand 223 D2
Kensington St. Derby 218 C3
Kensington St. Ilk 208 C3
Kent Ave. Sels 171 D2
Kent House Cl. Eck 58 C4
Kent Rd. Bu on T 254 C3
Kent Rd. Glos 10 B1
Kent Rd. Greas 195 E4
Kent Rd. Shef 43 D3
Kent St. Chest 115 E4
Kent St. Derby 219 F4
Kent's Bank Rd. Bux 85 E3
Kentmere Cl. Dron 56 C1
Kenwell Dr. Shef 56 A3
Kenyon Rd. Chest 96 C1
Keppel Ct. Ilk 194 C2
Kepple Gate. Ripley 180 C4
Kernel Cl. Derby 231 D4
Kerry Dr. Smal 192 C3
Kerry St. Derby 219 F4
Kerry's Yd. Kilb 191 F4
Kershaw St. Glos 17 E4
Kershope Dr. Derby 206 A2
Kerwin Cl. Totley 55 E4
Kerwin Dr. Totley 55 E4
Kerwin Rd. Totley 55 E4
Kestrel Ave. Wood 256 C2
Kestrel Cl. Ilk 208 C2
Kestrel Cl. Kill 60 A4
Kestrel Cl. Marple 23 D2
Kestrel Dr. Eck 59 D2
Kestrel Way. Bu on T 248 B2
Kestrels Croft. Derby 231 F2
Keswick Ave. Derby 231 F3
Keswick Cl. Ilk 208 B3
Keswick Ct. Lo Ea 223 D1
Keswick Dr. Chest 95 E4
Keswick Pl. Shef 56 C4
Ketton Ave. Shef 43 D2
Kevin Cl. Derby 220 A4
Kew Cres. Hean 182 A1
Kew Cres. Shef 44 A1
Kew Gdns. Derby 218 A3
Keyhaven Cl. Derby 219 E4
Keynsham Cl. Derby 232 C4
Keys Rd. Som 159 D1
Keys St. Derby 219 D3
Kibworth Cl. Derby 220 A4
Kidd Rd. Glos 17 F3
Kidsley Cl. Chest 95 D3
Kilburn La. Denby 179 F2
Kilburn Rd. Belper 179 E2
Kilburn Rd. Shef 56 C4
Kilburn Toll Bar. Kilb 179 F1
Kilburn Way. Swad 255 F3
Kildale Gdns. Mosb 59 E4
Kildare Rd. Derby 220 A2
Kildonan Gr. Shef 44 B2
Killingworth Ave. Derby 231 F2
Killis La. Belper 179 E1
Killis La. Holbr 191 E4
Kiln Bent Rd. Holme 3 D3
Kiln Cl. We Ha 193 F1
Kiln Croft. Etwall 229 E2
Kiln La. Glos 10 A3
Kiln La. Par 151 E1
Kiln Way. Swad 256 B2
Kilvington Ave. Shef 44 A4
Kilvington Cres. Shef 44 A4
Kilvington Rd. Shef 44 A4
Kimberley Cl. Kim 195 F3
Kimberley Dr. Bu on T 248 B2
Kimberley Rd. Ock 221 D1
Kinder Rd. Stav 97 D3
Kinder Cl. Glos 17 D4
Kinder Cres. Ripley 168 A3
Kinder Dr. Marple 23 D3
Kinder Gr. Bux 85 D3
Kinder Rd. Hay 25 E1
Kinder Row. Hay 25 F1
Kinder View. N Mills 33 E4
Kinder Way. Bux 85 F4
Kinder Wlk. Derby 218 C2
King Alfred St. Derby 218 C2
King Charles Ct. Glos 17 E4
King Ecgbert Rd. Totley 55 F3
King Edward Ave. Glos 10 B1
King Edward St. Sand 223 D3
King Edward St. Shireb 119 F2
King Edward St. Wirk 166 A4
King George Ave. Ilk 208 C4
King George St. S Wing 157 F4
King George St. Wirk 165 F4
King St N. Chest 96 A4
King St S. Chest 115 D4
King St. Alf 158 C2
King St. Ashb 173 E1
King St. Bake 109 E3
King St. Belper 178 C2
King St. Bu on T 254 B4
King St. Chest 77 F1
King St. Cl Cr 131 E2
King St. Clowne 80 C2
King St. Derby 219 D3
King St. Duff 190 C2
King St. East 182 C1
King St. Glos 17 E4
King St. Ilk 194 C1
King St. Lo Ea 236 B4
King St. M in L 9 E3
King St. M in L 16 A4
King St. Mans 136 B1
King St. Mar War 120 B3
King St. Mid 154 B3
King St. Pinx 160 B2
King St. S Norm 159 F3
King St. Tibs 148 A4
King St. Whit 82 B3
King William Centre. Iron 170 C2
King William St. Iron 170 C2
King's Cl. Bux 85 E4
King's Mead Cl. Derby 218 C3
King's Mead Wlk. Derby 218 C3
King's Mills La. We on T 245 F3
King's Rd. Bux 85 E4
Kingfisher Ave. Wood 256 C2
Kingfisher House. Chest 77 D2
Kingfisher Wlk. Derby 231 F1
Kings Cl. Cars 164 C4
Kings Cl. Clowne 80 C2
Kings Cl. Elmt 81 F1
Kings Coppice. Totley 55 E3
Kings Croft. Derby 204 C2
Kings Ct. Derby 219 D3
Kings Dr. Brin 182 C4
Kings Dr. Derby 218 A1
Kings Gate. C Don 247 F2
Kings Hill. Brass 153 D1
Kings Mews. Eck 59 F2
Kings Rd. Sand 223 D3
Kings Rd. Swad 256 A3
Kingsbury Rd. Derby 218 A3
Kingsclere Ave. Derby 206 A1
Kingscroft Cl. Totley 55 F4
Kingsdale Cl. Lo Ea 236 A3
Kingsfield Ind Es. Wirk 165 F3
Kingsfield Rd. Wirk 165 F4
Kingsgate. Calver 72 B1
Kingsland Cl. Derby 205 F1
Kingsley Ave. Chest 114 C4
Kingsley Ave. Mans 136 B3
Kingsley Cl. Mans 136 B2
Kingsley Cres. Lo Ea 236 A2
Kingsley Cres. Shirl 146 C2
Kingsley Ct. Mans 136 B3
Kingsley Rd. Derby 204 B2
Kingsley St. Derby 231 F3
Kingsmead Ave. Staple 209 E1
Kingsmead Ind Est. Derby 218 B3
Kingsmede Ave. Chest 95 E1
Kingsmoor Fields. Glos 10 B2
Kingsmoor Rd. Glos 10 B1
Kingsmuir Rd. Derby 217 E2
Kingsthorpe Cl. Mans 136 C1
Kingston Ave. Ilk 209 D2
Kingston Ct. We Ha 207 E4
Kingston Rd. Bu on T 248 B1
Kingston St. Derby 218 C4
Kingsway Cres. Kilb 192 A4
Kingsway Park Cl. Derby 218 B3
Kingsway. Derby 218 A3
Kingsway. Hean 181 E1
Kingsway. Ilk 209 D3
Kingswood Cl. Chest 95 E4
Kinross Ave. Derby 219 E4
Kipling Cl. Dron 76 B4
Kipling Dr. Derby 217 E1
Kipling Rd. Chest 95 F4
Kirby La. Wens 142 A4
Kirk Dale Ave. Derby 220 C2
Kirk Leys Ave N. Derby 220 C2
Kirk Leys Ave S. Derby 220 C2
Kirk St. Derby 219 D4
Kirk's La. Belper 179 D2
Kirkby Ave. Ilk 208 C3
Kirkby Ave. Shef 44 A2
Kirkby Dr. Shef 44 A2
Kirkby Rd. Shef 44 A2
Kirkby View. Shef 44 A2
Kirkby Way. Shef 44 A2
Kirkcroft Ave. Kill 60 B4
Kirkcroft Dr. Kill 60 B3
Kirkcroft La. Kill 60 B3
Kirkdale Cl. Chest 115 D4
Kirkdale Gdns. Lo Ea 236 A3
Kirkdale Rd. Lo Ea 236 A3
Kirkewhite Ave. Lo Ea 236 B4
Kirkfield Dr. Brea 235 E4
Kirkham Cl. Hean 181 E1
Kirkham Dr. Bees 223 F1
Kirkham La. Crich 168 A4
Kirkistown Cl. Derby 233 E3
Kirkland Cl. C Don 247 D2
Kirkman Rd. Hean 181 E2
Kirkstead Cl. Derby 206 A1
Kirkstead Cl. Pinx 160 B2
Kirkstead Rd. Pinx 160 B2
Kirkstone Ct. Lo Ea 223 D1
Kirkstone Rd. Bux 85 E2
Kirkstone Rd. Chest 95 E4
Kirton Ave. Lo Ea 236 B4
Kishfield La. Kettle 45 D3
Kitchener Ave. Derby 231 F4
Kitchener Terr. Scarc 101 D1
Kitson Ave. Sels 171 E2
Knab Rd. Da Da 127 F2
Knabhall La. Tans 144 B3
Knapp Ave. East 182 C1
Knifesmithgate. Chest 96 A2
Knight's La. Bretby 249 D3
Knight's La. Rep 249 D3
Knighton St. N Wing 131 F3
Knights Cl. Derby 231 F1
Knights Ct. Bu on T 240 C1
Knightsbridge. Derby 218 A3
Knightwake Rd. N Mills 33 D4
Kniveton La. Ashb 174 B2
Kniveton Park. Ilk 208 B4
Knob Fields. Linton 261 F4
Knob La. Spout 166 B3
Knoll Cl. Derby 231 D4
Knoll St. N Mills 33 D4
Knoll The. Chest 94 C1
Knoll The. Dron 57 E2
Knoll The. Shireb 119 E2
Knoll The. Swad 256 A3
Knoll The. Tans 144 A3
Knowes Cl. Bux 85 F4
Knowes Cres. Bux 85 E4
Knowl Ave. Belper 178 C3
Knowle Ave. C-Frith 47 D3
Knowle Rd. Marple 23 E3
Knowle Top. Mosb 59 F4
Knowles Hill. Rolle 240 A2
Knowleston Pl. Mat 143 E2
Knutsford Green. Derby 205 E1
Kyle Gr. Derby 206 A2
Kynance Cl. Derby 233 E3

Laburnam Cl. Elmt 81 F1
Laburnham Ct. Calow 97 D2
Laburnum Avenue. Shireb 119 F3
Laburnum Cl. Bols 99 E1
Laburnum Cl. Da Da 127 D2
Laburnum Cl. S Norm 160 A4
Laburnum Cl. Sand 223 D4
Laburnum Cres. Derby 204 B2
Laburnum Cres. Som 170 A4
Laburnum Gr. Derby 218 A3
Laburnum Gr. Kill 60 B3
Laburnum Gr. Mans 136 A2
Laburnum Rd. Bu on T 254 C3
Laburnum Rd. Swad 256 A3
Laburnum St. Stav 78 A1
Laburnum Way. Etwall 229 E2
Laceby Ct. Mans 136 C2
Lacey Fields Rd. Hean 182 A1
Ladbroke Gdns. Derby 217 F3
Ladies Spring Dr. Totley 56 A4
Ladies Spring Gr. Totley 56 A4
Ladle End La. Wa on T 253 E1
Lady Field Rd. Th Sa 62
Lady Grove Rd. Da Da 127
Lady Lea Rd. Hors 192
Lady Ley Hill. Hors 192
Lady Mantle Cl. Derby 232
Ladybank Rd. Derby 217
Ladybank Rd. Mosb 59
Ladybank View. Eck 59
Ladybower Ct. Shef 56
Ladybower La. Stav 97
Ladybower Rd. Derby 220
Ladycroft Paddock. Derby 204
Ladycroft. Bux 66
Ladyfields. Swad 256
Ladyflatts Rd. Wirk 165
Ladygrove Cotts. Derby 219
Ladylea Rd. Lo Ea 236
Ladypit Rd. N Mills 33
Ladysmith Rd. Ock 221
Ladythorne Ave. N Mills 23
Ladywell Cl. Bu on T 240
Ladywell Ct. Belper 179
Ladywood Ave. Belper 179
Ladywood Rd. Dale 208
Ladywood Rd. Ilk 208
Lake Ave. Hean 181
Lake Dr. Derby 231
Lake Dr. Dove 211
Lake Side. Dove 211
Lake Side. Glos 10
Lakeside Ave. Lo Ea 236
Lakeside Cres. Lo Ea 236
Lakeside. Ashb 173
Lakeside. Bake 109
Lakeside. Win 114
Lamb Cres. Ripley 169
Lamb Hill Cl. Shef 44
Lambcroft Rd. Pinx 160
Lambe Ct. Derby 219
Lambgates. Glos 10
Lambhouse La. Shot 177
Lambley Dr. Derby 204
Lambourn Ct. Derby 205
Lambourn Dr. Derby 205
Lambourne Ave. Ashb 185
Lambpart La. Bradw 50
Lambrook Cl. Derby 217
Lambton Cl. Ilk 194
Lampad Cl. Mel 252
Lampeter Cl. Derby 206
Lanark St. Derby 219
Lancaster Ave. Sand 223
Lancaster Ave. Staple 223
Lancaster Dr. Tut 239
Lancaster Rd. Chest 95
Lancaster St. Al Hv 117
Lancaster Wlk. Derby 221
Lancelot Cl. Chest 114
Lancelot Dr. Bu on T 240
Lancing Rd. Shef 43
Lander La. Belper 179
Landmere Cl. Ship 194
Landon Cl. Chest 114
Landsdown Gr. Lo Ea 223
Landseer Cl. Dron 56
Landseer Cl. Shef 43
Landseer Dr. Marple 23
Landseer Dr. Shef 43
Landseer Pl. Shef 43
Landseer Wlk. Shef 43
Lane Head Rd. Totley 55
Lane Head Rd. W Br 45
Lane Head. Long 121
Lane Head. St Mid 71
Lane The. Awsw 195
Lane The. Eck 60
Lanes The. Wirk 155
Lanesend Cotts. W Br 46
Laneside Ave. Bees 223
Laneside Cl. C-Frith 47
Laneside Rd. N Mills 24
Laneside Rd. N Mills 33
Lang Rd. Derby 232
Langdale Cl. Chest 94
Langdale Dr. Derby 205
Langdale Dr. Dron 57
Langdale Dr. Lo Ea 236
Langdale Sq. Chest 96
Langdon Cl. Lo Ea 223
Langer Field Ave. Chest 115
Langer La. Chest 114
Langer La. Win 114
Langford Rd. Derby 217
Langhurst Rd. Chest 95
Langley Ave. Ilk 194
Langley Ave. Som 170
Langley Cl. Chest 95
Langley Cl. Mans 135
Langley Ct. Glos 10
Langley Dr. Glos 17
Langley Park. La Mi 182
Langley Rd. Derby 220
Langley St. Derby 218
Langsett Dr. Derby 233
Langsett La. Glos 9
Langstone Ave. Bols 99
Langton Hollow. Sels 171
Langtree Ave. Chest 77

angwith Dr. Scarc 100 C1
angwith Maltings. Scarc 119 F4
angwith Rd. Bols 118 B4
angwith Rd. Shireb 119 F3
ansbury Ave. Pils 132 B1
ansbury Ave. Stav 79 D2
ansbury Dr. S Norm 160 A3
ansbury Rd. Eck 59 E2
anscombe Park Rd. Derby 204 C1
ansdowne Ave. Chest 95 F3
ansdowne Ave. Hello 232 A1
ansdowne Rd. Bran 253 F4
ansdowne Rd. Bux 66 A1
ansdowne Rd. Chest 96 B4
ansdowne Rd. Swad 256 A2
ansing Gdns. Derby 220 A3
ant La. Ash 144 A4
antern View. N Mills 24 A1
apwing Cl. Derby 231 F1
arch Ave. Kill 60 B3
arch Ave. Mans 136 A3
arch Ave. Ripley 169 E1
arch Ave. Shireb 119 E2
arch Cl. Derby 204 B2
arch Cres. East 182 C1
arch Dr. Sand 223 D4
arch Rd. Eck 59 D1
arch Rd. Kilb 192 A4
arch Rd. Swad 255 F3
arch Way. Chest 95 E3
arch Way. Glos 17 F4
archdale Cl. S Norm 160 A2
arges St. Derby 218 C3
ark Cl. Derby 231 E3
arkhill Cl. Som 169 F4
arkhill Cres. Derby 231 F2
arkhill. Som 169 F4
arkin Cl. Derby 232 A3
arklands Ave. Ilk 209 D4
arkspur Cl. Mans 136 B1
arkspur Cl. S Norm 160 A2
arkspur Ct. Derby 206 A2
arkstone La. Alst 149 D1
arpit Green. Whit 82 A3
ascelles Rd. Bux 85 D4
atham Cl. Bu on T 248 B1
athbury Cl. Derby 205 E1
athkil Dr. S Norm 159 F3
athkil Gr. Bux 85 E4
athkill Ave. Derby 233 E4
athkill Ave. Ilk 194 C3
athkill Ave. Stav 97 E3
athkill Cl. Shef 44 B4
athkill Cl. We Ha 207 F4
athkill Dale. Swad 255 F1
athkill Dr. Ripley 180 B3
athkill Dr. Sels 171 F4
athkill Gr. Cl Cr 131 E1
athkill Gr. Tibs 147 F3
athkill Rd. Derby 219 F4
athkill Rd. Shef 44 B4
athkilldale Cres. Lo Ea 236 A3
atimer Cl. Derby 230 C4
atimer St. Derby 232 B3
atrigg Cl. Derby 217 F1
auder Cl. Derby 231 F1
aunceston Rd. Derby 233 D3
aund Ave. Belper 179 D3
aund Cl. Belper 179 D3
aund Hill. Belper 179 D3
aund Nook. Belper 179 D3
aunds Ave. Sels 171 E4
aurel Ave. Mans 136 C1
aurel Ave. Ripley 169 E1
aurel Cl. Shireb 119 E3
aurel Cl. Som 170 A4
aurel Cres. Lo Ea 236 B3
aurel Cres. Smal 192 C3
aurel Cres. Stav 78 A1
aurel Dr. Kill 60 B3
aurel Garth Cl. Chest 77 D2
aurel Gr. Bu on T 254 C3
aurel Gr. S Norm 160 A2
aurence Cl. Chest 77 D1
aurie Pl. Derby 232 C4
avender Rd. Som 170 A4
avender Row. Derby 204 C1
averdene Ave. Totley 55 F2
averdene Cl. Totley 55 F2
averdene Dr. Totley 55 F2
averdene Rd. Totley 55 F2
averdene Way. Totley 55 F2
averick Rd. Sels 171 D2
awn Ave. Derby 204 B1
awn Ave. Etwall 229 E3
awn Cl. Hean 181 F1
awn Heads Ave. Derby 218 B1
awn Mill Rd. Kim 195 F4
awn The. Dron 57 D1
awn Villas. Calow 97 D1
awnfold. Glos 9 F2
awns The. As on T 246 A4
awns The. Rolle 240 A2
awns The. Utt 210 A1
awnside. Derby 220 C3
awnswood Cl. Derby 231 E4
awrence Ave. Awsw 195 E2
awrence Ave. Brea 235 E4
Lawrence Ave. Derby 220 A4
Lawrence Ave. East 182 C1
Lawrence Ave. Mans 136 A2
Lawrence Ave. N Wing 116 B1
Lawrence Ave. Ripley 180 B4
Lawrence Dr. Brin 182 B4
Lawrence St. Derby 231 F4
Lawrence St. Lo Ea 236 B4
Lawrence St. Sand 223 D4
Lawrence St. Staple 223 E3
Lawson Ave. Lo Ea 236 C4
Laxfield Cl. Chest 114 B4
Layton Dr. Chest 77 D1
Lea Cl. Derby 204 C2
Lea Cres. Som 170 B3
Lea Dr. Derby 217 F2
Lea Dr. Derby 219 F3
Lea La. Sels 171 F3
Lea Main Rd. Hollow 156 A4
Lea Moor Rd. Hollow 156 C4
Lea Rd. Dron 57 D1
Lea Rd. Hay 25 E2
Lea Rd. Hollow 156 A4
Lea Rd. Mat Ba 155 E3
Lea St. N Mills 33 D4
Lea Vale. S Norm 160 A2
Lea Wood Croft. Hollow 156 A3
Leabrook Rd. Shef 56 C4
Leabrooks Ave. Mans 136 B3
Leabrooks Rd. Som 170 B4
Leacroft Rd. Derby 219 D1
Leacroft Rd. Wins 141 E3
Leadale Ave. Som 170 A4
Leadale Cres. Mans 136 C3
Leadbeater Rd. Shef 44 A2
Leafenden Cl. Derby 205 D2
Leafield Rd. Disley 32 B3
Leafy La. Hean 181 F1
Leake St. Derby 218 B3
Leam Glen. Mans 136 B1
Leamington Cl. Derby 218 B1
Leamington Dr. S Norm 160 A3
Leamington Rd. Bran 253 F4
Leamington St. Ripley 169 F1
Leamoor Ave. Som 170 A4
Lean Town. Glos 17 E3
Leander Cl. Derby 231 E4
Leander Rise. Bu on T 255 D4
Leaper St. Derby 218 C3
Leapley La. Alk 199 E2
Leapley La. Yea 199 E2
Leas Ave. Plea 135 D3
Leas Rd. Mans 136 B2
Leashaw Rd. Crich 156 B2
Leashaw Rd. Hollow 156 B2
Leashaw. Crich 156 B2
Leashaw. Hollow 156 B2
Leathersley La. Scro 226 B1
Leathersley La. Sud 226 B1
Leaway The. Shireb 119 E2
Leawood Gdns. Derby 206 A2
Leawood Rd. Swad 256 B4
Leche Cft. Belper 179 E2
Lechlade Cl. We Ha 207 E4
Ledbury Chase. Derby 231 E1
Ledbury Pl. Derby 205 E1
Ledo Ave. Ripley 169 E1
Lee Cres. Ilk 209 D4
Lee Dale. Bux 85 E2
Lee Farm Cl. Derby 232 C1
Lee Head. Cha 16 B3
Lee La. Hean 182 A1
Lee Mount. Glos 17 E4
Lee Rd. Chest 96 C1
Lee Vale Dr. Cha 16 B4
Leebangs Rd. M in L 16 A4
Leech Ct. Greas 195 D4
Leedhams Croft. Wa on T 259 E4
Leeds Pl. Derby 219 E2
Leeds Rd. Shire 63 F4
Leefield Rd. C-Frith 47 D3
Leek Rd. Bux 84 C3
Leek Rd. Long 121 D3
Leeming La N. Mans 136 C3
Leeming La S. Mans 136 B1
Leeming La. Mar War 136 C4
Leeming Park. Mans 136 B2
Leen Valley Dr. Shireb 119 F2
Lees Hall Ave. Shef 43 D2
Lees Hall Pl. Shef 43 D3
Lees Hall Rd. Shef 43 D2
Lees House Ct. Shef 43 D2
Lees La. S Norm 159 F3
Lees Nook. Shef 43 D2
Lees Rd. St Pk 126 C2
Lees Row. Glos 10 B3
Leeside Rd. Bam 40 B2
Leeswood Cl. Chest 95 E4
Leeway. Derby 220 B2
Leicester Dr. Glos 17 F4
Leicester St. Bu on T 254 B4
Leicester St. Derby 218 C2
Leicester St. Lo Ea 236 C3
Leigh Rd. Bees 223 F2
Leigh Rd. Disley 32 A3
Leigh Way. N Wing 131 F4
Leighton Dr. Marple 23 E4
Leighton Dr. Shef 43 F2
Leighton Pl. Shef 43 F2
Leighton Rd. Shef 43 F2
Leisure La. Hartin 137 F3
Leman St. Derby 218 C2
Lemont Rd. Totley 55 F2
Leniscar Ave. Hean 181 E2
Lens Rd. Derby 204 B1
Lenton Ave. Derby 219 F3
Lenton St. Sand 223 E4
Leominster Dr. Derby 206 A1
Leonard Cl. Derby 219 D2
Leonard Cl. Shef 44 A4
Leonard St. Derby 219 D2
Leopold St. Derby 219 D2
Leopold St. Lo Ea 236 B4
Leslie Ave. Kim 195 F3
Leslie Cl. Derby 230 C4
Lesser La. Bux 85 F4
Level La. Bux 84 B3
Leven Cl. Derby 231 F1
Levens Way. Chest 95 F4
Lewcote La. WeHa 194 A1
Lewis St. Derby 218 C1
Lewiston Rd. Derby 220 A3
Lexington Rd. Derby 220 B3
Ley Ave. Alf 159 D2
Ley Croft. Hatton 227 E1
Ley Croft. Mans 136 B3
Ley Gdns. Alf 159 D2
Ley La. Mans 136 B2
Ley La. Marple 23 E4
Leyburn Cl. Chest 95 F3
Leycote Way. Belper 179 D3
Leyfield Rd. Totley 55 E4
Leygate View. N Mills 33 D4
Leyland Cl. Bees 223 F1
Leyland Ct. Derby 218 C4
Leyland Gdns. Derby 218 C4
Leyland St. Derby 218 C4
Leylands La. Marple 15 F4
Leylands. Derby 218 C4
Leys Ct. Belper 179 E2
Leys La. Bons 154 A4
Leys The. Lit Ea 191 E1
Leys The. Swad 255 F3
Leytonstone Dr. Derby 218 A3
Lichfield Rd. B-u-Ne 253 E2
Lichfield Rd. Bran 253 E2
Lichfield Rd. Dun 253 E2
Lichfield Ave. Swad 256 C3
Lichfield Cl. Bees 223 F2
Lichfield Dr. Derby 233 D4
Lichfield Rd. Chest 114 B4
Lichford Rd. Shef 43 E3
Lickpenny La. Ash 144 C2
Lid La. Rost 197 F4
Lidgate Cl. Derby 217 E1
Liffs Rd. A le Da 150 B4
Liffs Rd. Biggin 138 E1
Light Alders La. Disley 32 A3
Lightfoot Rd. Utt 210 A1
Lightwood Ave. Bux 85 E4
Lightwood La. Eck 43 F1
Lightwood La. Uns 77 F4
Lightwood Rd. Bux 66 A1
Lightwood Rd. Eck 58 C1
Lilac Ave. Derby 218 A3
Lilac Cl. Derby 233 D3
Lilac Cl. Heath 116 C1
Lilac Gr. Bols 99 E1
Lilac Gr. Bu on T 254 C3
Lilac Gr. Glap 134 A4
Lilac Gr. Mar War 120 C4
Lilac Gr. S Norm 160 A2
Lilac Gr. Shireb 119 F3
Lilac Mews. Ilk 194 B2
Lilac St. Stav 78 A1
Lilac St. Stav 97 D4
Lilac Way. Derby 204 B1
Lilac Way. Shirl 146 B1
Lilian Prime Cl. Derby 233 D4
Lilley St. Derby 233 D3
Lillymede Cl. Chest 114 C3
Lilybank Cl. Mat 143 E3
Lilypools The. Mel 252 A4
Limb La. Totley 55 E4
Limbersitch La. Ch Bro 227 F3
Lime Ave. Derby 205 E1
Lime Ave. Derby 218 C2
Lime Ave. Duff 190 C3
Lime Ave. La Mi 182 B1
Lime Ave. N Mills 24 B1
Lime Ave. Ripley 169 E1
Lime Ave. Stav 78 C1
Lime Cl. Calow 97 D2
Lime Cl. Dove 224 A4
Lime Cl. Hatton 227 E1
Lime Cl. Pinx 160 B2
Lime Cres. Belper 179 D1
Lime Cres. Mar War 120 C4
Lime Gr. Ashb 185 E4
Lime Gr. Bu on T 254 C3
Lime Gr. Da Da 127 E2
Lime Gr. Derby 220 A3
Lime Gr. Dray 234 C4
Lime Gr. Lo Ea 236 B4
Lime Gr. S Norm 160 A3
Lime Gr. Sand 223 D3
Lime Gr. Staple 223 E3
Lime Grove Ave. Mat 143 E3
Lime Grove Wlk. Mat 143 E3
Lime La. Derby 206 A2
Lime La. Morley 206 B3
Lime Rd. Eck 59 D1
Lime St. Ilk 208 C4
Lime Terr. Lo Ea 236 B4
Lime Tree Ave. Da Da 127 D2
Lime Tree Ave. Glap 134 A4
Lime Tree Ave. Kill 60 B3
Lime Tree Ave. Mans 136 A3
Lime Tree Ave. Swad 256 A4
Lime Tree Gr. Cl Cr 131 F1
Lime Tree Rd. Mat 143 E3
Lime Wlk. Derby 218 B1
Limecroft View. Win 115 D2
Limekiln Fields Rd. Bols 99 D2
Limerick Rd. Derby 220 A2
Limes Ave. Derby 217 E1
Limes Ave. Ne La 101 D1
Limes Cl The. Mat 143 E3
Limes Cres. Shireb 119 E3
Limes Park. Ripley 169 E1
Limes The. Mapp 193 F2
Limestone Terr. Mans 136 A2
Limetree Cl. Chest 96 C3
Limetree Rise. Ilk 208 B3
Linacre Ave. Cl Cr 131 E1
Linacre Rd. Chest 95 D3
Linacre Rd. O Bram 95 D3
Linacre Way. Glos 17 F4
Linacres Dr. Derby 233 D1
Linbery Cl. S Wing 158 A2
Lincoln Ave. Derby 233 D4
Lincoln Ave. Sand 223 D2
Lincoln Cl. Staple 209 F1
Lincoln Cl. Tibs 148 A3
Lincoln Dr. Derby 233 E3
Lincoln Dr. Mans 136 B2
Lincoln Green. Derby 232 C1
Lincoln Rd. Bu on T 254 B4
Lincoln St. Alf 158 C2
Lincoln St. Chest 115 D4
Lincoln St. Tibs 148 A3
Lincoln Way. Glos 17 F4
Lincoln Way. Swad 256 C3
Lindale Rd. Chest 76 B1
Linden Ave. Chest 95 D1
Linden Ave. Cl Cr 131 E1
Linden Ave. Dron 57 D2
Linden Cl. Kilb 192 A4
Linden Ct. Cl Cr 131 E1
Linden Dr. Chest 115 E3
Linden Gr. Mat 143 E3
Linden Gr. Sand 223 D4
Linden Gr. Shireb 119 F2
Linden Gr. Staple 223 F3
Linden Rd. Elmt 81 F1
Linden St. Mans 136 A1
Linden St. Shireb 119 F2
Linden Way. H La 32 A4
Lindford Cl. Derby 205 F2
Lindisfarne Ct. Chest 95 E1
Lindisfarne Rd. Dron 76 A4
Lindley St. Sels 171 E3
Lindrick Cl. Derby 217 F1
Lindrick Cl. Mans 136 B3
Lindrick Gdns. Chest 114 B4
Lindsey Cl. Derby 219 F3
Lindway La. Brack 145 D1
Lindway La. Crich 145 D1
Ling La. Scarc 118 B2
Ling Rd. Chest 114 B4
Lingfield Rd. Bran 253 F4
Lingfield Rise. Derby 217 E2
Lingfoot Ave. Shef 57 D3
Lingfoot Cl. Shef 57 D3
Lingfoot Cres. Shef 57 E3
Lingfoot Dr. Shef 57 E3
Lingfoot Pl. Shef 57 D3
Lingfoot Wlk. Shef 57 E3
Linglongs Ave. W Br 45 E3
Linglongs Rd. W Br 45 E3
Lings Cres. N Wing 132 A4
Linkmel Rd. East 182 B2
Links Cl. Derby 231 F2
Links Rd. C-Frith 46 C3
Links Rd. Dron 76 A4
Linley La. Shef 44 B3
Linnet Cl. Derby 220 C3
Linnet House. Chest 77 D2
Linscott Cl. Chest 95 E4
Linshaws Rd. Holme 3 F3
Linton Rd. Chest 114 B4
Linton Rd. Linton 261 F4
Linton Rd. Rosl 260 C3
Linwood Cres. East 182 C1
Linwood Ct. Mans 136 C2
Lipp Ave. Kill 60 B4
Liskeard Dr. Derby 204 B2
Lismore Gr. Bux 85 D4
Lismore Park. Bux 85 D4
Lismore Rd. Bux 85 D4
Lismore Rd. Shef 43 D3
Lissett Ave. Ilk 208 C4
Lister Ave. Shef 44 A2
Lister Cl. Derby 218 A2
Lister Cl. Shef 44 A2
Lister Cres. Shef 44 A2
Lister Dr. Shef 44 A2
Lister Pl. Shef 44 A2
Lister Way. Shef 44 A2
Liston Dr. Derby 218 C4
Litchen Cl. Ilk 194 C1
Litchfield Cl. Lo Ea 237 D4
Litchurch La. Derby 219 E1
Litchurch St. Derby 219 D2
Little Acre. Mans 136 C3
Little Bolehill. Wirk 155 D1
Little Breck. S Norm 160 A2
Little Bridge St. Derby 218 C3
Little Debdale La. Mans 135 F1
Little Fen. Tibs 147 F3
Little Hallam Hill. Ilk 208 C3
Little Hallam La. Ilk 209 D3
Little La. A in W 89 F1
Little La. Kim 195 F3
Little La. Litton 69 F2
Little La. Mans 135 D3
Little La. S in A 148 C1
Little La. Shef 44 A3
Little La. Shireb 119 E2
Little La. Th Sa 63 D3
Little London. Hollow 156 A3
Little Longstone Cl. Derby 217 F1
Little Lunnon. B in F 237 F3
Little Morton Rd. N Wing 132 A3
Little Norton Ave. Shef 57 D4
Little Norton Dr. Shef 57 D4
Little Norton La. Shef 57 D4
Little Norton Way. Shef 57 D4
Little Wood Dr. Shef 44 A2
Little Wood Rd. Shef 44 A2
Littlebrook Cl. Glos 10 A2
Littlefield La. Ella 183 D1
Littlefield La. Snel 184 A2
Littlefield Rd. Ch Bro 227 E4
Littlefields. M in L 9 D2
Littlemoor Cres. Chest 95 E4
Littlemoor La. Mat 143 F1
Littlemoor Rd. M in L 9 D1
Littlemoor. Chest 95 E4
Littlemoor. Eck 59 F2
Littleover Cres. Derby 218 B1
Littleover La. Derby 231 F4
Littlewell La. S-by-D 208 C1
Littlewood La. Mans 136 A3
Litton Cl. Belper 179 D3
Litton Cl. Ilk 194 C2
Litton Cl. Stav 97 E4
Litton Dr. Derby 220 C2
Litton Mews. Glos 9 F1
Litton Rd. Mans 136 C2
Liverpool St. Derby 219 F4
Liversage Pl. Derby 219 D2
Liversage Rd. Derby 219 D2
Liversage St. Derby 219 D2
Livingstone Rd. Derby 218 C1
Lloyd St. Derby 218 B3
Loads Rd. Holy 113 D4
Loadshead La. O Bram 112 E4
Lochinvar Cl. Derby 220 C2
Lock Cl. Ilk 208 B3
Lock La. Lo Ea 236 B2
Lock La. Sand 223 E2
Lockford La. Chest 96 A3
Lockington Cl. Derby 232 C1
Lockington Rd. C Don 247 E3
Locko Ct. Derby 220 B3
Locko La. Al Hu 132 C2
Locko Rd. Dale 220 C4
Locko Rd. Derby 220 C4
Locko Rd. Pils 132 B2
Lockoford La. Chest 96 B3
Lockside. Marple 23 D3
Lockton Ave. Hean 193 F4
Lockwood Rd. Derby 204 B2
Lode La. Alst 149 F2
Lodge Ave. Ashb 185 D4
Lodge Bank. Glos 10 A3
Lodge Cl. Calow 97 D2
Lodge Cl. Duff 190 C2
Lodge Cl. Etwall 229 E2
Lodge Ct. M in L 9 D2
Lodge Dr. Belper 178 C3
Lodge Dr. Win 115 D2
Lodge Estate. As on T 246 A4
Lodge Farm Cl. Chest 114 B4
Lodge Hill. Rolle 239 F2
Lodge La. Ald 181 F4
Lodge La. Alst 149 D2
Lodge La. Derby 218 C3
Lodge La. Derby 220 B2
Lodge La. Mack 203 E3
Lodge Lane. Shot 177 E4
Lodge Mews. As on T 246 A4
Lodge Moor Rd. Lod M 42 C4
Lodge Pl. Stav 97 E3
Lodge Rd. Greas 195 D4
Lodge Rd. Lo Ea 236 B3
Lodge Rd. Mapp 193 F2
Lodge Rd. Neth 261 E1
Lodge St. Dray 235 D4
Lodge The. Glos 10 A3
Lodge The. Tide 69 E1

Lodge Way. Derby 217 E1
Lodge Wlk. Stav 97 E3
Lohengrin Ct. Bu on T 240 C1
Lombard St. Derby 217 F3
Lomond Ave. Derby 231 F1
London Rd S. Shef 43 D4
London Rd. Bux 85 E3
London Rd. C Don 247 D4
London Rd. Derby 219 E1
London Rd. Shar 234 C1
London Rd. Shef 43 D3
London Rd. Shef 43 D4
London St. Uns 77 E3
Long Bridge La. Derby 232 B4
Long Croft. As on T 246 A4
Long Hill. Bux 65 E2
Long Hill. Da Da 127 E2
Long Hill. W Br 45 F1
Long Hill. W Br 65 E2
Long La. Alst 149 D3
Long La. Ash 130 A3
Long La. C-Frith 46 B2
Long La. C-Frith 47 D2
Long La. Cha 16 B4
Long La. K Lang 202 A1
Long La. Kill 60 C3
Long La. Lees 202 A1
Long La. Longf 200 C1
Long La. Ship 194 B3
Long La. Ship 194 C4
Long La. Shireb 119 F2
Long La. Tadd 87 F3
Long La. Thurv 201 E1
Long La. Trus 201 E1
Long La. Uns 77 E4
Long La. W Br 46 B2
Long Meadow Rd. Alf 158 C2
Long Meadow. Mans 136 B3
Long Rake. Middle 123 E2
Long Rake. Youl 124 B3
Long Row. Belper 178 C2
Long Row. Shar 235 D1
Long Shambles. Chest 96 A2
Long St. Bu on T 254 C4
Longacre Rd. Dron 76 A4
Longacre Way. Mosb 60 A4
Longbow Cl. Bu on T 240 B1
Longbow Gr. Bu on T 240 B1
Longbridge La. Bux 67 D2
Longclough Dr. Glos 17 D4
Longcourse La. L Duk 98 A1
Longcroft Ave. Dron 56 B1
Longcroft Cres. Dron 56 B1
Longcroft Rd. Dron 56 B1
Longcroft View. Whit 82 A3
Longdale Dr. M in L 9 D2
Longdale Gdns. M in L 9 D2
Longdale. Mans 136 C1
Longden Cl. Staple 209 F1
Longedge Gr. Win 115 D2
Longedge La. Win 114 C2
Longedge La. Win 115 D2
Longedge Rise. Win 115 D2
Longfield Cres. Ilk 208 C3
Longfield La. Ilk 208 C3
Longford Cl. Derby 204 B1
Longford Cl. Shef 56 A3
Longford Cres. Shef 56 A3
Longford Dr. Shef 55 F2
Longford La. 214 C3
Longford Rd. Shef 56 A2
Longford Spinney. Shef 55 F2
Longford St. Derby 218 C4
Longhedge La. Bu on T 239 F1
Longhedge La. Plea 134 C3
Longhurst La. Marple 23 E3
Longhurst View. Whit 81 F3
Longlands Dr. N Mills 33 D4
Longlands La. Fin 230 B1
Longlands Rd. N Mills 33 D4
Longlands Rd. Swad 256 B4
Longlands. Bols 99 D1
Longley La. Derby 220 B3
Longload La. Mid 154 C3
Longmeade Dr. C-Frith 47 D2
Longmoor Gdns. Lo Ea 223 D1
Longmoor La. Brea 222 C1
Longmoor La. Sand 223 D2
Longmoor Rd. Glos 17 D4
Longmoor Rd. Lo Ea 223 D1
Longnor Mews. Glos 9 E1
Longreave La. G Lo 90 B2
Longrose La. Kni 163 D1
Longshaw Cl. N Wing 131 F3
Longshaw Cl. Stav 97 E4
Longside Rd. Holy 112 F3
Longson Rd. C-Frith 47 E3
Longster La. Mar War 120 B2
Longstock Cl. Derby 205 F1
Longstone Wlk. Derby 218 C2
Longstone Cres. Shef 44 B2
Longstone La. A in W 89 F1
Longstone Rise. Belper 179 D3
Longwalls La. Belper 178 B3
Longwood Rd. Pinx 160 C1
Lonsdale Dr. Bees 223 F1
Lonsdale Gr. Da Da 142 C4
Lonsdale Pl. Derby 218 B2
Lonsdale Rd. Bran 254 A4
Lonsdale Rd. Pils 132 A1
Loosemore Dr. Shef 43 F3
Lord Haddon Rd. Ilk 194 C1
Lord Roberts Rd. Chest 96 A1
Lord St. Derby 232 B3
Lord St. Glos 10 B1
Lord St. M in L 9 E2
Lords Cl. Bols 99 D1
Lordsmill St. Chest 96 A1
Lorne Cl. Dron 56 B1
Lorne St. Derby 218 C2
Lorraine Cl. Derby 232 C2
Loscoe Grange. Hean 181 E2
Loscoe Rd. Derby 206 A1
Loscoe Rd. Hean 181 E1
Loscoe-denby La. Hean 181 D2
Losk Cnr. Scarc 118 B1
Losk La. Scarc 118 B2
Lothian Pl. C Don 247 D2
Lothian Pl. Derby 219 F4
Lothlorien Cl. Derby 231 D4
Loudon St. Derby 219 D2
Loudoun Pl. C Don 247 D2
Loundes Rd. Uns 76 C3
Loundsley Ct. O Bram 94 C2
Loundsley Green Rd. Chest 95 E3
Lount La. Bu on T 239 F1
Lousie Greaves La. Derby 220 C3
Louvain Rd. Derby 218 B1
Louwil Ave. Mans 136 C3
Lovatt Cl. Bu on T 240 C1
Love La. Tibs 147 E2
Low Comm. Barl 79 E4
Low Cl. W Und 189 D1
Low Lea Rd. Marple 23 D3
Low Leighton Rd. N Mills 33 E4
Low Meadow. W Br 45 E4
Low Pavement. Chest 96 A2
Low's La. S-by-D 209 D1
Lowburn Rd. Shef 44 B4
Lowe St. Derby 232 C3
Lowedges Cres. Shef 56 C3
Lowedges Dr. Shef 56 C3
Lowedges Pl. Shef 57 D3
Lowedges Rd. Shef 56 C3
Lower Bagthorpe. Sels 171 F2
Lower Bank. Glos 17 E4
Lower Barn Rd. Glos 9 F2
Lower Bloomsgrove Rd. Ilk 194 C1
Lower Brook St. Lo Ea 236 C4
Lower Chapel St. Ilk 194 C1
Lower Chapel St. Shirl 147 D2
Lower Clara Mount Rd.
Hean 182 A1
Lower Dale Rd. Derby 218 C1
Lower Dr. Som 169 E4
Lower Dunstead Rd. Ald ... 182 A2
Lower Dunstead Rd. La Mi 182 A2
Lower Eaves View. C-Frith .. 47 E3
Lower Eley St. Derby 218 C2
Lower Fold. Marple 23 D4
Lower Gladstone St. Hean 181 F1
Lower Granby St. Ilk 194 C1
Lower Green. Fin 230 B1
Lower Greenshall La. Disley 32 C3
Lower Grove Rd. Chest 95 F2
Lower Hague. N Mills 32 C4
Lower Hall Cl. Holbr 191 E3
Lower Hardwick St. Bux 85 D4
Lower High St. Tut 239 E4
Lower La. Chin 34 B1
Lower Macclesfield Rd. W Br 45 F3
Lower Mantle Cl. Cl Cr 131 E2
Lower Market St. M in L 16 A4
Lower Middleton St. Coss . 195 D1
Lower Nelson St. Hean 181 E1
Lower Orchard St. Staple .. 223 E4
Lower Park St. Staple 223 E3
Lower Rd. Mack 217 F4
Lower Somercotes. Som ... 170 C4
Lower Sq. Tint 10 A4
Lower St. Dove 224 A4
Lower Stanton Rd. Ilk 208 C3
Lower Strines Rd. Marple 23 D3
Lower Terr Rd. Tide 69 D3
Lower Whitworth Rd. Ilk 208 C3
Lowerlea. Disley 32 B3
Lowery Dr. Marple 23 D4
Lowes Hill. Ripley 169 E2
Lowes La. Swark 244 B4
Lowfield Ave. Eck 58 C4
Lowfield Ct. Shef 43 D4
Lowfields. Stav 79 D1
Lowgates. Stav 79 D1
Lowlands Lea. Hean 181 F1
Lowlands Rd. Belper 179 D2
Lowry Ct. M in L 9 D2
Lowry Dr. Dron 56 C1
Lowside Cl. Calver 72 A1
Lowside. Calver 72 B1
Loxley Cl. Chest 95 D2
Loxley Cl. Derby 206 A1
Loxton Ct. Derby 217 E2
Loyne Cl. Derby 231 F1
Lucas La. Hilton 228 C1
Lucas Rd. Chest 95 F3
Lucas Terr. Hay 25 E2
Luccombe Dr. Derby 233 E3
Lucerne Rd. Derby 206 B2
Ludborough Wlk. Mans 136 C2
Ludgate St. Tut 239 E3
Ludgate Wlk. Derby 217 F3
Ludham Cl. Chest 95 F4
Ludham Gdns. Chest 95 F4
Ludlam Ave. Greas 195 D4
Ludlow Cl. Derby 220 C3
Luke La. Brai 201 F4
Lullington Rd. C Camp 263 F2
Lullington Rd. Over 262 A2
Lulworth Cl. Derby 231 E3
Lulworth Ct. Kim 195 F4
Lum's Hill Rise. Mat 143 E3
Lumb La. Haz 178 A2
Lumb La. North 127 D3
Lumber Lane. H Ward 176 B1
Lumsdale Cres. Mat 143 E3
Lumsdale Rd. Stav 97 E4
Lumsdale. Mat 143 F3
Luna Croft. Shef 43 F1
Lundie Cl. Derby 231 E1
Lundy Rd. Dron 76 A4
Lune Meadow. Mans 136 C2
Lupin Cl. Derby 206 B2
Lupin Way. Calow 97 D2
Lupton Cres. Shef 56 C3
Lupton Dr. Shef 56 C3
Lupton Rd. Shef 56 C3
Lupton Wlk. Shef 57 D3
Lwr Bank Cl. Glos 9 F2
Lychgate Cl. Derby 205 E1
Lydden Cl. Chest 96 C4
Lydford Ave. Chest 77 D1
Lydford Rd. Alf 159 D3
Lydgate Dr. Win 114 C2
Lydgate. Eyam 71 F3
Lydstep Cl. Derby 206 B1
Lyle Cl. Kim 195 F4
Lyme Park. Chin 34 C1
Lyme Rd. Disley 32 A3
Lymefield Terr. M in L 16 A4
Lymewood Dr. Disley 32 B3
Lynam Pl. Cl Cr 131 F2
Lynam Rd. Crich 168 A4
Lynam Rd. S Wing 168 B4
Lyncroft Ave. Ripley 169 F1
Lyndale Dr. Codnor 181 D4
Lynden Ave. Lo Ea 236 B3
Lyndhurst Gr. Derby 220 A3
Lyndhurst St. Derby 219 D1
Lyne Ave. Glos 17 D4
Lynholmes Rd. Mat 143 E3
Lynmouth Dr. Ship 194 B2
Lynne Cl. Glos 17 F4
Lynton Cl. Ripley 169 E2
Lynton Rd. Ripley 168 A2
Lynton St. Derby 218 C2
Lynwood Cl. Bran 253 F4
Lynwood Cl. Shef 56 C4
Lynwood Rd. Bran 253 F4
Lynwood Rd. Derby 231 F2
Lytham Cl. Derby 205 E1
Lyttelton St. Derby 218 B3
Macaulay St. Derby 232 A3
Macclesfield Main Rd. Bux .. 84 B3
Macclesfield Old Rd. Bux 84 B3
Macclesfield Rd. Bux 85 D3
Macclesfield Rd. W Br 45 E3
Macdonald Cl. Gra 115 F2
Macdonald Sq. Ilk 208 B3
Machins Ct. Dron 57 D1
Mackenzie St. Derby 218 B3
Mackinley Ave. Staple 209 F1
Macklin St. Derby 219 D3
Macready Pl. Derby 232 C4
Macworth Rd. Derby 218 C3
Maddock La. Brass 153 D1
Madehurst Gdns. Shef 43 D4
Madehurst Rd. Shef 43 D4
Madehurst Rise. Shef 43 D4
Madehurst View. Shef 43 D4
Madeley Ct. Derby 217 E1
Madeley St. Derby 219 D1
Madin Dr. Stav 97 D3
Madin St. Chest 96 A2
Madin St. Tupton 131 E4
Madison Ave. Derby 219 F4
Madras Rd. Bu on T 248 B2
Mag La. Elmt 100 C4
Mag Lane. Idri 176 B3
Magnolia Way. Som 170 A4
Maidstone Dr. Derby 232 C3
Main Ave. Derby 204 C3
Main Ave. Totley 55 F2
Main Rd. Bam 40 A2
Main Rd. Bradw 51 D4
Main Rd. Brai 201 F4
Main Rd. Crich 156 B1
Main Rd. Eck 58 C2
Main Rd. Eck 58 C4
Main Rd. Eck 79 D4
Main Rd. Elv 234 A3
Main Rd. Flagg 106 C3
Main Rd. Grin 72 B4
Main Rd. Hath 53 D4
Main Rd. Heath 117 D1
Main Rd. Hol 75 D4
Main Rd. Morton 147 D3
Main Rd. Ne La 101 D1
Main Rd. O Bram 94 C4
Main Rd. Pent 169 E3
Main Rd. Ripley 169 D2
Main Rd. Sels 171 D2
Main Rd. Sels 171 F1
Main Rd. Shirl 146 B1
Main Rd. Shirl 146 B3
Main Rd. Smal 192 C2
Main Rd. Som 170 C3
Main Rd. Stret 146 B3
Main Rd. Sud 225 F3
Main Rd. Sud 226 A2
Main Rd. Tadd 88 A2
Main Rd. Uns 76 C4
Main Rd. Uns 77 E4
Main Rd. Wens 127 E1
Main St. Awsw 195 E3
Main St. Black 257 E1
Main St. Bols 117 F4
Main St. Br Hill 252 C1
Main St. Br Hill 252 C3
Main St. Brea 235 E4
Main St. Brin 171 E1
Main St. Bu on T 240 C1
Main St. Bu on T 254 C4
Main St. Burn 229 F3
Main St. C Camp 263 F1
Main St. C Don 247 E3
Main St. C Don 247 F3
Main St. C Elms 260 B2
Main St. Cald 260 C4
Main St. Calver 72 B1
Main St. Ch Bro 227 D4
Main St. Chel 106 A4
Main St. Dun 253 D4
Main St. East 182 C1
Main St. Eg 241 D3
Main St. Elv 234 B3
Main St. Etwall 229 D2
Main St. Fin 230 B1
Main St. G Lo 90 A2
Main St. G Low 89 F2
Main St. H Wood 192 B3
Main St. Harts 257 D3
Main St. Hilton 228 B1
Main St. K Ire 165 D1
Main St. Kim 195 F3
Main St. Linton 261 E3
Main St. Lo Ea 236 C4
Main St. Mapp 193 F2
Main St. Mel 245 E1
Main St. Mid 154 B2
Main St. Moira 256 B1
Main St. N Sol 248 C4
Main St. Neth 264 C4
Main St. Newt 148 A2
Main St. Over 262 A2
Main St. Rep 242 B1
Main St. Rep 243 D1
Main St. Rosl 260 B3
Main St. S in A 148 C2
Main St. S Norm 160 A3
Main St. S-by-D 222 C4
Main St. Scarc 101 D1
Main St. Scarc 118 A3
Main St. Scarc 118 C3
Main St. Shireb 119 E2
Main St. Smisby 257 F2
Main St. Swad 255 F3
Main St. Tick 251 D3
Main St. Wa on T 253 E1
Main St. We on T 245 F3
Main St. Wins 141 E3
Main St. Bran 253 F4
Maine Dr. Derby 220 A3
Mais Cl. Tans 144 A3
Makeney Rd. Belper 191 D3
Makeney Rd. Duff 190 C1
Makeney Rd. Holbr 191 E3
Malbon's Yd. Ashb 173 E1
Malcolm Gr. Derby 230 C4
Malcolm St. Derby 219 D1
Malham Cl. Chest 95 E3
Malia Rd. Chest 96 B3
Malin Cl. Derby 233 D3
Malinscommon La. Spout .. 166 B2
Malkin St. Chest 96 A2
Mallard Cl. Kill 60 A4
Mallard Cl. Shireb 119 F2
Mallatratt Pl. Mans 136 A3
Malmesbury Ave. Swad 256 B3
Malpas Rd. Mat 143 D3
Malson Way. Chest 95 F3
Maltby Ave. Morton 146 C3
Maltby Cl. Derby 204 C1
Malthouse Cl. East 182 C1
Malthouse Cl. Wirk 154 C2
Malthouse Ct. Ashb 173 E1
Malthouse La. Ash 129 F2
Malthouse La. Curbar 72 B3
Malthouse La. Hatton 227 E2
Malthouse La. Ripley 168 A1
Malthouse Rd. Whit 82 A3
Maltings The. Bu on T 248 A1
Maltings The. Shar .... 235 D
Malton Pl. Derby .... 205 E
Malvern Ave. Bu on T .... 248 A
Malvern Cl. Derby .... 217 E
Malvern Gdns. Lo Ea .... 236 A
Malvern Gdns. Mat .... 143 D
Malvern Rd. Chest .... 95 F
Malvern Rise. Glos .... 10 A
Malvern Way. Derby .... 205 E
Manchester La. Harts .... 257 E
Manchester Rd. Bux .... 65 F
Manchester Rd. C-Frith .... 46 C
Manchester Rd. M in L .... 9 F
Manchester Rd. Tide .... 69 D
Manchester Rd. Tint .... 9 F
Manchester St. Derby .... 218 B
Manchester St. Lo Ea .... 236 B
Manifold Ave. Ashb .... 173 E
Manifold Ave. Stav .... 97 E
Manifold Dr. Derby .... 233 D
Manifold Dr. Sels .... 171 F
Manitoba Way. Sels .... 171 F
Manknell Rd. Chest .... 96 A
Manners Ave. Ilk .... 194 B
Manners Cl. Chin .... 34 B
Manners Rd. Ilk .... 194 C
Manners St. Ilk .... 209 D
Manning View. Ilk .... 194 C
Mannion Cres. Lo Ea .... 236 A
Manor Ave. Chest .... 96 C
Manor Ave. Derby .... 218 B
Manor Ave. Staple .... 223 E
Manor Bungalows. Dron ...... 56 C
Manor Cl. Brass .... 153 D
Manor Cl. Newt .... 148 A
Manor Cl. Pils .... 132 B
Manor Cl. Swad .... 255 D
Manor Court Rd. Bols .... 98 C
Manor Cres. Bu on T .... 255 D
Manor Cres. Chest .... 95 E
Manor Cres. Dron .... 56 C
Manor Croft. Ripley .... 169 E
Manor Ct. Ba on T .... 244 A
Manor Ct. Brea .... 235 F
Manor Ct. Clowne .... 80 C
Manor Ct. Som .... 170 C
Manor Dr. Chest .... 95 E
Manor Dr. Chest .... 96 C
Manor Dr. Neth .... 264 C
Manor Farm Ct. Whit .... 81 F
Manor Farm Mews. Burn ... 229 F
Manor Farm Rd. As on T ... 246 A
Manor Fields Dr. Ilk .... 208 E
Manor Gr. Barl .... 80 A
Manor House Rd. Lo Ea ... 236 C
Manor Park Ct. Derby .... 218 A
Manor Park Rd. Glos .... 10 C
Manor Park View. Glos .... 10 C
Manor Park. Ock .... 221 D
Manor Rd. Ashb .... 173 E
Manor Rd. B in F .... 237 F
Manor Rd. Barl .... 80 A
Manor Rd. Belper .... 178 C
Manor Rd. Chest .... 95 E
Manor Rd. Chest .... 96 C
Manor Rd. Derby .... 218 B
Manor Rd. Derby .... 232 C
Manor Rd. East .... 182 C
Manor Rd. Ilk .... 194 C
Manor Rd. Kill .... 60 C
Manor Rd. Mans .... 136 A
Manor Rd. Ock .... 221 D
Manor Rd. S Wing .... 157 F
Manor Rd. Swad .... 255 D
Manor Rd. W Br .... 45 F
Manor St. Glos .... 10 B
Manor View. Mosb .... 59 F
Manse Ave. Elmt .... 100 E
Manse Cl. Elmt .... 100 E
Mansfeldt Cres. Chest .... 95 F
Mansfeldt Rd. Chest .... 95 F
Mansfield Dr. Shef .... 44 B
Mansfield Rd. Al Hv .... 117 F
Mansfield Rd. Alf .... 159 D
Mansfield Rd. Brin .... 182 C
Mansfield Rd. Chest .... 115 F
Mansfield Rd. Clowne .... 80 C
Mansfield Rd. Derby .... 219 D
Mansfield Rd. East .... 182 C
Mansfield Rd. Elmt .... 81 F
Mansfield Rd. Glap .... 134 B
Mansfield Rd. Gra .... 116 B
Mansfield Rd. Hean .... 182 A
Mansfield Rd. Heath .... 117 D
Mansfield Rd. Kill .... 60 C
Mansfield Rd. Kill .... 60 C
Mansfield Rd. Mans .... 136 B
Mansfield Rd. Mar War ..... 120 C
Mansfield Rd. S Norm .... 160 E
Mansfield Rd. Scarc .... 118 A
Mansfield Rd. Scarc .... 118 E
Mansfield Rd. Sels .... 171 F
Mansfield Rd. Shef .... 44 E
Mansfield Rd. Tibs .... 148 A
Mansfield Rd. Work .... 82 C
Mansfield St. Derby .... 219 D
Mansfield St. Som .... 170 B
Mansfields Croft. Etwall .... 229 D

Manton Cl. Swad 255 F3
Manvers Ave. Ripley 169 F1
Manvers Ct. Mar War 120 A2
Manvers Rd. Calow 97 D2
Manvers St. Mans 136 A2
Manvers St. Mar War 120 A2
Manvers St. Ripley 169 F1
Manystones La. Brass 153 D2
Maple Ave. Derby 231 E3
Maple Ave. Disley 33 D3
Maple Ave. Ripley 180 B4
Maple Ave. Sand 223 D4
Maple Cl. Mans 136 C1
Maple Dr. Ashb 185 E4
Maple Dr. Belper 179 D1
Maple Dr. Derby 233 D1
Maple Dr. Derby 233 D3
Maple Dr. Kill 60 B3
Maple Dr. S Norm 160 A2
Maple Gdns. Hean 181 E1
Maple Gr. Brea 235 F4
Maple Gr. Bu on T 254 C3
Maple Gr. Derby 204 B3
Maple Gr. Glap 134 A4
Maple Rd. Swad 256 A3
Maple St. Stav 97 D4
Maplebeck Ct. Derby 219 D4
Mapletoft Ave. Mans 136 A3
Mapleton Ave. Derby 205 F1
Mapleton Rd. Ashb 173 D1
Mapleton Rd. Dray 235 D4
Mapperley La. Mapp 193 F1
Mapperley Rd. Shef 56 C4
Marchington Cl. Derby 204 C1
Marchwood Cl. Chest 95 F2
Marcus St. Derby 219 D4
Mardale Cl. Chest 76 C1
Maree Cl. Derby 231 F2
Marfleet Cl. Derby 217 E2
Margaret Ave. Derby 219 F3
Margaret Ave. Ilk 208 C4
Margaret Ave. Lo Ea 223 F1
Margaret Ave. Sand 223 D2
Margaret St. Derby 219 D4
Margreave Rd. Derby 219 F4
Marigold Cl. Derby 206 A2
Marina Dr. Derby 220 B3
Marina Dr. Derby 232 C3
Marina Rd. Smal 193 D4
Marion Ct. Bux 85 E3
Marjorie Rd. Derby 219 F4
Marjory La. Ch Bro 213 E2
Mark St. Sand 223 E3
Mark's Cl. Derby 231 E3
Markeaton La. Derby 218 A4
Markeaton St. Derby 218 C3
Market Cl. S Norm 160 A3
Market Cl. Shireb 119 F2
Market Pl. Ashb 173 E1
Market Pl. Belper 179 D2
Market Pl. Bols 99 D1
Market Pl. Bux 85 D4
Market Pl. C-Frith 47 D3
Market Pl. Cas 38 B1
Market Pl. Chest 96 A2
Market Pl. Codnor 181 D4
Market Pl. Crich 156 C1
Market Pl. Ilk 208 C4
Market Pl. Iron 170 C2
Market Pl. Lo Ea 236 C4
Market Pl. Long 121 D3
Market Pl. M in L 9 D2
Market Pl. Mans 136 B2
Market Pl. Mat Ba 155 D3
Market Pl. Mel 252 A4
Market Pl. Ripley 169 E1
Market Pl. S in A 148 C2
Market Pl. S Norm 160 A3
Market Pl. Som 170 B4
Market Pl. Som 170 C3
Market Pl. Stav 78 C1
Market Pl. Tide 69 E2
Market Pl. Wirk 165 F4
Market Sq. Tide 69 E2
Market St. Bake 109 E3
Market St. Bux 85 D4
Market St. C Don 247 D2
Market St. C-Frith 47 D3
Market St. Cl Cr 131 E2
Market St. Disley 32 B3
Market St. Dray 235 D4
Market St. Eck 59 E2
Market St. Glos 10 B1
Market St. Hay 25 E2
Market St. Hean 181 F1
Market St. Ilk 208 C4
Market St. Iron 170 C2
Market St. M in L 9 D2
Market St. M in L 9 E3
Market St. M in L 16 A4
Market St. N Mills 33 D4
Market St. S in A 148 C2
Market St. S Norm 160 A3
Market St. Shireb 119 F2
Market St. Stav 78 C1
Market St. Swad 256 A1
Market St. Swad 256 A2
Market St. W Br 45 F4
Markham Cres. Stav 78 C1
Markham La. L Duk 98 A2
Markham La. Stav 98 A2
Markham Rd. Chest 96 A1
Markham Rd. Stav 98 A3
Markland Ave. Clowne 81 D2
Markland La. Elmt 81 D1
Markland View. Elmt 81 E2
Marlborough Cres. Bu on T 255 D4
Marlborough Dr. Belper 179 E3
Marlborough Rd. Brea 235 E4
Marlborough Rd. Bux 85 D4
Marlborough Rd. Derby 232 B4
Marlborough Rd. Lo Ea 223 F1
Marlborough Rd. Mans 135 F1
Marlow Brow. Glos 10 A2
Marlow Cres. We Ha 207 E4
Marlow St. Bux 85 E4
Marlow St. Glos 10 A2
Marlpit La. Bols 99 E2
Marlpit La. Dens 196 B3
Marlpit La. Ella 183 D1
Marlpit La. S Hill 228 A4
Marple Rd. Cha 16 A3
Marples Ave. Mans 136 C3
Marrison Dr. Kill 60 B3
Marsden Cl. Duff 190 C2
Marsden Pl. Chest 95 E1
Marsden St. Chest 96 A2
Marsden St. Derby 232 C4
Marsden St. Glos 10 A2
Marsh Ave. Dron 57 D2
Marsh Ave. Hope 38 C2
Marsh Cl. Mosb 59 E3
Marsh Green La. Ash 129 F2
Marsh Hall La. C-Frith 46 C3
Marsh Hollow. Holl 200 C3
Marsh La. Belper 179 D3
Marsh La. N Mills 33 E3
Marsh La. Stan 183 E4
Marsh Lane Cres. Belper 179 D2
Marsh View. Eck 59 D1
Marshall Dr. Staple 223 F4
Marshall St. Alf 159 D2
Marshall St. Hean 181 F1
Marsham Dr. Marple 23 D3
Marshaw Cl. Derby 217 F1
Marshes The. Hope 38 C2
Marshfield Gr. Stav 79 D1
Marshgreen Cl. Derby 233 E3
Marston Cl. Belper 179 E3
Marston Cl. Derby 231 E3
Marston Cl. Dron 75 E4
Marston Cres. Totley 55 F3
Marston La. Dove 211 E2
Marston La. Hatton 239 E4
Marston La. M on D 228 A1
Marston La. Rolle 240 A2
Marston Old La. Hatton 239 E4
Marston Rise. Bu on T 254 C4
Marston. Chel 106 A4
Martin Ct. Eck 59 E2
Martin Dr. Derby 220 A4
Martin Rise. Eck 59 E2
Martin's La. Han 238 A3
Martindale Ct. Belper 179 E3
Martins La. Win 131 D4
Martlet Ave. Disley 32 B3
Mary Ann St. Chest 76 C2
Mary St. Eck 59 E2
Mary St. Scarc 101 D1
Maryland Ct. Staple 209 F1
Maryland Ct. Swad 256 A4
Maryland Rd. Derby 220 A3
Marylebone Cres. Derby 218 A3
Masefield Ave. Derby 231 F4
Masefield Ave. N Wing 116 B1
Masefield Ave. Swad 256 B3
Masefield Rd. Shef 44 B4
Mason Cres. Shef 44 B4
Mason Gr. Shef 44 B4
Mason St. Whit 81 F3
Masson Cl. Chest 95 E3
Masson Rd. Mat Ba 143 D1
Mastin Ave. Clowne 80 B3
Mather's Way. Tupton 115 E1
Matlock Ct. Lo Ea 235 F3
Matlock Dr. Stav 97 E3
Matlock Green. Mat 143 E2
Matlock Rd. Ash 113 F2
Matlock Rd. Ash 129 F3
Matlock Rd. Ash 145 E1
Matlock Rd. Belper 178 C4
Matlock Rd. Brack 145 E1
Matlock Rd. Derby 205 F1
Matlock Rd. Derby 220 A4
Matlock Rd. Holy 114 A4
Matlock Rd. Ripley 167 F2
Matlock Rd. S Wing 157 F4
Matlock St. Bake 109 E3
Mattersey Ct. Mans 136 A1
Matthew Cl. Tint 9 F4
Matthew St. Derby 232 C3
Matthew Way. Derby 230 C4
Matthews Ct. Staple 209 F1
Matthews La. Shef 43 E1
Maude St. Eck 59 E2
Maugerhay. Shef 43 E1
Maunleigh. Mans 136 C1
Mawfa Ave. Shef 43 E1
Mawfa Cres. Shef 43 E1
Mawfa Dr. Shef 43 E1
Mawfa Rd. Shef 43 E1
Mawkin La. K in A 160 C3
Maws La. Kim 195 F4
Mawstone La. Youl 125 D2
Max Rd. Derby 219 F4
Maxey Pl. Shef 43 D3
Maxwell Ave. Derby 218 B4
Maxwell St. Brea 235 F4
May Ave. Uns 77 E3
May St. Derby 218 C2
May St. Ilk 194 C2
Maybank Rd. C-Frith 35 D1
Mayfair Cres. Derby 217 F3
Mayfair. Swad 255 F3
Mayfield Ave. Hean 181 F1
Mayfield Ave. Kilb 192 A4
Mayfield Ave. May 184 B4
Mayfield Dr. Bu on T 255 D4
Mayfield Dr. N Wing 131 F3
Mayfield Dr. Staple 209 F1
Mayfield Gr. Lo Ea 223 F1
Mayfield Rd. Ashb 173 D1
Mayfield Rd. Ashb 184 C4
Mayfield Rd. Bu on T 248 A2
Mayfield Rd. Chest 95 E1
Mayfield Rd. Derby 219 F4
Mayfield Rd. Lod M 42 C4
Mayfield Rd. Marple 15 D1
Mayfield Terr. Hath 53 D4
Mayfield Terr. May 184 B3
Mayflower Ct. Shireb 119 F2
Mayflower Rd. Greas 195 E4
Mayhall Ave. Mans 136 A2
Maylands Ave. Brea 235 F4
Maylands. Ock 221 D1
Maynard Rd. Chest 95 F1
Maynard Rd. Grin 53 E1
Maynestone Rd. Chin 34 C3
Maypole Hill. Swad 256 A3
Maypole La. Derby 230 C4
McGough Mews. Derby 232 A3
McMahon Ave. Stav 97 D3
McNeil Gr. Dray 235 D4
Mead Cl. Derby 231 F2
Mead Cres. Bu on T 255 D3
Mead Wlk. Bu on T 255 D3
Meadow Ave. Bux 67 D3
Meadow Ave. Codnor 181 D4
Meadow Bank. Glos 16 C4
Meadow Bank. M in L 9 E3
Meadow Bank. Mans 136 C3
Meadow Cl. Bols 118 A4
Meadow Cl. Brea 235 F4
Meadow Cl. C-Frith 47 F1
Meadow Cl. Chest 77 E1
Meadow Cl. Derby 220 C2
Meadow Cl. Dray 235 D4
Meadow Cl. Dron 57 E2
Meadow Cl. Fin 230 B1
Meadow Cl. Greas 182 C2
Meadow Cl. H Wood 192 B3
Meadow Cl. Rep 242 C1
Meadow Cl. St Mid 72 A2
Meadow Cl. Tibs 148 A4
Meadow Cl. W Br 45 E4
Meadow Cotts. Mans 136 B2
Meadow Cres. C Don 247 D1
Meadow Cres. Mosb 59 D4
Meadow Croft. N Wing 132 B4
Meadow Ct. Belper 178 C2
Meadow Ct. Kilb 192 A4
Meadow Ct. S Norm 159 F2
Meadow Gr. Newt 148 A2
Meadow Gr. Totley 55 F2
Meadow Grove Rd. Totley 55 E2
Meadow Head Ave. Shef 56 C4
Meadow Head Dr. Shef 56 C4
Meadow La. Bu on T 248 A4
Meadow La. C-Frith 47 F1
Meadow La. Derby 219 E3
Meadow La. Derby 219 F3
Meadow La. Disley 32 B3
Meadow La. Lo Ea 236 C4
Meadow La. Newt 159 F4
Meadow La. Rep 243 D2
Meadow La. Rost 197 E4
Meadow La. Swad 255 F3
Meadow La. Swad 256 A3
Meadow La. Tide 69 D1
Meadow Rd. Awsw 195 E3
Meadow Rd. Cl Cr 131 D3
Meadow Rd. Derby 219 D3
Meadow Rd. Derby 219 F1
Meadow Rd. Ripley 169 F1
Meadow Rise. Brass 153 D1
Meadow Rise. Ch Bro 227 D4
Meadow Rise. Glos 16 C4
Meadow Rise. O Bram 94 C2
Meadow St. Ilk 194 C1
Meadow St. Iron 170 C3
Meadow St. N Mills 33 E4
Meadow Vale. Duff 190 B2
Meadow View Rd. Shef 56 C4
Meadow View Rd. Swad 255 F3
Meadow View. Bols 80 C2
Meadow View. Chest 114 A4
Meadow View. Da Da 142 C4
Meadow View. N Wing 132 B4
Meadow View. Rolle 240 B2
Meadow View. S Wing 157 F3
Meadow Way. Derby 233 D1
Meadow Way. Swad 256 A3
Meadowbank Way. East 182 B2
Meadowbrook Ind Est. Mosb 60 A4
Meadowcroft Gdns. Mosb 59 F4
Meadowcroft Glade. Mosb 59 F4
Meadowcroft Rise. Mosb 59 F4
Meadowcroft. M in L 9 D2
Meadowfield Cl. Glos 9 F2
Meadowfield. W Br 45 E4
Meadowhead. Shef 57 D4
Meadowhill Rd. Chest 115 E4
Meadowlark Gr. Derby 206 A1
Meadows Croft. Duff 190 B2
Meadows Rd. Hay 25 E1
Meadows The. Chest 94 C3
Meadows The. Hean 181 F1
Meadows The. O Bram 95 D3
Meadows The. Som 169 F4
Meadows The. Utt 210 A1
Meadowside Cl. Shir 200 B4
Meadowside Cl. Win 115 D2
Meadowside. Disley 33 D3
Meadowside. May 184 B3
Meadowside. W Br 45 E4
Meads The. Shef 57 D4
Meadway Dr. Totley 55 E4
Meadway The. Totley 55 E4
Meakin St. Chest 115 E4
Meal Hill Rd. Holme 2 C4
Meal St. N Mills 33 E4
Mear Greaves La. Bu on T 248 A2
Mease La. C Camp 263 D1
Measham Rd. Donis 265 E3
Measham Rd. Moira 262 C2
Measham Rd. S Field 265 F1
Meath Ave. Derby 220 A2
Meden Ave. Plea 134 C4
Meden Bank. Mans 135 D3
Meden Cl. Mans 135 D3
Meden Rd. Mans 136 B2
Meden Sq. Mans 135 D3
Medina Cl. Derby 233 E3
Medlock Cl. Chest 114 A4
Medlock Rd. Chest 114 B4
Medway Dr. Derby 205 D3
Meerbrook Cl. Derby 206 A1
Meerbrook Pl. Ilk 208 B3
Meersbrook Park Rd. Shef 43 D3
Meersbrook Rd. Shef 43 D3
Megaloughton La. Derby 220 B2
Megdale. Mat 143 D3
Melandra Castle Rd. Glos 9 E1
Melandra Ct. Derby 218 C2
Melanie Cl. Glos 17 D4
Melbourn Cl. Duff 190 C2
Melbourne Ave. Bu on T 248 B2
Melbourne Ave. Dron 56 A1
Melbourne Cl. Belper 179 D1
Melbourne Cl. Derby 204 B1
Melbourne Cl. Derby 217 F2
Melbourne Ct. Lo Ea 235 F2
Melbourne La. Br Hill 252 C1
Melbourne La. Tick 251 E3
Melbourne Rd. Staple 209 F1
Melbourne St. Derby 219 D2
Melbourne St. Mans 136 B3
Melbreak Cl. Derby 217 F1
Melfort Cl. Derby 231 F1
Melling Cl. Chest 114 C4
Mellington Cl. Shef 43 E1
Mellor Dr. Utt 210 A1
Mellor La. Barlow 75 F1
Mellor La. C-Frith 47 D3
Mellor Rd. Bran 254 A4
Mellor Rd. N Mills 24 B2
Mellor St. Derby 232 C3
Mellor Way. Chest 115 D4
Mellor's La. Holbr 191 E3
Melrose Cl. Chest 95 E2
Melrose Cl. Derby 231 F1
Meltham La. Chest 96 A3
Melton Ave. Derby 231 E3
Melton Ave. Mel 252 A4
Melton Ct. Sand 223 D3
Melton Ct. Som 170 B3
Melville Cl. H Ward 175 F2
Melville Cres. Chest 96 C2
Melville Ct. Etwall 229 D2
Memorial Rd. Derby 204 B2
Mendip Cl. Lo Ea 223 D1
Mendip Cres. Chest 95 D2
Mendip Ct. Derby 205 F1
Menin Rd. Derby 204 B1
Mentmore Cl. Som 170 A4
Mercaston Cl. Chest 95 D3
Mercaston La. H Ward 188 A2
Mercaston La. Mack 203 D4
Mercaston La. W Und 203 D4
Mercaston Rd. Derby 219 F4
Mercer Cres. Alf 159 E2
Merchant Ave. Derby 220 B2
Merchant St. Derby 218 C3
Merchant St. Shireb 120 A2
Mercia Cl. Hatton 239 E4
Mercia Dr. Totley 55 F3
Mercia Dr. Will 242 A3
Mercian Mews. Derby 220 B2
Meredith Ct. Staple 209 F1
Mereoak La. Tick 257 F4
Merlin Cres. Bran 253 F4
Merlin Way. Ilk 208 C2
Merlin Way. Wood 256 C2
Merrial Cl. Bake 109 E2
Merrick Cl. Chest 95 E3
Merridale Rd. Derby 231 E4
Merrill Way. Derby 232 B3
Merrybower Cl. Derby 231 E2
Merrydale Rd. Bu on T 255 D4
Mersey Bank Rd. Glos 9 F2
Merthyr Ct. Derby 206 A1
Merton Ct. Staple 209 F1
Mervyn Rd. Bu on T 248 A2
Metcalfe Cl. Derby 233 D4
Metcalfe Way. Kill 60 B3
Methley Cl. Shef 43 F3
Metro Ave. Newt 148 A2
Mettesford. Mat 143 E3
Meverill Rd. Tide 69 E3
Mevril Rd. W Br 45 F3
Mewies Cl. Wa on T 253 E1
Mews The. Mel 252 A4
Meynell Cl. Bu on T 248 A1
Meynell Cl. Chest 95 E1
Meynell Rd. Lo Ea 236 B3
Meynell Rise. Ashb 173 E2
Meynell St. Derby 218 C1
Meynell St. Swad 256 A1
Meynell Way. Kill 60 B3
Michael Cl. Win 115 D3
Michael's La. Ella 183 E3
Michelle Cl. Derby 231 E2
Michigan Cl. Derby 220 B3
Michlow Dr. Bradw 51 D4
Michlow La. Bradw 51 D4
Micklecroft Gdns. Derby 230 C4
Mickledon Cl. Lo Ea 236 A4
Mickleross Cl. Derby 217 E2
Mickley La. Dron 55 F2
Mickley La. Shirl 146 B3
Mickley La. Totley 55 F2
Middle Hay Cl. Shef 43 F2
Middle Hay Pl. Shef 43 F2
Middle Hay Rise. Shef 43 F2
Middle Hay View. Shef 43 F2
Middle La. Cl Cr 131 F2
Middle Ox Gdns. Mosb 59 F3
Middle Pavement. Chest 96 A2
Middle Rd. Win 114 C1
Middle Shambles. Chest 96 A2
Middle St. Scarc 118 B4
Middlebeck Cl. Derby 232 C1
Middlecroft Rd. Stav 97 E4
Middlefield Cl. Totley 55 E4
Middlefield Croft. Totley 55 E4
Middlegate Field Dr. Whit 82 A3
Middleton Ave. Codnor 181 D3
Middleton Ave. Derby 218 B1
Middleton Dr. Chest 97 D3
Middleton La. St Mid 71 E2
Middleton Rd. Ilk 209 D3
Middleton Rd. Mans 136 B3
Middleton St. Awsw 195 D2
Middleton St. Coss 195 D1
Middleton St. Derby 219 D1
Midhill Rd. Shef 43 D4
Midland Ave. Staple 223 E3
Midland Ct. Chest 115 D4
Midland Pl. Derby 219 E2
Midland Rd. Derby 219 E2
Midland Rd. East 182 C1
Midland Rd. Hean 181 F1
Midland Rd. Swad 256 A2
Midland St. Lo Ea 236 C4
Midland Terr. Chest 115 D4
Midland Terr. N Mills 33 E4
Midland Terr. Newt 147 E1
Midland Terr. Ripley 167 F2
Midland Terr. Stav 78 A2
Midland View. N Wing 131 F4
Midway Rd. Swad 256 B3
Midway. Derby 204 C1
Mikado Rd. Lo Ea 236 B3
Milbank Cl. Derby 217 F3
Milburn Gdns. Derby 206 A2
Milbury Cl. Derby 205 F1
Mile Ash La. Derby 204 C1
Milford Ave. Lo Ea 223 D2
Milford Dr. Ilk 194 B2
Milford Rd. Duff 190 C2
Milford Rd. Stav 97 E3
Milford St. Derby 218 C4
Milford. Bake 109 E3
Milken La. Ash 130 A2
Mill Brow Rd. Marple 23 F4
Mill Brow. M in L 16 A4
Mill Brow. Marple 23 E4
Mill Cl. Fin 230 B1
Mill Cl. Kilb 192 A4

Mill Cl. N Sol 248 C4
Mill Cl. Ock 221 E1
Mill Cl. Som 169 F4
Mill Cl. Swad 256 B3
Mill Cliff. Bux 85 E4
Mill Cres. Whit 82 A3
Mill Cres. Win 115 E2
Mill Croft. Derby 217 E2
Mill Farm Cl. Calver 72 B1
Mill Green. Stav 78 C1
Mill Hill Dr. Bu on T 248 A2
Mill Hill La. Brea 222 C1
Mill Hill La. Bu on T 248 A2
Mill Hill La. Derby 218 C2
Mill Hill Rd. Derby 218 C2
Mill Hill. L Duk 117 D3
Mill La. Al Hu 133 E4
Mill La. Ashb 173 F1
Mill La. Belper 179 D2
Mill La. Bols 98 C4
Mill La. Bols 99 D2
Mill La. Brad 163 D3
Mill La. Cas 38 B2
Mill La. Chest 95 E1
Mill La. Cl Cr 131 D2
Mill La. Codnor 181 D4
Mill La. Coss 195 E1
Mill La. Derby 217 E2
Mill La. Dove 211 D1
Mill La. Dron 57 D1
Mill La. Eck 60 A1
Mill La. Eyam 71 F3
Mill La. Gra 115 E2
Mill La. Hartin 137 E3
Mill La. Hath 52 C4
Mill La. Heath 117 D1
Mill La. Hilton 228 B1
Mill La. Hol 74 C3
Mill La. Hollow 144 A1
Mill La. Hollow 156 A3
Mill La. Pinx 160 B1
Mill La. Rost 197 E4
Mill La. Sand 223 E3
Mill La. Scro 226 B4
Mill La. Scro 226 C1
Mill La. Shir 200 B4
Mill La. Totley 55 F3
Mill La. Whit 82 A3
Mill La. Win 115 E2
Mill La. Win 130 C3
Mill Meadow Way. Etwall 229 D2
Mill Moor Cl. Derby 232 C1
Mill Rd. Hean 194 A4
Mill Rd. Mat Ba 155 D3
Mill Rd. Staple 223 E4
Mill St. Bake 109 E3
Mill St. Barlow 75 E2
Mill St. Belper 179 D2
Mill St. C Elms 260 B2
Mill St. Chest 96 A2
Mill St. Clowne 80 C2
Mill St. Derby 218 C3
Mill St. Glos 10 B1
Mill St. Hay 25 E2
Mill St. Ilk 194 C1
Mill St. Roc 197 D2
Mill St. St Mid 72 A2
Mill Stream Cl. Chest 95 E1
Mill Wlk. Whit 82 A3
Mill Yd. Som 170 B4
Millash La. Whit 82 A2
Millbank Cl. Ship 194 B2
Millbank. Hean 194 A4
Millbrook. M in L 9 F3
Millcross La. Barlow 75 F2
Milldale Ave. Bux 84 C3
Milldale Cl. Chest 95 E3
Milldale Cl. Ripley 180 B3
Milldale Ct. Ashb 185 E4
Milldale Rd. Derby 220 C2
Milldale Rd. Lo Ea 236 A3
Milldale Rd. Totley 55 F3
Milldam La. Bradl 186 C4
Miller Ave. Stav 79 E2
Millers Dale Cl. Belper 179 E3
Millers Green. Wirk 165 F3
Millers La. Brack 145 F1
Millersdale Ave. Ilk 194 C3
Millersdale Cl. Bu on T 248 A3
Millersdale Ct. Glos 10 C1
Millfield Croft. Swad 256 A4
Millfield Rd. Ilk 209 D4
Millfield Rd. Kim 195 F4
Millfield St. Wood 257 D1
Millfield. Shar 235 D1
Millom Pl. Derby 205 E1
Mills Cl. Dray 235 D4
Mills Ct. Crich 156 C1
Millstone Cl. Dron 56 B1
Millstone La. Pent 169 E4
Millthorpe La. Hol 75 D3
Milltown. Glos 10 B1
Millway La. Alst 149 F2
Millway. Mans 136 B1
Milnbank Ave. Bux 85 E4
Milner Ave. Codnor 181 D4
Milner Ave. Dray 235 D4
Milner Rd. Lo Ea 236 B4
Milnhay Rd. Hean 182 B1
Milnhay Rd. La Mi 182 B1
Milton Ave. Alf 159 E2
Milton Ave. Ilk 194 C2
Milton Ave. Shirl 146 B2
Milton Ave. Swad 256 B3
Milton Cres. Chest 115 D4
Milton La. C-Frith 46 A3
Milton Pl. Stav 78 C1
Milton Rd. Derby 217 E2
Milton Rd. Ilk 194 C2
Milton Rd. Rep 242 B1
Milton St. Derby 218 B2
Milton St. Ilk 194 C2
Milton St. Lo Ea 236 B4
Milward Rd. Hean 181 E1
Miners Hill. Brass 153 D1
Minimum Terr. Chest 95 F1
Minster Rd. Derby 205 F1
Minster Way. Som 169 F4
Mires La. G Lo 90 A2
Mires La. Litton 70 A2
Mires The. Alst 149 D2
Mires The. Bir 126 A1
Miriam Ave. Chest 114 A4
Miry La. Scro 227 E2
Misterton Cl. Derby 204 C1
Misterton Ct. Mans 136 A1
Mitcham Wlk. Derby 218 A3
Mitchell Ave. La Mi 182 A2
Mitchell St. Clowne 80 C2
Mitchell St. Lo Ea 236 C4
Mitchell Terr. Ilk 209 D3
Mitchell Way. Chest 77 F2
Mitre Dr. Rep 242 B1
Moat Bank. Bu on T 248 B1
Moat St. Swad 256 A1
Moat The. C Don 247 D2
Model Village. Elmt 100 C4
Moffatt Rd. Shef 43 D4
Moira Cl. Derby 220 A4
Moira Dale. C Don 247 E2
Moira Rd. Donis 262 C1
Moira Rd. Moira 262 C4
Moira Rd. Over 262 A2
Moira Rd. Wood 256 C1
Moira St. Mel 252 A4
Moisty La. March 224 B2
Moisty La. St Mid 71 D2
Molineux Ave. Stav 78 B1
Molineux St. Derby 219 D1
Molloy Pl. Shef 43 D3
Molloy St. Shef 43 D3
Moncrieff Cres. Derby 220 A4
Mondello Dr. Derby 233 E3
Monk Rd. Som 159 D1
Monk St. Derby 218 C2
Monk St. Tut 239 E4
Monk's Rd. Glos 17 F3
Monks Cl. Derby 231 E2
Monks Cl. Ilk 209 D4
Monks' Rd. Glos 16 C3
Monksdale Cl. Tide 69 D2
Monksdale La. Tide 68 C1
Monkton Cl. Ship 194 B2
Monkwood Rd. Chest 95 E4
Monmouth St. Derby 219 E3
Monnies End. Clowne 80 B3
Monpelier Cl. Bran 254 A4
Monsal Ave. Bux 85 E4
Monsal Cres. Stav 97 D3
Monsal Cres. Tibs 147 F3
Monsal Dr. Derby 220 C2
Monsal Dr. S Norm 159 F3
Monsal Gr. Bux 85 E4
Monsaldale Cl. Bu on T 248 A2
Monsaldale Cl. Lo Ea 236 A3
Monsall Ave. Ilk 194 C3
Monsdale La. Par 151 F1
Monsom La. Rep 242 B2
Montagu St. Marple 15 D1
Monteith Pl. C Don 247 D2
Montpelier Pl. Bux 66 B1
Montpelier Rd. Ripley 167 F2
Montpelier. Quar 204 B4
Montrose Cl. Derby 231 F2
Montrose Ct. Staple 209 F1
Montrose Pl. Dron 56 B1
Montrose Sq. Mans 136 A3
Monument Hill. Iron 170 C2
Monument La. Iron 170 C2
Monyash Cl. Derby 220 A4
Monyash Cl. Ilk 194 C2
Monyash Mews. Glos 9 E1
Monyash Rd. Bake 109 E3
Monyash Rd. O Had 109 D1
Monyash Way. Belper 179 D3
Moonpenny Way. Dron 57 D1
Moor Cres. Mosb 59 E4
Moor Dr. Derby 233 D3
Moor End Rd. Marple 24 A3
Moor End. Derby 220 C3
Moor Farm Ave. Mosb 59 D4
Moor Farm Garth. Mosb 59 E4
Moor Farm Rd E. Ashb 185 F4
Moor Farm Rd W. Ashb 185 F4
Moor Farm Rise. Mosb 59 D4
Moor La. As on T 246 A4
Moor La. Ba on T 244 A4
Moor La. Bols 99 D1
Moor La. Bons 142 A1
Moor La. Callow 165 D2
Moor La. Calow 116 B4
Moor La. Chel 87 F1
Moor La. Da Da 127 E2
Moor La. Dale 207 F1
Moor La. Derby 232 B3
Moor La. Elton 140 C3
Moor La. Flagg 106 C2
Moor La. G Low 89 F3
Moor La. K Ire 165 D2
Moor La. K Lang 202 C1
Moor La. Lit Ea 191 F1
Moor La. Ock 221 E3
Moor La. Osm 185 F3
Moor La. Scarc 119 D4
Moor La. Tadd 87 F1
Moor La. Youl 125 D3
Moor Rd. Ash 129 F2
Moor Rd. Bread 205 F3
Moor Rd. Brin 182 C4
Moor Rise. Holbr 191 E4
Moor St. Derby 220 C3
Moor The. Brin 182 B4
Moor The. Mid 154 B2
Moor Valley. Mosb 59 D4
Moor Valley. Shef 44 C1
Moor View Rd. Stav 79 D1
Mooracre La. Bols 99 E1
Moorbridge La. Staple 209 E1
Moorbrook La. Bradw 50 C4
Moore St. Derby 219 D2
Mooredge Dr. Mat 143 E3
Mooredge Rd. Crich 157 D1
Moorend. Beeley 111 E2
Moores Ave. Sand 223 E4
Moorfield Ave. Bols 99 D1
Moorfield Ave. Holbr 191 E4
Moorfield Cres. Sand 223 D3
Moorfield Ct. Staple 209 F1
Moorfield La. Scarc 100 C2
Moorfield Prec. M in L 9 E3
Moorfield Sq. Bols 99 D1
Moorfield St. M in L 9 E3
Moorfield Terr. M in L 9 E3
Moorfield. Mat 143 E4
Moorfields Ave. East 182 C2
Moorgate Ave. Plea 134 C4
Moorgate Cres. Dron 76 A4
Moorgate. Derby 217 F3
Moorhaigh La. Mans 135 D2
Moorhall. Bake 109 E3
Moorhead Ave. Derby 232 C3
Moorings The. Disley 32 C3
Moorland Ave. Staple 223 E3
Moorland Dr. Heath 116 C1
Moorland Rd. Derby 217 E2
Moorland Rd. Hath 53 D4
Moorland View Rd. Chest 95 E1
Moorland View. Shef 44 A1
Moorland View. Uns 58 A1
Moorlands La. Bons 142 A2
Moorlands La. Curbar 72 B3
Moorlawn Ave. Holy 113 F4
Moorpark Ave. Chest 114 B4
Moorpool Cres. Holbr 191 E4
Moorside Cl. Mat Ba 155 D3
Moorside Cl. Mosb 59 E4
Moorside Cres. Derby 231 F2
Moorside La. Holbr 191 E4
Moorthorpe Gdns. Shef 44 C1
Moorthorpe Green. Shef 44 C1
Moorthorpe Way. Shef 44 C1
Moortop Rd. Uns 58 A1
Moorview Cl. Chest 96 B4
Moorview Cl. Win 115 D2
Moorway Croft. Derby 231 D4
Moorway La. Derby 231 D3
Moorway. Bread 205 F2
Moorwood Ave. Totley 55 E1
Moray Ct. Kim 195 F4
Moray Pl. Dron 56 B1
Mordaunt Rd. Shef 43 F3
Morden Green. Derby 218 A3
Morden Rd. Greas 195 E4
Morefern Dr. Derby 205 F1
Morland Cl. Shef 43 F2
Morland Dr. Shef 43 F2
Morland Pl. Shef 43 F2
Morland Rd. Hay 25 D1
Morland Rd. Shef 43 F2
Morledge. Derby 219 D3
Morleston St. Derby 219 D2
Morley Almshouses La. Morley 206 A4
Morley Ave. Chest 95 E2
Morley Cl. Belper 179 F3
Morley Cl. Shef 56 C4
Morley Dr. Ilk 194 B2
Morley La. Bread 205 F4
Morley La. Lit Ea 205 F4
Morley La. Stanl 207 D3
Morley Rd. Derby 206 B1
Morley St. Derby 218 B3
Morley St. Glos 17 E4
Morleyfields Cl. Ripley 169 F1
Morlich Dr. Derby 231 F3
Morningside Cl. Derby 232 B2
Mornington Cl. Sand 223 E3
Mornington Cres. Derby 218 A3
Mornington Rd. N Wing 132 B4
Mornington Rise. Mat 143 E2
Morpeth Gdns. Derby 205 E1
Morrell Wood Dr. Belper 179 E3
Morris Ave. Chest 95 F3
Morris Dr. Chest 95 F3
Mortimer St. Derby 232 B4
Morton Ave. Cl Cr 131 D2
Morton La. Uns 58 B1
Morton Rd. Pils 147 E4
Morton Road. Shirl 146 B3
Morton St. Mans 135 F1
Morven Ave. Bols 99 D1
Morven Ave. Mans 136 A1
Morven St. Elmt 100 C4
Mosborough Moor. Mosb 59 D4
Mosbrough Rd. Shef 44 A4
Moscar Croft Rd. Bradf 31 F3
Mosedale Cl. Derby 232 C4
Moseley St. Ripley 169 E1
Moses La. Morley 206 C3
Mosley Dr. Utt 210 A1
Mosley Rd. Bux 85 D3
Moss Dr. Kill 60 B3
Moss Edge Rd. Holme 3 E4
Moss La. H Ward 175 F2
Moss La. Marple 15 F4
Moss La. Ripley 169 E2
Moss Rd. Ilk 208 C4
Moss Rd. Totley 55 D2
Moss Rise Pl. Eck 59 E2
Moss St. Derby 218 C2
Moss St. M in L 9 E3
Moss View Rd. C-Frith 47 E3
Moss View. Mosb 59 E3
Moss Way. Mosb 59 E4
Mossbank Cl. Glos 9 F2
Mossborough Hall Dr. Mosb 59 F3
Mossdale Ave. Mosb 59 E4
Mostyn Ave. Derby 218 B1
Mottistone Cl. Derby 233 E3
Mottram Old Rd. Marple 15 D4
Mottram Rd. M in L 9 D2
Mottram Rd. M in L 16 A4
Mouldridge La. Aldw 139 F1
Mouldridge La. Ball 139 F1
Moult Ave. Derby 220 C2
Moulton Cl. Belper 179 E3
Moulton Cl. Som 169 F4
Mound Rd. Chest 96 A1
Mount Carmel St. Derby 218 C2
Mount Cres. S Norm 160 A2
Mount Pleasant Dr. Belper 178 C3
Mount Pleasant Dr. Ripley 179 F4
Mount Pleasant La. Neth 265 D4
Mount Pleasant Rd. Grin 72 B4
Mount Pleasant Rd. Linton 261 F4
Mount Pleasant Rd. Rep 242 C1
Mount Pleasant Rd. Swad 256 A1
Mount Pleasant. A in W 108 C4
Mount Pleasant. C Don 247 D2
Mount Pleasant. Ilk 194 C2
Mount Pleasant. Ripley 169 E1
Mount Pleasant. Som 170 B3
Mount Rd. Bretby 249 D2
Mount Rd. Harts 257 D2
Mount Rd. Linton 261 E4
Mount Rd. Marple 15 D3
Mount St. Brea 235 F4
Mount St. Bu on T 248 A2
Mount St. Derby 219 D2
Mount St. Glos 17 E4
Mount St. Hean 181 F1
Mount St. Mans 136 A1
Mount St. Staple 223 F4
Mount The. Staple 223 E3
Mount View Ave. Shef 43 D2
Mount View Gdns. Shef 43 D2
Mount View Rd. Shef 43 D2
Mountbatten Ct. Ilk 194 C2
Mountcastle St. Chest 95 F4
Mountcastle Wlk. Chest 95 F4
Mountfield Ave. Sand 223 D2
Mountford Ave. Wirk 165 F4
Mountford Cl. Derby 206 A1
Mountford Croft. Totley 55 F3
Mouselow Cl. Glos 9 F2
Mowbray St. Derby 232 B4
Moy Ave. Derby 231 F1
Moyne Gdns. Derby 245 D4
Mudhurst La. Disley 32 C1
Muirfield Cl. Chest 96 A3
Muirfield Dr. Derby 217 F1
Muirfield Way. Mans 136 C3
Mulberry Cl. Win 115 D2
Mulberry Mews. Ripley 180 B3
Mulberry Rd. Eck 59 D1
Mulberry Way. Kill 60 A3
Mullion Pl. Derby 233 D3
Mumford Dr. Ashb 185 E4
Mundella Pl. Shef 43 D2
Mundy Cl. Derby 218 C3
Mundy St. Derby 218 C3
Mundy St. Hean 181 F1
Mundy St. Ilk 194 C1
Mundy's Dr. Hean 193 F4
Munro Cl. Kill 60 B3
Murray Rd. Derby 217 F2
Murray Rd. Kill 60 C4
Murray St. Derby 232 C4
Murrayfield Dr. Mosb 59 F3
Musard Pl. Stav 78 B1
Musard Way. Kill 60 B3
Muse La. Boyl 213 D1
Muse La. Ch Bro 213 D1
Mushroom La. Moira 262 B4
Muskham Ave. Ilk 194 C2
Muskham Ct. Mans 136 A1
Musters St. Shireb 120 A2
Muswell Rd. Derby 217 F3
Mycock La. Flagg 106 C3
Myers Cl. Derby 231 F2
Mynd The. Mans 136 C3
Myrtle Ave. Lo Ea 236 B3
Myrtle Ave. Staple 223 F3
Myrtle Cl. Shireb 119 E3
Myrtle Gr. Stav 78 A1
Myrtle Rd. Shef 43 D4
Myrtle Springs. Shef 43 F3
Mytham Bridge. Bam 40 A1

Nabb La. Dens 196 A2
Nailers Way. Belper 179 E3
Nailor La. Bons 142 B2
Nairn Ave. Derby 219 E4
Nairn Cl. Derby 231 E2
Nairn Dr. Shef 56 C4
Namur Cl. Derby 218 B2
Nan Gell's Hill. Wirk 155 D2
Napier Cl. Derby 217 F2
Napier St. Derby 218 B3
Narlow La. Thorpe 161 F1
Narrow La. Dens 196 B3
Narrow La. Tick 250 C2
Narrowleys La. Ash 129 F2
Naseby Cl. Derby 217 E2
Naseby Dr. Lo Ea 236 C2
Naseby Rd. Belper 179 E2
Nathaniel Rd. Lo Ea 236 C3
Navan Rd. Shef 44 A4
Neal Ct. La Mi 182 A2
Neale Bank. Chest 96 B4
Neale St. Lo Ea 236 C4
Near Meadow. Lo Ea 236 C3
Nearwell Cl. C-Frith 46 C3
Nearwood Dr. Derby 205 F2
Needham St. Codnor 181 D4
Needwood Ave. Staple 209 E1
Needwood Ct. Tut 239 E3
Neighwood Cl. Bees 223 F1
Neilson St. Derby 232 C4
Nelper Cres. Ilk 209 D3
Nelson Cl. Derby 217 F2
Nelson Pl. Smisby 257 F2
Nelson St. Bu on T 248 B2
Nelson St. Chest 96 A3
Nelson St. Derby 219 E2
Nelson St. Ilk 194 C2
Nelson St. Lo Ea 236 B3
Nelson St. Swad 256 A3
Nene Cl. Bu on T 240 B1
Nesbit St. Scarc 118 A4
Nesfield Cl. Chest 95 E4
Nesfield Cl. Derby 233 E4
Nesfield Ct. Ilk 194 C1
Nesfield Rd. Ilk 194 C1
Ness Wlk. Derby 204 C2
Nether Ave. Kill 60 B3
Nether Blindlow La. Chel 106 A3
Nether Cl. Duff 190 C3
Nether Cl. Greas 182 C2
Nether Cl. Som 169 F4
Nether Cl. Win 115 D1
Nether Croft Cl. Chest 96 C4
Nether Croft Rd. Chest 96 C4
Nether Gdns. Wirk 165 F4
Nether La. Brass 163 F4
Nether La. Haz 190 A4
Nether La. Holbr 191 E3
Nether La. K Ire 176 A4
Nether Springs Rd. Bols 98 C2
Nether Thorpe Rd. Th Sa 63 D3
Netherclose St. Derby 219 D1
Nethercroft La. Cl Cr 131 F2
Netherdene Rd. Dron 57 D1
Netherfield Cl. Stav 79 D1
Netherfield La. C Don 247 F4
Netherfield Rd. C-Frith 47 E3
Netherfield Rd. Chest 114 A4
Netherfield Rd. Lo Ea 236 B2
Netherfield Rd. Sand 223 D2
Netherfields Cres. Dron 76 A4
Nethergreen Ave. Kill 60 B4
Nethergreen Gdns. Kill 60 B4
Netherleigh Ct. Chest 95 D2
Netherleigh Rd. Chest 95 D2
Nethermoor Ave. Kill 60 B4
Nethermoor Cl. Kill 60 B4
Nethermoor Dr. Kill 60 B4
Nethermoor La. Kill 60 B4
Nethermoor Rd. Tupton 115 D1
Nethermoor Rd. Tupton 131 E4

ethermoor Rd. Win 115 D1
etherseal Rd. C Camp 263 F1
etherseal Rd. Chil 264 C2
etherside. Bradw 51 D4
etherthorpe Cl. Stav 78 C1
etherthorpe La. Kill 60 B4
etherthorpe Rd. Stav 78 C1
etherthorpe. Stav 79 D1
etherwood Ct. Derby 204 B2
ettlefold Cres. Mel 245 D1
ettleton La. Bux 85 E2
eville Cl. Rolle 240 A2
evinson Ave. Derby 231 E4
evinson Dr. Derby 231 E4
evis Cl. Chest 95 E2
evis Cl. Derby 231 E1
ew Rd. Iron 170 C2
ew Barlborough Cl. Clowne 80 B3
ew Bath Rd. Mat Ba 155 D4
ew Beetwell St. Chest 96 A1
ew Breck Rd. Belper 179 D2
ew Church St. Bradw 51 D4
ew Cl. Eyam 71 E3
ew Cotts. Cuck 101 F2
ew Derby Rd. East 182 B1
ew Eaton Rd. Staple 223 F3
ew England Way. Mans 135 E2
ew Fall St. S in A 148 C2
ew Hall Rd. Chest 95 E1
ew High St. Bux 85 E4
ew Horwich Rd. W Br 45 F4
ew Inn La. Lit Ea 205 E4
ew La. Bradw 50 C3
ew La. Newt 148 B1
ew Lawn Rd. Ilk 208 C4
ew Linden St. Shireb 120 A2
ew Lumford. Bake 109 E4
ew Market St. Bux 85 D3
ew Mill La. Mans 136 C2
ew Mills Rd. Cha 16 A2
ew Mills Rd. Hay 25 D2
ew Mount Cl. Derby 231 E3
ew Queen St. Chest 96 A2
ew Rd (Baslow Rd).
A in W 108 C4
ew Rd. B in F 237 F3
ew Rd. Bam 40 A3
ew Rd. Barl 80 A4
ew Rd. Belper 178 C2
ew Rd. Belper 179 E4
ew Rd. Boyl 213 D2
ew Rd. Bradw 51 D2
ew Rd. C Elms 260 B2
ew Rd. Chin 34 A1
ew Rd. Crich 168 A4
ew Rd. Derby 205 D1
ew Rd. Eyam 71 F3
ew Rd. Grin 72 A3
ew Rd. Hilton 228 C1
ew Rd. Hol 75 D3
ew Rd. Holy 113 E4
ew Rd. Mid 154 A3
ew Rd. Ripley 168 A2
ew Rd. Ripley 179 E4
ew Rd. Som 170 B1
ew Rd. Staple 209 E1
ew Rd. Swad 255 F3
ew Rd. Tint 9 F4
ew Rd. Uns 58 A1
ew Rd. Utt 210 A1
ew Rd. W Br 45 F3
ew Rd. W Und 188 B1
ew Rd. Win 114 C2
ew Rd. Wirk 155 D2
ew Rd. Wood 256 C1
ew Rd. Youl 125 E3
ew Row. Sels 171 D3
ew Sq. Chest 96 A2
ew St Bus Link. Mosb 60 A4
ew St. Alf 158 C2
ew St. Alf 159 D2
ew St. Bake 109 E3
ew St. Bols 99 D2
ew St. Bux 67 D3
ew St. Chest 96 A1
ew St. Derby 219 D2
ew St. Donis 262 C1
ew St. Dray 235 D4
ew St. Gra 115 F2
ew St. Lit Ea 205 E4
ew St. Lo Ea 236 C4
ew St. M in L 16 A4
ew St. Mat 143 E3
ew St. Morton 147 D3
ew St. Mosb 60 A4
ew St. N Mills 33 E4
ew St. N Wing 131 F3
ew St. Newt 148 A2
ew St. Ock 221 E2
ew St. Pils 132 B1
ew St. Ripley 169 F1
ew St. Rosl 260 B3
ew St. S in A 148 C2
ew St. S Norm 160 A3
ew St. S Norm 160 B4
ew St. Shirl 146 B1
ew St. Som 169 F4
ew St. Som 170 B4
New St. Stanl 207 E3
New St. Swad 256 A1
New St. Whit 81 F3
New Station Rd. Bols 99 D1
New Terr. Plea 134 C3
New Terr. Sand 223 D3
New Tythe St. Lo Ea 236 C4
New Wye St. Bux 85 E4
New Zealand La. Duff 190 C1
New Zealand Sq. Derby 218 B3
Newark Rd. Derby 205 E1
Newark. Mosb 59 F4
Newbarn Cl. Shireb 119 E1
Newbery Ave. Lo Ea 236 C3
Newbold Ave. Chest 95 F3
Newbold Ave. Ock 221 E1
Newbold Back La. Chest 95 E3
Newbold Cl. Derby 232 C1
Newbold Ct. Chest 95 E4
Newbold Dr. C Don 247 D3
Newbold Rd. Chest 95 F3
Newbold Rd. Chest 95 E3
Newborough Rd. Derby 233 E3
Newbound La. S in A 134 B1
Newboundmill La. Plea 135 D3
Newbridge Cl. We Ha 207 E4
Newbridge Cres. Derby 232 C2
Newbridge Ct. Chest 77 D1
Newbridge Dr. Chest 96 B4
Newbridge La. Chest 77 D1
Newbridge Rd. Ripley 168 A1
Newbridge St. Chest 77 D1
Newburgh Terr. Calver 72 B1
Newbury Dr. Bu on T 240 B1
Newbury St. Derby 232 C4
Newby Rd. Chest 95 E4
Newcastle St. Mans 136 A2
Newcastle St. S in A 148 C2
Newdigate St. Derby 232 A4
Newdigate St. Ilk 209 D3
Newdigate St. Kim 195 F3
Newdigate St. We Ha 207 E4
Newfield Cres. Totley 55 E4
Newfield Croft. Totley 55 E4
Newfield Farm Cl. Shef 43 F3
Newfield Green Rd. Shef 43 E3
Newfield La. Totley 55 E4
Newfield Rd. Bu on T 248 A2
Newgates La. S in A 134 C1
Newhall Rd. Swad 256 B3
Newham Ave. Ripley 169 E1
Newham Cl. Hean 182 A1
Newhaven Ave. Mans 136 A2
Newhaven Cl. Chest 95 D1
Newhaven Rd. Derby 220 A3
Newland Dale. Chest 96 A2
Newland Gdns. Chest 95 F3
Newland St. Derby 218 C3
Newlands Ave. Chest 95 E2
Newlands Ave. Shef 44 A3
Newlands Cl. Swad 256 A1
Newlands Cres. Newt 148 A2
Newlands Dr. Glos 9 F2
Newlands Dr. Hean 181 F2
Newlands Dr. Shef 44 A3
Newlands Dr. Som 170 B3
Newlands Gr. Shef 44 A3
Newlands Rd. Shef 44 A3
Newlands Rd. Som 170 B2
Newlyn Dr. Derby 231 F4
Newlyn Pl. Shef 43 D2
Newman Dr. Bran 254 A4
Newmanleys Rd S. East 194 C4
Newmanleys Rd. East 194 C4
Newmarket Ct. Derby 219 F1
Newmarket Dr. Derby 232 C4
Newmarket La. Cl Gr 130 C2
Newmarket Way. Bees 223 F1
Newport Cres. Mans 135 F1
Newport Ct. Derby 233 E3
Newquay Pl. Derby 233 E3
Newshaw La. Glos 9 F2
Newstead Ave. Derby 219 F3
Newstead Ave. Shef 44 C2
Newstead Cl. Shef 44 C2
Newstead Cl. Shef 56 C4
Newstead Dr. Shef 44 C1
Newstead Gr. Shef 44 C2
Newstead Pl. Shef 44 C1
Newstead Rd S. Ilk 194 B2
Newstead Rd. Lo Ea 223 E2
Newstead Rd. Shef 44 C1
Newstead Rise. Shef 44 C1
Newstead Terr. Bux 85 D3
Newstead Way. Shef 44 C1
Newton Cl. N Sol 248 C4
Newton Dr. Staple 223 F3
Newton La. N Sol 248 C4
Newton Leys. Bu on T 248 B2
Newton Rd. Bu on T 248 A2
Newton Rd. N Sol 248 B4
Newton Rd. Tibs 147 F2
Newton's La. Awsw 195 D2
Newton's Wlk. Derby 218 C4
Newtondale Ave. Mans 136 C1
Newtonwood La. Tibs 148 A3
Nicholas Cl. Derby 220 C3
Nicholas St. Chest 115 E4
Nicholson Ct. Tide 69 E2
Nicholson Pl. Shef 43 D3
Nicholson Rd. Shef 43 D3
Nicholson's Row. Shireb 119 F2
Nicola Gdns. Derby 231 E2
Nicolas Cl. Bux 85 F4
Nidderdale Ct. Derby 233 E3
Nightingale Ave. Plea 135 D2
Nightingale Cl. Cl Cr 131 F1
Nightingale Cl. Hollow 155 F3
Nightingale Cl. Ripley 169 E1
Nightingale Dr. Mans 135 F1
Nightingale Dr. Wood 256 C2
Nightingale Rd. Derby 232 B4
Ninelands Rd. Hath 53 D4
No Man's Heath Rd. Chil 264 C2
No Man's La. Risley 222 B4
No Man's La. Som 222 B4
Nobel Cl. Elmt 81 F1
Noble St. Derby 219 E2
Nodder Rd. Shef 44 B4
Nodin Hill La. Ripley 168 A2
Noel St. Derby 218 B3
Nook End Rd. Hean 181 E1
Nook The. Ba on T 244 A3
Nook The. Hean 181 E2
Nook The. Holbr 191 E4
Nook The. Shireb 119 E2
Nook The. St Mid 72 A2
Nooning La. Dray 234 C4
Norbriggs Rd. Stav 79 E1
Norburn Dr. Kill 60 B3
Norbury Cl. Chest 95 D3
Norbury Cl. Derby 204 C1
Norbury Cl. Shef 56 C4
Norbury Cres. Derby 231 E3
Norbury Ct. Derby 204 B1
Norbury Hollow. Rost 183 E1
Norbury Way. Belper 179 E3
Norfolk Ave. Gra 115 F1
Norfolk Cl. Chest 114 A4
Norfolk Ct. Mans 136 C3
Norfolk Gdns. Derby 218 C4
Norfolk Rd. Bu on T 254 B4
Norfolk Rd. Lo Ea 223 F1
Norfolk Sq. Glos 10 B1
Norfolk St. Derby 219 D1
Norfolk St. Glos 10 B1
Norfolk Wlk. Sand 223 D3
Norgreave Way. Mosb 59 F4
Norman Ave. Derby 231 F4
Norman Cres. Ilk 194 C2
Norman Keep. Tut 239 E3
Norman Rd. Ripley 169 E1
Norman Rd. Som 170 C4
Norman Rd. Tut 239 E3
Norman St. Ilk 194 C2
Norman St. Kim 195 F4
Normanton Ave. Alf 159 E2
Normanton Gr. Shef 44 C3
Normanton Hill. Shef 44 B3
Normanton La. Derby 231 D4
Normanton Rd. Derby 219 D2
Normanton Spring Ct. Shef 44 C3
Normanton Spring Rd. Shef 44 C3
North Ave. Ashb 173 D1
North Ave. Derby 205 D2
North Ave. Derby 217 F1
North Ave. Sand 223 D3
North Brook Rd. Glos 9 F2
North Church St. Bake 109 E3
North Cl. Derby 217 F2
North Cl. S Norm 159 F3
North Cl. Tint 9 F4
North Cl. Uns 76 C3
North Cl. Will 242 A3
North Cres. Kill 60 C4
North Cres. Stav 98 A3
North End. Wirk 154 C1
North Gr. Stav 98 A3
North La. Belper 178 B1
North La. Belper 190 C4
North Leys. Ashb 173 D1
North Moor View. Chest 96 C4
North Par. Derby 219 D3
North Parade. Mat Ba 143 D1
North Rd. Bux 66 B1
North Rd. Calow 96 C2
North Rd. Clowne 80 C2
North Rd. Glos 10 B2
North Rd. Hay 25 E2
North Rd. Lo Ea 236 B3
North Row. Derby 205 D1
North Side. Tupton 115 E1
North St. Al Hv 117 E1
North St. Alf 159 D2
North St. Bu on T 248 A2
North St. Cl Cr 131 D3
North St. Derby 218 B1
North St. Derby 218 C4
North St. Ilk 194 C1
North St. La Mi 182 A2
North St. Mar War 120 B2
North St. Mat Ba 155 D3
North St. Mel 252 A4
North St. N Wing 131 F3
North St. Newt 147 F1
North St. Pinx 160 B2
North St. S Norm 159 F3
North St. Scarc 101 D1
North St. Som 170 B3
North St. Swad 256 A3
North Terr. Chest 115 D4
North View St. Bols 98 C2
North View. Crich 168 A4
North Wingfield Rd. Gra 115 F2
North La. Brai 187 F2
Northacre Rd. Derby 206 A1
Northam Dr. Ripley 169 E2
Northcliffe Rd. Ashb 173 D1
Northcote Ave. Shef 43 D3
Northcote Rd. Shef 43 D3
Northcote St. Lo Ea 236 C4
Northedge La. Ash 130 A4
Northern Ave. Shef 43 F4
Northern Comm. Dron 56 A1
Northern Dr. Staple 209 E2
Northern Rd. Hean 181 E1
Northfield Ave. Ilk 194 C1
Northfield Ave. Lo Ea 236 A2
Northfield Ave. Mans 136 A2
Northfield Ave. Roc 197 D2
Northfield Cl. Utt 210 A1
Northfield Cres. Bees 223 F2
Northfield La. Mans 135 F2
Northfield La. Mans 136 A3
Northfield La. Scarc 118 B3
Northfield Park. Mans 136 A3
Northfield Rd. Bees 223 F2
Northfield. Derby 231 E2
Northfield. Kilb 179 F1
Northfields. Clowne 80 C2
Northfields. Lo Ea 236 A2
Northgate St. Ilk 194 C1
Northlands. Hart 61 F4
Northmoor Cl. Chest 96 C4
Northumberland Rd.
Bu on T 254 B4
Northumberland St. Derby 218 C1
Northwood Ave. Da Da 127 E2
Northwood Ave. Derby 219 F4
Northwood La. Ella 183 E2
Northwood La. North 127 D3
Northwood St. Staple 223 E4
Norton Ave. Bols 98 C3
Norton Ave. Chest 114 A4
Norton Ave. Shef 43 E1
Norton Ave. Shef 43 F1
Norton Church Rd. Shef 43 D1
Norton Green Cl. Shef 43 E1
Norton La. Shef 57 D4
Norton Lawns. Shef 43 E1
Norton Lees Cl. Shef 43 D2
Norton Lees Cres. Shef 43 D2
Norton Lees La. Shef 43 D2
Norton Lees Rd. Shef 43 D2
Norton Lees Sq. Shef 43 D2
Norton Park Ave. Shef 57 D4
Norton Park Cres. Shef 57 D4
Norton Park Dr. Shef 57 D4
Norton Park Rd. Shef 57 D4
Norton Park View. Shef 57 D4
Norton Rd. Shef 44 A2
Norwell Ct. Mans 136 A1
Norwich Cl. Mans 136 B3
Norwich St. Derby 219 F4
Norwood Ave. Chest 115 F3
Norwood Cl. Chest 115 F3
Norwood Cl. Derby 218 A3
Norwood Cres. Kill 60 C4
Norwood Pl. Kill 60 C4
Nottingham Cl. Win 115 D2
Nottingham Dr. Win 115 D2
Nottingham La. Iron 170 C3
Nottingham La. Som 170 C3
Nottingham Rd. Alf 159 D1
Nottingham Rd. Ash-Z 258 C1
Nottingham Rd. Belper 179 D2
Nottingham Rd. Br Hill 252 B1
Nottingham Rd. Codnor 181 E4
Nottingham Rd. Derby 219 D3
Nottingham Rd. Derby 219 F3
Nottingham Rd. Derby 220 C2
Nottingham Rd. Drayc 221 F1
Nottingham Rd. East 182 C1
Nottingham Rd. Greas 195 E4
Nottingham Rd. Ilk 209 D3
Nottingham Rd. Lo Ea 236 C4
Nottingham Rd. Ock 221 E1
Nottingham Rd. Ripley 169 F1
Nottingham Rd. Sels 171 F3
Nottingham Rd. Som 159 D1
Nottingham Rd. Staple 209 F3
Nottingham Rd. Staple 223 F4
Nottingham Rd. Tans 144 A2
Nottingham Rd. Trow 209 F3
Nowill Ct. Shef 43 D3
Nowill Pl. Shef 43 D3
Nun's St. Derby 218 C3
Nunbrook Gr. Bux 85 E4
Nunn Brook Rd. S in A 148 C1
Nunn Brook Rise. S in A 148 C1
Nunn Cl. S in A 148 C1
Nunsfield Dr. Derby 233 D4
Nunsfield Rd. Bux 66 B1
Nursery Ave. Sand 222 C3
Nursery Ave. We Ha 207 F4
Nursery Cl. Glos 17 E4
Nursery Cl. Ock 221 D1
Nursery Cl. Swad 256 A3
Nursery Croft. Wirk 165 F3
Nursery Dr. Bux 66 B1
Nursery Gdns. S Norm 160 B2
Nursery Hollow. Ilk 208 C3
Nursery La. Bux 84 C3
Nutbrook Cres. Ilk 208 B2
Nuthall Circ. Ilk 208 B2
Nuttall Cl. Alf 158 C2
Nuttall St. Alf 158 C2
Nuttall Terr. Al Hv 117 E1
Nutwood Cl. Derby 205 D2

Oadby Rise. Derby 231 F3
Oak Ave. Ald 182 A3
Oak Ave. Disley 33 D3
Oak Ave. Ripley 180 B4
Oak Ave. Sand 223 D4
Oak Ave. Shireb 119 E2
Oak Bank Ave. Chest 77 D1
Oak Bank. Disley 33 D3
Oak Cl. C-Frith 47 E3
Oak Cl. Derby 204 C2
Oak Cl. Duff 190 C1
Oak Cl. Kill 60 B3
Oak Cl. Linton 261 F4
Oak Cl. M in L 9 D2
Oak Cl. Ock 221 E3
Oak Cl. Pinx 160 B2
Oak Cres. Ashb 185 E4
Oak Cres. Derby 231 E4
Oak Cres. Win 114 C2
Oak Dr. Alf 159 D2
Oak Dr. Derby 217 F1
Oak Dr. Derby 233 D3
Oak Dr. East 182 C1
Oak Dr. Hilton 228 B1
Oak Dr. Dove 211 D1
Oak La. Sud 212 B2
Oak Lodge Dr. Kim 195 F4
Oak Rd. Dens 196 B3
Oak Rd. Elv 233 F2
Oak Rd. Gra 115 F2
Oak Rd. Mat 143 E3
Oak Rd. Shef 44 A1
Oak St. Derby 219 D1
Oak St. Glos 10 B1
Oak St. Mosb 59 E4
Oak St. Shef 43 D4
Oak St. Stav 78 A1
Oak St. Swad 256 A1
Oak Tree Ave. Glap 134 A4
Oak Tree Cres. Mans 136 A2
Oak Tree Ct. Ock 221 E1
Oak Tree Gdns. Tans 144 A2
Oak Tree Rd. Clowne 80 C1
Oakamoor Cl. Chest 95 D3
Oakbank Ct. Totley 55 F3
Oakdale Cl. Cl Cr 131 F1
Oakdale Rd. S Norm 160 A2
Oakdell. Dron 57 E2
Oakerthorpe Rd. Wirk 155 D1
Oakes Park View. Shef 43 E1
Oakes's Row. Iron 170 C3
Oakfield Ave. Chest 95 D1
Oakfield Dr. Sand 223 D2
Oakfield Rd. Glos 9 F2
Oakfield Rd. Staple 223 E4
Oakfields. Han 238 A2
Oakham Cl. Derby 205 E1
Oakham Way. Ilk 194 C2
Oakhill Rd. Dron 57 E2
Oakhurst Cl. Belper 178 B3
Oakland Ave. Lo Ea 236 B3
Oakland Ave. S in A 148 C1
Oakland Cres. Som 170 B3
Oakland St. Alf 159 D2
Oakland Terr. Lo Ea 236 B3
Oaklands Ave. Derby 231 E3
Oaklands Ave. Hean 182 A1
Oaklands Ave. Marple 23 E4
Oaklands Cl. Denby 180 B1
Oaklands Rd. Etwall 229 E2
Oaklands Rd. Swad 256 A3
Oaklands The. S Norm 160 A2
Oaklands Way. Mel 252 A4
Oaklea Way. Cl Cr 131 D3
Oaklea. Bux 85 E3
Oakleigh Ave. Derby 219 F3
Oakleigh Ave. Swad 255 F3
Oakley Ave. Chest 95 F2
Oakley's Rd W. Lo Ea 236 B3
Oakley's Rd. Lo Ea 236 C4
Oakover Dr. Derby 204 B1
Oakridge Cl. Mans 136 C1
Oakridge. Derby 220 A4
Oaks Ave. Elmt 100 B4
Oaks Ave. Hay 25 E1
Oaks Farm La. Calow 97 D1
Oaks La. Ash 129 E3
Oaks La. O Bram 94 A4
Oaks Rd. Will 242 A3
Oaksedge La. Tans 144 A3
Oakstedge La. Ash 145 D4
Oaktree Ave. Derby 232 A4

Oaktree Cl. Som 170 A4
Oaktree Rd. Newt 148 B1
Oakwell Cres. Ilk 208 C4
Oakwell Dr. Ilk 208 C4
Oakwood Cl. Derby 231 E1
Oakwood District Centre. Derby 206 A1
Oakwood Dr. Derby 206 A1
Oakwood Rd. Disley 32 B3
Oakworth Cl. Mosb 59 F3
Oakworth Dr. Mosb 59 E3
Oakworth Gr. Mosb 59 E3
Oakworth View. Mosb 59 E3
Oarr La. Dron 56 B1
Oat Hill. Wirk 165 F4
Oats Orch. Mosb 59 E3
Occupation Cl. Barl 80 A3
Occupation La. N Wing 131 F4
Occupation La. Shef 44 C2
Occupation La. Wood 256 C1
Occupation Rd. Chest 95 F4
Occupation Rd. Moira 262 B4
Occupation Rd. Plea 134 C4
Ochard St. Ilk 208 C4
Ochbrook Ct. Ilk 194 C2
Oddfellows Cotts. Bux 85 D4
Oddfellows Rd. Hath 53 D4
Oddfellows Terr. Hath 53 D4
Oddford La. Da Da 127 E1
Odom Ct. Shef 43 D3
Offcote Cres. Ashb 173 E2
Offerton Ave. Derby 231 F4
Offridge Cl. Clowne 80 C1
Ogden St. M in L 16 A4
Ogston La. Brack 146 A2
Ogston La. Shirl 146 A2
Ogston New Rd. Brack 145 F2
Okeover Ave. Ashb 173 E1
Oker Ave. Da Da 127 D2
Oker Dr. Da Da 127 D2
Oker La. Wens 142 B3
Oker Rd. Wens 142 A4
Oker Terr. Wens 142 A4
Old Hall Ave. Derby 218 A1
Old La. H Ward 176 C2
Old Bakery Cl. Chest 77 D1
Old Bank. May 184 B4
Old Barn Cl. Lit Ea 205 E4
Old Chester Rd. Derby 219 D4
Old Church La. Quar 204 B3
Old Coach Rd. Tans 143 F2
Old Coalpit La. Chel 86 C1
Old Colliery La. N Wing 132 C4
Old Coppice Side. Hean 193 F4
Old Dam La. Pk F 49 E2
Old Derby Rd. Ashb 185 E4
Old Derby Rd. East 182 B2
Old End. S Field 265 F1
Old Gate Ave. We on T 245 F3
Old Gate. Holme 2 C4
Old Hackney La. Da Da 142 C4
Old Hall Ave. Derby 233 D4
Old Hall Ave. Duff 190 C2
Old Hall Ave. W Br 45 F2
Old Hall Cl. Glos 10 B1
Old Hall Dr. Will 242 A3
Old Hall Gdns. St Mid 72 A2
Old Hall Gdns. Swad 256 A1
Old Hall La. Ch Bro 227 D4
Old Hall La. M in L 9 D3
Old Hall La. Marple 23 E3
Old Hall Rd. Chest 95 E2
Old Hall Rd. Derby 218 B1
Old Hall Sq. Glos 10 A3
Old Hartshay Hill. Ripley 169 E1
Old Hay Gdns. Totley 55 E3
Old Hay La. Totley 55 E3
Old Highcliff La. Turn 177 D2
Old Hill. Ashb 173 E1
Old Hill. Bols 99 D1
Old La. Derby 205 D1
Old La. Mosb 60 A4
Old La. Shot 177 D3
Old La. Wirk 154 C1
Old Lime Ct. Mat 143 E3
Old Longhill Rd. W Br 65 D2
Old Manor Rd. Mans 136 B2
Old Mansfield Rd. Derby 205 E1
Old Market Pl. S Norm 160 A3
Old Mill Cl. Duff 190 C2
Old Mill Cl. Pils 132 B1
Old Mill Dr. Chest 95 D4
Old Mill La. Mans 136 C1
Old Park Ave. Shef 56 B4
Old Park Rd. Shef 56 B4
Old Peverel Rd. Stav 98 A2
Old Pit La. Smal 193 D3
Old Pond The. Hean 194 A4
Old Rd. Bran 253 F4
Old Rd. Bux 65 E3
Old Rd. Chest 95 E2
Old Rd. Da Da 127 E1
Old Rd. M in L 9 D3
Old Rd. O Bram 95 E2
Old Rd. Ripley 179 F4
Old Rd. Tint 10 A4
Old Rd. W Br 33 E2
Old Rd. W Br 45 F2
Old Rd. W Br 45 F3
Old Rd. W Br 65 E3
Old School Cl. Al Hv 117 E1
Old School La. Plea 135 D3
Old St. M in L 16 A4
Old Storth La. S Norm 160 A2
Old Terr. Plea 134 C2
Old Vicarage Cl. Derby 218 B1
Old Vicarage La. Quar 204 B3
Old Whittington La. Uns 76 C3
Oldbury Cl. Derby 206 A1
Olde Derwent Ave. Mat 143 D2
Oldfield Dr. Swad 256 B3
Oldfield La. Hilton 241 D4
Oldfield La. Hog 164 A1
Oldfield La. K Ire 164 C1
Oldfield La. Snel 184 A2
Oldfield La. Wens 142 A4
Oldhay Cl. Totley 55 E3
Oldicote La. Bretby 248 C2
Oldknow Rd. Marple 23 D3
Oldridge Cl. Chest 95 D3
Oldwell Cl. Totley 55 E2
Olive Ave. Lo Ea 223 F1
Olive Ave. Shireb 119 E3
Olive Cres. Shef 44 A1
Olive Gr. Derby 219 F3
Olive Grove Rd. Shef 43 D4
Olive Rd. Mosb 59 E4
Olive St. Derby 218 C2
Olive Terr. M in L 16 A4
Oliver Cl. Hean 182 A1
Oliver Rd. Ilk 208 B3
Olivet Rd. Shef 43 D2
Olivier St. Derby 219 D1
Ollersett Ave. N Mills 33 E4
Ollersett La. N Mills 24 C1
Olton Rd. Derby 217 E2
Onslow Rd. Derby 217 F2
Onward Cotts. Bux 85 E4
Opal Cl. Derby 206 A1
Openacre. Iron 170 C2
Openwood Rd. Denby 179 F2
Openwoodgate. Belper 179 E2
Orange Cl. Shireb 119 F3
Orange St. Alf 159 D2
Orchard Ave. C Don 247 D2
Orchard Ave. W Br 45 E4
Orchard Bsns Park. Sand 223 E3
Orchard Bsns Pk. Ilk 194 B1
Orchard Cl. Barl 80 A4
Orchard Cl. Belper 191 D4
Orchard Cl. Bols 99 D1
Orchard Cl. Brea 235 F4
Orchard Cl. Clowne 80 C2
Orchard Cl. Derby 231 E4
Orchard Cl. Mel 252 A4
Orchard Cl. Ock 221 E2
Orchard Cl. Ripley 181 D4
Orchard Cl. Shireb 119 F3
Orchard Cl. Utt 210 A1
Orchard Cl. Wa on T 253 E1
Orchard Cl. We Ha 207 F4
Orchard Cl. Will 242 A3
Orchard Cres. Glap 134 A4
Orchard Cres. Som 169 E4
Orchard Ct. Derby 220 C3
Orchard Ct. La Mi 182 A2
Orchard Dr. Elmt 81 F1
Orchard La. Da Da 142 C4
Orchard La. Wya 185 E1
Orchard Pl. Kill 60 B3
Orchard Rd. Marple 15 D1
Orchard Rd. Mat Ba 143 D1
Orchard Rd. Som 170 B3
Orchard Rd. W Br 45 E4
Orchard Rise. Hean 181 F1
Orchard Sq. Dron 56 B1
Orchard St. Derby 217 E1
Orchard St. Derby 218 C3
Orchard St. Kim 195 F3
Orchard St. La Mi 182 A2
Orchard St. Lo Ea 236 C4
Orchard St. Mans 136 A1
Orchard St. Staple 223 E4
Orchard St. Swad 255 F3
Orchard The. Belper 179 D2
Orchard The. Codnor 170 A1
Orchard The. H Wood 192 B3
Orchard The. S-by-D 222 C4
Orchard The. Utt 210 A2
Orchard The. Youl 125 E3
Orchard View Rd. Chest 95 E2
Orchard View. Bols 117 F4
Orchard View. Mans 136 A2
Orchard Way. Derby 232 C1
Orchard Way. Sand 223 D2
Orchards The. Derby 204 B2
Orchards The. Sels 171 D2
Orchards Way. Chest 95 E1
Orchid Cl. Bu on T 255 D4
Orchid Cl. Calow 97 D2
Ordish Ave. Derby 219 F3
Ordley La. Stan 183 F4
Oregon Way. Derby 220 B3
Orford Ave. Disley 32 B3
Organ Way. M in L 9 E3
Oriel Ct. Derby 219 D2
Orly Ave. C Don 247 D1
Ormesby Cl. Shef 56 C4
Ormond Cl. Chest 114 A4
Ormond Cl. Shef 57 D3
Ormond Dr. Shef 57 D3
Ormond Rd. Shef 57 D4
Ormond Way. Shef 57 D4
Ormonde St. Ald 182 A2
Ormonde Terr. Ald 182 A2
Ormsby Rd. Chest 95 F4
Ormskirk Rise. Derby 220 C2
Orpean Way. Bees 223 F1
Orpen Dr. Shef 43 F1
Orpen Way. Shef 43 F1
Orwins Cl. Chest 95 E4
Osborne Cl. Sand 223 D2
Osborne Pl. Glos 10 A3
Osborne Rd. Derby 219 E2
Osborne St. Bu on T 248 A2
Osmaston Cl. Lo Ea 235 F3
Osmaston Rd. Derby 219 D1
Osmaston St. Sand 223 E3
Osmond Rd. Eck 59 E2
Osprey Cl. Bu on T 248 B2
Osprey Cl. Derby 231 F1
Osterly Green. Derby 218 A3
Ostrich La. Kni 163 D1
Oswestry Cl. Derby 206 A2
Otter St. Derby 219 D4
Otterburn Dr. Derby 204 B1
Oulton Cl. Derby 232 B2
Oundle Dr. Ilk 209 D4
Oundle Dr. Mans 135 E1
Ousley La. Ella 183 E3
Out La. Al Hu 132 C3
Outfield Rd. Bu on T 254 C4
Outgang La. Mans 136 B2
Outgang La. Plea 135 D3
Outlands Rd. Bradw 50 C3
Outram Ct. Ripley 169 F1
Outram Rd. Chest 95 F3
Outram St. Ripley 169 F1
Outram Way. Derby 231 F1
Outseats Dr. Alf 159 D2
Oval Ct. Derby 231 E4
Oven Hill Rd. Chin 34 A3
Oven Hill Rd. N Mills 34 A3
Over La. Baslow 91 F3
Over La. Belper 179 F3
Over La. Haz 178 A1
Overcroft Rise. Totley 55 E2
Overdale Ave. Bux 85 E4
Overdale Cl. Lo Ea 236 A3
Overdale Gdns. Totley 55 E3
Overdale Rd. Derby 218 C1
Overdale Rd. Disley 32 C3
Overdale Rise. Totley 55 E3
Overdale. Mat 143 E3
Overend Cl. Shef 43 E2
Overend Dr. Shef 43 E2
Overend Rd. Shef 43 E2
Overend Way. Shef 43 E2
Overlees. Barlow 75 E2
Oversetts Ct. Swad 255 F3
Oversetts Rd. Swad 255 F3
Overstone Cl. Belper 179 E2
Overton Cl. Stav 78 C2
Owen Ave. Lo Ea 237 D3
Ower Bar Rd. Totley 54 A2
Owers Ave. Hean 193 F4
Owlcotes View. Bols 118 A4
Owler Car La. Eck 57 F3
Owlers La. Derby 218 B1
Owlston Cl. East 182 C2
Owlswick Cl. Derby 231 D4
Owlthorpe Ave. Mosb 59 D4
Owlthorpe Cl. Mosb 59 D4
Owlthorpe Dr. Mosb 59 D4
Owlthorpe La. Mosb 59 D4
Owlthorpe Rise. Mosb 59 D4
Ox Close Ave. Shef 56 A3
Oxbury Rd. Greas 195 F4
Oxclose Dr. Shef 56 C4
Oxclose La. A le Da 150 B1
Oxclose La. Mans 135 E2
Oxclose La. Mans 136 A2
Oxclose La. Shef 56 C4
Oxcroft Estate. Bols 99 E4
Oxcroft La. Bols 99 D3
Oxcroft La. Elmt 99 F4
Oxenhope Cl. Derby 230 C4
Oxford Cl. Chest 96 C4
Oxford St. Al Hv 117 F1
Oxford St. Derby 219 D2
Oxford St. Derby 220 C3
Oxford St. East 182 C1
Oxford St. Ilk 208 C4
Oxford St. Lo Ea 236 B4
Oxford St. Mans 136 B1
Oxford St. Newt 147 F1
Oxford St. Ripley 169 E1
Oxford St. Swad 256 A1
Oxley Rd. Bu on T 248 A2
Oxmead. May 184 B4
Oxpasture La. Elmt 100 A3
Oxwich Ct. Derby 206 A1
Ozier Holt. Lo Ea 236 B3
Pack Horse Rd. Mel 252 A4
Packer's Row. Chest 96 A2
Packman La. Hart 62 B3
Paddock Cl. C Don 246 C2
Paddock Cl. Win 114 C2
Paddock Cres. Shef 43 F3
Paddock Croft. Derby 205 F1
Paddock La. W Br 45 F3
Paddock The. Bols 99 D1
Paddock The. Bu on T 248 A2
Paddock The. Bux 84 C4
Paddock The. Glos 9 F3
Paddock The. M in L 9 F3
Paddock The. Newt 147 F1
Paddock The. Ock 221 E2
Paddock The. Rolle 240 A2
Paddock The. W Br 45 F3
Paddock Way. Dron 57 D2
Paddocks Cl. Pinx 160 B2
Paddocks The. Mans 136 C3
Paddocks The. Pils 132 B1
Paddocks The. Sand 223 D3
Paddocks The. Stav 79 E2
Paddocks The. Swad 255 F3
Paddocks View. Lo Ea 236 A4
Padfield Gate. Glos 17 E4
Padfield Main Rd. Glos 10 A3
Padley Cl. Derby 205 D3
Padley Cl. Ripley 169 E2
Padley Hill. Grin 53 F1
Padley Rd. Grin 53 E1
Padley Way. N Wing 131 F3
Padley Wood La. Pils 147 D4
Padley Wood Rd. Pils 132 B1
Padstow Cl. Derby 231 E2
Padstow Rd. Derby 233 E3
Painter's La. Osm 186 A2
Painters Way. Da Da 127 E1
Painters Way. Wins 141 E3
Paisley Cl. Stav 97 E4
Palace La. Shot 166 B1
Palace Rd. Bux 85 D4
Palatine Gr. Derby 230 C4
Palerow La. Alder 166 C2
Palerow La. Spout 166 C2
Pall Mall. Bread 205 F2
Palm Cl. Derby 218 A1
Palmer Cl. Bran 254 A4
Palmer Cres. Dron 57 D1
Palmer Dr. Som 169 F4
Palmer Dr. Staple 223 E3
Palmerston Ct. Mel 252 A4
Palmerston St. Derby 218 C1
Palmerston St. Sels 171 E2
Palmerston St. Sels 171 F1
Palterton La. L Duk 117 E3
Pamela's Cl. Derby 221 D3
Pankhurst Pl. Cl Cr 131 E2
Parade The. Derby 217 E1
Paradise St. Glos 10 A3
Parcel Terr. Derby 218 B3
Pares Way. Ock 221 E3
Park Ave. Ashb 173 E1
Park Ave. Awsw 195 D3
Park Ave. C Don 246 C2
Park Ave. Da Da 127 E2
Park Ave. Dron 57 D1
Park Ave. East 182 C2
Park Ave. Glap 118 B1
Park Ave. Hol 75 D4
Park Ave. Ilk 208 C4
Park Ave. Mans 136 B2
Park Ave. Ripley 169 F1
Park Ave. Shireb 119 F2
Park Ave. Stanl 207 E3
Park Ave. Utt 210 A1
Park Ave. W Br 33 E2
Park Cl. Chest 115 D4
Park Cl. Glos 10 B1
Park Cl. Linton 261 E3
Park Cl. Lit Ea 205 D4
Park Cl. Mat 143 E2
Park Cl. Pinx 160 B1
Park Cl. S-by-D 222 C4
Park Cl. Shirl 146 C1
Park Cres. C-Frith 47 D3
Park Cres. Dove 211 D1
Park Cres. Glos 10 A2
Park Cres. Greas 182 C2
Park Cres. Ilk 209 D4
Park Cres. Ripley 179 F4
Park Cres. W Br 33 E2
Park Ct. Hean 181 F1
Park Dr. Chest 96 A1
Park Dr. Derby 218 B1
Park Dr. Ilk 208 C4
Park Dr. Sand 223 D2
Park Dr. Som 169 F3
Park Edge. Hath 52 C4
Park Farm Centre. Derby 204 B1
Park Farm Dr. Derby 204 B1
Park Farm Mews. Eck 60 B1
Park Gr. Derby 218 C4
Park Grange Cl. Shef 43 E4
Park Grange Dr. Shef 43 E4
Park Grange Mount. Shef 43 E4
Park Grange Rd. Shef 43 E4
Park Grange View. Shef 43 E4
Park Hall Ave. Chest 114 A4
Park Hall Cl. Chest 114 A4
Park Hall Gdns. Chest 114 A4
Park Hall Gdns. Mans 136 B3
Park Hall La. We Ha 207 E4
Park Hall Rd. Denby 180 A2
Park Hall Rd. Mans 136 B3
Park Head Rd. Mat 143 D3
Park Hill Cl. N Mills 24 B1
Park Hill Dr. Derby 231 F4
Park Hill. Awsw 195 D3
Park Hill. Eck 59 F2
Park La. C Don 246 C2
Park La. Chest 95 F4
Park La. Da Da 127 E1
Park La. Derby 204 C2
Park La. Derby 218 B1
Park La. Holb 101 E3
Park La. O Had 110 B1
Park La. Pent 169 D4
Park La. Pinx 160 B1
Park La. S Wing 157 E1
Park La. Shir 200 B4
Park La. Shirl 159 D4
Park La. Tut 239 D1
Park La. We on T 245 F2
Park Leys Ct. Derby 220 C
Park Mews. Mans 136 B2
Park Mews. Som 170 B3
Park Mill Dr. Newt 159 E4
Park Pale The. Tut 239 E3
Park Rd. Ashb 173 E1
Park Rd. Bake 109 E3
Park Rd. Belper 179 D
Park Rd. Bux 85 D
Park Rd. C-Frith 47 D
Park Rd. Chest 95 F1
Park Rd. Chest 96 A
Park Rd. Derby 217 E1
Park Rd. Derby 220 B3
Park Rd. Disley 32 A
Park Rd. Duff 190 B2
Park Rd. Glos 10 A2
Park Rd. Ilk 208 C4
Park Rd. Linton 262 A3
Park Rd. Mans 136 A
Park Rd. N Mills 33 E4
Park Rd. N Wing 116 C
Park Rd. O Had 110 A
Park Rd. Ripley 169 F1
Park Rd. Ripley 179 F3
Park Rd. Shireb 119 F3
Park Rd. Staple 223 F4
Park Rd. Swad 255 E3
Park Rd. Swad 256 B
Park Rd. Tupton 131 E
Park Rd. W Br 45 E
Park Rise. Hol 75 D
Park Row. Cl Cr 131 E2
Park Side. Som 170 B
Park Spring Cl. Shef 43 E
Park Spring Dr. Shef 43 E
Park Spring Gr. Shef 43 E
Park Spring Pl. Shef 43 E
Park Spring Way. Shef 43 E
Park St. Alf 158 C
Park St. Barl 80 A
Park St. Brea 235 F
Park St. Chest 115 D
Park St. Derby 219 E
Park St. Hean 181 E
Park St. Lo Ea 223 E
Park St. Mans 136 A
Park St. Ripley 169 F
Park St. S Wing 157 F
Park St. Staple 223 E
Park St. Swad 256 A
Park St. Utt 210 B
Park Terr. Glos 17 E
Park Terr. North 127 D
Park The. May 184 B
Park View Ave. Mosb 59 F
Park View Cl. Derby 204 C
Park View Ct. Shef 43 D
Park View Dr. C-Frith 47 D
Park View Rise. N Mills 24 B
Park View. Bake 109 E
Park View. Barl 80 A
Park View. Chest 115 E
Park View. Clowne 80 C
Park View. Hean 181 E
Park View. Som 170 B
Park Way. Etwall 229 E
Parker Ave. Calow 96 C
Parker Centre. Derby 219 D
Parker Cl. Derby 218 C
Parker St. Derby 218 C
Parker's La. Mans 136 B
Parkers Cl. Black 257 D
Parkers La. Totley 55 E
Parkfield Cl. Shef 43 D
Parkfield Cres. S Field 265 F
Parkfield Ct. Bux 85 D
Parkfield La. Snel 184 B
Parkfields Dr. Derby 218 C
Parkgate Cl. Mosb 59 D
Parkgate Croft. Mosb 59 D
Parkgate Dr. Mosb 59 D

Parkgate La. Stav 77 F3
Parkgate La. Uns 77 F3
Parkham Rd. Kim 195 F4
Parkhill La. Barl 60 B1
Parkhouse Dr. S Norm 159 F3
Parkhouse Rd. Pils 132 A2
Parkin St. Alf 159 D2
Parkland Ave. N Mills 24 B1
Parkland Dr. Win 115 D1
Parks Ave. S Wing 157 F2
Parkside Ave. Lo Ea 236 A4
Parkside Cl. Iron 170 C2
Parkside Dr. Iron 170 C2
Parkside Dr. Lo Ea 236 A4
Parkside La. Marple 23 E3
Parkside Rd. Derby 220 A3
Parkside. Bux 85 D4
Parkside. Ripley 179 F4
Parkstone Ct. Derby 217 E1
Parkstone Delph. Shef 44 A1
Parkville Cl. Bux 85 E3
Parkway Ct. Shef 56 C4
Parkway The. Da Da 127 E2
Parkway. Derby 232 C1
Parkway. N Mills 24 B1
Parkway. Whit 82 A3
Parliament Cl. Derby 218 C2
Parliament St. Derby 218 C2
Parliament St. Swad 255 F3
Parsonage Cl. Mosb 59 E3
Parsonage Croft. Bake 109 E3
Parsonage Gdns. Marple 23 D2
Parsons Cl. Hartin 137 E3
Parsons Gate. Bam 40 A3
Partington Ct. Glos 10 C1
Partridge Cl. Eck 59 D2
Partridge Dr. Wood 256 C2
Partridge Way. Derby 218 A2
Parture Gr. Eck 59 E2
Parwich Cl. Chest 95 D3
Parwich La. Par 151 F4
Parwich Rd. N Wing 131 F3
Pasteur Ave. Ripley 169 E1
Pasture La. Brass 152 B1
Pasture La. Flagg 106 B3
Pasture La. Lo Ea 237 D3
Pasture La. Newt 148 B1
Pasture La. Shirl 147 D2
Pasture Rd. Staple 209 E1
Pastures Ave. Derby 230 C4
Pastures Hill. Derby 231 D4
Pastures The. Duff 190 C2
Pastures The. Greas 195 E4
Pastures The. Mans 136 C3
Pastures The. Rep 242 B1
Pastures The. Swad 255 F3
Paterson Ave. Derby 220 A3
Patmore Sq. Derby 231 F4
Paton Gr. Chest 96 B4
Patrick Cl. Linton 261 E3
Patten Cl. Derby 232 A3
Patterdale Cl. Dron 56 C1
Pattison St. Bols 98 C3
Pavilion Cl. Clowne 80 C1
Pavilion Gdns. Plea 134 C4
Pavilion Rd. Derby 231 E4
Pavilion Rd. Ilk 194 C3
Pavillion Workshops. N Wing 116 B1
Paxton Cl. Derby 217 E1
Paxton Cl. Mat 143 D3
Paxton Ct. Shef 43 F2
Paxton Rd. Chest 96 B3
Payler Cl. Shef 44 A4
Payne St. Derby 218 B3
Peach Ave. S Norm 160 A4
Peach Ave. Sels 171 F3
Peach St. Derby 218 B3
Peach St. Hean 181 E1
Peacock Cl. Glos 9 F2
Peacock Cl. Kill 60 B3
Peacock Pl. Ilk 194 B2
Peacroft La. Hilton 228 B1
Peafield La. Mans 136 C2
Peak Ave. Som 170 A3
Peak Pl. Stav 97 E4
Peak Rd. N Mills 33 E4
Peak The. Shireb 119 F2
Peak View Dr. Ashb 173 E1
Peak View Rd. Chest 95 E3
Peak View. S Norm 159 F3
Peakdale Cl. Lo Ea 236 A3
Peakdale Cl. Ripley 180 B3
Peakdale Cres. Shef 44 C3
Peakdale Rd. Glos 9 F2
Peakdale Rd. Marple 23 D2
Peakland View. Da Da 127 D2
Peaknaze Cl. Glos 17 D4
Peaktor La. Row 126 C4
Pear Tree Ave. Ripley 180 B4
Pear Tree Ave. Swad 255 F4
Pear Tree Cl. Glos 9 F2
Pear Tree Cl. Harts 257 D4
Pear Tree Cl. Kill 60 B3
Pear Tree Cl. Marple 23 D4
Pear Tree Cl. Stav 97 D4
Pear Tree Cres. Derby 232 A4
Pear Tree Dr. Linton 261 E3
Pear Tree Dr. Shireb 119 F3
Pear Tree Ind Pk. Derby 232 A4
Pear Tree Rd. Pils 132 B1
Pear Tree St. Derby 219 D1
Pearce La. Win 114 B2
Pearl Bank. M Mont 211 F4
Pearl Cl. Derby 206 A1
Pearl Way. M in L 9 D1
Peartree Ave. Win 114 C2
Peartree Cl. C Don 247 D2
Peartree Ct. Derby 205 E1
Peartree La. S in A 134 A1
Pease Cl. Alf 159 D2
Pease Hill. Alf 159 D2
Peasehill Rd. Ripley 180 C4
Peasehill. Ripley 180 C4
Peasunhurst La. Ash 113 D1
Peat La. Spout 166 B2
Peatburn Ave. Hean 181 E1
Peatfield Rd. Kill 60 C4
Peatfield Rd. Staple 209 E1
Peats Cl. K Ire 165 D1
Peckham Gdns. Derby 218 A3
Pedley Ave. Mosb 59 F4
Pedley Dr. Mosb 59 F4
Pedley St. Ilk 208 C4
Peebles Cl. Derby 231 F1
Peel Cres. Mans 135 E1
Peel St. Derby 218 B3
Peel St. Glos 10 B3
Peel St. La Mi 182 A2
Peel St. Lo Ea 236 C4
Peel St. S Norm 160 A3
Peers Cl. Derby 206 A1
Peet St. Derby 218 C2
Peggs Wlk. Derby 231 F4
Pegwell Cl. Derby 231 E4
Pelham Ave. Ilk 194 C1
Pelham St. Derby 218 C2
Pemberton The. S Norm 160 A2
Pembleton Dr. Mans 135 E1
Pembrey Cl. Staple 209 E1
Pembroke Cl. Chest 95 E1
Pembroke Rd. Dron 76 A4
Pembroke Rd. Shire 63 F4
Pembroke St. Derby 219 E4
Penalton Cl. Derby 232 C3
Pendean Cl. Newt 147 F1
Pendennis Cl. Derby 233 D3
Pendlebury Dr. Derby 217 F1
Pendleside Way. Derby 230 C4
Pendleton La. Alder 166 C4
Penfold Way. Morton 147 D3
Penge Rd. Derby 218 A4
Penhaligan's Cl. Derby 232 C1
Penine View. Ripley 179 F4
Peniston Rise. Mel 252 A4
Penistone Gdns. Cl Cr 131 E1
Penmore Cl. Chest 115 E4
Penmore Gdns. Chest 96 B1
Penmore La. Chest 115 E4
Penmore St. Chest 115 E4
Penn La. Mel 252 A4
Penn St. Belper 179 D2
Penncroft Dr. Cl Cr 131 E1
Penncroft La. Cl Cr 131 E2
Penniment La. Mans 135 D1
Pennine Ave. Som 170 B4
Pennine Cl. Lo Ea 223 D1
Pennine Cl. Lo Ea 236 B2
Pennine Cl. Mans 136 B2
Pennine Cl. Newt 148 A2
Pennine Cl. S in A 148 C2
Pennine Cl. Tibs 147 F3
Pennine Dr. S Norm 159 F3
Pennine Dr. Sels 171 F4
Pennine Rd. Glos 17 D4
Pennine View. Scarc 118 A3
Pennine Way. Chest 95 E3
Pennine Way. Gra 115 F2
Pennine Way. Swad 256 A2
Penns Rd. Shef 43 E3
Penny Engine La. Eck 59 F2
Penny Green. Whit 82 A3
Penny La. Totley 55 E3
Penny Long La. Derby 218 C4
Pennycroft La. Utt 210 B1
Pennycroft Rd. Utt 210 A1
Pennytown Ct. Som 159 E1
Pennyunk La. A in W 89 F1
Pennywell Dr. Holy 113 E4
Penrhyn Ave. Derby 218 B1
Penrith Pl. Derby 205 E1
Penrose St. L Duk 97 E1
Pentagon The. Derby 219 E3
Pentewen Cl. Derby 204 C1
Penthorpe Cl. Shef 44 A3
Pentland Cl. Chest 95 E3
Pentland Cl. Derby 206 A1
Pentland Gdns. Lo Ea 223 D1
Pentland Rd. Shef 56 C4
Pentrich Rd. Ripley 169 E1
Pentrich Rd. Som 169 F3
Penzance Rd. Derby 233 D3
Pepper La. S-by-D 222 C4
Percy St. Derby 218 C2
Percy St. Ilk 208 C4
Percy Wood Cl. Hilton 228 B1
Peregrine Cl. Bu on T 248 B2
Perlethorpe Ave. Mans 136 A1
Perth Cl. Bu on T 248 B1
Perth Cl. Derby 217 F2
Perth Cl. Mans 136 B3
Perth Dr. Staple 209 F1
Perth St. Derby 205 E1
Peter Baines Ind Est. Derby 218 C2
Peter More Hill. Whit 81 F2
Peter St. Ashb 173 E1
Peter St. Glos 10 A3
Peterborough St. Derby 219 F4
Peterdale Cl. Chest 96 C4
Peterdale Rd. Chest 96 C4
Peterhouse Terr. Derby 219 D1
Peterlee Pl. Derby 233 D3
Peters Ave. Cl Cr 131 D2
Petersgate Cl. Lo Ea 223 D1
Petersgate. Lo Ea 223 D1
Petersham Dr. Derby 233 E3
Petersham Rd. Lo Ea 223 D1
Peterway. Som 170 B4
Pettifor Terr. Newt 147 E1
Petty Close La. K Lang 202 B1
Pettyclose La. Chest 96 B3
Petworth Ave. Bees 223 F2
Pevensey Ave. Chest 95 F3
Pevensey Ct. Chest 95 F4
Peveril Ave. N Mills 24 B1
Peveril Ave. Ock 221 E1
Peveril Cl. Cas 38 B1
Peveril Cl. Som 170 B3
Peveril Cres. Lo Ea 235 F3
Peveril Cres. We Ha 207 F4
Peveril Ct. Glos 17 F4
Peveril Ct. Ripley 169 E1
Peveril Dr. Ilk 194 B1
Peveril Dr. Som 170 B3
Peveril Gdns. Disley 33 D3
Peveril Mews. Disley 33 D3
Peveril Rd. Bux 85 E4
Peveril Rd. Chest 95 F4
Peveril Rd. Eck 59 F2
Peveril Rd. Tibs 147 F3
Peveril St. Derby 232 B3
Peveril. Cas 38 B1
Peverill Rd. Bols 98 C2
Pewit Cl. N Wing 132 B4
Pewit La. Pils 147 E3
Pewit La. Tibs 147 E3
Pheasant Field Dr. Derby 221 D3
Pheasant Hill. Mans 136 A1
Philip Howard Rd. Glos 17 E4
Philips Croft. Duff 190 C2
Philipway. Som 170 B4
Phoenix Ct. Eck 44 C1
Phoenix Rd. Eck 44 C1
Phoenix St. Derby 219 D3
Phyllis Gr. Lo Ea 236 C4
Pic Tor La. Mat 143 D2
Piccadilly Cotts. Chest 96 B2
Piccadilly La. May 172 B1
Piccadilly Rd. Chest 96 B2
Pickard La. Ripley 168 B1
Pickering Ave. East 182 C1
Pickering Rise. Derby 205 E1
Pickford Pl. C-Frith 47 D3
Pickleys La. Dove 224 B4
Pickton Cl. Chest 95 E1
Pictor Gr. Bux 85 E4
Pictor Rd. Bux 85 E4
Piddocks Rd. Swad 255 D3
Pig La. Beeley 111 D2
Pighills La. Dron 57 D2
Pike Cl. Chest 95 D3
Pike View Cl. Chin 34 C1
Pike's La. Glos 17 D4
Pilgrims Way. Derby 231 E2
Pilhough La. St Pk 126 B3
Pilhough Rd. Row 126 C3
Pilkington's Yd. Eck 59 F2
Pillar Butts. Wirk 165 F4
Pilsley Rd. Cl Cr 131 F2
Pilsley Rd. Morton 147 D3
Pimlico. Derby 218 A3
Pimlico. Ilk 208 C4
Pimm's Rd. K Lang 217 D4
Pinch The. A le Da 150 A1
Pinchom's Hill Rd. Belper 179 D2
Pincot Rd. N Mills 33 E4
Pindale Ave. Stav 97 E4
Pindale Rd. Cas 38 C1
Pindale Rd. Hope 38 C1
Pine Ave. La Mi 182 A2
Pine Cl. Derby 220 A2
Pine Cl. Elmt 81 F1
Pine Cl. Etwall 229 E2
Pine Cl. Kill 60 B3
Pine Cl. Mans 136 B3
Pine Cl. Ripley 169 E1
Pine Cl. Shireb 119 F3
Pine Cl. Smal 192 C3
Pine Croft. Ashb 185 E4
Pine Gr. Swad 255 F3
Pine St. Stav 97 D4
Pine Tree Wlk. East 182 B1
Pine View. Chest 95 D2
Pine View. Cl Cr 131 F2
Pine Wlk. Linton 261 F4
Pinecroft Ct. Derby 206 A1
Pinewood Rd. Belper 178 C3
Pinewood Rd. Bu on T 254 C3
Pinewood Rd. Mat 143 D4
Pinewood. Codnor 181 D4
Pinfold Cl. Holy 113 F4
Pinfold Cl. Rep 242 B1
Pinfold Cl. Tut 239 E3
Pinfold Cres. Tide 69 E2
Pinfold Hill. Curbar 72 C1
Pinfold La. Bradl 187 D4
Pinfold La. Rep 242 B1
Pinfold La. Staple 223 F4
Pinfold Rd. Tide 69 E2
Pinfold St. Eck 59 E2
Pinfold The. Belper 179 E3
Pinfold The. Elv 233 F2
Pinfold The. Glap 118 A1
Pinfold The. Middle 124 C2
Pinfold View. Bake 109 E3
Pinfold. Glos 9 F2
Pingle Cres. Belper 178 C3
Pingle Farm Rd. Swad 255 F3
Pingle Grange. Chest 96 C4
Pingle La. Belper 178 C3
Pingle La. Cars 164 C4
Pingle Rd. Kill 60 C4
Pingle The. Derby 220 C2
Pingle The. Lo Ea 236 B4
Pingle The. Mel 252 A4
Pingle. Derby 204 C2
Pingott La. Glos 10 A3
Pinxton Green. K in A 160 C2
Pinxton La. K in A 160 C3
Pinxton La. S Norm 160 B3
Piper Ave. Cl Cr 131 F2
Piper La. Holy 94 C2
Piper La. O Bram 94 C2
Pipeyard La. Eck 59 E1
Pippenwell Rd. Chel 106 A4
Pippin Hill. Denby 180 C1
Pipworth La. Eck 59 F2
Pit Close La. Derby 233 D1
Pit La. Crich 157 D3
Pit La. Ripley 169 F1
Pit La. Ripley 181 D4
Pit La. Shef 44 A4
Pit La. Ship 194 A3
Pit La. Shirl 158 B4
Pitch Cl. Clowne 80 C1
Pitt Hill. Scarc 100 C1
Pitt St. Eck 59 E1
Pittar St. Derby 218 C2
Pittlemere La. Tide 50 A1
Pittywood Rd. Wirk 165 F4
Placket La. Wins 141 D3
Plackett Cl. Brea 235 E4
Plain The. Brai 201 F4
Plains La. Haz 178 A2
Plainspot Rd. Sels 171 F1
Plaistow Green Rd. Crich 156 C1
Plant La. Lo Ea 236 A2
Plantation Cl. Whit 81 F3
Plantation Rd. Shef 43 D3
Plantations The. Lo Ea 236 A4
Plantin Rise. Mosb 59 F4
Plantin The. Mosb 59 F4
Platt St. Glos 10 A3
Platt St. Pinx 160 B1
Platts Ave. Hean 181 E1
Pleasant Ave. Scarc 118 A4
Pleasant Cl. Shef 44 A3
Pleasant Pl. Chest 95 E2
Pleasant Rd. Shef 44 A3
Pleasant View. Marple 15 D2
Plimsoll St. Derby 218 B3
Plough Gate. Derby 204 C1
Ploughfield Cl. Derby 231 D3
Plover Ave. Wood 256 C2
Plover Way. Calow 96 C2
Plowman Ct. Staple 223 E3
Plowright Cl. Shef 43 E3
Plowright Dr. Shef 43 E3
Plowright Mount. Shef 43 E3
Plowright Way. Shef 43 E3
Plucksbridge Rd. Marple 23 D2
Plumbley Hall Mews. Mosb 59 E3
Plumbley Hall Rd. Mosb 59 E3
Plumbley La. Mosb 59 D3
Plumbley La. Mosb 59 F4
Plummer Rd. Swad 256 A3
Plumptre Cl. East 182 C1
Plumptre Way. East 182 C1
Plumptre. Ald 182 A3
Plymouth Ave. Pinx 160 C1
Pocknedge La. Holy 113 E4
Pole La. Marple 24 A2
Pole La. N Mills 24 A2
Pole's Rd. K Lang 217 D4
Polly Froggat La. Calver 72 A1
Polyfields La. Bols 118 A4
Pond La. Win 114 C2
Pond Rd. Holbr 191 E4
Pond St. Chest 96 A1
Pondwell Cnr. Chest 96 C4
Pondwell Dr. Chest 96 C4
Ponsonby Terr. Derby 218 C3
Pontefract St. Derby 232 B4
Pontypool Cl. Derby 206 A1
Pool Cl. Pinx 160 B1
Pool Rd. Mel 252 B3
Pool St. Swad 256 B1
Pool's La. Uns 77 E4
Poole St. Derby 232 C3
Poolsbrook Ave. Stav 98 A4
Poolsbrook Cres. Stav 98 A4
Poolsbrook Rd. Stav 98 A3
Poolsbrook Sq. Stav 98 A4
Poolsbrook View. Stav 98 A4
Pope Carr Rd. Mat 143 E3
Poplar Ave. Chest 95 D1
Poplar Ave. Derby 220 C3
Poplar Ave. Moira 262 C1
Poplar Ave. N Mills 24 B1
Poplar Ave. Ripley 180 B4
Poplar Ave. Sand 223 D4
Poplar Ave. Swad 256 A3
Poplar Cl. Derby 233 D4
Poplar Cl. Dron 76 B4
Poplar Cl. Kill 60 B3
Poplar Cres. Ashb 185 E4
Poplar Dr. Glap 134 A4
Poplar Dr. Mans 135 D2
Poplar Nook. Derby 204 C2
Poplar Rd. Brea 235 F4
Poplar Rd. Eck 59 E1
Poplar Rd. S Norm 160 A4
Poplar Row. Derby 205 D1
Poplar St. Mans 136 B2
Poplar Terr. C-Frith 47 D4
Poplar Way. H La 32 A4
Poplar Way. Ilk 208 B3
Poplars The. Derby 204 C2
Poplars The. Whit 82 A3
Porlock Cl. Lo Ea 236 A4
Porlock Ct. Derby 206 A1
Port Way. Holbr 191 E3
Porteous Cl. Da Da 127 E2
Porter La. Mat Ba 154 C2
Porter La. Mid 154 C2
Porter La. Wirk 154 C2
Porter Rd. Derby 218 C1
Porter St. Stav 78 C1
Porter's La. Derby 205 F2
Porter's La. Fin 230 B1
Porterhouse Rd. Ripley 169 F1
Porters Farm. March 224 C1
Porthcawl Pl. Derby 206 B1
Portland Ave. Bols 99 D1
Portland Ave. Bran 254 A4
Portland Ave. Elmt 81 F1
Portland Cl. Derby 217 E1
Portland Cres. Bols 99 D1
Portland Cres. Mans 136 B2
Portland Cres. Staple 223 F3
Portland Ct Mews. Mans 136 B2
Portland Gr. Chin 34 C1
Portland Rd. Bees 223 F1
Portland Rd. Greas 195 E4
Portland Rd. Ilk 194 C2
Portland Rd. Lo Ea 236 A2
Portland Rd. N Mills 24 B1
Portland Rd. Scarc 101 D1
Portland Rd. Shireb 119 F2
Portland Sq. Bake 109 E3
Portland St. Clowne 81 D2
Portland St. Derby 232 A4
Portland St. Etwall 229 D2
Portland St. Mans 136 B2
Portland St. Plea 135 D4
Portland St. Whit 81 F3
Portland Terr. Scarc 101 D1
Portman Chase. Derby 231 E1
Portreath Dr. Derby 204 C2
Portway Cl. Derby 205 D2
Portway Dr. Tut 239 E3
Post St. Glos 10 A3
Postmans La. Gra 116 B2
Posy La. As on T 246 A4
Potato Pit Hill. Dale 208 A1
Potlocks The. Will 242 B3
Potter St. Derby 220 B2
Potter St. Mel 252 A4
Potters La. Crich 157 D3
Potters Way. Ilk 209 D4
Pottery La. Chest 96 A4
Pottery La. Denby 180 B2
Poulter St. Scarc 100 C1
Pound La. Tupton 131 E4
Powell Dr. Kill 60 B3
Powell St. Derby 218 C1
Powtrell Pl. Ilk 209 D3
Poynter Cl. Hean 181 E1
Poynton Wood Cres. Shef 56 A3
Poynton Wood Glade. Shef 56 A3
Poyser Ave. Derby 220 A4
Poyser La. K Lang 203 D1
Pratt Cl. Mans 135 E1
Pratthall La. Wirk 166 A3
Prescot Cl. Derby 217 E1
Press La. Ash 130 B3
Prestbury Cl. Derby 206 A1
Prestom Ave. Alf 159 D2
Preston Ave. Alf 159 D2
Preston St. Shef 43 D4

Prestwood La. Dens 196 C4
Prestwood Park Dr. Swad 256 B3
Pretoria St. Bols 98 C3
Priestcliffe Rd. Tadd 87 F2
Priestland Ave. Derby 220 B2
Priestley Ave. Shirl 146 B3
Primary Cl. Belper 179 D2
Prime Ind Est. Derby 219 D1
Prime Ind Park. Derby 219 E1
Primrose Ave. Sels 171 F1
Primrose Cl. Derby 205 F2
Primrose Cl. Kill 60 C4
Primrose Cres. Glos 17 D4
Primrose Dr. Morley 206 B4
Primrose Hill. Glos 17 D4
Primrose Hill. Newt 147 F1
Primrose La. Glos 17 D4
Primrose La. Hay 25 E3
Primrose La. Kill 60 C4
Primrose La. Marple 24 A2
Primrose Meadow. Swad 256 A4
Primrose Rise. Greas 195 E4
Primrose St. Ilk 194 C2
Prince Charles Ave. Derby 218 A3
Prince of Wales Rd. Shef 44 A4
Prince St. Ilk 194 C2
Prince St. Lo Ea 236 B4
Prince's Rd. Bux 85 E4
Princes Dr. Derby 218 A1
Princes Rd. Chin 34 C1
Princes St. Derby 219 D1
Princess Ave. Linton 261 E3
Princess Ave. S Norm 160 A3
Princess Cl. Wood 256 C1
Princess Ct. Shef 44 A4
Princess Dr. Ock 221 D1
Princess Dr. Sand 223 D2
Princess Pl. Cl Cr 131 E1
Princess Rd. Dron 57 D1
Princess Rd. Utt 210 A1
Princess St. Chest 95 F2
Princess St. Chest 96 C4
Princess St. East 182 C2
Princess St. Glos 17 E4
Princess St. Lo Ea 236 B4
Princess St. Swad 261 F4
Princess Way. Bu on T 240 C1
Printers Fold. M in L 9 E3
Printers Park. M in L 9 F3
Priors Barn Cl. Ock 221 E1
Priorway Ave. Ock 221 E1
Priorway Gdns. Ock 221 E1
Priory Cl. Derby 233 D1
Priory Cl. Ilk 208 B3
Priory Cl. Swad 256 A3
Priory Cl. Tut 239 D3
Priory Cl. Yea 199 E3
Priory Gdns. Som 170 A4
Priory Lands. Bu on T 240 C1
Priory Rd. Alf 159 D3
Priory Rd. East 182 C1
Priory Rd. Mans 136 A2
Priory Sq. Mans 136 A2
Pritchard Dr. Staple 223 F3
Pritchett Dr. Derby 230 C4
Private Dr. Stav 78 A1
Progress Ct. Bake 109 E3
Prospect Ave. S Norm 159 F3
Prospect Ct. S in A 148 C1
Prospect Dr. Belper 178 C1
Prospect Dr. Mat 143 D3
Prospect Dr. Shef 55 F3
Prospect Dr. Shireb 119 F2
Prospect Pl. Shef 56 A3
Prospect Rd. Chest 76 C1
Prospect Rd. Denby 180 A1
Prospect Rd. Dron 57 E2
Prospect Rd. Hean 194 A4
Prospect Rd. Pils 132 B1
Prospect Rd. Shef 43 D4
Prospect Rd. Shef 56 A3
Prospect St. Alf 159 D2
Prospect Terr. Chest 95 F2
Prospect Terr. Crich 168 A4
Providence Ct. Wood 256 C1
Providence Pl. Ilk 194 C1
Providence Rd. Sels 171 D2
Providence St. Ripley 180 C4
Provident St. Derby 219 D1
Pudding Bag La. Ash 129 F2
Pullman Cl. Stav 78 C2
Pullman Rd. Derby 219 F2
Pump Cl. Mat 143 E2
Pump La. Dove 211 D1
Purbeck Ave. Chest 95 E2
Purbeck Cl. Lo Ea 236 A4
Purchase Ave. Hean 181 E1
Purdy Meadow. Lo Ea 235 F3
Purseglove Dr. Tide 69 E2
Purseglove Rd. Tide 69 E2
Putney Cl. Derby 217 F3
Pybus St. Derby 218 B3
Pye Bridge Ind Est. Som 170 C3
Pye Hill Rd. Sels 171 D2
Pyegrove Rd. Glos 10 C1
Pyegrove. Glos 10 C1
Pykestone Cl. Derby 205 F1
Pym Leys. Lo Ea 235 F3
Pynot Rd. Chest 77 D1
Pytchley Cl. Belper 179 E2

Quadrant The. Bux 85 D4
Quadrant The. Totley 55 F3
Quantock Cl. Derby 231 E1
Quantock Rd. Lo Ea 223 D1
Quantock Way. Chest 95 D3
Quarn Dr. Derby 204 B2
Quarn Gdns. Derby 218 C4
Quarn St. Derby 218 C4
Quarn Way. Derby 218 C3
Quarndon Hts. Derby 204 B2
Quarry Bank Rd. Chest 96 B1
Quarry Bank. Mat 143 D4
Quarry Berry La. Chil 264 C1
Quarry Cl. Glos 10 B1
Quarry Hill Rd. Ilk 208 C3
Quarry Hill. Eck 58 B1
Quarry Hill. Mosb 59 D4
Quarry Hill. S-by-D 223 D4
Quarry La. Ash 130 B3
Quarry La. Brack 145 E3
Quarry La. Chest 95 E1
Quarry La. Mat 143 F4
Quarry La. Shirl 146 C2
Quarry Rd. Belper 178 C1
Quarry Rd. Bols 99 D2
Quarry Rd. Kill 60 B4
Quarry Rd. Morley 192 A1
Quarry Rd. N Mills 24 C1
Quarry Rd. N Mills 33 E4
Quarry Rd. Som 170 B4
Quarry Rd. Totley 55 F3
Quarry Rd. Uns 58 A1
Quarry Vale Gr. Shef 44 B2
Quarry Vale Rd. Shef 44 B2
Queen Elizabeth Ct. Ashb 173 D1
Queen Elizabeth Way. Ilk 208 B3
Queen Mary Cl. Shef 44 A4
Queen Mary Cres. Shef 44 A4
Queen Mary Rd. Chest 95 D1
Queen Mary Rd. Shef 44 A4
Queen St N. Chest 96 A4
Queen St. Belper 179 D2
Queen St. Chest 77 F1
Queen St. Chest 95 F2
Queen St. Cl Cr 131 E2
Queen St. Derby 219 D3
Queen St. Eck 59 F2
Queen St. Elmt 81 F1
Queen St. Glos 10 A2
Queen St. Glos 17 D4
Queen St. Ilk 208 C4
Queen St. Iron 170 C2
Queen St. La Mi 182 B2
Queen St. Lo Ea 236 C4
Queen St. Long 121 D3
Queen St. Marple 23 D3
Queen St. Mid 154 B3
Queen St. Mosb 59 E4
Queen St. Pils 132 B1
Queen St. Pinx 160 B2
Queen St. Ripley 181 D4
Queen St. S Norm 159 F3
Queen St. Som 170 B4
Queen St. Stav 97 E4
Queen St. Swad 256 A1
Queen St. Tide 69 E2
Queen Victoria Rd. Shef 55 F3
Queen Victoria Rd. Totley 55 F3
Queen Victoria Rd. Tupton 115 E1
Queen's Ave. Bux 85 E4
Queen's Dr. Belper 178 C3
Queen's Dr. Glos 10 C1
Queen's Dr. Ilk 208 C4
Queen's Dr. Swad 256 A3
Queen's Rd. Bux 85 E4
Queen's Sq. East 182 C1
Queen's Way. Tupton 115 E1
Queen's Wlk. Ne La 101 D1
Queen's Wlk. Tupton 115 E1
Queens Ave. Hean 181 E1
Queens Ave. Ilk 209 D3
Queens Ave. Stanl 207 E3
Queens Cl. Whit 82 B3
Queens Ct. Dray 235 D4
Queens Ct. Elmt 81 F1
Queens Dr. Brin 182 C4
Queens Dr. Derby 218 B1
Queens Dr. Sand 223 D2
Queens Rd N. East 182 C1
Queens Rd S. East 182 C1
Queens Rd. Shef 43 D4
Queens Rd. Whit 82 B3
Queens Rise. Tut 239 E3
Queensferry Gdns. Derby 232 C2
Queensland Cl. Derby 217 F2
Queensland Cres. Bu on T 248 B1
Queensview Dr. Ripley 181 D4
Queensway. C Don 246 C2
Queensway. Derby 204 C1
Queensway. Mel 252 A4
Queensway. N Wing 116 C1
Queensway. Pils 132 B1
Queensway. Shirl 146 C2
Quentin Rd. C-Frith 47 E3
Quick Cl. Mel 252 A4
Quick Hill Rd. Derby 231 E1
Quillings Way. Ock 221 E1
Quilow La. Osm 185 F2
Quixhill Bank. Dens 196 C4
Quixhill La. Dens 196 C4
Quoit Green. Dron 57 D1
Quorn Cl. Bu on T 248 A1
Quorn Dr. Chest 95 D3
Quorn Rise. Derby 231 F3
Quorndon Cres. Lo Ea 236 B3

Rabown Ave. Derby 231 E4
Racecourse Ind Est. Derby 219 E4
Racecourse Mount. Chest 95 F4
Racecourse Rd E. Chest 96 A4
Racecourse Rd. Chest 95 F4
Racester Way. N Wing 131 F3
Rad Meadows. Lo Ea 236 B3
Radbourne La. Derby 217 F3
Radbourne St. Derby 218 B3
Radbourne St. Mans 136 C2
Radburn Ct. Staple 209 F1
Radcliffe Ave. Derby 219 F4
Radcliffe Dr. Derby 218 B2
Radford Rd. Smal 192 C3
Radford St. Derby 232 C4
Radmanthwaite Rd. Mans 135 E2
Radnor Pl. Mans 135 E2
Radnor St. Derby 219 E4
Radstock Gdns. Derby 205 F1
Radstone Cl. Derby 206 A1
Raeburn Cl. Shef 43 F1
Raeburn Dr. Bees 223 F1
Raeburn Dr. Marple 23 D4
Raeburn Pl. Shef 43 F2
Raeburn Rd. Shef 43 F2
Raeburn Way. Shef 43 F1
Raglan Ave. Derby 218 B3
Raglan St. Alf 159 D2
Railway Ave. Elmt 100 B4
Railway Cotts. Kim 195 F3
Railway Row. Iron 170 C2
Railway Side. Swad 256 A1
Railway St. Glos 10 A3
Railway St. Glos 10 B1
Railway Terr. Bux 85 E4
Railway Terr. Chest 115 D4
Railway Terr. Derby 219 E2
Rain's La. Mid 154 B2
Rainham Gdns. Derby 233 D3
Rainier Dr. Derby 220 A3
Rake Head Rd. Holme 2 C4
Rake La. Middle 124 B2
Rake The. Mo 123 D3
Rakes La. Tiss 162 A3
Rakes Rd. Mo 107 E1
Raleigh Cl. Ilk 194 C2
Raleigh St. Derby 218 B3
Raliegh Rd. Shef 43 D3
Ralph Dr. Som 170 B4
Ralph Rd. Stav 79 D1
Ralston Croft. Mosb 59 F3
Ralston Ct. Mosb 59 E3
Ralston Gr. Mosb 59 E3
Ralston Pl. Mosb 59 E3
Rambler Cl. Swad 256 A3
Ramblers Dr. Derby 206 B2
Ramper Ave. Clowne 80 C1
Ramscliff Ave. Donis 265 F4
Ramsdean Cl. Derby 219 E4
Ramsden Cl. Glos 10 B1
Ramsden La. Holme 3 D4
Ramsden Rd. Holme 3 E4
Ramsey Ave. Chest 95 E1
Ramsey Cl. Staple 209 F1
Ramshaw Rd. Uns 76 C3
Ramshaw Way. Derby 218 C2
Randall Dr. Swad 256 A2
Randall Pl. Shef 43 D4
Randall St. Eck 59 D1
Randolph Rd. Derby 231 F4
Ranelagh Gdns. Derby 218 A4
Raneld Mount. Chest 114 B4
Rangemoor La. Stan 183 E3
Rangemore Cl. Derby 217 F2
Ranmoor Cl. Chest 115 E4
Ranmoor Hill. Hath 52 C4
Rannoch Cl. Derby 204 C2
Rannoch Cl. Derby 220 C3
Ranworth Cl. Derby 232 B2
Ratcliffe St. East 182 C1
Rauche Ct. Derby 219 D2
Raven Ave. Tibs 147 F3
Raven Cl. Som 170 B3
Raven Oak Cl. Belper 179 D2
Raven St. Derby 218 C2
Ravencar Rd. Eck 59 D2
Ravenscourt Rd. Derby 218 B3
Ravenscroft Ave. Shef 44 C4
Ravenscroft Cl. Shef 44 C4
Ravenscroft Cres. Shef 44 C4
Ravenscroft Ct. Shef 44 C4
Ravenscroft Dr. Derby 219 F3
Ravenscroft Dr. Shef 44 C4
Ravenscroft Oval. Shef 44 C4
Ravenscroft Pl. Shef 44 C4
Ravenscroft Rd. Shef 44 C4
Ravenscroft Way. Shef 44 C4
Ravensdale Ave. Lo Ea 223 D1
Ravensdale Cl. Stav 97 E3
Ravensdale Rd. Derby 204 B2
Ravensdale Rd. Shef 56 C4
Ravenstor Rd. Wirk 154 C1
Ravenswood Rd. Chest 95 D3
Rawdon Cl. C Don 247 D2
Rawdon Rd. Moira 262 C3
Rawdon St. Derby 218 C1
Rawlins Ct. Dron 57 E2
Rawlinson Ave. Derby 232 A4
Rawson Green. Kilb 179 F1
Ray St. Hean 181 F1
Ray's Ave. Hean 181 F1
Rayleigh Ave. Chest 96 B4
Raynald Rd. Shef 44 A4
Rayneham Rd. Ilk 194 B2
Raynesway Park Dr. Derby 220 A1
Raynesway. Derby 220 A2
Reader St. Derby 220 C3
Recreation Cl. Clowne 80 C2
Recreation Cl. Newt 147 F1
Recreation Dr. Shireb 119 F1
Recreation Rd. Chest 96 C3
Recreation Rd. Plea 134 C4
Recreation Rd. Sand 223 D3
Recreation Rd. Shireb 119 F2
Recreation Rd. Tide 69 E2
Recreation Rd. Wirk 165 F4
Recreation St. Lo Ea 236 C4
Recreation Terr. Staple 223 E3
Recreation View. Shireb 119 F3
Rectory Cl. Br Hill 252 C1
Rectory Cl. Eck 59 F2
Rectory Cl. L Duk 98 A2
Rectory Dr. Win 114 C2
Rectory Farm Mews.
We on T 245 F2
Rectory Gdns. As on T 246 A4
Rectory Gdns. Kill 60 B3
Rectory La. Bread 205 E3
Rectory La. K Ire 165 D1
Rectory La. S Field 265 F1
Rectory Pl. B in F 237 F3
Rectory Rd. Brea 235 F4
Rectory Rd. Clowne 80 C2
Rectory Rd. Kill 60 B3
Rectory Rd. L Duk 98 A2
Rectory Rd. Stav 78 C1
Rectory Rd. Stav 98 A2
Reculver Cl. Derby 231 E4
Red Barn Cl. Newt 148 A2
Red Hill La. Tans 144 B2
Red Hill. Tans 144 B2
Red La. Belper 191 D3
Red La. Brin 171 F1
Red La. Disley 32 B3
Red La. Rep 249 F3
Red Lane. S Norm 159 F2
Red Lion Hill. Brass 153 D1
Red Lion Sq. Hean 181 F1
Redbarn La. Newt 148 A2
Redbrook Ave. Chest 115 D4
Redbury Cl. Derby 218 C2
Redcar Gdns. Derby 205 E1
Reddish Ave. W Br 45 E3
Reddish La. W Br 45 E3
Reddish Rd. W Br 45 E3
Redfern Ave. Ripley 169 F1
Redfern Rd. Utt 210 A1
Redfern St. Tupton 131 E4
Redgap La. Bux 86 A4
Redgate St. Pinx 160 B1
Redgate. Glos 10 B2
Redgrove Way. Chest 114 B4
Redhill La. Tut 239 D3
Redhouse Cl. Chest 77 E2
Redhouse La. Disley 32 C3
Redland Cl. Derby 231 F2
Redland Cl. Ilk 194 C2
Redmires Dr. Derby 233 D1
Redmires Rd. Hal M 42 A4
Redmoor Cl. Bu on T 248 A2
Redmoor Cl. Codnor 170 A1
Redmoor La. Disley 33 D2
Redmoor La. N Mills 33 D3
Rednall Cl. Chest 95 D3
Redruth Pl. Derby 233 E3
Redshaw St. Derby 218 C4
Redstart Cl. Derby 220 C3
Redthorn Rd. Shef 44 C4
Redvers Buller Rd. Chest 96 A1
Redway Croft. Mel 252 A4
Redwing Croft. Derby 231 E4
Redwood Dr. Bu on T 255 D4
Redwood Rd. Derby 231 F2
Reedman Rd. Lo Ea 236 A2
Reeves Rd. Derby 219 D1
Regency Cl. Derby 231 E4
Regent Ct. Iron 170 C2
Regent St. Clowne 80 B2
Regent St. Derby 219 D2
Regent St. Glos 10 A3
Regent St. Glos 10 B1
Regent St. Ilk 208 C4
Regent St. Kim 195 F3
Regent St. La Mi 182 A2
Regent St. Lo Ea 236 B4
Regent St. Staple 223 E3
Regent St. Swad 256 A1
Reginald Rd N. Derby 219 F4
Reginald Rd S. Derby 219 F3
Reginald St. Derby 219 D1
Regis Cl. Derby 206 A1
Reigate Dr. Derby 217 F3
Reigate Dr. Derby 218 A4
Rembrandt Dr. Dron 56 C1
Renals St. Derby 219 D2
Reney Ave. Shef 56 B3
Reney Cres. Shef 56 B3
Reney Dr. Shef 56 B3
Reney Rd. Shef 56 C4
Reney Wlk. Shef 56 B3
Renfrew St. Derby 219 F4
Renishaw Rd. Stav 79 E2
Renshaw Dr. Swad 255 F3
Rent Cl. Chest 95 F3
Repton Ave. Derby 218 B1
Repton Cl. Chest 95 D3
Repton Ct. Mans 136 C2
Repton Dr. Ilk 209 D4
Repton Pl. Shef 56 C4
Repton Rd. Harts 256 C4
Repton Rd. Lo Ea 235 F2
Repton Rd. N Sol 248 C4
Repton Rd. Will 242 A3
Reservoir Hill. Moira 262 B4
Reservoir Rd. W Br 45 E4
Reservoir Terr. Chest 95 F2
Resthaven. Swad 256 A3
Retford Cl. Derby 205 E1
Revill Cres. Staple 223 F4
Reynard Cres. Eck 79 D4
Reynards La. Hartin 137 F2
Reynolds Ave. Ripley 169 F1
Reynolds Cl. Dron 75 F4
Reynolds Dr. Marple 23 D4
Rhodes Ave. Chest 95 F3
Rhodes Cotts. Clowne 80 C2
Rhodes St. Glos 10 A3
Rhodesia Rd. Chest 95 E1
Rhuddlan Pl. Chin 34 B1
Ribblesdale Cl. Derby 204 B1
Ribblesdale Dr. Mosb 59 D4
Ribblesdale Rd. Lo Ea 236 A3
Ribblesdale. Ilk 208 B3
Riber Ave. Som 170 B4
Riber Bank. Glos 9 F1
Riber Cl. Lo Ea 236 B3
Riber Cl. Stav 97 E3
Riber Cl. We Ha 207 F4
Riber Cres. Cl Cr 131 D3
Riber Rd. Hollow 156 A4
Riber Rd. Mat 143 E1
Riber Terr. Chest 95 F1
Riber View Cl. Tans 144 A3
Richard La. Tide 69 E2
Richards Ct. Shef 43 D3
Richards Rd. Shef 43 D4
Richardson Dr. Smal 192 C3
Richardson St. Derby 218 B3
Richardsons La. Som 170 B3
Richmond Ave. Derby 231 E4
Richmond Ave. Ilk 194 C2
Richmond Ave. Lo Ea 236 A4
Richmond Ave. Sand 223 D2
Richmond Ave. Shef 44 C4
Richmond Cl. Chest 114 C4
Richmond Cl. Glos 10 A3
Richmond Cl. We Ha 207 E4
Richmond Ct. Rep 242 B1
Richmond Dr. Duff 190 B3
Richmond Dr. Mans 136 B1
Richmond Gr. Shef 44 C4
Richmond Hall Ave. Shef 44 B4
Richmond Hall Cres. Shef 44 B4
Richmond Hall Dr. Shef 44 B4
Richmond Hall Rd. Shef 44 B4
Richmond Hall Way. Shef 44 B4
Richmond Hill Rd. Shef 44 B4
Richmond Park Rd. Shef 44 C4
Richmond Pl. Shef 44 B4
Richmond Rd. Derby 219 D1
Richmond Rd. Derby 219 F3
Richmond Rd. Shef 44 B4
Richworth Rd. Shef 44 C4
Ricroft Rd. Marple 15 D2
Ridd Way. Win 115 D2
Riddings Cl. Shef 44 A4
Riddings La. Curbar 72 B2
Riddings St. Derby 218 C2
Riddings. Derby 204 C2
Ridge Ave. Marple 23 D2
Ridge Cl. Glos 9 F2
Ridge Cres. Marple 23 D2
Ridge End Fold. Marple 23 D1
Ridge La. C-Firth 65 E4
Ridge Rd. Eck 58 C1
Ridge Rd. Marple 23 D2
Ridge The. Marple 23 D2
Ridge The. Newt 147 F1
Ridge Top La. Hay 25 E1
Ridgedale Rd. Bols 118 A4
Ridgedale View. Ripley 169 E1
Ridgehill Ave. Shef 44 A3
Ridgehill Gr. Shef 44 A3

idgeway Ave. Derby 231 E3
idgeway Cres. Shef 44 A3
idgeway Dr. Ilk 208 A3
idgeway Dr. Shef 44 A3
idgeway La. Ripley 168 B2
idgeway Moor. Eck 58 C3
idgeway Rd. Bu on T 254 C4
idgeway Rd. Shef 44 A2
idgeway The . Disley 32 B3
idgeway. Derby 245 D4
idgeway. Dron 57 E2
idgeway. Hean 193 F4
idgeways. Hay 25 E1
idgewood Ct. Derby 205 F1
idgewood Dr. Mat Ba 155 E3
idgway W. Clowne 80 C1
idgway. Clowne 80 C1
iding Bank. Mel 251 F3
idings Rd. Glos 9 F3
idings The. Mans 136 C1
idings The. Ook 221 E3
igga La. Lit Ea 191 D1
iggotts Way. O Bram 94 C4
iggs La. M Mont 212 A4
igley Ave. Ilk 194 C1
igsby Ct. Derby 217 E2
iley Ave. S Wing 157 F4
iley Back La. Eyam 71 F3
iley La. Pent 169 D3
imsdale Cl. Derby 231 F2
ing-o-bells La. Disley 32 B3
inger La. Clowne 80 C2
inger Way. Clowne 80 C2
inginglow Rd. Hal M 42 C2
ingstone Way. W Br 45 E4
ingwood Ave. Chest 95 F4
ingwood Ave. Stav 97 E4
ingwood Cl. Derby 219 F4
ingwood Rd. Chest 96 C4
ingwood View. Chest 96 C4
ink Dr. Swad 256 A2
ipley Rd. Ripley 168 B3
ipley Rd. Ripley 168 C1
ipon Cres. Derby 219 F4
ipon Gdns. Bux 85 E3
ise The. Derby 204 C1
ise The. Swad 255 F3
ise The. W Br 45 E3
ises The. Glos 9 F3
isley Ct. Ilk 194 C2
isley La. Brea 222 B1
ivenhall Cl. Derby 230 C4
iver St. Derby 219 D3
iver View. Ald 171 D3
iver View. Belper 190 C4
iver View. Litton 88 B4
iverbank Way. Glos 17 F4
iverdale Cl. Bu on T 248 A3
iversfield Dr. Roc 196 C2
iverside Cl. Calver 72 B1
iverside Cl. Glos 10 B1
iverside Cres. Holy 113 F4
iverside Dr. Bran 253 F4
iverside Dr. Calver 72 B1
iverside Way. Mans 136 B3
iverside. Wa on T 253 E1
iverview Cotts. Glos 17 E4
ivington Rd. Bees 223 F1
oadmeadow Cl. Ashb 185 E4
obert Cl. Uns 76 C3
obert Rd. Shef 57 D4
obert St. Derby 219 D3
oberts Ave. S in A 148 C1
oberts Dr. Alf 159 D2
oberts St. Ilk 209 D3
obertson Rd. Bux 85 D3
obertson's Ave. Stav 98 A2
obey Dr. East 182 C2
obian Way. Swad 256 A2
obin Croft Rd. Derby 204 C2
obin Hood Cl. East 182 C1
obin Hood Pl. Swad 256 B1
obin Rd. Derby 218 C4
obin's Cross La. Rep 249 F4
obina Cl. Derby 206 B2
obina Dr. Greas 195 E4
obincroft Rd. Win 114 B2
obincroft. Chest 114 C4
obinettes La. Coss 195 E1
obinlands La. Cas 38 A2
obinscross. Ock 221 D1
obinson Ind Est. Derby 219 D1
obinson Rd. Swad 256 A3
obinson Way. Kill 60 B3
obinson's Hill. Mel 251 F3
obridding Rd. Ash 129 D2
obson Cl. Derby 233 D4
oche. Mosb 59 F4
ochester Cl. Derby 233 D3
ochley Cl. Derby 205 F2
ock Bank. Bux 85 E2
ock Bank. W Br 45 F3
ock Cres. Cl Cr 131 D3
ock La. L Duk 116 C3
ock St. N Mills 33 E4
ock Terr. Bake 109 E3
ock Terr. Bux 85 D3
ockbourne Cl. Derby 233 E3
Rockeries The. Ripley 168 C1
Rockfield Rd. Bux 85 E4
Rockford Ct. Staple 209 F1
Rockhall Terr. Hay 25 F1
Rockhouse Rd. Derby 233 D3
Rockingham Cl. Chest 95 E2
Rockingham Cl. Derby 205 D2
Rockingham Cl. Shef 56 C4
Rockingham. Mosb 59 F4
Rocklands The. Shireb 119 F2
Rockley Cl. Chest 114 C4
Rockley Way. Shireb 119 F2
Rocks The. Tans 144 A3
Rod Moor Rd. Shef 56 A2
Rodge Croft. Chest 77 D2
Rodger's La. Alf 159 D3
Rodknoll La. O Bram 93 E1
Rodney Way. Ilk 194 C2
Rodney Wlk. Derby 230 C4
Rodsley Cl. Chest 95 D3
Rodsley Cres. Derby 231 E3
Rodsley La. Rods 199 F4
Rodsley La. Wya 199 F4
Rodsley La. Yea 199 F3
Rodwood Ave. Barl 80 A4
Roe Cross Rd. M in L 9 D3
Roe Farm La. Derby 219 F4
Roe Wlk. Derby 219 D1
Roe's La. Crich 157 D1
Roebuck Pl. C-Frith 47 D3
Roecar Cl. Chest 77 D1
Roehampton Dr. Derby 218 A4
Roehampton Dr. Staple 209 E1
Rogers Ave. Elmt 81 E1
Rolaine Cl. Mans 136 B2
Rolleston Cres. Greas 195 F4
Rolleston Dr. Greas 195 E4
Rolleston La. Tut 239 E3
Rollet Cl. Shef 44 A4
Rollins La. Marple 15 D1
Roman Bank. Mans 136 B2
Roman Rd. Derby 219 D4
Romeley Cres. Clowne 80 B2
Romford Way. Stav 78 A2
Romney Dr. Dron 56 C1
Romney Gdns. Shef 43 D3
Romsley Cl. Derby 217 E2
Rona Cl. Derby 231 F2
Ronald Cl. Derby 230 C4
Rood La. Clowne 80 C2
Rood La. Idri 176 C3
Roosevelt Ave. Derby 220 A3
Roosevelt Ave. Lo Ea 236 B3
Roper Ave. Hean 193 F4
Roper Hill. Hal M 42 B4
Ropewalk The. Hean 193 F4
Ropewalk The. Ilk 195 D1
Ropewalk The. Stanl 193 D1
Ropework Seedbed Centre The. Ilk 195 D1
Rosamond Ave. Shef 56 A3
Rosamond Cl. Shef 56 A3
Rosamond Dr. Shef 56 A3
Rosamond Glade. Shef 56 A3
Rosamond Pl. Shef 56 A3
Rosamond's Ride. Derby 231 E4
Rose Ave. Bu on T 241 D1
Rose Ave. Calow 97 D2
Rose Ave. Clowne 81 D3
Rose Ave. Ilk 194 C1
Rose Ave. Ock 221 E1
Rose Bank Cl. M in L 9 E3
Rose Cottage Dr. S in A 148 C1
Rose Cotts. Chest 96 B1
Rose Cres. Stav 79 E2
Rose Ct. Cl Cr 131 D2
Rose Ct. Lo Ea 223 D1
Rose End Ave. Mat Ba 155 D3
Rose Hill E. Chest 96 A2
Rose Hill St. Derby 219 D1
Rose Hill W. Chest 95 F2
Rose Hill. Chest 96 A2
Rose Hill. Swad 256 C2
Rose La. Mans 136 B2
Rose La. Tick 251 D2
Rose Tree La. Swad 255 F4
Rose Valley. Swad 256 A3
Rose Way. Kill 60 B3
Rose Wood Cl. Chest 95 E4
Roseberry Ct. Derby 206 A1
Rosecroft Gdns. Swad 256 B2
Rosedale Ave. Chest 115 D4
Rosedale Ave. Derby 233 D3
Rosedale Cl. Lo Ea 236 A3
Rosedale View. Chest 114 A4
Rosedale Way. Mans 136 C1
Rosehill Ct. Bols 99 D1
Roseleigh Cres. Swad 255 F3
Rosemary Dr. Derby 233 D3
Rosemoor La. Derby 206 A1
Rosemount Ct. Derby 204 B2
Rosengrave St. Derby 219 D2
Rosette Cl. Derby 206 B2
Rosewood Cl. Derby 233 E4
Rosewood Cl. S Norm 160 A4
Rosewood Cres. Hean 182 A1
Rosewood Rd. Bu on T 254 C3
Rosier Cres. Som 170 A4
Rosling Cl. L Duk 97 E1
Rosliston Rd S. Swad 254 C3
Rosliston Rd. Bu on T 254 C4
Rosliston Rd. Wa on T 254 B2
Rosliston Rd. Wa on T 259 F4
Roslyn Cres. Hath 53 D4
Roslyn Rd. Hath 53 D4
Ross Wlk. Derby 205 F1
Rossell Dr. Staple 223 F3
Rossendale Cl. Chest 114 C4
Rossendale. Ilk 194 C2
Rosser Ave. Shef 43 F1
Rosslyn Gdns. Derby 233 D3
Roston Cl. Shef 56 C4
Rothay Cl. Dron 75 F4
Rothbourne Croft. Par 151 E1
Rothbury Ave. Staple 209 E1
Rothbury Pl. Derby 205 F1
Rother Ave. Chest 96 B4
Rother Cl. Chest 114 C4
Rother Croft. Tupton 131 E4
Rother St. Pils 132 B1
Rother Valley Way. Mosb 60 A4
Rother Way. Chest 96 A3
Rotherham Cl. Kill 60 C4
Rotherham Rd N. Mosb 59 F4
Rotherham Rd. Bols 99 F1
Rotherham Rd. Clowne 80 C3
Rotherham Rd. Eck 59 F3
Rotherham Rd. Kill 60 C4
Rotherham Rd. Mosb 59 F3
Rotherham Rd. Plea 134 C4
Rotherham Rd. Scarc 118 B2
Rotherside Rd. Eck 59 F2
Rothervale Rd. Chest 115 D4
Rotherwood Rd. Kill 60 C4
Rothesay Cl. Derby 231 F2
Rothey Gr. Chest 94 C3
Rothwell La. Belper 179 D2
Rothwell Rd. Derby 217 E2
Rough Heanor Rd. Derby 218 A1
Rough La. Osm 186 B3
Roughpiece La. Spout 166 B3
Roughton Cl. Derby 230 B4
Round Hill Cl. Glos 9 F2
Round Way. N Mills 33 E4
Rouse St. Pils 132 B1
Routh Ave. C Don 247 D1
Rowan Ave. Ripley 180 B4
Rowan Ave. Staple 209 F1
Rowan Cl. Da Da 127 D2
Rowan Cl. Derby 220 A3
Rowan Cl. Derby 231 E2
Rowan Cl. Elmt 81 F1
Rowan Cl. Mans 136 B1
Rowan Croft. S in A 148 C2
Rowan Dr. Kilb 192 A4
Rowan Dr. Sels 171 E4
Rowan Dr. Shireb 119 E3
Rowan Dr. Shirl 146 B1
Rowan Park Cl. Derby 231 E4
Rowan Rd. Eck 59 E1
Rowan Rd. Stav 79 E2
Rowan Tree Cl. Ashb 185 E4
Rowan Tree Cl. Kill 60 B3
Rowan Tree Dell. Totley 55 F2
Rowan Tree Rd. Kill 60 A3
Rowan Wlk. Glos 9 F2
Rowbury Dr. Bu on T 248 A1
Rowdale Cres. Shef 44 B3
Rowditch Ave. Derby 218 B2
Rowditch Pl. Derby 218 B2
Rowena Cl. Derby 232 C4
Rowland Ct. Alf 158 C2
Rowland Rd. Shef 43 D4
Rowland St. Alf 159 D2
Rowland St. Derby 232 C3
Rowley Ct. Swad 256 A2
Rowley Gdns. Derby 231 E4
Rowley La. Derby 231 E4
Rowsley Ave. Derby 231 E4
Rowsley Ave. Lo Ea 236 A3
Rowsley Cres. Stav 97 E4
Rowsley Mews. Glos 9 F1
Rowthorne Ave. Som 170 A4
Rowthorne La. Al Hu 134 A4
Rowthorne La. Glap 134 A4
Rowton Grange Rd. C-Frith 47 D3
Roxburgh Ave. Derby 219 F4
Roxton Ave. Shef 56 C4
Roxton Ct. Kim 195 F4
Royal Ave. Lo Ea 223 E1
Royal Croft Dr. Baslow 91 F3
Royal Hill Rd. Derby 220 B3
Royal Oak Pl. Bake 109 E3
Royal Rd. Disley 32 B3
Royale Cl. Eck 59 F2
Roydon Cl. Derby 217 E2
Royle Ave. Glos 10 B1
Royston Cl. Chest 114 A4
Royston Dr. Belper 179 E3
Rubens Cl. Dron 56 C1
Rubens Cl. Marple 23 E4
Ruby Paddocks. Kim 195 F3
Rudyard Ave. Derby 220 C3
Rufford Cl. Chest 95 F1
Rufford Dr. Mans 136 C2
Rufford Rd. Lo Ea 236 A2
Ruffstone Cl. Holbr 191 E4
Rugby Ave. Alf 159 E2
Rugby Cl. Bu on T 254 B4
Rugby St. Derby 219 F1
Rugeley Ave. Lo Ea 237 D4
Ruislip Cl. Kim 195 F4
Rupert Rd. Derby 220 A4
Rupert St. Ilk 195 D1
Rupert St. Pils 132 A2
Rush Leys. Lo Ea 236 B3
Rushcliffe Ave. Derby 219 F3
Rushdale Ave. Derby 231 E3
Rushdale Ave. Shef 43 D3
Rushdale Mount. Shef 43 D3
Rushdale Rd. Shef 43 D3
Rushdale Terr. Shef 43 D3
Rushen Mount. Chest 114 C3
Rushes The. Glos 9 F2
Rushes The. Mans 136 B3
Rushleigh Ct. Totley 55 E4
Rushley Ave. Totley 55 E4
Rushley Cl. Totley 55 E4
Rushley Dr. Totley 55 E4
Rushley Rd. Totley 55 E4
Rushpool Ave. Mans 136 B2
Rushton Cl. Marple 23 D3
Rushton Dr. Marple 23 D3
Rushup Cl. Derby 205 D3
Rushup La. C-Frith 48 B4
Rushy La. Sand 222 C3
Rushycroft. M in L 9 D2
Ruskin Ave. Lo Ea 236 A3
Ruskin Rd. Derby 218 C4
Ruskin Rd. Mans 135 E1
Ruskin Sq. Shef 43 D3
Ruskin Way. Derby 231 D4
Russell Gdns. Cl Cr 131 D3
Russell St. Derby 219 E1
Russell St. Lo Ea 223 E1
Russell St. Marple 15 D2
Russell St. Swad 256 B2
Russet Cl. Derby 206 A1
Russet Cl. Hatton 227 E1
Ruston Cl. Chest 95 D3
Ruston Cl. Swad 256 A2
Rutherford Dr. Derby 205 F1
Ruthyn Ave. Barl 80 A4
Rutland Ave. Bols 99 D1
Rutland Ave. Mat 143 E3
Rutland Ave. Ock 221 E1
Rutland Cl. Bu on T 254 B3
Rutland Dr. Derby 217 F2
Rutland Gr. Staple 223 E3
Rutland Pl. Ripley 168 A3
Rutland Rd. Chest 95 F2
Rutland Rd. Sels 171 E2
Rutland Sq. Bake 109 E3
Rutland St. Chest 77 D1
Rutland St. Derby 219 D1
Rutland St. Ilk 194 C1
Rutland St. Mat 143 E3
Rutland Terr. Ilk 194 C1
Rutland Way. Chin 34 B1
Ryal Cl. Ock 221 E3
Ryan Cl. Derby 231 F2
Rycroft Rd. C Don 247 E3
Rydal Ave. Lo Ea 223 D1
Rydal Cl. Derby 204 C2
Rydal Cl. Shef 56 C4
Rydal Cres. Chest 95 F4
Rydal Way. Cl Cr 131 D2
Ryder Cl. Swad 255 F1
Rye Butts. Derby 232 C1
Rye Cl. Derby 205 F2
Rye Cres. Cl Cr 131 E2
Rye Flatts La. Hatton 227 E1
Ryecroft Glen Rd. Totley 56 A4
Ryecroft St. Staple 223 F4
Ryecroft View. Totley 55 E4
Ryecroft. Da Da 127 E1
Ryegrass Cl. Belper 179 E2
Ryegrass Rd. Derby 206 B1
Ryehill Ave. Chest 95 D1
Ryemere Cl. East 182 C1
Rykneld Cl. Derby 230 C3
Rykneld Ct. Cl Cr 131 E2
Rykneld Dr. Derby 230 C4
Rykneld Rd. Derby 230 C3
Rykneld Rd. Fin 230 C3
Rykneld Rise. Win 115 D2
Rykneld Way. Derby 230 C3
Ryknield Ave. Kilb 192 A4
Ryknield Hill. Denby 180 A1
Rylah Hill. Scarc 117 F3
Rymill Dr. Derby 205 F1

Sacheveral La. Wins 140 C2
Sacheverall Ave. Pinx 160 B2
Sacheverel St. Derby 219 D2
Sackerville Tr. Kill 60 A4
Sackville Cl. Chest 114 A4
Sackville St. Derby 231 F4
Saddlers Cl. Mans 136 C1
Saddleworth Wlk. Derby 232 C2
Sadler Gate. Derby 219 D3
Saffron Dr. Derby 206 A1
Saint John's Rd. Chest 95 F4
St Agnes Ave. Derby 204 B2
St Aidan's Ave. Shef 43 E4
St Aidan's Cl. Shef 43 F4
St Aidan's Dr. Shef 43 F4
St Aidan's Mount. Shef 43 F4
St Aidan's Pl. Shef 43 F4
St Aidan's Rd. Shef 43 F4
St Aidan's Way. Shef 43 F4
St Albans Cl. N Wing 132 C4
St Albans Pl. N Mills 33 E4
St Albans Rd. Derby 218 B2
St Albans St. N Mills 33 E4
St Alkmund's Cl. Duff 190 C2
St Alkmund's Way. Derby 219 D3
St Andrew's Cl. C Camp 263 F1
St Andrew's Dr. Ilk 208 C4
St Andrew's Dr. Som 169 F4
St Andrews Cl. Som 170 A4
St Andrews Ct. Glos 10 A2
St Andrews Rise. Chest 114 B4
St Andrews View. Derby 205 F1
St Andrews Wlk. N Mills 33 E4
St Ann's Cl. C-Frith 46 C3
St Anne's Cl. Baslow 91 F3
St Anne's Cl. Derby 218 C3
St Anne's La. C Don 247 D2
St Annes St. M in L 16 A4
St Augustine St. Derby 218 C1
St Augustines Ave. Chest 115 D4
St Augustines Cres. Chest 115 D4
St Augustines Dr. Chest 96 A1
St Augustines Mnt. Chest 96 A1
St Augustines Rd. Chest 115 D4
St Augustines Rise. Chest 115 D4
St Barnabas La. Shef 43 D4
St Barnabas Rd. Shef 43 D4
St Bride's Wlk. Derby 218 A3
St Catherine's Rd. Swad 255 F3
St Chad's Cl. Dens 196 B3
St Chad's Cl. Dray 235 D4
St Chad's Rd. Derby 218 C1
St Charles Cl. Glos 9 F3
St Clare's Cl. Derby 218 B1
St Cuthbert's Rd. Derby 218 B2
St David's Cl. Derby 218 B2
St David's Rise. Chest 114 B4
St Davids Rd. C Camp 263 F1
St Edmund's Ave. Mans 136 B2
St Edmund's Cl. Derby 204 C2
St Edward's Rd. C Don 247 D1
St Edwards Ct. Swad 255 F3
St Elizabeth Cl. Shef 43 D4
St George's Pl. Belper 178 C2
St Georges Rd. N Mills 33 E4
St Giles Cl. Chest 115 D4
St Giles Rd. Derby 218 C1
St Giles Wlk. Mat 143 E2
St Helen's Cl. Chest 96 A2
St Helen's Cl. Da Da 127 D2
St Helen's Cl. Grin 72 B4
St Helen's Cres. Trow 209 E2
St Helen's Croft. Grin 72 B4
St Helen's Dr. Sels 171 E4
St Helen's La. Wirk 166 A4
St Helen's St. Chest 96 A2
St Helen's St. Derby 218 C3
St Helens Ave. Pinx 160 B2
St Hugh's Cl. Derby 205 D1
St James Ave. Ilk 209 D4
St James Cl. Belper 179 E2
St James Cl. Chest 96 B1
St James Cl. Glos 17 E4
St James Ct. Sand 223 D2
St James' Dr. Brin 182 B4
St James' Sq. N Mills 33 E4
St James' St. Bux 85 D4
St James' St. Derby 219 D1
St James' St. Derby 219 D3
St James' Terr. Bux 85 D4
St James's Ct. Bux 85 E2
St James's St. Staple 223 E3
St James's Terr. Staple 223 E3
St John St. Hay 25 E1
St John's Ave. Derby 220 A3
St John's Cl. Brin 171 E1
St John's Cl. Derby 204 B2
St John's Dr. Derby 220 A3
St John's Dr. Kilb 192 A4
St John's Dr. Swad 255 F3
St John's Mount. Chest 95 F4
St John's Rd. Belper 179 D2
St John's Rd. Bux 85 D4
St John's Rd. Dron 76 C4
St John's Rd. Ilk 209 D4
St John's Rd. Mat Ba 143 D2
St John's Rd. Smal 192 C3
St John's Rd. Tide 69 E2
St John's St. Ashb 173 E1
St John's St. Lo Ea 236 B4
St John's St. Wirk 165 F4
St John's Terr. Derby 218 C3
St Johns Cl. Bam 40 A2
St Johns Pl. Stav 78 B1
St Johns Rd. Stav 78 B1
St Jonn's Cres. Clowne 80 C2
St Joseph's St. Mat 143 E3
St Katherine's La. Row 110 C1
St Lawrence Ave. Bols 118 B4
St Lawrence Cl. Hean 181 F1

St Lawrence Rd. N Wing ... 131 F3
St Lawrence View. Whit ... 81 F3
St Leonards Dr. Chest ... 96 B1
St Leonards Pl. Shirl ... 146 C1
St Lukes Ct. Chest ... 95 F4
St Margaret's Dr. Chest ... 95 F2
St Mark's Cl. Mat Ba ... 155 D3
St Mark's Rd. Chest ... 95 F2
St Mark's Rd. Derby ... 219 E3
St Martin's Rd. Marple ... 23 D3
St Martin's Wlk. Whit ... 82 B3
St Mary St. Ilk ... 208 C4
St Mary's Ave. Dray ... 235 D4
St Mary's Cl. Derby ... 233 D3
St Mary's Cl. N Sol ... 248 C4
St Mary's Cres. Utt ... 210 A1
St Mary's Ct. Derby ... 219 D3
St Mary's Dr. Bu on T ... 240 C1
St Mary's Gate. Chest ... 96 A2
St Mary's Gate. Derby ... 219 D3
St Mary's Gate. Wirk ... 165 F4
St Mary's Rd. Disley ... 32 B3
St Mary's Rd. Glos ... 17 E4
St Mary's Rd. N Mills ... 33 D4
St Mary's Wlk. Sels ... 171 D2
St Matthew's St. Bu on T ... 254 B4
St Matthew's Wlk. Derby ... 204 C1
St Mawes Cl. Derby ... 204 B2
St Mellion Cl. Derby ... 217 F1
St Michael's Cl. Holbr ... 191 E3
St Michael's Cl. Shir ... 200 B4
St Michael's Cl. Will ... 242 A3
St Michael's Dr. S Field ... 265 F1
St Michael's Dr. S Norm ... 160 A4
St Michael's La. Derby ... 219 D3
St Michaels Cl. Crich ... 156 C1
St Michaels Cl. Derby ... 233 E4
St Michaels View. Derby ... 233 E4
St Nicholas Cl. Derby ... 204 B1
St Norbert Dr. Ilk ... 208 B2
St Oswald Cres. Ashb ... 173 E1
St Paul's Rd. Derby ... 219 D4
St Pauls Ave. Chest ... 115 E3
St Peter's Churchyard. Derby ... 219 D3
St Peter's Cl. Belper ... 178 C2
St Peter's Rd. Bux ... 66 B1
St Peter's Rd. Derby ... 233 D1
St Peter's Rd. Th Sa ... 62 C4
St Peter's St. Derby ... 219 D3
St Peters Cft. Belper ... 179 D2
St Peters Cl. Stav ... 98 A2
St Philip's Dr. Chest ... 115 D4
St Quentin Cl. Derby ... 218 B2
St Quentin Cl. Shef ... 56 A3
St Quentin Dr. Shef ... 56 A3
St Quentin Mount. Shef ... 56 A3
St Quentin Rise. Shef ... 56 A3
St Quentin View. Shef ... 56 A3
St Ronan's Ave. Duff ... 190 C1
St Stephen's Cl. Derby ... 231 E3
St Stephen's Ct. Wood ... 256 C2
St Swithin's Cl. Derby ... 218 B2
St Thomas Cl. Tibs ... 147 F3
St Thomas Rd. Derby ... 219 D1
St Thomas Rd. Derby ... 232 A4
St Thomas' St. Chest ... 95 E1
St Vincent Cl. Lo Ea ... 236 C3
St Werburgh's View. Derby ... 220 B3
St Wilfrid's Rd. Shef ... 43 D4
St Wilfrid's Rd. We Ha ... 207 F4
St Wystan's Rd. Derby ... 218 B2
Salcey Cl. Som ... 169 F4
Salcey Dr. Staple ... 209 E1
Salcey Sq. Chest ... 95 E1
Salcombe Rd. Alf ... 159 E3
Sale St. Derby ... 219 D1
Sales Ave. Tupton ... 131 E4
Sales La. Bu on T ... 248 B2
Salisbury Ave. Bu on T ... 248 B2
Salisbury Ave. Chest ... 95 F4
Salisbury Ave. Dron ... 76 A4
Salisbury Cl. Mans ... 136 B2
Salisbury Cres. Chest ... 95 F4
Salisbury Dr. Swad ... 256 C3
Salisbury La. Mel ... 252 A4
Salisbury Rd. Dron ... 76 A4
Salisbury St. Derby ... 219 D2
Salisbury St. Glos ... 10 A3
Salisbury St. Lo Ea ... 236 C4
Sallyfield Lane. Stan ... 183 F4
Sallywood Cl. Derby ... 231 E1
Saltburn Cl. Derby ... 205 E1
Salter Cl. C Don ... 246 C2
Saltergate La. Bam ... 40 B1
Saltergate. Chest ... 96 A2
Salters La. Mat Ba ... 142 C2
Salvin Cres. Clowne ... 80 C2
Samantha Ct. Derby ... 206 A1
Sampson's La. Mans ... 135 D2
Samuel Cl. Shef ... 43 E4
Samuel Dr. Shef ... 43 E4
Samuel Pl. Shef ... 43 E4
Samuel Rd. Shef ... 43 E4
Samuel St. M in L ... 9 E2
Sand La. Dove ... 211 D1
Sandalwood Cl. Derby ... 233 E4
Sandalwood Rd. Bu on T ... 254 C3
Sandbach Cl. Derby ... 206 A1
Sandbed La. Belper ... 179 E2
Sandby Croft. Shef ... 43 F1
Sandby Ct. Shef ... 43 F1
Sandby Dr. Marple ... 23 D4
Sandby Dr. Shef ... 43 F1
Sandcliffe Park. Swad ... 256 B4
Sandcliffe Rd. Swad ... 256 B3
Sandcroft Cl. Swad ... 256 B3
Sandcroft Rd. Derby ... 220 C3
Sanderson Rd. Derby ... 220 A3
Sandfield Cl. Derby ... 220 A4
Sandfield Rd. Bees ... 223 F1
Sandford Ave. Lo Ea ... 236 C4
Sandgate Ave. Mans ... 136 B2
Sandgate Cl. Derby ... 233 D3
Sandgate Rd. Mans ... 136 B2
Sandhall La. Spout ... 166 C3
Sandham La. Ripley ... 169 E1
Sandhill La. Cha ... 16 A1
Sandhill La. Marple ... 15 F1
Sandhills Rd. Bols ... 99 E1
Sandiacre Rd. Staple ... 223 E3
Sandiway. Chest ... 114 B4
Sandiway. Glos ... 17 F4
Sandlands The. Swad ... 256 B3
Sandown Ave. Derby ... 217 E2
Sandown Cl. Eck ... 59 D2
Sandown Rd. Bees ... 223 F1
Sandown Rd. Derby ... 232 C4
Sandringham Ave. Bu on T ... 248 A1
Sandringham Cl. Calow ... 97 D2
Sandringham Ct. Mans ... 136 A3
Sandringham Dr. Derby ... 220 C3
Sandringham Dr. Mans ... 136 A3
Sandringham Pl. Ilk ... 208 B3
Sandringham Rd. Calow ... 97 D2
Sandringham Rd. Derby ... 205 F1
Sandringham Rd. Mans ... 136 C3
Sandringham Rd. Sand ... 223 D2
Sands Cl. Shef ... 43 F2
Sandstone Ave. Chest ... 114 A4
Sandwood Cl. Newt ... 148 A2
Sandy Cl. Whit ... 81 F3
Sandy La. Cald ... 261 D4
Sandy La. Cha ... 16 A2
Sandy La. Crich ... 167 F4
Sandy La. Hors ... 192 A2
Sandy La. Mat ... 143 E4
Sandybank Cl. Glos ... 9 F2
Sandybrook Cl. Ashb ... 173 E2
Sandycliffe Cl. Mans ... 136 C1
Sandyford La. Alder ... 166 C2
Sandyford La. Spout ... 166 C2
Sandypits La. Etwall ... 229 E2
Sanforth St. Chest ... 96 A3
Santolina Dr. Derby ... 205 F1
Sapperton Cl. Derby ... 231 E3
Sapperton La. Boyl ... 213 F1
Sapperton La. Ch Bro ... 213 F1
Sarah Cl. Som ... 170 B4
Sark Rd. Shef ... 43 D4
Saundby Ave. Mans ... 135 E1
Saundersfoot Way. Derby ... 206 B1
Savage La. Totley ... 55 E4
Saville Cl. Staple ... 223 F4
Saw Pit La. Tibs ... 148 A3
Sawley Rd. Brea ... 235 F3
Sawley Rd. Dray ... 235 D4
Sawpit La. Hatton ... 227 E1
Saxon Cl. Bu on T ... 254 C4
Saxon Gr. Will ... 242 A3
Saxon Rd. Shef ... 43 D4
Saxon St. Bu on T ... 254 C4
Saxondale Ave. Derby ... 217 E2
Saxton Ave. Hean ... 181 F1
Scaddows La. Tick ... 250 C2
Scalby Cl. East ... 182 B1
Scaliot Cl. N Mills ... 33 D4
Scalpcliffe Rd. Bu on T ... 248 A1
Scarborough Ave. Ilk ... 208 C4
Scarborough Rise. Derby ... 205 E1
Scarcliffe Cl. Derby ... 232 C2
Scarcliffe La. Scarc ... 119 E4
Scarcliffe Terr. Scarc ... 101 D1
Scargill Rd. We Ha ... 207 F4
Scargill Wlk. East ... 182 C2
Scarsdale Ave. Derby ... 204 B2
Scarsdale Ave. Derby ... 218 B1
Scarsdale Cl. Dron ... 76 A4
Scarsdale Cres. Chest ... 96 B4
Scarsdale Cross. Dron ... 57 D1
Scarsdale Pl. Bux ... 85 D4
Scarsdale Rd. Chest ... 96 A4
Scarsdale Rd. Dron ... 57 D1
Scarsdale Rd. Duff ... 190 C2
Scarsdale St. Bols ... 117 F4
Scarthin. Mat Ba ... 155 D3
School Ave. Mosb ... 59 F4
School Board La. Chest ... 95 F2
School Cl. F Bent ... 162 A1
School Cl. Moira ... 256 B1
School Cl. Mosb ... 59 F4
School Cl. Newt ... 147 E1
School Cl. Shirl ... 146 B1
School Cl. Shirl ... 146 C2
School Croft. Som ... 170 B3
School House Hill. Ripley ... 168 B1
School La. Ashb ... 173 D1
School La. Baslow ... 91 F3
School La. Beeley ... 111 D2
School La. Brack ... 145 E1
School La. C Don ... 247 D2
School La. Derby ... 233 D1
School La. Dron ... 57 D1
School La. Eck ... 58 C2
School La. Hassop ... 90 C3
School La. Hath ... 53 D4
School La. Mans ... 136 B2
School La. Marple ... 15 D2
School La. O Bram ... 93 F2
School La. Ripley ... 168 B1
School La. Ripley ... 169 E1
School La. Rolle ... 240 B2
School La. Row ... 126 C4
School La. S Norm ... 160 A2
School La. S-by-D ... 222 C4
School La. Shef ... 56 C4
School La. Shef ... 57 E4
School La. St Pk ... 126 B3
School La. Sud ... 225 F2
School La. Tadd ... 87 F2
School Lane Cl. Shef ... 43 E1
School Rd. Bux ... 67 D3
School Rd. Chest ... 96 A4
School Rd. Mat ... 143 E3
School Rd. Utt ... 210 A1
School Sq. We Ha ... 207 F4
School St. Eck ... 59 E2
School St. Moira ... 262 C1
School St. Mosb ... 59 E4
School St. Swad ... 256 A1
Schoolpiece La. Ch Bro ... 227 E4
Scothches The. Belper ... 178 C3
Scotia Dr. Shef ... 43 F4
Scotland St. Whit ... 81 F3
Scotswood Rd. Mans ... 136 A3
Scott Cl. Gra ... 115 F2
Scott Cres. Shirl ... 146 C2
Scott Dr. Belper ... 179 F3
Scott Dr. Marple ... 23 D4
Scott Dr. Som ... 170 B4
Scott St. Derby ... 218 C1
Scott St. Scarc ... 101 D1
Scotts The. Linton ... 261 E4
Scowerdons Cl. Shef ... 44 C3
Scowerdons Dr. Shef ... 44 C3
Scratta La. Whit ... 63 E1
Screetham La. Ash ... 112 E1
Scropton Old Rd. Hatton ... 239 E4
Scropton Rd. Hatton ... 239 D4
Scropton Rd. Scro ... 226 C1
Scropton Wlk. Derby ... 232 C2
Sea Breeze Terr. Shef ... 44 C4
Seaburn Rd. Bees ... 223 F1
Seaford Way. Ilk ... 194 C3
Seagrave Ave. Shef ... 44 A2
Seagrave Cl. Derby ... 220 A4
Seagrave Cres. Shef ... 44 A2
Seagrave Dr. Shef ... 44 A2
Seagrave Rd. Shef ... 44 A2
Seal View. Linton ... 261 E3
Seale St. Derby ... 219 D4
Sealey Cl. Will ... 242 B3
Seals Rd. Donis ... 262 C1
Sealwood La. Neth ... 261 F2
Sealwood La. Neth ... 261 F3
Seamer Rd. Kim ... 195 F4
Seanor La. Pils ... 132 A2
Searl St. Derby ... 218 C3
Searson Ave. Bols ... 99 D1
Searston Ave. N Wing ... 132 B4
Seascale Cl. Derby ... 205 E1
Seaton Cl. Derby ... 217 E2
Second Ave. Derby ... 245 D4
Second Ave. Risley ... 222 C3
Sedbergh Cres. Chest ... 95 E4
Sedgebrook Cl. Derby ... 205 F1
Sedgebrook St. Mans ... 136 C2
Sedgefield Green. Derby ... 217 E1
Sedgemoor Cl. O Bram ... 95 D2
Sedgwick St. La Mi ... 182 A2
Sedgwick St. Sels ... 171 D2
Sefton Ave. Staple ... 223 F4
Sefton Cl. Bu on T ... 248 A1
Sefton Rd. Derby ... 219 F3
Sefton St. Glos ... 17 E4
Selborne St. Derby ... 219 E1
Selby Cl. Bees ... 223 F2
Selby Cl. Chest ... 114 B4
Selhurst Rd. Chest ... 95 F3
Selina Cl. C Don ... 247 D2
Selkirk St. Derby ... 219 F4
Selly Oak Gr. Shef ... 57 D2
Selly Oak Rd. Shef ... 57 E3
Selmer Ct. Chest ... 96 B4
Selston Rd. Sels ... 171 D3
Selworthy Cl. Derby ... 206 A1
Selwyn St. Derby ... 218 B3
Selwyn St. Scarc ... 118 B4
Senners La. Chel ... 87 D1
Serina Ave. Derby ... 231 E4
Setcup La. Eck ... 59 E1
Sett Cl. N Mills ... 33 D4
Settlement The. Ock ... 221 E3
Setts Way. Win ... 115 D2
Seven Oaks Rd. S-by-D ... 209 D1
Sevenoaks Ave. Derby ... 217 F3
Severals. Staple ... 223 F4
Severn Cl. Bu on T ... 240 B1
Severn Cres. N Wing ... 132 A3
Severn St. Derby ... 232 C4
Severnale Cl. Derby ... 205 D3
Sewell Rd. Mosb ... 59 F3
Sexton St. Tint ... 9 F4
Seymour Cl. Derby ... 218 B3
Seymour La. Stav ... 79 E1
Seymour Rd. East ... 182 C1
Shacklecross Cl. Ock ... 221 E1
Shady Gr. Hilton ... 228 B1
Shaftesbury Ave. Chest ... 95 E2
Shaftesbury Ave. Lo Ea ... 236 A2
Shaftesbury Ave. Mans ... 135 F1
Shaftesbury Ave. Sand ... 223 D3
Shaftesbury Cres. Derby ... 219 D1
Shaftesbury St S. Derby ... 219 D1
Shaftesbury St. Derby ... 219 D1
Shafton Cl. Cl Cr ... 131 F2
Shafton Wlk. Cl Cr ... 131 F2
Shakespeare Ave. Elmt ... 81 E1
Shakespeare Ave. Mans ... 136 A2
Shakespeare Ave. Shirl ... 146 B2
Shakespeare Cl. Cl Cr ... 131 D3
Shakespeare Cl. Swad ... 256 B3
Shakespeare Cres. Dron ... 76 B4
Shakespeare Dr. Alf ... 159 D2
Shakespeare Rd. Awsw ... 195 E3
Shakespeare St. Derby ... 232 A3
Shakespeare St. Gra ... 115 F2
Shakespeare St. Lo Ea ... 223 E1
Shakespeare St. N Wing ... 116 B1
Shaldon Dr. Derby ... 218 B1
Shalfleet Dr. Derby ... 233 E3
Shallcross Ave. W Br ... 45 F2
Shallcross Cres. W Br ... 45 F2
Shallcross Rd. W Br ... 45 F2
Shambles The. Chest ... 96 A2
Shamrock Pl. Stav ... 79 E2
Shamrock St. Derby ... 218 C1
Shanklin Dr. Staple ... 223 E4
Shannon Cl. Derby ... 231 E3
Shap Cl. Chest ... 95 E3
Shardlow Rd. As on T ... 246 B4
Shardlow Rd. Derby ... 233 E3
Sharman Cl. Uns ... 58 A1
Sharp Cl. Ilk ... 208 B3
Sharp Cl. Lo Ea ... 236 B3
Sharpe Ave. Shef ... 56 C4
Sharrard Cl. Shef ... 44 A3
Sharrard Dr. Shef ... 44 A3
Sharrard Gr. Shef ... 44 A3
Sharrard Rd. Shef ... 44 A3
Shatton La. Shat ... 51 F4
Shaw St. Glos ... 17 E4
Shaw La. Belper ... 191 D4
Shaw La. Glos ... 9 F2
Shaw La. Hollow ... 156 B4
Shaw La. M Mont ... 198 A1
Shaw St E. Ilk ... 209 D3
Shaw St W. Ilk ... 209 D3
Shaw St. Chest ... 96 A4
Shaw St. Derby ... 218 C3
Shaw St. Dron ... 57 E2
Shaw St. M in L ... 9 D2
Shaw St. N Wing ... 116 B1
Shaw St. Som ... 170 B3
Shaw's Row. Chest ... 95 E1
Shaw's Yd. Kilb ... 191 F4
Shawcroft Ave. Som ... 170 B3
Shawcroft. Ashb ... 173 E1
Shawfield Rd. Glos ... 9 F2
Shaws Green. Derby ... 218 C3
Shaws Hill. Crich ... 156 B1
Sheaf Bank. Shef ... 43 D4
Sheardhall Ave. Disley ... 32 C3
Sheards Cl.Dron ... 56 C1
Sheards Dr. Dron ... 56 C1
Sheards Way. Dron ... 56 C1
Shearwater Cl. Derby ... 231 E4
Sheepbridge La. Chest ... 76 C1
Sheepcote Rd. Kill ... 60 B3
Sheephill Rd. Totley ... 42 C1
Sheeplea La. Ash ... 129 F4
Sheepwash La. Ash ... 145 D4
Sheffield Pl. Derby ... 219 E2
Sheffield Rd. Barl ... 79 E4
Sheffield Rd. Baslow ... 92 A4
Sheffield Rd. C-Frith ... 47 F4
Sheffield Rd. Chest ... 76 C2
Sheffield Rd. Chest ... 96 A3
Sheffield Rd. Dron ... 56 C2
Sheffield Rd. Eck ... 59 F3
Sheffield Rd. Elmt ... 81 E2
Sheffield Rd. Glos ... 10 C1
Sheffield Rd. Hath ... 53 D4
Sheffield Rd. Kill ... 60 B4
Sheffield Rd. Mosb ... 59 F3
Sheffield Rd. Shef ... 44 C1
Sheffield Rd. Uns ... 76 C2
Sheffield Rd. Whit ... 81 E2
Sheldon Cl. Lo Ea ... 223 D2
Sheldon Ct. Derby ... 232 C2
Sheldon Mews. Glos ... 9 E1
Sheldon Rd. Chest ... 95 D3
Sheldon Rd. Hean ... 181 E3
Shelford Cl. Derby ... 217 E2
Shelley Ave. Mans ... 136 A2
Shelley Dr. Derby ... 232 A3
Shelley Dr. Dron ... 76 B4
Shelley Gr. Shirl ... 146 C2
Shelley St. N Wing ... 116 B1
Shelly Rd. Swad ... 256 B3
Shelmory Cl. Derby ... 232 C3
Shelton Cl. Mans ... 135 F1
Shelton Dr. Derby ... 232 C2
Shenington Way. Derby ... 206 A1
Shepherd St. Derby ... 218 B1
Shepherd's La. Tick ... 251 E3
Shepherd's Row. Uns ... 77 D4
Shepley St. Chest ... 95 E1
Shepley St. Glos ... 10 C1
Shepley's Yd. Chest ... 96 A2
Shepton Cl. Ship ... 194 B2
Sherbourne Ave. Chest ... 95 F4
Sherbourne Dr. Bran ... 254 A4
Sherbrook Gr. Bux ... 85 E3
Sherbrooke Rd. Disley ... 32 B3
Sheridan Ct. Staple ... 209 F1
Sheridan St. Derby ... 231 F3
Sheriff Dr. Mat ... 143 D3
Sherriff's Lea. Bees ... 223 F1
Sherston Cl. Derby ... 206 A1
Sherwin Rd. Staple ... 209 F1
Sherwin St. Derby ... 218 C4
Sherwood Ave. Derby ... 219 F4
Sherwood Ave. Derby ... 231 E3
Sherwood Ave. Elmt ... 81 E1
Sherwood Ave. Hope ... 39 D2
Sherwood Ave. Ock ... 221 E1
Sherwood Ave. Pinx ... 160 B2
Sherwood Ave. Shireb ... 119 F2
Sherwood Chase. Totley ... 55 F3
Sherwood Copse. Tide ... 69 E2
Sherwood Dr. Shireb ... 119 F2
Sherwood Fold. Cha ... 16 B4
Sherwood Pl. Dron ... 56 B1
Sherwood Rd. Bux ... 85 E3
Sherwood Rd. Kill ... 60 C4
Sherwood Rd. Mat ... 143 E2
Sherwood Rd. Shef ... 56 C4
Sherwood Rd. Tide ... 69 E2
Sherwood Rise. East ... 182 C1
Sherwood Rise. Mans ... 136 C2
Sherwood St. Bols ... 117 F4
Sherwood St. Chest ... 96 A1
Sherwood St. Derby ... 218 C2
Sherwood St. Mans ... 136 A1
Sherwood St. Newt ... 148 A2
Sherwood St. S in A ... 148 C2
Sherwood St. Shirl ... 146 B3
Sherwood St. Som ... 170 B4
Shetland Cl. Derby ... 219 E4
Shetland Cl. Mans ... 136 C1
Shetland Rd. Dron ... 76 A4
Shetland Rd. Tibs ... 147 F3
Shields Cres. C Don ... 246 C2
Shieling The. Hatton ... 227 E1
Shilling Way. Lo Ea ... 236 A4
Shiloh Rd. Marple ... 24 A3
Shinwell Ave. Stav ... 97 D4
Shipley Ct. Ilk ... 194 B1
Shipley La. Mapp ... 193 F3
Shipley La. Ship ... 193 F3
Shipley Wlk. Derby ... 232 C2
Shipman Ct. Mosb ... 59 E4
Shipstone St. Ilk ... 209 D3
Shire La. Heath ... 116 C2
Shire La. L Duk ... 116 C2
Shire Way. Glos ... 10 C2
Shirebrook Dr. Glos ... 17 F4
Shirebrook Rd. Shef ... 43 D3
Shireoaks Comm. Shire ... 63 F4
Shireoaks Rd. Dron ... 57 E1
Shireoaks Rd. Shire ... 63 F3
Shireoaks Row. Shire ... 63 F4
Shireoaks. Belper ... 178 B3
Shires The. Mans ... 136 C1
Shirland St. Chest ... 96 A2
Shirley Cl. C Don ... 247 D2
Shirley Cl. Chest ... 95 D
Shirley Cl. Hope ... 39 D
Shirley Cres. Brea ... 235 E4
Shirley Park. As on T ... 246 A4
Shirley Rd. Derby ... 205 F1
Shirley Rd. Ripley ... 169 E1
Shirley Rd. Som ... 169 F4
Shirley St. Lo Ea ... 236 A2
Shop La. Ripley ... 168 B1
Shop Stones. Ock ... 221 E
Shoreham St. Shef ... 43 D
Short Ave. Derby ... 204 C
Short Cl. Holy ... 113 E4
Short Hill. Br Hill ... 252 C
Short La. C Don ... 246 C
Short Lands. Belper ... 179 D
Short Row. Belper ... 178 C
Short St. Belper ... 179 D
Short St. Bu on T ... 254 C
Shortbrook Bank. Mosb ... 59 F4
Shortbrook Cl. Mosb ... 59 F4
Shortbrook Croft. Mosb ... 59 F4
Shortbrook Dr. Mosb ... 59 F4

Shortbrook Rd. Mosb 59 F4
Shortbrook Way. Mosb 59 F4
Shortbrook Wlk. Mosb 59 F4
Shortheath Rd. Moira 262 C2
Shortheath. Over 262 B2
Shortlands The. Mat 143 D2
Shorts La. Totley 55 D3
Shorwell Gdns. Derby 233 E3
Shottle Wlk. Derby 232 C2
Shotwoodhill La. Rolle 240 A3
Shrewsbury Cl. Derby 206 B1
Shrewsbury Rd. Bu on T 240 C1
Shrewsbury St. Glos 10 B1
Shropshire Ave. Derby 219 F4
Shropshire Ave. Sels 171 E2
Shropshire Dr. Glos 17 F4
Shrubbery The. Wood 257 D1
Shuckstone La. Crich 156 C3
Shudehill Cl. Hay 25 E2
Shuttlewood Rd. Bols 99 D2
Shutts La. Bake 109 E2
Sicklebrook La. Eck 57 F2
Sickleholme. Bam 40 A1
Siddals La. Derby 204 C2
Siddals Rd. Derby 219 D2
Siddals St. Bu on T 248 A2
Siddons St. Derby 233 D4
Side End La. Kettle 45 D1
Sides La. Snel 184 A3
Sidings The. Derby 220 A2
Sidings Way. Newt 147 E1
Sidlaw Cl. Chest 95 E3
Sidmouth Cl. Derby 233 E4
Sidney Cl. Derby 217 F2
Sidney St. Derby 219 D2
Sidney St. Kim 195 F3
Sidney St. Lo Ea 236 B3
Silk Hill. W Br 46 A4
Silk Mill La. Tut 239 E3
Silk St. Glos 10 C1
Silken Holme. S Norm 160 A2
Silkstone Cl. Shef 44 C2
Silkstone Cres. Shef 44 C2
Silkstone Pl. Shef 44 C2
Silkstone Rd. Shef 44 C2
Silver Birch Cres. Newt 159 E4
Silver Hill Rd. Derby 219 D1
Silver La. Elv 234 A3
Silver La. March 224 C1
Silver Mill Rd. Shef 43 D4
Silverburn Dr. Derby 206 A1
Silverdale Ave. Mans 136 A2
Silverdale Cl. Chest 76 C1
Silverdale. Staple 223 F3
Silverhill Cl. Bu on T 240 B1
Silverhill La. S in A 148 C4
Silverhill Rd. Derby 220 C2
Silverlands Cl. Bux 85 E4
Silverlands Park. Bux 85 E4
Silverlands. Bux 85 E4
Silverton Dr. Derby 231 E1
Silvey Gr. Derby 220 B2
Simcoe Leys. Derby 233 D1
Simcrest Ave. Kill 60 B3
Simmondley Gr. Glos 17 D4
Simmondley La. Glos 17 D4
Simmondley New Rd. Glos 17 D4
Simon Fields Cl. Stanl 193 D1
Simons Cl. Glos 17 D4
Simons Wlk. Glos 17 D4
Simpson St. Derby 232 C3
Sims Ave. Derby 218 C3
Sims Croft. Uns 77 E3
Sinclair Cl. Derby 231 F2
Sinfin Ave. Derby 232 B2
Sinfin Fields Cres. Derby 232 B3
Sinfin La. Ba on T 244 A3
Sinfin La. Derby 231 F2
Sinfin La. Derby 232 A3
Sinfin Moor La. Derby 231 F2
Sinfin Moor La. Derby 232 C1
Sir Frank Whittle Rd. Derby 219 E4
Sir Henry's La. Mel 252 A2
Sir Josephs La. Da Da 127 D2
Sir William Hill Rd. Eyam 71 E4
Sisley Ave. Staple 223 F3
Sister's La. Ock 221 E3
Sitch La. Callow 165 D2
Sitch La. N Mills 24 C2
Sitch Rd. Wens 142 B4
Sitwell Ave. Chest 95 F1
Sitwell Cl. Derby 220 B2
Sitwell Dr. Kilb 192 A4
Sitwell Grange La. Pils 147 E4
Sitwell Grange La. Tibs 147 E4
Sitwell St. Derby 219 D2
Sitwell St. Derby 220 C2
Sitwell St. Eck 59 E2
Sitwell Villas. Morton 146 C3
Sitwell. Mosb 59 F4
Skeavington's La. Ilk 194 C3
Skeldale Dr. Chest 115 D4
Skelton Rd. Shef 43 D3
Skelwith Cl. Chest 95 E4
Skiddaw Cl. Chest 95 E3
Skiddaw Dr. Derby 217 F1
Skinner St. Elmt 81 E1
Skipton Cl. Ship 194 B2
Skipton Green. Derby 205 E1
Skye Gdns. Tibs 147 F3
Slack La. Ash 129 E1
Slack La. Brai 187 E1
Slack La. Chest 95 D2
Slack La. Derby 204 C1
Slack La. Derby 218 B3
Slack La. Harts 257 D3
Slack La. May 184 B4
Slack La. Ripley 168 B2
Slack La. Ripley 169 E1
Slack La. S Wing 157 E4
Slack La. Ship 193 F4
Slack La. Som 170 B3
Slack's La. Pils 132 B1
Slackey La. Moira 262 B2
Slacks La. Hay 25 E3
Slade Cl. Etwall 229 E2
Slade Cl. S Norm 160 A2
Slade Fields. Utt 210 A1
Slade Hollow La. Holl 201 D2
Slade La. W Und 202 C4
Slag La. Uns 77 E3
Slaidburn Cl. Derby 217 F1
Slaley La. Bons 154 B4
Slaley View Rd. Barl 80 A3
Slaney Cl. Derby 232 C4
Slant Cl. Glos 17 E4
Slant La. Mans 136 A2
Slant The. Shireb 119 E2
Slate St. Shef 43 D4
Slatelands Ave. Glos 17 D4
Slatelands Rd. Glos 17 D4
Slatepit La. Barlow 93 E4
Slatepit La. O Bram 93 E4
Slater Ave. Derby 218 C3
Slater Cres. Wirk 165 F4
Slater St. Cl Cr 131 E2
Slayley Hill. Clowne 80 B2
Slayley View. Clowne 80 B3
Slaypit La. Th Sa 62 B3
Sledgegate La. Hollow 156 A4
Sledmere Cl. Derby 233 E4
Sleepy La. Mel 245 E1
Sleetmoor La. Som 170 A4
Sleights La. Pinx 160 B1
Slindon Croft. Derby 233 E3
Slipperlow La. Tadd 87 F1
Sloade La. Eck 58 B3
Sloane Rd. Derby 218 A3
Small Gate. Mans 136 C3
Small Knowle End. Wor 67 E3
Small Meer Cl. Derby 232 C1
Small Thorn Pl. Wood 256 C1
Smalldale Cotts. Wor 67 E4
Smalldale Head Rd. Bradw 50 C4
Smalldale Rd. Shef 44 B2
Smalldale Rd. Wor 67 E4
Smalley Dr. Derby 206 A2
Smalley Mill Rd. Hors 192 A2
Smalley Mill Rd. Smal 192 A2
Smeath Rd. Sels 171 F1
Smeckley Wood Cl. Chest 76 B2
Smedley Ave. Ilk 209 D4
Smedley Ave. Som 159 E1
Smedley Ct. Eg 241 D3
Smedley Pl. Glos 10 C1
Smedley St E. Mat 143 E3
Smedley St W. Mat 143 D4
Smedley St. Mat 143 D3
Smedley's Ave. Sand 223 D3
Smeeton St. Hean 182 A1
Smelter Wood Ave. Shef 44 C4
Smelter Wood Cl. Shef 44 C4
Smelter Wood Cres. Shef 44 C4
Smelter Wood Ct. Shef 44 C4
Smelter Wood Dr. Shef 44 C4
Smelter Wood La. Shef 44 C4
Smelter Wood Pl. Shef 44 C4
Smelter Wood Rd. Shef 44 C4
Smelter Wood Rise. Shef 44 C4
Smelter Wood Way. Shef 44 C4
Smeltinghouse La. Barlow 75 F2
Smisby Rd. Ash-Z 258 A1
Smisby Way. Derby 232 C2
Smith Ave. Codnor 170 A1
Smith Ave. Mel 245 D1
Smith Ave. Stav 97 E4
Smith Cres. Chest 96 B1
Smith Dr. La Mi 182 A2
Smith Rd. Mat 143 D3
Smith-Hall La. H Ward 188 A4
Smithfield Ave. Chest 115 E4
Smithfield Ave. Trow 209 E2
Smithfield Rd. Shef 44 A2
Smithson Ave. Bols 99 D1
Smithurst Rd. Greas 195 D4
Smithy Ave. Cl Cr 131 E2
Smithy Cl. Glos 10 B1
Smithy Cl. Par 151 E1
Smithy Croft. Dron 56 B1
Smithy Fold. Glos 10 B1
Smithy Hill. Bradw 51 D4
Smithy Knoll Rd. Calver 72 B1
Smithy La. C Camp 263 F1
Smithy La. Marple 15 F1
Smithy Meadows. Hath 53 D4
Smithy Pl. Gra 115 F1
Smuse La. Mat 143 F2
Snake La. Duff 190 C2
Snake Rd. Glos 18 B4
Snake Rd. High Peak 28 B4
Snape Hill Dr. Dron 57 D2
Snape Hill La. Dron 57 D1
Snape Hill. Dron 57 D1
Snapehill Cl. Dron 57 D2
Snapehill Cres. Dron 57 D2
Snapes La. Snel 184 A1
Snelsmoor La. Derby 233 D1
Snelston Cl. Shef 56 C4
Snelston Cres. Derby 218 B1
Snipe Cl. Holy 113 E4
Snipesmoor La. Ashb 185 F4
Snitterton Rd. Mat 143 D3
Snowdon La. Eck 58 A2
Snowdrop Valley. Crich 168 A4
Snowfield View. Wirk 165 F3
Soaper La. Dron 57 D1
Soarbank Cl. Kim 195 F4
Society Pl. Derby 219 D1
Soft Water La. Bradw 51 D4
Solney Cl. Swad 255 F2
Soloman Rd. Coss 195 D1
Solway Cl. Derby 206 A1
Solway Rise. Dron 56 B1
Somerby Way. Derby 205 F1
Somercotes Hill. Som 170 B4
Somercotes Rd. Shef 44 B3
Somersal Cl. Derby 232 C2
Somersall Cl. Chest 95 D1
Somersall La. Chest 95 D1
Somersall Park Rd. Chest 95 D1
Somersby Ave. Chest 114 A4
Somerset Cl. Bux 85 E2
Somerset Cl. Lo Ea 237 D4
Somerset Dr. Chest 97 D4
Somerset Rd. Bu on T 254 B3
Somerset St. Derby 219 E4
Somme Rd. Quar 204 A2
Sookholme Cl. Shireb 119 F2
Sookholme La. Mar War 120 C3
Sookholme Rd. Mar War 120 C1
Sookholme Rd. Shireb 119 F2
Soresby St. Chest 96 A2
Sough La. Tadd 87 E1
Sough La. Wirk 154 C1
Sough La. Wirk 155 D1
Sough Rd. S Norm 160 A4
Soughley La. Hal M 42 B4
South Ave. Bux 85 D4
South Ave. Derby 205 D2
South Ave. Derby 218 B1
South Ave. Derby 220 C2
South Ave. Derby 232 C2
South Ave. Shireb 119 F2
South Brae Cl. Derby 231 E4
South Broadway St. Bu on T 254 B4
South Church St. Bake 109 E3
South Cl. Tint 9 F4
South Cl. Uns 76 C3
South Cres. Bols 99 D1
South Cres. Kill 60 C4
South Cres. Stav 98 A3
South Dr. Derby 218 A1
South Dr. Derby 218 C4
South Dr. Derby 220 A3
South Dr. Derby 232 C2
South Dr. Swad 255 F3
South Hill La. Stret 145 F3
South Hill. Rolle 240 B2
South Hill. Stret 145 F4
South Lodge Ct. O Bram 95 D2
South Marlow St. Glos 10 A2
South Oak St. Bu on T 254 A4
South Parade. Mat Ba 143 D1
South Park Ave. Da Da 127 E2
South Pl. Chest 95 E1
South Pl. Chest 96 A1
South Pl. Ripley 169 E1
South St N. Uns 77 E3
South St. Ashb 173 E1
South St. Bux 85 D4
South St. Chest 96 A1
South St. Derby 218 C3
South St. Dray 235 D4
South St. East 182 C1
South St. Greas 195 E4
South St. Ilk 208 C4
South St. Lo Ea 236 C4
South St. Mel 252 A4
South St. Mosb 59 E3
South St. Newt 147 F1
South St. Pils 132 B1
South St. S Norm 160 A3
South St. Som 169 F4
South St. Som 170 B3
South St. Wood 257 D1
South Uxbridge St. Bu on T 254 A4
South View Rd. Glos 17 F4
South View Wlk. Roc 196 C2
South View. Bam 40 A2
South View. May 184 B3
South View. Mosb 60 A4
South View. N Mills 33 D4
South View. Whit 81 F3
Southall St. Shef 43 D3
Southard's La. Th Sa 62 C3
Southbrook Cl. Glos 9 F2
Southcote Dr. Shef 56 C4
Southcroft. Alf 159 D2
Southcroft. Bux 85 D4
Southcroft. Derby 231 E2
Southdown Ave. Chest 95 E3
Southdown Cl. Derby 231 E1
Southend. Gra 115 F1
Southfield Ave. Chest 115 E3
Southfield Cl. Whit 81 F3
Southfield Dr. Dron 76 B4
Southfield Dr. S Norm 160 B3
Southfield La. Whit 82 A2
Southfield Mount. Dron 76 B4
Southfields Ave. Pinx 160 B2
Southfields. Clowne 80 C2
Southfields. Lo Ea 236 C4
Southgate Cl. Derby 217 E2
Southgate Cres. Clowne 80 C3
Southgate Way. Stav 78 A2
Southgate. Eck 59 F2
Southmoor Cl. Chest 96 C2
Southwark Cl. Derby 218 A3
Southwood Ave. Dron 76 A4
Southwood Dr. Clowne 80 C2
Southwood St. Derby 232 C4
Sovereign Gr. Lo Ea 236 A4
Sovereign Way. Derby 206 B2
Sowbrook Brook. Ilk 208 B2
Sowbrook La. S-by-D 208 C2
Sowter Rd. Derby 219 D3
Spa Brook Cl. Shef 44 C2
Spa Brook Dr. Shef 44 C3
Spa Croft. Tibs 147 F3
Spa La. Chest 96 A1
Spa La. Derby 218 C2
Spa View Ave. Shef 44 C2
Spa View Dr. Shef 44 C2
Spa View Pl. Shef 44 C2
Spa View Rd. Shef 44 C2
Spa View Terr. Shef 44 C2
Spa View Way. Shef 44 C2
Spalden Ave. Ashb 173 E2
Spang La. S in A 148 C2
Spanker La. Ripley 168 A1
Spanker Terr. Ripley 168 B1
Speedwell Cl. Derby 206 B2
Speedwell Cl. Tint 9 F4
Speedwell. Tint 9 F4
Speighthill Cres. Win 114 C2
Spenbeck Dr. Derby 205 D3
Spencer Ave. Belper 179 D2
Spencer Ave. Derby 232 B2
Spencer Ave. Sand 223 D3
Spencer Ave. Stav 79 D1
Spencer Cl. Bu on T 240 B1
Spencer Cres. Staple 223 F4
Spencer Dr. Som 170 B4
Spencer Gr. Bux 85 D3
Spencer Rd. Belper 179 D2
Spencer Rd. Bux 85 D3
Spencer Rd. C-Frith 46 C3
Spencer Rd. Shef 43 D4
Spencer St. Bols 117 F4
Spencer St. Chest 96 A2
Spencer St. Derby 233 D4
Spencer St. Stanl 193 D1
Spend La. Mapple 173 D3
Spend La. Thorpe 161 F1
Spender Cl. Ashb 185 E4
Sperry Cl. Sels 171 F3
Spindletree Dr. Derby 205 F1
Spinkhill Ave. Shef 44 B4
Spinkhill Dr. Shef 44 B4
Spinkhill La. Eck 60 A1
Spinkhill Rd. Kill 60 C2
Spinkhill Rd. Shef 44 B4
Spinnerbottom. N Mills 24 C1
Spinney Cl. Derby 205 D1
Spinney Cl. Glos 10 B1
Spinney Cl. Mans 136 C3
Spinney Cres. Bees 223 F2
Spinney Dr. Lo Ea 223 E1
Spinney Hill. Mel 252 A4
Spinney Rd. Bran 253 F4
Spinney Rd. Derby 218 C2
Spinney Rd. Derby 219 F4
Spinney Rd. Ilk 208 C3
Spinney Rd. Lo Ea 223 E1
Spinney Rise. Bees 223 F2
Spinney The. Belper 179 D3
Spinney The. C Don 247 D2
Spinney The. Ock 221 E1
Spinney The. Ripley 169 E2
Spinney The. S-by-D 222 C4
Spinney The. Shireb 119 E2
Spire Hollin. Glos 10 B1
Spital Gdns. Chest 96 B1
Spital La. Chest 96 B1
Spitewinter La. Barlow 93 E4
Spittal Green. Bols 118 A4
Spittal Hill. C Don 247 D2
Spittal. C Don 247 D2
Spooner La. Curbar 72 B3
Sporton Cl. S Norm 160 A4
Sporton La. S Norm 160 A4
Spotswood Cl. Shef 43 F2
Spotswood Dr. Shef 43 F3
Spotswood Mount. Shef 43 F2
Spotswood Pl. Shef 43 E2
Spotswood Rd. Shef 43 E3
Spout La. Spout 166 B2
Spout La. Tans 144 A2
Spring Bank Rd. Chest 95 F2
Spring Bank Rd. N Mills 33 E4
Spring Bank. Bux 67 E2
Spring Bank. G Lo 90 A2
Spring Cl Dell. Shef 43 F2
Spring Cl Mount. Shef 43 F2
Spring Cl View. Shef 43 F2
Spring Cl. Belper 178 C3
Spring Cl. Bradw 51 D4
Spring Cl. Brea 235 E4
Spring Cl. Swad 256 A1
Spring Cottage Rd. Moira 262 B3
Spring Dale Gdns. Staple 209 E2
Spring Garden Terr. Ilk 194 C1
Spring Gdns. Bux 85 E4
Spring Gdns. Derby 219 F4
Spring Gdns. Glos 10 A3
Spring Hill. Kim 195 F3
Spring Hill. Mans 136 A2
Spring Hill. Whit 82 A3
Spring Hollow. Haz 190 B4
Spring House Cl. Chest 94 C3
Spring La. Elmt 99 F3
Spring La. Hean 181 F1
Spring La. Shef 43 F4
Spring La. Shire 63 F3
Spring Mount. N Mills 33 E4
Spring Pl. Chest 96 A2
Spring Rd. Som 170 C3
Spring Rise. Glos 16 C4
Spring St. Derby 218 C2
Spring St. Glos 10 A1
Spring St. M in L 9 E3
Spring St. M in L 16 A4
Spring St. Swad 262 A4
Spring St. Whit 82 A3
Spring The. Lo Ea 236 B3
Spring Vale Rd. Chest 96 C4
Spring Vale Rd. Hay 25 F1
Spring Wood Cl. Chest 95 E4
Springbank. Glos 9 F3
Springdale Ct. Derby 217 F1
Springfarm Rd. Bu on T 248 A1
Springfield Cl. Crich 157 D1
Springfield Ave. Ashb 185 E4
Springfield Ave. Chest 95 E2
Springfield Ave. Hean 181 D3
Springfield Ave. Lo Ea 236 C4
Springfield Ave. Sand 223 D2
Springfield Ave. Shireb 119 F3
Springfield Cl. Clowne 80 C2
Springfield Cl. Eck 59 E2
Springfield Cl. Glos 9 F2
Springfield Cl. Swad 256 A3
Springfield Cres. Bols 98 C2
Springfield Cres. Som 170 B4
Springfield Ct. Staple 209 F1
Springfield Dr. Duff 190 B2
Springfield Gdn. Ilk 194 C1
Springfield Rd. Barlow 75 E2
Springfield Rd. Bradw 51 D4
Springfield Rd. Derby 220 A3
Springfield Rd. Derby 232 C1
Springfield Rd. Etwall 229 D2
Springfield Rd. N Wing 132 C4
Springfield Rd. Rep 242 B1
Springfield Rd. Swad 256 A3
Springfield Rise. Mat 143 E3
Springfield Terr. Ripley 169 F1
Springfield View. Ripley 169 E1
Springfield. Cha 16 B3
Springfield. Derby 218 A1
Springhill Way. Codnor 181 D4
Springhill. Harts 257 D4
Springmeadow. Cha 16 B4
Springvale Cl. Cl Cr 131 E1
Springvale Rd. Cl Cr 131 E1
Springwell Hill. Uns 77 F3
Springwell St. S in A 148 C1
Springwood Dr. Derby 206 A1
Springwood Farm Rd. Swad 256 A4
Springwood Rd. Shef 43 D3
Springwood St. Gra 116 A2
Springwood. Glos 16 C4
Sprinkswoods La. Snel 184 C3
Spruce Ave. Sels 171 E3
Spruce Rise. Kill 60 B3
Spurr St. Shef 43 D4
Square The. Bretby 249 D2
Square The. Bux 85 D4
Square The. Cl Cr 131 F2
Square The. Derby 205 D1
Square The. Derby 217 E1
Square The. Eyam 71 F3
Square The. March 224 C1
Square The. Mo 107 E1
Squirrel La. Br Hill 252 C2
Springfield Terr. Hay 25 E1
Stable Cl. Hollow 156 A3
Stable La. Alst 149 D1

Stables Ct. Bols 99 E1
Stables St. Derby 218 B3
Stacey Rd. Mans 135 E1
Staden Bsns Pk. Bux 85 F3
Staden La. Bux 85 F2
Stadmoor Ct. Derby 232 C1
Staffa Dr. Tibs 147 F3
Stafford Cl. Dron 56 B1
Stafford Cl. Glos 17 F4
Stafford Cl. Smal 192 C3
Stafford Cres. Wirk 165 F4
Stafford St. Derby 218 C3
Stafford St. Lo Ea 236 C4
Stafford St. N Mills 24 B1
Staines Cl. Derby 217 E1
Stainforth St. Mans 136 B1
Stainsbro' La. Callow 165 D3
Stainsbro' La. Cars 165 D3
Stainsby Ave. H Wood 192 C3
Stainsby Ave. Hean 193 F4
Stainsby Cl. Heath 132 C4
Staithes Wlk. Derby 205 E1
Staker La. Burn 230 B3
Stalybridge Rd. M in L 9 D2
Stamford Cl. Lo Ea 236 C2
Stamford St. Awsw 195 E2
Stamford St. Derby 232 B3
Stamford St. Hean 181 F1
Stamford St. Ilk 194 C1
Stamps Cl. Bu on T 248 B2
Stanage Green. Derby 217 F1
Stanage Rise. Shef 44 C3
Stanage Way. Chest 94 C3
Stancliffe Ave. Da Da 127 E2
Stancliffe View. Da Da 127 D2
Stand Rd. Chest 95 F4
Standing Butts Cl. Wa on T 259 E4
Standlow La. Kni 163 E1
Stanedge Rd. Bake 109 D3
Stanford Rd. Shef 56 C4
Stanford Way. Chest 114 A4
Stanhope Glade. Bretby 255 A4
Stanhope Rd. Derby 217 F2
Stanhope Rd. Shef 44 B3
Stanhope Rd. Swad 256 A2
Stanhope St. Al Hv 117 F1
Stanhope St. Bu on T 248 A2
Stanhope St. Derby 218 C1
Stanhope St. Ilk 209 D3
Stanhope St. Lo Ea 236 B4
Stanhope St. S-by-D 222 C4
Staniforth Ave. Eck 59 D2
Stanleigh Rd. Over 262 A2
Stanley Ave. Ripley 169 F1
Stanley Ave. Stav 97 D4
Stanley Cl. Derby 218 C4
Stanley Cl. Ilk 208 C4
Stanley Cl. Neth 264 C4
Stanley Cl. Wood 256 C2
Stanley Cres. Utt 210 A1
Stanley Ct. Chest 96 B1
Stanley Dr. Bees 209 F1
Stanley Hall La. Disley 32 B3
Stanley La. S in A 133 E1
Stanley Rd. Derby 220 A3
Stanley Rd. Derby 232 C3
Stanley Rd. Shef 43 D3
Stanley St. Derby 218 B3
Stanley St. Ilk 208 C4
Stanley St. Kill 60 B4
Stanley St. Lo Ea 236 C4
Stanley St. Som 170 B4
Stanley St. Swad 256 B2
Stanshope La. Alst 149 E1
Stanstead Rd. Derby 217 E2
Stanton Ave. Belper 179 D2
Stanton Cl. Da Da 127 D2
Stanton Cres. Shef 44 B2
Stanton Gate. S-by-D 209 E1
Stanton Hill. Tick 251 E3
Stanton Moor View. Da Da 142 C4
Stanton Pl. Plea 134 C4
Stanton Rd. Ashb 185 E4
Stanton Rd. Bu on T 254 C4
Stanton Rd. Ilk 208 C4
Stanton Rd. Sand 223 D4
Stanton St. Derby 218 C1
Stanton St. Plea 134 C4
Stanton View. Bake 109 E2
Stantonhall La. St Pk 126 B4
Stanwood Dr. Chest 114 A4
Stanyforth St. Glos 10 A2
Stapleford La. Bees 223 F2
Stapleford Rd. Staple 209 E2
Stapleford Rd. Trow 209 E2
Stapleton Rd. Ilk 194 C2
Starch La. Sand 223 E4
Starcross Ct. Derby 217 E2
Starkholmes Rd. Mat 143 E1
Starkie Ave. C Don 246 C2
Start La. W Br 45 D4
Starthe Bank. Hean 181 F1
Statham Ave. Tupton 131 E4
Statham St. Derby 218 C4
Station Rd. B-u-Ne 253 D1
Station App. Bux 85 D4
Station App. Derby 219 D2
Station App. Duff 190 C2
Station Back La. Chest 96 A2
Station Cl. Derby 232 C1
Station Ct. Ilk 194 C1
Station Dr. Moira 262 C2
Station Hill. Mans 136 A2
Station La Ind Est. Chest 77 D1
Station La. Chest 77 E1
Station La. Codnor 181 D3
Station La. Iron 170 C2
Station La. Shat 40 A1
Station La. Uns 58 A1
Station La. Wa on T 253 E1
Station New Rd. Tupton 131 E4
Station Rd. Ashb 173 D1
Station Rd. Awsw 195 E3
Station Rd. Bake 109 F3
Station Rd. Bam 40 A1
Station Rd. Bols 98 C2
Station Rd. Bread 205 F2
Station Rd. Bux 85 E4
Station Rd. C Don 247 D3
Station Rd. C Don 247 E3
Station Rd. C-Frith 47 D3
Station Rd. C-Frith 47 F1
Station Rd. Chest 77 D1
Station Rd. Chest 96 A2
Station Rd. Chest 96 B4
Station Rd. Chin 34 A1
Station Rd. Chin 34 B1
Station Rd. Clowne 80 C2
Station Rd. Da Da 127 E1
Station Rd. Denby 180 A2
Station Rd. Derby 217 E2
Station Rd. Derby 220 B2
Station Rd. Derby 232 C1
Station Rd. Dray 235 D4
Station Rd. Duff 190 C2
Station Rd. Eck 59 F2
Station Rd. Eck 60 B1
Station Rd. G Low 89 F2
Station Rd. Glos 10 A3
Station Rd. Hath 53 D4
Station Rd. Hatton 227 E1
Station Rd. Hay 25 D1
Station Rd. Hean 182 A1
Station Rd. Hope 39 E2
Station Rd. Ilk 194 C1
Station Rd. Kill 60 A3
Station Rd. Kim 195 F3
Station Rd. La Mi 182 A1
Station Rd. Lit Ea 205 E4
Station Rd. Lo Ea 236 C4
Station Rd. Marple 23 D4
Station Rd. Marple 23 E1
Station Rd. Mel 252 B4
Station Rd. Morton 147 D3
Station Rd. Mosb 59 F4
Station Rd. N Mills 33 D4
Station Rd. N Wing 131 F3
Station Rd. Ock 221 D1
Station Rd. Pils 132 B1
Station Rd. Ripley 167 F2
Station Rd. Rolle 240 B2
Station Rd. Sand 223 E3
Station Rd. Scarc 118 C3
Station Rd. Sels 160 C1
Station Rd. Shireb 119 F3
Station Rd. Stanl 207 E3
Station Rd. Stav 78 A1
Station Rd. Tibs 147 F3
Station Rd. W Br 33 E2
Station Rd. We Ha 207 E4
Station Rd. Whit 82 A3
Station Rd. Wood 256 C1
Station St. Ashb 173 D1
Station St. Coss 195 D1
Station St. Glos 10 B1
Station St. Lo Ea 236 C4
Station St. Mans 136 A2
Station St. Swad 261 F4
Station View. Shireb 119 F2
Station Wlk. Bux 85 E4
Staunton Ave. Derby 231 F3
Staunton Cl. C Don 247 D2
Staunton La. Tick 251 D1
Staveley Cl. Derby 232 C2
Staveley La. Eck 59 F1
Staveley La. Eck 78 C4
Staveley La. Stav 78 A3
Staveley Rd. Chest 77 F2
Staveley Rd. L Duk 97 F2
Staveley Rd. Shef 43 D4
Staveley Rd. Stav 98 A4
Staverton Dr. Derby 217 E2
Stead St. Eck 59 E2
Steam Mill La. Ripley 181 D4
Steel La. Bols 99 D1
Steel's La. Scarc 118 A3
Steele Ave. Stav 97 D3
Steele Ct. Bux 85 D4
Steep La. Win 114 A2
Steep Turnpike. Mat 143 E3
Steeping Cl. Chest 96 C4
Steeple Cl. Derby 205 F1
Steeple Grange. Wirk 154 C2
Steetley La. Whit 63 F2
Steetley La. Work 63 F2
Stenson Ave. Derby 231 F3
Stenson Rd. Derby 231 E2
Stenson Rd. Twy 231 E2
Stenton Rd. Shef 56 C4
Stephenson Cl. Elmt 81 F1
Stephenson Pl. Chest 96 A2
Stephenson Pl. Cl Cr 131 D2
Stephenson Rd. Stav 78 C1
Stepping Cl. Derby 218 C3
Stepping La. Derby 218 C3
Sterland St. Chest 95 F2
Sterndale Cl. Litton 69 F2
Sterndale Moor. Chel 105 F3
Sterndale Rd. Lo Ea 236 A3
Sterry Cl. Clowne 80 C1
Steven Cl. Bees 223 F2
Stevenage Cl. Derby 232 C3
Stevens La. Brea 235 E4
Stevens Rd. Sand 223 D3
Stevenson Ave. Brea 235 D4
Stevenson Pl. Derby 231 D4
Stevenson Rd. Dove 224 A4
Steward Gate. Bam 40 A3
Stewart Cl. Derby 220 C3
Stewart St. Som 170 B3
Stile Croft. Mid 154 B3
Stiles Cl. Glos 9 F3
Stiles Rd. Derby 233 D4
Stillman Cl. Chest 115 E4
Stinting La. Mans 136 C1
Stinting La. Shireb 119 E1
Stirland St. Codnor 170 A1
Stirling Cl. Derby 219 E4
Stirling Gr. Kim 195 F4
Stock La. March 224 B1
Stockbrook Rd. Derby 218 B2
Stockbrook St. Derby 218 C2
Stocker Ave. Derby 233 E4
Stockley La. Glap 117 F1
Stockley View. Bols 118 A4
Stockport Rd. M in L 15 E4
Stockport Rd. Marple 23 D3
Stocks Green Ct. Totley 55 E2
Stocks Green Dr. Totley 55 E2
Stocks Rd. Kim 195 F4
Stocks The. Tint 10 A4
Stockton Dr. Chin 34 C1
Stoddard Dr. Hean 181 F1
Stoke Cl. Belper 179 F3
Stollard St. Cl Cr 131 E2
Stone Cl. Derby 220 C3
Stone Furlong Rd. Baslow 91 F3
Stone Hill Rd. Derby 218 C1
Stone La. Uns 77 E3
Stone Meadows. Lo Ea 236 C3
Stone Rd. Dron 57 E2
Stone Row. Chest 95 E1
Stone Row. Marple 23 D3
Stone St. Mosb 59 E4
Stonebench La. Flagg 106 B2
Stonebroom La. Tibs 147 D3
Stonebroom Wlk. Derby 232 C2
Stonechat Cl. Derby 218 A2
Stonecliff Terr. Bux 85 E4
Stonecroft Rd. Totley 55 F3
Stonedale Cl. Mosb 59 E4
Stonegravels Croft. Mosb 59 F3
Stonegravels La. Chest 96 A3
Stonegravels Way. Mosb 59 F3
Stoneheads Rise. W Br 45 E4
Stonehill. C Don 247 D1
Stoneholes Dr. Cl Cr 131 F1
Stoneleigh Way. Som 169 F4
Stoneley Cl. Shef 44 A1
Stoneley Cres. Shef 44 A1
Stonelow Cres. Dron 57 E1
Stonelow Green. Dron 57 D1
Stonelow Rd. Dron 57 E1
Stonepit La. Hog 164 A2
Stoneridge. Glos 9 F3
Stonerows La. Ash 145 E3
Stonesby Cl. Derby 205 F1
Stonesdale Ct. Derby 233 E3
Stonewell La. Hartin 137 E3
Stoney Cl. Bake 109 E2
Stoney Cross. Derby 220 C2
Stoney Flatts Cres. Derby 220 A4
Stoney Hill. Wirk 155 D1
Stoney La. Ash 130 B2
Stoney La. Brin 182 B3
Stoney La. Derby 220 C3
Stoney La. Hog 164 A1
Stoney La. S Field 265 F1
Stoney La. Sels 171 F4
Stoney La. Trow 209 D3
Stoney Way. Mat 143 E2
Stoney Wood Dr. Crich 156 B1
Stoneycroft La. Holy 114 A3
Stoneydale Cl. Swad 255 F3
Stoneyland Dr. N Mills 33 D4
Stony La. Holbr 191 E3
Stony Ridge Rd. Totley 54 B3
Stonyhurst Ct. Derby 232 C2
Stoodley Pike Gdns. Derby 204 B1
Storer La. Spout 166 A2
Stores Rd. Derby 219 D4
Storforth La Terr. Chest 115 E4
Storforth La. Chest 115 D4
Stormont Cl. S Norm 160 A2
Storrs Rd. Chest 95 D1
Stort Sq. Mans 136 B1
Storth Bank. Glos 16 C4
Storth La. S Norm 160 A2
Storth Meadow Rd. Glos 16 C4
Storthfield Way. S Norm 160 A2
Stour Cl. Chest 96 C4
Stourdale Cl. Lo Ea 236 A3
Stourport Dr. Derby 233 D2
Stow Ct. Mans 136 C2
Stowmarket Dr. Derby 219 E4
Stradbroke Ave. Shef 44 B4
Stradbroke Cl. Shef 44 C4
Stradbroke Cres. Shef 44 C4
Stradbroke Dr. Shef 44 C4
Stradbroke Pl. Shef 44 C4
Stradbroke Rd. Shef 44 C4
Stradbroke Rise. Chest 114 B4
Stradbroke Way. Shef 44 C4
Stradbroke Wlk. Shef 44 B4
Strand Arc. Derby 219 D3
Strand. Derby 219 D3
Stranfaer Cl. Som 170 A4
Stranraer Cl. Mans 136 B3
Stratford Cl. Rep 242 B1
Stratford Rd. Derby 205 E1
Stratford St. Ilk 194 C2
Strathallan Cl. Da Da 127 E2
Strathaven Ct. Derby 220 C3
Strathglen Cl. Kim 195 F4
Strathmore Ave. Derby 233 D3
Stratton Rd. Bols 99 D1
Straw La. Stret 146 B4
Strawberry Bank. S in A 148 C2
Strawberry La. Black 257 D1
Strawberry La. Rosl 260 B3
Strawberry Lee La. Totley 55 D3
Streatham Rd. Derby 218 A3
Street La. Denby 180 A3
Street La. Ripley 180 A3
Street The. Bux 64 B3
Streetfield Cres. Mosb 59 E3
Streetfield La. Mosb 59 F3
Streetfields. Mosb 59 F3
Strelley Ave. Ripley 180 B4
Stretfield Rd. Bradw 39 D1
Strettea La. Shirl 146 B1
Stretton Cl. Derby 217 E1
Stretton Rd. Cl Cr 131 E1
Stretton Rd. Morton 146 C3
Stretton Rd. Stret 146 B4
Stretton View. Donis 265 F3
Strines Rd. Marple 23 D2
Stroma Cl. Derby 231 F2
Strutt St. Belper 178 C2
Strutt St. Derby 219 D1
Stuart Cl. Chest 96 B3
Stuart St. Derby 219 D3
Stubben Edge La. Ash 130 B1
Stubbing Rd. Chest 114 C4
Stubbins La. Chin 34 B1
Stubbins Wood La. Shireb 119 F3
Stubbins Wood. Shireb 119 F3
Stubley Cl. Dron 56 C2
Stubley Croft. Shef 56 C4
Stubley Dr. Dron 56 C1
Stubley Hollow. Dron 56 C2
Stubley La. Dron 56 C1
Stubley Pl. Dron 56 C1
Stubwood Hollow. Dens 196 B3
Studbrook Cl. C Don 246 C2
Studfarm Cl. Br Hill 252 C1
Sturge Croft. Shef 43 D3
Sturges La. Elv 233 F2
Sturston Rd. Ashb 173 E1
Sudbury Ave. Ilk 209 D4
Sudbury Ave. Sand 223 D3
Sudbury Cl. Chest 95 D3
Sudbury Cl. Derby 218 C3
Sudbury Ct. Lo Ea 235 F2
Sudbury Mews. East 182 C1
Sudbury Park. Sud 225 E4
Sudbury St. Derby 218 C3
Sudhall Cl. Chest 95 E4
Suff La. Pinx 160 B2
Suffolk Ave. Derby 219 F4
Suffolk Rd. Bu on T 254 B4
Sugworth Rd. Bradf 31 F3
Summer Cross. Tide 69 D2
Summer Dr. Wirk 165 F4
Summer La. Totley 55 E2
Summer La. Wirk 165 E4
Summer Wood Ct. Derby 231 F4
Summerbottom. M in L 16 A4
Summerbrook Ct. Derby 218 C2
Summerfield Cres. Chest 96 C4
Summerfield Rd. Chest 95 F1
Summerfield Rd. Dron 57 D2
Summerfields Way. Ship 194 B2
Summerley Lower Rd. Uns 57 F1
Summerley Rd. Uns 57 F1
Summerskill Green. Stav 97 E4
Summerwood La. Dron 56 C1
Summerwood Pl. Dron 56 C1
Summit Dr. Shireb 119 F2
Sumner St. Glos 17 E4
Sumners Pl. Glos 10 A1
Sun Alley. Eden 91 E2
Sun La. Crich 156 C1
Sun St. Derby 218 C2
Sun St. Wood 256 C1
Sunart Cl. Derby 231 F1
Sundew Cl. Derby 220 C2
Sundown Ave. Derby 231 E3
Sundown Cl. N Mills 33 D4
Sundown Pl. Shef 44 C4
Sundown Rd. Shef 44 C4
Suningdale Cl. Bu on T 240 B1
Sunlaws St. Glos 17 D4
Sunlea Cres. Staple 223 F3
Sunningdale Ave. Derby 220 B3
Sunningdale Ave. Hean 193 F4
Sunningdale Cl. Chest 114 C4
Sunningdale Dr. Ilk 208 A3
Sunningdale Rise. Chest 114 B4
Sunninghill Cl. We Ha 207 E4
Sunny Bank Gdns. Belper 178 C1
Sunny Bank La. Tide 69 E2
Sunny Bank. G Lo 90 A2
Sunny Bank. Tibs 147 F3
Sunny Banks. Glos 17 D4
Sunny Brook Cl. Clowne 80 C2
Sunny Gr. Derby 220 A3
Sunny Hill. Belper 190 C4
Sunny Springs. Chest 96 A2
Sunnyfield. Bux 85 F1
Sunnyhill Ave. Derby 231 F3
Sunnyside Rd. Utt 210 A1
Sunnyside. Swad 255 F4
Sunnyside. Whit 82 A3
Sunnyvale Ave. Totley 55 F2
Sunnyvale Rd. Totley 55 E2
Surbiton Cl. Derby 218 A3
Surbiton Cl. Derby 218 A3
Surbiton Ct. We Ha 207 E4
Surgery La. Crich 157 D1
Surrey St. Derby 218 B3
Surrey St. Glos 10 B1
Sussex Cir. Derby 219 F4
Sussex Rd. Bu on T 254 C3
Sussex Way. Sand 223 D3
Sutherland Rd. Derby 219 D1
Sutton Ave. Derby 232 C2
Sutton Cl. Derby 218 B3
Sutton Cres. Stav 97 E4
Sutton Ct. East 182 C1
Sutton Dr. Derby 232 C2
Sutton Hall Rd. Bols 117 F4
Sutton La. Etwall 229 D3
Sutton La. Hatton 227 F2
Sutton La. Hilton 228 B2
Sutton La. L Duk 116 C4
Sutton Rd. Ch Bro 227 E4
Sutton Rd. S in A 148 C2
Sutton View. Scarc 118 A4
Sutton Way. Glos 10 A3
Suttons La. Marple 23 D3
Swaddale Ave. Chest 96 A3
Swadlincote La. Swad 255 F1
Swadlincote Rd. Swad 256 C2
Swalebank Cl. Chest 115 D4
Swaledale Ct. Derby 233 E3
Swallow Cl. Derby 218 A2
Swallow House Cres. Hay 25 E2
Swallow House La. Hay 25 D2
Swallow Rd. Wood 256 C
Swan La. Mans 136 A2
Swanbourne Cl. Chest 96 B1
Swanbourne Cl. Chest 115 E4
Swanmore Rd. Derby 231 D4
Swann Yd. S in A 148 C2
Swanson Ave. S in A 148 C2
Swanwick Ave. Shireb 119 F2
Swanwick Gdns. Derby 206 A1
Swanwick Hill. Som 169 F4
Swanwick Rd. Som 170 A4
Swanwick St. Chest 77 D1
Swarkestone Dr. Derby 231 E3
Swarkestone Rd. Ba on T 244 A
Swarkestone Rd. Derby 244 C
Swathwick Cl. Win 114 C2
Swathwick La. Win 114 B2
Swayfield Cl. Derby 217 E
Sweetbriar Cl. Derby 233 D
Swift Cl. Derby 218 A
Swift Cl. Wood 256 C
Swift Ct. East 182 C
Swinburne St. Derby 219 D
Swinderby Dr. Derby 206 A
Swindon Cl. Greas 195 E
Swiney Way. Bees 223 F
Swinger La. Ash 129 E
Swinney Bank. Belper 179 D
Swinney La. Belper 179 D
Swinscoe Hill. May 172 A
Swinscoe Way. Chest 95 D
Swinson Cl. Roc 197 D
Sycamore Ave. Chest 95 F
Sycamore Ave. Derby 204 B
Sycamore Ave. Dron 57 D
Sycamore Ave. Elmt 81 F
Sycamore Ave. Fin 230 C
Sycamore Ave. Glap 134 A
Sycamore Ave. Ripley 180 B
Sycamore Ave. Swad 256 A
Sycamore Cl. Bols 99 E

ycamore Cl. Etwall 229 E2
ycamore Cl. Linton 261 E3
ycamore Cl. Mapp 193 F2
ycamore Cl. N Mills 24 C1
ycamore Cl. Pinx 160 B2
ycamore Cl. Sels 171 E4
ycamore Cl. Shirl 146 B2
ycamore Cotts. Par 151 E1
ycamore Cres. Sand 223 D4
ycamore Dr. Chest 96 C2
ycamore Dr. Ilk 209 D4
ycamore Dr. Kill 60 B3
ycamore La. Stav 78 A1
ycamore Rd. Awsw 195 E3
ycamore Rd. Bu on T 254 C3
ycamore Rd. C Don 247 D3
ycamore Rd. C-Frith 47 D2
ycamore Rd. Lo Ea 236 B3
ycamore Rd. Mans 136 B3
ycamore Rd. Mat 143 D3
ycamore Rd. May 184 B4
ycamore Rd. N Mills 24 C1
ycamore Rd. Stav 78 A1
ycamore St. Mar War 120 C3
ycamore St. Mosb 59 E4
ycamores The. East 182 C1
ycamores The. Glos 9 F2
ycamores The. S Norm 160 A3
yda La. O Bram 93 F1
yday La. Barl 79 F4
ydenham Rd. Derby 218 A4
ydney Cl. Mans 136 B3
ydney St. Chest 95 F2
ydney St. Dray 235 D4
ydnope Hill. Da Da 128 D3
yerscote La. C Camp 263 D1
ylvan Cl. Chest 96 A1
ylvan Cliff. Bux 85 E4
ylvan Dr. Cl Cr 131 D3
ylvan Park. Bux 85 E3
ylvia Rd. Uns 76 B3
ywell Cl. Som 169 F4

abley Gdns. Marple 23 D2
addington Cl. Derby 219 F4
addington Rd. Chest 95 D3
addington Rd. Derby 205 F1
aft Ave. Sand 223 D3
agg La. Mo 107 D1
aggs Knoll. Bam 40 A2
aghole La. W Und 188 C1
ailby Dr. Will 242 A3
albot Cres. Chest 115 E4
albot Dr. Staple 209 E1
albot Pl. Donis 265 F4
albot Rd. Glos 10 B1
albot St. Chest 115 E4
albot St. Derby 218 C3
albot St. Glos 10 B1
albot St. Pinx 160 B1
albot St. Swad 256 A1
algarth Cl. Derby 206 B1
amar Ave. Derby 204 B2
amworth Rd. C Don 235 F1
amworth Rd. Lo Ea 236 B3
amworth Rd. S Field 265 F1
amworth St. Duff 190 C2
amworth Terr. Duff 190 C2
anner's La. Rep 242 B2
ansley Ave. Stanl 193 D1
ansley Rd. N Wing 131 F3
ansley Rise. Derby 205 F1
ansley Way. Stav 97 E3
ants Meadow. Hors 191 F3
antum Ave. Hean 181 E2
anyard Cl. C Don 247 D2
ap La. Chest 95 F2
aplow Cl. Derby 217 E1
apton La. Chest 96 A2
apton Terr. Chest 96 A2
apton Vale. Chest 96 B3
apton View Rd. Chest 95 F3
apton Way. Calow 96 C2
aptonn Lock Hill. Chest 96 A3
arina Cl. Derby 233 D1
arnside Fold. Glos 17 D4
asman Cl. Derby 217 F2
atenhill La. Bran 253 E4
atenhill La. Dun 253 D4
atham's La. Ilk 194 C1
attersall Wlk. Mans 136 C2
attle Hill. Dale 207 F1
aunton Cl. Derby 233 E4
averners Cres. Derby 231 E4
avistock Ave. Ripley 169 E1
avistock Cl. Derby 231 E2
avistock Sq. Alf 159 D3
awney Croft. Tans 144 A2
axal Moor Rd. W Br 45 E2
ay Cl. Derby 231 E1
ay Cl. Dron 56 B1
ay Wlk. Derby 204 C2
aylor Cres. Chest 96 B1
aylor Cres. Staple 223 F4
aylor La. Hean 181 E2
aylor St. Derby 219 F1
aylor St. Ilk 194 C1
aylor St. M in L 9 E2
Taylor's La. Spout 166 A2
Taylor's La. Trus 215 F3
Teal Cl. Shireb 119 E2
Tealby Wlk. Mans 136 C2
Tean Cl. Bu on T 248 A1
Tedder Ave. Bux 85 E2
Tedgness Rd. Grin 53 F1
Tedworth Ave. Derby 231 E1
Teesdale Rd. Lo Ea 236 A3
Teesdale Rd. Mosb 58 C4
Telford Cl. Derby 217 F1
Telford Cres. Stav 78 C1
Telford Rd. Marple 23 D2
Telmah Cl. Bu on T 240 B1
Temperance Hill. Stret 145 F4
Temperance St. M in L 16 A4
Templar Cl. Derby 231 E2
Temple Ave. Glos 10 B3
Temple Normanton Bsns Pk. Gra 116 A2
Temple Rd. Bux 85 D3
Temple Rd. Mat Ba 143 D1
Temple St. Derby 219 D2
Temple St. Glos 10 B3
Temple Wlk. Mat Ba 143 D1
Ten Foot Cl. Glos 10 A1
Tenant St. Derby 219 D3
Tennessee Rd. Derby 220 A4
Tennyson Ave. Chest 95 F2
Tennyson Ave. Mans 136 B1
Tennyson Ave. Swad 256 B3
Tennyson Rd. Elmt 81 E1
Tennyson Sq. Awsw 195 E2
Tennyson St. Derby 232 B4
Tennyson St. Ilk 194 C2
Tennyson St. N Wing 116 B1
Tennyson St. Shirl 146 B3
Tennyson Way. Gra 115 F2
Tenter Cl. Lo Ea 236 B3
Tenter La. Ripley 168 B1
Tern Ave. Wood 256 C2
Terrace La. Plea 134 C3
Terrace Rd. Bux 85 D4
Terrace Rd. C-Frith 47 D3
Terrace Rd. Tide 69 E2
Terrace The. Mat 143 F4
Terret Gr. Bux 84 B3
Terrey Rd. Totley 55 F3
Terry Pl. Derby 232 C4
Tetford Wlk. Mans 136 C2
Teversal Ave. Mans 135 D2
Tevery Cl. Staple 223 F4
Teviot Pl. Derby 206 A1
Tewkesbury Ave. Mans 136 B2
Tewkesbury Cres. Derby 219 E4
Tewkesbury Dr. Kim 195 F4
Tewkesbury Rd. Lo Ea 236 C3
Thackeray Rd. Shirl 146 C2
Thackeray St. Derby 232 A3
Thames Cl. Derby 217 F3
Thanet Dr. Derby 233 D3
Thanet St. Cl Cr 131 E2
Thatchers La. Tans 144 A2
Theatre La. Chest 96 A2
Theatre Yd. Chest 96 A2
Thickley Cl. Shireb 119 F2
Thirlmere Dr. Dron 57 D1
Thirlmere Ave. Derby 204 C2
Thirlmere Cl. Lo Ea 223 D1
Thirlmere Rd. Chest 95 E4
Thirlmere Rd. Lo Ea 223 D1
Thirlwell Rd. Shef 43 D3
Thirsk Pl. Derby 232 B4
Thirteen Row. Scarc 118 A3
Thistle Cl. Greas 195 E4
Thistle Green Cl. Hean 182 A1
Thistledown Cl. Derby 205 D1
Thomas Cook Cl. Mel 252 A4
Thomas St. Glos 10 C1
Thomas St. Marple 15 D1
Thompson Cl. Chest 96 A4
Thompson St. Chest 96 A4
Thompson St. La Mi 182 A2
Thomson Dr. Codnor 181 D4
Thoresby Ave. Shireb 119 F2
Thoresby Cl. Derby 206 A1
Thoresby Cres. Dray 234 C4
Thoresby Pl. Stav 97 E3
Thoresby Rd. Lo Ea 236 B3
Thoresby Rd. Mans 136 A2
Thoresey Ave. Clowne 81 D2
Thorn Ave. Mans 135 F1
Thorn Cl. Derby 204 B2
Thorn Dr. Greas 195 E4
Thorn St. Derby 218 C1
Thorn St. Wood 256 C1
Thorn Tree Gdns. Greas 182 C2
Thorn Tree La. Bretby 255 F4
Thorn Tree La. Swad 255 F4
Thornborough Cl. Shef 43 E4
Thornborough Pl. Shef 43 E4
Thornborough Rd. Shef 43 E4
Thornbridge Ave. Shef 44 B2
Thornbridge Cl. Shef 44 B2
Thornbridge Cres. Chest 115 D3
Thornbridge Cres. Shef 44 C2
Thornbridge Dr. Shef 44 B2
Thornbridge Gr. Shef 44 B2
Thornbridge Pl. Shef 44 B2
Thornbridge Rise. Shef 44 C2
Thornbridge Way. Shef 44 C2
Thornbrook Rd. C-Frith 47 E3
Thorncliffe Ave. North 127 D3
Thorncliffe Rd. Glos 9 F2
Thorndene Cl. Chest 96 A3
Thorndike Ave. Derby 233 D4
Thorndon Cl. Derby 230 B4
Thorndon Way. Chest 114 B4
Thorne Cl. O Bram 94 C2
Thornecliffewood. M in L 9 E3
Thornell Cl. C-Frith 47 E3
Thornescroft Gdns. Bran 254 A4
Thorness Cl. Derby 233 E3
Thornewill Dr. Bu on T 240 C1
Thorneywood Rd. Lo Ea 236 C4
Thornfield Ave. Chest 95 D1
Thornhill La. Thor 39 F2
Thornhill Rd. Derby 218 B1
Thornhill Rd. Derby 218 B2
Thornsett Ave. Bux 85 F4
Thornsett Cl. Bux 85 F4
Thornsett Gdns. Totley 55 F4
Thornsett. N Mills 24 C1
Thornton Pl. Shef 56 C4
Thorntree La. Derby 219 D3
Thornway. H La 32 A4
Thornwood Ct. Bux 85 D4
Thorp Cl. Shef 43 D4
Thorpe Ave. Dron 57 E2
Thorpe Ave. Whit 81 F3
Thorpe Cl. Chest 95 F4
Thorpe Cl. Staple 223 E4
Thorpe Croft. Hollow 156 A3
Thorpe Dr. Derby 217 F2
Thorpe Hill Dr. Hean 193 F4
Thorpe House Ave. Shef 43 D2
Thorpe House Rd. Shef 43 D2
Thorpe House Rise. Shef 43 D2
Thorpe La. Shire 63 E3
Thorpe Leys. Lo Ea 236 B3
Thorpe Rd. Greas 182 C2
Thorpe Rd. Hart 62 A4
Thorpe St. Glos 10 C1
Thorpe St. Ilk 194 C2
Thorpe Way. Belper 179 D3
Thorpe's Rd. Hean 181 E1
Thorpe's Rd. Ship 193 E4
Thorpelands Ave. Mans 136 C1
Thorpelands Dr. Derby 204 C1
Thorpleigh Rd. Stav 79 D1
Three Gates. Belper 178 C1
Throstle Nest Way. Brai 201 F4
Thrumpton Ave. Lo Ea 237 D4
Thrushton Cl. Fin 230 B1
Thruxton Cl. Derby 233 E3
Thunderpit La. St Mid 71 D2
Thurgarton Ct. Ashb 173 E1
Thurlby Ct. Mans 136 C2
Thurlow Ct. Derby 206 A1
Thurman St. Ilk 209 D3
Thurstan Ave. Shef 56 C4
Thurston Ave. Som 170 B4
Thurstone Furlong. Derby 232 C1
Thurvaston Rd. M Mont 197 F1
Tiber Cl. Derby 233 E3
Tibshelf Rd. Al Hu 132 C4
Tibshelf Rd. Newt 147 E1
Tickham Ave. Derby 231 E1
Ticknall La. Denby 180 A1
Ticknall La. Harts 257 D4
Ticknall Wlk. Derby 231 F3
Tideswell Cl. Stav 97 E4
Tideswell Green. Swad 255 F3
Tideswell La. Eyam 71 D3
Tideswell Rd. Derby 205 F1
Tiger Yd. Ashb 173 D1
Tilbury Pl. Derby 233 D3
Tillotson Cl. Shef 43 D3
Tillotson Rise. Shef 43 D3
Tilton Gr. Ilk 208 B3
Timber La. Al Hu 132 C3
Timbersbrook Cl. Derby 206 A1
Timsbury Ct. Derby 205 F1
Tinderbox La. Burn 229 F3
Tinkerley La. Idri 165 E1
Tinkerley La. K Ire 165 E1
Tinkley La. Ash 130 B2
Tinsley Rd. East 182 B1
Tintagel Cl. Bu on T 240 C1
Tintagel Cl. Derby 219 D1
Tip Tree Cl. Kim 195 F4
Tipnall Rd. C Don 247 D2
Tipper's La. Ch Bro 227 D4
Tiree Cl. Derby 231 F2
Tiree Cl. Staple 209 E1
Tiree Cl. Tibs 147 F3
Tissington Cl. Chest 95 D3
Titchfield Ave. Mans 136 B2
Titchfield St. Elmt 81 F1
Titchfield St. Whit 81 F3
Tithe Barn Cl. Tide 69 E2
Tithebarn La. Thurv 215 E3
Tiverton Cl. Derby 217 E2
Tivoli Gdns. Derby 218 C4
Toadmoor La. Ripley 167 F2
Todbrook Cl. W Br 45 E3
Todd St. Glos 17 E4
Toll Bar Ave. Shef 43 F3
Toll Bar Cl. Shef 43 F3
Toll Bar Dr. Shef 43 F3
Toll Bar Rd. Shef 43 F3
Tollbridge Rd. Stav 79 D1
Tollemache Cl. M in L 9 D3
Tollemache Rd. M in L 9 D3
Tom La. C-Frith 46 B3
Tom La. Stav 97 F3
Tonbridge Dr. Derby 233 D3
Tonge La. Br Hill 252 C2
Tongue La. Bux 85 F4
Tontine Rd. Chest 96 A1
Top Farm Ct. Kilb 191 F4
Top Fingle Cl. Chest 96 C4
Top Hag La. Crich 168 A3
Top La. Crich 156 B1
Top La. Mans 135 D1
Top La. O Bram 93 F2
Top La. Shot 166 B1
Top Manor Cl. Ock 221 E3
Top Meadow. Swad 256 A4
Top Rd. Calow 97 D2
Top Rd. Win 114 B1
Top Row. Sels 171 D3
Tophill La. Ible 153 E4
Tophole Rd. Bradw 50 C2
Topley Gdns. Derby 205 F1
Toppham Dr. Shef 56 C3
Toppham Rd. Shef 56 C3
Toppham Way. Shef 56 C3
Topshill La. K Ire 165 D1
Tor Ave. Som 170 B3
Tor Rise. Mat 143 D2
Tor View Rise. Mat Ba 155 D3
Torksey Wlk. Mans 136 C2
Torr St. Bux 85 D4
Torr Top St. N Mills 33 E4
Torridon Cl. Derby 231 F2
Torrvale Rd. N Mills 33 D4
Tors The. Crich 156 C1
Torwood Dr. Shef 56 C4
Totley Brook Cl. Totley 55 E3
Totley Brook Croft. Totley 55 E3
Totley Brook Glen. Totley 55 E3
Totley Brook Gr. Totley 55 E3
Totley Brook Rd. Totley 55 F3
Totley Brook Way. Totley 55 E3
Totley Grange Cl. Totley 55 E2
Totley Grange Dr. Totley 55 E2
Totley Grange Rd. Totley 55 E2
Totley Hall La. Totley 55 E2
Totley La. Shef 56 A3
Totley Mews. Glos 9 E1
Totley Mnt. Chest 96 B4
Toton La. Bees 223 F3
Toton La. Staple 223 F3
Toulmin Dr. Swad 256 A2
Tower Cl. Ock 221 E1
Tower Cl. Shef 43 E4
Tower Cl. Som 170 B4
Tower Cres. Bols 118 A4
Tower Dr. Shef 43 E4
Tower Rd. Bu on T 248 A1
Tower Rd. Harts 257 D3
Tower St. Derby 232 B4
Towers La. Hath 40 C1
Towle St. Lo Ea 236 A2
Towles Pastures. C Don 247 D2
Town End Rd. Dray 235 D4
Town End. Bols 99 D1
Town End. Bux 66 C1
Town End. Shirl 146 B1
Town End. Uns 58 A1
Town Gate. Bradw 51 D4
Town Hall Yd. Ashb 173 E1
Town La. Bradw 51 D4
Town La. Cha 16 B3
Town La. Newt 148 A2
Town St. Brass 153 D1
Town St. Duff 190 C2
Town St. Holbr 191 E3
Town St. Marple 23 D4
Town St. Pinx 160 C2
Town St. Sand 223 D3
Town The. Lit Ea 205 E4
Town View. Kim 195 F4
Townfield La. Shat 39 F1
Townhead La. Thor 39 F2
Townhead Rd. Totley 55 E4
Townscliffe La. Marple 23 E3
Townside Cl. Lo Ea 236 A2
Towson Ave. La Mi 182 B1
Trafalgar Rd. Lo Ea 236 B3
Trafalgar Sq. Lo Ea 236 C4
Traffic St. Derby 219 D2
Traffic Terr. Chest 115 D4
Traffic Terr. Stav 78 A2
Trafford Way. Derby 231 E4
Tranmere Ave. Cl Cr 131 E2
Transvaal Terr. Scarc 118 A3
Travers Rd. Sand 223 D3
Travey Rd. Shef 44 A4
Tredcroft St. Glos 17 D4
Tredegar Dr. Derby 206 A1
Treeneuk Cl. Chest 95 D2
Tregaron Cl. Derby 206 B1
Tregony Way. Derby 231 E2
Trelawney Rd. Cl Cr 131 E2
Trenchard Dr. Bux 85 E2
Trent Ave. Bux 85 E2
Trent Ave. Will 242 B3
Trent Bridge Ct. Derby 231 E4
Trent Cl. Derby 231 E1
Trent Cl. Will 242 B3
Trent Dr. Derby 231 E3
Trent Gr. Alf 159 D1
Trent Gr. Dron 57 D2
Trent La. C Don 247 D3
Trent La. Lo Ea 236 C3
Trent La. Mel 245 E1
Trent La. N Sol 248 C4
Trent La. We on T 245 F2
Trent Rd. Ilk 208 B2
Trent Rise. Derby 220 C2
Trent St. Derby 233 D4
Trent St. Lo Ea 236 C4
Trent Wlk. Mans 136 C2
Trenton Cl. Bees 209 F1
Trenton Dr. Lo Ea 237 D4
Trenton Green Dr. Derby 220 A3
Trenton Grn. Derby 220 A3
Tresillian Cl. Derby 204 C1
Tressall Cl. Ilk 209 D4
Trevelyn Cl. Bu on T 248 B1
Treveris Cl. Derby 220 C2
Trevone Ave. Staple 223 F3
Trevose Cl. Chest 114 B4
Triangle The. Ilk 209 D3
Trickett Cl. Cas 38 B2
Trinity Cl. Chest 95 F2
Trinity Cl. Ilk 194 C2
Trinity Gr. Swad 256 A2
Trinity St. Derby 219 D2
Trinkey La. St Mid 72 A2
Tristram Gr. Bu on T 240 C1
Troon Cl. Bu on T 240 B1
Troon Cl. Chest 114 B4
Troon Cl. Derby 231 D4
Troon Cl. Kim 195 F4
Trot La. Gr H 70 A3
Trough La. Greas 195 F4
Troughbrook Hill. Stav 97 D4
Troughbrook Rd. Stav 78 A1
Trowbridge Cl. Derby 205 F1
Trowell Ave. Ilk 209 D3
Trowell Gr. Lo Ea 223 E1
Trowell Gr. Staple 209 F2
Trowell Park Dr. Staple 209 E1
Trowell Rd. Staple 209 E1
Trowels La. Derby 218 B2
Trueman St. Ilk 194 C2
Truman St. Coss 195 D1
Truman St. Kim 195 E4
Truro Cl. Swad 256 C3
Truro Cres. Derby 219 F4
Trusley Gdns. Derby 231 E3
Trusley Wlk. Mans 136 C2
Tudor Cl. Lo Ea 223 F1
Tudor Falls. Hean 181 F2
Tudor Pl. Ilk 208 B3
Tudor Rd. Derby 220 A3
Tudor Rise. C Camp 263 F1
Tudor St. Stav 78 C1
Tudor Way. Swad 256 A3
Tudorhouse Cl. Swad 256 A4
Tuffolds Cl. Shef 44 A4
Tufnell Gdns. Derby 218 A4
Tulip Rd. Awsw 195 D3
Tulla Cl. Derby 231 F1
Tunnel Yd. Ashb 173 D1
Tunstall Green. Chest 95 E1
Tunstall Way. Chest 95 E1
Turf Lea Rd. Marple 23 D1
Turlowfields La. Hog 175 E4
Turnberry Cl. Chest 114 B4
Turncliffe Cl. Bux 84 C3
Turner Ave. La Mi 182 A2
Turner Cl. Dron 56 C1
Turner Cl. Staple 223 F3
Turner Dr. Greas 195 E4
Turner Dr. Stav 97 D4
Turner Rd. Lo Ea 236 B2
Turner St. Derby 232 C3
Turners La. Som 170 A4
Turnlee Cl. Glos 17 E4
Turnlee Dr. Glos 17 E4
Turnlee Rd. Glos 17 E4
Turnoaks La. Chest 115 D4
Turnpike Cl. Mat 143 E3
Turton Cl. La Mi 182 A2
Tutbury Rd. Bu on T 240 A1
Tutbury Rd. Rolle 240 A1
Tuxford Cl. Derby 206 A1
Twentylands. Rolle 240 B2
Twentywell Dr. Shef 56 A3
Twentywell La. Shef 56 A3
Twentywell Rd. Shef 56 A3
Twentywell Rise. Shef 56 A3
Twentywell View. Shef 56 A3
Twickenham Cl. Mosb 59 F3
Twickenham Cres. Mosb 59 F3
Twickenham Ct. Mosb 59 F3
Twickenham Dr. Derby 218 A3
Twickenham Glade. Mosb 59 F3

Twickenham Glen. Mosb 59 F3
Twickenham Gr. Mosb 59 F3
Twin Oaks Cl. Derby 230 C4
Twisses Bank. Ch Bro 213 D1
Twyford Cl. Hean 193 E4
Twyford Cl. Swad 255 F1
Twyford Cl. We Ha 207 E4
Twyford Cl. Will 242 B3
Twyford Rd. Ba on T 244 A3
Twyford Rd. Lo Ea 235 F2
Twyford Rd. Will 242 A3
Twyford St. Derby 219 D2
Tylney Rd. Chest 114 A4
Tyndale Chase. Derby 231 E1
Tynedale Cl. Lo Ea 236 A3
Tynefield Ct. Etwall 229 D1
Tynefield Mews. Etwall 229 D1
Tythe The. Swad 256 A4

Uffa Magna. Derby 217 E1
Ulley Cres. Shef 44 A4
Ulley Rd. Shef 44 A4
Ullswater Ave. Mosb 59 F3
Ullswater Cl. Derby 205 E1
Ullswater Cl. Dron 56 C1
Ullswater Cl. Mosb 59 F3
Ullswater Dr. Derby 220 C3
Ullswater Dr. Dron 56 C1
Ullswater Park. Dron 56 C1
Ullswater Pl. Dron 56 C1
Ulverston Rd. Chest 95 E4
Underhall. Da Da 127 E1
Underhill Ave. Derby 231 F4
Underhill Cl. Derby 231 F3
Underpass The. Derby 219 D3
Undertown La. Rost 197 E3
Underwood Terr. Da Da 143 D4
Union Rd. Ilk 208 C4
Union Rd. N Mills 33 E4
Union Rd. Swad 256 A3
Union St. Ashb 173 D1
Union St. Glos 17 E4
Union St. Lo Ea 236 C4
Union St. Mel 252 A4
Union St. S Norm 159 F3
Unity Cl. Swad 256 A1
Unity Wlk. Glos 17 E4
Unstone Dronfield By Pass. Dron 75 F4
Unstone Hill. Dron 76 B4
Unstone Rd. Chest 76 C2
Unthank La. Hol 74 B2
Upchurch Cl. Derby 217 E2
Upland Rise. Chest 95 E1
Uplands Ave. Derby 231 E3
Uplands Gdns. Derby 218 C1
Uplands Rd. Glos 17 E4
Uplands Rd. Marple 15 D3
Upper Albert Rd. Shef 43 D3
Upper Bainbridge St. Derby 219 D2
Upper Barn Cl. Hean 181 F1
Upper Blindlow La. Chel 106 A3
Upper Boundary Rd. Derby 218 C2
Upper Croft Cl. Chest 96 C4
Upper Croft. Cl Cr 131 F2
Upper Dale Rd. Derby 218 C1
Upper Dunstead Rd. Ald 182 A2
Upper End Rd. Bux 67 E2
Upper Hall Cl. Holbr 191 E3
Upper Hollow. Derby 218 B1
Upper King St. Chest 77 F1
Upper La. H Ward 175 F2
Upper Mantle Cl. Cl Cr 131 E2
Upper Marehay Rd. Ripley 180 B3
Upper Moor St. Chest 95 D1
Upper Nelson St. Hean 181 E1
Upper Newbold Cl. Chest 95 D4
Upper Orchard St. Staple 223 F4
Upper School La. Dron 76 A4
Upper Town La. Bir 126 A1
Upper Valley Rd. Shef 43 D3
Upper Wellington St. Lo Ea 223 E1
Upper Yeld Rd. Bake 109 E2
Uppermoor Rd. Derby 232 C3
Upperthorpe Rd. Kill 60 B3
Upperthorpe Villas. Kill 60 B3
Uppertown La. Bons 142 B1
Upperwood Rd. Mat Ba 143 D1
Upton Mount. Mans 135 F1
Upwood Cl. Chest 95 D3
Upwoods Rd. Dove 211 D1
Uttoxeter New Rd. Derby 218 B2
Uttoxeter Old Rd. Derby 218 C3
Uttoxeter Rd. Derby 217 F1
Uttoxeter Rd. Hatton 227 D1
Uttoxeter Rd. Scro 226 C2

Vale Cl. Bols 99 D1
Vale Cl. Dron 57 D1
Vale Dr. Shireb 119 F1
Vale Mills. Derby 218 C2
Vale Rd. Harts 257 D2
Vale Rd. Mans 136 A2
Vale Rd. Swad 256 A3
Vale The. Ilk 194 C2
Valentine Ave. Sels 171 F4
Valerie Rd. As on T 246 A4
Vallance St. Mans 136 A2
Valley Cl. Pils 132 A2
Valley Dr. Kill 60 B4
Valley Gdns. M in L 15 F4
Valley Rd. Barlow 75 E2
Valley Rd. Bols 118 A4
Valley Rd. Chest 96 B1
Valley Rd. Cl Cr 131 D2
Valley Rd. Derby 218 B1
Valley Rd. Derby 220 A3
Valley Rd. Hay 25 F1
Valley Rd. Ilk 208 C3
Valley Rd. Kill 60 B4
Valley Rd. Kim 195 E4
Valley Rd. M in L 15 F4
Valley Rd. Over 262 A2
Valley Rd. Shef 43 D3
Valley Rd. Shireb 119 F3
Valley Rd. Stav 79 E2
Valley Rise. Barlow 75 E2
Valley Rise. Swad 256 A3
Valley View Cl. Chest 115 F4
Valley View Cl. Eck 59 E1
Valley View Dr. Stanl 193 D1
Valley View Rd. Som 170 B2
Valley View. Belper 179 D1
Valley View. Ilk 208 C3
Vancouver Ave. Derby 220 B2
Vancouver Dr. Bu on T 248 B2
Vanguard Rd. Lo Ea 236 B3
Vanguard Trading Est. Chest 115 D4
Varley St. Derby 232 B3
Vaughan Pl. Shireb 119 F3
Vaughan Rd. W Br 45 F3
Vauxhall Ave. Derby 218 A4
Venture Cres. Som 159 D1
Vere Cl. Will 242 A3
Vermont Dr. Derby 220 B3
Verney St. Plea 134 C4
Verney Way. Plea 134 C4
Vernon Ct. Shireb 120 A2
Vernon Dr. Derby 220 C2
Vernon Green. Bake 109 D4
Vernon Rd. Chest 95 E2
Vernon Rd. Totley 55 F3
Vernon Rise. Gra 115 F1
Vernon St. Derby 218 C3
Vernon St. Ilk 194 C2
Vernon St. Shireb 120 A2
Veronica Dr. Greas 195 E4
Vestry Rd. Derby 205 F2
Vetchfield Cl. Derby 231 F1
Via Gellia Rd. Bons 154 B4
Vicar La. Chest 96 A2
Vicar La. Tibs 148 A3
Vicarage Ave. Derby 218 C1
Vicarage Ave. Ilk 194 B2
Vicarage Cl. Belper 179 D2
Vicarage Cl. Black 257 E1
Vicarage Cl. Bu on T 248 A2
Vicarage Cl. Heath 117 D1
Vicarage Cl. Hol 75 D4
Vicarage Cl. Shireb 119 F2
Vicarage Cl. Smal 192 C3
Vicarage Cl. Som 169 F4
Vicarage Ct. Derby 217 E1
Vicarage Dr. Derby 220 A4
Vicarage Dr. Utt 210 A2
Vicarage Gdns. Hean 181 F1
Vicarage La. A in W 108 C4
Vicarage La. Duff 190 C2
Vicarage La. Hay 25 E1
Vicarage La. Iron 170 C2
Vicarage La. Lit Ea 205 E4
Vicarage La. Row 110 C1
Vicarage La. Totley 55 E4
Vicarage Mews. Som 170 C3
Vicarage Rd. Belper 190 C4
Vicarage Rd. Derby 217 E1
Vicarage Rd. Derby 232 C1
Vicarage Rd. Swad 256 B2
Vicarage Rd. Wood 256 C1
Vicarage St. Ilk 194 B2
Vicarage Wlk. Rosl 260 B3
Vicarwood Ave. Derby 204 C1
Vicarwood Ave. Holbr 191 E4
Victor Ave. Derby 218 C4
Victor Cres. Sand 223 E2
Victor Rd. Totley 55 F4
Victoria Ave. Bux 85 E4
Victoria Ave. Dray 235 D4
Victoria Ave. Ock 221 D1
Victoria Ave. Stav 79 D2
Victoria Cl. Derby 217 F2
Victoria Cotts. Som 159 E1
Victoria Cres. Iron 170 C2
Victoria Ct. Ilk 194 C1
Victoria Ct. Mat 143 E3
Victoria Dr. Newt 147 F1
Victoria Gr. Chest 96 C3
Victoria Park Rd. Bux 85 E4
Victoria Park Rd. Chest 96 C3
Victoria Rd. Bam 40 A2
Victoria Rd. Dray 235 D4
Victoria Rd. Pinx 160 B2
Victoria Rd. Ripley 169 E1
Victoria Rd. Sand 223 D3
Victoria Rd. Sels 171 F3
Victoria Sq. Ashb 173 E1
Victoria St N. Chest 76 C1
Victoria St W. Chest 95 F1
Victoria St. Alf 159 D2
Victoria St. C Don 247 D3
Victoria St. Chest 77 F1
Victoria St. Chest 96 A2
Victoria St. Cl Cr 131 E2
Victoria St. Derby 219 D3
Victoria St. Dron 56 C1
Victoria St. Elmt 81 F1
Victoria St. Glos 17 E4
Victoria St. Ilk 194 C2
Victoria St. Iron 170 C2
Victoria St. La Mi 182 B2
Victoria St. Lo Ea 236 A3
Victoria St. Mel 252 A4
Victoria St. N Mills 33 D3
Victoria St. Ripley 169 F1
Victoria St. S Norm 160 A3
Victoria St. Scarc 118 A4
Victoria St. Shireb 119 F2
Victoria St. Som 170 B4
Victoria St. Staple 223 E4
Victoria Terr. Tibs 148 A4
Victoria Wlk. Tupton 115 E1
Victory Ave. Ripley 169 F1
Victory Cl. Lo Ea 236 B3
Victory Dr. Mans 136 C1
Victory Rd. Derby 232 A3
View Rd. Shef 43 D4
Viewdales Cl. H Ward 175 F1
Viking Bsns Centre. Wood 256 C2
Vikinglea Dr. Shef 44 A4
Vikinglea Rd. Shef 44 A4
Villa St. Dray 235 D4
Village Ct. Duff 190 C2
Village St. Derby 231 F4
Village The. Dale 207 F1
Village The. We Ha 207 F4
Villas Rd. Bols 98 C2
Villas Rd. Ripley 167 F2
Villiers Cl. Shef 43 F3
Villiers Dr. Shef 43 F3
Vincent Ave. Derby 220 C2
Vincent Ave. Ilk 208 C4
Vincent Cl. Kilb 192 A4
Vincent Cres. Chest 95 D1
Vincent St. Derby 218 C1
Vine Cl. Derby 231 D4
Vine Cres. Sand 223 D3
Vine Farm Cl. Ilk 208 B3
Viola Cl. Derby 206 B2
Violet La. Bu on T 254 C4
Violet St. Derby 218 C1
Violet Way. Bu on T 255 D4
Virginsalley La. Snel 184 B1
Vista The. Staple 223 F3
Vivian St. Bols 98 C3
Vivian St. Derby 219 D4
Vulcan St. Derby 219 D1
Vyse Dr. Lo Ea 236 B3

Wade Ave. Derby 218 B1
Wade Ave. Ilk 209 D4
Wade Dr. Derby 217 F1
Wade St. Derby 218 B1
Wadebridge Gr. Derby 233 E3
Wadsworth Ave. Shef 44 B3
Wadsworth Cl. Shef 44 B3
Wadsworth Dr. Shef 44 B3
Wadsworth Rd. Shef 44 B3
Wadsworth Rd. Staple 223 F4
Wagstaff La. Sels 171 E3
Wain Ave. N Wing 132 A4
Wain Way. N Wing 132 A4
Waingroves Rd. Codnor 181 D3
Waingroves Rd. Ripley 181 D4
Wainwright Ave. Shef 44 B4
Wainwright Cres. Shef 44 B4
Wakami Cres. Derby 233 D2
Wakefield Ave. Tut 239 D3
Wakelyn Cl. Shar 234 C1
Walbrook Rd. Derby 218 C1
Walden Rd. Shef 43 D4
Waldene Dr. Derby 233 D3
Waldley La. M Mont 211 E4
Waldorf Ave. Derby 233 D4
Waldorf Cl. Derby 233 D4
Walford Rd. Kill 60 B3
Walford Rd. Rolle 240 B2
Walgrove Ave. Chest 95 F1
Walgrove Rd. Chest 95 E1
Walk Cl. Dray 235 D4
Walk Mill Rd. Hay 25 E1
Walk The. Kilb 192 A4
Walker Ave. Ripley 169 F1
Walker Gr. Staple 223 F3
Walker La. Derby 218 C3
Walker St. Glos 10 A2
Walkers Ave. Brin 182 C3
Walkers La. Kill 60 B3
Wall Ditch. Alst 149 D1
Wall St. Bux 85 E4
Wall St. Ripley 169 E1
Wallace St. Derby 218 B3
Wallfields Cl. Fin 230 B1
Wallis Cl. Dray 235 D4
Walls La. Whit 81 D4
Walnut Ave. Derby 233 D4
Walnut Ave. Shire 63 F4
Walnut Cl. As on T 246 A4
Walnut Cl. Ba on T 244 A3
Walnut Cl. Burn 229 F3
Walnut Cl. Derby 245 D4
Walnut Cl. Ilk 209 D4
Walnut Cl. Rep 243 D1
Walnut Cl. Swad 256 A3
Walnut Dr. Kill 60 B3
Walnut St. Derby 232 B4
Walpole St. Derby 219 E3
Walseker La. Hart 61 E4
Walsham Ct. Derby 205 E1
Walter St. Derby 218 C4
Walter St. Dray 234 C4
Walters Cres. Sels 171 E3
Waltham Ave. Derby 231 F2
Walthamstow Dr. Derby 218 A3
Waltheof Rd. Shef 44 A4
Walton Ave. Derby 232 C2
Walton Back La. Chest 114 A4
Walton Back La. Holy 113 F4
Walton Cl. Chest 114 A4
Walton Cl. Dron 56 B1
Walton Cl. Swad 256 A2
Walton Cres. Ashb 173 E1
Walton Cres. Chest 95 F1
Walton Ct. Shef 56 C4
Walton Ct. We Ha 207 E4
Walton Dr Ct. Chest 95 F1
Walton Dr. Chest 95 F1
Walton Dr. Derby 231 F4
Walton Fields Rd. Chest 95 E1
Walton Hill. C Don 247 D2
Walton Rd. Chest 95 E1
Walton Rd. Derby 219 F3
Walton Rd. Wa on T 254 B3
Walton St. Lo Ea 223 E1
Walton Way. Win 114 C2
Walton Wlk. Chest 95 F1
Wansfell Cl. Derby 217 F1
Wapentake La. K Ire 165 E1
Warburton Cl. Shef 43 E4
Warburton Gdns. Shef 43 E4
Warburton Rd. Shef 43 E4
Ward Dr. Som 170 B4
Ward La. Barl 80 A4
Ward La. Disley 32 C2
Ward Pl. Shef 43 D4
Ward St. Derby 218 C2
Ward St. Tupton 131 E4
Ward's La. Brea 235 E4
Ward's La. Mel 244 C2
Ward's La. Mel 245 D1
Ward's Yd. Chest 96 A1
Wardgate Way. Chest 95 D3
Wardlow Ave. Derby 220 A4
Wardlow Cl. Chest 114 C4
Wardlow Mews. Glos 9 E1
Wardlow Rd. Ilk 194 C2
Wardlow Rd. Shef 44 B3
Wardwick. Derby 219 D3
Warehouse La. Hope 38 B2
Warhurst Fold. Glos 10 A3
Warmbrook Rd. C-Frith 47 E3
Warmbrook. Wirk 165 F4
Warminster Cl. Shef 43 D2
Warminster Cres. Shef 43 D2
Warminster Dr. Shef 43 D2
Warminster Gdns. Shef 43 D2
Warminster Pl. Shef 43 D1
Warminster Rd. Shef 43 D2
Warmwells La. Ripley 180 B3
Warner St. Chest 96 A1
Warner St. Derby 217 E1
Warner St. Derby 218 C2
Warney Rd. Da Da 127 E1
Warren Ave Ext. Staple 223 E4
Warren Ave. Staple 223 E4
Warren Cl. Pils 132 B1
Warren Cres. Shef 58 C1
Warren Ct. Staple 223 E4
Warren Dr. Linton 261 E3
Warren La. Bran 253 F4
Warren Lea. Marple 15 D1
Warren Rise. Dron 57 E2
Warren St. Derby 232 C4
Warren Wlk. Eck 58 C1
Warsop Rd. Mans 136 B2
Warwick Ave. Derby 218 B1
Warwick Cl. Bran 253 F4
Warwick Cl. Glos 17 E4
Warwick Cl. Swad 256 C3
Warwick Dr. Ship 194 B2
Warwick Rd. Lo Ea 237 D4
Warwick Rd. Som 159 E1
Warwick St. Chest 115 D4
Warwick St. Derby 219 E1
Wasdale Ave. Mosb 59 F3
Wash Green. Wirk 166 A4
Wash House La. Chest 95 E1
Washbrook La. Tiss 161 F2
Washhouse Bottom. G Huck 69 F4
Washington Ave. Derby 220 A3
Washington Cl. Mel 252 A4
Washington Dr. Staple 209 F1
Watburn Rd. N Mills 24 B1
Water La. Bake 109 E3
Water La. Bam 40 A2
Water La. Bols 117 F4
Water La. Eyam 71 F3
Water La. M in L 9 E3
Water La. Mans 135 D2
Water La. Mat Ba 155 D3
Water La. Mid 154 B3
Water La. Plea 118 C1
Water La. S Norm 160 A3
Water La. Tide 68 C3
Water La. Wirk 165 F4
Water Meadow La. Chest 95 D4
Water Meadows The. Swark 244 B3
Water Orton Cl. Bees 223 F2
Water St. Bake 109 E3
Water St. Bux 85 D4
Water St. Glos 10 C1
Watercress La. Cl Cr 131 E1
Waterfoot Cotts. M in L 9 D2
Waterfoot La. W Br 45 E3
Waterford Dr. Derby 220 A2
Watergo La. Burn 230 C4
Watering La. Holbr 191 E3
Wateringbury Gr. Stav 78 C1
Waterloo Cl. S Norm 160 B4
Waterloo La. Trow 209 F3
Waterloo Pl. Swad 256 A2
Waterloo Rd. Mat Ba 143 D1
Waterloo St. Al Hv 117 F1
Waterloo St. Cl Cr 131 E2
Watermeade. Eck 59 D1
Watermeadow Cl. Mans 136 B3
Watermeadow Rd. Derby 233 D3
Watermeadows The. Lo Ea 236 A4
Waterpark Rd. Dove 224 A4
Waterside Cl. Derby 205 D1
Waterside Cl. Sand 223 D2
Waterside Rd. Bu on T 254 B4
Waterside Rd. Disley 32 C4
Waterside Rd. N Mills 32 C4
Waterside Rd. Wa on T 254 B4
Waterside. Baslow 91 E3
Waterside. Bu on T 254 C
Waterside. Glos 10 A3
Waterside. Iron 170 C2
Waterside. Marple 23 D2
Waterside. Marple 23 D1
Waterswallows La. Bux 66 C2
Waterswallows Rd. Bux 66 C
Waterthorpe Cl. Mosb 59 F4
Waterthorpe Cres. Mosb 59 F4
Waterthorpe Gdns. Mosb 59 F4
Waterthorpe Glade. Mosb 59 F4
Waterthorpe Glen. Mosb 59 F4
Waterthorpe Rise. Mosb 59 F4
Waterway The. Sand 223 E
Watery La. Ashb 184 C
Watery La. Bretby 249 E
Watery La. Clif 184 C
Watery La. Ella 183 D
Watery La. Scro 226 C
Watery La. Swad 255 E
Watery La. Thurv 215 E
Watford Bridge Ind Est. N Mills 24 B
Watford Bridge Rd. N Mills 24 B
Watford La. N Mills 24 B
Watford Rd. Bux 84 C
Watford Rd. N Mills 24 B
Watkin Ave. Glos 9 F2
Watkinson St. Hean 181 E
Watnall Rd. Kim 195 F
Watson Ave. Hean 181 F1
Watson La. Win 114 B
Watson St. Derby 218 C
Watson St. Derby 218 C
Watten Cl. Derby 231 F1
Watts Green. A in W 108 C
Waveney Cl. Derby 205 D
Waverley St. Derby 232 B
Waverley St. Lo Ea 236 C
Waverley St. Tibs 148 A
Wayfaring Rd. Derby 206 A
Wayford Ave. Chest 96 A
Wayford Ave. Chest 115 D
Wayside Cl. N Wing 132 A
Wayside Ct. Chest 96 B
Wayside. Chest 96 B
Wayzgoose Dr. Derby 219 E
Weaddow La. Middle 124 C
Weakland Cl. Shef 44 C
Weakland Cres. Shef 44 C
Weakland Dr. Shef 44 C
Weakland Way. Shef 44 C
Weather Hill La. Holme 3 F
Weathern Field. Linton 261 E
Weaver Cl. Ashb 185 E
Weaver Rd. Utt 210 A
Weavers Cl. Ock 221 E
Weavers Green. Derby 217 E
Weavers The. Dens 196 B
Weaving Ave. Cas 38 B
Webster Ave. East 182 C
Webster Croft. Chest 77 D
Webster Ct. Chest 95 F

Webster St. Derby 218 C2
Wedgewood Cl. Bu on T 248 A1
Wedneshough. M in L 9 E3
Weightman Dr. Greas 195 D4
Weir Bank. Bu on T 254 C3
Weirfield Rd. Derby 205 D1
Weirside. May 184 B4
Welbeck Ave. Bux 85 E3
Welbeck Ave. Ilk 208 B3
Welbeck Cl. Dron 56 B1
Welbeck Cl. Stav 97 E3
Welbeck Cl. Clowne 80 C2
Welbeck Dr. Win 114 C2
Welbeck Gdns. Bees 223 F2
Welbeck Gr. Derby 204 B2
Welbeck Rd. Bols 99 D1
Welbeck Rd. Lo Ea 223 E2
Welbeck Rd. Mans 136 B2
Welbeck St. Elmt 81 F1
Welbeck St. Whit 82 A3
Welbury Gdns. Mosb 59 F3
Welch Ave. Staple 223 F4
Welfare Ave. Chest 95 E2
Welfare Cl. Shireb 119 F2
Welfitt Gr. Ne La 101 D1
Well Banks. K Ire 165 D1
Well Cl. H Ward 175 F2
Well Gate. Glos 10 C1
Well La. Belper 190 C4
Well La. Black 257 D1
Well La. Holy 112 F4
Well La. Rep 242 B1
Well La. Shirl 146 B2
Well Rd. Shef 43 D3
Well Row. M in L 16 A4
Well Spring Cl. Chest 96 C4
Well St. Brass 152 C1
Well St. Derby 219 D4
Well St. Elton 140 C4
Well St. N Mills 33 D4
Well St. Ripley 169 E1
Welland Cl. Bu on T 248 A3
Welland Cl. Derby 217 E2
Wellcarr Rd. Shef 43 D1
Welldon St. Hean 181 D2
Wellesley Ave. Derby 231 E4
Wellfield Cl. Eck 44 C1
Wellfield St. Mat 143 E3
Wellfield. Mat 143 E3
Wellgate La. O Had 109 D1
Wellhead Rd. Shef 43 D3
Wellington Cl. Mat 143 E4
Wellington Cres. Derby 219 E2
Wellington Ct. Belper 178 C2
Wellington Ct. Belper 178 C2
Wellington Pl. East 182 C1
Wellington Rd. Bran 253 F4
Wellington St. Derby 219 E2
Wellington St. East 182 C2
Wellington St. Hean 181 E2
Wellington St. Lo Ea 223 E1
Wellington St. Mat 143 E3
Wellington St. Ripley 169 F1
Wellington St. Staple 223 E3
Wellington St. Uns 77 E3
Wells Cl. Mans 136 B2
Wells Ct. Derby 230 C4
Wells Rd. Derby 217 F1
Wells St. Scarc 118 B4
Wellspring Cl. Win 115 D2
Wellspring Dale. Staple 223 F3
Wellwood Rd. Swad 256 A3
Welney Cl. Derby 230 B4
Welshpool Pl. Chest 95 E2
Welshpool Rd. Derby 205 E1
Welwyn Ave. Derby 204 B2
Welwyn Ave. Derby 232 C2
Welwyn Ave. Mans 136 C2
Welwyn Cl. Chest 95 E2
Welwyn Cl. Shef 44 A2
Welwyn Rd. Shef 44 A2
Wembley Gdns. Derby 218 A3
Wendover Cl. Derby 217 E1
Wenham La. S in A 148 C2
Wenlock Cl. Chest 95 E2
Wenlock Cl. Derby 217 F1
Wenlock Cl. Greas 195 E4
Wenlock Cres. Chest 95 E2
Wenlock Dr. Gra 115 F2
Wensley Dr. Derby 220 C2
Wensley Rd. N Wing 131 F3
Wensley Rd. Wins 141 E3
Wensley Way. Stav 97 E4
Wensleydale Cl. Mans 136 C1
Wensleydale Rd. Lo Ea 236 A3
Wensleydale Wlk. Derby 233 E4
Wentworth Ave. Chest 114 C4
Wentworth Cl. Derby 217 F1
Wentworth Cl. Mans 136 C1
Wentworth Croft. Hean 182 A2
Wentworth Ct. Kim 195 F3
Wentworth Dr. Bu on T 240 B1
Wentworth Rd. Shef 56 C4
Wentworth St. Coss 195 D1
Werburgh Cl. Derby 220 B2
Werburgh St. Derby 218 C2
Werneth Low Rd. Marple 15 D3
Werneth Rd. Glos 17 D4
Wesley La. Ock 221 E3
Wesley Pl. Staple 223 F4
Wesley Rd. Derby 233 D3
Wesley Rd. Ripley 167 F2
Wesley Rd. Shirl 146 C2
Wesley St. Glos 10 A3
Wesley St. Glos 10 C1
Wesley St. Ilk 194 C2
Wesley St. La Mi 182 B2
Wesleyan Chapel Wlk. Staple 223 E4
Wessex Gdns. Totley 55 E3
Wessington La. S Wing 158 A3
Wessington Mews. Derby 204 C1
Wessington Mews. Glos 9 F1
West Ave. Derby 218 C3
West Ave. Derby 232 C2
West Ave. Dray 234 C4
West Ave. Hilton 228 B1
West Ave. Ripley 169 E1
West Ave. Sand 223 D3
West Ave. Staple 223 F4
West Bank Ave. Crich 156 C1
West Bank Ave. Derby 218 C4
West Bank Cl. Derby 218 C4
West Bank Lea. Mans 136 A1
West Bank Link. Mans 136 A1
West Bank Rd. Derby 204 C3
West Bank. Mat Ba 143 D1
West Bank. Ripley 168 A1
West Bank. Wins 141 D3
West Bars. Chest 95 F2
West Cl. Derby 204 C1
West Cres. Mat 143 D3
West Cres. Stav 98 A3
West Croft Ave. Derby 231 E3
West Croft Cl. Youl 125 D3
West Dr. Derby 217 E1
West Dr. Dove 211 D1
West Dr. Tint 9 F4
West Edge Cl. Ash 129 E2
West End Cl. Alf 159 D2
West End Cres. Ilk 208 B4
West End Dr. Ilk 208 B4
West End Dr. Shar 234 C1
West End St. Staple 223 E3
West End View. Eck 59 E1
West End. Alf 159 D2
West End. Barl 80 A4
West End. Brass 152 C1
West End. Elton 140 C3
West End. M in L 15 F4
West End. Pinx 160 B2
West End. Wirk 165 F4
West Gate. Holme 3 F4
West Gate. Lo Ea 236 C4
West Gr. Derby 232 B3
West Hill Park. Mans 136 A2
West Hill. Codnor 181 D4
West Lawn. Fin 230 B1
West Lea Cotts. Clowne 80 B2
West Lea. Chest 95 D1
West Lees Rd. Bam 40 A2
West Park Rd. Derby 218 C4
West Rd. Bux 85 D3
West Rd. Derby 220 B3
West Row. Derby 205 D1
West Service Rd. Derby 220 A2
West St. Al Hv 117 E1
West St. Bu on T 248 A2
West St. Chest 95 F2
West St. Cl Cr 131 D2
West St. Clowne 81 D3
West St. Dron 56 C1
West St. Eck 59 E1
West St. Elmt 81 E1
West St. Hean 181 E1
West St. Ilk 208 C4
West St. La Mi 182 A2
West St. Mar War 120 B2
West St. S Norm 159 F3
West St. Scarc 101 D2
West St. Shirl 146 C2
West St. Som 170 B3
West St. Swad 256 A2
West St. Tint 9 F4
West Terr. Ilk 194 C1
West View Ave. Derby 231 D4
West View Cl. Totley 55 F3
West View La. Totley 55 F3
West View Rd. Chest 95 F3
West View. Barl 80 A3
West View. May 184 B3
West View. Roc 197 D2
West View. Scarc 118 A4
West View. Stav 78 B1
West Way. Som 159 E1
Westacre Dr. Swad 255 F1
Westbank Cl. Dron 57 D2
Westbourne Pk. Derby 217 F4
Westbourne Ave. Shirl 147 D2
Westbourne Gr. Chest 95 D2
Westbridge Rd. Barl 80 A4
Westbrook Cl. C-Frith 47 E3
Westbrook Cl. Chest 94 C1
Westbrook Dr. Chest 94 C1
Westbury Gdns. Belper 179 E3
Westbury St. Derby 218 C2
Westby La. Awsw 195 E2
Westby La. Kim 195 E2
Westcroft Cres. Mosb 59 F4
Westcroft Dr. Mosb 59 F4
Westcroft Gdns. Mosb 59 F4
Westcroft Glen. Mosb 59 F4
Westcroft Gr. Mosb 59 F4
Westcross Ave. Staple 223 F4
Westdale Cl. Lo Ea 236 A3
Westdale Rd. Mans 136 A1
Westdale Rd. Sels 171 E2
Westdene Ave. Derby 232 B3
Westerlands. Staple 223 F3
Western Ave. Som 169 E4
Western Dr. Hean 193 F4
Western La. W Br 46 A4
Western Rd. Derby 217 F1
Western Rd. Derby 219 D2
Westfield Ave. Chest 95 D1
Westfield Ave. Hean 181 F1
Westfield Bank. Barl 80 A4
Westfield Centre. Mosb 59 F4
Westfield Cl. Chest 95 D1
Westfield Cl. Ilk 208 B3
Westfield Cres. Mosb 59 E4
Westfield Dr. Newt 147 F1
Westfield Gdns. Chest 95 D1
Westfield La. Barl 79 F4
Westfield La. Uns 77 F4
Westfield Northway. Mosb 59 F4
Westfield Rd. Dron 76 B4
Westfield Rd. Kill 60 B3
Westfield Rd. Swad 256 A3
Westfield Southway. Mosb 59 F4
Westgreen Ave. Derby 232 B3
Westhall Rd. Derby 217 E2
Westhill La. Gra 115 F2
Westhorpe Dr. Lo Ea 236 B4
Westland Dr. Pinx 160 B2
Westland Gdns. Mosb 59 E4
Westland Gr. Mosb 59 F4
Westland Rd. Mosb 59 F4
Westleigh Ave. Derby 218 B3
Westleigh Ct. Chest 95 F3
Westleigh. Mans 136 B3
Westley Cres. Lit Ea 191 E1
Westminster Ave. Staple 223 E3
Westminster St. Derby 232 C4
Westmoor Rd. Chest 96 C2
Westmorland Cl. Derby 219 E3
Westmorland Way. Sels 171 D2
Weston Bank. M Mont 211 F4
Weston Cl. Chest 95 D3
Weston Cres. Lo Ea 235 F2
Weston Park Ave. Derby 232 C2
Weston Park Gdns. Derby 232 B2
Weston Rd. As on T 246 A4
Weston Rd. We on T 245 F3
Weston Rise. Derby 245 D4
Weston Spot Cl. Ripley 180 B4
Weston St. Hean 194 A4
Weston St. Swad 256 A2
Westthorpe Rd. Kill 60 B3
Westward Cl. Utt 210 A1
Westwell Pl. Mosb 59 E3
Westwick Cres. Shef 56 B4
Westwick Gr. Shef 56 C4
Westwick La. Holy 94 B1
Westwick Rd. Shef 56 C4
Westwick St. Ilk 209 D3
Westwood Ave. Stav 97 E4
Westwood Cl. Stav 97 E3
Westwood Dr. Derby 232 B3
Westwood La. Chest 96 C2
Westwood Park. Swad 255 F3
Westwood Rd. Calow 97 D2
Wetherby Cl. Kim 195 F4
Wetherby Rd. Derby 232 C4
Wetlands La. Chest 96 C2
Weybridge Cl. We Ha 207 E4
Whaley Comm. Scarc 100 B2
Whaley La. W Br 45 E4
Whaley Rd. Scarc 100 C1
Wharf La. Chest 96 A2
Wharf La. Stav 78 C2
Wharf Rd. Pinx 160 B1
Wharf Rd. W Br 45 F4
Wharf The. Shar 235 D1
Wharfdale Rd. Lo Ea 236 A3
Wharfedale Cl. Derby 205 D2
Wharmby Ave. Mans 135 E2
Wharncliffe Cl. Glos 9 F2
Wharncliffe Rd. Ilk 194 C1
Wharncliffe Rd. Ilk 208 C4
Wheal La. Shel 107 E4
Wheal La. Tadd 107 E4
Wheatbridge Rd. Chest 95 F2
Wheatcroft Cl. Cl Cr 131 E1
Wheatcroft Cl. Win 115 D2
Wheatcroft La. Crich 156 C4
Wheatcroft. Glos 9 F2
Wheatfield Cres. Mans 136 C3
Wheatfield Way. Chest 94 C3
Wheathill Cl. Chest 94 C3
Wheathill Cl. Chest 96 C2
Wheathill La. Chest 96 B2
Wheatland Cl. Derby 231 E1
Wheatlands La. Baslow 91 E3
Wheatlands Rd. Bu on T 254 C4
Wheatlands Rd. Win 114 C2
Wheatlands. Swad 256 A4
Wheatley Ave. Som 159 E1
Wheatley Cl. Mans 136 C1
Wheatley Gdns. Da Da 127 E1
Wheatley La. Bu on T 248 B2
Wheatley Rd. Da Da 127 E2
Wheatsheaf Cl. Derby 206 B1
Wheatsheaf La. Crich 156 C1
Wheatsheaf Rd. W Br 45 F3
Wheeldon Ave. Belper 179 D2
Wheeldon Ave. Derby 218 C4
Wheeldon Cres. Chest 96 B4
Wheeldon Way. H Ward 175 F2
Whenby Cl. Derby 217 E1
Whernside Cl. Derby 233 E3
Wheston Bank. Tide 69 D3
Whetmorhurst Rd. Marple 23 F2
Whilton Cres. We Ha 207 E4
Whilton Ct. Belper 179 E2
Whinacre Cl. Shef 57 D3
Whinacre Pl. Shef 57 D3
Whinacre Wlk. Shef 57 D3
Whinbush Ave. Derby 232 C3
Whinney Bank. Mans 136 B2
Whinney Hill. Mans 136 B2
Whiston St. Derby 219 D1
Whitaker Gdns. Derby 218 C1
Whitaker Rd. Derby 218 C1
Whitaker St. Derby 219 D1
Whitburn Rd. Bees 223 F2
Whitby Ave. Derby 205 E1
Whitcombe Pl. Ripley 169 E1
White Edge Cl. Chest 95 E3
White Edge Dr. Baslow 91 F3
White Gate Rd. Holme 3 E4
White Gates. Codnor 181 D4
White Hart Yd. Kilb 191 F4
White Horse La. Stret 145 E4
White Knowle Park. Bux 85 E3
White Knowle Rd. Bux 85 E3
White La. Eck 44 B1
White La. Shef 44 B1
White La. Shot 177 E2
White Leas Ave. N Wing 132 A4
White Leas. Chest 95 D2
White Lion Sq. Ilk 208 C4
White Lodge La. Baslow 91 F3
White Rd. N Mills 24 B1
White Rd. Stav 79 D2
White St. Derby 218 C4
White Thorns Cl. Shef 57 D3
White Thorns Dr. Shef 57 D3
White Thorns View. Shef 57 D3
White Tor Rd. Mat 143 E1
White Woods Way. Mat 143 D2
White's La. Som 170 A4
Whitebank Cl. Chest 96 A1
Whitecarr La. Ash 145 D2
Whitecarr La. Brack 145 D2
Whitecotes Cl. Chest 114 C4
Whitecotes La. Chest 114 C4
Whitecroft Rd. Marple 23 E1
Whitecroft View. Barl 80 A3
Whitecross Ave. Tide 69 E2
Whitecross Gdns. Derby 218 C4
Whitecross Rd. Tide 69 E3
Whitecross St. Derby 218 C3
Whitefield La. Ash 129 D3
Whitefield La. Chel 106 B4
Whitehall Terr. Chin 34 B1
Whitehead Dr. Brin 182 B4
Whitehead St. Stav 78 C1
Whitehough Head La. C-Frith 46 C4
Whitehouse Cl. Derby 232 B2
Whitehouse Rise. Belper 178 C3
Whitehouses. Chest 96 A1
Whitehurst St. Derby 232 B4
Whitelea La. Tans 144 A3
Whiteleas Rd. W Br 45 E2
Whiteley Rd. Ripley 180 C4
Whitelow La. Ible 153 F4
Whitelow La. Totley 55 D4
Whitely Cl. Staple 223 F4
Whitemoor La. Belper 179 E3
Whites Cl. Som 159 D1
Whiteway. Derby 204 C1
Whitewell Gdns. Derby 233 E3
Whitewells La. Alder 178 B4
Whitewells Rd. Alder 167 F1
Whitfield Ave. Glos 17 E4
Whitfield Cross. Glos 17 E4
Whitfield La. Middle 124 C1
Whiting Ave. Bees 223 F1
Whiting St. Shef 43 D3
Whitle Bank Rd. N Mills 24 A1
Whitle Rd. N Mills 24 B1
Whitley Way. Ashb 185 F4
Whitmore Ave. Gra 115 F1
Whitmore Rd. Derby 219 F3
Whitstable Cl. Derby 231 E4
Whittaker La. Lit Ea 191 E1
Whitting Valley Rd. Chest 77 D1
Whittington Hill. Chest 77 D1
Whittington La. Uns 76 C3
Whittington Rd. Stav 77 F2
Whittington St. Derby 232 B3
Whittlebury Dr. Derby 230 C4
Whitton Pl. Stav 98 A3
Whitwell Rd. Th Sa 63 D2
Whitworth Ave. Da Da 127 E2
Whitworth Rd. Chest 96 A3
Whitworth Rd. Da Da 127 D2
Whitworth Rd. Ilk 208 C3
Whitworth Rd. North 127 D2
Whysall St. Hean 181 F1
Whyteleafe Gr. Derby 206 A1
Wickens Pl. Stav 79 D2
Wickersley Cl. Derby 204 C1
Wickets The. Bu on T 254 C4
Wickfield Cl. Shef 44 C3
Wickfield Dr. Shef 44 C3
Wickfield Gr. Shef 44 C2
Wickfield Pl. Shef 44 C3
Wickfield Rd. Shef 44 C3
Wicksteed Cl. Belper 179 E3
Widdop Cl. Shef 44 B4
Widdop Croft. Shef 44 B4
Widdybank Cl. Derby 204 B1
Wideshaft. Swad 256 B2
Widmerpool St. Pinx 160 B1
Wigley Rd. Stav 97 E3
Wigmore Cl. Derby 217 E2
Wilberforce Rd. Mans 135 E1
Wilbury Dr. Shef 44 A3
Wilcox Ave. Mans 136 A3
Wild Hill. S in A 148 C4
Wild La. S Wing 157 D2
Wild St. Derby 218 B3
Wildaygreen La. Barlow 75 D1
Wilderbrook La. Shot 178 A4
Wilders Lea Ct. Belper 179 D1
Wildhay La. Stan 183 E4
Wildpark La. W Und 202 B3
Wildsmith St. Derby 233 D4
Wilfred St. Derby 219 D1
Wilhallow La. Sels 171 F1
Wilkin Hill. Barlow 75 F1
Wilkins Dr. Derby 232 C4
Wilkinson Cl. Chest 115 D3
Wilkinson Cl. Plea 135 D3
Wilkinson Dr. Stav 97 D4
Will Shore's La. Wens 142 B3
Willerbley Rd. Mat 143 E1
Willersley Ct. Chest 95 E4
Willersley Rd. Mat Ba 155 E4
Willesden Ave. Derby 218 A4
Willetts Rd. Derby 220 A4
William Ave. East 182 C1
William Cl. Mosb 59 E3
William Cres. Mosb 59 E3
William Newton Cl. Eg 241 D3
William Rd. Staple 223 E4
William St N. Chest 76 C1
William St. Belper 178 C2
William St. Chest 96 A3
William St. Derby 218 C3
William St. Eck 59 E2
William St. Lo Ea 223 E1
Williams Cl. Som 170 B3
Williamson Ave. Bux 66 B1
Williamson Cres. W Br 45 E4
Williamson Rd. W Br 45 E4
Williamthorpe Cl. N Wing 132 A4
Williamthorpe Rd. N Wing 132 A4
Willington Rd. Etwall 229 E2
Willington Rd. Fin 242 B4
Willington Rd. Rep 242 A2
Willn St. Derby 218 C1
Willoughby Ave. Lo Ea 223 E2
Willoughby Cl. Brea 235 F4
Willoughby St. Coss 195 D1
Willow Ave. Lo Ea 223 E1
Willow Ave. Ripley 180 B4
Willow Ave. Shireb 119 E3
Willow Ave. Staple 223 E3
Willow Brook Cl. Hilton 228 B1
Willow Cl. Alf 159 D3
Willow Cl. As on T 246 A4
Willow Cl. Derby 204 C1
Willow Cl. Elmt 81 F1
Willow Cl. Pils 132 B1
Willow Cl. S Norm 160 A3
Willow Ct. Calow 97 D2
Willow Dr. C-Frith 47 D3
Willow Dr. Stav 79 E2
Willow Dr. Swad 255 F4
Willow Garth Rd. Chest 95 E4
Willow Gr. Belper 179 D1
Willow Gr. Will 242 A3
Willow Meadow Rd. Ashb 185 E4
Willow Pl. Bu on T 254 C4
Willow Rd. C Don 247 D3
Willow Rd. Kill 60 B3
Willow Rise. Sand 223 D3
Willow Row. Derby 218 C3
Willow St. Shirl 146 B1
Willow Terr. Clowne 80 C1
Willow Way. Da Da 127 D2
Willowbath La. Wirk 165 F4
Willowcroft Rd. Derby 220 C2
Willowfields. Hilton 228 B1
Willowherb Cl. Derby 231 F1
Willowpit La. Hilton 228 C3

Willows Ave. Alf 159 D3
Willows The. H Ward 175 F2
Willowsend Cl. Fin 230 B1
Willridding La. Stan 183 E4
Willson Ave. Derby 231 E4
Willson Rd. Derby 231 E4
Wilmington Ave. Derby 233 D3
Wilmore Rd. Derby 232 A3
Wilmot Ave. Derby 219 F3
Wilmot Ave. We on T 245 F3
Wilmot Dr. Smal 192 C3
Wilmot Rd. Belper 179 D2
Wilmot Rd. Swad 256 A2
Wilmot St. Derby 219 D2
Wilmot St. Hean 181 F1
Wilmot St. Ilk 194 C1
Wilmot St. Lo Ea 236 A3
Wilmot St. Mat 143 D3
Wilmslow Dr. Derby 206 A1
Wilne Ave. Lo Ea 236 A2
Wilne Cl. Lo Ea 235 F2
Wilne La. Brea 235 E2
Wilne La. Shar 235 D1
Wilne Rd. Dray 235 D3
Wilne Rd. Lo Ea 235 F2
Wilshaw Cl. C-Frith 47 E3
Wilson Ave. Clowne 80 C3
Wilson Ave. Hean 181 D2
Wilson Ave. Newt 147 F1
Wilson Cl. Burn 230 B4
Wilson Cl. Cl Cr 131 E1
Wilson Dr. Som 170 B4
Wilson La. Heath 117 D1
Wilson Pl. Shef 43 D4
Wilson Rd. Derby 219 F4
Wilson Rd. Dron 57 E2
Wilson Rd. East 182 C1
Wilson Rise. Br Hill 252 C3
Wilson St. Alf 159 D2
Wilson St. Derby 219 D2
Wilson St. Dron 76 A4
Wilson St. Mans 135 E1
Wilson St. Pinx 160 B2
Wilson's Terr. Glos 17 D4
Wilsthorpe Rd. Brea 235 F4
Wilsthorpe Rd. Derby 220 A4
Wilsthorpe Rd. Lo Ea 236 A3
Wilton Cl. Derby 231 E1
Wilton Pl. Ilk 194 C1
Wiltshire Ave. Sels 171 D2
Wiltshire Rd. Derby 219 F4
Wimbledon Rd. Derby 218 A4
Wimborne Cres. Chest 95 F4
Wimbourne Cl. Derby 233 D1
Wimpole Gdns. Derby 218 A3
Wimsey Way. Som 159 D1
Wincanton Cl. Derby 219 E1
Winchcombe Dr. Bu on T 248 A1
Winchcombe Way. Derby 206 A1
Winchester Cres. Ilk 209 D4
Winchester Dr. Bu on T 254 B4
Winchester Dr. Linton 261 E3
Winchester Dr. Mans 136 B2
Winchester Dr. Swad 256 B3
Winchester Rd. Chest 95 F4
Windermere Ave. Dron 56 C1
Windermere Ave. Ilk 208 B3
Windermere Cres. Derby 204 C2
Windermere Dr. Derby 220 C3
Windermere Gdns. Lo Ea 223 D1
Windermere Rd. Chest 95 E4
Windermere Rd. Cl Cr 131 D2
Windermere Rd. Lo Ea 223 D1
Windlea Rd. Som 170 B3
Windley Cres. Derby 204 C1
Windley Dr. Ilk 194 B2
Windley La. Idri 176 C3
Windley La. Wind 189 F4
Windmill Ave. Kilb 192 A4
Windmill Cl. Bols 99 D2
Windmill Cl. C Don 247 D1
Windmill Cl. Ock 221 E3
Windmill Dr. March 224 C2
Windmill Greenway. Mosb 59 F3
Windmill Hill La. Derby 218 B3
Windmill La. Alder 166 C3
Windmill La. Ashb 173 E2
Windmill La. Belper 179 D2
Windmill La. Eyam 71 E3
Windmill La. Snel 184 C1
Windmill La. Uns 77 D3
Windmill Rd. Etwall 229 D2
Windmill Rise. Belper 179 D3
Windmill Rise. S Norm 159 F3
Windmill Rise. Som 170 B4
Windmill St. Swad 256 A1
Windmill View. Ripley 179 F4
Windrush Cl. Derby 205 D3
Windses Est. Grin 53 E1
Windsmoor Rd. Brin 182 B4
Windsor Ave. Derby 231 D4
Windsor Ave. Mel 252 A4
Windsor Cl. Ashb 173 E2
Windsor Cl. Chest 95 E1
Windsor Cl. Hean 181 F2
Windsor Cl. Ock 221 E1
Windsor Cl. Som 170 A4
Windsor Cl. Swad 256 A3
Windsor Cl. Trow 209 D3
Windsor Cres. Ilk 208 C2
Windsor Cres. Staple 223 F4
Windsor Ct. Sand 223 D2
Windsor Ct. We Ha 207 E4
Windsor Dr. Derby 221 D3
Windsor Dr. Shef 56 C4
Windsor Dr. Win 114 C2
Windsor Park Rd. Bux 85 E4
Windsor Rd. Bux 85 E4
Windsor Rd. Linton 261 E3
Windsor Rd. Utt 210 A1
Windsor St. Staple 223 F4
Windsor Wlk. Chest 115 E4
Windy Fields Rd. Holy 113 E4
Windy House La. Shef 44 A4
Windy La. Lit Ea 191 E1
Windyridge. Long 121 D3
Winfield Gr. Marple 15 D1
Wingerworth Ave. Shef 56 B4
Wingerworth Cotts. Gra 115 F2
Wingerworth Park Rd. Derby 220 C3
Wingerworth St. Gra 115 F2
Wingfield Cl. Shef 56 C4
Wingfield Cres. Shef 44 B3
Wingfield Dr. Derby 205 F1
Wingfield Dr. Ilk 194 B2
Wingfield Gr. Glos 17 F4
Wingfield Rd. Alf 158 C2
Wingfield Rd. Tupton 131 E4
Winhill Rd. N Mills 24 B1
Winn La. Atlow 174 C4
Winnat Pl. Stav 97 E4
Winnats Cl. Chest 95 E3
Winnats Cl. Glos 17 F4
Winnats. Cas 37 F1
Winnington Rd. Marple 23 D4
Winslow Ave. M in L 9 D1
Winslow Grn. Derby 220 B3
Winster Cl. Belper 179 D3
Winster Cl. Cl Cr 131 D3
Winster Gr. Bux 85 F4
Winster La. Elton 140 C3
Winster Mews. Glos 9 F1
Winster Rd. Derby 205 F1
Winster Rd. Stav 97 E4
Winster Sq. Bux 85 F4
Winster Way. Lo Ea 235 F3
Winston Cl. Staple 223 F4
Winter Closes. Sels 171 F1
Winterbourne Dr. Staple 209 F1
Wintercroft La. Thorpe 161 F1
Wire La. Newt 148 A2
Wirksmoor Rd. N Mills 33 D4
Wirksworth Rd. Duff 190 B2
Wirksworth Rd. Idri 176 C3
Wirksworth Rd. Ilk 208 B2
Wirksworth Rd. K Ire 165 D1
Wirksworth Rd. Shot 177 E2
Wirksworth Rd. Wind 177 E2
Wirksworth Rd. Wind 189 F4
Wisbech Cl. Chest 114 C4
Wisgreaves Rd. Derby 232 C4
Wishing Stone Way. Mat 143 F3
Witham Cl. Chest 96 B3
Witham Ct. Chest 95 E2
Witham Dr. Derby 231 E3
Witney Cl. Derby 232 B4
Witney St. Shef 43 D4
Woburn Cl. Newt 147 F1
Woburn Cl. Som 169 F4
Woburn Croft. Sand 223 D2
Woburn La. Mans 135 E2
Woburn Pl. Derby 218 A3
Woburn Pl. Mans 135 E2
Woburn Rd. Mans 135 E2
Wolds Rise. Mat 143 E4
Wolfa St. Derby 218 C2
Wolfcote Cl. Cl Cr 131 E1
Wolfe Cl. Chest 95 E1
Wolfscote Dale. Swad 255 F1
Wollaton Ave. Shef 56 A3
Wollaton Dr. Shef 56 A3
Wollaton Rd S. Derby 205 F1
Wollaton Rd. Derby 219 F4
Wollaton Rd. Shef 56 A3
Wollen Cl. Elmt 81 F1
Wolseley Rd. Shef 43 D4
Wolverley Grange. Derby 233 E3
Wood Ave. Elmt 81 E1
Wood Ave. Sand 223 D3
Wood Cl. Win 114 B2
Wood Croft. Derby 231 E4
Wood End Rd. Hean 181 F1
Wood Gdns. Hay 25 E2
Wood La. Belper 190 C4
Wood La. Elmt 100 B4
Wood La. H Wood 192 B3
Wood La. Han 238 A2
Wood La. Hollow 144 A1
Wood La. Ible 153 F3
Wood La. Idri 176 C4
Wood La. Kni 163 D1
Wood La. Mar War 120 C4
Wood La. Pent 169 D2
Wood La. Plea 119 F1
Wood La. Scarc 118 C3
Wood La. Shireb 119 F1
Wood La. Smal 192 B3
Wood La. Swad 256 A4
Wood Nook Cl. Sels 171 F3
Wood Rd. Derby 205 F1
Wood Rd. Derby 220 A4
Wood Rd. Derby 221 D3
Wood St N. Alf 159 E3
Wood St. Alf 159 E3
Wood St. Codnor 181 D4
Wood St. Derby 219 D3
Wood St. East 182 C2
Wood St. Glos 17 E4
Wood St. Ilk 194 C1
Wood St. M in L 9 E3
Wood St. N Mills 33 D4
Wood St. N Wing 116 C1
Wood St. Ripley 169 E1
Wood St. Som 170 B4
Wood St. Swad 256 A1
Wood St. Wirk 165 F4
Woodale Cl. Derby 230 C3
Woodall Rd. Kill 60 C3
Woodbeck Ct. Derby 206 A1
Woodborough Rd. Mans 135 F1
Woodbourne Rd. N Mills 33 D3
Woodbridge Cl. Derby 232 C1
Woodbridge Rise. Chest 114 A4
Woodbrook Ct. W Br 45 F4
Woodbrook. W Br 45 F4
Woodchester Dr. Derby 233 E3
Woodcock Gr. Glos 10 C1
Woodcock Rd. Glos 11 D1
Woodfall La. Wind 189 F2
Woodfield Cl. Glos 9 F3
Woodfield Dr. Ripley 181 D4
Woodfield Dr. Swad 256 B3
Woodfield Rd. Pinx 160 B2
Woodford Rd. Derby 218 A4
Woodford Way. Stav 78 A2
Woodhall Dr. Derby 230 C4
Woodhead La. Stret 130 B1
Woodhead Rd. Glos 10 B3
Woodhead Rd. Holme 2 C3
Woodhead Rd. Shef 43 D4
Woodhead Rd. Tint 10 A4
Woodhouse Ct. Mans 136 B1
Woodhouse La. Barl 79 F3
Woodhouse La. Bols 98 C2
Woodhouse La. Eck 79 E3
Woodhouse La. Row 126 C4
Woodhouse La. S Norm 159 F3
Woodhouse La. Scro 226 C4
Woodhouse La. Wins 141 E3
Woodhouse Rd. Kilb 191 F4
Woodhouse Rd. Kilb 192 A4
Woodhouse St. Swad 256 B2
Woodhurst Cl. Derby 219 E4
Woodland Ave. Ilk 194 B2
Woodland Ave. Ock 221 E1
Woodland Ave. S in A 148 C2
Woodland Dr. Scro 226 B2
Woodland Dr. Shef 44 A1
Woodland Gr. Clowne 81 D2
Woodland Gr. Mans 136 B2
Woodland Pl. Shef 55 F3
Woodland Rd. Derby 218 C4
Woodland Rd. Shef 43 D2
Woodland Rd. Swad 255 D2
Woodland View. Scarc 101 D2
Woodland View. Shef 44 A1
Woodland View. Totley 56 A4
Woodland Views. March 224 C1
Woodland Way. Cl Cr 131 D3
Woodland Way. East 182 C1
Woodland Wlk. Chest 94 C3
Woodlands Ave. Brea 235 F4
Woodlands Ave. Derby 232 C2
Woodlands Brow. Ashb 173 E2
Woodlands Cl. Lit Ea 205 D4
Woodlands Cl. Mel 252 A4
Woodlands Cl. Tint 9 F3
Woodlands Cres. Over 262 A2
Woodlands Gr. Cl Cr 131 D3
Woodlands La. Derby 245 D4
Woodlands La. Quar 204 B3
Woodlands Rd. C-Frith 47 D2
Woodlands Rd. Derby 204 C3
Woodlands Rd. Disley 32 A3
Woodlands Rd. N Mills 33 D4
Woodlands Rd. Over 262 A2
Woodlands The. Mans 136 A1
Woodlands The. Mel 252 A4
Woodlands The. Scarc 101 D2
Woodlands Way. Mel 252 A4
Woodlands. Chest 96 B4
Woodlands. Wirk 165 F4
Woodleigh Cl. Chest 94 C3
Woodmans Croft. Hatton 227 E1
Woodminton Dr. Derby 232 C2
Woodnook Cl. O Bram 95 D2
Woodnook La. O Bram 94 C3
Woodnook Way. O Bram 94 C2
Woodpecker Hill. Dale 208 A1
Woodrising Cl. Derby 206 A2
Woodroffe Wlk. Derby 231 F4
Woodrove Ave. Shef 44 A4
Woodrove Cl. Shef 44 A4
Woods La. Bu on T 248 A1
Woods La. Bu on T 254 C4
Woods La. Derby 218 C2
Woodseats Rd. Cha 16 A3
Woodshop La. Swark 244 B3
Woodside Ave. Hol 75 D4
Woodside Ave. Kill 60 C4
Woodside Cl. Bake 109 E3
Woodside Cl. Chest 95 D2
Woodside Cres. Ilk 194 B3
Woodside Cres. Lo Ea 236 A4
Woodside Dr. Bake 109 E3
Woodside Dr. Derby 205 D2
Woodside Pl. Cl Cr 131 D2
Woodside Rd. Sand 223 D3
Woodside Rd. Shire 63 F4
Woodside Rd. Shireb 119 F3
Woodside St. N Mills 33 D3
Woodside View. Hol 75 D4
Woodside. East 182 C2
Woodside. Hors 192 A2
Woodsorrel Dr. Derby 206 A2
Woodstock Cl. Derby 204 B2
Woodstock Dr. Chest 115 E4
Woodstock Rd. Bees 223 F2
Woodstock Rise. Chest 115 E4
Woodthorpe Ave. Cl Cr 131 D2
Woodthorpe Ave. Derby 219 F3
Woodthorpe Ave. Derby 232 C2
Woodthorpe Cl. Bols 98 C4
Woodthorpe Cl. Shef 44 A4
Woodthorpe Cres. Shef 44 B4
Woodthorpe Rd. Bols 98 C4
Woodthorpe Rd. Shef 44 B4
Woodthorpe Rd. Stav 79 E1
Woodvale Cl. Chest 114 A4
Woodview Cl. Win 114 C1
Woodview Rd. Swad 255 F3
Woodville Rd. Harts 256 C2
Woodville Rd. Harts 257 D3
Woodville Rd. Over 262 A2
Woodward's Pl. Swad 256 B2
Woodwards Cl. Ock 221 E1
Woodyard La. Scro 226 C3
Woolaton La. Biggin 138 E1
Woolley Bridge Rd. Glos 9 F3
Woolley Cl. M in L 9 E2
Woolley La. M in L 9 E2
Woolley La. M in L 9 E3
Woolley Mill La. Tint 9 F4
Woolley Rd. Mat 143 D3
Woolley Yd. Wins 141 E3
Woolrych St. Derby 218 C1
Woolsthorpe Cres. Ilk 208 B2
Worcester Ave. Mans 136 B3
Worcester Cres. Derby 219 F4
Worcester Gr. Glos 17 F4
Worcester Mews. Mans 136 B3
Worcester Rd. Bu on T 254 C3
Wordsworth Ave. Derby 231 F3
Wordsworth Ave. Mans 136 A2
Wordsworth Ave. Swad 256 B3
Wordsworth Dr. Derby 232 A3
Wordsworth Pl. Dron 76 B4
Wordsworth Rd. Awsw 195 E3
Wordsworth Rd. Chest 95 F4
Works La. L Duk 97 D2
Works Rd. Stav 78 A1
Worksop Rd. Barl 79 E2
Worksop Rd. Stav 79 E2
Worksop Rd. Th Sa 62 C4
Worksop Rd. Whit 81 F3
Worrall Ave. Lo Ea 223 F1
Worthington La. Br Hill 252 C1
Wortley Cl. Ilk 209 D4
Wortley Ave. Staple 209 E2
Wortley Ct. Bradw 51 D4
Wragley Way. Derby 231 E1
Wreakes La. Dron 56 C1
Wren Cl. Wood 256 C2
Wren Nest Rd. Glos 10 A1
Wren Nest Terr. Glos 10 B1
Wren Park Cl. Belper 178 B3
Wren Park Cl. Chest 114 C4
Wren Park Cl. Fin 230 B1
Wren Pk Cl. Eck 58 C4
Wrenpark Rd. Win 114 B2
Wretham Cl. Derby 230 B4
Wright Ave. Ripley 169 F1
Wright St. Codnor 181 D4
Wroxham Cl. Derby 232 B2
Wulfric Cl. Shef 43 F4
Wulfric Pl. Shef 43 F4
Wulfric Rd. Eck 59 E2
Wulfric Rd. Shef 43 F4
Wulfric Rd. Shef 44 A4
Wyaston Cl. Derby 204 C1
Wyaston Rd. Ashb 185 E3
Wyaston Rd. Osm 185 E3
Wybersley Rd. H La 32 A4
Wybersley Rd. Marple 23 D1
Wychwood Dr. Staple 209 E1
Wycliffe Rd. Alf 159 D2
Wye Bank Gr. Bake 109 F2
Wye Bank. Bake 109 F3
Wye Dale. Swad 255 F1
Wye Gr. Bux 85 D4
Wye Head Cl. Bux 84 C4
Wye St. Bux 85 E
Wye St. Derby 233 D
Wye Terr. Row 126 C
Wyedale Cl. Bake 109 F
Wyedale Cres. Bake 109 F
Wyedale Ct. Chest 95 F
Wyedale Dr. Bake 109 F
Wyedale View. Bake 109 F
Wyelands Cl. Bux 84 C
Wyming Brook Dr. Hal M 42 A
Wynd The. Barl 79 E
Wyndale Dr. Ilk 208 B
Wyndham Cres. Bu on T 248 B
Wyndham St. Derby 233 D
Wynton Ave. Derby 232 C
Wyntor Ave. Wins 141 E
Wynward Cl. Ilk 194 B
Wysall Cl. Mans 135 F
Wystan Ct. Rep 242 B
Wythburn Rd. Chest 95 E
Wyver La. Belper 178 C
Wyvern Ave. Lo Ea 236 B
Wyvern Cl. Greas 195 D
Wyvern Cl. Mat 143 D
Wyvern Gdns. Totley 55 F
Wyvern Way. Derby 220 A

Yardley Cl. Som 169 F
Yardley Way. Belper 179 E
Yarncliff Cl. Chest 95 E
Yarrow Cl. Derby 231 F
Yates Ave. We on T 246 A
Yates Rd. N Mills 33 E
Yates St. Derby 219 D
Yeardsley Ave. W Br 33 E
Yeardsley Green. W Br 45 E
Yeardsley La. W Br 33 E
Yeld Cl. Bake 109 E
Yeld Rd. Bake 109 E
Yeld The. Bake 109 E
Yeldersley Cl. Chest 95 D
Yeldersley La. Brai 187 D
Yeldersley La. Osm 186 C
Yelt La. Dove 224 B
Yeoman St. Bons 142 E
Yeovil Cl. Derby 233 E
Yerley Hill. Swin 172 B
Yew Tree Ave. Ock 221 E
Yew Tree Cl. Ash 129 F
Yew Tree Dr. Chest 114 A
Yew Tree Dr. Cl Cr 131 D
Yew Tree Dr. Kill 60 B
Yew Tree Dr. S in A 148 C
Yew Tree Dr. Shireb 119 E
Yew Tree Gdns. Rosl 260 B
Yew Tree Hill. Hollow 156 A
Yew Tree La. Bradl 186 C
Yew Tree La. Elv 233 F
Yew Tree Rd. Hatton 227 E
Yew Tree Rd. Rosl 260 E
Yew Tree Rd. Swad 255 F
Yews Cl. Derby 233 D
Yewtree Cl. Derby 233 E
Yewtree Cres. Bu on T 254 C
Yokecliffe Ave. Wirk 165 F
Yokecliffe Cres. Wirk 165 F
Yokecliffe Dr. Wirk 165 F
Yokecliffe Hill. Wirk 165 F
York Ave. Sand 223 D
York Ave. Sels 171 D
York Cl. Swad 256 B
York Cres. Al Hv 117 F
York Pl. N Wing 132 A
York Pl. Shire 63 F
York Rd. Derby 219 F
York Rd. Lo Ea 223 E
York Rd. Shireb 119 F
York Rd. Swad 256 A
York St. Chest 115 E
York St. Derby 218 C
York St. Glos 10 C
York Terr. Glos 17 E
York Terr. Pinx 160 F
Yorke St. Mans 136 A
Yorkshire Way. Glos 17 F
Youlgreave Cl. Derby 205 F
Youlgreave Cres. Glos 9 E
Youlgreave Dr. Shef 44 E
Young St. Derby 218 C
Ypres Rd. Derby 204 E

Zetland Cres. Derby 231 E

OS STREET ATLASES ORDER FORM

T506N99C	Hardback QUANTITY	Hardback TOTAL	Softback QUANTITY	Softback TOTAL	Pocket QUANTITY	Pocket TOTAL	➤
	£12.99		£8.99		£4.99		
Berkshire	ISBN 0-540-05992-7		ISBN 0-540-05993-5		ISBN 0-540-05994-3		
Buckinghamshire	ISBN 0-540-05989-7		ISBN 0-540-05990-0		ISBN 0-540-05991-9		
East Essex	ISBN 0-540-05848-3		ISBN 0-540-05866-1		ISBN 0-540-05850-5		
West Essex	ISBN 0-540-05849-1		ISBN 0-540-05867-X		ISBN 0-540-05851-3		
North Hampshire	ISBN 0-540-05852-1		ISBN 0-540-05853-X		ISBN 0-540-05854-8		
South Hampshire	ISBN 0-540-05855-6		ISBN 0-540-05856-4		ISBN 0-540-05857-2		
Hertfordshire	ISBN 0-540-05995-1		ISBN 0-540-05996-X		ISBN 0-540-05997-8		
East Kent	ISBN 0-540-06026-7		ISBN 0-540-06027-5		ISBN 0-540-06028-3		
West Kent	ISBN 0-540-06029-1		ISBN 0-540-06031-3		ISBN 0-540-06030-5		
Nottinghamshire	ISBN 0-540-05858-0		ISBN 0-540-05859-9		ISBN 0-540-05860-2		
Oxfordshire	ISBN 0-540-05986-2		ISBN 0-540-05987-0		ISBN 0-540-05988-9		
Surrey	ISBN 0-540-05983-8		ISBN 0-540-05984-6		ISBN 0-540-05985-4		
East Sussex	ISBN 0-540-05875-0		ISBN 0-540-05874-2		ISBN 0-540-05873-4		
West Sussex	ISBN 0-540-05876-9		ISBN 0-540-05877-7		ISBN 0-540-05878-5		
	£12.99		£9.99		£4.99		
Bristol and Avon	ISBN 0-540-06140-9		ISBN 0-540-06141-7		ISBN 0-540-06142-5		
Cheshire	ISBN 0-540-06143-3		ISBN 0-540-06144-1		ISBN 0-540-06145-X		
Derbyshire	ISBN 0-540-06137-9		ISBN 0-540-06138-7		ISBN 0-540-06139-5		
Staffordshire	ISBN 0-540-06134-4		ISBN 0-540-06135-2		ISBN 0-540-06136-0		
	£10.99						
Warwickshire	ISBN 0-540-05642-1						

Name ____________________

Address ____________________

____

____________________ *Postcode*

◆ ***Free postage and packing*** ◆ *All available titles will normally be dispatched within 5 working days of receipt of order but please allow up to 28 days for delivery*

☐ *Please tick this box if you do not wish your name to be used by other carefully selected organisations that may wish to send you information about other products and services*

I enclose a cheque / postal order, for a ***total*** *of* ☐

made payable to ***Reed Book Services****, or please debit my*

☐ *Access* ☐ *American Express* ☐ *Visa*

account by ☐

Account no ☐☐☐☐ ☐☐☐☐ ☐☐☐☐ ☐☐☐☐

Expiry date ☐☐ ☐☐

Signature ____________________